American Constitutionalism

Volume I Structures of Government

Howard Gillman
University of Southern California

Mark A. Graber
University of Maryland

Keith E. Whittington
Princeton University

New York Oxford
Oxford University Press

Oxford University Press, Inc., publishes works that further Oxford University's objective of excellence in research, scholarship, and education.

Oxford New York
Auckland Cape Town Dar es Salaam Hong Kong Karachi
Kuala Lumpur Madrid Melbourne Mexico City Nairobi
New Delhi Shanghai Taipei Toronto

With offices in
Argentina Austria Brazil Chile Czech Republic France Greece
Guatemala Hungary Italy Japan Poland Portugal Singapore
South Korea Switzerland Thailand Turkey Ukraine Vietnam

For titles covered by Section 112 of the US Higher Education Opportunity Act, please visit www.oup.com/us/he for the latest information about pricing and alternate formats.

Published by Oxford University Press, Inc.
198 Madison Avenue, New York, New York 10016
http://www.oup.com

Library of Congress Cataloging-in-Publication Data
Gillman, Howard.
American constitutionalism / Howard Gillman, Mark A. Graber, Keith E. Whittington.
p. cm.
Includes bibliographical references and index.
ISBN 978-0-19-975126-6 (v. 1)
1. Constitutional history—United States. I. Graber, Mark A. II. Whittington, Keith E. III. Title.
KF4541.G55 2012
342.7302′9—dc23 2012001321

9 8 7 6 5 4 3 2 1

Printed in the United States of America
on acid-free paper

Brief Contents

Contents

Appendices

Topical Outline of Volume I

Tables, Figures, and Illustrations

Preface

This textbook pioneers a new approach to American constitutionalism. Our target audience consists of professors, students, and readers interested in researching, teaching, and learning about constitutional politics in the United States. This subject matter explains four crucial features of the material that follows.

- We discuss *all important debates* in American constitutional history.
- We include readings from *all prominent participants* in these constitutional debates.
- We organize these constitutional debates by *historical era*.
- Chapter introductions clearly lay out the *political and legal contexts*.

Our goal is to familiarize readers with the central constitutional issues that have excited Americans over the years—and that are still vigorously debated in our time. We hope to break the habit of equating American constitutionalism with the decisions of the Supreme Court of the United States. Constitutionalism in the United States covers more topics, is more complex, and is more interesting than one would gather from merely reading essays by judges in law reports.

American Constitutionalism is directed at all persons who hope to be sophisticated observers and informed participants in a constitutional regime, not just the very few who make arguments before federal judges or the extraordinary few who become federal judges. Our text provides readers with the materials they need to form educated opinions on the fundamental questions of American constitutionalism.

Constitutional norms pervade all of American politics, and all of us participate in that constitutional politics. The very vocabulary that ordinary Americans use when talking politics reflects the language chosen by long-dead framers. When we think that government is treating us unfairly, we complain that we have been denied "the equal protection of the laws." We insist or deny that national health care is a legitimate exercise of the congressional power under Article I "to regulate commerce among the several states." We debate whether it is a "necessary and proper" exercise of the constitutional power "to lay and collect Taxes and provide for the general welfare of the United States."

Sophisticated observers and informed participants need a different introduction to American constitutionalism than lawyers practicing before the Supreme Court of the United States. Both should be exposed to such judicial landmarks as *McCulloch v. Maryland* (1819), the decision which defined the scope of national powers, and *Brown v. Board of Education* (1954), the decision which declared the laws unconstitutional that mandated racial segregation in public schools. For this reason, *American Constitutionalism* includes generous selections from the most important cases decided by the Supreme Court of the United States.

Participants in constitutional politics should be familiar with important constitutional issues that are *not* being litigated, and may never have been litigated, before the Supreme Court of the United States. They should know the basic arguments for and against presidential power to initiate military action in foreign countries, even if that constitutional question has not been decided by the Supreme Court of the United States. Sophisticated observers should be aware of the ways in which Supreme Court rulings may be consequences of previous constitutional choices made by other constitutional authorities. The *Brown* decision, for example, occurred only after Presidents Roosevelt, Truman, and Eisenhower packed the federal courts with racial liberals who believed Jim Crow unconstitutional.

American Constitutionalism seeks to make readers more sophisticated observers and informed participants in constitutional politics. If our goal is to understand American constitutionalism, then we should be open to the full range of the American constitutional experience. If our goal is to engage the fundamental questions that have roiled American politics and understand the dynamics of constitutional development, then we must widen our perspective. We must incorporate the constitutional politics underlying landmark Supreme Court decisions, and we must include landmark constitutional decisions made by elected officials and state courts. *American Constitutionalism* provides these materials.

Constitutional arguments are as much the stuff of politics as the pork barrel and the log roll. The interplay of legal principles, moral values, partisan interests, and historical development is a central feature of our constitutional system. Basic constitutional institutions provide normative and procedural frameworks that allow political debate and decision making to move forward in ways that both political winners and losers alike usually consider legitimate. At the same time, preexisting constitutional commitments confer advantages on some political movements and partisan coalitions relative to others.

With the materials that follow we hope to provide an understanding of how constitutionalism actually works in the United States. We reject the simple view that constitutionalism has nothing to do with politics—and the equally simple view that constitutionalism is nothing more than a dressed-up version of ordinary politics. American constitutionalism is a distinctive form of politics with distinctive goals and modes of justification. Understanding the interplay between all the different elements of constitutional law and politics is a precondition for any realistic assessment of how American constitutionalism actually works, how that system of governance should work, and how our political order might work better.

All Important Constitutional Debates

American Constitutionalism covers the major constitutional controversies that have excited Americans from the colonial era to the present. Readings range from protests that the Stamp Act violated the unwritten English Constitution to the arguments made in the contemporary controversy over "enhanced" methods of interrogating suspected terrorists. Along the way, we include the constitutional debates over the Bill of Rights, the Louisiana Purchase, the Emancipation Proclamation, prohibition, women's suffrage, the New Deal, and presidential power to order troops into foreign countries.

When determining what materials to include, we look to the impact of the controversy on American constitutional development. We devote space to the constitutional disputes over the annexation of Texas and the proposed Human Life Amendment. Both debates were central to the constitutional politics of the time and provide foundations for contemporary constitutional politics. We spend less time on technical legal questions primarily of interest to lawyers with a federal courts practice. We believe that scarce space in a textbook aimed at providing a deeper understanding of the workings of our constitutional system is better spent covering such issues as the constitutional debates during the 1920s over federal anti-lynching laws than the precise details of the state market exception to the dormant commerce clause. The former tells us more about the politics and principles of American constitutionalism than the latter.

All Important Constitutional Participants

American Constitutionalism examines the contributions of all Americans to important constitutional debates. These contributions include the judicial opinions in such landmark Supreme Court cases as *Marbury v. Madison* (1803) and *Roe v. Wade* (1973). The major contributions to important constitutional debates also include the arguments lawyers made before the Supreme Court, the judicial opinions and legal arguments in lower federal court and state court cases, presidential speeches and opinions of the attorney general, congressional debates and legislative reports, party manifestos, pamphlets produced by interest groups, and scholarly commentaries. A comprehensive education in American constitutionalism should include Salmon Chase's argument that Congress had no constitutional power to pass a fugitive slave act, the prominent state court decisions interpreting provisions in state bills of rights, President Nixon's veto of the War Powers Resolution, the congressional debates over the ratification of the post–Civil War Amendments, and the Margold Report outlining the NAACP's strategy during the 1930s and 1940s for securing a Supreme Court decision ending "separate but equal."

We include these materials because we recognize that American constitutionalism takes shape in the legislature and the executive branches of government, as well as in the judiciary. Constitutional provisions and principles are elaborated within the national government, by state and local officials, and on the streets and in meeting places throughout the United States. Constitutional meaning is determined by government officials, party platforms, campaign speeches, legal treatises, and newspaper articles.

Our emphasis on all participants is closely related to our concern with presenting all major constitutional debates. Consider the constitutional issues raised by national expansion and presidential war-making powers. These matters were debated and settled by elected officials. We would only skim the surface of the constitutional controversies raised during the contemporary war against terror if we limited materials to Supreme Court rulings. Even when courts make constitutional rulings, those rulings are typically preceded and structured by constitutional politics outside the judiciary. The Supreme Court in *Planned Parenthood v. Casey* (1992) refrained from overruling *Roe v. Wade* in part because pro-choice Democrats in 1986 were able to prevent President Reagan from appointing Robert Bork, a vigorous critic of *Roe*, to the Supreme Court. The Supreme Court in *McCulloch v. Maryland* declared that congressional decisions made during the preceding decade had partly settled questions about the constitutionality of the national bank. Elected officials often decide the fate of judicial decisions once they are handed down. If we pay too much attention to *Brown v. Board of Education* (1954), we will overlook the crucial role the Civil Rights Act of 1964 played in securing desegregation. If we concentrate too narrowly on the words of the Court in *Brown*, we miss the equally significant and diverse words of Harry Truman, Dwight Eisenhower, the Southern Manifesto, and Martin Luther King, Jr.

Historical Organization

American Constitutionalism is organized historically. It respects the traditional division into two volumes, on the structures of government and rights and liberties. However, within each volume, we divide American constitutional development into ten relatively distinct and stable political regimes: Colonial (before 1776), Founding (1776–1788), Early National (1789–1828), Jacksonian (1829–1860), Civil War/Reconstruction (1861–1876), Republican (1877–1932), New Deal/Great Society (1933–1968), Liberalism Divided (1969–1980), Reagan (1981–1993), and Contemporary (1994–present). These ten eras are characterized by important constitutional stabilities that mark that period off from previous and later eras.

Constitutional questions about secession and slavery were settled by the Civil War. Americans during the Jacksonian Era bitterly debated the constitutional issues associated with national territorial expansion, banking, and internal improvements. Americans after Reconstruction were far more concerned with national power to regulate railroads and drinking. New Dealers temporarily settled the constitutional questions over national power to regulate the economy that divided Americans from 1876 to 1932. Many of these issues reemerged in transmuted and muted form during the contemporary era. *Brown v. Board of Education* was hotly contested during the New Deal and Great Society. Americans after 1968 celebrated *Brown* and debated whether that decision supported or undermined affirmative action.

Approaching American constitutionalism historically provides a sound framework for understanding crucial episodes in American constitutional politics. Consider struggles over constitutional authority. Thomas Jefferson, Andrew Jackson, Abraham Lincoln, and Franklin Roosevelt maintained that the president, when making constitutional decisions, should not always be bound by past Supreme Court decisions. Other presidents have accepted judicial rulings as authoritative. Our period divisions enable readers to see patterns in this cycle of presidential assertion and deference.

The historical approach also enables students to see vital connections between different constitutional issues. Debates over slavery ranged from the scope of the federal power to regulate the interstate slave trade under the interstate commerce clause to whether the Sixth Amendment gave alleged fugitive slaves a right to a jury trial. The movement for racial equality during the 1950s and 1960s challenged existing constitutional understandings of the First Amendment, constitutional criminal procedure, cruel and unusual punishment, equal protection, the scope of federal power over interstate commerce, and state power to regulate interstate commerce in the absence of federal power.

We risk losing the vital connections between constitutional provisions when we cabin American constitutionalism into artificial doctrinal categories and treat them as timeless abstractions.

The Political and Legal Contexts

In all these ways, *American Constitutionalism* provides readers with information about the political and legal contexts in which constitutional controversies arise, are debated, and are settled. A concise introduction to each chapter identifies the central features of American constitutional politics during a particular era. These crucial elements are both political and legal.

The *political elements* include the most important partisan coalitions that fought for electoral supremacy, the main interests that supported those coalitions, the positions those coalitions took on the most important issues that divided Americans, and the extent to which one coalition was more successful than others at gaining control of the national government. The *Dred Scott* decision (1857), which declared that Congress could not ban slavery in American territories, articulated the constitutional commitments of the Jacksonian Democrats, who usually controlled the national government from 1828 to 1860.

The *legal elements* include the most important schools of constitutional and legal thought in a particular era. They include the general principles that most people believed best justified the constitutional order and were the best methods for interpreting the Constitution. Last, they include the available precedents that could be invoked to justify future constitutional developments. New Deal liberals, when justifying extensive government regulation of the national economy, relied heavily on notions of a "living constitution" that had become increasingly prominent in legal thought during the early twentieth century.

Pedagogical Framework

The context presented in chapter introductions is part of a consistent pedagogical framework:

- An opening chapter lays out the nature of American constitutionalism—starting with the five basic questions beneath constitutional debates. We believe that this chapter is an essential introduction for students unfamiliar with the nature of a constitution, constitutional interpretation, constitutional authority, and constitutional change.
- Each historical chapter is divided into a consistent set of topical sections.
- After the period introduction, sections within each subsequent chapter summarize the major issues. Each section begins with a bulleted list of major developments, for ease of reference and to facilitate understanding.
- All readings are prefaced with explanatory headnotes, and all headnotes to court cases end with questions. We believe that this more effectively creates engaged readers and engaged citizens.
- Occasional "Notes" explain particularly vexing constitutional debates.
- Period illustrations, such as political cartoons, further suggest controversies and contexts.
- Tables throughout the volume summarize key issues and court cases.
- All chapters end with suggested readings.

We hope the materials provided here allow readers to think about questions of constitutional interpretation and what the text that we have means, but also to think about questions of constitutional design and practice. If resolving fundamental disputes was merely a matter of consulting a neutral referee, such as a Supreme Court, whose authority was acknowledged by all players, then constitutional politics would be a simple matter of appeals, decisions, and essays in law books. Because our system does not work in this way, we have written this book.

For ease of use, the readings in the text are modernized, and we generally use modern terminology to refer to political and constitutional concepts. Since U.S. Supreme Court cases can now be easily found, we have generally cited them only by party names and decision date. Other court cases are referenced by full legal citation. Footnotes appearing in case excerpts are from the original source, unless otherwise indicated.

Supplements

However hard we tried, two volumes alone could not have space for literally all the participants in all the debates, without growing so large as to be costly and intimidating. While we have kept chapters flexible, so that instructors can skip around, we nonetheless took a further step: we have made many more readings available on the Web, as part of the extensive supplements available with this book.

We also make available correlation guides—to match our coverage to more traditional sequences. We wish to make our unusual range of coverage suitable to *any* class. Yet we also hope in this way to make the transition to a new approach easier. We believe that a historical organization best reflects the lived experience of the political actors who challenged existing constitutional practices and the constitutional authorities who determined the validity of those challenges.

Acknowledgments

American Constitutionalism was inspired by and is for our teachers and our students. Walter Murphy, Sanford Levinson, Mark Tushnet, Stephen Elkins, Lou Fisher, Bruce Ackerman, Martin Shapiro, and Rogers Smith are foremost among our many teachers. From them and others we learned that American constitutionalism was about the construction of a political regime and not limited to close analysis of a few Supreme Court opinions. Leslie Goldstein, Judith Baer, Gary Jacobsohn, H. W. Perry, Gordon Silverstein, Paul Frymer, Julie Novkov, George Lovell, Daniel Carpenter, Cornell Clayton, Michael McCann, Barry Friedman, Jack Balkin, Randy Barnett, Douglas Reed, Steve Griffin, Pamela Brandwein, Kevin McMahon, Tom Keck, Keith Bybee, Shep Melnick, Ken Kersch, Ron Kahn, Stephen Skowronek, and many others have simultaneously been our teachers and students. For the past quarter century we have participated in a common project devoted to elaborating new constitutional histories, new constitutional theories, and new constitutional visions all aimed at exploring the ways in which the study of American constitutional politics might differ from the study of constitutional law. We are particularly grateful for the opportunities to teach and learn from Kim Scheppele, Ran Hirschl, Gary Jacobsohn, Leslie Goldstein, and Thomas Ginsburg, who have consistently reminded us that we can understand American constitutionalism only by understanding constitutionalism outside of the United States. Over the past decade, we have welcomed Mariah Zeisberg, Tom Clark, Bradley Hays, Steve Simon, Beau Breslin, Doug Edlin, Helen Knowles, David Erdos, Justin Crowe, David Glick, and Emily Zackin to this constitutionalist fellowship. Each of these talented scholars has been tolerant of our foibles while diligently pointing out the many mistakes made in the initial elaboration of this new American constitutionalism. Finally, we should acknowledge the debt we owe to our students at Princeton University, the University of Southern California, and the University of Maryland. They will inherit American constitutionalism, if not *American Constitutionalism*. From them, we have learned that less is often more. We have experienced firsthand the hunger in younger Americans for ways to better understand and reform the American constitutional order.

The three of us owe a special debt of gratitude to the many persons who directly assisted the actual writing of *American Constitutionalism*. The list of friends and colleagues who responded promptly when we asked for advice about such matters as executive privilege in the Jacksonian Era or Sunday laws in the 1920s is probably longer than this volume, if that can be imagined. Nevertheless, we ought to single out Rogers Smith and Sandy Levinson for being particularly helpful with their comments and assistance. A legion of research assistants worked diligently finding cases, making tables, correcting typos, and inserting periods. They include Deborah Beim, David Bridge, Benjamin Bruins, Jonathan Cheng, Colleen Clary, Ina Cox, Danny Frost, David Glick, Abigail Graber, Ayana Mayberry, April Morton, David Myers, Herschel Nachlis, Benjamin Newton, David Nohe, Amanda Radke, Jennifer Ratcliff, Jessica Rebarber, Edward Reilly, Ryan Palmer, Clara Shaw, Michael Sullivan, Thaila Sundaresan, Jeff Tessin, and Katie Zuber.

Many friends and colleagues helped us test earlier iterations of *American Constitutionalism*. Each of them provided vital encouragement to us at initial stages of the project, but also gave us plain hard truths about the difficult choices we needed to make in order to bring this book to market. We thank them profusely for their counsel, as well as their students, whose comments on earlier editions we did our best to incorporate in the later volumes.

This project would not exist if not for Jennifer Carpenter and John Haber, our editors at Oxford University Press. They combined consistent encouragement, meticulous editing, and the patience of Job. Most important, they kept the faith that what we had to say mattered if said right and clearly. Other members of Oxford University Press demonstrated the same standard of exemplary professionalism and friendship.

We must also thank the many reviewers who closely examined each chapter to ensure its scholarly integrity and suitability to their course in constitutional law: David Gray Adler, Idaho State University; John M. Aughenbaugh, Virginia Commonwealth University; Steven P. Brown, Auburn University; Ericka Christensen, Washington State University; John Feldmeier, Wright State University; Greg Goelzhauser, Coastal Carolina University; Hans J. Hacker, Arkansas State University; Jeffrey D. Hockett, University of Tulsa; Robert M. Howard, Georgia State University; Thomas R. Hunter, University of West Georgia; Thomas Keck, Syracuse University; John C. Kilwein, West Virginia University; Barbara Kirby, University of North Texas; Drew Lanier, University of Central Florida; Carolyn N. Long, Washington State University Vancouver; David S. Mann, College of Charleston; Banks Miller, University of Texas at Dallas; Lisa L. Miller, Rutgers University; Jason Pierceson, University of Illinois Springfield; Heather Marie Rice, University of Pittsburgh; Howard Schweber, University of Wisconsin–Madison; Chris Shortell, Portland State University; Steven Tauber, University of South Florida; Douglas Telling, Framingham State University; Michael C. Tolley, Northeastern University; David Upham, University of Dallas; Chad Westerland, University of Arizona; Darren Wheeler, Ball State University; Teena Wilhelm, University of Georgia.

Still others have class tested drafts of this text with their students: Rogers M. Smith, University of Pennsylvania; Julie Novkov, University at Albany; Alice Hearst, Smith College; Justin Crowe, Williams College.

Before, during, and after writing this book, we drew inspiration from our families, who seem appropriately amused with our fascination for American constitutional development. Mark Graber wishes to extend his love and appreciation to his mother, Anita Wine Graber, and his spouse, Julia Bess Frank, and children—Naomi, Abigail, and Rebecca. Keith Whittington thanks Tracey and Taylor for their great patience and love. Howard Gillman thanks Ellen, Arielle, and Danny. The good news for our families is that, if they are reading this, the volume is finally done. The bad news is that we are probably still down in the basement, obsessed by some other project on which we have already missed a deadline.

Part 1 **Themes**

Chapter 1

Introduction to American Constitutionalism

On May 10, 1776, the Second Continental Congress passed what John Adams called "the most important resolution that was ever taken in America."[1] The resolution recommended that each colony draft and ratify a state constitution. Citizens were requested to "adopt such government as shall, in the opinions of the representatives of the people, best conduce to the happiness and safety of their constituents in particular, and America in general."[2] The reaction was overwhelming. Americans paraded in joy on the streets of Philadelphia, eager to get on with the work of self-government. Within a year, every colony but Rhode Island and Connecticut established a new constitution.

These celebrations highlight the American commitment to constitutionalism. Government in the United States is constitutional government. A written constitution, citizens of all political persuasions agree, is fundamental law. Constitutional law is higher than ordinary law made by legislatures or common law announced by justices. Federal, state, and local authorities exercise power legitimately only when the constitution authorizes their actions and decisions. America's commitment to constitutionalism extends far beyond traditional governing institutions. Student governments, the P.T.A., such civic organizations as the Knights of Columbus, and even many chess clubs have constitutions that create, empower, and limit their leaders and members.

Five Basic Questions. This shared American commitment to constitutionalism masks disputes over what that commitment to constitutionalism entails. Consider the controversy over *Roe v. Wade* (1973), the Supreme Court decision which held that the Constitution protects abortion rights. We might initially see that dispute as limited to the proper interpretation of such constitutional provisions as the due process clause of the Fourteenth Amendment. On closer inspection, the debate over *Roe* is rooted in more basic debates over the nature of constitutionalism. Persons who support that decision often speak of "a living constitution" that incorporates social and political changes. Opponents of *Roe* often champion "strict construction," and insist that constitutions limit government only when constitutional provisions are interpreted consistently with their original meaning.

Five basic questions lie beneath most constitutional disputes.

1. What is a constitution?
2. What purposes should constitutions serve?
3. How should constitutions be interpreted?
4. How should constitutional disputes be resolved?
5. How are constitutions ratified, changed, and repudiated?

Many Americans think that four of these questions have easy answers.

1. The Constitution of the United States consists of the written text ratified in 1787–88 and amendments passed according to the procedures set out in Article V. That Constitution is the fundamental law of the land.
2. The purpose of that Constitution is to limit government and protect basic rights.
4. The Supreme Court has the final say on all constitutional controversies. Those judicial decisions bind all other governing officials.

1. David McCullough, *John Adams* (New York: Simon & Schuster, 2001), 109.

2. *Journal of the Second Continental Congress*, vol. 5 (1776), 342.

5. Article VII details the necessary procedures for ratifying the Constitution.[3] Article V details the only legitimate means for passing constitutional amendments. Constitutional amendments are the only legitimate means for constitutional change.[4]

The only constitutional questions most Americans think are open to serious public debate are the proper method for interpreting the constitution and the meaning of such broad constitutional phrases as "equal protection" and "due process of law."

These common answers are rooted in a broadly shared vision of constitutionalism and the central place of the Constitution in the American ideal of government. Americans venerate the Constitution. We believe the Constitution is the primary source of our prosperity and liberty. Most people agree that constitutional controversies should be resolved by the Supreme Court whose justices have life tenure. This commitment to judicial supremacy guarantees that the exercise of government authority will rest on sound constitutional principles and not on the short-term political needs that too often motivate elected officials. Government officials should respect the Constitution because the Constitution is the law. We worry that politicians and some judges too often substitute their preferences for what the Constitution commands.

In fact, the five basic constitutional questions are more difficult than these common answers suggest.

1. The Constitution may not be limited to the words the framers ratified in 1787–88, 1868, and at other times when the constitution was amended. From the first, Americans have asserted that unwritten constitutional principles limit governing officials.
2. The Constitution does more than limit government. Such provisions as the interstate commerce clause empower Congress. The constitutional text expresses national aspirations and establishes processes for making laws that enable persons with very different politics to share the same civic space.
3. How the Constitution is best interpreted depends on the best answers to the other basic constitutional questions.
4. Constitutionalism does not require judicial supremacy, the view that courts resolve all constitutional controversies. The framers thought that our system of government and basic rights would better be maintained by well-designed constitutional institutions than by written declarations of constitutional law enforced by a life-tenured judiciary. Elected officials in the United States have played important roles settling major constitutional disputes. In some cases, most notably the constitutional disputes over American expansion, courts played almost no role in constitutional debates.
5. Article V does not explain all or even most constitutional change in the United States. Americans have frequently adopted new constitutional practices without using the textually prescribed process for constitutional amendment.

American constitutional history and the experience of other constitutional democracies demonstrate that many practices that Americans now take for granted are not necessary elements of constitutional government. Federal courts presently enjoy a near monopoly on constitutional decision making, but that preeminence was the product of a long historical struggle. Most constitutional decision makers in the United States think the notion of an "unconstitutional constitutional amendment" is legal nonsense. Courts in India and Germany, by comparison, have declared some constitutional amendments unconstitutional. Most troubling perhaps, the conventional view that the Constitution is responsible for what is good about the United States may be wrong. Leading scholars have recently asserted that the Constitution of the United States is responsible for many ills of American society.[5] Constitutional defects may even have caused the Civil War.[6]

---

3. "The Ratification of the Conventions of nine States shall be sufficient for the Establishment of this Constitution between the States so ratifying the Same."

4. "The Congress, whenever two thirds of both Houses shall deem it necessary, shall propose Amendments to this Constitution, or, on the Application of the Legislatures of two thirds of the several States, shall call a Convention for proposing Amendments, which, in either Case, shall be valid to all Intents and Purposes, as part of this Constitution, when ratified by the Legislatures of three fourths of the several States or by Conventions in three fourths thereof, as the one or the other Mode of Ratification may be proposed by the Congress."

5. See Sanford Levinson, *Our Undemocratic Constitution: Where the Constitution Goes Wrong (and How We the People Can Correct It)* (New York: Oxford University Press, 2006).

6. See Mark A. Graber, *Dred Scott and the Problem of Constitutional Evil* (New York: Cambridge University Press, 2006).

Constitutionalism as Governance. The basic questions of constitutionalism are difficult because constitutionalism is more than textual interpretation. Constitutionalism is a distinctive form of politics and governance. Constitutions structure ordinary politics and politics structures how constitutional systems operate. Consider contemporary campaigns for the White House. Candidates for the presidency spend huge amounts of money and time in a few swing states because Article II requires a majority of electoral votes rather than a majority of popular votes. Change the constitutional rules for electing the president and the politics of presidential elections will change. Presidential candidates would spend more time in New York and Los Angeles if the Constitution required them to gain a majority of the popular vote. The constitutional rules for making laws structure politics by encouraging legislative compromises and privileging the status quo. Article I and Article II require policy proposals to run a difficult obstacle course before becoming settled law. Divided government, threats of presidential veto, and judicial review may slow the policy-making process and moderate policy swings. At the same time, the Constitution gives great power to a few political actors. The difficulty of passing legislation often vests presidents and justices with the practical power to resolve constitutional controversies. For the past forty years, neither pro-life nor pro-choice advocates in the elected branches of government have gained the political power necessary to reverse any Supreme Court decision on abortion.

How the Constitution is interpreted at any time is influenced significantly by ordinary politics. Since the beginning of the Republic, arguments about the meaning and purpose of the Constitution have reflected the partisan divisions of their time period. The Constitution declares that government institutions may not lawfully impose "cruel and unusual punishments," but liberals and conservatives have different views on whether the death penalty constitutes cruel treatment. Political processes determine how those disputes get resolved. Presidents and senators use mostly partisan criteria when considering appointments to the Supreme Court, precisely so that justices will advance their distinctive understanding of how the Constitution should be interpreted. The Supreme Court has become more conservative in recent years because political conservatives have appointed a majority of the justices on the Supreme Court. Elections have had an extraordinary influence on constitutional development. Abraham Lincoln had very different understandings about the constitutionality of secession and slavery than the other three candidates for president in 1860. Change the result of the national election that year and American constitutional history would likely have taken a very different path.

Students of constitutional systems must accept as natural these relationships between constitutional politics and ordinary politics. Constitutional study should illuminate these relationships, not disguise them by focusing solely on how to find right answers to disputes over the meaning of particular constitutional words. Rather than obsess about whether constitutionalism is pure law or pure politics, we should study the distinctive ways American constitutionalism blends legal and political considerations.

I. What Is a Constitution?

Although constitutionalism has a long tradition in politics and political theory, substantial disagreement exists over the history and substance of that tradition. Many commentators believe the constitutional tradition began in ancient Greece. They see Aristotle's *Politics* as the first great work of constitutionalism and identify constitutionalism with the study of political regimes. Others find the first seeds of constitutionalism in ancient Rome and the Middle Ages. Constitutional regimes developed as rulers became committed to governing consistently with certain fundamental legal principles and the rule of law. A third understanding of constitutionalism developed in England and the United States during the seventeenth and eighteenth centuries. The liberal constitutionalism of the Enlightenment was committed to limited government and individual liberty, to the notion that governing institutions could not pass certain kinds of laws.

Contemporary constitutionalism is committed to law and legality. The constitutional commitment to the rule of law requires that governing officials be chosen on the basis of preexisting legal standards and that government officials may act only when their conduct is sanctioned by preexisting legal standards. Consider what Mary Jones must demonstrate in order to veto a bill passed by both houses of Congress requiring states to recognize same-sex marriages.

- Ms. Jones must demonstrate that she is president as the qualifications for the presidency are set out in Article II.
- Ms. Jones must demonstrate that Article II vests her with the power to veto bills passed by Congress.
- Ms. Jones must demonstrate that the veto does not violate any other rule laid down in the Constitution.

Political actors have no legal authority when they take actions that are inconsistent with constitutional standards. You have a right to disobey all unconstitutional laws passed by your state legislature (although you take the risk that the law will not be declared unconstitutional).

Ancient Constitutionalism. Political thinkers in ancient Greece and Rome used the term *politeia* or *constitutio* to refer "to the total composition, the shape or form of the state."[7] Ancient constitutionalism focused on the *telos* of a polity, the particular goods and vision of the good life that the polity sought to promote. The first sentence of Aristotle's *Politics* declares, "Every state is a community of some kind, and every community is established with a view to some good."[8] Ancient constitutionalists studied how social institutions were internally organized and interacted with other social institutions to generate a good society. They were particularly interested in political socialization, the practices by which citizens developed political identities, interests, and values.

American constitutionalism, in this view, is characterized by a two-party system and consumerism, as well as by the institutions explicitly laid out in Articles I, II, and III. Constitutional analysis, from an Aristotelian perspective, must take as a given both the Bill of Rights and the Super Bowl. Aristotelians further contend that American constitutional institutions and practices must be rooted in the broader political culture of the United States, and not be designed for some mythical people who live a life of unadulterated virtue. Steven Elkin points out that while "a commercial republican regime" may not be "the best regime," such a society may be "the best regime for the kind of people we are with our history and capacities."[9] An ideal people might be less concerned with material prosperity than Americans, but any political coalition which fails to "grow the economy" is unlikely to survive in the United States.

Constitutions as Fundamental Law. Constitutions are commonly regarded as higher or fundamental law. Constitutions authorize the making of ordinary law and determine how ordinary law is made. Constitutions provide the foundations for ordinary lawmaking by establishing the rules for determining who makes the law. They set out the processes by which governing officials may make laws and they limit the laws those governing officials may enact. Article I provides for a House of Representatives that is elected every two years, requires all bills to pass the House (and Senate) by a majority vote, and forbids the House from creating titles of nobility. These constitutional principles and rules are legally binding. No person has a legal obligation to obey an official decree not sanctioned by the Constitution. Charles McIlwain observes that in constitutional government "any exercise of authority beyond these limits by any government is an exercise of 'power without right.'"[10]

The constitutional commitment to fundamental law entails a commitment to the rule of law. Rule following, Frederick Schauer points out, fosters

> the interrelated virtues of reliance, predictability, and certainty.... [D]ecision-makers who follow rules even when other results appear preferable enable those affected to predict in advance what the decisions are likely to be. Consequently, those affected by the decisions of others can plan their activities more successfully under a regime of rules than under more particularistic decision-making.[11]

Persons in regimes that respect the rule of law at all times know the legal consequences of contemplated actions. All citizens are capable of learning in advance what conduct government permits, what conduct government sanctions, and how severely government sanctions that conduct. This legal regularity enables people to preserve their liberty by acting consistently with known laws.

---

7. Graham Maddox, "A Note on the Meaning of 'Constitution,'" *American Political Science Review* 76 (1982):806.

8. Aristotle, *The Politics and the Constitution of Athens* (New York: Cambridge University Press, 1996), 11.

9. Stephen L. Elkin, *Reconstructing the Commercial Republic* (Chicago: University of Chicago, 2006), 10.

10. Charles Howard McIlwain, *Constitutionalism* (Ithaca: Cornell University Press, 1947), 11.

11. Frederick Schauer, *Playing by the Rules* (New York: Oxford University Press, 1991), 254.

Liberal Constitutionalism. Liberal constitutionalists identify constitutionalism with a system of "protected freedom for the individual." Constitutions protect rights. Giovanni Sartori regards a constitution as "a fundamental law, or a fundamental set of principles, and a correlative institutional arrangement, which would restrict arbitrary power and ensure a 'limited government.'"[12] Prominent contemporary thinkers reject claims that just *any* plan of government amounts to a constitution. Constitutions establish textual and practical protections for certain liberties. "For a constitutionalist," Walter Murphy and his co-authors insist, "a law enacted by a Congress chosen after open public debate and free elections and signed by a President similarly chosen would still be illegitimate if it violated a fundamental guarantee, such as the right to free exercise of religion."[13]

Liberal constitutions protect two kinds of rights. The first are *fundamental or natural rights.* These exist apart from the constitution. Political liberalism is committed to some version of universal rights, the claim that persons have some rights simply by virtue of being persons. These rights may be "endowed by their Creator," as Thomas Jefferson maintained, or inherent in some aspect of the human condition, as many philosophers believe. Liberal constitutions recognize and guarantee these fundamental rights but do not "create" them.

The second kind of rights are *positive rights*. They are created by the constitution or laws passed under the constitution. Positive rights are contingent, rather than essential, features of a liberal constitutional scheme. State legislatures routinely establish new positive rights such as the right to swim in a public pool or the right to deduct charitable contributions when paying income taxes. Unlike fundamental rights, no constitutional problem exists when positive rights are repealed by statutory revision or constitutional amendment. Rights created by government may be abolished by government.

12. Giovanni Sartori, "Constitutionalism: A Preliminary Discussion," *American Political Science Review* 56 (1962):855.

13. Walter F. Murphy, James E. Fleming, Sotirios A. Barber, and Stephen Macedo, *American Constitutional Interpretation*, 3rd ed. (New York: Foundation Press, 2003), 48–49.

II. Constitutional Purposes

Fundamental laws that limit government serve many purposes. Good constitutions provide governing officials with necessary power and organize politics. They enable governments to make credible commitments to investors and foreign powers, prevent governing officials from enriching and entrenching themselves, promote deliberation on the public interest, enable a society to realize national aspirations, and facilitate compromises among persons who disagree on national aspirations.

Constitutionalism also entails some rule by the dead, not normally considered a virtue in a democracy.[14] Americans are not constitutionally free to decide whether an established state religion, all things considered, promotes the public good. We must instead determine whether that policy is consistent with words ratified more than two hundred years ago by men who owned slaves and wore wigs. New Yorkers may blame equal state representation in the Senate for inefficient and unjust allocations of federal funds.[15] Nevertheless, New Yorkers are not free to secure alternative arrangements by ordinary democratic means. If we want to change those rules, we have to change the Constitution.

Empowering Officials and Organizing Politics. Constitutions both limit and empower government. Constitutions empower government by establishing the background rules that enable ordinary politics to take place. Stephen Holmes points out that "constitutions may be usefully compared to the rules of a game."[16] Just as the rules of baseball enable persons to play that game and the rules of grammar enable persons to speak English, so constitutional rules enable persons to engage in democratic politics. Constitutional rules help us determine when someone's idea becomes a

14. The U.S. Constitution was mostly written in 1789, but it would pose the same obstacle of dead political majorities obstructing present ones if it had been written in 1989. For a provocative discussion, see Andrei Marmor, "Are Constitutions Legitimate?" *Canadian Journal of Law and Jurisprudence* 20 (2007): 69.

15. Frances E. Lee and Bruce I. Oppenheimer, *Sizing Up the Senate: The Unequal Consequences of Equal Representation* (Chicago: University of Chicago Press, 1999).

16. Stephen Holmes, *Passions and Constraints* (Chicago: University of Chicago Press, 1995), 163.

statute with the force of law and whether a government official has lost his right to rule. We know who the president is because Article II provides the rules that enable us to identify the winner of a presidential election.

Constitutions empower government by resolving background issues in ways that facilitate debate on more important matters. If every political question were open at all times, little could be accomplished. Before having a vote on whether to raise taxes, we might have to vote on whether majorities should have the power to raise taxes. Nothing would ever be settled. By settling such questions as how to elect a president, whether to have a state religion, or whose orders army officers must follow, the Constitution enables our politics to revolve around such substantive issues as health care and the proper level of taxation. The absence of constitutional rules would not result in unlimited legal power, but anarchy.

Rule of Law and Credible Commitments. The rule of law facilitates prosperity, international relations, and peaceful cooperation. Political regimes need to secure cooperation from many parties, from ordinary citizens to private investors to foreign officials. Governments can always promise that they will respect rights, repay loans, and honor treaties. Constitutional institutions that respect the rule of law make those promises more credible. Credible commitments are particularly important for nations with market economies. Governments must make the constitutional guarantees necessary to entice private investors and lay the foundations for commercial development. When constitutional commitments are credible, skeptics buy into a new political system and a society may achieve gains in overall welfare.

Credible constitutional commitments promote numerous social goods. Douglass North and Barry Weingast insist that for "economic growth to occur the sovereign or government must not merely establish the relevant set of rights, but must make a credible commitment to them."[17] Persons considering buying government bonds must have some confidence they will be repaid. Soldiers must have some confidence they will receive promised wages. Financiers and entrepreneurs must have some confidence that their investments will not be expropriated or annulled. Foreign nations must have some confidence that international agreements will be respected. Political minorities must have some confidence that they will not be oppressed by political majorities.

Many constitutional provisions seek to reassure various constituencies. The supremacy clause of the Constitution of the United States reassured foreign governments that treaty obligations would be enforced in federal courts. The Bill of Rights reassured some anxious anti-Federalists that the national government would respect fundamental rights. The proposed apportionment of the seats in Senate and House of Representatives convinced representatives of small states and slave states that their interests would be protected in the powerful national government created by the Constitution.

Preventing Self-Dealing by Governing Official. Many constitutional rules and practices are designed to prevent *self-dealing* by governing officials, efforts by governing officials to either enrich themselves or entrench their power. Robert Michels' famous "iron law of oligarchy" postulated that official self-dealing is likely because all political leaders have different interests than their constituents.[18] The average member of Congress, for example, has far more money invested in the stock market than the average American. For this reason, we have good reason to fear that majorities in Congress may adopt securities regulations that promote the interests of the wealthy few at the expense of popular majorities.

Well-designed constitutions help guarantee that when conflicts arise between the rulers and the ruled, they are resolved in the public interest. Fixed constitutional rules prevent incumbents from unfairly entrenching themselves in office by manipulating electoral arrangements. The First Amendment recognizes that elected officials may not be the best judges of whether speech criticizing their performance should be prohibited.

Some constitutional rules and practices prevent self-dealing by popular majorities. Constitutional guarantees of equality require that popular and legislative majorities govern by general rules that apply to

17. Douglass C. North and Barry R. Weingast, "Constitutions and Commitment: The Evolution of Institutions Governing Public Choice in Seventeenth-Century England," *Journal of Economic History* 49 (1989):803.

18. Robert Michels, *Political Parties* (New York: Free Press, 1968).

majorities and minorities alike. Majorities determine whether abortion should be banned or whether troops shall be sent into combat, but they may not prohibit only Baptists from terminating pregnancies or draft only poor persons to fight a war. "There is no more effective practical guarantee against arbitrary and unreasonable government," Justice Robert Jackson declared, "than to require that the principles of law which government impose upon a minority must be imposed generally."[19]

Promoting the Public Interest. All constitutions seek to facilitate intelligent policy through a political structure that encourages deliberation. Americans want a government that respects rights and a government that promotes general prosperity. We want an economic system that provides jobs for college graduates, but we recognize that we cannot simply mandate by constitutional law that the gross domestic product will grow by 4 percent every year. Instead, the constitutional rules for staffing the government and making laws must establish the sort of political process that fosters consistent economic growth.

The constitutional system for selecting governing officials is the first means by which the Constitution of the United States promotes deliberation and intelligent policy. The framers thought that particularly capable rulers would most likely gain office under Article I and Article II. "The aim of every political constitution," James Madison wrote, is "first to obtain for rulers men who possess most wisdom to discern, and most virtue to pursue, the common good of the society."[20] Madison defended large legislative districts because he thought that they increased the number of worthy candidates. Large election districts also forced voters to transcend narrow concerns. More cosmopolitan representatives, in turn, would make better laws.

The division of power among the national executive, legislature, and judiciary is the second means for promoting intelligent legislation in the public interest. If two, three, and four heads are better than one, then requiring legislation to be approved by the Senate, House of Representatives, President, and Supreme Court is likely to yield particularly intelligent laws. "The separation of powers," Elkin writes, "sets up an institutional structure in which national lawmaking must revolve around the efforts of the branches to convince one another of the merits of its views."[21]

Federalism is the third constitutional means for promoting intelligent decision making. The division of power between the federal government and the states ideally enables policy to be made by legislators most familiar with the relevant issues and with the incentives to act on them in the public interest. National issues are resolved by national officials who have developed expertise in national problems. Local issues are resolved by local officials who have expertise in local problems. Federalism allows for policy experimentation and diversity as local officials respond to local conditions, pressures, and sentiment.

National Aspirations. Constitutions embody national aspirations. We may aspire to be the sort of people who protect fundamental rights, have a vigorous economy, or rule the world. Our constitution should remind us of those aspirations, declare these aspirations to the world, and provide a framework for achieving those aspirations. Consider the First Amendment, which protects the right to free speech. That provision promotes democratic aspirations in several ways. Political leaders must explain why their actions do not violate that cherished liberty. The more citizens who exercise free speech rights, the more likely public debate will be intelligent and diverse.

Constitutions may also serve as a bulwark against temptations to act in ways inconsistent with our notions of the best life. Just as students aspiring to law school have been known to miss class or skimp on their readings, so nations have been known to adopt policies that, on reflection, do not seem consistent with their notions of justice. Few Americans today think that interning Japanese-Americans during World War II reflected the best American values. A constitution, by reminding us of our values as a nation, may help return us to those values. Just as a New Year's resolution written on the wall of a dorm may remind students that they must somehow finish their assignment to read this chapter, so the equal protection clause may remind Americans

19. *Railway Express Agency, Inc. v. New York*, 336 U.S. 106, 112–13 (1949) (Jackson, J., concurring).

20. James Madison, "No. 57," in Alexander Hamilton, James Madison and John Jay, *The Federalist Papers*, ed. Clinton Rossiter (New York: Mentor, 1961), 350.

21. Elkin, 35.

and their governors that we must treat people of all races and ethnicities equally.

Abraham Lincoln in 1857 emphasized the aspirational function of the Constitution when articulating a constitutional commitment to the abolition of slavery. The assertion that "all men are created equal," he stated,

> was of no practical use in effecting our separation from Great Britain; and it was placed in the Declaration, nor for that, but for future use. Its authors meant it to be, thank God, it is now proving itself, a stumbling block to those who in after times might seek to turn a free people back into the hateful paths of despotism. They knew the proneness of prosperity to breed tyrants, and they meant when such should reappear in this fair land and commence their vocation they should find left for them at least one hard nut to crack.[22]

Lincoln's constitution did not immediately abolish slavery. Rather, the text consistently reminded Americans that slavery was inconsistent with their most fundamental values.

Constitutions as Compromises. Successful constitutions are compromises between people and political movements with very different aspirations and very different interests. The price of national unity or peaceful coexistence is often a less coherent constitution. We may have to make concessions to those we regard as less virtuous than ourselves in order to achieve more common goals such as a government strong enough to prevent foreign invasion. Article IV, Section 2, required citizens of a free state to return fugitive slaves to their Southern owners. The "federal ratio" compromised slave- and free-state interests by allowing slaves to count as three-fifths of a person when apportioning House seats and Electoral College votes.[23] Northern opponents of slavery accepted such injustices to build support for a constitution that would be broadly acceptable. They believed the benefits of Union outweighed the costs of slavery. Whether they were right is a bitterly disputed question.

22. Abraham Lincoln, "Speech at Springfield, Illinois, June 26, 1857," in *The Collected Works of Abraham Lincoln*, ed. Roy P. Basler, vol. 2 (New Brunswick, NJ: Rutgers University Press, 1953), 406.

23. In the apportionment of seats to the House of Representatives, states received a number of seats based on the population of their free inhabitants and three-fifths of their enslaved inhabitants. States receive the number of votes in the Electoral College equal to their number of seats in the House and the Senate.

III. Constitutional Interpretation and Decision Making

Americans engage in two distinctive debates over constitutional interpretation. *Normative* controversies concern the best way to ascertain what the Constitution of the United States means. Law professors, justices, and others debate whether constitutional provisions mean what they meant when ratified, how one determines that meaning, and how decisions about constitutional issues ought to be made. The second debate is over whether any of these normative theories actually explains constitutional decision making. Prominent political scientists insist that constitutional decision makers are interested only in making good policy. Their constitutional arguments merely mask conclusions reached on other grounds.

The stakes in these debates are the influence of constitutionalism on politics. At one extreme is the view that legal and policy arguments are completely distinct. Proponents of this position think notions of good policy should and do play no role in constitutional analysis. At the other extreme is the view that no practical difference exists between legal and policy arguments. Proponents of this position think people can use common methods of constitutional interpretation to support whatever policies they believe best. We believe that the relationship between law and politics is more complex than either position suggests. Constitutional arguments are best understood as practices that constrain and structure the influence of policy preferences on legal decisions, but are not devices that assure a complete separation of law and politics.

Constitutional Arguments. The constitutional text plainly resolves some matters, while leaving others open for debate and investigation. The president, Article II plainly states, must be at least thirty-five years old. No one seriously claims that the best high-school newspaper editor in the nation is constitutionally eligible to be the next president of the United States. The constitutional status of federal laws imposing capital punishment is harder to discern. The Eighth Amendment forbids "cruel and unusual punishments" without specifying what punishments are cruel and unusual. The amendment also fails to elaborate any elements of a cruel and unusual punishment. Constitutional decision makers and commentators have developed six approaches to interpreting such constitutional provisions.[24]

Originalism. Historical or originalist arguments maintain that constitutional provisions mean what they meant when they were ratified. Thomas Jefferson advised Supreme Court Justice William Johnson, "On every question of construction, carry ourselves back to the time when the Constitution was adopted, recollect the spirit manifested in the debates and, instead of trying what meaning may be squeezed out of the text or invented against it, conform to the probable one in which it was passed."[25]

Proponents of originalism sometimes refer to the original *intentions* underlying constitutional provisions, but most now emphasize original *meanings*. As Randy Barnett describes the original meaning approach, "Each word must be interpreted the way a normal speaker of English would have read it when it was enacted."[26] What matters is the public meaning of the constitutional text at the time the provision was ratified—not private understandings between particular framers, specific goals or applications the framers had in mind, or what that constitutional language might mean in the present. That most framers expected George Washington to be the first president has no bearing on the proper interpretation of the provisions in Article II discussing the constitutional qualifications for that office.

Originalists dispute how to interpret more abstract clauses in the Constitution, such as the declaration that "Congress shall make no law ... abridging the freedom of speech." Some insist that this provision should be interpreted as protecting only those free speech rights that persons in 1791 believed were constitutionally protected. Others believe that such provisions should be interpreted as stating a general principle, but not any specific application of that principle. According to Jack Balkin, a leading advocate of the latter approach, "The task of interpretation is to look to original meaning and underlying principle and decide how best to apply them in current circumstances."[27] Consider abortion rights. Some originalists consider only whether the framers of any constitutional provision believed that provision protected abortion rights. Balkin considers what the framers of the Fourteenth Amendment meant by the principle of equal protection. He would have us make an independent judgment as to how that principle applies to abortion.

Textualism. Textualist arguments emphasize the specific language of the Constitution. This includes the relationship among the terms used, along with the common meaning of those terms. Justice Joseph Story was a leading nineteenth century champion of textualism. In Story's view, interpreters should look only to "what is written," not to "scattered documents" and "probable guesses" about what those who adopted the Constitution meant. "It is obvious, that there can be no security to the people in any constitution of government," he wrote, "if they are not to judge of it by the fair meaning of the words of the text."[28] Leslie Goldstein, a leading contemporary textualist, adopts a similar position. She "believes it is inappropriate for judges to strike down statutes on the basis of anything other than a principle fairly inferable from the constitutional text (although such principle need not have been present in the conscious minds of the framers)."[29]

Textualists dispute the best ways of reading the Constitution. Some textualists place constitutional language in a historical context, looking to usages at the time constitutional words were ratified. They make use of eighteenth-century dictionaries when interpreting the meaning of "commerce" in the interstate commerce

24. There is no single typology of methods of constitutional interpretation, but a useful discussion of some common forms of constitutional argument can be found in Philip Bobbitt, *Constitutional Fate* (New York: Oxford University Press, 1982), 3–119.

25. Thomas Jefferson, "To William Johnson, Jun 12, 1823," in *The Writings of Thomas Jefferson*, ed. Paul Leicester Ford, vol. 10 (New York: G.P. Putnam's Sons, 1899), 231.

26. Randy E. Barnett, *Restoring the Lost Constitution* (Princeton: Princeton University Press, 2004) xiii.

27. Jack M. Balkin, "Original Meaning and Abortion," *Constitutional Commentary* 24 (2007):293. Note that, like many recent scholars, Balkin attempts to ground a right to abortion, in part, in an equality argument rather than a right-to-privacy argument as the Court did in *Roe v. Wade*. See also, Mark A. Graber, *Rethinking Abortion* (Princeton: Princeton University Press, 1996).

28. Joseph Story, *Commentaries on the Constitution of the United States*, vol. 1 (Boston: Hillard, Gray, 1833), 391.

29. Leslie Friedman Goldstein, *In Defense of the Text* (Savage, MD: Rowman & Littlefield, 1991), 3.

clause.[30] Other textualists focus on the language without regard to any particular historical context. They are willing to use modern dictionaries. When determining whether secularism is a religion for First Amendment purposes, these textualists look to the contemporary meaning of "religion," without worrying whether people in 1791 relied on similar definitions.

The most famous textual argument in American constitutional history is probably Justice Hugo Black's claim that the First Amendment prohibits *all* regulations of speech, no matter how dangerous the speech. The relevant text reads, "Congress shall make no law ... abridging the freedom of speech." "'No law,'" Black bluntly stated, "means no law."[31] Black did not do extensive historical research on free speech practices in 1791 or on the framers' general principles. That the text said "no law" was good enough for him.

Doctrinalism. Doctrinal arguments resolve contemporary controversies by interpreting past precedents. Rather than focus on the constitutional text or on what various provisions meant when adopted, doctrinalism emphasizes what government officials, particularly judges, have said about the Constitution over time. The Constitution is interpreted in light of previous constitutional decisions or precedents.

Doctrinal arguments often rely on analogies to previous constitutional decisions. If the justices have declared the Constitution protects the right to burn the flag of the United States, then the justices should declare that the Constitution protects the right to burn a map of the United States or the Texas state flag. All three cases treat burning certain objects as a form of political speech.

Extending principles articulated in one case to analogous cases characterizes the *common law* method of reasoning, which the United States inherited from England. Common law practice allows the law to develop over time as new cases arise. Common law justices apply inherited principles to new facts, sometimes subtly altering those principles in light of social developments. Justice Oliver Wendell Holmes stated, "when we are dealing with words that are also a constituent act, like the Constitution of the United States, we must realize that they have called into life a being the development of which could not have been foreseen completely by the most gifted of its begetters."[32] The framers said nothing explicitly about state and federal power to regulate trains. The Supreme Court in the late nineteenth century determined that train lines were subject only to federal regulation after a series of precedents clarified state and federal power over interstate commerce.

Doctrinalists often debate what constitutional principles were announced in past decisions. Consider present controversies over the meaning of *Brown v. Board of Education* (1954). Chief Justice John Roberts in 2007 insisted that that past precedent forbade local officials from using race when assigning children to various high schools. In "*Brown v. Board of Education* ...," he argued, "we held ... government classification and separation on grounds of race themselves denoted inferiority." Justice Breyer responded with a contrary doctrinal argument. He declared that race-conscious assignments "represent local efforts to bring about the kind of racially integrated education that *Brown v. Board of Education* ... long ago promised."[33] Both justices relied on *Brown*, but disputed the best interpretation of that precedent.

Doctrinal arguments may also cite past legislative and executive decisions. The justices in *Youngstown Sheet & Tube Company v. Sawyer* (1952) did so after President Harry Truman seized steel mills without congressional authorization. Several judicial opinions analyzed at great length past presidential decisions to act without congressional authorization. The majority of justices concluded that the few instances when presidents seized property on their initiative did not provide sufficient precedential support for Truman's decision to take possession of the steel mines.

Precedents do not have the same binding force as text. The doctrine of *stare decisis* states that courts should generally adhere to the principles laid down in previous rulings, but *stare decisis* is not absolute.

30. For historically oriented textualist approaches, see Antonin Scalia, *A Matter of Interpretation* (Princeton: Princeton University Press 1997); Akhil Reed Amar, *The Bill of Rights* (New Haven: Yale University Press, 1998).

31. Edmund Cahn, "Justice Black and First Amendment 'Absolutes': A Public Interview," *New York University Law Review* 37 (1962):549, 553–54.

32. *Missouri v. Holland*, 252 U.S. 416, 433 (1920). See also, David A. Strauss, "Common Law Constitutional Interpretation," *University of Chicago Law Review* 63 (1996): 877; Stephen M. Griffin, "Rebooting Originalism," *University of Illinois Law Review* 2008 (2008):1185.

33. *Parents Involved in Community Schools v. Seattle School District*, 127 S. Ct. 2738, 2767, 2800 (2007).

Constitutional decision makers may overrule precedents they believe wrongly decided. The Supreme Court during the New Deal overruled several past decisions limiting congressional power to regulate the economy. The Supreme Court in *Lawrence v. Texas* (2003) overruled *Bowers v. Hardwick* (1986) which had decided that states had the power to prohibit sexual relations between adults of the same gender.

Structuralism. Structural arguments rely on the general principles that best explain the structure of and relationships between governing institutions. Structural arguments, Charles Black noted, provide an "inference from the structures and relationships created by the constitution in all its parts or in some principal part."[34] Such basic principles as the "separation of powers," "democracy," or "federalism" are not stated explicitly in the constitutional text. Nevertheless, those principles help us understand the constitutional institutions established by Articles I, II, and III. When determining whether the president should have a line item veto, a structuralist will look at the general principles underlying the separation of powers. Structuralists will decide whether states may constitutionally regulate interstate commerce on the basis of their understanding of the constitutional commitment to federalism.

Justice Scalia's opinion in *Printz v. United States* (1997) is a good example of a structural argument. *Printz* struck down a federal requirement that local officials implement a federal gun control regulation. Scalia acknowledged that "there is no constitutional text speaking to this precise question," but he insisted that Congress could not mandate that state officials enforce federal laws. He began with a general principle. Scalia declared that the Constitution "contemplates that a State's government will represent and remain accountable to its own citizens." He then applied that principle to the issue before the court. Preventing the federal government from "impress[ing] into its service—at no cost to itself" the police officers to which local citizens have assigned other tasks, Scalia concluded, is essential to maintaining a "healthy balance of power between the States and the Federal Government."

34. Charles L. Black, Jr., *Structure and Relationship in Constitutional Law* (Baton Rouge: Louisiana State University, 1969), 7.

Prudentialism. Prudential arguments examine the costs and benefits of different constitutional policies. Justice Robert Jackson made a prudential argument in a dissent in *Terminiello v. City of Chicago* (1949) when he criticized a decision protecting speakers who directed abusive language at their audience. "[I]f the Court does not temper its doctrinaire logic with a little practical wisdom," Jackson warned, "it will convert the constitutional Bill of Rights into a suicide pact." Given several plausible interpretations of the Constitution, prudentialists claim, decision makers should choose the interpretation with the best consequences.

Prudential arguments are often employed when constitutional decision makers believe that their decisions are likely to be disobeyed. Legal scholar Alexander Bickel, a leading proponent of prudentialism, called on justices to avoid hot-button constitutional issues by employing various legal technicalities either to dismiss cases or decide on much narrower grounds.[35] Justice Jackson made this kind of prudential argument in *Korematsu v. United States* (1944) when urging his colleagues, unsuccessfully, to avoid determining the constitutionality of the executive decision detaining Japanese-Americans during World War II. "If we cannot confine military expedients by the Constitution," he wrote, "neither would I distort the Constitution to approve all that the military may deem expedient." The Court was under great pressure to uphold the government's actions. The question for Jackson was how to allow the government to act without creating damaging constitutional precedents.

Aspirationalism. Aspirational arguments interpret constitutional provisions in light of the fundamental principles of justice underlying the Constitution. Ronald Dworkin, the leading proponent of aspirationalism, insists that constitutional decision makers have an obligation to make the Constitution "the best it can be."[36] They do so, he believes, by discerning what general principles best justify American constitutional practice. They then determine whether particular governmental practices are consistent with that normative commitment. Justice William Brennan, a long-time leader of the liberal wing of the Court, was a vocal

35. Alexander M. Bickel, *The Least Dangerous Branch* (Indianapolis: Bobbs-Merrill Company, 1962), 111–98.

36. Ronald Dworkin, *Law's Empire* (Cambridge: Harvard University Press, 1986), 53.

advocate of the aspirationalist approach. In his view, the "Constitution is a sublime oration on the dignity of man, a bold commitment by the people to the ideal of libertarian dignity protected through law." Constitutional interpreters, Brennan believed, should interpret constitutional provisions in light of these aspirations.[37]

Justice Anthony Kennedy's opinion in *Lawrence v. Texas* (2003) provides a good example of an aspirationalist argument. As Scalia did in *Printz*, Kennedy began with a general principle. "In our tradition the State is not omnipresent in the home," he wrote. From these principles, Kennedy deduced that government could not prohibit consenting adults from engaging in private homosexual acts.

The Politics of Constitutional Argument. Scholars debate whether any theory of constitutional decision making actually influences constitutional practice. Two reasons exist for doubting whether constitutional forms actually constrain constitutional arguments. Legitimate constitutional arguments may exist for practically any policy. Two prominent law professors claim, "The range of permissible constitutional arguments now extends so far that a few workable ones are always available in a pinch."[38] Both proponents and opponents of abortion, health care, or federal aid to cities, in this view, can make intellectually respectable constitutional arguments for their preferred policy. Political actors may not make good-faith efforts to interpret the Constitution when they know the best interpretation is inconsistent with their policy preferences. Conservatives charge liberal pro-choice advocates with manufacturing a right to abortion out of thin jurisprudential air. Liberals charge conservatives with grossly distorting precedent in *Bush v. Gore* (2000) in order to hand George W. Bush the 2000 presidential election.

Lawyers and political scientists have developed four different models for thinking about the way judges and other constitutional authorities reach decisions. The attitudinal and strategic models claim that justices are far more concerned with policy than law. The legal model claims that constitutional decision makers place greater emphasis on legal criterion than proponents of the attitudinal or strategic model recognize. Historical institutionalists seek to combine the best insights of the attitudinal, strategic, and legal models of constitutional decision making.

The Attitudinal Model. Many prominent political scientists point to evidence that constitutional arguments do not constrain constitutional decision makers. Jeffrey Segal and Harold Spaeth are the two leading proponents of the attitudinal model of judicial decision making. They insist that Supreme Court decisions are based almost entirely on policy preferences. "Justices," they write, "make decisions by considering the facts of the case in light of their ideological attitudes and values."[39] Supreme Court justices, in this view, are particularly well positioned to act on their ideology and values. Unlike legislators, they cannot easily be held accountable for their decisions by voters or other political actors. Unlike lower court judges, their decisions are not reviewed by other courts and cannot be easily overturned. The cases that reach the Supreme Court are precisely those in which the law is unclear and political values might matter. As a result, justices are likely to decide cases in a manner consistent with their political values.

Proponents of the attitudinal model point out that justices routinely form conservative and liberal voting blocs. These blocs hold together across a range of issues and legal contexts. The same justices who consistently cast liberal votes in free speech cases also cast liberal votes in cases concerning federalism and the meaning of the commerce clause. If they know that the Roberts Court voted 5–4 on some case, that Justice Ruth Bader Ginsburg was in the majority and Justice Clarence Thomas was in the minority, court watchers (and students taking constitutional law classes) can normally predict with a high degree of accuracy how the other seven justices voted.

37. William J. Brennan, "The Constitution of the United States: Contemporary Ratification," *South Texas Law Review* 27 (1986):438.

38. Pamela S. Karlan and Daniel R. Ortiz, "Constitutional Farce," *Constitutional Stupidities, Constitutional Tragedies* (New York: New York University Press, 1998), 180.

39. Jeffrey A. Segal and Harold J. Spaeth, *The Supreme Court and the Attitudinal Model Revisited* (New York: Cambridge University Press, 2002), 110.

Figure 1-1 Left-Right Distribution of Justices, Congress, and President in 1974

Sources: Lee Epstein, Andrew D. Martin, Jeffrey A. Segal, and Chad Westerland, "Judicial Common Space", http://epstein.law.northwestern.edu/research/JCS.html; Keith T. Poole, "Common Space Scores, Congress 75–108," http://voteview.com/basic.htm.

Note: House and Senate reflect the median members of the chamber.

The Supreme Court makes decisions by majority rule, which magnifies the power of the justice occupying the ideological center. Figure 1-1 places the nine justices from most liberal on the left to most conservative on the right, based on their voting behavior during the 1974 Court term. The justices on what was then the Burger Court formed three distinctly visible blocs. Justices William O. Douglas, William Brennan, and Thurgood Marshall occupied the liberal wing. At the other end of the spectrum, Chief Justice Warren Burger and Justice William Rehnquist formed a looser conservative bloc. In the center, Harry Blackmun and Lewis Powell formed a more conservative pairing, and Potter Stewart and Byron White shared space at the median. This alignment was typical. We can see who the swing voters on the Court were and which justices tended to vote together. As important, we can see whose votes were necessary to form a majority. Centrist justices control judicial decision making because the more ideologically extreme justices must appeal to the more moderate justices in order to get the five votes necessary to decide a case. In recent terms, Justice Anthony Kennedy has been in the majority on almost all 5–4 votes because he occupied the center of the Roberts Court on almost all major constitutional issues. This gave Kennedy the power to make his particular constitutional vision the law of the land.

Figure 1-1 also helps us see the potential importance of changing a justice and how policy attitudes influence the judicial selection process. Justice Douglas in 1975 was replaced by John Paul Stevens. Stevens voted just to the left of Stewart. His replacing Douglas meant the Court traded a strong liberal for a centrist liberal. On those issues in which Stevens was the median justice, his appointment meant the Court would hand down more conservative decisions after 1975 than before. That the Republican President Ford and the Democratic Senate in 1975 would agree on a justice more like Stevens than Douglas is not surprising. Stevens had policy views far closer to President Ford and the Senate majority in 1975 than Douglas, who had been appointed by Franklin Roosevelt during the New Deal in 1939.[40]

Changing the composition of the Court has major consequences only when replacements have different values than their predecessors. William Brennan and Thurgood Marshall voted in favor of civil liberty claims more than three-quarters of the time. They consistently supported expanded rights for criminal defendants, a broad right to privacy, robust protections for free speech, and a sharp separation of church and state. When Brennan and Marshall left the bench in the early 1990s, the Court lost major voices (and votes) for constitutional liberalism. Supreme Court decisions moved rightward when Brennan was replaced by the less liberal David Souter and Marshall was replaced by the very conservative Clarence Thomas. The departure

40. By the time of Douglas's departure from the Court in 1975, the Senate had shifted to the left and Gerald Ford had replaced Richard Nixon in the White House. After Watergate, the president was not well positioned to push for a justice closer to his preferences rather than to the Senate's.

of Chief Justice William Rehnquist in 2005 had less influence on the Supreme Court. Rehnquist voted in favor of liberal rights claims less than a quarter of the time.[41] His replacement, John Roberts, was just as conservative a constitutional decision maker.

The Strategic Model. The strategic model suggests that justices seek to achieve their policy preferences by adjusting their behavior to take into account the behavior of other actors. Constitutional decision makers vote and write strategically, rather than sincerely. Persons engage in sincere voting when they vote solely on the basis of their personal preferences. An opponent of the death penalty votes sincerely when voting to declare all death sentences unconstitutional. Persons engage in sophisticated voting or vote strategically when they vote in the way they believe will achieve the best feasible policy under the circumstances. An opponent of the death penalty might sign an opinion holding that capital punishment may be constitutionally imposed, but only when the condemned person was represented at trial by a criminal defense specialist if this was the practical alternative the justice believed would result in the fewest executions.

Majority opinions are often the subject of negotiation among the justices. Justices compromise their best interpretation of the Constitution in order to unite on a view of the law that a majority will find acceptable. Justice Brennan famously joked that with five votes he could do anything. Brennan was not satisfied with voicing his vision of the law in dissent if he could make a majority to implement a slightly less ideal doctrine. Brennan in 1974 could easily write an opinion that would win the support of Thurgood Marshall. The question was how many compromises Brennan would make to win the support of Stewart and White—or even Blackmun or Powell. For example, Brennan believed that laws making gender discriminations should be evaluated using the same strict standard as laws making racial discriminations. Nevertheless, he signed an opinion in *Craig v. Boren* (1976) declaring that gender discriminations would be evaluated using a slightly less strict standard. Brennan did so because he knew the Court using *Craig* precedent would strike down most (not all) gender discriminations he thought unconstitutional. Three-quarters of a loaf, he decided, was better than none.

Justices need the cooperation of colleagues on the bench, lower court judges, legislators, executive branch officials, and ultimately the citizenry to achieve policy and legal goals. Governing officials implement judicial decisions, appoint like-minded justices to the bench, and preserve the constitutional and statutory foundations of judicial independence. Justices interested in making good policy must make accommodations to win that cooperation. As Lee Epstein and Jack Knight observe:

> If their objective is to see their favored policies become the law of the land, they must take into account the preferences of other actors and the actions they expect them to take. Failing to do so may have undesirable consequences: Congress could replace their most preferred position with their least, or the public may refuse to comply with a ruling, in which case their policy fails to take on the force of law.[42]

When justices act too far outside the political mainstream, they invite backlash. After the justices in *Furman v. Georgia* (1972) declared all laws imposing the death penalty unconstitutional, two-thirds of the states passed new death penalty statutes. As a result, more people were executed during the 1980s than during the 1960s. Perhaps a more strategically minded justice should have made a narrower ruling in the *Furman* case. Such a ruling might have prohibited William Furman from being executed, but not declared all death penalty laws unconstitutional.[43]

Considerable evidence exists that justices engage in strategic decision making. The Supreme Court

41. Jeffrey A. Segal, Lee Epstein, Harold J. Spaeth, and Thomas G. Walker, *The Supreme Court Compendium*, 4th ed. (Washington, DC: CQ Press, 2006), 534–35. For details on Rehnquist and Brennan, see Keith E. Whittington, "William H. Rehnquist: Nixon's Strict Constructionist, Reagan's Chief Justice," in *Rehnquist Justice*, ed. Earl M. Maltz (Lawrence: University Press of Kansas, 2003); Frank I. Michelman, *Brennan and Democracy* (Princeton: Princeton University Press, 2005).

42. Lee Epstein and Jack Knight, *The Choices Justices Make* (Washington, DC: CQ Press, 1998), 15.

43. Edward Keynes, with Randall K. Miller, *The Court vs. Congress* (Durham, NC: Duke University Press, 1989); Donald Grier Stephenson Jr., *Campaigns and the Court* (New York: Columbia University Press, 1999), 163–89; Gerald N. Rosenberg, "Judicial Independence and the Reality of Political Power," *Review of Politics* 54 (1992): 369; Lee Epstein and Joseph F. Kobylka, *The Supreme Court and Legal Change* (Chapel Hill, NC: University of North Carolina Press, 1992).

refrained from deciding whether Lincoln's use of martial law during the Civil War was constitutional until after General Lee surrendered. John Marshall refused to issue a writ of mandamus in *Marbury v. Madison* (1803) because he believed that such an order would not be obeyed. Marshall explicitly engaged in strategic behavior when, as a circuit justice, he refused to discuss the constitutionality of a Virginia law forbidding black seaman from entering the state. "I am not fond of butting against a wall in sport," he informed Justice Joseph Story.[44]

The Legal Model. Proponents of the legal model believe that history, text, and precedent influence constitutional decision makers, even when they do not provide answers to all constitutional questions.[45] Legalists ask whether and how legal materials shape and influence judicial outcomes. If Justice Scalia says that judges should be guided by the original meaning of the Constitution, legalists are interested in determining whether he is willing to follow the historical evidence that privileges liberal results. To the extent Scalia remains an originalist when history supports liberal causes, law is influencing his constitutional decisions. In fact, Scalia has shown a real liberal streak in criminal justice cases, sometimes emphasizing historical arguments on behalf of defendant rights. Nevertheless, he has also been criticized for ignoring historical evidence, as with the constitutionality of affirmative action under the Fourteenth Amendment.

American constitutional history is littered with instances in which law influenced constitutional decisions. Felix Frankfurter, before joining the Court, was a prominent proponent of free speech rights. Frankfurter was also committed to judicial restraint. When on the Court, he often voted to sustain what he thought were unwise legislative decisions regulating speech. Abraham Lincoln believed that slavery was an atrocious evil, but he also thought that the Constitution did not allow Congress to interfere with slavery in the states. Lincoln similarly recognized the constitutional authority of the fugitive slave clause. Free state citizens, he claimed throughout his career, were constitutionally obliged to return fugitive slaves to their masters.

Historical Institutionalism. The historical institutionalist school of political science insists that these three models take too narrow a perspective on constitutional decision making.[46] Constitutional authorities are neither automatons that leave all personal considerations out of decisions or single-minded policy entrepreneurs. Rather, historical institutionalists think judges and others try to make the best decision from a value or policy perspective that is permitted by legal text, history, and precedent.

Most constitutional decisions are based on a complex mix of attitudinal, strategic, and legal factors. These factors cannot be neatly isolated. Some constitutional rules permit strategic voting. The justices may deny for any reason a writ of certiorari, the writ needed to have the Supreme Court decide a case. When justices refuse to hear a case they think too politically explosive, they are acting both legally (the law permits them to deny certiorari) and strategically (they are trying to avoid antagonizing elected officials). Many commentators insist that decision makers have a *legal* obligation to act on their best understanding of abstract principles. Justice Thurgood Marshall's insistence that the death penalty was cruel and unusual punishment was simultaneously legal (the law required him to act on his best understanding of "cruel") and attitudinal (Justice Marshall believed capital punishment was unjust).

Historical institutionalists are interested in why people with particular policy preferences and constitutional visions had constitutional authority at a particular time. Rather than ask what particular Supreme Court justices thought about pornography or originalism, they ask why did obscenity issues arise during the time period when those particular justices were on the Court. This approach explains constitutional decisions as consequences of their political, historical, ideological, and institutional contexts. The liberalism of the Warren Court, for instance, was deeply rooted in the liberalism of the New Deal and Great Society coalition

44. John Marshall, quoted in Charles Warren, *The Supreme Court in United States History*, vol. 1 (Boston: Little, Brown, 1922), 86.

45. For an extended discussion, see Lief Carter and Thomas Burke, *Reason in Law*, 8th ed. (New York: Longman, 2009); Howard Gillman, "What's Law Got to Do With It? Judicial Behavioralists Test the 'Legal Model' of Judicial Decision Making," *Law and Social Inquiry* 26 (2001):465.

46. For an extended discussion, see Rogers M. Smith, "Historical Institutionalism and the Study of Law," in *The Oxford Handbook of Law and Politics*, eds. Keith E. Whittington, R. Daniel Kelemen, and Gregory A. Caldeira (New York: Oxford University Press, 2008); Ronald Kahn and Ken I. Kersch, *The Supreme Court and American Political Development* (Lawrence: University Press of Kansas, 2006).

that dominated American politics from 1932 to 1968. Liberals staffed the Supreme Court because liberals controlled the branches of the national government that appointed and confirmed Supreme Court justices. Constitutional decisions in the nineteenth century were as rooted in political and social contexts. Justice Brown, when sustaining laws mandating racial segregation in *Plessy v. Ferguson* (1897), wrote that "[l]egislation is powerless to eradicate racial instincts, or to abolish distinctions based upon physical differences." His decision was rooted in the common assumption of the time that "stateways cannot change folkways."

Both historical and institutional factors influence constitutional practice. History creates some constitutional options while foreclosing others. Consider the reason why states at present may not violate free speech rights. An initial reading of the Constitution might suggest that the provision in the Fourteenth Amendment prohibiting states from abridging the "privileges and immunities" of American citizens provides the best grounds for declaring unconstitutional state restrictions on free speech. A series of precedents dating from the *Slaughter-House Cases* (1873) foreclosed that constitutional basis for protecting political dissent. During the early twentieth century, a different line of precedents interpreted the due process clause of the Fourteenth Amendment as protecting fundamental rights. For this reason, free-speech advocates at present speak of "due process" rather than "privileges and immunities" when challenging the constitutionality of state measures that restrict expression. Institutional positions similarly influence constitutional perspectives. Justices are more familiar with the criminal process than other governing officials. Perhaps for this reason, judges have historically cared more about the rights of criminal suspects than have elected officials. Judges are also, unsurprisingly, more committed to the constitutional powers of the federal courts than legislators or members of the executive branch.

IV. Constitutional Authority

Throughout this book, you will see constitutional disputes arise and be settled. One such dispute is whether the Constitution permits a person to be executed. Another dispute was whether President Jefferson had the constitutional authority to purchase Louisiana from France. In each case, some governing official, governing institution, or governing officials had to determine authoritatively whether a proposed action was constitutional. That decision need not have established a principle that binds all constitutional actors for all time. Sometimes, there is a virtue in "leaving things undecided."[47] Nevertheless, what to do in the immediate present must always be resolved. Some decisions cannot be reversed. Whether a condemned prisoner may be executed without delay cannot be left unsettled, even if future controversies over capital punishment are decided differently. Americans who believe that President Jefferson acted unconstitutionally when purchasing Louisiana cannot easily declare that the regions west of the Mississippi River are no longer a part of the United States.

Everyone interprets the Constitution, but not everyone has the authority to settle constitutional disputes. In principle, any of the three branches of government could be the ultimate interpreter of the Constitution.[48] Prominent Americans before the Civil War insisted that individual states had the power to determine whether national legislation was constitutional. After the Civil War, most persons abandoned claims that states, the national executive, or the national legislature had the power to settle constitutional disputes. Judicial review, the judicial power to declare laws unconstitutional, is now entrenched. How that power can be justified and how courts should exercise that power remains unsettled.

Debates about constitutional authority for the past 150 years have been between proponents of two doctrines—*judicial supremacy* and *departmentalism*. Proponents of each view offer competing understandings of democracy and constitutionalism. Proponents of judicial supremacy emphasize the fundamental constitutional commitment to limited government. Proponents of departmentalism emphasize the fundamental democratic commitment to majority rule.

Judicial Supremacy. Most Americans support judicial supremacy, the view that the Supreme Court is the institution authorized to resolve disputes over the Constitution. With few exceptions, Supreme Court

47. See Cass R. Sunstein, *One Case at a Time* (Cambridge: Harvard University Press, 1999).

48. Mechanisms, such as constitutional amendments or referenda, that would put this role outside the three branches of government are also possible.

justices have aggressively asserted that their institution has the final authority to determine what the Constitution means. Judicial supremacy includes the judicial power to ignore unconstitutional acts when resolving specific cases, and the judicial power to establish principles that bind all other actors. When state officials in Arkansas questioned the correctness of *Brown v. Board of Education* (1954), Chief Justice Earl Warren treated them to a stern civics lecture. "The federal judiciary is supreme in the exposition of the law of the Constitution," he stated, "and that principle has ... been respected by this Court and the Country as a permanent and indispensable feature of our constitutional system."[49]

Proponents claim that judicial supremacy is a necessary ingredient of constitutionalism. If the Constitution is fundamental law, they believe, then the primary responsibility for interpreting the Constitution should be vested in the institution responsible for interpreting the law, the judiciary. As Justice Kennedy recently asserted, "If Congress could define its own powers by altering the Fourteenth Amendment's meaning, no longer would the Constitution be 'superior paramount law, unchangeable by ordinary means.'"[50]

Departmentalism. Departmentalists believe that all institutions have an equal right to interpret the Constitution. Most favor judicial review, the judicial power to make constitutional decisions that bind the particular parties before the court. Proponents of departmentalism reject the position that elected officials must always adhere to the principles justices announce in those decisions. They maintain that the judicial supremacy subverts constitutionalism by inviting politicians to ignore their constitutional responsibilities and allowing unchecked judges to warp constitutional principles through abuse and misinterpretation.

Throughout American history, prominent political leaders have asserted an equal right to constitutional authority. James Madison explained, "As the legislative, executive, and judicial departments are co-ordinate, and each equally bound to support the Constitution, it follows that each must, in the exercise of its functions, be guided by the text of the Constitution according to its own interpretation of it."[51] President Lincoln vigorously denied that his administration had a constitutional obligation to respect *Dred Scott v. Sandford* (1856), which ruled that the federal government could not ban slavery in the territories. "The candid citizen must confess that if the policy of the government ... is to be irrevocably fixed by decisions of the Supreme Court," he contended in first inaugural, "the people will have ceased to be their own rulers." Lincoln thought that his administration was bound by the legal decision in the court case between Dred Scott and John Sanford. Lincoln admitted that his government could not forcibly free Dred Scott if the courts held that he was legally bound. But the government did not have to accept the "political rule" that the Supreme Court had laid down in the case. When in power, Republicans did not hesitate to ban slavery in the federal territories and the District of Columbia.

The Countermajoritarian Difficulty. Debates over constitutional authority for the last fifty years have been shaped by a concern with what has become known as "the countermajoritarian difficulty." Alexander Bickel introduced this problem to American constitutionalism when he declared, "[W]hen the Supreme Court declares unconstitutional a legislative act or the action of an elected executive, it thwarts the will of representatives of the actual people of the here and now; it exercises control, not in behalf of the prevailing majority, but against it."[52] Bickel and others regard judicial review as antidemocratic because the practice empowers a small, elite body of electorally unaccountable individuals to undo the policies that have emerged from the democratic process. Judicial review is also undemocratic, they think, because the justices often assume that they should resist democratic majorities and their policy preferences.

Proponents of judicial power offer several responses to the countermajoritarian difficulty. One approach provides a democratic foundation for judicial review. Arguments in this vein contend that the courts should use the power of judicial review only to enforce

---

49. *Cooper v. Aaron*, 358 U.S. 1, 18 (1958).

50. *City of Boerne v. Flores*, 521 U.S. 507, 529 (1997). For a leading scholarly defense of judicial supremacy, see Larry Alexander and Frederick Schauer, "On Extrajudicial Constitutional Interpretation," *Harvard Law Review* 110 (1997):1359.

51. James Madison, "To Mr. __, 1834," in *Letters and Other Writings of James Madison*, vol. 4 (Philadelphia: J.B. Lippincott, 1867), 349.

52. Bickel, 17.

principles that the people have clearly endorsed.[53] A second approach claims judicial review makes democracy work better. Judges act democratically, in this view, when they prevent politicians from silencing critics. Chief Justice Harlan Fiske Stone argued that "legislation which restricts those political processes which can ordinarily be expected to bring about repeal of undesirable legislation" should "be subjected to more exacting judicial scrutiny" than other types of legislation.[54] A third approach embraces the antidemocratic character of courts. In this view, majority rule is not the only political value that our society should protect and uphold. Judges should stand up for substantively important rights and values, even when those values are not popular.[55]

Critics of judicial power are more skeptical of these efforts to reconcile democracy and judicial review. Some argue that the courts should exercise "judicial restraint" and use the power of judicial review only when the political branches have made a clear constitutional mistake.[56] Others argue that "the people" should play a more active role in constitutional interpretation and in checking judges.[57] A few voices contend that judicial review cannot be squared with democracy. Jeremy Waldron concludes, "When citizens or their representatives disagree about what rights we have or what those rights entail, it seems something of an insult to say that this is not something they are to be permitted to sort out by majoritarian processes, but that the issue is to be assigned instead for final determination to a small group of judges."[58]

Counter-Majoritarian, Majoritarian, or Non-Majoritarian. Many political scientists question whether the countermajoritarian difficulty provides the right framework for thinking about constitutional authority and judicial power. They think judicial decisions are (almost) as consistent with majoritarian sentiments as decisions made by other governing officials. A half century ago Robert Dahl observed that "it would appear ... somewhat unrealistic to suppose that a Court whose members are recruited in the fashion of Supreme Court Justices would long hold to norms of Right or Justice substantially at odds with the rest of the political elite."[59] Both political and sociological factors explain the judicial tendency to remain in the mainstream of American politics. Federal judges are nominated and confirmed through a political process. Presidents are unlikely to select individuals for the bench whose constitutional philosophies are at odds with their own. When liberals control the White House and Senate, as they did in the 1930s and 1960s, they appoint liberals to the Supreme Court. When conservatives hold greater sway, as they did in the 1920s and 1980s, they appoint conservatives to the Court. With some lag, the center of the Court tends to sit in the political mainstream of the particular historical era. The *Dred Scott* case reflected the pro-slavery and racist views of the reigning Jacksonian majority. Moreover, the sitting justices tend to share the common prejudices and values of their time. As Justice Benjamin Cardozo observed, the "great tides and currents which engulf the rest of men do not turn aside in their course and pass the judges by."[60] The Supreme Court became more liberal on race at approximately the same time most American elites became more liberal on race.

The Court does not simply stand outside or against political movements. The same events that move electoral politics often move the courts, though often at different speeds and times. Figure 1-2 maps the overall liberal tendency of public opinion and the liberalism of Supreme Court decisions in the latter half of the twentieth century.[61] The Court followed the public's more conservative mood in the 1970s, although judicial deci-

---

53. This was Bickel's own solution to the difficulty. For some recent efforts of this sort, see Bruce Ackerman, *We the People* (Cambridge: Harvard University Press, 1991); Keith E. Whittington, *Constitutional Interpretation* (Lawrence: University Press of Kansas, 1999).

54. *United States v. Carolene Products Co.*, 304 U.S. 144, 152n4 (1938). The classic scholarly elaboration of this argument is John Hart Ely, *Democracy and Distrust* (Cambridge: Harvard University Press, 1980).

55. See Ronald Dworkin, *A Matter of Principle* (Cambridge: Harvard University Press, 1985).

56. A modern version of this view can be found in Robert H. Bork, *The Tempting of America* (New York: Free Press, 1990).

57. See Larry D. Kramer, *The People Themselves* (New York: Oxford University Press, 2004).

58. Jeremy Waldron, *Law and Disagreement* (New York: Oxford University Press, 1999), 15.

59. Robert A. Dahl, "Decision making in a Democracy: The Supreme Court as a National Policy Maker," *Journal of Public Law* 6 (1957):291.

60. Benjamin N. Cardozo, *The Nature of the Judicial Process* (New Haven: Yale University Press, 1921), 168.

61. See also Kevin T. McGuire and James A. Stimson, "The Least Dangerous Branch Revisited: New Evidence on Supreme Court Responsiveness to Public Preferences," *Journal of Politics* 66 (2004):1018.

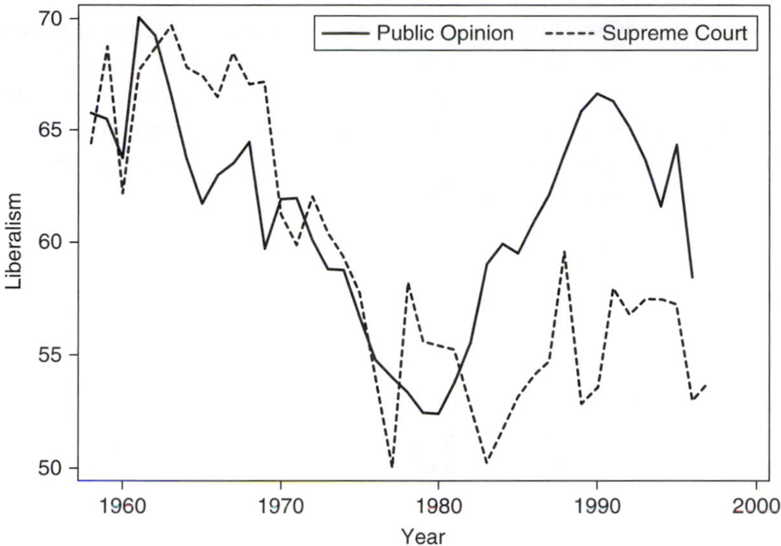

Figure 1-2 The Supreme Court and Public Opinion, 1957–1997

Source: Kevin T. McGuire, "The Least Dangerous Branch Revisited," Replication Data, http://www.unc.edu/~kmcguire/data.opinion.zip. Copyright © Cambridge University Press 2011.

Note: The two series are a public mood score and percentage of Supreme Court decisions in a liberal direction in cases reversing lower courts across three issue domains. The two series are scaled to public mood for presentation.

sion did not turn as sharply in a more liberal direction as public opinion did in the late 1980s and early 1990s.

When justices declare laws unconstitutional, they are often acting consistently with values shared by members of the dominant political coalition. Elected officials frequently encourage the Court to exercise the power of judicial review and to take the lead in interpreting the Constitution. Congress during the 1850s passed legislation facilitating a judicial decision on the constitutional status of slavery in the territories. Political leaders lay the groundwork for the justices to develop particular lines of doctrine. Archibald Cox, the solicitor general for the Kennedy Administration, developed the arguments used by the Supreme Court in *Baker v. Carr* (1962) in support of giving courts the power to determine whether malapportioned state legislatures violated the equal protection clause. The Court often acts when there are divisions among political leaders over the policy at issue or relatively little political support for the policy that is being struck down. The judicial majority in *Lawrence v. Texas* (2003), when ruling that consenting adults had a right to same-sex intimate behavior, pointed out that the vast majority of states had already repealed prohibitions on gay and lesbian behavior. Judicial review still raises important and difficult questions, but the politics of judicial review is more complicated than the countermajoritarian image of an isolated Court standing up against a united political majority.[62]

The Politics of Constitutional Authority. For more than two hundred years, Americans have witnessed contests for constitutional authority. Sometimes these struggles pit judges against elected officials. More often, elected officials empower the courts to interpret the Constitution. They staff courts with justices willing

62. See, for example, Mark A. Graber, "The Non-Majoritarian Difficulty: Legislative Deference to the Judiciary," *Studies in American Political Development* 7 (1993): 35; Howard Gillman, "How Parties Can Use the Courts to Advance Their Agendas: Federal Courts in the United States, 1875–1891," *American Political Science Review* 96 (2002): 511; Keith E. Whittington, "'Interpose Your Friendly Hand': Political Foundations of Judicial Review by the United States Supreme Court," *American Political Science Review* 99 (2005):583.

to declare limits on government power. They pass laws making constitutional challenges to federal and state laws easier. They pass vague legislation that may force courts to make policy in the guise of statutory or constitutional interpretation. Presidents do not nominate individuals to the Supreme Court who are pledged to uphold all laws against constitutional challenge.

Elected officials have various reasons for supporting judicial power. National government officials may want to keep local political majorities in line. Political moderates may want to avoid difficult decisions that divide their political coalitions. Party leaders with a tenuous hold on elected office may want to ensure that courts will protect their interests when they are out of power. As you read later chapters, you should consider whose interests are being served by appeals to the courts. You should also consider the implications of the judiciary's actions for other political actors.

Struggles for constitutional authority do not end when the judiciary speaks. Justices do not enforce their decrees. Elected officials often do not comply with constitutional orders in cases they believe wrongly decided. "Where there is local hostility to change," Gerald Rosenberg concludes, "court orders will be ignored." In his view, "community pressure, violence, or threats of violence, and lack of market response all serve to curtail actions to implement court decisions."[63] Many famous judicial decisions declaring laws unconstitutional had almost no immediate consequence. Ten years after *Brown v. Board of Education* was decided, less than 2 percent of African-American children in the Deep South were attending integrated schools.[64] Judicial decisions prohibiting state organized prayer in public schools had little immediate effect on that religious practice in schools across the United States.[65]

Judicial decisions shape, but do not end, political struggles over constitutional meaning. Political movements hardly ever fold their tents after judicial defeats. The Republican Party after *Dred Scott* remained committed to prohibiting slavery in the territories. Contemporary pro-life forces remain committed to reversing Supreme Court decisions prohibiting bans on abortion. Contemporary pro-choice forces remain committed to reversing Supreme Court decisions sustaining regulations on abortion. Constitutional conflicts are settled politically, not legally. Constitutional politics come to an end only when the forces backing the losing issue concede defeat and lose political interest in the issue.

V. Constitutional Change

Problems of constitutional change seem simpler than problems of constitutional interpretation and authority. "The Ratification of the Conventions of Nine States," Article VII plainly declares, "shall be sufficient for the Establishment of this Constitution between the States so ratifying the Same." Article V declares that when two-thirds of both Houses propose a constitutional amendment, that amendment becomes constitutional law if ratified by three-fourths of all State legislatures or by Conventions in three-fourths of all states, with Congress choosing the mode of state ratification. Two-thirds of the States may call a convention to propose amendments that, again, must be ratified by three-quarters of all states. These apparently plain requirements for ratification and amendment, however, mask difficult issues.

Creating Constitutions. Constitutions do not become authoritative sources of fundamental law merely because their stated conditions for ratification are satisfied. Otherwise, the authors of this book could write a new Constitution of the United States and condition legitimacy on our approval plus the approval of our five best friends. Federalists in 1787 acknowledged that their proposal to require ratification by nine states was quite different from the unanimous state approval for constitutional change set out in the Articles of Confederation. James Madison in *Federalist* 40 maintained that popular ratification compensated for any legal irregularities in the drafting process. The persons who framed the Constitution of the United States, he wrote,

> must have reflected, that ... since it is impossible for the people spontaneously and universally to move in concert towards their object; and it is therefore essential that such changes be instituted by some INFORMAL AND UNAUTHORIZED PROPOSITIONS, made by some patriotic and respectable citizen or number of citizens.... They must have borne in mind, that as the plan to be framed and

63. Gerald N. Rosenberg, *The Hollow Hope* (Chicago: University of Chicago Press, 1991), 337.

64. Rosenberg, 50.

65. Kenneth M. Dolbeare and Phillip E. Hammond, *The School Prayer Decisions* (Chicago: University of Chicago Press, 1971).

> proposed was to be submitted TO THE PEOPLE THEMSELVES, the disapprobation of this supreme authority would destroy it forever; its approbation blot out antecedent errors and irregularities.[66]

Akhil Amar has suggested that a new constitution would be legitimate today if a bare majority of American voters signed a petition for a national constitutional convention, a majority of the delegates at that convention approved the constitution, and that constitution was then approved by a national electoral majority.[67] Amar and Madison recognize that constitutions take hold and are considered legitimate because they are embraced by the people and accepted as legitimate, not because constitutional founders followed preexisting rules for constitutional change.

Limits on Constitutional Change. Conventional wisdom in the United States insists that Americans are free to adopt any constitutional amendment that does not abolish state equality in the Senate. Justice Frank Murphy in *Schneiderman v. United States* (1943) insisted that the constitutional amendment process allows citizens to fundamentally alter the constitutional regime, including transforming the United States into a communist dictatorship. "Article V," he wrote, "contains procedural provisions for constitutional change by amendment without any present limitation whatsoever except that no State may be deprived of equal representation in the Senate without its consent."[68] On this view, Americans could amend the constitution to establish a state religion or a monarchy.

Walter Murphy disagrees. He points out that the "word *amend* comes from the Latin *emendere*, to correct." For this reason, Murphy maintains, "abolishing constitutional democracy and substituting a different system would not be an amendment at all, but a re-creation, a re-forming, not simply of political structures but also of the people themselves."[69] On this view, not even a supermajority could constitutionally repeal the free speech clause or the Thirteenth Amendment's prohibition of slavery.

This possibility of unconstitutional constitutional amendments is not hypothetical outside of the United States. Constitutional courts in Germany, Nepal, South Africa, and India have declared constitutional amendments void on the ground that they are inconsistent with fundamental constitutional principles. Some Americans have sought to persuade the Supreme Court to make similar decisions. Opponents of the Nineteenth Amendment, which gave women the right to vote, asserted that principles of federalism implied that a majority of states could not change the voting requirements in states that did not ratify that amendment. The Supreme Court rebuffed this claim in *Leser v. Garnett* (1922).

Amending the Constitution Outside of Article V. Whether Article V provides the only procedures for constitutional amendment is controversial. Bruce Ackerman maintains that a combination of political mobilization, elections, judicial decisions, and "superstatutes" should be treated as valid constitutional amendments. The Jeffersonian victory in 1800, the success of the New Deal in 1930s, and the victory of the civil rights movement in the 1960s are all examples of "constitutional moments." The policies adopted during these periods of sweeping political change, Ackerman thinks, should trump the constitutional text. Future judges should take their guidance from these policies as if they were written into the Constitution.[70]

Ackerman's critics insist that Article V sets out the exclusive processes for constitutional amendment. As one critic argues, the constitutional provisions for amendment are "an example of yet another text the meaning of which is essentially clear." Permitting committed popular majorities to amend the constitution without going through the Article V process might weaken the constitutional commitment to liberty. "If the Constitution is to continue to be the ultimate source that protects individual rights against encroachment by government power and political majorities," David Dow contends, "then the affirmative words in Article V must be understood to negative other conceivable modes of amendment."[71]

---

66. Madison, "No. 40," 253.

67. Akhil Reed Amar, "Amending the Constitution Outside Article V," *University of Chicago Law Review* 55 (1988):1064–65.

68. *Schneiderman v. United States*, 320 U.S. 118, 137 (1943).

69. Walter F. Murphy, *Constitutional Democracy* (Baltimore: Johns Hopkins University Press, 2007), 506.

70. Bruce Ackerman, *We the People* (Cambridge: Harvard University Press, 1991).

71. David R. Dow, "The Plain Meaning of Article V," in *Responding to Imperfection*, ed. Sanford Levinson (Princeton: Princeton University Press, 1995), 127.

Constitutional Change without Constitutional Amendments. Constitutional changes do not always require constitutional amendment. The framers recognized that time would clarify some constitutional meanings. "All new laws, though penned with the greatest technical skill, and passed on the fullest and most mature deliberation," Madison wrote in *Federalist* 37, "are considered as more or less obscure and equivocal, until their meaning be liquidated and ascertained by a series of particular discussions and adjudications." The Constitution left undefined how executive-branch officials were to be removed from office. Presidential power to cashier an executive branch employee was debated by the First Congress and not clearly settled until the twentieth century. The understanding that federal judges should not engage in partisan politics dates from the failed impeachment of Justice Samuel Chase in 1805, not the drafting of Article III of the Constitution in 1787. New practices and principles may take on constitutional significance, such as the tradition that presidents would serve no more than two terms of office. When Franklin Roosevelt violated that tradition, Americans quickly formalized the prohibition by ratifying the Twenty-Second Amendment.

The status of state-mandated segregation in the United States provides a good example for thinking about the nature of constitutional change. In 1900, all but a few well-trained lawyers thought that state-mandated racial segregation was an acceptable practice under the equal protection clause of the Fourteenth Amendment. Within two decades after *Brown v. Board of Education* (1954), every well-trained lawyer recognized that government-sponsored racial segregation was hardly ever constitutionally valid. Effective constitutional requirements had radically changed, but no new constitutional text had been adopted.

Consider the different ways of describing this change in constitutional practice. Some would argue that "the Constitution" had not changed, but earlier judges, government officials and lawyers had simply misinterpreted the equal protection clause. Others would argue that the underlying constitutional principles stayed the same, but the implications of those constitutional principles changed over time given new circumstances or even new thinking. The Constitution does not change, in this view, but doctrines applying the Constitution do. Americans learned that separate was not equal. Still others would argue that the Court and other constitutional decision makers simply changed the constitutional rules. Perhaps the segregation question was like the question of executive removal, a matter to be "liquidated and ascertained" after a series of adjudications such as *Brown*. Perhaps segregation was acceptable under the original Fourteenth Amendment and *Brown* was part of a process of altering the meaning of that amendment.

The Merits of Constitutional Change. The framers debated the virtues of frequent constitutional change. Most believed fundamental constitutional change should be difficult. Prominent founders declared that constitutional change should take place only when society agreed on the constitutional flaw to be repaired. James Madison worried that frequent constitutional changes or constitutional conventions would "deprive the government of that veneration which time bestows on every thing."[72] His friend Thomas Jefferson thought constitutional change should take place more often. Jefferson declared, "Laws and institutions must go hand in hand with the progress of the human mind." In Jefferson's view, "as new discoveries are made, new truths disclosed, and manners and opinions change with the change of circumstances, institutions must advance also, and keep pace with the times."[73]

These debates over the merits of frequent constitutional change remain vibrant. Contemporary Madisonians insist that experience demonstrates why constitutions should be difficult to amend. Kathleen Sullivan writes,

> it is a bad idea to politicize the Constitution. The very idea of a constitution turns on the separation of the legal and political realms. The Constitution sets up the framework of government. It also sets forth a few fundamental political ideas (equality, representation, individual liberties) that place limits on how far any temporary majority may go. This is our higher law. All the rest is left to politics. Losers in the short run yield to the winners out of respect for the constitutional framework set up for the long run. This makes the peaceful conduction of ordinary politics possible. Without such respect for the constitutional framework, politics would degenerate into fractious war. But the more a constitution is politicized, the

72. Madison, "No. 49," 314.

73. Jefferson, "To Samuel Kercheval, July 12, 1816," in *Writings*, 10:43.

> less it operates as a fundamental charter of government. The more a constitution is amended, the more it seems like ordinary legislation.[74]

Contemporary Jeffersonians insist on a more majoritarian process for constitutional change. Sanford Levinson condemns "the ability of thirteen houses in as many states to block constitutional amendments desired by the overwhelming majority of Americans as well as, possibly, eighty-six out of the ninety-nine legislative houses in the American states.... [N]o other country—nor, for that matter, any of the fifty American states," he observes, "makes it so difficult to amend its constitution."[75] Both Sullivan and Levinson agree that the Constitution of the United States is presently one of the most difficult and most rarely amended constitutions still in use.[76] They dispute whether this longevity is a virtue.

VI. Constitutional Politics and Law

Constitutions work (when they work) not by announcing clear rules that people can simply obey, but by constraining, constructing, and constituting politics. Constitutions *constrain* politics when citizens and governing officials subordinate their policy preferences to constitutional norms. Constitutions *construct* politics when citizens and governing officials follow the rules that determine whose policy preferences and constitutional understandings are the official law of the land. Constitutions *constitute* politics when citizens and elected officials internalize constitutional values, so that they regard constitutional processes as the only legitimate means for resolving legal and policy disputes.

In healthy constitutional regimes, the constructive and constitutive functions play a far greater role than the constraining function. The Constitution shapes politics by creating a language for talking and thinking about such issues as abortion. Instead of discussing "Should abortion be legal?" we discuss "Should *Roe* be overruled?" and "Does the due process clause of the Fourteenth Amendment encompass the right to terminate a pregnancy?" and "Do women need a right to abortion to enjoy the equal protection of those laws?" These questions are answered by governing officials selected according to constitutional rules. The Supreme Court established by Article III decides whether to overrule *Roe*. The president established by Article II nominates Supreme Court justices. The Senate established by Article I confirms those nominations. Candidates for those offices articulate very different constitutional visions on the campaign trail. These visions include beliefs about whether *Roe* and other cases were rightly decided, but also beliefs about legitimate methods of constitutional decision making, about what institutions have the right to make authoritative constitutional decisions, and about the legitimate forms of constitutional change. Who decides whether *Roe* should be overruled depends both on ordinary partisan processes and on the rules laid out by the Constitution. A Senate whose members are elected in particular states may have very different views about abortion than a Senate whose members were elected by a national majority.

In the past fifty years, countries as diverse as Nepal, South Africa, Hungary, and Israel have ratified new constitutions and established institutions for implementing them. Most have adopted such features as a Bill of Rights and judicial review.[77] Few countries have as strict a separation of powers as the United States or as difficult an amendment process. Whether these constitutions will endure is an open question. In sharp contrast to the Constitution of the United States, which is over two hundred years old, the average national constitution lasts only seventeen years.[78]

These developments abroad cast light on American constitutionalism. By comparison with other nations, we can become more aware of our own assumptions. Often in this book, you will encounter assertions that some distinctive American practice is necessary

---

74. Kathleen Sullivan, "What's Wrong with Constitutional Amendments?" in *The New Federalist Papers* (New York: W.W. Norton, 1997), 63–64.

75. Levinson, *Our Undemocratic Constitution*, 7, 160.

76. Donald S. Lutz, "Toward a Theory of Constitutional Amendment," *American Political Science Review* 88 (1994):355.

77. The specific form of constitutional review adopted in most other countries differs from the American form of judicial review, however. Most nations have created a specific constitutional court separate from their regular judicial system, operating under different rules, and usually staffed with more politically accountable officials.

78. Zachary Elkins, Thomas Ginsburg, and James Melton, *The Endurance of National Constitutions* (New York: Cambridge University Press, 2009).

for human flourishing, the rule of law, or preventing tyranny. That may not always be true. Constitutional democracies that do without judicial supremacy or federalism do not routinely send dissenters to the gulag or execute more innocent people than the United States. Constitutional practices in the United States may nevertheless fit Americans best, even if they are not rooted in universal norms. Comparative analysis may shed light on the political and social factors that explain why practices that are good for Americans may nevertheless not be easy to export to other countries. We may also learn that some foreign constitutional practices may thrive on American soil.

Veneration must be earned. Whether we should venerate the Constitution of the United States depends on the results of a close encounter with the American constitutional experience. The first step is to know how the American constitutionalism system has operated over time, what purposes and interests that system has served, how that system has been maintained, and how that system has been reformed. This is what we hope to illuminate in the chapters to come.

Suggested Readings

Ackerman, Bruce A. "The Living Constitution," *Harvard Law Review* 120 (2007):1737.

Ackerman, Bruce A. *We the People: Foundations*. (Cambridge, MA: Harvard University Press, 1991).

Balkin, Jack M., and Sanford A. Levinson, "Understanding the Constitutional Revolution," *Virginia Law Review* 87 (2001):1045.

Barber, Sotirios A. *On What the Constitution Means*. (Baltimore, MD: Johns Hopkins University Press, 1983).

Barber, Sotirios A., and Robert P. George, eds., *Constitutional Politics: Essays on Constitutional Making, Maintenance, and Change*. (Princeton, NJ: Princeton University Press, 2001).

Barnett, Randy. *Restoring the Lost Constitution: The Presumption of Liberty*. (Princeton, NJ: Princeton University Press, 2004).

Bickel, Alexander M. *The Least Dangerous Branch: The Supreme Court at the Bar of Politics*. (Indianapolis: IN: Bobbs-Merrill Company, 1962).

Clayton, Cornell W., and Howard Gillman, eds., *Supreme Court Decision Making: New Institutionalist Approaches*. (Chicago: University of Chicago Press, 1999).

Dahl, Robert A. "Decision making in a Democracy: The Supreme Court as a National Policymaker," *Journal of Public Law* 6 (1957):279.

Devins, Neal, and Louis Fisher, *The Democratic Constitution*. (New York: Oxford University Press, 2004).

Dworkin, Ronald. *Law's Empire*. (Cambridge, MA: Harvard University Press, 1986).

Dworkin, Ronald. *Taking Rights Seriously*. (Cambridge, MA: Harvard University Press, 1977).

Ely, John Hart. *Democracy and Distrust: A Theory of Judicial Review*. (Cambridge, MA: Harvard University Press, 1980).

Epp, Charles. *The Rights Revolution: Lawyers, Activists, and Supreme Courts in Comparative Perspectives*. (Chicago: University of Chicago Press, 1998).

Epstein, Lee, and Jack Knight. *The Choices Justices Make*. (Washington, DC: CQ Press, 1998).

Eskridge, William N., and Sanford A. Levinson. *Constitutional Stupidities, Constitutional Tragedies*. (New York: New York University Press, 1998).

Fisher, Louis. *Constitutional Dialogues: Interpretation as Political Process*. (Princeton, NJ: Princeton University Press, 1988).

Friedman, Barry. "Dialogue and Judicial Review," *Michigan Law Review* 91 (1993):577–682.

Gillman, Howard. "How Political Parties Can Use the Courts to Advance Their Agendas: Federal Courts in the United States, 1875–1891," *American Political Science Review* 96 (2002):511

Ginsburg, Thomas. *Judicial Review in New Democracies: Constitutional Courts in Asian Cases*. (New York: Cambridge University Press, 2003).

Graber, Mark A. *Dred Scott and the Problem of Constitutional Evil*. (New York: Cambridge University Press, 2006).

Graber, Mark A. "The Non-Majoritarian Difficulty: Legislative Deference to the Judiciary," *Studies in American Political Development* 7 (1993):35–73.

Griffith, Stephen. *American Constitutionalism: From Theory to Practice*. (Princeton, NJ: Princeton University Press, 1996).

Holmes, Stephen. *Passions and Constraint*. (Chicago: University of Chicago Press, 1995).

Kahn, Ronald, and Ken I. Kersch, eds. *The Supreme Court and American Political Development*. (Lawrence: University Press of Kansas, 2006).

Keck, Tom. "Party, Policy, or Duty: Why Does the Supreme Court Invalidate Federal Statutes?" *American Political Science Review* 101(2007):321.

Kersch, Ken I. *Constructing Civil Liberties: Discontinuities in the Development of American Constitutional Law*. (New York: Cambridge University Press, 2004).

Klarman, Michael. *From Jim Crow to Civil Rights: The Supreme Court and the Struggle for Racial Equality*. (New York: Oxford University Press, 2004).

Kramer, Larry D. *The People Themselves: Popular Constitutionalism and Judicial Review*. (New York: Oxford University Press, 2004).

Levinson, Sanford A., ed. *Responding to Imperfection: The Theory and Practice of Constitutional Amendment*. (Princeton, NJ: Princeton, 1995).

Levinson, Sanford A. *Our Undemocratic Constitution: Where the Constitution Goes Wrong (and How We the People Can Correct It)*. (New York: Oxford University Press, 2006).

McIlwain, Charles Howard. *Constitutionalism: Ancient and Modern*. Rev. Ed. (Ithaca, NY: Cornell University Press, 1947).

McMahon, Kevin. *Reconsidering Roosevelt on Race: How the Presidency Paved the Road to* Brown. (Chicago: University of Chicago Press, 2003).

North, Douglas, and Barry Weingast, "Constitutions and Commitment: The Evolution of Institutions Governing Public Choice in Seventeenth-Century England," *Journal of Economic History* 49 (1989):803.

Peretti, Terri Jennings. *In Defense of a Political Court*. (Princeton, NJ: Princeton University Press, 2001).

Rosenberg, Gerald N. *The Hollow Hope: Can Courts Bring about Social Change?* 2nd ed. (Chicago: University of Chicago Press, 2008).

Scalia, Antonin. *A Matter of Interpretation: Federal Courts and the Law*. (Princeton, NJ: Princeton University Press, 1997).

Schauer, Frederick. *Playing by the Rules: A Philosophical Examination of Rule-Based Decision making in Law and in Life*. (New York: Oxford University Press, 1991).

Schweber, Howard. *The Language of Liberal Constitutionalism*. (New York: Cambridge University Press, 2007).

Segal, Jeffrey A., and Harold J. Spaeth, *The Supreme Court and the Attitudinal Model Revisited*. (New York: Cambridge University Press, 2002).

Sunstein, Cass A. *One Case at a Time: Judicial Minimalism on the Supreme Court*. (Cambridge, MA: Harvard University Press, 1999).

Tamanaha, Brian. *On the Rule of Law: History, Politics, Theory*. (New York: Cambridge University Press, 2004).

Tushnet, Mark A. *Taking the Constitution Away From the Courts*. (Princeton, NJ: Princeton University Press, 1999).

Tushnet, Mark A. *Weak Courts, Strong Rights: Judicial Review and Social Welfare Rights in Comparative Constitutional Law*. (Princeton, NJ: Princeton University Press, 2007).

Waldron, Jeremy. *Law and Disagreement*. (New York: Oxford University Press, 1999).

Whittington, Keith E. *Constitutional Construction: Divided Powers and Constitutional Meaning*. (Cambridge, MA: Harvard University Press, 1999).

Whittington, Keith E. *Constitutional Interpretation: Textual Meaning, Original Intent, and Judicial Review*. (Lawrence, KA: University Press of Kansas, 1999).

Whittington, Keith E. *Political Foundations of Judicial Supremacy: The Presidency, the Supreme Court, and Constitutional Leadership in U.S. History*. (Princeton, NJ: Princeton University Press, 2007).

Part 2 **Development**

Chapter 2

The Colonial Era: Before 1776

I. Introduction

American constitutionalism had a history even before fifty-five men assembled in Philadelphia in 1787 to draft a new federal constitution. There were constitutional debates in America even before there was a United States. The origins of American constitutionalism lie in colonial experience and in British traditions, Enlightenment thought, and classical and religious influences.

The thirteen colonies that would become the United States were established in three different ways. The *royal colonies*, the most common, were ruled directly by the British crown through appointed governors. *Proprietary colonies* were the products of royal grants to private owners (such as William Penn [1644–1718] in Pennsylvania), who established a local government of their choosing. Finally, *corporate colonies* were based on royal charters to self-governing settlers.

Despite these differences, the colonies shared some basic features. The American colonists were British subjects, and they shared the rights and privileges of British subjects, under the constitution of the British Empire. Each colony developed elected assemblies to make local policy (usually joined by an upper house selected by a royal governor). These local governments were subject to oversight and control from London. In particular, the king's Privy Council routinely reviewed and struck down colonial laws.

While each of the colonies was tied to Britain, there were no formal connections among them. Proposals to organize the colonies as a collective hardly got off the ground until the eve of the American Revolution. The most notable plan emerged from a 1754 conference in Albany, New York. Largely the brainchild of Benjamin Franklin (1706–1790), it would have created a continental government to conduct war and trade, with the power to raise its own taxes and army. Despite the threat of war with the French and their Native American allies, jealousies among the colonies and nervousness in Britain doomed the planned union. "Everybody cries, a Union is absolutely necessary," Franklin complained, "but when they come to the Manner and Form of the Union, their weak Noodles are perfectly distracted." The next year he proposed that the British *impose* a union on the colonies; otherwise they could "never expect to see an American War carried on as it ought to be." London declined.[1] It would be another two decades before the colonists found a common enemy that would pull them together.

The first constitutional debates in America were debates about the British constitution and its meaning for the colonies. The Declaration of Independence may be the beginning of the United States; yet it was the last move in an extended dialogue between the partisans of colonies in North America and the partisans of the English authorities in London. The colonists and imperial officials offered competing interpretations of the British constitution to justify their actions—both to one another and to interested observers in North America and in the British Isles. As that dialogue progressed, the two sides found themselves drifting further apart. Their disagreements over taxes and trade soon exposed deeper constitutional disagreements. The Americans came to think that the English government had violated the British constitution—and that constitution no longer suited their needs. They would have to adopt a new one.

1. Benjamin Franklin, *The Writings of Benjamin Franklin*, ed. Albert H. Smyth, vol. 3 (New York: Macmillan, 1905), 242, 267.

Table 2-1 Major Issues and Statements of the Colonial Era

Major Political Issues	Major Constitutional Issues
French-Indian War	Closer union of colonies
Closer union of colonies	Parliamentary taxation power in colonies
Sugar Act of 1764	Parliamentary trade regulation power in colonies
Stamp Act of 1765	Power of the purse in colonial government
Quartering Act of 1765	Appointment power in colonial government
Townshend Revenue Act of 1767	Privy Council view of colonial laws
Boston Port Act of 1774	Judicial review of Parliament
Massachusetts Government Act of 1774	Martial law
Independence of colonies	Independence of colonies

Legacies. The central debate was over the limits on the authority of Parliament in the colonies. On that issue, constitutional interpretation eventually gave way to revolution. The Americans stopped trying to live within the British constitution. Instead, in 1776, they drew on the British constitutional tradition to explain why they could no longer accept being bound by its terms. The Declaration of Independence gave the final American position: Parliament could have no authority in the thirteen colonies. From that point on, the constitutional debate would be exclusively American. It would focus on why revolution was justified and what a constitution drafted in America should look like.

The single greatest legacy of earlier debates is the United States as an independent nation. The Americans did not reach that decision quickly or easily. Many of those living in the American colonies did not agree with the decision to declare independence. Even earlier, in colonial debates, the process of constitutional interpretation did not settle disagreements. Rather, the two sides were no longer willing to live under a single constitutional system.

The long political struggle with Britain before 1776 deepened American constitutional thought and practice. Americans developed their ideas about democracy and representation, federalism (the division of power between a central authority and regional or local governments), separation of powers (the responsibilities of the executive, legislative, and judicial branches), rights and liberties, and the nature of constitutionalism itself. By the 1770s, established political leaders like Benjamin Franklin and John Dickinson (1732–1808) of Pennsylvania, Samuel Adams (1722–1803) and James Otis (1725–1783) of Massachusetts, and Patrick Henry (1736–1799) and Edmund Pendleton (1721–1803) of Virginia were joined by young lawyers like John Adams (1735–1826) and Thomas Jefferson (1743–1826). Together, they pressed the case for the rights of the American colonies, first within the British constitution and if necessary outside of it. Their ideas, arguments, and experience in the decades leading up to independence continued to shape American constitutionalism as the Revolution was being fought and after it had been won. They became core features of the Constitution, and they continue to influence American politics today.

The American constitutional tradition is a "written" one. Both the states and the federal government have a single document that empowers the government and defines its structure and limits. Constitutional debate revolves around the interpretation of that foundational document, although that process creates new materials for interpretation. By contrast, the British constitution is "unwritten." The British constitutional tradition includes the Magna Carta of 1215 and the Bill of Rights of 1689, but no single document stands as a source of government authority or the limits of government power. Rather, the British constitutional system is built on prior governmental practice and precedent. The best constitutional objection to government policy was often that nothing like it had ever been done before. It was thus important for the colonists to make known their objections to British policies that seemed to change the rules of the constitutional game. Even if new taxes were small, the principle established by an

Box 2-1 A Partial Cast of Characters of the Colonial Era

Thomas Hutchinson	■ Loyalist ■ Member and speaker of the colonial Massachusetts legislature (1737–1740, 1742–1749) ■ Chief justice of Massachusetts colony (1760–1769) ■ Last civilian governor of Massachusetts colony (1771–1774) ■ Author of multivolume history of the Massachusetts colony ■ Attempted to reconcile English and colonial forces during the tax act crises leading to the Revolution
Samuel Adams	■ Anti-Federalist ■ Newspaper writer critical of Parliament ■ Popular leader of protests against parliamentary taxes in the colonies ■ Member of the colonial Massachusetts assembly ■ Member of the Continental Congress ■ Governor of Massachusetts (1793–1797) ■ Opposed ratification of the U.S. Constitution
John Adams	■ Federalist ■ Author of important works on parliamentary authority over the colonies and constitutional government in the new republic ■ Influential member of the Continental Congress ■ First vice president under Federalist George Washington (1789–1797) ■ Last Federalist president of the United States (1797–1801) ■ Only president to be defeated for reelection until John Quincy Adams (1828)
James Otis	■ Patriot ■ Lawyer who argued against the legality of general writs of assistance before Massachusetts colonial court ■ Wrote prominent pamphlets on limits of parliamentary authority over colonies ■ Early proponent of judicial review

unchallenged law would be woven into the constitutional fabric for the future.

The American experience after independence built on colonial and Revolutionary experience. As Justice John Marshall Harlan once observed, the United States has been defined by "the traditions from which it developed as well as the traditions from which it broke."[2] The Americans learned from their earlier experiences, altering some institutions and keeping others. Colonial-era debates shed light on how the founding generation understood their constitutional choices. They also set the tone for the future. These debates spilled across legislatures, courts, newspapers, and meeting halls. Political actors used the best arguments available to them to advance their interests and ideals.

Pre-Revolutionary debates centered on the powers of the national government, separation of powers, judicial power, and other issues. They involve the proper limits on central government power, the boundaries between the central government and the provincial governments, and the problems of representation and diversity. Unlike in later chapters, the "national" government here is the British government, but the same issues arise again and again after independence.

2. *Poe v. Ullman*, 367 U.S. 497, 542 (1961).

II. Judicial Power and Constitutional Authority

MAJOR DEVELOPMENTS

- Debate over the supreme legal authority of Parliament
- Suggestion that courts have right to declare statutes unconstitutional

Everyone recognized that it was possible to debate whether Parliament had reached too far and the British constitution had been violated. What were not generally recognized in Britain in the mid-eighteenth century were legal limits on Parliament that could be judicially enforced. In other words, there was no *judicial review.* There were things that Parliament *should* not do, but there was nothing that Parliament *could* not do.

The colonists challenged that basic assumption. Rather, many argued, colonial and British courts could refuse to enforce an act of Parliament that they thought violated the Constitution. This suggestion was not universally accepted even in the colonies, but it was at least taken seriously. If judicial review is one of the great innovations of American constitutionalism, it was contemplated more than a decade before the Revolution.

Some form of judicial review felt natural—in part because the colonists had already experienced it. Colonial charters routinely guaranteed the liberties that the settlers would have enjoyed in England. The charters also prohibited the colonial assembly from making policies that were contrary to the laws of England. And they allowed appeals in legal cases from colonial courts to the Privy Council, a precursor to the modern British cabinet. This group of advisors to the monarch served as a kind of supreme court. More important, colonial assemblies were required to send a copy of their laws to the Privy Council for its approval. The Council was concerned to ensure the supremacy of English law across the empire, along with a reasonable uniformity. It wished to prevent the colonies from making policies that would undercut the policies being pursued by England.

In addition to looking out for English interests, the Council was also active in blocking the colonial assemblies from violating traditional English liberties. Criminalizing "Devilish practices," for example, was too vague to satisfy the requirements of due process. The Council also agreed with Quaker complaints when Connecticut required that they be taxed to support Puritan ministers; this violated the charter's protection of liberty of conscience. And the Council slapped down assemblies that tried to impose outcomes in legal cases or to issue *bills of attainder*, which impose criminal punishments on individuals without trials.[3]

This is not to say that colonial governments welcomed higher review, and in fact they were creative in finding ways to minimize it. In the 1670s, the Massachusetts General Assembly boldly informed the king, "the laws of England are bounded within the four seas, and do not reach America." (The assembly was willing to enact the very same laws—at least under the threat that the king might revoke their charter.)[4] Earlier, colonial legislatures simply refused to print a statute book, on the theory that the Privy Council could not strike down laws it could not see. They also tried sending the Council mere summaries of the laws, laws written in code and abbreviations, and statute books that were oddly organized or incomplete. Temporary laws were also popular, as were laws that had their effect before word could get back from England. But Council review familiarized the colonies with the idea that legislatures had legally limited authority—and that statutes were void when they violated fundamental law.[5]

To bolster their view that Parliament was hedged in by legal boundaries, the colonists also reached back into English legal history. Pride of place was given to a controversial 1610 judicial opinion by Lord Edward Coke (1552–1634) in *Dr. Bonham's Case*. One of the great innovators of English law, Coke argued that "it appears in our books, that in many cases, the common law will control acts of parliament, and sometimes adjudge them to be utterly void: for when an act of parliament is against common right and reason, or repugnant, or impossible to be performed, the common law will control it, and adjudge such act to be void."[6] Yet by the end of the seventeenth century—after the Glorious Revolu-

3. Elmer Beecher Russell, *The Review of American Colonial Legislation by the King in Council* (New York: Columbia University Press, 1915), 141—152.

4. *Records of the Governor and Company of the Massachusetts Bay in New England*, ed. Nathaniel B. Shurtleff, vol. 5 (Boston: W. White, 1854), 200.

5. See also Mary Sarah Bilder, *The Transatlantic Constitution: Colonial Legal Culture and the Empire* (Cambridge: Harvard University Press, 2004); Daniel J. Hulsebosch, *Constituting Empire: New York and the Transformation of Constitutionalism in the Atlantic World, 1664—1830* (Chapel Hill: University of North Carolina Press, 2005).

6. *Dr. Bonham's Case*, 8 Co. Rep. 107a, 118a (1610).

tion in which Parliament had won its supremacy over the king—there was still no notion of constitutional review of Parliament. At least from the perspective of the Chief Justice John Holt (1642–1710), sitting on the King's Bench in 1702, "an act of Parliament can do no wrong, though it may do several things that look pretty odd."[7] The law professor William Blackstone (1723–1780) captured the consensus in England at the time of the American Revolution: The authority of Parliament was absolute and could not be questioned in any court.

To stop what they saw as parliamentary abuses, the colonists took the first tentative steps toward inventing judicial review. Full realization of that power would have to await independence, when legal charters could not be set aside at the whim of a foreign sovereign. But it was a powerful idea about what the role of a judge in a constitutional system might be. The colonists appealed to colonial judges to refuse to enforce laws that were inconsistent with the constitution. Coke at least hinted that "acts of parliament" could be judged "void" in a court of law. The Massachusetts lawyer James Otis made use of *Bonham's Case* to contend that what the English were doing was illegal and that the colonial courts should intervene.

In *Dr. Bonham's Case*, Lord Coke quotes a medieval predecessor, Sir William Herle (1270–1347): "Some statutes are made against law and right, which those who made them perceiving, would not have put them into execution," in support of Coke's contention that such statutes are void.[8] How far would this argument extend? Could it form the foundation of modern judicial review?

But the British constitution was based on principles derived from government practice. Consequently, precedents assumed particular importance. Constitutional disputes turned on whether the action being questioned was similar to unchallenged actions taken in the past. The colonists lacked either a written constitution, to specify what the limits of government power were, or an established judicial process capable of declaring government actions void. They could only demonstrate *politically* that they regarded some government action as innovative and illegitimate. Symbolic actions ranged from resolutions passed by legislatures and town meetings protesting a law, to the publication of pamphlets arguing against a law, to the organization of vandalizing mobs (such as the Sons of Liberty who destroyed the taxed tea in the "Boston Tea Party").

All these kept alive colonial claims that parliamentary acts were unconstitutional. The burden was therefore on political leaders to mobilize support for collective action. Was the effort of mobilizing such protests worth it in any particular case? Has the art of voicing constitutional objections through political protest gone away with the adoption of a written constitution and the rise of judicial review?

7. *City of London v. Wood*, 12 Mod. 669, 688 (1702).

8. *Dr. Bonham's Case*, 8 Co. Rep. 107a, 114a (1610).

William Blackstone, **Commentaries on the Laws of England** (1765)[9]

William Blackstone was a professor of law at Oxford University, and his lectures there became the basis of the Commentaries. *The* Commentaries *aimed to synthesize the English law, and though it attracted some critics the treatise was quickly taken as authoritative throughout the British Empire. The* Commentaries *was the cornerstone of American understandings of the British common law that they had inherited and incorporated into their own legal and constitutional system, but Blackstone's understanding of legislative activity was not so easily accepted in America.*

St. George Tucker (1752–1827) was variously a state and federal judge in Virginia after independence, a professor of law at the College of William and Mary, and a states' rights Jeffersonian. He published a popular American edition of Blackstone's commentaries in 1803 that included an extended commentary on the U.S. Constitution by Tucker, along with critical notes on Blackstone. We include some of Tucker's footnotes here, along with Blackstone's text. Blackstone argued that there were no legal limits on the power of the English Parliament of the late eighteenth century. Parliamentary power was absolute. The colonists struggled with Blackstone's claim during the revolutionary era, but after the Revolution they were free to take a different path. In a footnote to Blackstone, St. George Tucker argued that the American constitutions can be distinguished from the British by being "acts of the people, and not of government." Is this difference enough to support judicial review? Is Tucker successful in his effort to separate American constitutionalism from these parts of Blackstone?

9. Excerpt taken from *Blackstone's Commentaries*, ed. St. George Tucker (Philadelphia: William Young Birch and Abraham Small, 1803), 1:108–110, 2:160–162.

...I know it is generally laid down more largely, that acts of parliament contrary to reason are void.[10] But if the parliament will positively enact a thing to be done which is unreasonable, I know of no power in the ordinary forms of the constitution, that is vested with authority to control it; and the examples usually alleged in support of this sense of the rule do none of them prove, that, where the main object of a statute is unreasonable, the judges are at liberty to reject it; for that were to set the judicial power above that of the legislature, which would be subversive of all government. But where some collateral matter arises out of the general words, and happens to be unreasonable; there the judges are in decency to conclude that this consequence was not foreseen by the parliament, and therefore they are at liberty to expound the statute by equity, and only *quoad hoc* [to this extent] disregard it....[T]here is no court that has power to defeat the intent of the legislature, when couched in such evident and express words, as leave no doubt whether it was the intent of the legislature or no.

...

...[O]ur more distant plantations [colonies] in America, and elsewhere, are also in some respect subject to English laws....But this must be understood with very many and very great restrictions. Such colonists carry with them only so much of the English law, as is applicable to their own situation and the condition of an infant colony; such, for instance, as the general rules of inheritance, and of protection from personal injuries....The artificial refinements and distinctions incident to the property of a great and commercial people, the laws of police and revenue, (such especially as are enforced by penalties)...are neither necessary nor convenient for them, and therefore are not in force. What shall be admitted and what rejected, at what times, and under what restrictions, must, in case of dispute, be decided in the first instance by their own provincial judicature, subject to the revision and control of the king in council: the whole of their constitution being also liable to be new-modeled and reformed by the general superintending power of the legislature in the mother country....

...

The power and jurisdiction of parliament, says Sir Edward Coke, is so transcendent and absolute, that it cannot be confined, either for causes or persons, within any bounds....It hath sovereign and uncontrollable authority in the making, confirming, enlarging, restraining, abrogating, repealing, reviving and expounding of laws, concerning matters of all possible denominations, ecclesiastical, or temporal, civil, military, maritime, or criminal; this being the place where that absolute despotic power, which must, in all governments,[11] reside somewhere, is entrusted by the constitution of these kingdoms. All mischiefs and grievances, operations and remedies, that transcend the ordinary course of the laws, are within the reach of this extraordinary tribunal. It can regulate or new model the succession to the crown....It can alter the established religion of the land....It can change and create afresh even the constitution of the kingdom and of parliaments themselves; as was done by the act of union, and the several statutes for triennial and septennial elections. It can, in short, do everything that is not naturally impossible; and, therefore, some have not scrupled to call it's power, by a figure rather too bold, the omnipotence of parliament.[12] True it is, that what the parliament doth, no authority upon earth can

10. One would imagine that it could not be deemed any great stretch of the freedom of opinion, to pronounce that any legislative act which prescribes a thing contrary to reason, is void; yet the caution of the learned commentator [Blackstone] on this occasion is certainly conformable to the principles of the British government; in which, it seems to be agreed by all their Jurists, the authority of parliament is absolute and uncontrollable; insomuch that it may alter or change the constitution itself. But, in America, the constitutions, both of the individual states, and of the federal government, being the acts of the people, and not of the government...the legislature can possess, no power, or obligation over the other branches of government, in any case, where the principles of the Constitution, may be in any degree infringed by an acquiescence under the authority of the legislative department...[Footnote by Tucker]

11. In the United States this absolute power is not delegated to the government: it remains with the people, whose safety requires that the government which they have themselves established, should be limited. "The powers not delegated to the United States by the constitution, nor prohibited by it to the states, are reserved to the states respectively, or to the people." Amendments to the C. U.S. Art. 12 [now the 10th Amendment]. [Footnote by Tucker]

12. Since, according to the fundamental principles of both the Federal and State Constitution, and Government, the supreme power...resides in the people, it follows that it is the right of the people to make laws. But as the exercise of that Right by the people at large would be equally inconvenient and impracticable, the constitution of the State has vested that power in the General Assembly of the Commonwealth....It is from these express provisions both in the State, and Federal Constitutions, and not from metaphysical deduction, that the State, and Federal Legislatures derive the power of making Laws....[Footnote by Tucker]

undo. So that it is a matter most essential to the liberties of this kingdom, that such members be delegated to this important trust, as are most eminent for their probity, their fortitude, and their knowledge....

It must be owned that Mr. Locke, and other theoretical writers, have held that "there remains still inherent in the people a supreme power to remove or alter the legislative, when they find the legislative act contrary to the trust reposed in them: for, when such trust is abused, it is thereby forfeited, and devolves to those who gave it."[13] But, however, just this conclusion may be, in theory, we cannot practically adopt it, nor take any *legal* steps for carrying it into execution, under any dispensation of government at present actually existing. For this devolution of power, to the people at large, includes in it a dissolution of the whole form of government established by the people.... So long, therefore, as the English constitution lasts, we may venture to affirm, that the power of parliament is absolute and without control.

Massachusetts Assembly Memorial (1764)[14]

On behalf of a public meeting in Boston in 1764, Samuel Adams drafted instructions to the Boston delegates to the Massachusetts House of Representatives calling on them to work for the immediate repeal of the Sugar Act. The instructions expressed particular concern with the precedent that the Sugar Act was setting: "If our trade may be taxed, why not our lands?... This we apprehend annihilates our charter right to govern and tax ourselves."[15] James Otis was one of those delegates, and he in turn drafted the Memorial, which was passed by the House and sent to London. The Memorial includes the development of a theory of judicial review that did not depend on the existence of a written constitution.

James Otis had been the advocate general for the vice-admiralty court in the Massachusetts colony, whose jurisdiction included the enforcement of the navigation acts that regulated colonial overseas trade. His father, the speaker of the house, had expected to be appointed to the colonial superior court, but when a vacancy arose in 1760 the governor passed him by. Lieutenant Governor Thomas Hutchinson (1711–1780) was appointed chief judge instead. The younger Otis broke completely with the administration over use of writs of assistance, which authorized customs agents looking for smugglers to conduct forcible searches on their own initiative of private property throughout the Boston area. In 1761, Otis appealed to the Superior Court, asking it to refuse to issue such writs on the grounds that they were unconstitutional. The argument of Otis stood out for its reference to Dr. Bonham's Case *as an English precedent for a power of judicial review. Hutchinson rejected the idea that the court had such a power. The reference in the writs of assistance case was brief, but Otis extended the argument in the Memorial and later pamphlets.*

Thomas Hutchinson later recounted, "The Stamp duty, although I always feared the consequence of it would be bad, both to the nation & colonies, and privately & publicly declared my thoughts upon it, yet after the passing the act I could not avoid considering it legally right, the Parliament being beyond dispute the supreme legislature of the British dominions; but our friends to liberty take advantage of a maxim they find in Lord Coke that an act of Parliament against Magna Charta or the peculiar rights of Englishmen is ipso facto void. This, taken in the latitude the people are often disposed to take it, must be fatal to all Government & it seems to have determined great part of the colonies to oppose the execution of the act with force & to show their resentment against all in authority who will not join with them."[16] Why did both Blackstone and Thomas Hutchinson think that the doctrine that "an act of Parliament against Magna Charta or the peculiar right of Englishmen is ipso facto void" would be "fatal to all government"? What are the dangers of such a doctrine? Within the British constitutional system, who would have the right to say that an act of Parliament was unconstitutional?

...

The absolute rights of Englishmen, as frequently declared in Parliament, from Magna Charta to this time, are the rights of *personal security, personal liberty*, and of *private property*.

...

It is presumed, that upon these principles, the colonists have been by their several charters declared natural subjects, and entrusted with the power of

13. This principle is expressly recognized in our government. Amendments to C. U.S. Art. 11, 12. See Declaration of Independence, and Virginia Bill of Rights, Art. 3. [Footnote by Tucker]

14. Excerpt taken from the appendix to James Otis, *The Rights of the British Colonies Asserted and Proved* (Boston: Edes and Gill, 1764), 70–80.

15. John Adams, in *The Works of John Adams*, ed. Charles Francis Adams, vol. 10 (Boston: Little, Brown and Company, 1856), 294.

16. Quoted in Horace Gray, "Appendix," in Josiah Quincy, ed., *Reports of Cases* (Boston: Little, Brown and Co., 1865), 415, 441.

making *their own local laws*, not repugnant to the laws of England, and with *the power of taxing themselves*.

This legislative power is subject by the same charter to the King's negative, as in Ireland. This effectually secures the *dependence* of the colonies on Great-Britain....

...

...The common law is received and practiced upon here, and in the rest of the colonies; and all ancient and modern acts of Parliament that can be considered as part of, or in amendment of the common law, together with all such acts of Parliament as expressly name the plantations; so that the power of the British Parliament is held as sacred and as uncontrollable in the colonies as in England. The question is not upon the general power or right of the Parliament, but whether right it is not circumscribed within some equitable and reasonable bounds? It is hoped it will not be considered a new doctrine, that even the authority of the Parliament of *Great-Britain* is circumscribed by certain bounds, which if exceeded, their acts become those of mere *power* without *right*, and consequently void. The judges of England have declared in favor of these sentiments when they expressly declare, that *acts of Parliament against natural equity are void*. That *acts against the fundamental principles of the British constitution are void*.[17] This doctrine is agreeable to the law of nature and nations, and to the divine dictates of natural and revealed religion. It is contrary to reason that the supreme power should have right to alter the constitution. This would imply that those who are entrusted with sovereignty by the people have a right to do as they please. In other words, that those who are invested with power to protect the people, and support their rights and liberties, have a right to make slaves of them. This is not very remote from a flat contradiction....

It is now near three hundred years since the continent of North America was first discovered, and that by British subjects. Ten generations have passed away through infinite toils and bloody conflicts in settling this country. None of those ever dreamed but that they were entitled at least to equal privileges with those of the same rank born within the realm.

17. Here Otis inserted a long footnote citing *Dr. Bonham's Case* and other authorities.

John Dickinson, **Letters from a Farmer in Pennsylvania** (1768)[18]

John Dickinson was a philosophically attuned lawyer and politician in Philadelphia. Though a defender of the proprietary government of Pennsylvania against critics such as Benjamin Franklin, he was an early and influential critic of parliamentary taxation of the colonies. He was slow to embrace the call for American independence, but he became a key drafter of the first federal constitution after independence, the Articles of Confederation. These newspaper articles, published pseudonymously as "Letters from a Farmer," were particularly concerned with the Townshend Act. In this letter, Dickinson addresses the issue of whether the taxes were too small to justify the level of protest that was building in the colonies. When can constitutional violations be overlooked? What are the consequences of accepting a constitutional violation? Should we be as concerned about constitutionally questionable legislation that is of little or no practical consequence? Is Dickinson right to think that how power is "checked and controlled" is more important than how it is actually "exercised"?

Letter VII

...

...[I]n truth, all men are subject to frailties of nature; and therefore whatever regard we entertain for *persons* of those who govern us, we should always remember that their conduct as *rulers*, may be influenced by human infirmities.

...Where these laws are to bind *themselves*, it may be expected, that the House of Commons will very carefully consider them: But when they are making laws that are not designed to bind *themselves*, we cannot imagine that their deliberations will be as cautious and scrupulous, as in their own case.

...

Some persons may think this act of no consequence, because the duties are so *small*. A fatal error. *That* is the very circumstance most alarming to me. For I am convinced, that the authors of this law would never have obtained an act to raise so trifling a sum as it must do, had they not intended by *it* to establish a *precedent* for future use. To console ourselves with the *smallness* of

18. Excerpt taken from John Dickinson, *Letters from a Farmer in Pennsylvania, to the Inhabitants of the British Colonies* (Philadelphia: David Hall and William Sellers, 1768), 33–38.

the duties, is to walk deliberately into the snare that is set for us, praising the *neatness* of the workmanship. Suppose the duties imposed by the late act could be paid by these distressed colonies with the utmost ease, and that the purposes to which they are to be applied, were the most reasonable and equitable that can be conceived... yet even in such a supposed case, these colonies ought to regard the act with abhorrence. For WHO ARE A FREE PEOPLE? Not *those*, over whom government is reasonably and equitably exercised, but those, who live under a government so *constitutionally checked and controlled*, that proper provision is made against its being otherwise exercised.

The late act is founded on the destruction of this constitutional security. If the Parliament has a right to lay a duty of four shillings and eight-pence on a hundred weight of glass, or a ream of paper, they have a right to lay a duty of any other sum on either.... In short, if they have a right to levy a tax of *one penny* upon us, they have a right to levy a *million* upon us: For where does their right stop?...

III. Powers of the National Government

MAJOR DEVELOPMENTS

- The debate over the scope of English authority over the internal policy of the colonies
- The struggle over Parliament's right to represent the colonists and impose internal taxes
- The question of whether the colonies should be independent of England

The primary constitutional debate of the colonial period—the one that drove all others and that eventually led to the Declaration of Independence—was over the extent of Parliament's policymaking authority over the colonies. In this, there were two closely intertwined issues.

The first issue was the precursor to the federalism debate that has echoed down through all of American history. How much power does and should the central government have? In the imperial context prior to 1776, this meant how much control the British government should have over public policy in the North American colonies. Was British authority absolute? Could the Parliament or the monarch dictate any policy in the colonies, or were there constitutional limits on their authority in North America? Were there areas of public policy or particular governmental powers that were under the exclusive control of local colony governments? Was it possible to draw a line between the scope of British authority and the scope of colonial authority? Or would any attempt give way in one direction or the other—either to absolute British domination or to colonial independence? Could there be federalism within the constitution of the British Empire?

The second issue arose from the first. This was essentially a debate about the nature and meaning of representative government. Were the colonies adequately represented in Parliament, and did that make a difference for how much policymaking authority Parliament had over colonial affairs? This is what the cry of "no taxation without representation" was about. If the colonists were not represented in Parliament, then the principles of the British constitution dictated that Parliament did not have the right to tax the colonists. Since the colonists did not elect any members of Parliament, the challenge for the defenders of parliamentary authority was to show that the British legislature adequately represented their interests anyway. Taxation was the flashpoint for the debate, but the colonists had thus begun to question whether their interests were represented in more than just local assemblies. And once they did, it did not take long for them to begin asking whether Parliament should have any say in North American affairs at all. If Parliament did not represent American interests, then Parliament should not tax Americans. But if that was true, then should Parliament make trade, military, or social policy for Americans either?

The debate began when Parliament passed the Sugar Act of 1764, but it reached crisis proportions after passage of the Stamp Tax in 1765. The global British war with the French, including operations in North America, had left the government with a massive debt. The colonies in the western hemisphere had always been a source of imperial wealth, but now London wanted the colonists to pay taxes to defray the expenses of empire as well. The taxes collected in the colonies, however, had generally been assessed and spent locally. Trade between the colonies and Europe had always been closely regulated by Britain. Parliament's control over commerce across the empire was a well-understood feature of the British constitution, and Parliament used a system of tariffs to regulate the flow of trade. The Sugar and Molasses Act of 1733 set high duties on foreign sugar and rum and was designed to stop the trade in those goods altogether so that sugar would be purchased from British sources instead. Nonetheless, smuggling of French sugar was rampant in the colonies. The Sugar Act of 1764 cut the tariffs but cracked down on smuggling. If the Americans could not be forced to buy British sugar, London at least wanted to collect revenue on the French sugar trade. The result in practice was to make several basic goods both less available and more expensive than they had been.

The Stamp Act of 1765 imposed imperial taxes on a wide variety of printed paper, including newspapers, calendars, playing cards, and legal documents. When passing the Stamp Act, Parliament made special reference to the previous year's Sugar Act as providing a precedent for its actions. Both statutes were designed to tax the colonists to raise revenue for the crown. The Stamp Act was financially burdensome, but the colonists were particularly disturbed that the Act imposed a clear and direct tax unrelated to the regulation of their international trade. The tax crossed a line, but did that make it unconstitutional?

Colonial thinking evolved over the course of the 1760s and 1770s. It went first from emphasizing that certain kinds of taxes imposed by the British Parliament were unconstitutional to arguing that Parliament had no authority in the colonies. Finally, it went from arguing that the colonists were subject only to the king to concluding that the Americans owed no allegiance to England at all. Samuel Adams in Massachusetts helped push the line, later joined by such young lawyers as John Adams and Thomas Jefferson. As early as 1768, Samuel Adams helped pen a public letter protesting the Townshend Revenue Act by arguing that "their local circumstances cannot by any possibility be represented in the Parliament."[19] As tensions mounted and London declared martial law in Boston to enforce English taxes, the possibility and legitimacy of English rule in the American colonies was increasingly put into question. A debate over centralization gave way to a debate over independence.

This debate is represented in the exchange between English Secretary of Treasury Thomas Whately (1726–1772) and Maryland lawyer Daniel Dulany (1722–1797) in the 1760s. Whately was one of the architects of the British tax policy and an able defender of it as a just and legitimate policy. Dulany was deeply skeptical of the parliamentary authority to tax the colonies, but he hoped to find a middle ground that would protect American interests within the empire.

Thomas Whately, **The Regulations Lately Made** (1765)[20]

Thomas Whately, who had previously served on the British Board of Trade that oversaw colonial affairs, was a Member of Parliament and Secretary of Treasury in 1765, and he was the principal author of the Stamp Act. This pamphlet was a sweeping vindication of the British colonial system, including the Sugar Act of the year before. It concluded with an argument in favor of the Stamp Act then being considered in Parliament. The pamphlet was a leading defense of the policy and constitutionality of parliamentary taxation of the colonies. Whately denied that the power to impose the stamp tax was different in kind than any other type of power that Parliament exercised over the colonies. He also examined the doctrine of virtual representation—the view that legislators represent the populace generally and not just their particular electorates. Virtual representation *was Parliament's explanation of how it could represent, and therefore tax, the colonists, even though the colonists did not vote for any members of Parliament. As Whately points out, the theory of virtual representation was crucial to parliamentary democracy as it operated in England itself as well as the colonies. Against those who thought that the colonists could only be represented in their local assemblies, Whately argued in favor of what he called "double representation" in both the local assembly and the British Parliament. The empire allowed for a kind of federal structure.*

As you read Whately's argument, think about what assumptions he relies upon in making his arguments for virtual representation. Does he, for example, rely upon an assumption of shared interests between representatives and those they represent to make virtual representation work?

The Revenue that may be raised by the duties which have been already, or by these if they should be hereafter imposed, are all equally applied by Parliament, *towards defraying the necessary Expenses of defending, protecting, and securing, the British Colonies and Plantations*

19. Samuel Adams, "Massachusetts Circular Letter, February 11, 1768," in *The Writings of Samuel Adams*, ed. Harry Alonzo Cushing, vol. 1 (New York: G.P. Putnam's Sons, 1904), 188.

20. Excerpt taken from Thomas Whately, *The Regulations Lately Made concerning the Colonies, and the Taxes Imposed upon Them, Considered*, 3rd ed. (London: J. Wilkie, 1775), 101–110.

in America: Not that on the one hand an *American* Revenue might not have been applied to different purposes; or on the other, that *Great Britain* is to contribute nothing to these.... *Great Britain* has a right at all times, she is under a necessity, upon this occasion, to demand their assistance....

The reasonableness, and even the necessity of requiring an *American* revenue being admitted, the right of the mother country to impose such a duty upon her colonies, if duly considered, cannot be questioned: they claim, it is true, the privilege, which is common to all *British* Subjects, of being taxed only with their own consent, given by their representatives; and may they ever enjoy the privilege in all its extent: May this sacred pledge of liberty be preserved inviolate, to the utmost verge of our Dominions, and to the latest page of our history! But let us not limit the legislative rights of the *British* people to subjects of taxation only: No new law whatever can bind us that is made without the concurrence of our representatives. The acts of trade and navigation, and all the other acts that relate either to ourselves or to the colonies, are founded upon no other authority; they are not obligatory if a Stamp Act is not, and every argument in support of an exemption from the superintendence of the *British* Parliament in the one case, is equally applicable to the others. The constitution knows no distinction; the colonies have never attempted to make one; but have acquiesced under several parliamentary taxes. [The Molasses Act of 1733] lays heavy duties on all foreign rum, sugar, and molasses, imported into the *British* Plantations: the amount of the impositions has been complained of; the policy of the laws has been objected to; but the right of making such a law, has never been questioned....

It is in vain to call these only regulations of trade; the trade of *British* Subjects may not be regulated by such means, without the concurrence of their representatives. Duties laid for these purposes, as well as for the purposes of revenue, are still levies of money upon the people. The constitution again knows no distinction between Impost duties and internal taxation; and if some speculative difference should be attempted to be made, it certainly is contradicted by fact; for an internal tax also was laid on the colonies by the establishment of a post office there; which, however it may be represented, will... appear to be essentially a tax, and that of the most authoritative kind; for it is enforced by provisions, more peculiarly prohibitory and compulsive, than others are usually attended with.... These provisions are indeed very proper, and even necessary; but certainly money levied by such methods, the effect of which is intended to be a monopoly of the carriage of letters to the officers of this revenue, and by means of which the people are forced to pay the rates imposed upon all their correspondence, is a public tax to which they must submit, and not merely a price required of them for a private accommodation....

The instances that have been mentioned prove, that the right of the Parliament of *Great Britain* to impose taxes of every kind on the colonies, has been always admitted; but were there no precedents to support the claim, it would still be incontestable, being founded on the principles of our constitution; for the fact is, that the inhabitants of the colonies are represented in Parliament; they do not indeed choose the members of that assembly; neither are nine tenths of the people of *Britain* electors; for the right of election is annexed to certain species of property, to peculiar franchises, and to inhabitancy in some particular places; but these descriptions comprehend only a very small part of the land, the property, and the people of this island.... Women and persons under age be their property ever so large, and all of it freehold, have [no vote]. The merchants of *London*, a numerous and respectable body of men, whose opulence exceeds all that *America* could collect... are all in the same Circumstances; none of them choose their representatives; and yet are they not represented in Parliament? Is their vast property subject to taxes without their consent? Are they all arbitrarily bound by laws to which they have not agreed? The colonies are in exactly the same Situation; All *British* Subjects are really in the same; none are actually, all are virtually represented in Parliament; for every Member of Parliament sits in the House not as a representative of his own constituents, but as one of that august Assembly by which all the commons of *Great Britain* are represented. Their rights and their interests, however his own borough may be affected by general dispositions, ought to be the great Objects of his Attention, and the only rules for his conduct; and to sacrifice these to a partial advantage in favor of the place where he was chosen, would be a departure from his duty....

The inhabitants of the colonies however have by some been supposed to be excepted, because they are represented in their respective assemblies. So are the citizens of *London* in their common council; and yet so far from excluding them from the national representation, it does not impeach their right to choose Members of Parliament: it is true, that the powers vested in the common council of *London*, are not equal to those which the assemblies in the Plantations [colonies] enjoy; but still they are legislative powers, to be exercised within their district, and over their citizens; yet not exclusively of the general superintendence of the great council of the nation... and indeed what contradiction, what absurdity, does a double representation imply? What difficulty is there in allowing both, though both should even be vested with equal legislative powers, if the one is to be exercised for local, and the other for general purposes? And where is the necessity that the subordinate power must derogate from the superior authority?...

Daniel Dulany, Considerations of the Propriety of Imposing Taxes in the British Colonies (1765)[21]

Daniel Dulany was trained in law in England before returning to his native Maryland. Regarded as one of the best lawyers in the colonies, he had served there on the Governor's Council. His pamphlet was one of the first and most cutting critiques of the Stamp Act and the doctrine of virtual representation. He later refused to join the movement for American independence, however, which he regarded as too radical.

As you read Dulany's argument against virtual representation, consider whether we can dispense entirely with the notion even in modern democracies. What might be the difficulties with taking his argument to its logical conclusions? The colonists contended that the principle of "no taxation without consent" required that only local legislatures had the authority to impose taxes. If the colonists had been able to vote for any of the members of Parliament, would that have also satisfied the principle? What line does he try to draw between the powers of Parliament and the colonial assemblies? Does the debate between Whately and Dulany provide a basis for justifying a congressional power to impose taxes? To make other policies? For justifying a state legislature's power to impose taxes on the residents of that state?

... [I]n framing the late Stamp Act, the commons acted in the character of representative of the colonies. They assumed it as the principle of that measure and the propriety of it must therefore stand, or fall, as the principle is true, or false: For the preamble sets forth, that the commons of *Great-Britain* had resolved to *give and grant* the several rates and duties imposed by the act; but what Right had the Commons of *Great-Britain* to be thus munificent at the expense of the commons of *America*?—To give property not belonging to the giver, and without the consent of the owner, is such evident and flagrant injustice, in *ordinary cases*, that few are hardy enough to avow it; and therefore, when it really happens, the fact is disguised and varnished over by the plausible pretences the ingenuity of the giver can suggest.—But it is alleged that there is a *virtual*, or *implied representation* of the colonies springing out of the constitution of the *British* government: And it must be confessed on all hands, that, as the representation is not actual, it is virtual, or it doth not exist at all; for no third kind of representation can be imagined. The colonies claim only the privilege, which is common to all *British subjects*, of being taxed *only* with their own consent given by their representatives, and all the advocates for the *Stamp Act* admit this claim. Whether, therefore, upon the whole matter, the imposition of the *Stamp Duties* is a *proper* exercise of constitutional authority, or not, depends upon the single question, Whether the commons of *Great-Britain* are *virtually* the representatives of the commons of *America*, or not.

...

I shall undertake to disprove the supposed similarity of situation, whence the same kind of representation is deduced, of the inhabitants of the colonies, and of the British non-electors; and, if I succeed, the notion of a virtual representation of the colonies must fail.... I would be understood: I am upon a question of *propriety*, not of power; and, though some may be inclined to think it is to little purpose to discuss the one, when the other is irresistible, yet are they different considerations....

...

...The electors, who are inseparably connected in their interests with the non-electors may be justly deemed to be the representatives of both. This is the only rational explanation for the expression, *virtual representation*....

21. Excerpt taken from Daniel Dulany, *Considerations of the Propriety of Imposing Taxes in the British Colonies for the Purposes of Raising Revenue*, 2nd ed. (London: J. Almon, 1766), 1–10, 17–18, 40–41, 46–47.

...

There is not that intimate and inseparable relation between the *electors* of Great-Britain, and the *Inhabitants of the colonies*, which must inevitably involve both in the same taxation; on the contrary, not a single *actual* elector in *England*, might be immediately affected by a taxation in *America*, imposed by a statute which would have general operation and effect, upon the properties of the inhabitants of the colonies. The latter might be oppressed in a thousand shapes, without any Sympathy, or exciting any alarm in the former. Moreover, even acts, oppressive and injurious to the colonies in an extreme degree, might become popular in *England*, from the promise or expectation, that the very measures which depressed the colonies would give ease to the Inhabitants of *Great-Britain*.

...

By their constitutions of government, the colonies are empowered to impose internal taxes. This power is compatible with their dependence, and hath been expressly recognized by *British* Ministers and the *British* Parliament, upon many occasions; and it may be exercised effectually without striking at, or impeaching, in any respect, the superintendence of the *British* Parliament. May not then the line be distinctly and justly drawn between such acts as are necessary, or proper, for preserving or securing the dependence of the colonies, and such as are not necessary or proper for that very important purpose?

...

The origin of other governments is covered by the veil of antiquity, and is differently traced by the fancies of different men; but, of the colonies, the evidence of it is as clear and unequivocal as any other fact.

By these declaratory charters the inhabitants of the colonies claim an exemption from *all* taxes not imposed by their own consent....

...

It appears to me, that there is a clear and necessary distinction between an act imposing a tax for *the single purpose of revenue*, and those acts which have been made for the regulation of trade, and have produced some revenue *in consequence of their effect* and operation as *regulations of trade*.

The colonies claim the privileges of *British* subjects—It has been proved to be inconsistent with those privileges, to tax them *without their own consent*, and it hath been demonstrated that a tax imposed by Parliament, is a tax *without their consent*.

The subordination of the colonies, and the authority of Parliament to preserve it, have been fully acknowledged. Not only the welfare, but perhaps the existence of the mother country, as an independent kingdom, may depend upon her trade and navigation, and these so far upon her intercourse with the colonies, that if this should be neglected, there would soon be an end to that commerce, whence her greatest wealth is derived, and upon which her maritime power is principally founded. From these considerations, the right of the *British Parliament* to regulate the trade of the colonies, may be justly deduced; a denial of it would contradict the admission of the subordination, and of the authority to preserve it, resulting from the nature of the relation between the mother country and her colonies. It is a common, and frequently the most proper method to regulate trade by duties on imports and exports. The authority of the mother country to regulate the trade of the colonies, being unquestionable, what regulations are most proper, are to be of course submitted to the determination of the Parliament; and if an *incidental revenue* should be produced by such regulations, these are not unwarrantable.

A right to impose an internal tax on the colonies, without their consent, *for the single purpose of revenue*, is denied; a right to regulate their trade without their consent is admitted. The imposition of a duty may, in some instances, be the proper regulation.

IV. Separation of Powers

MAJOR DEVELOPMENTS

- Use of the power of the purse by legislature to check colonial governors

British authorities generally exercised their influence over the colonies most directly through the governor, the personal representative of the crown (in the royal colonies) or the proprietor (in the proprietary colonies). The governor in turn was usually advised by a council, or upper legislative chamber, and had the power to appoint judges and executive officers within the colony.

The colonists were generally represented in a lower legislative chamber, the members of which were locally elected. Laws, taxes and appropriations from the colonial treasury had to pass through the legislature, but were subject to an absolute gubernatorial veto (it could not be overridden by a subsequent legislative vote).

The popular assembly held the power of the purse in the colonial government, but the governor held the power of appointment and veto. Colonial governors not only needed to run the government, but also hoped to be compensated generously for their public service. The assemblies therefore jealously controlled the purse strings and used their authority, modeled on Parliament's, to keep the governor in check. The governors in turn sometimes called on English authorities to grant them fiscal independence from the assembly. London declined to do so until the colonies were nearly in open revolt against the crown in the 1770s. The power of the purse was the central legislative check on the executive in the British system of government, and the colonists used that power to its maximum effect and guarded it jealously. As resistance to the enforcement of the Townshend Act and the collection of its taxes grew, Massachusetts Governor Thomas Hutchinson, on the basis of royal instructions, suspended the General Assembly. In the summer of 1772, he announced that the assembly would no longer control his salary and that the colonial government would now be funded out of the parliamentary tax. Under pressure of the tax crisis, the English authorities had finally made the governor financially independent of the colonial legislature. Within two years, Parliament suspended the Massachusetts charter and replaced Hutchinson with a military governor.

English lawyer Richard Jackson (1721–1787) described how the colonial legislature of Pennsylvania used its control over the budget to influence the governor in the pre-revolutionary period. As the debate over English taxes was heating up in the 1770s, Samuel Adams helped guide a public meeting in Boston to adopt a widely circulated "list of infringements" detailing the ways in which the English government was violating the rights of the Americans. A key complaint was that the new tax system was weakening the assemblies' power of the purse and freeing the colonial governments from the political control of the locally elected legislatures.

Boston List of Infringements (1772)[22]

When Massachusetts's governor disbanded the assembly and announced in 1772 that the colonial government would be funded directly by Parliament out of the new taxes being collected in the colonies, public protests erupted. Under the guidance of Samuel Adams a public meeting in Boston adopted a series of resolutions denouncing the government. The resolutions were soon endorsed by towns throughout the state.

The colonial legislators thought the power of the purse was essential to the maintenance of constitutional government. Is this still critical to the constitutional equilibrium outside the colonial context? President Richard Nixon (1913–1994) argued for an independent presidential authority to impound, or refuse to spend, funds that Congress had appropriated for projects that the president thought were unwise or wasteful. State courts have argued that their effectiveness in performing their own constitutional duties requires their "fiscal independence" from state legislatures. Is the legislature's exclusive power of the purse a relic of a time of monarchy and empire, inappropriate to a republican government?

We cannot help thinking, that an enumeration of some of the most open infringements of our rights, will by every candid person be judged sufficient to justify whatever measures have been already taken, or may be thought proper to be taken, in order to obtain a redress of the grievances under which we labor....

...

3dly. A number of new officers, unknown in the charter of this province, have been appointed to superintend this revenue [deriving from the Townshend Act]; whereas by our charter, the great and General Court or Assembly of this province, has the sole right of appointing all civil officers, excepting only such officers, the election and constitution of whom is, in said charter, expressly excepted....

...

6thly. The revenue arising from this tax unconstitutionally laid, and committed to the management of persons arbitrarily appointed and supported by an armed force quartered in a free city has been in part applied to the most destructive purposes. It is absolutely necessary in a mixed government, like that of this province, that a due proportion or balance of power should be established among the several branches of the legislative. Our ancestors received from King William and Queen Mary a charter, by which it was understood by both parties in the contract, that such a proportion or balance was fixed; and therefore every thing which renders any one branch of

22. Excerpt taken from *The Votes and Proceedings of the Freeholders and other Inhabitants of the Town of Boston* (Boston: Edes and Gill, 1772), 13–20.

the legislative more independent of the other two than it was originally designed, is an alteration of the constitution as settled by the charter; and as it has been, until the establishment of this revenue, the constant practice of the general assembly to provide for the support of government, so it is an essential part of our constitution, as it is a necessary means of preserving an equilibrium, without which we cannot continue a free state.

In particular it has always been held, that the dependence of the governor of this province upon the general assembly for his support, was necessary for the preservation of this equilibrium; nevertheless his Majesty has been pleased to apply fifteen hundred pounds sterling annually, out of the American revenue, for the support of the governor of this province independent of the assembly; whereby the ancient connection between him and this people is weakened, the confidence in the governor lessened, the equilibrium destroyed, and the constitution essentially altered.

And we look upon it highly probable, from the best intelligence we have been able to obtain, that not only our governor and lieutenant governor, but the judges of the Superior Court of Judicature, as also the king's attorney and solicitor general are to receive their support from this grievous tribute. This will, if accomplished, complete our slavery: For if taxes are to be raised from us by the Parliament of Great Britain without our consent, and the men on whose opinions and decisions our properties, liberties, and lives, in a great measure depend, receive their support from the revenues arising from these taxes, we cannot, when we think on the depravity of mankind, avoid looking with horror on the danger to which we are exposed!

The Declaration of Independence (1776)

In 1773, with colonial assemblies in Massachusetts and New York suspended by imperial officials, Virginia called on extralegal committees of correspondence to form in the various colonies to coordinate the protests against Britain. In 1774, representatives of those committees met in a Continental Congress in Philadelphia. In May 1776, a convention in Virginia instructed the colony's delegates to propose independence from Britain and seek an alliance with the other colonies to secure that independence. The Declaration, principally drafted by Thomas Jefferson, was one of a string of documents that the Congress produced arguing the American case against British transgressions on the rights of the colonies. It was one of numerous resolutions adopted by towns and assemblies across the colonies explaining their reasons for declaring independence. Thus, after the famous opening paragraphs appealing to natural law and the right of revolution, there is a long list of particular abuses, most of which the colonists regarded as not merely oppressive but as unconstitutional. Notably, the Declaration broke from both Parliament and the King. The British monarch now emerged as a relatively new object of American constitutional and political criticism.

The Unanimous Declaration of the Thirteen United States of America,

When in the Course of human events, it becomes necessary for one people to dissolve the political bands which have connected them with another, and to assume among the powers of the earth, the separate and equal station to which the Laws of Nature and of Nature's God entitle them, a decent respect to the opinions of mankind requires that they should declare the causes which impel them to the separation.

We hold these truths to be self-evident, that all men are created equal, that they are endowed by their Creator with certain unalienable Rights, that among these are Life, Liberty and the pursuit of Happiness. —That to secure these rights, Governments are instituted among Men, deriving their just powers from the consent of the governed, —That whenever any Form of Government becomes destructive of these ends, it is the Right of the People to alter or to abolish it, and to institute new Government, laying its foundation on such principles and organizing its powers in such form, as to them shall seem most likely to effect their Safety and Happiness. Prudence, indeed, will dictate that Governments long established should not be changed for light and transient causes; and accordingly all experience hath shown, that mankind are more disposed to suffer, while evils are sufferable, than to right themselves by abolishing the forms to which they are accustomed. But when a long train of abuses and usurpations, pursuing invariably the same Object evinces a design to reduce them under absolute Despotism, it is their right, it is their duty, to throw off such Government, and to provide new Guards for their future security. —Such has been the patient sufferance of these Colonies; and such is now the necessity which constrains them to alter their former Systems of Government. The history of the present King of Great Britain is a history of repeated injuries and usurpations, all having in direct object the establishment of an absolute Tyranny over these States. To prove this, let Facts be submitted to a candid world.

He has refused his Assent to Laws, the most wholesome and necessary for the public good.

He has forbidden his Governors to pass Laws of immediate and pressing importance, unless suspended in their operation till his Assent should be obtained; and when so suspended, he has utterly neglected to attend to them.

He has refused to pass other Laws for the accommodation of large districts of people, unless those people would relinquish the right of Representation in the Legislature, a right inestimable to them and formidable to tyrants only.

He has called together legislative bodies at places unusual, uncomfortable, and distant from the depository of their public Records, for the sole purpose of fatiguing them into compliance with his measures.

He has dissolved Representative Houses repeatedly, for opposing with manly firmness his invasions on the rights of the people.

He has refused for a long time, after such dissolutions, to cause others to be elected; whereby the Legislative powers, incapable of Annihilation, have returned to the People at large for their exercise; the State remaining in the mean time exposed to all the dangers of invasion from without, and convulsions within.

He has endeavored to prevent the population of these States; for that purpose obstructing the Laws for Naturalization of Foreigners; refusing to pass others to encourage their migrations hither, and raising the conditions of new Appropriations of Lands.

He has obstructed the Administration of Justice, by refusing his Assent to Laws for establishing Judiciary powers.

He has made Judges dependent on his Will alone, for the tenure of their offices, and the amount and payment of their salaries.

He has erected a multitude of New Offices, and sent hither swarms of Officers to harass our people, and eat out their substance.

He has kept among us, in times of peace, Standing Armies without the consent of our legislatures.

He has affected to render the Military independent of and superior to the civil power.

He has combined with others to subject us to a jurisdiction foreign to our constitution and unacknowledged by our laws; giving his Assent to their Acts of pretended Legislation:

For quartering large bodies of armed troops among us:

For protecting them, by a mock Trial, from punishment for any Murders which they should commit on the Inhabitants of these States:

For cutting off our Trade with all parts of the world:

For imposing Taxes on us without our Consent:

For depriving us, in many cases, of the benefits of Trial by Jury:

For transporting us beyond Seas to be tried for pretended offences:

For abolishing the free System of English Laws in a neighboring Province, establishing therein an arbitrary government, and enlarging its Boundaries so as to render it at once an example and fit instrument for introducing the same absolute rule into these Colonies:

For taking away our Charters, abolishing our most valuable Laws, and altering fundamentally the Forms of our Governments:

For suspending our own Legislatures, and declaring themselves invested with power to legislate for us in all cases whatsoever.

He has abdicated Government here, by declaring us out of his Protection and waging War against us.

He has plundered our seas, ravaged our Coasts, burnt our towns, and destroyed the lives of our people.

He is at this time transporting large Armies of foreign Mercenaries to complete the works of death, desolation and tyranny, already begun with circumstances of Cruelty and perfidy scarcely paralleled in the most barbarous ages, and totally unworthy the Head of a civilized nation.

He has constrained our fellow Citizens taken Captive on the high Seas to bear Arms against their Country, to become the executioners of their friends and Brethren, or to fall themselves by their Hands.

He has excited domestic insurrections amongst us, and has endeavored to bring on the inhabitants of our frontiers, the merciless Indian Savages, whose known rule of warfare, is an undistinguished destruction of all ages, sexes and conditions.

In every stage of these Oppressions We have petitioned for Redress in the most humble terms: Our repeated Petitions have been answered only by repeated injury. A Prince whose character is thus marked by every act which may define a Tyrant, is unfit to be the ruler of a free people.

Nor have we been wanting in attentions to our British brethren. We have warned them from time to time of attempts by their legislature to extend an unwarrantable jurisdiction over us. We have reminded them of the circumstances of our emigration and settlement here. We have appealed to their native justice and magnanimity, and we have conjured them by the ties of our common kindred to disavow these usurpations, which, would inevitably interrupt our connections and correspondence. They too have been deaf to the voice of justice and of consanguinity. We must, therefore, acquiesce in the necessity, which denounces our Separation, and hold them, as we hold the rest of mankind, Enemies in War, in Peace Friends.

We, therefore, the Representatives of the united States of America, in General Congress, Assembled, appealing to the Supreme Judge of the world for the rectitude of our intentions, do, in the Name, and by the Authority of the good People of these Colonies, solemnly publish and declare, That these United Colonies are, and of Right ought to be Free and Independent States; that they are Absolved from all Allegiance to the British Crown, and that all political connection between them and the State of Great Britain, is and ought to be totally dissolved; and that as Free and Independent States, they have full Power to levy War, conclude Peace, contract Alliances, establish Commerce, and to do all other Acts and Things which Independent States may of right do. And for the support of this Declaration, with a firm reliance on the protection of divine Providence, we mutually pledge to each other our Lives, our Fortunes and our sacred Honor.

Suggested Readings

Bailyn, Bernard. *The Ideological Origins of the American Republic* (Cambridge: Harvard University Press, 1967).

Bilder, Mary Sarah. *The Transatlantic Constitution: Colonial Legal Culture and the Empire* (Cambridge: Harvard University Press, 2004).

Breen, T. H. *American Insurgents, American Patriots: The Revolution of the People* (New York: Hill and Wang, 2010).

Brewer, John. *The Sinews of Power: War, Money, and the English State, 1688–1783* (Cambridge: Harvard University Press, 1990).

Greene, Jack P. *Peripheries and Center: Constitutional Development in the Extended Polities of British Empire and the United States, 1607–1788* (Athens: University of Georgia Press, 1986).

Hamburger, Philip. *Law and Judicial Duty* (Cambridge: Harvard University Press, 2008).

Hatfield, April Lee. *Atlantic Virginia: Intercolonial Relations in the Seventeenth Century* (Philadelphia: University of Pennsylvania Press, 2007).

Hulsebosch, Daniel J. *Constituting Empire: New York and the Transformation of Constitutionalism in the Atlantic World, 1664–1830* (Chapel Hill: University of North Carolina Press, 2005).

Kammen, Michael G. *Deputyes and Libertyes: The Origins of Representative Government in Colonial America* (New York: Knopf, 1969).

LaCroix, Alison L. *The Ideological Origins of American Federalism* (Cambridge: Harvard University Press, 2010).

Lutz, Donald S. *The Origins of American Constitutionalism* (Baton Rouge: Louisiana State University Press, 1988).

Maier, Pauline. *American Scripture: Making the Declaration of Independence* (New York: Vintage, 1997).

McIlwain, Charles Howard. *The American Revolution: A Constitutional Interpretation* (New York: Macmillan, 1923).

McLaughlin, Andrew C. *The Foundations of American Constitutionalism* (New York: New York University Press, 1932).

Morgan, Edmund. *The Birth of the Republic, 1763–89* (Chicago: University of Chicago Press, 1956).

Pocock, J. G. A., ed. *Three British Revolutions: 1641, 1688, 1776* (Princeton: Princeton University Press, 1980).

Reid, Thomas Phillip. *The Constitutional History of the American Revolution*, four volumes (Madison: University of Wisconsin Press, 1986–1993).

Russell, Elmer Beecher. *The Review of American Colonial Legislation by the King in Council* (New York: Columbia University Press, 1915).

Smith, Joseph Henry. *Appeals to the Privy Council from the American Plantations* (New York: Columbia University Press, 1950).

Stoner, James R. *The Common Law and Liberal Theory: Coke, Hobbes, and the Origins of American Constitutionalism* (Lawrence: University Press of Kansas, 1992).

Chapter 3

The Founding Era: 1776–1788

I. Introduction

Once the "thirteen united States of America" declared their independence from Great Britain in 1776, the authority to govern within those states had shifted. Now Parliament, they claimed, had no authority at all—not over taxes, not over trade, not over anything. With no more allegiance to the king, there would be no need for American laws to be consistent with English law or English liberties. If "absolute despotic power" (as William Blackstone, the English jurist, had called the sovereign power) over the Americans was going to reside somewhere, it was now going to reside in America.

The Declaration of Independence also brought to a head an issue that was already becoming critical: the need to form a new government. It was time for the Americans to "institute new Government, laying its foundations on such principles and organizing its powers in such form, as to them shall seem most likely to effect their Safety and Happiness." The colonial governments were generally derived not from "we the people," but from the British crown. With independence, these foundations were washed away. More practically, colonial governments were themselves in disarray. In some places, they had been suspended entirely and replaced with military governments under royal command. In others, the governors, upper legislative chambers, and courts still took their direction from England. "The people," or at least the people who declared themselves Americans and no longer Britons, had therefore withdrawn from the colonial governments. Revolutionary "committees of correspondence" therefore had more political legitimacy than the government institutions recognized by the colonial charters. The Americans would no longer seek to interpret the British constitution. They would now create their own.

State Constitution Making. The task of governing the former colonies could not be put off, but the effort at constitution making stretched across more than a decade. From its beginning, however, it proceeded on two tracks. One track played out in the individual states, as the Americans shook off their colonial governments. After 1776—and, if the Revolution were a success, long into the future—new republican governments would provide for law and order in the states. Even as the military struggle for independence continued, individuals continued to get married, to make contracts, to commit crimes, to die and pass their property on to their heirs. Even during war, the Americans needed law and government. The state governments also played an important part in fighting the war, and they needed to organize themselves to play that part well.

This first decade of American constitutionalism was a time of experiment. In several states, the first revolutionary constitutions were soon judged inadequate, and new constitutions were written to replace them. The first state constitutions often did not distinguish very clearly between the state legislature and the constitutional convention. Often, in fact, one elected assembly both wrote the constitution and governed under it. It is no surprise that these constitutions emphasized the power of the legislature. The powerful governors of the colonial era were swept away, and the new state governors were weak and highly constrained. The executives had few powers of their own. In many states, the executive could be appointed and removed by the legislative branch. Governors were hemmed in by executive councils, appointed by the legislature, who acted as a further check on the governor's decisions.

Legislatures were also becoming more active. They once primarily limited themselves to holding the purse strings and monitoring how the government was run. By the late eighteenth century, legislatures started to take over more of the policymaking role of government. They passed more and more important statutes, which the executive and the judges were expected to implement. Frequent elections and term limits on legislators were the primary checks on legislative power in the first constitutions. Many of these state governments were designed to be highly responsive to the electorate, even if the electorate was somewhat skewed or limited. But at least in theory, many argued, the legislature should be a "mirror" of the people, and the new republican governments strove to realize this ideal of clearly reflecting public opinion in the legislature.

By 1800, the thirteen original states, plus the two new states of Kentucky and Tennessee, had among them adopted twenty-four different constitutions. The two corporate colonies, Connecticut and Rhode Island, simply continued to use their colonial charters as constitutions. This was easier for them to do since they did not have royal governors or councils who needed to be thrown overboard. They merely needed to ignore old charter provisions regarding British supremacy and Privy Council review. The other states had to build up new governments from scratch, and this required fresh thinking about what a republican government should look like and how it should be formed.

In some cases, states had second thoughts about revolutionary constitutions that relied too exclusively on elections to limit the power of the legislature, and a second wave of constitutions emphasized checks and balances. Governors were given a little more independence. State courts discovered the power of judicial review. Constitutional reformers worried that state legislatures did not sufficiently respect minority or individual rights. State constitutional revision was a first step toward reining in state legislatures, but for reformers like James Madison state-level revision was not enough. National constitutional reform would be needed as well.

National Constitutional Reform. The second track of constitution making played out at the "continental" level. The thirteen colonies had all declared their separation from Britain. (Others declined the invitation to revolt and remained loyal to the crown—including the five North American colonies that would eventually become Canada.) Just as important, they had declared independence *together*. They were, according to the Declaration of Independence, "Free and Independent States," with "full Power" to do all the "Things which Independent States may of right do." But they had also pledged "to each other" their lives, their fortunes, and their honor to make independence a reality. And they needed to be constituted not just as thirteen individual bodies, but as united states. This complicated relationship between the states after independence would provide fodder for both nationalists and advocates of states rights after the adoption of the Constitution.

For much of this founding era, the groups that participated in the politics of constitution-making were fluid. In the first years of this period, the war for American independence took center stage, and the political world was primarily divided between patriots and loyalists. Loyalists, including some who had been prominent colonial participants in American constitutionalism such as Thomas Hutchinson of Massachusetts and Daniel Dulany of Maryland, were now irrelevant to the process of making new constitutions. This was a matter to be resolved among the patriots. The patriots could be more radical or more conservative, more elite or more provincial, but these were not hard divisions. After the Revolution, sharper lines began to develop. In the states, politics was often more personal and geographic than ideological. In the country as a whole, a group of more nationally and internationally minded leaders began to emerge, and they would thump for a constitutional reform to make a stronger union. They would become the Federalists.

Federalists emerged in every state, but its leaders were national politicians who had become convinced that the promise of the Revolution was being frittered away, perhaps to the point of endangering independence itself. The efforts at piecemeal constitutional reform at the national level had proven unavailing, and by 1787 the Federalists were prepared for a bolder departure. Many of the Federalist leaders had played leading roles in the national government during the Revolution and afterwards. Those who ultimately opposed the Constitution, known generally as the anti-Federalists, included a number of the high-profile leaders of the early revolutionary movement of the 1770s, such as Samuel Adams and Patrick Henry, as well as state government leaders such as New York governor George Clinton.

The first federal constitution, the Articles of Confederation, had been cobbled together during the Revolution. Benjamin Franklin, advocate of union since the Albany Congress of 1754, had proposed a set of articles to the Continental Congress in 1775. John Dickinson introduced a draft of the Articles of Confederation to the Congress on July 12, 1776. With more urgent matters on the agenda, the Articles were not approved by Congress until 1777 and not ratified in the last state until 1781. The first constitution was immediately problematic, and James Madison, among others, began to lobby for reform before the ink was even dry on the Articles. Like many of the revolutionary state constitutions, the Articles reflected the Americans' extreme distrust of governors and kings. It provided for no national executive or judicial branches. All national powers were held by the Confederation Congress, to be delegated out to appointed committees, commissions, or individuals as the legislature saw fit. Congress's authority was limited, and it had little muscle to put behind its decisions. Each state held an equal number of seats in Congress, and most important decisions required a supermajority or unanimity. Its enforcement powers, short of mustering the Continental Army, were limited. Its revenues were dependent on borrowing and requisitions to the states, and by the end of its life the Confederation had exhausted its credit and no state was willing to send it money. The national government, James Madison later observed, had sunk into a "state of imbecility" and "impotency."[1]

The Articles of Confederation were inadequate and had to be changed. Well before 1787, there was little disagreement about that. There was, however, disagreement over what changes were needed. The challenge for the Federalists was to force a choice between their favored solution, the new Constitution, and the status quo that no one was willing to defend. They could force this choice because critical and more modest constitutional amendments proved impossible. Any alteration in the Articles required unanimous consent of the states.

Taxes on imports were the most logical source of revenue for the federal government, but the states with the busiest ports jealously guarded access to those treasure troves. In 1781, Rhode Island vetoed a proposal to give the Confederation government the power to tax imports. In 1783, New York balked at a modified tax amendment. As the 1780s progressed, the fiscal situation only worsened, while other structural deficiencies were becoming more apparent and problematic. Peace and trade treaties proved difficult to negotiate and even harder to enforce. War debt and paper currency fed internal tensions in the states, which boiled over in the anti-tax Shay's Rebellion in Massachusetts in 1787. Secession or violent conflict among the states over such strategic resources as land and access to trade routes seemed increasingly likely to many, and it was unclear whether the United States could effectively defend itself if attacked by any of the European powers. Further constitutional amendments to give Congress the power to regulate trade were not ratified, and the Annapolis Convention which met in 1786 to consider that issue was sparsely attended. Any particular reform aimed at improving the overall situation threatened to hurt some particular states or interests.

What was needed was sweeping reform—a grand compromise that could package several issues at once. Members of the failed Annapolis Convention—including Alexander Hamilton, James Madison, and George Washington—asked Congress to call a new convention to address a broader set of defects in the Articles. This became the agenda of the better-attended Philadelphia Constitutional Convention in 1787. While obstructionist states like Rhode Island stayed home, and New York barely attended, others set to work drafting a new constitution to replace the Articles of Confederation.

James Madison took the initiative, drafting what became known as the Virginia Plan, for a completely restructured and more powerful national government. The delegates generally agreed about the goal—that was, after all, why they were there—so they quickly sat down to serious negotiation over the details of what the government would look like. They faced two critical and related issues: Who would dominate the new national government, and what powers would it exercise? If they knew who could be expected to control the government, they would know, too, what powers they could safely entrust to it. Those who could expect to be well endowed with seats in the House of Representatives, seats in the Senate, and electoral votes for the president could afford to be generous with national power. Those who could foresee themselves in the national minority were likely to be more cautious. Across multiple policy

1. Annals of Congress, 1st Cong., 1st sess., 1:107 (9 April 1789) (Madison, J.).

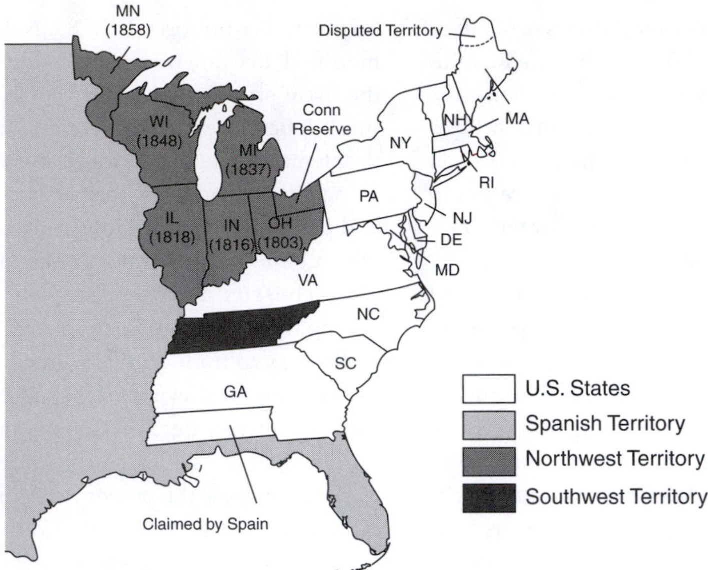

Figure 3-1 Territorial Map of the United States, 1789

issues of tax and trade, foreign policy and slavery and the design of the several branches of government, the necessary compromises and adjustments could be made to satisfy almost everyone in attendance.

The Ratification Struggle. It also helped to change the rules of the game. The rule that constitutional changes required the unanimous agreement of the thirteen states had proved fatal to the Confederation. The Philadelphia Convention itself operated by majority rule, and even then it helped that the delegates in attendance were Federalist in their basic sympathies. But they wanted to give their proposal the best start possible. The proposed Constitution would go into effect, and the old Confederation would be dissolved, with the approval of only nine states. Moreover, ratification would be by popular conventions in the states, not by the state legislatures. The Federalists wanted a fresh election on their proposal, as well as to put their new federal government on the firmer footing of popular sovereignty. This would be a Constitution of the people in the states, not an agreement among the state governments. Looking to the future, the Constitution allowed amendments with a mere supermajority of Congress and the states. Rhode Island had lost its veto.

Even with this ratification procedure, adoption of the Constitution was no sure thing. The Federalists had a head start on organizing, and they had chosen their name to sound reassuring. Their opponents had no national organization, were soon stuck with the unappealing moniker of anti-Federalists, and did not have a clear alternative to the failed Articles of Confederation to offer. The anti-Federalists did have effective local organizations, since their leaders were often leading figures in state government and politics, and their central message that the Constitution was an untried experiment in distant, centralized government had a great deal of popular resonance. The Americans had not shaken off the British Empire only to give up self-government to a continental empire.

The anti-Federalist strategy was to demand a second constitutional convention to revise the proposed Constitution in light of the ongoing public discussion. The Federalists, fearful that all their carefully negotiated compromises would be undone in a second convention without anything emerging to take their place, insisted on a straight up-or-down vote on the Constitution as written. The anti-Federalists raised complaints about the Constitution: Too much power was given to the national government, the national government

Table 3-1 Ratification of the U.S. Constitution by State

State	Convention Majority	Ratification Date	Final Vote
Delaware	Federalist	Dec. 7, 1787	100%
Pennsylvania	Federalist	Dec. 12, 1787	67%
New Jersey	Federalist	Dec. 19, 1787	100%
Georgia	Federalist	Jan. 2, 1788	100%
Connecticut	Federalist	Jan. 9, 1788	76%
Massachusetts	Anti-Federalist	Feb. 6, 1788	53%
Maryland	Federalist	April 28, 1788	85%
South Carolina	Federalist	May 23, 1788	67%
New Hampshire	Anti-Federalist	June 21, 1788	55%
Constitution meets Article VII requirement for ratification			
Virginia	Evenly Split	June 25, 1788	53%
New York	Anti-Federalist	July 26, 1788	53%
George Washington inaugurated as first president April 30, 1789 Bill of Rights passed by Congress Sept. 25, 1789			
North Carolina	Federalist	Nov. 21, 1789	71%
Rhode Island	Anti-Federalist	May 29, 1790	52%

would be insufficiently representative and violated a strict separation of powers, the national government was given excessive and dangerous powers over taxation and the military, and the new Constitution did not include a bill of rights.

The Federalists gained quick victories in several small states that had much to gain from an improved union. The struggle for ratification was harder fought elsewhere. Although most states, in their ratification, reserved powers not delegated to the new federal government, the Federalist strategy was to postpone considering any amendments until after ratification. The election of an anti-Federalist majority to the Massachusetts ratification convention forced an adjustment to that approach. The Federalists secured ratification in Massachusetts by agreeing to recommend a list of constitutional amendments to Congress. Similar deals were made in Virginia and New York. Those two large and wealthy states were essential to a successful union, and the Federalists could not breathe easy until they had ratified the Constitution. John Jay, Alexander Hamilton, and James Madison collaborated to write an anonymous series of newspaper articles advocating ratification in order to swing the debate in New York. The New York convention voted before the newspaper series was completed, but the essays were later repackaged as a much-discussed book, *The Federalist Papers*. North Carolina and Rhode Island were left outside the new union, but once the new government was up and running, it was widely expected that those two reluctant states would come along. With ratification accomplished and the new federal government apparently successful, the anti-Federalists either committed themselves to participating within the new constitutional system or to drifting out of politics entirely.[2]

2. For accounts of the constitutional drafting and ratification, see Max Farrand, *The Framing of the Constitution of the United States* (New Haven: Yale University Press, 1913); Catherine Drinker Bowen, *Miracle at Philadelphia* (Boston: Little, Brown and Company, 1966); Robert Allen Rutland, *The Ordeal of the Constitution* (Norman: University of Oklahoma Press, 1966); Jack N. Rakove, *Original Meanings* (New York: Vintage, 1996).

Box 3-1 Partial Cast of Characters of the Founding Era

Alexander Hamilton	■ Federalist ■ Proponent of strong presidency and national power ■ Leader of Federalist forces in New York during ratification debate and an author of the "Federalist" essays ■ Secretary of Treasury for Federalist George Washington (1789–1795) ■ Helped create the Federalist Party ■ Killed in a duel with Vice President Aaron Burr
James Madison	■ Moderate Republican ■ Leading figure in the Philadelphia Constitutional Convention ■ An author of the "Federalist" essays supporting ratification ■ Authored the Bill of Rights ■ Advocated a moderate form of strict constructionism in constitutional interpretation ■ Secretly authored the Virginia Resolutions of 1798 ■ Helped create the Jeffersonian Republican Party ■ Secretary of State for Republican Thomas Jefferson (1801–1809) ■ President of the United States (1809–1817)
James Wilson	■ Federalist ■ Author of important revolutionary pamphlet on legal authority of Parliament over the colonies ■ Signer of the Declaration of Independence ■ Pennsylvania delegate to the Philadelphia Constitutional Convention ■ Appointed by Federalist George Washington to be one of the first members of the U.S. Supreme Court (1789–1798) ■ Delivered the founding lectures on law at the University of Pennsylvania
William Paterson	■ Moderate Federalist ■ New Jersey attorney general (1776–1783) ■ Delegate to Philadelphia Constitutional Convention and author of the small-state "New Jersey Plan" ■ New Jersey governor (1790–1793) ■ Appointed by Federalist George Washington to be an Associate Justice of the U.S. Supreme Court (1793–1806)
Robert Yates	■ Anti-Federalist ■ Chief judge of New York Supreme Court (1790–1798) ■ Delegate to Philadelphia Constitutional Convention but left early in opposition to the powerful national government ■ Likely authored the "Brutus" essays criticizing the Constitution

James Madison himself thought that the Constitution that emerged from Philadelphia was imperfect, and he was honest in saying so. He also admitted that the constitutional text was murky in places. "All new laws, though penned with the greatest technical skill, and passed on the fullest and most mature deliberation, are considered as more or less obscure and equivocal, until their meaning be liquidated and ascertained by a series of particular discussions and adjudications."[3] Yet he argued that it was the best that anyone could hope to achieve.

Debating the Constitution. What kind of constitution had the Federalists made? The anti-Federalists argued that it was it was a "consolidated" and "aristocratic" constitution. It created a government that absorbed extraordinary powers to itself and yet was distant from the people. Progressive scholars at the turn of the twentieth century became newly fascinated by the anti-Federalist concerns. Most prominently, the historian Charles Beard argued that the creation of the Constitution was one battle in the long-running war between commercial and agricultural interests in the United States. The personal economic interests of the Convention delegates, he claimed, motivated reform and the details of the proposed Constitution. Those who supported the Constitution were creditors and business interests, he argued, and those opposed were debtors and heavily invested in land. The details of Beard's argument did not hold up, but other scholars have also emphasized the importance of real interests, whether economic or political, in shaping the constitutional politics of the founding era.[4]

Over the past few decades, scholars have also emphasized the importance of ideas to the constitutional debates. A central theme is the tension between liberal and republican ideas in the founding era. Liberalism, in the tradition of English philosophers John Locke and later John Stuart Mill, emphasizes individualism and rights against government power. Republicanism, in the tradition of the Italian writer Niccolo Machiavelli and the English writer James Harrington, emphasizes civic virtue, political community, and skepticism of government corruption. The traditions can be reinforcing; both value democracy and limited government. But the constitutional reforms of the 1780s can be seen as a shift in emphasis toward liberalism and away from the more republican constitutions of the revolutionary era. The Constitution created a more distant, less accountable and more complex machinery of government. It would refine the sentiments of the people rather than mirror them, and provide more institutional protections of rights, especially the rights of property.[5]

Through history, many constitutional commentators have insisted that constitutional provisions be interpreted consistently with their original meaning. Critics claim that no clear agreement existed on the meaning of crucial constitutional provisions or on more general constitutional principles.[6] This chapter discusses how the meaning of the constitutional text was understood, as well as disagreements over what it meant and even whether it was desirable. Later chapters illuminate the debates that have emerged or continued over time about the meaning of the Constitution.

Four main points of contention shaped constitutional debate during this period:

1. The role of the federal judiciary in the new Republic.
2. The scope of the powers of the national government.
3. The nature of federal–state relations.
4. The proper understanding of separation of powers.

As you become familiar with these debates, you should also consider some more general questions about the challenges associated with building a successful constitutional system. What is the point of the activity? Grounding the Republic in sound principles of good government? Legitimating the political system by creating a mechanism of consent? Hammering out a bargain that would be considered acceptable by people with diverse interests, perspectives, and values? Do you think that these particular debates are representative of the politics of constitution making in other settings? Is there something about the nature of constitution making that makes it a distinctive way of creating a working political system?

---

3. Alexander Hamilton, James Madison, and John Jay, *The Federalist Papers*, ed. Clinton Rossiter (New York: Mentor Books, 1961), No. 37, 229.

4. Charles A. Beard, *An Economic Interpretation of the Constitution of the United States* (New York: Free Press, 1986); Forrest McDonald, *We the People* (Chicago: University of Chicago Press, 1958); John Patrick Diggins, "Power and Authority in American History: The Case of Charles Beard and His Critics," *American Historical Review* 86 (1981): 701; Robert A. McGuire, *To Form a More Perfect Union* (New York: Oxford University Press, 2003).

5. Gordon S. Wood, *The Creation of the American Republic, 1776–1787* (New York: Norton, 1972): Forrest McDonald, *Novus Ordo Seclorum* (Lawrence: University Press of Kansas, 1985).

6. On the originalism debate, see Keith E. Whittington, *Constitutional Interpretation* (Lawrence: University Press of Kansas, 1999); Jack N. Rakove, ed., *Interpreting the Constitution* (Boston: Northeastern University Press, 1990).

Finally, consider what, if anything, made this act of nation building legitimate. After all, the national constitution in force at the time of the Philadelphia Convention required that changes be authorized by the unanimous consent of the states. If the framers could legitimately depart from this requirement then would it also be appropriate for us to change our Constitution by virtue of a process that is not authorized by the document?

II. Judicial Power and Constitutional Authority

MAJOR DEVELOPMENTS

- Establishment of an independent federal judiciary
- Development of judicial review in the state courts
- Debate over the value of constitutional interpretation by federal judges

The judicial power was not quite an afterthought in the decade after the declaration of independence, but it was close. No one questioned the importance of the courts to maintaining law and order and to keeping society running smoothly. Judges had important work to perform in the United States, just as they had in the colonies. It was, however, thought to be pretty much the *same* work as they had performed in the colonies. The basic transition from empire to independence, from monarchy to republic required a transformation in constitutional forms and a transformation in the laws, but the courts seemed little affected by those transformations. The founding generation did not think very much about the courts. They thought that the role of these courts was fairly uncontroversial.

If the federal government were to have the power to enforce its own laws directly on the people, however, then it would need its own courts. However, these courts then needed to be tied down with the familiar common law forms and liberties. They should not generally be allowed to operate without juries, for example. They should be given rules that they should follow and boundaries that they should not exceed, such as not imposing excessive bail on criminal defendants and not holding trials in inconvenient places.

The courts were also charged with adhering to the Constitution when its requirements otherwise became relevant to the performance of their duties. Pennsylvania had experimented, less than satisfactorily, with a council of censors to "enquire whether the constitution has been preserved inviolate" in its state constitution of 1776. James Madison had unsuccessfully urged the federal constitutional convention to make all state laws subject to something like Privy Council review in Congress. The Convention responded instead with the supremacy clause, which specified that the Constitution and federal law had legal priority over state law. State and federal courts were both expected to recognize that priority when deciding whether and how to apply state laws in the cases that came before them. There was general agreement that judges would have the power to declare state laws void if they violated the U.S. Constitution. Meanwhile, some argued that *all* constitutions were legally superior to *all* statutes, and that judges were obliged to ignore laws that violated constitutional requirements. Legislators did not always accept the idea that judges were entitled to look in back of the law and determine whether the legislature was authorized to pass them in the first place. In the absence of a special institution like a council of censors, perhaps it was up to the conscience of the legislators, or to the people themselves, to measure the consistency of the law with the constitution and to determine what action, if any, might be needed. This was a judicial power that would become of greater interest over time.

A. Judicial Review

Some form of judicial review was anticipated during the founding era debates. State courts had already exercised a power of judicial review by the time of the Philadelphia Convention of 1787. Federalists wanted federal and state courts to be able to enforce federal commitments against the states. What was less certain was the form and importance that such judicial activity might take. The institution of judicial review had little precedent, and there were few guidelines to suggest how American courts and constitutional law might look after constitution writers had done their work. The very idea of judicial review of state and federal statutes generated some controversy during the founding era, but there was even more debate over how best to justify and imagine such a practice.

Robert Yates, "Brutus" (1787)[7]

Robert Yates was a judge on the New York Supreme Court, later serving as chief justice. He had been a delegate to the federal Constitutional Convention, but left when it became obvious that the Convention would not limit itself to minor revisions of the Articles of Confederation. He became a prominent and influential anti-Federalist in New York.

Yates was likely the author of the "Brutus" essays published in the New York newspapers during the ratification debates. The quality of the Brutus essays helped spur Alexander Hamilton to mount a response with the Federalist essays. Several of the Brutus essays focused on the proposed federal judiciary. Among his criticisms was a concern with how the federal courts might interpret the Constitution. Brutus was convinced that federal judges would find it in their interest to interpret the terms of the Constitution broadly so as to expand their own jurisdiction and influence, and that Congress would be supportive of such loose interpretations because they would ultimately expand federal legislative power as well. Judicial interpretation would become the vehicle for expanding federal power. Is Brutus worried about the anti-democratic or "countermajoritarian" nature of judicial review, or does he have other concerns about judicial interpretation of the Constitution?

No. 11

. . .

The judicial are not only to decide questions arising upon the meaning of the constitution in law, but also in equity.

By this they are empowered, to explain the constitution according to the reasoning spirit of it, without being confined to the words or letter.

. . .

They will give the sense of every article of the constitution, that may from time to time come before them. And in their decisions they will not confine themselves to any fixed or established rules, but will determine, according to what appears to them, the reason and spirit of the constitution. The opinions of the supreme court, whatever they may be, will have the force of law; because there is no power provided in the constitution, that can correct their errors, or control their adjudications. From this court there is no appeal. And I conceive the legislature themselves, cannot set aside a judgment of this court, because they are authorized by the constitution to decide in the last resort. The legislature must be controlled by the constitution, and not the constitution by them. They have therefore no more right to set aside any judgment pronounced upon the construction of the constitution, than they have to take from the president, the chief command of the army and navy, and commit it to some other person. The reason is plain; the judicial and executive derive their authority from the same source, that the legislature do theirs; and therefore in all cases, where the constitution does not make the one responsible to, or controllable by the other, they are altogether independent of each other.

The judicial power will operate to effect, in the most certain, but yet silent and imperceptible manner, what is evidently the tendency of the constitution:—I mean, an entire subversion of the legislative, executive and judicial powers of the individual states. Every adjudication of the supreme court, on any question that may arise upon the nature and extent of the general government, will affect the limits of the state jurisdiction. In proportion as the former enlarge the exercise of their powers, will that of the latter be restricted.

That the judicial power of the United States, will lean strongly in favor of the general government, and will give such an explanation to the constitution, as will favor an extension of its jurisdiction, is very evident from a variety of considerations.

1st. The constitution itself strongly countenances such a mode of construction. Most of the articles in this system, which convey powers of any considerable importance, are conceived in general and indefinite terms, which are either equivocal, ambiguous, or which require long definitions to unfold the extent of their meaning. . . .

This constitution gives sufficient color for adopting an equitable construction, if we consider the great end and design it professedly has in view—these appear from its preamble to be, "to form a more perfect union, establish justice, insure domestic tranquility, provide for the common defense, promote the general welfare, and secure the blessings of liberty to ourselves and posterity." The design of this system is here expressed, and it is proper to give such a meaning to the various parts, as will best promote the accomplishment of the end; this idea suggests itself naturally upon reading the preamble, and will countenance the court in giving the

7. Excerpt taken from *New York Journal* (January 31–February 7, 1788).

several articles such a sense, as will the most effectually promote the ends the constitution had in view—how this manner of explaining the constitution will operate in practice, shall be the subject of future enquiry.

2d. Not only will the constitution justify the courts in inclining to this mode of explaining it, but they will be interested in using this latitude of interpretation. Every body of men invested with office are tenacious of power; they feel interested, and hence it has become a kind of maxim, to hand down their offices, with all its rights and privileges, unimpaired to their successors; the same principle will influence them to extend their power, and increase their rights; this of itself will operate strongly upon the courts to give such a meaning to the constitution in all cases where it can possibly be done, as will enlarge the sphere of their own authority. Every extension of the power of the general legislature, as well as of the judicial powers, will increase the powers of the courts; and the dignity and importance of the judges, will be in proportion to the extent and magnitude of the powers they exercise.... From these considerations the judges will be interested to extend the powers of the courts, and to construe the constitution as much as possible, in such a way as to favor it; and that they will do it, appears probable.

...

No. 12

...

First. Let us enquire how the judicial power will effect an extension of the legislative authority.

Perhaps the judicial power will not be able, by direct and positive decrees, ever to direct the legislature, because it is not easy to conceive how a question can be brought before them in a course of legal discussion, in which they can give a decision, declaring, that the legislature have certain powers which they have not exercised, and which, in consequence of the determination of the judges, they will be bound to exercise. But it is easy to see, that in their adjudications they may establish certain principles, which being received by the legislature, will enlarge the sphere of their power beyond all bounds.

It is to be observed, that the supreme court has the power, in the last resort, to determine all questions that may arise in the course of legal discussion, on the meaning and construction of the constitution. This power they will hold under the constitution, and independent of the legislature. The latter can no more deprive the former of this right, than either of them, or both of them together, can take from the president, with the advice of the senate, the power of making treaties, or appointing ambassadors.

In determining these questions, the court must and will assume certain principles, from which they will reason, in forming their decisions. These principles, whatever they may be, when they become fixed, by a course of decisions, will be adopted by the legislature, and will be the rule by which they will explain their own powers. This appears evident from this consideration, that if the legislature pass laws, which, in the judgment of the court, they are not authorized to do by the constitution, the court will not take notice of them; for it will not be denied, that the constitution is the highest or supreme law. And the courts are vested with the supreme and uncontrollable power, to determine, in all cases that come before them, what the constitution means; they cannot, therefore, execute a law, which, in their judgment, opposes the constitution, unless we can suppose they can make a superior law give way to an inferior. The legislature, therefore, will not go over the limits by which the courts may adjudge they are confined. And there is little room to doubt but that they will come up to those bounds, as often as occasion and opportunity may offer, and they may judge it proper to do it. For as on the one hand, they will not readily pass laws which they know the courts will not execute, so on the other, we may be sure they will not scruple to pass such as they know they will give effect, as often as they may judge it proper.

From these observations it appears, that the judgment of the judicial, on the constitution, will become the rule to guide the legislature in their construction of their powers.

What the principles are, which the courts will adopt, it is impossible for us to say; but taking up the powers as I have explained them in my last number, which they will possess under this clause, it is not difficult to see, that they may, and probably will, be very liberal ones.

...

The Federalist, No. 78[8]

The Federalist Papers *were originally written as a series of essays under the pen name of "Publius" for the New York*

8. Excerpt taken from *The Federalist: A Collection of Essays, Written in Favour of the New Constitution, as Agreed Upon by the Federal Convention, September 17, 1787, in two volumes* (New York: J. and A. McLean, 1788).

newspapers during the New York ratification debates. They were also collected and published in book form, originally in two volumes, for wider distribution. Within a decade, the authors of the collection, but not the authors of the individual essays, were publicly identified as Alexander Hamilton, James Madison, and John Jay. The Federalist *was immediately recognized as a great and influential commentary on the meaning of the Constitution, and it has long been used as a prominent statement of the promises made about and the public understandings of the Constitution at the time of its ratification.*

The essays were organized by Alexander Hamilton, who was fighting an uphill battle for ratification in New York. Secretary of Foreign Affairs John Jay was to be the other major contributor, but illness prevented him from writing. Hamilton turned to James Madison as a replacement. As a leading Federalist politician in New York, Jay was a natural contributor to the project. Madison, who was bogged down in his own closely fought ratification battle in his home-state of Virginia, was in some ways a less obvious choice. But Madison was a fast and effective writer and had been orchestrating the national Federalist ratification campaign already, and Hamilton knew that he could be persuasive to moderates on the merits of the proposed Constitution.

Hamilton specifically responded to the Brutus essays on the judiciary in a group of late essays that were only included in the book form of The Federalist. *The first of these, Number 78, is among the most influential of all the* Federalist *essays. Here Hamilton tries to reassure the anti-Federalists that the federal courts will not be oppressive. What is more, Hamilton discusses how the courts will interpret the Constitution. In doing so, he, like Brutus, anticipates the power of judicial review and offers a justification for it. How effective is this as a response to Brutus? Hamilton argues that the judiciary is the "least dangerous branch." Why does he think that is true, and how persuasive is he?*

No. 78 (Alexander Hamilton)

...The standard of good behavior for the continuance in office of the judicial magistracy, is certainly one of the most valuable of the modern improvements in the practice of government. In a monarchy it is an excellent barrier to the despotism of the prince; in a republic it is a no less excellent barrier to the encroachments and oppressions of the representative body. And it is the best expedient which can be devised in any government, to secure a steady, upright, and impartial administration of the laws.

Whoever attentively considers the different departments of power must perceive, that, in a government in which they are separated from each other, the judiciary, from the nature of its functions, will always be the least dangerous to the political rights of the Constitution; because it will be least in a capacity to annoy or injure them. The Executive not only dispenses the honors, but holds the sword of the community. The legislature not only commands the purse, but prescribes the rules by which the duties and rights of every citizen are to be regulated. The judiciary, on the contrary, has no influence over either the sword or the purse; no direction either of the strength or of the wealth of the society; and can take no active resolution whatever. It may truly be said to have neither FORCE nor WILL, but merely judgment; and must ultimately depend upon the aid of the executive arm even for the efficacy of its judgments.

...[T]he judiciary is beyond comparison the weakest of the three departments of power;...it can never attack with success either of the other two; and...all possible care is requisite to enable it to defend itself against their attacks....[T]hough individual oppression may now and then proceed from the courts of justice, the general liberty of the people can never be endangered from that quarter; I mean so long as the judiciary remains truly distinct from both the legislature and the Executive. For I agree, that "there is no liberty, if the power of judging be not separated from the legislative and executive powers."...[A]s liberty can have nothing to fear from the judiciary alone, but would have every thing to fear from its union with either of the other departments; that as all the effects of such a union must ensue from a dependence of the former on the latter, notwithstanding a nominal and apparent separation; that as, from the natural feebleness of the judiciary, it is in continual jeopardy of being overpowered, awed, or influenced by its co-ordinate branches; and that as nothing can contribute so much to its firmness and independence as permanency in office, this quality may therefore be justly regarded as an indispensable ingredient in its constitution, and, in a great measure, as the citadel of the public justice and the public security.

The complete independence of the courts of justice is peculiarly essential in a limited Constitution. By a limited Constitution, I understand one which contains certain specified exceptions to the legislative authority; such, for instance, as that it shall pass no bills of attainder, no ex-post-facto laws, and the like. Limitations of this kind can be preserved in practice no other way than through the medium of courts of justice, whose duty it must be to declare all acts contrary to the manifest tenor of the Constitution void. Without this, all the reservations of particular rights or privileges would amount to nothing.

Some perplexity respecting the rights of the courts to pronounce legislative acts void, because contrary to the Constitution, has arisen from an imagination that the doctrine would imply a superiority of the judiciary to the legislative power. It is urged that the authority which can declare the acts of another void, must necessarily be superior to the one whose acts may be declared void. As this doctrine is of great importance in all the American constitutions, a brief discussion of the ground on which it rests cannot be unacceptable.

There is no position which depends on clearer principles, than that every act of a delegated authority, contrary to the tenor of the commission under which it is exercised, is void. No legislative act, therefore, contrary to the Constitution, can be valid. To deny this, would be to affirm, that the deputy is greater than his principal; that the servant is above his master; that the representatives of the people are superior to the people themselves; that men acting by virtue of powers, may do not only what their powers do not authorize, but what they forbid.

If it be said that the legislative body are themselves the constitutional judges of their own powers, and that the construction they put upon them is conclusive upon the other departments, it may be answered, that this cannot be the natural presumption, where it is not to be collected from any particular provisions in the Constitution. It is not otherwise to be supposed, that the Constitution could intend to enable the representatives of the people to substitute their WILL to that of their constituents. It is far more rational to suppose, that the courts were designed to be an intermediate body between the people and the legislature, in order, among other things, to keep the latter within the limits assigned to their authority. The interpretation of the laws is the proper and peculiar province of the courts. A constitution is, in fact, and must be regarded by the judges, as a fundamental law. It therefore belongs to them to ascertain its meaning, as well as the meaning of any particular act proceeding from the legislative body. If there should happen to be an irreconcilable variance between the two, that which has the superior obligation and validity ought, of course, to be preferred; or, in other words, the Constitution ought to be preferred to the statute, the intention of the people to the intention of their agents.

Nor does this conclusion by any means suppose a superiority of the judicial to the legislative power. It only supposes that the power of the people is superior to both; and that where the will of the legislature, declared in its statutes, stands in opposition to that of the people, declared in the Constitution, the judges ought to be governed by the latter rather than the former. They ought to regulate their decisions by the fundamental laws, rather than by those which are not fundamental.

...It not uncommonly happens, that there are two statutes existing at one time, clashing in whole or in part with each other, and neither of them containing any repealing clause or expression....So far as they can, by any fair construction, be reconciled to each other, reason and law conspire to dictate that this should be done; where this is impracticable, it becomes a matter of necessity to give effect to one, in exclusion of the other. The rule which has obtained in the courts for determining their relative validity is, that the last in order of time shall be preferred to the first....

But in regard to the interfering acts of a superior and subordinate authority, of an original and derivative power, the nature and reason of the thing indicate the converse of that rule as proper to be followed. They teach us that the prior act of a superior ought to be preferred to the subsequent act of an inferior and subordinate authority; and that accordingly, whenever a particular statute contravenes the Constitution, it will be the duty of the judicial tribunals to adhere to the latter and disregard the former.

It can be of no weight to say that the courts, on the pretense of a repugnancy, may substitute their own pleasure to the constitutional intentions of the legislature. This might as well happen in the case of two contradictory statutes; or it might as well happen in every adjudication upon any single statute. The courts must declare the sense of the law; and if they should be disposed to exercise WILL instead of JUDGMENT, the consequence would equally be the substitution of their pleasure to that of the legislative body. The observation, if it prove any thing, would prove that there ought to be no judges distinct from that body.

...If, then, the courts of justice are to be considered as the bulwarks of a limited Constitution against legislative encroachments, this consideration will afford a strong argument for the permanent tenure of judicial offices, since nothing will contribute so much as this to that independent spirit in the judges which must be essential to the faithful performance of so arduous a duty.

This independence of the judges is equally requisite to guard the Constitution and the rights of individuals from the effects of those ill humors, which the arts of designing men, or the influence of particular conjunctures, sometimes disseminate among the people themselves, and which, though they speedily give place to better information, and more deliberate reflection, have a tendency, in the meantime, to occasion dangerous innovations in the government, and serious oppressions of the minor party in the community. Though I trust the friends of the proposed Constitution will never concur with its enemies, in questioning that fundamental principle of republican government, which admits the right of the people to alter or abolish the established Constitution, whenever they find it inconsistent with their happiness, yet it is not to be inferred from this principle, that the representatives of the people, whenever a momentary inclination happens to lay hold of a majority of their constituents, incompatible with the provisions in the existing Constitution, would, on that account, be justifiable in a violation of those provisions; or that the courts would be under a greater obligation to connive at infractions in this shape, than when they had proceeded wholly from the cabals of the representative body. Until the people have, by some solemn and authoritative act, annulled or changed the established form, it is binding upon themselves collectively, as well as individually; and no presumption, or even knowledge, of their sentiments, can warrant their representatives in a departure from it, prior to such an act. But it is easy to see, that it would require an uncommon portion of fortitude in the judges to do their duty as faithful guardians of the Constitution, where legislative invasions of it had been instigated by the major voice of the community.

There is yet a further and a weightier reason for the permanency of the judicial offices, which is deducible from the nature of the qualifications they require. It has been frequently remarked, with great propriety, that a voluminous code of laws is one of the inconveniences necessarily connected with the advantages of a free government. To avoid an arbitrary discretion in the courts, it is indispensable that they should be bound down by strict rules and precedents, which serve to define and point out their duty in every particular case that comes before them;...and must demand long and laborious study to acquire a competent knowledge of them. Hence it is, that there can be but few men in the society who will have sufficient skill in the laws to qualify them for the stations of judges....[A] temporary duration in office, which would naturally discourage such characters from quitting a lucrative line of practice to accept a seat on the bench, would have a tendency to throw the administration of justice into hands less able, and less well qualified, to conduct it with utility and dignity....

B. The Absence of a Bill of Rights

The U.S. Constitution as it emerged out of the Philadelphia Convention of 1787 did not have an explicit Bill of Rights. This was unusual. The state constitutions had bills of rights, which were understood to justify and legitimate the constitution and to limit the powers of the government formed under the constitution. The original U.S. Constitution included some rights provisions, but the preamble did not declare a long list of rights that were to be held fundamental and secure nor did it end with an inventory of rights that citizens could expect to be protected.

The anti-Federalists jumped on the omission as a critical mistake. They argued that the absence of a bill of rights opened the door to a powerful, abusive government. Worse yet, the fact that the Federalists had not included a bill of rights suggested that the authors of the Constitution did not hold traditional American liberties as particularly important and so could not be trusted to create a new government. It was an important talking point for the anti-Federalists as they sought to derail ratification of the proposed Constitution.

When the Constitution ran into serious opposition in states like Pennsylvania, Virginia and New York, the Federalists needed an answer to the bill of rights problem in order to win ratification. James Wilson in Pennsylvania and Alexander Hamilton in New York offered two of the major responses to the anti-Federalists concerns. They argued that the Constitution should not include a bill of rights and that anti-Federalist fears were misplaced. That response proved inadequate. James Madison of Virginia helped lead an alternative strategy of proposing that the Constitution be adopted without a bill of rights with an understanding that amendments would be considered later. Many of the state ratification conventions then proposed constitutional amendments at the same time that they voted on the U.S. Constitution, and Madison took the lead in the First Congress in drafting a set of amendments that became the Bill of Rights. Politically, Madison's solution worked. Was it the best approach to designing the Constitution? Are Wilson and Hamilton persuasive that the original Constitution would have worked well without a bill of rights?

James Wilson, **State House Yard Speech** (1787)[9]

One prominent objection to the ratification of the Constitution was that it failed to include a bill of rights. In states such as Pennsylvania and New York, where anti-Federalist forces were strong enough to forcefully raise their objections, the Federalists were obliged to explain why the absence of a bill of rights should not prevent ratification. The issue absorbed the attention of some of the most brilliant Federalists, including James Wilson and Alexander Hamilton. Although every state constitution included a bill of rights, the Federalists did not argue that the absence of a bill of rights in the U.S. Constitution was an oversight or something to be corrected through amendment. Instead, they argued that a bill of rights was inappropriate to the Constitution and would warp its structure if added to it.

As you read these arguments, consider whether the Bill of Rights as eventually added to the Constitution reinforced or subverted the original constitutional design. Are their concerns general to any bill of rights, or could their concerns be addressed through the choices made in drafting a bill of rights?

...

It will be proper...to mark the leading discrimination between the State constitutions and the constitution of the United States. When the people established the powers of legislation under their separate governments, they invested their representatives with every right and authority which they did not in explicit terms reserve; and therefore upon every question respecting the jurisdiction of the House of Assembly, if the frame of government is silent, the jurisdiction is efficient and complete. But in delegating federal powers, another criterion was necessarily introduced, and the congressional power is to be collected, not from tacit implication, but from the positive grant expressed in the instrument of the union. Hence, it is evident, that in the former case everything which is not reserved is given; but in the latter the reverse of the proposition prevails, and everything which is not given is reserved.

This distinction being recognized, will furnish an answer to those who think the omission of a bill of rights a defect in the proposed constitution; for it would have been superfluous and absurd to have stipulated with a federal body of our own creation, that we should enjoy those privileges of which we are not divested, either by the intention or the act that has brought the body into existence. For instance, the liberty of the press, which has been a copious source of declamation and opposition—what control can proceed from the Federal government to shackle or destroy that sacred palladium of national freedom? If, indeed, a power similar to that which has been granted for the regulation of commerce had been granted to regulate literary publications, it would have been as necessary to stipulate that the liberty of the press should be preserved inviolate, as that the impost should be general in its operation.... In truth, then, the proposed system possesses no influence whatever upon the press, and it would have been merely nugatory to have introduced a formal declaration upon the subject—nay, that very declaration might have been construed to imply that some degree of power was given, since we undertook to define its extent.

Another objection that has been fabricated against the new constitution, is expressed in this disingenuous form—"The trial by jury is abolished in civil cases." I must be excused, my fellow citizens, if upon this point I take advantage of my professional experience to detect the futility of the assertion. Let it be remembered then, that the business of the Federal Convention was not local, but general—not limited to the views and establishments of a single State, but co-extensive with the continent, and comprehending the views and establishments of thirteen independent sovereignties. When, therefore, this subject was in discussion, we were involved in difficulties which pressed on all sides, and no precedent could be discovered to direct our course. The cases open to a trial by jury differed in

9. Excerpt taken from *Independent Gazetteer* (October 11, 1787).

the different States. It was therefore impracticable, on that ground, to have made a general rule. The want of uniformity would have rendered any reference to the practice of the States idle and useless; and it could not with any propriety be said that, "The trial by jury shall be as heretofore," since there has never existed any federal system of jurisprudence, to which the declaration could relate. Besides, it is not in all cases that the trial by jury is adopted in civil questions; for cases depending in courts of admiralty, such as relate to maritime captures, and such as are agitated in courts of equity, do not require the intervention of that tribunal. How, then was the line of discrimination to be drawn? The Convention found the task too difficult for them, and they left the business as it stands, in the fullest confidence that no danger could possibly ensue, since the proceedings of the Supreme Court are to be regulated by the Congress, which is a faithful representation of the people; and the oppression of government is effectually barred, by declaring that in all criminal cases the trial by jury shall be preserved.

This constitution, it has been further urged, is of a pernicious tendency, because it tolerates a standing army in the time of peace. This has always been a topic of popular declamation; and yet I do not know a nation in the world which has not found it necessary and useful to maintain the appearance of strength in a season of the most profound tranquility. Nor is it a novelty with us; for under the present articles of confederation, Congress certainly possesses this reprobated power, and the exercise of that power is proved at this moment by her cantonments along the banks of the Ohio....

...

The power of direct taxation has likewise been treated as an improper delegation to the federal government; but when we consider it as the duty of that body to provide for the national safety, to support the dignity of the union, and to discharge the debts contracted upon the collected faith of the States for their common benefit, it must be acknowledged that those upon whom such important obligations are imposed, ought in justice and in policy to possess every means requisite for a faithful performance of their trust. But why should we be alarmed with visionary evils? I will venture to predict that the great revenue of the United States must, and always will, be raised by impost, for, being at once less obnoxious and more productive, the interest of the government will be best promoted by the accommodation of the people. Still, however, the objects of direct taxation should be within reach in all cases of emergency; and there is no more reason to apprehend oppression in the mode of collecting a revenue from this resource, than in the form of an impost, which by universal assent, is left to the authority of the federal government....

The Federalist, No. 84[10]

No. 84 (Alexander Hamilton)

...

...The Constitution proposed by the convention contains...a number of such provisions.

...The establishment of the writ of habeas corpus, the prohibition of ex-post-facto laws, and of TITLES OF NOBILITY, TO WHICH WE HAVE NO CORRESPONDING PROVISION IN OUR CONSTITUTION, are perhaps greater securities to liberty and republicanism than any it contains. The creation of crimes after the commission of the fact, or, in other words, the subjecting of men to punishment for things which, when they were done, were breaches of no law, and the practice of arbitrary imprisonments, have been, in all ages, the favorite and most formidable instruments of tyranny....

...

It has been several times truly remarked that bills of rights are, in their origin, stipulations between kings and their subjects, abridgements of prerogative in favor of privilege, reservations of rights not surrendered to the prince. Such was MAGNA CARTA, obtained by the barons, sword in hand, from King John....It is evident, therefore, that, according to their primitive signification, they have no application to constitutions professedly founded upon the power of the people, and executed by their immediate representatives and servants. Here, in strictness, the people surrender nothing; and as they retain every thing they have no need of particular reservations. "WE, THE PEOPLE of the United States, to secure the blessings of liberty to ourselves and our posterity, do ORDAIN and ESTABLISH this Constitution for the United States of Amer-

10. Excerpt taken from *The Federalist: A Collection of Essays, Written in Favour of the New Constitution, as Agreed Upon by the Federal Convention, September 17, 1787, in two volumes* (New York: J. and A. McLean, 1788).

ica." Here is a better recognition of popular rights, than volumes of those aphorisms which make the principal figure in several of our State bills of rights, and which would sound much better in a treatise of ethics than in a constitution of government.

. . .

I go further, and affirm that bills of rights, in the sense and to the extent in which they are contended for, are not only unnecessary in the proposed Constitution, but would even be dangerous. They would contain various exceptions to powers not granted; and, on this very account, would afford a colorable pretext to claim more than were granted. For why declare that things shall not be done which there is no power to do? Why, for instance, should it be said that the liberty of the press shall not be restrained, when no power is given by which restrictions may be imposed? I will not contend that such a provision would confer a regulating power; but it is evident that it would furnish, to men disposed to usurp, a plausible pretense for claiming that power. They might urge with a semblance of reason, that the Constitution ought not to be charged with the absurdity of providing against the abuse of an authority which was not given, and that the provision against restraining the liberty of the press afforded a clear implication, that a power to prescribe proper regulations concerning it was intended to be vested in the national government. This may serve as a specimen of the numerous handles which would be given to the doctrine of constructive powers, by the indulgence of an injudicious zeal for bills of rights.

On the subject of the liberty of the press, as much as has been said, I cannot forbear adding a remark or two: in the first place, I observe, that there is not a syllable concerning it in the constitution of this State; in the next, I contend, that whatever has been said about it in that of any other State, amounts to nothing. What signifies a declaration, that "the liberty of the press shall be inviolably preserved"? What is the liberty of the press? Who can give it any definition which would not leave the utmost latitude for evasion? I hold it to be impracticable; and from this I infer, that its security, whatever fine declarations may be inserted in any constitution respecting it, must altogether depend on public opinion, and on the general spirit of the people and of the government. And here, after all, as is intimated upon another occasion, must we seek for the only solid basis of all our rights.

There remains but one other view of this matter to conclude the point. The truth is, after all the declamations we have heard, that the Constitution is itself, in every rational sense, and to every useful purpose, A BILL OF RIGHTS. The several bills of rights in Great Britain form its Constitution, and conversely the constitution of each State is its bill of rights. And the proposed Constitution, if adopted, will be the bill of rights of the Union. Is it one object of a bill of rights to declare and specify the political privileges of the citizens in the structure and administration of the government? This is done in the most ample and precise manner in the plan of the convention; comprehending various precautions for the public security, which are not to be found in any of the State constitutions. Is another object of a bill of rights to define certain immunities and modes of proceeding, which are relative to personal and private concerns? This we have seen has also been attended to, in a variety of cases, in the same plan. Adverting therefore to the substantial meaning of a bill of rights, it is absurd to allege that it is not to be found in the work of the convention. It may be said that it does not go far enough, though it will not be easy to make this appear; but it can with no propriety be contended that there is no such thing. It certainly must be immaterial what mode is observed as to the order of declaring the rights of the citizens, if they are to be found in any part of the instrument which establishes the government. And hence it must be apparent, that much of what has been said on this subject rests merely on verbal and nominal distinctions, entirely foreign from the substance of the thing.

III. Powers of the National Government

MAJOR DEVELOPMENTS

- The compromise over the basis of representation in the national government
- The decision to give the national government taxing and regulatory authority
- The debate over how extensive the powers delegated to the national government should be

As in the colonial debate, the primary constitutional issue of the founding period was over the scope and powers of the central government. Independence had freed the colonies from British control and oversight, but the thirteen colonies had embarked on independence together and they were well aware that "united we stand, divided we fall." But just how united did they need to be, and what did union mean?

The Articles of Confederation was minimalist in its approach. The Articles mostly put into writing the relationship that the Continental Congress had to the pre-revolutionary Committees of Correspondence. The federal government was mostly just to coordinate the relationship between the United States and the rest of the world. To serve that function, it only needed a single house of Congress composed of an equal number of delegates—really, ambassadors—to represent the governments of the individual states.

Proposals to strengthen the federal government were concerned with insuring that the federal government was given the tools it would need to adequately perform the tasks it had been assigned. Experience had suggested to the Federalists that the federal government would need a drastic overhaul if it were to be effective. The anti-Federalists were convinced that a few modest adjustments would be sufficient to do the job. Anything more, to their way of thinking, was to invite more dangers than those they already faced. What powers needed to be entrusted to the federal government, and who would get to control those powers?

This section includes some of the key documents in the debate surrounding the creation of the Constitution that address the powers of the national government. The Articles of Confederation created a weak national government with few powers and equal representation for the states. The Philadelphia Convention in 1787 revolved around two competing plans to change the Articles: the Virginia Plan introduced by Edmund Randolph at the beginning of the Convention and the New Jersey Plan introduced by William Paterson as a response to it. The Virginia Plan proposed scrapping the Articles of Confederation and creating a more powerful national government with democratic representation. The New Jersey Plan proposed making more modest changes to the Confederation, adding some important powers to the national government but keeping equal state representation. The Philadelphia Convention compromised between the two plans, but the Virginia Plan set the agenda. Nationalists like Alexander Hamilton, James Madison, and James Wilson would strongly defend bold constitutional change both inside the Convention and during the ratification debates in the states. Some "small-state" Federalists like Roger Sherman looked for compromise inside the Convention, but defended the Constitution during ratification. Anti-Federalists like Patrick Henry became strong opponents of the Constitution during the ratification debates.

Articles of Confederation (1777)

The Articles of Confederation were the first federal constitution of the United States. It was largely drafted by Delaware's John Dickinson and Virginia's Richard Henry Lee and, after substantial negotiation, unanimously passed by the Continental Congress in 1777. It was then sent to the state legislatures for ratification and was formally ratified by the last of the thirteen legislatures (Maryland) in 1781. Between 1776 and 1781, the Continental Congress operated without the benefit of a formal constitution, though the government largely acted as if the terms of the Articles applied. Compared to the later U.S. Constitution, the structure of the Articles of Confederation created a weak central government and emphasized legislative supremacy. The Confederation Congress had responsibility for national security and foreign affairs, but had no power to raise taxes, raise an army, or punish those who violated its decisions.

. . .

II.

Each state retains its sovereignty, freedom, and independence, and every power, jurisdiction, and right, which is not by this Confederation expressly delegated to the United States, in Congress assembled.

III.

The said States hereby severally enter into a firm league of friendship with each other, for their common defense, the security of their liberties, and their mutual and general welfare, binding themselves to assist each other, against all force offered to, or attacks made upon them, or any of them, on account of religion, sovereignty, trade, or any other pretense whatever.

. . .

V.

For the most convenient management of the general interests of the United States, delegates shall be annually appointed in such manner as the legislatures of each State shall direct, to meet in Congress on the first Monday in November, in every year, with a power reserved to each State to recall its delegates, or any of them, at any time within the year, and to send others in their stead for the remainder of the year.

...

Each State shall maintain its own delegates in a meeting of the States, and while they act as members of the committee of the States.

In determining questions in the United States in Congress assembled, each State shall have one vote.

...

VII.

When land forces are raised by any State for the common defense, all officers of or under the rank of colonel, shall be appointed by the legislature of each State respectively, by whom such forces shall be raised, or in such manner as such State shall direct, and all vacancies shall be filled up by the State which first made the appointment.

VIII.

All charges of war, and all other expenses that shall be incurred for the common defense or general welfare, and allowed by the United States in Congress assembled, shall be defrayed out of a common treasury, which shall be supplied by the several States in proportion to the value of all land within each State....

The taxes for paying that proportion shall be laid and levied by the authority and direction of the legislatures of the several States within the time agreed upon by the United States in Congress assembled.

IX.

The United States in Congress assembled, shall have the sole and exclusive right and power of determining on peace and war...—of sending and receiving ambassadors—entering into treaties and alliances, provided that no treaty of commerce shall be made whereby the legislative power of the respective States shall be restrained from imposing such imposts and duties on foreigners, as their own people are subjected to, or from prohibiting the exportation or importation of any species of goods or commodities whatsoever—of establishing rules for deciding in all cases, what captures on land or water shall be legal, and in what manner prizes taken by land or naval forces in the service of the United States shall be divided or appropriated—of granting letters of marque and reprisal in times of peace—appointing courts for the trial of piracies and felonies committed on the high seas and establishing courts for receiving and determining finally appeals in all cases of captures, provided that no member of Congress shall be appointed a judge of any of the said courts.

The United States in Congress assembled shall also be the last resort on appeal in all disputes and differences now subsisting or that hereafter may arise between two or more States concerning boundary, jurisdiction or any other causes whatever....

...

The United States in Congress assembled shall also have the sole and exclusive right and power of regulating the alloy and value of coin struck by their own authority, or by that of the respective States—fixing the standards of weights and measures throughout the United States—regulating the trade and managing all affairs with the Indians, not members of any of the States, provided that the legislative right of any State within its own limits be not infringed or violated—establishing or regulating post offices from one State to another, throughout all the United States, and exacting such postage on the papers passing through the same as may be requisite to defray the expenses of the said office—appointing all officers of the land forces, in the service of the United States, excepting regimental officers—appointing all the officers of the naval forces, and commissioning all officers whatever in the service of the United States—making rules for the government and regulation of the said land and naval forces, and directing their operations.

...

The United States in Congress assembled shall never engage in a war, nor grant letters of marque or reprisal in time of peace, nor enter into any treaties or alliances, nor coin money, nor regulate the value thereof, nor ascertain the sums and expenses necessary for the defense and welfare of the United States, or any of them, nor emit bills, nor borrow money on the credit of the United States, nor appropriate money, nor agree upon the number of vessels of war, to be built or purchased, or the number of land or sea forces to be raised, nor appoint a commander in chief of the army or navy, unless nine States assent to the same: nor shall a question on any other point, except for adjourning from day to day be determined, unless by the votes of the majority of the United States in Congress assembled.

...

XIII.

Every State shall abide by the determination of the United States in Congress assembled, on all questions which by this confederation are submitted to them. And the Articles of this Confederation shall be inviolably observed by every State, and the Union shall be perpetual; nor shall any alteration at any time hereafter be made in any of them; unless such alteration be agreed to in a Congress of the United States, and be afterwards confirmed by the legislatures of every State.

The Virginia Plan, presented to the Constitutional Convention (1787)[11]

The "Virginia Plan" was presented by eminent Virginia delegate Edmund Randolph in the opening days of the Philadelphia Convention and set the agenda for the rest of the Convention's work. It immediately dispensed with the auspices under which the Convention had been assembled—to propose amendments to the existing Articles of Confederation—and instead outlined a completely new constitution for the United States. Although presented by Randolph, the plan was prepared by the young James Madison. Madison had insisted to Randolph that constitutional reform could not be contemplated in a piecemeal fashion. Only a negotiated package would win national support and solve the problems of the Confederation.

Madison anticipated that Randolph, and others, "will think this project, if not extravagant, absolutely unattainable and unworthy of being attempted." In particular Madison proposed to shift the United States from a confederated basis of equal state representation to a "republican" basis of representation by population, a federal government empowered to legislate on all national issues, and a national veto over state laws. But he expected that the "northern States will be reconciled to it [the principle of proportional representation] by the actual superiority of their populousness; the Southern by their expected superiority on this point. This principle established, the repugnance of the large States to part with power will in a great degree subside, and the smaller States must ultimately yield to the predominant will. It is also already seen by many, and must by degrees be seen by all, that, unless the Union be organized efficiently on republican principles, innovations of a much more objectionable form may be obtruded, or, in the most favorable event, the partition of the Empire, into rival and hostile confederacies will ensue."[12]

1. Resolved that the Articles of Confederation ought to be so corrected and enlarged, as to accomplish the objects proposed by their institution, namely common Defense Security of Liberty and general welfare.

2. Resolved therefore that the right of Suffrage in the National Legislature ought to be, proportioned to the quotas of Contribution, or to the number of free inhabitants, as the one or the other, may serve best in different cases.

3. Resolved that the National Legislature ought to consist of two branches.

4. Resolved that the Members of the first Branch of the National Legislature ought to be elected by the people of the several States every—for the term of three years, to be of the age of—at least. To receive liberal stipends, by which they may be compensated for the devotion of their time to public service—to be ineligible to any office established by a particular State, or under the authority of the United States, (except those peculiarly belonging to the functions of the first Branch) during the term of service, and for the space of one—after the expiration; to be incapable of re-election for the space of—after the expiration of their term of service, and to be subject to recall.

5. Resolved that the members of the second Branch of the Legislature, ought to be elected by the individual Legislatures: to be of the age of—years at least; to hold their Offices for a term sufficient to ensure their independency. . . .

6. Resolved that each Branch ought to possess the right of originating acts, that the National Legislature ought to be empowered to enjoy, the Legislative rights vested in Congress. by the Confederation, and moreover to Legislate all cases to which the Separate States are incompetent; or in which the harmony of the United States may be interrupted, by the exercise of individual Legislation—to negative all Laws passed by the several States, contravening, in the opinion of the National Legislature, The articles of Union; or any Treaty subsisting under the Authority of the Union—and to call forth the force of the Union, against any Member of the Union, failing to fulfill its duties under the articles thereof.

7. Resolved that a national Executive be instituted to consist of a single person, with powers to carry into execution the National Laws, and to appoint to Offices, in cases not otherwise provided for, to be chosen by the

---

11. Excerpt taken from *The Documentary History of the Constitution of the United States of America*, vol. 1 (Washington, D.C: Department of State, 1894), 332–35.

12. James Madison, "To Edmund Randolph, April 8, 1787," in *The Writings of James Madison*, ed. Gaillard Hunt, vol. 2 (New York: G. P. Putnam's Sons, 1904), 340.

National Legislature, for the term of seven years—to receive punctually at stated times a fixed compensation, for the services rendered, in which no increase or diminution shall be made, so as to affect the Magistracy existing at the time of such increase or diminution, and to be ineligible a second time.

8. Resolved that the Executive and a convenient number of the National Judiciary ought to compose a Council of revision, with authority to examine every act of the National Legislature, before it shall operate, and every act of a particular Legislature before a negative thereon shall be final; and that the dissent of the said council shall amount to a rejection, unless the act of the National Legislature, be again passed, or that of a particular Legislature be again negatived by—of the Members of each Branch.

9. Resolved that a National Judiciary be established to Consist of one Supreme Tribunal, to hold their Offices during good behavior, and to receive punctually at stated times fixed compensation for their services, in which no increase or diminution shall be made, so as to affect the persons actually in office at the time of such increase or diminution.

That the jurisdiction of the inferior Tribunals, shall be to hear and determine in the first instance, and of the Supreme Tribunal to hear and determine in the dernier resort; all piracies and felonies on the high Seas, Captures from an Enemy; cases in which Foreigners, or Citizens of other States applying to such jurisdictions, may be interested, or which respect the collection of the national Revenue, Impeachment of any national officer and questions which may involve, the National peace and harmony.

10. Resolved that provision ought to be made for the admission of States lawfully arising within the limits of the United States whether from a voluntary junction of Government and Territory or otherwise, with the Consent of a number of Voices in the National Legislatures less than the whole.

11. Resolved that a republican Government of each State (except in the Voluntary junction of Government and Territory) ought to be guaranteed by the United States to each State.

. . .

13. That provision ought to be made for the amendment of the Articles of the Union, whensoever it shall seem necessary (and that the assent of the National Legislature, ought to be required).

14. Resolved that the Legislative, Executive and judicial powers of the several States, ought to be bound by oath to support the Articles of Union.

15. Resolved that the amendments which shall be offered to the Confederation, by the Convention, ought at a proper time, or times, after the approbation of Congress, to be submitted to an assembly or assemblies of representatives, recommended by the several Legislatures, to be expressly chosen by the people to consider and decide thereon.

The New Jersey Plan, presented to the Constitutional Convention (June 15, 1787)[13]

The New Jersey Plan was presented to the Philadelphia Convention by William Paterson of New Jersey on behalf of the "small," or less populous, states. It was a hastily drafted alternative to the Virginia Plan that had dominated the Convention's initial deliberations. The New Jersey Plan challenged Madison's basic assumption that the governance of the United States should be shifted to a "republican" basis, with representation determined by population. Instead, it proposed to keep the basic plan of the Confederation and represent each state equally in Congress. The New Jersey Plan proposed relatively modest revisions of the existing Articles of Confederation, addressing some long-standing problems of concern to the Federalists but leaving many of the basic structural assumptions of the Confederation in place. The conflict between the two plans was eventually compromised ("the Connecticut Compromise") in the creation of the U.S. Senate as a second congressional chamber in which each state would have an equal representation. What other differences are there between these two plans?

1. Resolved that the articles of Confederation ought to be so revised, corrected & enlarged, as to render the federal Constitution adequate to the exigencies of Government, & the preservation of the Union.

2. Resolved that in addition to the powers vested in the United States in Congress, by the present existing articles of Confederation, they be authorized to pass acts for raising a revenue, by levying a duty or duties on all goods or merchandizes of foreign growth or manufacture, imported into any part of the United States, by

13. Excerpt taken from *The Documentary History of the Constitution of the United States of America*, vol. 1 (Washington, DC: Department of State, 1894), 322–26.

Stamps on paper, vellum or parchment, and by a postage on all letters or packages passing through the general post-Office, to be applied to such federal purposes as they shall deem proper & expedient; to make rules & regulations for the collection thereof; and the same from time to time, to alter & amend in such manner as they shall think proper: to pass Acts for the regulation of trade & commerce as well with foreign nations as with each other: provided that all punishments, fines, forfeitures & penalties to be incurred for contravening such acts rules and regulations shall be adjudged by the Common law Judiciaries of the State in which any offence contrary to the true intent & meaning of such Acts rules & regulations shall have been committed or perpetrated, with liberty of commencing in the first instance all suits & prosecutions for that purpose in the superior Common law Judiciary in such State, subject nevertheless, for the correction of all errors, both in law & fact in rendering judgment, to an appeal to the Judiciary of the United States.

3. Resolved that whenever requisitions shall be necessary, instead of the rule for making requisitions mentioned in the articles of Confederation, the United States in Congress be authorized to make such requisitions in proportion to the whole number of white & other free citizens & inhabitants of every age sex and condition including those bound to servitude for a term of years & three fifths of all other persons not comprehended in the foregoing description, except Indians not paying taxes; that if such requisitions be not complied with, in the time specified therein, to direct the collection thereof in the noncomplying States & for that purpose to devise and pass acts directing & authorizing the same; provided that none of the powers hereby vested in the United States in Congress shall be exercised without the consent of at least—States, and in that proportion if the number of Confederated States should hereafter be increased or diminished.

4. Resolved that the United States in Congress be authorized to elect a federal Executive to consist of persons, to continue in office for the term of years, to receive punctually at stated times a fixed compensation for their services, in which no increase or diminution shall be made so as to affect the persons composing the Executive at the time of such increase or diminution, to be paid out of the federal treasury; to be incapable of holding any other office or appointment during their time of service and for years thereafter; to be ineligible a second time, & removable by Congress on application by a majority of the Executives of the several States; that the Executives besides their general authority to execute the federal acts ought to appoint all federal officers not otherwise provided for, & to direct all military operations; provided that none of the persons composing the federal Executive shall on any occasion take command of any troops, so as personally to conduct any enterprise as General, or in other capacity.

5. Resolved that a federal Judiciary be established to consist of a supreme Tribunal the Judges of which to be appointed by the Executive, & to hold their offices during good behavior, to receive punctually at stated times a fixed compensation for their services in which no increase or diminution shall be made, so as to affect the persons actually in office at the time of such increase or diminution; that the Judiciary so established shall have authority to hear & determine in the first instance on all impeachments of federal officers, & by way of appeal in the dernier resort in all cases touching the rights of Ambassadors, in all cases of captures from an enemy, in all cases of piracies & felonies on the high seas, in all cases in which foreigners may be interested, in the construction of any treaty or treaties, or which may arise on any of the Acts for regulation of trade, or the collection of the federal Revenue: that none of the Judiciary shall during the time they remain in Office be capable of receiving or holding any other office or appointment during their time of service, or for thereafter.

6. Resolved that all Acts of the United States in Congress made by virtue & in pursuance of the powers hereby & by the articles of confederation vested in them, and all Treaties made & ratified under the authority of the United States shall be the supreme law of the respective States so far forth as those Acts or Treaties shall relate to the said States or their Citizens, and that the Judiciary of the several States shall be bound thereby in their decisions, any thing in the respective laws of the Individual States to the contrary notwithstanding; and that if any State, or any body of men in any State shall oppose or prevent the carrying into execution such acts or treaties, the federal Executive shall be authorized to call forth the power of the Confederated States, or so much thereof as may be necessary to enforce and compel an obedience to such Acts, or an Observance of such Treaties.

7. Resolved that provision be made for the admission of new States into the Union.

8. Resolved the rule for naturalization ought to be the same in every State.

9. Resolved that a Citizen of one State committing an offence in another State of the Union, shall be deemed guilty of the same offence as if it had been committed by a Citizen of the State in which the Offence was committed.

Article I, Section 8 of the Constitution of the United States (1787)

The Virginia Plan simply said that Congress should have the power to act when the several states were "incompetent." Like the Articles of Confederation, the New Jersey Plan gave Congress a specific but limited list of powers. The U.S. Constitution adopted the strategy of the New Jersey Plan, but the powers granted to the new national government were more extensive than what Paterson had proposed. This "enumeration of powers" was contained in Section 8 of Article I of the Constitution. During the ratification debates, Federalists like James Madison and James Wilson would emphasize this comprehensive list of powers given to the national government, but not just as a significant expansion of national power. They also called the list a limit on the power of government. They saw it as an alternative to a bill of rights.

Section 8 included provisions that would soon become especially controversial, so-called "sweeping" clauses that perhaps swept in more, not yet clearly known powers that the federal government could exercise. The "necessary and proper" provision at the end of Section 8 dropped the word "expressly" from a similar provision in the Articles of Confederation (and from the proposed amendments that emerged out of many state ratifying conventions), which some would argue was a signal that the clause should be read broadly as a grant of "implied" powers. Some saw the "general welfare" clause at the beginning of Section 8 as an echo of the Virginia Plan, empowering Congress to take whatever actions might be in the national interest. The significance of the list of powers in Section 8 is still up for debate. Some argue that it imposed important limits on national powers, while others contend that it does not significantly constrain Congress from acting in the national interest.

Article I, Section 8

The Congress shall have Power To lay and collect Taxes, Duties, Imposts and Excises, to pay the Debts and provide for the common Defence and general Welfare of the United States; but all Duties, Imposts and Excises shall be uniform throughout the United States;

To borrow Money on the credit of the United States;

To regulate Commerce with foreign Nations, and among the several States, and with the Indian Tribes;

To establish an uniform Rule of Naturalization, and uniform Laws on the subject of Bankruptcies throughout the United States;

To coin Money, regulate the Value thereof, and of foreign Coin, and fix the Standard of Weights and Measures;

To provide for the Punishment of counterfeiting the Securities and current Coin of the United States;

To establish Post Offices and post Roads;

To promote the Progress of Science and useful Arts, by securing for limited Times to Authors and Inventors the exclusive Right to their respective Writings and Discoveries;

To constitute Tribunals inferior to the supreme Court;

To define and punish Piracies and Felonies committed on the high Seas, and Offences against the Law of Nations;

To declare War, grant Letters of Marque and Reprisal, and make Rules concerning Captures on Land and Water;

To raise and support Armies, but no Appropriation of Money to that Use shall be for a longer Term than two Years;

To provide and maintain a Navy;

To make Rules for the Government and Regulation of the land and naval Forces;

To provide for calling forth the Militia to execute the Laws of the Union, suppress Insurrections and repel Invasions;

To provide for organizing, arming, and disciplining, the Militia, and for governing such Part of them as may be employed in the Service of the United States, reserving to the States respectively, the Appointment of the Officers, and the Authority of training the Militia according to the discipline prescribed by Congress;

To exercise exclusive Legislation in all Cases whatsoever, over such District (not exceeding ten Miles square) as may, by Cession of particular States, and the Acceptance of Congress, become the Seat of the Government of the United States, and to exercise like Authority over all Places purchased by the Consent of the Legislature of the State in which the Same shall be, for the Erection of Forts, Magazines, Arsenals, dock-Yards, and other needful Buildings;—And

To make all Laws which shall be necessary and proper for carrying into Execution the foregoing Powers, and all other Powers vested by this Constitution in the Government of the United States, or in any Department or Officer thereof.

Samuel Adams, Letter to Richard Henry Lee (1787)[14]

*Samuel Adams of Massachusetts and Richard Henry Lee of Virginia had both been leaders of the revolutionary movements in their respective states and architects of the confederation that emerged out of the Revolution. Neither attended the Philadelphia Convention, and both were skeptical of the new Constitution and ultimately helped mobilize the anti-Federalist opposition to its ratification. Significant opposition to the Constitution emerged in both Massachusetts and Virginia, with Massachusetts providing an early test for the Federalists and Virginia providing a difficult obstacle late in the ratification process. Both state ratification conventions produced an extended debate over the wisdom of the proposed Constitution, and both conventions produced numerous amendments that they recommended be swiftly adopted. In this letter, written shortly after the Constitution was forwarded to the states for their consideration, Samuel Adams laid out some of the central anti-Federalist objections to the new national government and suggested that domestic peace and freedom could only be maintained if the central government were given its necessary powers "*and no more.*"*

...

I confess, as I enter the Building I stumble at the threshold; I meet with a national government, instead of a federal union of sovereign states. I am not able to conceive why the Wisdom of the Convention led them to give the preference to the former, before the latter. If the several states in the union, are to become one entire nation, under one legislature, the powers of which shall extend to every subject of legislation, and its laws be supreme, and control the whole, the idea of sovereignty in these states, must be lost. Indeed I think, upon such a supposition, those sovereignties ought to be eradicated from the mind; for they would be *imperia in imperia*, justly deemed a solecism in politics, and they would be highly dangerous, and destructive of the peace, union, and safety of the nation. And can this national legislature be competent to make laws for the *free* internal government of one people, living in climates so remote and whose "habits and particular interests" are, and probably always will be, so different. Is it to be expected, that general laws can be adapted to the feelings of the more eastern, and the more southern parts of so extensive a nation? It appears to me difficult, if practicable; hence then, may we not look for discontent, mistrust, disaffection to government and frequent insurrections, which will require standing armies to suppress them in one place & another, where they may happen to arise; or, if laws could be made, adapted to the local habits, feelings, views, and interests of those distant parts, would they not cause jealousies of partiality in government, which would excite envy and other malignant passions productive of wars and fighting? But, should we continue distinct sovereign states, confederated for the purposes of mutual safety and happiness, each contributing to the federal head, such a part of its sovereignty, as would render the government fully adequate to those purposes, and *no more*, the people would govern themselves more easily, the laws of each state being well adapted to its own genius and circumstances, and the liberties of the United States would be more secure than they can be, as I humbly conceive, under the proposed new constitution....

The Federalist, Nos. 1, 10, and 23[15]

These particular essays by Hamilton and Madison develop the argument for shifting at least some important powers to the national government. Federalist 10 *is perhaps Madison's most important work and the culmination of his thinking about the flaws in the Articles of Confederation. The essay became particularly prominent in the twentieth century as its analysis of factions took on new relevance in an era of interest groups, but it garnered less attention in the early republic.*[16]

14. Excerpt taken from *Memoir of the Life of Richard Henry Lee*, vol. 2 (Philadelphia: M. C. Carey and I. Lea, 1825), 130–131.

15. Excerpts taken from *The Federalist: A Collection of Essays, Written in Favour of the New Constitution, as Agreed Upon by the Federal Convention, September 17, 1787, in two volumes* (New York: J. and A. McLean, 1788).

16. Larry D. Kramer, "Madison's Audience," *Harvard Law Review* 112 (1998):611.

Is there a principle guiding the allocation of powers to the national government? How did the allocation of powers to the national government in the U.S. Constitution differ from the allocation of powers to Parliament in the constitution of the British Empire? Were the Articles of Confederation more consistent with revolutionary principles and concerns than the U.S. Constitution? Are there any "national interests" that the federal government cannot reach?

No. 1 (Alexander Hamilton)

...AFTER an unequivocal experience of the inefficiency of the subsisting federal government, you are called upon to deliberate on a new Constitution for the United States of America. It has been frequently remarked that it seems to have been reserved to the people of this country, by their conduct and example, to decide the important question, whether societies of men are really capable or not of establishing good government from reflection and choice, or whether they are forever destined to depend for their political constitutions on accident and force.

...

...To judge from the conduct of the opposite parties, we shall be led to conclude that they will mutually hope to evince the justness of their opinions, and to increase the number of their converts by the loudness of their declamations and the bitterness of their invectives. An enlightened zeal for the energy and efficiency of government will be stigmatized as the offspring of a temper fond of despotic power and hostile to the principles of liberty....[I]t will be equally forgotten that the vigor of government is essential to the security of liberty; that, in the contemplation of a sound and well-informed judgment, their interest can never be separated; and that a dangerous ambition more often lurks behind the specious mask of zeal for the rights of the people than under the forbidden appearance of zeal for the firmness and efficiency of government....

No. 10 (James Madison)

AMONG the numerous advantages promised by a well constructed Union, none deserves to be more accurately developed than its tendency to break and control the violence of faction....The instability, injustice, and confusion introduced into the public councils, have, in truth, been the mortal diseases under which popular governments have everywhere perished; as they continue to be the favorite and fruitful topics from which the adversaries to liberty derive their most specious declamations....Complaints are everywhere heard from our most considerate and virtuous citizens, equally the friends of public and private faith, and of public and personal liberty, that our governments are too unstable, that the public good is disregarded in the conflicts of rival parties, and that measures are too often decided, not according to the rules of justice and the rights of the minor party, but by the superior force of an interested and overbearing majority. However anxiously we may wish that these complaints had no foundation, the evidence, of known facts will not permit us to deny that they are in some degree true....

By a faction, I understand a number of citizens, whether amounting to a majority or a minority of the whole, who are united and actuated by some common impulse of passion, or of interest, adverse to the rights of other citizens, or to the permanent and aggregate interests of the community.

There are two methods of curing the mischiefs of faction: the one, by removing its causes; the other, by controlling its effects.

There are again two methods of removing the causes of faction: the one, by destroying the liberty which is essential to its existence; the other, by giving to every citizen the same opinions, the same passions, and the same interests.

It could never be more truly said than of the first remedy, that it was worse than the disease. Liberty is to faction what air is to fire, an aliment without which it instantly expires. But it could not be less folly to abolish liberty, which is essential to political life, because it nourishes faction, than it would be to wish the annihilation of air, which is essential to animal life, because it imparts to fire its destructive agency.

The second expedient is as impracticable as the first would be unwise. As long as the reason of man continues fallible, and he is at liberty to exercise it, different opinions will be formed. As long as the connection subsists between his reason and his self-love, his opinions and his passions will have a reciprocal influence on each other; and the former will be objects to which the latter will attach themselves. The diversity in the faculties of men, from which the rights of property originate, is not less an insuperable obstacle to a uniformity of interests. The protection of these faculties is the first object of government. From the protection of different and unequal faculties of acquiring property, the possession of different degrees and kinds of property immediately results; and from the influence of these on the sentiments and views of the respective proprietors, ensues a division of the society into different interests and parties. The latent causes of faction are thus sown in the nature of man; and we see them everywhere brought into different degrees of activity, according to the different circumstances of civil society. A zeal for different opinions concerning religion, concerning government, and many other points, as well of speculation as of practice; an attachment to different leaders ambitiously contending for pre-eminence and power; or to persons of other descriptions whose fortunes have been interesting to the human passions, have, in turn, divided mankind into parties, inflamed them with mutual animosity, and rendered them much more disposed to vex and oppress each other than to cooperate for their common good. So strong is this propensity of mankind to fall into mutual animosities, that where no substantial occasion presents itself, the most frivolous and fanciful distinctions have been sufficient to kindle their unfriendly passions and excite their most violent conflicts. But the most common and durable source of factions has been the various and unequal distribution of property. Those who hold and those who are without property have ever formed distinct interests in society. Those who are creditors, and those who are debtors, fall under a like discrimination. A landed interest, a manufacturing interest, a mercantile interest, a moneyed interest, with many lesser interests, grow up of necessity in civilized nations, and divide them into different classes, actuated by different sentiments and views. The regulation of these various and interfering interests forms the principal task of modern legislation, and involves the spirit of party and faction in the necessary and ordinary operations of the government.

...

It is in vain to say that enlightened statesmen will be able to adjust these clashing interests, and render them all subservient to the public good. Enlightened statesmen will not always be at the helm. Nor, in many cases, can such an adjustment be made at all without taking into view indirect and remote considerations, which will rarely prevail over the immediate interest which one party may find in disregarding the rights of another or the good of the whole. The inference to which we are brought is, that the CAUSES of faction cannot be removed, and that relief is only to be sought in the means of controlling its EFFECTS.

If a faction consists of less than a majority, relief is supplied by the republican principle, which enables the majority to defeat its sinister views by regular vote. It may clog the administration, it may convulse the society; but it will be unable to execute and mask its violence under the forms of the Constitution. When a majority is included in a faction, the form of popular government, on the other hand, enables it to sacrifice to its ruling passion or interest both the public good and the rights of other citizens. To secure the public good and private rights against the danger of such a faction, and at the same time to preserve the spirit and the form of popular government, is then the great object to which our inquiries are directed....

By what means is this object attainable? Evidently by one of two only. Either the existence of the same passion or interest in a majority at the same time must be prevented, or the majority, having such coexistent passion or interest, must be rendered, by their number and local situation, unable to concert and carry into effect schemes of oppression. If the impulse and the opportunity be suffered to coincide, we well know that neither moral nor religious motives can be relied on as an adequate control. They are not found to be such on the injustice and violence of individuals, and lose their efficacy in proportion to the number combined together, that is, in proportion as their efficacy becomes needful.

From this view of the subject it may be concluded that a pure democracy, by which I mean a society consisting of a small number of citizens, who assemble and administer the government in person, can admit of no cure for the mischiefs of faction. A common passion or interest will, in almost every case, be felt by a majority of the whole; a communication and concert result from the form of government itself; and there is nothing to check the inducements to sacrifice the weaker party or an obnoxious individual. Hence it is that such democracies have ever been spectacles of turbulence and contention; have ever been found incompatible with personal security or the rights of property; and have in general been as short in their lives as they have been violent in their deaths....

A republic, by which I mean a government in which the scheme of representation takes place, opens a different prospect, and promises the cure for which we are seeking. Let us examine the points in which it varies from pure democracy, and we shall comprehend both the nature of the cure and the efficacy which it must derive from the Union.

The two great points of difference between a democracy and a republic are: first, the delegation of the government, in the latter, to a small number of citizens elected by the rest; secondly, the greater number of citizens, and greater sphere of country, over which the latter may be extended.

The effect of the first difference is, on the one hand, to refine and enlarge the public views, by passing them through the medium of a chosen body of citizens, whose wisdom may best discern the true interest of their country, and whose patriotism and love of justice will be least likely to sacrifice it to temporary or partial considerations. Under such a regulation, it may well happen that the public voice, pronounced by the representatives of the people, will be more consonant to the public good than if pronounced by the people themselves, convened for the purpose. On the other hand, the effect may be inverted. Men of factious tempers, of local prejudices, or of sinister designs, may, by intrigue, by corruption, or by other means, first obtain the suffrages, and then betray the interests, of the people. The question resulting is, whether small or extensive republics are more favorable to the election of proper guardians of the public weal; and it is clearly decided in favor of the latter by two obvious considerations:

In the first place, it is to be remarked that, however small the republic may be, the representatives must be raised to a certain number, in order to guard against the cabals of a few; and that, however large it may be, they must be limited to a certain number, in order to guard against the confusion of a multitude. Hence, the number of representatives in the two cases not being in proportion to that of the two constituents, and being proportionally greater in the small republic, it follows that, if the proportion of fit characters be not less in the large than in the small republic, the former will present a greater option, and consequently a greater probability of a fit choice.

In the next place, as each representative will be chosen by a greater number of citizens in the large than in the small republic, it will be more difficult for unworthy candidates to practice with success the vicious arts by which elections are too often carried; and the suffrages of the people being more free, will be more likely to centre in men who possess the most attractive merit and the most diffusive and established characters.

It must be confessed that in this, as in most other cases, there is a mean, on both sides of which inconveniences will be found to lie. By enlarging too much the number of electors, you render the representatives too little acquainted with all their local circumstances and lesser interests; as by reducing it too much, you render him unduly attached to these, and too little fit to comprehend and pursue great and national objects. The federal Constitution forms a happy combination in this respect; the great and aggregate interests being referred to the national, the local and particular to the State legislatures.

The other point of difference is, the greater number of citizens and extent of territory which may be brought within the compass of republican than of democratic government; and it is this circumstance principally which renders factious combinations less to be dreaded in the former than in the latter. The smaller the society, the fewer probably will be the distinct parties and interests composing it; the fewer the distinct parties and interests, the more frequently will a majority be found of the same party; and the smaller the number of individuals composing a majority, and the smaller the compass within which they are placed, the more easily will they concert and execute their plans of oppression. Extend the sphere, and you take in a greater variety of parties and interests; you make it less probable that a majority of the whole will have a common motive to invade the rights of other citizens; or if such a common motive exists, it will be more difficult for all who feel it to discover their own strength, and to act in unison with each other. Besides other impediments, it may be remarked that, where there is a consciousness of unjust or dishonorable purposes, communication is always checked by distrust in proportion to the number whose concurrence is necessary.

Hence, it clearly appears, that the same advantage which a republic has over a democracy, in controlling the effects of faction, is enjoyed by a large over a small republic,—is enjoyed by the Union over the States composing it. Does the advantage consist in the substitution of representatives whose enlightened views and virtuous sentiments render them superior to local prejudices and schemes of injustice? It will not be denied that the representation of the Union will be most likely to possess these requisite endowments. Does it consist in the greater security afforded by a greater variety of parties, against the event of any one party being able to outnumber and oppress the rest? In an equal degree does the increased variety of parties comprised within the Union, increase this security. Does it, in fine, consist in the greater obstacles opposed to the concert and accomplishment of the secret wishes of an unjust and interested majority? Here, again, the extent of the Union gives it the most palpable advantage.

The influence of factious leaders may kindle a flame within their particular States, but will be unable to spread a general conflagration through the other States. A religious sect may degenerate into a political faction in a part of the Confederacy; but the variety of sects dispersed over the entire face of it must secure the national councils against any danger from that source. A rage for paper money, for an abolition of debts, for an equal division of property, or for any other improper or wicked project, will be less apt to pervade the whole body of the Union than a particular member of it; in the same proportion as such a malady is more likely to taint a particular county or district, than an entire State.

In the extent and proper structure of the Union, therefore, we behold a republican remedy for the diseases most incident to republican government. And according to the degree of pleasure and pride we feel in being republicans, ought to be our zeal in cherishing the spirit and supporting the character of Federalists.

No. 23 (Alexander Hamilton)

...

THE necessity of a Constitution, at least equally energetic with the one proposed, to the preservation of the Union, is the point at the examination of which we are now arrived.

...

The principal purposes to be answered by union are these: the common defense of the members; the preservation of the public peace as well against internal convulsions as external attacks; the regulation of commerce with other nations and between the States; the superintendence of our intercourse, political and commercial, with foreign countries.

The authorities essential to the common defense are these: to raise armies; to build and equip fleets; to prescribe rules for the government of both; to direct their operations; to provide for their support. These powers ought to exist without limitation, BECAUSE IT IS IMPOSSIBLE TO FORESEE OR DEFINE THE EXTENT AND VARIETY OF NATIONAL EXIGENCIES, OR THE CORRESPONDENT EXTENT AND VARIETY OF THE MEANS WHICH MAY BE NECESSARY TO SATISFY THEM. The circumstances that endanger the safety of nations are infinite, and for this reason no constitutional shackles can wisely be imposed on the power to which the care of it is committed....

...

Whether there ought to be a federal government entrusted with the care of the common defense, is a question in the first instance, open for discussion; but the moment it is decided in the affirmative, it will follow, that that government ought to be clothed with all the powers requisite to complete execution of its trust. And unless it can be shown that the circumstances which may affect the public safety are reducible within certain determinate limits; unless the contrary of this position can be fairly and rationally disputed, it must be admitted, as a necessary consequence, that there can be no limitation of that authority which is to provide for the defense and protection of the community, in any matter essential to its efficacy: that is, in any matter essential to the FORMATION, DIRECTION, or SUPPORT of the NATIONAL FORCES.

...

...The same must be the case in respect to commerce, and to every other matter to which [federal] jurisdiction is permitted to extend....Not to confer in each case a degree of power commensurate to the end, would be to violate the most obvious rules of prudence and propriety, and improvidently to trust the great interests of the nation to hands which are disabled from managing them with vigor and success.

...

Note: Slavery and the Constitution

Slave-owning interests were accommodated in the U.S. Constitution in various ways. There was little question that some accommodation would be necessary if the union were to be maintained and a stronger national government created. The economies of the southern states were built on slavery, and those states were determined that they alone would have the authority to decide the fate of the "peculiar institution" within their boundaries. The northern states in the 1780s did not have much interest in challenging that commitment. The revolutionary era had encouraged greater interest the morality of slavery and had inspired some movement toward ending slavery. Even so, slavery had already proven itself to be a difficult political

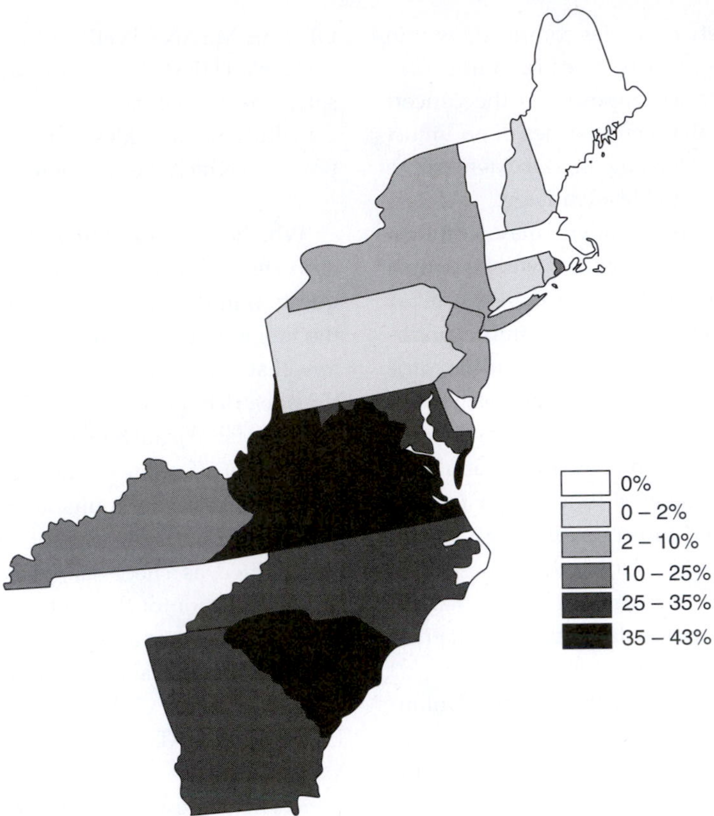

Figure 3-2 Slaves as Percentage of State Population, 1790

Source: Historical Statistics of the United States (New York: Cambridge University Press, 2006). Copyright © Cambridge University Press 2011

issue, and abolitionism was not yet a powerful political movement and did not enjoy widespread political support.

Political emancipation (as opposed to the emancipation of slaves by individual slave-owners) had been controversial even in the northern states. In 1790, slaves were roughly 18 percent of the total population of the United States. Less than one percent of those slaves were in New England, and just over five percent were in the mid-Atlantic states. The rest of the slave population was in the South, but even there the importance of slavery and the presence of slaves varied greatly, with relatively small populations in Delaware, Tennessee, and Kentucky and high populations in Georgia, Virginia, and the Carolinas. As Figure 3-2 illustrates, few states at the opening of the republic were untouched by slavery, and some northern states had a significant number of slaves. Unsurprisingly, emancipation efforts were more successful in New England and the mid-Atlantic than in the South. Vermont led the way with a constitutional ban on slavery in 1777, but even in the North, where slaves were a tiny fraction of the population, emancipation was politically difficult. State legislatures in those states often rejected proposals for immediate abolition. Over the next quarter century, most northern states adopted policies of gradual emancipation, which usually freed the future children of slaves when they reached an age of maturity. At the same time, the southern states had their own variations. Virginia and South Carolina had a much larger concentration of slaves than did the other slave states, and at least initially they fought the hardest for the slaveholder interests.

In the Philadelphia Convention, the southern states fought for and won five constitutional provisions directly affecting slavery. The three-fifths clause for representation allocated seats in the House of Representatives to the states in accord with their total population of free persons and three-fifths of their population of slaves. The three-fifths clause for taxation allocated head taxes and direct taxes in the same way as House seats. Congress was barred from

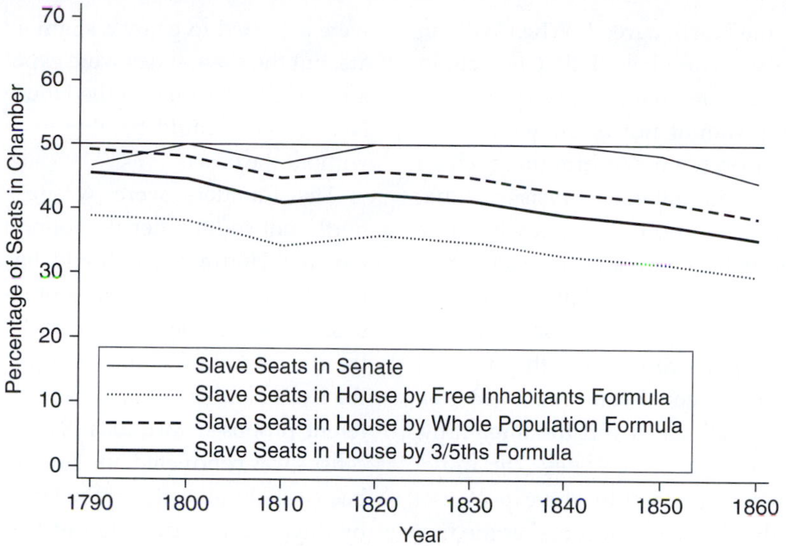

Figure 3-3 Slave-State Representation in Congress, 1790–1860

Source: Calculated from *Historical Statistics of the United States* (New York: Cambridge University Press, 2006), various tables.

Note: "Slave Seats" includes all states where slavery as an ongoing practice was legal.

interfering with the importation of new slaves into the United States until 1808. The fugitive slave clause required that escaped slaves who had crossed state lines "shall be delivered up on claim of the party to whom such service or labor may be due." The importation or taxation provisions could not be altered by constitutional amendment before 1808. Slave states expected to benefit as well from such provisions as the requirement that the federal government assist in suppressing "insurrections" within any state. At the same time, the Constitution neither prohibited or guaranteed slavery anywhere, and it imposed no explicit limitations on congressional power to affect slavery except in these tax and trade clauses. The Constitution was silent on some issues that had already proven controversial when they touched on slavery, such as the status of slavery in the territories (which had already shown itself to be relevant in the passage of the Northwest Ordinance) or whether slaves could be recruited into military service (which had been proposed during the Revolution).[17]

The critical question for slavery, as it was for many other issues, was how representation in Congress would be determined and thus who would control national policy under the Constitution. The Virginia Plan called for apportioning seats in Congress by "free inhabitants" (or, alternatively, by the proportion of tax revenue collected in each state, which was understood to be equivalent to the whole population). It mattered a great deal how slaves were to be counted. If House seats were allocated by the whole population in each state, then Virginia would be the biggest state and the South (including slave-holding Maryland and Delaware) would receive 50 percent of the seats. If House seats were allocated by free inhabitants only, then Pennsylvania would be the biggest state and the North would receive 60 percent of the seats. (These percentages are based on the 1790 census, but the drafters had a fairly accurate understanding of the distribution of the population in 1787.) Many southern delegates urged the Convention to count slaves or taxes in allocating seats in the House, otherwise the southern states would "form so considerable a minority, and the regulation of trade is to be given to the General Government, they will be nothing more than overseers for the Northern States." To protect its interests, the South needed "something like an equality" in

17. Philip A. Klinkner, with Rogers M. Smith, *The Unsteady March* (Chicago: University of Chicago Press, 1999), 17–20; Paul Finkelman, "Slavery and the Northwest Ordinance: A Study in Ambiguity," *Journal of the Early Republic* 6 (1986):343.

Congress.[18] Some in the North agreed. When William Paterson of New Jersey complained that he "could regard negroes [sic] slaves in no light but as property" and argued that they should not be represented in Congress, James Madison reminded him that such an argument was at odds with Paterson's insistence that small states be given equal representation with large states.[19] In both cases, in that of the small states and that of the slaveholding states, the states that feared being an endangered minority in the new, more powerful Congress were given the representation they needed to protect their interests—equal-state representation in the Senate for the small states and the three-fifths clause in the House for the slave states. The initial allocation of House seats, guided by the expectation of what the three-fifths clause would do after the first census, gave the North a small majority.

Southern Federalists returned home able to reassure their states that their interests were protected in the proposed Constitution. South Carolina's Charles Cotesworth Pinckney concluded that there was nothing to fear.

> We have a security that the general government can never emancipate them, for no such authority is granted; and it is admitted, on all hands, that the general government has no powers but what are expressly granted by the Constitution, and that all rights not expressed were reserved by the several states. . . . In short, considering all circumstances, we have made the best terms for the security of this species of property it was in our power to make. We would have made better if we could; but on the whole, I do not think them bad.[20]

In 1787, it was expected that the population in the South would grow over time. As long as the South was given enough seats in the initial creation of the House to protect its interests in the short term, the natural growth of population in sparsely populated but agriculturally fertile states such as Georgia would secure the South's interests in the long term. The free states were expected to enjoy a slight advantage in the Senate, but the slave states were expected to enjoy a slight advantage over time in the House of Representatives. Neither side would be able to make national policy without the other.

The founders were wrong. Population flowed north, not south, after the founding. The debate over whether House seats should be allocated by whole population, free inhabitants, or something in between soon became irrelevant. Figure 3-3 demonstrates these trends, tracking the allocation of seats across time in the two chambers of Congress in accord with the different proposed formulas. By the time the first 1790 census was conducted, the southern states would have been a slight minority in the House of Representatives by any formula, even under the most generous one of representation by whole population. Even so, differences in the allocation of seats to the South would likely have made a difference in such close elections as 1796 and 1800 and to how controversial legislation was put together and passed in the early republic.[21] The slave states' situation in the House deteriorated over time, and the free states' small majority became a substantial majority. The House would prove to be the most antislavery institution in the national government in the antebellum era. Instead, it was the Senate with its equal representation for each state that became the bastion for protecting southern interests. Only in the Senate did the South maintain "something like an equality" throughout the early decades of the nineteenth century. But not all the "slave states" were the same, and border states with relatively small slave populations, such as Delaware and Maryland, did not always share the same interests as the states of the Deep South. When even the official slave states could no longer claim equality in the Senate, it no longer trusted that its interests would be protected within the national government. Since the Electoral College mirrored the composition of the House and the Senate, the opening had emerged for a purely sectional party like Lincoln's Republican Party to capture the White House, perhaps permanently. Once it did, the South seceded from the union.

---

18. Charles Cotesworth Pinckney of South Carolina, quoted in James Madison, *Notes of Debates in the Federal Convention of 1787* (New York: W. W. Norton, 1987), 261.

19. Ibid., 259.

20. Charles Cotesworth Pinckney, in Jonathan Elliott, ed., *Debates in the Several State Conventions on the Adoption of the Federal Constitution*, 2nd Rev. ed., vol. 4 (Philadelphia: J. B. Lippincott, 1891), 286.

21. For an analysis, see Brian D. Humes et al., "Representation of the Antebellum South in the House of Representatives: Measuring the Impact of the Three-Fifths Clause," in David W. Brady and Mathew D. McCubbins, *Party, Process, and Political Change in Congress* (Stanford: Stanford University Press, 2002).

IV. Federalism

MAJOR DEVELOPMENTS

- The decision not to include a congressional veto over state legislation in the Constitution
- The inclusion of a supremacy clause in the Constitution and judicial review of state legislation that conflicted with the terms of the Constitution
- The adoption of six-year terms for U.S. Senators without possibility of recall between elections

In addition to determining what powers the national government should have, a constitutional union also required determining what the proper relationship should be between the federal government and the states and among the states. The colonial experience provided both an example and a warning. On the one hand, the British Empire had operated on something like federal principles, with constitutional boundaries separating the issues normally subject to resolution by local legislatures and issues normally addressed by the central government. Policy decisions on international trade and war were clearly decided in London; the regulation of the internal affairs of the colony was, in the first instance, the responsibility of the colonial government. On the other hand, the debates of the 1770s were precisely over how stable such a constitutional boundary could be. The alleged logical impossibility of an *imperium in imperio* (of a sovereign within a sovereign) fed both assertions of parliamentary supremacy over all matters of public policy that might arise within the Empire and claims of American autonomy from any effective English supervision. The friction along that boundary between the central government and the local government and between those competing claims ultimately sparked a revolution.

The choices were stark. The former colonies could abandon union and deal with each other as independent sovereign governments. Most thought war, and with it despotism, lay down that path. The political map could be redrawn, erasing the former colonies and starting over with a new nation that would govern their territory. Proposals had been made for consolidating the separate North American colonies into one or more larger colonies, but Parliament had never acted. After the Revolution, when only American opinion mattered, no such proposal was realistic. In affection and politics, the people of the United States were citizens of their individual states first, and only secondarily Americans. Only one option was realistic, making union work, and that required finding a way to live together.

The Articles of Confederation tried to establish a fairly loose union. The national government had little independent existence. The legislators who ran the national government were chosen by, and paid by, the state governments for short terms and could be recalled at any time if they strayed too far. The national government was dependent on the states for the money and enforcement powers to implement any decisions that it might make. The restrictions on the states were the bare essentials needed to make the union meaningful (e.g., states were not supposed to conduct their own foreign policy), but the central government could only try to mediate conflicts when they arose.

The Constitution sought to create a tighter, "more perfect," union. The national government was given more autonomy from the states, both in making and in implementing its policy decisions. The state governments were to be represented in only one chamber of the legislature, and those senators were to have the longest of any elected term of office and could not be recalled. The U.S. senators were to be as independent as possible from their state governments. The states were guaranteed no role in financing or implementing national policy, and thus were given less opportunity to obstruct or ignore national policy. The central government was now to be responsive to and to act directly on the individual citizens, not the states as the Confederation government did. At the same time, more restrictions were placed on the states and those restrictions were made legally binding, that is, enforceable in court.

Some thought the Constitution went too far. Others thought it did not go far enough.

In the Philadelphia Convention, the delegates considered but ultimately voted down a proposal to allow Congress to review and veto any and all state laws. In the ratification debates, James Madison argued that the state governments would retain the affections of the people. New York politician Melancton Smith was more skeptical. He was among those who wanted a constitutional amendment that would make U.S. senators more responsive to the state governments.

A. Representation of State Interests

A key issue for the creation of a federal constitution is how best to represent the interests of the states. The issue was particularly pressing for the United States, where the union of states was itself somewhat fragile and the existing federal constitution (the Articles of Confederation) gave the states a great deal of power. The states expected their social and political interests to be taken into account in any new federal arrangement. At the same time, those various interests could easily conflict, and the federal government needed to be able to act in the collective interests of the whole. Finding the right balance of securing the self-interest of the individual state and creating a workable union was a primary challenge of the Philadelphia Convention. The problem of representing state interests within the new federal government appeared at various points over the course of the Convention debates. In the end, neither side was completely happy with the results.

Debate in the Constitutional Convention (1787)[22]

The Virginia Plan included a provision for a congressional veto of state laws, which James Madison regarded as essential to the success of any federal system. The congressional veto over state laws would both protect national interests from local interference and protect individual and local minorities from abuses by state governments. At the end of this debate, the provision was deleted by a vote of seven states to three.

Madison thought this was one of the great failures of the Convention. The proposal for a congressional veto was replaced with the supremacy clause in Article VI of the Constitution, which made the federal Constitution, treaties and federal statutes legally superior to conflicting state constitutions and laws and that supremacy would be enforceable in state and federal court. The supremacy clause largely borrows from the New Jersey Plan, and relies on the courts, rather than Congress, to monitor the states for compliance with the Constitution. Madison's proposed veto would have also given Congress a wide-ranging authority to veto state laws for any reason that it wanted. The supremacy clause narrowed the federal veto to those instances in which the states ran afoul of federal authority.

How did Madison's proposed national veto on state laws differ from the power of judicial review that we know today? Why would its proponents view it as the cornerstone of a national government? Were they right?

June 8th

Mr. CHARLES PINCKNEY (South Carolina) moved "that the National Legislature should have authority to negative all laws which they should judge to be improper." He urged that such a universality of the power was indispensably necessary to render it effectual; that the States must be kept in due subordination to the nation; that if the States were left to act of themselves in any case, it would be impossible to defend the national prerogatives, however extensive they might be on paper; that the acts of Congress had been defeated by this means; nor had foreign treaties escaped repeated violations; that this universal negative was in fact the corner stone of an efficient national Government; that under the British Government the negative of the Crown had been found beneficial, and the States are more one nation now, than the *Colonies* were then.

Mr. JAMES MADISON (Virginia) seconded the motion. He could not but regard an indefinite power to negative legislative acts of the States as absolutely necessary to a perfect system. Experience had evinced a constant tendency in the States to encroach on the federal authority; to violate national Treaties; to infringe the rights & interests of each other; to oppress the weaker party within their respective jurisdictions. A negative was the mildest expedient that could be devised for preventing these mischiefs. The existence of such a check would prevent attempts to commit them. Should no such precaution be engrafted, the only remedy would lie in an appeal to coercion. Was such a remedy eligible? Was it practicable? Could the national resources, if exerted to the utmost enforce a national decree against Massachusetts abetted perhaps by several of her neighbors? It would not be possible. A small proportion of the Community, in a compact situation, acting on the defensive, and at one of its extremities might at any time bid defiance to the National authority. Any Government for the United States formed on the supposed practicability of using force against the unconstitutional proceedings of the States, would prove as visionary & fallacious as the Government of Congress. The negative would render the use of force unnecessary. The States could of themselves then pass no operative act, any more than one branch of a Legislature where there are two branches, can proceed without the other. But in order to give the negative this efficacy, it must extend to all cases. A discrimination would only be a fresh source of contention between the

22. Excerpt taken from *The Papers of James Madison* (Washington, DC: Langtree & O'Sullivan, 1840).

two authorities. In a word, to recur to the illustrations borrowed from the planetary system. This prerogative of the General Government is the great pervading principle that must control the centrifugal tendency of the States; which, without it, will continually fly out of their proper orbits and destroy the order & harmony of the political System.

Mr. HUGH WILLIAMSON (North Carolina) was against giving a power that might restrain the States from regulating their internal police.

Mr. ELBRIDGE GERRY (Massachusetts) could not see the extent of such a power, and was against every power that was not necessary. He thought a remonstrance against unreasonable acts of the States would reclaim them. If it should not force might be resorted to. He had no objection to authorize a negative to paper money and similar measures. When the confederation was depending before Congress, Massachusetts was then for inserting the power of emitting paper money among the exclusive powers of Congress. He observed that the proposed negative would extend to the regulations of the Militia, a matter on which the existence of a State might depend. The National Legislature with such a power may enslave the States. Such an idea as this will never be acceded to. It has never been suggested or conceived among the people.... The States too have different interests and are ignorant of each other's interests. The negative therefore will be abused....

Mr. ROGER SHERMAN (Connecticut) thought the cases in which the negative ought to be exercised, might be defined. He wished the point might not be decided till a trial at least should be made for that purpose.

Mr. JAMES WILSON (Pennsylvania)... We are now one nation of brethren. We must bury all local interests & distinctions.... [But] No sooner were the State Governments formed than their jealousy and ambition began to display themselves. Each endeavored to cut a slice from the common loaf, to add to its own morsel, till at length the confederation became frittered down to the impotent condition in which it now stands.... To correct its vices is the business of this convention. One of its vices is the want of an effectual control in the whole over its parts. What danger is there that the whole will unnecessarily sacrifice a part? But reverse the case, and leave the whole at the mercy of each part, and will not the general interest be continually sacrificed to local interests?

...

Mr. GUNNING BEDFORD (Delaware). In answer to his colleague's question where would be the danger to the States from this power, would refer him to the smallness of his own State which may be injured at pleasure without redress. It was meant he found to strip the small States of their equal right of suffrage. In this case Delaware would have about 1/90 for its share in the General Councils, whilst Pennsylvania and Virginia would posses 1/3 of the whole. Is there no difference of interests, no rivalry of commerce, of manufactures? Will not these large States crush the small ones whenever they stand in the way of their ambitious or interested views? This shows the impossibility of adopting such a system as that on the table, or any other founded on a change in the principle of representation. And after all, if a State does not obey the law of the new System, must not force be resorted to as the only ultimate remedy, in this as in any other system.... Besides, how can it be thought that the proposed negative can be exercised? Are the laws of the States to be suspended in the most urgent cases until they can be sent seven or eight hundred miles, and undergo the deliberations of a body who may be incapable of Judging of them? Is the National Legislature too to sit continually in order to revise the laws of the States?

Mr. MADISON observed that the difficulties which had been started were worthy of attention and ought to be answered before the question was put. The case of laws of urgent necessity must be provided for by some emanation of the power from the National Government into each State so far as to give a temporary assent at least. This was the practice in Royal Colonies before the Revolution and would not have been inconvenient, if the supreme power of negativing had been faithful to the American interest, and had possessed the necessary information. He supposed that the negative might be very properly lodged in the Senate alone, and that the more numerous & expensive branch therefore might not be obliged to sit constantly.—He asked Mr. Bedford what would be the consequence to the small States of a dissolution of the Union which seemed likely to happen if no effectual substitute was made for the defective System existing, and he did not conceive any effectual system could be substituted on any other basis than that of a proportional suffrage? If the large States possessed the avarice & ambition with which they were charged, would the small ones in their neighborhood, be more secure when all control of a General Government was withdrawn?

Melancton Smith, Speech to the New York Ratification Convention (1788)[23]

The New York state ratification convention was the last great test for the proposed Constitution. The powerful state of New York had vetoed earlier proposals to amend the Articles of Confederation, and its delegates boycotted the Philadelphia Convention once it became clear that sweeping reforms were on the agenda. The anti-Federalists won a majority of the delegates to the state ratification convention, but they did not push for an early meeting. By the time it convened in June of 1788, eight states had already ratified and two more were well into their deliberations. Alexander Hamilton spearheaded the Federalist forces in New York. Melancton Smith, a businessman and experienced politician, emerged as one of the most thoughtful anti-Federalists in the convention. He often concentrated his attention on possible amendments to the Constitution, and in this excerpt he defended a proposal that would impose a then-popular form of term limits, or mandatory "rotation," on U.S. senators (barring them from serving more than six years in any twelve year period) and that would allow states to recall and replace their senators before the expiration of their six-year terms. The proposal was designed to make senators less independent of state governments and keep them focused on their home states.

...We think the amendment will place the senate in a proper medium between a fluctuating and perpetual body. As the clause now stands, there is no doubt that the senators will hold their office perpetually; and in this situation, they must of necessity lose their dependence and attachment to the people. It is certainly inconsistent with the established principles of republicanism, that the senate should be a fixed and unchangeable body of men. There should be then some constitutional provision against this evil. A rotation I consider as the best possible mode of affecting a remedy. The amendment will not only have a tendency to defeat any plots, which may be formed against the liberty and authority of the state governments, but will be the best means to extinguish the factions which often prevail, and which are sometimes so fatal in legislative bodies. This appears to me an important consideration. We have generally found, that perpetual bodies have either combined in some scheme of usurpation, or have been torn and distracted with cabals....

...

With respect to the second part of the amendment, I would observe that as the senators are the representatives of the state legislatures, it is reasonable and proper that they should be under their control. When a state sends an agent commissioned to transact any business, or perform any service, it certainly ought to have a power to recall him. These are plain principles, and so far as they apply to the case under examination, they ought to be adopted by us. Form this government as you please, you must at all events lodge in it very important powers: These powers must be in the hands of a few men, so situated as to produce a small degree of responsibility. These circumstances ought to put us upon our guard; and the inconvenience of this necessary delegation of power should be corrected, by providing some suitable checks.

...

An honorable gentleman from New York [Alexander Hamilton] observed yesterday, that the states should always maintain their importance and authority, on account of their superior influence over the people. To prove this influence, he mentioned the aggregate number of the state representatives throughout the continent. But I ask him, how long the people will retain their confidence for two thousand representatives, who shall meet once in a year to make laws for regulating the height of your fences and the repairing of your roads?...The state governments, without object or authority, will soon dwindle into insignificance, and be despised by the people themselves. I am, sir, at a loss to know how the state legislatures will spend their time....Another reason offered by the gentleman is, that by the states will have a greater number of officers than the general government. I doubt this. Let us make a comparison. In the first place, the federal government must have a complete set of judicial officers of different ranks throughout the continent: Then, a numerous train of executive officers....Add to this, their salaries will probably be larger and better secured than those of any state officers. If these numerous officers are not at once established, they are in the power of congress, and will all in time be created. Very few offices will be the objects of ambition in the states....But the whole reasoning of the gentleman rests upon the principle that the states will be able to check the general government,

23. Excerpt taken from Jonathan Elliot, ed., *Debates in the Several State Conventions on the Adoption of the Federal Constitution, as Recommended by the General Convention at Philadelphia, in 1787*, vol. 2 (Philadelphia: J. B. Lippincott, 1891), 309.

by exciting the people to opposition. . . . This kind of check, I contend, would be a pernicious one; and certainly ought to be prevented. Checks in government ought to act silently, and without public commotion. I think that the harmony of the two powers should by all means be maintained: If it be not, the operation of the government will be baneful—One or the other of the parties must finally be destroyed in the conflict. The constitutional line between the authority of each should be so obvious, as to leave no room for jealous apprehensions or violent contests.

V. Separation of Powers

MAJOR DEVELOPMENTS

- Establishment of a unitary executive with a single president
- Establishment of an independently elected president who was not accountable to the legislature
- Emphasis on checks and balances in the constitutional scheme

Everyone agreed that separation of powers is a good thing. There was less agreement over what that meant.

The Americans had practical experience with the separation of powers from their own colonial history and, less directly, from English history. The struggles between Parliament and the king in seventeenth-century England had produced a welter of political and legal thinking about the respective powers of representative assembly and monarch. The British constitutional tradition was one of divided political power, not one of absolutism, as the colonists were well aware and keen to argue. Within the colonies themselves, the firm grip of the elected assembly on the power of the purse was understood to be the cornerstone of effective limitations on government power. The French writer Baron de Montesquieu's influential book, *On the Spirit of the Laws*, entrenched the notion that there were three basic branches of government—the legislative, the executive, and the judicial—and that this separation was essential to British liberty. About that, the Americans had no doubt.

Even so, both the idea and the practice of the separation of powers were in their infancy. For many, the British example echoed the classical idea that good government was characterized by a "balance of powers." In this conception, the powers that had to be balanced were social interests, particularly the wealthy and the poor. A balanced or mixed constitution was one that incorporated each of these constituencies into the political system, most commonly by representing them in different institutions. Thus, a three-part balance of powers might include the king (representing himself or perhaps the nation as a collective), the House of Lords (representing the aristocracy), and the House of Commons (representing "the people"). For some, this was the ideal to be reconstituted in America, even if in a more republican form.

What Montesquieu and some other political thinkers of the seventeenth and eighteenth centuries introduced was a modern separation of functional powers. Within this theory, there were three basic types of functions that governmental officials might perform, and those functions should and could be entrusted to different government officials. Traditionally, the king made, applied, and enforced the law. It was only with the creation of representative assemblies or autonomous councils of advisors, like the Parliament, that it was possible to begin to think of *setting* policy (the job of the legislature), as distinct from *implementing* that policy (the job of the executive). The two tasks could then be performed by different institutions—or "branches" of government. A strict separation of powers would insist that different powers or functions of government should be carefully classified and placed in different hands. Safety for liberty came from preventing the executive from having any share of the legislative power, and vice versa. There would be a rule of law and not of men only if the same person did not both make and apply the law. The separation of powers also built a fail-safe into the government. The abuse of government power would require the cooperation of all the branches of government. The legislature could do nothing without the executive, and the executive could do nothing without the prior authorization of the legislature.

Checks and balances modified the strict separation of powers. The argument for a strict separation of powers held that no person should ever perform more than one type of function. The executive could not "share" in the legislative power if the system was to be stable and the separation of powers was to do its work of preventing the abuse of power. A concern soon developed, however, that one branch could pull the powers into itself if the other branches were not empowered to resist that encroachment. The legislature might entice or coerce the executive into going along with its plans, unless the executive was both rendered sufficiently independent of the legislature and armed with weapons to resist the legislature. Care had to be taken not only to separate the powers but also to insure that they stayed separated. Ironically, the solution to this problem was the careful mixing of powers, the creation of checks and balances by which one branch might interfere with the other. Thus, the executive might be given a share of the "legislative" power in the form of a veto on proposed laws, and the legislature might be given a share of the "executive" power in the form of a veto over the appointment of executive officers. Powers would no longer be strictly separated by function, but the branches of government would be counterbalanced. The creation of checks and balances required forgetting some of the lessons that the theory of separation of powers had taught.

The theory and practice of separation of powers was also complicated by the difficulty in identifying what the "powers" were and in which category they belonged. The theory began in the seventeenth century by distinguishing between the legislative and the executive power, but it was only much later in the eighteenth century that the judicial power of interpreting the law and applying it to particular cases was distinguished from the executive power of enforcing the law. Even if the application of the law and its enforcement can be readily distinguished, other government actions do not always fall neatly into these three categories. Some theorists, such as John Locke, carved out separate categories to take into account the possibility of action by "the executive" that did not simply involve enforcing preexisting rules, such as making war or conducting foreign policy or acting out of immediate necessity. The boundaries between powers were sometimes murky, such as the oversight of how laws were implemented or the definition of the job description of individual government officials.

There was room for disagreement about the details, but the founding generation knew that a true government had three branches exercising distinct powers. The Confederation was, in this sense, not a true government, since it only possessed a legislative branch. It was consequently extremely weak. The national government could only be *strengthened* if it were given additional powers and the appropriate institutions to exercise them and exercise them well. The government could only be strengthened *safely* if those powers were carefully distributed and counterbalanced. The state governments had always been committed to the ideal of separation of powers, but they had begun with relatively strong legislatures. As time went on, the writers of state constitutions also looked to strengthen the relative power and capacities of the other institutions of government.[24]

In the Philadelphia Convention, the delegates disagreed among themselves over how best to structure the executive branch. Crucial issues to be decided included whether there would be one president or a plural executive, whether the president should be accountable to the legislature or only to the people, and how long the president should serve in office. During the ratification debates, James Madison defended the principle of checks and balances while Alexander Hamilton advocated an "energetic" executive. Anti-Federalists such as "Centinel" were more critical of constitutional checks and balances and instead argued that the Constitution should have emphasized term limits and frequent elections to keep government officials under control.

Debate in the Constitutional Convention (1787)[25]

The delegates to the Philadelphia Convention had very vague ideas of how the executive branch should be organized. They were convinced that the national government needed an executive branch—even the New Jersey Plan included executive officers. But that left open the question of what kind of executive branch should be established. For some, the federal constitution should follow the example of the states and their weak governors, multiple executive officeholders, and close accountability of the executive to the legislature. For others, this was something to be avoided and a more powerful, independent executive would be more likely to provide an effective check on the legislature and good administration for the government. Should there be one chief executive, or should there be an executive council with no one at the top? Should

24. On separation of powers in the founding era, see Keith E. Whittington, "The Separation of Powers at the Founding," in *Separation of Powers*, ed. Katy J. Harriger (Washington, DC: CQ Press, 2003); M. J. C. Vile, *Constitutionalism and the Separation of Powers*, 2nd ed. (Indianapolis: Liberty Fund, 1998).

25. Excerpt taken from *The Papers of James Madison* (Washington, DC: Langtree & O'Sullivan, 1840).

the executive be independent of the legislature, or should the executive be a tool of the legislature? Alexander Hamilton shook up the Convention by proposing the creation of a monarchy, elected for life, which he thought would be no more powerful than the president already being contemplated by the Convention but would spare the nation the "tumults" of the frequent competition for high office. The Convention eventually favored a strong, unified executive, but even within that agreement there were details to be settled, such as whether and under what conditions the president could be removed from office and whether the president should have a veto power.

June 2nd

Mr. JOHN DICKINSON (Delaware)... A limited Monarchy he considered as one of the best Governments in the world. It was not certain that the same blessings were derivable from any other form. It was certain that equal blessings had never yet been derived from any of the republican form. A limited Monarchy however was out of the question. The spirit of the times—the state of our affairs, forbade the experiment, if it were desirable. Was it possible moreover in the nature of things to introduce it even if these obstacles were less insuperable? A House of Nobles was essential to such a Government could these be created by a breath, or by a stroke of the pen? No. They were the growth of ages, and could only arise under a complication of circumstances none of which existed in this Country. But though a form the most perfect perhaps in itself be unattainable, we must not despair. If ancient republics have been found to flourish for a moment only & then vanish for ever, it only proves that they were badly constituted; and that we ought to seek for every remedy for their diseases. One of these remedies he conceived to be the accidental lucky division of this Country into distinct States; a division which some seemed desirous to abolish altogether....

Mr. EDMUND RANDOLPH (Virginia) opposed it with great earnestness, declaring that he should not do justice to the Country which sent him if he were silently to suffer the establishment of a Unity in the Executive department. He felt an opposition to it which he believed he should continue to feel as long as he lived. He urged 1. that the permanent temper of the people was adverse to the very semblance of Monarchy. 2. that a unity was unnecessary a plurality being equally competent to all the objects of the department. 3. that the necessary confidence would never be reposed in a single Magistrate. 4. that the appointments would generally be in favor of some inhabitant near the center of the Community, and consequently the remote parts would not be on an equal footing. He was in favor of three members of the Executive to be drawn from different portions of the Country.

Mr. PIERCE BUTLER (South Carolina) contended strongly for a single magistrate as most likely to answer the purpose of the remote parts. If one man should be appointed he would be responsible to the whole, and would be impartial to its interests. If three or more should be taken from as many districts, there would be a constant struggle for local advantages. In Military matters this would be particularly mischievous....

June 4th

DOC. BENJAMIN FRANKLIN (Pennsylvania), said he... had some experience of this check in the Executive on the Legislature, under the proprietary Government of Pennsylvania. The negative [veto] of the Governor was constantly made use of to extort money. No good law whatever could be passed without a private bargain with him. An increase of his salary, or some donation, was always made a condition; till at last it became the regular practice, to have orders in his favor on the Treasury, presented along with the bills to be signed, so that he might actually receive the former before he should sign the latter.... This was a mischievous sort of check.... He was afraid, if a negative should be given as proposed, that more power and money would be demanded, till at last enough would be gotten to influence and bribe the Legislature into a complete subjection to the will of the Executive.

Mr. ROGER SHERMAN (Connecticut) was against enabling any one man to stop the will of the whole. No one man could be found so far above all the rest in wisdom. He thought we ought to avail ourselves of his wisdom in revising the laws, but not permit him to overrule the decided and cool opinions of the Legislature.

Mr. JAMES MADISON (Virginia) supposed that if a proper proportion of each branch should be required to overrule the objections of the Executive, it would answer the same purpose as an absolute negative. It would rarely if ever happen that the Executive constituted as ours is proposed to be would, have firmness enough to resist the legislature, unless backed by a certain part of the body itself....

Mr. JAMES WILSON (Pennsylvania) believed as others did that this power would seldom be used. The Legislature would know that such a power existed, and would refrain from such laws, as it would be sure to defeat. Its silent operation would therefore preserve harmony and prevent mischief. The case of Pennsylvania formerly was very different from its present case. The Executive was not then as now to be appointed by the people. It will not in this case as in the one cited be supported by the head of a Great Empire, actuated by a different & sometimes opposite interest.... The requiring a large proportion of each House to overrule the Executive check might do in peaceable times; but there might be tempestuous moments in which animosities may run high between the Executive and Legislative branches, and in which the former ought to be able to defend itself.

Mr. GUNNING BEDFORD (Delaware) was opposed to every check on the Legislative.... He thought it would be sufficient to mark out in the Constitution the boundaries to the Legislative Authority, which would give all the requisite security to the rights of the other departments. The Representatives of the people were the best Judges of what was for their interest, and ought to be under no external control whatever. The two branches would produce a sufficient control within the Legislature itself.

June 18th

Mr. HAMILTON (NEW YORK)... In his private opinion he had no scruple in declaring, supported as he was by the opinions of so many of the wise and good, that the British Government was the best in the world: and that he doubted much whether any thing short of it would do in America. He hoped Gentlemen of different opinions would bear with him in this, and begged them to recollect the change of opinion on this subject which had taken place and was still going on. It was once thought that the power of Congress was amply sufficient to secure the end of their institution. The error was now seen by everyone. The members most tenacious of republicanism, he observed, were as loud as any in declaiming against the vices of democracy. This progress of the public mind led him to anticipate the time, when others as well as himself would... praise... it [as] the only Government in the world "which unites public strength with individual security."—In every community where industry is encouraged, there will be a division of it into the few & the many. Hence separate interests will arise. There will be debtors, and creditors, etc. Give all power to the many, they will oppress the few. Give all power to the few, they will oppress the many. Both therefore ought to have power, that each may defend itself against the other. To the want of this check we owe our paper money, installment laws, etc. To the proper adjustment of it the British owe the excellence of their Constitution. Their house of Lords is a most noble institution. Having nothing to hope for by a change, and a sufficient interest by means of their property, in being faithful to the national interest, they form a permanent barrier against every pernicious innovation, whether attempted on the part of the Crown or of the Commons. No temporary Senate will have firmness enough to answer the purpose.... Gentlemen differ in their opinions concerning the necessary checks, from the different estimates they form of the human passions. They suppose seven years a sufficient period to give the senate an adequate firmness, from not duly considering the amazing violence & turbulence of the democratic spirit. When a great object of Government is pursued, which seizes the popular passions, they spread like wild fire, and become irresistible. He appealed to the gentlemen from the New England States whether experience had not there verified the remark.—As to the Executive, it seemed to be admitted that no good one could be established on Republican principles. Was not this giving up the merits of the question: for can there be a good Government without a good Executive? The English model was the only good one on this subject. The Hereditary interest of the King was so interwoven with that of the Nation, and his personal emoluments so great, that he was placed above the danger of being corrupted from abroad—and at the same time was both sufficiently independent and sufficiently controlled, to answer the purpose of the institution at home. One of the weak sides of Republics was their being liable to foreign influence and corruption. Men of little character, acquiring great power become easily the tools of intermeddling Neighbors.... What is the inference from all these observations? That we ought to go as far in order to attain stability and permanency, as republican principles will admit. Let one branch of the Legislature hold their places for life or at least during good behavior. Let the Executive also be for life.... But is this a Republican Government, it will be asked? Yes if all the Magistrates are appointed, and vacancies are filled, by the people, or a process of election originating with the people.... An Executive for life has not this motive for forgetting his fidelity, and will therefore be a safer depository of power. It will be objected probably, that such an Executive will be an elective Monarch, and will give birth to the tumults which characterize that form of Government. He would reply that Monarch is an indefinite term. It marks not either the degree or duration of power. If this Executive Magistrate would be a monarch for life—the other proposed by the Report from the Committee of the whole, would be a monarch for seven years. The circumstance of being elective was also applicable to both. It had been observed by judicious writers that elective monarchies would be the best if they could be guarded against the tumults excited by the ambition and intrigues of competitors. He was not sure that tumults were an inseparable evil.... But will such a plan be adopted out of doors? In return he would ask will the people adopt the other plan? At present they will adopt neither. But he sees the Union dissolving or already dissolved—he sees evils operating in the States which must soon cure the people of their fondness for democracies—he sees that a great progress has been already made & is still going on in the public mind. He thinks therefore that the people will in time be unshackled from their prejudices....

June 20th

Mr. MADISON thought it indispensable that some provision should be made for defending the Community against the incapacity, negligence or perfidy of the chief Magistrate. The limitation of the period of his service, was not a sufficient security. He might lose his capacity after his appointment. He might pervert his administration into a scheme of peculation or oppression. He might betray his trust to foreign powers. The case of the Executive Magistracy was very distinguishable, from that of the Legislature or of any other public body, holding offices of limited duration. It could not be presumed that all or even a majority of the members of an Assembly would either lose their capacity for discharging, or be bribed to betray, their trust. Besides the restraints of their personal integrity and honor, the difficulty of acting in concert for purposes of corruption was a security to the public. And if one or a few members only should be seduced, the soundness of the remaining members, would maintain the integrity and fidelity of the body. In the case of the Executive Magistracy which was to be administered by a single man, loss of capacity or corruption was more within the compass of probable events, and either of them might be fatal to the Republic.

Mr. CHARLES PINCKNEY (South Carolina) did not see the necessity of impeachments. He was sure they ought not to issue from the Legislature who would in that case hold them as a rod over the Executive and by that means effectually destroy his independence. His revisionary power in particular would be rendered altogether insignificant.

Mr. ELBRIDGE GERRY (Massachusetts) urged the necessity of impeachments. A good magistrate will not fear them. A bad one ought to be kept in fear of them. He hoped the maxim would never be adopted here that the chief magistrate could do no wrong.

Mr. RUFUS KING (Massachusetts) expressed his apprehensions that an extreme caution in favor of liberty might enervate the Government we were forming. He wished the House to recur to the primitive axiom that the three great departments of Governments should be separate and independent.... Would this be the case, if the Executive should be impeachable?... The Executive was to hold his place for a limited term like the members of the Legislature: Like them... he would periodically be tried for his behavior by his electors, who would continue or discontinue him in trust according to the manner in which he had discharged it. Like them therefore, he ought to be subject to no intermediate trial, by impeachment.... But under no circumstances ought he to be impeachable by the Legislature. This would be destructive of his independence and of the principles of the Constitution. He relied on the vigor of the Executive as a great security for the public liberties.

Mr. RANDOLPH. The propriety of impeachments was a favorite principle with him. Guilt wherever found ought to be punished. The Executive will have great opportunities of abusing his power; particularly in time of war when the military force, and in some respects the public money will be in his hands. Should no regular punishment be provided, it will be irregularly inflicted by tumults and insurrections. He is aware of the necessity of proceeding with a cautious hand, and of excluding as much as possible the influence of the Legislature from the business. He suggested for consideration an idea which had fallen [from Col. Hamilton] of composing a forum out of the Judges belonging to the States: and even of requiring some preliminary inquest whether just grounds of impeachment existed.

The Federalist, Nos. 51, 70, and 71[26]

As The Federalist *explained it, the Constitution created a system of checks and balances among multiple institutions while also placing different powers where they could be best used in the new government. They justify the organization and details of each component of the proposed government. Often these justifications provided rationales for what Hamilton and Madison knew had been ad hoc compromises in the Convention itself, but in hindsight and in public they argued that the design of the Constitution was not merely acceptable but desirable. These essays include some of the most sophisticated discussions of the idea of checks and balances ever written, but they are also trying to imagine how the system will operate once put into motion. As you read, you should consider how well these expectations conform to our experience. The founders did not anticipate highly organized, mass political parties, but they were familiar with and critical of short-lived or personality-based factions that operated inside and outside of legislative assemblies. Do party ties fulfill, subvert, or work alongside the constitutional separation of powers that the founding generation put in place?*

No. 51 (James Madison)

TO WHAT expedient, then, shall we finally resort, for maintaining in practice the necessary partition of power among the several departments, as laid down in the Constitution? The only answer that can be given is, that... the defect must be supplied, by so contriving the interior structure of the government as that its several constituent parts may, by their mutual relations, be the means of keeping each other in their proper places....

In order to lay a due foundation for that separate and distinct exercise of the different powers of government, which to a certain extent is admitted on all hands to be essential to the preservation of liberty, it is evident that each department should have a will of its own; and consequently should be so constituted that the members of each should have as little agency as possible in the appointment of the members of the others. Were this principle rigorously adhered to, it would require that all the appointments for the supreme executive, legislative, and judiciary magistracies should be drawn from the same fountain of authority, the people, through channels having no communication whatever with one another. Perhaps such a plan of constructing the several departments would be less difficult in practice than it may in contemplation appear. Some difficulties, however, and some additional expense would attend the execution of it. Some deviations, therefore, from the principle must be admitted. In the constitution of the judiciary department in particular, it might be inexpedient to insist rigorously on the principle: first, because peculiar qualifications being essential in the members, the primary consideration ought to be to select that mode of choice which best secures these qualifications; secondly, because the permanent tenure by which the appointments are held in that department, must soon destroy all sense of dependence on the authority conferring them.

It is equally evident, that the members of each department should be as little dependent as possible on those of the others, for the emoluments annexed to their offices. Were the executive magistrate, or the judges, not independent of the legislature in this particular, their independence in every other would be merely nominal.

But the great security against a gradual concentration of the several powers in the same department, consists in giving to those who administer each department the necessary constitutional means and personal motives to resist encroachments of the others. The provision for defense must in this, as in all other cases, be made commensurate to the danger of attack. Ambition must be made to counteract ambition. The interest of the man must be connected with the constitutional rights of the place. It may be a reflection on human nature, that such devices should be necessary to control the abuses of government. But what is government itself, but the greatest of all reflections on human nature? If men were angels, no government would be necessary. If angels were to govern men, neither external nor internal controls on government would be necessary. In framing a government which is to be administered by men over men, the great difficulty lies in this: you must first enable the government to control the governed; and in the next place oblige it to control itself. A dependence on the people is, no doubt, the primary control on the government; but experience has taught mankind the necessity of auxiliary precautions.

But it is not possible to give to each department an equal power of self-defense. In republican government,

26. Excerpt taken from *The Federalist: A Collection of Essays, Written in Favour of the New Constitution, as Agreed Upon by the Federal Convention, September 17, 1787, in two volumes* (New York: J. and A. McLean, 1788).

the legislative authority necessarily predominates. The remedy for this inconveniency is to divide the legislature into different branches; and to render them, by different modes of election and different principles of action, as little connected with each other as the nature of their common functions and their common dependence on the society will admit. It may even be necessary to guard against dangerous encroachments by still further precautions. As the weight of the legislative authority requires that it should be thus divided, the weakness of the executive may require, on the other hand, that it should be fortified. An absolute negative on the legislature appears, at first view, to be the natural defense with which the executive magistrate should be armed. But perhaps it would be neither altogether safe nor alone sufficient.... May not this defect of an absolute negative be supplied by some qualified connection between this weaker department and the weaker branch of the stronger department, by which the latter may be led to support the constitutional rights of the former, without being too much detached from the rights of its own department?

...

...In a single republic, all the power surrendered by the people is submitted to the administration of a single government; and the usurpations are guarded against by a division of the government into distinct and separate departments. In the compound republic of America, the power surrendered by the people is first divided between two distinct governments, and then the portion allotted to each subdivided among distinct and separate departments. Hence a double security arises to the rights of the people. The different governments will control each other, at the same time that each will be controlled by itself....

No. 70 (Alexander Hamilton)

...Energy in the Executive is a leading character in the definition of good government. It is essential to the protection of the community against foreign attacks; it is not less essential to the steady administration of the laws; to the protection of property against those irregular and high-handed combinations which sometimes interrupt the ordinary course of justice; to the security of liberty against the enterprises and assaults of ambition, of faction, and of anarchy....

...A feeble Executive implies a feeble execution of the government. A feeble execution is but another phrase for a bad execution; and a government ill executed, whatever it may be in theory, must be, in practice, a bad government.

...

The circumstances which constitute safety in the republican sense are, 1st. a due dependence on the people, secondly a due responsibility.

...

...Decision, activity, secrecy, and dispatch will generally characterize the proceedings of one man, in a much more eminent degree, than the proceedings of any greater number, and in proportion as the number is increased, these qualities will be diminished.

...

No. 71 (Alexander Hamilton)

...

There are some who would be inclined to regard the servile pliancy of the Executive to a prevailing current, either in the community or in the legislature, as its best recommendation. But such men entertain very crude notions, as well of the purposes for which government was instituted, as of the true means by which the public happiness may be promoted. The republican principle demands that the deliberate sense of the community should govern the conduct of those to whom they entrust the management of their affairs; but it does not require an unqualified complaisance to every sudden breeze of passion, or to every transient impulse which the people may receive from the arts of men, who flatter their prejudices to betray their interests. It is a just observation, that the people commonly INTEND the PUBLIC GOOD. This often applies to their very errors. But their good sense would despise the adulator who should pretend that they always REASON RIGHT about the MEANS of promoting it....When occasions present themselves, in which the interests of the people are at variance with their inclinations, it is the duty of the persons whom they have appointed to be the guardians of those interests, to withstand the temporary delusion, in order to give them time and opportunity for more cool and sedate reflection. Instances might be cited in which a conduct of this kind has saved the people from very fatal consequences of their own mistakes, and has procured lasting monuments of their gratitude to the men who had courage and magnanimity enough to serve them at the peril of their displeasure.

But however inclined we might be to insist upon an unbounded complaisance in the Executive to the inclinations of the people, we can with no propriety contend for a like complaisance to the humors of the legislature. The latter may sometimes stand in opposition to the former, and at other times the people may be entirely neutral. In either supposition, it is certainly desirable that the Executive should be in a situation to dare to act his own opinion with vigor and decision.

The same rule which teaches the propriety of a partition between the various branches of power, teaches us likewise that this partition ought to be so contrived as to render the one independent of the other. To what purpose separate the executive or the judiciary from the legislative, if both the executive and the judiciary are so constituted as to be at the absolute devotion of the legislative? Such a separation must be merely nominal, and incapable of producing the ends for which it was established. It is one thing to be subordinate to the laws, and another to be dependent on the legislative body. The first comports with, the last violates, the fundamental principles of good government; and, whatever may be the forms of the Constitution, unites all power in the same hands.... The representatives of the people, in a popular assembly, seem sometimes to fancy that they are the people themselves, and betray strong symptoms of impatience and disgust at the least sign of opposition from any other quarter; as if the exercise of its rights, by either the executive or judiciary, were a breach of their privilege and an outrage to their dignity. They often appear disposed to exert an imperious control over the other departments; and as they commonly have the people on their side, they always act with such momentum as to make it very difficult for the other members of the government to maintain the balance of the Constitution.

...

"Centinel," Letter No. 1 (1787)[27]

Centinel was the pen-name for one of the most significant anti-Federalist writers during the ratification debates. His letters were first published in the Philadelphia newspapers during the weeks leading up to the ratification vote in Pennsylvania, but they were widely circulated across the state and the country. The Centinel letters may not have all been written by the same person, but the first letter is now commonly attributed to Samuel Bryan, an up-and-coming state government official. Bryan was also a primary force behind a minority report of the Pennsylvania anti-Federalists at the state ratification convention. The Centinel essays were particularly class-conscious, critical of the "wealthy and ambitious, who in every community think they have a right to lord it over their fellow creatures" and who now hoped that the people could be led to adopt "any extreme of government."[28] *Rather than a complicated scheme of checks and balances, Centinel emphasized the importance of clear lines of accountability between the governors and the governed, with term limits ("rotation"), a free press, and frequent elections as the key to maintaining liberty.*

...

...I believe it will be found that the form of government, which holds those entrusted with power, in the greatest responsibility to their constituents, the best calculated for freemen. A republican, or free government, can only exist where the body of the people are virtuous, and where property is pretty equally divided; in such a government the people are the sovereign and their sense or opinion is the criterion of every public measure; for when this ceases to be the case, the nature of the government is changed, and an aristocracy, monarchy or despotism will rise on its ruin. The highest responsibility is to be attained, in a simple structure of government, for the great body of the people never steadily attend to the operations of government, and for want of due information are liable to be imposed on—If you complicate the plan by various orders, the people will be perplexed and divided in their sentiments about the sources of abuses or misconduct, some will impute it to the senate, others to the house of representatives, and so on, that the interposition of the people may be rendered imperfect or perhaps wholly abortive. But if, imitating the constitution of Pennsylvania, you vest all the legislative power in one body of men (separating the executive and the judicial) elected for a short period, and necessarily excluded by rotation from permanency, and guarded from precipitancy and surprise by delays imposed on its proceedings, you will create the most perfect responsibility for then, whenever the people feel a grievance they cannot

27. Excerpt taken from Centinel, *To the People of Pennsylvania* (Philadelphia: Eleazer Oswald, 1787).

28. Ibid.

mistake the authors, and will apply the remedy with certainty and effect, discarding them at the next election. This tie of responsibility will obviate all the dangers apprehended from a single legislature, and will the best secure the rights of the people.

. . .

. . . [I]f the United States are to be melted down into one empire, it becomes you to consider, whether such a government, however constructed, would be eligible in so extended a territory; and whether it would be practicable, consistent with freedom? It is the opinion of the greatest writers, that a very extensive country cannot be governed on democratical principles, on any other plan, than a confederation of a number of small republics, possessing all the powers of internal government, but united in the management of their foreign and general concerns.

It would not be difficult to prove, that any thing short of despotism, could not bind so great a country under one government; and that whatever plan you might, at first setting out, establish, it would issue in a despotism.

. . .

. . . [W]e see, the house of representatives, are on the part of the people to balance the senate, who I suppose will be composed of the *better sort*, the *well born*, etc. The number of the representatives (being only one for every 30,000 inhabitants) appears to be too few, either to communicate the requisite information, of the wants, local circumstances and sentiments of so extensive an empire, or to prevent corruption and undue influence, in the exercise of such great powers; the term for which they are to be chosen, too long to preserve a due dependence and accountability to their constituents; and the mode and places of their election not sufficiently ascertained, for as Congress have the control over both, they may govern the choice, by ordering the *representatives* of a *whole* state, to be *elected* in *one* place, and that too may be the most *inconvenient*.

The senate, the great efficient body in this plan of government is constituted on the most unequal principles. The smallest state in the union has equal weight with the great states of Virginia, Massachusetts, or Pennsylvania—The Senate, besides its legislative functions, has a very considerable share in the Executive; none of the principal appointments to office can be made without its advice and consent. The term and mode of its appointment, will lead to permanency; the members are chosen for six years, the mode is under the control of Congress, and as there is no exclusion by rotation, they may be continued for life, which, from their extensive means of influence, would follow of course. The President, who would be a mere pageant of state, unless he coincides with the views of the Senate, would either become the head of the aristocratic junto in that body, or its minion; besides, their influences being the most predominant, could the best secure his re-election to office. And from his power of granting pardons, he might screen from punishment the most treasonable attempts on the liberties of the people, when instigated by the Senate.

From this investigation into the organization of this government, it appears that it is devoid of all responsibility or accountability to the great body of the people, and that so far from being a regular balanced government, it would be in practice a *permanent* ARISTOCRACY.

Suggested Readings

Adams, Willi Paul. *The First American Constitutions: Republican Ideology and the Making of the State Constitutions in the Revolutionary Era* (Chapel Hill: University of North Carolina Press, 1980).

Amar, Akhil Reed. *America's Constitution: A Biography* (New York: Random House, 2005).

Bowen, Catherine Drinker. *Miracle at Philadelphia: The Story of the Constitutional Convention, May to September 1787* (Boston: Little, Brown and Company, 1966).

Cornell, Saul. *The Other Founders: Anti-Federalism and the Dissenting Tradition in America, 1788–1828* (Chapel Hill: University of North Carolina Press, 1999).

Dougherty, Keith L. *Collective Action under the Articles of Confederation* (New York: Cambridge University Press, 2006).

Edling, Max M. *A Revolution in Favor of Government: Origins of the U.S. Constitution and the Making of the American State* (New York: Oxford University Press, 2003).

Hendrickson, David C. *Peace Pact: The Lost World of the American Founding* (Lawrence: University Press of Kansas, 2006).

Holton, Woody. *Unruly Americans and the Origins of the Constitution*. (New York: Hill and Wang, 2007).

Jillson, Calvin C. *Constitution Making: Conflict and Consensus in the Federal Convention of 1787* (New York: Agathon Press, 1988).

Kramer, Larry D. *The People Themselves: Popular Constitutionalism and Judicial Review* (New York: Oxford University Press, 2004).

Kruman, Marc W. *Between Liberty and Authority: State Constitution Making in Revolutionary America* (Chapel Hill: University of North Carolina Press, 1997).

Lutz, Donald S. *Popular Consent and Popular Control: Whig Political Theory in the Early State Constitution* (Baton Rouge: Louisiana State University, 1980).

McDonald, Forrest. *Novus Ordo Seclorum: The Intellectual Origins of the Constitution* (Lawrence: University Press of Kansas, 1985).

Maier, Pauline. *Ratification: The People Debate the Constitution, 1787–1788* (New York: Simon and Schuster, 2010).

Morgan, Edmund S. *Inventing the People: The Rise of Popular Sovereignty in America* (New York: W. W. Norton, 1988).

Onuf, Peters S. *The Origins of the Federal Republic: Jurisdictional Controversies in the United States, 1775–1787* (Philadelphia: University of Pennsylvania Press, 1983).

Rakove, Jack N. *Original Meanings: Politics and Ideas in the Making of the Constitution* (New York: Knopf, 1996).

Rakove, Jack N. *The Beginnings of National Politics: An Interpretive History of the Continental Congress* (New York: Knopf, 1979).

Robertson, David Brian. *The Constitution and America's Destiny* (New York: Cambridge University Press, 2005).

Wood, Gordon S. *The Creation of the American Republic, 1776–1787* (Chapel Hill: University of North Carolina, 1969).

Chapter 4

The Early National Era: 1789–1828

I. Introduction

The Constitution of the United States took effect on March 4, 1789, with the start of a new form of government. It was a stunning success. Significant opposition ceased almost immediately. Former Federalists and anti-Federalists alike welcomed clear constitutional rules—and dutifully followed them. National elections were held every two years in the manner prescribed. Elected officials from all regions of the United States agreed that Congress could regulate interstate commerce and that no state could establish titles of nobility. Few forms of government can claim the institutional stability of the United States. Fewer still experienced the almost complete disappearance of criticism of their constitution shortly after its ratification.

The Constitution, it was widely agreed, contained the right answer to all vital political questions. But this consensus came at a price: vigorous disagreement over *what the right answer was*. Controversies broke out under the first president, George Washington, over the powers of the national government, the status of states in the union, the powers of the national executive, and the judicial authority to declare laws unconstitutional. And most of these controversies were not fully resolved by the end of the early national period. Many remain unsettled today, but the Constitution's achievement was real. What Americans did from 1789 to 1829 was to establish the terms on which all these questions, and more, would be debated. How that first generation of Americans thought about these basic constitutional problems remains central, but they did not settle how to frame the issues once and for all. Rather, they launched debates that have often been transformed by events and by new ways of thinking about the Constitution.

These disagreements were fueled by the constitutional text and the rise of partisan coalitions. The Constitution provided an outline of the national government, but the framers did not specify every detail. No provision explicitly determines whether Congress may grant corporate charters, whether the President may claim executive privilege when Congress requests certain documents, or whether the Supreme Court may declare laws unconstitutional. When disputes over these issues arose, political leaders often disagreed. The founding generation believed that political parties (or "factions") were dangerous in a republic, but their dream of nonpartisan politics lasted longer than the reality. National political leaders almost immediately began to form political parties, starting in the late 1790s with the Federalists and the Republicans. When controversies arose, these parties looked to both constitutional principle and concrete political interest. Federalists generally construed national powers more broadly than Republicans, but not always. When it came to the Louisiana Purchase in 1803, Republicans were far more likely to claim a constitutional power to acquire new territory. At least in part, that was because most people believed the new territories would increase the strength of the Republican coalition.

On some important matters, members of the First Congress sometimes admitted, the Constitution was silent. Could the President constitutionally remove a cabinet officer without Congressional approval? "Perhaps this is an omitted case," James Madison confessed.[1] By 1800 Federalists and Republicans were more confident in their own views and less generous about their opponents. Both were convinced that their rivals were sacrificing law to politics. Republicans feared Federal-

1. *Annals of Congress* 1st Cong., 1st Sess. (1789):500.

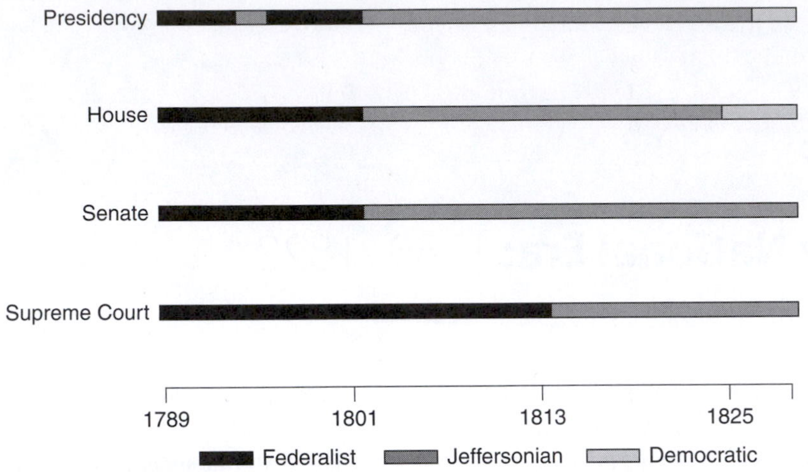

Figure 4-1 Partisan Control of the U.S. Government, 1789–1828

ists were manipulating the text in order to establish an English-style aristocracy. Federalists were as fearful of what they perceived as Republican efforts to create a French-style Jacobean government.

Developments. The federal government was successfully launched under the new U.S. Constitution during this period, but the process was not an easy one. After the constitutional ratification debates of 1787 and 1788, the country mostly rallied around the election of George Washington to the presidency in 1789.[2] Much was accomplished, but new disagreements also broke out. The outlines of the federal government were established. A system of taxes was put in place, though internal taxes were so controversial that they gave rise to violent tax protests and one of the first exercises of judicial review in *Hylton v. United States* (1796). Over great protest, the Bank of the United States was chartered to help finance the federal government and spur the economy. A modest military was built, and diplomatic issues with Britain were settled. But as the government built new institutions and made new policy, Americans divided over what direction the government should take. Debate turned into protest, which turned into the formation of an opposition party. For a founding generation that regarded protests and parties as dangerous to the health of a republic, these developments were an ominous sign, and the government took steps to crush the opposition by force in the late 1790s.

When the Jeffersonians won both houses of Congress and the presidency in the 1800 elections, many Federalists feared that constitutional government would not survive. The Jeffersonians did cut taxes and spending, shrink the military, and engage in a brief struggle with the courts. The Federalists had tried to pack the courts with their allies before leaving office, and the Jeffersonians responded by undoing what the Federalists had done and impeaching two federal judges, including a Supreme Court justice. On the whole, however, the Jeffersonians built on Federalist accomplishments. They added huge swaths of new territory with the Louisiana Purchase. They accepted the first Bank of the United States and eventually chartered a Second Bank in 1816. They opened the door to protectionist tariffs and federal support for "internal improvements" or transportation projects, though they disagreed among themselves about how far those policies could go. Especially after the War of 1812 with Britain, many Jeffersonian leaders accepted that the federal government would need to be active and strong enough to protect the nation. Congress occupied the center of government, and the Senate was just emerging from the shadow of the House of Representatives as an important political force. By the end of the early national period, the foundations of the government were secure, the size and circumstances of the nation had significantly changed, and the terms of constitutional debate had become familiar.

2. The lingering holdouts of North Carolina and Rhode Island from the union were the notable exceptions.

Partisan Coalitions in the Early National Period. The Federalists were initially the stronger of the two coalitions during the 1790s, in no small part because they enjoyed the support of President Washington. Led by Treasury Secretary Alexander Hamilton, Federalists favored a liberal, broad, or expansive construction of national powers. They insisted that the Constitution was an agreement among the people of the United States, not a compact between formerly sovereign states. Federalists supported giving the president independent powers to conduct foreign policy. After some initial hesitation, they became strong supporters of a powerful judiciary, with the power to declare federal laws unconstitutional. Federalists acted on these constitutional commitments when they controlled the national government from 1789 to 1800. They were committed to economic development, a posture of national strength, and a relatively friendly attitude toward Britain. Congress passed legislation incorporating a national bank; it also assumed outstanding state debts from the American Revolution, imposed tariffs on imported goods, and created an extensive federal judiciary. President Washington acted independently from Congress when he issued the Neutrality Proclamation, which announced that the United States would not take sides in the ongoing war between England and France.

The Federalists borrowed their name from supporters of the Constitution during ratification debates. However, some leaders of the movement for a new constitution, such as James Madison (now a member of Congress), broke from Hamilton and his allies in the 1790s. Conversely, some prominent anti-Federalists from the ratification debates (such as Maryland's Samuel Chase) rallied to the support of the administration.

Jeffersonians, often known as Republicans or Democratic-Republicans, opposed the Federalists in both their constitutional vision and policies. Led by Secretary of State Thomas Jefferson and James Madison, Republicans favored a strict or narrow construction of the powers of the new national government in the 1790s. They believed that the separate states were the crucial parties to the Constitution. Jefferson and his political allies favored a weaker president than the Federalists. After some initial hesitation, they also favored a weaker federal judiciary. They favored a more agrarian, laissez-faire economic policy, smaller government, and friendlier relations with France.

Federalists in the 1790s enjoyed the strong support of coastal towns, while Republicans were electorally stronger in the interior farmlands. Neither party was exclusively sectional. South Carolina was initially a bastion of Federalism, while Republicans tended to win elections in western Massachusetts. Sectional divisions during the first years of constitutional life were as much between the east (the immediate Atlantic coast) and the west (the Appalachian region and beyond) as between the North and the South. But as time wore on, the Federalists found their greatest strength in New England, while the Republican base was in the South.

A Shift in Dominance. Jeffersonians replaced the Federalists as the dominant national coalition in 1800. The Federalists were swept out of national elected office in the 1800 elections, and they were never able to recover. The "Revolution of 1800" marked the first time a national coalition was voted out of office, and the Jeffersonians proclaimed that they were returning government to its true principles. Within a few years, the Jeffersonians were also able to appoint a majority of the Supreme Court, though it remained under the leadership of the moderate Federalist Chief Justice John Marshall through the end of the early national era.

No sooner had Jeffersonians gained unified control of the national government, however, than the coalition splintered. Almost immediately after Jefferson's inauguration, some doctrinaire Republicans complained that the administration made too many compromises with federal power. This faction became known as Old Republicans or Tertium Quids (literally "third something"). Led by John Randolph in Congress, Chief Justice Spencer Roane of the Virginia Court of Appeals, the Virginia writer and politician John Taylor of Caroline, and Thomas Ritchie, editor of the influential *Richmond Enquirer*, they insisted on a sharper narrowing of federal power. Often encouraged by Jefferson himself once he left the White House, they opposed most federal efforts to develop the national economy and challenged federal judicial authority over the states.

Other Jeffersonians became more comfortable with national power. This faction, which became known as National Republicans, included Henry Clay of Kentucky, John C. Calhoun of South Carolina, and Daniel Webster of Massachusetts. A younger generation of political leaders, they were dismayed by weaknesses in the national government exposed by the War of

Table 4-1 Major Issues and Decisions of the Early National Era

Major Political Issues	Major Constitutional Issues	Major Court Decisions
Incorporation of Bank of the United States	Scope of necessary and proper clause	*Hayburn's Case* (1792)
Imposition of federal taxes	Presidential removal power	*Chisholm v. Georgia* (1793)
Relations with England and France	Treaty powers	*Hylton v. United States* (1796)
Judiciary Act of 1801 and its repeal	Executive privilege	*Marbury v. Madison* (1803)
Embargo	Free speech	*Stuart v. Laird* (1803)
Louisiana Purchase	Adoption of Bill of Rights	*Martin v. Hunter's Lessee* (1816)
Yazoo Land Scandal	Judicial independence	*McCulloch v. Maryland* (1819)
Burr Conspiracy	Regulation of commerce	*Cohens v. Virginia* (1821)
War of 1812	Spending power	*Gibbons v. Ogden* (1824)
Internal improvements	Contract clause	*Fletcher v. Peck* (1810)
Missouri Compromise	Judicial review	*Dartmouth College v. Woodward* (1819)

1812, and they sponsored aggressive federal efforts to develop the economic infrastructure. By 1820, National Republicans were enthusiastic proponents of a more powerful national state and federal judicial authority.

The Federalist Era lasted 12 years, or just one presidential term after Washington's. The Jeffersonian Era lasted nearly three times as long, but it too had difficulty surviving the retirement of its founders. The "Virginia dynasty" consisted of two presidential terms each for the Virginians Jefferson, Madison, and James Monroe. Monroe presided over the Era of Good Feelings after the final collapse of the Federalists, but there was no clear successor. The informal practice of having party members in Congress "nominate" the presidential candidate (a practice derided as "King Caucus") failed to unify the Jeffersonian party in 1824. The result was a multi-candidate race that was finally decided in Congress. John Quincy Adams, the first committed National Republican, claimed victory. But he was limited to a single, controversial term of office before being unseated by Andrew Jackson.

The Federal Judiciary in the Early National Era. The federal judiciary went through a difficult period of transition in the early years under the Constitution. The Judiciary Act of 1789, creating the federal judiciary, was a compromise measure: It limited judicial power and forced the Supreme Court justices to spend time "riding circuit"—or hearing cases while sitting as members of federal trial courts throughout the country. Supreme Court justice was not necessarily an attractive position, and Chief Justice John Jay busied himself with diplomatic missions before resigning his seat to become governor of New York. The federal judiciary won some early support from the Jeffersonians by claiming the power of judicial review, but not for long. It lost that support when Federalist judges upheld controversial policies on taxes and oversaw sedition prosecutions against Jeffersonian newspapers.

When the Federalists lost the elections of 1800, they immediately passed the Judiciary Act of 1801, expanding the size and power of the federal courts. These judges became known as the "midnight appointments," because the Federalists worked until the very last minute of their term of office, leaving no vacancies on the bench when Jefferson assumed the presidency. When they assumed power, the Jeffersonians repealed the Judiciary Act of 1801 in its entirety and pursued impeachment charges against two federal judges, including Justice Samuel Chase.

Despite the seismic shift in 1800, the Marshall Court was able to issue important opinions upholding national power, by focusing on rulings that could gain the support of other national officials. Presidents Washington and Adams established the practice of appointing only justices committed to the Federalist vision of the Constitution. Chief Justice John Marshall, an Adams appointee in 1800, implemented that vision in a series of bold opinions—handed down after the Federalists fell from power:

- *Marbury v. Madison* (1803) explained that federal courts had the power to declare federal laws unconstitutional.
- *Fletcher v. Peck* (1810) emphasized that the federal courts had the power to declare state laws unconstitutional.
- *Martin v. Hunter's Lessee* (1816) asserted that federal courts could review the rulings of state courts on matters involving federal law.
- *McCulloch v. Maryland* (1819) held that Congress had "implied powers" as well; these could be exercised whenever they were reasonable means of achieving a constitutional end, such as collecting taxes or providing for the national defense.
- *Gibbons v. Ogden* (1824) determined that Congress, under the interstate commerce clause, could regulate all forms of "commercial intercourse" that influenced more than one state.

Marshall was able to retain control of the Court after 1800, in part by force of personality. In addition, Presidents Jefferson, Madison, and Monroe tended to appoint justices sympathetic to this constitutional vision. Justice Joseph Story, a Madison appointee in 1812, was particularly committed to a nationalist understanding of the Constitution.

The differences between the federal courts and the elected branches of the government resulted in two parallel constitutional tracks by the 1820s. The first track was official constitutional law as found in Supreme Court decisions. This track, as articulated in *Marbury v. Madison*, *McCulloch v. Maryland*, and *Gibbons v. Ogden*, vested the national government with broad powers. It also rejected claims that states retained any independent sovereignty and claimed that the federal judiciary was the institution responsible for determining the meaning of ambiguous constitutional provisions.

The second track was the dominant constitutional understandings of elected officials. This track, as articulated by Presidents Jefferson, Madison, and Monroe, suggested sharp constitutional limits on federal power. It insisted that states retained vital constitutional roles, and it claimed that elected officials had independent power to interpret the Constitution. The clash between these two constitutional tracks would intensify during the Jacksonian Era, as the Old Republicans became Democrats and the National Republicans became the Whigs.

Legacies. The early national period established the terms of debate for the rest of American constitutional history. This debate has been over the meaning of the Constitution, not whether the Constitution should be amended, modified, or abandoned. Presidents from George Washington to George W. Bush and Barack Obama insist that they are exercising *existing* constitutional powers. They have not generally thought it necessary to call for changes in the Constitution to augment their power. Rather, political coalitions have fought for control over the institutions responsible for declaring the *meaning* of the Constitution. While federal courts have played a major role in this, other officials have contested that meaning as well, often successfully. Could George Washington constitutionally withhold documents from Congress? Could Bill Clinton be impeached for lying under oath? These and other controversies have been resolved without judicial participation.

Many precedents established during the early national period are now considered authoritative. Two are particularly important: *Marbury v. Madison* (1803) and *McCulloch v. Maryland* (1819). *Marbury* is commonly said to have established judicial review. *McCulloch*, most would agree, gives the federal government the power to respond to all national crises. (Whether *Marbury* and *McCulloch* had the same meaning and authority in the early national period is less clear.) Other precedents were set outside the Court. The First Congress has in fact been referred to as a "continuing constitutional convention." An extraordinary number of constitutional questions, big and small, transformed the constitutional text into a working government.[3] Among the most notable was the "great debate" over the president's power to remove lower executive branch officials, but what exactly was resolved has been the subject of recurrent debate. As you read this and later chapters, you will want to consider what these documents said, what they accomplished, and how they have been used ever since.

3. David P. Currie, *The Constitution in Congress: The Federalist Period* (Chicago: University of Chicago Press, 1997), 3.

Box 4-1 A Partial Cast of Characters of the Early National Era

Thomas Jefferson	■ Republican ■ Author of the Declaration of Independence ■ Secretary of State to Federalist George Washington (1790–93) ■ Vice president to Federalist John Adams (1797–1801) ■ President of the United States (1801–09) ■ Founder of the Jeffersonian Republican Party ■ Secret author of the Kentucky Resolution of 1798 ■ Leading political proponent of "strict constructionism" in constitutional interpretation
John Marshall	■ Moderate Federalist ■ Secretary of State to Federalist John Adams (1800–01) ■ Chief Justice of the U.S. Supreme Court (1801–35), appointed to the Supreme Court by John Adams after the election of 1800 ■ Leading judicial proponent of broad, nationalist interpretation of the Constitution ■ Author of most of the Court's important constitutional opinions in the early republic
Joseph Story	■ National Republican ■ Massachusetts Speaker of the House (1811) ■ Associate Justice of the U.S. Supreme Court (1812–45) ■ Harvard law professor ■ Madison's fourth choice to fill a vacancy on the Supreme Court, opposed by Jefferson who regarded Story was too much of a Federalist ■ Close ally of John Marshall and a leading treatise writer in the early republic
Spencer Roane	■ Republican ■ Chief judge of the Virginia Court of Appeals (1794–1822) ■ Leading states' rights activist in the state courts during the early republic ■ Part of the "Richmond Junto" that surrounded the influential *Richard Enquirer* newspaper and criticized any deviations from strict constructionist philosophy
James Monroe	■ Republican ■ Anti-Federalist in the Virginia ratification convention ■ Favored as an alternative candidate for president to James Madison by strict constructionist Republicans in 1808 ■ Secretary of State to Republican James Madison (1811–17) ■ Last president of the United States in the "Virginia Dynasty" and last president of the revolutionary generation (1817–25) ■ Presided over the "Era of Good Feelings" and the final collapse of the Federalist Party

The War of 1812 and the events of the 1810s finally brought the United States out of the shadow of conflicts between France and England. National politics could then turn fully to domestic policy, especially development of the vast territory that the United States possessed. The Jeffersonians struggled with the legacy of the War of 1812 and the growing demands for greater use of national governmental power, which helped fracture the party in the 1820s. The effort to partition the territory gained through the Louisiana Purchase also exposed serious sectional tensions. It foreshadowed the conflicts over slavery and territory that would consume America for decades to come. Even as the issues evolved, however, lawyers and politicians continued to understand the terms of debate within the framework developed in the early republic.

Alexander Hamilton, Report on Manufacturers (1791)[4]

Alexander Hamilton was the political leader who best articulated the Federalist constitutional vision during the 1790s. As Washington's first Secretary of the Treasury, he produced several reports, all urging Congress to promote various commercial enterprises in the United States. Hamilton's "Report on Manufacturers," presented to Congress on December 5, 1791, is one of his most famous state papers. That Report had two objectives. The first was to explain why encouraging commercial enterprise was an important objective. The second was to lay out a broad federal program that would encourage commercial enterprises.

The expediency of encouraging manufactures in the United States, which was not long since deemed very questionable, appears at this time to be pretty generally admitted. The embarrassments, which have obstructed the progress of our external trade, have led to serious reflections on the necessity of enlarging the sphere of our domestic commerce: the restrictive regulations, which in foreign markets abridge the vent of the increasing surplus of our Agricultural produce, serve to beget an earnest desire, that a more extensive demand for that surplus may be created at home....

...

[T]he greatest obstacle of all to the successful prosecution of a new branch of industry in a country, in which it was before unknown, consists, as far as the instances apply, in the bounties premiums and other aids which are granted, in a variety of cases, by the nations, in which the establishments to be imitated are previously introduced. It is well known (and particular examples in the course of this report will be cited) that certain nations grant bounties on the exportation of particular commodities, to enable their own workmen to undersell and supplant all competitors, in the countries to which those commodities are sent. Hence the undertakers of a new manufacture have to contend not only with the natural disadvantages of a new undertaking, but with the gratuities and remunerations which other governments bestow. To be enabled to contend with success, it is evident, that the interference and aid of their own government are indispensable.

...

The introduction of Banks, as has been shown on another occasion has a powerful tendency to extend the active Capital of a Country....

...

The want of a Navy to protect our external commerce, as long as it shall continue, must render it a peculiarly precarious reliance, for the supply of essential articles, and must serve to strengthen prodigiously the arguments in favor of manufactures.

...

Ideas of a contrariety of interests between the northern and southern regions of the Union, are in the Main as unfounded as they are mischievous. The diversity of Circumstances on which such contrariety is usually predicated, authorizes a directly contrary conclusion. Mutual wants constitute one of the strongest links of political connection, and the extent of these bears a natural proportion to the diversity in the means of mutual supply.

...

...If the northern and middle states should be the principal scenes of such establishments, they would immediately benefit the more southern, by creating a demand for productions; some of which they have in common with the other states, and others of which are either peculiar to them, or more abundant, or of better quality, than elsewhere....

...

Good roads, canals, and navigable rivers, by diminishing the expense of carriage, put the remote parts of a country more nearly upon a level with those in the neighborhood of the town. They are, upon that account, the greatest of all improvements....

Thomas Jefferson, First Inaugural Address (1801)[5]

Jefferson's ascension to the presidency marked the first peaceful transition of power in a modern republic. Washington

4. Excerpt taken from *American State Papers: Finance*, vol. 1 (Washington, DC: Seaton and Gales, 1832), 123.

5. Excerpt taken from *A Compilation of the Messages and Papers of the Presidents*, ed. James D. Richardson, vol. 1 (New York: Bureau of National Literature, 1897), 309.

had voluntarily set aside the office in 1796, and Adams had been his favored successor. By contrast, the election of 1800 had been extremely bitter and hard-fought, and passions were running high. The country had taken an important step toward becoming a stable democracy, but it was not clear what the future would bring.

Jefferson's inaugural address was designed to celebrate that milestone, reassure the nervous Federalists, and announce the principles that would guide his own administration and unite his followers. On the one hand, it emphasized national reconciliation and respecting majority rule, a common "attachment to union and representative government." On the other hand, it laid down the new public philosophy. The "sum of good government," Jefferson intoned, was a government that "shall restrain men from injuring one another," but "shall leave them otherwise free to regulate their own pursuits of industry and improvement, and shall not take from the mouth of labor the bread it has earned."[6]

...

During the contest of opinion through which we have passed the animation of discussions and of exertions has sometimes worn an aspect which might impose on strangers unused to think freely and to speak and to write what they think; but this being now decided by the voice of the nation, announced according to the rules of the Constitution, all will, of course, arrange themselves under the will of the law, and unite in common efforts for the common good. All, too, will bear in mind this sacred principle, that though the will of the majority is in all cases to prevail, that will to be rightful must be reasonable; that the minority possess their equal rights, which equal law must protect, and to violate would be oppression. Let us, then, fellow-citizens, unite with one heart and one mind.... [E]very difference of opinion is not a difference of principle. We have called by different names brethren of the same principle. We are all Republicans, we are all Federalists. If there be any among us who would wish to dissolve this Union or to change its republican form, let them stand undisturbed as monuments of the safety with which error of opinion may be tolerated where reason is left free to combat it.... I believe this... the strongest Government on earth. I believe it the only one where every man, at the call of the law, would fly to the standard of the law, and would meet invasions of the public order as his own personal concern. Sometimes it is said that man can not be trusted with the government of himself. Can he, then, be trusted with the government of others? Or have we found angels in the forms of kings to govern him? Let history answer this question.

...

About to enter, fellow-citizens, on the exercise of duties which comprehend everything dear and valuable to you, it is proper you should understand what I deem the essential principles of our Government, and consequently those which ought to shape its Administration. I will compress them within the narrowest compass they will bear, stating the general principle, but not all its limitations. Equal and exact justice to all men, of whatever state or persuasion, religious or political; peace, commerce, and honest friendship with all nations, entangling alliances with none; the support of the State governments in all their rights, as the most competent administrations for our domestic concerns and the surest bulwarks against antirepublican tendencies; the preservation of the General Government in its whole constitutional vigor, as the sheet anchor of our peace at home and safety abroad; a jealous care of the right of election by the people—a mild and safe corrective of abuses which are lopped by the sword of revolution where peaceable remedies are unprovided; absolute acquiescence in the decisions of the majority, the vital principle of republics...; a well-disciplined militia, our best reliance in peace and for the first moments of war till regulars may relieve them; the supremacy of the civil over the military authority; economy in the public expense, that labor may be lightly burdened; the honest payment of our debts and sacred preservation of the public faith; encouragement of agriculture, and of commerce as its handmaid; the diffusion of information and arraignment of all abuses at the bar of the public reason; freedom of religion; freedom of the press, and freedom of person under the protection of the habeas corpus, and trial by juries impartially selected.... They should be the creed of our political faith, the text of civic instruction, the touchstone by which to try the services of those we trust; and should we wander from them in moments of error or of alarm, let us hasten to retrace our steps and to regain the road which alone leads to peace, liberty, and safety....

6. Ibid, 311.

II. Judicial Power and Constitutional Authority

MAJOR DEVELOPMENTS

- Creation of the federal judicial system
- Federal courts staffed largely by justices committed to broad interpretation of the Constitution
- Courts assert right to declare statutes unconstitutional
- U.S. Supreme Court affirms its right to review state court rulings on federal law

Article III of the U.S. Constitution, like Article II, begins with a vesting clause. It vests "judicial power" in the Supreme Court and any inferior courts that Congress might create. Like Article II, Article III says little more about this power. A great deal was left to be fleshed out.

The Judiciary Act of 1789. That process of adding flesh to the bones of Article III began with the Judiciary Act of 1789, which launched the federal court system. The Judiciary Act insured that there would be a federal court system and that federal judges would have a chance to interpret the U.S. Constitution, implement treaties, and apply federal law. Article III of the Constitution gives Congress the power to establish lower federal courts. It also gives the power, subject to important exceptions, to determine the conditions under which the Supreme Court hears appeals from lower federal and state courts.

Drafted largely by future Chief Justice Oliver Ellsworth, the Judiciary Act of 1789 was the first major piece of legislation passed by Congress and signed into law by President Washington. It provided for a Supreme Court with one chief justice and five associate justices, three Circuit Courts of Appeals presided over by two justices from the Supreme Court and one district judge, and thirteen District Courts, one in each state, each with a single presiding judge. Supreme Court justices would spend most of their time "riding circuit," or acting as circuit court judges. That left them relatively little time for sitting with their fellow justices to hear cases as the Supreme Court.

Both Article III of the Constitution and the Judiciary Act of 1789 detail the types of cases over which the federal judicial power "shall extend." This defines the *jurisdiction* of the federal courts—the set of cases that those courts have the legal power to hear and resolve. Federal jurisdiction is established either by the type of party involved (e.g., "cases affecting ambassadors" or "between citizens of different states") or by the type of law involved (e.g., "cases...arising under this Constitution [or] the laws of the United States"). Article III specifies that the U.S. Supreme Court has original jurisdiction in a small number of cases. Those cases begin in the Supreme Court. In all other cases, the Supreme Court only has appellate jurisdiction. Those cases only reach the Supreme Court after they have been initiated in some other court.

Appellate Jurisdiction. The limits Congress placed on the federal court system in 1789 began a controversy over federal jurisdiction that has never been settled. Article III, Section 1, declares, "The judicial Power of the United States, shall be vested in one supreme Court, and in such inferior Courts as the Congress may from time to time ordain and establish." Proponents of mandatory federal jurisdiction emphasize the word "shall." They insist that Congress must enable some federal court to hear all cases involving federal law, or what is known as diversity of citizenship. Proponents of discretionary federal jurisdiction disagree. They note a provision in Article III, Section 2: "In all Cases affecting Ambassadors, other public Ministers and Consuls, and those in which a State shall be Party, the supreme Court shall have original Jurisdiction. In all...other Cases..., the supreme Court shall have appellate Jurisdiction,...with such Exceptions,...as the Congress shall make." In their view, Congress may make exceptions to the appellate jurisdiction by permitting some cases involving federal law or diversity of citizenship to be resolved entirely by state courts.

The stakes in this debate are high. If Congress may deprive the Supreme Court of appellate jurisdiction in most cases, then Congress has the power to prevent federal courts from hearing almost all appeals from constitutional cases. In effect, by depriving the federal courts of jurisdiction, Congress ensures that each state court system has the final say on whether federal or state laws are constitutional. If Virginia courts rule a federal tax unconstitutional, no appeal exists, because Congress had not empowered federal courts with the jurisdiction necessary to hear those cases.

Those who supported the Judiciary Act of 1789 clearly believed that Congress was not constitutionally obligated to provide appellate jurisdiction. They need not, they assumed, establish a federal court system that could hear all cases involving the federal constitution, federal law, and federal treaties. The Judiciary Act permitted appeals to the U.S. Supreme Court only when a state court declared a federal law unconstitutional, declared a state law constitutional, or rejected a claim of constitutional right. If, for example, a Virginia court declared that a federal tax was consistent with the U.S. Constitution, the losing litigant in 1795 could not appeal that decision to a federal court.

Unfortunately, we do not have detailed records of the debate over the Judiciary Act. For this reason, we do not know whether members of Congress in 1789 thought that they could deprive federal courts of jurisdiction over most questions of federal constitutional law. Perhaps they thought that Section 25, which provided for a limited set of appeals to the U.S. Supreme Court, provided sufficient protection for federal interests. As it stood, however, Section 25 would become an important vehicle for bringing constitutional cases before the Supreme Court through much of the nineteenth century.

Judicial Review. Unlike the constitutions of many countries today, the U.S. Constitution does not say anything explicit about judicial review. Some have argued that judicial review is implicit in the "judicial power" vested in the Supreme Court in Article III. Others have argued that it is inherent in the overall constitutional design. State constitutions were equally silent on the subject. Yet in both the state and the federal courts, judges heard arguments that the laws that they were asked to apply were unconstitutional. And they responded by refusing to apply statutes in ways that would violate constitutional requirements. The U.S. Supreme Court case of *Marbury v. Madison*, decided in 1803, has become famous as the origin of the power of judicial review. By the time of *Marbury*, however, the power of the courts to take into account the Constitution when deciding cases was widely accepted. Nonetheless, judges offered a variety of different justifications for this power. They also had different explanations for why and how the power should be used.

The rise of partisanship raised doubts about the constitutional commitment to a judiciary that would be above politics. As we have seen, Federalists and Jeffersonians during the 1790s advanced different constitutional visions. Their partisan struggles created opportunities for the exercise of judicial power, but also threats to judicial independence. At different times, both Federalists and Jeffersonians suggested that the federal judiciary might have a vital role to play in keeping the national government within constitutional limits. But both sides also feared that a "faction" might install its adherents in the judiciary and abuse the powers of the courts.

Thomas Jefferson had been an early advocate of a federal bill of rights precisely because he anticipated that it would be judicially enforceable. Writing from France, he had helped persuade Madison that a bill of rights could be useful in part because of "the legal check which it puts in the hands of the judiciary. This is a body, which if rendered independent & kept strictly to their own department merits great confidence for their learning & integrity."[7] Even in 1798, Jefferson reassured one correspondent that "the laws of the land, administered by upright judges, would protect you from any exercise of power unauthorized by the Constitution of the United States."[8] After the Federalists lost the elections of 1800, they passed the Judiciary Act of 1801 to strengthen and expand the federal courts. President John Adams filled these seats with loyal Federalists, the "midnight appointments," in the days and hours before Jefferson's inauguration. Jefferson thought that this was a "fraudulent use of the constitution," and that these "useless judges" had been put in place simply to preserve Federalist policies and attack "all the works of republicanism."[9] The Jeffersonian response was to repeal the Judiciary Act of 1801 and impeach two federal judges.

The position of the courts was generally considered stronger at the end of the early republic than at the beginning. The role and membership of the state and federal courts had stabilized. They routinely interpreted state and federal constitutions, and they sometimes refused to apply statutory provisions as unconstitutional. The U.S. Supreme Court under Chief Justice John Marshall frequently provoked controversy, but it steered a relatively moderate path. The Court avoided issuing decisions that would be ignored or opposed by major Jeffersonian leaders.

7. Thomas Jefferson, "To James Madison, March 15, 1789," in *The Writings of Thomas Jefferson*, ed. Paul Leicester Ford, vol. 5 (New York: G.P. Putnam's Sons, 1904), 461.

8. Jefferson, "To Archibald Hamilton Rowan, September 26, 1798," in *Writings*, vol. 7, 281.

9. Thomas Jefferson, *Memoir, Correspondence, and Miscellanies, from the Papers of Thomas Jefferson*, ed. Thomas Jefferson Randolph, vol. 3 (Charlottesville, VA: F. Carrington and Co., 1829).

Table 4-2 Some Early Cases of Judicial Review in American Courts

Case	Court	Decision
Ten-Pound Act Cases (1786)	New Hampshire Inferior Court	Struck down state statute expanding the set of civil suits that could be tried without a jury as violating state constitution
Bayard v. Singleton, 1 N.C. 5 (1787)	North Carolina Supreme Court	Struck down state statute denying loyalists the right to challenge state seizure of property as violating state constitution
Cases of the Judges, 8 Va. 135 (1788)	Virginia Court of Appeals	Declaration that state law requiring court of appeals judges to also sit on district courts violated the state constitution
Bowman v. Middleton, 1 S.C.L. 252 (1792)	South Carolina Supreme Court	Struck down as "against common right...[and] the Magna Carta" an act transferring a land title without trial by jury
Hayburn's Case, 2 U.S. 408 (1792)	U.S. Circuit Court	First instance in which a law of Congress was declared unconstitutional. Federal Circuit Court of Pennsylvania struck down a federal statute requiring judges to review pension applications as violating the federal Constitution
Kamper v. Hawkins, 3 Va. 20 (1793)	Virginia General Court	Struck down state statute transferring some powers of chancery courts to district courts as violating state constitution
Vanhorne's Lessee v. Dorrance, 2 U.S. 297 (1795)	U.S. Circuit Court	Struck down a state statute regarding property claims as violating state constitution, upheld two others as not violating federal Constitution. Articulated argument for judicial review
Hylton v. United States, 3 U.S. 171 (1796)	U.S. Supreme Court	First instance of Supreme Court review of a federal statute. Upheld a federally imposed tax as not violating federal Constitution
United States v. La Vengeance, 3 U.S. 297 (1796)	U.S. Supreme Court	Upheld use of admiralty courts for enforcing embargo statutes as not violating federal right to trial by jury
Calder v. Bull, 3 U.S. 386 (1798)	U.S. Supreme Court	Upheld state statute altering probate rules as not violating federal Constitution
Cooper v. Telfair, 4 U.S. 14 (1800)	U.S. Supreme Court	Upheld a state statute regarding penalties and property confiscation of persons convicted of treason as not violating state constitution
Mossman v. Higginson, 4 U.S. 12 (1800)	U.S. Supreme Court	Struck down a section of the Judiciary Act of 1789 for being in conflict as applied with the federal Constitution
Stidger v. Rogers, 2 Ky. 52 (1801)	Kentucky Supreme Court	Struck down an act of assembly allowing the court, rather than juries only, to ascertain the value of property as violating the state constitution
Marbury v. Madison, 5 U.S. 137 (1803)	U.S. Supreme Court	Struck down a section of the Judiciary Act of 1789 that expanded original jurisdiction as violating the federal Constitution
Stuart v. Laird, 5 U.S. 299 (1803)	U.S. Supreme Court	Upheld the Judiciary Act of 1802 as not in conflict with the federal Constitution

A. Judicial Review

Judicial review is usually understood to include the power of courts to interpret a constitution and refuse to apply statutes that would violate it. State and federal courts began to interpret constitutions in the United States soon after they were written. Those courts soon emphasized that their duty was to follow the constitution when deciding cases, even when statutory requirements were in conflict with it. State courts, federal judges, and eventually the U.S. Supreme Court all asserted such a power in the first years of the republic.

The power of judicial review was anticipated at the time of the founding, but was not well understood. No American constitution granted such a power explicitly, though provisions such as the supremacy clause of Article VI seemed to imply a form of it: "The Constitution . . . shall be the supreme Law of the Land; and the Judges of every State shall be bound thereby, any Thing in the Constitution or Laws of any State to the Contrary notwithstanding." Controversy surrounded some of the earliest exercises of judicial review. Still, by the 1790s the courts were widely regarded as useful for interpreting constitutions and remedying some constitutional violations. As Table 4-2 indicates, many courts struggled with and asserted the power of judicial review in the first years of the republic.

There was less agreement about when the courts could do that—and what effects such decisions might have. In *Calder v. Bull* (1798), Justices Samuel Chase and James Iredell disagreed on how the Court should interpret constitutions and when it should strike down laws. Chase implied that judges should be guided by the "very nature of our free Republican governments"; Iredell stressed that judges should not appeal to "natural justice" when evaluating statutes.

In *Marbury v. Madison* (1803), Chief Justice John Marshall provided a detailed justification for the power of judicial review. Marshall's opinion declared that Jefferson had acted illegally when his administration refused to deliver a judicial commission to William Marbury. Marshall also maintained that federal courts could order the administration to deliver the commission. Finally, he stated that the Supreme Court had the power to declare federal laws unconstitutional. His lengthy defense of judicial authority seemed a powerful rebuke to the Jefferson administration. The force of *Marbury*, however, was substantially muted. Marshall had declared unconstitutional only an obscure provision in the Judiciary Act of 1789. This provision gave the Supreme Court jurisdiction to issue the writ ordering the Jefferson administration to deliver the commission. Lacking jurisdiction, Marshall concluded that the Court could issue no order in *Marbury*. Soon after *Marbury*, the Marshall Court had another opportunity to consider the constitutionality of Jeffersonian policies toward the courts. In *Stuart v. Laird* (1803), the Court heard a challenge to the repeal of the Judiciary Act of 1801 and the dismissal of numerous Federalist judges. The stakes were much higher in *Stuart*, and in that case the Court simply issued a brief opinion upholding the repeal. In short, the Marshall Court was more willing in *Marbury* than in *Stuart* to deliver a lecture on Federalist constitutional principles. Yet in both cases the justices avoided directly challenging Jefferson or the Republican Congress.

The Jeffersonians did not generally disagree with Marshall's reasoning on the power of judicial review. Where they and the Federalists split was over importance of constitutional interpretation by judges. Federalists insisted that constitutional controversies were best resolved in the courts. Jeffersonians frequently questioned whether judges could have the final word on constitutional meaning.

Calder v. Bull, 3 U.S. 386 (1798)

Norman Morrison wrote a will which left his estate to his grandson, Caleb Bull. In 1793, the Court of Probate for Hartford, Connecticut, concluded that the will was void. The Connecticut legislature two years later passed a law setting aside that decree, and granting a new hearing. At this second hearing, the court approved the original will. The Calder family, who stood to inherit under the first probate decision, appealed to the Supreme Court of the United States. They maintained that the legislation setting aside the first probate ruling was an ex post facto law, prohibited by the Constitution of Connecticut and the Constitution of the United States.

The Supreme Court unanimously rejected that claim. All four justices who heard the case agreed that the ex post facto clause only banned retrospective criminal laws and not laws adjusting property rights. Justices Chase and Iredell engaged in an important debate over the role of natural law and unwritten principles in constitutional decision making.

Justice Iredell asserted that courts had no business striking down laws solely on the ground that the legislation was inconsistent with natural justice. Justice Chase asserted that no people would empower a legislature to violate certain fundamental rights and that constitutions should be interpreted as protecting those fundamental rights.

Chase did not make clear whether he believed that fundamental law provided independent grounds to void legislation. Perhaps it merely provided a standard justices should use when interpreting the Constitution. If the first, courts should void laws that violate fundamental rights, even when the Constitution explicitly sanctions that violation. If the second, a presumption exists that a constitution does not give the legislature power to violate fundamental rights. Although the justices had previously done so, Chase's opinion also claimed that Supreme Court justices should not determine whether state laws violated the state constitution.

JUSTICE CHASE delivered the opinion of the Court.

...I cannot subscribe to the omnipotence of a State Legislature, or that it is absolute and without control; although its authority should not be expressly restrained by the Constitution, or fundamental law, of the State. The people of the United States erected their Constitutions, or forms of government, to establish justice, to promote the general welfare, to secure the blessings of liberty; and to protect their persons and property from violence. The purposes for which men enter into society will determine the nature and terms of the social compact; and as they are the foundation of the legislative power, they will decide what are the proper objects of it: The nature, and ends of legislative power will limit the exercise of it. This fundamental principle flows from the very nature of our free Republican governments, that no man should be compelled to do what the laws do not require; nor to refrain from acts which the laws permit. There are acts which the Federal, or State, Legislature cannot do, without exceeding their authority. There are certain vital principles in our free Republicans governments, which will determine and over-rule an apparent and flagrant abuse of legislative power; as to authorize manifest injustice by positive law; or to take away that security for personal liberty, or private property, for the protection whereof the government was established. An ACT of the Legislature (for I cannot call it a law) contrary to the great first principles of the social compact, cannot be considered a rightful exercise of legislative authority. The obligation of a law in governments established on express compact, and on republican principles, must be determined by the nature of the power, on which it is founded. A few instances will suffice to explain what I mean. A law that punished a citizen for an innocent action, or, in other words, for an act, which, when done, was in violation of no existing law; a law that destroys, or impairs, the lawful private contracts of citizens; a law that makes a man a Judge in his own cause; or a law that takes property from A. and gives it to B: It is against all reason and justice, for a people to entrust a Legislature with SUCH powers; and, therefore, it cannot be presumed that they have done it. The genius, the nature, and the spirit, of our State Governments, amount to a prohibition of such acts of legislation; and the general principles of law and reason forbid them. The Legislature may enjoin, permit, forbid, and punish; they may declare new crimes; and establish rules of conduct for all its citizens in future cases; they may command what is right, and prohibit what is wrong; but they cannot change innocence into guilt; or punish innocence as a crime; or violate the right of an antecedent lawful private contract; or the right of private property. To maintain that our Federal, or State, Legislature possesses such powers, if they had not been expressly restrained; would, in my opinion, be a political heresy, altogether inadmissible in our free republican governments.

...

Without giving an opinion, at this time, whether this Court has jurisdiction to decide that any law made by Congress, contrary to the Constitution of the United States, is void; I am fully satisfied that this court has no jurisdiction to determine that any law of any state Legislature, contrary to the Constitution of such state, is void. Further, if this court had such jurisdiction, yet it does not appear to me, that the resolution (or law) in question, is contrary to the charter of Connecticut, or its constitution, which is said by counsel to be composed of its acts of assembly, and usages, and customs. I should think, that the courts of Connecticut are the proper tribunals to decide, whether laws, contrary to the constitution thereof, are void....

JUSTICE IREDELL, concurring in part.

...It is true, that some speculative jurists have held, that a legislative act against natural justice must, in itself, be void; but I cannot think that, under such a government, any Court of Justice would possess a power to declare it so....

...[I]t has been the policy of all the American states, which have, individually, framed their state constitutions since the revolution, and of the people of the United States, when they framed the Federal Constitution, to define with precision the objects of the legislative power, and to restrain its exercise within marked and settled boundaries. If any act of Congress, or of the Legislature of a state, violates those constitutional provisions, it is unquestionably void; though, I admit, that as the authority to declare it void is of a delicate and awful nature, the Court will never resort to that authority, but in a clear and urgent case. If, on the other hand, the Legislature of the Union, or the Legislature of any member of the Union, shall pass a law, within the general scope of their constitutional power, the Court cannot pronounce it to be void, merely because it is, in their judgment, contrary to the principles of natural justice. The ideas of natural justice are regulated by no fixed standard: the ablest and the purest men have differed upon the subject; and all that the Court could properly say, in such an event, would be, that the Legislature (possessed of an equal right of opinion) had passed an act which, in the opinion of the judges, was inconsistent with the abstract principles of natural justice. There are then but two lights, in which the subject can be viewed: 1st. If the Legislature pursue the authority delegated to them, their acts are valid. 2d. If they transgress the boundaries of that authority, their acts are invalid. In the former case, they exercise the discretion vested in them by the people, to whom alone they are responsible for the faithful discharge of their trust: but in the latter case, they violate a fundamental law, which must be our guide, whenever we are called upon as judges to determine the validity of a legislative act.

Marbury v. Madison, 5 U.S. 137 (1803)

The lame-duck Federalist Congress was busy after the elections of 1800. In addition to passing the Judiciary Act of 1801, it also passed a law organizing the District of Columbia. Section 11 of that statute authorized the president to appoint an unspecified number of justices of the peace. John Adams nominated William Marbury to one of those new justiceships. The Senate confirmed his appointment the day before the Jeffersonians took control of the national government.

Marbury's commission was signed and sealed, but not delivered during the haste and confusion that marked the last hours of the Adams administration. Such tasks fell to Adams's Secretary of State, John Marshall, who in turn employed his brother, James, to make the deliveries. (Obviously Marshall thus knew the situation well.) Thomas Jefferson, outraged by these last-minute appointments, ordered that the leftover commissions remain undelivered. Determined to hold office, Marbury in December 1801 asked the Supreme Court for a writ of mandamus ordering Jefferson's Secretary of State, James Madison, to deliver his commission. The administration refused to recognize the Court's jurisdiction in the matter. In fact, it declined to send an attorney to argue the case or to even admit that a commission for Marbury had ever existed.

The central issue of the Marbury *litigation was thought to be whether the justices could order the executive to deliver the commission. Whether the justices had the power to declare laws unconstitutional was not as clearly at issue. To most people, a more pressing test of that power might involve the law repealing the Judiciary Act of 1801. The Court heard a challenge to that repeal at about the same time in* Stuart v. Laird *(1803). Federalists failed to preserve their circuit court justiceships or secure Marbury his office. They neither persuaded elected officials to restore the Judiciary Act of 1801, nor convinced the Supreme Court to declare the repeal unconstitutional. Marbury never obtained his commission.*

Marshall organized his Marbury *opinion in what might seem an unorthodox fashion. Justices typically first consider whether they have jurisdiction to hear a case. Only after determining that the have to power to adjudicate do they turn to the substantive dispute.* Marbury *has a different structure. The first sections of John Marshall's opinion decided that Marbury had a right to the commission and that a writ of mandamus was the appropriate remedy. Only after deciding the substantive issue did Marshall turn to the jurisdictional issue, which had not been argued at any length before the justices. Marshall determined that Section 13 of the Judiciary Act of 1789 was unconstitutional. This section was interpreted as giving the Court the power to issue a writ of mandamus in a case of original jurisdiction, a case originating in the Supreme Court itself. If Section 13 was unconstitutional, then the Court did not have the legal power to issue the order to the executive branch to force the delivery of the commission in this case.*

Last, Marshall turned to whether justices should nevertheless be guided by an unconstitutional law. Here he made his argument for judicial review of federal law. Many commentators think that Marshall had strategic reasons for structuring the Marbury *opinion in this way. He was able both to declare that the Jefferson administration's actions were illegal and to defend the power of judicial review. Yet he could still avoid having to issue a judicial order that the president would almost certainly have ignored.*

Marshall's argument in Marbury *became the canonical defense of judicial review in the United States. The argument in defense of the power of judicial review was neither surprising nor original by 1803. Nevertheless,* Marbury *was the first time the U.S. Supreme Court had fully defended the right to declare federal laws unconstitutional. As you read, consider how persuasive Marshall's argument is. How else might judicial review be defended? What exactly is the power that Marshall is defending? Is the power outlined in* Marbury *limited to laws that are clearly unconstitutional? Is it limited to laws affecting the judiciary, or could the Court strike down any type of law? Are the other branches of government obliged to follow the conclusions about constitutional meaning that the Court reaches, or do those conclusions only guide the actions of the judges?*

CHIEF JUSTICE MARSHALL delivered the opinion of the Court.

. . .

In the order in which the court has view this subject, the following questions have been considered and decided.

1st. Has the applicant a right to the commission he demands?

2d. If he has a right, and that right has been violated, do the laws of this country afford him a remedy?

3d. If they do afford him a remedy, is it a mandamus issuing from this court?

. . .

1st Has the applicant a right to the commission he demands?

. . .

In order to determine whether he is entitled to this commission, it becomes necessary to inquire whether he has been appointed to this office. For if he has been appointed, the law continues him in office for five years, and he is entitled to the possession of those evidences of office, which, being completed, became his property.

. . .

. . . [T]he clauses of the constitution and laws of the United States, which affect this part of the case . . . seem to contemplate three distinct operations:

1st. The nomination. This is the sole act of the president, and is completely voluntary.

2d. The appointment. This is also the act of the president, and is also a voluntary act, though it can only be performed by and with the advice and consent of the senate.

3d. The commission. To grant a commission to a person appointed, might, perhaps, be deemed a duty enjoined by the constitution. "He shall," says that instrument, "commission all the officers of the United States."

. . .

The last act to be done by the president is the signature of the commission. He has then acted on the advice and consent of the senate to his own nomination. The time for deliberation has then passed. He has decided. His judgment, on the advice and consent of the senate concurring with his nomination, has been made, and the officer is appointed. . . .

Some point of time must be taken when the power of the executive over an officer, not removable at his will, must cease. The point of time must be when the constitutional power of appointment has been exercised. And the power has been exercised when the last act, required from the person possessing the power, has been performed. This last act is the signature of the commission. . . .

. . .

The commission being signed, the subsequent duty of the secretary of state is prescribed by law and not to be guided by the will of the president. He is to affix the seal of the United States to the commission, and is to record it.

This is not a proceeding which may be varied, if the judgment of the executive shall suggest one more eligible; but is a precise course accurately marked out by law, and is to be strictly pursued. It is the duty of the secretary of state to conform to the law, and in this he is an officer of the United States, bound to obey the laws. He acts, in this respect . . . under the authority of the law, and not by the instructions of the president. It is a ministerial act which the law enjoins on a particular officer for a particular purpose.

If it should be supposed, that the solemnity of affixing the seal is necessary not only to the validity of the commission, but even to the completion of an appointment, still when the seal is affixed the appointment is made, and the commission is valid. No other solemnity is required by law; no other act is to be performed on the part of the government. All that the executive can do to invest the person with his office is done....

...

Mr. Marbury, then, since his commission was signed by the President and sealed by the Secretary of State, was appointed, and as the law creating the office gave the officer a right to hold for five years independent of the Executive, the appointment was not revocable, but vested in the officer legal rights which are protected by the laws of his country.

To withhold the commission, therefore, is an act deemed by the Court not warranted by law, but violative of a vested legal right.

This brings us to the second inquiry, which is:

2d. If he has a right, and that right has been violated, do the laws of this country afford him a remedy?

The very essence of civil liberty certainly consists in the right of every individual to claim the protection of the laws whenever he receives an injury. One of the first duties of government is to afford that protection. In Great Britain, the King himself is sued in the respectful form of a petition, and he never fails to comply with the judgment of his court.

...

The Government of the United States has been emphatically termed a government of laws, and not of men. It will certainly cease to deserve this high appellation if the laws furnish no remedy for the violation of a vested legal right.

If this obloquy is to be cast on the jurisprudence of our country, it must arise from the peculiar character of the case.

It behooves us, then, to inquire whether there be in its composition any ingredient which shall exempt from legal investigation or exclude the injured party from legal redress....

...

By the Constitution of the United States, the President is invested with certain important political powers, in the exercise of which he is to use his own discretion, and is accountable only to his country in his political character and to his own conscience. To aid him in the performance of these duties, he is authorized to appoint certain officers, who act by his authority and in conformity with his orders.

In such cases, their acts are his acts; and whatever opinion may be entertained of the manner in which executive discretion may be used, still there exists, and can exist, no power to control that discretion. The subjects are political. They respect the nation, not individual rights, and, being entrusted to the Executive, the decision of the Executive is conclusive. The application of this remark will be perceived by adverting to the act of Congress for establishing the Department of Foreign Affairs. This officer, as his duties were prescribed by that act, is to conform precisely to the will of the President. He is the mere organ by whom that will is communicated. The acts of such an officer, as an officer, can never be examinable by the Courts.

But when the Legislature proceeds to impose on that officer other duties; when he is directed peremptorily to perform certain acts; when the rights of individuals are dependent on the performance of those acts; he is so far the officer of the law, is amenable to the laws for his conduct, and cannot at his discretion, sport away the vested rights of others.

The conclusion from this reasoning is that, where the heads of departments are the political or confidential agents of the Executive, merely to execute the will of the President, or rather to act in cases in which the Executive possesses a constitutional or legal discretion, nothing can be more perfectly clear than that their acts are only politically examinable. But where a specific duty is assigned by law, and individual rights depend upon the performance of that duty, it seems equally clear that the individual who considers himself injured has a right to resort to the laws of his country for a remedy.

...

It is then the opinion of the Court:

1st. That, by signing the commission of Mr. Marbury, the President of the United States appointed him a justice of peace for the County of Washington in the District of Columbia, and that the seal of the United States, affixed thereto by the Secretary of State, is conclusive testimony of the verity of the signature, and of the completion of the appointment, and that the appointment conferred on him a legal right to the office for the space of five years.

2d. That, having this legal title to the office, he has a consequent right to the commission, a refusal to deliver which is a plain violation of that right, for which the laws of his country afford him a remedy.

It remains to be inquired whether,

3d. He is entitled to the remedy for which applies. This depends on,

1st. The nature of the writ applied for; and,

2d. The power of this court.

. . .

. . . [T]o render the mandamus a proper remedy, the officer to whom it is to be directed, must be one to whom, on legal principles, such a writ may be directed; and the person applying for it must be without any other specific and legal remedy.

1st. With respect to the officer to whom it would be directed. The intimate political relation, subsisting between the President of the United States and the heads of departments, necessarily renders any legal investigation of the acts of one of those high officers peculiarly irksome, as well as delicate, and excites some hesitation with respect to the propriety of entering into such investigation. Impressions are often received without much reflection or examination, and it is not wonderful that, in such a case as this, the assertion by an individual of his legal claims in a court of justice, to which claims it is the duty of that court to attend, should, at first view, be considered by some as an attempt to intrude into the cabinet and to intermeddle with the prerogatives of the Executive.

It is scarcely necessary for the Court to disclaim all pretensions to such a jurisdiction. An extravagance so absurd and excessive could not have been entertained for a moment. The province of the Court is solely to decide on the rights of individuals, not to inquire how the Executive or Executive officers perform duties in which they have a discretion. Questions, in their nature political or which are, by the Constitution and laws, submitted to the Executive, can never be made in this court.

But, if this be not such a question; if, so far from being an intrusion into the secrets of the cabinet, it respects a paper which, according to the law, is upon record, and to a copy of which the law gives a right . . . ?

. . .

It is not by the office of the person to whom the writ is directed, but the nature of the thing to be done, that the propriety or impropriety of issuing a mandamus is to be determined. Where the head of a department acts in a case in which Executive discretion is to be exercised, in which he is the mere organ of Executive will, it is again repeated, that any application to a court to control, in any respect, his conduct, would be rejected without hesitation.

But where he is directed by law to do a certain act affecting the absolute rights of individuals, in the performance of which he is not placed under the particular direction of the President, and the performance of which the President cannot lawfully forbid, and therefore is never presumed to have forbidden—as for example, to record a commission, or a patent for land, which has received all the legal solemnities; or to give a copy of such record—in such cases, it is not perceived on what ground the Courts of the country are further excused from the duty of giving judgment that right to be done to an injured individual than if the same services were to be performed by a person not the head of a department.

. . .

This, then, is a plain case of a mandamus, either to deliver the commission or a copy of it from the record, and it only remains to be inquired:

Whether it can issue from this Court.

The act to establish the judicial courts of the United States authorizes the Supreme Court "to issue writs of mandamus, in cases warranted by the principles and usages of law, to any courts appointed, or persons holding office, under the authority of the United States."

The Secretary of State, being a person, holding an office under the authority of the United States, is precisely within the letter of the description, and if this Court is not authorized to issue a writ of mandamus to such an officer, it must be because the law is unconstitutional, and therefore absolutely incapable of conferring the authority and assigning the duties which its words purport to confer and assign.

The Constitution vests the whole judicial power of the United States in one Supreme Court, and such inferior courts as Congress shall, from time to time, ordain and establish. This power is expressly extended to all cases arising under the laws of the United States . . .

In the distribution of this power it is declared that "The Supreme Court shall have original jurisdiction in all cases affecting ambassadors, other public ministers and consuls, and those in which a state shall be a party. In all other cases, the Supreme Court shall have appellate jurisdiction."

. . .

If it had been intended to leave it in the discretion of the Legislature to apportion the judicial power between the Supreme and inferior courts according to the will of that body, it would certainly have been useless to have proceeded further than to have defined the judicial power and the tribunals in which it should be vested. The subsequent part of the section is mere surplusage—is entirely without meaning—if such is to be the construction. If Congress remains at liberty to give this court appellate jurisdiction where the Constitution has declared their jurisdiction shall be original, and original jurisdiction where the Constitution has declared it shall be appellate, the distribution of jurisdiction made in the Constitution, is form without substance.

Affirmative words are often, in their operation, negative of other objects than those affirmed, and, in this case, a negative or exclusive sense must be given to them or they have no operation at all.

It cannot be presumed that any clause in the Constitution is intended to be without effect, and therefore such construction is inadmissible unless the words require it.

. . .

When an instrument organizing fundamentally a judicial system, divides it into one supreme, and so many inferior courts as the legislature may ordain and establish; then enumerates its powers, and proceeds so far to distribute them, as to define the jurisdiction of the supreme court by declaring the cases in which it shall take original jurisdiction, and that in others it shall take appellate jurisdiction; the plain import of the words seems to be, that in one class of cases its jurisdiction is original and not appellate; in the other it is appellate, and not original. . . .

To enable this court then to issue a mandamus, it must be shown to be an exercise of appellate jurisdiction, or to be necessary to enable them to exercise appellate jurisdiction.

. . .

It is the essential criterion of appellate jurisdiction that it revises and corrects the proceedings in a cause already instituted, and does not create that case. Although, therefore, a mandamus may be directed to courts, yet to issue such a writ to an officer for the delivery of a paper is, in effect, the same as to sustain an original action for that paper, and therefore seems not to belong to appellate, but to original jurisdiction. . . .

The authority, therefore, given to the Supreme Court by the act establishing the judicial courts of the United States to issue writs of mandamus to public officers appears not to be warranted by the Constitution, and it becomes necessary to inquire whether a jurisdiction so conferred can be exercised.

The question, whether an act, repugnant to the constitution, can become the law of the land, is a question deeply interesting to the United States; but, happily, not of an intricacy proportioned to its interest. It seems only necessary to recognize certain principles, supposed to have been long and well established, to decide it.

That the people have an original right to establish, for their future government, such principles as, in their opinion, shall most conduce to their own happiness, is the basis, on which the whole American fabric has been erected. The exercise of this original right is a very great exertion; nor can it, nor ought it to be frequently repeated. The principles, therefore, so established, are deemed fundamental. And as the authority, from which they proceed, is supreme, and can seldom act, they are designed to be permanent.

This original and supreme will organizes the government, and assigns, to different departments, their respective powers. It may either stop here; or establish certain limits not to be transcended by those departments.

The government of the United States is of the latter description. The powers of the legislature are defined, and limited; and that those limits may not be mistaken, or forgotten, the constitution is written. To what purpose are powers limited, and to what purpose is that limitation committed to writing, if these limits may, at any time, be passed by those intended to be restrained? The distinction, between a government with limited and unlimited powers, is abolished, if those limits do not confine the persons on whom they are imposed, and if acts prohibited and acts allowed, are of equal obligation. It is a proposition too plain to be contested, that the constitution controls any legislative act repugnant to it; or, that the legislature may alter the constitution by an ordinary act.

Between these alternatives there is no middle ground. The constitution is either a superior, paramount law, unchangeable by ordinary means, or it is on a level with ordinary legislative acts, and like other acts, is alterable when the legislature shall please to alter it.

If the former part of the alternative be true, then a legislative act contrary to the constitution is not law: if the latter part be true, then written constitutions are absurd attempts, on the part of the people, to limit a power, in its own nature illimitable.

Certainly all those who have framed written constitutions contemplate them as forming the fundamental and paramount law of the nation, and consequently the theory of every such government must be, that an act of the legislature, repugnant to the constitution, is void.

This theory is essentially attached to a written constitution, and is consequently to be considered, by this court, as one of the fundamental principles of our society. It is not therefore to be lost sight of in the further consideration of this subject.

If an act of the legislature, repugnant to the constitution, is void, does it, notwithstanding its invalidity, bind the courts, and oblige them to give it effect? Or, in other words, though it be not law, does it constitute a rule as operative as if it was a law? This would be to overthrow in fact what was established in theory; and would seem, at first view, an absurdity too gross to be insisted on. It shall, however, receive a more attentive consideration.

It is emphatically the province and duty of the judicial department to say what the law is. Those who apply the rule to particular cases, must of necessity expound and interpret that rule. If two laws conflict with each other, the courts must decide on the operation of each.

So if a law be in opposition to the constitution; if both the law and the constitution apply to a particular case, so that the court must either decide that case conformably to the law, disregarding the constitution; or conformably to the constitution, disregarding the law; the court must determine which of these conflicting rules governs the case. This is of the very essence of judicial duty.

If then the courts are to regard the constitution; and the constitution is superior to any ordinary act of the legislature; the constitution, and not such ordinary act, must govern the case to which they both apply.

Those then who controvert the principle that the constitution is to be considered, in court, as a paramount law, are reduced to the necessity of maintaining that courts must close their eyes on the constitution, and see only the law.

This doctrine would subvert the very foundation of all written constitutions. It would declare that an act, which, according to the principles and theory of our government, is entirely void; is yet, in practice, completely obligatory. It would declare, that if the legislature shall do what is expressly forbidden, such act, notwithstanding the express prohibition, is in reality effectual. It would be giving to the legislature a practical and real omnipotence, with the same breath which professes to restrict their powers within narrow limits. It is prescribing limits, and declaring that those limits may be passed at pleasure.

That it thus reduces to nothing what we have deemed the greatest improvement on political institutions—a written constitution—would of itself be sufficient, in America, where written constitutions have been viewed with so much reverence, for rejecting the construction. But the peculiar expressions of the constitution of the United States furnish additional arguments in favor of its rejection.

The judicial power of the United States is extended to all cases arising under the constitution.

Could it be the intention of those who gave this power, to say that, in using it, the constitution should not be looked into? That a case arising under the constitution should be decided without examining the instrument under which it arises?

This is too extravagant to be maintained.

In some cases then, the constitution must be looked into by the judges. And if they can open it at all, what part of it are they forbidden to read, or to obey?

There are many other parts of the constitution which serve to illustrate this subject.

It is declared that "no tax or duty shall be laid on articles exported from any state." Suppose a duty on the export of cotton, of tobacco, or of flour; and a suit instituted to recover it. Ought judgment to be rendered in such a case? Ought the judges to close their eyes on the constitution, and only see the law?

The constitution declares that "no bill of attainder or ex post facto law shall be passed."

If, however, such a bill should be passed and a person should be prosecuted under it; must the court condemn to death those victims whom the constitution endeavors to preserve?

"No person," says the constitution, "shall be convicted of treason unless on the testimony of two witnesses to the fame overt act, or on confession in open court."

Here the language of the constitution is addressed especially to the courts. It prescribes, directly for them, a rule of evidence not to be departed from. If the legislature should change that rule, and declare one witness, or a confession out of court, sufficient for conviction, must the constitutional principle yield to the legislative act?

From these, and many other selections which might be made, it is apparent, that the framers of the constitution contemplated that instrument, as a rule for the government of courts, as well as of the legislature.

Why otherwise does it direct the judges to take an oath to support it? This oath certainly applies, in an especial manner, to their conduct in their official character. How immoral to impose it on them, if they were to be used as the instruments, and the knowing instruments, for violating what they swear to support!

The oath of office, too, imposed by the legislature, is completely demonstrative of the legislative opinion on the subject. It is in these words, "I do solemnly swear that I will administer justice without respect to persons, and do equal right to the poor and to the rich; and that I will faithfully and impartially discharge all the duties incumbent on me as according to the best of my abilities and understanding, agreeably to the constitution, and laws of the United States."

Why does a judge swear to discharge his duties agreeably to the constitution of the United States, if that constitution forms no rule for his government? If it is closed upon him, and cannot be inspected by him?

If such be the real state of things, this is worse than solemn mockery. To prescribe, or to take this oath, becomes equally a crime.

It is also not entirely unworthy of observation, that in declaring what shall be the supreme law of the land, the constitution itself is first mentioned; and not the laws of the United States generally, but those only which shall be made in pursuance of the constitution, have that rank.

Thus, the particular phraseology of the constitution of the United States confirms and strengthens the principle, supposed to be essential to all written constitutions, that a law repugnant to the constitution is void; and that courts, as well as other departments, are bound by that instrument.

The rule must be discharged.

B. Judicial Supremacy

Thomas Jefferson on Departmentalism[10]

In the Virginia and Kentucky Resolutions of 1798, the Jeffersonians had claimed the authority of the states to interpret the U.S. Constitution and evaluate the constitutionality of federal statutes. (They left unclear what the consequences would be if a federal law were found unconstitutional by one or more states.) In Marbury, *Chief Justice John Marshall argued that an unconstitutional law was necessarily null and void. An invalid law could not be binding on the courts, for the "courts, as well as other departments, are bound by" the Constitution. The Constitution was, said Marshall, "a rule for the government of courts, as well as of the legislature."*

Thomas Jefferson and his supporters developed a different approach—sometimes called the departmentalist *(or coordinate) view of constitutional interpretation. Each branch (or department) of government would have equal authority to interpret the Constitution for itself when performing its duties. The courts must be guided by their own best understandings of constitutional requirements when meeting their responsibilities. Nonetheless, judicial interpretations of the Constitution are not necessarily supreme over the competing interpretations offered by Congress or the president.*

Jefferson articulated this principle on various occasions, and three are excerpted here. The first two excerpts are from letters President Jefferson sent to former first lady Abigail Adams. In these letters, the president explained his policy of pardoning everyone who had been convicted under the Sedition Act of 1798. The later letter to Judge Spencer Roane of the Virginia Supreme Court of Appeals contains Jefferson's reaction to Roane's Hampden essays criticizing John Marshall's opinion in McCulloch v. Maryland. *Although Roane was concerned with the relationship between the U.S. Supreme Court and the states, Jefferson thought the Virginia judge had not been careful enough to recognize the limited authority that the Supreme Court had to dictate constitutional meaning to the other branches of the federal government and to the states.*

To Abigail Adams, July 22, 1804

...[You wrote] that I "liberated a wretch who was suffering for a libel against Mr. Adams." I do not know who was the particular wretch alluded to; but I discharged every person under punishment or prosecution under the sedition law, because I considered, and now consider, that law to be a nullity, as absolute and as palpable as if Congress had ordered us to fall down and worship a golden image; and that it was as much my duty to arrest its execution in every stage, as it would have been to have rescued from the fiery furnace those who should have been cast into it for refusing to worship their image. It was accordingly done in every instance, without asking what the offenders had done, or against whom they had offended, but whether the pains they were suffering were inflicted under the pretended sedition law....

10. Excerpt taken from *The Writings of Thomas Jefferson*, ed. Paul Leicester Ford, vol. 10 (New York: G. P. Putnam's Sons, 1899), 86, 88; and vol. 12, 135.

To Abigail Adams, September 11, 1804

. . . You seem to think it devolved on the judges to decide on the validity of the sedition law. But nothing in the Constitution has given them a right to decide for the Executive, more than to the Executive to decide to them. The judges, believing the law constitutional, had a right to pass a sentence of fine and imprisonment; because the power was placed in their hands by the Constitution. But the Executive, believing the law to be unconstitutional, was bound to remit the execution of it; because that power has been confided to him by the Constitution. That instrument meant that its co-ordinate branches should be checks on each other. But the opinion which gives to the judges the right to decide what laws are constitutional, and what not, not only for themselves in their own sphere of action, but for the Legislative and Executive also, in their spheres, would make the judiciary a despotic branch. Nor does the opinion of unconstitutionality, and consequent nullity of that law, remove all restraint for the overwhelming torrent of slander, which is confounding all vice and virtue, all truth and falsehood, in the U.S. The power to do that is fully possessed by the several State Legislatures. It was reserved to them, and was denied to the General Government, by the Constitution, according to our construction of it.

To Spencer Roane, September 6, 1819

. . . In denying the right they [the federal judiciary] usurp of exclusively explaining the constitution, I go further than you do, if I understand rightly your quotation from the Federalist, of an opinion that "the judiciary is the last resort in relation *to the other departments* of the government, but not in relation to the rights of the parties to the compact under which the judiciary is derived." If this opinion be sound, then indeed is our constitution a complete *felo de se* [suicide]. For intending to establish three departments, co-ordinate and independent, that they might check and balance one another, it has given, according to this opinion, to one of them alone, the right to prescribe rules for the government of the others, and to that one too, which is unelected by, and independent of the nation. For experience has already shown that the impeachment it has provided is not even a scare-crow. . . . The constitution, on this hypothesis, is a mere thing of wax in the hands of the judiciary, which they may twist and shape into any form they please. It should be remembered, as an axiom of eternal truth in politics, that whatever power in any government is independent, is absolute also; in theory only, at first, while the spirit of the people is up, but in practice, as fast as that relaxes. Independence can be trusted nowhere but with the people in mass. They are inherently independent of all but moral law. My construction of the constitution is very different from that you quote. It is that each department is truly independent of the others, and has an equal right to decide for itself what is the meaning of the constitution in the cases submitted to its action; and especially, where it is to act ultimately and without appeal. . . .

. . .

C. Federal Review of the States

Federal judicial review of state law was taken for granted during most of the early national period. No one in 1789 seems to have made a serious objection to Section 25 of the Judiciary Act, which authorized the Supreme Court of the United States to overturn state court decisions on federal constitutional issues. When the Supreme Court in the 1790s challenged states, the response was to amend the Constitution (or ignore the court), not to abolish judicial review.

Controversies over the judicial power to strike down state laws first broke out during the 1810s. Proponents of state sovereignty raised two objections to Section 25 of the Judiciary Act. The first was rooted in the more radical interpretation of the Virginia and Kentucky Resolutions. If the Constitution was a compact between otherwise sovereign states, then the state courts were the proper authorities for determining whether state laws were consistent with the federal Constitution. Second, and more technical, even if federal courts had the right to declare state laws unconstitutional, federal courts had no right to review the rulings of state supreme courts and overrule them. If Congress permitted state supreme courts to resolve constitutional issues, then Congress had to allow those state courts to have the final word on the cases that they heard. In this view, Congress could empower the federal courts to strike down state laws, but not by accepting those cases on appeal from the state courts.

The argument against federal judicial review of state laws (vertical judicial review) differed from the argument against judicial review of laws from the same level of government (horizontal judicial review). In the early republic, leading opponents of federal judicial review of federal laws insisted that elected officials should be trusted to make the most important constitutional decisions. Most of those critics of horizontal judicial review were legislators. By comparison, many leading opponents of federal judicial review of state laws, most notable Spencer Roane of Virginia, were judges on state supreme courts. These judges often vigorously supported state judicial review of state laws. Their argument against vertical judicial review was based on federalism, not the separation of powers. In a federal republic, Roane and others insisted, the judges of each state ought to have the authority to determine whether the laws of their state violated the national Constitution.

The U.S. Supreme Court rejected both positions in *Martin v. Hunter's Lessee* (1816). Justice Story's unanimous opinion ruled that federal courts could declare state laws unconstitutional and that Congress could give federal courts the power to reverse state court decisions. The *Martin* decision emphasized the importance of uniformity. If each state could determine the meaning of the federal Constitution, Story reasoned, the result would be constitutional chaos. Virginia might pass laws taxing the national bank that Massachusetts thought unconstitutional.

Throughout this period, the U.S. Supreme Court consistently maintained that the federal courts could not hear cases unless Congress had provided proper jurisdiction through statute. Article III may have authorized federal jurisdiction, and created an obligation in Congress to create courts to exercise that jurisdiction, but the courts could not act without Congress. In *Martin v. Hunter's Lessee* (1816), Justice Joseph Story emphasized this obligation on Congress:

> The third article of the constitution is that which must principally attract our attention....
>
> ...The language of the article throughout is manifestly designed to be mandatory upon the legislature. Its obligatory force is so imperative, that congress could not, without a violation of its duty, have refused to carry it into operation. The judicial power of the United States shall be vested (not may be vested) in one supreme court, and in such inferior courts as congress may, from time to time, ordain and establish. Could congress have lawfully refused to create a supreme court, or to vest in it the constitutional jurisdiction?...
>
> If, then, it is a duty of congress to vest the judicial power of the United States, it is a duty to vest the whole judicial power. The language, if imperative as to one part, is imperative as to all. If it were otherwise, this anomaly would exist, that congress might successively refuse to vest the jurisdiction in any one class of cases enumerated in the constitution, and thereby defeat the jurisdiction as to all....
>
> ...It would seem, therefore, to follow, that congress are bound to create some inferior courts, in which to vest all that jurisdiction which, under the constitution, is exclusively vested in the United States, and of which the supreme court cannot take original cognizance....[T]he whole judicial power of the United States should be, at all times, vested either in an original or appellate form, in some courts created under its authority....

Nevertheless, the Supreme Court consistently refused to hear cases when Congress had not provided the necessary jurisdiction. The justices in *Wiscart v. Dauchy* (1796) held that the Supreme Court could not adjudicate any appeal without statutory permission. Chief Justice Ellsworth declared, "[i]f Congress has provided no rule to regulate our proceedings, we cannot exercise an appellate jurisdiction." *Durousseau v. United States* (1810) agreed. The "affirmative description" of the jurisdiction laid out in the Judiciary Act of 1789, Chief Justice Marshall declared, "has been understood to imply a negative on the exercise of such appellate power as is not comprehended within it." Congress could give, and take away, jurisdiction over cases covered by Article III from the federal courts. Congress did not begin to give the federal courts significantly more jurisdiction over Article III cases until after the Civil War.

Federal courts in the early republic reviewed the constitutionality of state laws more often than federal laws. Some of the most important decisions in this period, *Fletcher v. Peck* (1810) and *Dartmouth College v. Woodward* (1819), relied on the contracts clause in Article I to prevent states from rescinding land grants or corporate charters. Other decisions, such as *McCulloch v. Maryland* (1819) and *Gibbons v. Ogden* (1824), focused on the ways in which state laws interfered with the powers of the federal government. Constitutional politics permitted the Court to wield more power when striking down state laws than when striking down federal laws. A judicial decision declaring the Repeal Act of 1802 unconstitutional would have brought the wrath of the Jeffersonian national majority down upon the Supreme

Court. By comparison, the judicial decision in *Fletcher* was accepted as a painful necessity. In some instances, most national politicians did not care how the Supreme Court ruled on a local law. In other instances, many national politicians stood to gain from a Supreme Court decision that struck down a local law, especially one that interfered with out-of-state interests.

Martin v. Hunter's Lessee, 14 U.S. 304 (1816)

In 1781, Denny Martin inherited Lord Thomas Fairfax's property in Virginia. During the Revolution, Virginia had confiscated those lands, after Fairfax fled to England. The state had then sold the land to David Hunter. Martin claimed that the original confiscation was invalid under the peace treaties the United States had signed with Great Britain.

After long delay, the Virginia Court of Appeals finally ruled in favor of Hunter in 1810, but in 1813 the U.S. Supreme Court overruled the Virginia court. The U.S. Supreme Court held that Fairfax's American property was protected under the Jay Treaty of 1794. The Supreme Court's decision was formed on the basis of a mere three-justice majority, with one justice dissenting, two abstaining (including John Marshall, who had purchased some of the land from Martin), and one absent. In a strongly worded opinion by Justice Story, the Supreme Court sent a writ of mandamus to the Virginia court, directing it to issue a new decision favoring Martin.

The Virginia court took offense. The Virginia Court of Appeals responded by declaring Section 25 of the Judiciary Act of 1789 an unconstitutional infringement on states' rights. Section 25 empowered the U.S. Supreme Court to hear appeals from the state supreme courts when federal treaty or constitutional rights were questioned. The Virginia court found particularly objectionable the Supreme Court's assumption that it could issue a writ of mandamus to the Virginia court. (Thomas Jefferson had earlier objected to the assertion that the Supreme Court could issue such a writ to cabinet officials.) The court contended that the two judicial systems were completely independent of one another, and hence the Supreme Court had no authority to supervise or direct the Virginia judges as the mandamus writ implied. More generally, it argued that the Virginia Court of Appeals was not an "inferior court" over which the U.S. Supreme Court could exercise appellate jurisdiction.

The case then, came back to the U.S. Supreme Court to determine the constitutionality of Section 25 of the Judiciary Act. Justice Story again wrote the majority opinion (with Chief Justice Marshall not participating). And this time he wrote a sweeping nationalist vision of the Constitution that would anticipate John Marshall's similar effort in McCulloch.

At stake was the critical issue of whether the federal government could exercise any control over what the state courts did. At a time when the federal court system was very small, and the federal government often relied on the state courts to enforce federal statutes, this issue had significant implications for federal policy as well. That includes how much control the federal government would have over how federal policy was implemented—or whether it would be enforced at all. As Martin *itself indicated, it also had significant implications for how effectively the federal government could enforce its international treaties or insure that the states met their constitutional obligations.*

Although Judge Spencer Roane on the Virginia court was influential in Jeffersonian circles for his doctrinaire constitutional philosophy, national Republican leaders had little interest in repealing Section 25. Repeal was sometimes discussed during the Jeffersonian period, but Congress took no action to support the Virginia court and overturn Martin. *As you read* Martin, *consider whether Congress could, according to Story, constitutionally repeal Section 25 of the Judiciary Act of 1789. Compare Justice Story's opinion in* Martin *to Chief Justice Marshall's opinion in* Marbury. *How do they differ in their discussions of judicial review? One hundred years later, Justice Holmes asserted, "I do not think the United States would come to an end if we lost our power to declare an Act of Congress void. I do think the Union would be imperiled if we could not make that declaration as to the laws of the several States."*[11] *Do you agree?*

JUSTICE STORY delivered the opinion of the Court.

...

The constitution of the United States was ordained and established, not by the states in their sovereign capacities, but emphatically, as the preamble of the constitution declares, by "the people of the United States." There can be no doubt that it was competent to the people to invest the general government with all the powers which they might deem proper and necessary; to extend or restrain these powers according to their own good pleasure, and to give them a paramount and supreme authority. As little doubt can

11. Oliver Wendell Holmes, Jr., "Law and the Court, Speech at a Dinner of the Harvard Law School Association of New York on February 13, 1913," in *Collected Legal Papers*, ed. Learned Hand (New York: Harcourt, Brace, and Company, 1921), 295–296.

there be, that the people had a right to prohibit to the states the exercise of any powers which were, in their judgment, incompatible with the objects of the general compact; to make the powers of the state governments, in given cases, subordinate to those of the nation, or to reserve to themselves those sovereign authorities which they might not choose to delegate to either. The constitution was not, therefore, necessarily carved out of existing state sovereignties, nor a surrender of powers already existing in state institutions, for the powers of the states depend upon their own constitutions; and the people of every state had the right to modify and restrain them, according to their own views of policy or principle. On the other hand, it is perfectly clear that the sovereign powers vested in the state governments, by their respective constitutions, remained unaltered and unimpaired, except so far as they were granted to the government of the United States.

These deductions do not rest upon general reasoning, plain and obvious as they seem to be. They have been positively recognized by one of the articles in amendment of the constitution, which declares, that "the powers not delegated to the United States by the constitution, nor prohibited by it to the states, are reserved to the states respectively, or to the people."

The government, then, of the United States, can claim no powers which are not granted to it by the constitution, and the powers actually granted, must be such as are expressly given, or given by necessary implication. On the other hand, this instrument, like every other grant, is to have a reasonable construction, according to the import of its terms; and where a power is expressly given in general terms, it is not to be restrained to particular cases, unless that construction grow out of the context expressly, or by necessary implication. The words are to be taken in their natural and obvious sense, and not in a sense unreasonably restricted or enlarged.

The constitution unavoidably deals in general language. It did not suit the purposes of the people, in framing this great charter of our liberties, to provide for minute specifications of its powers, or to declare the means by which those powers should be carried into execution. It was foreseen that this would be a perilous and difficult, if not an impracticable, task. The instrument was not intended to provide merely for the exigencies of a few years, but was to endure through a long lapse of ages, the events of which were locked up in the inscrutable purposes of Providence. It could not be foreseen what new changes and modifications of power might be indispensable to effectuate the general objects of the charter; and restrictions and specifications, which, at the present, might seem salutary, might, in the end, prove the overthrow of the system itself. Hence its powers are expressed in general terms, leaving to the legislature, from time to time, to adopt its own means to effectuate legitimate objects, and to mould and model the exercise of its powers, as its own wisdom, and the public interests, should require.

...

But, even admitting that the language of the constitution is not mandatory, and that congress may constitutionally omit to vest the judicial power in courts of the United States, it cannot be denied that when it is vested, it may be exercised to the utmost constitutional extent....

As, then, by the terms of the constitution, the appellate jurisdiction is not limited as to the supreme court, and as to this court it may be exercised in all other cases than those of which it has original cognizance, what is there to restrain its exercise over state tribunals in the enumerated cases? The appellate power is not limited by the terms of the third article to any particular courts. The words are, "the judicial power (which includes appellate power) shall extend to all cases," etc., and "in all other cases before mentioned the supreme court shall have appellate jurisdiction." It is the case, then, and not the court, that gives the jurisdiction. If the judicial power extends to the case, it will be in vain to search in the letter of the constitution for any qualification as to the tribunal where it depends....

...If state tribunals might exercise concurrent jurisdiction over all or some of the other classes of cases in the constitution without control, then the appellate jurisdiction of the United States might, as to such cases, have no real existence, contrary to the manifest intent of the constitution....

...

A moment's consideration will show us the necessity and propriety of this provision in cases where the jurisdiction of the state courts is unquestionable....Suppose an indictment for a crime in a state court, and the defendant should allege in his defense that the crime was created by an ex post facto act of the state, must not the state court, in the exercise of a jurisdiction which has already rightfully attached, have a right to pronounce on the validity and sufficiency of the defense? It would be extremely difficult, upon any legal principles, to give a negative answer to these inquiries....

It must, therefore, be conceded that the constitution not only contemplated, but meant to provide for cases within the scope of the judicial power of the United States, which might yet depend before state tribunals. It was foreseen that in the exercise of their ordinary jurisdiction, state courts would incidentally take cognizance of cases arising under the constitution, the laws, and treaties of the United States....

...

It is a mistake that the constitution was not designed to operate upon states, in their corporate capacities. It is crowded with provisions which restrain or annul the sovereignty of the states in some of the highest branches of their prerogatives.... The courts of the United States can, without question, revise the proceedings of the executive and legislative authorities of the states, and if they are found to be contrary to the constitution, may declare them to be of no legal validity. Surely the exercise of the same right over judicial tribunals is not a higher or more dangerous act of sovereign power....

...

It is further argued, that no great public mischief can result from a construction which shall limit the appellate power of the United States to cases in their own courts:... because state judges are bound by an oath to support the constitution of the United States, and must be presumed to be men of learning and integrity.... The constitution has presumed (whether rightly or wrongly we do not inquire) that state attachments, state prejudices, state jealousies, and state interests, might sometimes obstruct, or control, or be supposed to obstruct or control, the regular administration of justice. Hence, in controversies between states; between citizens of different states; between citizens claiming grants under different states; between a state and its citizens, or foreigners, and between citizens and foreigners, it enables the parties, under the authority of congress, to have the controversies heard, tried, and determined before the national tribunals....

This is not all. A motive of another kind, perfectly compatible with the most sincere respect for state tribunals, might induce the grant of appellate power over their decisions. That motive is the importance, and even necessity of uniformity of decisions throughout the whole United States, upon all subjects within the purview of the constitution. Judges of equal learning and integrity, in different states, might differently interpret a statute, or a treaty of the United States, or even the constitution itself....

There is an additional consideration, which is entitled to great weight. The constitution of the United States was designed for the common and equal benefit of all the people of the United States. The judicial power was granted for the same benign and salutary purposes. It was not to be exercised exclusively for the benefit of parties who might be plaintiffs, and would elect the national forum, but also for the protection of defendants who might be entitled to try their rights, or assert their privileges, before the same forum. Yet, if the construction contended for be correct, it will follow, that as the plaintiff may always elect the state court, the defendant may be deprived of all the security which the constitution intended in aid of his rights. Such a state of things can, in no respect, be considered as giving equal rights....

On the whole, the court are of opinion, that the appellate power of the United States does extend to cases pending in the state courts; and that the 25th section of the judiciary act, which authorizes the exercise of this jurisdiction in the specified cases, by a writ of error, is supported by the letter and spirit of the constitution. We find no clause in that instrument which limits this power; and we dare not interpose a limitation where the people have not been disposed to create one.

Strong as this conclusion stands upon the general language of the constitution, it may still derive support from other sources. It is an historical fact, that this exposition of the constitution, extending its appellate power to state courts, was, previous to its adoption, uniformly and publicly avowed by its friends, and admitted by its enemies, as the basis of their respective reasonings, both in and out of the state conventions. It is an historical fact, that at the time when the judiciary act was submitted to the deliberations of the first congress, composed, as it was, not only of men of great learning and ability, but of men who had acted a principal part in framing, supporting, or opposing that constitution, the same exposition was explicitly declared and admitted by the friends and by the opponents of that system. It is an historical fact... that no state tribunal has ever breathed a judicial doubt on the subject, or declined to obey the mandate of the supreme court, until the present occasion. This weight of contemporaneous exposition by all parties, this acquiescence of enlightened state courts, and these judicial decisions of the supreme court through so long a period, do, as we think, place the doctrine upon a foundation of authority which cannot be shaken, without delivering over the subject to perpetual and irremediable doubts.

...

It is the opinion of the whole court, that the judgment of the court of appeals of Virginia, rendered on the mandate in this case, be reversed, and the judgment of the district court, held at Winchester be, and the same is hereby affirmed.

JUSTICE JOHNSON, concurring.

...

III. Powers of the National Government

MAJOR DEVELOPMENTS

- The struggle between broad and strict construction of national powers
- The establishment of a national power to acquire and govern new territories
- Interstate commerce defined to include navigation and all forms of commercial intercourse that concern more states than one

Constitutional disputes over the powers of the national government divided Americans during the early national period. Everyone recognized that the federal government established by the Constitution was far more powerful than the one established by the Articles of Confederation. Article I vested Congress with the power to raise revenues by taxation, the power to regulate interstate commerce, the power to raise armies, and other powers that the national government had previously lacked. However, Americans who agreed that the Constitution established a more powerful government still disagreed over just how powerful that government could be. Members of the First Congress debated when and whether Congress could pass laws that promoted the abolition of slavery. Members of the Second Congress debated whether Congress had the power to incorporate a national bank. Over the next forty years, debates broke out over whether Congress had the power to impose a military draft, acquire new territories, attach conditions to the admission of a new state, forbid speech criticizing the national government, build roads and canals within a state, and forbid exports to foreign countries.

Liberal or Strict Construction. The central issue in each of these debates was how liberally or strictly constitutional powers should be construed. This concern with liberal or strict construction, in turn, had three aspects. The first was the proper *definition of a constitutional power*. Article I permitted Congress to regulate "interstate commerce." Read very broadly, the clause permitted the federal government to regulate any activity that affected commerce in more than one state. Read very narrowly, that clause permitted the federal government to regulate only the actual act of transporting commercial goods across state lines.

The second source of controversy was whether the federal government had *implied powers*. The Constitution nowhere stated that the federal government could build canals. Interpreted broadly, the Constitution nevertheless permitted the federal government to build canals whenever doing so was a means to promote interstate commerce or some other explicit constitutional power. Interpreted narrowly, the Constitution did not permit Congress to exercise any power not explicitly enumerated in Article I, Section 8 of Article I of the U.S. Constitution enumerated the powers of Congress, but it also gave the national legislature the power to pass all laws that were "necessary and proper" to carrying out the powers vested in the federal government. Was the necessary and proper clause a substantive grant of its own, a "sweeping clause" that gave Congress an expansive set of additional powers? Or did it just state the obvious, that Congress could pass laws to carry out its responsibilities?

Legislative purposes were a third source of controversy. Article I permitted the Congress to "lay taxes." Interpreted broadly, that clause empowered Congress to pass exorbitant taxes on specific goods, perhaps slaves, for the purpose of prohibiting that good. Read narrowly, that clause empowered Congress to lay taxes only for the purpose of obtaining revenue.

The Tenth Amendment. The Tenth Amendment to the Constitution was ratified along with the rest of the Bill of Rights in 1791. It stated, "The powers not delegated to the United States by the Constitution, nor prohibited by it to the States, are reserved to the States respectively, or to the people." The Tenth Amendment did not play a very direct role in debates over the scope of national power in the 1790s. Both sides saw the amendment as confirming what the Federalists had said during the ratification debates of 1787–1788: The national government was one of limited, enumerated powers. It emphasized, rather than altered, the meaning of the Constitution.

For the Republicans, the Tenth Amendment reinforced their view that the powers of the national government had to be strictly construed so that it did not encroach on the proper, reserved powers of the states. For the Federalists, it was significant that the Tenth Amendment did not refer to powers "*expressly* delegated" to the national government, which was the formulation of a similar provision in Article II of the Articles of Confederation. The Federalists took that change of language to imply that the powers of the national government should not be read narrowly. Instead, they should be read as expansively as necessary to realize the aspirations and goals of the new nation.

Debates under the Republicans. As the Federalists gradually disappeared as a significant political force, and the Republicans coped with the demands of governing, new debates arose. New circumstances and new policy proposals expanded the range of important debates over national power. Moreover, many of these new debates did not pit the Republicans against the Federalists. Instead, they were debates among the Republicans themselves. Each faction claimed its own commitment to Jeffersonian orthodoxy, but what did Republican principles require?

Federalists and, later, National Republicans insisted that the powers granted to the new government should be interpreted liberally, with a broad construction. They were opposed by advocates of strict construction, who thought that the powers granted to the federal government should be interpreted so as not to interfere with the reserved rights of the states or the people. As you read, consider the extent to which and when political actors seem to deviate from their expected constitutional commitments. Do constitutional philosophies justify, constrain, or refine social and partisan interests?

The Jeffersonians, in turn, insisted that national powers be read strictly, in accord with the constitutional enumeration of powers. This meant that many new policies raised constitutional questions that had to be overcome, and not all were easily answered. Some of the most intense debates revolved around the necessary and proper clause and the notion of implied powers. There were basic tensions between implied powers and the idea of enumerated powers, and the issue arose in such varied contexts as the debate over the creation of the Bank of the United States, the passage of the Sedition Act of 1798, and the proposal for a military draft during the War of 1812.

The same issues lurked in the background of other debates as well. The Louisiana Purchase and the Missouri Compromise both raised questions about the federal government's power to acquire and govern new territory. The Jeffersonian embargo and *Gibbons v. Ogden* (1824) both raised questions about the scope of congressional power over commerce. And the recurrent debate over internal improvements led presidents and members of Congress to examine the breadth of the federal spending power.

A. General Principles

Note: Strict Construction

Looking back from the late nineteenth century, the English historian and politician James Bryce observed,

> The interpretation of the Constitution has at times become so momentous as to furnish a basis for the formation of political parties.... Soon after the formation of the National government in 1789 two parties grew up, one advocating a strong central authority, the other championing the rights of the States. Of these parties the former naturally came to insist on a liberal, an expansive, perhaps a lax construction of the words of the Constitution, because the more wide is the meaning placed upon the grants of powers, so much the wider the powers themselves. The latter party, on the other hand, was acting in protection both of the States and of the individual citizen against the central government, when it limited by a strict and narrow interpretation of the fundamental instrument the powers which that instrument conveyed. The distinction which began in those early days has never since vanished.[12]

The Republican challenge to the constitutional vision of the Federalists of the 1790s has framed much of American constitutional debate ever since. Constitutional debate has been understood, in no small part, as a divide between those who would recognize the Constitution as authorizing broad government powers and those who would interpret the constitutional

12. James Bryce, *The American Commonwealth*, vol. 1 (New York: Macmillan, 1888), 378.

grants more narrowly. To use modern labels, it was a debate between a party of "big government" and a party of "small government." Moreover, as Bryce noted, these divisions have not been limited to particular constitutional provisions: They often defined broad constitutional philosophies. One side read the "necessary and proper clause" of Article I expansively, and they tended to read the interstate commerce clause or the spending clause expansively as well. Others have adopted narrowing interpretations across the board.

The Origins of Strict Construction. The Jeffersonians gave us the phrase "strict construction," which still runs through debates today. They believed that grants of power in the Constitution should be read narrowly, or "strictly." A Virginia law professor and judge, St. George Tucker, popularized the term in his influential edition of William Blackstone's *Commentaries on the Laws of England* in 1803. In a lengthy appendix, Tucker explained that the U.S. Constitution is to be understood as a "written contract," or "a federal compact, or alliance between the states." He also sharply distinguished between the sovereign people who made constitutions and the governments that were created by them, the mere "*servants* and *agents*" of the people. To preserve the distinction between the servants and their masters, the powers of government were "pretty accurately defined, and limited" by the Constitution.

> But to guard against, encroachments on the powers of the several states, in their political character, and of the people, both in their individual and sovereign capacity, an amendatory article was added, immediately after the government was organized, declaring; that the powers not delegated to the United States, by the constitution, nor prohibited by it to the states, or reserved to the states, respectively, or to the people [in the Tenth Amendment]. And, still further, to guard the people against constructive usurpations and encroachments on their rights, another article declares; that the enumeration of certain rights in the constitution, shall not be construed to deny, or disparage, others retained by the people [in the Ninth Amendment]. The sum of all which appears to be, that the powers delegated to the federal government, are, in all cases, to receive the most strict construction that the instrument will bear, where the rights of a state or of the people, either collectively, or individually, may be drawn in question.[13]

This was not a completely new turn. An earlier editor of Blackstone observed, "It is a fundamental rule of construction, that penal statutes shall be construed strictly, and remedial statutes shall be constructed liberally. It was one of the laws of the twelve tables of Rome, that whenever there was a question between liberty and slavery, the presumption should be on the side of liberty. This excellent principle our law has adopted in the construction of penal statutes: for whenever any ambiguity arises in a statute introducing a new penalty or punishment, the decision shall be on the side of lenity and mercy; or in favor of natural right and liberty: or, in other words, the decision shall be according to the strict letter in favor of the subject."[14] But note how Tucker was reworking the old maxims for this new context: the grants of power in a constitution were to be understood as analogous to a criminal statute. In both cases, "liberty" required reading the terms of the law narrowly, against the claimed exertion of government power.

Tucker's approach to constitutional interpretation was commonplace among the Republicans at that time. The "Revolution of 1800" was fought and won for the principle that federal powers would be strictly construed. Jefferson reminded his followers that it would be better to seek a constitutional amendment when questionable powers are necessary, rather "than assume it by a construction which would make our powers boundless. Our peculiar security is in the possession of a written constitution. Let us not make it a blank paper by construction."[15] This touchstone of the Jeffersonian Republicans was carried over by the Jacksonian Democrats. In 1838, for example, the Democrats in Congress issued an address to the people at the launch of the campaign season: "We adhere to the constitutional doctrines of the republican party of 1798–9; we adopt the rule of strict construction they maintained, as the only true and safe one, applicable to our constitution."[16] The Mississippi Democrat Jefferson

13. St. George Tucker, *Blackstone's Commentaries*, vol. 1 (Philadelphia: Birch and Small, 1803), 153, 154.

14. Tucker, *Blackstone's Commentaries*, vol. 1, 87n14.

15. Thomas Jefferson, "To Wilson C. Nicholas, September 7, 1803," in *The Writings of Thomas Jefferson*, ed. Paul Leicester Ford, vol. 8 (New York: G. P. Putnam's Sons, 1897), 247.

16. "Address of the Republican Members of Congress," *Niles' National Register* (1 September 1838), 4.

Davis carried the doctrine of strict construction with him into secession. In his first inaugural address as President of the southern Confederate States of America, he declared that "all offices are but trusts held for the people, and . . . delegated powers are to be strictly construed."[17] It remained a routine part of Democratic political rhetoric through the rest of the nineteenth century.

The Federalist Reply. Federalists, National Republicans, and later Whigs and Republicans all denounced the principle of strict construction. Chief Justice John Marshall took the lead in responding to the Jeffersonian argument. A moderate Federalist, Marshall had been appointed to the Supreme Court by President John Adams after the Federalists lost the election of 1800 and would preside over the Court throughout the Jeffersonian period. When the Court was urged by a lawyer in the case of *Gibbons v. Ogden* (discussed later in this chapter) to adopt a strict construction of congressional power, Marshall responded that such an interpretation was not justified by the constitutional text and would make government unworkable:

> What do gentlemen mean, by a strict construction? If they contend only against that enlarged construction, which would extend words beyond their natural and obvious import, we might question the application of the term, but should not controvert the principle. If they contend for that narrow construction which, in support of some theory not found in the constitution, would deny to the government those powers which the words of the grant, as usually understood, import, and which are consistent with the general views and objects of the instrument; for that narrow construction, which would cripple the government, and render it unequal to the object for which it is declared to be instituted, and to which the powers given, as fairly understood, render it competent; then we cannot perceive the propriety of this strict construction, nor adopt it as the rule, by which the constitution is to be expounded.[18]

Justice Joseph Story, a scholarly advocate of Marshall's nationalism and a Madison appointee, sought to specifically rebut Tucker in his own influential treatise on constitutional law. Story insisted that the commitment to popular sovereignty required that constitutional powers be liberally construed:

> [The question] is, how are we to construe the words as used, whether in the most confined, or in the more liberal sense properly belonging to them. Now, in construing a grant, or surrender of powers by the people to a monarch, for his own benefit or use, it is not only natural, but just, to presume, as in all other cases of grants, that the parties had not in view any large sense of the terms, because the objects were a derogation permanently from their rights and interests. But in construing a constitution of government, framed by the people for their own benefit and protection for the preservation of their rights, and property, and liberty; where the delegated powers are not, and cannot be used for the benefit of their rulers, who are but their temporary servants and agents; but are intended solely for the benefit of the people, no such presumption of an intention to use the words in the most restricted sense necessarily arises.[19]

Later, John Quincy Adams, by then a committed Whig, celebrated the fiftieth anniversary of Washington's first inaugural with a speech condemning "the system of strict construction of state rights" as a "substitute for the opposition to the Constitution itself." At "the head of this opposition Mr. Jefferson was in the cabinet, and Mr. Madison in the house of representatives."[20] The Whigs took glee in accusing their opponents of hypocrisy whenever the Democrats seemed to take actions that stretched the bounds of what might be thought a strict construction of the Constitution. To the Whigs, such examples were just more evidence that strict construction was a misguided and unrealistic doctrine.

The Debate Today. A great Michigan scholar and judge, Thomas Cooley, observed near the end of the nineteenth century that there had always been two

17. Jefferson Davis, "First Inaugural Address, February 18, 1861," in *The Papers of Jefferson Davis*, eds. Lynda L. Crist and Mary S. Dix, vol. 7 (Baton Rouge: Louisiana State University, 1992), 416.

18. *Gibbons v. Ogden*, 22 U.S. 1, 188 (1824).

19. Joseph Story, *Commentaries on the Constitution of the United States*, vol. 1 (Boston: Hilliard, Gray, 1833), 396–397.

20. John Quincy Adams, *The Jubilee of the Constitution* (New York: Samuel Colman, 1839), 111.

parties with "conflicting views" as to the construction of the Constitution. One "looks on government as a necessary evil, whose powers should be abridged as much as possible, and whose conduct should be watched with jealousy.... Hence the doctrine, that the Constitution should be strictly construed, that no power should be held to exist unless conveyed in unmistakable terms." The "opposing party is impressed with the belief, that the government of a great nation must have ample powers, and that the want of power in emergencies is more dangerous than its liability to abuse," hence giving the Constitution a "liberal construction."

Cooley noted that, while the parties "have been largely based on these opposing views, but the opinions, or at least the practice, of the party controlling the government, always tend to enlarged views of their powers, and the party in opposition has been generally disposed to charge the administration with unconstitutional acts."[21] As you read, you might consider how accurate Cooley's assessment is. Does the party in power always tend to adopt arguments in favor of big government, and vice versa? If he was right, what are the implications?

In the late twentieth century, Richard Nixon helped revitalize the language of strict construction. On the campaign trail in 1968 and while in office as president, Nixon regularly promised to appoint judges who shared that philosophy. Nixon's emphasis was rather different from Tucker's, however. To Nixon, such "strict constructionists" would see "their duty as interpreting law and not making law. They would see themselves as caretakers of the Constitution and servants of the people, not super-legislators with a free hand to impose their own social and political viewpoints on the American people."[22]

This too has its roots in the Jeffersonian Era. Jefferson himself complained, "The constitution... is a mere thing of wax in the hands of the judiciary, which they may twist and shape into any form they please," but would Jefferson have endorsed Nixon's formulation?[23] Are there any "strict constructionists" in the original Jeffersonian sense on the contemporary political scene? Is there still a battle between a party constitutionally committed to small government and one committed to expansive government powers? Why did the rhetoric of strict construction shift between the nineteenth and twentieth centuries?

B. Necessary and Proper Clause

The necessary and proper clause is sometimes called "the sweeping clause" or "the elastic clause" because it can potentially be used to do so much to extend the reach of the national government. The potential significance of the clause was recognized immediately in the early republic. The U.S. Constitution included an enumeration of powers delegated to Congress, but it also authorized Congress to pass all laws "necessary and proper" to carrying out the powers granted elsewhere in the document. Was this an independent grant of power, or did it merely express a truism? Were there implied powers, and how could they be identified? The debate soon focused on the meaning of the word "necessary." What did the word mean? Did it matter that constitutional text does not modify the requirement of "necessary" with a term like "expressly"?

Arguments about the necessary and proper clause fit within broader constitutional philosophies about how to interpret the Constitution and what the purpose of the Constitution might be. In the debate over the creation of the Bank of the United States in the House of Representatives, James Madison offered a strict constructionist view. He argued that the interpreter should be careful not to find implied powers that would alter the basic character of the government. These powers must not go against the understanding of those who adopted the Constitution. Treasury Secretary Alexander Hamilton countered that the national government should be able to take all reasonable actions to meet its responsibilities that are not specifically prohibited. Two decades later, Chief Justice Marshall would largely endorse Hamilton's views in *McCulloch v. Maryland*, which provoked a public rebuke from the Jeffersonian Judge Spencer Roane of the Virginia high court. The Bank debate was perhaps the most important and long-lasting debate over the necessary and proper clause in the early republic, but it was not the only one. The clause was also central to efforts to criticize and defend the Sedition Act of 1798. It was also used to justify and

---

21. Thomas M. Cooley, *Constitutional History of the United States* (New York: G. P. Putnam's Sons, 1889), 208.

22. Richard M. Nixon, quoted in "E. E. Kensworthy, "Nixon Scores Indulgence," *New York Times*, November 3, 1968, 1.

23. Jefferson, "To Judge Spencer Roane, September 6, 1819," in *Writings*, vol. 10, 141.

denounce President James Monroe's proposal for a military draft during the War of 1812.

As Table 4-3 illustrates, the federal courts have heard a wide range of challenges to federal laws since the early nineteenth century that have contended that Congress has not acted in a way that is necessary and proper to exercising a constitutionally enumerated power. The U.S. Supreme Court has usually upheld federal statutes against such challenges. But not always. John Marshall offered a broad reading of the necessary and proper clause as early as *United States v. Fisher* (1805), and he influentially argued along with other nationalists that Congress could act so long as the purpose of a law was legitimate and the means used were "appropriate" and "plainly adapted" to that legitimate end and were not themselves prohibited. There were implied powers within the enumerated powers. Subsequent debates have shown just how various those implied powers can be.

Debate on the Bank of the United States

The debate over whether Congress could incorporate a national bank was the most important and sustained constitutional controversy in the early republic over how strictly constitutional powers should be construed. Secretary of Treasury Alexander Hamilton initiated the controversy at the end of 1790 when he proposed that Congress create a national bank. In a cash-poor country with no national currency, Hamilton hoped that the Bank would provide a common means of exchange and would pull together the wealth needed to finance the growth of a private manufacturing sector in the economy, as well as the needs of the federal government.

The constitutional debate was initially taken up in Congress. The resulting controversy helped solidify a partisan split between the loyal friends of the Washington administration, who believed the bank was wise policy and a legitimate exercise of constitutional power, and representatives such as James Madison, who had grown increasingly sus-

Table 4-3 Selection of U.S. Supreme Court Cases Reviewing Federal Laws under the Necessary and Proper Clause

Case	Vote	Outcome	Decision
United States v. Fisher, 6 U.S. (2 Cranch) 358 (1805)	5–0	Upheld	Federal law prioritizing the United States in the payment of all insolvent debtors or estates is a valid means of paying government debt
McCulloch v. Maryland, 17 U.S. (14 Wheat) 316 (1819)	7–0	Upheld	Federal law establishing a bank of the United States is legitimately grounded in the government's power to tax and spend
United States v. Coombs, 37 U.S. (12 Pet.) 72 (1838)	9–0	Upheld	Federal statute punishing looting from ships stranded on shore is a valid extension of the power to regulate interstate commerce
United States v. Fox, 95 U.S. 670 (1877)	9–0	Struck down	Federal law criminalizing past fraudulent acts of those who file bankruptcy petitions is not a valid use of the bankruptcy power
Legal Tender Cases, 79 U.S. 457 (1871)	5–4 (1 concurrence)	Upheld	Federal law declaring paper notes to be legal tender in payment of debts is a valid extension of the power to coin money and regulate currency
Ex parte Yarbrough, 110 U.S. 651 (1884)	9–0	Upheld	Federal law punishing those who conspire to intimidate voters in federal elections is valid means to regulate elections
United States v. Gettysburg Electric Railroad Co., 160 U.S. 668 (1896)	9–0	Upheld	Federal law condemning land in order to create Gettysburg memorial is valid means of exercising the war power

Continued

Table 4-3 *Continued*

Case	Vote	Outcome	Decision
Selective Draft Law Cases, 245 U.S. 366 (1918)	9–0	Upheld	Federal law compelling military service is a valid means of raising an army
Lambert v. Yellowley, 272 U.S. 581 (1926)	5–4	Upheld	Federal law restricting the use of medically prescribed liquor is valid incident of power to prohibit alcohol under the Eighteenth Amendment
Schechter Poultry Corp. v. United States, 295 U.S. 495 (1935)	9–0 (1 concurrence)	Struck down	Federal law empowering the President to develop industrial codes of fair competition is not a valid means of exercising the legislative power
Carter v. Carter Coal Company, 298 U.S. 238 (1936)	5–4	Struck down	Federal law regulating employee wages and hours in the coal industry is not a valid means of regulating interstate commerce
United States v. Classic, 313 U.S. 299 (1941)	4–3	Upheld	Federal law regulating state primaries for national office is a valid means to regulate elections
Lichter v. United States, 334 U.S. 742 (1948)	8–1	Upheld	Federal law regulating excessive profits on the production of war goods is a valid means of raising armies
United States ex rel. Toth v. Quarles, 350 U.S. 11 (1955)	6–3	Struck down	Federal law allowing for the prosecution of discharged servicemen in military courts-martial, is not a valid means of regulating the military
Katzenbach v. McClung, 379 U.S. 294 (1964)	9–0	Upheld	Federal law prohibiting discrimination in public restaurants is a valid means of regulating interstate commerce
Oregon v. Mitchell, 400 U.S. 112 (1970)	5–4 (4 concurring in part and dissenting in part)	Upheld/Struck down	Federal law fixing the voting age at eighteen is a valid means for regulating elections when applied to federal elections but not when applied to state and local elections.
Printz v. United States, 521 U.S. 898 (1997)	5–4 (2 concurrences)	Struck down	Federal law requiring state officials to perform background checks of prospective handgun purchasers is not a proper exercise of a federal power
Gonzales v. Raich, 545 U.S. 1 (2005)	6–3 (1 concurrence)	Upheld	Federal law regulating the manufacture or use of marijuana within a state that overrides conflicting local regulation is a valid means to regulate interstate commerce
United States v. Comstock, 130 S. Ct. 1949 (2010)	7–2 (2 concurrences)	Upheld	Federal law allowing civil commitment of dangerously mentally ill federal prisoners beyond their sentences is valid means to care for federal prisoners

picious of Hamilton's economic program. Federalists won the first round when Congress passed a bill to incorporate a national bank by a nearly two-to-one margin.

President George Washington took the constitutional objections raised in Congress seriously, however. He requested opinions from the members of the Cabinet on the constitutional question. Alexander Hamilton prepared an efficient defense of the measure. Thomas Jefferson, serving as Secretary of State, and Attorney General Edmund Randolph argued against it. Washington was persuaded by Hamilton and his supporters and signed the bill into law, launching the first Bank of the United States with a twenty-year charter.

The constitutional controversy over the national bank remained vibrant after the Bank Bill became law. When he became president, Jefferson directed his own reluctant treasury secretary, Albert Gallatin, to provide no special assistance to the Bank:

> *This institution is one of the most deadly hostility existing, against the principles and form of our Constitution.... An institution like this, penetrating by its branches every part of the Union, acting by command and in phalanx, may, in a critical moment, upset the government. I deem no government safe which is under the vassalage of any self-constituted authorities, or any other authority than that of the nation, or its regular functionaries. What an obstruction could not this bank of the United States, with all its branch banks, be in time of war! It might dictate to us the peace we should accept, or withdraw its aids. Ought we then to give further growth to an institution so powerful, so hostile?*[24]

A Republican-dominated Congress initially refused to renew the Bank's charter when the first charter expired in 1811. The War of 1812, however, convinced many more Republicans that a national bank was more vital to national security and commercial prosperity than Jefferson had once thought. President Madison vetoed a bill incorporating a Second Bank of the United States, but his message indicated that his objections were no longer constitutional. Madison's veto message "[w]aiv[ed] the question of the constitutional authority of the Legislature to establish an incorporated bank as being precluded in my judgment by repeated recognitions under varied circumstances of the validity of such an institution in acts of the legislative, executive, and judicial branches of the Government, accompanied by indications, in different modes, of a concurrence of the general will of the nation."[25] *For mainstream national Republicans, the question of the constitutionality of the Bank was settled by precedent and popular acquiescence. The country had lived with the Bank for two decades. The people had accepted that exercise of federal power. When Congress passed a modified bill incorporating a national bank in 1816, Madison signed the measure into law.*

The constitutional controversy shifted to the federal courts after Madison signed the bill incorporating the Second Bank of the United States. Many Old Republicans felt betrayed. They charged that mere precedent could not overturn the constitutional principles that had helped launch the Republican movement in the 1790s. Local officials, tied politically and economically to state-chartered banks that competed with the national bank, joined that campaign against the Bank. In the midst of a recession that threw many states into a fiscal crisis, several states adopted laws either prohibiting or heavily taxing any bank other than a state-operated bank.

The Marshall Court, to the delight of many National Republicans, ruled these measures unconstitutional with strong support from the executive and legislative branches of the national government. In McCulloch v. Maryland *(1819), the justices unanimously declared that Congress was constitutionally authorized to incorporate a national bank and that no state could pass any law that interfered with the exercise of that power. Opposition to the national bank remained intense in many local communities during the 1820s. Nevertheless, National Republicans on the Supreme Court and in Congress through the rest of the early national period had the power to prevent any serious attack on the Second Bank of the United States.*

Whether constitutional powers should be liberally or narrowly construed was the central question in the Bank debate. Federalists and Republicans recognized that no constitutional provision explicitly declared that Congress had the power to incorporate a national bank—or, for that matter, grant corporate charters. Proponents of the national bank did not find this omission constitutionally troublesome. Hamilton and Marshall regarded the Bank as a useful means to implementing an enumerated power, particularly the power to borrow money. Madison and Jefferson insisted that the doctrine of implied powers called into question the very idea of a government of enumerated powers. The Bank was a major exercise of national power. Yet creating a Bank

24. Thomas Jefferson, "To Albert Gallatin, December 13, 1803," in *The Writings of Thomas Jefferson*, ed. Paul Leicester Ford, vol. 8 (New York: G. P. Putnam's Sons, 1897), 285.

25. James Madison, "Veto Message, January 30, 1815," in *A Compilation of the Messages and Papers of the Presidents*, ed. James D. Richardson, vol. 2 (New York: Bureau of National Literature, 1897), 540.

or chartering corporations was not among the enumerated powers of the federal government.

When reading the constitutional debates over the Bank of the United States, keep these considerations in mind. Proponents of the Bank insisted that Congress had implied as well as explicit powers. How did they justify those implied powers? How far could such implied powers extend without subverting the constitutional scheme? The Bank debate raised basic questions about how to interpret the Constitution. How do various participants in the debate treat the significance of the drafting history? Did the ratification debates and the recently proposed Ninth and Tenth Amendments affect how the Constitution should be interpreted? The Bank debate took place in Congress, in the President's cabinet, in the Supreme Court, and in the newspapers. Do you detect any differences in the constitutional arguments that were made in different settings? To what extent were participants in the debate over the Bank in one institution willing to defer to a constitutional decision reached by persons in another governing institution?

House Debate on the Bank (1791)[26]

Mr. James Madison (Republican, Virginia)...

...

In making these remarks on the merits of the bill, he had reserved to himself the right to deny the authority of Congress to pass it. He had entertained this opinion from the date of the Constitution. His impression might, perhaps, be the stronger, because he well recollected that a power to grant charters of incorporation had been proposed in the General Convention and rejected.

...

As preliminaries to a right interpretation, he laid down the following rules:

An interpretation that destroys the very characteristics of the Government cannot be just.

Where a meaning is clear, the consequences, whatever they may be, are to be admitted—where doubtful, it is fairly triable by its consequences.

In controverted cases, the meaning of the parties to the instrument, if to be collected by reasonable evidence, is a proper guide.

26. Excerpt taken from *Annals of the Debates in Congress*, 1st Cong., 3rd sess. (Feb. 2, 4, 1791), 1944–1951, 1960–1962.

Contemporary and concurrent expositions are a reasonable evidence of the meaning of the parties.

In admitting or rejecting a constructive authority, not only the degree of its incidentality to an express authority is to be regarded, but the degree of its importance also; since on this will depend the probability or improbability of its being left to construction.

Reviewing the Constitution with an eye to these positions, it was not possible to discover in it the power to incorporate a Bank....

...

From the view of the power of incorporation exercised in the bill, it could never be deemed an accessory or subaltern power to be deduced by implication, as a means of executing another power; it was in its nature a distinct, an independent and substantive prerogative, which not being enumerated in the Constitution, could never have been meant to be included in it, and not being included, could never be rightfully exercised.

...

But the proposed Bank could not even be called necessary to the Government; at most it could be but convenient. Its uses to the Government could be supplied by keeping taxes a little in advance; by loans from individuals; by other Banks....

He proceeded next to the contemporary expositions given to the Constitution.

The defense against the charge founded on the want of a bill of rights pre-supposed, he said, that the powers not given were retained; and that those given were not to be extended by remote implications. On any other supposition, the power of Congress to abridge the freedom of the press, or the rights of conscience, etc. could not have been disproved.

The explanations in the State Conventions all turned on the same fundamental principle, and on the principle that the terms necessary and proper gave no additional powers to those enumerated.

...

The explanatory amendments proposed by Congress themselves, at least, would be good authority with them; all these renunciations of power proceeded on a rule of construction, excluding the latitude now contended for. These explanations were the more to be respected, as they had not only been proposed by Congress, but ratified by nearly three-fourths of the States. He read several of the articles proposed, remarking particularly on the [9th] and [10th]; the former, as guarding against a latitude of interpretation; the latter, as excluding every source of power not within the Constitution itself.

...

Mr. Theodore Sedgwick (Federalist, Massachusetts) said...

He would only observe, in answer to everything which has been said of the danger of extending construction and implication, that the whole business of Legislation was a practical construction of the powers of the Legislature; and that probably no instrument for the delegation of power could be drawn with such precision and accuracy as to leave nothing to necessary implication. That all the different Legislatures in the United States had, and this, in his opinion, indispensably must construe the powers which had been granted to them, and they must assume such auxiliary powers as are necessarily implied in those which are expressly granted. In doing which, it was no doubt their duty to be careful not to exceed those limits to which it was intended they should be restricted. By any other limitation the Government would be so shackled that it would be incapable of producing any of the effects which were intended by its institutions.

Thomas Jefferson, Opinion on the Constitutionality of the Bill for Establishing a National Bank (1791)[27]

...

I consider the foundation of the Constitution as laid on this ground that "all powers not delegated to the U.S. by the Constitution, not prohibited by it to the states, are reserved to the states or to the people" [10th Amendment]. To take a single step beyond the boundaries thus specially drawn around the powers of Congress, is to take possession of a boundless field of power, no longer susceptible of any definition.

The incorporation of a bank, and other powers assumed by this bill have not, in my opinion, been delegated to the U.S. by the Constitution.

I. They are not among the powers specially enumerated, for these are

1. A power to lay taxes for the purpose of paying the debts of the U.S. But no debt is paid by this bill, nor any tax laid....
2. "to borrow money." But this bill neither borrows money, nor ensures the borrowing it. The proprietors of the bank will be just as free as any other money holders, to lend or not to lend their money to the public....
3. "to regulate commerce with foreign nations, and among the states, and with the Indian tribes." To erect a bank, and to regulate commerce, are very different acts. He who erects a bank creates a subject of commerce in its bills: so does he who makes a bushel of wheat, or digs a dollar out of the mines. Yet neither of these persons regulates commerce thereby. To erect a thing which may be bought and sold, is not to prescribe regulations for buying and selling. Besides; if this was an exercise of the power of regulating commerce, it would be void, as extending as much to the internal commerce of every state, as to its external....

Still less are these powers covered by any other of the special enumerations.

II. Nor are they within either of the general phrases, which are the two following.

1. "To lay taxes to provide for the general welfare of the U.S." that is to say "to lay taxes for the purpose of providing for the general welfare." For the laying of taxes is the power and the general welfare the purpose for which the power is to be exercised. They are not to lay taxes ad libitum for any purpose they please; but only to pay the debts or provide for the welfare of the Union. In like manner they are not to do anything they please to provide for the general welfare, but only to lay taxes for that purpose. To consider the latter phrase, not as describing the purpose of the first, but as giving a distinct and independent power to do any act they please, which might be for the good of the Union, would render all the preceding and subsequent enumerations of power completely useless....
2. The second general phrase is "to make all laws necessary and proper for carrying into execution the enumerated powers." But they can all be carried into execution without a bank. A bank therefore is not necessary, and consequently not authorized by this phrase.

It has been much urged that a bank will give great facility, or convenience in the collection of taxes.

27. Excerpt taken from Thomas Jefferson, "Opinion on the Constitutionality of a National Bank," in *The Writings of Thomas Jefferson*, ed. Paul Leicester Ford, vol. 5 (New York: G. P. Putnam's Sons, 1897), 284.

Suppose this were true: yet the constitution allows only the means which are "necessary" not those which are merely "convenient" for effecting the enumerated powers. If such a latitude of construction be allowed to this phrase as to give any non-enumerated power, it will go to everyone, for [there] is no one which ingenuity may not torture into a convenience, in some way or other, to some one of so long a list of enumerated powers. It would swallow up all the delegated powers, and reduce the whole to one phrase as before observed. Therefore it was that the constitution restrained them to the necessary means, that is to say, to those means without which the grant of the power would be nugatory.

...

The Negative of the President is the shield provided by the constitution to protect against the invasions of the legislature 1. the rights of the Executive 2. of the Judiciary 3. of the states and state legislatures. The present is the case of a right remaining exclusively with the states and is consequently one of those intended by the constitution to be placed under his protection.

It must be added however, that unless the President's mind on a view of everything which is urged for and against this bill, is tolerably clear that it is unauthorized by the constitution, if the pro and the con hang so even as to balance his judgment, a just respect for the wisdom of the legislature would naturally decide the balance in favor of their opinion. It is chiefly for cases where they are clearly misled by error, ambition, or interest, that the constitution has placed a check in the negative of the President.

Alexander Hamilton, Opinion as to the Constitutionality of the Bank of the United States (1791)[28]

...

...[P]rinciples of construction like those espoused by the Secretary of State and Attorney General, would be fatal to the just and indispensable authority of the United States.

...

Now it appears to the Secretary of the Treasury that this general principle is inherent in the very definition of government, and essential to every step of progress to be made by that of the United States, namely: That every power vested in a government is in its nature sovereign, and includes, by force of the term, a right to employ all the means requisite and fairly applicable to the attainment of the ends of such power, and which are not precluded by restrictions and exceptions specified in the Constitution, or not immoral, or not contrary to the essential ends of political society.

...

The circumstance that the powers of sovereignty are in this country divided between the National and State governments, does not afford the distinction required. It does not follow from this, that each of the portion of powers delegated to the one or to the other, is not sovereign with regard to its proper objects. It will only follow from it, that each has sovereign power as to certain things, and not as to other things. To deny that the government of the United States has sovereign power, as to its declared purposes and trusts, because its power does not extend to all cases would be equally to deny that the State governments have sovereign power in any case, because their power does not extend to every case....

...

This general and indisputable principle puts at once an end to the abstract question, whether the United States have power to erect a corporation....For it is unquestionably incident to sovereign power to erect corporations....

...

...It is conceded that implied powers are to be considered as delegated equally with express ones. Then it follows, that as a power of erecting a corporation may as well be implied as any other thing, it may as well be employed as an instrument or mean of carrying into execution any of the specified powers, as any other instrument or mean whatever. The only question must be in this, as in every other case, whether the mean to be employed or in this instance, the corporation to be erected, has a natural relation to any of the acknowledged objects or lawful ends of the government....

...

It is certain that neither the grammatical nor popular sense of the term requires that construction [offered by Jefferson and Randolph]. According to both, necessary often means no more than needful, requisite, incidental, useful, or conducive to. It is a common mode of expression to say, that it is necessary for a government

28. Excerpt taken from Paul Leicester Ford, *The Federalist* (New York: Henry Holt and Co., 1898), 655.

or a person to do this or that thing, when nothing more is intended or understood, than that the interests of the government or person require, or will be promoted by, the doing of this or that thing. The imagination can be at no loss for exemplifications of the use of the word in this sense. And it is the true one in which it is to be understood as used in the Constitution. The whole turn of the clause containing it indicates, that it was the intent of the Convention, by that clause, to give a liberal latitude to the exercise of the specified powers. The expressions have peculiar comprehensiveness. They are "to make all laws necessary and proper for carrying into execution the foregoing powers, and all other powers vested by the Constitution in the government of the United States, or in any department or officer thereof."

To understand the word as the Secretary of State does, would be to depart from its obvious and popular sense, and to give it a restrictive operation, an idea never before entertained. It would be to give it the same force as if the word absolutely or indispensably had been prefixed to it.

Such a construction would beget endless uncertainty and embarrassment. The cases must be palpable and extreme, in which it could be pronounced, with certainty, that a measure was absolutely necessary, or one, without which, the exercise of a given power would be nugatory. There are few measures of any government which would stand so severe a test. To insist upon it, would be to make the criterion of the exercise of any implied power, a case of extreme necessity; which is rather a rule to justify the overleaping of the bounds of constitutional authority, than to govern the ordinary exercise of it.

...

This restrictive interpretation of the word necessary is also contrary to this sound maxim of construction, namely, that the powers contained in a constitution of government, especially those which concern the general administration of the affairs of a country, its finances, trade, defense, etc., ought to be construed liberally in advancement of the public good. This rule does not depend on the particular form of a government, or on the particular demarcation of the boundaries of its powers, but on the nature and object of government itself. The means by which national exigencies are to be provided for, national inconveniences obviated, national prosperity promoted, are of such infinite variety, extent, and complexity, that there must of necessity be great latitude of discretion in the selection and application of those means. Hence, consequently, the necessity and propriety of exercising the authorities entrusted to a government on principles of liberal construction.

...

[The doctrine which is contended for] leaves... a criterion of what is constitutional, and of what is not so. This criterion is the end, to which the measure relates as a mean. If the end be clearly comprehended within any of the specified powers, and if the measure have an obvious relation to that end, and is not forbidden by any particular provision of the Constitution, it may safely be deemed to come within the compass of the national authority. There is also this further criterion, which may materially assist the decision: Does the proposed measure abridge a pre-existing right of any State or of any individual? If it does not, there is a strong presumption in favor of its constitutionality, and slighter relations to any declared object of the Constitution may be permitted to turn the scale.

...

McCulloch v. Maryland, 17 U.S. 316 (1819)

James McCulloch was the cashier of the Baltimore branch of the Bank of the United States. The Maryland state legislature imposed a tax on the notes of any bank not incorporated by the state of Maryland. When McCulloch refused to pay, Maryland brought suit in state court to collect the unpaid taxes. The Maryland government won at trial, and the ruling was affirmed by the Maryland supreme court. As expected, McCulloch then appealed to the U.S. Supreme Court.

The case received extensive newspaper coverage, and the courtroom was jammed. The Bank's legal team was led by Daniel Webster. A member of the House of Representatives, Webster was a rising star among the lawyers who regularly argued cases before the U.S. Supreme Court. The United States attorney general, William Wirt, also argued on behalf of the Bank. They argued that Maryland's tax was an unconstitutional interference with the policies of the federal government. Maryland's legal team included Luther Martin, the elderly state attorney general and a delegate to the Philadelphia Constitutional Convention. They argued that the Bank itself was unconstitutional, and the states had full authority to tax any business operating within their borders. The federal bank could hardly expect to compete with state banks while contributing nothing to state coffers.

Oral argument lasted for days. There was little doubt, however, about how the Court would rule. Chief Justice John Marshall's views on the subject were well known, and there was no reason to believe that a majority of his brethren on the Court disagreed with him. Opponents of the Bank therefore looked to open other fronts in their war against the Bank. They convinced the U.S. House of Representatives to investigate charges that the directors of the Bank and its branches (including McCulloch himself) had manipulated Bank operations to enrich themselves and damage the state banks. The investigating committee (which included future president John Tyler) found that the charges were largely accurate. While the Supreme Court was hearing oral arguments in the McCulloch *case, the Republican House overwhelmingly voted down resolutions to revoke the Bank's charter. Congress would not take action against the Bank. Shortly thereafter, the Supreme Court unanimously upheld the constitutionality of the Bank charter and struck down the state tax as unconstitutional.*

The opinion that Marshall wrote for the Court was more surprising. Marshall was not content to declare that the bank was constitutional. His unanimous opinion asserted that the necessary and proper clause permitted the national government to pass any *reasonable means to secure a legitimate constitutional end. Marshall also indicated that any state effort to interfere with the national bank would be unconstitutional. "The power to tax," he declared, "involves the power to destroy." Under this ruling, even a tax aimed at all banks might be unconstitutional. Former President Madison complained that this broad interpretation of the necessary and proper clause and the implied powers of Congress obliterated "the landmarks intended by a specification of the powers of Congress." He hoped that "sound arguments & conciliatory expostulations addressed both to Congress & to their Constituents" might yet keep Congress within its original constitutional bound. Such arguments might cause it to "abstain" from the powers that the Court was attempting to give it.*[29]

Some states initially remained resistant to the Bank and to the Court's decision. Ohio, for example, forcibly entered the Bank's vaults and seized the money owed under taxes of the same sort that the Court had struck down in McCulloch. *The Bank sued, and the Ohio legislature eventually backed down, appropriating money to repay the Bank for what the state government had confiscated.*[30]

McCulloch v. Maryland *is one of the most important constitutional decisions in American history. Marshall's analysis of implied powers and the meaning of the necessary and proper clause had enormous influence. How does Marshall understand the constitutional meaning of necessary and proper? What is the constitutional foundation for that understanding? Is he correct that a "stricter" construction would make government in the United States unworkable? The law incorporating the national bank did not forbid (or sanction) state taxes on that institution. Marshall nevertheless declared the Maryland tax unconstitutional. On what basis did he do so? Why did he assert that a state tax on a national bank is particularly constitutionally problematic?*

CHIEF JUSTICE MARSHALL delivered the opinion of the Court.

In the case now to be determined, the defendant, a sovereign state, denies the obligation of a law enacted by the legislature of the Union, and the plaintiff, on his part, contests the validity of an act which has been passed by the legislature of that state. The constitution of our country, in its most interesting and vital parts, is to be considered; the conflicting powers of the government of the Union and of its members, as marked in that constitution, are to be discussed; and an opinion given, which may essentially influence the great operations of the government. No tribunal can approach such a question without a deep sense of its importance, and of the awful responsibility involved in its decision. But it must be decided peacefully, or remain a source of hostile legislation, perhaps, of hostility of a still more serious nature; and if it is to be so decided, by this tribunal alone can the decision be made. On the supreme court of the United States has the constitution of our country devolved this important duty.

The first question made in the cause is, has Congress power to incorporate a bank? It has been truly said, that this can scarcely be considered as an open question, entirely unprejudiced by the former proceedings of the nation respecting it....

...An exposition of the constitution, deliberately established by legislative acts, on the faith of which an

29. Quoted in Keith E. Whittington, "The Road Not Taken: *Dred Scott*, Judicial Authority, and Political Questions," *Journal of Politics* 63 (2001):373.

30. On the background and aftermath of *McCulloch*, see Mark R. Killenbeck, *M'Culloch v. Maryland* (Lawrence: University Press of Kansas, 2006); Richard E. Ellis, *Aggressive Nationalism* (New York: Oxford University Press, 2007).

immense property has been advanced, ought not to be lightly disregarded.

The power now contested was exercised by the first Congress elected under the present constitution. The bill for incorporating the bank of the United States did not steal upon an unsuspecting legislature, and pass unobserved. Its principle was completely understood, and was opposed with equal zeal and ability. After being resisted, first in the fair and open field of debate, and afterwards in the executive cabinet, with as much persevering talent as any measure has ever experienced, and being supported by arguments which convinced minds as pure and as intelligent as this country can boast, it became a law. The original act was permitted to expire; but a short experience of the embarrassments to which the refusal to revive it exposed the government, convinced those who were most prejudiced against the measure of its necessity, and induced the passage of the present law. It would require no ordinary share of intrepidity to assert that a measure adopted under these circumstances was a bold and plain usurpation, to which the constitution gave no countenance.

These observations belong to the cause; but they are not made under the impression that, were the question entirely new, the law would be found irreconcilable with the constitution.

. . .

This government is acknowledged by all to be one of enumerated powers. The principle, that it can exercise only the powers granted to it, would seem too apparent to have required to be enforced by all those arguments which its enlightened friends, while it was depending before the people, found it necessary to urge. That principle is now universally admitted. But the question respecting the extent of the powers actually granted, is perpetually arising, and will probably continue to arise, as long as our system shall exist.

. . .

Among the enumerated powers, we do not find that of establishing a bank or creating a corporation. But there is no phrase in the instrument which, like the Articles of Confederation, excludes incidental or implied powers; and which requires that every thing granted shall be expressly and minutely described. Even the 10th amendment, which was framed for the purpose of quieting the excessive jealousies which had been excited, omits the word "expressly." . . . The men who drew and adopted this amendment had experienced the embarrassments resulting from the insertion of this word in the articles of confederation, and probably omitted it to avoid those embarrassments. A constitution, to contain an accurate detail of all the subdivisions of which its great powers will admit, and of all the means by which they may be carried into execution, would partake of the prolixity of a legal code, and could scarcely be embraced by the human mind. It would probably never be understood by the public. Its nature, therefore, requires, that only its great outlines should be marked, its important objects designated, and the minor ingredients which compose those objects be deduced from the nature of the objects themselves. . . . In considering this question, then, we must never forget, that it is a constitution we are expounding.

Although, among the enumerated powers of government, we do not find the word "bank" or "incorporation," we find the great powers to lay and collect taxes; to borrow money; to regulate commerce; to declare and conduct a war; and to raise and support armies and navies. The sword and the purse, all the external relations, and no inconsiderable portion of the industry of the nation, are entrusted to its government. It can never be pretended that these vast powers draw after them others of inferior importance, merely because they are inferior. Such an idea can never be advanced. But it may with great reason be contended, that a government, entrusted with such ample powers, on the due execution of which the happiness and prosperity of the nation so vitally depends, must also be entrusted with ample means for their execution. The power being given, it is the interest of the nation to facilitate its execution. . . .

. . .

. . . Congress is not empowered by it to make all laws, which may have relation to the powers conferred on the government, but such only as may be "necessary and proper" for carrying them into execution. The word "necessary," is considered as controlling the whole sentence, and as limiting the right to pass laws for the execution of the granted powers, to such as are indispensable, and without which the power would be nugatory. That it excludes the choice of means, and leaves to Congress, in each case, that only which is most direct and simple.

Is it true, that this is the sense in which the word "necessary" is always used? Does it always import an absolute physical necessity, so strong, that one thing, to which another may be termed necessary, cannot exist without that other? We think it does not. If reference be had to its use, in the common affairs of the world, or in approved authors, we find that it frequently imports no more than that one thing is convenient, or useful, or essential to another. To employ the means necessary to an end, is generally understood as employing any means calculated to produce the end.... The word "necessary"... has not a fixed character peculiar to itself. It admits of all degrees of comparison; and is often connected with other words, which increase or diminish the impression the mind receives of the urgency it imports. A thing may be necessary, very necessary, absolutely or indispensably necessary.... This comment on the word is well illustrated, by the passage cited at the bar, from the 10th section of the 1st article of the constitution. It is, we think, impossible to compare the sentence which prohibits a State from laying "imposts, or duties on imports or exports, except what may be absolutely necessary for executing its inspection laws," with that which authorizes Congress "to make all laws which shall be necessary and proper for carrying into execution" the powers of the general government, without feeling a conviction that the convention understood itself to change materially the meaning of the word "necessary," by prefixing the word "absolutely." This word, then, like others, is used in various senses; and, in its construction, the subject, the context, the intention of the person using them, are all to be taken into view.

Let this be done in the case under consideration. The subject is the execution of those great powers on which the welfare of a nation essentially depends. It must have been the intention of those who gave these powers, to insure, as far as human prudence could insure, their beneficial execution. This could not be done by confining the choice of means to such narrow limits as not to leave it in the power of Congress to adopt any which might be appropriate, and which were conducive to the end. This provision is made in a constitution intended to endure for ages to come, and, consequently, to be adapted to the various crises of human affairs. To have prescribed the means by which government should, in all future time, execute its powers, would have been to change, entirely, the character of the instrument, and give it the properties of a legal code. It would have been an unwise attempt to provide, by immutable rules, for exigencies which, if foreseen at all, must have been seen dimly, and which can be best provided for as they occur. To have declared that the best means shall not be used, but those alone without which the power given would be nugatory, would have been to deprive the legislature of the capacity to avail itself of experience, to exercise its reason, and to accommodate its legislation to circumstances....

...

We admit, as all must admit, that the powers of the government are limited, and that its limits are not to be transcended. But we think the sound construction of the constitution must allow to the national legislature that discretion, with respect to the means by which the powers it confers are to be carried into execution, which will enable that body to perform the high duties assigned to it, in the manner most beneficial to the people. Let the end be legitimate, let it be within the scope of the constitution, and all means which are appropriate, which are plainly adapted to that end, which are not prohibited, but consist with the letter and spirit of the constitution, are constitutional.

...

...Should Congress, in the execution of its powers, adopt measures which are prohibited by the constitution; or should Congress, under the pretext of executing its powers, pass laws for the accomplishment of objects not entrusted to the government; it would become the painful duty of this tribunal, should a case requiring such a decision come before it, to say that such an act was not the law of the land. But where the law is not prohibited, and is really calculated to effect any of the objects entrusted to the government, to undertake here to inquire into the degree of its necessity, would be to pass the line which circumscribes the judicial department, and to tread on legislative ground. This court disclaims all pretensions to such a power.

...

It being the opinion of the Court, that the act incorporating the bank is constitutional; and that the power of establishing a branch in the State of Maryland might be properly exercised by the bank itself, we proceed to inquire —

2. Whether the State of Maryland may, without violating the constitution, tax that branch?

...

[T]he constitution and the laws made in pursuance thereof are supreme;... they control the constitution and laws of the respective States, and cannot be controlled by them. From this, which may be almost termed an axiom, other propositions are deduced as corollaries.... These are, 1st. that a power to create implies a power to preserve. 2nd. That a power to destroy, if wielded by a different hand, is hostile to, and incompatible with these powers to create and to preserve. 3d. That where this repugnancy exists, that authority which is supreme must control, not yield to that over which it is supreme.

...

...It is admitted that the power of taxing the people and their property is essential to the very existence of government, and may be legitimately exercised on the objects to which it is applicable, to the utmost extent to which the government may choose to carry it. The only security against the abuse of this power, is found in the structure of the government itself. In imposing a tax the legislature acts upon its constituents. This is in general a sufficient security against erroneous and oppressive taxation.

The people of a State, therefore, give to their government a right of taxing themselves and their property, and as the exigencies of government cannot be limited, they prescribe no limits to the exercise of this right, resting confidently on the interest of the legislator, and on the influence of the constituents over their representative, to guard then against its abuse. But the means employed by the government of the Union have no such security, nor is the right of a State to tax them sustained by the same theory....

...

If we measure the power of taxation residing in a State, by the extent of sovereignty which the people of a single State possess, and can confer on its government, we have an intelligible standard, applicable to every case to which the power may be applied. We have a principle which leaves the power of taxing the people and property of a State unimpaired; which leaves to a State the command of all its resources, and which places beyond its reach, all those powers which are conferred by the people of the United States on the government of the Union, and all those means which are given for the purpose of carrying those powers into execution. We have a principle which is safe for the States, and safe for the Union....

We find, then, on just theory, a total failure of this original right to tax the means employed by the government of the Union, for the execution of its powers. The right never existed, and the question whether it has been surrendered, cannot arise.

...

That the power to tax involves the power to destroy; that the power to destroy may defeat and render useless the power to create; that there is a plain repugnance, in conferring on one government a power to control the constitutional measures of another, which other, with respect to those very measures, is declared to be supreme over that which exerts the control, are propositions not to be denied. But all inconsistencies are to be reconciled by the magic of the word CONFIDENCE. Taxation, it is said, does not necessarily and unavoidably destroy. To carry it to the excess of destruction would be an abuse, to presume which, would banish that confidence which is essential to all government.

But is this a case of confidence? Would the people of any one State trust those of another with a power to control the most insignificant operations of their State government? We know they would not. Why, then, should we suppose that the people of any one State should be willing to trust those of another with a power to control the operations of a government to which they have confided their most important and most valuable interests? In the legislature of the Union alone, are all represented. The legislature of the Union alone, therefore, can be trusted by the people with the power of controlling measures which concern all, in the confidence that it will not be abused. This, then, is not a case of confidence, and we must consider it as it really is.

...

It has also been insisted, that, as the power of taxation in the general and State governments is acknowledged to be concurrent, every argument which would sustain the right of the general government to tax banks chartered by the States, will equally sustain the right of the States to tax banks chartered by the general government.

But the two cases are not on the same reason. The people of all the States have created the general government, and have conferred upon it the general power of taxation. The people of all the States, and the States themselves, are represented in Congress, and, by their representatives, exercise this power. When they tax the chartered institutions of the States, they tax their constituents; and these taxes must be uniform. But, when a State taxes the operations of the government of the United States, it acts upon institutions created, not by their own constituents, but by people over whom they claim no control. It acts upon the measures of a government created by others as well as themselves, for the benefit of others in common with themselves. The difference is that which always exists, and always must exist, between the action of the whole on a part, and the action of a part on the whole—between the laws of a government declared to be supreme, and those of a government which, when in opposition to those laws, is not supreme.

...

We are unanimously of opinion, that the law passed by the legislature of Maryland, imposing a tax on the Bank of the United States, is unconstitutional and void.

This opinion does not deprive the States of any resources which they originally possessed. It does not extend to a tax paid by the real property of the bank, in common with the other real property within the State, nor to a tax imposed on the interest which the citizens of Maryland may hold in this institution, in common with other property of the same description throughout the State. But this is a tax on the operations of the bank, and is, consequently, a tax on the operation of an instrument employed by the government of the Union to carry its powers into execution. Such a tax must be unconstitutional.

Spencer Roane and John Marshall on McCulloch v. Maryland[31]

John Marshall's opinion in McCulloch v. Maryland *was immediately recognized as having historic significance, and orthodox Republicans, including Thomas Jefferson and James Madison, did not like it. Neither Jefferson nor Madison doubted that the Bank of the United States had to be accepted. Madison had, after all, signed the Second Bank of the United States into law. Yet they recognized that* McCulloch *was not just about the Bank. It was about the shape of the union and the basic nature of the federal Constitution.*

Marshall had already, anonymously, defended the McCulloch *opinion in the newspapers. In the spring of 1819, a "furious hurricane" broke in the form of the "Hampden essays," anonymously authored by Virginia chief judge Spencer Roane and printed in the influential* Richmond Enquirer. *Marshall and Roane had fought a lengthy battle over the supremacy of the Supreme Court to state courts in interpreting the Constitution in the* Hunter's Lessee *cases (discussed elsewhere in this chapter), and Marshall easily recognized the author of the Hampden essays. Roane's essays challenged the liberal construction of federal power. He was particularly concerned with language in* McCulloch *that he believed would enable the federal government to deprive state governments of their traditional functions. Eager to blunt the force of Roane's arguments, Marshall hurriedly prepared a response under the pen name "A Friend of the Constitution."*

In the end, the controversy over the McCulloch *decision passed without the serious attacks on the Court that Marshall feared, and Marshall and Roane moved on to disagreeing over other cases. The Hampden essay may be read as a missing Jeffersonian dissent from the* McCulloch *decision. How much did Roane and Marshall disagree?*

Spencer Roane, "Hampden" (1819)

...

...*They* have not dared to break down the barriers of the constitution, by a *general* act declaratory of their power. That measure would be too bold for these ephemeral deputies of the people.—That people hold them in check, by a short rein, and would consign them to merited infamy, at the next election...They have adopted a safer course....[T]hey have succeeded in seeing the constitution expounded, not by what it actually contains, but by the *abuses* committed under it. A new mode of amending the constitution has been added to the ample ones provided in that instrument, and the strongest checks established in it, have been made to yield to the force of precedents! The time will soon arrive, if it is not already at hand, when the constitution may be expounded without ever looking into it!—by merely reading the acts of a renegade congress....

The warfare waged by the judicial body has been of a bolder tone and character....They resolved...to put down all discussions of the kind, in future, by a judicial *coup de main*: to give a *general* letter of attorney to the future legislators of the union: and to tread under foot all those parts and articles of the constitution which had been, heretofore, deemed to set limits to the power of the federal legislature. That man must be a deplorable idiot who does not see that there is no earthly difference between an *unlimited* grant of power, and a grant limited in its terms, but accompanied with *unlimited* means of carrying it into execution.

31. Excerpt taken from *John P. Branch Historical Papers of Randolph-Macon College* 4 (1904):357–363.

...It was only necessary, in that case, to decide whether or not the bank law was "necessary and proper," within the meaning of the constitution, for carrying into effect some of the granted powers; but the court have, in effect, expunged those words from the constitution....

...

If, in relation to the powers of the general government, the express grants...do not confer on the government power sufficiently ample, let those powers be extended by amendment to the constitution. Let us now do what our convention did in 1789, in relation to the articles of confederation. Let us extend their powers, but let this be the act of the people, and not that of subordinate agents. But let us see how far the amendments are to extend, and not, by opening wide the door of implied or constructive powers, grant we know not how much, nor enter into a field of indeterminable limits. Let us...extend the powers of the general government, if it be necessary; but until they are extended, let us only exercise such powers as are clear and undoubted....

...

The principle of the common law, is, that when any one grants a thing he grants also that *without which* the grant cannot have its effect; as, if I grant you my trees in a wood, you may come with carts over my land to carry the wood off. So a right of way arises on the same principle of necessity, by operation of the law...[W]hen the law giveth any thing to any one, it impliedly giveth whatever is necessary for taking or enjoying the same: it giveth "what is convenient, vis. entry, egress and regress as much as is necessary." The term "convenient" is here used in a sense convertible with the term "necessary," and is not allowed the latitude of meaning given to it by the supreme court. It is so restricted in tenderness to the rights of the other party. The right of way, passing in the case above mentioned, is also that, merely, of a private way, and does not give a high road, or avenue, through another's land, though such might be most convenient to the purposes of the grantee. It is also a principle of the common law that the incident is to be taken according to "a reasonable and easy sense," and not strained to comprehend things remote, "unlikely or unusual." The connection between the grant and the incident must be easy and clear: the grant does not carry with it as incidents things which are remote or doubtful.

...

The court is pleased to remind us...that it is a *constitution* that we are expounding. That constitution, however, conveys only *limited* and specified powers to the government, the extent of which must be traced in the instrument itself. The residuary powers abide in the state governments, and the people. If it is a constitution, it is also a *compact* and a limited and defined compact. The states have also constitutions, and their people rights, which ought also to be respected. It is on behalf of these constitutions, and these rights, that the enlarged and boundless power of the general government is objected to...

...

The supreme court seems to consider it as quite unimportant, so long as the great principles involving human liberty are not invaded, by which set of the representatives of the people, the powers of government are to be exercised. I beg leave to say, on the other hand, that the adjustment of those powers made by the constitution, between the general and state governments, is beyond their power, and ought not to be set aside. That adjustment has been made by the *people* themselves, and they only are competent to change it....[F]or the powers of the general government are few and defined, and relate chiefly to external objects, while the states retain a residuary and inviolable sovereignty over all other subjects; over all those great subjects which immediately concern the prosperity of the people. Are these last powers of so trivial a character that it is entirely unimportant which of the governments act upon them? Are the representatives of Connecticut in congress, best qualified to make laws, on the subject of our negro population? Or ought the South Carolina nabobs to regulate *their* steady habits? Is it the wish of any state, or at least of any of the larger states, that the whole circle of legislative powers should be confined to a body in which, in one branch at least, the small state of Delaware has as much weight as the great state of New York; having fourteen times its population?...

...[T]he great fault of the present times is, in considering the constitution as perfect. It is considered as a nose of wax, and is stretched and contradicted at the arbitrary will and pleasure of those who are entrusted to administer it. It is considered as *perfect*, in contravention of the opinion of those who formed it. Their opinion is greatly manifested, in the ample provisions it contains for its amendment. It is so considered in contravention of everything that is human: for nothing made by man is perfect. It is construed to this effect, by the *in's*, to the prejudice of the *out's*, by the agents of one government in prejudice of the rights of another; and by those who, possessing power, will not fail to "feel it, and forget right."

...

How...in this contest between the head and one of the members of our confederacy, in this vital contest for power, between them, can the supreme court assert its *exclusive* right to determine the controversy. It is not denied but that the judiciary of this country is in the daily habit of far outgoing that of any other. It often puts its veto upon the acts of the immediate representatives of the people.... [In the present case] it claims the right, in effect, to change the government: to convert a federal into a consolidated government. The supreme court is also pleased to say, that this important right and duty has been devolved upon it by the *constitution*.

If there is a clause to that effect in the constitution, I wish the supreme court had placed their finger upon it....

John Marshall, "A Friend of the Constitution" (1819)

...

The zealous and persevering hostility with which the constitution was originally opposed, cannot be forgotten. The deep rooted and vindictive hate, which grew out of unfounded jealousies, and was aggravated by defeat, though suspended for a time, seems never to have been appeased. The desire to strip the government of those effective powers, which enable it to accomplish the objects for which it was created; and, by construction, essentially to reinstate that miserable confederation, whose incompetency to the preservation of our union, the short interval between the treaty of Paris and the meeting of the general convention at Philadelphia, was sufficient to demonstrate, seems to have recovered all its activities. The leaders of this plan, like skillful engineers, batter the weakest part of the citadel.... The judicial department, being without power, without patronage, without the legitimate means of ingratiating itself with the people, forms the weakest part; and is, at the same time, necessary to the very existence of the government and to the effectual execution of its laws....

...

...The constitution has defined the powers of the government, and has established that division of power which its framers, and the American people, believed to be most conducive to the public happiness and to public liberty. The equipoise thus established is as much disturbed by taking weights out of the scale containing the powers of the government, as by putting weights into it. His hand is unfit to hold the state balance who occupies himself entirely in giving a preponderance to one of the scales.

...

The object of language is to communicate the intention of him who speaks, and the great duty of a judge who construes an instrument, is to find the intention of its makers. There is no technical rule applicable to every case, which enjoins us to interpret arguments in a more restricted sense than their words import. The nature of the instrument, the words that are employed, the object to be effected, are all to be taken into consideration, and to have their due weight.

...

It can scarcely be necessary to say, that no one of the circumstances which might seem to justify rather a strict construction in the particular cases quoted by Hampden, apply to a constitution. It is not a contract between enemies seeking each other's destruction, and anxious to insert every particular, lest a watchful adversary should take advantage of the omission.— Nor is it a case where implications in favor of one man impair the vested rights of another. Nor is it a contract for a single object, every thing relating to which, might be recollected and inserted. It is the act of a people, creating a government, without which they cannot exist as a people. The powers of this government are conferred for their own benefit, are essential to their own prosperity, by persons chosen for that purpose by themselves. The object of the instrument is not a single one which can be minutely described, with all its circumstances. The attempt to do so, would totally change its nature, and defeat its purposes. It is intended to be a general system for all future times, to be adapted by those who administer it, to all future occasions that may come within its own view.... The legislature is an emanation from the people themselves. It is a part chosen to represent the whole, and to mark, according to the judgment of the nation, its course, within those great outlines which are given in the constitution. It is impossible to construe such an instrument rightly, without adverting to its nature, and marking the points of difference which distinguish it from ordinary contracts.

...

If we were now making, instead of a controversy, a constitution, where else could this important duty of deciding questions which grow out of the constitution, and the laws of the union, be safely or wisely placed? Would any sane mind prefer to the peaceful and quiet mode of carrying the laws of the union into execution by the judicial arm, that they should be trampled under foot, or enforced by the sword?...

...

To whom more safely than to the judges are judicial questions to be referred?... Their paramount interest is the public prosperity, in which is involved their own and that of their families.—*No* tribunal can be less liable to be swayed by unworthy motives from a conscientious performance of duty. It is not then the party sitting in his own cause. It is the application of individuals by one department to the acts of another department of the government. The people are the authors of all; the departments are their agents; and if the judge be personally disinterested, he is as exempt from any political interest that might influence his opinion, as imperfect human institutions can make him....

Debate on the Military Draft

James Monroe, Proposal for a Military Draft (1814)[32]

During the War of 1812, the British sacked Washington, D.C. Soon after, an angry Congress passed a resolution demanding that the Secretary of War, James Monroe, detail "the defects in the present military establishment," and outline "(w)hat future provisions, by law, are deemed necessary to remedy such defects."[33] *Monroe responded by advocating a draft, to draw four percent of the male population between 18 and 45 into national military service. The states were understood to have the power to require service in the militia, and they had used conscriptions during the Revolutionary War. The U.S. Constitution gave the federal government the power to "raise and support" its own army. Monroe's proposal was the first to test whether a national draft was a "necessary and proper" means for "raising" an army, an implied power of the federal government. The controversial proposal was not adopted, however, and a draft would not be tested again until the Civil War.*

Monroe had been an anti-Federalist during the constitutional ratification debates, and he had sometimes been considered by more radical Jeffersonians as a possible challenger to James Madison. It was Monroe, not Madison, who was sent by the Virginia legislature to the U.S. Senate for the first Congress. But in the end, the younger Monroe waited his turn to be president, first serving in the critical offices of secretary of state and secretary of war for President Madison. Does he propose a constricted or expansive reading of federal power here?

...

[T]here [does not] appear to be any well founded objection to the right in Congress to adopt this plan, or to its equality in its application to our fellow-citizens individually. Congress have a right, by the constitution, to raise regular armies, and no restraint is imposed on the exercise of it, except in the provisions which are intended to guard generally against the abuse of power, and none of which does this plan interfere. It is proposed that it shall operate on all alike; that none shall be exempted from it except the Chief Magistrate of the United States, and the Governors of the several States.

It would be absurd to suppose that Congress could not carry this power into effect, otherwise than by accepting the voluntary service of individuals. It might happen that an army could not be raised in that mode, whence the power would have been granted in vain. The safety of the State might depend on such an army. Long continued invasions, conducted by regular, well disciplined troops, can best be repelled by troops kept constantly in the field, and equally well disciplined. Courage in an army is, in a great measure, mechanical. A small body, well trained, accustomed to action, gallantly led on, often breaks three or four times the number of more respectable and more brave, but raw and undisciplined troops.... The grant to Congress to raise armies, was made with a knowledge of all these circumstances, and with an intention that it should take effect. The framers of the constitution, and the States who ratified it, knew the advantage which an enemy might have over us, by regular forces, and intended to place their country on an equal footing.

32. Excerpt from James Monroe to William Branch Giles, October 17, 1814, *American State Papers: Military Affairs*, vol. 1 (Washington, DC: Seaton and Gales, 1832), 14–16.

33. William Branch Giles to James Monroe, September 23, 1814, *American State Papers: Military Affairs*, vol. 1 (Washington, DC: Seaton and Gales, 1832), 14.

The idea that the United States cannot raise a regular army in any other mode than by accepting the voluntary service of individuals, is believed to be repugnant to the uniform construction of all grants of power, and equally so to the first principles and leading objects of the federal compact. An unqualified grant of power gives the means necessary to carry it into effect. This is an universal maxim, which admits of no exception. Equally true is it, that the conservation of the State is a duty paramount to all others. The commonwealth has a right to the service of all its citizens; or, rather, the citizens composing the commonwealth have a right, collectively and individually, to the service of each other, to repel any danger which may be menaced. The manner in which the service is to be apportioned among the citizens, and rendered by them, are objects of legislation. All that is to be dreaded in such case, is, the abuse of power; and, happily, our constitution has provided ample security against that evil.

...

Daniel Webster, Speech on the Proposed Military Draft (1814)[34]

Congress debated the proposed draft bill during the winter of 1814. On December 9, 1814, the young Federalist congressman Daniel Webster from the ardently anti-war New England made a powerful speech against the constitutionality of the draft bill. Was the bill defeated because of such opposition—or simply because the Treaty of Ghent ending the war was signed while the debate was taking place? What is clear is that no draft took place during the War of 1812. The issue of the federal draft did not arise again until the Civil War.

Daniel Webster would soon become known as one of the most ardent nationalists in Congress. His legal arguments on behalf of the Bank of the United States in the McCulloch *case offered a broad reading of the necessary and proper clause for the Marshall Court to adopt. But during the unpopular war he emphasized limitations on federal power. This speech was left out of the collected papers published during and immediately after Webster's own lifetime. Does Monroe's argument, or Webster's, fit better with Marshall's opinion in* McCulloch? *Can Webster's argument on the draft be reconciled with* McCulloch? *Notice that in ridiculing the constitutional argument in favor of the draft, he compares it to an argument in favor of legal tender. That issue would rise again during the Civil War.*

...

Congress having, by the Constitution a power to raise armies, the Secretary contends that no restraint is to be imposed on the exercise of this power, except such as is expressly stated in the written letter of the instrument. In other words, that Congress may execute its power, by any means it chooses, unless such means are particularly prohibited. But the general nature and object of the Constitution impose as rigid a restriction on the means of exercising power, as could be done by the most explicit injunctions. It is the first principle applicable to such a case, that no construction shall be admitted which impairs the general nature and character of the instrument. A free constitution of Government is to be construed upon free principles, and every branch of its provisions is to receive such an interpretation as is full of its general spirit. No means are to be taken by implication, which would strike us absurdly, if expressed. And what would have been more absurd, that for this constitution to have said, that to secure the great blessings of liberty it gave to Government an uncontrolled power of military conscription?...

But it is said, that it might happen that an army would not be raised by voluntary enlistment, in which case the power to raise armies would be granted in vain, unless they might be raised by compulsion. If this reasoning could prove any thing, it would equally show, that whenever the legitimate powers of the Constitution should be so badly administered as to cease to answer the great ends intended by them, such new powers may be assumed or usurped, as any existing administration deem expedient. This is a result of his own reasoning, to which the Secretary does not profess to go. But it is a true result. For it is to be assumed, that all powers were granted, which might by possibility become necessary, and that Government itself is the judge of this possible necessity, then the powers of Government are precisely what it chooses they should be. Apply the same reasoning to any other power granted to Congress, test its accuracy by the result. Congress has the power to borrow money. How is it to exercise this power? Is it confined to voluntary loans? There is no express limitation to

34. Excerpt taken from Daniel Webster, "Speech on the Conscription Bill, December 9, 1814," in *The Writings and Speeches of Daniel Webster*, ed. Edward Everett, vol. 14 (Boston: Little, Brown, 1903), 55.

that effect, and, in the language of the Secretary, it might happen, indeed, it has happened, that persons could not be found willing to lend. Money might be borrowed then in any other mode. In other words, Congress might resort to a *forced* loan. It might take the money of any man, by force, and give him in exchange Exchequer notes or Certificate of Stock. Would this be quite constitutional, Sir?...

...

Sir, in granting Congress the power to raise armies, the People have granted all the means which are ordinary and usual, and which are consistent with the liberties and security of the People themselves; and they have granted no others. To talk about the unlimited power of the Government over the means to execute its authority, is to hold a language which is true only in regard to despotism. The tyranny of Arbitrary Government consists as much in its means as in its ends; and it would be a ridiculous and absurd constitution which should be less cautious to guard against abuses in the one case than in the other....

C. Territorial Acquisition and Governance

National expansion raised additional questions about broad and strict construction of national powers. Participants in the debate over the Louisiana Purchase disputed whether and when the United States could acquire new territories. Participants in the debate over Missouri raised questions about congressional power to govern territories and whether Congress could attach conditions to statehood. The Constitution provided few clear rules to guide governing officials. Article IV, Section 3, declares, "New States may be admitted by the Congress into this Union." Article IV, Section 4, declares, "The Congress shall have the Power to dispose of and make all needful Rules and Regulations of the Territory or other Property of the United States." Neither provision mentions any federal power to purchase additional territory beyond what the United States already possessed at the time of the founding. Section 3 does not state explicitly whether Congress may require people in a territory to agree to certain conditions before being allowed to become a state. Section 4 does not state explicitly whether that provision authorizes the United States to establish territorial governments.

National expansion was more politically explosive than most issues involving federal power. The debate over the bank divided Federalists from Republicans. National expansion divided the North from the South. Each section was terrified that the other section would control the West. New Englanders in 1803 feared that the Louisiana Purchase would give southern interests permanent control over the national government. Southerners in 1820 feared that states that had or were abolishing slavery would soon control the national government if Missouri was required to emancipate slaves as a condition for statehood.

How helpful is the familiar framework of strict and broad construction of constitutional powers in this context? What new issues are raised when thinking about the power of adding territory and citizens to a republic? Is the power to acquire new territory omitted

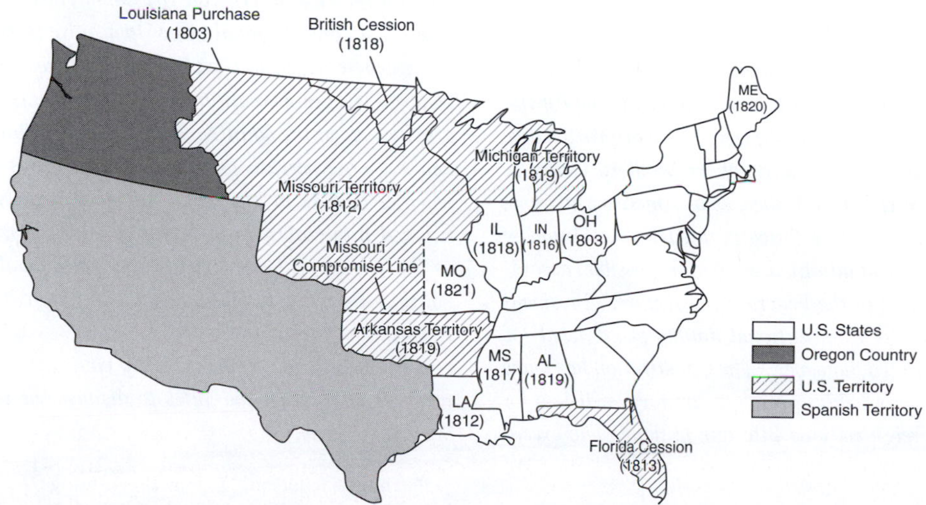

Figure 4-2 Map of Louisiana Purchase and Missouri Compromise

from the Constitution, an essential attribute of a sovereign government, or implied by one or more of the enumerated powers?

Senate Debate on the Louisiana Purchase (1803)[35]

The Louisiana Purchase offered the first chance for the United States to acquire additional territory since the Treaty of Paris (1783) ended the American Revolution. The United States emerged from the Revolution with large territorial holdings, and the federal government's role grew when the states agreed to cede control over western lands to the federal government after independence. By the time of the Louisiana Purchase, the territories in the southwest had already become the states of Kentucky and Tennessee, and the Northwest Territories had just produced the state of Ohio. Americans had long anticipated further territorial expansion. But the direction and the means by which this would occur had not always been clear. Unfortunately, the Constitution did not explicitly provide for the acquisition of new territories.

Control over the Mississippi River had been a longtime concern. It was well recognized that the river, and the port of New Orleans, would be important instruments of commerce in the coming decades, and that American economic growth would be severely hampered if access to the river were to be blocked by hostile European powers. Moreover, there was often unrest among the settlers in the west, who complained that the distant government on the Atlantic seaboard did not understand or care about their interests. They sometimes threatened to leave the Union and seek better terms from the English or the French.

American envoys in France, hoping to purchase New Orleans, were stunned when Napoleon offered to sell for $15 million all French possessions in North America. The American delegation quickly agreed. The treaty they negotiated provided that the current inhabitants of the territory would be guaranteed all the rights and liberties of American citizens, and the territory would be "incorporated in the Union of the United States, and admitted as soon as possible, according to the principles of the Federal constitution." President Jefferson had serious constitutional doubts about what his envoys had negotiated, however. "The Constitution has made no provision for our holding foreign territory, still less for incorporating foreign nations into our Union." The executive had "done an act beyond the Constitution." He considered proposing a narrowly drawn constitutional amendment that would explicitly authorize the treaty. Doing so would have the dual benefit of winning public confirmation for what they had done and of clarifying the terms of the Constitution.[36] The president was advised, however, that Napoleon was already getting cold feet about the deal and would use the constitutional tangle to renege on the agreement. Others in the administration assured the president that there were no constitutional problems with the deal in any case. Jefferson gave in. He submitted the treaty for Senate ratification without any mention of his constitutional doubts.

The treaty was quickly and easily ratified. When it came time to pass legislation implementing the terms of the treaty, however, the Federalists in New England raised constitutional objections. They were convinced that western expansion would reduce the economic and political clout of New England within the union. Even if the federal government could legitimately purchase new territory, they argued, it should hold those lands in perpetual territorial status. Further, new states could not be added to the union from that "foreign" territory without the consent of every other state. The Republicans had the numbers in Congress, however, and overrode the Federalist objections.

Jefferson saw the Louisiana Purchase as not only securing commercial access to the Mississippi River and protecting the American flank from hostile powers. It also, he believed, opened a vast new home to independent farmers and could reduce the political obstacles to ending slavery. By diffusing the population of slaves across a wider area, some hoped that the South would then look more like the mid-Atlantic states and move toward gradual emancipation. Republicans believed the Federalists' constitutional objections were mistaken. The constitutional power to acquire territory, in their view, was inherent in the power to make war and negotiate treaties. The Louisiana Purchase radically expanded the geographic size of the country, and it laid the foundations for a new era of American politics. As those lands were settled, whether opened or closed for slavery, they were also partitioned into states, to be admitted into the union as soon as possible by majority vote. These states would have equal political rights to the states that had fought the American Revolution.

Was President Jefferson overly cautious in this case, or were his supporters too quick to dismiss the constitutional

35. Excerpt taken from *Annals of Congress*, 8th Cong., 1st Sess. (November 3, 1803), 49.

36. Thomas Jefferson, "To John Breckenridge, August 12, 1802," in *The Writings of Thomas Jefferson*, ed. Paul Leicester Ford, vol. 8 (New York: G. P. Putnam's Sons, 1897), 244.

concerns given their strict constructionist philosophy? Should Jefferson have submitted the treaty to the Senate given his views on the Constitution? Did the Federalists adopt the Jeffersonian position, or did they develop a distinctive position of their own for restricting national power in this case? What might be the implications of the Federalist argument for other sorts of cases? Are there implications for secession—or for national decisions about citizenship and suffrage? Imagine a proposal today to admit the territory and citizens of Canada and Mexico into the United States. How would that alter the current political balance of the United States? Would such a proposal raise constitutional concerns?

Mr. John TAYLOR (Republican, Virginia):

. . .

Before a confederation, each State in the Union possessed a right, as attached to sovereignty, of acquiring territory, by war, purchase, or treaty. This right must be either still possessed, or forbidden both to each State and to the General Government, or transferred to the General Government. It is not possessed by the States separately because war and compacts with foreign Powers and with each other are prohibited to a separate State; and no other means of acquiring territory exist. By depriving every State of the means of exercising the right of acquiring territory, the Constitution has deprived each separate State of the right itself. Neither the means nor the right of acquiring territory are forbidden to the United States.... The means of acquiring territory consist of war and compact; both are expressly surrendered to Congress and forbidden to the several States.... The means of acquiring and the right of holding territory, being both given to the United States, and prohibited to each State, it follows that these attributes of sovereignty once held by each State are thus transferred to the United States....

. . .

To prove the treaty unconstitutional, a member from Massachusetts, [Mr. Pickering,] has quoted from the sixth article of the Constitution these words: "This Constitution, and the laws of the United States which shall be made in pursuance thereof, and all treaties made, or which shall be made, under the authority of the United States, shall be the supreme law of the land;" and he has reasoned upon the ground, that the words "in pursuance thereof," referred to treaties as well as to laws. But the difference between the phraseology in relation to laws and to treaties, is plain and remarkable; laws were to be made "in pursuance of the Constitution;" treaties "under the authority of the United States." This difference, probably, arises from the following consideration. The objects of the Legislative power could be foreseen and defined; therefore laws are limited to be made "in pursuance of" the definitions of the objects of Legislative power in the Constitution. But the objects of the treaty-making power could not be foreseen, and are not defined.... But if the words, "under the authority of the United States," are considered as being applied to treaties, in place of these "in pursuance of the Constitution," which are applied to laws; because the objects of treaties are not defined; then the treaty-making power retains all the political attributes belonging to it, not inconsistent with the principle of agency or subordination interwoven with our policy in all its parts— Among these is the right or attribute of acquiring territory. And it was probably the absence of a definition as to the objects of the treaty-making power, which suggested the precaution of checking it by two-thirds of the Senate; thus subjecting it, in this body, to the same restraint imposed upon amendments to the Constitution....

Mr. Uriah TRACY (Federalist, Connecticut):

Mr. President: I shall vote against this bill, and will give some of the reasons which govern my vote in this case. It is well known that this bill is introduced to carry into effect the treaty between the United States and France, which has been lately ratified. If that treaty be an unconstitutional compact, such a one as the President and Senate had no rightful authority to make, the conclusion is easy, that it creates no obligation on any branch or member of the Government to vote for this bill, or any other, which is calculated to carry into effect such unconstitutional compact.

. . .

It is well known that in Europe, any part of a country may be ceded by treaty, and the transfer is considered valid, without the consent of the inhabitants of the part thus transferred. Will it be said that the President and Senate can transfer Connecticut by treaty to France or to any other country? I know that a nation may be in war, and reduced to such necessitous circumstances, as that giving up a part or half the territory to save the remainder, may be inevitable: the United States may be in this condition; but necessity knows no law nor constitution either; such a case might be the result of extreme necessity, but it would never make it constitutional; it is a state of things which cannot, in its own nature, be governed by law or constitution. But if the President and Senate should, in ordinary peaceable times, transfer Connecticut, against her consent, would the Government be bound to make laws to carry such a treaty into effect?...

A number of States, or independent sovereignties, entered into a voluntary association, or, to familiarize the subject, it may be called a partnership, and the Constitution was agreed to as the measure of power delegated by them to the Federal Government, reserving to themselves every other power not by them delegated. In this Constitution they have restricted the powers of Congress, or the Federal Government, in a number of instances. In all these, I think the treaty-making power is clearly restricted, as much as if it had been mentioned in the restriction. For instance, Congress can lay no tax or duty on articles exported from any State. If this restriction should be violated by treaty, could it be thought valid?...

...

It is agreed, by the friends to the treaty, that the President and Senate cannot transfer a State. Let us examine the power of introducing a State. Suppose Louisiana contain ten millions of inhabitants; or, for the sake of argument, let it be supposed that we had a President inclined to monarchical principles, and he lived in the northern part of the Union, say in Connecticut or Massachusetts, and that two-thirds of the Senate were with him in sentiment, and that the four northern provinces of Great Britain contained ten millions of inhabitants, and were all determined monarchists, would the parties of the Union say it was competent and Constitutional for the President and Senate to introduce these ten millions of monarchists, who could at once out vote us all; and even give fifteen millions of dollars for the benefit of having them?

The principles of our Government, the original ideas and rights of the partners to the compact, forbid such a measure; and without the consent of all the partners, no such thing can be done.

The principle of admission, in the case of Louisiana, is the same as if it contained ten millions of inhabitants; and the principles of these people are probably as hostile to our Government, in its true construction, as they can be, and the relative strength which this admission gives to a Southern and Western interest, is contradictory to the principles of our original Union, as any can be, however strongly stated.

...

I shall be asked, sir, what can be done? To this question I have two answers: one is, that nothing unconstitutional can or ought to be done; and if it be ever so desirable that we acquire foreign States, and the navigation of the Mississippi, etc., no excuse can be formed for violating the Constitution; and if all those desirable effects cannot take place without violating it, they must be given up. But another and more satisfactory answer can be given. I have no doubt but we can obtain territory either by conquest or compact, and hold it, even all Louisiana, and a thousand times more, if you please, without violating the Constitution. We can hold territory; but to admit the inhabitants into the Union, to make citizens of them, and States, by treaty, we cannot constitutionally do; and no subsequent act of legislation, or even ordinary amendment to our Constitution, can legalize such measures. If done at all, they must be done by universal consent of all the States or partners to our political association. And this universal consent I am positive can never be obtained to such a pernicious measure as the admission of Louisiana, of a world, and such a world, into our Union. This would be absorbing the Northern States, and rendering them as insignificant in the Union as they ought to be, if by their own consent, the measure should be accepted.

House Debate on the Missouri Compromise (1819)[37]

Sectional tensions intensified in 1818, when the people of the Missouri Territory petitioned for admission into the Union. Republican Representative James Tallmadge of New York proposed that Missouri be admitted only if the state agreed to pass laws that would require the gradual emancipation of slavery. Opponents claimed that Congress had no authority to prevent the introduction of a new slave state into the Union or require any other special condition for statehood that was not demanded of existing states. The House voted 82 to 78 to require the exclusion of slavery in the new state of Missouri. When the Senate rejected the restriction, the Fifteenth Congress ended without an agreement on admitting Missouri.

By 1819 the Missouri question became the chief political issue facing the country. State legislatures bombarded the Congress with petitions on all sides of the issue. An

37. Excerpt taken from *Annals of Congress*, House, 15th Congress, 2nd Session (1819), 1169–1213.

opportunity for compromise arose when Maine applied for admission as a state. On February 16, 1820, the Senate agreed to unite the Maine and Missouri bills into one bill. The following day the Senate agreed to an amendment that would prohibit slavery in the Louisiana Territory north of latitude 36°30′—a line south of such existing and proposed slave states as Missouri, Kentucky, and Virginia. The House initially rejected the compromise that was proposed by the Senate, passing a bill that admitted Missouri without slavery. However, after a House-Senate conference agreed to the Senate version, the House voted 90 to 87 to allow slavery in Missouri. It then voted 134 to 42 to prohibit slavery in the Louisiana Territory north of latitude 36°30′.

Most of the constitutional debate focused on Congress' authority to impose a "restriction" on a new state, and whether new states must be admitted on "equal footing" with existing states (as provided by the Northwest Ordinance). We take for granted that new states have the same control over their internal affairs as older states, and are no more or less subject to federal authority or supervision. But heated exchanges took place on this fundamental question of what it means to admit new states into this Union. Could they be admitted conditionally or on more restricted terms than other states?

On the issue of Congress's authority to regulate slavery in the territories there was significantly less attention and division. The vote in the Senate on accepting the territorial ban was 34–10. Southerners generally supported the territorial restriction. In their view, the northern regions of the Louisiana Purchase were unlikely to be settled in the foreseeable future. Tolerating limits on slavery where slaveholders were unlikely to settle seemed, at least in 1820, a small price to pay for obtaining Missouri as a slave state. Nevertheless, virtually all southerners who spoke on the matter insisted that Congress had no power to ban slavery in the territories. Many anticipated arguments that would later be used when the constitutional status of slavery in the territories heated up again in the Jacksonian Era. Before signing the compromise legislation, President Monroe asked his Cabinet whether Congress could impose such a ban in the territories. Everyone agreed that the answer was yes.

The Missouri Compromise successfully managed a serious political crisis, but it did not resolve the underlying conflict. A little more than a month after the resolution, Jefferson wrote: "The momentous question, like a fire bell in the night, awakened and filled me with terror. I considered it at once as the knell of the Union. It is hushed, indeed, for the moment. But this is a reprieve only, not a final sentence. A geographical line, coinciding with a marked principle, moral and political, once conceived and held up to the angry passions of men, will never be obliterated; and every new irritation will mark it deeper and deeper."[38]

Mr. John W. Taylor (Republican, New York)

Mr. Chairman, . . . those whom we shall authorize to set in motion the machine of free government beyond the Mississippi, will, in many respects, decide the destiny of millions. . . . Our votes this day will determine whether the high destinies of this region, and of these generations, shall be fulfilled, or whether we shall defeat them by permitting slavery, with all its baleful consequences, to inherit the land. . . .

. . .

. . . The third section of the fourth article declares, that "the Congress shall have power to dispose of and make all needful rules and regulations respect the territory, or other property, belonging to the United States." It would be difficult to devise a more comprehensive grant of power. . . . Until admitted into the Union, this political society is a territory; all the preliminary steps relating to its admission are territorial regulations. Hence, in all such cases, Congress has exercised the power of determining by whom the constitution should be made, how its framers should be elected, when and where they should meet, and what propositions should be submitted to their decisions. After its formation, the Congress examine its provisions, and, if approved, admit the State into the Union, in pursuance of a power delegated by the same section of the Constitution, in the following words: "New States may be admitted by the Congress into the Union." . . . [I]f Congress has the power of altogether refusing to admit new States, much more has it the power of prescribing such conditions of admission as may be judged reasonable. The exercise of this power, until now, has never been questioned. The act of 1802, under which Ohio was admitted into the Union, prescribed the condition that its constitution should not be repugnant to the ordinance of 1787. The sixth article of that ordinance declares, "There shall be neither slavery nor involuntary servitude in the said Territory, otherwise than in the punishment of crimes whereof the party shall have been duly convicted." The same condition was imposed by Congress on the people of Indiana and

38. Thomas Jefferson, "To John Holmes, April 22, 1820," in *The Writings of Thomas Jefferson*, ed. Paul Leicester Ford, vol. 10 (New York: G. P. Putnam's Sons, 1899), 157.

Illinois. These States have all complied with it, and framed constitutions excluding slavery. Missouri lies in the same latitude. Its soil, productions, and climate are the same, and the same principles of government should be applied to it.

...

Mr. P. P. Barbour (Republican, Virginia)

[W]e have no Constitutional right to enact the provision.... [W]hilst the proposed State continued a part of our territory, upon the footing of a Territorial government, it would have been competent for us, under the power expressly given, to make needful rules and regulations—to have established the principle now proposed; yet, the question assumes a totally different aspect when that principle is intended to apply to a State. This term State has a fixed and determinate meaning; in itself, it imports the existence of a political community, free and independent, and entitled to exercise all the rights of sovereignty, of every description whatever.... It is true that slavery does not exist in many of the original States; but why does it not? Because they themselves, in the exercise of their legislative power, have willed that it shall be so. But, though it does not now exist, it is competent for them, by a law of their own enactment, to authorize it—to call it into existence whenever they shall think fit. Sir, how different would be the situation of Missouri, if the proposed amendment be adopted.....

...But it has been said that we imposed conditions on the admission of the State of Louisiana into the Union. What were these conditions? That civil and religious liberty should be established, and the trial by jury secured. It cannot be necessary to remind the House, that these several provisions attached also to the original States, by the most explicit declaration to that effect, in the first, fifth, and seventh amendments to the Constitution of the United States.... All that he contended for was, that we could impose no condition upon the new States, which the Constitution had not imposed upon the old ones;....

...

Mr. James Tallmadge (Republican, New York)

Sir, the ... gentleman, from Georgia [Mr. Cobb], ... has said, "that, if we persist, the Union will be dissolved;" and, with a look fixed on me, has told us, "we have kindled a fire which all the waters of the ocean cannot put out, which seas of blood can only extinguish."

...

Sir, if a dissolution of the Union must take place, let it be so! If civil war, which gentlemen so much threaten, must come, I can only say, let it come! ... If blood is necessary to extinguish any fire which I have assisted to kindle, I can assure gentlemen, while I regret the necessity, I shall not forbear to contribute my mite.... An evil so fraught with such dire calamities to us as individuals, and to our nation, and threatening, in its progress, to overwhelm the civil and religious institutions of the country, with the liberties of the nation, ought at once to be met, and to be controlled. If its power, its influence, and its impending dangers have already arrived at such a point that it is not safe to discuss it on this floor, and it cannot now pass under consideration as a proper subject for general legislation, what will be the result when it is spread through your widely extended domain? Its present threatening aspect, so far from inducing me to yield to its progress, prompts me to resist its march. Now is the time. It must now be met, and the extension of the evil must now be prevented, or the occasion is irrecoverably lost, and the evil can never be contracted.

...

...Whenever the United States have had the right and the power, they have heretofore prevented the extension of slavery. The States of Kentucky and Tennessee were taken off from other States, and were admitted into the Union without condition, because their lands were never owned by the United States. The Territory Northwest of the Ohio is all the land which ever belonged to them. Shortly after the cession of those lands to the Union, Congress passed, in 1787, a compact which was declared to be unalterable, the sixth article of which provides that "there shall be *neither slavery nor involuntary servitude* in the said territory, otherwise than in the punishment for crimes, whereof the party shall have been duly convicted." ...

...

Sir, there is yet another, and an important point of view in which this subject ought to be considered. We have been told by those who advocate the extension of slavery into the Missouri, that any attempt to control this subject by legislation is a violation of that faith and mutual confidence upon which our Union was formed and our Constitution adopted. This argument might be considered plausible, if the restriction was attempted to be enforced against any of the slaveholding States, which had been a party in the adoption of the Constitution. But it can have no reference or application to a new district of country recently acquired.... The

Constitution provides that the Representatives of the several States to this House shall be according to their numbers, including three-fifths of the slaves in the respective States. This is an important benefit yielded to the slaveholding States, as one of the mutual sacrifices of the Union....

But none of the causes which induced the sacrifice of this principle, and which now produce such an unequal representation of the free population of the country, exist as between us and the newly acquired territory across the Mississippi. That portion of the country has no claims to such an unequal representation, unjust in its results upon the other States.... Abstract from the moral effects of slavery, its political consequences in the representation under this clause of the Constitution demonstrate the importance of the proposed amendment.

D. Power to Regulate Commerce

Section 8 of Article I of the U.S. Constitution gives Congress the power to "regulate Commerce with foreign Nations, and among the several States, and with the Indian Tribes." Many thought that the inability of Congress to effectively regulate commerce was one of the flaws of the Articles of Confederation that needed to be remedied with the drafting of a new constitution. This included the power to regulate both international and interstate trade. But that power affected fundamental economic interests, and they had been reluctant to entrust it to the national government. In the end, Congress was given the power to regulate commerce by simple statute, to be passed by majority rule. But what did the power to regulate include? What was part of commerce? What was commerce "with foreign nations" and "among the several states"?

Over time, the so-called interstate commerce clause ("among the several states") has been the source of the most controversy. It has also opened the greatest exercise of congressional power. The Marshall Court's decision in *Gibbons v. Ogden* (1824) was a landmark in examining the meaning of the clause. As *Gibbons* highlights, the commerce clause has two sides. Most explicitly, it is a grant of power to the federal government to regulate commerce in each of these three domains. But the other side of the commerce clause is as an implicit restriction on the states. If the Constitution *em*powers the federal government to regulate some forms of commerce, how far does it go in *dis*empowering the states from regulating commerce?

The question becomes all the more important if the federal commerce power is large, and Marshall read the commerce power relatively broadly in *Gibbons*. This "power, like all others vested in congress, is complete in itself, may be exercised to its utmost extent, and acknowledges no limitations, other than are prescribed by the constitution," and "[c]ommerce among the states cannot stop at the external boundary line of each state, but may be introduced into the interior."[39] Commerce that "extend[s] to or affect[s] other States" or "concerns more States than one" were open to federal regulation.[40]

Marshall did not have to wrestle with the question of what was included in the power to "regulate" in *Gibbons*. Other early debates did raise that question. In the winter of 1807–08, Congress passed, at the urging of President Jefferson, the embargo acts, which barred all foreign trade. The Jeffersonians hoped that the embargo would keep the United States out of the ongoing war between England and France. First, it would put economic pressure on the European powers. Second, it would prevent a diplomatic crisis if an American trading ship were to be seized at sea. The embargo put a severe strain on the domestic economy, particularly in New England and parts of the South that were heavily involved in the international trade. Could an absolute prohibition on commerce qualify as a "regulation"? As Boston congressman Josiah Quincy asked, is textualism enough to guide constitutional interpretation? Or should we consider the circumstances in which text was adopted and the interests of all who live under it? Debates over internal improvements (see "Taxing and Spending Power" later in this chapter) often raised a different issue: Does the power to "regulate" include a power to promote and encourage commerce by building roads and canals? Days before the Court handed down its decision in *Gibbons*, Jeffersonian congressman John Randolph complained in the House that bills to provide for roads and canals required an excessively "*liberal* construction" of the power "to regulate" commerce. If Congress were to adopt such an approach, then "they may not only enact

39. *Gibbons v. Ogden*, 22 U.S. 1, 196, 194 (1824).

40. Ibid., 194.

a sedition law,...but they may emancipate every slave in the United States."[41]

United States v. The William, 28 F. Cas. 614 (D. Mass. 1808)

When several ships, including The William, *were seized by federal officers for violating the Jeffersonian embargo, their owners argued at trial in Massachusetts that Congress did not have the constitutional authority to pass the embargo acts. The case was brought before Federalist district court judge John Davis, one of John Adams's appointments. The challenge led Judge Davis to consider not only the scope of federal power under the commerce clause but also the reality and limits of the power of judicial review. Although Judge Davis upheld the embargo, juries frequently refused to convict those who were prosecuted for violating it, and many writers and politicians continued to assert that it was unconstitutional.*

JUDGE DAVIS delivered the opinion of the Court.

...

...[I]s a mere exceeding of the powers of congress, in legislation, without a repugnancy to express provisions of the constitution, among the proper objects of cognizance in the federal judiciary?

...

...[I]t is evident, that the judicial authority, is...precisely limited, in regard to deciding on the validity of legislative acts; and that the power to declare them void exists, only, in cases of contravention, opposition or repugnancy, to some express restrictions or provisions contained in the constitution. The examples and the argument [offered in earlier discussions of judicial review] apply only to cases of legislative action, which their powers forbid; not to those, which their powers may be supposed not to authorize....

...To extend this censorial power further, and especially to extend it to the degree, contended for in the objections to the act now under consideration, would be found extremely difficult, if not impracticable, in execution. To determine where the legitimate exercise of discretion ends, and usurpation begins, would be a task most delicate and arduous....

It is contended, that congress is not invested with powers, by the constitution, to enact laws, so general and so unlimited, relative to commercial intercourse with foreign nations, as those now under consideration. It is well understood, that the depressed state of American commerce, and complete experience of the inefficacy of state regulations, to apply a remedy, were among the great, procuring causes of the federal constitution. It was manifest, that other objects, of equal importance, were exclusively proper for national jurisdiction; and that under national management and control, alone, could they be advantageously and efficaciously conducted. The constitution specifies those objects. A national sovereignty is created. Not an unlimited sovereignty, but a sovereignty, as to the objects surrendered and specified, limited only by the qualifications and restrictions, expressed in the constitution. Commerce is one of those objects....Such is the declaration in the constitution. Stress has been laid, in the argument, on the word "regulate," as implying, in itself, a limitation. Power to regulate, it is said, cannot be understood to give a power to annihilate. To this it may be replied, that the acts under consideration, though of very ample extent, do not operate as a prohibition of all foreign commerce. It will be admitted that partial prohibitions are authorized by the expression; and how shall the degree, or extent, of the prohibition be adjusted, but by the discretion of the national government, to whom the subject appears to be committed?...I say nothing of the policy of the expedient. It is not within my province. But, on the abstract question of constitutional power, I see nothing to prohibit or restrain the measure.

Further, the power to regulate commerce is not to be confined to the adoption of measures, exclusively beneficial to commerce itself, or tending to its advancement; but, in our national system, as in all modern sovereignties, it is also to be considered as an instrument for other purposes of general policy and interest....The situation of the United States, in ordinary times, might render legislative interferences, relative to commerce, less necessary; but the capacity and power of managing and directing it, for the advancement of great national purposes, seems an important ingredient of sovereignty. It was perceived, that, under the power of regulating commerce, congress would be authorized to abridge it, in favor of the great principles of humanity and justice. Hence the introduction of a clause, in the constitution, so framed, as to interdict a prohibition of the slave trade, until 1808....

41. *Annals of Congress*, 18th Cong. 1st Sess. (1824) 1306, 1308.

It has been said, in the argument, that the large commercial states, such as New York and Massachusetts, would never have consented to the grant of power, relative to commerce, if supposed capable of the extent now claimed. On this point, it is believed, there was no misunderstanding. The necessity of a competent national government was manifest. Its essential characteristics were considered and well understood; and all intelligent men perceived, that a power to advance and protect the national interests, necessarily involved a power, that might be abused....

...

Notes

1. A case challenging the constitutionality of the embargo was also heard in the busy port city of Charleston, South Carolina. The Embargo Act authorized customs collectors to detain any vessel "ostensibly bound with a cargo to some other port of the United States, whenever in their opinions, the intention is to violate and evade" the embargo. Interpreting the requirements of that statutory provision, the Secretary of Treasury, acting for President Jefferson, had instructed the collector of the port of Charleston to detain vessels with "unusual shipments" of particular goods, including flour and lumber, or destined "for a place where they cannot be wanted for consumption." *The Resource* was scheduled to set sail from Charleston to Baltimore loaded with rice and cotton, and the port collector refused to provide clearance for *The Resource* to leave port.

The owner of *The Resource* sought a writ of mandamus from Justice William Johnson, then sitting in circuit court in Charleston. Johnson had been Jefferson's first appointee to the Supreme Court, but in *Gilchrist v. Collector of Charleston*, 10 F. Cas. 355 (So. Car. Cir. Ct. 1808) Johnson commanded that the collector give a clearance to *The Resource*. Johnson avoided the issue of whether the embargo itself was constitutional. Instead he focused on whether a correct interpretation of the Embargo Act covered the case of *The Resource* and whether the president could direct how the port collectors implemented the statute. The owner of *The Resource* denied that the ship was intended for foreign ports, asserting rather that it was simply being moved from Charleston to Baltimore (an admittedly unusual port for that cargo) to avoid a seasonal wood rot in South Carolina. The Charleston port collector admitted that he did not himself think *The Resource* intended to evade the embargo, but he believed the president's instructions required him to detain the ship. Johnson concluded that the statute had placed discretion in the port collector, and thus the Treasury Secretary's letter could only speak "in the language of recommendation, not of command" and could not authorize "an unsanctioned encroachment upon individual liberty."

The Federalist press in the North and South celebrated the opinion as evidence of an independent judiciary maintaining "the predominancy of the law over Executive usurpations." The administration responded by publicly releasing an opinion by Attorney General Caesar Rodney denying that the circuit court had jurisdiction to issue a writ of mandamus countermanding the instructions of the president to an executive branch officer, though it could later hear motions to "redress" any wrong that might have been committed by those officers (by, for example, suing the port collectors personally for monetary damages). Stung by the public rebuke, Justice Johnson himself took to the newspapers to defend his actions in the case. It was, he insisted, the courts that "are the constitutional expositors, and every department of government must submit to their exposition; for laws have no legal meaning but what is given them by the Courts to whose exposition they are submitted." If the courts interpreted the Embargo Act more narrowly than did the administration, the judges were entitled to intervene and command the port collectors to follow the judicial interpretation.[42]

Jefferson later convinced Congress to provide the president with explicit authority to instruct the port collectors on how to implement the embargo, but *Gilchrist* reflected a variety of obstacles that federal and state judges threw up to the enforcement of the embargo. Although Judge Davis in *The William* was alone in addressing the basic constitutionality of the Embargo Act, various judges interpreted the statute narrowly so as to limit its enforcement.

2. In 1833, Justice Joseph Story published his *Commentaries on the Constitution of the United States*, which offered a comprehensive examination of the meaning of the Constitution. Story had been placed on the bench by President James Madison on the eve of the War of 1812 and had become a staunch ally of Chief Justice John Marshall and a brilliant advocate of na-

---

42. See also Charles Warren, *The Supreme Court in United States History*, vol. 1 (Boston: Little, Brown, and Company, 1926), 324–341; H. Jefferson Powell, *A Community Built on Words* (Chicago: University of Chicago Press, 2002), 110–116.

tional power in the early republic. Like most New Englanders, however, he had opposed the embargo on policy grounds and was still ambivalent about it in the *Commentaries*. By the 1830s, however, New England strongly favored a broad reading of the federal power to regulate international trade, while southerners questioned the constitutionality of protectionist trade barriers that aided northern industries. With the *Commentaries* appearing just after the South Carolina nullification crisis,[43] Story took the opportunity to encourage regions of the country unhappy with federal trade policy to nonetheless submit to judicial supremacy in the interpretation of the Constitution and defer to the greater interests of federal union.

> [The embargo] was avowedly recommended, as a measure of safety for our vessels, our seamen, and our merchandise, from the then threatening dangers from the belligerents of Europe.... It was in no sense, then, a war measure. If it could be classed at all, as flowing from, or as an incident to, any of the enumerated powers, it was to that of regulating commerce....
>
> No one can reasonably doubt, that the laying of an embargo, suspending commerce for a limited period, is within the scope of the constitution. But the question of difficulty was, whether congress... could constitutionally suspend and interdict it wholly for an unlimited period.... An appeal was made to the judiciary upon the question; and it having been settled to be constitutional by that department of the government, the decision was acquiesced in, though the measure bore with almost unexampled severity upon the Eastern state.... The argument was, that the power to regulate did not include the power to annihilate commerce, by interdicting it permanently and entirely with foreign nations. The decision was, that the power of congress was sovereign, in relation to commercial intercourse, qualified by the limitations and restrictions contained in the constitution itself. Non-intercourse and Embargo laws are within the range of legislative discretion....
>
> That this measure went to the utmost verge of constitutional power, and especially of implied power, has never been denied. That it could not be justified by any, but the most liberal construction of the constitution, is equally undeniable. It was the favorite measure of those, who were generally the advocates of the strictest construction. It was sustained by the people from a belief, that it was promotive of the interests, and important to the safety of the Union.[44]

Josiah Quincy, Speech on Foreign Relations (1808)[45]

Josiah Quincy was a Massachusetts Federalist from Boston, the center of the opposition to the Jeffersonian embargo. Bills and resolutions relating to the embargo came before Congress repeatedly. Congress repeatedly reconsidered such details of the embargo policy as whether it should be extended for a limited duration or whether the president should be authorized to suspend it as circumstances permit. Congress also revisited the basic wisdom and constitutionality of the embargo policy. When resolutions were introduced to bolster the Jefferson administration in its defense of "the rights, honor, and independence" of the nation against England and France, Josiah Quincy used the occasion to again denounce the embargo. He pointed to its effects on the merchants and shippers of New England and, in his eyes, its dubious constitutionality.

As you read this excerpt, you might consider how consistent it seems with Federalist arguments on behalf of the Bank of the United States nearly twenty years before. Consider, too, the relationship between political circumstances and constitutional commitments. What distinguishes Representative Quincy from Judge Davis in the case of The William? *During the Philadelphia Convention, the New Englanders had pushed to give national majorities a power to regulate commerce. Quincy now complained that the Constitution never would have been ratified had New England foreseen the adoption of the Embargo Act. Is this a reasonable approach to trying to understand what powers had been given to the federal government? Does the Embargo Act*

43. In the winter of 1832–33, South Carolina declared that the federal protective tariff was unconstitutional and null and void. The state then threatened to block the collection of tariff revenues within its borders. A military stand-off was avoided through a congressional compromise.

44. Joseph Story, *Commentaries on the Constitution of the United States*, vol. 2 (Boston: Little, Brown, and Company, 1873), 170.

45. Excerpt taken from *Annals of Congress*, 10th Cong., 2nd Sess. (November 28, 1808), 541–542.

simply illustrate how hard it is to anticipate future needs when making constitutional agreements?

But there is another obstacle to a long and effectual continuance of this law—the doubt which hangs over its constitutionality, I know I shall be told that the sanction of the Judiciary has been added to this act of the Legislature. Sir, I honor that tribunal. I revere the individual whose opinion declared in this instance the constitutionality of the law. But it is one thing to venerate our courts of justice; it is one thing to deem this law obligatory upon the citizen, while it has all these sanctions; it is another, on this floor, in the high court of the people's privileges, to advocate its repeal on the ground that it is an invasion of their rights. The embargo laws have unquestioned sanction—they are laws of this land. Yet, who shall deny to a representative of the people the right, in their own favorite tribunal, of bringing your laws to the test of the principles of the Constitution?

. . .

I ask, in what page of the Constitution you find the power of laying an embargo? Directly given, it is nowhere. You have it, then, by construction or precedent. By construction, of the power to regulate. I lay out the question the common place argument, that regulation cannot mean annihilation, and that what is annihilated cannot be regulated. I ask this question, Can a power be ever obtained by construction, which had never been exercised at the time of the authority given, the like of which had never entered into human imagination, I will not say in this country but in the world? Yet such is the power which, by construction, you assume to exercise. Never before did society witness a total prohibition, like this, in a commercial nation. Did the people of the United States invest this House with a power of which at the time of investment, that people had not and could not have had any idea?... I appeal to the history of the times when this national compact was formed. This Constitution grew out of our necessities, and it was, in every stage of its formation, obstructed by the jealousies and diverse interests of the different States.... In this state of things, would the people of New England consent to convey to a Legislature, constituted as this in time must be, a power not only to regulate commerce, but to annihilate it, for a time unlimited, or altogether? Suppose, in 1788, in the convention of Massachusetts, while debating upon the adoption of this Constitution, some hoary sage had arisen, and with an eye looking deep into futurity, with a prophet's ken, had thus addressed the Assembly: "Fellow-citizens of Massachusetts: To what ruin are you hastening? Twenty years shall not elapse, before, under a strict and dubious construction of the instrument now proposed for your adoption, your commerce shall be annihilated. The whole of your vast trade prohibited. Not a boat shall cross your harbors, not a coaster shall be permitted to go out of your ports, unless under permission of the distant head of your nation, and after a grievous visitation of a custom-house officer."

Sir, does any man believe that, with such a prospect into futurity, the people of that State would have for one moment listened to its adoption? Rather, would they not have rejected it with indignation?

Gibbons v. Ogden, 22 U.S. 1 (1824)

New York required a license for steamships operating in its waters, and a monopoly on issuing such licenses was awarded to Robert Livingston and Robert Fulton in reward for their innovations in developing the steam engine. Aaron Ogden, the outgoing governor of New Jersey, persuaded the New Jersey legislature to grant him a similar "monopoly"; his aim was to cut into Livingston's steamer business between New York City and New Jersey. When Ogden's political opponents succeeded in repealing his New Jersey monopoly, he jumped the border. He managed to convince the heirs of the recently deceased Fulton and Livingston to grant him a New York license to run ships between New York City and New Jersey. Meanwhile, Thomas Gibbons, Ogden's former business partner, had started up a competing ferry business, running two steamships on an unannounced schedule between Elizabethtown, New Jersey, and New York City. Seeking to keep the case in the friendly New York courts, Ogden sought an injunction against Gibbons and won on the basis of his New York state steamship license. Gibbons responded that he had been licensed by the federal government to operate in coastal waters, however. He appealed to the U.S. Supreme Court.

The case raised two basic issues. First, did the Constitution implicitly prohibit or exclude the states from passing laws of this sort? Did the states have a concurrent power to regulate interstate commerce, or was this an exclusive power of the federal government? Even if the states could not "regulate interstate commerce," could they pass laws for other purposes that affected interstate commerce? Second, did the Constitution authorize Congress to preempt state laws of this sort with regulations of its own, and had Congress in fact done so in this case? New York's laws granting a steamboat monopoly were adopted soon after the Constitution and had been approved by Governor John Jay, among others. The state had long sought to exploit its position as the leading hub of imports into the United States. Tensions had built between New York and neighboring states over the taxation and regulation of commerce passing through the New York ports, fueling the movement to alter the Articles of Confederation.

The steamboat license was seen as a new variation on that old problem, but it was less clear whether it was a variation that the Constitution covered. Ogden relied on the services of two former New York state attorneys general to argue his case; Gibbons turned to Daniel Webster. Although a private suit, the U.S. attorney general was also given time to present arguments in the case, intervening on behalf of Gibbons and urging the Supreme Court to "interpose your friendly hand" to end New York's obstruction of interstate commerce.

The Supreme Court unanimously declared that Gibbons had a right to operate a ferry between New Jersey and New York. Chief Justice Marshall's majority opinion ruled that the commerce clause gave the federal government the power to license ships operating in coastal waters. New York thus could not prohibit a ship with a federal license from operating in state waters. Justice Johnson's concurring opinion declared unconstitutional the New York law granting Ogden a monopoly on a second ground. Johnson asserted that the commerce power was exclusive. *In his view, states could not pass laws regulating interstate commerce, even when the state law was not inconsistent with an existing federal law. Marshall maintained this position had "great force," but was content to rest his decision on his finding that the New York law authorizing the monopoly was inconsistent with federal law.*

The result in Gibbons *was highly popular, but Marshall's opinion was more controversial. Few were sorry that the Supreme Court declared unconstitutional New York's effort to monopolize the interstate steamship trade. But in doing so, Marshall took time to give a relatively broad reading to the interstate commerce clause. How far does Marshall's reading of the interstate commerce clause extend? What might the implications for contemporary debates over internal improvements or slavery have been? How much support does* Gibbons *provide for modern regulatory policy?*

CHIEF JUSTICE MARSHALL delivered the opinion of the Court.

...

This [Constitution] contains an enumeration of powers expressly granted by the people to their government. It has been said, that these powers ought to be construed strictly. But why ought they to be so construed? Is there one sentence in the constitution which gives countenance to this rule? In the last of the enumerated powers, that which grants, expressly, the means for carrying all others into execution, Congress is authorized "to make all laws which shall be necessary and proper" for the purpose. But this limitation on the means which may be used, is not extended to the powers which are conferred; nor is there one sentence in the constitution, which has been pointed out by the gentlemen of the bar, or which we have been able to discern, that prescribes this rule. We do not, therefore, think ourselves justified in adopting it. What do gentlemen mean, by a strict construction? If they contend only against that enlarged construction, which would extend words beyond their natural and obvious import, we might question the application of the term, but should not controvert the principle. If they contend for that narrow construction which, in support of some theory not to be found in the constitution, would deny to the government those powers which the words of the grant, as usually understood, import, and which are consistent with the general views and objects of the instrument; for that narrow construction, which would cripple the government, and render it unequal to the object, for which it is declared to be instituted, and to which the powers given, as fairly understood, render it competent; then we cannot perceive the propriety of this strict construction, nor adopt it as the rule by which the constitution is to be expounded. As men, whose intentions require no concealment, generally employ the words which most directly and aptly express the ideas they intend to convey, the enlightened patriots who framed our constitution, and the people who adopted it, must be understood to have employed words in their natural sense, and to have intended what they have said. If, from the imperfection of human language, there should be serious doubts respecting the extent of any given power, it is a well settled rule, that the objects for which it was given, especially when those objects are expressed in the instrument itself, should have great influence in the construction. We know of no reason for excluding this rule from the present case....

The words are, "Congress shall have power to regulate commerce with foreign nations, and among the several States, and with the Indian tribes."

The subject to be regulated is commerce; and . . . it becomes necessary to settle the meaning of the word. The counsel for the appellee would limit it to traffic, to buying and selling, or the interchange of commodities, and do not admit that it comprehends navigation. . . . Commerce, undoubtedly, is traffic, but it is something more: it is intercourse. It describes the commercial intercourse between nations, and parts of nations, in all its branches, and is regulated by prescribing rules for carrying on that intercourse. The mind can scarcely conceive a system for regulating commerce between nations, which shall exclude all laws concerning navigation, which shall be silent on the admission of the vessels of the one nation into the ports of the other, and be confined to prescribing rules for the conduct of individuals, in the actual employment of buying and selling, or of barter.

If commerce does not include navigation, the government of the Union has no direct power over that subject, and can make no law prescribing what shall constitute American vessels, or requiring that they shall be navigated by American seamen. Yet this power has been exercised from the commencement of the government, has been exercised with the consent of all, and has been understood by all to be a commercial regulation. All America understands, and has uniformly understood, the word "commerce," to comprehend navigation. It was so understood, and must have been so understood, when the constitution was framed. The power over commerce, including navigation, was one of the primary objects for which the people of America adopted their government, and must have been contemplated in forming it. The convention must have used the word in that sense, because all have understood it in that sense; and the attempt to restrict it comes too late.

. . .

The subject to which the power is next applied, is to commerce "among the several States." The word "among" means intermingled with. A thing which is among others, is intermingled with them. Commerce among the States, cannot stop at the external boundary line of each State, but may be introduced into the interior.

It is not intended to say that these words comprehend that commerce, which is completely internal, which is carried on between man and man in a State, or between different parts of the same State, and which does not extend to or affect other States. Such a power would be inconvenient, and is certainly unnecessary.

Comprehensive as the word "among" is, it may very properly be restricted to that commerce which concerns more States than one. The phrase is not one which would probably have been selected to indicate the completely interior traffic of a State, because it is not an apt phrase for that purpose; and the enumeration of the particular classes of commerce, to which the power was to be extended, would not have been made, had the intention been to extend the power to every description. . . . The genius and character of the whole government seem to be, that its action is to be applied to all the external concerns of the nation, and to those internal concerns which affect the States generally; but not to those which are completely within a particular State, which do not affect other States, and with which it is not necessary to interfere, for the purpose of executing some of the general powers of the government. The completely internal commerce of a State, then, may be considered as reserved for the State itself.

. . .

We are now arrived at the inquiry—What is this power?

It is the power to regulate; that is, to prescribe the rule by which commerce is to be governed. This power, like all others vested in Congress, is complete in itself, may be exercised to its utmost extent, and acknowledges no limitations, other than are prescribed in the constitution. . . . The wisdom and the discretion of Congress, their identity with the people, and the influence which their constituents possess at elections, are, in this, as in many other instances, as that, for example, of declaring war, the sole restraints on which they have relied, to secure them from its abuse. They are the restraints on which the people must often rely solely, in all representative governments.

. . .

The grant of the power to lay and collect taxes is, like the power to regulate commerce, made in general terms, and has never been understood to interfere with the exercise of the same power by the States; and hence has been drawn an argument which has been applied to the question under consideration. But the two grants are not, it is conceived, similar in their terms or their nature. Although many of the powers formerly exercised by the States, are transferred to the government of the Union, yet the State governments remain, and constitute a most important part of our system. The power of taxation is indispensable to their existence, and is a power which, in its own nature, is capable of residing in, and being exercised by, different authorities at the same time. We are accustomed to see it placed, for different purposes, in different hands.... When, then, each government exercises the power of taxation, neither is exercising the power of the other. But, when a State proceeds to regulate commerce with foreign nations, or among the several States, it is exercising the very power that is granted to Congress, and is doing the very thing which Congress is authorized to do. There is no analogy, then, between the power of taxation and the power of regulating commerce.

In discussing the question, whether this power is still in the States, in the case under consideration, we may dismiss from it the inquiry, whether it is surrendered by the mere grant to Congress, or is retained until Congress shall exercise the power. We may dismiss that inquiry, because it has been exercised, and the regulations which Congress deemed it proper to make, are now in full operation. The sole question is, can a State regulate commerce with foreign nations and among the States, while Congress is regulating it?

...

[T]he inspection laws are said to be regulations of commerce, and are certainly recognized in the constitution, as being passed in the exercise of a power remaining with the States.

That inspection laws may have a remote and considerable influence on commerce, will not be denied; but that a power to regulate commerce is the source from which the right to pass them is derived, cannot be admitted. The object of inspection laws, is to improve the quality of articles produced by the labor of a country.... They act upon the subject before it becomes an article of foreign commerce, or of commerce among the States, and prepare it for that purpose. They form a portion of that immense mass of legislation, which embraces every thing within the territory of a State, not surrendered to the general government.... Inspection laws, quarantine laws, health laws of every description, as well as laws for regulating the internal commerce of a State, and those which respect turnpike roads, ferries, etc. are component parts of this mass.

No direct general power over these objects is granted to Congress; and, consequently, they remain subject to State legislation....

...

It has been contended by the counsel for the appellant, that, as the word ""to regulate" implies in its nature, full power over the thing to be regulated, it excludes, necessarily, the action of all others that would perform the same operation on the same thing.... It produces a uniform whole, which is as much disturbed and deranged by changing what the regulating power designs to leave untouched, as that on which it has operated.

There is great force in this argument, and the Court is not satisfied that it has been refuted.

Since, however, in exercising the power of regulating their own purely internal affairs, whether of trading or police, the States may sometimes enact laws, the validity of which depends on their interfering with, and being contrary to, an act of Congress passed in pursuance of the constitution, the Court will enter upon the inquiry, whether the laws of New York, as expounded by the highest tribunal of that State, have, in their application to this case, come into collision with an act of Congress, and deprived a citizen of a right to which that act entitles him. Should this collision exist, it will be immaterial whether those laws were passed in virtue of a concurrent power "to regulate commerce with foreign nations and among the several States," or, in virtue of a power to regulate their domestic trade and police. In one case and the other, the acts of New York must yield to the law of Congress; and the decision sustaining the privilege they confer, against a right given by a law of the Union, must be erroneous.

...

This section [of the act of Congress] seems to the Court to contain a positive enactment, that the vessels it describes shall be entitled to the privileges of ships or vessels employed in the coasting trade. These privileges cannot be separated from the trade, and cannot be enjoyed, unless the trade may be prosecuted. The grant of the privilege is an idle, empty form, conveying nothing, unless it convey the right to which the privilege is attached, and in the exercise of which its whole value consists. To construe these words otherwise than as entitling the ships or vessels described, to carry on the coasting trade, would be, we think, to disregard the apparent intent of the act.

...

JUSTICE JOHNSON, concurring.

In attempts to construe the constitution, I have never found much benefit resulting from the inquiry, whether the whole, or any part of it, is to be construed strictly, or literally. The simple, classical, precise, yet comprehensive language, in which it is couched, leaves, at most, but very little latitude for construction; and when its intent and meaning is discovered, nothing remains but to execute the will of those who made it, in the best manner to effect the purposes intended....

...

For a century the States had submitted, with murmurs, to the commercial restrictions imposed by the parent State [Britain]; and now [after the Revolution], finding themselves in the unlimited possession of those powers over their own commerce, which they had so long been deprived of, and so earnestly coveted, that selfish principle which, well controlled, is so salutary, and which, unrestricted, is so unjust and tyrannical, guided by inexperience and jealousy, began to show itself in iniquitous laws and impolitic measures, from which grew up a conflict of commercial regulations, destructive to the harmony of the States, and fatal to their commercial interests abroad.

This was the immediate cause, that led to the forming of a convention [to draft the Constitution and grant a power over commerce for "the purpose of remedying those evils"].

...

The "power to regulate commerce," here meant to be granted, was that power to regulate commerce which previously existed in the States....And since the power to prescribe the limits to its freedom, necessarily implies the power to determine what shall remain unrestrained, it follows, that the power must be exclusive; it can reside but in one potentate; and hence, the grant of this power carries with it the whole subject, leaving nothing for the State to act upon.

...

But, it is almost laboring to prove a self-evident proposition, since the sense of mankind, the practice of the world, the contemporaneous assumption, and continued exercise of the power, and universal acquiescence, have so clearly established the right of Congress over navigation, and the transportation of both men and their goods, as not only incidental to, but actually of the essence of, the power to regulate commerce....

It is impossible, with the views which I entertain of the principle on which the commercial privileges of the people of the United States, among themselves, rests, to concur in the view which this Court takes of the effect of the coasting license in this cause. I do not regard it as the foundation of the right set up in behalf of the appellant. If there was any one object riding over every other in the adoption of the constitution, it was to keep the commercial intercourse among the States free from all invidious and partial restraints. And I cannot overcome the conviction, that if the licensing act was repealed to-morrow, the rights of the appellant to a reversal of the decision complained of, would be as strong as it is under this license....

...[T]his Court doth further DIRECT, ORDER, and DECREE, that the bill of the said Aaron Ogden be dismissed, and this same is hereby dismissed accordingly.

E. Taxing and Spending Power

Whether the United States could sponsor internal improvements was one of the sustained constitutional debates of the early national period. This debate did not truly begin until the Federalists had largely passed from the national political scene and Jeffersonians competed among themselves for control over the government. During this period Congress considered numerous proposals for federally sponsored lighthouses, roads, and canals. Many Americans were particularly enthusiastic about the National or Cumberland Road, a turnpike connecting the Potomac and Mississippi Rivers that began construction in 1811. Demands for federally sponsored improvements increased after the War of 1812, with young nationalists like Henry Clay and John C. Calhoun leading the charge.

The constitutional debates over internal improvements that took place in the early nineteenth century were similar to the constitutional debate over the national bank. National Republicans argued for a broad construction of constitutional provisions that could give Congress a power to build roads and canals in existing states. Old Republicans argued for a strict construction of the enumerated powers, which made many internal improvement projects difficult to justify. There was no explicit federal power to build roads in the Constitution. Anticipating the logic of *McCulloch v. Maryland*, advocates of construction projects argued that federally funded internal improvements were an implied power. They were necessary and proper means for exercising one of the enumerated powers, whether delivering the mails or regulating interstate commerce.

The "general welfare" clause, or spending provision of the Constitution, seemed to provide another option for authorizing internal improvements. Section 8 of Article I gave Congress the "power to lay and collect taxes...to pay debts and provide for the common defense and general welfare of the United States." Advocates of internal improvements argued that the general welfare clause gave Congress broad discretion in how it spent federal funds. Strict constructionists argued that the general welfare clause had to be read in the context of the overall constitutional design. To them, the mere power to spend funds did not imply other regulatory powers that were essential to internal improvements (such as the power to seize land, or eminent domain).

No major internal improvements bills became law during this period after 1810. Advocates of internal improvements thought that President James Madison's approval of the Second Bank of the United States meant that he would also accept other parts of the National Republican program. They were taken by surprise when Madison reaffirmed his strict constructionist views and vetoed a major internal improvements bill on his last day in office.

> To refer the power in question to the clause "to provide for the common defense and general welfare" would be contrary to the established and consistent rules of interpretation, as rendering the special and careful enumeration of powers which follow the clause nugatory and improper. Such a view of the Constitution would have the effect of giving to Congress a general power of legislation instead of the defined and limited one hitherto understood to belong to them, the terms "common defense and general welfare" embracing every object and act within the purview of a legislative trust.[46]

The Bank was an exception to the rule for Madison. President James Monroe, Madison's successor, took much the same view and was willing to use his veto pen to back it up.

House Report on Internal Improvements (1817)[47]

The House of Representatives appointed a committee to respond to Madison's veto of the internal improvements bill. The committee was led by Henry St. George Tucker, a Republican from an influential Virginia family of judges and politicians. In the extended debate that followed, Tucker expressed exasperation with the charge that he and his allies

> *are deserting the great principles of the Republicans of 1798, and subverting the acknowledged rights of the States, by a construction too latitudinous.... In the construction of this Constitution, there is not, there cannot be, a system of orthodoxy. Agreeing, as we do, in principle, there must always be a variety of application. The instrument, conferring upon us incidental, as well as express powers, there must always be great differences of opinion, as to the "direct relationship," and "real necessity" of the accessory powers. Sir, with these things before your eyes, who shall pretend to say what is orthodoxy—what is heterodoxy? It is impossible. It remains to us to act according to our consciences, without attempting a conformity to any particular sect or persuasion.*[48]

Tucker, a veteran of the War of 1812 and serving only his second term of office in the House, allied himself with other young insurgents such as Henry Clay and John Calhoun who were willing to take a more vigorous view of federal power and what was necessary to avoid a repeat of the indignities that had befallen the United States in that war. Proponents insisted that, particularly with state approval, such policies were necessary given the congressional power to raise armies and regulate interstate commerce.

...

It is true that the wants of the Union cannot confer power under the Constitution; but they may justly be touched upon as affording aid in its construction. They must have clearly foreseen, and must have been supposed to be provided for. If the power to carry on war implies "the necessary and proper" means of conducting it to a safe and proper issue, and if, without the use of these means, the burdens, and the privations, and the miseries of war, are to be infinitely increased, and its issue (always doubtful) rendered yet more precarious and unprosperous, are we not justified in presuming those means to have been contemplated as being

46. H.R. Rep. No. 11, 15th Cong., 1st sess. (1817).

47. Excerpt taken from *Annals of Congress*, 15th Cong., 1st sess. (December 15, 1817), 453–460.

48. *Annals of Congress*, 15th Cong., 1st sess. (March 13, 1818), 1323.

vested in the General Government? Are we not justified in asserting that "necessary" power—the power of constructing roads and canals—at least with the assent of the States?

If your committee have not erred in attributing to Congress a Constitutional power to make roads and canals, either as an original or accessory power, it would seem that no doubt could remain of the right of applying our revenues to these purposes. If, indeed, the power was denied to the General Government of constructing roads and canals themselves, a question might still arise, whether it had not power to appropriate part of the revenue "to aid in the construction of roads and canals by the States."

There is perhaps no part of the Constitution more unlimited than that which relates to the application of the revenues which are to be raised under its authority. That power is given to "lay and collect taxes to pay the debts and provide for the common defense and general welfare of the United States;" and though it be really admitted, that, as this clause is only intended to designate the objects for which revenue is to be raised, it cannot be construed to extend the specified powers of Congress, yet it would be difficult to reconcile either the generality of the expression or the course of administration under it, with the idea that Congress has not a discretionary power over its expenditures, limited by their application "to the common defense and general welfare."

. . .

Nor, is there any danger that such power will be abused, while the vigor of representative responsibility remains unimpaired. It is on this principle that the framers of the Constitution mainly relied for protection of the public purse. It was a safe reliance. It was manifest that there was no other subject on which representative responsibility would be so great. On the other hand, while this principle is calculated to prevent abuses in the appropriation of public money, it was equally necessary to get an extensive discretion to the legislative body in the disposition of the revenues; since no human foresight could discern, nor human industry enumerate, the infinite variety of purposes to which the public money might advantageously and legitimately be applied. The attempt would have been to *legislate*, not frame a *Constitution*; to foresee and provide specifically for the wants of future generations, not to frame a rule of conduct for the legislative body. . . .

James Monroe, "Views of the President of the United States on the Subject of Internal Improvements" (1822)[49]

President James Monroe continued Madison's opposition to internal improvements without a constitutional amendment. After he vetoed legislation that would have expanded the national road, Monroe wrote a long state paper detailing why he regarded internal improvements to be unconstitutional. Like more moderate national Republicans, Monroe believed the national government could fund state government projects, when those internal improvements had national significance. He emphatically rejected, however, claims that various enumerated powers sanctioned federal control of the internal transportation system or the federal power to build its own.

Monroe made sure that a copy of his essay was delivered to the justices of the Supreme Court. Justice William Johnson informed the president that the McCulloch *opinion had already settled the issue—in favor of congressional power as well. The news apparently had no influence on Monroe.*

It may be presumed that the proposition relating to internal improvements by roads and canals, which has been several times before Congress, will be taken into consideration again. . . . It seems to be the prevailing opinion that great advantage would be derived from the exercise of such a power by Congress. Respecting the right [of Congress to do so] there is much diversity of sentiment. It is of the highest importance that this question should be settled. If the right exists, it ought forthwith to be exercised. If it does not exist, surely those who are friends to the power ought to unite in recommending an amendment to the Constitution to obtain it. I propose to examine this question.

. . .

If the United States possesses this power, it must be either because it has been specifically granted or that it is incidental and necessary to carry into effect some specific grant. . . .

49. Excerpt taken from James Monroe, "Views of the President of the United States on the Subject of Internal Improvements," in *A Compilation of the Messages and Papers of the Presidents*, ed. James D. Richardson, vol. 2 (New York: Bureau of National Literature, 1897), 713.

The first of these grants is in the following words: "Congress shall have the power to establish post-offices and post-roads." What is the just import of these words and the extent of the grant?... If we were to ask any number of our most enlightened citizens, who had no connection with public affairs and whose minds were unprejudiced, what was the import of the word "establish" and the extent of the grant which it controls, we do not think there would be any difference of opinion among them.... The use of the existing road... in passing it as others do is all that would be thought of, the jurisdiction and soil remaining to the State, with a right in the State or those authorized by its legislature to change the road at pleasure.

...

The next object of inquiry is whether the right to declare war includes the right to adopt and execute this system of improvement....

...

...[N]o war with any great power can be prosecuted with success without the command of the resources of the Union in all these respects.... But these powers have all been granted specifically with many others, in great detail, which experience has shown were necessary for the purposes of war. By specifically granting, then, these powers it is manifest that every power was thus granted which it was intended to grant for military purposes, and that it was also intended that no important power should be included in this grant by way of incident, however useful it might be for some of the purposes of the grant.

...

I come next to the right to regulate commerce, the third source from whence the right to make internal improvement is claimed.... Commerce between independent powers or communities is universally regulated by duties and imposts. It was so regulated by the states before the adoption of this Constitution equally in respect to each other and to foreign powers. The goods and vessels employed in the trade are the only subjects of regulation. It can act on none other. A power, then, to impose such duties and imposts in regard to foreign nations and to prevent any on the trade between the States was the only power granted.

...

The fourth claim is founded on the right of Congress to "pay the debts and provide for the common defense and general welfare" of the United States....

...

... Have Congress a right to raise and appropriate the money to any and to every purpose according to their will and pleasure? They certainly have not. The Government of the United States is a limited Government, instituted for great national purposes, and for those only. Other interests are committed to the States, whose duty it is to provide for them. Each government should look to the great and essential purposes for which it was instituted, and confine itself to those purposes. A State government will rarely if ever apply money to national purposes without making it a charge to the nation. The people of the state would not permit it. Nor will Congress be apt to apply money in aid of the State administrations for purposes strictly local in which the nation at large has no interest, although the state should desire it. The people of the other states would condemn it. They would declare that Congress has no right to tax them for such a purpose, and would dismiss at the next election such of their representatives as had voted for that measure, especially if it should be severely felt....

...

The right of appropriation is nothing more than a right to apply the public money to this or that purpose. It has no incidental power, nor does it draw after it any consequences of that kind. All that Congress could do under it in the case of internal improvements would be to appropriate the money necessary to make them. For every act requiring legislative sanction or support the State authority must be relied on. The condemnation of the land, if the proprietors should refuse to sell it, the establishment of turnpikes and tolls, and the protection of the work when finished must be done by the State. To these purposes the powers of the General Government are believed to be utterly incompetent.

...

IV. Federalism

MAJOR DEVELOPMENTS

- The Eleventh Amendment prohibits federal courts from adjudicating lawsuits against a state brought by a citizen of another state or country
- The compact theory of the relationship between states and national government

Ratification left open many important constitutional questions about the place of states in the national union. General agreement existed that all states had surrendered certain vital powers. Article I clearly forbade New Jersey from declaring war on France, or North Carolina from granting titles of nobility. Other constitutional questions were less clear. In particular, Americans disputed whether states or the people of the United States were the parties to the Constitution. The answer to that question influenced how constitution decision makers understood the proper balance of power between state governments and the national government. It also affected what governing institutions were authorized to resolve constitutional disputes between the states and the national government, as well as whether states could be sued in federal court.

Sovereignty. Many of the materials in this section speak of sovereignty when discussing the respective powers of the state and federal governments. *Sovereignty* is a term of international law that refers to the authority to make law or govern a particular territory. Sovereign nations in international law have various powers, including the power to make war, form alliances, determine citizenship, and govern a population. Several sovereign powers were particularly important during the early national period. When sovereign nations make treaties, each sovereign has the independent right to determine what treaty obligations were agreed upon. If the United States and France sign a treaty agreeing to ban the killing of large fish, each nation has the power to determine what constitute "large fish." If the two nations disagree, they must accept the disagreement, negotiate a new treaty, declare the treaty void, or agree to submit the controversy to an arbiter. No independent body has the right to arbitrate a dispute between two sovereignties. Sovereign nations may not be sued without their permission. You cannot sue the United States unless Congress has passed a law giving you permission. This is known as *sovereign immunity*. Sovereign nations have the right to determine whether maintaining alliances remains in the national interest. If the United States believes that our allies have violated treaty commitments, we may unilaterally pull out of NATO or the United Nations.

The state governments were clearly not fully sovereign after the ratification of the U.S. Constitution. There was less certainty over whether they possessed some measure of sovereignty. Even if they were not fully sovereign, they seemed to possess important legal and political characteristics of sovereignty. The states certainly had a powerful interest in asserting that they still possessed some attributes of sovereign governments. Thus, many were surprised when the U.S. Supreme Court ruled in *Chisholm v. Georgia* (1793) that a citizen of South Carolina could sue the state of Georgia in federal court. Bipartisan majorities in Congress proposed the Eleventh Amendment in response, and the states quickly ratified it. The amendment barred federal courts from hearing suits against a state filed by a citizen of some other state or country, giving constitutional recognition to some measure of state sovereign immunity.

Many Jeffersonians believed that the Constitution formed a "compact" between sovereign states. As Jefferson conceived of it, "the constitution of the United States is a compact of independent nations subject to the rules acknowledged in similar cases, as well that of amendment provided within itself, as, in case of abuse, justly dreaded but unavoidable *ultimo ratio gentium* [the last argument of nations]."[50] The compact theory of union implied a strict construction of national powers. The sovereign states that formed the union should not easily be understood to have given up powers to the general government. To Jefferson and many of his allies, the states were also necessarily the ultimate interpreters of the Constitution. (Madison was more ambivalent on this point.) Since these parties constituted the union and delegated powers to the national government, they must be able to interpret the terms of that grant of power.

What this might mean in practice was not immediately clear. It at least suggested that the states should be vigilant watchdogs, ready to sound the alarm if the federal government were to slip its constitutional constraints. It might also mean that the states could take positive action to prevent the federal government from abusing its powers. This might include directing its senators to stop the abuse, as well as refusing to comply with judicial decisions that were not adequately grounded in the Constitution. It might extend to interposing its own forces between those of the federal government and its citizens—or even seceding from the union. The Virginia and Kentucky Resolutions of 1798, secretly drafted by James Madison and Thomas Jefferson in response to the congressional Alien and Sedition

50. Thomas Jefferson, "To Edward Everett, April 8, 1826," in *Writings*, vol. 10, 385.

Acts passed that same year, became the touchstones for the compact theory of the Constitution.

Federalists and National Republicans rejected the compact theory of the Constitution. In their view, the Constitution was an agreement among the people of the United States. Chief Justice John Marshall went out of his way in *McCulloch v. Maryland* (1819) to reject the compact theory. He declared, "The government of the Union, then (whatever may be the influence of this fact on the case), is, emphatically and truly, a government of the people. In form, and in substance, it emanates from them. Its powers are granted by them, and are to be exercised directly on them, and for their benefit." Justice Joseph Story agreed. His opinion in *Martin v. Hunter's Lessee* (1816) asserted, "The constitution of the United States was ordained and established, not by the states in their sovereign capacities, but emphatically, as the preamble of the constitution declares, by 'the people of the United States.'" In the early republic, rejecting compact theory opened the door to a broad construction of congressional powers. If the Constitution was made by and for the people of the nation as a whole, then the best repository of their power and guardian of their interest were their elected representatives in Congress.

If the compact theory provided an overarching perspective on federalism and the constitutional relationship between the states and the national government, there remained a further question: How should the states relate to one another, and how had their powers been limited by their entry into the union? Madison was acutely aware of the problems posed by the clashing of the states among themselves and of abuses of power by the state governments. And this too was part of the Republican inheritance.

The first line of defense against such problems was, of course, the constitutions and governments of the states themselves. But Madison had failed in the Philadelphia Convention to win his congressional veto over state laws. The second line of defense was the federal judiciary, which had the power to uphold the supremacy of the federal government within its appropriate sphere. The judiciary could also enforce the limits on state power that were contained within the U.S. Constitution. The Fourteenth Amendment would later vastly expand these federal constitutional limits on the states, but interpreting and applying the original limits on the states was challenge enough during the Jeffersonian Era. (Perhaps the most notable of those limitations during this period was the contracts clause, which is considered in Volume Two.)

A. Sovereign Immunity

Sovereign states enjoy "sovereign immunity." They cannot be sued or otherwise be subject to court proceedings. Sovereignties can be sued only when they choose to waive that immunity.

The Articles of Confederation had declared that each state retained its "sovereignty, freedom, and independence." The U.S. Constitution did not. The Constitution imposed new obligations and restrictions on the states, and it directed state and federal judges to enforce those constitutional requirements. The states under the Articles of Confederation, like all governments, had traditionally enjoyed "sovereign immunity." They could not be subjected against their will to court proceedings that could result in financial losses. The state governments could be sued in state courts, and their treasuries imperiled, only if they chose to waive that immunity.

The Constitution of the United States complicated traditional notions of sovereign immunity. All agreed the federal government enjoyed sovereign immunity. No one can sue the United States unless a federal statute permits that lawsuit. Whether state governments can be sued in federal courts raised more difficult issues. Sovereign governments cannot be sued without their permission in their courts or foreign courts. Federal courts are neither state courts nor foreign courts. Did immunity principles apply there as well? Article III of the Constitution explicitly anticipated that states would be parties in lawsuits heard in federal courts. But did that include suits that the states did not initiate? And could individuals sue states for monetary damages?

Both the federal government and the states during the late eighteenth century had financial reasons for being concerned with the status of sovereign immunity. During the Revolutionary War, states had borrowed money freely from citizens of other states and other countries. Most Federalists wanted to ensure that creditors were paid back. Repayment would demonstrate that the United States was a trustworthy economic partner and ease tensions between the United States and foreign countries. States, many of whom had limited capacity to repay debts, wanted to keep the option to repudiate those obligations. Needless to say, federal courts were more likely to issue orders on behalf of creditors against the debtor states than were state courts.

The issue of state sovereign immunity was controversial from the moment that the Constitution was proposed. During the ratification debates, Federalists such as Alexander Hamilton reassured skeptics that nothing in the Constitution would alter state sovereign immunity. Creditors quickly tested this theory, however. In one of its earliest important decisions, the U.S. Supreme Court ruled in *Chisholm v. Georgia* (1793) that the states did not enjoy sovereign immunity in federal court. Chief Justice Jay observed simply, "the people are the sovereign of this country." In a republican government, he wrote, "justice is the same whether due from one man or a million." *Chisholm* was immediately reversed by the actions of the elected branches. The Eleventh Amendment to the Constitution was drafted specifically to overturn the result in *Chisholm*. It was quickly ratified by the necessary number of states. The entire episode leaves open whether *Chisholm* correctly interpreted the original Constitution, or whether *Chisholm* was itself a mistake that was "corrected." What then are the larger implications for whether the states have sovereign immunity, and under what circumstances? What are the lessons for the Court as it seeks to interpret the Constitution? Why did the Court "fail" in *Chisholm*, but not in other controversial cases?

Chisholm v. Georgia, 2 U.S. 419 (1793)

This case was the first important decision of the U.S. Supreme Court. It is also the first example of how judicial opinions do not always settle constitutional disputes. Alexander Chisholm was a citizen of South Carolina and the executor of the estate of a South Carolina merchant. He believed the state of Georgia owed the merchant's estate some money, arising out of a contract to supply Georgia with clothing during the Revolutionary War. Chisholm sued the state in federal court, relying on the language in Article III, Section 2 of the Constitution, which declared that the jurisdiction of federal courts extended to controversies between "a State and Citizens of another State."

However, the state of Georgia refused to appear in court, claiming that it was sovereign state and thus (by definition) immune from the legal processes of another government. From the state's point of view, the language in Article III was intended to give states recourse as plaintiffs in federal courts against citizens in other states. It was not, the state believed, intended to force states to act as defendants in federal courts against creditors from other states.

The Attorney General of the United States urged the Supreme Court to assert its jurisdiction over Georgia, and the Court was accommodating. The decision of this five-member Court was 4 to 1 against the state's assertion of sovereign immunity. James Wilson and John Jay wrote in strong, nationalist terms that sovereignty resided only in the people of the United States. Justice Iredell was the only dissenting vote, but even he did not assert a theory of state sovereignty. He emphasized merely the absence of a congressional statute authorizing this kind of lawsuit.

Before John Marshall became Chief Justice in 1801, the justices each wrote their own opinions in every case, a practice known as "seriatim" opinions. They are presented here after the argument made by the Attorney General, beginning with Iredell's dissenting view. Consider whether the justices were basing their arguments on a literal reading of the text, or structural considerations, or general principles of the constitutional system. Possessing sovereign immunity is part of what it meant to be a government. What role does such a legal background play in constitutional interpretation? Can it be assumed that the Constitution overturned such a basic principle by mere implication? What are possible justifications for sovereign immunity? Is it consistent with a democratic government?

Mr. RANDOLPH [Attorney General of the United States], for the plaintiff....

1st. The Constitution vests a jurisdiction in the Supreme Court over a State, as a defendant, at the suit of a private citizen of another State. Consult the letter of the Constitution, or rather the influential words of the cause in question. The judicial power is extended to controversies between a State and citizens of another State.... Human genius might be challenged to restrict these words to a plaintiff state alone....

With the advantage of the letter on our side, let us now advert to the spirit of the Constitution, or rather its genuine and necessary interpretation....

Are States...to enjoy the high privilege of acting...eminently wrong, without control; or does a remedy exist? The love of morality would lead us to wish that some check should be found; if the evil, which flows from it, be not too great for the good contemplated.... Government itself would be useless, if a pleasure to obey or transgress with impunity should be substituted in the place of a sanction to its laws....

What is to be done, if in consequence of a bill of attainder, or an ex post facto law, the estate of a citizen shall be confiscated, and deposited in the treasury of a State? What, if a State should adulterate or coin money below the Congressional standard, emit bills of credit, or enact unconstitutional tenders, for the purpose of extinguishing its own debts? What if a State should impair her own contracts? These evils, and others which might be enumerated like them, cannot be corrected without a suit against the State....

...

With this discussion, though purely legal, it will be impossible to prevent the world from blending political considerations. Some may call this an attempt to consolidate. But before such an imputation shall be pronounced, let them examine well, if the fair interpretation of the Constitution does not vindicate my opinions. Above all, let me personally assure them, that the prostration of State-rights is no object with me; but that I remain in perfect confidence, that with the power, which the people and the Legislatures of the States indirectly hold over almost every movement of the National Government, the States need not fear an assault from bold ambition, or any approaches of covered stratagem....

JUSTICE IREDELL, dissenting.

This is the first instance wherein the important question involved in this cause has come regularly before the Court....What controversy of a civil nature can be maintained against a State by an individual?...

...

...So much, however, has been said on the Constitution, that it may not be improper to intimate that my present opinion is strongly against any construction of it, which will admit, under any circumstances, a compulsive suit against a State for the recovery of money. I think every word in the Constitution may have its full effect without involving this consequence, and that nothing but express words, or an insurmountable implication (neither of which I consider, can be found in this case) would authorize the deduction of so high a power. This opinion I hold, however, with all the reserve proper for one, which, according to my sentiments in this case, may be deemed in some measure extra-judicial. With regard to the policy of maintaining such suits, that is not for this Court to consider, unless the point in all other respects was very doubtful. Policy might then be argued from with a view to preponderate the judgment. Upon the question before us, I have no doubt. I have therefore nothing to do with the policy. But I confess, if I was at liberty to speak on that subject, my opinion on the policy of the case would also differ from that of the Attorney General. It is, however, a delicate topic....

JUSTICE BLAIR, concurring.

...

JUSTICE WILSON, concurring.

...

To the Constitution of the United States the term SOVEREIGN, is totally unknown. There is but one place where it could have been used with propriety. But, even in that place it would not, perhaps, have comported with the delicacy of those, who ordained and established that Constitution. They might have announced themselves "SOVEREIGN" people of the United States: But serenely conscious of the fact, they avoided the ostentatious declaration....

...[A State] is an artificial person. It has its affairs and its interests: It has its rules: It has its rights: And it has its obligations. It may acquire property distinct from that if its members: It may incur debts to be discharged out of the public flock, not out of the private fortunes of individuals. It may be bound by contracts; and for damages arising from the breach of those contracts.... A State, like a merchant, makes a contract. A dishonest State, like a dishonest merchant, willfully refuses to discharge it: The latter is amenable to a Court of Justice: Upon general principles of right, shall the former when summoned to answer the fair demands of its creditor, be permitted, proteus-like, to assume a new appearance, and to insult him and justice, by declaring I am a SOVEREIGN State? Surely not....

...

But, in my opinion, this doctrine rests not upon the legitimate result of fair and conclusive deduction from the Constitution: It is confirmed, beyond all doubt, by the direct and explicit declaration of the Constitution itself. "The judicial power of the United States shall extend, to controversies between two States."...Can the most consummate degree of professional ingenuity devise a mode by which this "controversy between two States" can be brought before a Court of law; and yet neither of those States be a Defendant? "The judicial power of the United States shall extend to controversies, between a State and citizens of another State." Could the strictest legal language; could even that language, which is peculiarly appropriated to an art, deemed, by a great master, to be one of the most honorable, laudable, and profitable things in our law; could this strict and appropriated language, describe, with more precise accuracy, the cause now depending before the tribunal? Causes, and not parties to causes, are weighed by justice, in her equal scales: On the former solely, her attention is fixed: To the latter, she is, as she is painted, blind....

JUSTICE CUSHING, concurring.

...

CHIEF JUSTICE JAY, concurring.

In determining the sense in which Georgia is a sovereign State, it may be useful to turn our attention to the political situation we were in, prior to the Revolution, and to the political rights which emerged from the Revolution....

The Revolution, or rather the Declaration of Independence, found the people already united for general purposes, and at the same time providing for their more domestic concerns by State conventions, and other temporary arrangements. From the crown of Great Britain, the sovereignty of their country passed to the people of it...."We the people of the United States, do ordain and establish this Constitution." Here we see the people acting as sovereigns of the whole country; and in the language of sovereignty, establishing a Constitution by which it was their will, that the State Governments should be bound, and to which the State Constitutions should be made to conform....

Let us now proceed to enquire whether Georgia has not, by being a party to the national compact, consented to be suable by individual citizens of another State. This enquiry naturally leads our attention, 1st. To the design of the Constitution. 2d. To the letter and express declaration in it.

Prior to the date of the Constitution, the people had not any national tribunal to which they could resort for justice; the distribution of justice was then confined to State judicatories, in whose institution and organization the people of the other States had no participation, and over whom they had not the least control....There was danger that from this source animosities would in time result; and as the transition from animosities to hostilities was frequent in the history of independent States, a common tribunal for the termination of controversies became desirable, from motives both of justice and of policy.

Prior also to that period, the United States had, by taking a place among the nations of the earth, become amenable to the laws of nations; and it was their interest as well as their duty to provide, that those laws should be respected and obeyed; in their national character and capacity, the United States were responsible to foreign nations for the conduct of each State, relative to the laws of nations, and the performance of treaties; and there the inexpediency of referring all such questions to State Courts, and particularly to the Courts of delinquent States became apparent....

These were among the evils against which it was proper for the nation, that is, the people of all the United States, to provide by a national judiciary, to be instituted by the whole nation, and to be responsible to the whole nation.

Let us now turn to the Constitution....

The question now before us renders it necessary to pay particular attention to that part of the 2d section, which extends the judicial power "to controversies between a State and citizens of another State." It is contended, that this ought to be construed to reach none of these controversies, excepting those in which a State may be Plaintiff. The ordinary rules for construction will easily decide whether those words are to be understood in that limited sense.

This extension of power is remedial, because it is to settle controversies. It is therefore, to be construed liberally. It is politic, wise, and good that, not only the controversies, in which a State is Plaintiff, but also those in which a State is Defendant, should be settled; both cases, therefore, are within the reason of the remedy; and ought to be so adjudged, unless the obvious, plain, and literal sense of the words forbid it. If we attend to the words, we find them to be express, positive, free from ambiguity, and without room for such implied expressions....If the Constitution really meant to extend these powers only to those controversies in which a State might be Plaintiff, to the exclusion of those in which citizens had demands against a State, it is inconceivable that it should have attempted to convey that meaning in words, not only so incompetent, but also repugnant to it; if it meant to exclude a certain class of these controversies, why were they not expressly excepted; on the contrary, not even an intimation of such intention appears in any part of the Constitution....

...

For my own part, I am convinced that the sense in which I understand and have explained the words "controversies between States and citizens of another State," is the true sense. The extension of the judiciary power of the United States to such controversies, appears to me to be wise, because it is honest, and because it is useful. It is honest, because it provides for doing justice without respect of persons, and by securing individual citizens as well as States, in their respective rights, performs the promise which every free Government makes to every free citizen, of equal justice and protection. It is useful, because it is honest, because it leaves not even the most obscure and friendless citizen without means of obtaining justice from a neighboring State; because it obviates occasions of quarrels between States on account of the claims of their respective citizens; because it recognizes and strongly rests on this great moral truth, that justice is the same whether due from one man or a million, or from a million to one man; because it teaches and greatly appreciates the value of our free republican national Government, which places all our citizens on an equal footing, and enables each and every of them to obtain justice without any danger of being overborne by the weight and number of their opponents; and, because it brings into action, and enforces this great and glorious principle, that the people are the sovereign of this country, and consequently that fellow citizens and joint sovereigns cannot be degraded by appearing with each other in their own Courts to have their controversies determined. The people have reason to prize and rejoice in such valuable privileges; and they ought not to forget, that nothing but the free course of Constitutional law and Government can ensure the continuance and enjoyment of them....

Note: The Passage of the Eleventh Amendment

The justices' references to popular sovereignty, combined with their reliance on the literal meaning of Article III, Section 2, make a persuasive case. However, it is another question whether this outcome reflected the original understanding of the authority of federal courts over states. During the ratification debates, there were concerns over whether creditors could force the heavily indebted states, against their will, to be defendants in federal courts. Alexander Hamilton attempted to allay these concerns in his essay in *Federalist* 81:

> ...I shall take occasion to mention here a supposition which has excited some alarm upon very mistaken grounds. It has been suggested that an assignment of the public securities of one State to the citizens of another, would enable them to prosecute that State in the federal courts for the amount of those securities; a suggestion which the following considerations prove to be without foundation.
>
> It is inherent in the nature of sovereignty not to be amenable to the suit of an individual *without its consent*. This is the general sense, and the general practice of mankind; and the exemption, as one of the attributes of sovereignty, is now enjoyed by the government of every State in the Union. Unless, therefore, there is a surrender of this immunity in the plan of the convention, it will remain with the States, and the danger intimated must be merely ideal.... The contracts between a nation and individuals are only binding on the conscience of the sovereign, and have no pretensions to a compulsive force. They confer no right of action, independent of the sovereign will. To what purpose would it be to authorize suits against States for the debts they owe? How could recoveries be enforced? It is evident, it could not be done without waging war against the contracting State; and to ascribe to the federal courts, by mere implication, and in destruction of a pre-existing right of the State governments, a power which would involve such a consequence, would be altogether forced and unwarrantable.[51]

Not surprisingly, *Chisholm* did not resolve the nature of our federal system. In fact, it ignited fears that the new national government would attempt to consolidate power at the expense of the states. Some feared it might also put the treasuries of states at risk from lawsuits by out-of-state creditors. The Massachusetts Legislature declared that the decision was "repugnant to the first principles of a federal government." It called on the State's Senators and Representatives to take steps to "remove any clause or article of the Constitution, which can be construed to imply or justify a decision, that, a State is compellable to answer in any suit by an individual or individuals in any Court of the United States." The state of Georgia—the defendant in the lawsuit—expressed itself even more strongly. Its lower house passed a bill declaring that anyone who attempted to enforce the *Chisholm* decision would be

51. *The Federalist: A Collection of Essays, Written in Favour of the New Constitution, as Agreed Upon by the Federal Convention, September 17, 1787, in two volumes* (New York: J. and A. McLean, 1788).

"guilty of felony and shall suffer death, without benefit of clergy, by being hanged."[52]

A day after the decision was announced, a proposal to amend the Constitution was introduced into the House of Representatives. Congress finally proposed a constitutional amendment on March 4, 1794: "The Judicial power of the United States shall not be construed to extend to any suit in law or equity, commenced or prosecuted against one of the United States by Citizens of another State, or by Citizens or Subjects of any Foreign State." It was ratified by the required three-fourths of state legislatures by February 7, 1795, almost exactly two years after the *Chisholm* decision was handed down. It became the Eleventh Amendment to the Constitution—the first amendment after the ratification of the promised Bill of Rights.

The Eleventh Amendment demonstrated that the status of states in the new republic was far from settled. Many states continued to defend their sovereign prerogatives as co-equal centers of governance, despite the efforts of Federalist judges and administration officials to articulate theories of popular sovereignty and national authority. Federalist concerns with securing the property rights of creditors did not prevent the interests of property from taking a backseat to local political interests. With respect to disputes about the proper scope of federal judicial power, Congress and the states arrived at a political solution that everyone considered agreeable. Other disputes would prove more difficult to resolve. Did the Eleventh Amendment make more explicit what the Constitution always meant, or did it alter the meaning of the Constitution? Does the Eleventh Amendment represent a retreat from the purposes and goals of the Constitution? Should the Eleventh Amendment be read literally and strictly, or does it represent an affirmation of the general principle of state sovereign immunity?

The aftermath of *Chisholm v. Georgia* also represented the first time that a U.S. Supreme Court decision was reversed through the amendment process. Given that this was the Court's first important opinion, it is tempting to say that this was not an auspicious beginning. After all, the Eleventh Amendment represented a clear, decisive, and across-the-board rebuke of the Court's understanding of the Constitution. On the other hand, it is noteworthy that opposition to the decision took the form of a constitutional amendment, rather than a denial of the Court's authority to interpret the Constitution. As Hamilton had suggested, enforcing judicial decisions was not going to be easy. Neither state nor federal politicians were eager to see repeated showdowns either. Would states like Georgia carry out their threat to execute anyone attempting to make good on a federal court order to collect a debt against a state? Better to make such lawsuits go away. By changing the Constitution, rather than declaring the Court's opinion to be irrelevant, the opponents of *Chisholm* helped to establish a precedent: Justices had the final say over the meaning of the document.

B. State Authority to Interpret the Constitution

Political tensions increased during the 1790s. Newspapers were filled with scandalous, and often anonymous, gossip and opinion about political leaders. An anti-administration faction led by Thomas Jefferson formed in Congress and was organizing in the states. War with France seemed increasingly likely. With anti-French passions peaking, Federalists in Congress hoped to put an end to the "factions" that they believed were dividing the nation and encouraging enemies of the United States.

The Alien and Sedition Acts of 1798 were passed in this politically explosive environment. The Alien Act expanded presidential power to detain and deport aliens and increased the residency requirements for citizenship. The Sedition Act prohibited speech and writings that brought the government into contempt. Once these measures became law, the Adams administration launched a series of prosecutions that shut down many Jeffersonian newspapers. One congressman was even jailed. Jeffersonians responded with a public campaign against the Acts.

Their most visible and significant protest came in the Virginia and Kentucky Resolutions of 1798. The Virginia Resolutions were secretly drafted by Congressman James Madison and adopted by the Virginia state legislature. The Kentucky Resolutions were secretly drafted by Vice President Thomas Jefferson and adopted by the Kentucky state legislature. Those were the only two state legislatures firmly in Republican control in 1798. Several states responded, particularly in New England, by criticizing Virginia and

52. In Herman Ames, ed., *State Documents on Federal Relations* (Philadelphia: Department of History at the University of Pennsylvania, 1900–1906), 10.

Kentucky for claiming the right to judge the constitutionality of acts of Congress. Congress responded with a report of its own defending the Alien and Sedition Acts. James Madison left the U.S. House of Representatives in order to win a seat in the Virginia legislature, and once there he authored a 1799 report for that body defending and elaborating on the 1798 resolutions.

The Resolutions were somewhat vague about the appropriate remedies for the constitutional violations that they identified. However, the immediate goal was to rally electoral opposition to the Federalists and seek legislative repeal of the measures. The Resolutions were widely circulated in pamphlet form and became important campaign documents for the Jeffersonians in 1800. They remained central constitutional documents throughout the early nineteenth century.

General agreement exists that these texts assert that states have some authority to interpret what the Constitution means. Americans before the Civil War would dispute, however, what actions states could take after concluding that the federal government had passed an unconstitutional law. What is the source of this state authority to interpret the Constitution? What actions may states take when they conclude the federal government has passed an unconstitutional law? Do the Virginia and Kentucky Resolutions take the same position on this issue? Thirty years later, Madison insisted that nothing in the Virginia and Kentucky Resolutions justified *nullification*—the state power to declare a federal law null and void. Do you believe that is the correct interpretation of what he wrote in 1798 and 1799? Others argued that the Resolutions sowed the seeds for secession.

Virginia and Kentucky Resolutions of 1798[53]

Resolutions of the Virginia Legislature (1798)

1. Resolved, That the General Assembly of Virginia doth unequivocally express a firm resolution to maintain and defend the Constitution of the United States, and the Constitution of this State, against every aggression, either foreign or domestic, and that it will support the government of the United States in all measures warranted by the former.

2. That this Assembly most solemnly declares a warm attachment to the union of the States, to maintain which, it pledges all its powers; and that for this end it is its duty to watch over and oppose every infraction of those principles, which constitute the only basis of that union, because a faithful observance of them can alone secure its existence, and the public happiness.

3. That this Assembly doth explicitly and peremptorily declare that it views the powers of the Federal Government as resulting from the compact, to which the States are parties, as limited by the plain sense and intention of the instrument constituting that compact; as no further valid than they are authorized by the grants enumerated in that compact, and that in case of a deliberate, palpable, and dangerous exercise of other powers not granted by the said compact, the States, who are the parties thereto, have the right, and are in duty bound, to interpose for arresting the progress of the evil, and for maintaining within their respective limits, the authorities, rights, and liberties appertaining to them.

4. That the General Assembly doth also express its deep regret that a spirit has in sundry instances been manifested by the Federal Government, to enlarge its powers by forced constructions of the constitutional charter which defines them; and that indications have appeared of a design to expound certain general phrases (which, having been copied from the very limited grant of powers in the former articles of confederation, were the less liable to be misconstrued), so as to destroy the meaning and effect of the particular enumeration, which necessarily explains and limits the general phrases, and so as to consolidate the States by degrees into one sovereignty, the obvious tendency and inevitable result of which would be to transform the present republican system of the United States into an absolute, or at best, a mixed monarchy.

5. That the General Assembly doth particularly protest against the palpable and alarming infractions of the Constitution, in the two late cases of the "alien and sedition acts," . . . [which] exercises in like manner a power not delegated by the Constitution, but on the contrary expressly and positively forbidden by one of the amendments thereto; a power which more than any other ought to produce universal alarm, because it is leveled against that right of freely examining public characters and measures, and of free communication among the people thereon, which has ever been justly deemed the only effectual guardian of every other right.

53. Excerpt taken from Herman V. Ames, ed., *State Documents on Federal Relations* (Philadelphia: Department of History at the University of Pennsylvania, 1900–1906).

6. That this State having by its convention which ratified the federal Constitution, expressly declared, "that among other essential rights, the liberty of conscience and of the press cannot be cancelled, abridged, restrained, or modified by any authority of the United States," and from its extreme anxiety to guard these rights from every possible attack of sophistry or ambition, having with other States recommended an amendment for that purpose, which amendment was in due time annexed to the Constitution, it would mark a reproachful inconsistency and criminal degeneracy, if an indifference were now shown to the most palpable violation of one of the rights thus declared and secured, and to the establishment of a precedent which may be fatal to the other.

7. That the good people of this commonwealth having ever felt, and continuing to feel the most sincere affection to their brethren of the other States, the truest anxiety for establishing and perpetuating the union of all, and the most scrupulous fidelity to that Constitution which is the pledge of mutual friendship, and the instrument of mutual happiness, the General Assembly doth solemnly appeal to the like dispositions of the other States, in confidence that they will concur with this commonwealth in declaring, as it does hereby declare, that the acts aforesaid are unconstitutional, and that the necessary and proper measure will be taken by each, for co-operating with this State in maintaining unimpaired the authorities, rights, and liberties reserved to the States respectively, or to the people.

...

Resolutions of the Kentucky Legislature (1798)

1. Resolved, That the several states composing the United States of America, are not united on the principle of unlimited submission to their general government; but that by compact, under the style and title of a Constitution for the United States, and of amendments thereto, they constituted a general government for special purposes, delegated to that government certain definite powers, reserving, each state to itself the residuary mass of right to their own self-government; and that whensoever the general government assumes undelegated powers, its acts are unauthoritative, void, and of no force: That to this compact each state acceded as a state, and is an integral party, its co-states forming as to itself, the other party: That the government created by this compact was not made the exclusive or final judge of the extent of the powers delegated to itself; since that would have made its discretion, and not the Constitution, the measure of its powers; but that, as in all other cases of compact among parties having no common judge, each party has an equal right to judge for itself, as well of infractions, as of the mode and measure of redress.

...

3. Resolved, That it is true as a general principle, and is also expressly declared by one of the amendments to the Constitution, that "the powers not delegated to the United States by the Constitution, nor prohibited by it to the states, are reserved to the states respectively, or to the people;" and that no power over the freedom of religion, freedom of speech, or freedom of the press, being delegated to the United States by the Constitution, nor prohibited by it to the states, all lawful powers respecting the same did of right remain, and were reserved to the states, or to the people; that thus was manifested their determination to retain to themselves the right of judging how far the licentiousness of speech and of the press may be abridged without lessening their useful freedom, and how far those abuses which cannot be separated from their use, should be tolerated rather than the use be destroyed;...and that in addition to this general principle and express declaration, another and more special provision has been made by one of the amendments to the Constitution, which expressly declares, that "Congress shall make no law respecting an establishment of religion, or prohibiting the free exercise thereof, or abridging the freedom of speech, or of the press,"...therefore the act of the Congress of the United States, passed on the 14th day of July, 1798, entitled, "an act in addition to the act for the punishment of certain crimes against the United States," which does abridge the freedom of the press, is not law, but is altogether void and of no effect.

...

9. Resolved, lastly, That the Governor of this commonwealth be, and is hereby authorized and requested to communicate the preceding resolutions to the legislatures of the several states, to assure them that this commonwealth considers union for specified national purposes, and particularly for those specified in their late federal compact, to be friendly to the peace, happiness, and prosperity of all the states: that, faithful to that compact, according to the plain intent

and meaning in which it was understood and acceded to by the several parties, it is sincerely anxious for its preservation: that it does also believe, that to take from the states all the powers of self-government, and transfer them to a general and consolidated government, without regard to the special obligations and reservations solemnly agreed to in that compact, is not for the peace, happiness or prosperity of these states: and that therefore, this commonwealth is determined, as it doubts not its co-states are, tamely to submit to undelegated and consequently unlimited powers in no man or body of men on earth:... that these and successive acts of the same character, unless arrested on the threshold, may tend to drive these states into revolution and blood, and will furnish new calumnies against republican governments, and new pretexts for those who wish it to be believed, that man cannot be governed but by a rod of iron:... In questions of power, then, let no more be heard of confidence in man, but bind him down from mischief, by the chains of the Constitution. That this commonwealth does, therefore, call on its co-states for an expression of their sentiments on the acts concerning aliens, and for the punishment of certain crimes herein before specified, plainly declaring whether these acts are or are not authorized by the Federal compact. And it doubts not that their sense will be so announced, as to prove their attachment unaltered to limited government, whether general or particular, and that the rights and liberties of their co-states, will be exposed to no dangers by remaining embarked on a common bottom with their own: That they will concur with this commonwealth in considering the said acts as so palpably against the Constitution, as to amount to an undisguised declaration, that the compact is not meant to be the measure of the powers of the general government, but that it will proceed in the exercise over these states of all powers whatsoever: That they will view this as seizing the rights of the states, and consolidating them in the hands of the general government with a power assumed to bind the states, (not merely in cases made federal,) but in all cases whatsoever, by laws made, not with their consent, but by others against their consent: That this would be to surrender the form of government we have chosen, and to live under one deriving its powers from its own will, and not from our authority; and that the co-states, recurring to their natural right in cases not made federal, will concur in declaring these acts void and of no force and will each unite with this commonwealth, in requesting their repeal at the next session of Congress.

Resolution of the State of Rhode Island and Providence Plantations to Virginia (February, 1799)

...

1. *Resolved*, That, in the opinion of this legislature, the second section of the third article of the Constitution of the United States, in these words, to wit,—"The judicial power shall extend to all cases arising under the laws of the United States,"—vests in the Federal Courts, exclusively, and in the Supreme Court of the United States, ultimately, the authority of deciding on the constitutionality of any act or law of the Congress of the United States.

2. *Resolved*, That for any state legislature to assume that authority would be —

1st. Blending together legislative and judicial powers;

2d. Hazarding an interruption of the peace of the states by civil discord, in case of a diversity of opinions among the state legislatures; each state having, in that case, no resort, for vindicating its own opinions, but the strength of its own arm;

3d. Submitting most important questions of law to less competent tribunals; and,

4th. An infraction of the Constitution of the United States expressed in plain terms.

3. *Resolved*, That, although, for the above reasons, this legislature, in their public capacity, do not feel themselves authorized to consider and decide on the constitutionality of the Sedition and Alien laws, (so called,) yet they are called upon, by the exigency of this occasion, to declare that, in their private opinions, these laws are within the powers delegated to Congress, and pro-motive of the welfare of the United States.

V. Separation of Powers

MAJOR DEVELOPMENTS

- Creation of the executive branch of the national government
- First debates over the power of the president to act independently in foreign and domestic affairs
- First assertions of executive privilege

Americans during the early national period converted the constitutional outline into a working government. This challenge was particularly difficult when determining the relationship between the legislative and executive branches of the government. Article II of the Constitution states that the "executive power" is vested in the president. It does not say what the executive power is. On one interpretation, the vesting clause simply authorizes the president to implement whatever laws the Congress passes. If Congress passes a law which declares that a postmaster shall be appointed in every district, the president may hire the postmaster. On another interpretation, the vesting clause is one source of so-called "inherent" powers of the president. These powers are said to be implicit in the Constitution, bound up with and implied by the explicit terms of the Constitution. As part of the Article II powers of the president, they exist independent of any statute. The president does not need authorization from Congress to exercise them, and Congress cannot attempt to deny or restrict those powers by statute. The president may issue executive orders to the members of the executive branch, instructing them on administration policy and on how to perform their duties.

Sources of Presidential Power. Section 3 of Article II requires that the president "shall take Care that the Laws be faithfully executed." This "take care" clause imposes some responsibility on the president to insure that the laws are administered and enforced. Proponents of presidential power have read the take care clause to have a number of particular implications. It might suggest that presidents must exercise independent judgment on what the meaning of the law is in order to "faithfully" execute it. It might suggest that presidents must have broad control over the executive branch and its officers, to insure that the law is being appropriately followed.

Other provisions of Article II have been the source of further implied powers for the president as well. Section 2 of Article II indicates that the president "shall be Commander in Chief of the Army and Navy of the United States." The president's role as commander in chief has been a frequent reference point for claims of "presidential war powers"—or implied powers over foreign policy generally. This is so especially when combined with other provisions, such as the president's role in receiving diplomats or negotiating treaties. Article II also specifies the presidential oath of office, which includes the promise to "preserve, protect and defend the Constitution of the United States." This might be thought to carry with it implicit powers needed to fulfill that responsibility in a crisis.

These constitutional provisions of Article II could be interpreted either broadly or narrowly, just like the provisions of Article I. A broad interpretation of the provisions of Article II tended to favor implied presidential powers. A narrow interpretation tended to restrict presidential power. The debate over separation of powers was not usually framed as a debate between the strict and broad construction of constitutional powers, but the effects were similar. At least initially, the participants were similar as well. Alexander Hamilton advocated a broad interpretation of presidential powers for the Federalists. Some of the Jeffersonians were more critical.

The Politics of Presidential Power. Constitutional ambiguities, institutional affiliations, and partisan politics all influenced early debates over the separation of powers. Americans quickly discovered that the constitutional text did not provide as detailed instructions for constructing the executive branch of the government as for constructing the national legislature. Under what conditions, for example, could a president remove a cabinet officer? No explicit constitutional text guided the members of the first Congress here.

When debating the scope of independent presidential power, presidents unsurprisingly tended to take a broader view of executive authority than did many members of Congress. President Washington did not wait for Congress before declaring American neutrality in the war between France and England. The framers did not anticipate, however, how partisan considerations would influence constitutional debates over the separation of powers. *Federalist* 51, excerpted in Chapter 3, predicted that elected officials would consistently side with their home institutions when conflict occurred between the branches of the national government. Presidents would seek to augment executive power. Senators would promote the powers of the Senate.

Partisanship added a different consideration. Federalist members of the House of Representatives during the Jay Treaty, for example, supported the prerogatives of the Federalist Washington administration rather than the powers of the House of Representatives to derail the treaty. Once the questions of institutional authority and power were tangled up in questions of substantive public policy and partisan loyalties, constitutional deliberations and outcomes were necessarily affected.

The Early Republic. Many of the most basic issues of separation of powers arose during the early republic. Some were rather decisively resolved, such as the question of what to call to the president in official documents. (A simple "President of the United States" was deemed adequate.) So was whether the president should treat the Senate like an executive council and consult with it in person on such matters as treaty negotiations. (After a brief, unhappy experiment, President Washington vowed not to return to the Senate chamber—ratification of completed treaties would be sufficient.) Others were less firmly settled. Thomas Jefferson, for example, decided to deliver the State of the Union address to Congress in writing rather than in person (a practice that endured for a century).

The early republic saw brushes with partisan turmoil. These led a Republican Congress to test the limits of the impeachment power (aimed at Federalist judges) and a Federalist president to test the limits of executive privilege (aimed at a Republican House of Representatives). Congress and the president debated how much unilateral power the president had over foreign policy, as well as the scope of executive privilege that might keep government documents secret from Congress. The early republic also struggled with the task of setting up a new government and making it function well. That entailed grappling with policy crises in both the foreign and domestic arenas. Legislators and executive branch officials debated over who possessed the power to remove lower level executive branch officers, how the president should use the veto power, and how much oversight and control the president could and should exercise over the executive branch.

A. General Principles

Note: The Power to Act beyond the Constitution

One purpose of constitutional government is to subject politics to rules, to limit the scope of the discretion of government officials. The Constitution seeks to define ahead of time what powers the government as a whole, and specific officers within it, possess and how those powers can be used. At the same time, it rules out some acts as constitutionally impermissible, or permissible only under certain specified conditions. Constitutional politics is a politics confined within law. As Thomas Paine announced during the American Revolution, "in absolute governments the King is law," but "in America THE LAW IS KING."[54]

Politics is not so simple, however. Even those who believe in constitutional government in normal circumstances have often been forced to concede that there may be extraordinary circumstances when the rules have to be broken. The ideas of John Locke, the English philosopher of limited government, have permeated American constitutional thought since before the founding. Locke argued that such exceptions have to be built into any adequate political theory. He called this the prerogative power, which he lodged in executive. "Many things there are, which the Law can by no means provide for, and those must necessarily be left to the discretion of him, that has the Executive Power in his hands, to be ordered by him, as the public good and advantage shall require." The executive must sometimes be able to act "without the prescription of the Law, and sometimes even against it."[55] Some constitutional systems have made explicit room for governing in a state of emergency. The ancient Roman Republican allowed for a creation of a "dictator," who could wield absolute power during an emergency but for only six months. Some modern political systems have made similar provision for dealing with emergencies. Most famously, Article 48 of the constitution of Weimar Germany between the First and Second World Wars authorized the president to suspend various liberties and employ the military if necessary to restore "public safety and order."[56]

The U.S. Constitution does not make explicit provision for its own suspension during times of emergency or in circumstances where its requirements no longer seem to serve the public good.[57] But the concept was well understood by the founders. *The Federalist* pointed out, "It is in

54. Thomas Paine, *Common Sense* (New York: Penguin, 1976), 98.

55. John Locke, "The Second Treatise of Government," in *Two Treatises of Government*, ed. Peter Laslett (New York: Cambridge University Press, 1988), § 159, 160.

56. For background, see Clinton Rossiter, *Constitutional Dictatorship* (New Brunswick, NJ: Transaction, 2002); Brian Loveman, *The Constitution of Tyranny* (Pittsburgh: University of Pittsburgh Press, 1993).

57. The Constitution does make reference to a power to suspend the writ of habeas corpus (Art. I, Section 9). Habeas corpus allows judges to question the circumstances of and justification for holding a prisoner.

vain to oppose constitutional barriers to the impulse of self-preservation," but also warned that, "It is worse than vain; because it plants in the Constitution itself necessary usurpations of power, every precedent of which is a germ of unnecessary and multiplied repetitions."[58]

There have been two basic models for addressing this problem within American constitutionalism.[59] The first model is associated most closely with Thomas Jefferson. His strict construction of the Constitution implied that government officials should be acutely aware of the proper limits of their power. Yet the Constitution may not provide for all acts in the public good. The best response in such situations would be to seek a constitutional amendment. Jefferson contemplated this course of action as president, faced with his own doubts about the constitutionality of the Louisiana Purchase. James Madison and James Monroe advocated the same path in regard to a federal power to fund internal improvements. As Jefferson explained to one of his political lieutenants before the Louisiana Purchase:

> When an instrument admits two constructions, the one safe, the other dangerous, the one precise, the other indefinite, I prefer that which is safe & precise. I had rather risk an enlargement of powers from the nation [by constitutional amendment], where it is found necessary, than to assume it by construction that would make our powers boundless. Our peculiar security is in possession of a written Constitution. Let us not make it a blank paper by construction.[60]

But Jefferson also recognized that constitutional amendments are not always feasible. In such circumstances, the president must maintain a strict construction of the Constitution but, if necessary, frankly act "beyond the constitution." The president can then only "rely on the nation to sanction an act done for its great good, without its previous authority."[61] As he told another correspondent, in reference to a different event:

> A strict observance of the written laws is doubtless one of the high duties of a good citizen, but it is not the highest. The laws of necessity, of self-preservation, of saving our country when in danger, are of higher obligation. To lose our country by a scrupulous adherence to written law, would be to lose the law itself, with life, liberty, property and all those who are enjoying them with us; thus absurdly sacrificing the ends to the means. . . . The officer who is called to act on this superior ground, does indeed risk himself on the justice of the controlling powers of the constitution, and his station makes it is his duty to incur that risk. But those controlling powers, and his fellow citizens generally, are bound to judge according to the circumstances under which he acted.[62]

In other words, presidents sometimes have an obligation to violate the Constitution in the name of the greater good. To maintain a strict construction of the Constitution in normal times, they must leave open the possibility of a power outside the Constitution in extraordinary times. They will then "throw themselves on their country" and seek absolution from their constitutional sins.[63] There are echoes of this reasoning in Abraham Lincoln's first annual message to Congress. There he sought to justify the actions that he had taken to deal with secession:

> These measures, whether strictly legal or not, were ventured upon under what appeared to be a popular demand and a public necessity, trusting then, as now, that Congress would readily ratify them. . . . To state the question more directly, are all the laws, but one, to go unexecuted, and the government should be overthrown, when it was believed that disregarding the single law, would tend to preserve it?"[64]

---

58. James Madison, "No. 41," in Alexander Hamilton, James Madison, and John Jay, *The Federalist Papers*, ed. Clinton Rossiter (New York: Mentor, 1961), 257.

59. For background, see Clement Fatovic, "Constitutionalism and Presidential Prerogative: Jeffersonian and Hamiltonian Perspectives," *American Journal of Political Science* 48 (2004): 429. Also useful are George Thomas, "As Far as Republican Principles Will Admit: Presidential Prerogative and Constitutional Government," *Presidential Studies Quarterly* 30 (2000): 534; Jeremy D. Bailey, *Thomas Jefferson and Executive Power* (New York: Cambridge University Press, 2007); Harvey C. Mansfield, Jr., *Taming the Prince* (Baltimore: Johns Hopkins University Press, 1993).

60. Thomas Jefferson, "To Wilson C. Nicholas, September 7, 1803," in *The Writings of Thomas Jefferson*, ed. Paul Leicester Ford, vol. 8 (New York: G. P. Putnam's Sons, 1897), 247.

61. Jefferson, "To John Dickinson, August 9, 1803," in *Writings*, vol. 8, 262.

62. Jefferson, "To John B. Colvin, September 20, 1810," in *Writings*, vol. 9, 280, 281.

63. Jefferson, "To John C. Breckenridge, August 12, 1803," in *Writings*, vol. 8, 244.

64. Abraham Lincoln, "Message to Congress in Special Session, July 4, 1861," in *A Compilation of the Messages and Papers of the Presidents*, ed. James D. Richardson, vol. 7 (New York: Bureau of National Literature, 1897), 3225, 3226.

The other model for addressing this problem is most closely associated with Alexander Hamilton. Hamilton, of course, was no friend to the strict constructionists. He was quite comfortable with broad and flexible interpretations of government power. He thus did not have to face the intellectual difficulty that confronted the Jeffersonians as they attempted to govern. Moreover, Hamilton was acutely aware of the need to meet crises as and when they develop. He saw them as routine features of human society, the norm rather than the exception. It was the day-to-day challenge of government to deal with the unexpected and restore order in a chaotic world. This combination of broad constructionism and crisis government implied a quite different understanding of the prerogative power. From his contributions to the *Federalist Papers* to his Pacificus essays, Hamilton defended the need for "energy" in the executive branch. The executive need not ever turn to extraconstitutional powers, because the prerogative power was built into the Hamiltonian Constitution. There was no need for special justifications or absolutions. The president could simply *act*.

B. Appointment and Removal Powers

The first important constitutional debate in American history was over whether the President could remove a cabinet official, such as the Secretary of State, without Senate approval. The Constitution plainly declares that the Senate must approve cabinet officials. Article II, Section 2, declares that the President "shall nominate, and by and with the Advice and Consent of the Senate, shall appoint Ambassadors, other public Ministers and Consuls, Judges of the Supreme Court, and all other Officers of the United States." The only provision relating to the removal of "Officers of the United States" is the impeachment power, which is entrusted Congress in the case of high crimes and misdemeanors. The framers did not provide for more ordinary removals. The omission has generated controversy ever since.

James Madison initiated the first debate over the removal power when he drafted the bills establishing what became the State, Treasury, and War Departments. His legislative proposal declared that these three departments should each be headed by a Secretary "who shall be appointed by the President, by and with the advice of the Senate; and to be removable by the President." Some argued that this language in the statute did not add to or change the powers that the president already had. They insisted that a unilateral presidential removal power was implicit in the presidential office. Other supporters of the provision contended that Congress had discretionary authority when legislatively creating an office to specify the procedure by which an officeholder might be removed. On this reading, the president could remove lower level executive officers if and only if Congress empowered him to do so through statute.

Some opponents of the provision argued that impeachment was the *only* constitutional option for removing officials. More commonly, opponents reasoned that executive officers could be removed only by the bodies that had appointed them. Given the constitutional requirement that the Senate approve the cabinet official, this meant that both the president and the Senate must concur to remove an official. The "executive power" of appointment was shared by the president and Senate, and by implication the executive power of removal was also shared.

A congressional majority supported Madison's proposal, but the significance of that decision was unclear. Even representatives who supported unilateral presidential removal power did not agree why. Were they delegating that power or merely recognizing that the Constitution authorized it? As you read the debates, consider these questions. Did the congressional inclusion of a unilateral presidential removal power in the law creating the first cabinet officers have any constitutional significance as a precedent that might bind future constitutional decision makers? Could Congress have adopted a different procedure for removing executive officers? Was the removal power a constitutional oversight, or was there an implicit answer in the text of the Constitution?

House Debate on Removal of Executive Officers (1789)[65]

Mr. James MADISON (Republican, Virginia)

I look upon every constitutional question, whatever its nature may be, as of great importance. I look upon the present to be doubly so, because its nature is of the highest moment to the well-being of the Government. I

65. Excerpt taken from *Annals of Congress*, 1st Cong., 1st sess. (May 19; June 17, 1789), 393–395, 521–525.

have listened with attention to the objections which have been stated, and to the replies that have been made, and I think the investigation of the meaning of the constitution has supported the doctrine I brought forward. If you consult the expediency, it will be greatly against the doctrine advanced by gentlemen on the other side of the question.... It has been said, we may guard against the inconveniency of that construction, by limiting the duration of the office to a term of years; but, during that term, there is no way of getting rid of a bad officer but by impeachment. During the time this is depending, the person may continue to commit those crimes for which he is impeached, because if his construction of the constitution is right, the President can have no more power to suspend than he has to remove.

...

It is said, that it comports with the nature of things, that those who appoint should have the power of removal; but I cannot conceive that this sentiment is warranted by the constitution; I believe it would be found very inconvenient in practice. It is one of the most prominent features of the constitution, a principle that pervades the whole system, that there should be the highest degree of responsibility in all the executive officers thereof; any thing, therefore, which tends to lessen this responsibility, is contrary to its spirit and intention, and, unless it is saddled upon us expressly by the letter of that work, I shall oppose the admission of it into any act of the Legislature. Now, if the heads of the executive departments are subjected to removal by the President alone, we have in him security for the good behavior of the officer. If he does not conform to the judgment of the President in doing the executive duties of his office, he can be displaced. This makes him responsible to the great executive power, and makes the President responsible to the public for the conduct of the person he has nominated and appointed to aid him in the administration of his department. But if the President shall join in a collusion with the officer, and continue the bad man in office, the case of impeachment will reach the culprit, and drag him forth to punishment. But if you take the other construction, and say he shall not be displaced by and with the advice and consent of the Senate, the President is no longer answerable for the conduct of the officer; all will depend on the Senate. You here destroy a real responsibility without obtaining even the shadow; for no gentleman will pretend to say the responsibility of the Senate can be of such a nature as to afford substantial security. But why, it may be asked, was the Senate joined with the President in appointment to office, if they have responsibility? I answer, merely for the sake of advising, being supposed, from their nature, better acquainted with the characters of the candidates than an individual; yet even here the President is held to the responsibility he nominates, and, with their consent, appoints. No person can be forced upon him as an assistant by any other branch of the Government.

...

Mr. Elbridge GERRY (Republican, Massachusetts)

I wish, sir, to consider this question so far, as to ascertain whether it is, or is not, unconstitutional. I have listened with attention to the arguments which have been urged on both sides; and it does appear to me, that the clause [the statutory provision specifying presidential removal] is as inconsistent with the constitution as any set of words which could possibly be inserted in the bill.

...The gentlemen will agree, that this House has not the power of removal; they will also agree that it does not vest in the Judiciary; then it must vest in the President, or the President by and with the advice and consent of the Senate; in either of these cases, the clause is altogether useless and nugatory. It is useless if the power vests in the President; because, when the question comes before him, he will decide upon the provision made in the constitution, and not on what is contained in this clause. If the power vests in the President and Senate, the Senate will not consent to pass the bill with this clause in it; therefore the attempt is nugatory. But if the Senate will assent to the exercise of the power of removal by the President alone, whenever he thinks proper to use it so, then in that case the clause is, as I said before, both useless and nugatory.

...The gentlemen in favor of this clause have not shown that, if the construction that the power vests in the President and Senate is admitted, it will be an improper construction. I call on gentlemen to point out the impropriety, if they discover any. To me, it appears to preserve the unity of the several clauses of the constitution; while their construction produces a clashing of powers, and renders of none effect some powers the Senate by express grants possess. What becomes of their power of appointing, when the President can remove at discretion?...

It is said, that the President shall be subject to an impeachment for dismissing a good man. This in my mind involves an absurdity. How can the House impeach the President for doing an act which the Legislature has submitted to his discretion?

But what consequence may result from giving the President an absolute control over all officers? Among the rest, I presume he is to have an unlimited control over the officers of the Treasury. I think if this is the case, you may as well give him at once the appropriation of the revenue; for of what use is it to make laws on this head, when the President, by looking at the officer, can make it his interest to break him? We may expect to see institutions arising under the control of the revenue, and not of the law.[66]

. . .

But if we give the President the power to remove, (though I contend if the constitution has not given it him, there is no power on earth that can except the people, by an alteration of the constitution, though I will suppose it for argument's sake,) you virtually give him a considerable power over the appointment, independent of the Senate; for if the Senate should reject his first nomination, which will probably be his favorite, he must continue to nominate until the Senate concur; then immediately after the recess of the Senate, he may remove the officer, and introduce his own creature, as he has this power expressly by the constitution. The influence created by this circumstance, would prevent his removal from an office which he held by a temporary appointment from his patron.

This has been supposed by some gentlemen to be an omitted case, and that Congress have the power of supplying the defect. Let gentlemen consider the ground on which they tread. If it is an omitted case, an attempt in the Legislature to supply the defect, will be in fact an attempt to amend the constitution. But this can only be done in the way pointed out by the fifth article of that instrument, and an attempt to amend it in any other way may be a high crime or misdemeanor, or perhaps something worse. . . .

. . .

The system, it cannot be denied, is in many parts obscure; if Congress are to explain and declare what it shall be, they certainly will have it in their power to make it what they please. It has been a strong objection to the constitution, that it was remarkably obscure; nay, some have gone so far as to assert that it was studiously obscure, that it might be applied to every purpose by Congress. By this very act the House are assuming a power to alter the constitution. The people of America can never be safe, if Congress have a right to exercise the power of giving constructions to the constitution different from the original instrument. Such a power would render the most important clause in the constitution nugatory, and one without which, I will be bold to say, this system of Government would never have been ratified. If the people were to find that Congress meant to alter it in this way, they would revolt at the idea; it would be repugnant to the principles of the revolution, and to the feelings of every freeman in the United States.

It is said, that the power to advise the President in appointment officers, is an exception to a general rule. To what general rule? That the President, being an executive officer, has the right of appointment. From whence is this general rule drawn? Not from the constitution, nor from custom, because the State Governments are generally against it. . . .

It is said to be the duty of the President to see the laws faithfully executed, and he could not discharge this trust without the power of removal. I ask the gentleman, if the power of suspension, which we are willing to give, is not sufficient for that purpose? In case the Senate should not be sitting, the officer could be suspended, and at their next session the causes which require his removal might be inquired into.

. . .

The dangers which lie against investing this power jointly in the Senate and President have been pointed out; but I think them more than counterbalanced by the dangers arising from investing it in the President alone. . . . It is said, that if the Senate should have this power, the Government would contain a two-headed monster; but it appears to me, that if it consists in blending the power of making treaties and appointing officers, as executive powers, with their legislative powers, the Senate is already a two-headed monster; if it is a two-headed monster, let us preserve it as a consistent one; for surely it will be a very inconsistent monster, while it has the power of appointment, if you deprive it of the power of removing. It was said, that the judges could not have the power of deciding on this subject, because the constitution is silent; but I ask, if the judges are not *ex officio* judges of the law; and whether they would not be bound to declare the law a nullity, if this clause is continued in it and is inconsistent with the constitution? There is a clause in this system of government that makes it their duty. I allude to that which

66. In this connection, consider the debate over Jackson's removal of the deposits in Chapter Five of this volume.

authorizes the President to obtain the opinions of the heads of departments in writing; so the President and Senate may require the opinion of the judges respecting this power, if they have any doubts concerning it.

...

C. Executive Privilege

Executive privilege is the claim that certain documents and information can be kept confidential and do not normally have to be revealed to the judicial or legislative branch. Executive privilege might be used to explain why documents or conversations should not be revealed to informal requests for information. Executive privilege might also be invoked to refuse to comply with a formal subpoena for documents or testimony.

There is no explicit provision for executive privilege in the Constitution. The privilege is argued to be an implied power of the executive, rooted in provisions such as the vesting clause and in structural necessity of the smooth operation of the executive branch and the separation of powers. The very concept of executive privilege has been controversial, though it has long been recognized by various government officials, including judges. The proper scope and application of executive privilege have been even more controversial than its existence. How far does the privilege extend, and under what circumstances might it be asserted? When might it be overridden?

The first substantial debate over executive privilege occurred during the Washington administration. It focused on a claim of executive privilege against Congress, and involved documents from international negotiations that the House of Representatives wanted to inform its own policy-making process. But the broader context of both the House's demands and the administration's refusal to release its internal records was a partisan dispute and a controversial trade agreement. In refusing to release documents from American negotiations with Great Britain, President Washington emphasized the value of "secrecy" to diplomatic exchanges and the irrelevance of such communications to any decisions that Congress might need to make. In response, Representative James Madison emphasized the need for Congress to make its own assessment of the evidence supporting a policy, while respecting the sensitive nature of diplomatic affairs. In the end, both Congress and the president made their constitutional points, but they moved forward without full agreement on who was right.

In 1795, President Washington submitted the Jay Treaty for ratification. The treaty negotiated with Great Britain by Chief Justice John Jay resolved several outstanding issues from the Revolution, including terms of trade. The Federalist majority in the Senate pushed the treaty through, despite strong objections from the Republican minority. In 1796, the president sent a message to the House and Senate promulgating the signed and ratified treaty, with the expectation that Congress would appropriate the necessary funds to implement the treaty. Instead, Representative Edward Livingston introduced a resolution requesting that the president provide the House with all documents and communications relating to the treaty.

Unlike the Senate, the House had a Republican majority. This resolution set off a prolonged debate. Did the House have discretion in implementing the treaty? Did it have a constitutionally valid reason to request the documents from the executive? And did the president have the right to withhold executive documents from the House of Representatives? The Republicans raised a variety of constitutional and policy objections to the treaty and the process by which it had been negotiated and ratified, but there was no clear alternative to implementing it. The Republican majority in the House resolved to request the materials from the White House. When the president refused to supply them, the House reaffirmed its initial position, but also passed the bill appropriating funds to implement the Jay Treaty.

As you read the exchange between Washington and Madison, you will note a disagreement not only about what the Constitution means, but also about how to interpret the Constitution. Both Washington and Madison appeal to the original meaning of the Constitution, but they differ on how it should be assessed. What is the basis of their disagreement? What other forms of constitutional argument do you see in these readings? Does the claim of executive privilege have a constitutional basis, or is the argument for the privilege simply a prudential one?

House Debate on the Jay Treaty (1796)[67]

Mr. Albert GALLATIN (Republican, Pennsylvania)

...[T]he House had a *right* to ask for the papers proposed to be called for, because their co-operation and

67. Excerpt taken from *Annals of Congress*, 4th Cong., 1st sess. (March 9, 1796), 464–474.

sanction was necessary to carry the Treaty into full effect, to render it a binding instrument, and to make it, properly speaking, a law of the land; because they had a full discretion either to give or to refuse that co-operation; because they must be guided, in the exercise of that discretion, by the merits and expediency of the Treaty itself, and therefore had a *right* to ask for every information which could assist them in deciding that question.

. . . [Mr. Gallatin] would say what he conceived constituted the unconstitutionality of a Treaty. A Treaty is unconstitutional if it provides for doing such things, the doing of which is forbidden by the Constitution; but if a Treaty embraces objects within the sphere of the general powers delegated to the Federal Government, but which have been exclusively and specially granted to a particular branch of Government, say to the Legislative department, such a Treaty, though not unconstitutional, does not become the law of the land until it has obtained the sanction of that branch. In this case, and to this end, the Legislature have a right to demand the documents relative to the negotiation of the Treaty, because that Treaty operates on objects specially delegated to the Legislature. . . .

. . .

George Washington, Response to the House on the Jay Treaty (1796)[68]

Gentlemen of the House of Representatives:

. . .

I trust that no part of my conduct has ever indicated a disposition to withhold any information which the Constitution has enjoined upon the President, as a duty, to give, or which could be required of him by either House of Congress as a right; and, with truth, I affirm, that it has been, as it will continue to be, while I have the honor to preside in the Government, my constant endeavor to harmonize with the other branches thereof, so far as the trust delegated to me by the people of the United States, and my senses of the obligation it imposes, to "preserve, protect, and defend the Constitution," will permit.

The nature of foreign negotiations requires caution; and their success must often depend on secrecy; and even, when brought to a conclusion, a full disclosure of all the measures, demands, or eventual concessions which may have been proposed or contemplated would be extremely impolitic: for this might have a pernicious influence on future negotiations; or produce immediate inconveniences, perhaps danger and mischief, in relation to other Powers. The necessity of such caution and secrecy was one cogent reason for vesting the power of making Treaties in the President with the advice and consent of the Senate; the principle on which the body was formed confining it to a small number of members. To admit, then, a right in the House of Representatives to demand, and to have, as a matter of course, all the papers respecting a negotiation with a foreign Power, would be to establish a dangerous precedent.

. . .

The course which the debate has taken on the resolution of the House, leads to some observations on the mode of making Treaties under the Constitution of the United States.

Having been a member of the General Convention, and knowing the principles on which the Constitution was formed, I have ever entertained but one opinion on this subject. . . . [E]very Treaty so made, and promulgated, thenceforward becomes the law of the land. It is thus that the Treaty-making power has been understood by foreign nations, and in all the Treaties made with them, *we* have declared, and *they* have believed, that when ratified by the President, with the advice and consent of the Senate, they become obligatory. In this construction of the Constitution every House of Representatives has heretofore acquiesced, and until the present time not a doubt or suspicion has appeared to my knowledge that this construction was not the true one. Nay, they have more than acquiesced; for until now, without controverting the obligation of such Treaties, they have made all the requisite provisions for carrying them into effect.

. . .

If other proofs than these, and the plain letter of the Constitution itself, be necessary to ascertain the point under consideration, they may be found in the Journals of the General Convention, which I have deposited in the office of the Department of State. In those Journals it will appear, that a proposition was made, "that no Treaty should be binding on the United States which was not ratified by a law," and that the proposition was explicitly rejected.

As, therefore, it is perfectly clear to my understanding, that the assent of the House of Represen-

68. Excerpt taken from *Annals of Congress*, 4th Cong., 1st sess. (March 30, 1796), 760–762.

tatives is not necessary to the validity of a Treaty; as the Treaty with Great Britain exhibits in itself all the objects requiring Legislative provision, and on these the papers called for can throw no light; and as it is essential to the due administration of the Government, that the boundaries fixed by the Constitution between the different departments should be preserved—a just regard to the Constitution and to the duty of my office, under all the circumstances of this case, forbid a compliance with your request.

James Madison, Response to the President's Message (1796)[69]

Mr. MADISON (Republican, Virginia)

The Message related to two points: First. The application made for the papers. . . .

On the first point, [Mr. Madison] observed, that the right of the House to apply for any information they might want, had been admitted by a number in the minority, who had opposed the exercise of the right in this particular case. He thought it clear that the House must have a right, in all cases, to ask for information which might assist their deliberations on the subjects submitted to them by the Constitution; being responsible, nevertheless, for the propriety of the measure. He was as ready to admit that the Executive had a right, under a due responsibility, also, to withhold information, when of a nature that did not permit a disclosure of it at the time. And if the refusal of the PRESIDENT had been founded simply on a representation, that the state of the business within his department, and the contents of the papers asked for, required it, although he might have regretted the refusal, he should have been little disposed to criticize it. But the Message had contested what appeared to him a clear and important right of the House; and stated reasons for refusing the papers, which, with all the respect he should feel for the Executive, he could not regard as satisfactory or proper.

One of the reasons was, that it did not occur to the Executive that the papers could be relative to any purpose under the cognizance, and in the contemplation of the House. . . .

[This argument] implied that the Executive was not only to judge of the proper objects and functions of the Executive department, but, also, of the objects and functions of the House. He was not only to decide how far the Executive trust would permit a disclosure of information, but how far the Legislative trust could derive advantage from it. It belonged, he said, to each department to judge for itself. If the Executive conceived that, in relation to his own department, papers could not be safely communicated, he might, on that ground, refuse them, because he was the competent though a responsible judge within his own department. If the papers could be communicated without injury to the objects of his department, he ought not to refuse them as irrelative to the objects of the House of Representatives; because the House was, in such cases, the only proper judge of its own objects. . . .

The second object to which the measure related, was the Constitutional power of the House on the subject of Treaties. . . .

. . .

[W]hatever veneration might be entertained for the body of men who formed our Constitution, the senses of that body could never be regarded as the oracular guide in expounding the Constitution. As the instrument came from them it was nothing more than a draft of a plan, nothing but a dead letter, until life and validity were breathed into it by the voice of the people, speaking through the several State Conventions. If we are to look, therefore, for the meaning of the instrument beyond the face of the instrument, we must look for it, not in the General Convention, which proposed, but in the State conventions, which accepted and ratified the Constitution. . . .

In referring to the debates of the State Conventions as published, he wished not to be understood as putting entire confidence in the accuracy of them. . . . The amendments proposed by the several Conventions were better authority, and would be found, on a general view, to favor the sense of the Constitution which had prevailed in this House. But even here it would not be reasonable to expect a perfect precision and system in all their votes and proceedings. . . .

. . .

It was certainly to be regretted, as had often been expressed, that different branches of the Government should disagree in the construction of their powers; but when this could not be avoided, each branch must judge for itself; and the judgment of the Executive in

69. Excerpt taken from *Annals of Congress*, 4th Cong., 1st sess. (April 6, 1796), 772–773.

this case be no more an authority for overruling the judgment of the House than the judgment of the House could be an authority for overruling that of the Executive. It was also to be regretted that any foreign nation should at any time proceed under a misconception of the meaning of our Constitution [but e]ach nation must adjust the forms and operations of its own Government, and all others are bound to understand them accordingly. . . .

[I]t might be sufficient to remark, that this was the first instance in which a foreign Treaty had been made since the establishment of the Constitution; and that this was the first time the Treaty-making power had come under formal and accurate discussion. Precedents, therefore, would readily be perceived to lose much of their weight.

D. Legislative Powers of the President

Note: The Veto Power and the Legislative Role of the President

Under strict "separation of powers," the President's role would be limited to exercising "the executive power." His principal obligation would be to "take care that the laws be faithfully executed" (Article II, Section 3). However, the American constitutional system rejected the notion of strict separation in favor of a blending of some institutional responsibilities. One consequence of this blending was that the American chief executive was given some role in the legislative process.

One simple task was that, "from time to time," the president was to "give to the Congress information of the state of the union, and recommend to their consideration such measures as he shall judge necessary and expedient" (Article II, Section 3). During the first session of the first Congress, President Washington declined to propose "particular measures." He was concerned that he not be perceived as exerting inappropriate influence on the legislative branch. However, by January 1790, Washington shook off the excessive caution and was making recommendations on the need for legislation. This included such matters as weights and measures, currency, naturalization, and the promotion of learning. A few legislators initially grumbled at what they considered the "servile" practice by which the Congress would often respond immediately to presidential recommendations. Nevertheless, such recommendations became a routine and uncontroversial feature of annual State of the Union addresses.[70]

The presidential *veto power* has been more significant and more controversial. Article I, Section 7, reads that "Every bill which shall have passed the House of Representatives and the Senate, shall, before it become a law, be presented to the President of the United States; if he approve he shall sign it, but if not he shall return it, with his objections to that House in which it shall have originated, who shall enter the objections at large on their journal, and proceed to reconsider it." Any bill returned to the Congress with presidential objections can only become a law if two-thirds of both Houses approve it over those objections. This is known as a "qualified" veto, because it can be overridden by the legislature. An absolute veto is not subject to an override vote.

In the early republic, presidents took a relatively narrow view of the circumstances in which they could veto legislation. By contrast, modern presidents feel free to exercise this influence over the lawmaking process whenever they have a policy disagreement with Congress. During the early period, most believed that presidents should primarily veto bills that they considered to be *unconstitutional* or otherwise clearly improper; they should not veto a bill merely because they considered it unwise. The reasoning had to do with separation of powers: Congress was considered the policy-making branch, and it was assumed that presidents should defer to their policy judgments except in the most extraordinary cases. They might, say, need to take action to satisfy their oath to "defend the Constitution of the United States." Even when concerned about the constitutionality of a bill, Jefferson had suggested to President Washington that the veto should only be used when the violation was "tolerably clear" (see Jefferson's Opinion on the Constitutionality of the Bank discussed in Chapter Three).[71]

George Washington vetoed only two bills in eight years. The first was a bill apportioning congressional seats, and Washington believed that the scheme in the

---

70. *Documentary History of the First Federal Congress*, vol. 9 (Baltimore: Johns Hopkins University Press, 1972), 181.

71. On the early veto power, see also Bruce Peabody, "Recovering the Political Constitution: Nonjudicial Interpretation, Judicial Supremacy, and the Separation of Powers" (Ph.D. diss., University of Texas, 2000); Nolan McCarty, "Presidential Vetoes in the Early Republic," *Journal of Politics* 71 (2009): 369; Robert J. Spitzer, *The Presidential Veto* (Albany: SUNY Press, 1988).

bill failed to meet constitutional requirements. The second veto rejected a bill reducing the size of the army, a reduction that the president thought would be "injurious to the public."[72] The army bill particularly affected the president's ability to carry out the duties of his own office, but Washington made no constitutional arguments in vetoing it. His successors, John Adams and Thomas Jefferson, vetoed no bills. The next president, James Madison, used the regular veto just five times: four for constitutional reasons (involving the separation of church and state, the scope of Congress' power to promote internal improvements, and the president's appointment powers) and another because he considered the bill so poorly crafted as to be fatally flawed.

This cramped conception of the appropriate use of the veto power was not inevitable. In *Federalist* 73, Hamilton justified granting this power to the president—and not merely to protect the Constitution and the executive branch against legislative encroachment. It would also furnish "additional security against the enaction of improper laws. It establishes a salutary check upon the legislative body, calculated to guard the community against the effects of faction, precipitancy, or of any impulse unfriendly to the public good, which may happen to influence a majority of that body." It would protect the community against "bad laws, through haste, inadvertence, or design."

Nevertheless, up through the first quarter of the nineteenth century, constitutional norms led to a more restrictive understanding of the veto power. With rare exception, the president's role in blocking legislation was considered analogous to the judiciary's role: Each was to focus primarily on constitutional considerations rather than policy.

E. Presidential Power to Execute the Law

Jeffersonians maintained that Congress was the primary institution of government. The president, they believed, served primarily to implement the will of the national legislature. For this reason, they often conceived of executive branch officials as having similar responsibilities as contemporary independent agencies. Presidents appointed governing officials, but were not expected to supervise their daily activities. Jeffersonians thought executive branch officials who were implementing congressional problems were at least as responsible to Congress as the President.

Legal opinions by the attorneys general have been one of the main instruments for working out the relationship between the president and lower level executive officials. William Wirt was one of the great Jeffersonian attorneys general, serving in that role under both President James Monroe and President John Quincy Adams. Unlike many of the early attorneys general, Wirt was first and foremost a lawyer and litigator rather than a politician. (He had earlier been entrusted by Thomas Jefferson with prosecuting the treason trial of former vice president Aaron Burr.) Wirt's 1823 opinion on the accounting officers was among his most important. In that opinion, he examined the meaning of the take care clause of Article II. Wirt's opinion focuses on presidential responsibility in cases of routine administration, and implicitly elaborates on a distinction that Chief Justice John Marshall had made two decades earlier in *Marbury*.

In *Marbury v. Madison* (1803), Marshall distinguished between discretionary and ministerial duties of the executive branch. He indicated that courts could only examine how executive officials performed merely ministerial duties. When a statute required the Secretary of State to deliver a document to an individual, he was acting "under the authority of law, and not by the instructions of the president. It is a ministerial act which the law enjoins on a particular officer for a particular purpose."[73] Presidential discretion and oversight were minimal in such cases. Wirt's opinion also expresses an institutional fear that the president could be overwhelmed by the minutia of running the government. At the time government was fairly informal, and the executive branch was small. (The office of attorney general was itself still only a part-time job, and Wirt was the first attorney general to be provided with office space and a clerk.) It was easy to imagine the president spending most of his time running the day-to-day affairs of the government, rather than making and conducting domestic and foreign policy.

President Harry Truman famously declared that "the buck stops here." He wrote, "Our government is fixed on the basis that the President is the only person in the executive branch who has the final authority....

72. George Washington, "Veto Message of February 28, 1797," in *A Compilation of the Messages and Papers of the Presidents*, ed. James D. Richardson, vol. 1 (New York: Bureau of National Literature, 1897), 211.

73. *Marbury v. Madison*, 5 U.S. 137, 158 (1803).

Every President in our history has been faced with this problem: how to prevent career men from circumventing presidential policy.... [T]he President [has to] keep his hands on the reins and know exactly what goes on in each department."[74] The Jeffersonian presidents faced the problem of controlling the members of the executive branch as well, and they sent directives to executive branch officials on how to interpret and apply the law. But Jeffersonian ideology emphasized an important role for Congress and statutes in defining the duties of executive officers and the policies they should carry out.

William Wirt, Opinion on the President and Accounting Officers (1823)[75]

Major Joseph Wheaton was a former quarter-master in the army who had supplied whiskey to the navy during the War of 1812. He had sought reimbursement from the Treasury Department for those expenses but was dissatisfied with the accounting of the Treasury's auditor. After exhausting his appeals within the Treasury Department, he had petitioned Congress for an adjustment of his account but to no avail. He now turned to President Monroe to go through his receipts, and Monroe sought an opinion from his attorney general. Was he obliged to consider Wheaton's appeal as part of his constitutional responsibilities to take care that the laws are faithfully executed?

Wirt's opinion let President Monroe off the hook from becoming the "accountant general of the government." However, in doing so he also drew a sharp line between the president and the executive branch. Wirt would treat ordinary executive officials in a manner similar to how we now think of independent agencies. In Wirt's view, the executive departments were ultimately tools of Congress for implementing its policies. Was Wirt's opinion empowering or limiting of the president, or both? Did it weaken presidential control over the executive branch? Is this view that the executive departments are tools of Congress consistent with Article II's assertion that the executive power is vested in the president? Is it consistent with the president's responsibility to take care that the laws are faithfully executed?

...

1. It appears to me that you [the president] have no power to interfere [with the decision of an accounting officer in the Treasury Department].

The constitution of the United States requires the President, in general terms, to take care that the laws be faithfully executed; that is, it places the officers engaged in the execution of the laws under his general superintendence: he is to see that they do their duty faithfully; and on their failure, to cause them to be displaced, prosecuted, or impeached, according to the nature of the case. In case of forcible resistance to the laws, too, so as to require the interposition of the power of the government to overcome the illegal resistance, he is to see that the power be furnished. But it could never have been the intention of the constitution, in assigning the general power to the President to take care that the laws be executed, that he should in person execute them himself.... [T]o call upon him to perform such duties himself, would be not only to require him to perform an impossibility himself, but take upon himself the responsibility of all the subordinate executive officers of the government—a construction too absurd to be seriously contended for. But the requisition of the constitution is, that he shall *take care* that the *laws* be executed. If the laws, then, require a particular officer by name to perform a duty, not only is that officer bound to perform it, but no other officer can perform it without a violation of the law; and were the President to perform it, he would not only be taking care that the laws were faithfully executed, but he would be violating them himself. The constitution assigns to Congress the power of designating the duties of particular officers: the President is only required to take care that they execute them faithfully.... He is not to perform the duty, but to see that the officer assigned by law performs his duty *faithfully*—that is, *honestly*: not with perfect correctness of judgment, but *honestly*....

It would be strange, indeed, if it were otherwise. The office of President is ordained for very different purposes than that of settling individual accounts. The constitution has committed to him the care of the great interests of the nation, in all its foreign and domestic relations.... How will it be possible for the President to perform these great duties, if he is also to exercise the appellate power of revising and correcting the settlement of all the individual accounts which pass through the hands of the accounting officers? Let it be remem-

74. Harry Truman, *Memoirs*, vol. 2 (Garden City, NY: Double Day, 1956), 165.

75. Excerpt taken from William Wirt, *The President and Accounting Officers, October 20, 1823,* 1 Op. Att'y Gen. 624 (1854).

bered that, out of the vast multitude of these accounts which are annually settled by these officers, there are very few which are settled to the entire satisfaction of the claimants; and if every dissatisfied claimant has a right to appeal to the President, and call upon him to revise and correct the settlement, the President would be constrained to abandon the great national objects which are committed to his peculiar care, and become the accountant general of the government....

Notes

1. The Jacksonians took a stronger view of presidential power than did the Jeffersonians. President Franklin Pierce's attorney general, Caleb Cushing, disagreed with Wirt on the relationship between the president and lower officials of the executive branch. In numerous official opinions, Cushing detailed his view that the president was the chief executive of the federal government, and that empowered him to exercise authority over all of the executive branch. In contrast to the Jeffersonian Wirt, Cushing laid out the Jacksonian doctrine of a unitary executive. In this view, the subordinate officers in the executive branch were always answerable to their superiors, right up to the president of the United States:

> Question has existed as to the relation of the President and the respective heads of departments to the chiefs of bureaus, and especially the accounting officers of the Treasury.
>
> It is not the duty of the President, and in general it is not convenient for him, to entertain appeals from the departments on the various matters of business, and especially the private claims, on which they have occasion from time to time to pass....
>
> Now, from the fact that the executive agents ... are assigned by law to particular duties, it has been somewhat hastily inferred, that while it is indubitably true that he may direct the heads of departments, yet he has no authority over the chiefs of bureaus, and especially those in the department of Treasury....
>
> Such a doctrine was against common sense, which assumes that the superior shall overrule the subordinate, not the latter the former. It was contrary to settled constitutional theory. That theory ... while it supposes that in all matters not purely ministerial, that executive discretion exists, and that judgment is continually to be exercised, yet requires unity of executive action, and, of course, unity of executive decision; which, by the inexorable necessity of the nature of things, cannot be obtained by means of a plurality of persons wholly independent of one another ... and released from subjection to one determining will....
>
> ... [I]f an opinion delivered many years ago by Mr. Wirt is now to be received as law ... [an] auditor is wholly above the authority of the President.... Such an assumed anomaly of relation, therefore, as this idea supposes, resting upon mere opinion or exposition, must, of course, yield to better reflection, whenever it comes to be a practical question demanding the consideration of any Attorney General.[76]

F. Elections and Political Parties

Note: The Constitution and the Election of 1800

The election of 1800—or what Jefferson referred to as the "Revolution of 1800"—is notable for many reasons. It represented the development of competitive national political parties in the United States (although not the mass-based electoral machines that developed in the period of Jacksonian democracy). It was the first example in modern history of the peaceful transfer of governing authority from a party in power to an opposition party. It also ushered in a generation of Jeffersonian-Republican rule in the presidency and Congress, and it foreshadowed the eventual demise of the Federalist Party. Last, it set up a series of unprecedented battles between the federal judiciary (still controlled by Federalists) and the other branches of the national government.

The event was also a case study in the complicated relationship between constitutional politics and conventional politics. For one thing, it revealed flaws in the original design of the Constitution. It exposed the ways in which political developments in the 1790s had already overrun important features of the framers' plan. It proved the importance for presidential politics of the framers' decision to give a political bonus to slave states. It showed how an urgent political context might make it easy to ignore constitutional technicalities that seem insignificant under the circumstances.

76. Caleb Cushing, *Opinion on the Offices and Duties of the President, March 8, 1854*, 6 Op. Att'y Gen. 326, 342–345 (1854).

And it demonstrated that the Constitution provided splendid opportunities for repudiated officeholders to protect their interests.

Even more pressingly, the structure of the Electoral College contributed to a deadlocked outcome. Under the original design, members of the Electoral College each cast two votes for President; the presidential contender who came in second would be Vice President. This made sense at a time before the rise of political parties. At that time, one might assume that this process would simply identify the two most respected leaders in the country. But it became extremely problematic the minute opposite political camps began organizing "tickets" made up of presumptive presidential and vice-presidential nominees. Suppose a majority of Electoral College members cast one vote for the person they wanted to be president and the other for the person they wanted to be vice president. Despite their clear preferences, the system would then produce a tie for the presidential vote and throw the election into Congress.

By 1800 the Federalists understood the problem. They arranged for John Adams to receive one more electoral vote than their vice-presidential candidate, Charles Cotesworth Pinckney, by instructing one elector to cast his second vote for John Jay.[77] In contrast, all Republican electors cast one vote for their presidential candidate, Thomas Jefferson, and another for their vice-presidential candidate, Aaron Burr. Rather than a clear victory for Jefferson, the Constitution led to a tie.[78]

Jefferson, as (outgoing) Vice President and therefore President of the Senate, was responsible for overseeing the counting of the Electoral College votes.[79] When things run smoothly, this is a relatively straightforward responsibility, but in 1800 nothing was running smoothly. In particular, Jefferson came upon the official record of the votes submitted from the state of Georgia, a solidly Republican state. It became clear that the paper did not have all the constitutionally required information. The Constitution mandates that a state's electors submit a "List of all the Persons voted for, and of the Number of Votes for each; which list they shall sign and certify." The Georgia document contained a list, but it did not say that these were the persons "voted for." In addition, the electors did not sign and certify that the list was an accurate statement of their preferences.

The person who presided over the counting of the ballots could have drawn the attention of the House to these irregularities, and this might have opened up a discussion of whether the ballots should be disqualified. Were that to have happened Jefferson and Burr would have only had 69 valid electoral votes—one shy of the required majority. That would have thrown the election into the House, and allowed the members of the House of Representatives to choose the next president from the top five candidates who had received votes in the Electoral College. In that case, it would have been a contest among Jefferson (with 69 votes in the Electoral College), Burr (69), Adams (65) Pickney (65), and Jay (1), and the Federalists would have had many more options for resolving the situation. However, the person who did preside over the counting, Thomas Jefferson, simply recorded Georgia's votes as for Jefferson and Burr, thus leading to the tie and making the existing mess a bit less complicated—if also a bit less in conformity with constitutional technicalities.

Under the original rules, the tie would have to be resolved in the House of Representatives, where each state delegation was given one vote. This process could easily have favored Jefferson. After all, his supporters won a clear victory in 1800, and in the Seventh Congress (1801–03) they enjoyed a 68–38 majority over the Federalists. However, the framers decided that this decision was to be made by the *outgoing* (lame-duck) Congress—in this case, the Sixth Congress. It had been elected in 1798, when Federalists won a 60–46 majority over the Jeffersonians.

This might have been fatal for Jefferson, but for one further fact: Votes came from state delegations rather than individual members. Because Federalist support was disproportionately concentrated in the North,

77. The Federalists were less well organized in 1796. John Adams won the presidency with 71 electoral votes, but 12 Federalist electors chose favorite sons (candidates from their own states) rather than the vice presidential candidate, Thomas Pinckney. This allowed Jefferson to squeeze into the vice presidency with 68 votes.

78. Jeffersonians were not the only ones who made political mistakes during this period. After the election the Federalists had a 17–15 majority in the incoming Senate. However, Adams agreed to nominate two Federalist senators nearing the end of their six-year terms, Ray Greene of Rhode Island and Elijah Paine of Vermont, for positions as district court judges. They were replaced by Republicans, thus giving Jefferson's party complete control of the presidency and the Congress.

79. See Bruce Ackerman, *The Failure of the Founding Fathers* (Cambridge: Harvard University Press, 2005), 55–76.

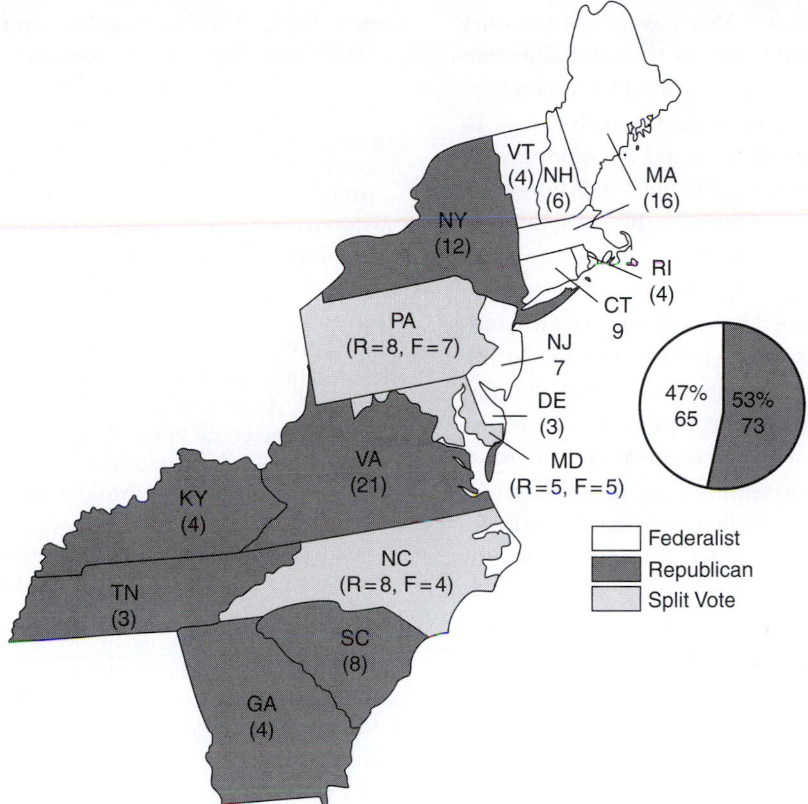

Figure 4-3 Electoral Map of the United States, 1800

Note: Electoral Votes cast in 1800 presidential elections.

Federalists were a majority in only six out of sixteen state delegations. Jeffersonians controlled eight state delegations. Two others (Vermont and Maryland) were split evenly and thus not initially in a position to cast a ballot.

Under the rules, the tie would be resolved only when a candidate received the support of a majority of the state delegations. With a total of sixteen states, this meant that someone needed nine votes. If the Federalists remained determined to deny Jefferson the presidency they needed only to hold firm and convince just a few state delegates that the Republican Burr was an acceptable alternative to Jefferson. Republicans complained that this would be inconsistent with the popular will, but Federalists were not swayed. They pointed out that Jefferson disproportionately benefited from another undemocratic feature of the Constitution: Under the "three-fifths compromise," southern states received more votes in the Electoral College than if only free men were counted for the purpose of apportioning seats in the House. As far as the Federalists were concerned, a majority of free men voted for Adams. Consequently, to them Jefferson had no special claim on the presidency.

Over the course of seven days (February 11–17), the House cast a total of thirty-five ballots, with Jefferson receiving eight state delegations each time. The logjam was broken up in part because Alexander Hamilton convinced some Federalists that Burr, his political rival in New York politics, was dangerous and would be bad for the country. It helped as well that the federal government did not have a standing army under the command of the Federalists. Meanwhile the Republican governors of Virginia and Pennsylvania did have control of state militias—and were willing to use them if the Federalists did not relent.

Jefferson's victory on the thirty-sixth ballot resolved the question of who would be the next president. However, his presidency would be deeply influenced by one more feature of the Constitution's electoral system. Not only did the document give the outgoing Congress the authority to break a logjam in the Electoral College. It also allowed that body to hold a legislative session for an extended period of time after those lawmakers had suffered electoral defeat.[80] This gave the lame-duck Federalist President and Congress time after the selection of Jefferson to take steps to protect their members, and their constitutional vision. They quickly did so, by expanding the federal judiciary and appointing loyal Federalists to key positions. The need to address this turn of events dominated politics during Jefferson's first administration.

The election of 1800 demonstrates how deeply the political system is shaped by constitutional structure. Implicated in this crisis were the various rules of the Electoral College, the three-fifths compromise, and the lame-duck authority given repudiated officeholders. Of all these features, only one was considered so deeply problematic as to require constitutional change, and that was the provision that had presidential electors cast two votes for president. The rule was simply inconsistent with political developments in the 1790s. An amendment to provide for separate votes for president and vice president was proposed by the Congress on December 9, 1803; it was ratified on June 15, 1804. The Twelfth Amendment represented formal acknowledgment in the constitutional text that, despite the framers' hopes, political parties, presidential slates, and pledged electors had become a permanent feature of the American republic.

Suggested Readings

Ackerman, Bruce A. *The Failure of the Founding Fathers: Jefferson, Marshall, and the Rise of Presidential Democracy* (Cambridge: Harvard University Press, 2005).

Banning, Lance. *The Sacred Fire of Liberty: James Madison and the Founding of the American Republic* (Ithaca: Cornell University Press, 1995).

Baxter, Maurice J. *The Steamboat Monopoly: Gibbons v. Ogden, 1824* (Boston; Knopf, 1972).

Brown, Everett S. *The Constitutional History of the Louisiana Purchase, 1803–1812* (Berkeley: University of California Press, 1920).

Brown, Roger H. *Redeeming the Republic: Federalists, Taxation, and the Origins of the Constitution* (Baltimore: Johns Hopkins University Press, 2000).

Clinton, Robert L. *Marbury v. Madison and Judicial Review* (Lawrence: University Press of Kansas, 1989).

Cornell, Saul. *The Other Founders: Anti-Federalism & the Dissenting Tradition in America, 1788–1828* (Chapel Hill: University of North Carolina Press, 1999).

Cunningham, Noble E., Jr. *The Process of Government under Jefferson* (Princeton: Princeton University Press, 1978).

Currie, David P. *The Constitution in Congress: The Federalist Period, 1789–1801* (Chicago: University of Chicago Press, 1997).

Currie, David P. *The Constitution in Congress: The Jeffersonians* (Chicago: University of Chicago Press, 2001).

Elkins, Stanley, and Eric McKitrick. *The Age of Federalism: The Early American Republic, 1788–1800* (New York: Oxford University Press, 1995).

Ellis, Richard E. *Jeffersonian Crisis: Courts and Politics in the Young Republic* (New York: Oxford University Press, 1971).

Freeman, Joanne B. *Affairs of Honor: National Politics in the New Republic* (New Haven: Yale University Press, 2001).

Graber, Mark. A. "Federalist or Friends of Adams: The Marshall Court and Party Politics." *Studies in American Political Development* 12 (1998): 229–266.

Hobson, Charles F. *The Great Chief Justice: John Marshall and the Rule of Law* (Lawrence: University Press of Kansas, 1996).

Hofstadter, Richard. *The Idea of a Party System: The Rise of Legitimate Opposition in the United States, 1780–1840* (Berkeley: University of California Press, 1970).

Kastor, Peter J. *The Nation's Crucible: The Louisiana Purchase and the Creation of America* (New Haven: Yale University Press, 2004).

Ketcham, Ralph Louis. *Presidents above Party: The First American Presidency, 1789–1829* (Chapel Hill: University of North Carolina Press, 1984).

Killenbeck, Mark R. *M'Culloch v. Maryland: Securing a Nation* (Lawrence: University Press of Kansas, 2006).

Kramer, Larry D. *The People Themselves: Popular Constitutionalism and Judicial Review* (New York: Oxford University Press, 2004).

Kuroda, Tadahisa. *The Origins of the Twelfth Amendment: The Electoral College in the Early Republic, 1787–1804* (Westport, CT: Greenwood Press, 1994).

Larson, John Lauritz. *Internal Improvements: National Public Works and the Promise of Popular Government in the Early United States* (Chapel Hill: University of North Carolina Press, 2000).

Levy, Leonard W. *Emergence of a Free Press* (New York: Oxford University Press, 1985).

Marcus, Maeva, ed. *Origins of the Federal Judiciary: Essays on the Judiciary Act of 1789* (New York: Oxford University Press, 1992).

80. The First Congress did not commence its first proceedings until March 4, 1789. Since representatives were given two or six year terms of office, it was decided that old officeholders would lose their power on March 4 and the new government would then begin. This would be the rule for the next 150 years, until a new political calendar was established by the Twentieth Amendment in 1933.

Mayer, David N. *The Constitutional Thought of Thomas Jefferson* (Charlottesville: University of Virginia Press, 1994).

McDonald, Forrest. *The Presidency of George Washington*. (Lawrence: University Press of Kansas, 1974).

Nelson, William E. *Marbury v. Madison: The Origins and Legacy of Judicial Review* (Lawrence: University Press of Kansas, 2000).

Newmyer, R. Kent. *John Marshall and the Heroic Age of the Supreme Court* (Baton Rouge: Louisiana State University, 2002).

Read, James H. *Power Versus Liberty: Madison, Hamilton, Wilson, and Jefferson* (Charlottesville: University of Virginia Press, 2000).

Risjord, Norman K. *The Old Republicans: Southern Conservatism in the Age of Jefferson* (New York: Columbia University Press, 1965).

Rosen, Gary. *American Compact: James Madison and the Problem of Founding* (Lawrence: University Press of Kansas, 1999).

Scalia, Laura J. *America's Jeffersonian Experiment: Remaking State Constitutions, 1820–1850* (De Kalb: Northern Illinois University Press, 1999).

Siemers, David J. *Ratifying the Republic: Antifederalists and Federalists in Constitutional Time* (Stanford: Stanford University Press, 2002).

Stourzh, Gerald. *Alexander Hamilton and the Idea of Republican Government* (Stanford: Stanford University Press, 1970).

White, G. Edward. *The Marshall Court and Cultural Change, 1815–1835* (New York: Oxford University Press, 1988).

Wirls, Daniel, and Stephen Wirls. *The Invention of the United States Senate* (Baltimore: Johns Hopkins University Press, 2004).

Chapter 5

The Jacksonian Era: 1829–1860

Illustration 5-1 The first inauguration of President Andrew Jackson was known as an unusually raucous affair. The White House and the surrounding streets were packed with people for hours. Witnesses described a joyful mob that broke dishes, furniture, and noses during the celebration.
Source: Cruikshank, Robert, 1789–1856, artist. Library of Congress. Rare Book and Special Collections Division.

I. Introduction

Andrew Jackson's (1767–1845) inauguration in 1829 turned into a drunken revelry. Twenty thousand admirers stormed the White House, destroying furniture and carpets in a desperate effort to greet the new President. Order was restored only when an intrepid member of Jackson's coterie arranged for free whiskey on the White House lawn. Traditional Washingtonians were horrified by what they saw. Margaret Bayard Smith, a prominent Washington socialite, complained that "the Majesty of the People had disappeared," replaced by "a rabble, a mob, of boys, negros, women, children, scrambling, fighting, romping."[1] Looking at the debris and carnage, Supreme Court Justice Joseph Story

1. Margaret Bayard Smith, *First Forty Years of Washington Society*, ed. Gaillard Hunt (New York: C. Scribner's Sons: 1906), 295.

(1779–1845) and Senator Daniel Webster (1782–1852) of Massachusetts concluded that the old order was dead. "The reign of King Mob," Story wrote, "seemed triumphant."[2]

Webster and Story were right to note that Jackson's inaugural marked the coming to power of a new generation of constitutional politicians. The first five presidents played prominent roles in either the American Revolution or the constitutional convention. John Quincy Adams, the sixth president, was both by blood and temperament allied with the framing generation. Andrew Jackson and his successors came of age during the early national era. Jackson lacked personal or familial relationships with any founders. He was from the west, calling home a state that did not exist at the time of the Revolution. The persons responsible for the Constitution of 1787 who witnessed the Jackson phenomenon were appalled by the state of American constitutional politics. James Madison in 1834 fervently hoped that "the danger and even existence of the parties which have grown up under the auspices of [Jackson's] name will expire with his natural or official life."[3]

Webster correctly observed at Jackson's inaugural in 1828 that the President's supporters thought "that the country is rescued from some dreadful danger."[4] Jackson and his supporters believed that a political and economic aristocracy was corrupting the Constitution. Many thought such Federalist/National Republican initiatives as the national bank, federally federal internal improvements and protective tariffs were unconstitutional usurpations that were transforming the national government into a vehicle for enriching the privileged few at the expense of the common citizen.

Jacksonians thought the "corrupt bargain" that allegedly settled the presidential election of 1824 was the most immediate manifestation of this political depravity. Although Andrew Jackson received a plurality of the popular votes, he did not obtain the Electoral College majority necessary to gain the presidency. As mandated by Article I, Section 1, the House of Representatives determined whether to select Jackson, Adams, or William Crawford for the presidency. Henry Clay of Kentucky, the fourth candidate in the race, urged his supporters to favor Adams, who most closely shared Clay's National Republican values. After Adams was victorious, he appointed Clay as his Secretary of State, the traditional stepping stone to the presidency. National Republicans regarded the political maneuvering responsible for Adams' triumph over Jackson as vindicating the framing hope that well-designed constitutional institutions would successfully refine popular opinions. Jackson and his supporters interpreted these political maneuverings as further proof that constitutional institutions had come under the control of a self-perpetuating elite.

Different beliefs about the constitutional status of democracy were at the heart of the generation gap between Jacksonians and the framers. Most persons responsible for the Constitution took great pains to emphasize that the United States was a "republic," not a "democracy." Governing would be done by a "natural aristocracy," chosen by a voting system designed to privilege the "best persons." "The aim of every political constitution," Madison wrote in 1788, "is … first to obtain for rulers men who possess most wisdom to discern, and most virtue to pursue, the common good of the society."[5] Jacksonians rejected this elitist politics. Their Constitution was unashamedly democratic. Andrew Jackson expressed this sentiment when in his first inaugural address he declared that the "duties of all public offices are, or at least admit of being made, so plain and simple that men of intelligence may readily qualify themselves for their performance."[6]

Developments. The Jacksonian democratizing imperative influenced every governing institution in the United States. The deferential politics of congressional

2. Joseph Story, To Mrs. Joseph Story, March 3, 1829, in *The Life and Letters of Joseph Story*, ed. William W. Story, vol. 1 (Boston: Little and Brown, 1851), 563.

3. James Madison, To Edward Coles, August 29, 1834, in *The Letters and Other Writings of James Madison*, vol. 4 (Philadelphia: Lippincott, 1865), 357.

4. Daniel Webster, To Achsah Pollard, March 4, 1829, in *The Papers of Daniel Webster*, ed. Charles M. Wiltse and Harold D. Moser, vol. 2 (Hanover, NH: University Press of New England, 1974–89), 405.

5. Alexander Hamilton, James Madison, and John Jay, *The Federalist Papers*, ed. Clinton Rossiter (New York: Mentor, 1969), No. 37.

6. Andrew Jackson, First Annual Message, *Compilation of the Messages and Papers of the Presidents*, eds. James Richardson, vol. 2 (New York: Bureau of National Literature and Art, 1908), 449. Jacksonians were "democratic" and committed to majority rule only by the cribbed democratic standards of antebellum American which prioritized white males.

Table 5-1 Major Issues and Decisions of the Jacksonian Era

Major Political Issues	Major Constitutional Issues	Major Court Decisions
Continuance of the Second Bank of the United States	Admission of New States	*Prigg v. Pennsylvania* (1842)
Internal Improvements	Territorial Governance	*Willson v. Black Bird Creek Marsh Co.* (1829)
Protective Tariffs	Spending Power	*Mayor of New York v. Miln* (1837)
Slavery in Territories	Regulation of Commerce	*Cooley v. Board of Wardens* (1852)
Mexican War	Necessary and Proper Clause	*Worcester v. Georgia* (1832)
Nullification	Fugitive Slave Clause	
Native American Removal	Nullification	
Spoils System	Presidential Veto Power	*Luther v. Borden* (1849)
	Suffrage	*Dred Scott v. Sandford* (1857)

elections in Jeffersonian America was replaced by a partisan free-for-all in which elections were typically won by the candidate who secured the most alcohol and voters (sometimes more than the number of persons actually eligible to vote).[7] The Senate, originally conceived of as republican aristocracy that would advise the president, increasingly behaved as the second house of the national legislature.[8] Jacksonian presidents such as Martin Van Buren and James Polk claimed to be the best representatives of the people and refrained from adopting the Washingtonian pose of leaders above the political fray. Their cabinets consisted of presidential loyalists, who implemented presidential policy and mobilized support for the president. An increasing number of states opted for elective judiciaries. Federal courts were the only governing institution not fundamentally transformed by the democratic spirit.

Jackson and his followers cheered institutional changes that promoted more direct democratic engagement and decision making. Committed to majority rule, Jacksonian Democrats interpreted the Constitution, whenever plausible, as promoting majoritarianism. Their constitutional vision emphasized a strong president (by nineteenth-century standards) who wielded the veto power in the name of national majorities against the special interests that sometimes controlled the national legislature. Constitutional authority was primarily vested in elected officials and not in mandarin justices.

Jackson's leading opponents were less excited about these institutional developments. Prominent National Republicans and Whigs regarded aggressive presidential vetoes as usurping the authority of the more republican national legislature. They championed the courts as the institution responsible for determining official constitutional meanings.

Slowly, an institutional reapproachment occurred. Jackson and his followers made their peace with a strong judiciary. Daniel Webster, Henry Clay and their followers eventually made their peace with the Jacksonian presidency. After the Mexican War, Jackson's opponents sought to capitalize on the democratized presidency by nominating two war heroes, William Henry Harrison and Zachary Taylor, for that office. Jacksonians in the national government began insisting that the federal judiciary was the national institution charged with determining the constitutional status of slavery.

Partisan Coalitions during the Jacksonian Era. Jacksonian constitutional politics was a contest between the first two mass political parties in American history, Jacksonian Democrats and Whigs. Both were well organized by the late 1830s. Each provided voters with distinctive constitutional visions on national issues. Jacksonian Democrats inherited a version of the strict constructionist constitutional philosophy that guided the Jeffersonian Republicans. They were deeply fearful of corruption and faction in the government.

7. Richard Franklin Bensel, *The American Ballot Box in the Mid-Nineteenth Century* (New York: Cambridge University Press, 2004).

8. Elaine K. Swift, *The Making of an American Senate* (Ann Arbor: University of Michigan Press, 2002).

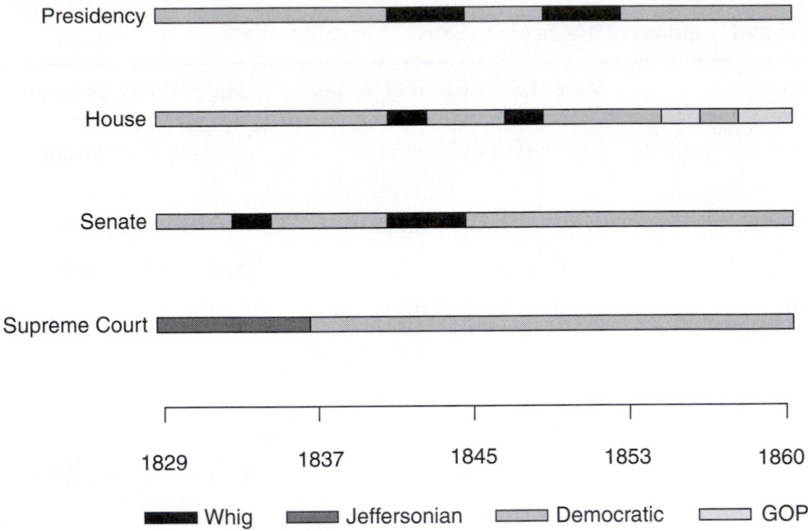

Figure 5-1 Partisan Control of the U.S. Government, 1829–1860

Democrats were always on the lookout for "class legislation" and monopolies that used government power to enrich particular interests in society at the expense of the people at large. Most Whigs were former National Republicans committed to a broad interpretation of federal powers. They often championed a partnership between government and private interests in order to encourage economic development and civic virtue.

National debate for most of the Jacksonian Era was over western expansion and the "American System," an interrelated set of Whig proposals for a protective tariff, national banking, and federally funded internal improvements. Democrats insisted that the Constitution prohibited each element of the American System, but permitted the annexation of Texas by joint resolution and President Polk's decision to provoke the Mexican War. Whigs thought the annexation of Texas unconstitutional and claimed President Polk unconstitutionally provoked the Mexican War, but maintained that Congress had the power to enact every element of the American System.

Whigs and Democrats were national parties that competed as near equals in both the free and slave states. While Whigs were slightly stronger in the North and Democrats had a pronounced southern tilt, both parties enjoyed strong support in all regions of the United States. The winning candidate in every election contested between a Whig and a Democrat carried at least seven free states and seven slave states. The losing candidate in every close election carried at least five free states and five slave states. This was the first era of frequent divided government. More often than not, each party controlled at least one of the three elected bodies of the national government.

Although elections were close, Democrats generally got the better of the Whigs. Democrats won seven out of the nine presidential elections held between 1828 and 1856. Their political base were the small craftsmen, farmers, and immigrants who formed a majority of the voters. The Whigs enjoyed more support from the upper middle class. They were often less comfortable with the aggressively partisan and populist organizing that the Democrats pioneered.

The Constitution placed substantial barriers to Whig efforts. In order to pass their cherished American System, Whigs had to control all branches of the national government. Time and time again, Whigs passed their measures in Congress, only to have them vetoed by a Jacksonian president. When Whigs successfully elected a president (William Henry Harrison) who pledged to put away the veto pen, he died thirty days after taking the oath of office. He was replaced by a politician (John Tyler) more committed to Jacksonian understandings of federal power and presidential prerogatives.

The Federal Judiciary in the Jacksonian Era. One consequence of the repeated Whig failure to pass their legislative program was that the Supreme Court of the United States rarely spoke on the constitutional issues that divided Democrats and Whigs. This silence surprised some observers who expected a reconstituted bench to overturn such landmark decisions of the early national period of *McCulloch v. Maryland* (1819). By the end of the 1830s, the federal judiciary had passed into Democratic hands. The new judicial majority was composed of men who had previously championed strict construction in Congress or in Jackson's cabinet. Roger Taney, Andrew Jackson's close political advisor, replaced John Marshall as Chief Justice. Taney and his judicial allies nevertheless had no opportunity to revisit *McCulloch* because Jackson and President Tyler vetoed Whig bills rechartering the national bank. Had Jackson or Tyler signed those bills, most politically astute commentators believed the Taney Court would have declared that Congress had no power to incorporate a national bank. The Supreme Court did not consider whether the internal improvements bill passed by Congress in 1846 was constitutional for the same reason. President Polk vetoed the bill, preventing the passage of a law the justices might have declared unconstitutional.

Slavery was the great exception in Jacksonian constitutional politics. Human bondage loomed over most major constitutional debates. Nevertheless, Jacksonians had difficulty fitting the constitutional politics of slavery into the general structure of Jacksonian constitutional politics. Mass political parties took strong stands on the constitutional issues of the day, except on those constitutional issues that concerned slavery. Sharp partisan differences vanished when sectional issues were on the table. All Whigs and Democrats with national ambitions asserted that agitation on slavery would destroy the Union. The slavery question was to be a local or a legal issue, but preferably not one resolved in Congress or in national elections. Parties were national in Jacksonian American, except the political party that took a clear stand on slavery. The Republican Party, which formed in 1854, attracted only free-state voters with a platform dedicated to preventing the westward expansion of slavery. The Supreme Court played a limited role in Jacksonian constitutional politics, except when constitutional controversies erupted over slavery. The two most important constitutional decisions handed down from 1825 to 1860 by the Supreme Court sustained the Fugitive Slave Act of 1793 and declared unconstitutional federal laws prohibiting slavery in the territories. Many prominent southerners championed strict construction, except when defending broad federal powers to pass fugitive slave laws. Many prominent northerners championed nationalism, except when defending state power to nullify federal fugitive slave laws.

Legacies. Mass political parties were the most important Jacksonian contribution to American constitutionalism. The framers sought to prevent parties from arising. Jeffersonians regarded parties as a necessary evil. Americans during the Jacksonian age celebrated parties as the best vehicle for ensuring mass participation in politics and guaranteeing that political decisions would reflect popular opinions. An influential Jacksonian journal spoke for both Democrats and, eventually, Whigs when declaring, "When men are governed by a common principle, which is fully indulged and equally operative in all parts of the country, the agency of party conduces to the public good."[9]

The modern presidency is rooted in Jacksonian practice. During the early national period, Americans debated whether cabinet officials had obligations to be loyal to the president and whether presidents could use the veto to influence policymaking in Congress. These issues were largely, but not completely, settled by 1860. President Andrew Jackson established durable precedents when he made routine use of the veto and insisted that his cabinet officials either carry out his orders or be removed from office. Abraham Lincoln, a Whig in the 1840s, adopted the Jacksonian conception of the presidency upon taking office in 1861.

Jacksonians entrenched the Constitution of the United States. New political leaders in many countries rise to power by condemning and replacing older constitutions. The Jacksonian generation of political leaders pledged allegiance to the Constitution written and ratified by the previous republican generation of political leaders. The young Lincoln spoke for virtually all prominent political leaders when in 1838 he declared

> We find ourselves under the government of a system of political institutions, conducing more essentially to the ends of civil and religious liberty, than any of which the history of former times tells us. We, when mounting the stage of existence, found

9. Michael Wallace, "Changing Concepts of Party in the United States: New York, 1815–1828," *Am. Hist. Rev.* 74 (1968):490 (quoting Albany Argus).

> ourselves the legal inheritors of these fundamental blessings. We toiled not in the acquirement or establishment of them—they are a legacy bequeathed us, by a once hardy, brave, and patriotic, but now lamented and departed race of ancestors. Their's was the task (and nobly they performed it) to possess themselves, and through themselves, us, of this goodly land; and to uprear upon its hills and its valleys, a political edifice of liberty and equal rights; 'tis ours only, to transmit these, the former, unprofaned by the foot of an invader; the latter, undecayed by the lapse of time, and untorn by usurpation—to the latest generation that fate shall permit the world to know. This task of gratitude to our fathers, justice to ourselves, duty to posterity, and love for our species in general, all imperatively require us faithfully to perform.[10]

Andrew Jackson during his 1837 Farewell Address demanded the same fidelity to the Constitution. "Our Constitution is no longer a doubtful experiment," he declared, "and at the end of nearly half a century we find that it has preserved unimpaired the liberties of the people, secured the rights of property, and that our country has improved and is flourishing beyond any former example in the history of nations." With the exception of a few abolitionists, Americans of all political persuasions claimed to revere the framers and the Constitution they ratified. Americans disputed the proper understanding, but not the authority, of that text.

"An Introductory Statement of the Democratic Principle," *The Democratic Review* (1837)[11]

The Democratic Review *was the ideological torch bearer for Jacksonian Democrats. Founder John L. O'Sullivan (1813–1895) established that journal in 1837 to be a more radical alternative to the established and more conservative political journals that were critical of the Jacksonian movement. This "introductory statement" was published in the inaugural issue.*

...

We believe...in the principle of democratic republicanism, in its strongest and purest sense. We have an abiding confidence in the virtue, intelligence, and full capacity for self-government, of the great mass of our people, our industrious, honest, manly, intelligent millions of freemen. We are opposed to all self-styled "wholesome restraints" on the free action of the popular opinion and will, other than those which have for their sole object the prevention of precipitate legislation. This latter object is to be attained by the expedient of the division of power, and by causing all legislation to pass through the ordeal of successive forms; to be sifted through the discussions of coordinate legislative branches with mutual suspensive veto powers....We cannot, therefore, look with an eye of favor on any such forms of representation as, by length of tenure of delegated power, tend to weaken that universal and unrelaxing responsibility to the vigilance of public opinion which is the true conservative principle of our institutions.

...

...[T]he greatest number are more likely, at least, as a general rule, to understand and follow their own greatest good, than is the minority.

...[A] minority is much more likely to abuse power for the promotion of its own selfish interests, at the expense of the majority of numbers, the substantial and producing mass of the nation, than the latter is to oppress unjustly the former....

...

It is under the word *government* that the subtle danger lurks. Understood as a central consolidated power, managing and directing the various general interests of the society, all government is evil, and the parent of evil. A strong and active democratic government, in the common sense of the term, is an evil, differing only in degree and mode of operation, and not in nature, from a strong despotism....

The best government is that which governs least. No human depositories can, with safety, be trusted with the power of legislation upon the general interests of society so as to operate directly or indirectly on the industry and property of the community. Such power must be perpetually liable to the most pernicious abuse, from the natural imperfection, both in wisdom of judgment and purity of purpose, of all human legislation, exposed constantly to the pressure of partial interests....Government should have as little as possible to do with the general business and

10. Isaac N. Arnold, *The Life of Abraham Lincoln* (Chicago: Jansen, McClurg, and Company, 1885), 62.

11. Excerpt taken from *The United States Magazine and Democratic Review* (October 1837).

Box 5-1 A Partial Cast of Characters of the Jacksonian Era

Andrew Jackson	■ Democrat ■ Brief political career in Tennessee ■ Popular military leader in War of 1812 and in Indian wars in Georgia and Spanish Florida ■ Lost controversial presidential election of 1824 that was settled in the House of Representatives ■ President of the United States (1829–1837) ■ Founder of the Democratic Party ■ Advocate of presidential power, nationalism, popular democracy, and strict constructionism
Roger Taney	■ Democrat ■ Entered politics as a Maryland Federalist ■ U.S. Attorney General under Democrat Andrew Jackson (1831–1833) ■ Authored important presidential papers, including Bank Veto message ■ U.S. Secretary of Treasury under Jackson (1833–1834), removed federal funds from Bank of the United States ■ Nomination as associate justice, defeated by Whig Senate, confirmed as chief justice by Democratic Senate to succeed John Marshall (1836–1864) ■ Advocate of states' rights and strict constructionism, known as a defender of slave interests, and the author of *Dred Scott* decision
Daniel Webster	■ Whig ■ Began career as Massachusetts Federalist ■ Member of the U.S. House of Representatives (1813–1817, 1823–1827) ■ Member of U.S. Senate (1827–1841, 1845–1850) ■ Whig candidate for president in 1836 ■ U.S. Secretary of State under several Whig presidents (1841–1843, 1850–1852) ■ Leading Supreme Court litigator and advocate of property rights, national union, and broad construction of congressional powers
Henry Clay	■ Whig ■ Began career as Kentucky "War Hawk" and National Republican ■ Member of the U.S. House of Representatives (1811–1821, 1823–1825), usually serving as Speaker of the House ■ Member of the U.S. Senate (1806–1807, 1810–1811, 1831–1842, 1849–1852) ■ U.S. Secretary of State under Republican John Quincy Adams (1825–1829) ■ Three-time unsuccessful presidential candidate ■ Advocate of "American System" of national banking, infrastructure, protectionist tariffs and broad construction of congressional powers
John C. Calhoun	■ Democrat ■ Began career as South Carolina "War Hawk" and National Republican ■ Member of U.S. House of Representatives (1811–1817) ■ Member of U.S. Senate (1832–1843, 1845–1850) ■ U.S. Secretary of War under Republican James Monroe (1817–1825) ■ U.S. Vice President under Republican John Quincy Adams and Democrat Andrew Jackson (1825–1832) ■ U.S. Secretary of State under Whig John Tyler (1844–1845) ■ Broke with Jackson and flirted with Whig and local states' rights parties ■ Advocate of states' rights and Southern sectional interests, known as leading theorist of state nullification

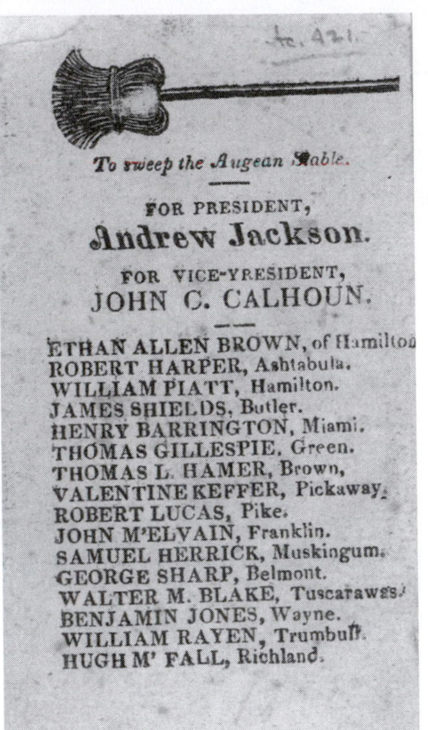

Illustration 5-2 A Democratic Party ticket ballot for the presidential election of 1828 for Ohio, with a list of presidential electors. The ballot was distributed to voters by the party, often by printing them in party newspapers. Voters carried the ballot with them and cast it at the polling place. The government did not print ballots until the late nineteenth century.

Source: Library of Congress: Broadsides, leaflets, and pamphlets from America and Europe.

interests of the people.... It will be impossible to confine it to the public interests of the commonwealth. It will be perpetually tampering with private interests, and sending forth seeds of corruption which will result in the demoralization of the society. Its domestic action should be confined to the administration of justice, for the protection of the natural equal rights of the citizen and the preservation of social order.

...

Such is, then, our democracy. It of course places us in the school of the strictest construction of the Constitution.... One necessary inference from the views expressed above is that we consider the preservation of the present ascendancy of the Democratic party as of great, if not vital, importance to the future destinies of this holy cause....

John Quincy Adams, First Annual Message (1825)[12]

John Quincy Adams (1767–1848) was the last president with close personal ties to the framers. His first State of the Union message announced a bold National Republican program. The orthodox Jeffersonians and the Jacksonian insurgents who together controlled Congress in 1825 rejected this vision of national power to promote commercial prosperity and civic virtue. Adams and his supporters, such as Henry Clay and Daniel Webster, soon formed the Whig Party, which advanced the policies and sense of national purpose that Adams sketched out during his administration.

... The great object of the institution of civil government is the improvement of the condition of those who are parties to the social compact, and no government, in whatever form constituted, can accomplish the lawful ends of its institution but in proportion as it improves the condition of those over whom it is established. Roads and canals, by multiplying and facilitating the communications and intercourse between distant regions and multitudes of men, are among the most important means of improvement. But moral, political, intellectual improvement are duties assigned by the Author of Our Existence to social no less than to individual man. For the fulfillment of those duties governments are invested with power, and to the attainment of the end—the progressive improvement of the condition of the governed—the exercise of delegated powers is a duty as sacred and indispensable as the usurpation of powers not granted is criminal and odious. Among the first, perhaps the very first, instrument for the improvement of the condition of men is knowledge, and to the acquisition of much of the knowledge adapted to the wants, the comforts, and enjoyments of human life public institutions and seminaries of learning are essential....

...

Connected with the establishment of a university, or separate from it, might be undertaken the erection of an astronomical observatory, with provision for the support of an astronomer, to be in constant attendance of

12. Excerpt taken from John Quincy Adams, "First Annual Message," (Dec. 6, 1825), in *A Compilation of the Messages and Papers of the President 1789–1897*, ed. James D. Richardson, vol. 2 (Washington, DC: Government Printing Office, 1896), 299.

observation upon the phenomena of the heavens, and for the periodical publication of his observations....

...

The Constitution under which you are assembled is a charter of limited powers. After full and solemn deliberation upon all or any of the objects which, urged by an irresistible sense of my own duty, I have recommended to your attention should you come to the conclusion that, however desirable in themselves, the enactment of laws for effecting them would transcend the powers committed to you by that venerable instrument which we are all bound to support, let no consideration induce you to assume the exercise of powers not granted to you by the people. But if... [the powers] enumerated in the Constitution may be effectually brought into action by laws promoting the improvement of agriculture, commerce, and manufactures, the cultivation and encouragement of the mechanic and of the elegant arts, the advancement of literature, and the progress of the sciences, ornamental and profound, to refrain from exercising them for the benefit of the people themselves would be to hide in the earth the talent committed to our charge—would be treachery to the most sacred of trusts.

The spirit of improvement is abroad upon the earth. It stimulates the hearts and sharpens the faculties not of our fellow-citizens alone, but of the nations of Europe and of their rulers. While dwelling with pleasing satisfaction upon the superior excellence of our political institutions, let us not be unmindful that liberty is power; that the nation blessed with the largest portion of liberty must in proportion to its numbers be the most powerful nation upon earth, and that the tenure of power by man is, in the moral purposes of his Creator, upon condition that it shall be exercised to ends of beneficence, to improve the condition of himself and his fellowmen. While foreign nations less blessed with that freedom which is power than ourselves are advancing with gigantic strides in the career of public improvement, were we to slumber in indolence or fold up our arms and proclaim to the world that we are palsied by the will of our constituents, would it not be to cast away the bounties of Providence and doom ourselves to perpetual inferiority?... [C]an we, the representative authorities of the whole Union, fall behind our fellow-servants [in the states] in the exercise of the trust committed to us for the benefit of our common sovereign by the accomplishment of works important to the whole and to which neither the authority nor the resources of any one State can be adequate?

II. Judicial Power and Constitutional Authority

MAJOR DEVELOPMENTS

- Most elected officials support the judicial power to declare laws unconstitutional.
- Jacksonians reorganize the federal judicial system in ways that guarantee a slave state majority on the Supreme Court.
- Most states adopt constitutional provisions requiring state judges to be elected.

The constitutional authority of state and federal courts was well established by the end of the Jacksonian Era. The Supreme Court of the United States in *Ableman v. Booth* (1858) strongly reasserted the judicial power to declare federal and state laws unconstitutional, bluntly stated that state courts were bound by federal judicial interpretations of the Constitution, and indicated that elected officials in the national government were similarly bound to obey federal judicial rulings. Most state courts before the Civil War successfully asserted the power to declare that state laws violated the state constitution. These assertions of judicial authority enjoyed bipartisan support. Whigs historically favored strong courts. Democrats became more partial to federal courts as those courts became staffed with justices appointed by Democrats.

Occasional flare-ups of court-curbing occurred, but federal and state courts survived them largely unscathed. In 1824, the Kentucky legislature disbanded the state supreme court after the justices struck down a popular mortgage relief law. Over the next two elections, supporters of the courts and judicial review won decisive victories at the polls. The state judiciary was reinstated, much to the satisfaction of watchful national leaders.[13] Judge William Gibson of the Pennsylvania Supreme Court sharply criticized *Marbury v. Madison* (1803) when dissenting in *Eakin v. Raub* (1825). President Jackson pointedly passed over Gibson when later considering appointments to the Supreme Court of the United States. Southern Jacksonians in 1831 sought to repeal Section 25 of the Judiciary Act, the provision that gave the Supreme Court the power to review constitutional decisions made by state courts. A coalition of

13. See generally, Theodore W. Ruger, "'A Question Which Convulses a Nation': The Early Republic's Greatest Debate About the Judicial Review Power," *Harvard Law Review* 117 (2004):826.

Whigs and northern Democrats defeated that proposal by a 3–1 margin. When anti-slavery advocates during the 1840s and 1850s bitterly condemned the pro-southern bias of federal judicial decisions in fugitive slave cases, Democrats in all three branches of the national government reiterated commitments to judicial power.

The more important debates over constitutional authority in Jacksonian America were over who would control the courts and how judges should use the power of judicial review. The Judiciary Act of 1837 expanded the membership of the Supreme Court by two justices. This measure enabled Democrats to secure a majority on the Court for the next thirty years. The Judiciary Act of 1837 also reorganized the federal judiciary so that the majority of justices on the Supreme Court resided in the slaveholding states. The justices Democrats appointed to the Supreme Court had substantial experience in legislatures and in high-level executive office before being nominated to the bench (see Figure 7-4). They understood politics and party commitments, sometimes leaking valuable information to the supporters in Congress or the White House. At the state level, the Jacksonian Era saw extensive debates over whether judges should be appointed or elected, and, if elected, whether for a short or long term of office. Elected judiciaries made judges accountable directly to the people, but in an increasingly partisan era judicial elections took the appointment process out of the hands of politicians.

As you read, consider the kinds of judicial reform that were debated and adopted at the state and federal levels during this period. The U.S. Constitution has particularly strong safeguards for judicial independence. State-level reforms have often been concerned with getting more accountability from the courts. Is the design of the federal judiciary contained in the U.S. Constitution antiquated? Has the Constitution been effective in maintaining judicial independence? If we were to design a federal judiciary today, would we choose something close to the system that we have now—or would we create something quite different?

A. Judicial Structure and Selection

Note: Jacksonians Reorganize the Federal Judiciary

In the early republic, seats on the Supreme Court were tightly connected to federal judicial circuits. Supreme Court seats were treated as "local" positions, just like regular circuit court judges. Presidents were expected to nominate individuals from the states in the appropriate circuit. Individual justices oversaw their circuits and spent much time acting as circuit court judges. Many circuit court cases involved state law and procedures. Local citizens bringing these suits expected federal judges to have local expertise. As a result of these conventions, the number of seats on the Supreme

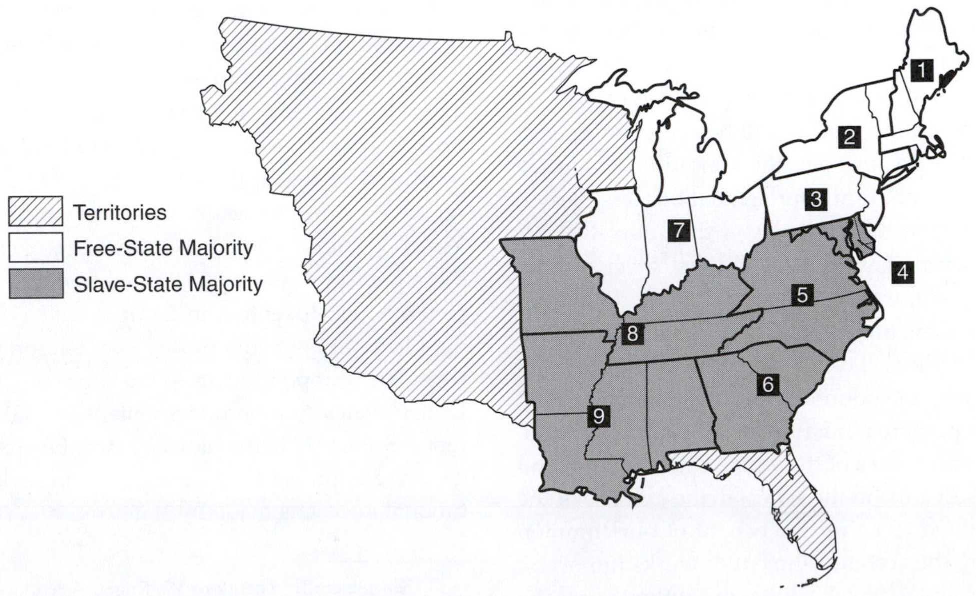

Figure 5-2 Map of Federal Judicial Circuits, 1837

Table 5-2 Supreme Court Justices and Federal Judicial Circuits, 1842–1860

Federal Judicial Circuits	Supreme Court Justices
Free State Circuits	
First Circuit ME, MA, NH RI	Joseph Story (MA) (1812–1845) Levi Woodbury (NH) (1845–1851) Benjamin Curtis (MA) (1851–1857) Nathan Clifford (ME) (1858–1881)
Second Circuit CT, NY, VT	Smith Thompson (NY) (1823–1843) Samuel Nelson (NY) (1845–1872)
Third Circuit NJ, PA	Henry Baldwin (PA) (1830–1844) Robert Grier (PA) (1846–1870)
Seventh Circuit IL, IN, MI, OH	John McLean (OH) (1829–1861)
Slave State Circuits	
Fourth Circuit DE, MD	Roger B. Taney (MD) (1836–1864)
Fifth Circuit NC, VA	Peter Daniel (VA) (1842–1860)
Sixth Circuit GA, SC	James Wayne (GA) (1835–1867)
Eighth Circuit MO, KY, TN	John Catron (TN) (1837–1865)
Ninth Circuit AL, AR, LA, MS	John McKinley (AL) (1838–1852) John Campbell (AL) (1853–1861)

Court equaled the number of federal circuits, and the location of those circuits determined the balance of judicial power between the free and slave states.

Jacksonians inherited a federal court system with seven circuits. The first three circuits were entirely within free states, the next three were entirely within slave states, and the mixed Seventh Circuit contained Ohio (free), Kentucky (slave), and Tennessee (slave). Many new western states were not included. Congress repeatedly failed during the 1820s and early 1830s to expand the federal judicial system. Divided government ensured that members of one party did not provide the president of another party with the opportunity to make additional judicial appointments. Representatives from the free and slave states were also concerned with the balance of sectional power in the federal judiciary.

This impasse was broken after the national elections of 1834 and 1836 left Democrats in control of both Houses of Congress and the White House. The Judiciary Act of 1837 reorganized the federal judiciary so that a majority of the circuits were located entirely within slave states. The Seventh Circuit was transformed from a mixed circuit to a non-slave circuit by replacing Kentucky and Tennessee with Illinois and Indiana. The new Eighth (Missouri, Kentucky, and Tennessee) and Ninth (Alabama, Louisiana, Mississippi, and Arkansas) Circuits were composed entirely of slave states. Some additional adjustments were made in 1842. Virginia moved from the all-slave Fifth to the all-slave Fourth, Alabama and Louisiana moved to the all-slave Fifth, North Carolina was added to the all-slave Sixth, and Michigan was added to the free Seventh. In 1855, a Tenth Circuit was created for California, but for the first time no Supreme Court seat was associated with that circuit. The Judiciary Act also created two new seats on the Supreme Court. President Jackson filled those seats with justices representing the newly created Eighth and Ninth Circuits. With these reforms in place, the slave states were assured a five-to-four advantage on the Supreme Court for the rest of the antebellum period.

The Judiciary Act of 1837, by practically guaranteeing a slaveholding majority on the Supreme Court, provided additional structural protection for southern interests. Jacksonian judicial appointees were relatively moderate when compared to some of the more extreme voices heard in the House and the Senate. Only one member, Justice Peter Daniel, was a southern extremist; one other, Justice John Campbell, was a reluctant secessionist. Nevertheless, the justices of the slave-state circuits could always be counted on to act as a reliable "veto point" in the event that the elected branches of the national government or the free states became more hostile to the interests of the slave states. Judicial majorities during the Jacksonian Era repeatedly sustained federal fugitive slave laws, struck down northern personal liberty laws that southerners perceived as interfering with efforts to capture escaped slaves, declared that free persons of color were not American citizens, and ruled that Congress had no power to ban slavery in American territories. *United States v. The Amistad* (1841), the case made famous by the Stephen Spielberg movie, is the only major Supreme Court decision made during the Jacksonian Era which rejected strong slaveholding demands.

Debate on the Electoral Accountability of the Judiciary, Ohio Constitutional Convention (1850)[14]

By the end of the Jacksonian Era, almost three-quarters of the states chose judges by popular election. Nineteen of the twenty-one state constitutional conventions held between 1846 and 1850 adopted elective judiciaries. Other states shifted to elected judiciaries by specific constitutional amendment, rather than as part of a larger constitutional reform. In most states, the adoption of elective judiciaries was bipartisan and relatively uncontroversial. Most Democrats and some Whigs regarded appointed judiciaries as instruments of partisan mobilization rather than as instruments of justice. Judicial offices were awarded as the political spoils of electoral victory. Appointment fights were bruising and often left judicial seats vacant. Justice in court was neither reliable nor fast. Making judges electorally accountable to the people, proponents of elected judiciaries hoped, would promote courts that served the public's interest.[15]

Ohio was among the states that adopted an elective judiciary. The 1850 state constitution, which remains in effect today, provided for five-year terms for the judges of the state supreme court. The debate in the Ohio convention was not over whether judges should be elected. All sides admitted that there was no other politically realistic option. The delegates instead debated how long the judicial term of office should be. Democrats, the majority party in Ohio, favored shorter terms of office than Whigs. Who had the better argument? Should judges face the voters frequently or infrequently? Which better advances the will of the people?

Mr. M. H. MITCHELL (Democrat)...As to how far I would have the popular sentiment, or impulse, as some have expressed it, to operate on the court, I beg leave to say, that I have such confidence in the great mass of mankind, as to believe that they will come to right conclusions at last; and that the settled opinions of the popular mind may be always safely trusted. But I also know that the masses of mankind, like the waves of the ocean, are subject to fluctuation; and if you could find the true criterion by which to judge of what really is the popular sentiment, you must take more than a mere period—you must take a reasonable, perhaps I might say considerable period together, so as to get their settled opinion....

This is the proper process of reasoning to follow, when inquiring as to what is really the character and feeling of the community at large. And this is what the judge should have always in his mind. Acting upon this rule, he would ever be preserved from the influence of the sudden emotions and impulses and excitement of the day or any short period of time. He would always take a survey of the popular feeling for an extended period of time....Neither should a judge forget that it is his great duty to discharge with fidelity every trust which is committed to him by the community. So, then, he should hold himself accountable, not that he should obey the impulses of their excited minds, or the ebullitions of their passions, but that he should always be

---

14. Excerpt taken from Report of the Debates and Proceedings of the Convention for the Revision of the Constitution of the State of Ohio, 1850–51, vol. 1 (Columbus: S. Medary, 1851), 681–691.

15. On elected judiciaries, see Kermit L. Hall, "The Judiciary on Trial: State Constitutional Reform and the Rise of an Elected Judiciary, 1846–1860," *The Historian* 45 (1983):337; F. Andrew Hanssen, "Learning about Judicial Independence: Institutional Change in the State Courts," *Journal of Legal Studies* 33 (2004):431; Jed Shugerman, "Economic Crisis and the Rise of Judicial Elections and Judicial Review," *Harvard Law Review* 123 (2010):1061.

obedient to their sober judgment, and with studied reference to that he should always act. It is in this manner that the impulses and sentiments of mankind should always act upon a judicial tribunal....

...

Mr. CHARLES REEMELIN (Democrat)...I [am] in favor of impartial courts, at the same time that I said I was opposed to independent courts. Impartial between man and man, and not independent of public opinion, popular feeling, and even, if you please, popular impulses. I want no balance wheel in our government, but the balance wheel of public opinion. I have confidence in the public opinion; I want it to have its due, frequent, and unbiased influence on every part of our government. I do not want a judge to go out into the streets, and ask himself whether the man whose case he is adjudicating upon is a whig, or a democrat, but I want a judge above him, to whom he must soon render an account, and that judge is the people of Ohio.

...

Mr. REUBEN HITCHCOCK (Whig)...[W]e have been informed...as to what the object is. It is to make a political court, to decide the causes according to the political dogmas of the day. The gentleman says, to be sure, we would not have the principle prevail where individuals are before the court as suitors, but where the public is concerned, or where a corporation is concerned, the court is to carry out, not the law but the political opinions of those who appointed them. That I understand to be the object of the gentlemen, and now I ask, is it the desire of this body to have the court so constituted, that it shall not in all cases be controlled by the law of the land but shall be controlled by the political dogmas of any political party? What does the gentleman desire? A political court not to be controlled by law—not to decide cases according to the constitution and the law but to decide cases as shall be dictated them by those who appointed them. Is that the object?...

...

Why Mr. Chairman, if such is to be the case, it may operate upon us all. This popular prejudice at one time may be running in one direction; and thus those who to-day gain their rights, or succeed in that which they pretend to be right, through popular prejudice, may to-morrow, by a change of parties, be placed in a situation to lose as much or still more than they have gained. Now it seems to me, Mr. Chairman, this is worthy of the utmost consideration. We should reflect upon this subject before we act.

...

Mr. HENRY STANBERY (Whig)...I did not know that our judges performed their duties more faithfully than in other countries. The judges of England, though appointed by the Crown, had been faithful and impartial in discharging the duties of their high station. None more so. The judges, in many of the States of the Union, appointed by the Executive, and holding by a life tenure, are equally faithful and honest.

Mr. DANIEL ROBERTSON (Democrat). Then the gentleman is in favor of the appointment of judges by the Executive, is he not?

Mr. STANBERY. Not at all. I am in favor of their election by the people. But that is not the point. I was answering the assertion that frequent elections of the judges, and short terms of office, would insure more capable and impartial officers. That is what I very much doubt. I may say, it is what I do not expect. I fear the contrary.

...In the history of the world, not an instance can be found, in which the liberties of the people have been taken away by the judiciary. It holds neither the sword nor the purse. It wields no patronage. We must protect it, rather than guard against it. It is our safeguard, when properly constituted, against political power, wherever that power may be lodged. We must make it independent, to secure impartiality and honesty. From the earliest times—from the times when man first conceived a right idea of the judicial character, independence and impartiality have been deemed its essential attributes. In the early ages, when the virtues were deified, justice was well personified, a bandage was drawn over her eyes, and even balances put into her hands, to indicate perfect impartiality—complete independence of all extraneous influences.

I never want to see a judge upon the bench, who must look to the people before he can decide a case—who must constantly consult and be governed by popular impulses—who shall be always under a fear of accountability to those who make and unmake him. How can such a judge take a solemn oath to discharge his high office without fear, favor or affection; he who is constantly in dread—who is trembling at every step, lest his decisions may not be acceptable to a popular majority.

. . .

Mr. BENJAMIN STANTON (Whig). I will trust to the influence of reason and authority upon an upright and intelligent judge. If I differ with him upon a constitutional question; if he holds that the constitution means one thing and I hold that it means or ought to mean another, I will seek to change it by amendment, and not by judicial construction. When a constitution, or law has received a settled judicial construction I will abide by it, until it is changed by the proper authority and not seek to work a revolution by an appeal from the court to the ballot box upon the construction of a law. I will never consent that the independence of the judiciary shall be destroyed, and the constitution changed by construction of an appeal to the people in the election of judges—*never*, NEVER! . . .

[I]f I had the making of the constitution, I would elect the judges of the court of last resort for a long term, and make them ineligible for a re-election.

It seems to be imagined by some gentlemen that the majority, which is the governing power, should be at all times absolutely omnipotent. That there should be no obstacles or restraints to prevent them from sacrificing the most sacred rights of individuals at pleasure. That the life, liberty, reputation and property of every individual in community should at all times be at the mercy of the governing power.

An upright and independent judiciary would be an effectual protection to the inalienable rights of individuals, and hence it must be got rid of. There must be an appeal from the court to the ballot box. Everything must be sacrificed to a domineering partisan majority. Sir, I demure most earnestly to any such doctrine. I ought not to hold my life, liberty, and property at the mercy of the majority. . . .

. . .

Mr. JOSEPH McCORMICK (Democrat) . . .

I hold, sir, that democracy looks to a pure and disinterested judiciary; that democracy seeks for the sacrifice of no right; that it seeks for the promotion of law and order, and for a proper and consistent state of things; that it asks not for the government of lynch law; that it asks not to make the judiciary subservient in the wishes and caprices of individuals or cliques—all these things I openly disclaim as constituting any part of my democracy; yet I am in favor of the election of judges by the people, and not only so, but I am in favor of a short term of office.

B. Constitutional Litigation

Luther v. Borden (1849) is commonly regarded as the starting point for the political question doctrine. The case made explicit that some constitutional questions were non-justiciable. This means those issues can not be decided by the courts. The "political question" doctrine does not prohibit justices from deciding cases that are controversial or involve matters of public policy. Political questions have some characteristic or element that makes them best suited for elected officials. The Court in *Marbury v. Madison* (1803) stated that federal judges had no power to adjudicate substantive questions that had been entrusted to the discretionary authority of another branch of government. Chief Justice Roger Taney in *Luther v. Borden* expanded this notion into a full-blown doctrine that there were some issues that were simply inappropriate for judicial resolution. Such questions were non-justiciable because they had been specifically delegated to a different institution, were intrinsically mixed up with policy judgments, or lacked an adequate standard that could guide judges. The particular concern in *Luther v. Borden* was whether the Court could decide cases based on the republican guarantee clause of the Article IV of the U.S. Constitution—specifically, could it determine whether the government exercising power within a state met the requirements of a republican government. Taney argued that such issues could not be decided by the federal courts and had instead been entrusted to the political branches of the national government.

Luther v. Borden, 48 U.S. 1 (1849)

The state of Rhode Island in 1841 was governed by the same charter granted to the Rhode Island colony in 1663. That charter extended suffrage to landholders and heavily favored the rural areas of the state in the apportionment of legislative seats. As the state urbanized, many citizens demanded that the state adopt a new constitution that expanded the suffrage. The state legislature resisted calls for reform, and the royal charter included no provisions for amendment. Frustrated, reformers sponsored a popular convention that drafted a new constitution. That constitution was promulgated and "ratified" in town meetings across the state. A government, led by Thomas Dorr, was elected by universal, white, male suffrage under the new radical constitution. The charter government refused to recognize the new constitution. Members of the established government of Rhode Island in 1842 sponsored a separate constitutional convention which adopted a modestly reformed constitution. The old charter government, led by Samuel King, was reelected under that new reformed constitution. This left Rhode Island with two separate groups of elected officials claiming to be the legitimate government of the state under two different constitutions.

The King government triumphed by declaring martial law and successfully disbursing the Dorr government. While Rhode Island was under martial law, official government troops led by Luther Borden raided the house of Martin Luther, a shoemaker and a bit player in the Dorr reform movement. Luther sued Borden for trespass in federal court. He claimed that the King government was not the lawful authority in 1842. The federal circuit court rejected Luther's argument, and he appealed to the U.S. Supreme Court.

The Supreme Court ruled that federal courts could not determine the lawful government of Rhode Island. Chief Justice Taney maintained that the question of which government was the lawful government of a state was a political question entrusted to elected officials. The judicial majority in Luther v. Borden *then determined that Governor King was constitutionally authorized to declare martial law. Justice Woodbury dissented on that issue only.*

You might consider the following questions when reading Chief Justice Taney's opinion. Are there constitutional questions that cannot be answered by the courts? What considerations might lead the courts to stay out of a constitutional controversy? What practical considerations might explain why the Taney Court was reluctant to intervene in the Dorr War?

CHIEF JUSTICE TANEY delivered the opinion of the Court.

. . .

. . . [T]he question presented is certainly a very serious one: For, if this court is authorized to enter upon this inquiry as proposed by the plaintiff, and it should be decided that the charter government had no legal existence during the period of time above mentioned,—if it had been annulled by the adoption of the opposing government,—then the laws passed by its legislature during that time were nullities; its taxes wrongfully collected; its salaries and compensation to its officers illegally paid; its public accounts improperly settled; and the judgments and sentences of its courts in civil and criminal cases null and void, and the officers who carried their decisions into operation answerable as trespassers, if not in some cases as criminals.

When the decision of this court might lead to such results, it becomes its duty to examine very carefully its own powers before it undertakes to exercise jurisdiction.

Certainly, the question which the plaintiff proposed to raise by the testimony he offered has not heretofore been recognized as a judicial one in any of the State courts. In forming the constitutions of the different States, after the Declaration of Independence, and in the various changes and alterations which have since been made, the political department has always determined whether the proposed constitution or amendment was ratified or not by the people of the State, and the judicial power has followed its decision. In Rhode Island, the question has been directly decided. . . .

. . .

[T]he Constitution of the United States, as far as it has provided for an emergency of this kind, and authorized the general government to interfere in the domestic concerns of a State, has treated the subject as political in its nature, and placed the power in the hands of that department.

The fourth section of the fourth article of the Constitution of the United States provides that the United States shall guarantee to every State in the Union a republican form of government, and shall protect each of them against invasion; and on the application of the legislature or of the executive (when the legislature cannot be convened) against domestic violence.

Under this article of the Constitution it rests with Congress to decide what government is the established one in a State. For as the United States guarantee to each State a republican government, Congress must necessarily decide what government is established in the State before it can determine whether it is republican or not. And when the senators and representatives of a State are admitted into the councils of the Union, the authority of the government under which they are appointed, as well as its republican character, is recognized by the proper constitutional authority. And its decision is binding on every other department of the government, and could not be questioned in a judicial tribunal. . . .

. . .

By this act [of Congress of February 28, 1795 for calling out the militia], the power of deciding whether the exigency had arisen upon which the government of the United States is bound to interfere, is given to the President. He is to act upon the application of the legislature or of the executive, and consequently he must determine what body of men constitute the legislature, and who is the governor, before he can act.... And the President must, of necessity, decide which is the government, and which party is unlawfully arrayed against it, before he can perform the duty imposed upon him by the act of Congress.

After the President has acted and called out the militia, is a Circuit Court of the United States authorized to inquire whether his decision was right? Could the court, while the parties were actually contending in arms for the possession of the government, call witnesses before it and inquire which party represented a majority of the people? If it could, then it would become the duty of the court (provided it came to the conclusion that the President had decided incorrectly) to discharge those who were arrested or detained by the troops in the service of the United States or the government which the President was endeavoring to maintain. If the judicial power extends so far, the guarantee contained in the Constitution of the United States is a guarantee of anarchy, and not of order....

...

It is said that this power in the President is dangerous to liberty, and may be abused. All power may be abused if placed in unworthy hands. But it would be difficult, we think, to point out any other hands in which this power would be more safe, and at the same time equally effectual. When citizens of the same State are in arms against each other, and the constituted authorities unable to execute the laws, the interposition of the United States must be prompt, or it is of little value. The ordinary course of proceedings in courts of justice would be utterly unfit for the crisis. And the elevated office of the President, chosen as he is by the people of the United States, and the high responsibility he could not fail to feel when acting in a case of so much moment, appear to furnish as strong safeguards against a willful abuse of power as human prudence and foresight could well provide. At all events, it is conferred upon him by the Constitution and laws of the United States, and must therefore be respected and enforced in its judicial tribunals.

...

Much of the argument on the part of the plaintiff turned upon political rights and political questions, upon which the court has been urged to express an opinion. We decline doing so. The high power has been conferred on this court of passing judgment upon the acts of the State sovereignties, and of the legislative and executive branches of the federal government, and of determining whether they are beyond the limits of power marked out for them respectively by the Constitution of the United States. This tribunal, therefore, should be the last to overstep the boundaries which limit its own jurisdiction. And while it should always be ready to meet any question confided to it by the Constitution, it is equally its duty not to pass beyond its appropriate sphere of action, and to take care not to involve itself in discussions which properly belong to other forums. No one, we believe, has ever doubted the proposition, that, according to the institutions of this country, the sovereignty in every State resides in the people of the State, and that they may alter and change their form of government at their own pleasure. But whether they have changed it or not by abolishing an old government, and establishing a new one in its place, is a question to be settled by the political power. And when that power has decided, the courts are bound to take notice of its decision, and to follow it.

The judgment of the Circuit Court must therefore be affirmed.

JUSTICE WOODBURY, dissenting.

...

III. Powers of the National Government

MAJOR DEVELOPMENTS

- Jackson and his successors veto on constitutional grounds bills incorporating a national bank and providing federal funding for internal improvements.
- Congress annexes Texas by joint resolution.
- The Supreme Court sustains federal fugitive slave acts, but rules that Congress has no power to ban slavery in the western territories.

The scope of congressional authority to promote commercial prosperity, aquire new territories, and protect slavery remained the most important constitutional controversies over the powers of the national government during the Jacksonian Era. Debates over congressional power to promote commercial prosperity focused on the constitutionality of the national bank, federally funded internal improvements, and protective tariffs. Whether Congress could annex, by a joint resolution, the Republic of Texas was the primary constitutional debate over national expansion. Slaveholders and antislavery activists disputed whether Congress could prohibit slavery in American territories and whether Congress could pass a fugitive slave law.

Most prominent political actors championed broad national powers during some of these debates and rejected national power in others. Democrats opposed and Whigs favored broad national power to promote commercial prosperity. The parties reversed position on national expansion. Most Democrats thought Texas could be annexed by a joint resolution passed by majorities in both the Senate and the House. Most Whigs insisted that Texas could be annexed only by a treaty ratified by a two-thirds majority of the Senate. Many antislavery activists maintained that Congress could ban slavery in the territories, but could not pass a fugitive slave law. Many slaveholders maintained that Congress could not ban slavery in the territories, but could pass a fugitive slave law.

Southern Democrats triumphed during most of these constitutional debates. President Jackson and his successors vetoed bills incorporating the national bank and providing federal funds for internal improvements. Congress reduced tariffs. Texas was admitted to the Union by a joint resolution of both Houses of Congress. The Supreme Court in *Prigg v. Pennsylvania* (1842) ruled that Congress could pass fugitive slave laws. Congress passed a controversial fugitive slave law in 1850. Congress in 1854 repealed the provision in the Missouri Compromise prohibiting slavery in all territories above the 36°30′ parallel line. The Supreme Court in *Dred Scott v. Sandford* (1857) declared that provision had always been unconstitutional, that Congress had no power to ban slavery in the territories.

Jacksonian Democrats during these constitutional debates maintained they were the true heirs to the strict constructionist philosophy of the Jeffersonian Republicans. Whigs disagreed. As you read, consider the extent to which Democratic thinking about federal power was simply an extension of Jeffersonian thinking about federal power. Are there significant modifications or contradictions? What about American politics might encourage Democratic–Whig debates to be a replay of Jeffersonian–Federalist debates, and to what degree do politics not simply repeat the debates of the past? How did participants in the constitutional debates of the Jacksonian Era justify claims that the Constitution vested the national government with broad powers to regulate some matters, but not others? What significance did the judiciary or other institutions have in defining national power during this period? Why did they play those roles? What issues helped drive the specification of national power under the Constitution, and why?

A. Necessary and Proper Clause

Jacksonians inherited from the early national period ongoing constitutional controversies over the Bank of the United States and internal improvements. The Democratic Party that formed around Andrew Jackson was the home for the ideological heirs of the Old Republicans who had raised constitutional objections to National Republican efforts to use national power during the first two decades of the nineteenth century. The national platform of the Democratic Party in 1844 declared:

> the Federal Government is one of limited powers, derived solely from the Constitution, and the grants of power shown therein ought to be strictly construed by all the departments and agents of the government, and that it is inexpedient and dangerous to exercise doubtful constitutional powers.
>
> [T]he Constitution does not confer upon the General Government the power to commence or carry on a general system of internal improvements.
>
> [T]he Constitution does not confer authority upon the Federal Government, directly or indirectly, to assume the debts of the several States, contracted for local internal improvements or other State purposes; nor would such assumption be just or expedient.
>
> . . .
>
> Congress has no power to charter a United States Bank, that we believe such an institution one of deadly hostility to the best interests of the country, dangerous to our republican institutions and the liberties of the people, and calculated to place the business of the country within the control of a concentrated money power, and above the laws and the will of the people.

The Whig leadership was made up of former National Republicans who were comfortable with previous uses of federal power and broader constructions of federal authority. During the 1830s, Whigs championed the national bank. After 1840, Whigs united behind a program of federally funded internal improvements. Their 1852 national platform declared,

> The Constitution vests in Congress the power to open and repair harbors, and remove obstructions from navigable rivers, whenever such improvements are necessary for the common defence, and for the protection and facility of commerce with foreign nations, or among the States, said improvements being, in every instance, national and general in their character.

Jackson and his successors in the White House successfully prevented Whigs from implementing their vision of national power. Democrats during the decades before the Civil War made extensive use of the Presidential veto power to maintain a strict construction of national authority:

- Andrew Jackson vetoed bills providing federal funds for local roads and incorporating a national bank.
- John Tyler vetoed bills providing federal support to improve the navigation of rivers and incorporating a national bank.
- James Polk vetoed a bill providing federal funds to improve local rivers and harbors.
- Franklin Pierce vetoed bills providing federal funds to build hospitals and federal funds to make internal improvements.
- James Buchanan vetoed bills providing federal funds for education, federal funds for internal improvements, and giving federal lands to settlers.

Each of these vetoes was accompanied by a lengthy message explaining why the legislation was unconstitutional.

These presidential vetoes explain why the Supreme Court during the Jacksonian Era did not reconsider the Marshall Court's decision in *McCulloch v. Maryland* (1819) that the necessary and proper clause supported construing federal powers broadly. The Supreme Court under the leadership of Chief Justice Roger Taney might have overruled *McCulloch* and adopted a narrower reading of congressional power in an appropriate case. Taney helped write Jackson's veto declaring the national bank unconstitutional. Other Jacksonians on the Court had previously given speeches in Congress declaring the national bank unconstitutional. That case did not occur because Jacksonian presidents from 1828 to 1860 prevented Whig proposals from becoming law. Nevertheless, sophisticated politicians understood that *McCulloch* was no longer a vital precedent. Jackson's Bank veto message, not Marshall's *McCulloch* opinion, was the canonical document of the Jacksonian Era on the scope of the necessary and proper clause. The unconstitutionality of the Bank was an article of faith among Democrats. Presidents ignored *McCulloch* when writing their veto messages. Legislators in congressional debates admitted that the Taney Court would not sustain *McCulloch*. Abraham Lincoln in his 1858 debates with Stephen Douglas acknowledged that Jackson and his successors in the White House had effectively established that Congress had no power to incorporate a national bank.

Andrew Jackson, Veto Message Regarding the Bank of the United States (1832)[16]

The Second Bank of the United States was given a 20-year charter in 1816. Jackson's political opponents decided they could embarrass the President by seeking an early recharter of that institution before the 1832 election. President Jackson surprised many by vetoing the bill and offering powerful constitutional arguments against the bank. Jackson was far more astute than his opponents, who thought the bank veto would destroy Jackson politically. Jacksonians trumpeted their opposition to the Bank in the 1832 presidential election and won a landslide victory.

Jackson's veto message established that McCulloch v. Maryland *(1819) did not settle the constitutionality of the national bank. The first part argued that the constitutionality of the Bank was still a live issue that could be determined only by the elected officials. Jackson then argued that the Bank was not necessary and proper to the exercise of federal powers. The President concluded his message by denouncing the Bank bill as factional legislation, creating a monopoly to benefit the rich.*

Whigs made an effort to charter a third national bank of the United States after gaining control of all three branches of

16. Excerpt taken from Andrew Jackson, "Veto Message Regarding the Bank of the United States," (July 10, 1832), in *A Compilation of the Messages and Papers of the President 1789–1897*, ed. James D. Richardson, vol. 2 (Washington, DC: Government Printing Office, 1896), 576.

the national government in 1840. Unfortunately, President Harrison died before legislation was passed. His successor, Vice President John Tyler, had a more narrow understanding of federal power than Jackson. When Congress presented Tyler with a bank bill he rejected the measure on the ground that the bank would have the power to establish branches in the states without state approval. When Congress passed a national bank bill that confined the offices of that Bank to the District of Columbia, President Tyler vetoed the measure on the ground that the measure unconstitutionally "invested" a "local bank" with "general powers to operate over the Union."[17] *Whigs never again made a serious effort to charter a national bank.*

How do these events help you understand the constitutional status of McCulloch *after the Bank veto? What did the necessary and proper clause "mean" in the late 1830s? What would have been the best "authority" to cite when fashioning a constitutional argument for a lawyer in the 1840s?*

. . .

A bank of the United States is in many respects convenient for the Government and useful to the people. Entertaining this opinion, and deeply impressed with the belief that some of the powers and privileges possessed by the existing bank are unauthorized by the Constitution, subversive of the rights of the States, and dangerous to the liberties of the people, I felt it my duty at an early period of my Administration to call the attention of Congress to the practicability of organizing an institution combining all its advantages and obviating these objections. I sincerely regret that in the act before me I can perceive none of those modifications of the bank charter which are necessary, in my opinion, to make it compatible with justice, with sound policy, or with the Constitution of our country.

. . .

It is maintained by the advocates of the bank that its constitutionality in all its features ought to be considered as settled by precedent and by the decision of the Supreme Court. To this conclusion I can not assent. Mere precedent is a dangerous source of authority, and should not be regarded as deciding questions of constitutional power except where the acquiescence of the people and the States can be considered as well settled. So far from this being the case on this subject, an argument against the bank might be based on precedent. One Congress, in 1791, decided in favor of a bank; another, in 1811, decided against it. One Congress, in 1815, decided against a bank; another, in 1816, decided in its favor. Prior to the present Congress, therefore, the precedents drawn from that source were equal. If we resort to the States, the expressions of legislative, judicial, and executive opinions against the bank have been probably to those in its favor as 4 to 1. There is nothing in precedent, therefore, which, if its authority were admitted, ought to weigh in favor of the act before me.

If the opinion of the Supreme Court covered the whole ground of this act, it ought not to control the coordinate authorities of this Government. The Congress, the Executive, and the Court must each for itself be guided by its own opinion of the Constitution. Each public officer who takes an oath to support the Constitution swears that he will support it as he understands it, and not as it is understood by others. It is as much the duty of the House of Representatives, of the Senate, and of the President to decide upon the constitutionality of any bill or resolution which may be presented to them for passage or approval as it is of the supreme judges when it may be brought before them for judicial decision. The opinion of the judges has no more authority over Congress than the opinion of Congress has over the judges, and on that point the President is independent of both. The authority of the Supreme Court must not, therefore, be permitted to control the Congress or the Executive when acting in their legislative capacities, but to have only such influence as the force of their reasoning may deserve.

But in the case relied upon the Supreme Court have not decided that all the features of this corporation are compatible with the Constitution. It is true that the court have said that the law incorporating the bank is a constitutional exercise of power by Congress. . . .

[But t]he principle here affirmed is that the "degree of its necessity," involving all the details of a banking institution, is a question exclusively for legislative consideration. A bank is constitutional, but it is the province of the Legislature to determine whether this or that particular power, privilege, or exemption is "necessary and proper" to enable the bank to discharge its duties to the Government, and from their decision there is no appeal to the courts of justice. Under the decision of the Supreme Court, therefore, it is the exclusive province of Congress and the President to decide whether the particular features of this

17. John Tyler, "Veto Messages," supra, Vol. 4, 70.

act are *necessary* and *proper* in order to enable the bank to perform conveniently and efficiently the public duties assigned to it as a fiscal agent, and therefore constitutional, or *unnecessary* and *improper*, and therefore unconstitutional.

Without commenting on the general principle affirmed by the Supreme Court, let us examine the details of this act in accordance with the rule of legislative action which they have laid down. It will be found that many of the powers and privileges conferred on it can not be supposed necessary for the purpose for which it is proposed to be created, and are not, therefore, means necessary to attain the end in view, and consequently not justified by the Constitution.

The original act of incorporation...enacts "that no other bank shall be established by any future law of the United States during the continuance of the corporation hereby created, for which the faith of the United States is hereby pledged...."

If Congress possessed the power to establish one bank, they had power to establish more than one if in their opinion two or more banks had been "necessary" to facilitate the execution of the powers delegated to them in the Constitution....It was possessed by one Congress as well as another, and by all Congresses alike....But the Congress of 1816 have taken it away from their successors....It can not be "*necessary*" or "*proper*" for Congress to barter away or divest themselves of any of the powers vested in them by the Constitution to be exercised for the public good....This restriction on themselves and grant of a monopoly to the bank is therefore unconstitutional.

...

This act authorizes and encourages transfers of its stock to foreigners and grants them an exemption from all State and national taxation. So far from being "*necessary and proper*" that the bank should possess this power to make it a safe and efficient agent of the Government in its fiscal operations, it is calculated to convert the Bank of the United States into a foreign bank, to impoverish our people in time of peace, to disseminate a foreign influence through every section of the Republic, and in war to endanger our independence.

...

The Government of the United States have no constitutional power to purchase lands within the States except "for the erection of forts, magazines, arsenals, dockyards, and other needful buildings," and even for these objects only "by the consent of the legislature of the State in which the same shall be." By making themselves stockholders in the bank and granting to the corporation the power to purchase lands for other purposes they assume a power not granted in the Constitution and grant to others what they do not themselves possess. It is not *necessary* to the receiving, safe-keeping, or transmission of the funds of the Government that the bank should possess this power, and it is not *proper* that Congress should thus enlarge the powers delegated to them in the Constitution.

...

By its silence, considered in connection with the decision of the Supreme Court in the case of McCulloch against the State of Maryland, this act takes from the States the power to tax a portion of the banking business carried on within their limits, in subversion of one of the strongest barriers which secured them against Federal encroachments....

Upon the formation of the Constitution the States guarded their taxing power with peculiar jealousy. They surrendered it only as it regards imports and exports. In relation to every other object within their jurisdiction, whether persons, property, business, or professions, it was secured in as ample a manner as it was before possessed....Every private business, whether carried on by an officer of the General Government or not, whether it be mixed with public concerns or not, even if it be carried on by the Government of the United States itself, separately or in partnership, falls within the scope of the taxing power of the State....Over this whole subject-matter it is just as absolute, unlimited, and uncontrollable as if the Constitution had never been adopted, because in the formation of that instrument it was reserved without qualification.

The principle is conceded that the States can not rightfully tax the operations of the General Government. They can not tax the money of the Government deposited in the State banks, nor the agency of those banks in remitting it; but will any man maintain that their mere selection to perform this public service for the General Government would exempt the State banks and their ordinary business from State taxation? Had the United States, instead of establishing a bank at Philadelphia, employed a private banker to keep and transmit their funds, would it have deprived Pennsylvania of the right to tax his bank and his usual banking operations? It will not be pretended. Upon what principal, then, are the banking establishments of the Bank of the United States and their usual banking operations to be exempted from taxation?...

It can not be *necessary* to the character of the bank as a fiscal agent of the Government that its private business should be exempted from that taxation to which all the State banks are liable, nor can I conceive it *"proper"* that the substantive and most essential powers reserved by the States shall be thus attacked and annihilated as a means of executing the powers delegated to the General Government....

If our power over means is so absolute that the Supreme Court will not call in question the constitutionality of an act of Congress...it becomes us to proceed in our legislation with the utmost caution....

...

It is to be regretted that the rich and powerful too often bend the acts of government to their selfish purposes. Distinctions in society will always exist under every just government. Equality of talents, of education, or of wealth can not be produced by human institutions. In the full enjoyment of the gifts of Heaven and the fruits of superior industry, economy, and virtue, every man is equally entitled to protection by law; but when the laws undertake to add to these natural and just advantages artificial distinctions, to grant titles, gratuities, and exclusive privileges, to make the rich richer and the potent more powerful, the humble members of society—the farmers, mechanics, and laborers—who have neither the time nor the means of securing like favors to themselves, have a right to complain of the injustice of their Government. There are no

Illustration 5-3 President Andrew Jackson, wielding a cane marked "veto," attacks the monster Bank of the United States and its many branches. The largest head on the monster is that of Nicholas Biddle, the president of the Bank. Jackson is aided by Vice President Martin Van Buren and "Major Jack Downing," a popular fictional companion to Jackson.

Source: Division of Home and Community Life, National Museum of American History, Smithsonian Institution. Harry T. Peters, "America on Stone" Lithography Collection.

necessary evils in government. Its evils exist only in its abuses. If it would confine itself to equal protection, and, as Heaven does its rains, shower its favors alike on the high and the low, the rich and the poor, it would be an unqualified blessing. In the act before me there seems to be a wide and unnecessary departure from these just principles.

Nor is our Government to be maintained or our Union preserved by invasions of the rights and powers of the several States. In thus attempting to make our General Government strong we make it weak. Its true strength consists in leaving individuals and States as much as possible to themselves—in making itself felt, not in its power, but in its beneficence; not in its control, but in its protection; not in binding the States more closely to the center, but leaving each to move unobstructed in its proper orbit.

Experience should teach us wisdom. Most of the difficulties our Government now encounters and most of the dangers which impend over our Union have sprung from an abandonment of the legitimate objects of Government by our national legislation, and the adoption of such principles as are embodied in this act. Many of our rich men have not been content with equal protection and equal benefits, but have besought us to make them richer by act of Congress. By attempting to gratify their desires we have in the results of our legislation arrayed section against section, interest against interest, and man against man, in a fearful commotion which threatens to shake the foundations of our Union. It is time to pause in our career to review our principles, and if possible revive that devoted patriotism and spirit of compromise which distinguished the sages of the Revolution and the fathers of our Union. If we can not at once, in justice to interests vested under improvident legislation, make our Government what it ought to be, we can at least take a stand against all new grants of monopolies and exclusive privileges, against any prostitution of our Government to the advancement of the few at the expense of the many, and in favor of compromise and gradual reform in our code of laws and system of political economy.

B. Fugitive Slave Clause

Slavery gradually replaced the American System as the most politically divisive controversy about national power. Constitutional debates raged over congressional power to regulate the interstate slave trade, the international slave trade, and slavery in Washington, DC. Debate over two issues was particularly intense: federal power to pass fugitive slave laws and federal power to prohibit slavery in American territories. Both raised complex and intertwined issues concerning national powers, federalism, judicial power, and individual rights. Critics of federal fugitive slave laws insisted that Congress was not authorized to regulate the rendition process and that federal laws denied alleged slaves the right to trial by jury. Critics of federal laws prohibiting slavery in the territories claimed that Congress had no power to pass such measures and that such laws deprived slaveholders of their property without due process of law. This section focuses on the constitutional debates over federal fugitive slave laws. The next section details the constitutional debates over slavery in American territories.

Article IV, Section 2, of the U.S. Constitution requires states to return escaped slaves. That provision declares, "No Person held to Service or Labour in one State, under the Laws thereof, escaping into another, shall, in Consequence of any Law or Regulation therein, be discharged from such Service or Labour, But shall be delivered up on Claim of the Party to whom such Service or Labour may be due." The fugitive slave clause did not clarify several matters. The first was congressional power over the rendition process, the process by which fugitive slaves were identified, captured, and returned. Article I, some antislavery commentators observed, enumerated congressional powers. By placing the fugitive slave clause in Article IV, they argued, the framers intended merely to enumerated state obligations to other states. The second was whether, if the federal government could regulate the rendition process, that power was exclusive or concurrent. Antislavery advocates insisted that free states retained the power to hold a hearing to determine whether an alleged fugitive was actually an escaped slave. Slave state representatives claimed that the fugitive slave clause prohibited any state law that might interfere in any way with the rendition process determined by Congress.

Federal and state legislation in the early national era did more to aggravate than resolve possible confusion about the fugitive slave clause. The Fugitive Slave Act of 1793 allowed masters to recover slaves on their own with a minimal legal hearing before taking them back to their home states. Many northern states adopted "personal liberty" laws requiring masters to rely on state officials (rather than private slave catchers) to locate and detain fugitives. These laws typically provided captured individuals with extensive hearings in which they could demonstrate their legally free status. Led by Salmon Chase, abolitionists claimed that Congress lacked the power to pass fugitive slave laws. Slaveholders responded that personal liberty laws unconstitutionally interfered with constitutional federal fugitive slave laws.

Democrats from all regions of the country and many moderate Whigs (known as the Cotton Whigs) supported the southern understanding of federal power over fugitive slaves. Supreme Court Justice Joseph Story in *Prigg v. Pennsylvania* (1842) issued an opinion sustaining the Fugitive Slave Law of 1793 and declaring unconstitutional state personal liberty laws. Eight years later, Congress passed an even tougher Fugitive Slave Law. Attorney General John Crittenden immediately issued an opinion declaring that measure constitutional. The Supreme Court in *Ableman v. Booth* (1858) agreed with Crittenden's assessment.

Salmon Chase, Speech in the Case of the Colored Woman Matilda (1837)[18]

Matilda Lawrence escaped from her master (and father) while they were on a trip to Cincinnati, Ohio. She was soon captured and detained according to the provisions of the Fugitive Slave Act of 1793. In later years, Lawrence might have claimed that she became free when her master voluntarily took her to a free state. Her lawyer in this case, future Chief Justice of the United States Salmon Chase (1808–1873), made a different argument. Chase maintained that the Constitution gave Congress no power to pass the Fugitive Slave Act.

The Ohio Court of Common Pleas rejected Chase's argument that the Fugitive Slave Act was unconstitutional. Almost immediately after the decision, Matilda was taken back to Kentucky and then to New Orleans, where she was sold.

...

...The leading object of the framers of our federal constitution was to create a national government, and confer upon it adequate powers. A secondary object was to adjust and settle certain matters of right and duty, between the states and between the citizens of different states, by permanent stipulations having the force and effect of a treaty.

...Now what is the clause in the constitution in regard to fugitives from labor, but an article of agreement between the states? It is expressed in these words, "No person held to service or labor in one state, under the laws thereof, escaping into another, shall, in consequence of any law or regulation thereof, be discharged from such service or labor; but shall be delivered up on claim of the party to whom such service or labor may be due." Does this clause confer any power on government, or on any officer or department of government?—Clearly not. It says nothing about the government, or its officers, or its departments. It declares that the citizens of no state in the Union, legally entitled to the service of any person, shall be deprived of that right to service, by the operation of the laws of any state into which the servant may escape; and it requires such state to deliver him up, on the claim of the lawful master. The clause, then, restrains the operation of state constitutions and state laws in a particular class of cases; and it obliges, so far as a compact can oblige, each state to the performance of certain duties towards the citizens of other states. The clause has nothing to do with the creation of a form of government. It is, in the strictest sense, a clause of compact. The parties to the agreement are the states. The general government is not a party to it, nor affected by it. If the clause stood alone in the constitution, it would mean precisely what it does now, and would be just as obligatory as it is now. Nothing can be plainer, then, than that this clause cannot be construed as vesting any power in the government, or in any of its departments, or in any of its officers; and this is the only provision in the constitution which at all relates to fugitives from labor.

Now the whole legislative power of congress is derived, either from the general grant of power, "to make all laws, necessary and proper for carrying into execution all the powers vested by the constitution in the government of the United States, or in any department or officer thereof;" or from special provisions in relation to particular subjects. If congress has any power to legislate upon the subject of fugitives from labor, it must be derived from one of these

18. Excerpt taken from Salmon Chase, *Speech of Salmon P. Chase in the Case of the Colored Woman Matilda* (Cincinnati: Pugh & Dodd, 1837).

sources,—from the general grant, or from some special provision. It cannot be derived from the general grant, because the clause in regard to fugitives from labor, vests no power in the national government, or in any of its departments or officers; and the general grant of legislative power is expressly confined to the enactment of laws, necessary and proper to carry into execution the powers so vested. Nor can it be derived from any special provision: for none is attached to the clause relating to fugitives from service. The conclusion seems inevitable, that the constitution confers on congress no power to legislate in regard to escaping servants. Where then is this power? Undoubtedly it is reserved to the states; for "all powers not delegated to the United States, nor prohibited to the states, are reserved to the states or to the people." The constitution restrains the operation of the state constitutions and the state laws, which would enfranchise the fugitive. It also binds the states to deliver him up on the claim of the master, and by necessary inference, it obliges them to provide a tribunal before which such claim may be asserted and tried, and by which such claims may be decided upon, and, if valid, enforced: but it confers no jot of legislative power on congress.

...

Prigg v. Pennsylvania, 41 U.S. 539 (1842)

Edward Prigg was a professional slave catcher hired to find and capture Margaret Morgan, who had allegedly fled to Pennsylvania from slavery in Maryland. After local officials refused his requests for help, Prigg and his associates abducted Morgan and her family. Pennsylvania charged Prigg with a felony for forcibly removing a black person from the state to be kept as a slave. Prigg was convicted by a state jury and his conviction was upheld by the Pennsylvania Supreme Court. He appealed that decision to the U.S. Supreme Court. Prigg claimed that the Pennsylvania law violated the U.S. Constitution. Both Pennsylvania and Maryland officials cooperated in order to make sure the Supreme Court adjudicated this test case.

The Supreme Court reversed Prigg's conviction. Justice Joseph Story's opinion for the Court held that owners were free to engage in self-help when capturing escaped slaves, that the Fugitive Slave Act of 1793 was constitutional, and that federal power over the rendition process was exclusive. States, Story maintained, could not pass any laws regulating the rendition of fugitive slaves. Chief Justice Roger Taney, Justice Peter Daniel, and Justice Smith Thompson rejected Story's claim that the federal power over fugitive slaves was exclusive. They believed that states were empowered to pass laws that assisted masters seeking to recover fugitive slaves. Justice John McLean's dissent rejected claims that owners could rely on self-help when capturing fugitive slaves.[19]

As you read, consider what a strict constructionist reading of the fugitive slave clause might be. How would a person read provisions relating to slavery narrowly? Note the similarities between Justice Story's broad construction of federal power over fugitive slaves and John Marshall's broad interpretation in McCulloch v. Maryland *(1819) of the necessary and proper clause. Does this demonstrate principled jurisprudence or a failure to recognize important distinctions between the two constitutional issues? Justice Story maintained that his opinion in* Prigg *was actually a "triumph of freedom." Why might he have thought that? Was he correct?*

JUSTICE STORY delivered the opinion of the Court.

...

...Historically, it is well known, that the object of [the Fugitive Slave Clause] was to secure to the citizens of the slaveholding states the complete right and title of ownership in their slaves, as property, in every state in the Union into which they might escape from the state where they were held in servitude. The full recognition of this right and title was indispensable to the security of this species of property in all the slaveholding states; and, indeed, was so vital to the preservation of their domestic interests and institutions, that it cannot be doubted that it constituted a fundamental article, without the adoption of which the Union could not have been formed. Its true design was to guard against the doctrines and principles prevalent in the non-slaveholding states, by preventing them from intermeddling with, or obstructing, or abolishing the rights of the owners of slaves.

By the general law of nations, no nation is bound to recognize the state of slavery, as to foreign slaves found within its territorial dominions, when it is in opposition to its own policy and institutions, in favor of the subjects of other nations where slavery is recognized. If it does it, it is as a matter of comity, and not as a matter of international right. The state of slavery is deemed

19. On the background to *Prigg*, see also Paul Finkelman, "Story Telling on the Court: *Prigg v. Pennsylvania* and Justice Joseph Story's Judicial Nationalism," *Supreme Court Review 1994* (1995):247.

to be a mere municipal regulation, founded upon and limited to the range of the territorial laws.... It is manifest from this consideration, that if the Constitution had not contained this clause, every non-slave-holding state in the Union would have been at liberty to have declared free all runaway slaves coming within its limits, and to have given them entire immunity and protection against the claims of their masters; a course which would have created the most bitter animosities, and engendered perpetual strife between the different states. The clause was, therefore, of the last importance to the safety and security of the southern states; and could not have been surrendered by them without endangering their whole property in slaves. The clause was accordingly adopted into the Constitution by the unanimous consent of the framers of it; a proof at once of its intrinsic and practical necessity.

...

The clause manifestly contemplates the existence of a positive, unqualified right on the part of the owner of the slave, which no state law or regulation can in any way qualify, regulate, control, or restrain.... Now, certainly, without indulging in any nicety of criticism upon words, it may fairly and reasonably be said, that any state law or state regulation, which interrupts, limits, delays, or postpones the right of the owner to the immediate possession of the slave, and the immediate command of his service and labor, operates, protanto, a discharge of the slave therefrom....

...[U]nder and in virtue of the Constitution, the owner of a slave is clothed with entire authority, in every state in the Union, to seize and recapture his slave, whenever he can do it without any breach of the peace, or any illegal violence. In this sense, and to this extent this clause of the Constitution may properly be said to execute itself; and to require no aid from legislation, state or national.

...

And this leads us to the consideration of the other part of the clause, which implies at once a guaranty and duty. It says, "But he (the slave) shall be delivered up on claim of the party to whom such service or labor may be due." Now, we think it exceedingly difficult, if not impracticable, to read this language and not to feel that it contemplated some further remedial redress than that which might be administered at the hands of the owner himself.... The slave is to be delivered up on the claim. By whom to be delivered up? In what mode to be delivered up? How, if a refusal takes place, is the right of delivery to be enforced? Upon what proofs?...

These, and many other questions, will readily occur upon the slightest attention to the clause; and it is obvious that they can receive but one satisfactory answer. They require the aid of legislation to protect the right, to enforce the delivery, and to secure the subsequent possession of the slave. If, indeed, the Constitution guarantees the right, and if it requires the delivery upon the claim of the owner, (as cannot well be doubted,) the natural inference certainly is, that the national government is clothed with the appropriate authority and functions to enforce it.... The states cannot... be compelled to enforce them; and it might well be deemed an unconstitutional exercise of the power of interpretation, to insist that the states are bound to provide means to carry into effect the duties of the national government, nowhere delegated or entrusted to them by the Constitution. On the contrary, the natural, if not the necessary conclusion is, that the national government, in the absence of all positive provisions to the contrary, is bound, through its own proper departments, legislative, judicial, or executive, as the case may require, to carry into effect all the rights and duties imposed upon it by the Constitution....

...

Congress has taken this very view of the power and duty of the national government. As early as the year 1791, the attention of Congress was drawn to it.... The result of their deliberations was the passage of the [Fugitive Slave Act of 1793].

[T]his act may be truly said to cover the whole ground of the Constitution.... If this be so, then it would seem, upon just principles of construction, that the legislation of Congress, if constitutional, must supersede all state legislation upon the same subject; and by necessary implication prohibit it.... [T]he legislation of Congress, in what it does prescribe, manifestly indicates that it does not intend that there shall be any further legislation to act upon the subject-matter....

But it has been argued, that the act of Congress is unconstitutional, because it does not fall within the scope of any of the enumerated powers of legislation confided to that body; and therefore it is void.... No one has ever supposed that Congress could, constitutionally, by its legislation, exercise powers, or enact laws beyond the powers delegated to it by the Constitution; but it has, on various occasions, exercised powers which were necessary and proper as means to carry into effect rights expressly given, and duties expressly enjoined thereby. The end being required, it has been deemed a just and necessary implication, that the means to accomplish it are given also; or, in other words, that the power flows as a necessary means to accomplish the end.

...

The remaining question is, whether the power of legislation upon this subject is exclusive in the national government, or concurrent in the states, until it is exercised by Congress. In our opinion it is exclusive....

...

It is scarcely conceivable that the slaveholding states would have been satisfied with leaving to the legislation of the non-slaveholding states, a power of regulation, in the absence of that of Congress, which would or might practically amount to a power to destroy the rights of the owner....[C]onstrue the right of legislation as exclusive in Congress, and every evil, and every danger vanishes....But, upon the other supposition, the moment he passes the state line, he becomes amenable to the laws of another sovereignty, whose regulations may greatly embarrass or delay the exercise of his rights; and even be repugnant to those of the state where he first arrested the fugitive. Consequences like these show that the nature and objects of the provision imperiously require, that, to make it effectual, it should be construed to be exclusive of state authority....

...

JUSTICE WAYNE, concurring.

...

My object, and the only object which I have in view, in what I am about to say, is, to establish the position that Congress has the exclusive right to legislate upon this provision of the Constitution....

...

It is admitted, that the provision raises what is properly termed a perfect obligation upon all of the states to abstain from doing any thing which may interfere with the rights secured. Will this be so, if any part of what may be necessary to discharge the obligation is reserved by each state, to be done as each may think proper?...That was not anticipated by the representatives of the slaveholding states in the convention, nor could it have been intended by the framers of the Constitution.

Is it not more reasonable to infer, as the states were forming a government for themselves, to the extent of the powers conceded in the Constitution, to which legislative power was given to make all laws necessary and proper to carry into execution all powers vested in it—that they meant that the right for which some of the states stipulated, and to which all acceded, should, from the peculiar nature of the property in which only some of the states were interested—be carried into execution by that department of the general government in which they were all to be represented, the Congress of the United States.

...But it is said, all that is contended for, is, that the states may legislate to aid the object, and that such legislation will be constitutional if it does not conflict with the remedies which Congress may enact. This is a cautious way of asserting the right in the states, and it seems to impose a limitation which makes it unobjectionable. But the reply to it is, that the right to legislate a remedy, implies so much indefinite power over the subject, and such protracted continuance, as to the mode of finally determining whether a fugitive owes service and labor, that the requirements of the remedy, without being actually in conflict with the provision or the enactments of Congress might be oppressive to those most interested in the provision, by interposing delays and expenses more costly than the value of the fugitive sought to be reclaimed.

...

CHIEF JUSTICE TANEY, concurring.

...I think the states are not prohibited; and that, on the contrary, it is enjoined upon them as a duty to protect and support the owner when he is endeavoring to obtain possession of his property found within their respective territories.

...[T]he laws of the different states, in all other cases, constantly protect the citizens of other states in their rights of property, when it is found within their respective territories; and no one doubts their power to do so. And in the absence of any express prohibition, I perceive no reason for establishing, by implication, a different rule in this instance; where, by the national compact, this right of property is recognized as an existing right in every state of the Union.

...

...There are other clauses in the Constitution in which other individual rights are provided for and secured in like manner; and it never has been suggested that the states could not uphold and maintain them, because they were guarantied by the Constitution of the United States. On the contrary, it has always been held to be the duty of the states to enforce them;

and the action of the general government has never been deemed necessary except to resist and prevent their violation.

...

JUSTICE THOMPSON, concurring.

...

...The provision in the Constitution under consideration, is one under which such conflicting legislation may arise; and harmony is produced by making the state law yield to that of the United States. But to assert that the states cannot legislate on the subject at all, in the absence of all legislation by Congress, is, in my judgment, not warranted by any fair and reasonable construction of the provision.... [W]hat becomes of the right where there is no law on the subject? Should Congress repeal the law of 1793, and pass no other law on the subject, I can entertain no doubt that state legislation, for the purpose of restoring the slave to his master, and faithfully to carry into execution the provision of the Constitution, would be valid.

JUSTICE DANIEL, concurring.

...

...I cannot regard the third clause of the fourth article as falling either within the definition or meaning of an exclusive power....

...

If there is a power in the states to authorize and order their arrest and detention for delivery to their owners, not only will the probabilities of recovery be increased by the performance of duties enjoined by law upon the citizens of those states, as well private persons as those who are officers of the law; but the incitements of interest, under the hope of reward, will in a certain class of persons powerfully co-operate to the same ends.... But those who argue from such possible or probable abuses against all regulations by the states touching this matter, should dismiss their apprehensions, under the recollection that should those abuses be attempted, the corrective may be found, as it is now about to be applied to some extent, in the controlling constitutional authority of this Court.

...

JUSTICE McLEAN, dissenting.

...

...That the Constitution was adopted in a spirit of compromise, is matter of history. And all experience shows that to attain the great objects of this fundamental law, it must be construed and enforced in a spirit of enlightened forbearance and justice....

...

The nature of the power shows that it must be exclusive.

...

The necessity for this provision was found in the views and feelings of the people of the states opposed to slavery; and who, under such an influence, could not be expected favorably to regard the rights of the master. Now, by whom is this paramount law to be executed?

It is contended that the power to execute it rests with the states. The law was designed to protect the rights of the slaveholder against the states opposed to those rights; and yet, by this argument, the effective power is in the hands of those on whom it is to operate.

This would produce a strange anomaly in the history of legislation. It would show an inexperience and folly in the venerable framers of the Constitution, from which, of all public bodies that ever assembled, they were, perhaps, most exempt.

...

It is contended, that the power to legislate on this subject is concurrently in the states and federal government. That the acts of the latter are paramount, but that the acts of the former must be regarded as of authority, until abrogated by the federal power. How a power exercised by one sovereignty can be called concurrent, which may be abrogated by another, I cannot comprehend....

...

John J. Crittenden, Opinion on the Constitutionality of the Fugitive Slave Bill (1850)[20]

The Fugitive Slave Act of 1850 was part of the Compromise of 1850. That Compromise included the admission of California as a free state and the organization of the New Mexico and Utah territories without any specific rule on slavery. The Fugitive Slave Act empowered federal commissioners to recapture runaway slaves, empowered federal marshals to order "bystanders" to assist in the recapture, and made aiding fugitive slaves a federal crime. Congress authorized slave owners to obtain from their local magistrate a certificate for a fugitive slave and required courts in other states to accept that certificate as "conclusive" proof of a person's fugitive

20. Excerpt taken from 5 Op. Atty. Gen. 254 (September 18, 1850).

status. If a Virginian had a certificate from a Virginia court declaring that Fred and Mary were escaped slaves, and the Virginian located Fred and Mary in New York, Fred and Mary could not contest their status as slaves in a New York legal proceeding.

President Millard Fillmore asked Attorney General John Crittenden (1787–1863) to provide an official opinion on the constitutionality of the fugitive slave bill. Crittenden concluded that the bill was sanctioned by Prigg v. Pennsylvania *(1842). His opinion claimed that the rendition process did not deny persons the right to contest their slave status in a habeas corpus or other legal proceeding. All Congress had done, Crittenden declared, was determine that the state courts where the slaveholder resided were the proper tribunals for resolving debates over whether a person was an escaped slave.*

...

The Supreme Court of the United States has decided that the owner, independent of any aid from State or national legislation, may, in virtue of the constitution, and his own right of property, seize and recapture his fugitive slave in whatsoever State he may find him, and carry him back to the State or Territory from which he escaped. (*Prigg v. Commonwealth of Pennsylvania*.) This bill, therefore, confers no right on the owner of the fugitive slave. It only gives him an appointed and peaceable remedy in place of the more exposed and insecure, but not less lawful mode of self redress: and as to the fugitive slave, he has no cause to complain of this bill—it adds no coercion to that which his owner himself might, at his own will, rightfully exercise; and all the proceedings which it institutes are but so much of orderly judicial authority interposed between him and his owner, and consequently of protection to him, and mitigation of the exercise directly by the owner himself of his personal authority. This is the constitutional and legal view of the subject, as sanctioned by the decisions of the Supreme Court, and to that I limit myself.

...

Congress, in the case of fugitive slaves, as in all other cases within the scope of its constitutional authority, has the unquestionable right to ordain and prescribe for what causes, to what extent, and in what manner persons may be taken into custody, detained, or imprisoned. Without this power they could not fulfill their constitutional trust, nor perform the ordinary and necessary duties of government. It was never heard that the exercise of that legislative power was any encroachment upon or suspension of the privilege of the writ of habeas corpus. It is only by some confusion of ideas that such a conflict can be supposed to exist. It is not within the province or privilege of this great writ to loose those whom *the law* has bound....

The condition of one in custody as a fugitive slave is, under this law, so far as respects the writ of habeas corpus, precisely the same as that of all other prisoners under the laws of the United States. The "privilege" of that writ remains alike to all of them, but to be judged of—granted, or refused—discharged or enforced—by the proper tribunal, according to the circumstances of each case, and as the commitment and detention may appear to be legal or illegal.

...

C. Territorial Acquisition and Governance

Territorial Acquisition. Slavery was at or just beneath the surface during Jacksonian disputes over territorial acquisition and governance. Slavery issues were explicit when Americans debated whether Congress could ban human bondage in the territories. Slavery issues were implicit when Americans debated the constitutionality of the means by which Americans acquired new territories. Whether politicians favored or opposed the annexation of Texas and the acquisition of new territories from Mexico depended largely on estimates about how such decisions would affect slavery in existing states and the sectional balance of power.

Northern and southern Democrats united on annexing Texas, acquiring more territory from Mexico, and removing bans on slavery in the territories. Texas was annexed by a joint resolution of Congress in 1845. The Treaty of Guadalupe Hidalgo in 1848 added more than a half million square miles in the Southwest to the United States. Congress in 1854 repealed the Missouri Compromise, which had prohibited slavery in federal territory above the southern border of the state of Missouri. That ban on slavery in the northwestern territories was then declared unconstitutional in *Dred Scott*. Southern Democrats favored all these policies because they wished to open up more territories for slavery. Northern Whigs, some northern Democrats, and all Republicans opposed these polices for that reason.

Northern Democrats supported annexation, expansion, and opening up more territories to slavery because they perceived these policies were part of a more general program of westward national expansion that would guarantee more land for free- and slave-state citizens. Many southern Whigs opposed these policies because they feared that Texas would drain slaves from the eastern states and that recently acquired western territories would in practice prove inhospitable to slavery, even when human bondage was nominally legal.

Slavery in the Territories. Whether Congress could prohibit slavery in the territories was the most explosive constitutional question in Jacksonian politics. The stakes were political and economic. Conventional wisdom maintained that the congressional decision to ban or permit human bondage in the territories determined the balance of power in Congress between the free and slave states. Most slaveholders and abolitionists agreed that slave territories invariably became slave states and free territories invariably became free states. Conventional wisdom also maintained that slavery could survive economically only by expanding into new territories. Slaveholders and abolitionists agreed that slavery would eventually wither away if the practice was confined to the original slave states and slave territories.

Slaveholders and their northern political allies combined arguments about national powers, federalism, and individual rights when claiming that Congress could not constitutionally prohibit slavery in American territories. Their most common constitutional arguments were

- *Common Property*. Congressional bans on slavery in the territories practically excluded slave state citizens from regions that were the common property of all states.
- *No Power.* The Constitution gave the federal government no power to ban slavery in the territories. The congressional power in Article IV, Section 4 "to dispose of and make all needful Rules and Regulations respecting the Territory or other Property belong to the United States" gave the national government power only to sell public lands.
- *Due Process.* Congressional bans on slavery in the territories deprived slaveholders of their property without due process of law.
- *Popular Sovereignty.* Congressional bans on slavery in the territories violated the constitutional commitment to giving the people of each state and territories the right to regulate their internal affairs.

Southerners preferred the common property, no power, and due process arguments. These positions entailed that neither Congress nor a territorial legislature could prohibit slavery in the territories. Northern Democrats more often defended popular sovereignty. That position permitted territorial legislatures, but not Congress, to ban slavery.

Opponents of slavery insisted that Congress was constitutionally empowered to ban slavery in the territories. They interpreted Article IV, Section 4 as vesting Congress with the same authority over a territory as a state legislature exercised within a state. Everyone in Jacksonian America agreed that state legislatures could choose whether to ban slavery. Hence, antislavery advocates concluded, Congress could choose to ban slavery in the territories. Some abolitionists claimed that Congress was constitutionally obligated to ban slavery in the territories. Federal laws that permitted slavery in the territories, they claimed, deprived enslaved persons of liberty without due process.

During the 1830s and 1840s, the Missouri Compromise remained the law of the land. Slavery was permitted in territories south of the 36°30′ parallel line (the southern border of Missouri) and prohibited in all territories north of that line. Moderates in both parties successfully defeated attempts by slaveholders and antislavery advocates to have the national government take a stronger pro-slavery or antislavery stand. Mainstream Democrats and Whigs in 1837 tabled Senator John C. Calhoun's proposal that Congress foreswear any effort to ban slavery in American territories. Calhoun's rejected resolutions declared:

> *Resolved*, That this Government was instituted and adopted by the several States of this Union as a common agent,... and that it is the solemn duty of the Government to resist all attempts by one portion of the Union to use it as an instrument to attack the domestic institutions of another, or to weaken or destroy such institutions, instead of strengthening and upholding them, as it is in duty bound to do.
>
> *Resolved*, That the intermeddling of any State or States, or their citizens, to abolish slavery in [the District of Columbia], or any of the Territories, on

the ground, or under the pretext, that it is immoral or sinful, or the passage of any act or measure of Congress, with that view, would be a direct and dangerous attack on the institutions of all the slaveholding States.

Resolved, That the union of these States rests on an equality of rights and advantages among its members, and that whatever destroys that equality, tends to destroy the Union itself; and that it is the solemn duty of all, and more especially of [the Senate], which represents the States in their corporate capacity, to resist all attempts to discriminate between the States in extending the benefits of the Government to the several portions of the Union; and that to refuse to extend to the southern and western States any advantage which would tend to strength, or render them more secure, or increase their limits or population by the annexation of new territory or States, on the assumption or under the pretext that the institution of slavery, as it exists among them, is immoral or sinful, or otherwise obnoxious, would be contrary to that equality of rights and advantages which the Constitution was intended to secure alike to all the members of the Union, and would, in effect, disenfranchise the slaveholding States, withholding from them the advantages, while it subjecting them to the burdens, of the Government.[21]

A decade later, Whig and Jacksonian political leaders prevented Congress from passing Representative David Wilmot's proposal to ban slavery from all territories acquired from Mexico as a consequence of the Mexican War. The failed Wilmot Proviso declared:

Provided, That as an express and fundamental condition to the acquisition of any territory from the Republic of Mexico by the United States, by virtue of any treaty which may be negotiated between them, and to the use by the Executive of the moneys herein appropriated, neither slavery nor involuntary servitude shall ever exist in any part of said territory, except for crime, whereof the party shall first be duly convicted.

Congress in the Compromise of 1850 organized the New Mexico territory without reference to slavery. Eager to avoid further divisive debates over slavery, party moderates included a provision expediting Supreme Court review of any case raising constitutional questions about the status of slavery in those territories. A judicial decision, many mainstream Democrats and Whigs hoped, might provide a more peaceful settlement to the constitutional controversy.

Southerners overturned the Missouri Compromise during the 1850s, but at the cost of first destroying the Whigs and then the Democrats as national political parties. The Kansas-Nebraska Act of 1854 declared that, contrary to the Missouri Compromise, slavery would be permitted in the Kansas and Nebraska territories. The Whig Party failed to survive the bitter legislative debate over that measure. Most northern Whigs and some northern Democrats almost immediately formed the Republican Party, the first major political party in American history united by an antislavery platform. The Supreme Court in *Dred Scott v. Sandford* (1857) antagonized antislavery northerners by ruling that Congress could not constitutionally ban slavery in any territory. Senator Stephen Douglas of Illinois attempted to maintain Democratic unity by insisting that *Dred Scott* left the people of each territory with the power to abolish slavery. Southerners found this position unacceptable, particularly after Douglas led the fight to prevent Kansas from being admitted as a slave state. When the Democratic Party in 1860 rejected a southern demand that the party platform include a call for a federal slave code in the territories, slave state representatives walked out of the national convention. Divided into southern and northern wings, the Democrats were conquered. Abraham Lincoln in 1860 became the first person elected president without a single electoral vote from a state in which slavery was legal.

Congressional Debate on the Annexation of Texas (1844)[22]

The annexation of Texas in 1845 was politically and constitutionally controversial. The political controversy began when Texas petitioned to join the Union in 1836 immediately after gaining independence from Mexico. Americans were initially hesitant. Texas would add at least one more slave state to the Union. Annexation risked war with Mexico, which continued to contest both Texas independence

21. *Congressional Globe*, 25th Cong., 2nd Sess., p. 55.

22. Excerpt taken from *Congressional Globe*, 28th Cong., 2nd Sess., App., pp. 234, 378–82.

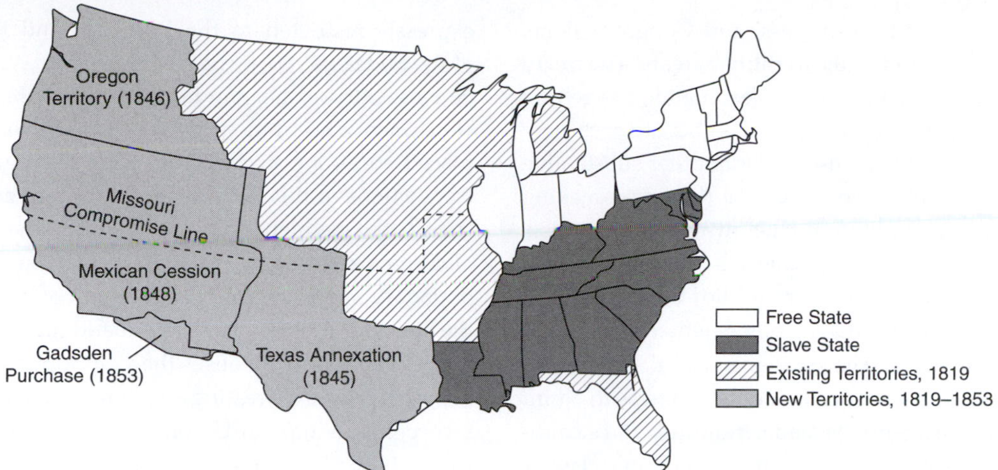

Figure 5-3 Map of the Territorial Acquisitions of the Jacksonian Era

and the location of Texas's borders. The constitutional controversy began when President Tyler submitted an annexation treaty to the U.S. Senate in the spring of 1844. The treaty failed by a wide margin to win the two-thirds vote needed for ratification. Once the treaty failed, supporters of annexation proposed admitting Texas by a joint resolution. The joint resolution only needed support from a simple majority of those voting in both the House and the Senate.

Both the House and Senate engaged in lengthy debates over whether Texas could constitutionally be annexed by a joint resolution. Jacksonian proponents of the joint resolution insisted that Article IV, Section 3, which declares "New States may be admitted by the Congress," permitted majorities in both Houses of Congress to admit as states both American territories and foreign countries. Whig opponents asserted that a treaty was the only constitutional means by which the United States could make any agreement with a foreign country.

Proponents of annexation gained a strong majority in the House and a weaker majority in the Senate. The annexation of Texas was almost immediately followed by a war with Mexico, which led to the acquisition of an even greater amount of land in the West, completing manifest destiny (see Figure 5-3).

Senator LEVI WOODBURY (Democrat, New Hampshire)

. . . The friends of the resolution maintained that Congress could admit new States, whether the territory out of which they were formed ever had previously been in the Union or not. . . . The friends of the resolution said that Congress could organize States in what had been foreign territory, whether acquired by the treaty-making power or by legislation. They denied a treaty was indispensable. . . . Its friends relied on the simple letter of the constitution, plain, and in accordance with its spirit, without any implication or forced construction in the matter. The constitution said that *new States may be admitted by the Congress into the Union*. And what were those States? Did not a State consist of lands and people? The clause then meant the *new lands and people* may be admitted into the Union. Gentlemen denied this, and insisted that before we could admit a State we must interpolate a requirement to go to a foreign government by means of the treaty power, and thus buy the territory out of which it was to be formed. How must these conflicting views strike the country in respect to principle? The friends of the measure on his side of the House stood now just where they had always stood. They supported the constitution in its express grants of power; while the gentlemen on the other side relied upon construction and implication for destroying one of these express grants of power. We go for the plain common-sense meaning of words, while you resort to refinements and subtleties. . . .

. . .

. . . I will remind you of an important difference between the treaty as submitted to the Senate, and the joint resolution now proposed for adoption. It was by treaty proposed to annex Texas as a *Territory*; now it was proposed to admit Texas as a State. It never had been proposed to admit a State by the treaty power. The treaty was to obtain it as a Territory; and even then it was held that, if we got the territory first, still the State must be admitted by Congress, and Congress alone. We did not now undertake to ratify a treaty. The treaty had been repudiated and its subject matter, the getting of Texas merely as a Territory. The Senate was now asked to act with the House under another substantive power in the constitution.... Could the treaty-making power by mere implication take away from Congress an express grant made to Congress alone in the constitution?... [W]hat express grant [did] the constitution contain[] to the treaty-making power either to buy territory or admit States? The gentleman could show none, while we could show such a one to Congress to admit States. Thus the attempt is made, indirectly and stealthily, to strip Congress of this express grant, in a class of cases which come plainly within its language.

...

Senator WILLIAM RIVES (Whig, Virginia)

... What would it profit us should we gain Texas, if thereby we lost our regard for that sacred instrument which was the palladium of our liberty and happiness? The mode in which Texas was to be acquired, in its aspect upon the principles of our political compact, was, with him, a vital and paramount consideration. We had heretofore made important acquisitions of foreign territory, more than doubling the area of our original limits; but we had made the acquisition by means of the treaty power, and in the case of Texas, too, the treaty power had been called into action to achieve the measure of annexation, but the treaty not having received the constitutional sanction of two-thirds of this body, it was now at last discovered that all this reference to the treaty-making power was a mere useless ceremony; a work of supererogation; an idle, unmeaning formality; and that the object could be better accomplished by a mere majority of the two Houses of Congress. Under these circumstances, the question now put to the judgment and conscience of every senator was, whether this summary mode of proceeding was warranted by the constitution, and in conformity with that good faith which the people of the several States had pledged to each other when they adopted the constitution and promised to abide by it.

...

... Under the power of Congress to admit new States into the Union, it was contended that a mere majority of the two Houses of Congress could enter into stipulations and agreements with foreign States for their incorporation into our political system, although the power of treating with foreign States had been expressly restricted to the President and two-thirds of the States, as represented in this body. Would it not be most extraordinary, indeed, that the wise and sagacious men who framed the constitution should have placed so strong a check on the most unimportant transactions of this government with foreign powers, such as the payment of a sum of money, the surrender of criminals, the fixing of some small and unimportant boundary line, by requiring the assent of two-thirds of the States, and yet should have abandoned to a simple majority of the two Houses the vast, formidable, transcendent power of treating with a foreign nation for its incorporation into our Union?

...

... [W]e must obtain foreign territory by the treaty-making power; then we might admit new States from that territory by the legislative power. This was the law and constitution of our land....

Let us now, Mr. President, attempt to follow out in the visions of the future what was likely to occur, if, in the face of the remonstrances of those who took their stand upon the plighted faith of the constitution, this should be consummated by a mere majority of the two Houses of Congress.... The same legislative majority which passed the joint resolution might repeal it.... Who could say how future elections might turn out? What security had gentlemen that the next Congress, by their majority power, might not repeal the act of the present Congress, and, when Texas came for admission, the door be slammed in her face—what then?

...

And he now turned to his southern friends on that floor, and he would invoke their sober attention to what he should submit to their consideration. The entire slaveholding portion of this Union could place themselves for safety only on the sacredness of the constitution....

... Would the senators representing that interest set the example of trampling on the guarantees of the constitution, and of admitting the absolute and unlimited power of the majority?

Dred Scott v. Sandford, 60 U.S. 394 (1857)

Dred Scott was the slave of John Emerson, an army doctor. Emerson took Scott to military forts in the free state of Illinois and in the Wisconsin Territory (where slavery was barred by the Missouri Compromise) before returning to

St. Louis, Missouri (where slavery was legal). Some time after Emerson's death, Scott sued Emerson's widow and her brother, John Sanford,[23] *for his freedom. Scott claimed he had been freed by his travels in free territory. Sanford claimed that slavery reattached once Scott returned to Missouri. A trial court declared Scott free, but the Missouri Supreme Court reversed that decision. Scott then filed a similar lawsuit in federal court. That federal lawsuit raised two new constitution questions. The first was whether Scott, if free, was a citizen of the United States entitled to sue another citizen of the United States in federal court. The second was whether Congress had the power to ban slavery in the territories. After the federal district court rejected Scott's freedom suit, he appealed to the U.S. Supreme Court.*

The Supreme Court held that former slaves could not become American citizens and that Congress could not prohibit slavery in American territories acquired after the Constitution was ratified. Chief Justice Taney's opinion for the Court insisted that Article IV was either limited to the territory the United States possessed in 1787 or merely vested Congress with the power to hold and sell public lands. The concurring opinions in Dred Scott *maintained that bans on slavery in the territories unconstitutionally discriminated against slaveholders and the slaveholding states. The dissenting opinions in* Dred Scott *asserted that Article IV vested Congress with the same power to govern the territories as the national legislature had to govern the District of Columbia or as state governments had to govern their states.*

As you read, consider how these arguments over the power to regulate slavery in the territories compare with arguments over the necessary and proper clause. Many commentators contend that Dred Scott *was the worst decision ever made by the Supreme Court. Was Justice Taney guilty of poor legal reasoning, or is the main flaw with* Dred Scott *the judicial decision to protect slavery and racism?*

Chief Justice TANEY delivered the opinion of the court.

...

The counsel for the plaintiff has laid much stress upon that article of the Constitution which confers on Congress the power "to dispose and make all needful rules and regulations respecting the territory or other property belonging to the United States;" but, in the judgment of the court, that provision has no bearing on the present controversy, and the power there given, whatever it may be, is confined, and was intended to be confined, to the territory which at that time belonged to, or was claimed by, the United States.... It was a special provision for a known and particular territory, and to meet a present emergency, and nothing more.

...

The language used in this clause, the arrangement and combination of the powers, and the somewhat unusual phraseology it uses...all indicate the design and meaning of the clause to be such as we have mentioned. It does not speak of *any* territory, nor of *Territories*, but uses language which, according to its legitimate meaning, points to a particular thing. The power is given in relation only to *the* territory of the United States.... It begins its enumeration of powers by that of disposing, in other words, making sale of the lands, or raising money from them, which, as we have already said, was the main object of the cession and which is accordingly the first thing provided for in the article. It then gives the power which was necessarily associated with the disposition and sale of the lands—that is, the power of making needful rules and regulations respecting the territory....

...

The words "needful rules and regulations" would seem, also, to have been cautiously used for some definite object. They are not the words usually employed by statesmen, when they mean to give the powers of sovereignty, or to establish a Government, or to authorize its establishment....

...

There is certainly no power given by the Constitution to the Federal Government to establish or maintain colonies bordering the United States or at a distance, to be ruled and governed at its pleasure; nor to enlarge its territorial limits in any way, except by admission of new States....

...

Taking this rule to guide us, it may be safely assumed that citizens of the United States who migrate to a Territory belonging to the people of the United States, cannot be ruled as a mere colonists, dependent upon the will of the General Government, and to be governed by any laws it may think proper to impose.... Whatever it acquires, it acquires for the benefit of the people of the several States who created it. It is their trustee acting for them, and charged with the duty of promoting the

23. The Court reporter misspelled Sanford's name.

interests of the whole people of the Union in the exercise of the powers specifically granted.

...

Upon these considerations, it is the opinion of this court that the act of Congress which prohibited a citizen from holding and owning property of this kind in the territory of the United States north of the line therein mentioned, is not warranted by the Constitution, and is therefore void; and that neither Dred Scott himself, nor any his family, were made free by being carried into this territory; even if they had been carried there by the owner, with the intention of becoming a permanent resident.

...

JUSTICE WAYNE...

JUSTICE NELSON...

JUSTICE GRIER...

JUSTICE DANIEL

...

But whatever power vested in Congress, and whatever the precise subject to which that power extended, it is clear that the power related to a subject appertaining to the *United States*, and one to be disposed of and regulated for the benefit and under the authority of the *United States*. Congress was made simply the agent or *trustee* for the United States, and could not, without a breach of trust and a fraud, appropriate the subject of the trust to any other beneficiary... than the United States, or to the people of the United States, upon equal grounds, legal or equitable. Congress could not appropriate that subject to any one class or portion of the people, to the exclusion of others, politically and constitutionally equals; but every citizen would, if any *one* could claim it, have the like rights of purchase, settlement, occupation, or any other right, in the national territory.

Nothing can be more conclusive to show the equality of this with every other right in all the citizens of the United States, and the iniquity and absurdity of the pretension to exclude or to disenfranchise a portion of them because they are the owners of slaves, than the fact that the same instrument, which imparts to Congress its very existence and its every function, guarantees to every slaveholder the title to his property, and gives him the right to its reclamation throughout the entire extent of the nation; and, further, that the only private property which the Constitution has *specifically recognized*, and has imposed it as a direct obligation both on the States and the Federal Government to protect and enforce, is the property of the master in his slave....

...

JUSTICE CAMPBELL

...

Whatever these [state] Constitutions and laws validly determine to be property, it is the duty of the Federal Government, through the domain of jurisdiction merely Federal, to recognize to be property.

And this principle follows from the structure of the respective Governments, State and Federals, and their reciprocal relations.... A proscription, therefore, of the Constitution and the laws of one or more States, determining property, on the part of the Federal Government, by which the stability of its social system may be endangered, is plainly repugnant to the conditions on which the Federal Constitution was adopted, or which the Government was designed to accomplish.... Wherever a master is entitled to go within the United States, his slave may accompany him, without any impediment from, or fear of, Congressional legislation or interference....

...

JUSTICE CATRON...

JUSTICE McLEAN [dissenting]

...The power to make all needful rules and regulations is a power to legislate. This no one will controvert, as Congress cannot make "rules and regulations," except by legislation. But is argued that the word territory is used as synonymous with the word land.... That this is not the true construction of the section appears from the fact that in the first line of the section "the power to dispose of the public lands" is given expressly, and, in addition, to make all needful rules and regulations. The power to dispose of is complete in itself, and requires nothing more....

...

But, if it be admitted that the word territory as used means land, and nothing but land, the power of Congress to organize a temporary Government is clear. It has power to make all needful regulations respecting the public lands, and the extent of those "needful regulations" depends upon the direction of Congress, where the means are appropriate to the end, and do not conflict with any of the prohibitions of the Constitution. If a temporary Government be deemed needful, necessary, requisite, or is wanted, Congress has the power to establish it....

If Congress should deem slaves or free colored persons injurious to the population of a free Territory, as conducing to lessen the value of the public lands, or on any other ground connected with the public interest, they have the power to prohibit them from becoming settlers in it. This can be sustained on the ground of a sound national policy.... [I]t is only necessary to say that... the repugnancy to slavery would probably prevent fifty or a hundred freemen from settling in a slave Territory, where one slaveholder would be prevented from settling in a free Territory.

...

JUSTICE CURTIS [dissenting]

...

No reason has been suggested why any reluctance should have been felt, by the framers of the Constitution, to apply this ["needful rules and regulations"] provision to all the territory which might belong to the United States, or why any distinction should have been made, founded on the accidental circumstances of the dates of the cessions; a circumstance in no way material as respects the necessity for rules and regulations, or the propriety of conferring on the Congress power to make them. And if we look at the course of the debates in the Convention on this article, we shall find that the then unceded lands [belonging to North Carolina and Georgia], so far from having been left out of view in adopting this article, constituted, in the minds of members, a subject of paramount importance.

...

If, then, this clause does contain a power to legislate respecting the territory, what are the limits of that power?

To this I answer, that, in common with all the other legislative powers of Congress, it finds limits in the express prohibitions on Congress not to do certain things; that, in the exercise of the legislative power, Congress cannot pass an ex post facto law or bill of attainder, and so in respect to each of the other prohibitions contained in the Constitution.

Besides this, the rules and regulations must be needful. But undoubtedly the question whether a particular rule or regulation be needful, must be finally determined by Congress itself. Whether a law be needful, is a legislative or political, not a judicial, question. Whatever Congress deems needful is so, under the grant of power.

...

The Constitution declares that Congress shall have power to make "*all* needful rules and regulations" respecting the territory belonging to the United States.

The assertion is, though the Constitution says all, it does not mean all—though it says all, without qualification, it means all except such as allow or prohibit slavery. It cannot be doubted that it is incumbent on those who would introduce an exception not found in the language of the instrument, to exhibit some solid and satisfactory reason, drawn from the subject-matter or the purposes and objects of the clause, the context, or from other provisions of the Constitution, showing that the words employed in this clause are not to be understood according to their clear, plain, and natural signification.

The subject-matter is the territory of the United States out of the limits of every State, and consequently under the exclusive power of the people of the United States. Their will respecting it, manifested in the Constitution, can be subject to no restriction....

A practical construction, nearly contemporaneous with the adoption of the Constitution, and continued by repeated instances through a long series of years, may always influence, and in doubtful cases should determine, the judicial mind, on a question of the interpretation of the Constitution.

...

I consider the passage of this law [the law confirming the Northwest Ordinance] to have been an assertion by the first Congress of the power of the United States to prohibit slavery within this part of the territory of the United States....

...

With the weight of... considerations [of natural right or the political equality of the sections of the nation], when presented to Congress to influence its action, this court has no concern. One or the other may be justly entitled to guide or control the legislative judgment upon what is a needful regulation. The question here is, whether they are sufficient to authorize this court to insert into the clause of the Constitution an exception of the exclusion or allowance of slavery, not found in it, must be admitted to be a matter attended with great difficulty.... To allow this to be done with the Constitution, upon reasons purely political, renders its judicial interpretation impossible—because judicial tribunals, as such, cannot decide upon political considerations. Political reasons have not the requisite certainty to afford rules of judicial interpretation. They are different in different men. They are different in the same men at different times. And when a strict interpretation of the Constitution, according to the fixed rules which govern the interpretation of law, is abandoned, and the theoretical opinions of individuals are allowed to control its meaning, we have no longer a Constitution; we are under the government of individual men, who for the time being have power to declare what the Constitution is, according to their own views of what it ought to mean. When such a method of interpretation of the Constitution obtains, in place of a republican Government, with limited and defined powers, we have a Government which is merely an exponent of the will of Congress; or what, in my opinion, would not be preferable, an exponent of the individual political opinions of the members of this court.

. . .

Abraham Lincoln, Speech on Slavery in the Territories (1860)[24]

Abraham Lincoln (1809–1865) emerged after the passage of the Kansas-Nebraska Act of 1854 as a prominent organizer of the Republican Party in Illinois and popular speaker for the antislavery cause. Lincoln made opposition to the Kansas-Nebraska Act and to the Dred Scott *decision the centerpiece of his 1858 campaign to unseat Democratic Senator Stephen A. Douglas. For Lincoln, Congress had both the constitutional authority and the moral obligation to exclude slavery from the territories. He lost the Senate election in 1858. Nevertheless, the national prominence Lincoln achieved during his famous debates with Douglas made him a frontrunner for the Republican presidential nomination.*

The following excerpt is taken from a speech Lincoln gave on February 27, 1860, at the Cooper Institute in New York. Lincoln was not an official candidate for the presidency at this time. Nineteenth-century politicians did not publicly seek the White House. That was considered bad form. Nevertheless, the Cooper Institute address was part of a series of speeches that Lincoln and his political advisors thought would foster eastern Republican support for his nomination in the summer party convention.

24. Excerpt taken from Abraham Lincoln, "Address at Cooper Institute, New York City," in *The Collected Works of Abraham Lincoln*, ed. Roy P. Basler, vol. 3 (New Brunswick, NJ: Rutgers University Press, 1953).

. . .

Does the proper division of local from federal authority, or anything in the Constitution, forbid *our Federal Government* to control as to slavery in *our Federal Territories?*

. . .

In 1789, by the first Congress which sat under the Constitution, an act was passed to enforce the Ordinance of '87, including the prohibition of slavery in the Northwestern Territory. . . . It went through all its stages without a word of opposition, and finally passed both branches without yeas and nays, which is equivalent to a unanimous passage. In this Congress there were sixteen of the thirty-nine fathers who framed the original Constitution. . . .

This shows that, in their understanding, no line dividing local from federal authority, nor anything in the Constitution, properly forbade Congress to prohibit slavery in the federal territory; else both their fidelity to correct principle, and their oath to support the Constitution, would have constrained them to oppose the prohibition.

Again, George Washington, another of the "thirty-nine," was then President of the United States, and, as such, approved and signed the bill; thus completing its validity as a law, and thus showing that, in his understanding, no line dividing local from federal authority, nor anything in the Constitution, forbade the Federal Government, to control as to slavery in federal territory.

. . .

[After finishing a survey of congressional votes on slavery in the territories between 1784 and the Missouri Compromise in 1820, Lincoln declared,] [h]ere, then, we have twenty-three out of our thirty-nine fathers "who framed the Government under which we live," . . . and twenty-one of them—a clear majority of the whole "thirty-nine"—so acting upon it as to make them guilty of gross political impropriety and willful perjury, if, in their understanding, any proper division between local and federal authority, or anything in the Constitution they had made themselves, and sworn to support, forbade the Federal Government to control as to slavery in the federal territories. Thus the twenty-one acted; and, as actions speak louder than words, so actions, under such responsibility, speak still louder.

. . .

Now, and here, let me guard a little against being misunderstood. I do not mean to say we are bound to follow implicitly in whatever our fathers did. To do so, would be to discard all the lights of current experience—to reject all progress—all improvement. What I do say is, that if we would supplant the opinions and policy of our fathers in any case, we should do so upon evidence so conclusive, and argument so clear, that even their great authority, fairly considered and weighed, cannot stand; and most surely not in a case whereof we ourselves declare they understood the question better than we.

But enough! Let all who believe that "our fathers, who framed the Government under which we live, understood this question just as well, and even better, than we do now," speak as they spoke, and act as they acted upon it. This is all Republicans ask—all Republicans desire—in relation to slavery. As those fathers marked it, so let it be again marked, as an evil not to be extended, but to be tolerated and protected only because of and so far as its actual presence among us makes that toleration and protection a necessity. Let all the guaranties those fathers gave it, be, not grudgingly, but fully and fairly maintained. For this Republicans contend, and with this, so far as I know or believe, they will be content.

...

Will they be satisfied if the Territories be unconditionally surrendered to them? We know they will not. In all their present complaints against us, the Territories are scarcely mentioned. Invasions and insurrections are the rage now. Will it satisfy them, if, in the future, we have nothing to do with invasions and insurrections? We know it will not. We so know, because we know we never had anything to do with invasions and insurrections; and yet this total abstaining does not exempt us from the charge and the denunciation.

...

[W]hat will convince them? This, and this only: cease to call slavery *wrong*, and join them in calling it *right*.... Wrong as we think slavery is, we can yet afford to let it alone where it is, because that much is due to the necessity arising from its actual presence in the nation; but can we, while our votes will prevent it, allow it to spread into the National Territories, and to overrun us here in these Free States?...

...

IV. Federalism

MAJOR DEVELOPMENTS

- The Supreme Court permits states to regulate the local incidents of interstate commerce.
- President Jackson vigorously opposes nullification.
- Georgia ignores a Supreme Court decision declaring that states may not exercise sovereignty over Native American lands.

The relationship between the federal government and the states presented Jacksonians with difficult constitutional problems. At the most basic level was the question of union. Most National Republicans and Whigs believed that the people were the constituent units of the United States and that the American Union was permanent. John Marshall in *McCulloch v. Maryland* (1819), they maintained, provided the canonical statement of American nationality when he declared, the "government of the Union... is emphatically, and truly, a government of the people. In form and in substance it emanates from them. Its powers are granted by them, and are to be exercised directed on them, and for their benefit." Most Democrats thought that states were the constitutive units of the United States. Thomas Jefferson in the Kentucky Resolutions (1798), they maintained, provided the canonical statement of state rights when he declared, "the several States composing the United States of America... delegated to [the federal] government certain definite powers, reserving, each State to itself, the residual mass of right to their own self-government." Proponents of state rights in Jacksonian America disputed the best interpretation of this language. Mainstream proponents of state rights asserted that Republicans in 1798 meant to assert only that the federal government was one of limited powers. Proponents of nullification insisted that, as the constituent units of the national union, states were entitled to decide for themselves whether federal laws were constitutional.

These disagreements over the place of states in the national Union roiled American politics from the beginning of the Jacksonian Era. In January of 1830, Daniel Webster concluded a strongly nationalist speech by linking union to the most fundamental American value. He declared on the floor of the Senate, "Liberty and Union, Now and Forever, One and Inseparable." Webster's gambit bore fruit when the

Democratic Party elite gathered at a Jefferson Day dinner later that year. The "states' rights" faction of the Democratic Party hoped to pull President Jackson into their orbit. The president had resolved to side with Webster, on this issue at least. After an evening filled with toasts to the memory of Jefferson and Virginia's resistance to the federal sedition laws, President Jackson pointedly offered a toast to "Our Union: It must be preserved." No one was more surprised than Jackson's vice president, John C. Calhoun, whose own political future depended on holding the support of the "states' rights" faction within his home state of South Carolina and in the national Democratic Party. Visibly disturbed, Calhoun countered: "The Union, next to our liberty, most dear. May we all remember that it can be preserved by respecting the rights of the States and by distributing equally the benefits and burdens of Union." South Carolina Senator Robert Hayne quickly persuaded the president to amend his toast to "Our *Federal* Union—It must be preserved." The amendment gave the southerners something they could spin in their favor, but no one mistook the president's sentiment. Secretary of State Martin Van Buren, who had helped set the president's strategy for the dinner, offered a more conciliatory toast emphasizing the virtues of "mutual forbearance and reciprocal concessions" and the "patriotic spirit" that would allow them to preserve the Union.[25]

Most Jacksonians sought to toe the fine line President Jackson walked between nationalism and state rights. Jackson repeatedly insisted that federal power was supreme and that federal authorities determined the balance of power between the federal government and the states. He rejected claims by more extreme state rights proponents that the Constitution was a compact with the states that permitted each state to nullify perceived unconstitutional laws. Nevertheless, when questions about state control over Native Americans and commercial enterprise arose, Jackson, his Democratic Party successors, and the Democratic majority on the Taney Court consistently declared that the Constitution vested far more power in state governments than the Marshall Court had been willing to recognize.

25. Martin Van Buren, *The Autobiography of Martin Van Buren*, vol. 2 (Washington, DC: Government Printing Office, 1920), 415–16.

A. States and the Commerce Clause

Debates over the commerce clause after the 1820s shifted from federal to state power. The Marshall Court interpreted federal commercial power broadly. *Gibbons v. Ogden* (1824) and *Brown v. Maryland* (1827) established that federal power over interstate commerce "cannot be stopped at the external boundary of a State, but must enter its interior." Congress from 1825 to 1860 rarely tested the limits of this power. The issue that occupied the late Marshall and Taney Courts was the extent to which states could regulate interstate commerce in the absence of any conflicting federal law.

The materials presented in this subsection discuss the constitutional issues associated with the "dormant" commerce clause or the "negative radiations" of the commerce clause. Justice Joseph Story and many Whigs claimed that the federal power over interstate commerce was exclusive. They interpreted the commerce clause as declaring that Congress and only Congress could regulate interstate commerce. State laws that affected interstate commerce were unconstitutional, even when no federal law regulated the matter. Chief Justice Roger Taney and many Democrats maintained that the federal government and state governments had concurrent power over commercial activity. They interpreted the commerce clause as permitting the states to regulate at will, unless state law conflicted with a valid federal law. Moderates strove to find a middle ground between the exclusive and concurrent interpretations of the commerce power. They claimed that, in the absence of federal regulation, the constitutionality of state laws that affected interstate commerce depended on particular circumstances.

The Supreme Court during the 1830s and 1840s was usually sharply divided when adjudicating dormant commerce clause cases, in part because many raised explosive political issues. *Groves v. Slaughter* (1841) raised questions about whether the Mississippi Constitution could bar persons from importing slaves into the state for sale. The justices ducked the issue by noting that the state legislature had never implemented that constitutional prohibition. Several justices wrote opinions discussing at great length both federal and state power under the commerce clause to regulate the interstate slave trade. In *The License Cases* (1847), the justices entered the fray over state temperance laws. Six justices wrote separate opinions. The end result was a 5–4 majority sustaining state laws requiring hard or impossible to obtain local licenses for the sale of alcoholic beverages. *The Passenger Cases* (1849) likewise fractured the Court. The justices produced a welter of opinions discussing whether the commerce clause prohibited state laws imposing special taxes on alien passengers brought by ship into the state. A narrow majority struck down these statutes as an unconstitutional interference with congressional power over foreign and interstate commerce. Justice Wayne, in the majority, qualified the effect of the decision. Wayne stated that the states retained a police power to remove "paupers, vagabonds and fugitives" from their territory. Of crucial interest to the south, he made clear that the slave states could exclude "all such as are, from a common ancestry and country, of the same class of men" as their slaves. In short, states could prohibit free blacks. Many did, in both the South and the Northwest.

The Taney Court gave some coherence to commerce clause doctrine in *Cooley v. Board of Wardens of the Port of Philadelphia* (1852). *Cooley* directed the Court's attention away from the volatile issues of state sovereignty and whether the federal commerce power was exclusive or concurrent to the more pragmatic issue of regulatory effectiveness. Justice Benjamin Curtis's opinion distinguished between objects of regulation that were "in their nature national" and required nationally uniform solutions and objects of regulation that do not require uniform rules but instead can benefit from "local knowledge and experience." Although some justices continued to assert the exclusivity of the congressional commerce power and others the supremacy of the state police power, *Cooley* provided a clear channel between these shoals. The federal government had exclusive power over all commercial matters of national importance. States retained concurrent power to regulate local aspects of interstate commerce in the absence of federal law.

Willson v. Black Bird Creek Marsh Company, 27 U.S. 245 (1829)

Thompson Willson was the owner of a federally licensed sloop, the Sally. While sailing, Willson partially dismantled a dam built by the Black Bird Creek Marsh Company. The Company, which had been incorporated by Delaware to erect the dam and embank the surrounding marshland, sued Willson for damages. Willson responded that the dam unlawfully obstructed a navigable creek and that he had the right to restore the public way. The Delaware courts found against Willson, and a jury awarded the requested damages. Willson appealed that decision to the Supreme Court of the United States. He argued that he had a federal constitutional right to navigate coastal streams, that states had no power to close navigable streams, and that the state's action in this case was motivated by private profits rather than by public health. The Company responded that clearing the marsh fell within the legitimate police powers of the state, that their action was consistent with existing federal law, and that Congress could not legitimately prevent a state from undertaking such public health measures.

The Supreme Court declared that Delaware had acted constitutionally. Chief Justice John Marshall's opinion found no conflict between federal and state power, even though he noted that the dam might interfere with interstate commerce. What reason did Marshall give for sustaining the Maryland law?

CHIEF JUSTICE MARSHALL delivered the opinion of the Court.

. . .

The act of assembly by which the plaintiffs were authorized to construct their dam, shows plainly that this is one of those many creeks, passing through a deep level marsh adjoining the Delaware, up which the tide flows for some distance. The value of the property on its banks must be enhanced by excluding the water from the marsh, and the health of the inhabitants probably improved. Measures calculated to produce these objects, provided they do not come into collision with the powers of the general government, are undoubtedly within those which are reserved to the states. But the measure authorized by this act stops a navigable creek, and must be supposed to abridge the rights of those who have been accustomed to use it. But this abridgement, unless it comes in conflict with the constitution or a law of the United States, is an affair between the government of Delaware and its citizens, of which this Court can take no cognizance.

The counsel for the plaintiffs in error insist that it comes in conflict with the power of the United States "to regulate commerce with foreign nations and among the several states."

If congress had passed any act which bore upon the case; any act in execution of the power to regulate commerce, the object of which was to control state legislation over those small navigable creeks into which the tide flows, and which abound throughout the lower country of the middle and southern states; we should feel not much difficulty in saying that a state law coming in conflict with such act would be void. But congress has passed no such act. The repugnancy of the law of Delaware to the constitution is placed entirely on its repugnancy to the power to regulate commerce with foreign nations and among the several states; a power which has not been so exercised as to affect the question.

We do not think that the act empowering the Black Bird Creek Marsh Company to place a dam across the creek, can, under all the circumstances of the case, be considered as repugnant to the power to regulate commerce in its dormant state, or as being in conflict with any law passed on the subject.

There is no error, and the judgment is affirmed.

City of New York v. Miln, 36 U.S. 102 (1837)

George Miln was the master of the Emily. *On August 27, 1829, the* Emily *arrived in New York from Liverpool, England, with 100 passengers aboard. New York law required the masters of ships arriving in the port of New York City to provide a written record of information on all ship passengers from out of state, post a bond for each passenger, and indemnify the city for any passengers that accepted poor relief from the city within two years of their arrival. Miln neither provided New York City with the legally required written record nor posted bond for each passenger. When the city initiated proceedings in local court to collect penalties, Miln had the case removed to a federal circuit court. That lower court was divided, and the constitutional question was certified for hearing by the Supreme Court. The city argued that the law was a valid exercise of the state police powers. Miln argued that the law was an unconstitutional infringement on the congressional authority to regulate foreign and interstate commerce.*

The Supreme Court ruled that the New York City law was constitutional. Justice Philip Barbour declared that the commerce clause did not prohibit states from exercising their traditional police powers to regulate for the health, safety, welfare, and morals of the community. The decision in Miln *had implications for similar passenger laws targeting poor immigrants in the North, and for southern laws prohibiting free black sailors in state ports. The Marshall Court had long avoided addressing such issues. The Taney Court was inclined to give room to the states to manage the people who came within their borders.*

JUSTICE BARBOUR delivered the opinion of the Court.

...

We shall not enter into any examination of the question whether the power to regulate commerce, be or be not exclusive of the states, because the opinion which we have formed renders it unnecessary: in other words, we are of opinion that the act is not a regulation of commerce, but of police; and that being thus considered, it was passed in the exercise of a power which rightfully belonged to the states.

...

Now, we hold that both the end and the means here used, are within the competency of the states, since a portion of their powers were surrendered to the federal government. Let us see what powers are left with the states. The Federalist, in the 45th number, speaking of this subject, says; the powers reserved to the several states, will extend to all the objects, which in the ordinary course of affairs, concern the lives, liberties, and properties of the people; and the internal order, improvement, and prosperity of the state.

And this Court, in the case of *Gibbons v. Ogden* (1824)... in speaking of the inspection laws of the states, say; they form a portion of that immense mass of legislation which embraces every thing within the territory of a state, not surrendered to the general government, all which can be most advantageously exercised by the states themselves. Inspection laws, quarantine laws, health laws of every description, as well as laws for regulating the internal commerce of a state, and those which respect turnpike roads, ferries, etc. are component parts of this mass.

...If we look at the place of [the act's] operation, we find it to be within the territory, and, therefore, within the jurisdiction of New York. If we look at the person on whom it operates, he is found within the same territory and jurisdiction. If we look at the persons for whose benefit it was passed, they are the people of New York, for whose protection and welfare the legislature of that state are authorized and in duty bound to provide.

If we turn our attention to the purpose to be attained, it is to secure that very protection, and to provide for that very welfare. If we examine the means by which these ends are proposed to be accomplished, they bear a just, natural, and appropriate relation to those ends.

...

. . . We choose . . . to plant ourselves on what we consider impregnable positions. They are these: That a state has the same undeniable and unlimited jurisdiction over all persons and things, within its territorial limits, as any foreign nation; where that jurisdiction is not surrendered or restrained by the constitution of the United States. That, by virtue of this, it is not only the right, but the bounden and solemn duty of a state, to advance the safety, happiness and prosperity of its people, and to provide for its general welfare, by any and every act of legislation, which it may deem to be conducive to these ends; where the power over the particular subject, or the manner of its exercise is not surrendered or restrained, in the manner just stated. That all those powers which relate to merely municipal legislation, or what may, perhaps, more properly be called internal police, are not thus surrendered or restrained; and that, consequently, in relation to these, the authority of a state is complete, unqualified, and exclusive.

. . .

Now in relation to the section in the act immediately before us, that is obviously passed with a view to prevent her citizens from being oppressed by the support of multitudes of poor persons, who come from foreign countries without possessing the means of supporting themselves. There can be no mode in which the power to regulate internal police could be more appropriately exercised. New York, from her particular situation, is, perhaps more than any other city in the Union, exposed to the evil of thousands of foreign emigrants arriving there, and the consequent danger of her citizens being subjected to a heavy charge in the maintenance of those who are poor. It is the duty of the state to protect its citizens from this evil; they have endeavored to do so, by passing, amongst other things, the section of the law in question. We should, upon principle, say that it had a right to do so.

. . .

JUSTICE THOMPSON, concurring.

. . .

It is not necessary, in this case, to fix any limits upon the legislation of congress and of the states, on this subject; or to say how far congress may, under the power to regulate commerce, control state legislation in this respect. It is enough to say that whatever the power of congress may be, it has not been exercised so as, in any manner, to conflict with the state law; and if the mere grant of the power to congress does not necessarily imply a prohibition of the states to exercise the power, until congress assumes to exercise it; no objection, on that ground, can arise to this law.

. . .

JUSTICE STORY, dissenting.

. . .

. . . If then the regulation of passenger ships, be in truth a regulation of trade and commerce, it seems very difficult to escape from the conclusion, that the act in controversy is, in the sense of the objection, an act which assumes to regulate trade and commerce between the port of New York and foreign parts. It requires a report, not only of passengers who arrive at New York, but of all who have been landed at any places out of the territorial limits of New York, whether in foreign ports or in the ports of other states. It requires bonds to be given by the master or owner for all passengers not citizens; and it compels them to remove, or pay the expenses of removal of all passengers, who are citizens, and are deemed likely to become chargeable to the city, under severe penalties. If these enactments had been contained in any act passed by congress, it would not have been doubted that they were regulations of passenger ships engaged in foreign commerce. Is their character changed by their being found in the laws of a state?

I admit, in the most unhesitating manner, that the states have a right to pass health laws and quarantine laws, and other police laws, not contravening the laws of congress rightfully passed under their constitutional authority. I admit, that they have a right to pass poor laws, and laws to prevent the introduction of paupers into the state, under the like qualifications. I go further, and admit, that in the exercise of their legitimate authority over any particular subject, the states may generally use the same means which are used by congress, if these means are suitable to the end. But I cannot admit that the states have authority to enact laws, which act upon subjects beyond their territorial limits, or within those limits, and which trench upon the authority of congress in its power to regulate commerce. . . .

. . .

It has been argued that the power of congress to regulate commerce is not exclusive, but concurrent with that of the states. If this were a new question in this Court, wholly untouched by doctrine or decision; I should not hesitate to go into a full examination of all the grounds upon which concurrent authority is attempted to be maintained. But in point of fact, the whole argument on this very question, as presented by the learned counsel on the present occasion, was presented by the learned counsel who argued the case of *Gibbons*... and it was then deliberately examined and deemed inadmissible by the Court. Mr. Chief Justice Marshall, with his accustomed accuracy and fullness of illustration, reviewed at that time the whole grounds of the controversy; and from that time to the present, the question has been considered (as far as I know) to be at rest. The power given to congress to regulate commerce with foreign nations, and among the states, has been deemed exclusive; from the nature and objects of the power, and the necessary implications growing out of its exercise. Full power to regulate a particular subject implies the whole power, and leaves no residuum; and a grant of the whole to one, is incompatible with a grant to another of a part....

Cooley v. Board of Wardens of the Port of Philadelphia, 53 U.S. 299 (1852)

In 1789, Congress passed a statute adopting the state laws then in force regarding the use of pilots to assist in navigating ships through local rivers and ports. In 1803, Pennsylvania passed a law requiring that foreign or large coastal ships arriving or departing from Philadelphia employ a local pilot. The board of wardens for the port of Philadelphia brought action in state court to collect pilot fees from Aaron Cooley, who had failed to employ a pilot for two ships making use of the port. After losing in state court, Cooley appealed to the U.S. Supreme Court. He argued that the Pennsylvania pilot law was either an unconstitutional regulation of interstate commerce or in conflict with the 1789 federal statute. Pennsylvania responded that the pilot law was a constitutional exercise of a concurrent power to regulate commerce that did not conflict with any existing federal regulation.

The Supreme Court ruled that Pennsylvania could constitutionally require that ships hire local pilots. Justice Benjamin Curtis's majority opinion distinguished between situations requiring a national, uniform regulation and situations better addressed by divergent, local regulations. Pilotage, he concluded, was a matter best addressed by local law. Cooley's *distinction between national and local concerns became the leading approach to dormant commerce issues during the rest of the nineteenth century. How useful does this formulation seem for resolving commerce clause disputes?*

JUSTICE CURTIS delivered the opinion of the Court.

...

That the power to regulate commerce includes the regulation of navigation, we consider settled. And when we look to the nature of the service performed by pilots, to the relations which that service and its compensations bear to navigation between the several States, and between the ports of the United States and foreign countries, we are brought to the conclusion, that [such regulations] do constitute regulations of navigation, and consequently of commerce, within the just meaning of this clause of the Constitution.

...

If the law of Pennsylvania, now in question, had been in existence at the date of this act of Congress [leaving in place state laws regarding pilots], we might hold it to have been adopted by Congress, and thus made a law of the United States, and so valid....

But the law on which these actions are founded was not enacted till 1803. What effect then can be attributed to so much of the act of 1789, as declares, that pilots shall continue to be regulated in conformity, "with such laws as the States may respectively hereafter enact for the purpose, until further legislative provision shall be made by Congress"?

If the States were divested of the power to legislate on this subject by the grant of the commercial power to Congress, it is plain this act could not confer upon them power thus to legislate. If the Constitution excluded the States from making any law regulating commerce, certainly Congress cannot regrant, or in any manner reconvey to the States that power. And yet this act of 1789 gives its sanction only to laws enacted by the States. This necessarily implies a constitutional power to legislate.... Entertaining these views we are brought directly and unavoidably to the consideration of the question, whether the grant of the commercial power to Congress, did per se deprive the States of all power to regulate pilots.... If they are excluded it must be because the nature of the power, thus granted to Congress, requires that a similar authority should not exist in the States....

The diversities of opinion... which have existed on this subject, have arisen from the different views taken of the nature of this power. But when the nature of a power like this is spoken of, when it is said that the nature of the power requires that it should be exercised exclusively by Congress, it must be intended to refer to the subjects of that power, and to say they are of such a nature as to require exclusive legislation by Congress. Now the power to regulate commerce, embraces a vast field, containing not only many, but exceedingly various subjects, quite unlike in their nature; some imperatively demanding a single uniform rule, operating equally on the commerce of the United States in every port; and some, like the subject now in question, as imperatively demanding that diversity, which alone can meet the local necessities of navigation.

Either absolutely to affirm, or deny that the nature of this power requires exclusive legislation by Congress, is to lose sight of the nature of the subjects of this power, and to assert concerning all of them, what is really applicable but to a part. Whatever subjects of this power are in their nature national, or admit only of one uniform system, or plan of regulation, may justly be said to be of such a nature as to require exclusive legislation by Congress. That this cannot be affirmed of laws for the regulation of pilots and pilotage is plain. The act of 1789 contains a clear and authoritative declaration by the first Congress, that the nature of this subject is such, that until Congress should find it necessary to exert its power, it should be left to the legislation of the States; that it is local and not national; that it is likely to be the best provided for, not by one system, or plan of regulations, but by as many as the legislative discretion of the several States should deem applicable to the local peculiarities of the ports within their limits.

. . .

JUSTICE McLEAN, dissenting.

. . .

That a State may regulate foreign commerce, or commerce among the States, is a doctrine which has been advanced by individual judges of this court; but never before, I believe, has such a power been sanctioned by the decision of this court. In this case, the power to regulate pilots is admitted to belong to the commercial power of Congress; and yet it is held, that a State, by virtue of its inherent power, may regulate the subject, until such regulation shall be annulled by Congress. This is the principle established by this decision. Its language is guarded, in order to apply the decision only to the case before the court. But such restrictions can never operate, so as to render the principle inapplicable to other cases. And it is in this light that the decision is chiefly to be regretted. The power is recognized in the State, because the subject is more appropriate for State than Federal action; and consequently, it must be presumed the Constitution cannot have intended to inhibit State action. This is not a rule by which the Constitution is to be construed. It can receive but little support from the discussions which took place on the adoption of the Constitution, and none at all from the earlier decisions of this court.

. . .

I think the charge of half-pilotage is correct under the circumstances, and I only object to the power of the State to pass the law. Congress, to whom the subject peculiarly belongs, should have been applied to, and no doubt it would have adopted the act of the State.

JUSTICE DANIEL, concurring.

. . . The power delegated to Congress by the Constitution relates properly to the terms on which commercial engagements may be prosecuted; the character of the articles which they may embrace; the permission or terms according to which they may be introduced; and do not necessarily nor even naturally extend to the means of precaution and safety adopted within the waters or limits of the States by the authority of the latter for the preservation of vessels and cargoes, and the lives of navigators or passengers. These last subjects are essentially local—they must depend upon local necessities which call them into existence, must differ according to the degrees of that necessity. It is admitted, on all hands, that they cannot be uniform or even general, but must vary so as to meet the purposes to be accomplished. They have no connection with contract, or traffic, or with the permission to trade in any subject, or upon any conditions. . . . This is a power which is deemed indispensable to the safety and existence of every community. It may well be made a question, therefore, whether it could, under any circumstances, be surrendered; but certainly it is one which cannot be supposed to have been given by mere implication, and as incidental to another, to the exercise of which it is not indispensable. It is not just nor philosophical to argue from the possibility of abuse against the rightful existence of this power in the States; such an argument would, if permitted, go to the overthrow of all power in either the States or in the federal government, since there is no power which may not be abused. . . . I am forced to conclude that this is an original and inherent power in the States, and not one to be merely tolerated, or held subject to the sanction of the federal government.

B. State Authority to Interpret the Constitution

Compact theory was an article of faith for many southerners and some northerners during the Jacksonian Era. Proponents of this theory maintained that the Constitution was a compact or a treaty between otherwise independent states. These states did not surrender central elements of sovereignty when joining the union. In particular, proponents of compact theory maintained that each state had the power to determine whether a federal law was unconstitutional. They revered the passage in Thomas Jefferson's Kentucky Resolutions of 1798 which declared, "as in all other cases of compact among powers having no common judge, each party has an equal right to judge for itself, as well of infractions as of the mode and measure of redress." Nullification was the means by which a state could exercise this sovereign power to "judge for itself" whether the federal government was acting constitutionally. Compact theorists believed that states could declare federal laws null and void. When that happened, the federal government had no power to enforce the law within the boundaries of the nullifying state.

South Carolina in 1832 put compact theory into practice. A state nullification convention was called, and the federal protectionist tariff was declared to be unconstitutional in November. The South Carolina Nullification Ordinance of 1832 declared,

> We, therefore, the people of the State of South Carolina, in convention assembled, do declare and ordain...that the several acts and parts of acts of the Congress of the United States, purporting to be laws for the imposing of duties and imposts on the importation of foreign commodities...are unauthorized by the constitution of the United States, and violate the true meaning and intent thereof and are null, void, and no law, nor binding upon this State, its officers or citizens....
>
> And it is further ordained, that it shall not be lawful for any of the constituted authorities, whether of this State or of the United States, to enforce the payment of duties imposed by the said acts within the limits of this State; but it shall be the duty of the legislature to adopt such measures and pass such acts as may be necessary to give full effect to this ordinance, and to prevent the enforcement and arrest the operation of the said acts and parts of acts of the Congress of the United States within the limits of this State, from and after the first day of February next....

President Andrew Jackson condemned nullification. When the Governor of South Carolina mustered the state militia, Jackson threatened to march on the state at the head of an army and hang the nullifiers as guilty of secession and treason. He issued a strong nationalistic proclamation denouncing nullification. Jackson believed the Constitution strictly limited the powers of the federal government. Nevertheless, his Nullification Proclamation asserted that federal authorities determined the proper balance of power between the states and the central government.

Congress quickly hammered out a compromise that empowered the president to collect the revenue by force, but phased out the protectionist tariff. Both sides declared victory, but there was little enthusiasm among states' rights advocates for calling a nullification convention again. The elderly James Madison was among the critics of nullification. He objected to using the Kentucky Resolution of 1798 as a precedent. In his view, allowances had to be made for "a habit in Mr. Jefferson as in others of great genius of expressing in strong and round terms, impressions of the moment."[26] Was Madison right?

John C. Calhoun, **"Fort Hill Address"** (1831)[27]

John C. Calhoun (1782–1850) of South Carolina started his career as a "War Hawk" during the War of 1812. He made common cause with other young nationalists such as Henry Clay and Daniel Webster. The three supported federal policies such as protective tariffs and internal improvements aimed at building national strength. By the 1820s, tariff rates had been raised to unprecedented levels. They were no longer justified as short-term measures to nurture "infant industries" but as permanent features of American political economy. South Carolina turned hostile to federal economic policies that subsidized northern manufacturing interests. Calhoun turned as well. He became the leading spokesman

26. James Madison, Letter to N. P. Trist (May, 1832), in Gaillard Hunt, ed. *The Writings of James Madison*, vol. 9, (New York: G. P. Putnam's Sons, 1910), 478.

27. Excerpt taken from John C. Calhoun, "Address on the Relation Which the States and the Federal Government Bear to Each Other," 26 July 1831, in Richard C. Cralle, *Works of John C. Calhoun*, Vol. 6 (New York: D. Appleton and Company, 1855), 59.

and theorist of conservative southern constitutionalism and compact theory.

The "Fort Hill Address" was Calhoun's first public statement on nullification. He presented nullification as the natural extension of the Virginia and Kentucky Resolutions of 1798. In contrast to Jefferson, Calhoun's theory required a special, popular state convention (rather than the state legislature) to determine whether the federal law in question was unconstitutional and to determine the appropriate action that the state could make. Is nullification a natural extension of the Virginia and Kentucky Resolutions of 1798? Is state nullification a less reasonable inference from the constitutional scheme than the power of judicial review?

...

The great and leading principle is, that the General Government emanated from the people of the several States, forming distinct political communities, and acting in their separate and sovereign capacity, and not from all of the people forming one aggregate political community; that the Constitution of the United States is, in fact, a compact, to which each State is a party, in the character already described; and that the several States, or parties, have a right to judge of its infractions; and in case of a deliberate, palpable, and dangerous exercise of power not delegated, they have the right, in the last resort, to use the language of the Virginia Resolutions, "to interpose for arresting the progress of the evil, and for maintaining, within their respective limits, the authorities, rights, and liberties appertaining to them." This right of interposition, thus solemnly asserted by the State of Virginia, be it called what it may—State-right, veto, nullification, or by any other name—I conceive to be the fundamental principle of our system, resting on facts historically as certain as our revolution itself, and deductions as simple and demonstrative as that of any political, or moral truth whatever; and I firmly believe that on its recognition depend the stability and safety of our political institutions.

...

It has been well said by one of the most sagacious men of antiquity, that the object of a constitution is, to *restrain the government, as that of laws* is to restrain *individuals.* The remark is correct; nor is it less true, where the government is vested in a majority, than where it is in a single or a few individuals—in a republic, than a monarchy or aristocracy. No one can have a higher respect for the maxim that the majority ought to govern than I have, taken in its proper sense, subject to the restrictions imposed by the Constitution, and confined to objects in which every portion of the community have similar interests; but it is a great error to suppose, as many do, that the right of a majority to govern is a natural and not a conventional right; and, therefore absolute and unlimited. By nature, every individual has the right to govern himself; and governments, whether founded on majorities or minorities, must derive their right from the assent, expressed or implied, of the governed, and be subject to such limitations as they may impose. Where the interests are the same, that is, where the laws that may benefit one, will benefit all, or the reverse, it is just and proper to place them under the control of the majority; but where they are dissimilar, so that the law that may benefit one portion may be ruinous to another, it would be, on the contrary, unjust and absurd to subject them to its will; and such, I conceive to be the theory on which our Constitution rests.

...

Should the General Government and a State come into conflict, we have a higher remedy: the power which called the General Government into existence, which gave it all of its authority, and can enlarge, contract, or abolish its powers at its pleasure, may be invoked. The States themselves may be appealed to—three-fourths of which, in fact, form a power, whose decrees are the Constitution itself, and whose voice can silence all discontent [by amending the Constitution]....[T]o avoid the supposed dangers of [appealing to the states], it is proposed to resort to the novel, the hazardous, and, I must add, fatal project of giving to the General Government the sole and final right of interpreting the Constitution—thereby reversing the whole system, making that instrument the creature of its will, instead of a rule of action impressed on it at its creation, and annihilating, in fact, the authority which imposed it, and from which the Government itself derives its existence.

...

In examining this point, we ought not to forget that the Government, through all its departments, judicial as well as others, is administered by delegated and responsible agents; and that *the power which really controls, ultimately, all the movements is not in the agents, but those who elect or appoint them.* To understand, then, its real character, and what would be the action of the system in any supposable case, we must raise our view from the mere agents to this high controlling power, which finally impels every movement of the machine.... The judges are, in fact, as truly the judicial representatives of this united majority, as the majority of Congress itself, or the President, is its legislative or executive representative; and to confide the power to the Judiciary to determine finally and conclusively, what powers are delegated, and what reserved, would be, in reality, to confide it to the majority, whose agents they are, and by whom they can be controlled in various ways; and, of course, to subject (against the fundamental principle of our system and all sound political reasoning) the reserved powers of the States, with all of the local and peculiar interests they were intended to protect, to the will of the very majority against which the protection was intended. Nor will the tenure by which the judges hold their office, however valuable the provision in many other respects, materially vary the case. Its highest possible effect would be to *retard,* and not *finally* to *resist,* the will of a dominant majority.

...

...Stripped of all its covering, the naked question is, whether ours is a federal or a consolidated government; a constitutional or absolute one; a government resting ultimately on the solid basis of the sovereignty of the States, or on the unrestrained will of a majority; a form of government, as in all other unlimited ones, in which injustice, and violence, and force must finally prevail. *Let it never be forgotten that, where the majority rules, the minority is the subject;* and that, if we should absurdly attribute to the former, the exclusive right of construing the Constitution, there would be, in fact, between the sovereign and subject, under such a government, no Constitution; or, at least, nothing deserving the name, or serving the legitimate object of so sacred an instrument.

...

Andrew Jackson, Proclamation on Nullification (December 10, 1832)

President Andrew Jackson's reaction to the nullification crisis was crucial and not easily predicted from his previous actions and pronouncements. Jackson was not a strong supporter of protectionist tariffs, but neither had he opposed them. For nearly a decade, the federal government tolerated South Carolina's negro seamen's laws, despite the opinion of a Supreme Court justice and an attorney general that they effectively nullified federal law and American treaties. Jackson publicly stood by while Georgia ignored such Supreme Court decisions as Worcester v. Georgia *(1832), which asserted federal supremacy over Indian tribes within the state borders. These actions gave South Carolinians reason for thinking that Jackson might look the other way during the nullification crisis. His 1832 State of the Union message, delivered on December 4, praised states' rights and recommended that tariffs be slashed. Now-Congressman John Quincy Adams declared the message "a complete surrender to the Nullifiers of South Carolina."*[28]

Adams was almost immediately proven wrong. Jackson leaped into the fray a week later. He sharply condemned nullification. Nullification of the tariff directly challenged the president's responsibility to collect the federal revenue. The South Carolina government also miscalculated when calling out the state militia to support the nullification ordinance, hoping a show of force would encourage the federal government to back down. Instead, the former general who lived in the White House denounced the action as "positive treason" and threatened to raise an army of "two hundred thousand men" that would crush the opposition. Spurning his usual advisors (who were sympathetic to states' rights even if critical of nullification), Jackson drafted a boldly nationalist proclamation. Nullification was equivalent to secession, and secession was equivalent to treason. Congress was to be checked by the presidential veto, not state nullification. Why didn't Jackson point to the courts as a check on national power?

...

The [state nullification] ordinance is founded, not on the indefeasible right of resisting acts which are plainly unconstitutional and too oppressive to be endured, but on the strange position that any one State may not only declare an act of Congress void, but prohibit its execution; that they may do this consistent with the Constitution....

If this doctrine had been established at an earlier day, the Union would have been dissolved in its infancy. The excise law in Pennsylvania, the embargo and nonintercourse law in the Eastern States, the carriage tax in Virginia, were all deemed unconstitutional, and were more unequal in their operation than any of the laws now complained of; but, fortunately, none of

28. Quoted in Richard E. Ellis, *The Union at Risk* (New York: Oxford University Press, 1989), 83.

those States discovered that they had the right now claimed by South Carolina.[29] . . .

In our colonial state, although dependent on another power, we very early considered ourselves as connected by common interest with each other. Leagues were formed for common defense, and before the declaration of independence we were known in our aggregate character as the *United Colonies of America*. That decisive and important step was taken jointly. We declared ourselves a nation by a joint, not by several acts. . . .

. . .

I consider, then, the power to annul a law of the United States, assumed by one State, incompatible with the existence of the Union, contradicted expressly by the letter of the Constitution, unauthorized by its spirit, inconsistent with every principle on which it was founded, and destructive of the great object for which it was formed.

. . .

The Constitution has given, expressly, to Congress the right of raising revenue and of determining the sum the public exigencies will require. The States have no control over the exercise of this right other than that which results from the power of changing the representatives who abuse it, and thus procure redress. Congress may undoubtedly abuse the discretionary power; but the same may be said of others with which they are vested. Yet the discretion must exist somewhere. The Constitution has given it to the representatives of all the people, checked by the representatives of the States and by the Executive power. The South Carolina construction gives it to the legislature or the convention of a single State, where neither the people of the different States, nor the States in their collective capacity, nor the Chief Magistrate elected by the people have any representation. Which is the most discreet disposition of the power? I do not ask you, fellow-citizens, which is the constitutional disposition; that instrument speaks in a language not to be misunderstood. . . .

. . .

. . . [The nullification ordinance not only asserts] the right to annul the laws of which it complains, but to enforce it by a threat of seceding from the Union if any attempt is made to execute them.

. . .

The Constitution of the United States . . . forms a government, not a league; and whether it be formed by compact between the States or in any other manner, its character is the same. It is a Government in which all the people are represented, which operates directly on the people individually, not upon the States; they retained all the power they did not grant. But each State, having expressly parted with so many powers as to constitute, jointly with the other States, a single nation, can not, from that period, possess any right to secede, because such secession does not break a league, but destroys the unity of a nation; and any injury to that unity is not only a breach which would result from the contravention of a compact, but it is an offense against the whole Union.

. . .

C. States and Native American Sovereignty

The national government and several southern states heatedly disputed sovereignty over Native American lands during the first part of the Jacksonian Era. The United States during the early national period made numerous treaties with Native Americans. These treaties granted the tribes rights to exercise sovereignty on lands within existing states. National Republicans, particularly from the North, insisted that these agreements were valid exercises of the national power to make treaties. Democrats, particularly from the South, insisted that Native American tribes were not sovereign nations and that states had sovereign rights over all lands within their borders.

Georgia was particularly aggressive when asserting rights over Cherokees. The state legislature in 1828 passed legislation imposing various restrictions on whites who entered Cherokee territory and regulating the internal affairs of the Cherokees. Georgia prosecuted a Cherokee Indian named Corn Tassels in state court for murdering another Cherokee. After the Supreme Court took jurisdiction to consider whether the state's proceedings violated federal treaties, Georgia quickly executed Corn Tassels. Congress supported Georgia's initiative. The national legislature, backed by the Jackson administration, passed the Indian Removal

29. The "excise tax in Pennsylvania" refers to the tax that led to several tax protests in Pennsylvania during the Washington administration, including the "Whiskey Rebellion." On the Jeffersonian "embargo and nonintercourse law," see *United States v. The William*, 28 F. Cas. 614 (D. Mass. 1808). On the Federalist carriage tax, see *Hylton v. United States* (1796).

Act of 1830. That measure authorized the president to negotiate land-exchange treaties with tribes that lived within the borders of existing U.S. states, "encouraging" them to relocate west of the Mississippi in what would become known as "Indian territory."

Federal courts slowed but could not prevent Georgia from removing the Cherokees and other Native Americans. The Supreme Court in *Worcester v. Georgia* (1832) ruled that states could not exercise jurisdiction over lands that federal treaties set aside for Native Americans. The Jackson Administration, however, made little effort to enforce that decision. In 1835, a faction of Cherokees signed the Treaty of New Echota, which, in 1838, led to their forcible relocation by the U.S. army to "Indian territory." Thousands of Cherokees died on the "trail of tears" during the winter they were relocated from Georgia to what is now Oklahoma.

Worcester v. Georgia, 31 U.S. 515 (1832)

Samuel Austin Worcester was one of several missionaries arrested by Georgia authorities for violating a state statute that required white persons living on Cherokee soil to obtain a license. At trial, Worcester was convicted, and sentenced to four years hard labor. After the Supreme Court of Georgia sustained the trial ruling, Worcester appealed to the Supreme Court. Leading National Republicans, hoping to slow down Jacksonian efforts at Native American removal, came to Worcester's defense. William Wirt, the attorney general in the Monroe and Adams administrations, was Worcester's counsel. Wirt claimed the Georgia law was inconsistent with federal treaties. Georgia claimed that the federal government was not empowered to grant Native Americans sovereignty over lands within a state.

The Supreme Court ruled that Worcester's conviction was invalid. Chief Justice Marshall's opinion declared that the federal government was empowered to make treaties with Native American tribes and that the states could not exercise sovereignty over lands these treaties set aside for the tribes. Marshall's strongly worded opinion was a clear rebuke to Democratic policy on the eve of Jackson's reelection campaign. Jackson, however, had the more popular side of that argument. Resistance to Georgia's efforts was politically untenable. Jackson has sometimes been quoted as responding to the Worcester *decision with the quip, "John Marshall has made his decision; now let him enforce it." He may never have said those particular words, but Jackson did say, "The decision of the supreme court has fell stillborn, and they find that it cannot coerce Georgia to yield to its mandate." Jackson made no special effort to execute the Court's judgment.*[30] *Georgia ignored the ruling. State officials kept Worcester (and others) in prison until 1833, when a new governor, Wilson Lumpkin, persuaded the missionaries to accept pardons on condition that they left the state.*

CHIEF JUSTICE MARSHALL delivered the opinion of the Court.

...

The extra-territorial power of every legislature being limited in its action, to its own citizens or subjects, the very passage of this act is an assertion of jurisdiction over the Cherokee nation, and of the rights and powers consequent on jurisdiction.

...

From the commencement of our government, congress has passed acts to regulate trade and intercourse with the Indians; which treat them as nations, respect their rights, and manifest a firm purpose to afford that protection which treaties stipulate. All these acts,... manifestly consider the several Indian nations as distinct political communities, having territorial boundaries, within which their authority is exclusive, and having a right to all the lands within those boundaries, which is not only acknowledged, but guaranteed by the United States.

...

The treaties and laws of the United States contemplate the Indian territory as completely separated from that of the states; and provide that all intercourse with them shall be carried on exclusively by the government of the union.... The constitution, by declaring treaties already made, as well as those to be made, to be the supreme law of the land, has adopted and sanctioned the previous treaties with the Indian nations, and consequently admits their rank among those powers who are capable of making treaties. The words "treaty" and "nation" are words of our own language, selected in our diplomatic and legislative proceedings, by ourselves, having each a definite and well understood meaning. We have applied them to Indians, as we have applied them to the other nations of the earth. They are applied to all in the same sense.

Georgia, herself, has furnished conclusive evidence that her former opinions on this subject concurred

30. See Keith E. Whittington, *Political Foundations of Judicial Supremacy* (Princeton: Princeton University Press, 2007), 33.

with those entertained by her sister states, and by the government of the United States. Various acts of her legislature . . . , including the contract of cession made in the year 1802, all tending to prove her acquiescence in the universal conviction that the Indian nations possessed a full right to the lands they occupied, until that right should be extinguished by the United States, with their consent: that their territory was separated from that of any state within whose chartered limits they might reside, by a boundary line, established by treaties: that, within their boundary, they possessed rights with which no state could interfere: and that the whole power of regulating the intercourse with them, was vested in the United States. . . . Her new series of laws, manifesting her abandonment of these opinions, appears to have commenced in December 1828.

. . .

The Cherokee nation, then, is a distinct community occupying its own territory, with boundaries accurately described, in which the laws of Georgia can have no force, and which the citizens of Georgia have no right to enter, but with the assent of the Cherokees themselves, or in conformity with treaties, and with the acts of congress. The whole intercourse between the United States and this nation, is, by our constitution and laws, vested in the government of the United States.

The act of the state of Georgia, under which the plaintiff in error was prosecuted, is consequently void, and the judgment a nullity. . . .

JUSTICE BALDWIN, dissenting.

. . .

JUSTICE McLEAN, concurring.

. . .

V. Separation of Powers

MAJOR DEVELOPMENTS

- President Jackson claims the right to remove cabinet officials at will.
- The Senate censures President Jackson.
- Democrats and Whigs debate the constitutional powers of the president during wartime.
- Americans debate the proper use of the veto power.

The Democratic and Whig parties had sharp differences over the proper constitutional balance of power between the President and Congress. These differences were partly rooted in politics. During the early years of the Jacksonian Era, Andrew Jackson occupied the White House, and his opponents controlled or significantly influenced at least one House of Congress. Perhaps as an accident of these circumstances, the Democratic Party became ideologically committed to a strong presidency, and the Whigs became equally committed to a weak presidency.[31] Long after Jackson left office, Democrats continued to believe in a strong presidency that could take independent action when warranted. Whigs continued to complain about the strong presidency and to press their presidential candidates to pledge to be more deferential to Congress should they occupy the Oval Office.

Disputes over executive powers stretched across a multitude of issues. Most famously, Jackson and his successors made aggressive use of the presidential veto to block the policies of their legislative opponents. They exercised a broad authority to determine how federal policy was implemented. President Jackson claimed constitutional authority to remove federal deposits from the national bank and fire cabinet officials who refused to carry out his orders. President James Polk claimed constitutional authority to move United States troops into territories whose ownership was disputed by Mexico. Whigs rejected these claims and developed contrasting theories of limited executive power. As the minority party in the national government, Whigs could often do little more than complain, but they did complain very loudly. Senate Whigs censured Jackson after he removed the deposits from the banks. Whigs in the House of Representatives sought to impeach President Tyler for an improper use of the veto power. Abraham Lincoln first attracted national attention when he claimed that Polk unconstitutionally provoked the Mexican War.

Whigs were more successful when disputes over the separation of powers broke out in the states. Jacksonians in the national government established the principle that cabinet officers were subordinate to the president. Whigs in many states successfully vested such officers as the Secretary of State with terms of office and powers independent from the Governor. Both national and state practices established in the Jacksonian Era were enduring. Twenty-first-century presidents may remove cabinet officials at will. Some

31. The Whigs took their party name from the English opponents of executive power during the reign of King James II of England (1685–1688).

members of the executive branch of most state governments are elected by the general public, have independent powers, and may not be removed by the governor.

As you read, consider whether general principles help resolve separation-of-powers questions, or whether each question raises unique concerns? How important are principles to resolving these disputes? Do the political parties have consistent and coherent views on the powers and relationships of the various branches of the government? Do they have more consistent views about separation of powers than they do about other constitutional questions, such as the powers of the national government? The Whigs are sometimes associated with the constitutional philosophies of such nationalist Federalists as John Marshall and Alexander Hamilton. Is that true of their views about separation of powers as well as their views about national powers? Does the Whig view of a strong legislature and a weak executive make sense? These Whig arguments are not often heard in modern politics. Could they be revived?

A. Presidential Power to Execute the Law

Congress makes the law, and the president executes the law. But what authority and discretion is included in the power to "execute" the law? The question had been contested since the early days of the republic when Alexander Hamilton emphasized a broad discretionary authority on the part of the executive and various Jeffersonians responded by emphasizing the importance of the legislature in setting policy.

Although the Jacksonians borrowed a great deal from Jeffersonian constitutional philosophy, they embraced a strong executive. One key feature of that Jacksonian belief was a relatively broad understanding of the presidential power to execute the law. The canonical statements of those beliefs came in the debate over the removal of the federal deposits from the Bank of the United States. Once Congress had passed a statute, Jackson believed, the president alone had the authority and the ultimate responsibility for determining what the statute required and how best to implement that statute. Lower level executive officials were expected to take their directives from the president, not from Congress, when deciding how to execute the law.

The Debate over the Removal of the Deposits

President Jackson's decision to remove federal deposits from the Bank of the United States triggered vigorous and wide-ranging constitutional disputes over the separation of powers. After vetoing the recharter of the national bank in 1832 and being resoundingly vindicated for that decision during the 1832 national election, Jackson determined to drive a stake through the heart of the "Monster Bank." He was convinced that the Bank's director, Nicholas Biddle, was using his position of power to corrupt politics. Although the charter granted to the bank in 1816 did not expire until 1836, Jackson realized that Biddle would be crippled if all of the federal government's money was withdrawn from the Bank. His decision to remove the deposits triggered three distinct constitutional debates:

- *Could the president without congressional authorization remove the deposits?*
- *Could the president without congressional authorization remove the Secretary of the Treasury after he refused to remove the deposits?*
- *Could the Senate censure the President for these actions?*

The initial constitutional debates over removal took place within in Jackson's Cabinet. Jackson first urged the Secretary of the Treasury, William Duane, to remove the deposits from the national bank. Duane refused. He maintained that Congress had conferred on the Secretary of the Treasury alone the power to move government deposits. Jackson then ordered Duane to remove the deposits. He insisted that cabinet officials had a duty to implement presidential decrees. Jackson bluntly informed Duane, "A secretary, sir, is merely an executive agent, a subordinate" to the president. Congress, Jackson continued, required no further explanation than that the removal was done at the direction of the president. When Duane again refused to act, the president informed him that "your services as Secretary of the Treasury are no longer required."[32] Attorney General Roger Taney, the only cabinet member who supported removal, was appointed acting Secretary of the Treasury. Taney promptly carried out the president's will.

The congressional reaction to the removal order was immediate and furious. Such strict constructionists as John

32. Quoted in Robert V. Remini, *Andrew Jackson and the Bank War* (New York: W.W. Norton, 1967), 123, 124.

C. Calhoun and John Tyler joined forces with such nationalists as Henry Clay and Daniel Webster to denounce what they took to be a lawless abuse of presidential power. Clay, recognizing that the Democratic majority in the House of Representatives would not impeach President Jackson, introduced a formal resolution of censure in the Senate. Clay's speech defending the censure resolution condemned Jackson for removing the deposits and for treating the Secretary of the Treasury as a mere subordinate with no responsibility to Congress. His censure resolution passed 26–20 on a largely party-line vote. The Whig-controlled Senate then refused to confirm Taney as Secretary of the Treasury, the first time the Senate refused to confirm a Cabinet nominee. A few months later, the Senate refused to confirm Taney when Jackson nominated him to be an associate justice on the Supreme Court.

Jackson and his allies had the last laugh. Jackson's "Protest of the Censure Resolution" provided a strong defense of presidential power and a sharp criticism of the constitutionality of the Censure Resolution. Democrats won control of the Senate in the 1834 midterm elections. The newly elected Senate confirmed Jackson's choice of Roger Taney to serve as chief justice and voted to expunge the censure resolution from the journal of the Senate just before Martin Van Buren was inaugurated as Jackson's successor as president.

Andrew Jackson, Paper on the Removal of the Deposits (1833)[33]

...

Can it now be said that the question of a recharter of the bank was not decided at the election which ensued? Had the veto been equivocal, or had it not covered the whole ground; if it had merely taken exceptions to the details of the bill or the time of its passage; if it had not met the whole ground of constitutionality and expediency, then there might have been some plausibility for the allegation that the question was not decided by the people. It was to compel the President to take his stand that the question was brought forward into which his adversaries sought to force him, and frankly declared his unalterable opposition to the bank as being both unconstitutional and inexpedient. On that ground the case was argued to the people; and now that the people have sustained the President, notwithstanding the array of influence and power which was brought to bear upon him, it is too late, he confidently thinks, to say that the question has not been decided. Whatever may be the opinions of others, the President considers his reelection as a decision of the people against the bank....

...

It is for the wisdom of Congress to decide upon the best substitute to be adopted in the place of the Bank of the United States, and the President would have felt himself relieved from a heavy and painful responsibility if in the charter to the bank Congress had reserved to itself the power of directing at its pleasure the public money to be elsewhere deposited, and had not devolved that power exclusively on one of the Executive Departments. It is useless now to inquire why this high and important power was surrendered by those who are peculiarly and appropriately the guardians of the public money. Perhaps it was an oversight. But as the President presumes that the charter to the bank is to be considered a contract on the part of the Government, it is now not in the power of Congress to disregard its stipulations; and by the terms of that contract the public money is to be deposited in the bank during the continuance of its charter unless the Secretary of the Treasury shall otherwise direct. Unless, therefore, the Secretary of the Treasury first acts, Congress have no power over the subject, for they can not add a new clause to the charter or strike one out of it without the consent of the bank, and consequently the public money must remain in that institution until the last hour of its existence unless the Secretary of the Treasury shall remove it at an earlier day. The responsibility is thus thrown upon the executive branch of the Government of deciding how long before the expiration of the charter the public interest will require the deposits to be placed elsewhere; and although according to the frame and principle of our Government this decision would seem more properly to belong to the legislative power, yet as the law has imposed it upon the executive department the duty ought to be faithfully and firmly met, and the decision made and executed upon the best lights that can be obtained and the best judgment that can be formed.... And while the President anxiously wishes to abstain from the exercise of doubtful powers and to avoid all interference with the rights and duties

33. Excerpt taken from Andrew Jackson, "Removal of the Public Deposits, September 18, 1833," in *A Compilation of the Messages and Papers of the Presidents*, ed. James D. Richardson, vol. 3 (New York: National Bureau of Literature, 1897), 1224.

of others, he must yet with unshaken constancy discharge his own obligations, and can not allow himself to turn aside in order to avoid any responsibility which the high trust with which he has been honored requires him to encounter; and it being the duty of one of the Executive Departments to decide in the first instance... the President has felt himself bound to examine the question carefully and deliberately in order to make up his judgment on the subject, and in his opinion the near approach of the termination of the charter and the public considerations heretofore mentioned are of themselves amply sufficient to justify the removal of the deposits, without reference to the conduct of the bank or their safety in its keeping.

...

In conclusion, the President must be permitted to remark that he looks upon the pending question as of higher consideration than the mere transfer of a sum of money from one bank to another. Its decision may affect the character of our Government for ages to come. Should the bank be suffered longer to use the public moneys in the accomplishment of its purposes, with the proofs of its faithlessness and corruption before our eyes, the patriotic among our citizens will despair of success in struggling against its power, and we shall be responsible for entailing it upon our country forever. Viewing it as a question of transcendent importance, both in the principles and consequences it involved, the President could not, in justice to the responsibility which he owes the country, refrain from pressing upon the Secretary of the Treasury his view of the considerations which impel to immediate action. Upon him has been devolved by the Constitution and the suffrages of the American people the duty of superintending the operations of the Executive Departments of the Government and seeing that the laws are faithfully executed. In the performance of this high trust it is his undoubted right to express to those whom the laws and his own choice have made his associates in the administration of the Government his opinion of their duties under circumstances as they arise. It is this right which he now exercises. Far be it from him to expect or require that any member of the Cabinet should at his request, order, or dictation do any act which he believes unlawful or in his conscience condemn. From them and from his fellow-citizens in general he desires only that aid and support which their reason approves and their conscience sanctions.

In the remarks he has made on this all-important question he trusts the Secretary of the Treasury will see only the frank and respectful declarations of the opinions which the President has formed on a measure of great national interest deeply affecting the character and usefulness of his Administration, and not a spirit of dictation, which the President would be as careful to avoid as ready to resist....

The President again repeats that he begs his Cabinet to consider the proposed measure as his own, in the support of which he shall require no one of them to make a sacrifice of opinion or principle. Its responsibility had been assumed after the most mature deliberation and reflection as necessary to preserve the morals of the people, the freedom of the press, and the purity of the elective franchise, without which all will unite in saying that the blood and treasure expended by our forefathers in the establishment of our happy system of government will have been vain and fruitless. Under these convictions he feels that a measure so important to the American people can not be commenced too soon, and he therefore names the 1st day of October next as a proper period for the change of the deposits, or sooner, provided the necessary arrangements with the State banks can be made.

Henry Clay, Speech on the Removal of the Deposits (1833)[34]

1. *Resolved*, That, by dismissing the late Secretary of the Treasury because he would not, contrary to his sense of his own duty, remove the money of the United States in deposit with the Bank of the United State and its branches, in conformity with the President's opinion; and by appointing his successor to effect such removal, which has been done, the President has assumed the exercise of a power over the treasury of the United States, not granted to him by the constitution and laws, and dangerous to the liberties of the people.

...

...We are... in the midst of a revolution, hitherto bloodless, but rapidly tending towards a total change of the pure republican character of the Government, and to the concentration of all power in the hands

34. Excerpt taken from Henry Clay, *Speech of The Honorable Henry Clay on the Subject of the Removal of the Deposits* (Washington, DC: Duff Green, 1834).

of one man. The powers of Congress are paralyzed, except when exerted in conformity with his will, by frequent and an extraordinary exercise of the executive veto, not anticipated by the founders of the constitution, and not practiced by any of the predecessors of the present Chief Magistrate.... The constitutional participation of the Senate in the appointing power is virtually abolished, by the constant use of the power of removal from office without any known cause, and by the appointment of the same individual to the same office, after his rejection by the Senate....

...

Up to the period of the termination of the last session of Congress, the exclusive constitutional power of Congress over the treasury of the United States had never been contested. Among its earliest acts was one to establish the Treasury Department, which provided for the appointment of a Treasurer.... When the existing bank was established, it was provided that the public moneys should be deposited with it, and consequently that bank became the treasury of the United States....

...

...Th[e] [Constitution] confers on the President the right to require the opinion, in writing, of the principal officers of the executive departments, separately, on subjects appertaining to their respective offices. Instead of conforming to this provision, the President reads to those officers, collectively, his opinion and decision, in writing, upon an important matter which related only to one of them, and to him exclusively. This paper is afterwards formally promulgated to the world, with the President's authority. And why? Can it be doubted that it was done under the vain expectation that *a name* would quash all inquiry, and secure the general approbation of the people? Those who now exercise power in this country appear to regard all the practices and usages of their predecessors as wrong. They look upon all precedents with contempt, and, casting them scornfully aside, appear to be resolved upon a new era of administration....

...

...What power has the President over the public treasury? Is it in the bank charter?... The Secretary of the Treasury alone is designated. The President is not, by the remotest allusion, referred to. And, to put the matter beyond all controversy, whenever the Secretary gives an order or direction for the removal, he is to report his reasons—to whom? To the President? No! directly to Congress.... The constitution had ordained that no money should be drawn from the treasury but in consequence of appropriations made by law. It remained for Congress to provide *how* it should be drawn. And that duty is performed by the act constituting the Treasury Department. According to that act, the Secretary of the Treasury is to prepare and sign, the Comptroller to countersign, the Register to record, and, finally, the Treasurer to pay a warrant issued, *and only issued*, in virtue of a prior act of appropriation. Each is referred to the law as the guide of his duty; each acts on his own separate responsibility; each is a check upon every other; and all are placed under the control of Congress. The Secretary is to report to Congress, and to each branch of Congress. The great principle of division of duty, and of control and responsibility—that principle which lies at the bottom of all free government—that principle, without which there can be no free government—is upheld throughout....

Thus is it evident that the President, neither by the act creating the Treasury Department, nor by the bank charter, has any power over the public treasury. Has he any by the constitution? None, none. We have already seen that the constitution positively forbids any money from being drawn from the treasury but in virtue of a previous act of appropriation. But the President himself says that "upon him has been devolved, by the constitution, and the suffrages of the American people, the duty of superintending the operation of the executive departments of the Government, and seeing that the laws are faithfully executed." If there existed any such double source of executive power, it has been seen that the Treasury Department is not an executive department; but that, in all that concerns the public treasury, the Secretary is the agent or representative of Congress, acting in obedience to their will, and maintaining a direct intercourse with them. By what authority does the President derive power from the mere result of an election? In another part of the same cabinet paper he refers to the suffrages of the people as a source of power independent of the constitution, if not overruling it. At all events, he seems to regard the issue of the election as an approbation of all constitutional opinions previously expressed by him, no matter in what ambiguous language. I differ, sir, entirely from the President. No such conclusions can be legitimately drawn from his re-election. He was re-elected from his presumed merits generally, and from the attachment and confidence of the people, and also from the unworthiness of his competitor. The people had no idea, by that exercise of their suffrage, of expressing their approbation of all the opinions which the President held....

...

...[H]e is charged by the constitution to "take care that the laws be faithfully executed." And the question is, what does this injunction really import?...[The] enormous pretension of the Executive claims that if a treaty or law exists, contrary to the constitution, in the President's opinion; or if a judicial opinion be pronounced, in his opinion repugnant to the constitution, to a treaty, or to a law, he is not bound to afford the executive aid in the execution of any such treaty, law, or decision. If his be sound doctrine, it is evident that every thing resolves itself into the President's opinion. There is an end to all constitutional government, and a sole functionary engrosses the whole power supposed hitherto to have been assigned to various responsible officers, checking and checked by each other. Can this be true? Is it possible that there is any one so insensible to the guaranties of civil liberty as to subscribe to this monstrous pretension?...

...

The eyes and hopes of the American people are anxiously turned to Congress. They feel that they have been deceived and insulted; their confidence abused; their interests betrayed; and their liberties in danger. They see a rapid and alarming concentration of all power in one man's hands. They see that, by the exercise of the positive authority of the Executive, and his negative power exerted over Congress, the will of one man alone prevails, and governs the republic. The question is no longer what laws will Congress pass, but what will the Executive not veto? The President and not Congress, is addressed for legislative action. We have seen a corporation, charged with the execution of a great national work, dismiss an experienced, faithful, and zealous president, afterwards testify to his ability by a voluntary resolution, and reward his extraordinary services by a large gratuity, and appoint in his place an executive favorite, totally inexperienced and incompetent, to propitiate the President. We behold the usual incidents of approaching tyranny. The land is filled with spies and informers; and detraction and denunciation are the orders of the day. People, especially official incumbents in this place, no longer dare speak in the fearless tones of manly freemen, but in the cautious whispers of trembling slaves. The premonitory symptoms of despotism are upon us; and if Congress do not apply an instantaneous and effective remedy, the fatal collapse will soon come on, and we shall die—ignobly die—base, mean, and abject slaves; the score and contempt of mankind; unpitied, unwept; unmourned!

Andrew Jackson, **Protest of the Censure Resolution** (1834)[35]

...

The whole executive power being vested in the President, who is responsible for its exercise, it is a necessary consequence that he should have a right to employ agents of his own choice to aid him in the performance of his duties, and to discharge them when he is no longer willing to be responsible for their acts. In strict accordance with this principle, the power of removal, which, like that of appointment, is an original executive power, is left unchecked by the Constitution in relation to all executive officers, for whose conduct the President is responsible while it is taken from him in relation to judicial officers, for whose acts he is not responsible....

But if there were any just ground for doubt on the face of the Constitution whether all executive officers are removable at the will of the President, it is obviated by the cotemporaneous construction of the instrument and the uniform practice under it.

The power of removal was a topic of solemn debate in the Congress of 1789 while organizing the administrative departments of the Government, and it was finally decided that the President derived from the Constitution the power of removal so far as it regards that department for whose acts he is responsible. Here, then, we have the concurrent authority of President Washington, the Senate, and the House of Representatives, members of whom had taken an active part in the convention which framed the Constitution and in the State conventions which adopted it, that the President

35. Excerpt taken from Andrew Jackson, "Protest, April 15, 1834," in *A Compilation of the Messages and Papers of the Presidents*, ed. James D. Richardson, vol. 3 (New York: National Bureau of Literature, 1897), 1288–1312.

derived an unqualified power of removal from that instrument itself, which is "beyond the reach of legislative authority." Upon this principle the Government has now been steadily administered for about forty-five years, during which there have been numerous removals made by the President, or by his direction, embracing every grade of executive officers from the heads of Departments to the messengers of bureaus.

The Treasury Department in the discussions of 1789 was considered on the same footing as the other Executive Departments, and in the act establishing it were incorporated the precise words indicative of the sense of Congress that the President derives his power to remove the Secretary from the Constitution, which appear in the act establishing the Department of Foreign Affairs....

The custody of public property, under such regulations as may be prescribed by legislative authority, has always been considered an appropriate function of the executive department in this and all other Governments....

Public money is but a species of public property. It can not be raised by taxation or customs, nor brought into the Treasury in any other way except by law; but whenever or howsoever obtained, its custody always has been and always must be, unless the Constitution be changed, entrusted to the executive department. No officer can be created by Congress for the purpose of taking charge of it whose appointment would not by the Constitution at once devolve on the President and who would not be responsible to him for the faithful performance of his duties. The legislative power may undoubtedly bind him and the President by any laws they may think proper to enact; they may prescribe in what place particular portions of the public property shall be kept and for what reason it shall be removed, as they may direct that supplies for the Army or Navy shall be kept in particular stores, and it will be the duty of the President to see that the law is faithfully executed; yet will the custody remain in the executive department of the Government. Were the Congress to assume, with or without a legislative act, the power of appointing officers, independently of the President, to take the charge and custody of the public property contained in the military and naval arsenals, magazines, and storehouses, it is believed that such an act would be regarded by all as a palpable usurpation of executive power, subversive of the form as well as the fundamental principles of our Government. But where is the difference in principle whether the public property be in the form of arms, munitions or war, and supplies or in gold and silver or bank notes? None can be perceived; none is believed to exist. Congress can not, therefore, take out of the hands of the executive department the custody of the public property or money without an assumption of executive power and a subversion of the first principles of the Constitution.

...

It can not be doubted that it was the legal duty of the Secretary of the Treasury to order and direct the deposits of the public money to be made elsewhere than in the Bank of the United States *whenever sufficient reasons existed for making the change*. If in such a case he neglected or refused to act, he would neglect or refuse to execute the law. What would be the sworn duty of the President? Could he say that the Constitution did not bind him to see the law faithfully executed because it was one of his Secretaries and not himself upon whom the service was specially imposed? Might he not be asked whether there was any such limitation to his obligations prescribed in the Constitution? Whether he is not equally bound to take care that the laws be faithfully executed, whether they impose duties on the highest officer of State or the lowest subordinate in any of the Departments? Might not he be told that it was for the sole purpose of causing all executive officers, from the highest to the lowest, faithfully to perform the services required of them by law that the people of the United States have made him their Chief Magistrate and the Constitution has clothed him with the entire executive power of this Government? The principles implied in these questions appear too plain to need elucidation.

...

Thus was it settled by the Constitution, the laws, and the whole practice of the Government that the entire executive power is vested in the President of the United States; that as incident to that power the right of appointing and removing those officers who are to aid him in the execution of the laws, with such restrictions only as the Constitution prescribes, is vested in the President; that the Secretary of the Treasury is one of those officers; that the custody of the public property and money is an Executive function which, in relation to the money, has always been exercised through the Secretary of the Treasury and his subordinates; that in the performance of these duties he is subject to the supervision and control of the President, and in all important measures having relation to them consults the Chief Magistrate and obtains his approval and sanction; that the law establishing the bank did not, as it could not, change the relation between the President and the Secretary—did not release the former from his obligation to see the law faithfully executed nor the latter from the President's supervision and control; that afterwards and before the Secretary did in fact consult and obtain the sanction of the President to transfers and removals of the public deposits, and that all the departments of the Government, and the nation itself, approved or acquiesced in these acts and principles as in strict conformity with our Constitution and laws.

...

B. Presidential War and Foreign Affairs Powers

Relationships between the United States and Mexico sharply deteriorated after the United States annexed Texas in March 1845. Mexico, which still did not recognize Texas's independence, insisted that the United States had no right to annex Mexican territory. Jacksonians insisted that Texas was now part of the United States. Mexico and the United States also disputed the southern boundary of Texas. Mexico claimed sovereignty over all lands south of the Nueces River. The United States claimed sovereignty over all lands north of the Rio Grande River. A few hundred square miles of disputed scrublands were in between these rivers. President James K. Polk in December 1845 ordered troops under the command of Zachary Taylor to move from Corpus Christi to the bank of the Rio Grande. Polk claimed he moved troops into the disputed territories to protect American soil. Abraham Lincoln and other Whigs insisted that the move was made to provoke Mexico, that Polk had no constitutional power to move troops into foreign territory without congressional permission, and that, even if the territory was merely contested, his actions provoked a war that could be declared only by Congress. Shortly after the American troops were moved into position, they were attacked by Mexican troops. Congress responded by declaring war.

The Mexican War raised two constitutional issues. The first was whether President Polk was constitutionally authorized to order General Taylor to move troops to the Rio Grande. This raised questions both about how the boundary of the United States was determined and the scope of presidential power over military affairs in peacetime. The second, which would become quite familiar, concerned presidential power in wartime. President Polk and most Democrats insisted that presidential war power was broad. Congress had the power to declare war, but once war was declared, the president was expected to direct the war without congressional interference. Whigs asserted that, outside of giving battlefield orders, Congress could determine war objects and demand that the president obey basic legislative prerogatives.

The Democratic vision of presidential war powers prevailed. Polk's "little war" was a political success. The United States achieved a quick victory over Mexico. Mexico in the Treaty of Guadalupe Hidalgo (1848) ceded to the United States more than 500,000 square miles of land that would become California, New Mexico, and Arizona, as well as parts of Colorado, Utah, and Nevada. Whigs were reduced to passing resolutions declaring the war unconstitutional.

As you read, consider the scope of the presidential war powers being defended by the Whigs and Democrats. May presidents control the movement of troops in peacetime, even if the result might make war more likely? May Congress hamper how the president chooses to conduct a war after hostilities have been declared? What are the responsibilities of a legislator who believes that a president has involved the United States in an unjust war?

James Polk, Second Annual Message (1846)[36]

James K. Polk was a Jackson protégé, serving as Speaker of the U.S. House of Representatives during Andrew Jackson's presidency and then moving on to become governor of Tennessee. Jackson threw his support to Polk for the Democratic presidential nomination in 1844. Polk leaped ahead of his rivals by embracing the immediate annexation of Texas and promising to serve only one term of office. The Democratic convention passed over the former president Martin Van Buren, who opposed the annexation of Texas, when supporting the dark horse Polk. Polk went on to defeat the Whig Henry Clay in the general election, becoming the youngest president to hold office to that date.

36. Excerpt taken from James K. Polk, "Second Annual Message, December 8, 1846," in *A Compilation of the Messages and Papers of the Presidents: 1789–1897*, ed. James D. Richardson, vol. 6 (New York: National Bureau of Literature, 1897), 2321.

Polk was also among the most important presidents of the nineteenth century. His status rests on his willingness to fight the Mexican War and his ability to bring it to a successful resolution. As a result, the United States vastly expanded and took its current shape in extending to the Pacific Ocean. Later presidents looked back to Polk's example as helping to establish modern presidential war powers. Polk used his second annual message to Congress to justify his actions in moving the United States army into Mexican territory.

...

The existing war with Mexico was neither desired nor provoked by the United States. On the contrary, all honorable means were resorted to avert it. After years of endurance of aggravated and unredressed wrongs on our part, Mexico, in violation of solemn treaty stipulations and of every principle of justice recognized by civilized nations, commenced hostilities, and thus by her own act forced the war upon us. Long before the advance of our Army to the left bank of the Rio Grande we had ample cause of war against Mexico, and had the United States resorted to this extremity we might have appealed to the whole civilized world for the justice of our cause....

...

The annexation of Texas to the United States constituted no just cause of offense to Mexico. The pretext that it did so is wholly inconsistent and irreconcilable with well-authenticated facts connected with the revolution by which Texas became independent of Mexico....

...

But there are those who, conceding all this to be true, assume the ground that the true western boundary of Texas is the Nueces instead of the Rio Grande, and that therefore in marching our Army to the east bank of the latter river we passed the Texan line and invaded the territory of Mexico. A simple statement of facts known to exist will conclusively refute such an assumption. Texas, as ceded to the United States by France in 1803, has been always claimed as extending west to the Rio Grande or Rio Bravo....

...

...The Republic of Texas always claimed [the Rio Grande] as her western boundary, and in her treaty made with Santa Anna in May, 1836, he recognized it as such. By the constitution which Texas adopted in March, 1836, senatorial and representative districts were organized extending west of the Nueces....That the Congress of the United States understood the State of Texas which they admitted into the Union to extend beyond the Nueces is apparent from the fact that on the 31st of December, 1845, only two days after the act of admission, they passed a law "to establish a collection district in the State of Texas," by which they created a port of delivery at Corpus Christi, situated west of the Nueces....In view of all these facts it is difficult to conceive upon what ground it can be maintained that in occupying the country west of the Nueces with our Army, with a view solely to its security and defense, we invaded the territory of Mexico....

...

But Mexico herself has never placed the war which she has waged upon the ground that our Army occupied the intermediate territory between the Nueces and the Rio Grande. Her refuted pretension that Texas was not in fact an independent state, but a rebellious province, was obstinately persevered in, and her avowed purpose in commencing a war with the United States was to reconquer Texas and to restore Mexican authority over the whole territory—not to the Nueces only, but to the Sabine. In view of the proclaimed menaces of Mexico to this effect, I deemed it my duty, as a measure of precaution and defense, to order our Army to occupy a position on our frontier as a military post, from which our troops could best resist and repel any attempted invasion which Mexico might make. Our Army had occupied a position at Corpus Christi, west of the Nueces...without complaint from any quarter...many months before it advanced to the eastern bank of the Rio Grande....

...[During the winter of 1845–46], [t]he reconquest of Texas and war with the United States were openly threatened. These were the circumstances existing when it was deemed proper to order the Army under the command of General Taylor to advance to the western frontier of Texas and occupy a position on or near the Rio Grande....

...

House Debate on the Constitutionality of the Mexican War (1847–1848)[37]

The Democrats who controlled Congress during Polk's presidency were united in supporting the war with Mexico.

37. Excerpt taken from *Congressional Globe*, 30th Cong., 1st Sess. (1848), 154–56; *Cong. Globe*, 29th Cong., 2nd Sess. (1847), 430–31, 489–90.

In 1846, with troops already engaged on the field of battle, Congress by large majorities voted a declaration of war with Mexico. Nonetheless, the war was controversial. Whigs denounced the conflict as a war of choice rather than a war of necessity, one that the president had initiated without proper authorization from Congress. Many Northerners saw the work of slave interests behind the effort to defend Texas and fight with Mexico. The speedy and dramatic success of American troops on the battlefield cut short the debate. With American troops occupying Mexico City, a treaty ending the war was signed less than two years after the declaration of war. The Whigs continued to dismiss Polk as a bad president, but they later turned to military heroes from the war such as General Zachary Taylor and General Winfield Scott to carry their party banner.

Consider the principle that North Carolina's George Badger lays out for the congressional war power. Does that provide a workable basis for controlling the presidential use of military force? Would it prevent the type of situation that arose in Texas? Could it be applied in modern contexts?

Mr. LINCOLN (Whig, Illinois),

...

...The President seemed to attach great importance to the assumed fact that the soil was our own where hostilities commenced. He...agreed with him on the importance of it, if he understood the President. It was his opinion that that was the very point on which rightfully the President should be justified or condemned....

...

He now wished to state briefly what he understood to be the true rule for the purpose of determining what was the boundary between Texas and Mexico....In the exercise of that right [to revolution], the Texans shook off the Mexican yoke. But how far? Did the nation, did the people revolutionize by lines? Certainly not. They revolutionized exactly to the extent that they took part in it. When they rose up and shook off the old Government, so much of the country was theirs. And where were the people that did not rise? They remained with the old Government. It was this right of revolution, and it could not be a perfect right if it could not be exercised until every individual inhabitant was in favor of it. It would be no right. Minorities must submit to majorities.

Just such was the case with the Tories in the American revolution. They were obliged to submit to the majority—the great body of the people, who rose and put them down by force. Now, he said, when the Texan people rose up and shook off the Mexican Government, they put down the minority among them who were not disposed to go with them and became owners of the soil themselves; the country belonged to Texas. But if there were an isolated portion of people who took no part in the movement, over whom the revolutionary party, by force or otherwise, had never been able to extend their power, then that people and the country they occupied were not included within the boundaries of the territory revolutionized. No rule could be more just, more republican, more in conformity with natural right. Why, under the rule that one portion of the people have the right to rise and shake off their Government, another portion have precisely the same right to remain as they were. When they rise up, they have a right to put down the minority. But if there were on the Rio Grande a portion of people who had never been disturbed by them—at least successfully—who had never consented to go, it seemed to him in violation of common sense to claim that the people who chose to remain there, and who did remain there notwithstanding all the force that could be brought to bear upon them, belonged to the revolutionary government.

Mr. BADGER (Whig, North Carolina)

...

He held...that Congress had a right to control every operation of this war—not to direct the army in the field, but, as the war-making power of the Government was vested in Congress, Congress had a constitutional right to declare with whom we should be at war, and for what, and to determine when the objects of the war had been accomplished. Congress had a right to say to the President of the United States, the purposes for which we authorized this war are accomplished; there is no need of prosecuting an offensive war any further. Congress had a right to give directions as to the end and purposes of the war; and according to his humble judgment, it was the duty of the President to yield a respectful attention to the advice of Congress, and to govern himself as commander-in-chief of the army at the direction of Congress.

He agreed also...that if the President sought in defiance of the will of Congress, obstinately to prosecute the war and to use the public forces for this purpose, Congress in such case, he held, had the right to exercise the only remaining constitutional power of controlling the Executive by withholding the supplies, because otherwise it would follow that one branch of the Government would be able to usurp the power belonging to another branch, thereby placing that branch whose power it had usurped under the necessity of absolute submission.

But he had voted these supplies for the war. Why? Not because he thought the war was necessary; he thought it was unnecessary. Not because it was commenced by Mexico; he believed it was commenced by the President of the United States. But he had voted the supplies because the interests of the country were at stake in the actual condition of things; because the remedy of withholding the supplies, that *ultima ratio* which was never to be applied until all others failed in controlling the too great extension of executive power, might produce mischievous consequences....

...

Mr. DROMGOOLE (Democrat, Virginia)

...

...I say, upon the question of the appropriations for the support of the army and the prosecution of the war, it is unnecessary to go further back than to inquire whether this war does legally and constitutionally exist, and whether we mean to support it....That inquiry is answered by the act of Congress; and this is the answer about all these preliminary causes and the conduct of the President; it is; that the war is legally and constitutionally declared to exist by the people's Representatives here assembled, with only fourteen dissentients upon this floor....

...

...[I]t is true that the appropriation is to enable the President, as is his duty to do, to prosecute the war; and I would ask any gentleman here or elsewhere, whether he declares that the legislative power can interfere at all with the manner of prosecuting the war after we have once authorized it? The Executive power, the Executive power alone, is entrusted with conducting it, and any attempt upon the part of Congress to designate the mode in which it is to be conducted, what country shall be overrun, to what part our army shall be withdrawn, is a legislative usurpation, an encroachment upon the Executive power. Will you do the injustice to the President of holding him accountable for the prosecution of the war and the success of our arms, and then undertake, pragmatically and in violation of the Constitution, by the legislative power, to control the exercise of his power?

Sir, this is no new question. It was agitated in the Convention which formed the Constitution, whether Congress should have the power to direct the prosecution of war—for that was the original draft of the Constitution; and, upon motion and solemn arguments, it was decided that the President alone should be entrusted with the prosecution of war. Congress, then, has only the power to declare war, to authorize it, and furnish supplies for conducting it. The President, as commander-in-chief of the army, supported by those supplies, is to exercise his discretion in prosecuting this war, according to the constitutional powers vested in him, according to the established usages of nations, and the principles of international law.

...

...So long, then, Mr. Chairman, as the war does exist, and so long as supplies of men and money are given for its prosecution, we are to look to the Executive alone for the prosecution of the war; and the only mode by which the legislative power can check him is by the extreme resort of withholding supplies, of refusing to pass acts for the raising of men and the appropriation of money.

C. Legislative Powers of the President

Democrats and Whigs engaged in sharp disputes over the presidential veto power. Jackson and his successors vetoed more laws and more important laws than any president in the early national period. Democrats defended aggressive use of the veto as the primary means by which the one national figure elected by the people could defend the Constitution against the entrenched interests that sometimes controlled the national legislature. Whigs condemned that stream of vetoes as undue executive policy making.

The constitutional debate over the veto power heated up in the 1840s. The first Whig President, William Henry Harrison, promised to limit vetoes to the rare occasion when Congress violated the Constitution or endangered the nation. When Harrison died thirty days later, he was replaced by John Tyler. Tyler shared Andrew Jackson's broad conception of the veto power. His vetoes gutted the Whig legislative program. Whigs in Congress attempted to impeach Tyler for making too aggressive use of the veto. That effort failed. Whigs were no more successful when they proposed constitutional amendments repealing the presidential power to veto legislation. By 1860, the veto had become a major instrument by which presidents influenced legislation.

Illustration 5-4 Whigs were scandalized by Andrew Jackson's assertive use of his veto power. This Whig cartoon portrays Jackson as exercising monarchical power, trampling underfoot the Bank and internal improvements, judicial decisions, and the Constitution.

Source: American political prints, 1766–1876 / Bernard F. Reilly. Boston : G.K. Hall, 1991, entry 1833–4. American cartoon print filing series (Library of Congress).

House Debate on the Veto Power (1842)[38]

After William Henry Harrison died, Vice President John Tyler (1790–1862) ascended to the presidency. Tyler was a Jeffersonian Old Republican who had broken with Jackson over the administration's handling of nullification and the removal of the deposits from the Bank. Regarding the "exercise of some independence of judgment" as the responsibility of holding office, Tyler resolved as president to carry out the duties of his office as he understood them.[39] *He vetoed bills that would revive the Bank of the United States, impose protective tariffs and provide federal funding for internal improvements. Although Whigs held majorities in both chambers of Congress when Tyler first took office, they did not have the votes needed to override those vetoes.*

After Tyler vetoed a second tariff bill, former president John Quincy Adams, now serving in the House of Representatives, moved that the veto be referred to a select committee chaired by Adams. The House complied. Adams produced a report denouncing Tyler's use of the veto power and reaffirming Whig commitments to legislative supremacy in policymaking. The report called for Tyler's impeachment and a constitutional amendment allowing a simple majority in both Houses of Congress to override a presidential veto. Both recommendations failed. Are there circumstances under which the use of the presidential veto would be inappropriate? Does the president ever have an obligation to defer to the legislative majority?

Majority Report delivered by John Quincy Adams (Whig, Massachusetts)

. . .

. . . In the spirit of the Constitution of the United States, the executive is not only separated from the legislative power, but made dependent upon, and responsible to it. Until a very recent period of our history, all reference, in either house of Congress, to the opinions or wishes of the President, relating to any subject in deliberation before them, was regarded as an outrage upon the rights of the deliberative body, among the first of whose duties it is to spurn the influence of the dispenser of patronage and power. Until very recently, it was sufficient greatly to impair the influence of any member to be suspected of personal subserviency to the Executive; and any allusion to his wishes, in debate, was deemed a departure not less from decency than from order. . . .

. . . [T]he measures among those deemed by the Legislature of the Union indispensably necessary for the salvation of its highest interests, and for the restoration of its credit, its honor, its prosperity, was prostrated, defeated, annulled, by the weak and wavering obstinacy of one man, accidentally, and not by the will of the people, invested with that terrible power—as if prophetically described by one of his own chosen ministers, at this day, as "the right to deprive the people of self-government."

. . .

They perceive that the whole legislative power of the Union has been, for the last fifteen months, with regard to the action of Congress upon measures of vital importance, in a state of suspended animation, strangled by the *five* times repeated stricture of the executive cord. They observe that, under these unexampled obstructions to the exercise of their high and legitimate duties, they have hitherto preserved the most respectful forbearance towards the executive chief; that while he has, time after time, annulled, by the mere act of his will, their commission from the people to enact laws for the common welfare, they have forborne even the expression of their resentment for these multiplied insults and injuries. They believed they have a high destiny to fulfill, by administering to the people, in the form of law, remedies for the suffering which they had too long endured. The will of one man had frustrated all their labors, and prostrated all their powers. The majority of the committee believed that the case has occurred, in the annals of our Union, contemplated by the founders of the Constitution by the grant to the House of Representatives of the power to impeach the President of the United States; but they are aware that the resort to that expedient might, in the present condition of public affairs, prove abortive. They see that the irreconcilable difference of opinion and of action between the legislative and executive department of the Government is but sympathetic with the same discordant views and feelings among the people. To them alone the final issue of the struggle must be left. . . .

. . . [T]he abusive exercise of the constitutional power of the president to arrest the action of Congress upon measures vital to the welfare of the people, has wrought conviction upon the minds of the majority of the committee, that the veto power in itself must be

38. Excerpt taken from *Report on Veto of New Tariff of Duties*, 27th Cong., 2nd sess., August 16, 1842, H.R. Rept. 998.

39. John Tyler, "Veto Message, August 9, 1842," in *A Compilation of the Messages and Papers of the Presidents*, ed. James D. Richardson, vol. 5 (New York: National Bureau of Literature, 1897), 2037.

restrained and modified by an amendment of the Constitution itself: a resolution for which they accordingly herewith respectfully report.

...

Instead of the words "two-thirds," twice repeated in the second paragraph of the said seventh section [of Article I], substitute, in both cases, the words "a majority of the whole number."

Protest and Counter Report of Thomas W. Gilmer (Whig, Virginia)

...

...Under the specious pretext of defending Congress from what is imagined to be an attack on their constitutional right, it is sought to strip the other departments of Government of powers which the Constitution has confided to them; to remove every constitutional obstruction to the arbitrary will of Congress; to destroy the equilibrium of our well-considered system of government; and to assume unlimited jurisdiction, not only over the co-ordinate branches, but over the States and the people. Encouraged by the present embarrassed condition of the country and our public affairs, deriving fresh political hopes from the general gloom and despondency which their own proceedings have cast over the union, it is attempted to extort from the sufferings of the people some sanction for principles of government which their judgment has never failed to repudiate. The history of our Government abounds in examples of conflicts between the several departments. It has sometimes happened that all the departments combined to overthrow Constitution, and, but for the intelligence of the people, and the controlling power of the suffrage, in restoring the supremacy of the Constitution over the Legislature, the Executive, and the Judiciary, such combinations must have been fatal to our institutions. While it is the privilege and the duty of every citizen to arraign either department of the government, or any public officer, for infidelity to the Constitution and the laws, it is neither wise, just, nor patriotic, for one of those departments to impair the confidence or the harmony which should subsist between the separate branches of the public service, by fomenting prejudices and discord. They are all agents of the people. Their duties are prescribed by a law which all acknowledge as supreme.

...Zeal in the pursuit of some cherished object of interest or ambition induces some men not only to complain when they are thwarted by what they easily believe to be an improper exercise of power, but to make war on the established forms of government, and to seek, by revolution or radical change, what they cannot lawfully obtain. The disposition, which has been recently manifested to some extent, to disturb the well-adjusted checks of the Constitution, by claiming powers for Congress which that instrument does not confer, or by denying to a co-ordinate branch of Government powers which it does confer, in order to establish a particular system of party policy, or to carry an election, must be regarded with deep regret and serious apprehension by the people—those whose province it is to judge, and who, free from the bias of mere party politics, can think and feel and act under the superior influences of patriotism. Our government has survived the shock of many severe political contests, because hitherto to these contests have involved only a difference of opinion as to the principle and policy of the Government, as organized. It has been deemed unwise, as well as dangerous, to exasperate local or general prejudices against the acknowledged forms of Government, and to enlist the spirit of revolution as an auxiliary to the spirit of party.

...

Has the president either assumed a power which does not belong to his office, or has he abused a power which does belong to it? It has not been denied that the power in question exists under the Constitution. Indeed, it has been proposed to abolish it by amendment. If it has been abused, it was done either corruptly and wantonly, or under an error of Executive judgment. If there is evidence of the least corruption in the President's conduct, he should be impeached. The power of impeachment has been confided to the House of Representatives. It is the duty, therefore, of the majority, who accuse the president, to arraign him under the articles of impeachment before the Senate, if they believe him to be guilty of any impeachable offense. If he has neither assumed power, nor abused it corruptly, then the issue dwindles to a mere question—who is right as to a measure of policy?...If the charge preferred by this majority is understood, it involves no breach of the Constitution, or of any law on the part of the President; but they accuse him of obstructing *their* will. The accusation implies either a general infallibility on the part of the accusers, or a particular exemption from error on this occasion; or it denies the President the right and the responsibility of judging on a subject which Congress submitted to his judgment. They will find that there are two sides to this question. The Executive is a co-ordinate department of the Government. The President is under no obligation implicitly to approve every bill which the Legislature may pass. He is commanded either to approve, or, if he cannot approve, to return, with objections, *all bills* sent to him; and Congress are required to send to him *all bills* which they pass....

...

Minority Report of Mr. INGERSOLL (Democrat, Pennsylvania) and Mr. ROOSEVELT (Democrat, New York)

Free government depends on constitutional checks; otherwise, democracy is despotism. Each house of Congress has an absolute negative upon the other. The American Judiciary exercise the power to annul laws. The Union and the States, respectively, in some instances, nullify each other's legislation; the sovereign arbiter, being the people, never yet, in more than fifty years of prosperous experience, failing to interpose their political omnipotence, peacefully, intelligently, and for the general welfare. In addition to these fundamental principles, which are the conservative bases of our free institutions, the Constitution of the United States required the Executive Magistrate, if he disapproves an act of Congress, to return it, with his objections, to its authors, and call upon them to reconsider, before it can become a law....What has been passionately stigmatized as the one-man power in this country, is, in principle, the same thing as the separation of Congress into two bodies, to correct the errors of each other; though much less powerful, because the power of the majority, by a single vote in either House, is absolute, while that of the Executive is merely suspensive and subordinate. Had all the members of the House of Representatives voted on the tariff bill, it would have either been carried or lost by one vote—and that, the casting vote of the Speaker. There is much of one-man power in all free government.

...

Suggested Readings

Allen, Austin. *Origins of the Dred Scott Case: Jacksonian Jurisprudence and the Supreme Court, 1837–1857* (Athens: University of Georgia Press, 2006).

Bestor, Arthur. "State Sovereignty and Slavery: A Reinterpretation of Proslavery Constitutional Doctrine, 1846–1860," *Journal of the Illinois State Historical Society* 54 (1961):117.

Carpenter, Jesse T. *The South as a Conscious Minority, 1789–1861: A Study in Political Thought* (New York: New York University Press, 1930).

Currie, David P. *The Constitution in Congress: Democrats and Whigs, 1829–1861* (Chicago: University of Chicago Press, 2005).

Currie, David P. *The Constitution in Congress: Descent into the Maelstrom, 1829–1861* (Chicago: University of Chicago Press, 2005).

Ellis, Richard E. *The Union at Risk: Jacksonian Democracy, States' Rights, and the Nullification Crisis* (New York: Oxford University Press, 1987).

Fehrenbacher, Don E. *Constitutions and Constitutionalism in the Slaveholding South* (Athens: University of Georgia Press, 1989).

Fehrenbacher, Don E. *The Dred Scott Case: Its Significance in American Law and Politics* (New York: Oxford University Press, 1978).

Frankfurter, Felix. *The Commerce Clause under Marshall, Taney, and Waite* (Chapel Hill: University of North Carolina Press, 1937).

Freehling, William H. *Prelude to Civil War: The Nullification Controversy in South Carolina, 1816–1836* (New York: Oxford University Press, 1966).

Freyer, Tony A. *Harmony and Dissonance: The Swift and Erie Cases in American Federalism* (New York: New York University Press, 1981).

Graber, Mark A. *Dred Scott and the Problem of Constitutional Evil* (New York: Cambridge University Press, 2006).

Graber, Mark A. "Resolving Political Questions into Judicial Questions: Tocqueville's Thesis Revisited," *Constitutional Commentary* 16 (2004):485.

Howe, Daniel Walker. *The Political Culture of the American Whigs* (Chicago: University of Chicago Press, 1979).

Hyman, Harold M, and William M. Wiecek. *Equal Justice Under Law: Constitutional Development, 1835–1876* (New York: Harper & Row, 1982).

Larson, John Lauritz. *Internal Improvement: National Public Works and the Promise of Popular Government in the United States* (Chapel Hill: University of North Carolina Press, 2001).

Leonard, Gerald F. *The Invention of Party Politics: Federalism, Popular Sovereignty, and Constitutional Development in Jacksonian Illinois* (Chapel Hill: University of North Carolina Press, 2002).

Magliocca, Gerald N. *Andrew Jackson and the Constitution: The Rise and Fall of Generational Regimes* (Lawrence: University Press of Kansas, 2007).

McCoy, Drew R. *The Last of the Fathers: James Madison and the Republican Legacy* (New York: Cambridge University Press, 1989).

Mushkat, Jerome, and Joseph G. Rayback. *Martin Van Buren: Law, Politics, and Republican Ideology* (Lanham, MD: Rowman & Littlefield, 1997).

Newmeyer, R. Kent. *The Supreme Court under Marshall and Taney* (New York: Thomas Y. Crowell Company, 1968).

Norgren, Jill. *The Cherokee Cases: The Confrontation of Law and Politics* (New York: McGraw-Hill, 1996).

Peterson, Merrill D. *The Great Triumvirate: Webster, Clay, and Calhoun* (New York: Oxford University Press, 1987).

Remini, Robert V. *Andrew Jackson and the Bank War: A Study in the Growth of Presidential Power* (New York: W. W. Norton, 1967).

Remini, Robert V. *Andrew Jackson*, thee volumes (New York: Harper & Row, 1977–1984).

Remini, Robert V. *Henry Clay: Statesman for the Union* (New York: W. W. Norton, 1991).

Richards, Leonard I. *The Slave Power: The Free North and Southern Domination, 1780–1860* (Baton Rouge: Louisiana State University, 2000).

Swisher, Carl B. *Roger B. Taney* (New York: Macmillan, 1936).

White, Leonard D. *The Jacksonians: A Study in Administrative History, 1829–1860* (New York: Macmillan, 1954).

Whittington, Keith E. *Constitutional Construction: Divided Powers and Constitutional Meaning* (Cambridge: Harvard University Press, 1999).

Whittington, Keith E. "The Road Not Taken: *Dred Scott*, Constitutional Law, and Political Questions," *Journal of Politics* 63 (2001):365.

Chapter 6

Secession, Civil War, and Reconstruction: 1861–1876

I. Introduction

The Civil War was the greatest constitutional crisis in the history of the United States. The crisis was constitutional in that the survival of the constitutional order established in 1789 was at stake. The crisis was also constitutional in that each section of the country advanced very different interpretations of the Constitution. The sectional differences over the constitutional status of slavery are discussed in the previous section on Jacksonian constitutional politics. The debate over secession presented in this chapter highlights a second major difference between northern and southern constitutional understandings. Abraham Lincoln and his political allies insisted that secession was unconstitutional because "we, the people" formed the United States in 1776 and no state was constitutionally authorized to destroy the resulting nation. Jefferson Davis and his political allies insisted that the Constitution was an agreement between the states, all of which retained the sovereign power to determine whether that agreement had been violated.

Lincoln's decision to resupply Fort Sumter in the Charleston harbor and the subsequent beginning of the Civil War ended constitutional debates over secession and slavery while beginning new ones over war powers and individual liberties. During the Civil War, martial law was declared in many northern communities, habeas corpus was frequently suspended, southern ports were blockaded, southern property was confiscated, the federal government printed paper money, a draft was instituted, and most slaves were declared free. In some instances, as was the case with legal tender and the draft, the constitutional debate resembled previous debates over national power between Whigs and Democrats. Republicans championed the broader Whig notion of national powers. Democrats insisted on a more limited national government. Other matters, most notably habeas corpus and martial law, internally divided the dominant Republican coalition. Most supported Lincoln's belief that the Constitution provided the president with whatever power the president thought necessary to wage war successfully. Others, following earlier Whig logic, insisted that Congress should play a primary role in setting war-time policy. The Supreme Court for the most part stayed on the sidelines, intervening only in *The Prize Cases* (1863) to sanction the blockade.

Robert E. Lee's surrender at Appomattox helped transform the constitutional politics of the Civil War into the constitutional politics of Reconstruction. Reconstruction witnessed military rule throughout the south, frequent exercises of congressional power under the post–Civil War Amendments to prohibit slavery, protect certain fundamental rights, and prevent racial discrimination in voting, and the first impeachment trial of a sitting president in American history. Prominent Republicans insisted that the Constitution vested Congress with broad powers to remake the former Confederate states as Congress saw fit. Many northern Democrats and President Andrew Johnson maintained that the new Constitution permitted Congress to pass only laws that abolished slavery or, after the Fourteenth Amendment was ratified, laws that granted persons of color formal legal equality. The result was intense struggles over the constitutional meaning of the Civil War, over the meaning of the post–Civil War constitutional amendments, and over which government institution was constitutionally authorized to decide those contested issues.

Partisan Coalitions in the Civil War Era. The combination of Republican success at the polls in the North and the secession of the South gave Republicans command over the national government from 1860 to 1876.

This Republican dominance was no sure thing in 1860. Abraham Lincoln won the presidency that year with just under 40 percent of the popular vote. Republicans retained control of the House, but gained a Senate majority only when the senators from seceding states resigned, leaving their offices vacant. The Supreme Court when Lincoln took office was the only national institution staffed by a Democratic majority. Although Republicans maintained control of the federal government during the Civil War and Reconstruction, they could not take political success for granted. Even with the South sitting out of national politics, Democrats were a significant electoral threat, especially when military affairs went badly. Lincoln tried to build a broader political base for his constitutional vision by bringing many "War Democrats" into his administration. In 1864, Lincoln ran under the "Union Party" banner, including former Tennessee Democrat Andrew Johnson as his vice presidential nominee. After the war took a positive turn, Lincoln won a popular majority for reelection. With the help of a few judicial resignations, deaths, and the creation of two new northern seats, Republicans gained control of the Supreme Court in 1864.

The dominant Republican Party was united only on a commitment to fight the Civil War to the finish and to achieve at least formal racial equality during Reconstruction. Party members were internally divided between radicals and moderates, with the radicals often willing to push more aggressively than moderates legislation and constitutional amendments that expanded national and congressional power to fight slavery, promote racial equality in practice, and otherwise reconstruct the South. These divisions created opportunities for Democrats, including President Andrew Johnson, to slow the pace of reform or win compromises.

Developments. Republicans governed largely unopposed during the Civil War. Congress passed and Lincoln signed constitutionally controversial legislation mandating a military draft and making paper money legal tender. Congress retroactively ratified Lincoln's decision to blockade southern ports, only slightly modified his decisions to suspend habeas corpus and impose martial law, and tacitly approved the Emancipation Proclamation. The Supreme Court questioned only President Lincoln's decision to impose martial law in the North, and did so in *Ex parte Milligan* (1866) after the Civil War had ended and martial law in the North was abandoned.

During the first years of Reconstruction, Republican congressional understandings of the constitutional order generally prevailed over the Democratic understandings championed by President Johnson. Congress proposed and states quickly ratified the Thirteenth, Fourteenth, and Fifteenth Amendments. The first abolished slavery. The second asserted that states could not deny persons of color (and others) certain fundamental rights. The third forbade voters from being discriminated against for racial reasons. Each amendment declared, "Congress shall have power to enforce, by appropriate legislation, the provisions of this article." Congressional majorities construed those powers

Table 6-1 Major Issues and Decisions of the Civil War and Reconstruction

Major Political Issues	Major Constitutional Issues	Major Court Decisions
Secession	Secession	*Legal Tender Cases* (1871)
Slavery	Suspension of Habeas Corpus	*Texas v. White* (1869)
Taxation	Confiscation	*In re Tarble* (1871)
Military Draft	Emancipation	*Tennessee v. Davis* (1880)
Western Settlement	Civil Rights	*Ex parte Merryman* (1861)
War	Legal Tender	*Ex parte Milligan* (1866)
Black Civil Rights	Martial Law	*The Prize Cases* (1863)
Martial Law	Reconstruction of the South	*Mississippi v. Johnson* (1867)
Black Suffrage	Test Oaths	*Ex parte McCardle* (1868)
	Black Suffrage	*Slaughterhouse Cases* (1872)
		United States v. Cruikshank (1875)

broadly when passing such measures as the Civil Rights Act of 1866, which prohibited racial discrimination in contract, property, and criminal law, and the Civil Rights Act of 1875, which guaranteed equal access regardless of race to all inns, theaters, and public transportation. When other branches interfered with Reconstruction, Congress cleared out those obstructions. When doubts were raised about the constitutionality of martial law in the South, Congress voted to strip the Supreme Court's jurisdiction to hear a case raising the issue. When President Andrew Johnson repeatedly vetoed Reconstruction measures and hampered enforcement efforts, the House of Representatives impeached him in 1868.

President Johnson, by slowing the pace of Reconstruction, successfully limited what Republicans achieved in the decade after the Civil War. The Republican effort to remake the South did not last long. Republicans suffered severe political losses in the 1867 state elections and the 1874 national elections, reversing the gains they had made in 1866. The more radical Republicans lacked the votes to convict President Johnson at his impeachment trial before the Senate and had increasing difficulty passing and implementing their racially egalitarian program. As time went on, more and more Republicans asserted that their party would be better off emphasizing economic policy rather than the rights of former slaves. After barely hanging on to the presidency in the disputed election of 1876, Republicans ended Reconstruction. Significant voices were still heard for federal efforts on behalf of blacks after 1876, but federal power would not be exercised on their behalf for almost a century.

Legacies. The Civil War and Reconstruction made permanent changes in the American constitutional order. Secession and compact theory as practical alternatives did not survive the Confederate military defeat. No major political movement after 1865 endorsed the right to secede. Compact theory remained moribund until revived only very briefly by southern segregationists in the wake of the Supreme Court's decision in *Brown v. Board of Education* (1954). The post–Civil War Amendments became permanent sources of Congressional power. The Thirteenth, Fourteenth, and Fifteenth Amendments reshaped national powers and constitutional federalism, vesting Congress with far greater authority to regulate local affairs than was constitutionally permissible before the Civil War. The Supreme Court in the *Legal Tender Cases* (1871) asserted a broad construction of national power under the necessary and proper clause of Article I, Section 8. Although no one made the prediction in 1871, that case consigned to history the more narrow construction of national power articulated before the Civil War by Jeffersonians and Jacksonians.

Americans from 1860 to 1876 created as many new constitutional controversies as they settled. Presidents for more than a century have pointed to Lincoln's decision to impose a blockade, suspend habeas corpus, and impose martial law when defending their unilateral exercises of executive power. Opponents point to the prominent Republicans in Congress who criticized those exercises of executive power and the Supreme Court decision in *Ex parte Milligan* (1868), which unanimously declared unilateral presidential imposition of martial law unconstitutional. The post–Civil War amendments ignited ongoing controversies over what substantive rights those provisions protect and over Congressional power to enforce those substantive rights.

As you read the materials below, think of the following questions. First, to what extent, if any, are the debates between Republicans and Democrats similar to the debates between Whigs and Jacksonians? Did the Republican Party become more attracted to federal power when a former Whig, Abraham Lincoln, was president? Were the Democrats consistent in their criticism of the Lincoln presidency, given their history of support for presidential power since the time of Andrew Jackson? Second, to what extent did the debates during the Civil War reflect sincere constitutional beliefs or attitudes toward the sectional conflicts? Did Democrats oppose the draft because of their traditional Jacksonian hostility to national power or because they were less committed to defeating southern secession? Third, to what extent did the structure of government practically doom radical Reconstruction? Did Republicans need to control all branches of the national government for radical Reconstruction to succeed while such an effort was likely to fail if opponents controlled any one governing institution?

II. Constitutional Authority and Judicial Power

MAJOR DEVELOPMENTS

- Republicans restructure the federal judiciary.
- Lincoln challenges judicial authority.
- The Supreme Court finds jurisdictional reasons not to rule on whether crucial Reconstruction Acts are constitutional.

Box 6-1 A Partial Cast of Characters of the Civil War and Reconstruction

Abraham Lincoln	■ Whig and Republican ■ Representative from Illinois (1847–1849) ■ President of the United States (1861–1865), assassinated 1865 ■ Known for his dedication to preserving the Union, and his success in leading the North to victory in the Civil War ■ Believed secession was unconstitutional and, despite his Whig background, defended executive power during his administration
Jefferson Davis	■ Democrat ■ President of the Confederacy (1861–1865) ■ Representative (1845–1846) and Senator (1847–1851, 1857–1861) from Mississippi ■ Secretary of War under President Pierce (1853–1857) ■ Known as a states' rights strict constructionist
Salmon Chase	■ Free Soiler and Republican ■ Senator from Ohio (1849–1855) ■ Rival for leadership of Republican Party ■ Secretary of the Treasury under Lincoln (1861–1864) ■ Appointed by Lincoln to be Chief Justice of the United States (1864–1873) ■ Oversaw key wartime policies as both treasury secretary and justice, and sometimes skeptical of the scope of national power
Charles Sumner	■ Free Soiler and Republican ■ Radical abolitionist Senator from Massachusetts (1851–1874) ■ Opposed secession and remained in the Senate when Tennessee left the union ■ Helped galvanize Northern public opinion against the expansion of slavery in the antebellum period, and led efforts to take a hard-line view against the South during the war and Reconstruction
Andrew Johnson	■ Democrat and Unionist ■ Representative (1843–1853) and Senator (1857–1862; 1875) from Tennessee ■ Governor of Tennessee (1853–1857) ■ Opposed secession and remained in the Senate when Tennessee left the Union ■ Appointed by Lincoln to be Military Governor of Tennessee after Union troops recaptured the state (1862–1865) ■ Vice President under Lincoln's second term on "Union Party" ticket (1865) ■ President of the United States upon Lincoln's assassination (1865–1869) ■ Opposed congressional Reconstruction, and impeached by the House in 1868

The Republican Party that controlled the national government during the Civil War and Reconstruction had a love-hate relationship with the federal judiciary. Most Republicans began their careers as Whigs, and most Whigs before the Civil War were strong supporters of federal judicial power. Abraham Lincoln repeatedly defended judicial supremacy when a young Whig member of the Illinois legislature. Judges, he believed, had the final authority to settle constitutional questions. An early Lincoln speech asserted "that the individuals composing our [state] Supreme Court have, in an official capacity, decided in favor of the constitutionality of the Bank, would, in my mind, seem a sufficient answer" to any continuing doubts about the constitutionality of that state bank. The state judiciary, Lincoln stated, is the "tribunal, by which and which alone, the constitutionality of the Bank can ever be settled."[1] Northern Whig and Republican faith in the judiciary was shaken late in the Jacksonian Era. Federal courts repeatedly sustained federal fugitive slave laws. The U.S. Supreme Court further earned the wrath of Republicans throughout the nation by holding in *Dred Scott v. Sandford* (1857) that slavery could not be banned in American territories. While many Republicans were content to attack particular Supreme Court decisions, some began questioning past commitments to judicial power.

Jacksonian justices controlled the federal judiciary when Lincoln took the presidential oath in 1861. The Supreme Court was undermanned, with only six justices remaining on the bench.[2] Five of those remaining justices had been in the *Dred Scott* majority. The other, Nathan Clifford, joined the Court after *Dred Scott* was handed down but was on record as supporting that decision. Republicans had good reason to believe that these holdover justices would not look favorably on their policies.

Lincoln, his political allies, and his political successors adopted various strategies to prevent federal judges from interfering with Republican policies. Republican officials sometimes ignored judicial decrees. Republicans in Congress manipulated federal jurisdiction to keep risky cases away from the Court. Lincoln placed reliable allies on the federal bench. The Judiciary Act of 1862 reorganized the federal judiciary to guarantee a free-state majority on the Supreme Court. Republicans from 1863 to 1871 alternately added and subtracted seats on the Supreme Court to gain and maintain a friendly tribunal.

Republican challenges to judicial authority began the moment that party took power. During his first inaugural, Lincoln asserted that the Supreme Court lacked the power to settle forever such vital issues as the constitutional status of slavery. Less than two months later, Lincoln refused to honor a writ of habeas corpus issued by Chief Justice Roger Taney. One year later, Congress prohibited slavery in all territories. That measure, which overturned *Dred Scott*, was not challenged in federal court. During the Civil War, Republicans made every effort to prevent the justices from hearing cases challenging the constitutionality of such Civil War measures as the Legal Tender Act of 1862 and President Lincoln's decision to suspend habeas corpus. The justices in these years exhibited little enthusiasm for challenging the Lincoln administration. In several cases, the justices avoided reaching the merits of constitutional attacks on national policies by denying jurisdiction on dubious legal grounds. *The Prize Cases* were the only instance when the Supreme Court adjudicated a Civil War policy while the war was ongoing. The judicial majority in that case sustained administration policy.

Republican attitudes toward the federal judiciary fluctuated during the decade after the Civil War. Republicans in Congress initially regarded federal courts staffed increasingly by Lincoln appointees as allies in their effort to reconstruct the South. The Joint Committee on Reconstruction revised the text of the Fourteenth Amendment to give courts the power to protect privileges and immunities, due process, and equal protection rights, even in the absence of a federal law. The Civil Rights Act of 1866 and the Habeas Corpus Act of 1867 enabled former slaves and southern Unionists to litigate in federal courts their new statutory and constitutional rights. Republican confidence in the federal judiciary soon faded. Justice David Davis's majority opinion in *Ex parte Milligan* cast considerable doubt on whether the Supreme Court would support crucial Reconstruction measures, most notably the imposition of martial law in the South. Republicans were outraged. Many questioned their initial support for empowering federal courts.

Buoyed by *Milligan* and rumors that several justices were prepared to declare crucial Reconstruction measures unconstitutional, prominent Democrats looked for a test case to bring before what they perceived as a sympathetic judiciary. Their initial efforts failed on jurisdictional grounds. In *Mississippi v. Johnson* (1867), the Supreme Court ruled that judges could not issue an injunction prohibiting a president from enforcing federal law. In *Georgia v. Stanton* (1867), the Court ruled that a state lacked standing to make a general attack on Reconstruction measures. Democrats finally appeared to hit pay dirt when the jus-

1. Abraham Lincoln, *The Collected Works of Abraham Lincoln*, ed. Roy P. Basler, vol. 1 (New Brunswick, NJ: Rutgers University Press, 1953), 62–63.

2. Justices John McLean and Peter Daniel had recently died. Justice John Campbell resigned his seat when Alabama seceded.

tices scheduled arguments to determine whether James McCardle, a racist newspaper editor from Mississippi, could be constitutionally tried by a military commission for encouraging resistance to Reconstruction.

Faced with the possibility that military rule in the South might be declared unconstitutional, Republicans in Congress took several steps to protect their legislative handiwork. First, they passed legislation shrinking the size of the court from ten to eight justices. This measure prevented President Andrew Johnson from filling any vacancies with a nominee hostile to Reconstruction. Second, Congress, over a presidential veto, repealed the Habeas Corpus Act of 1867. That repeal stripped the Court of the jurisdiction necessary to decide McCardle's case. The repeal was passed after the Supreme Court had already heard arguments in *Ex parte McCardle* (1869). Nevertheless, the justices delayed their decision until the Repealer Act became law. The justices then sustained the Repealer Act and dismissed McCardle's case for want of jurisdiction. The justices never determined whether Congress could impose martial law in the Reconstruction South.

These tensions between the Court and Congress did not simmer long. Shortly after President Grant took office, Congress voted to increase the number of Supreme Court justices to nine. Although this broke with the practice of having one justice for every circuit, the extra appointment combined with the resignation of Justice Grier in 1870 enabled President Grant to appoint two orthodox Republicans to the bench. Within a year, the justices overruled *Hepburn v. Griswold* (1870) and sustained Republican legislation passed during the Civil War which required creditors to accept paper money. As a federal bench augmented by Republican appointments became more sympathetic to Congress (and Congress less enthusiastic about racial equality), Republicans in Congress again became more interested in expanding than in contracting judicial power. The Judiciary Act of 1875, passed by a lame duck Republican Congress, was the first federal law since the repealed Federalist Judiciary Act of 1801 that gave federal courts the jurisdiction necessary to resolve virtually all federal questions.

A. Judicial Structure and Selection

Note: The Republicans Reorganize the Judiciary

Republicans, after gaining a national majority in the 1860 elections, quickly moved to reconstitute the federal judicial system. After a motion to abolish the Supreme Court failed, Congress in 1862 rearranged the federal judicial circuits and in 1863 added a new California circuit.[3] The size of the Supreme Court was increased to ten members to match the number of judicial circuits. These maneuvers, combined with the tradition of appointing one Supreme Court justice who resided in each of the federal circuits, ensured that at the end of the Civil War seven of the ten justices on the Supreme Court resided in the more northern and western states that abolished slavery long before the Civil War.

Senator John. P. Hale of New Hampshire, a leading abolitionist, made a motion in December 1861 for "the Committee on the Judiciary [to] be instructed to inquire into the expediency and propriety of abolishing the present Supreme Court of the United States, and establishing, instead thereof, another Supreme Court."[4] Defending this proposition, Hale asserted,

> I undertake to say that the Supreme Court of the United States, as at present established, has utterly failed. It is bankrupt in everything that was intended by the creation of such a tribunal. It has lost public confidence [and] it does not enjoy public respect....
>
> ...
>
> ...This court have not been careful to study and find out and declare the law; but they have been careful to declare what was agreeable to the party in power, and have declared it. The party which was then in power has gone out of power, and it seems to me it is not incumbent on us, now that they have abandoned the ground, to hold up and maintain what they have built up, as the citadel in our midst, to wit, the present Supreme Court of the United States.[5]

Most Republicans found abolishing the Supreme Court too radical. Senator Lafayette Foster from Connecticut insisted that Congress ought not further diminish public respect for the federal judiciary by tying courts too closely to partisan politics.

---

3. California briefly had a free-standing circuit court without a Supreme Court justice, but it was abolished when Congress created the Tenth Circuit in 1863.
4. *Congressional Globe*, 37th Cong., 2nd Sess. (1861), 26.
5. Ibid., 26–27.

Table 6-2 Reorganization of Federal Judicial Circuits, 1862–1863

Old Circuits	New Circuits
1. Rhode Island, Massachusetts, New Hampshire, Maine	1. Same
2. New York, Vermont, Connecticut	2. Same
3. Pennsylvania, New Jersey	3. Same
4. Maryland, Delaware, Virginia	4. Maryland, Delaware, Virginia, North Carolina
5. Alabama, Louisiana	5. Alabama, Mississippi, South Carolina, Georgia, Florida
6. North Carolina, South Carolina, Georgia	6. Louisiana, Texas, Arkansas, Kentucky, Tennessee
7. Ohio, Indiana, Illinois, Michigan	7. Ohio, Indiana
8. Kentucky, Tennessee, Missouri	8. Michigan, Wisconsin, Illinois
9. Mississippi, Arkansas	9. Missouri, Iowa, Kansas, Minnesota
	10. California, Oregon

> If by legislation we can get rid of this court and legislate these judges out of office, a new set of judges will be appointed in the same manner that the old ones were; and they will be appointed by a fallible President, and their confirmation or rejection will be voted on by a fallible Senate; and we shall be subject, I apprehend, to very much the same evils that we have been subject to for eighty years past....
>
> ...
>
> ...Would it be wise or desirable to have each department of the Government attacking and censuring every other department, and thus destroy the respect and confidence of the people in every department, one after another, belonging to our system of Government....[6]

Senator Orville Browning of Illinois, a confidant of President Lincoln, endorsed these sentiments. "If you repeal the Supreme Court out of existence to-day for the purpose of getting rid of obnoxious judges, and reorganize it, and have new judges appointed," he maintained, "the very moment there is a change in the political complexion of Congress the same 'town-meeting proceeding' recurs, and the court is again abolished, and it will be abolished as often, as the political complexion of Congress changes."[7]

The Republican majority on the Senate Judiciary Committee preferred to reorganize rather than abolish the federal court system. They proposed and Congress passed the Judiciary Act of 1862. This judicial reorganization placed six circuit courts entirely in free states and three entirely in slave states. That distribution contrasted sharply with the five–four advantage the slave states enjoyed when Lincoln took office. The free-state advantage became seven to three in 1863 when Congress approved a new circuit for California and Oregon. Three years later, the Judicial Circuit Act created seven circuit courts entirely or mostly within the North and West and only two entirely within former slave states.

Figure 6-1 reflects the shape of the federal judiciary and the Supreme Court after Republicans passed these measures. Good nonpartisan reasons existed for creating a new circuit court whose justices would have special expertise in the distinctive legal problems of the west. Still, Republicans were well aware that adding a tenth circuit in 1863 enabled President Lincoln to appoint immediately another pro-administration justice to the Supreme Court.

6. Ibid., 27.

7. Ibid., 28.

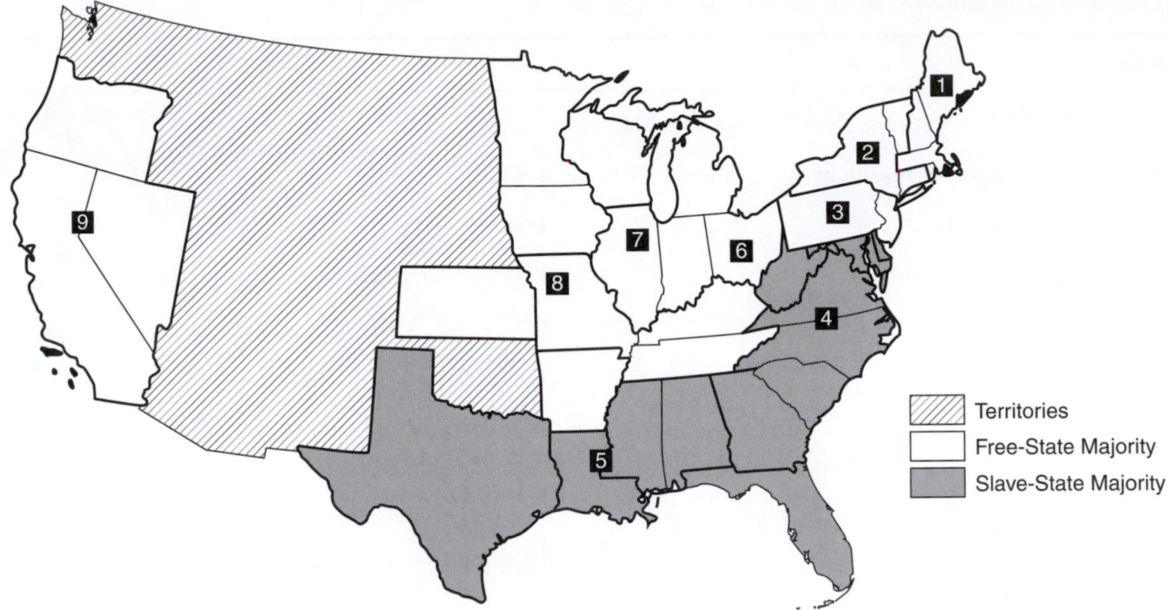

Figure 6-1 Map of Federal Judicial Circuits, 1866

As the old federal circuit system empowered the South, the new federal circuit system empowered the West. The 8th, 9th, and 10th circuits, in particular, were far less populated than the first seven.

Lincoln solidified the reconstitution of the federal bench by selecting justices who met his key litmus tests. He sought and appointed justices he believed were opposed to slavery and committed to the policies Republicans believed necessary to successfully fight the Civil War. As the president explained, "We cannot ask a man what he will do [if appointed to the Court], and if we should, and he should answer us, we should despise him for it. Therefore we must take a man whose opinions are known."[8] All five of Lincoln's Supreme Court appointees—Noah Swayne, Samuel Miller, Stephen Field, David Davis, and Salmon Chase—were committed opponents of slavery before the war and were committed to a northern victory during the war. Lincoln was quite willing to appoint Democrats or former Democrats whose credentials were otherwise suitable. Stephen Field was a Democrat and Salmon Chase was a former Democrat. Both were staunch Unionists while the Civil War raged. After the war, Field opposed virtually all Reconstruction measures. Both Chase and Field in *Hepburn v. Griswold* (1870) and in the *Legal Tender Cases* (1871) articulated the traditional Jacksonian antipathy to paper money.

8. George S. Boutwell, *Reminiscences of Sixty Years in Public Affairs*, vol. 2 (New York: McClure, Phillips, 1902), 29.

B. Judicial Supremacy

Lincoln on Departmentalism

Abraham Lincoln rose to fame attacking the *Dred Scott* decision. During the Lincoln–Douglas debates (1858) he repeatedly asserted that *Dred Scott* was part of a Democratic conspiracy to make slavery national. Stephen Douglas declared that such comments made "war" on the Supreme Court. Abandoning previous Jacksonian criticisms of judicial power, Douglas stated,

> I am content to take that decision as it stands delivered by the highest judicial tribunal on earth, a tribunal established by the Constitution of the United States for that purpose, and hence that decision becomes the law of the land, binding on you, on me, and on every other good citizen, whether we like it or not. Hence I do not choose to go into an argument to prove, before this audience, whether or not Chief Justice Taney understood the law better than Abraham Lincoln.[9]

9. Stephen Douglas, "Third Debate with Stephen A. Douglas at Jonesboro, Illinois (Sept. 15, 1858)," in *The Collected Works of Abraham Lincoln*, ed. Roy P. Basler, vol. 3 (New Brunswick, NJ: Rutgers University Press, 1953), 102, 112.

Lincoln responded to this charge by distinguishing between judicial review, which is the judicial power to interpret the Constitution when deciding the legal rights of the parties before the Court, and judicial supremacy, which is the judicial power to determine forever official constitutional meanings. The future president maintained that respect for the rule of law entailed a commitment to the first but not to the second. "We do not propose that when Dred Scott has been decided to be a slave by the court," he stated,

> we, as a mob, will decide him to be free. We do not propose that, when any other one, or one thousand, shall be decided by that court to be slaves, we will in any violent way disturb the rights of property thus settled; but we nevertheless do oppose that decision as a political rule which shall be binding on the voter, to vote for nobody who thinks it wrong, which shall be binding on the members of Congress or the President to favor no measure that does not actually concur with the principles of that decision. We do not propose to be bound by it as a political rule in that way, because we think it lays the foundation not merely of enlarging and spreading out what we consider an evil, but it lays the foundation for spreading that evil into the States themselves. We propose so resisting it as to have it reversed if we can, and a new judicial rule established upon this subject.[10]

When taking the presidential oath in 1861, Lincoln reiterated his commitment to reversing the result in *Dred Scott* and his opposition to judicial supremacy.

> I do not forget the position assumed by some that constitutional questions are to be decided by the Supreme Court, nor do I deny that such decisions must be binding in any case upon the parties to a suit as to the object of that suit.... At the same time, the candid citizen must confess that if the policy of the Government upon vital questions affecting the whole people is to be irrevocably fixed by decisions of the Supreme Court, the instant they are made, in ordinary litigation between parties, in personal actions, the people will have ceased to be their own rulers, having to that extent practically resigned their Government into the hands of that eminent tribunal. Nor is there in this view any assault upon the court or the judges. It is a duty from which they may not shrink to decide cases properly brought before them, and it is no fault of theirs if others seek to turn their decisions to political purposes.[11]

The anticipated clash between President Lincoln and the Supreme Court over slavery never arose. Republicans did not ban human bondage in the territories until 1862. That prohibition was not challenged in federal court. The Lincoln administration also rejected *Dred Scott*'s holding that free blacks were not citizens of the United States. Attorney General Edward Bates (1793–1869) routinely issued passports to persons of color, but no one had standing to challenge such decisions in court. Lincoln's most direct confrontation with the federal courts came weeks after his inaugural when he refused to obey, or even respond to, a federal judicial decision declaring that the president had no power to suspend habeas corpus.[12] When Lincoln and Attorney General Bates eventually defended presidential suspensions of habeas corpus, their comments concentrated on the separation of powers rather than judicial authority.

C. Constitutional Litigation

The most important controversies over federal jurisdiction and standing from 1860 to 1876 took place when Democrats launched a litigation campaign to declare crucial Reconstruction measures unconstitutional. Congress after the Civil War passed a series of Reconstruction Acts that divided the South into military districts, mandated that the army supervise elections, and authorized local military commanders to use military commissions to try civilians suspected of fomenting insurrection or disturbing the public peace. Such prominent Democrats as Jeremiah Black (1819–1883), the Attorney General under President Buchanan, insisted that these policies violated state sovereignty

10. Abraham Lincoln, *The Collected Works of Abraham Lincoln*, ed. Roy P. Basler, vol. 3 (New Brunswick, NJ: Rutgers University Press, 1953), 245.

11. Ibid., 4:268.

12. On Lincoln's departmentalism, see Keith E. Whittington, *Political Foundations of Judicial Supremacy* (Princeton: Princeton University Press, 2007); Michael Stokes Paulsen, "The *Merryman* Power and the Dilemma of Autonomous Executive Branch Interpretation," *Cardozo Law Review* 15 (1993): 84; Hadley Arkes, *First Things* (Princeton: Princeton University Press, 1986), 419–22; Larry D. Kramer, *The People Themselves* (New York: Oxford University Press, 2004), 212–17.

and individual rights. Black and his political allies brought three separate cases before the Supreme Court in their effort to secure a judicial ruling striking down Congressional Reconstruction.

The Supreme Court refused to reach the merits in each of these cases. In *Mississippi v. Johnson* (1867), the Court ruled that federal judges could not issue an injunction to the President of the United States. In *Georgia v. Stanton* (1867), the justices ruled that a state did not have standing to challenge the constitutionality of Reconstruction measures. Justice Samuel Nelson's majority opinion concluded that these matters "call for the judgment of the court upon political questions, and upon rights not of persons and property, but of a political character... rights of sovereignty, of political jurisdiction, of government, of corporate existence as a State, with all its constitutional powers and privileges." He concluded, the Court "possesses no jurisdiction over the subject-matter presented in the bill for relief." In *Ex parte McCardle* (1869), the justices refused to issue a ruling on Reconstruction when, after oral argument on the merits of the case had already taken place, Congress repealed the Habeas Corpus Act of 1867, the measure which had initially authorized jurisdiction in that case.

Chief Justice Salmon Chase's opinion in *McCardle* provided one last glimmer of hope for opponents of Reconstruction by suggesting that the Court might have jurisdiction over a case challenging martial law that took a different procedural route. That path was soon taken.[13] In Jackson, Mississippi, Edward Yerger killed Major Joseph Crane when Crane attempted to seize Yerger's piano in payment for overdue city taxes. After Yerger was held for trial before a military commission, he sought a writ of habeas corpus from District Judge Robert Hill, the same district judge in Jackson who heard McCardle's case. Chief Justice Chase suggested to Judge Hill that were he to remand Yerger back into the custody of the military, Yerger could then appeal to the Supreme Court of the United States based on an unrepealed provision of the Judiciary Act of 1789. After this maneuvering, Chase wrote, "a decision of the Supreme Court upon the legality of the imprisonment can be had."[14] The federal government agreed not to execute a sentence against Yerger before the case could be decided by the Supreme Court. When the Supreme Court ruled in *Ex parte Yerger* (1869) that jurisdiction existed to hear the case, the federal government quickly released Yeager to the state authorities for his murder trial. Yerger was never successfully prosecuted, and he soon left the state. With his release by the military, the case was mooted and could not proceed to the merits. The Court never ruled on the constitutionality of the detention and trial of civilians by military commissions in the South. Military rule in the South was eventually abandoned by executive decree and federal legislation, not by judicial order.

Consider the interplay of law and politics when reading the excerpts from these cases. To what extent do you believe existing law compelled the Supreme Court not to reach the merits in any of these cases? To what extent to you believe the justices made a purely strategic decision not to challenge Congress? To what extent do the decisions presented here integrate legal and political considerations?

13. *Ex parte Yerger*, 75 U.S. 85 (1869).

14. Quoted in Charles Fairman, *Reconstruction and Reunion, 1864–88* (New York: Macmillan, 1971), 572.

Mississippi v. Johnson, 71 U.S. 475 (1867)

The state of Mississippi sought an injunction from the Supreme Court prohibiting President Andrew Johnson from implementing the Reconstruction Acts on the grounds that legislatively mandated military rule in the South violated state sovereignty and individual rights. Attorney General Henry Stanbery (1803–1881) objected to the motion seeking the injunction. He claimed the president could not be made the subject of judicial proceedings. Furthermore, Stanbery insisted, courts could not issue injunctions to presidents which compelled them to execute or refrain from executing a law. Members of the Johnson Administration thought the Reconstruction Acts were unconstitutional, but they did not welcome this form of judicial intervention. With Congress considering impeachment and the Reconstruction laws not yet declared unconstitutional, President Johnson could not afford to have his hands tied by the courts over whether and how congressional mandates were implemented.

The justices unanimously ruled that the Supreme Court could not issue an injunction to the President requiring him to refrain from implementing an unconstitutional law. The Supreme Court in Marbury v. Madison *(1803) had ruled that courts were empowered to order executive officials to deliver a judicial commission. Chief Justice Salmon Chase's opinion in* Mississippi v. Johnson *distinguished* Marbury v. Madison, *a case in which Chief Justice John Marshall had ruled that courts were empowered to order executive offi-*

cials to deliver a judicial commission, by claiming that, in Marbury, *"nothing was left to discretion." The Court could not issue an injunction in* Mississippi v. Johnson *because the duty to faithfully execute the law was political and discretionary. Such presidential duties could not be reviewed by courts. There was no legal duty owed to any particular individual to be enforced in court, and thus no judicial case to be heard.*

Mr. STANBERY, Attorney General, contra [arguing on behalf of President Johnson]:

...

The allegation is, that he is about to execute certain laws passed by Congress; that he considers it his duty to execute those laws; but that this court is a better judge of his duty as President than the President himself; and that when he seeks to execute a law, and to avoid impeachment and denouncement as unfaithful to his duty as Executive, this court is to interfere and tell him what his duty is in the premises, and compel him to perform it.

...

It is not upon any peculiar immunity that the individual has who happens to be President; upon any idea that he cannot do wrong; upon any idea that there is any particular sanctity belonging to him as an individual, as is the case with one who has royal blood in his veins; but it is on account of the office that he holds that I say the President of the United States is above the process of any court or the jurisdiction of any court to bring him to account as President. There is only one court or quasi court that he can be called upon to answer to for any dereliction of duty, for doing anything that is contrary to law or failing to do anything which is according to law, and that is not this tribunal but one that sits in another chamber of this Capitol. There he can be called and tried and punished, but not here while he is President; and after he has been dealt with in that chamber and stripped of the robes of office, and he no longer stands as the representative of the government, then for any wrong he has done to any individual, for any murder or any crime of any sort which he has committed as President, then and not till then can he be subjected to the jurisdiction of the courts. Then it is the individual they deal with, not the representative of the people.

...

Now let us suppose the case to go so far as it must go in order to give the relief that is claimed; what sort of a spectacle have we? One great department of this government has arraigned another, and the executive department of the government, represented by the President, brought before the judicial department—for what purpose? To be punished criminally; for if he stands out and makes no apology to the court, and does not purge himself of the contempt in failing to obey its orders, the court is bound to put him in jail or to fine him; ordinarily to put him in jail, and, if he still persists, to keep him in jail without any remedy....

...

But although counsel, in their bill, have said that the President have vetoed these acts of Congress as unconstitutional, I must say, in defense of the President, this, that when the President did that he did everything he intended to do in opposition to these laws. From the moment they were passed over his veto there was but one duty in his estimation resting upon him, and that was faithfully to carry out and execute these laws. He has instructed me to say that in making this objection, it is not for the purpose of escaping from any responsibility either to perform or to refuse to perform.

Mr. Robert J. WALKER[15], in reply [arguing on behalf of the State of Mississippi]:

...

The Attorney-General has said that if this court, in the performance of its duty, should proceed under its oath of office to defend the Constitution of the United States from violation, even by the hands of the President, the President could not obey its order, and that there would be brought on a direct and fearful conflict between the President and this great tribunal.

But who has contended more strongly and with more ability than this very President of the United States, in various veto messages, for the final character of the decisions of the Supreme Court of the United States in all cases involving a construction of its Constitution? Who has urged, from time to time, with more ability and force than this President the great doctrine that all the departments of this government are sworn to support the Constitution of the United States, and that this great tribunal, this arbiter, was created by the Constitution to avoid just such a result as the Attorney-General has referred to; was created for the peaceful and final and ultimate decision of all such questions as this? What! The President of the United States not obey

15. Former U.S. Senator and Secretary of the Treasury.

the mandate of this court? If he does not, he disobeys the mandate of the Constitution.

. . .

If there is anything that is definitely settled for three-fourths of a century by repeated and manifest decisions of this court, the opinions of the framers of the Constitution, and the great statesmen of the day, it is that this is the tribunal and the only tribunal created by the Constitution whose decision is final and conclusive upon the interpretation of the Constitution. . . .

. . .

The Attorney-General has shown a picture of the calamities which would follow, if the President of the United States should disobey the mandate of this court. Let us look at the calamities that might follow, on the other hand, if this court declines to exercise the power which I think is granted by the Constitution, and permits these military laws to go into effect. What then? According to the President's own opinion, as expressed in his veto messages, the Constitution of the United States is, by the Reconstruction Acts, subverted and overthrown, and a military despotism is erected upon its ruins. Ten States are to be expelled from the Union; ten millions of people are to be deprived of all the benefits of the Constitution; deprived of the right of trial by jury. These ten States are cut up into five military districts; people are to be tried outside of their States for offences unknown and undefined, merely at the will of a military officer. . . .

CHIEF JUSTICE CHASE delivered the opinion of the Court.

. . .

The single point which requires consideration is this: Can the President be restrained by injunction from carrying into effect an act of Congress alleged to be unconstitutional?

It is assumed by the counsel for the State of Mississippi, that the President, in the execution of the Reconstruction Acts, is required to perform a mere ministerial duty. In this assumption there is, we think, a confounding of the terms ministerial and executive, which are by no means equivalent in import.

A ministerial duty, the performance of which may, in proper cases, be required of the head of a department, by judicial process, is one in respect to which nothing is left to discretion. It is a simple, definite duty, arising under conditions admitted or proved to exist, and imposed by law.

The case of *Marbury v. Madison, Secretary of State*, furnishes an illustration. A citizen had been nominated, confirmed, and appointed a justice of the peace for the District of Columbia, and his commission had been made out, signed, and sealed. Nothing remained to be done except delivery, and the duty of delivery was imposed by law on the Secretary of State. It was held that the performance of this duty might be enforced by mandamus issuing from a court having jurisdiction.

[N]othing was left to discretion. There was no room for the exercise of judgment. The law required the performance of a single specific act; and that performance, it was held, might be required by mandamus.

Very different is the duty of the President in the exercise of the power to see that the laws are faithfully executed, and among these laws the acts named in the bill. By the first of these acts he is required to assign generals to command in the several military districts, and to detail sufficient military force to enable such officers to discharge their duties under the law. By the supplementary act, other duties are imposed on the several commanding generals, and these duties must necessarily be performed under the supervision of the President as commander-in-chief. The duty thus imposed on the President is in no just sense ministerial. It is purely executive and political.

An attempt on the part of the judicial department of the government to enforce the performance of such duties by the President might be justly characterized, in the language of Chief Justice Marshall, as "an absurd and excessive extravagance."

It is true that in the instance before us the interposition of the court is not sought to enforce action by the Executive under constitutional legislation, but to restrain such action under legislation alleged to be unconstitutional. But we are unable to perceive that this circumstance takes the case out of the general principles which forbid judicial interference with the exercise of Executive discretion.

. . .

The Congress is the legislative department of the government; the President is the executive department. Neither can be restrained in its action by the judicial department; though the acts of both, when performed, are, in proper cases, subject to its cognizance.

The impropriety of such interference will be clearly seen upon consideration of its possible consequences.

Suppose the bill filed and the injunction prayed for allowed. If the President refuse obedience, it is needless to observe that the court is without power to enforce its process. If, on the other hand, the President complies with the order of the court and refuses to execute the acts of Congress, is it not clear that a collision may occur between the executive and legislative departments of the government? May not the House of Representatives impeach the President for such refusal? And in that case could this court interfere, in behalf of the President, thus endangered by compliance with its mandate, and restrain by injunction the Senate of the United States from sitting as a court of impeachment? Would the strange spectacle be offered to the public world of an attempt by this court to arrest proceedings in that court?

These questions answer themselves.

. . . [W]e are fully satisfied that this court has no jurisdiction of a bill to enjoin the President in the performance of his official duties; and that no such bill ought to be received by us.

. . .

The motion for leave to file the bill is, therefore, denied.

Ex parte McCardle, 74 U.S. 506 (1868)[16]

The Union army in 1867 arrested William McCardle, a newspaper editor in Vicksburg, Mississippi. McCardle was charged with inciting insurrection by writing inflammatory editorials about Reconstruction. While awaiting trial by a military tribunal, McCardle filed for a writ of habeas corpus under the terms of the Habeas Corpus Act of 1867. That statute empowered federal courts to issue the writ in "all cases where any person may be restrained of his or her liberty in violation of the constitution, or of any treaty or law of the United States." While Congress intended the Habeas Corpus Act to extend federal court protection to former slaves and southern unionists, opponents of Reconstruction quickly recognized that the text also authorized federal courts to adjudicate cases challenging the constitutionality of martial law in the South. The district judge who upheld McCardle's detention expressed gratitude that the Supreme Court would review the case "where any error I may have committed may be corrected."

The Supreme Court placed McCardle on the docket at the same time that the Senate was considering whether to impeach President Johnson. Immediately before and during oral arguments, Republicans became concerned that the Supreme Court might declare the Reconstruction Acts unconstitutional. Acting quickly, Congress repealed that part of the Habeas Corpus Act of 1867 on which McCardle relied for jurisdiction, and applied the repeal to pending cases (like McCardle's). In other words, in order to prevent the Supreme Court from striking down Reconstruction, the Republicans in Congress took away the Court's authority to hear McCardle's case.

President Johnson vetoed the Repealer Act. His veto message argued

> *The legislation proposed in the second section, it seems to me, is not in harmony with the spirit and intention of the Constitution. It cannot fail to affect most injuriously the just equipoise of our system of government; for it establishes a precedent which, if followed, may eventually sweep away every check on arbitrary and unconstitutional legislation. Thus far, during the existence of the government, the Supreme Court of the United States has been viewed by the people as the true expounder of their Constitution, and in the most violent party conflicts its judgments and decrees have always been sought and deferred to with confidence and respect. . . . [This bill] will be justly held by a large portion of the people as an admission of the unconstitutionality of the act on which its judgment may be forbidden or forestalled, and may interfere with that willing acquiescence in its provisions which is necessary for the harmonious and efficient execution of any law.*[17]

Both the House and the Senate overrode the veto. The Supreme Court delayed making a decision on the merits in McCardle *until the Repealer Act became law and then unanimously denied jurisdiction. Chief Justice Salmon Chase's opinion ruled that the congressional power to determine the appellate jurisdiction of the Supreme Court included the power to strip the court of jurisdiction over cases pending before that tribunal. Some commentators suggest that the justices behaved strategically in* McCardle, *using the jurisdictional excuse to avoid having to rule on the merits of the case and inviting congressional reprisal. Others argue that Congress*

16. *Ex parte McCardle* was actually handed down on April 12, 1869. Supreme Court practice during the mid-nineteenth century cited cases by the beginning date of the Supreme Court term, in this case December 1868, rather than the date the decision was announced.

17. *A Compilation of the Messages and Papers of the Presidents*, ed. James D. Richardson, vol. 6 (Washington, DC: Government Printing Office, 1897), 648.

took advantage of existing rules governing the Court's appellate jurisdiction to prevent a direct confrontation between the two branches over the constitutionality of martial law in the South. Most commentators agree that the judicial majority would have declared crucial Reconstruction measures unconstitutional had Congress not repealed the offending provisions of the Habeas Corpus Act of 1867. Chief Justice Chase informally reported to the district judge in the case that "the Court would doubtless have held that [McCardle's] imprisonment for trial before a military commission was illegal" had the justices reached the merits.[18] *But what is the significance of the last paragraph in the opinion?*

CHIEF JUSTICE CHASE delivered the opinion of the Court.

The first question necessarily is that of jurisdiction; for, if the act of March, 1868, takes away the jurisdiction defined by the act of February, 1867, it is useless, if not improper, to enter into any discussion of other questions.

It is quite true, as was argued by the counsel for the petitioner, that the appellate jurisdiction of this court is not derived from acts of Congress. It is, strictly speaking, conferred by the Constitution. But it is conferred "with such exceptions and under such regulations as Congress shall make."

...

...In the case of *Durousseau v. The United States* (1810)...the court held, that while "the appellate powers of this court are not given by the [Judiciary Act of 1789], but are given by the Constitution," they are, nevertheless, "limited and regulated by that act, and by such other acts as have been passed on the subject." The court said, further, that the judicial act was an exercise of the power given by the Constitution to Congress "of making exceptions to the appellate jurisdiction of the Supreme Court." "They have described affirmatively," said the court, "its jurisdiction, and this affirmative description has been understood to imply a negation of the exercise of such appellate power as is not comprehended within it."

...

The exception to appellate jurisdiction in the case before us, however, is not an inference from the affirmation of other appellate jurisdiction. It is made in terms. The provision of the act of 1867, affirming the appellate jurisdiction of this court in cases of habeas corpus is expressly repealed. It is hardly possible to imagine a plainer instance of positive exception.

We are not at liberty to inquire into the motives of the legislature. We can only examine into its power under the Constitution; and the power to make exceptions to the appellate jurisdiction of this court is given by express words.

What, then, is the effect of the repealing act upon the case before us? We cannot doubt as to this. Without jurisdiction the court cannot proceed at all in any cause. Jurisdiction is power to declare the law, and when it ceases to exist, the only function remaining to the court is that of announcing the fact and dismissing the cause. And this is not less clear upon authority than upon principle.

...

...[T]he effect of repealing acts upon suits under acts repealed, has been determined by the adjudications of this court. In [two previous cases] it was held that no judgment could be rendered in a suit after the repeal of the act under which it was brought and prosecuted.

It is quite clear, therefore, that this court cannot proceed to pronounce judgment in this case, for it has no longer jurisdiction of the appeal; and judicial duty is not less fitly performed by declining ungranted jurisdiction than in exercising firmly that which the Constitution and the laws confer.

Counsel seem to have supposed, if effect be given to the repealing act in question, that the whole appellate power of the court, in cases of habeas corpus, is denied. But this is an error. The act of 1868 does not except from that jurisdiction any cases but appeals from Circuit Courts under the act of 1867. It does not affect the jurisdiction which was previously exercised.

The appeal of the petitioner in this case must be DISMISSED FOR WANT OF JURISDICTION.

III. Powers of the National Government

MAJOR DEVELOPMENTS

- Congress enacts the first national military draft.
- Congress finances the Civil War by printing paper money and making that currency legal tender for all public and private debts.

18. Quoted in Fairman, 494.

- The post–Civil War Amendments provide Congress with increased, but vague, powers to regulate what had been traditionally local affairs.
- Americans debate whether the Constitution provides the national government with adequate powers.

The national government exercised unprecedented powers during the Civil War and Reconstruction. Congress during the Civil War passed legislation making paper money legal tender for existing debts, confiscating confederate property, and conscripting northerners for the Union army. These measures tested the limits of congressional power under Article I, Section 8, to make laws that were "necessary and proper" for fulfilling national responsibilities. Congress during Reconstruction passed legislation providing freedmen with land and educational opportunities, prohibiting racial discrimination in state contract, property, and criminal laws, and mandating severe sentences for private persons who denied or conspired with others to deny "the privileges and immunities of citizens of the United States." These measures tested the limits of the congressional power to "enforce" the Thirteenth, Fourteenth, and Fifteenth Amendments "by appropriate legislation." Republicans who supported these policies insisted that the Constitution empowered the national government to take all steps necessary to win the Civil War, abolish slavery, and secure racial justice. Democrats claimed that these policies violated a Constitution that granted very limited powers to the national government.

State and federal judges more often passively acquiesced in, rather than enthusiastically supported, Republican claims for broad national powers. As noted in Section I, the Supreme Court for jurisdictional and strategic reasons did not issue rulings on whether crucial Civil War and Reconstruction measures were constitutional. Two judicial decisions ruling that the federal government had exercised unconstitutional powers were immediately overruled. The Supreme Court of Pennsylvania overruled within months an initial decision declaring the federal conscription law unconstitutional. The Supreme Court in *Hepburn v. Griswold* (1870) declared that the Legal Tender Act was neither constitutionally necessary nor proper. One year later, augmented by two Republican judicial appointees, the Supreme Court in *The Legal Tender Cases* (1871) declared that requiring creditors to accept paper money was a necessary and proper means for enabling the federal government to borrow the money necessary for fighting the Civil War.

The Republican justices appointed to the Supreme Court during Reconstruction interpreted more broadly the federal powers ratified in 1787 than the federal powers ratified in 1868. Justice Strong's majority opinion in *The Legal Tender Cases* relied heavily on the expansive Hamiltonian interpretation of the necessary and proper clause, abandoning the more narrow Jeffersonian construction that prevailed throughout most of the Jacksonian Era. "[T]he whole history of the government and of congressional legislation has exhibited the use of a very wide discretion," he wrote, "in the selection of the necessary and proper means to carry into effect the great objects for which the government was framed." Republican judicial appointees more narrowly interpreted federal power under the post–Civil War Amendments. *U.S. v. Reese* (1875) ruled that Sections 3 and 4 of the Enforcement Act of 1870 were unconstitutional. Those provisions prohibiting state officials and private actors from interfering with voting did not make explicit that the wrong had to be "on account of race, color, or previous condition of servitude." "It is only when the wrongful refusal at such an election is because of race, color, or previous condition of servitude, that Congress can interfere," Chief Justice Morrison Waite stated. "If, therefore, the third and fourth sections of the act are beyond that limit, they are unauthorized."

When reading the following materials, consider the extent to which constitutional arguments about national power reflected preexisting constitutional beliefs, new ideas connected to a more fundamental goal of winning the Civil War, or partisan maneuvering to gain an upper hand in electoral and institutional politics. To what extent did the debates between Republicans and Democrats over national powers from 1860 to 1876 resemble previous debates between Whigs and Democrats? How did the Civil War influence attitudes toward national power? Was the use of national power during Reconstruction a good faith effort to implement new constitutional values or a partisan effort to increase Republican Party strength in the South, or both?

A. Necessary and Proper Clause

Chief Justice John Marshall gave voice to the nationalist reading of the necessary and proper clause during the late Jeffersonian period, but the more strict constructionist views of the Jeffersonians and Jacksonians dominated politics in the first part of the nineteenth century. Strict constructionists were skeptical of the broad reading of the necessary and proper clause and the possibilities that it held for increasing congressional power and shrinking the sphere of state power.

The Civil War changed the dynamics of that debate. The 1860 elections and secession gave nationalists in the Republican and Democratic parties the upper hand. The strict constructionists in the Democratic Party were in the minority in the U.S. government and among the secessionists in the South. The war gave new life to the broad reading of the necessary and proper clause. Just as the War of 1812 created a generation of "War Hawks" in the Jeffersonian party who were more supportive of congressional power, so the Civil War pushed politicians and judges to think seriously about how much constitutional power Congress could draw upon to fight and win a war for national survival. The necessary and proper clause became a key feature in the debate over congressional war powers. What tools did the Constitution provide to Congress to fight a war? Were there implicit limits to the congressional war power, or could Congress do anything that might be useful to win a war?

Legal Tender

The Civil War was longer and more expensive than anyone anticipated. As early as 1861, President Lincoln was forced to call up additional troops, and Treasury Secretary Salmon Chase was struggling to find new ways to pay for the war. By the end of the year, the government faced a financial crisis. Major northern banks that had already committed $150 million in gold were having trouble making final payments and were in danger of collapsing.

Republicans solved this financial crisis by printing paper money to finance the Civil War. The Legal Tender Act of 1862 authorized the government to issue up to $50,000,000 in Treasury notes and made those notes legal tender for all private and public debts. This proposal was extremely controversial. No one in 1862 doubted that the national government could issue paper currency that national officials would accept for payment of taxes and debts to that government. The controversy was over whether the national government could constitutionally require that others—laborers, shopkeepers, bankers, state governments—also accept paper currency instead of other forms of payment. Republican leaders in Congress insisted that making paper money legal tender was a necessary and proper means for exercising the constitutional power "to borrow money." Democrats claimed that no enumerated power authorized Congress to make paper money legal tender and that the Legal Tender Act unconstitutionally interfered with existing contractual obligations. Republicans suffered some defections in the Senate, but not enough to jeopardize passage of the bill.

The Legal Tender Act was successful in the short term. Printing paper money gave an immediate boost to government finances in the early stages of the Civil War. State courts during the Civil War sustained federal power to make paper money legal tender. The Supreme Court ducked appeals from those decisions, making dubious arguments that those cases did not meet jurisdictional requirements.[19] Chief Justice Taney, unhappy with that state of affairs, privately wrote a draft opinion declaring the Legal Tender Act unconstitutional. Taney, however, died in 1864. He was replaced by Salmon Chase, who as Secretary of the Treasury had reluctantly endorsed proposals to make paper money legal tender for all debts.

Political and constitutional controversies over the Legal Tender Act intensified after the Civil War. The treasury notes proved inflationary. Creditors were repaid in notes far less valuable than the cash they previously lent, the goods they previously sold, or the services they previously performed. The Supreme Court in *Hepburn v. Griswold* (1870) surprised many observers by declaring the Legal Tender Act unconstitutional. That decision was a judicial move to defend hard money and contract rights.

Hepburn aggravated constitutional disputes over the means by which the national government financed the Civil War. While many in the business constituency of the post-bellum Republican Party believed in the sanctity of contract, their Whig heritage also left them sympathetic to the banks and fiat money, money that had value only by government decree. By contrast, Democrats were skeptical of banks and financial speculation. Both parties were internally torn by ideology and economic interests over whether and how quickly to remove legal tender from the economy. Before the Supreme Court decided *Hepburn*, the Grant administra-

19. *Roosevelt v. Meyer*, 68 U.S. 512 (1863).

Illustration 6-1 "Milk Tickets for Babies, In Place of Milk"

Sources: David A. Wells, *Robinson Crusoe's Money*, with illustrations by Thomas Nast (New York: Harper & Brothers, 1876), 97.

tion had reached an uneasy compromise that left over $300 million greenbacks in circulation. Raising these policies to the constitutional level threatened to tie the hands of the federal government in managing the money supply and national finances. The Court's decision also raised the immediate prospect of a rush on hard currency and a rash of defaults as debtors found that they could no longer afford to meet their obligations if they could not rely on the inflated greenbacks.

President Grant made two nominations to the Supreme Court on the same day *Hepburn* was announced. One nominee filled the seat of Justice Robert Grier, who had resigned. The other nominee filled a new, ninth seat on the Court, the seat that had been temporarily eliminated during the Johnson presidency. Grant had some difficulty filling the seats (one nominee was defeated, another died), but soon added two reliable Republican voices to the high bench. William Strong and Joseph Bradley became the sixth and seventh justices appointed to the Court since Lincoln. This gave the Republican Party six justices on a nine-member bench (Justice Field was a War Democrat). Of more immediate importance, Grier was a member of the *Hepburn* majority.

With a full complement of nine justices, the Court first ordered a new hearing on the legal tender laws and then, in *The Legal Tender Cases*, overruled *Hepburn v. Griswold*. Chief Justice Chase and the other three remaining members of the *Hepburn* majority publicly dissented from the order to rehear the case and the final decision. The narrow 5–4 decision in *The Legal Tender Cases* nevertheless endured. Opponents raised constitutional objections to making paper money legal tender throughout the late nineteenth century, but this critique gradually disappeared. Few Americans at present are aware that many distinguished constitutional decision makers in the nineteenth century thought unconstitutional the notation on the contemporary dollar bill declaring, "This Note is Legal Tender for All Debts, Public and Private."

Congressional Debate on the Legal Tender Bill[20]

Elbridge Spaulding, the chair of the House Ways and Means Committee, believed that the Union could solve the financial crisis by printing paper money. He proposed "for temporary purposes" that Congress authorize the Lincoln administration to issue up to $50 million in Treasury notes "on the faith of the United States." "Such Treasury notes," he added, "shall also be a legal tender in payment of all debts, public or private, within the United States."[21]

Before presenting the bill to the House of Representatives, Spaulding and other members of the Ways and Means committee asked members of the Lincoln Administration for their opinions on the constitutional issues. Attorney General Bates refused to offer an official opinion. He did write that as a private citizen he thought the measure constitutional: "Certainly the Constitution contains no direct verbal prohibition, and I think it contains no inferential or argumentative prohibition that can be fairly drawn from its expressed terms."[22] *Secretary of Treasury Salmon Chase was initially less forthcoming. He informed the Ways and Means Committee that he "regrett[ed] exceedingly that it is found necessary to resort to the measure of making fundable notes of the United States a legal tender, but heartily desir[ed] to co-operate with the Committee in all measures to meet existing necessities."*[23]

The Legal Tender Act became law after a fairly contentious congressional debate. Democrats were united in their opposition to the legal tender bill in both the House and the Senate. Representative George Pendleton and others insisted that the requirement that private creditors accept paper money "impair[s] the obligation of every contract of that kind." Spaulding and Republican proponents of the bill insisted legal tender was "necessary and proper" because the government could finance the Civil War effectively only "by issuing Treasury notes payable on demand, and making them a legal tender in payment of all debts, public and private." The Legal Tender Act passed both houses of Congress, although the vote was close in the Senate. Lincoln signed the first legal tender bill into law in February 1862.

Representative ELBRIDGE SPAULDING (Republican, New York)

. . .

The bill before us is a war measure, a measure of *necessity*, and not of choice, presented by the Committee of Ways and Means to meet the most pressing demands upon the Treasury to sustain the army and navy, until they can make a vigorous advance upon the traitors, and crush out the rebellion. These are extraordinary times, and extraordinary measures must be resorted to in order to save our Government, and preserve our nationality.

. . .

If you cannot borrow the money on the credit of the United States, except at ruinous rates of discount, and cannot make the new banking system available in time, and cannot realize the amount required from your tariff and tax bills, in what mode can the means be obtained, and the Government be carried on? It is believed that the only way in which it can be done is by issuing Treasury notes payable on demand, and making them a legal tender in payment of all debts, public and private, and by adequate taxation, to be imposed by new bills. This will bring into full exercise all the higher powers of Government under the Constitution. The Constitution confers on Congress the power (Art. I, Sec. 8).

. . .

If a certain means to the exercise of any of the powers expressly given by the Constitution to the Government of the Union be an appropriate measure, not prohibited by the Constitution, the degree of its necessity is a question of *legislative discretion*; not of judicial cognizance.

20. Excerpt taken from *Congressional Globe*, 37th Cong., 2nd Sess., 523–26, 549–51.

21. Elbridge G. Spaulding, *History of the Legal Tender Paper Money* (Buffalo: Express Printing Company, 1869), 14.

22. Ibid., 15.

23. Ibid., 27.

...

It is plainly within the scope of the Constitution that the Government should maintain itself; that the army should be supported; that the navy should be maintained. The ways and means of doing this are left to Congress to provide. Congress may do this entirely by taxation. It may provide by law to levy and collect taxes enough every year to pay the whole expenses of the war during each current year, and so "pay as we go." It may issue six percent bonds and sell them on the market for what they will bring... to raise money to carry on the war. It may issue Treasury notes payable on demand, and make them a legal tender in payment of debts. Either one or all of these modes of paying the expenses of the Government is left to the discretion of Congress. Either mode is constitutional; and it is left to the *sound discretion* of Congress to decide which mode it will adopt, or whether it will adopt a part of each, as being the best in the present crisis.

Representative GEORGE PENDLETON (Democrat, Ohio)

...I believe this Government has reached a crisis in its history. I believe that it is approaching a period in the history of its legislation which may determine the question of its continuance. By wisdom it may overcome the evils of secession; by its great powers and resources it may be able to defend itself against those in arms against it; but I firmly believe that it cannot maintain itself against the shock of the accumulated and manifold dangers which follow inevitably, closely in the wake of an illegal, unsound, and depreciated Government paper currency.

...Every contract for the payment of money is in legal contemplation a contract for the payment of gold and silver coin....

The provisions of this bill contemplate impairing the obligation of every contract of that kind....I am sure I need only state the proposition to shock the mind of the legal profession of the country, so thoroughly has it been imbued with the idea of the sanctity of the obligation of contracts by those who have taught it the beneficent maxims of constitutional law.

...

The gentleman spoke quite at large in reference to the sovereign power of the Government. He told us that this power was not prohibited in the Constitution. He told us that in times of great emergency everything may be done except that which is prohibited....Sir, I repudiate this whole idea. I think it has no solid foundation in the Constitution. In all its external relations, standing among the nations of the earth, the Government of the United States is sovereign, and is invested with all the attributes of sovereignty; but in its relations to its own citizens, in its relations to the States, in its relations to its own constituents, it has no power except that which is granted....

...

Hepburn v. Griswold, 75 U.S. 603 (1870)

Mrs. Hepburn in 1860 made a promissory note to Henry Griswold to pay over eleven thousand "dollars." When the contract was made, the parties understood that "dollars" meant gold and silver coins. Days after the note came due, Congress passed the Legal Tender Act. That bill required that creditors take the paper money printed by the United States as payment for all debts. Griswold in 1864 filed suit to collect the unpaid debt. Hepburn immediately tendered U.S. notes in payment of the debt. Griswold refused to receive that paper currency. The Louisville trial court accepted the notes as satisfying the debt and closed the case. Griswold appealed that verdict to the Kentucky Court of Errors. Two months after Lee's surrender, the Kentucky Court ruled the Legal Tender Act could not be constitutionally enforced when the contract was made before that measure became law. Hepburn appealed that decision to the U.S. Supreme Court.

The Supreme Court, by a 5–3 majority, declared the Legal Tender Act unconstitutional. Chief Justice Salmon Chase's majority opinion ruled that requiring creditors to accept paper money for payment of debts was neither constitutionally necessary nor constitutionally proper. Chase was the only Republican in the majority in the Hepburn *decision. He was joined by all four of the Democrats on the Court, including the only "War Democrat" that Lincoln appointed to the Court, Stephen Field. Lincoln's other three appointees dissented. One of the justices in the majority, Robert Grier, was senile and may not have understood the significance of his vote.*

The Hepburn *case revived* McCulloch v. Maryland *(1819). The Taney Court studiously ignored John Marshall's opinion in the Bank Case. Most Jacksonians regarded as a dead letter both the judicial decision that Congress had the power to incorporate a national bank and Chief Justice John Marshall's broad interpretation of the necessary and proper clause. The opinions in* Hepburn v. Griswold *include the first judicial discussions in over fifty years of the passages in the* McCulloch *opinion examining national power. How does Chief Justice Chase interpret* McCulloch? *Compare his interpretation to Justice Strong's interpretation in the* Legal Tender Cases. *Do they both capture aspects of John Marshall's legacy?*

CHIEF JUSTICE CHASE delivered the opinion of the Court.

. . .

We must inquire then whether [requiring that government notes be accepted as legal tender in payment of debts] can be done in the exercise of an implied power.

The rule for determining whether a legislative enactment can be supported as an exercise of an implied power was stated by Chief Justice Marshall, speaking for the whole court, in the case of *McCullough v. The State of Maryland*; and the statement then made has ever since been accepted as a correct exposition of the Constitution. His words were these: "Let the end be legitimate, let it be within the scope of the Constitution, and all means which are appropriate, which are plainly adapted to that end, which are not prohibited, but consistent with the letter and spirit of the Constitution, are constitutional." . . .

. . .

It is said that this is not a question for the court deciding a cause, but for Congress exercising the power. But the decisive answer to this is that the admission of a legislative power to determine finally what powers have the described relation as means to the execution of other powers plainly granted, and, then, to exercise absolutely and without liability to question, in cases involving private rights, the powers thus determined to have that relation, would completely change the nature of American government. . . .

Undoubtedly among means appropriate, plainly adapted, really calculated, the legislature has unrestricted choice. But there can be no implied power to use means not within the description.

. . .

We are unable to persuade ourselves that an expedient of this sort is an appropriate and plainly adapted means for the execution of the power to declare and carry on war. . . .

But there is another view, which seems to us decisive, to whatever express power the supposed implied power in question may be referred. In the rule stated by Chief Justice Marshall, the words appropriate, plainly adapted, really calculated, are qualified by the limitation that the means must be not prohibited, but consistent with the letter and spirit of the Constitution. Nothing so prohibited or inconsistent can be regarded as appropriate, or plainly adapted, or really calculated means to any end.

Let us inquire, then, first whether making bills of credit a legal tender, to the extent indicated, is consistent with the spirit of the Constitution.

Among the great cardinal principles of that instrument, no one is more conspicuous or more venerable than the establishment of justice. And what was intended by the establishment of justice in the minds of the people who ordained it is, happily, not a matter of disputation. . . .

. . .

But we think it clear that those who framed and those who adopted the Constitution, intended that the spirit of this prohibition should pervade the entire body of legislation, and that the justice which the Constitution was ordained to establish was not thought by them to be compatible with legislation of an opposite tendency. In other words, we cannot doubt that a law not made in pursuance of an express power, which necessarily and in its direct operation impairs the obligation of contracts, is inconsistent with the spirit of the Constitution.

. . .

But there is another provision in the same amendment, which, in our judgment, cannot have its full and intended effect unless construed as a direct prohibition of the legislation which we have been considering. It is that which declares that "no person shall be deprived of life, liberty, or property, without due process of law."

. . .

We confess ourselves unable to perceive any solid distinction between such an act and an act compelling all citizens to accept, in satisfaction of all contracts for money, half or three-quarters or any other proportion less than the whole of the value actually due, according to their terms. It is difficult to conceive what act would take private property without process of law if such an act would not.

We are obliged to conclude that an act making mere promises to pay dollars a legal tender in payment of debts previously contracted, is not a means appropriate, plainly adapted, really calculated to carry into effect any express power vested in Congress; that such an act is inconsistent with the spirit of the Constitution; and that it is prohibited by the Constitution.

It is not surprising that amid the tumult of the late civil war, and under the influence of apprehensions for the safety of the Republic almost universal, different views, never before entertained by American statesmen or jurists, were adopted by many. The time was not favorable to considerate reflection upon the constitutional limits of legislative or executive authority. If power was assumed from patriotic motives, the assumption found ready justification in patriotic hearts. Many who doubted yielded their doubts; many who did not doubt were silent. Some who were strongly averse to making government notes a legal tender felt themselves constrained to acquiesce in the views of the advocates of the measure. Not a few who then insisted upon its necessity, or acquiesced in that view, have, since the return of peace, and under the influence of the calmer time, reconsidered their conclusions, and now concur in those which we have just announced. These conclusions seem to us to be fully sanctioned by the letter and spirit of the Constitution.

We are obliged, therefore, to hold that the defendant in error was not bound to receive from the plaintiffs the currency tendered to him in payment of their note, made before the passage of the act of February 25th, 1862.

JUSTICE MILLER (with SWAYNE and DAVIS), dissenting.

. . .

Legal Tender Cases (Knox v. Lee; Parker v. Davis), 79 U.S. 457 (1871)

Mrs. Lee in 1861 was a loyal citizen of Pennsylvania who owned sheep in Texas. The Confederate government in 1863 confiscated the sheep and sold them to Knox. After the Civil War, Lee sued Knox for the purchase price of the sheep. When the trial court ruled that Knox was liable, he offered to pay his debt in paper currency. Lee insisted that the debt be paid in gold and silver coin, which after the Civil War were worth far more than the face value of the greenbacks the United States had printed. The trial court rejected her claim and permitted Knox to pay his debt in paper notes. Both Knox and Lee appealed to the Supreme Court. Knox insisted he should not be held responsible for the Confederate decision to confiscate the sheep. Lee maintained that she should either be paid in gold and silver, or in the actual dollars equal to the value of the sheep in gold and silver.

The Supreme Court in The Legal Tender Cases *overruled* Hepburn v. Griswold. *Justice William Strong's opinion declared that persons gained no legally enforceable property rights when they purchased the goods of loyal citizens that were confiscated by the Confederacy and that the government could require creditors to take paper currency, even an inflated paper currency, as payment for debts.* The Legal Tender Cases *were decided by a narrow 5–4 majority. That majority was soon augmented by additional Republican appointees to the Supreme Court. Justice Field was eventually the last member on the bench from the* Hepburn *majority. Field's retirement in 1897 ended for all practical purposes the constitutional attack on making paper money legal tender.*

JUSTICE STRONG delivered the opinion of the Court.

. . .

It would be difficult to overestimate the consequences which must follow our decision. They will affect the entire business of the country, and take hold of the possible continued existence of the government. If it be held by this court that Congress has no constitutional power, under any circumstances, or in any emergency, to make treasury notes a legal tender for the payment of all debts (a power confessedly possessed by every independent sovereignty other than the United States), the government is without those means of self-preservation which, all must admit, may, in certain contingencies, become indispensable, even if they were not when the acts of Congress now called in question were enacted. It is also clear that if we hold the acts invalid as applicable to debts incurred, or transactions which have taken place since their enactment, our decision must cause, throughout the country, great business derangement, widespread distress, and the rankest injustice. . . .

The consequences of which we have spoken, serious as they are, must be accepted, if there is a clear incompatibility between the Constitution and the legal tender acts. But we are unwilling to precipitate them upon the country unless such an incompatibility plainly appears. A decent respect for a coordinate branch of the government demands that the judiciary should presume, until the contrary is clearly shown, that there has been no transgression of power by Congress. . . . Such has always been the rule. . . .

Nor can it be questioned that, when investigating the nature and extent of the powers, conferred by the Constitution upon Congress, it is indispensable to keep in view the objects for which those powers were granted.... In no other way can the intent of the framers of the instrument be discovered....

...

And here it is to be observed it is not indispensable to the existence of any power claimed for the Federal government that it can be found specified in the words of the Constitution, or clearly and directly traceable to some one of the specified powers. Its existence may be deduced fairly from more than one of the substantive powers expressly defined, or from them all combined. It is allowable to group together any number of them and infer from them all that the power claimed has been conferred....

...

[T]he whole history of the government and of congressional legislation has exhibited the use of a very wide discretion, even in times of peace and in the absence of any trying emergency, in the selection of the necessary and proper means to carry into effect the great objects for which the government was framed, and this discretion has generally been unquestioned, or, if questioned, sanctioned by this court. This is true not only when an attempt has been made to execute a single power specifically given, but equally true when the means adopted have been appropriate to the execution, not of a single authority, but of all the powers created by the Constitution. Under the power to establish post-offices and post-roads Congress has provided for carrying the mails, punishing theft of letters and mail robberies, and even for transporting the mails to foreign countries. Under the power to regulate commerce, provision has been made by law for the improvement of harbors, the establishment of observatories, the erection of lighthouses, break-waters, and buoys, the registry, enrolment, and construction of ships, and a code has been enacted for the government of seamen....

...

It was...in *McCulloch v. Maryland* (1819) that the fullest consideration was given to this clause of the Constitution granting auxiliary powers, and a construction adopted that has ever since been accepted as determining its true meaning.... [T]his court then held that the sound construction of the Constitution must allow to the national legislature that discretion with respect to the means by which the powers it confers are to be carried into execution, which will enable that body to perform the high duties assigned to it in the manner most beneficial to the people....

With these rules of constitutional construction before us, settled at an early period in the history of the government, hitherto universally accepted, and not even now doubted, we have a safe guide to a right decision of the questions before us. Before we can hold the legal tender acts unconstitutional, we must be convinced they were not appropriate means, or means conducive to the execution of any or all of the powers of Congress, or of the government, not appropriate in any degree (for we are not judges of the degree of appropriateness), or we must hold that they were prohibited....

...

It may be conceded that Congress is not authorized to enact laws in furtherance even of a legitimate end, merely because they are useful, or because they make the government stronger. There must be some relation between the means and the end; some adaptedness or appropriateness of the laws to carry into execution the powers created by the Constitution. But when a statute has proved effective in the execution of powers confessedly existing, it is not too much to say that it must have had some appropriateness to the execution of those powers....

...[W]e proceed to inquire whether it was forbidden by the letter or spirit of the Constitution.... To assert...that the clause enabling Congress to coin money and regulate its value tacitly implies a denial of all other power over the currency of the nation, is an attempt to introduce a new rule of construction against the solemn decisions of this court. So far from its containing a lurking prohibition, many have thought it was intended to confer upon Congress that general power over the currency which has always been an acknowledged attribute of sovereignty in every other civilized nation than our own, especially when considered in connection with the other clause which denies to the States the power to coin money, emit bills of credit, or make anything but gold and silver coin a tender in payment of debts....

...

We come next to the argument much used, and, indeed, the main reliance of those who assert the unconstitutionality of the legal tender acts. It is that they are prohibited by the spirit of the Constitution because they indirectly impair the obligation of contracts.... The argument assumes two things,—first, that the acts do, in effect, impair the obligation of contracts, and second, that Congress is prohibited from taking any action which may indirectly have that effect.... We have been asked whether Congress can declare that a contract to deliver a quantity of grain may be satisfied by the tender of a less quantity. Undoubtedly not. But this is a false analogy. There is a wide distinction between a tender of quantities, or of specific articles, and a tender of legal values. Contracts for the delivery of specific articles belong exclusively to the domain of State legislation, while contracts for the payment of money are subject to the authority of Congress, at least so far as relates to the means of payment. They are engagements to pay with lawful money of the United States, and Congress is empowered to regulate that money. It cannot, therefore, be maintained that the legal tender acts impaired the obligation of contracts.

...

Closely allied to the objection we have just been considering is the argument pressed upon us that the legal tender acts were prohibited by the spirit of the Fifth Amendment, which forbids taking private property for public use without just compensation or due process of law. That provision has always been understood as referring only to a direct appropriation, and not to consequential injuries resulting from the exercise of lawful power. It has never been supposed to have any bearing upon, or to inhibit laws that indirectly work harm and loss to individuals. A new tariff, an embargo, a draft, or a war may inevitably bring upon individuals great losses; may, indeed, render valuable property almost valueless. They may destroy the worth of contracts....

...

But, without extending our remarks further, it will be seen that we hold the acts of Congress constitutional as applied to contracts made either before or after their passage. In so holding, we overrule so much of what was decided in *Hepburn v. Griswold*, as ruled the acts unwarranted by the Constitution so far as they apply to contracts made before their enactment. That case was decided by a divided court, and by a court having a less number of judges than the law then in existence provided this court shall have. These cases have been heard before a full court, and they have received our most careful consideration. The questions involved are constitutional questions of the most vital importance to the government and to the public at large. We have been in the habit of treating cases involving a consideration of constitutional power differently from those which concern merely private right. We are not accustomed to hear them in the absence of a full court, if it can be avoided. Even in cases involving only private rights, if convinced we had made a mistake, we would hear another argument and correct our error. And it is no unprecedented thing in courts of last resort, both in this country and in England, to overrule decisions previously made. We agree this should not be done inconsiderately, but in a case of such far-reaching consequences as the present, thoroughly convinced as we are that Congress has not transgressed its powers, we regard it as our duty so to decide and to affirm both these judgments.

...

JUSTICE BRADLEY, concurring.

...

The doctrine so long contended for, that the Federal Union was a mere compact of States, and that the States, if they chose, might annul or disregard the acts of the National legislature, or might secede from the Union at their pleasure, and that the General government had no power to coerce them into submission to the Constitution, should be regarded as definitely and forever overthrown. This has been finally effected by the National power, as it had often been before, by overwhelming argument.

...

Such being the character of the General government, it seems to be a self-evident proposition that it is invested with all those inherent and implied powers which, at the time of adopting the Constitution, were generally considered to belong to every government as such, and as being essential to the exercise of its functions....

...

...[T]he historical fact [is] that when the Constitution was adopted, the employment of bills of credit was deemed a legitimate means of meeting the exigencies of a regularly constituted government, and that the affixing to them of the quality of a legal tender was regarded as entirely discretionary with the legislature....

...

This power is entirely distinct from that of coining money and regulating the value thereof. It is not only embraced in the power to make all necessary auxiliary laws, but it is incidental to the power of borrowing money. It is often a necessary means of anticipating and realizing promptly the national resources, when, perhaps, promptness is necessary to the national existence....

...

No one supposes that these government certificates are never to be paid—that the day of specie payments is never to return. And it matters not in what form they are issued.... But it is the prerogative of the legislative department to determine when the fit time for payment has come. It may be long delayed, perhaps many may think it too long after the exigency has passed. But the abuse of a power, if proven, is no argument against its existence. And the courts are not responsible therefore. Questions of political expediency belong to the legislative halls, not to the judicial forum....

...

It is absolutely essential to independent national existence that government should have a firm hold on the two great sovereign instrumentalities of the sword and the purse, and the right to wield them without restriction on occasions of national peril. In certain emergencies government must have at its command, not only the personal services—the bodies and lives—of its citizens, but the lesser, though not less essential, power of absolute control over the resources of the country....

...

But the creditor interest will lose some of its gold! Is gold the one thing needful? Is it worse for the creditor to lose a little by depreciation than everything by the bankruptcy of his debtor? Nay, is it worse than to lose everything by the subversion of the government? What is it that protects him in the accumulation and possession of his wealth? Is it not the government and its laws? And can he not consent to trust that government for a brief period until it shall have vindicated its right to exist? All property and all rights, even those of liberty and life, are held subject to the fundamental condition of being liable to be impaired by providential calamities and national vicissitudes.... There are times when the exigencies of the state rightly absorb all subordinate considerations of private interest, convenience, or feeling....

...

I do not say that it is a war power, or that it is only to be called into exercise in time of war; for other public exigencies may arise in the history of a nation which may make it expedient and imperative to exercise it. But of the occasions when, and of the times how long, it shall be exercised and in force, it is for the legislative department of the government to judge. Feeling sensibly the judgments and wishes of the people, that department cannot long (if it is proper to suppose that within its sphere it ever can) misunderstand the business interests and just rights of the community.

...

Regarding the question of power as so important to the stability of the government, I cannot acquiesce in the decision of *Hepburn v. Griswold*. I cannot consent that the government should be deprived of one of its just powers by a decision made at the time, and under the circumstances, in which that decision was made.... Where the decision is recent, and is only made by a bare majority of the court, and during a time of public excitement on the subject, when the question has largely entered into the political discussions of the day, I consider it our right and duty to subject it to a further examination, if a majority of the court are dissatisfied with the former decision....

CHIEF JUSTICE SALMON CHASE, dissenting

...

JUSTICE STEPHEN FIELD, dissenting

...

B. Federal Power to Enforce Civil Rights

The national government gained important new constitutional powers immediately after the Civil War. The last sections of the Thirteenth, Fourteenth, and Fifteenth Amendments declare, "Congress shall have power to enforce this article by appropriate legislation." Congress immediately exercised that authority.

- The Freedmen's Bureau Act of 1866 provided former slaves and other refugees with land and educational opportunities.
- The Civil Rights Act of 1866 forbade states from engaging in race discrimination when passing or enforcing contract, property, or criminal laws.
- The Enforcement Act of 1870 prohibited private conspiracies to deny persons the right to vote and other privileges and immunities of United States citizenship.
- The Ku Klux Klan Act of 1871 provided both criminal and civil sanctions for private persons who deprived other persons of their constitutional rights.
- The Civil Rights Act of 1875 prohibited inns, public conveyances, and places of public amusement from engaging in racial discrimination.

The scope of the congressional power to enforce the post–Civil War Amendments has been controversial since their ratification. Read narrowly, these provisions do little more than empower Congress to provide remedies for persons deprived of judicially identified constitutional rights. Courts determine the legal meaning of slavery. Congress is limited to passing laws that decree the proper punishment for slaveholders and provide remedies for their victims. Read broadly, these provisions empower Congress to pass whatever measures legislative majorities believe will eradicate slavery, promote fundamental rights, and bring about a more egalitarian society. Congress might enforce the Thirteenth and Fourteenth Amendments by mandating that states provide all children with an adequate education, even if a court in an ordinary lawsuit might not be authorized to find a constitutional right to an education. The federal statute might nevertheless be constitutional if Congress determined that slave children were not educated, that persons have a fundamental right to an education, or that educated persons are better able to protect their constitutional rights.

Controversies over the congressional power to enforce the post–Civil War amendments broke out immediately after these amendments were ratified. Republican political leaders insisted that each statute listed previously was a legitimate exercise of national power under the post–Civil War Amendments. Democrats claimed that each bill went far beyond enforcing the rights protected by the Thirteenth, Fourteenth and Fifteenth Amendments. Over time, more Republicans became increasingly sympathetic to narrower interpretations of the congressional power granted by the Thirteenth, Fourteenth, and Fifteenth Amendments. Senator Lyman Trumbull of Illinois was the leading sponsor of the Civil Rights Act of 1866 and a leading opponent of the Enforcement Act of 1870. Republican opposition doomed efforts to place a ban on school segregation in the Civil Rights Act of 1875.

The Supreme Court at the end of Reconstruction imposed limits on Congressional power to enforce the post–Civil War Amendments. In *United States v. Reese* (1875), the Supreme Court quashed an indictment against several election judges in Kentucky who refused to allow an African-American to cast a ballot. Chief Justice Morrison Waite's majority opinion declared unconstitutional the provision in the Enforcement Act of 1870 authorizing punishments for "any person who shall . . . hinder, delay, prevent, or obstruct, any citizen . . . from voting at any election." This was not "appropriate legislation" under the Fifteenth Amendment, he declared, because "It is only when the wrongful refusal at such an election is because of race, color, or previous condition of servitude that Congress can interfere and provide for its punishment."

When reading the following excerpts, consider the extent to which Republican proponents of civil rights measures relied on the first section of the Thirteenth, Fourteenth and Fifteenth Amendments and the extent to which their arguments relied on the last section of these amendments. To what extent were Republicans claiming that they were merely protecting rights that were also judicially enforceable? To what extent were they relying on a special congressional power to enforce the post–Civil War Amendments?

Senate Debate over the Civil Rights Act of 1866[24]

The Civil Rights Act of 1866 was designed to outlaw the Black Codes passed by southern legislatures in the wake of the Thirteenth Amendment and guarantee civic equality to persons of color. The crucial provision of the measure required that persons of color enjoy the same rights and liberties "for the security of persons and property as is enjoyed by white citizens." This guarantee nullified laws enacted by southern legislatures immediately after the Civil War that limited African-American employment and housing opportunities, restricted their rights to testify in courts, and provided special punishments when they were convicted of criminal offenses. Persons of color who claimed that their rights were violated could remove lawsuits from state to federal courts, where they were more likely to gain a sympathetic hearing. The Civil Rights Act of 1866 did not outlaw all forms of racial discrimination. Such radical Republicans as Charles Sumner failed to convince fellow partisans to include voting rights in the Civil Rights Act or pass additional legislation enfranchising free persons of color. Most Republicans agreed that the measure did not prohibit laws banning interracial marriages.

Republicans and Democrats engaged in a lengthy partisan dispute over whether the Civil Rights Act of 1866 was constitutional. President Johnson, when vetoing the measure on March 27, 1866, complained that the bill was "an absorption and assumption of power by the General Government which, if acquiesced in, must sap and destroy our federative

24. Excerpt taken from *Congressional Globe*, 39th Cong., 1st Sess. (1866).

system of limited powers, and break down the barriers which preserve the rights of the States."

> *Hitherto every subject embraced in the enumeration of rights contained in this bill has been considered as exclusively belonging to the States. They all relate to the internal police and economy of the respective States. They are matters which in each State concern the domestic condition of its people, varying in each according to its own peculiar circumstances and the safety and well-being of its own citizens. I do not mean to say that upon all these subjects there are not federal restraints—as, for instance, in the State power of legislation over contracts.... If it be granted that Congress can repeal all State laws discriminating between whites and blacks in the subjects covered by this bill, why, it may be asked, may not Congress repeal, in the same way, all State laws discriminating between the two races on the subject of suffrage and office?...*
>
> ...
>
> *...It cannot...be justly claimed that, with a view to the enforcement of this article of the Constitution [the Thirteenth Amendment], there is at present any necessity for the exercise of all the powers which this bill confers. Slavery has been abolished, and at present nowhere exists within the jurisdiction of the United States; nor has there been, nor is likely there will be, any attempt to revive it by the people or the States. If, however, any such attempt shall be made, it will then become the duty of the General Government to exercise any and all incidental powers necessary and proper to maintain inviolate this great constitutional law of freedom.*[25]

Several weeks later, Senator Lyman Trumbull responded that the Civil Rights Act was well within the powers granted to Congress by the Thirteenth Amendment.

> *Whatever may have been the opinion of the President at one time as to "good faith requiring the security of the freedmen in their liberty and their property" it is now manifest from the character of his objections to this bill that he will approve no measure that will accomplish the object. That the second clause of the [Thirteenth] Amendment gives this power there can be no question. Some have contended that it gives the power even to confer the right of suffrage. I have not thought so, because I have never thought suffrage any more necessary to the liberty of a freedman than of a non-voting white, whether child or female. But his liberty under the Constitution he is entitled to, and whatever is necessary to secure it to him he is entitled to have, be it the ballot or the bayonet. If the bill now before us, and which goes no further than to secure civil rights to the freedman, cannot be passed, then the constitutional amendment proclaiming freedom to all the inhabitants of the land is a cheat and a delusion.*[26]

A two-thirds majority in both the House of Representatives and the Senate almost immediately overrode Johnson's veto. This was the first veto override on an important piece of legislation in American history.

The Civil Rights Act of 1866 sought to protect the rights of free persons of color by intertwining those rights with the rights of white persons. Rather than declare that persons of color have certain substantive rights, the law declares that persons of color will enjoy the same rights as white persons. This was thought to guarantee a robust set of rights and liberties because white voters could restrict the liberty of persons of color only by restricting their liberty to the same degree. What do you think of this strategy for using equal protection to protect substantive rights? Is this strategy likely to be an effective means for protecting the rights of persons who cannot vote? If you were in Congress in 1866, would you have reluctantly settled for "half a loaf" or would you have insisted that the Civil Rights Act include voting rights?

Republican Congressman John Bingham was one of the few Republicans who thought Congress did not have power under the Thirteenth Amendment to pass the Civil Rights Act of 1866. Bingham would soon become one of the major architects of the Fourteenth Amendment. How should his speech on the Civil Rights Act influence interpretation of both post–Civil War Amendments?

Senator LYMAN TRUMBULL (Republican, Illinois)

...

Mr. President, I regard the bill to which the attention of the Senate is now called as the most important measure that has been under its consideration since the adoption of the constitutional amendment abolishing slavery. That amendment declared that all persons in the United States should be free. This measure is

25. *A Compilation of the Messages and Papers of the Presidents*, ed. James D. Richardson, vol. 6 (Washington, DC: Government Printing Office, 1897), 405.

26. *Congressional Globe*, 39th Cong., 1st Sess., 1761.

intended to give effect to that declaration and secure to all persons within the United States practical freedom. There is very little importance in the general declaration of abstract truths and principles unless they can be carried into effect, unless the persons who are to be affected by them have some means of availing themselves of their benefits.... [O]f what avail will it now be that the Constitution of the United States has declared that slavery shall not exist, if in the late slaveholding States laws are to be enacted and enforced depriving persons of African descent of privileges which are essential to freemen?

...

...[T]he question will arise, has Congress authority to pass such a bill? Has Congress authority to give practical effect to the great declaration that slavery shall not exist in the United States? If it has not, then nothing has been accomplished by the adoption of the constitutional amendment....

...

[U]nder the constitutional amendment which we have now adopted, and which declares that slavery shall no longer exist, and which authorizes Congress by appropriate legislation to carry this provision into effect, I hold that we have a right to pass any law which, in our judgment, is deemed appropriate, and which will accomplish the end in view, secure freedom to all people in the United States. The various State laws to which I have referred—and there are many others—although they do not make a man an absolute slave, yet deprive him of the rights of a freeman; and it is perhaps difficult to draw the precise line, to say where freedom ceases and slavery begins, but a law that does not allow a colored person to go from one county to another is certainly a law in derogation of the rights of a freeman. A law that does not allow a colored person to hold property, does not allow him to teach, does not allow him to preach, is certainly a law in violation of the rights of a freeman, and being so may properly be declared void.

...

Senator CHARLES SUMNER (Republican, Massachusetts)

...Whatever legislation seems "appropriate" to "enforce" the abolition of Slavery, whatever means seem proper to this end, must be within the powers of Congress under the Constitutional Amendment. You cannot deny this principle without setting aside those most remarkable judgments which stand as landmarks of constitutional history. But who can doubt that the abolition of the whole Black Code, in all its oligarchical pretensions, civil and political, is "appropriate" to "enforce" the abolition of Slavery? Mark the language of the grant. Congress may "enforce" abolition, and nobody can question the "means" it thinks best to employ. Let it not hesitate to adopt the "means" that promise to be most effective. As the occasion is extraordinary, so the "means" employed must be extraordinary.

But the Senate has already by solemn vote affirmed this very jurisdiction. You have, Sir, decreed that blacks shall enjoy the same civil rights as whites,—in other words, that with regard to civil rights there shall be no oligarchy, aristocracy, caste, or monopoly, but that all shall be equal before the law, without distinction of color. And this great decree you have made, as "appropriate legislation" under the Constitutional Amendment, to "enforce" the abolition of Slavery. Surely you have not erred. Beyond all question, the protection of the colored race in civil rights is essential to complete the abolition of Slavery; but the protection of the colored race in political rights is not less essential, and the power is as ample in one case as in the other. In each you legislate for the maintenance of that Liberty so tardily accorded, and the legislation is just as "appropriate" in one case as in the other. Protection in civil rights by Act of Congress will be a great event. It will be great in itself. It will be greater still, because it establishes the power of Congress, without further amendment of the National Constitution, to protect every citizen in all his rights, including of course the elective franchise....

...

Senator EDGAR COWAN (Republican, Pennsylvania)

...Where do we get the power to pass this bill? From what clause of the Constitution is it extracted? Where is it? Has anybody satisfied this Senator, or that one, or all of them, that there is such a power in the Constitution?

What is the fair construction of that amendment of the Constitution abolishing slavery? That amendment declares that "neither slavery nor involuntary servitude, except as a punishment for crime whereof the party shall have been duly convicted...shall exist within the United States or any place subject to its jurisdiction." What was the slavery mentioned there? What was the involuntary servitude mentioned there? Was it the service that was due from the minor to his parent? Was it the right the husband had to the services of his wife? Nobody can pretend that those things were within the purview of that amendment; nobody believes it....The true meaning and intent of that amendment was simply to abolish negro slavery. That was the whole of it. What did it give to the negro? It abolished his slavery. Wherein did his slavery consist? It consisted in the restraint that another man had over his liberty, and the right that that other had to take the proceeds of his labor. This amendment deprived the master of that right, and conferred it upon the negro. What more did it do? Nothing, by the terms of it, and nobody can construe its terms to extend it beyond that. It gave to the negro that which is described in the elementary books as the right of personal liberty. What is that right of personal liberty? The right to go wherever one pleases without restraint or hindrance on the part of any other person.

That is followed by a subsequent clause, in which, it is stated that Congress shall have a right to enforce this provision by "appropriate legislation." What is the appropriate legislation? The appropriate legislation is that legislation which allows a personal liberty to the negro and prevents anybody from restraining him in that liberty....

...

...I suppose it will not be pretended by any lawyer in the world that the subject-matter of that amendment extended to anybody but slaves. We have seen that it did not extend to minors, it did not extend to apprentices, it did not extend to married women. We know that it did not extend to anybody who before that time was free. Did anybody ever suppose that it had any operation whatever upon the *status* of the free negro, a negro who was born free or who had been emancipated ten years before it was passed? Certainly not. Nobody ever dreamed of such a thing. Its operation was wholly confined to the slave; it made the slave free; it did not affect anybody else except the master by depriving him of his slave.

Now what does this bill do? This bill, pretending to be based upon the amendment of the Constitution, whose subject-matter was slaves, and which cannot be extended beyond that, proposes to legislate for a very large number of persons who were not slaves, and who were not within its purview or its operation. I mean this bill purports to give power to Congress to legislate in regard to free negroes and mulattoes. To my mind that is as clear and conclusive an objection to it upon the score of constitutionality as ever was made to a bill in the world. However constitutional it might be with regard to the emancipated slave, clearly it is as unconstitutional to all other people not embraced within that amendment.

Civil Rights Act of 1866[27]

An Act to Protect All Persons in the United States in their Civil Rights, and Furnish the Means for the Vindication

Be it Enacted...That all persons born in the United States and not subject to any foreign power, excluding Indians, not taxed, are hereby declared to be citizens of the United States; and such citizens of every race and color, without regard to any previous condition of slavery or involuntary servitude, except as a punishment for crime whereof the party shall have been duly convicted, shall have the same right in every State and Territory in the United States to make and enforce contracts; to sue, be parties, and give evidence; to inherit, purchase, lease, sell, hold, and convey real and personal property; and to full and equal benefit of all laws and proceedings for the security of persons and property as is enjoyed by white citizens, and shall be subject to like punishment, pains, and penalties, and to none other, any law, statute, ordinance, regulation, or custom, to the contrary notwithstanding.

...

SEC. 3. That the district courts of the United States, within their respective districts, shall have, exclusively of the courts of the several States, cognizance of all crimes and offenses committed against the provisions of this act, and also, concurrently with the circuit courts of the United States, of all causes, civil and criminal, affecting persons who are denied or cannot enforce in the courts or judicial tribunals of the State or locality where they may be any of the rights secured to them by the first section of this act; and if any suit or prosecution, civil or criminal, has been or shall be commenced in any State court against any such person, for any cause whatsoever, or against any officer, civil or military, or other person, for any arrest or imprisonment, trespasses, or wrongs done or committed by virtue or under color of authority derived from this act...such defendant shall have the right to remove such cases for trial to the proper district or circuit court....

27. Excerpt taken from Civil Rights Act of 1866, 14 Stat. 27 (1866).

IV. Federalism

MAJOR DEVELOPMENTS

- Americans debate the constitutionality of secession.
- Americans debate the constitutional status of those states that seceded from the Union.
- The Supreme Court declares that the United States is an "indestructible Union, composed of indestructible States."

Both the Civil War and Reconstruction raised fundamental questions about the relationship between the states and the federal government. The central question at the heart of the Civil War was whether secession was constitutional. The central question at the heart of Reconstruction was the extent to which the Civil War changed the relationship between the states and the federal government. The debates over these issues combined appeals to shared constitutional norms and appeals to political advantage. Southerners who endorsed secession sought to justify their actions in terms of the compact theory they believed underlay the Declaration of Independence and the Constitution of 1787. Northern proponents of Radical Reconstruction sought to refashion southern society in terms of the organic nationalism they believed underlay the Declaration of Independence and the Constitution of 1787. While political actors made references to these high political principles, they always kept in mind the perceived beneficiaries of increased national or state power. Southerners became more committed and northerners less committed to federalism when control of national institutions shifted from the slave to the free states.

A. Secession

The idea of secession was nothing new in 1860. Some prominent Federalists during the War of 1812 suggested that New England states might justifiably leave the Union. Prominent southerners threatened secession during the debates over the Compromise of 1850. Still, disunion from 1789 to 1860 tended to be an abstract possibility, a political threat, or a flight of rhetorical fancy.

Abraham Lincoln's election to the presidency in 1860 changed the constitutional debate over secession. The prospect of disunion became immediate and real. The election of a Republican president dedicated to the antislavery cause was of immediate concern to southern slave states. More broadly, the election of 1860 indicated that the era of national coalitions committed to satisfying the demands of slaveholding interests was over. Many southerners and their political allies feared that the Republican majority would promote only northern interests. New York's Samuel Tilden expressed the common viewpoint of Jacksonian party leaders on the eve of Lincoln's election: "If such an organization as the Republican Party should acquire complete possession of the federative government, what sort of system would it be? To the people of the fifteen States it would be a foreign government.... None of their citizens would have concurred in bringing the Administration into existence; none of their public opinion would be represented in that Administration." "Inevitable disunion," Tilden feared, would be the result.[28] The price of union for slaveholders seemed too high if they were consigned to being a permanent minority.

The following excerpts include both general arguments about secession in a democratic system of government and specific arguments about the legitimacy of secession in the particular circumstances of 1861. As you read, consider both the specific political and constitutional arguments concerning the secession of the southern states, but also think about the broader theoretical possibility of secession. Is secession ever justified? Is there a constitutionally appropriate procedure for legitimate secession? Could a right and process for secession be included in a constitutional text? Suppose the constitutional differences between the north and the south reflected the differences between an increasingly industrial society and an agrarian society. Would secession have been justified in this circumstance?

South Carolina Ordinance of Secession (1860)[29]

South Carolina seceded from the Union almost immediately after Abraham Lincoln won the 1860 presidential election.

28. Samuel J. Tilden, *The Writings and Speeches of Samuel J. Tilden*, ed. John Bigelow, vol. 1 (New York: Harper and Brothers, 1885), 292, 297.

29. Excerpt taken from *Declaration of the Immediate Causes Which Induce and Justify the Secession of South Carolina From the Federal Union and the Ordinance of Secession* (Charleston: Evans & Cogswell, 1860).

Secession ordinances were soon adopted in Florida, Mississippi, Georgia, Alabama, Louisiana, and Texas. Virginia, North Carolina, Arkansas, and Tennessee adopted secession ordinances after the military action at Fort Sumter. Substantial secession sentiment existed in Maryland, Kentucky, and Missouri, but through a combination of political and military maneuvering, unionist forces maintained control in those states. "I want God on my side," Lincoln declared before the Civil War, "but I must have Kentucky."[30]

That South Carolina was the first state to secede is not surprising. Politically and economically dominated by large plantation owners, South Carolina had the highest proportion of slaves to citizens of any state in the union. South Carolina politicians and activists had long been the leading voices of disunionist and proslavery sentiment. John C. Calhoun, Robert Barnwell Rhett, George McDuffie, James Henry Hammond, and other South Carolinians instigated many antebellum controversies between the North and the South.

The South Carolina Secession Ordinance relied on both appeals to natural law and appeals to constitutional right. The argument from natural law relied on the natural right of revolution articulated in the Declaration of Independence. The argument from the Constitution built on the Jeffersonian commitment to the compact theory of the federal government. South Carolinians who relied on compact theory emphasized the "secession" of the states in 1787 from the union created by the Articles of Confederation and the unenumerated, reserved powers of the states recognized in the Tenth Amendment.

Declaration of the Immediate Causes Which Induce and Justify the Secession of South Carolina from the Federal Union

. . .

In the year 1765, that portion of the British Empire embracing Great Britain, undertook to make laws for the government of that portion composed of the thirteen American Colonies. A struggle for the right of self-government ensued, which resulted, on the 4th of July, 1776, in a Declaration, by the Colonies, "that they are, and of right ought to be, FREE AND INDEPENDENT STATES; and that, as free and independent States, they have full power to levy war, conclude peace, contract alliances, establish commerce, and to do all other acts and things which independent States may of right do."

They further solemnly declared that whenever any "form of government becomes destructive of the ends for which it was established, it is the right of the people to alter or abolish it, and to institute a new government."...

In pursuance of this Declaration of Independence, each of the thirteen States proceeded to exercise its separate sovereignty.... For purposes of defense, they united their arms and their counsels; and, in 1778, they entered into a League known as the Articles of Confederation, whereby they agreed to entrust the administration of their external relations to a common agent, known as the Congress of the United States, expressly declaring, in the first Article "that each State retains its sovereignty, freedom and independence, and every power, jurisdiction and right which is not, by this Confederation, expressly delegated to the United States in Congress assembled."

. . .

The parties to whom th[e] Constitution was submitted, were the several sovereign States; they were to agree or disagree, and when nine of them agreed the compact was to take effect among those concurring; and the General Government, as the common agent, was then invested with their authority.

If only nine of the thirteen States had concurred, the other four would have remained as they then were—separate, sovereign States, independent of any of the provisions of the Constitution....

By this Constitution, certain duties were imposed upon the several States, and the exercise of certain of their powers was restrained, which necessarily implied their continued existence as sovereign States. But to remove all doubt, an amendment was added, which declared that the powers not delegated to the United States by the Constitution, nor prohibited by it to the States, are reserved to the States, respectively, or to the people....

. . .

We hold that the Government thus established is subject to the two great principles asserted in the Declaration of Independence; and we hold further, that the mode of its formation subjects it to a third fundamental principle, namely: the law of compact. We maintain that in every compact between two or more parties, the obligation is mutual; that the failure of one of the contracting parties to perform a material part of the agreement, entirely releases the obligation of the other; and that where no arbiter is provided, each party is

30. Lowell Harrison, *Lincoln of Kentucky* (Lexington: University Press of Kentucky, 2000).

remitted to his own judgment to determine the fact of failure, with all its consequences.

In the present case, that fact is established with certainty. We assert that fourteen of the States have deliberately refused, for years past, to fulfill their constitutional obligations, and we refer to their own Statutes for the proof.

The Constitution of the United States, in its fourth Article, provides as follows: "No person held to service or labor in one State, under the laws thereof, escaping into another, shall, in consequence of any law or regulation therein, be discharged from such service or labor, but shall be delivered up, on claim of the party to whom such service or labor may be due."

This stipulation was so material to the compact, that without it that compact would not have been made....

...

...For many years these laws were executed. But an increasing hostility on the part of the non-slaveholding States to the institution of slavery, has led to a disregard of their obligations, and the laws of the General Government have ceased to effect the objects of the Constitution...Thus the constituted compact has been deliberately broken and disregarded by the non-slaveholding States, and the consequence follows that South Carolina is released from her obligation.

...

For twenty-five years this agitation has been steadily increasing, until it has now secured to its aid the power of the common Government. Observing the forms of the Constitution, a sectional party has found within that Article establishing the Executive Department, the means of subverting the Constitution itself. A geographical line has been drawn across the Union, and all the States north of that line have united in the election of a man to the high office of President of the United States, whose opinions and purposes are hostile to slavery. He is to be entrusted with the administration of the common Government, because he has declared that that "Government cannot endure permanently half slave, half free," and that the public mind must rest in the belief that slavery is in the course of ultimate extinction.

...

On the 4th day of March next, this party will take possession of the Government. It has announced that the South shall be excluded from the common territory, that the judicial tribunals shall be made sectional, and that a war must be waged against slavery until it shall cease throughout the United States.

The guaranties of the Constitution will then no longer exist; the equal rights of the States will be lost. The slaveholding States will no longer have the power of self-government, or self-protection, and the Federal Government will have become their enemy.

...

We, therefore, the People of South Carolina, by our delegates in Convention assembled, appealing to the Supreme Judge of the world for the rectitude of our intentions, have solemnly declared that the Union heretofore existing between this State and the other States of North America, is dissolved, and that the State of South Carolina has resumed her position among the nations of the world, as a separate and independent State; with full power to levy war, conclude peace, contract alliances, establish commerce, and to do all other acts and things which independent States may of right do.

Jeremiah Black, **Opinion on the Power of the President in Executing the Laws** (1860)[31]

James Buchanan was the first president who confronted secession. Seven southern states withdrew from the Union after Lincoln's election but before his inauguration. Previous Jacksonian Democrats had been both pro-slavery and pro-Union. President Andrew Jackson urged Congress to prohibit persons from sending abolitionist materials in the mail, but threatened to use military force when faced with South Carolina's nullification movement. Buchanan amply demonstrated his commitment to the pro-slavery cause during his administration, most notably by vigorously championing a disputed pro-slavery constitution in the Kansas territory. Buchanan's response to the secession crisis of 1860 was much more tepid. In sharp contrast to Jackson's behavior in the nullification crisis, Buchanan during the secession crisis emphasized that the president should not predetermine how events play out before Congress took a stand on the issue. His main goal was to prevent a civil war from breaking out during the last weeks of his presidency. Buchanan explained in his final state of the union address,

> *the Executive has no authority to decide what shall be the relations between the Federal Government and South Carolina. He has been invested with no such discretion. He possesses no power to change the relations heretofore*

31. Excerpt taken from 9 Op. Atty. Gen. 516 (November 20, 1860).

existing between them, much less to acknowledge the independence of that State. This would be to invest a mere executive officer with the power of recognizing the dissolution of the Confederacy among our thirty-three sovereign States. It bears no resemblance to the recognition of a foreign de facto government—involving no such responsibility. Any attempt to do this would, on his part, be a naked act of usurpation. It is therefore my duty to submit to Congress the whole question in all its bearings.[32]

Several weeks before giving that address, Buchanan delivered a message to Congress expressing his official opinion of the president's constitutional role in the crisis. That message was actually written by Attorney General Jeremiah Black, who had emerged as a powerful anti-secessionist voice within Buchanan's cabinet. Buchanan and Black opposed secession. Nevertheless, both were convinced that the president could not launch an offensive war against the seceding states.

...

The existing laws put and keep the Federal Government strictly on the defensive. You can use force only to repel an assault on the public property, and aid the courts in the performance of their duty....

If one of the States should declare her independence, your action cannot depend upon the rightfulness of the cause upon which such declaration is based. Whether the retirement of a State from the Union be the exercise of a right reserved in the Constitution, or a revolutionary movement, it is certain that you have not in either case the authority to recognize the independence or to absolve her from her federal obligations. Congress, or the other States in convention assembled, must take such measures as may be necessary and proper....

Whether Congress has the constitutional right to make war against one or more States, and require the Executive of the Federal Government to carry it on by means of force to be drawn from the other States, is a question for Congress itself to consider. It must be admitted that no such power is expressly given, nor are there any words in the Constitution which imply it....Our forefathers do not seem to have thought that war was calculated "to form a more perfect union, establish justice, insure domestic tranquility, provide for the common defense, promote the general welfare, and secure the blessings of liberty to ourselves and our posterity." There was undoubtedly a strong and universal conviction among the men who framed and ratified the Constitution, that military force would not only be useless, but pernicious, as a means of holding the States together.

If it be true that war cannot be declared, nor a system of general hostilities carried on by the Central Government against a State, then it seems to follow that an attempt to do so would be *ipso facto* an expulsion of such State from the Union. Being treated as an alien and an enemy, she would be compelled to act accordingly....

The right of the General Government to preserve itself in its whole constitutional vigor, by repelling a direct and positive aggression upon its property or its officers, cannot be denied. But this is a totally different thing from an offensive war, to punish the people for the political misdeeds of their State Government, or to prevent a threatened violation of the Constitution, or to enforce an acknowledgement that the Government of the United States is supreme. The States are colleagues of one another, and if some of them shall conquer the rest and hold them as subjugated provinces, it would totally destroy the whole theory upon which they are now connected.

If this view of the subject be correct, as I think it is, then the Union must utterly perish at the moment when Congress shall arm one part of the people against another for any purpose beyond that of merely protecting the General Government in the exercise of its proper constitutional function.

Abraham Lincoln, First Inaugural Address (1861)[33]

President Abraham Lincoln agreed with Buchanan that secession was not constitutional, but they sharply disagreed on whether and how the president should respond in the absence of congressional instruction. Lincoln in his first inaugural address asserted that secession had no constitutional foundation. In sharp contrast to Buchanan, who believed that the Republican Party had unconstitution-

32. *The Works of James Buchanan*, ed. James Bassett Moore, vol. 11 (Philadelphia: J. B. Lippincott & Co., 1910), 18.

33. Excerpt taken from *A Compilation of the Messages and Papers of the Presidents*, ed. James D. Richardson, vol. 6 (Washington, DC: Government Printing Office, 1897), 5–12.

ally provoked secession, Lincoln insisted that no legitimate excuse existed for secession. Lincoln maintained that the Government had the power to meet secession with military force. Although for political reasons, Lincoln sought to provoke the South into firing the first shots at Fort Sumter, he had no constitutional qualms about treating secession as inaugurating a civil war.

Lincoln elaborated on the unconstitutionality of secession in his July 4, 1861, address to Congress. That speech declared,

> *Much is said about the "sovereignty" of the States; but the word, even, is not in the national Constitution; nor, as is believed, in any of the State constitutions. What is a "sovereignty," in the political sense of the term? Would it be far wrong to define it "A political community, without a political superior"? Tested by this, no one of our States, except Texas, ever was a sovereignty. And even Texas gave up the character on coming into the Union; by which act, she acknowledged the Constitution of the United States, and the laws and treaties of the United States made in pursuance of the Constitution, to be, for her, the supreme law of the land. The States have their status IN the Union, and they have no other legal status. If they break from this, they can only do so against law, and by revolution. The Union, and not themselves separately, procured their independence, and their liberty. By conquest, or purchase, the Union gave each of them, whatever of independence, and liberty, it has. The Union is older than any of the States; and, in fact, it created them as States. Originally, some dependent colonies made the Union; and, in turn, the Union threw off their old dependence, for them, and made them States, such as they are. Not one of them ever had a State constitution, independent of the Union. Of course, it is not forgotten that all the new States framed their constitutions, before they entered the Union; nevertheless, dependent upon, and preparatory to, coming into the Union.*[34]

Fellow-Citizens of the United States:

. . .

Apprehension seems to exist among the people of the Southern States that by the accession of a Republican Administration their property and their peace and personal security are to be endangered. There has never been any reasonable cause for such apprehension. Indeed, the most ample evidence to the contrary has all the while existed and been open to their inspection. It is found in nearly all the published speeches of him who now addresses you. I do but quote from one of those speeches when I declare that—"I have no purpose, directly or indirectly, to interfere with the institution of slavery in the States where it exists. I believe I have no lawful right to do so, and I have no inclination to do so."

. . .

I hold that in contemplation of universal law and of the Constitution the Union of these States is perpetual. Perpetuity is implied, if not expressed, in the fundamental law of all national governments. It is safe to assert that no government proper ever had a provision in its organic law for its own termination. Continue to execute all the express provisions of our National Constitution, and the Union will endure forever, it being impossible to destroy it except by some action not provided for in the instrument itself.

. . .

Descending from these general principles, we find the proposition that in legal contemplation the Union is perpetual confirmed by the history of the Union itself. The Union is much older than the Constitution. It was formed, in fact, by the Articles of Association in 1774. It was matured and continued by the Declaration of Independence in 1776. It was further matured, and the faith of all the then thirteen States expressly plighted and engaged that it should be perpetual, by the Articles of Confederation in 1778. And finally, in 1787, one of the declared objects for ordaining and establishing the Constitution was "to form a more perfect Union."

But if destruction of the Union by one or by a part only of the States be lawfully possible, the Union is less perfect than before the Constitution, having lost the vital element of perpetuity.

It follows from these views that no State upon its own mere motion can lawfully get out of the Union; that resolves and ordinances to that effect are legally void, and that acts of violence within any State or States against the authority of the United States are insurrectionary or revolutionary, according to circumstances.

. . .

All profess to be content in the Union if all constitutional rights can be maintained. Is it true, then, that any right plainly written in the Constitution has been denied? I think not. Happily, the human mind is so con-

34. *A Compilation of the Messages and Papers of the Presidents*, ed. James D. Richardson, vol. 6 (Washington, DC: Government Printing Office, 1897), 27.

stituted that no party can reach to the audacity of doing this. Think, if you can, of a single instance in which a plainly written provision of the Constitution has ever been denied. If by the mere force of numbers a majority should deprive a minority of any clearly written constitutional right, it might in a moral point of view justify revolution; certainly would if such right were a vital one. But such is not our case. All the vital rights of minorities and of individuals are so plainly assured to them by affirmations and negations, guaranties and prohibitions, in the Constitution that controversies never arise concerning them. But no organic law can ever be framed with a provision specifically applicable to every question which may occur in practical administration. No foresight can anticipate nor any document of reasonable length contain express provisions for all possible questions. Shall fugitives from labor be surrendered by national or by State authority? The Constitution does not expressly say. May Congress prohibit slavery in the Territories? The Constitution does not expressly say. Must Congress protect slavery in the Territories? The Constitution does not expressly say.

From questions of this class spring all our constitutional controversies, and we divide upon them into majorities and minorities. If the minority will not acquiesce, the majority must, or the Government must cease. There is no other alternative, for continuing the Government is acquiescence on one side or the other. If a minority in such case will secede rather than acquiesce, they make a precedent which in turn will divide and ruin them, for a minority of their own will secede from them whenever a majority refuses to be controlled by such minority. For instance, why may not any portion of a new confederacy a year or two hence arbitrarily secede again, precisely as portions of the present Union now claim to secede from it? All who cherish disunion sentiments are now being educated to the exact temper of doing this.

...

Plainly the central idea of secession is the essence of anarchy. A majority held in restraint by constitutional checks and limitations, and always changing easily with deliberate changes of popular opinions and sentiments, is the only true sovereign of a free people. Whoever rejects it does of necessity fly to anarchy or to despotism. Unanimity is impossible. The rule of a minority, as a permanent arrangement, is wholly inadmissible; so that, rejecting the majority principle, anarchy or despotism in some form is all that is left.

...

I am loath to close. We are not enemies, but friends. We must not be enemies. Though passion may have strained it must not break our bonds of affection. The mystic chords of memory, stretching from every battlefield and patriot grave to every living heart and hearthstone all over this broad land, will yet swell the chorus of the Union, when again touched, as surely they will be, by the better angels of our nature.

B. Federalism During the Civil War

Federalism in the North

Conscription and the creation of West Virginia were the most important federalism issues that arose in the North during the Civil War. Some Democrats argued that Lincoln administration policies, most notably the military draft, violated states' rights. The Supreme Court of Pennsylvania in *Kneedler v. Lane I* (1863) declared that the national conscription law was inconsistent with a constitutional commitment to state militia. The Pennsylvania Court reversed that decision the next year in *Kneedler v. Lane II* (1864). More often than not, northern state governors of both parties cooperated with the national government in implementing federal policy. Secession threw into disrepute more extreme challenges to national authority. Arguments that state courts could defy U.S. Supreme Court interpretations of the U.S. Constitution gained little traction in the North during the Civil War era.

Note: The Creation of West Virginia

The constitutional status of West Virginia was the other important constitutional question concerning states' rights that Union officials considered during the Civil War. Republicans and Democratic Unionists who denied the legitimacy of state secession embraced secession within a state when the mountainous northwestern counties of Virginia embarked on a course of action that eventually led to their separation from Virginia and the creation of West Virginia.

Virginia politics had historically been structured by contests for power between the slave-rich eastern counties and the slave-poor western counties. The eastern counties consistently proved more successful, dominating politics in part through gerrymandering and malapportionment. Secession provided another occasion for these sectional disputes. Most Virginians strongly supported secession from the Union after the attack on Fort Sumter. The state's "Ordinance of Secession" was adopted by the delegates to a state convention on April 17, 1861. The people from the northwest counties of the state were strongly opposed to secession. The disappointed pro-Union delegates to the state convention quickly recommended that dissident counties send representatives to a separate constitutional convention in Wheeling, Virginia. This First Wheeling Convention met from May 13 through May 15. The representatives delayed action until the outcome of the popular vote on the Ordinance of Secession. The next week, Virginians voted 132,201 to 37,451 to secede from the Union.

Once the secession ordinance was adopted, a Second Wheeling Convention was convened on June 11. Two days later John Carlile introduced "A Declaration of the People of Virginia." That proposal called for the government of Virginia to be reorganized on the grounds that the existing state officeholders had abandoned their legitimate positions by attempting to secede. The Wheeling Convention debated whether the four northwestern counties should secede from the state or simply re-form the Loyal Government of Virginia. Carlile pointed out that simple secession from the state was not an option. Article IV, Section 3, of the U.S. Constitution provided that "no new states shall be formed or erected within the jurisdiction of any other state...without the consent of the legislatures of the states concerned as well as of the Congress." The convention approved a two-step plan they believed consistent with the Constitution. Members of the convention first re-formed the legitimate government of Virginia. They then sought congressional permission to create a new state out of Virginia's northwestern counties.

The delegates to the Second Wheeling Convention formed what they regarded as the legitimate government of Virginia. Francis H. Pierpont became the new governor of the state and various delegates from the Wheeling Convention constituted the new state legislature. On July 1, 1861, the newly appointed Virginia legislature met at Wheeling, filled other state offices, and elected two United States senators, John Carlile and Waitman T. Willey. The U.S. Senate recognized these representatives of the so-called "Pierpont Government" as the legitimate representatives of the state of Virginia. The Wheeling Convention reassembled on August 20 to organize a popular vote on the formation of a new state. The election was held on October 24. The citizens voted in favor of a new state by a margin of 18,489 to 781. A constitutional convention later presented a document to the people of the western part of the state on February 18, 1862. The new state constitution was overwhelmingly ratified. The "loyal" state legislature of Virginia quickly approved the formation of this new state within its boundaries, now dubbed "West Virginia." On December 31, 1862, Abraham Lincoln signed the enabling act that admitted West Virginia on the condition that citizens in the new state amend the proposed state constitution to provide for the gradual end of slavery. Six months later, the president issued a proclamation recognizing the admission of West Virginia into the Union.[35]

Prominent political leaders had quite different views on the secession of Virginia from the United States and the "secession" of West Virginia from Virginia. Confederate President Jefferson Davis condemned the latter effort at secession. He wrote,

> The legally expressed decision of the majority was the true voice of the state. When, therefore, disorderly persons in the northwest counties assembled and declared the ordinance of secession "to be null and void," they rose up against the authority of the state.... The subsequent organization of the state of West Virginia and its separation from the state of Virginia were acts of secession. Thus we have, in their movements, insurrection, revolution and secession.... To admit a state under such a government is entirely unauthorized, revolutionary, subversive of the constitution and destructive of the Union of States.[36]

Lincoln had a different view:

> We can scarcely dispense with the aid of West Virginia in this struggle, much less can we afford to have her against us, in Congress and in the field. Her brave and good men regard her admission into the union as a matter of life and death. They have been true to the union under many severe trials.

35. On the history of the formation of West Virginia, see generally Otis K. Rice and Stephen W. Brown, *West Virginia: A History* (Lexington: University of Kentucky Press, 1993) and Richard Orr Curry, *A House Divided: A Study of Statehood Politics and the Copperhead Movement in West Virginia* (Pittsburgh: University of Pittsburgh Press, 1964).

36. Jefferson Davis, *The Rise and Fall of the Confederate Government*, vol. 2 (New York: Appleton and Company, 1881), 306.

> The division of a state is dreaded as a precedent but a measure expedient by a war is no precedent for times of peace.
>
> It is said that the admission of West Virginia is secession, and tolerated only because it is our secession. Well, if we call it by that name, there is still difference enough between secession against the constitution and secession in favor of the constitution. I believe the admission of West Virginia into the union is expedient.[37]

Is there a difference between secession against the constitution and secession in favor of the constitution? Did Virginia forfeit its right not to consent to the formation of West Virginia by adopting the Secession Resolution? Did the delegates at Wheeling have a claim to be the legitimate government of Virginia in 1861 and a right to exercise the powers of a state government under the U.S. Constitution?

Federalism in the South

The Confederate Congress in 1861, acting as a constitutional convention, quickly debated and approved a permanent constitution drafted by a select committee. In keeping with the southern view that the slave states had been faithful to the original Constitution, the persons responsible for the Constitution of the Confederate States of America largely copied the Constitution of the United States. The resulting constitution was soon ratified by the secessionist states.

The Confederate Constitution only slightly modified the Constitution of the United States. The Confederate president was limited to a single, six-year term of office but was given a more powerful role in setting fiscal policy with a line-item veto and a privileged role in initiating appropriations. The Confederate Congress was prohibited from adopting protective tariffs, passing internal improvements or interfering with slavery. The post office was required to be self-sufficient. The Constitution reduced the number of states required to force Congress to call a constitutional convention for considering constitutional amendments. The Confederate Constitution said little new about states' rights. No explicit right of secession or nullification was written into the Confederate Constitution.

The troublesome "necessary and proper" clause from Article I, Section 8, of the U.S. Constitution was carried over unchanged into Article I, Section 18, of the Confederate Constitution. The Tenth Amendment of the U.S. Constitution was incorporated into the body of the Confederate Constitution in Article VI, Section 6, without any substantive alteration of language. The Confederate Constitution did drop the "general welfare" clause, which was part of Article I, Section 8, of the U.S. Constitution. In the antebellum period, Federalists and Whigs relied on that clause when advocating protectionism and internal improvements. The Confederate Congress was empowered to collect taxes "for revenue necessary to pay the debts, provide for the common defense, and carry on the Government of the Confederate States."

States' rights played a greater role in the preamble and implementation of the Confederate Constitution. The preamble to the Confederate Constitution declared,

> We, the people of the Confederate States, each State acting in its sovereign and independent character, in order to form a permanent federal government, establish justice, insure domestic tranquility, and secure the blessings of liberty to ourselves and our posterity invoking the favor and guidance of Almighty God do ordain and establish this Constitution for the Confederate States of America

Although authorized to do so by the Constitution, the Confederate Congress never established a Supreme Court. Proponents of states' rights blocked efforts to create a Supreme Court for the Confederacy that would have the same appellate power over state courts that Section 25 of the Judiciary Act of 1789 had given to the U.S. Supreme Court. As a result, the several state supreme courts were able to reach independent decisions on the constitutionality of actions taken by the Confederate government. Fortunately for the Confederate government, the state supreme courts declared very few national laws unconstitutional.[38]

---

37. Opinion on the Admission of West Virginia into the Union. In *Collected Works of Abraham Lincoln*, ed. Roy P. Basler, vol. 6 (New Brunswick, NJ: Rutgers University Press, 1953), 28.

38. On the Confederate Constitution and judicial review, see Marshall L. DeRosa, *The Confederate Constitution of 1861* (Columbia: University of Missouri Press, 1991); Curtis Arthur Amlund, *Federalism in the Southern Confederacy* (Washington, DC: Public Affairs Press, 1966).

State governments in the Confederacy during the Civil War more vigorously challenged national authority than did either Confederate state courts or state governments in the Union. In a particularly famous exchange of letters, Georgia Governor Joseph E. Brown in 1862 accosted President Davis over the constitutionality of the military draft. The Confederate Constitution had the same provisions for military affairs as the U.S. Constitution. Brown claimed that the first conscription act passed by the Confederate Congress "disorganize[d]" the state militia and pulled the troops that the governor deemed necessary to the proper defense of the state out of Georgia. Worse, he complained, the law did not make an exemption for the officers of the state government. This threatened to "destroy her State Government by disbanding her law-making power." If necessary, Brown asserted, he would "use all the remaining military force of the State" to prevent the arrest of state legislators, judges and other essential personnel who might refuse to comply with the draft law, and he would otherwise offer no assistance in implementing a law of such dubious constitutionality.[39] Davis responded by observing that the Confederate Congress was given a clear power "to raise armies" and that the draft was "not only necessary, but…it was absolutely indispensable." So long as the draft was "calculated and intended to 'raise armies,'" and so long as conscription did not conflict with some other provision in the Constitution, Davis claimed, the draft was a "necessary and proper" law.[40] The grousing of governors like Brown led a generation of historians to argue that states' rights played a significant role in undermining the Confederacy during the Civil War. More recent work has emphasized the extent to which national leaders like Jefferson Davis won these constitutional and political arguments over military affairs.[41]

C. The Status of the Southern States during Reconstruction

The status of the states that passed secession ordinances in 1860 and 1861 created constitutional problems during the Civil War. The Confederate government contended that these states had formed an independent nation. The North rejected this theory. Lincoln justified the use of military force on the grounds that secession was unconstitutional and illegitimate. If southern secession ordinances were null and void and the southern states were still in the Union after 1861, however, then the constitutional basis on which the North waged a "war" against them was not clear. If the slave states were still members of the Union, were they entitled to representation in Congress?

Questions about the status of the seceding states became even more pressing during Reconstruction. After the surrender of the Confederate armies, the southern states no longer claimed to be outside the Union. They once again asserted their constitutional status as states, entitled to all the constitutional powers and privileges those states possessed before they passed secession ordinances. Most northerners disputed this contention. General agreement existed that states forfeited some powers and privileges by attempting to secede, but this consensus broke down when Americans considered what powers were forfeited and why.

President Andrew Johnson and the Reconstruction Congress bitterly contested basic questions about the constitutional status of former Confederate states after the Civil War. Johnson believed that the aim of the war was to restore as soon as possible the southern states as loyal and equal members of the United States. He and his supporters insisted that the southern states should be immediately represented in Congress and that local authorities should be trusted to administer the law in the former Confederate states. Proponents of Congressional Reconstruction maintained that states forfeited crucial constitutional powers and privileges when they attempted to secede. On this ground, the Republican majority voted to deny the southern states representation in Congress and placed them under military government.

The participants in these debates offered numerous theories about the constitutional status of the southern states. The competing theories all justified some federal intervention in the South, but they differed in their implications for the scope, pace, and administration of that intervention. Each had conceptual difficulties. The main theories were:

- Secession had no effect on the constitutional status of any state because secession was null and void.
- Secession suspended normal government operations, but only until the federal government reestab-

39. Joseph E. Brown, in *Correspondence between Governor Brown and President Davis on the Constitutionality of the Conscription Act* (Atlanta, GA: Atlanta Intelligencer, 1862), 4, 7.

40. Ibid., 17, 18.

41. For a review, see Richard E. Beringer, et al., *Why the South Lost the Civil War* (Athens, GA: University of Georgia Press, 1986).

lished loyal governments in the former Confederate states.

- States forfeited their political rights by attempting to secede, but not their territorial integrity.
- States that attempted to secede reverted to territorial status.
- The former Confederate states were conquered provinces with no constitutional status, rights or powers.

William T. Sherman, "Memorandum" (1865)[42]

General William T. Sherman (1820–1891) received the surrender of General Joseph Johnston's Confederate army in North Carolina in April 1865. At that time, Sherman believed that Lincoln administration policy treated secession as illegal and void, but regarded the seceding states as forfeiting no rights as states by seceding. President Lincoln in his First Inaugural Address and July 4, 1861, Message to Congress gave credence to this interpretation of his postwar intentions. Both indicated that the southern states would immediately resume their former status as soon as peace was established and loyalty oaths were taken. Sherman sought to implement this "southern" theory of secession. His memorandum on the surrender of the armies made no explicit adjustment in the federal role over slavery and black civil rights. With peace restored, the southern view suggested that such domestic matters remained exclusively in the hands of the states.

Although Sherman believed that he had acted consistently with administration policy, his memorandum was outdated when issued. Lincoln had already instructed General Ulysses S. Grant "not to decide, discuss or confer upon any political question" when negotiating the surrender of the Confederate armies but to leave all such questions to later presidential decision.[43] Those orders had not reached Sherman when Johnston surrendered.

...

2. The Confederate armies now in existence to be disbanded and conducted to their several State capitals, there to deposit their arms and public property in the State Arsenal; and each officer and man to execute and file an agreement to cease from acts of war, and to abide the action of the State and Federal authority....

3. The recognition, by the Executive of the United States, of the several State governments, on their officers and Legislatures taking the oaths prescribed by the Constitution of the United States, and, where conflicting State governments have resulted from the war, the legitimacy of all shall be submitted to the Supreme Court of the United States.

4. The reestablishment of all the Federal Courts in the several States, with powers as defined by the Constitution of the United States and of the States respectively.

5. The people and inhabitants of all the States to be guaranteed, so far as the Executive can, their political rights and franchises, as well as their rights of person and property, as defined by the Constitution of the United States and the States respectively.

6. The Executive authority of the Government, of the United States not to disturb any of the people by reason of the late war, so long as they live in peace and quiet, abstain from acts of armed hostility, and obey the laws in existence at the place of their residence.

7. In general terms—the war to cease; a general amnesty, so far as the Executive of the United States can command, on condition of the disbandment of the Confederate armies....

Not being fully empowered by our respective principals to fulfill these terms, we individually and officially pledge ourselves to promptly obtain the necessary authority, and to carry out the above program.

Andrew Johnson, First Annual Message (1865)[44]

President Andrew Johnson maintained that secession suspended the political functions of the states. The duty of the federal government was to reestablish lawful civil government in the South, while effectuating the freedom of the former slaves on the principle of " 'equal and exact justice to all men,' special privileges to none."[45] In his first State of the Union message to Congress after Lincoln's death and Lee's

42. Excerpt taken from *Memoirs of General W. T. Sherman*, vol. 2 (New York: Charles L. Webster & Co., 1891), 356–57.

43. Letter to Grant of March 3, 1865, in *Collected Works of Abraham Lincoln*, ed. Roy P. Basler, vol. 8 (New Brunswick, NJ: Rutgers University Press, 1953), 330–31.

44. Excerpt taken from *A Compilation of the Messages and Papers of the Presidents*, ed. James D. Richardson, vol. 6 (Washington, DC: Government Printing Office, 1897), 353–60.

45. Andrew Johnson, in *A Compilation of the Messages and Papers of the Presidents*, ed. James D. Richardson, vol. 6 (Washington, DC: Government Printing Office, 1897), 362.

surrender, Johnson explained the basis for his organization of provisional governments in the southern states and their readiness to rejoin the Union on an equal basis with the states of the North. Johnson required that the provisional governments ratify the Thirteenth Amendment banning slavery as part of their restoration. At the same time, he insisted that secession was fundamentally a problem of large-scale treason and, as such, was a law enforcement problem.[46]

...

The maintenance of the Union brings with it "the support of the State governments in all their rights," but it is not one of the rights of any State government to renounce its own place in the Union or to nullify the laws of the Union....

...

States, with proper limitations of power, are essential to the existence of the Constitution of the United States. At the very commencement, when we assumed a place among the powers of the earth, the Declaration of Independence was adopted by States; so also were the Articles of Confederation: and when "the people of the United States" ordained and established the Constitution it was the assent of the States, one by one, which gave it vitality....The best security for the perpetual existence of the States is the "supreme authority" of the Constitution of the United States. The perpetuity of the Constitution brings with it the perpetuity of the States; their mutual relation makes us what we are, and in our political system their connection is indissoluble. The whole cannot exist without the parts, nor the parts without the whole. So long as the Constitution of the United States endures, the States will endure. The destruction of the one is the destruction of the other; the preservation of the one is the preservation of the other.

...

I found the States suffering from the effects of a civil war. Resistance to the General Government appeared to have exhausted itself. The United States had recovered possession of their forts and arsenals, and their armies were in the occupation of every State which had attempted to secede. Whether the territory within the limits of those States should be held as conquered territory, under military authority emanating from the President as the head of the Army, was the first question that presented itself for decision.

Now military governments, established for an indefinite period, would have offered no security for the early suppression of discontent, would have divided the people into the vanquishers and the vanquished, and would have envenomed hatred rather than have restored affection. Once established, no precise limit to their continuance was conceivable....

Besides, the policy of military rule over a conquered territory would have implied that the States whose inhabitants may have taken part in the rebellion had by the act of those inhabitants ceased to exist. But the true theory is that all pretended acts of secession were from the beginning null and void. The States cannot commit treason nor screen the individual citizens who may have committed treason any more than they can make valid treaties or engage in lawful commerce with any foreign power. The States attempting to secede placed themselves in a condition where their vitality was impaired, but not extinguished; their functions suspended, but not destroyed.

But if any State neglects or refuses to perform its offices there is the more need that the General Government should maintain all its authority and as soon as practicable resume the exercise of all its functions. On this principle I have acted, and have gradually and quietly, and by almost imperceptible steps, sought to restore the rightful energy of the General Government and of the States. To that end provisional governors have been appointed for the States, conventions called, governors elected, legislatures assembled, and Senators and Representatives chosen to the Congress of the United States. At the same time the courts of the United States, as far as could be done, have been reopened, so that the laws of the United States may be enforced through their agency. The blockade has been removed and the custom-houses reestablished in ports of entry, so that the revenue of the United States may be collected. The Post-Office Department renews its ceaseless activity, and the General Government is thereby enabled to communicate promptly with its officers and agents....

46. "We all agree that the seceded States, so called, are out of their proper practical relation with the Union; and that the sole object of the government, civil and military, in regard to those States, is to again get them into their proper practical relation. I believe it is not only possible, but in fact, easier, to do this, without deciding or even considering, whether those States have ever been out of the Union, than with it." —Abraham Lincoln, "Last Public Address, April 11, 1865," in *Collected Works of Abraham Lincoln*, ed. Roy P. Basler, vol. 8 (New Brunswick, NJ: Rutgers University Press, 1953), 403.

I know very well that this policy is attended with some risk; that for its success it requires at least the acquiescence of the States which it concerns; that it implies an invitation to those States, by renewing their allegiance to the United States, to resume their functions as States of the Union. But it is a risk that must be taken. In the choice of difficulties it is the smallest risk; and to diminish and if possible to remove all danger, I have felt it incumbent on me to assert one other power of the General Government—the power of pardon. As no State can throw a defense over the crime of treason, the power of pardon is exclusively vested in the executive government of the United States. In exercising that power I have taken every precaution to connect it with the clearest recognition of the binding force of the laws of the United States and an unqualified acknowledgment of the great social change of condition in regard to slavery which has grown out of the war.

...

Henry Winter Davis, "No Peace Before Victory" (1863)[47]

Henry Winter Davis (1817–1865) and many Radical Republicans in Congress contended that the southern states became "disorganized" and "forfeited" their rights as states when they attempted to secede. States could not remove themselves from the Union, but they could lose their political status. A rebel state did not lose "its territorial character or defined boundaries or subdivisions," but lost the "rights or powers of government as [a] State[] of this Union."[48] Although embraced by many Radicals, Davis advanced a moderate alternative to the "states' rights" position favored by the Democrats and President Johnson and the conquered province theory favored by other Radical Republicans. The disorganized states theory placed the responsibility and obligation in Congress to secure "republican governments" in the southern states, while imposing implicit limits on what Congress could do in and to those states in the process of erecting new republican governments. The theory became the basis of the U.S. Supreme Court's opinion in Texas v. White *(1869).*

...

I turn to consider that other great power and duty—the guarantee of republican governments to the States. That touches a question which ought to have been decided by the last Congress, which our friends are so singularly timid about meeting.... I regret that, in dealing with the question of reorganizing the State governments, eminent gentlemen have used words which they, I think, will regret hereafter. They speak of the Southern men in arms as being alien enemies. The President has never so called them. Congress has never so called them. No law upon the statute-book so treats them. No official document has ever hinted at that character. To call them alien enemies admits that their secession was effectual to give them the right of independence in the eye of the world. It admits they are not traitors, but enemies. I say they are traitors and not enemies (applause); citizens under the law, against which they are illegally waging war, not foreigners waging a war upon equal terms with men who are foreigners to them. They war with the rope around their necks. (Applause.)... And when the right of conquest is referred to, as it has been by a very distinguished and very able gentleman, to find out the methods of dealing with the reorganization of the State governments, I desire to say that any man or any party that claims over the Southern States, after the insurrection has been repressed... [that we should] consider them a conquered people, that party will destroy itself, or, if it be successful, it will destroy republican liberty....

Do those men now in authority in the Southern States constitute the State governments under the Constitution that they repudiate, that they say is annulled, that they have taken up arms to destroy? On the contrary, the very first act in secession was not to carry their territory from beneath the laws of the United States, but to tear down their own State governments and institute others. Those that they tore down were republican governments in the sense of the Constitution. Those that they have established are a mob in the form of the government, and the rebellion organized to execute its purpose, entitled to recognition by nobody.... In the absence of a State government, there must be either anarchy, or a legislative and executive power somewhere. Those that have abdicated can no longer be the government of the State. The right and the duty to guarantee a republican government is vested in Congress. Congress is

---

47. Excerpt taken from Henry Winter Davis, "No Peace Before Victory," in *Speeches and Addresses Delivered Before Congress* (New York: Harper and Brothers, 1867), 317–28.

48. Sen. Samuel Shellabarger, *Congressional Globe*, 39th Cong., 1st sess., 142 (1866).

therefore charged to take every measure that is necessary to restore republican government. Pending the interregnum, Congress is the only legislative power for the State, the President is the only executive power for the State. They can... pass any law in their judgment necessary to consolidate the republican government which they are about to establish, and they have the sole and absolute discretion of determining who shall and who shall not be recognized as the government of the State....

Charles Sumner, "State Rebellion, State Suicide" (1862)[49]

Massachusetts Senator Charles Sumner (1811–1874), one of the most radical anti-slavery and anti-southern advocates in the Republican Party, maintained that the states had committed "suicide" in attempting to secede. They had "returned" to the status of mere territories, to be governed by Congress like other territorial holdings. Sumner's "state suicide" theory empowered Congress to reconfigure the former Confederate states before they were readmitted to the Union. As he wrote in an article published in the Atlantic *magazine, "The whole broad Rebel region is tabula rasa, or 'a clean slate,' where Congress, under the Constitution of the United States, may write the laws."[50] Although endorsed by some, the notion that states could commit "suicide" and that they could be reduced to territorial status seemed too radical to most national elected officials.*

...

Whereas certain States, rightfully belonging to the Union of the United States, have, through their respective Governments, wickedly undertaken to abjure all those duties by which their connection with the Union was maintained, to renounce all allegiance to the Constitution, to levy war upon the National Government, and, for the consummation of this treason, have unconstitutionally and unlawfully confederated together with the declared purpose of putting an end, by force, to the supremacy of the Constitution within their respective limits;

...

And whereas the Constitution, which is the supreme law of the land, cannot be displaced within this territory, but must ever continue the supreme law thereof, notwithstanding the doings of any pretended Governments, acting singly or in confederation, hostile to its supremacy: Therefore, —

1. *Resolved*. That any vote of secession, or other act, by a State hostile to the supremacy of the Constitution within its territory, *is inoperative and void against the Constitution*, and, when sustained by *force*, becomes a practical abdication by the State of all rights under the Constitution, while the treason it involves works instant forfeiture of all functions and powers essential to the continued existence of the State as a body politic; so that from such time forward the territory falls under the exclusive jurisdiction of Congress, as other territory, and the State becomes, according to the language of the law, *felo de se*.

...

4. That Slavery, being a peculiar local institution, derived from local law, *without any origin in the Constitution or in natural right*, is upheld by the sole and exclusive authority of the State, and must therefore cease, legally and constitutionally, when the State on which it depends has lapsed; for the incident must follow the principal.

...

9. That the duty cast upon Congress... by the positive injunction of the Constitution, addressed to the Nation, that "the United States shall guaranty to every State in this Union a republican form of government"; and that, in pursuance of this duty cast upon Congress, and further enjoined by the Constitution, *Congress will assume complete jurisdiction of such vacated territory, where such unconstitutional and illegal things have been attempted, and will proceed to establish therein republican forms of government under the Constitution*, and, in the execution of this trust, will provide carefully for the protection of all the inhabitants thereof, for the security of families, the organization of labor, the encouragement of industry, and the welfare of society, and will in every way discharge the duties of a just, merciful, and paternal Government.

49. Excerpt taken from Charles Sumner, "State Rebellion, State Suicide; Emancipation and Reconstruction, Resolutions in the Senate, February 11, 1862," in *The Works of Charles Sumner*, vol. 6 (Boston: Lee and Shepard, 1874), 301–305.

50. Charles Sumner, "Our Domestic Relations: Power of Congress over the Rebel States," in ibid., 7:534. See also, Orestes Brownson, *American Republic* (New York: P. O'Shea, 1866), 277–347.

Thaddeus Stevens, **Speech on Reconstruction** (1865)[51]

Congressman Thaddeus Stevens (1792–1868) of Pennsylvania, the leader of the radical faction in the House of Representatives, declared that southern states were "conquered provinces" under the laws of war. This theory frankly admitted that the southern states had left the Union. In defeat, they could be treated as a conquered nation. As vanquished enemies, the southern states and their people had no constitutional status or rights to be asserted or respected. Stevens had ambitious plans for summary mass executions and dramatic confiscation of private wealth. Confiscation, he calculated, would provide forty acres to each freedman, "pay the damages done to loyal men North and South" and pay off the national debt without the necessity of raising northern taxes. "What loyal man can object to this?" he asked.[52] *Successful realization of the ideals of the Republican Party required that the South be remade in the northern image. The authority to do so, Stevens declared, required that the territory and population of the former Confederacy be held outside the protection and requirements of the Constitution.*

...

How can such punishments be inflicted and such forfeitures produced without doing violence to established principles?

Two positions have been suggested.

1st—To treat those States as never having been out of the Union, because the Constitution forbids secession, and, therefore, a fact forbidden by law could not exist.

2nd—To accept the position in which they placed themselves as severed from the Union; an independent government *de facto*, and an alien enemy to be dealt with according to the laws of war.

...

...It is idle to deny that we treated them as a belligerent entitled to all the rights and subject to all the liabilities of an alien enemy....The Confederate States were for four years what they claimed to be as alien enemy in all their rights and liabilities....It will I suppose at least be conceded that the United States if not obliged so to do, have a right to treat them as an alien enemy now conquered, and subject to all the liabilities of a vanquished foe.

...

...In reconstruction, therefore, no reform can be effected in the Southern States if they have never left the Union. But reformation *must* be effected; the foundation of their institutions, both political, municipal, and social *must* be broken up and *relaid*, or all our blood and treasure have been spent in vain. This can only be done by treating and holding them as a conquered people. Then all things which we can desire to do, follow with logical and legitimate authority....

...

In short, all writers agree that the victor may inflict punishment upon the vanquished enemy even to the taking of his life, liberty, or the confiscation of all his property; but that this extreme right is never exercised except upon a cruel, barbarous, obstinate, or dangerous foe who has waged an unjust war.

Upon the character of the belligerent, and the justice of the war, and the manner of conducting it, depends our right to take the lives, liberty and property of the belligerent. The war had its origin in treason without one spark of justice....

Surely, these things are sufficient to justify the exercise of extreme rights of war—"to execute, to imprison, to confiscate."...

...

But, it is said, by those who have more sympathy with rebel wives and children than for the widows and orphans of loyal men, that this stripping the rebels of their estates and driving them to exile or to honest labor would be harsh and severe upon innocent women and children. It may be so, but that is the result of the necessary laws of war. But it is revolutionary, say they. This plan would, no doubt, work a radical reorganization in southern institutions, habits and manners. It is intended to revolutionize their principles and feelings. This may alarm feeble minds and shake weak nerves. So do all great improvements in the political and moral world....

...

Texas v. White, 74 U.S. 700 (1869)

The federal government in 1851, as part of a settlement over state boundaries, issued to Texas $5,000,000 in Government bonds. The bonds paid 5 percent interest and could be

51. Excerpt taken from Thaddeus Stevens, *Reconstruction: Speech of the Hon. Thaddeus Stevens, Delivered in the City of Lancaster, September 7, 1865* (Lancaster, PA: Examiner & Herald Print, 1865).

52. Ibid., 5.

redeemed for their face value after December 31, 1864. In an effort to raise revenue during the Civil War, the Texas legislature in 1862 directed that all the remaining bonds be sold. George White in 1865 purchased $210,000 worth of bonds from the Confederate State of Texas. After the war, the provisional and Reconstruction governments of Texas renounced the bond sale as part of an illegal conspiracy to overthrow the federal government. In February 1867, Texas asked the U.S. Supreme Court for an injunction prohibiting the United States from redeeming or paying interest on the Texas indemnity bonds sold by the Texas legislature during the Civil War. Texas argued that, as secession was null and void, all acts performed by the Confederate state of Texas, including the bond sales, were also null and void.

Texas v. White *presented several difficulties for the Supreme Court. The first was jurisdictional, whether the Reconstruction government in Texas was a "state" that could initiate a lawsuit directly in the Supreme Court. Simply deciding whether the Supreme Court could hear the case seemingly required the justices to rule on the legal status and constitutionality of the Reconstruction governments. With congressional Reconstruction already well under way and the impeachment of Andrew Johnson still a fresh memory, the Court was ill-positioned to regard the legitimacy of the Reconstruction governments as an open question. Nevertheless, how to explain their status under the Constitution was hardly clear.*

The merits of the case were no easier than the jurisdictional issue. Texas v. White *raised the classic legal problem of regime change: What was the status of actions taken by the* ancien regime *after the revolution? What was the legal status of the secessionist governments during the Civil War itself? Were any actions valid? If the old government had disposed of public property, whether for good, bad, or corrupt reasons, did the new government have to respect those arrangements?*

On the one hand, something was wrong with the idea that the U.S. government was obliged to pay those who had financed the southern "rebellion." On the other hand, there was long-term value in stabilizing property rights and not subjecting the legitimacy of a government to judicial scrutiny. If the bond sales of the "illegal" government were open to question, what about other routine acts of that government, such as granting marriage licenses or executing wills?

The Supreme Court in Texas v. White *granted the injunction prohibiting the federal government from paying bondholders who purchased from Texas during the Civil War. Chief Justice Salmon Chase's majority opinion declared that Texas was a state entitled to bring a lawsuit in federal courts and that all state legislative actions from 1861 to 1865 intended to facilitate secession and the war effort were void. All the justices were clear that in 1869 there was only one right answer to the question of the legitimacy of secession: The Union was "indissoluble" and "perpetual." Chase wrote that the United States was an "indestructible Union, composed of indestructible States." The court was otherwise divided 5–3, even on issues of style. Polk's appointee Justice Robert Grier, writing in dissent, kept the old habits. He referred to the "United States" as a plural noun. Lincoln's appointee, Chief Justice Salmon Chase, adopted the new style. His nation was no longer "these United States," but "the United States."*

CHIEF JUSTICE CHASE delivered the opinion of the Court.

...

...It is not to be questioned that this court has original jurisdiction of suits by States against citizens of other States, or that the States entitled to invoke this jurisdiction must be States of the Union. But, it is equally clear that no such jurisdiction has been conferred upon this court of suits by any other political communities than such States.

If, therefore, it is true that the State of Texas was not at the time of filing this bill, or is not now, one of the United States, we have no jurisdiction of this suit, and it is our duty to dismiss it.

...

In the Constitution the term state most frequently expresses the combined idea... of people, territory, and government. A state, in the ordinary sense of the Constitution, is a political community of free citizens, occupying a territory of defined boundaries, and organized under a government sanctioned and limited by a written constitution, and established by the consent of the governed. It is the union of such states, under a common constitution, which forms the distinct and greater political unit, which that Constitution designates as the United States, and makes of the people and states which compose it one people and one country.

...

It is needless to discuss, at length, the question whether the right of a State to withdraw from the Union for any cause, regarded by herself as sufficient, is consistent with the Constitution of the United States.

The Union of the States never was a purely artificial and arbitrary relation. It began among the Colonies, and grew out of common origin, mutual sympathies, kindred principles, similar interests, and geographical relations. It was confirmed and strengthened by the necessities of war, and received definite form, and character, and sanction from the Articles of Confederation. By these the Union was solemnly declared to "be perpetual." And when these Articles were found to be inadequate to the exigencies of the country, the Constitution was ordained "to form a more perfect Union." It is difficult to convey the idea of indissoluble unity more clearly than by these words. What can be indissoluble if a perpetual Union, made more perfect, is not?

But the perpetuity and indissolubility of the Union, by no means implies the loss of distinct and individual existence, or of the right of self-government by the States. Under the Articles of Confederation each State retained its sovereignty, freedom, and independence, and every power, jurisdiction, and right not expressly delegated to the United States. Under the Constitution, though the powers of the States were much restricted, still, all powers not delegated to the United States, nor prohibited to the States, are reserved to the States respectively, or to the people.... [I]t may be not unreasonably said that the preservation of the States, and the maintenance of their governments, are as much within the design and care of the Constitution as the preservation of the Union and the maintenance of the National government. The Constitution, in all its provisions, looks to an indestructible Union, composed of indestructible States.

When, therefore, Texas became one of the United States, she entered into an indissoluble relation. All the obligations of perpetual union, and all the guaranties of republican government in the Union, attached at once to the State. The act which consummated her admission into the Union was something more than a compact; it was the incorporation of a new member into the political body. And it was final....

Considered therefore as transactions under the Constitution, the ordinance of secession, adopted by the convention and ratified by a majority of the citizens of Texas, and all the acts of her legislature intended to give effect to that ordinance, were absolutely null.... If this were otherwise, the State must have become foreign, and her citizens foreigners. The war must have ceased to be a war for the suppression of rebellion, and must have become a war for conquest and subjugation.

...

But in order to the exercise, by a State, of the right to sue in this court, there needs to be a State government, competent to represent the State in its relations with the National government, so far at least as the institution and prosecution of a suit is concerned.

And it is by no means a logical conclusion, from the premises which we have endeavored to establish, that the governmental relations of Texas to the Union remained unaltered.... All admit that, during this condition of civil war, the rights of the State as a member, and of her people as citizens of the Union, were suspended. The government and the citizens of the State, refusing to recognize their constitutional obligations, assumed the character of enemies, and incurred the consequences of rebellion.

These new relations imposed new duties upon the United States. The first was that of suppressing the rebellion. The next was that of re-establishing the broken relations of the State with the Union. The first of these duties having been performed, the next necessarily engaged the attention of the National government.

The authority for the performance of the first had been found in the power to suppress insurrection and carry on war; for the performance of the second, authority was derived from the obligation of the United States to guarantee to every State in the Union a republican form of government. The latter, indeed, in the case of a rebellion which involves the government of a State, and for the time excludes the National authority from its limits, seems to be a necessary complement to the former.

...

In the exercise of the power conferred by the guaranty clause, as in the exercise of every other constitutional power, a discretion in the choice of means is necessarily allowed. It is essential only that the means must be necessary and proper for carrying into execution the power conferred, through the restoration of the State to its constitutional relations, under a republican form of government, and that no acts be done, and no authority exerted, which is either prohibited or unsanctioned by the Constitution.

...

Whether the action then taken was, in all respects, warranted by the Constitution, it is not now necessary to determine. The power exercised by the President was supposed, doubtless, to be derived from his constitutional functions, as commander-in-chief; and, so long as the war continued, it cannot be denied that he might institute temporary government within insurgent districts, occupied by the National forces, or take measures, in any State, for the restoration of State government faithful to the Union, employing, however, in such efforts, only such means and agents as were authorized by constitutional laws.

But, the power to carry into effect the clause of guaranty is primarily a legislative power, and resides in Congress....

...

The action of the President must, therefore, be considered as provisional, and, in that light, it seems to have been regarded by Congress....

...

...The necessary conclusion is that the suit was instituted and is prosecuted by competent authority.

The question of jurisdiction being thus disposed of, we proceed to the consideration of the merits as presented by the pleadings and the evidence.

...

The legislature of Texas, at the time of the [sale of the bonds], constituted one of the departments of a State government, established in hostility to the Constitution of the United States. It cannot be regarded, therefore, in the courts of the United States, as a lawful legislature, or its acts as lawful acts. And, yet, it is an historical fact that the government of Texas, then in full control of the State, was its only actual government; and certainly if Texas had been a separate State, and not one of the United States, the new government, having displaced the regular authority, and having established itself in the customary seats of power, and in the exercise of the ordinary functions of administration, would have constituted, in the strictest sense of the words, a de facto government, and its acts, during the period of its existence as such, would be effectual, and, in almost all respects, valid. And, to some extent, this is true of the actual government of Texas, though unlawful and revolutionary, as to the United States.

It is not necessary to attempt any exact definitions, within which the acts of such a State government must be treated as valid, or invalid. It may be said, perhaps with sufficient accuracy, that acts necessary to peace and good order among citizens, such for example, as acts sanctioning and protecting marriage and the domestic relations, governing the course of descents, regulating the conveyance and transfer of property, real and personal, and providing remedies for injuries to person and estate, and other similar acts, which would be valid if emanating from a lawful government, must be regarded in general as valid when proceeding from an actual, though unlawful government; and that acts in furtherance or support of rebellion against the United States, or intended to defeat the just rights of citizens, and other acts of like nature, must, in general, be regarded as invalid and void.

...

[The agency that sold the bonds to White] was organized not for the defence of the State against a foreign invasion or for its protection against domestic violence, within the meaning of these words as used in the National Constitution, but for the purpose, under the name of defence, of levying war against the United States. This purpose was undoubtedly unlawful, for the acts which it contemplated are, within the express definition of the Constitution, treasonable.

...

It follows that the title of the State was not divested by the act of the insurgent government in entering into this contract.

...

On the whole case, therefore, our conclusion is that the State of Texas is entitled to the relief sought by her bill, and a decree must be made accordingly.

JUSTICE GRIER, dissenting.

...

The original jurisdiction of this court can be invoked only by one of the United States. The Territories have no such right conferred on them by the Constitution, nor have the Indian tribes who are under the protection of the military authorities of the government.

Is Texas one of these United States? Or was she such at the time this bill was filed, or since?

This is to be decided as a political fact, not as a legal fiction. This court is bound to know and notice the public history of the nation.

If I regard the truth of history for the last eight years, I cannot discover the State of Texas as one of these United States....

...

Is Texas a State, now represented by members chosen by the people of that State and received on the floor of Congress? Has she two senators to represent her as a State in the Senate of the United States? Has her voice been heard in the late election of President? Is she not now held and governed as a conquered province by military force? The act of Congress of March 2d, 1867, declares Texas to be a "rebel State," and provides for its government until a legal and republican State government could be legally established. It constituted Louisiana and Texas the fifth military district, and made it subject, not to the civil authority, but to the "military authorities of the United States."

It is true that no organized rebellion now exists there, and the courts of the United States now exercise jurisdiction over the people of that province. But this is no test of the State's being in the Union; Dakota is no State, and yet the courts of the United States administer justice there as they do in Texas. The Indian tribes, who are governed by military force, cannot claim to be States of the Union. Wherein does the condition of Texas differ from theirs?

...I do not consider myself bound to express any opinion judicially as to the constitutional right of Texas to exercise the rights and privileges of a State of this Union, or the power of Congress to govern her as a conquered province, to subject her to military domination, and keep her in pupilage. I can only submit to the fact as decided by the political position of the government; and I am not disposed to join in any essay to prove Texas to be a State of the Union, when Congress have decided that she is not. It is a question of fact, I repeat, and of fact only. Politically, Texas is not a State in this Union. Whether rightfully out of it or not is a question not before the court.

...

...The contest now is between the State of Texas and her own citizens. She seeks to annul a contract with the respondents, based on the allegation that there was no authority in Texas competent to enter into an agreement during the rebellion....She now sets up the plea of insanity, and asks the court to treat all her acts made during the disease as void.

...

...She cannot, like the chameleon, assume the color of the object to which she adheres, and ask this court to involve itself in the contradictory positions, that she is a State in the Union and was never out of it, and yet not a State at all for four years, during which she acted and claims to be "an organized political body," exercising all the powers and functions of an independent sovereign State....

...

JUSTICE SWAYNE, with whom JUSTICE MILLER joins, dissenting.

I concur with my brother Grier as to the incapacity of the State of Texas, in her present condition, to maintain an original suit in this court. The question, in my judgment, is one in relation to which this court is bound by the action of the legislative department of the government.

Upon the merits of the case, I agree with the majority of my brethren.

...

D. Constitutional Amendment and Ratification

Note: The Validity of the Fourteenth Amendment

The process by which the Fourteenth Amendment was ratified raises difficult questions about the role of states as agents of formal constitutional change and the conditions under which constitutional amendments are legitimate. The Congress that proposed the Fourteenth Amendment had previously excluded almost all senators and congressmen representing the states that had seceded from the Union on the ground that these representatives could not take an oath swearing that they had always been loyal to the United States. The Fourteenth Amendment passed the two chambers of Congress by the required two-thirds vote only because representatives from the southern states did not participate. Before transmitting the proposed Fourteenth Amendment to the states for ratification in June of 1866, President Andrew Johnson voiced a repeated theme of his: Could a "rump Congress" that included representatives of only twenty-five of the thirty-six states make such a fundamental decision?

After excluding the South from the congressional vote to propose the Fourteenth Amendment, Republicans included the South in the state vote to ratify the amendment. Radicals worried that northern votes might not be enough to secure ratification of the Fourteenth Amendment. Moderates hoped that southern votes would lend legitimacy to the Reconstruction Amendments. Members of all Republican factions held out the prospect that southern states by ratifying would regain full political status in the Union (Republicans voted to seat representatives from Tennessee immediately after the state convention ratified).

The Fourteenth Amendment had a rough passage through the states. Most southern states initially refused to ratify, often by large margins. By March of 1867, only twenty-one states had ratified (including Tennessee) and thirteen had rejected the amendment (including three Union states). The new Congress then passed the Military Reconstruction Act. That statute disbanded the existing southern governments, organized new ones with different suffrage rules, and required that the reconstructed state legislatures approve the Fourteenth Amendment in order to gain seats in Congress. The new southern state governments reversed earlier decisions and voted to ratify. At the same time, Democratic electoral victories in Ohio and New Jersey led those states to rescind their earlier ratification of the amendment. Secretary of State William Seward immediately gave Congress a list of all the states that had passed ratifying resolutions, but noted that there was some "doubt and uncertainty whether such resolutions are not irregular, invalid, and therefore ineffectual."[53] Congress did not hesitate. The House and Senate on July 9, 1868, adopted a concurrent resolution declaring that the Fourteenth Amendment had been ratified.[54]

No present question exists that the Fourteenth Amendment is a part of the effective Constitution and will continue to be interpreted and enforced.[55] Democrats abandoned their attacks on the legitimacy of the post–Civil War Amendments by the end of the nineteenth century. The more extreme opponents of *Brown v. Board of Education* (1954) were unable to convince most Americans that the Fourteenth Amendment was illegitimate. Nevertheless, consideration of the process by which the Fourteenth Amendment was ratified raises questions about constitutional change. Why exactly is the Fourteenth Amendment a valid part of the U.S. Constitution? Was the process by which that amendment was ratified consistent with Article V? May constitutional amendments be ratified by some process other than that mandated in Article V? Bruce Ackerman maintains that Reconstruction Republicans successfully convinced Americans to adopt a more nationally centered process for constitutional change, one that largely cuts states out of the constitutional amendment process. Is Ackerman correct when he claims that Congress under certain conditions may effectively coerce state ratification of constitutional amendments? What is the appropriate state role in the amendment process after the ratification of the Fourteenth Amendment?

V. Separation of Powers

MAJOR DEVELOPMENTS

- President Lincoln unilaterally orders a blockade, suspends habeas corpus, imposes martial law, and issues the Emancipation Proclamation.
- Congress ratifies the blockade, empowers the President to suspend habeas corpus, but limits presidential power to impose martial law.
- The Supreme Court sustains President Lincoln's decision to order a blockade, but declares unconstitutional President Lincoln's decision to impose martial law in places where federal courts are open.
- The Senate fails by one vote to impeach President Johnson after Johnson violates the Tenure of Office Act by unilaterally removing a cabinet official from office.

Separation of powers problems intensified during the Civil War with a new twist. When Jacksonians and Whigs debated the separation of powers, Jacksonians championed far more presidential powers than Whigs. Among the less notable Whigs who objected to Jacksonian exercises of presidential prerogatives was a one-term congressman from Illinois, Abraham Lincoln. Lincoln as president frequently acted unilaterally. He insisted that as Commander in Chief he had power to raise troops, blockade southern ports, declare martial law, suspend habeas corpus, and issue the Emancipation Proclamation. Sometimes, he maintained that presidential powers were necessary because Congress was not in session. Other times, as was the case with the Emancipation Proclamation, Lincoln declared that his actions did not require subsequent legislative ratification. While most Democrats and some Republicans carped at Lincoln's tendency to act unilaterally, legislative majorities during the Civil War usually either supported or did not aggressively challenge Lincoln's actions.

President Andrew Johnson was less fortunate during Reconstruction. The national legislature and

53. "Certificate Respecting the Ratification of the Fourteenth Amendment to the Constitution. July 20, 1868," in Horace Greeley et al. *The Tribune Almanac and Political Register* (New York: Tribune Association, 1868), 47.

54. On the process of ratifying the Fourteenth Amendment, see David E. Kyvig, *Explicit & Authentic Acts* (Lawrence: University Press of Kansas, 1996), 163–76; Bruce Ackerman, *We the People*, vol. 2 (Cambridge: Harvard University Press, 1998), 99–119.

55. See Wayne D. Moore, "The Fourteenth Amendment's Initial Authority: Problems of Constitutional Coherence," *Temple Political and Civil Rights Law Review* 13 (2004):515.

national executive from 1865 to 1868 bitterly disputed the constitutionality of military Reconstruction and federal legislation protecting persons of color. Johnson was a Jacksonian Democrat from Tennessee who, while a firm Union supporter during the Civil War, believed that Reconstruction should be largely limited to the abolition of slavery. The Republicans who controlled Congress insisted that persons of color be treated as political equals. While much of the struggle between the president and Congress was over national powers, separation of powers arose when Johnson refused to obey a federal law prohibiting the president from removing cabinet officials without congressional approval. Johnson was impeached by the House of Representatives. The Senate failed to remove him from office by one vote.

A. General Principles

Abraham Lincoln, Fourth of July Message to Congress (1861)[56]

When Lincoln was first inaugurated as President of the United States on March 4, 1861, Congress was not in session. The newly elected Congress was not scheduled to meet until the first Monday of December. Presidents are empowered by the Constitution to call Congress into special session "on extraordinary occasions." Lincoln, however, waited until April before issuing a call, and he designated July 4th as the date on which Congress could legally assemble.

The days when the newly inaugurated President Lincoln sat in Washington, DC, without Congress were eventful ones. In the months before Congress arrived, Lincoln launched and fought a war on American soil. He issued a call for troops, ordered the navy to blockade southern ports, and suspended habeas corpus in some jurisdictions. When Congress assembled on July 4, 1861, Lincoln delivered a message to them explaining the authority for his unilateral actions. The president asked Congress to ratify some of his actions with statutes. Other actions, Lincoln suggested, required no congressional support and rested entirely on presidential power.

Consider what the respective obligations of Congress and the president were in this situation. What would have been the status of Lincoln's actions had Congress refused them legislative sanction? Why might Lincoln have waited until July but not later before having Congress assemble? Did the founders err in leaving the power to call the legislature into special session in the hands of the executive?

...At the beginning of the present Presidential term, four months ago, the functions of the Federal Government were found to be generally suspended within the several States of South Carolina, Georgia, Alabama, Mississippi, Louisiana, and Florida, excepting only those of the Post Office Department. Within these States, all the Forts, Arsenals, Dock-yards, Customhouses, and the like...had been seized, and were held in open hostility to this Government, excepting only...Fort Sumter, in Charleston harbor, South Carolina....Simultaneously, and in connection, with all this, the purpose to sever the Federal Union, was openly avowed....Finding this condition of things, and believing it to be an imperative duty upon the incoming Executive, to prevent, if possible, the consummation of such attempt to destroy the Federal Union, a choice of means to that end became indispensable....

...

Recurring to the action of the government, it may be stated that, at first, a call was made for seventy-five thousand militia; and rapidly following this, a proclamation was issued for closing the ports of the insurrectionary districts by proceedings in the nature of Blockade. So far all was believed to be strictly legal....Other calls were made for volunteers, to serve three years, unless sooner discharged; and also for large additions to the regular Army and Navy. These measures, whether strictly legal or not, were ventured upon, under what appeared to be a popular demand, and a public necessity; trusting, then as now, that Congress would readily ratify them. It is believed that nothing has been done beyond the constitutional competency of Congress. Soon after the first call for militia, it was considered a duty to authorize the Commanding General, in proper cases, according to his discretion, to suspend the privilege of the writ of habeas corpus; or, in other words, to arrest, and detain, without resort to the ordinary processes and forms of law, such individuals as he might deem dangerous to the public safety. This authority has purposely been exercised but very sparingly. Nevertheless, the legality and propriety of what has been done under it, are questioned; and the attention of the country has been called to the proposition that one who is sworn to "take care that the laws be faithfully executed,"' should not himself violate

56. Excerpt taken from *A Compilation of the Messages and Papers of the Presidents*, ed. James D. Richardson, vol. 6 (Washington, DC: Government Printing Office, 1897), 20–31.

them....It was not believed that any law was violated. The provision of the Constitution that "The privilege of the writ of habeas corpus, shall not be suspended unless when, in cases of rebellion or invasion, the public safety may require it," is equivalent to a provision—is a provision—that such privilege may be suspended when, in cases of rebellion, or invasion, the public safety *does* require it. It was decided that we have a case of rebellion, and that the public safety does require the qualified suspension of the privilege of the writ which was authorized to be made. Now it is insisted that Congress, and not the Executive, is vested with this power. But the Constitution itself, is silent as to which, or who, is to exercise the power; and as the provision was plainly made for a dangerous emergency, it cannot be believed the framers of the instrument intended, that in every case, the danger should run its course, until Congress could be called together; the very assembling of which might be prevented, as was intended in this case, by the rebellion....Whether there shall be any legislation upon the subject, and if any, what, is submitted entirely to the better judgment of Congress....

B. Martial Law and Habeas Corpus

Abraham Lincoln frequently suspended habeas corpus and declared martial law during the Civil War. Less than two months after taking the oath of office, he ordered habeas corpus suspended in Maryland to secure the safe transportation of troops from the northern states to the nation's capital. Lincoln subsequently either directly ordered habeas corpus suspended in various locations in the United States or authorized military officials to suspend habeas corpus when they thought doing so necessary to war effort. On September 24, Lincoln suspended habeas corpus and imposed martial law throughout the United States for persons suspected of "disloyal practices," broadly defined. His Proclamation declared:

> That, during the existing insurrection, and as a necessary measure for suppressing the same, all rebels and insurgents, their aiders and abettors, within the United States, and all persons discouraging volunteer enlistments, resisting militia drafts, or guilty of any disloyal practice, affording aid and comfort to the rebels against the authority of the United States, shall be subject to martial law, and liable to trial and punishment by courts-martial or military commission.
>
> That the writ of habeas corpus is suspended in respect to all persons arrested, or who are now, or hereafter during the rebellion shall be, imprisoned in any fort, camp, arsenal, military prison, or other place of confinement, by any military authority, or by the sentence of any court-martial or military commission.[57]

Congress authorized presidential suspensions by passing the Habeas Corpus Act of 1863. The Republican majority in Congress also sanctioned the use of military tribunals when passing the Conscription Act of 1863. Lincoln, claiming inherent executive authority, sometimes sanctioned military tribunals in circumstances not authorized by Congress.

Lincoln's decisions to suspend habeas corpus and impose martial law enabled his administration to imprison and punish persons government officials or military officers feared were disloyal, dangerous, or otherwise a threat to the general public. By suspending habeas corpus, the Lincoln Administration could arrest and detain without trial persons suspected of assisting the confederate cause. The best recent estimate is that government officials arrested and detained approximately 14,000 persons during the Civil War.[58] By imposing martial law, the Lincoln administration could have military commissions rather than juries try persons suspected of interfering with the war effort. The best recent estimate is that appropriately 1,500 persons were tried by military commissions during the Civil War and another 1,500 persons were tried by military commissions during Reconstruction. Most persons detained and tried by military commissions were charged with such crimes as desertion, trading with the enemy, and selling liquor to soldiers. Others were suspected of more political offenses. Members of the Lincoln administration ordered or approved the detention of and military trials for leading administration critics, most notably former Congressman Clement Vallandigham. The persons who plotted with John Wilkes Booth to assassinate Abraham Lincoln were tried by a military commission.[59]

---

57. *A Compilation of the Messages and Papers of the Presidents*, ed. James D. Richardson, vol. 6 (Washington, DC: Government Printing Office, 1897), 98.

58. Mark E. Neely, *The Fate of Liberty* (New York: Oxford University Press, 1992).

59. Booth was killed before he could be brought to trial.

Illustration 6-2 Chief Justice Roger Taney

Source: Roger Brooke Taney, 1777–1864 / Brady, N.Y. Library of Congress Prints and Photographs Division, LC-BH82–402.

Many prominent Americans challenged the constitutionality of official decisions to suspend habeas corpus and declare martial law. During the Civil War, most constitutional objections were based on the separation of powers. Chief Justice Roger Taney and many members of Congress believed that President Lincoln acted unconstitutionally when he suspended habeas corpus and declared martial law without congressional authorization. Democrats during the debate over the Habeas Corpus Act of 1863 further asserted that only Congress could suspend habeas corpus, that Congress could not delegate to the President the power to determine when suspending habeas corpus or declaring martial law was appropriate. Other constitutional objections were based on individual rights. Lincoln's critics maintained that federal laws imposing martial law in places where the courts were open violated such constitutional liberties as the right to trial by jury.

Constitutional debates over habeas corpus and martial law during the Civil War took place almost entirely in elected institutions, the states and the popular press. Both Republicans and Democrats in Congress sharply challenged Lincoln's claim that the Constitution gave the president the power to suspend habeas corpus and impose martial law. The few federal court interventions in this constitutional debate were ineffective. Abraham Lincoln ignored Roger

Taney when, acting as a circuit court judge, Taney in *Ex parte Merryman* (1861) declared that the President could not suspend habeas corpus without congressional authorization.

The full Supreme Court never ruled on a habeas corpus case during the Civil War. The justices in *Ex parte Vallandigham* (1864) found jurisdictional reasons to avoid hearing an appeal challenging the constitutionality of habeas suspensions and trials by military tribunals.[60] This use of jurisdiction seems strategic. Justice Samuel Miller, a Lincoln appointee, informed a friend, "strenuous efforts were made to use the Court in such a way to embarrass the Government in its conduct of operations by endeavoring to get decisions upon such questions," but the justices found a way "to prevent interference" by remaining silent on the constitutional issues.[61]

After the Civil War, the justices in *Ex parte Milligan* (1866) ruled that neither the president nor Congress could declare martial law in loyal states where courts were open. By then, the constitutional controversies over suspending habeas corpus and imposing martial law were more concerned with individual rights and federalism than with the separation of powers. Justice David Davis's majority opinion in *Milligan* asserted that President Lincoln violated the Sixth Amendment by imposing martial law in Indiana during the war. Martial law, he wrote,

> can never be applied to citizens in states which have upheld the authority of the government, and where the courts are open and their process unobstructed.... [N]o usage of war could sanction a military trial there for any offence whatever of a citizen in civil life, in nowise connected with the military service. Congress could grant no such power; and to the honor of our national legislature be it said, it has never been provoked by the state of the country even to attempt its exercise. One of the plainest constitutional provisions was, therefore, infringed when Milligan was tried by a court not ordained and established by Congress, and not composed of judges appointed during good behavior.

60. *Ex parte Vallandigham,* 68 U.S. 243 (1863); *Roosevelt v. Meyer,* 68 U.S. 512 (1863).

61. Quoted in Charles Fairman, *Mr. Justice Miller and the Supreme Court, 1862–1890* (Cambridge: Harvard University Press, 1939), 88–89.

Chief Justice Salmon Chase, in a concurring opinion, maintained that President Lincoln's decision to impose martial law violated only the constitutional separation of powers. He wrote,

> when the nation is involved in war, and some portions of the country are invaded, and all are exposed to invasion, it is within the power of Congress to determine in what states or districts such great and imminent public danger exists as justifies the authorization of military tribunals for the trial of crimes and offences against the discipline or security of the army or against the public safety.

Congress by statute in 1867 imposed military rule in the South. The Supreme Court in *Ex parte McCardle* (1869) and other cases discussed in Section II held that the justices did not have jurisdiction to determine whether that measure was constitutional.

Ex parte Merryman, 17 F. Cas. 144 (1861)

John Merryman was a prominent Marylander and proponent of secession. Republicans believed he was secretly conspiring with other secessionists to prevent northern state militias from coming to Washington, DC. Worried about the safety of the nation's capital, Abraham Lincoln on April 27, 1861, suspended habeas corpus in Baltimore. That suspension enabled the Union Army to detain persons suspected of aiding the confederacy for any period of time without charging them with a crime. Merryman was one of the first persons arrested under this order. He was held at Fort McHenry, outside of Baltimore. Merryman's friends asked Chief Justice Roger Taney, who was also the local federal circuit court judge, for a writ of habeas corpus. Such a writ required the federal government to produce Merryman in an open courtroom and either charge him with a crime or release him. When the Lincoln administration refused to produce Merryman, Taney issued an opinion declaring unconstitutional the presidential suspension of habeas corpus. After issuing his opinion, the Chief Justice of the United States told friends that he expected that he would soon be arrested and imprisoned by the army. Taney was never arrested, but Merryman remained in prison until July 12, 1861. He was subsequently indicted for treason, but never tried.

A similar incident took place in Missouri later in 1861. Union military officers arrested several Missouri citizens believed to be conspiring to attack St. Louis. Federal District Court Judge Samuel Treat issued a writ of habeas corpus. His decree ordered the military to release one of the detained citizens, Emmett McDonald. General William Harney refused. Harney first claimed that McDonald was not in his custody. This was consistent with a Lincoln Administration strategy to avoid adjudication. Writs of habeas corpus are traditionally directed to the jailor of the person in custody. By moving detainees to different places overseen by different jailors, federal officials prevented courts from exercising authority over the jailor actually holding the detained person. General Harney nevertheless declared that he could not in good conscience obey the writ, even should he be the custodian of the detained person. He wrote, "I must take to what I am compelled to regard as the higher law, even by doing so my conduct shall have the appearance of coming in conflict with the forms of the law."[62]

Why does Chief Justice Taney reject presidential power to suspend habeas corpus? Is he too quick to reject emergency powers?

CHIEF JUSTICE TANEY delivered the opinion for the Court.

...

As the case comes before me, therefore, I understand that the president not only claims the right to suspend the writ of habeas corpus himself, at his discretion, but to delegate that discretionary power to a military officer, and to leave it to him to determine whether he will or will not obey judicial process that may be served upon him. No official notice has been given to the courts of justice, or to the public, by proclamation or otherwise, that the president claimed this power, and had exercised it in the manner stated in the return. And I certainly listened to it with some surprise, for I had supposed it to be one of those points of constitutional law upon which there was no difference of opinion, and that it was admitted on all hands, that the privilege of the writ could not be suspended, except by act of congress.

...

The clause of the constitution, which authorizes the suspension of the privilege of the writ of habeas corpus, is in the 9th section of the first article. This article is devoted to the legislative department of the United States, and has not the slightest reference to the executive department....

...

62. L. U. Reavis, *The Life and Military Services of William Selby Harney* (St. Louis: Bryan, Brand & Co., 1878), 369.

It is the second article of the constitution that provides for the organization of the executive department, enumerates the powers conferred on it, and prescribes its duties. And if the high power over the liberty of the citizen now claimed, was intended to be conferred on the president, it would undoubtedly be found in plain words in this article; but there is not a word in it that can furnish the slightest ground to justify the exercise of the power.

...The short term for which [the president] is elected, and the narrow limits to which his power is confined, show the jealousy and apprehension of future danger which the framers of the constitution felt in relation to that department of the government, and how carefully they withheld from it many of the powers belonging to the executive branch of the English government which were considered as dangerous to the liberty of the subject; and conferred (and that in clear and specific terms) those powers only which were deemed essential to secure the successful operation of the government.

...

Even if the privilege of the writ of habeas corpus were suspended by act of congress, and a party not subject to the rules and articles of war were afterwards arrested and imprisoned by regular judicial process, he could not be detained in prison, or brought to trial before a military tribunal, for the article in the amendments to the constitution immediately following the one above referred to (that is, the sixth article) provides, that "in all criminal prosecutions, the accused shall enjoy the right to a speedy and public trial by an impartial jury of the state and district wherein the crime shall have been committed, which district shall have been previously ascertained by law; and to be informed of the nature and cause of the accusation; to be confronted with the witnesses against him; to have compulsory process for obtaining witnesses in his favor; and to have the assistance of counsel for his defence."

...

With such provisions in the constitution, expressed in language too clear to be misunderstood by any one, I can see no ground whatever for supposing that the president, in any emergency, or in any state of things, can authorize the suspension of the privileges of the writ of habeas corpus, or the arrest of a citizen, except in aid of the judicial power. He certainly does not faithfully execute the laws, if he takes upon himself legislative power, by suspending the writ of habeas corpus, and the judicial power also, by arresting and imprisoning a person without due process of law.

. . .

The right of the subject to the benefit of the writ of habeas corpus, it must be recollected, was one of the great points in controversy, during the long struggle in England between arbitrary government and free institutions, and must therefore have strongly attracted the attention of the statesmen engaged in framing a new and, as they supposed, a freer government than the one which they had thrown off by the revolution. From the earliest history of the common law, if a person were imprisoned, no matter by what authority, he had a right to the writ of habeas corpus, to bring his case before the king's bench; if no specific offence were charged against him in the warrant of commitment, he was entitled to be forthwith discharged; and if an offence were charged which was bailable in its character, the court was bound to set him at liberty on bail. . . .

. . .

[N]o power in England short of that of parliament can suspend or authorize the suspension of the writ of habeas corpus. I quote again from Blackstone: "But the happiness of our constitution is, that it is not left to the executive power to determine when the danger of the state is so great as to render this measure expedient. It is the parliament only or legislative power that, whenever it sees proper, can authorize the crown by suspending the habeas corpus for a short and limited time, to imprison suspected persons without giving any reason for so doing." If the president of the United States may suspend the writ, then the constitution of the United States has conferred upon him more regal and absolute power over the liberty of the citizen, than the people of England have thought it safe to entrust to the crown. . . .

. . .

Edward Bates, Opinion on the Suspension of the Privilege of the Writ of Habeas Corpus (1861)[63]

Abraham Lincoln's message to Congress on July 4, 1861, responded to Taney's accusation of lawlessness in Ex parte Merryman. *While defending the constitutionality of his decision to suspend habeas corpus, Lincoln indicated that he may have had supra-constitutional reasons taking unilateral executive action.*

> *Soon after the first call for militia, it was considered a duty to authorize the Commanding General, in proper cases, according to his discretion, to suspend the privilege of the writ of habeas corpus; or, in other words, to arrest, and detain, without resort to the ordinary processes and forms of law, such individuals as he might deem dangerous to the public safety. This authority has purposely been exercised but very sparingly. Nevertheless, the legality and propriety of what has been done under it, are questioned; and the attention of the country has been called to the proposition that one who is sworn to "take care that the laws be faithfully executed," should not himself violate them. Of course some consideration was given to the questions of power, and propriety, before this matter was acted upon. The whole of the laws which were required to be faithfully executed, were being resisted, and failing of execution, in nearly one-third of the States. Must they be allowed to finally fail of execution, even had it been perfectly clear, that by the use of the means necessary to their execution, some single law, made in such extreme tenderness of the citizen's liberty, that practically, it relieves more of the guilty, than of the innocent, should, to a very limited extent, be violated? To state the question more directly, are all the laws, but one, to go unexecuted, and the government itself go to pieces, lest that one be violated? Even in such a case, would not the official oath be broken, if the government should be overthrown, when it was believed that disregarding the single law, would tend to preserve it? But it was not believed that this question was presented. It was not believed that any law was violated.*[64]

Bates followed up Lincoln's speech with an official opinion justifying the president's suspension of the writ of habeas corpus as consistent with the Constitution. Bates insisted that impeachment is the only remedy for an abusive suspension of habeas corpus. Was he correct as a constitutional matter? Was he correct as a practical matter? President Lincoln was unwilling to obey the judicial order in Merryman. *During times of national crisis, is the judiciary likely to be able to impose constitutional limitations on the president without legislative support? What are the constitutional*

63. Excerpt taken from 10 Op. Atty Gen. 74, July 5, 1861.

64. *A Compilation of the Messages and Papers of the Presidents*, ed. James D. Richardson, vol. 6 (Washington, DC: Government Printing Office, 1897), 24.

means for challenging a president during wartime? How many of these means are politically feasible? Suppose you believed that Merryman and his allies were a serious threat to efforts to move Union troops from New York to the defense of Washington, DC. What would you have done in Lincoln's place?

...

...I am clearly of opinion that, in a time like the present, when the very existence of the nation is assailed, by a great and dangerous insurrection, the President has the lawful discretionary power to arrest and hold in custody persons known to have criminal intercourse with the insurgents, or persons against whom there is probable cause for suspicion of such criminal complicity....

The Constitution requires the President, before he enters upon the execution of his office, to take an oath that he "will faithfully execute the office of President of the United States, and will, to the best of his ability, preserve, protect and defend the Constitution of the United States."

The duties of the office comprehend all the executive power of the nation, which is expressly vested in the President by the Constitution, (Article II, Sec. 1,) and, also, all the powers which are specially delegated to the President, and yet are not, in their nature, executive powers. For example, the veto power; the treaty making power; the appointing power; the pardoning power. These belong to that class which, in England, are called prerogative powers, inherent in the crown. And yet the framers of our Constitution thought proper to preserve them, and to vest them in the President, as necessary to the good government of the country. The executive powers are granted generally, and without specification; the powers not executive are granted specially, and for purposes obvious in the context of the Constitution. And all these are embraced within the duties of the President, and are clearly within that clause of his oath which requires him to "faithfully execute the office of President."

The last clause of the oath is peculiar to the President. All the other officers of the Government are required to swear only "to support this Constitution;" while the President must swear to "preserve, protect, and defend" it, which implies the power to perform what he is required in so solemn a manner to undertake. And then follows the broad and compendious injunction to "take care that the laws be faithfully executed." And this injunction, embracing as it does all the laws—Constitution, treaties, statutes—is addressed to the President alone, and not to any other department or officer of the Government. And this constitutes him, in a peculiar manner, and above all other officers, the guardian of the Constitution—its preserver, protector, and defender.

It is the plain duty of the President (and his peculiar duty, above and beyond all other departments of the Government) to preserve the Constitution and execute the laws all over the nation; and it is plainly impossible for him to perform this duty without putting down rebellion, insurrection, and all unlawful combinations to resist the General Government....

The argument may be briefly stated thus: It is the President's bounden duty to put down the insurrection, as...the "combinations are too powerful to be suppressed by the ordinary course of judicial proceedings, or by the powers vested in the marshals." And this duty is imposed upon the President for the very reason that the courts and the marshals are too weak to perform it. The manner in which he shall perform that duty is not prescribed by any law, but the means of performing it are given, in the plain language of the statutes, and they are all means of force—the militia, the army, and the navy. The end, the suppression of the insurrection, is required of him; the means and instruments to suppress it are lawfully in his hands; but the manner in which he shall use them is not prescribed, and could not be prescribed, without a foreknowledge of all the future changes and contingencies of the insurrection. He is, therefore, necessarily, thrown upon his discretion, as to the manner in which he will use his means to meet the varying exigencies as they rise. If the insurgents assail the nation with an army, he may find it best to meet them with an army, and suppress the insurrection in the field of battle. If they seek to prolong the rebellion, and gather strength by intercourse with foreign nations, he may choose to guard the coast and close the ports with a navy, as one of the most efficient means to suppress the insurrection. And if they employ spies and emissaries, to gather information, to forward rebellion, he may find it both prudent and humane to arrest and imprison them. And this may be done, either for the purpose of bringing them to trial and condign punishment for their crimes, or they may be held in custody for the milder end of rendering them powerless for mischief, until the exigency is past.

In such a state of things, the President must, of necessity, be the sole judge, both of the exigency which requires him to act, and of the manner in which it is most prudent for him to employ the powers entrusted to him, to enable him to discharge his constitutional and legal duty—that is, to suppress the insurrection and execute the laws....

This is a great power in the hands of the chief magistrate; and because it is great, and is capable of being perverted to evil ends, its existence has been doubted and denied. It is said to be dangerous, in the hands of an ambitious and wicked President, because he may use it for the purposes of oppression and tyranny. Yes, certainly it is dangerous—all power is dangerous—and for the all-pervading reason that all power is liable to abuse; all the recipients of human power are men, not absolutely virtuous and wise. Still it is a power necessary to the peace and safety of the country, and undeniably belongs to the Government, and therefore must be exercised by some department or officer thereof.

Why should this power be denied to the President, on the ground of its liability to abuse, and not denied to the other departments on the same grounds? Are they more exempt than he is from the frailties and vices of humanity? Or are they more trusted by the law than he is trusted, in their several spheres of action? If it be said that a President may be ambitious and unscrupulous, it may be said with equal truth, that a legislature may be factious and unprincipled, and a court may be venal and corrupt. But these are crimes never to be presumed, even against a private man, and much less against any high and highly-trusted public functionary. They are crimes, however, recognized as such, and made punishable by the Constitution; and whoever is guilty of them, whether a President, a senator, or a judge, is liable to impeachment and condemnation.

The Habeas Corpus Act of 1863[65]

The Habeas Corpus Act of 1863 was originally conceived as a measure to prevent persons arrested and detained by the Lincoln administration from suing government officials. The bill proposed in the House of Representatives provided that persons acting under government orders would not be liable for damages in either trespass or false arrest suits. Senator Lyman Trumbull of Illinois, a moderate Republican, saw the bill as an opportunity to both modify Lincoln administration policy on suspending habeas corpus and to place that modified policy on firmer legal grounds. Trumbull's bill authorized the president to suspend habeas corpus, but provided that persons so detained be quickly brought before federal judges who would determine whether they were legally imprisoned. Democrats and radical Republicans sharply challenged Trumbull's proposal. Democrats insisted that Congress could not delegate power to the president to suspend habeas corpus and that Congress should provide strong remedies to persons they believed had been unconstitutionally arrested and detained by the Lincoln Administration. Many Republicans believed the Trumbull bill too weak. They maintained that the Lincoln Administration should have the power to detain indefinitely persons suspected of aiding the Confederate effort. Through deft political maneuvering, the middle held. Trumbull's version of the Habeas Corpus Act became law on March 3, 1863.

The excerpts that follow are from the bill, the Democratic alternative, and the debate in the Senate. How did the various parties to the debate over habeas corpus justify their constitutional arguments? In particular, how did they combine positions about the separation of powers with positions about individual rights? What do you believe best explains why Republicans did not present a united constitutional front during the Civil War on suspending habeas corpus and imposing martial law?

The Habeas Corpus Act

...That, during the present rebellion, the President of the United States, whenever, in his judgment, the public safety may require it, is authorized to suspend the privilege of the writ of habeas corpus in any case throughout the United States, or any part thereof....

SEC. 2. That the Secretary of State and the Secretary of War be, and they are hereby, directed, as soon as may be practicable, to furnish to the judges of the circuit and district courts of the United States and of the District of Columbia a list of the names of all persons, citizens of states in which the administration of the laws has continued unimpaired in the said Federal courts, who are now, or may hereafter be, held as prisoners of the United States, by order or authority of the President of the United States or either of said Secretaries, in any fort, arsenal, or other place, as state or political prisoners, or otherwise than as prisoners of war....And in all cases where a grand jury, having attended any of said courts having jurisdiction in the

65. Excerpt taken from 12 *U.S. Stat.* 755, 755–56 (1863); *Congressional Globe*, 37th Cong., 3rd Sess., 1092, 1191–1208.

premises, after the passage of this act, and after the furnishing of said list, as aforesaid, has terminated its session without finding an indictment or presentment, or other proceeding against any such person, it shall be the duty of the judge of said court forthwith to make an order that any such prisoner desiring a discharge from said imprisonment be brought before him to be discharged; and every officer of the United States having custody of such prisoner is hereby directed immediately to obey and execute said judge's order... That no person shall be discharged by virtue of the provisions of this act until after he or she shall have taken an oath of allegiance to the Government of the United States, and to support the Constitution thereof; and that he or she will not hereafter in any way encourage or give aid and comfort to the present rebellion, or the supporters thereof....

SEC. 3. That in case any of such prisoners shall be under indictment or presentment for any offence against the laws of the United States, and by existing laws bail or a recognizance may be taken for the appearance for trial of such person, it shall be the duty of said judge at once to discharge such person upon bail or recognizance for trial as aforesaid....

SEC. 4... That any order of the President, or under his authority, made at any time during the existence of the present rebellion, shall be a defense in all courts to any action or prosecution, civil or criminal, pending, or to be commenced, for any search, seizure, arrest, or imprisonment, made, done, or committed, or acts omitted to be done, under and by virtue of such order, or under color of any law of Congress, and such defense may be made by special plea, or under the general issue.

...

The Democratic Alternative

From and after the passage of this act, and during the present rebellion, it shall not be lawful for any officer or servant of the United States to arrest or detain any citizen of the United States who may be supposed or alleged to be disloyal thereto, or for any other cause, except upon oath or affirmation of some person or persons well known to be loyal to the United States, and particularly describing in said oath or affirmation the act of disloyalty or other cause for which the said citizen should be arrested and detained.

... That any and every officer or servant of the United States who shall arrest or detain any citizen of the United States in contravention of the provisions of the first section of this act, shall, on conviction thereof in any court having jurisdiction in the case, suffer a fine of not less than $10,000, or imprisonment in the penitentiary for a term not less than five years.

... That all persons arrested under the provision of this act upon the charge of disloyalty to the Government of the United States, or for any other cause, shall have the privilege of the writ of *habeas corpus*; and the said writ shall not be suspended in any time, so far as the same may relate to persons arrested as aforesaid.

...

Senator LAZARUS POWELL (Democrat, Kentucky)

...

I did say that where the courts were open and were in the exercise of all their functions, I did not believe the writ of *habeas corpus* should ever be suspended, and I am now clearly of that opinion. If you have a virtuous and intelligent judiciary, let those who are arrested be brought before the courts, and let them be punished if they be guilty. Let the man that is arrested come before the judges. If he has committed no crime, let him be discharged. If the case be bailable, let him give bond for his appearance at court. Where the courts are open and none of their functions obstructed, and the judges are upright and honest men, in my judgment a free people should never allow this great remedial writ to be suspended....

...

Mr. President, I do not believe that we have any power under the Constitution to delegate to the President of the United States the power to suspend the writ of *habeas corpus*; it is a power conferred upon us which we cannot delegate to another. We have as much right to delegate it to one of the judges of the Supreme Court or to any other individual, either indicated by his office or by his name, as we have to delegate to the President of the United States. We cannot delegate our functions. I hold that the power belongs to us, and whenever the writ is lawfully suspended, in my judgment, it must be done by Congress, for Congress alone, under the Constitution, has authority to suspend the writ....

I think it would be a dangerous precedent for this Congress or any other Congress to delegate to any other power on earth this privilege of suspending this great writ. A people who love their liberties and who are jealous of their personal rights, in my judgment, never should enter upon any such hazardous enterprise.... If the President of the United States should be a wicked or corrupt man, he could by one stroke of his pen compel every citizen who might be arrested by the minions of power, however unlawfully, to languish in prison, until he should see fit, not by virtue of the law, but in the exercise of his will and pleasure, to discharge him.... I would not confer it on any man, I care not how great, how good, how wise, how virtuous he may be, and I do not concede that those who are the real and true friends of constitutional and civil liberty ever will part with this power....

I am not one of those who believe that any great good in distempered times ever did or ever will result from the suspension of the writ of *habeas corpus*. Suppose you suspend it, what then? What is the effect of the suspension? All it does is to prevent a man who conceives that he is unlawfully imprisoned from being brought before the judicial tribunals of the country to have the causes of imprisonment investigated. That is all. The mere suspension of the writ of *habeas corpus* does not authorize the President or anybody else to arrest a citizen. The arrest is a separate and distinct thing from taking a man out of prison on a writ of *habeas corpus*. The power to arrest a citizen is confided not to the Executive or to any of his agencies or to any of his heads of Departments. It is confided by the Constitution to a separate and distinct body of magistracy, to wit, the judiciary, through the instrumentality and aid of the marshals and sheriffs of the country. You may suspend the writ of *habeas corpus* tonight if you please, and then the President of the United States, the Secretary of War, or one of your generals in the field, or your hands of Departments, would not be authorized to make an arrest of a citizen not in the military service; and if any of them did make an arrest he would be liable as a trespasser in the courts for that encroachment on the personal rights of the citizen. An arrest under the Constitution can only be made on warrant, sued out for just and proper cause on affidavit. That is the Constitution of your country....

...

I do not think the Senator's bill... is as it should be. It allows those persons to be kept for twenty days. Sir, a free citizen of a free country should not be detained and deprived of his liberty a single moment after he demands to be brought before the judicial tribunals of the country to have the charges against him investigated; and that is not a free country which will allow a man to be deprived for one moment of his liberty longer than he can apply to the proper tribunals to have the cause of his confinement investigated. I would vote for no law that would authorize any power on earth to keep any man twenty days or twenty hours, unless he was committed in obedience to the laws of his country. If you arrest him on a sudden emergency, which under the law you have a right to do in a large number of cases, hand him immediately over to the judicial magistrates to have the case investigated, and if he is guilty, punished; if innocent, acquitted. That is our duty, and whenever we fall short of that we are delinquent.

... You admit that thousands of people have been arrested without warrant of law. You admit that persons have ordered arrests who had no authority under the Constitution and laws to make arrests; and, so far from facilitating the people thus injured in having their remedies and rights of action against those who have acted thus wrongfully, we are engaged in passing laws to prevent, hinder, and delay these persons in appeals to the proper judicial tribunals to have their wrongs righted....

Senator JAMES DOOLITTLE (Republican, Wisconsin)

...

Mr. President, the necessity for the suspension of this writ is absolute; it is immediate; the only question is—and that is the disputed one—who has the power to suspend it, who shall judge when it shall be suspended? On that subject we all know there has been a great difference of opinion. Some of the very best legal minds of the country, and I will say some of the best legal minds in this Chamber, maintain, and earnestly maintain, that the suspension of *habeas corpus* in time of war is of necessity an executive power, and they put it on the ground of the very nature of the power. If it depends upon the Congress to suspend it, Congress is not in session for one half the year. The Executive is always in session, is always active, and always ready to exert his power. Not so with Congress. Before Congress could be called together, an insurrection might seize your seat of Government, seize your archives, seize your public offices, and prevent the assembling of Congress which is necessary to the suspension of the writ. But, sir, on the other hand it is maintained that the jealousies of our people are such that they are unwilling to place in the hands of a single individual this immense power to imprison a man in time of war and insurrection; and hence it is contended that it should be in the legislative power, it should belong to Congress, and to Congress alone to judge the necessity of when this writ should be suspended.

> Now, in that, which is the practical state of this case, what shall we do? The bill of the honorable Senator from Illinois is drawn in such a manner that those who maintain that the power is in the President can vote for that section for it amounts to but a declaratory section, declaring that the President is authorized; and those who maintain that the power is in Congress can vote for that section, for if the President does not have it under the Constitution, that section will clothe him with the power....
>
> ...
>
> ...I have no doubt, no misgiving as to the validity of this act, nor have I any doubt or any misgiving as to the beneficial effects which it will exercise throughout the lands; and then, under this act, the President clothed with this power upon his responsibility to suspend this writ, will be authorized to seize those who are guilty of the crime of treason, or those who are lending the rebellion aid or comfort, or those whom he knows, or has every reason to believe, are about to join the enemy, or give them aid or comfort; for it is to reach that class of men that it is necessary that the Executive should be clothed with this power. It is not enough that he may be permitted to arrest those who have been guilty of actual crime. In times of war it is necessary to arrest those who are about the engage in crime....

C. Presidential War and Foreign Affairs Powers

President Lincoln in his first eighteen months in office repeatedly insisted that the Civil War was being fought solely to preserve national union, and not for emancipating slaves. Responding to an editorial in the New York *Tribune* urging him to push more aggressively for emancipation, Lincoln on August 22, 1862, declared,

> I would save the Union. I would save it the shortest way under the Constitution. The sooner the national authority can be restored; the nearer the Union will be "the Union as it was." If there be those who would not save the Union, unless they could at the same time save slavery, I do not agree with them. If there be those who would not save the Union unless they could at the same time destroy slavery, I do not agree with them. My paramount object in this struggle is to save the Union, and is not either to save or to destroy slavery. If I could save the Union without freeing any slave I would do it, and if I could save it by freeing all the slaves I would do it; and if I could save it by freeing some and leaving others alone I would also do that. What I do about slavery, and the colored race, I do because I believe it helps to save the Union; and what I forbear, I forbear because I do not believe it would help to save the Union. I shall do less whenever I shall believe what I am doing hurts the cause, and I shall do more whenever I shall believe doing more shall help the cause.[66]

At the very time he issued that statement, Lincoln was planning on issuing a presidential proclamation emancipating slaves. He refrained from making his intentions public until after the Union armies at the Battle of Antietam successfully prevented a Confederate invasion of the North.

On September 22, 1862, Lincoln declared that "all persons held as slaves within any State...in rebellion against the United States shall be...forever free" as of January 1, 1863. The Emancipation Proclamation redefined the northern war effort as directed at securing freedom as well as maintaining union. The Proclamation had an important foreign policy aim. By converting a war for Union into a war for human freedom, Lincoln put public pressure on European powers not to recognize or aid the Confederacy.

As Table 6-3 suggests, the Civil War raised many new judicial challenges to the scope of the president's power as "commander in chief" under Article II of the U.S. Constitution. Many constitutional debates over the scope of the commander-in-chief clause, including the debate over the constitutionality of the Emancipation Proclamation, never reached the U.S. Supreme Court or were never addressed on their merits. But the justices have weighed in on some questions of presidential power over time. The Civil War created some new challenges, but by the 1860s the justices could already rely on decisions they had made stemming from the war with Mexico in the 1840s. Those precedents from the mid-nineteenth century continued to inform the Court as the justices grappled with problems of American imperialism at the turn of the twentieth century and the transformation of the United States into a global superpower a century after the Civil War.

---

66. Abraham Lincoln, *Collected Works of Abraham Lincoln*, ed. Roy P. Basler, vol. 5 (New Brunswick, NJ: Rutgers University Press, 1953), 388.

Table 6-3 Selection of U.S. Supreme Court Cases Reviewing Presidential Powers as Commander in Chief

Case	Vote	Outcome	Decision
Brown v. United States, 12 U.S. 110 (1814)	5–2	Struck down	President has no independent authority to seize alien enemies or their property within the United States
Cross, Hobson & Co. v. Harrison, 57 U.S. 164 (1854)	9–0	Upheld	President has independent authority to form a civil government and collect taxes in a conquered territory
The Prize Cases, 67 U.S. 635 (1863)	5–4	Upheld	President "bound to accept the challenge" of a de facto war and exercise war powers on his own authority
Ex parte Milligan, 71 U.S. 2 (1866)	9–0	Struck down	President cannot declare martial law where civilian courts are operating
The Grapeshot, 76 U.S. 129 (1869)	8–0	Upheld	President has independent authority to establish civil courts in a conquered territory
Totten v. United States, 92 U.S. 105 (1875)	9–0	Upheld	President has independent authority to employ covert operatives
Swaim v. United States, 165 U.S. 553 (1897)	9–0	Upheld	Statutes supplement president's own power to convene a court martial
Dooley v. United States, 182 U.S. 222 (1901)	5–4	Struck down	Power of president to set tariff rates in conquered territory ended with ratification of peace treaty
Santiago v. Nogueras, 214 U.S. 260 (1909)	9–0	Upheld	Power of president to maintain civilian courts in conquered territory continues after ratification of peace treaty
Ex parte Quirin, 317 U.S. 1 (1942)	9–0	Upheld	President has power to try war saboteurs by military commission
Youngstown Sheet & Tube Co. v. Sawyer, 343 U.S. 579 (1952)	6–3	Struck down	President does not have power to seize industrial plants to support war effort
Orloff v. Willouhby, 345 U.S. 83 (1953)	6–3	Upheld	President has discretion over commissioning military officers
United States ex rel. Toth v. Quarles, 350 U.S. 11 (1955)	6–3	Struck down	Neither president nor Congress can extend jurisdiction of courts martial to include veterans
Cafeteria & Restaurant Workers Unions v. McElroy, 367 U.S. 886 (1961)	5–4	Upheld	President has power to regulate and control access to military bases
Department of the Navy v. Egan, 484 U.S. 518 (1988)	5–3	Upheld	President can control identification of and access to classified materials
Hamdan v. Rumsfeld, 548 U.S. 557 (2006)	5–3	Struck down	President cannot create tribunals for trial and punishment of war criminals except in necessity

Abraham Lincoln, **"Emancipation Proclamation"** (1862)[67]

The Emancipation Proclamation freed only those slaves in areas not under Union military control on January 1, 1863. A broader emancipation act might have had political and legal problems. Politically, the act would have created problems in the border states, where slavery was still legal. The Thirteenth Amendment was necessary to abolish slavery in Maryland, Delaware, Missouri, and Kentucky. Moreover, Lincoln did not believe a general emancipation order was constitutional. Lincoln and most Republicans believed that Congress had no power to emancipate slaves in existing states. This limit on congressional power explains why Lincoln turned to his Article II power as commander in chief to justify depriving the Confederacy of a vital labor force. This Presidential power extended only over the seceding states. Slaves in such states as Maryland and Kentucky were not contributing to the Confederate war effort. Hence, Lincoln could not have issued an order as commander in chief freeing all slaves in those states.

The Emancipation Proclamation enjoyed a mixed reception in the North. African-Americans were overjoyed. Black abolitionists in Boston spontaneously began singing "Blow Ye the Trumpet Blow" when the Proclamation was promulgated.[68] Lincoln's critics were less exuberant. Former Supreme Court Justice Benjamin Curtis spoke of "military despotism." Many Democrats complained that uncompensated emancipation deprived loyal southerners of their property without due process of law.

The Emancipation Proclamation is presently one of the most celebrated documents in American constitutional history. Consider when reading the following materials the reason for the celebration. Should we celebrate Lincoln's constitutional reasoning? Should we care whether an order freeing slaves is constitutional?

Whereas, on the twenty-second day of September, in the year of our Lord one thousand eight hundred and sixty-two, a proclamation was issued by the President of the United States, containing, among other things, the following, to wit:

> "That on the first day of January, in the year of our Lord one thousand eight hundred and sixty-three, all persons held as slaves within any State or designated part of a State, the people whereof shall then be in rebellion against the United States, shall be then, thenceforward, and forever free; and the Executive Government of the United States, including the military and naval authority thereof, will recognize and maintain the freedom of such persons, and will do no act or acts to repress such persons, or any of them, in any efforts they may make for their actual freedom.
>
> "That the Executive will, on the first day of January aforesaid, by proclamation, designate the States and parts of States, if any, in which the people thereof, respectively, shall then be in rebellion against the United States. . . ."

Now, therefore I, Abraham Lincoln, President of the United States, by virtue of the power in me vested as Commander-in-Chief, of the Army and Navy of the United States in time of actual armed rebellion against the authority and government of the United States, and as a fit and necessary war measure for suppressing said rebellion, do . . . designate as the States and parts of States wherein the people thereof respectively, are this day in rebellion against the United States, the following [at this point Lincoln listed all areas not under Union control]. And by virtue of the power, and for the purpose aforesaid, I do order and declare that all persons held as slaves within said designated States, and parts of States, are, and henceforward shall be free; and that the Executive government of the United States, including the military and naval authorities thereof, will recognize and maintain the freedom of said persons.

. . .

And upon this act, sincerely believed to be an act of justice, warranted by the Constitution, upon military necessity, I invoke the considerate judgment of mankind, and the gracious favor of Almighty God.

Benjamin Curtis, **Executive Power** (1862)[69]

Benjamin Curtis (1809–1874) was a leading northern critic of the Emancipation Proclamation. When on the Supreme Court, Curtis wrote a powerful dissent in Dred Scott *which temporarily made him a hero to the anti-slavery movement. Curtis resigned from the Court the next year to return to*

67. Excerpt taken from *A Compilation of the Messages and Papers of the Presidents*, ed. James D. Richardson, vol. 6 (Washington, DC: Government Printing Office, 1897), 157–59.

68. See Ronald Garet, "'Proclaim Liberty,'" *Southern California Law Review* 74 (2000):158.

69. Excerpt taken from Benjamin Curtis, *Executive Power* (Boston: Little, Brown, 1862).

private legal practice. During the Civil War, the former Whig became a vocal opponent of expanded presidential power. Curtis targeted the Emancipation Proclamation as one of Lincoln's worse abuses of power. He paired that proclamation with Lincoln's proclamations suspending habeas corpus and setting up trials by military commissions in the North. These proclamations, Curtis believed, could not be constitutionally justified by the president's power as commander in chief.

. . .

This [emancipation] proclamation . . . proposes to repeal and annul valid State laws which regulate the domestic relations of their people.

. . . [T]his executive decree holds out this proposed repeal of State laws as a threatened penalty for the continuance of a governing majority of the people of each State, or part of a State, in rebellion against the United States. So that the President hereby assumes to himself the power to denounce it as a punishment against the entire people of a State, that the valid laws of that State which regulate the domestic condition of its inhabitants shall become null and void, at a certain future date, by reason of the criminal conduct of a governing majority of its people.

This penalty, however . . . is not to be inflicted on those persons who have been guilty of treason. The freedom of their slaves was already provided for by the act of Congress, recited in a subsequent part of the Proclamation. It is upon the slaves of loyal persons, or of those who, from their tender years, or other disability, cannot be either disloyal or otherwise, that the proclamation is to operate, if at all; and it is to operate to set them free, in spite of the valid laws of their States . . .

. . .

The only supposed source or measure of these vast powers appears to have been designated by the President, in his reply to the address of the Chicago clergymen, in the following words: "Understand, I raise no objection against it on legal or constitutional grounds; for, as commander-in-chief of the army and navy, in time of war, I suppose I have a right to take any measure which may best subdue the enemy."

. . . [I]f the President of the United States has an implied constitutional right, as commander-in-chief of the army and navy in time of war, to disregard any one positive prohibition of the Constitution, or to exercise any one power not delegated to the United States by the Constitution, because, in his judgment, he may thereby "best subdue the enemy," he has the same right, for the same reason, to disregard each and every provision of the Constitution, to exercise all power needful, in his opinion, to enable him "best to subdue the enemy."

. . .

The necessary result of this interpretation of the Constitution is that, in time of war, the President has any and all power which he may deem it necessary to exercise, to subdue the enemy; and that every private and personal right of individual security against mere executive control, and every right reserved to the States or the people, rests merely upon executive discretion.

. . .

He is general-in-chief; but can a general-in-chief disobey any law of his own country? When he can, he superadds to his rights as commander the powers of a usurper; and that is military despotism. . . . And that, under the Constitution and laws of the United States, no more than under the government of Great Britain, or under any free or any settled government, the mere authority to command an army is not an authority to disobey the laws of the country.

. . . [A]ll the powers of the President are executive merely. He cannot make a law. He cannot repeal one. He can only execute of the laws. He can neither make nor suspend nor alter them. . . .

. . .

In time of war, a military commander, whether he be the commander-in-chief or one of his subordinates, must possess and exercise powers both over the persons and the property of citizens which do not exist in time of peace. But he possesses and exercises such powers, not in spite of the Constitution and laws of the United States, or in derogation from their authority, but in virtue thereof and in strict subordination thereto. The general who moves his army over private property in the course of his operations in the field, or who impresses into the public service means of transportation or subsistence, to enable him to act against the enemy, or who seizes persons within his lines as spies, or destroys supplies in immediate danger of falling into the hands of the enemy, uses authority unknown to the Constitution and laws of the United States in time of peace, but not unknown to that Constitution and those laws in time of war. The power to declare war includes the power to use the customary and necessary means effectually to carry it on. . . . And, in time of war without any special legislation, not the commander-in-chief only, but every commander of an expedition or of a military post is lawfully empowered by the Constitution and laws of the United States to do whatever is necessary, and is sanctioned by the laws of war to accomplish the lawful objects of his command. But it is obvious that this implied authority must find early limits somewhere. If it were admitted that a commanding general in the field might do whatever in his discretion might be necessary to subdue the enemy, he could levy contributions to pay his soldiers; he could force conscripts in to his service; he could drive out of the entire country all persons not desirous to aid him: in short, he would be the absolute master of the country for the time being.

No one has ever supposed—no one will now undertake to maintain—that the commander-in-chief, in time of war, has any such lawful authority as this.

What, then, is his authority over the persons and property of citizens? I answer, that...over all persons and property within the sphere of his actual operations in the field, he may lawfully exercise such restraint and control as the successful prosecution of his particular military enterprise may, in his honest judgment, absolutely require....And there his lawful authority ends.

But when the military commander controls the persons or property of citizens who are beyond the sphere of his actual operation in the field, when he makes laws to govern their conduct, he becomes a legislator....

It is manifest that, in proclaiming these edicts, the President is not acting under the authority of military law: first, because military law extends only over the persons actually enlisted in the military service; and, second, because these persons are governed by laws enacted by the legislative power. It is equally manifest that he is not acting under that implied authority which grows out of particular actual military operations; for these executive decrees do not spring from the special emergencies of any particular military operations, and are not limited to any field in which any such operations are carried on.

...

These conclusions concerning the powers of the President cannot be shaken by the assertion that "rebels have no rights."

It is not true of those States; for the Government of the United States has never admitted, and cannot admit, that as States, they are in rebellion....

Nor is the assertion that "rebels have no rights" applicable to the people of those States...When many millions of people are involved in civil war, humanity, and that public law which in modern times is humane, forbid their treatment as outlaws. And if public law and the Constitution and laws of the United States are now their rules of duty towards us, on what ground shall we deny that public law and the Constitution, and the laws made under it, are also our rules of duty towards them?

But, if it were conceded that "rebels have no rights," there would still be matter demanding the gravest consideration. For the inquiry which I have invited is not what are their rights, but what are our rights.

Whatever may be thought of the wisdom of the proclamation of the President, concerning the emancipation of slaves, no one can doubt its practical importance, if it is to take effect. To set free about four millions of slaves, at an early fixed day, with absolutely no preparation for their future, and with no preparation for our future, in their relations with us, and to do this by force, must be admitted to be a matter of vast concern, not only to them and to their masters, but to the whole continent on which they must live. There may be great diversities of opinion concerning the effects of such an act. But that its effects must be of stupendous importance, extending not only into the border loyal States, but into all the States, North as well as South...It is among the rights of all of us that the powers of each State to govern its own internal affairs should not be trespassed on by any department of the Federal power; and it is a right essential to the maintenance of our system of government. It is among the rights of all of us that the executive power should be kept within its prescribed constitutional limits, and should not legislate, but its decrees, upon subjects of transcendent importance to the whole people.

A leading and influential newspaper, while expressing entire devotion to the President, and approbation of his proclamation of emancipation, says: "The Democrats talk about 'unconstitutional acts.' Nobody pretends that this act is constitutional, and nobody cares whether it is or not."

Among all the causes of alarm which now distress the public mind, there are few more terrible to reflecting men, than the tendency to lawlessness which is manifesting itself in so many directions. No stronger evidence of this could be afforded than the open declaration of a respectable and widely circulated journal, that "nobody cares" whether a great public act of the President of the United States is in conformity with or is subversive of the supreme law of the land....

...

The Prize Cases, 67 U.S. 635 (1863)

President Lincoln responded to the attack on Fort Sumter by ordering a blockade of southern ports and calling for military volunteers. The blockade was particularly crucial to Union military success. The states that seceded had little industrial capacity and were dependent on foreign trade for the supplies necessary to fight a war. Confederate leaders were convinced that European demand for cotton would eventually lead to European support for and recognition of southern independence. Thus, the blockade was both a military and political necessity. If successful, the Union blockade would isolate the South both economically and diplomatically, helping to starve the Confederacy into submission.

On July 10, 1861, the Quaker City *captured the* Amy Warwick. *The* Quaker City *was a Union ship, enforcing the blockade against the South. The* Amy Warwick *was owned by several merchants who lived in Richmond, Virginia. The captain and crew of the* Quaker City *claimed the cargo of the* Amy Warwick. *This was consistent with the traditional right of a captain and crew to claim as a prize any ship they captured attempting to run a lawful blockade. The owners of the* Amy Warwick *insisted the blockade was unlawful. They pointed out that Lincoln initially acted without congressional approval, ordering the blockade before Congress was in session. Although Congress in July ratified the blockade, the owners questioned whether that ratification could be retroactively applied to ships captured before the ratifying legislation was passed. Lincoln and the Republican Congress insisted that the national government could blockade the South because blockades were legitimate under international law. Opponents of the blockade rejected assertions that the Constitution incorporated international law. They also contested claims that international law authorized blockades during a civil war.*

The judicial majority in The Prize Cases *affirmed both presidential authority and national power. Justice Robert Grier ruled that the president had the power under both the Constitution and international law to order a blockade in response to an insurrection, although his majority opinion did not make clear the constitutional consequences had Congress not affirmed presidential policy. The newly constituted nine-member Court was closely divided, voting 5–4 on the case. Judicial appointments proved decisive. The surviving members of the Taney Court voted 4–2 against the constitutionality of the blockade. The three Lincoln appointees supported the blockade.*

JUSTICE GRIER delivered the opinion of the Court.

...

Had the President a right to institute a blockade of ports in possession of persons in armed rebellion against the Government, on the principles of international law, as known and acknowledged among civilized States?

...

By the Constitution, Congress alone has the power to declare a national or foreign war. It cannot declare war against a State, or any number of States, by virtue of any clause in the Constitution. The Constitution confers on the President the whole Executive power. He is bound to take care that the laws be faithfully executed. He is Commander-in-chief.... He has no power to initiate or declare a war either against a foreign nation or a domestic State. But by the Acts of Congress of February 28th, 1795, and 3d of March, 1807, he is authorized to call out the militia and use the military and naval forces of the United States in case of invasion by foreign nations, and to suppress insurrection against the government of a State or of the United States.

If a war be made by invasion of a foreign nation, the President is not only authorized but bound to resist force by force. He does not initiate the war, but is bound to accept the challenge without waiting for any special legislative authority. And whether the hostile party be a foreign invader, or States organized in rebellion, it is none the less a war, although the declaration of it be "unilateral."...

...

It is not the less a civil war, with belligerent parties in hostile array, because it may be called an "insurrection" by one side, and the insurgents be considered as rebels or traitors. It is not necessary that the independence of the revolted province or State be acknowledged in order to constitute it a party belligerent in a war according to the law of nations. Foreign nations acknowledge it as war by a declaration of neutrality. The condition of neutrality cannot exist unless there be two belligerent parties....

...

Whether the President in fulfilling his duties, as Commander-in-chief, in suppressing an insurrection, has met with such armed hostile resistance, and a civil war of such alarming proportions as will compel him to accord to them the character of belligerents, is a question to be decided by him, and this Court must be governed by the decisions and acts of the political department of the Government to which this power was entrusted.... The proclamation of blockade is itself official and conclusive evidence to the Court that a state of war existed....

...

If it were necessary to the technical existence of a war, that it should have a legislative sanction, we find it in almost every act passed at the extraordinary session of the Legislature of 1861, which was wholly employed in enacting laws to enable the Government to prosecute the war with vigor and efficiency. And finally, in 1861, we find Congress... in anticipation of such astute objections, passing an act "approving, legalizing, and making valid all the acts, proclamations, and orders of the President, etc., as if they had been issued and done under the previous express authority and direction of the Congress of the United States."

Without admitting that such an act was necessary under the circumstances, it is plain that if the President had in any manner assumed powers which it was necessary should have the authority or sanction of Congress,... this ratification has operated to perfectly cure the defect....

...

On this first question therefore we are of the opinion that the President had a right, jure belli, to institute a blockade of ports in possession of the States in rebellion, which neutrals are bound to regard.

...

JUSTICE NELSON, with whom CHIEF JUSTICE TANEY, JUSTICE CATRON and JUSTICE CLIFFORD join, dissenting.

...

By our constitution... Congress shall have power "to declare war, grant letters of marque and reprisal, and make rules concerning captures on land and water."

...

In the case of a rebellion or resistance of a portion of the people of a country against the established government, there is no doubt, if in its progress and enlargement the government thus sought to be overthrown sees fit, it may by the competent power recognize, or declare the existence of a state of civil war, which will draw after it all the consequences and rights of war between the contending parties as in the case of a public war.... But before this insurrection against the established Government can be dealt with on the footing of a civil war, within the meaning of the law of nations and the Constitution of the United States, and which will draw after it belligerent rights, it must be recognized or declared by the war-making power of the Government. No power short of this can change the legal status of the Government or the relations of its citizens from that of peace to a state of war, or bring into existence all those duties and obligations to neutral third parties growing out of a state of war. The war power of the Government must be exercised before this changed condition of the Government and people and of neutral third parties can be admitted. There is no difference in this respect between a civil or a public war.

...

An idea seemed to be entertained that all that was necessary to constitute a war was organized hostility in the district of country in a state of rebellion—that conflicts on land and on sea—the taking of towns and capture of fleets—in fine, the magnitude and dimensions of the resistance against the Government—constituted war with all the belligerent rights belonging to civil war....

Now, in one sense, no doubt this is war, and may be a war of the most extensive and threatening dimensions and effects, but it is a statement simply of its existence in a material sense, and has no relevancy or weight when the question is what constitutes war in a legal sense, in the sense of the law of nations, and of the Constitution of the United States. For it must be a war in this sense to attach to it all the consequences that belong to belligerent rights. Instead, therefore, of inquiring after armies and navies, and victories lost and won, or organized rebellion against the general Government, the inquiry should be into the law of nations and into the municipal fundamental laws of the Government. For we find there that to constitute a civil war in the sense in which we are speaking, before it can exist, in contemplation of law, it must be recognized or declared by the sovereign power of the State, and which sovereign power by our Constitution is lodged in the Congress of the United States—civil war, therefore, under our system of government, can exist only by an act of Congress, which requires the assent of two of the great departments of the Government, the Executive and Legislative.

We have thus far been speaking of the war power under the Constitution of the United States, and as known and recognized by the law of nations. But we are asked, what would become of the peace and integrity of the Union in case of an insurrection at home or invasion from abroad if this power could not be exercised by the President in the recess of Congress, and until that body could be assembled?

The framers of the Constitution fully comprehended this question, and provided for the contingency....

...

...The whole military and naval power of the country is put under the control of the President to meet the emergency. He may call out a force in proportion to its necessities, one regiment or fifty, one ship-of-war or any number at his discretion.... But whatever its numbers, whether great or small, that may be required, ample provision is here made; and whether great or small, the nature of the power is the same. It is the exercise of a power under the municipal laws of the country and not under the law of nations; and, as we see, furnishes the most ample means of repelling attacks from abroad or suppressing disturbances at home until the assembling of Congress, who can, if it be deemed necessary, bring into operation the war power, and thus change the nature and character of the contest. Then, instead of being carried on under the municipal [militia] law of 1795, it would be under the law of nations, and the Acts of Congress as war measures with all the rights of war.

...

The Acts of 1795 and 1807 did not, and could not under the Constitution, confer on the President the power of declaring war against a State of this Union, or of deciding that war existed, and upon that ground authorize the capture and confiscation of the property of every citizen of the State whenever it was found on the waters.... This great power over the business and property of the citizen is reserved to the legislative department by the express words of the Constitution. It cannot be delegated or surrendered to the Executive. Congress alone can determine whether war exists or should be declared; and until they have acted, no citizen of the State can be punished in his person or property, unless he had committed some offence against a law of Congress passed before the act was committed, which made it a crime, and defined the punishment. The penalty of confiscation for the acts of others with which he had no concern cannot lawfully be inflicted.

...

Congress on the 6th of August, 1862, passed an Act confirming all acts, proclamations, and orders of the President, after the 4th of March, 1861, respecting the army and navy, and legalizing them, so far as was competent for that body.... An ex post facto law is defined, when, after an action, indifferent in itself, or lawful, is committed, the Legislature then, for the first time, declares it to have been a crime and inflicts punishment upon the person who committed it. The principle is sought to be applied in this case. Property of the citizen or foreign subject engaged in lawful trade at the time, and illegally captured... may be held and confiscated by subsequent legislation....

...Here the captures were without any Constitutional authority, and void; and, on principle, no subsequent ratification could make them valid.

Upon the whole... I am compelled to the conclusion that... the President had no power to set on foot a blockade under the law of nations, and that the capture of the vessel and cargo in this case, and in all cases before us in which the capture occurred before the 13th of July, 1861 [when Congress first authorized a blockade], for breach of blockade, or as enemies' property, are illegal and void, and that the decrees of condemnation should be reversed and the vessel and cargo restored.

D. Impeaching and Censuring the President

Note: The Impeachment of Andrew Johnson

Andrew Johnson was the first president to face impeachment by the Senate. The roots of that impeachment lay in Republican efforts to broaden their political coalition during the Civil War. Eager to present a united front against the Confederates, Republicans renamed themselves the Union Party and actively sought support from former Democrats who were committed to fighting until the Confederate army surrendered. Placing Andrew Johnson on the ticket as Vice-President was the most important step Lincoln and his political allies took to secure this broader support. Andrew Johnson had served Tennessee as a Jacksonian Democrat in a variety of offices, from the state legislature to the governorship, during the years preceding the Civil War. Johnson was serving in the Senate of the United States when Tennessee seceded. Unlike many of his southern colleagues, he chose to remain in Washington, DC, rather than return to his home state and join the Confederate cause. Johnson's dedication to the Union and his antipathy to the large slaveowners, whom he blamed for secession, led President Lincoln to appoint him as the military governor of Tennessee when the state was retaken by the Union army in 1862. Needing to persuade Democrats to cross party lines in order to win reelection, Lincoln added Johnson to the presidential ticket of the "Union Party" in 1864. When Lincoln was assassinated days after Robert E. Lee's surrender at Appomattox, Johnson became the president.

Conflicts broke out between the former Jacksonian Johnson and the Republican majority in both the houses of Congress almost immediately after Johnson assumed the presidency. Rather than calling Congress into session early, Johnson oversaw the end of the war and the beginning of peace on his own. Following what he took to be Lincoln administration policy and constitutional requirements, Johnson sought to restore the seceding states to the union as soon as possible. He regarded secession as the treasonous plot of a few powerful slaveholders who had overthrown lawful governments in the states. Using the threat of treason trials and the carrot of presidential pardons, Johnson induced southern political leaders to swear loyalty to the Union, ratify the Thirteenth Amendment outlawing slavery, and reorganize state governments. By the time Congress came into session in late 1865, southerners had held elections for state and federal offices and expected to reenter national political life.

Republicans in Congress had other plans. They refused to seat the representatives from the former Confederate states and launched their own investigations into the situation in the South. By February 1866, the president had broken with Congress. He accused Radical Republicans of being as hostile to the inherited Constitution as the secessionists. Johnson successfully vetoed the first major piece of Reconstruction legislation, the Freedmen's Bureau Bill, which was designed to provide assistance to the former slaves and dispose of "abandoned" or confiscated land in the South. His veto of the Civil Rights Act of 1866 was overridden. Breaking with presidential tradition, Johnson hit the campaign trail during the midterm elections of 1866, trying to drum up support for his conservative understanding of Reconstruction. This effort was a dramatic failure. Republicans in 1866 gained a veto-proof majority in both Houses of Congress and began the process of Reconstruction over the president's objections and obstruction.

The new Congress immediately challenged Johnson's authority to shape Reconstruction. The Republican majority launched military Reconstruction, imposing martial law in the South and dismantling the civilian governments. Federal officials in the South were directed to make decisions without presidential input. General Ulysses S. Grant was put in charge of the army's operations in the South, and Congress directed that all presidential orders go through Grant. Congress passed federal statutes that prevented the president from removing or transferring military officers, including Grant. The Tenure of Office Act protected civilian executive branch officials from being removed from office without the consent of the Senate. Johnson believed that these restrictions on the power of the president were unconstitutional.

The new Congress also sought to prevent presidential interference with Reconstruction by removing Johnson from office. The House of Representatives in 1867 launched three impeachment investigations, but none mustered a majority in that chamber. In February 1868, Johnson removed Secretary of War Edwin Stanton (a Lincoln appointee) without the prior approval of the Senate. This decision violated the recently adopted Tenure of Office Act, which Johnson believed unconstitutional. Stanton's removal provided the boost that impeachment forces needed. Johnson was quickly impeached on a party line vote in the House. Nine articles of impeachment turned on his violation of the Tenure of Office Act, a tenth charged him with impeachable offenses for trying to call Congress into public contempt before the election of 1866, and an eleventh charged him with general resistance to congressional policies. If two-thirds of the Senate agreed, Johnson would be removed from office. The Radical Republican and president *pro tempore* of the Senate Benjamin Wade would ascend to the Oval Office (since the vice presidency had been vacant since Lincoln's death).

Controversies over Reconstruction fueled the Johnson impeachment, even though such matters were rarely explicitly addressed during the actual impeachment debates. Senator Simon Cameron told his Pennsylvania constituents that Johnson had not been "fit to become President...Why suffer him to remain there if we can put him out?" Massachusetts Senator

Charles Sumner took a broad view of the impeachment power, putting the burden on the president to prove that his "continuance in office is not inconsistent with the *Public Safety*."[70] Both congressional Republicans and the President feared a renewal of the Civil War if the other set the terms for Reconstruction. Johnson accused Republicans of establishing General Grant as a second commander in chief and instituting repressive measures in the South. Republicans accused Johnson of questioning the legitimacy of the "rump Congress" and inviting resistance to Congressional Reconstruction in the South.

The impeachment managers from the House of Representatives and the defense attorneys representing the president offered distinctive visions of both the presidency and the impeachment power during President Johnson's impeachment trial before the Senate. The House managers championed legislative supremacy. They maintained that the "sovereign power in this republic is the Congress of the United States" and that the national legislature was given the "controlling influence... even to regulating the executive and the judiciary." The president's function was to "follow and enforce the legislative will," nothing more.[71] Republican proponents of impeachment insisted that impeachment was a political decision. They regarded "the high court of impeachment" as "the highest court known to the Constitution of the Republic" and the only appropriate tribunal for resolving the political and constitutional disagreements between the president and the Congress.[72] Representative Benjamin Butler, a former army general and Republican leader, declared that "any malversation in office, highly prejudicial to the public interest, or subversive of some fundamental principle of government by which the safety of a people may be in danger, is a high crime against the nation" and justification for impeachment and removal. Impeachment was a political inquest to evaluate "political offenses," not merely the violation of a law.[73]

The president's defenders maintained that the impeachment of Johnson was a grave threat to the independence of the executive branch. Former Supreme Court Justice Benjamin Curtis and other members of Johnson's legal team insisted that the Reconstruction Congress was interfering with "the necessary means and instruments of performing the executive duty expressly imposed on [the president] by the Constitution of taking care that the laws be faithfully executed." By insulating the military and civilian officers of the executive branch from the command of the president, Congress was erecting "a new Executive" that exercised the executive power that Article II of the Constitution had vested in the president alone. The president, Johnson and his lawyers declared, was the "tribune of the People," who alone represented the nation as a whole.[74] The president was the "chief executive officer of the land" with distinctive rights and duties under the Constitution, not the "passive instrument of Congress." President Johnson's defenders regarded the congressional power of impeachment as limited to purely legal questions. During an impeachment, they insisted, the House and Senate had to give up their character as legislative bodies that made new law and sit in a "judicial capacity" free from "party spirit" and constrained by law. The president was accountable to the electorate for his political failings. He was impeachable only for committing serious violations of the ordinary criminal law that applied to every citizen.[75]

The Senate voted on only three of the eleven articles of impeachment lodged against the president. Each received an identical thirty-five to nineteen vote. This was one short of the two-thirds majority necessary to convict and remove Johnson. Seven Republican senators crossed party lines to vote against conviction. They spoke for a larger bloc of moderate Republicans who wished to send a strong message to Johnson but were leery of permanently damaging the presidency by removing him from office.

Johnson and his successors got the message. Johnson had previously communicated to moderates that he would stop resisting congressional Reconstruction, leaving administrative matters in the hands of General Grant, who during the impeachment process was nominated for the presidency by the

70. Quoted in Keith E. Whittington, *Constitutional Construction* (Cambridge: Harvard University Press, 1999), 142, 151.

71. *Trial of Andrew Johnson, President of the United States, Before the Senate of the United States, on Impeachment by the House of Representatives for High Crimes and Misdemeanors*, 2 vols. (Washington, DC: Government Printing Office, 1868), 2:28, 2:228, 1:685.

72. *Congressional Globe*, 40th Cong., 2nd sess. (1868), 1387.

73. *Trial of Johnson*, 1:88–89, 3:253.

74. *Trial of Johnson*, 1:39; 1:207; Edward McPherson, *The Political History of the United States of America during the Period of Reconstruction* (Washington, DC: Solomons and Chapman, 1875), 172.

75. *Trial of Johnson*, 2:166, 2:136, 1:377.

Republican Party. Upon winning election in 1868, Grant promptly professed that he regarded the presidency as "a purely administrative officer."[76] Johnson served out the rest of his term quietly and in political irrelevance.

The failed impeachment of Andrew Johnson had long-term consequences for American efforts to achieve racial equality. Johnson successfully stalled Reconstruction during the years immediately after the Civil War when northern support for the rights of persons of color peaked. When Johnson in 1868 finally agreed to accept Republican policy, the window for substantially reconstructing southern politics was closing. Northern opposition to black civil rights increased significantly after 1866. The Republican share of the national vote dropped sharply during elections held in 1867 and 1868. By the end of Johnson's term of office, many Republicans had moderated their commitment to securing racial justice in the South. Almost one-hundred years would pass before congressional majorities were as committed as Republicans were in 1866 to improving the lot of persons of color.

The failed impeachment also had long-term consequences for the impeachment process and the balance of power between the national legislature and national executive. Nineteenth-century Americans recognized that the Senate's failure to convict Johnson did not vindicate his policies or his presidency. Johnson was disciplined and his actions repudiated, even if he was not removed. The Senate majority found a path between the competing views of the impeachment power offered by House Republicans and Johnson's lawyers. The impeachment power remained available to check abuses of office, but was not to be used to remove incompetent or disagreeable presidents. The House impeachment team received more support from the Senate when they championed the idea of a weak president primarily dedicated to implementing the will of Congress. Johnson's failed presidency contributed to the birth of an era of "congressional government." Decades passed before presidents reasserted the Jacksonian vision of a strong national executive armed with inherent powers to take decisive action.

76. McPherson, 365.

Suggested Readings

Ackerman, Bruce. *We the People. Vol. 2: Transformations* (Cambridge, Mass.: Belknap Press of Harvard University Press, 1991).

Belz, Herman. *A New Birth of Freedom: The Republican Party and Freedmen's Rights 1861 to 1866* (Westport, Conn.: Greenwood Press, 1976).

Benedict, Michael Les. *A Compromise of Principle; Congressional Republicans and Reconstruction, 1863–1869* (New York: Norton, 1974).

Benedict, Michael Les. *Preserving the Constitution: Essays on Politics and the Constitution in the Reconstruction Era* (New York: Fordham University Press, 2006).

Brandon, Mark. *Free in the World: American Slavery and Constitutional Failure* (Princeton: Princeton Univeristy Press, 1998).

Brandwein, Pamela. *Reconstructing Reconstruction: The Supreme Court and the Production of Historical Truth* (Durham: Duke University Press, 1999).

DeRosa, Marshall. *The Confederate Constitution of 1861: An Inquiry into American Constitutionalism* (Columbia: University of Missouri Press, 1991).

Fairman, Charles. *Reconstruction and Reunion, 1864–88* (New York: Macmillan, 1971).

Farber, Daniel. *Lincoln's Constitution* (Chicago: University of Chicago Press, 2003).

Fletcher, George. *Our Secret Constitution: How Lincoln Redefined American Democracy* (New York: Oxford University Press, 2001).

Foner, Eric. *Reconstruction: America's Unfinished Revolution, 1863–1877* (New York: Harper & Row, 1988).

Graber, Mark A. Dred Scott *and the Problem of Constitutional Evil* (New York: Cambridge University Press, 2006).

Hyman, Harold M. *A More Perfect Union: The Impact of the Civil War and Reconstruction on the Constitution* (New York: Knopf, 1973).

Hyman, Harold M., and William M. Wiecek. *Equal Justice Under Law: Constitutional Development, 1835–1875* (New York: Harper & Row, 1982).

Kaczorowski, Robert J. *The Politics of Judicial Interpretation: The Federal Courts, Department of Justice and Civil Rights, 1866–1876* (Dobbs Ferry, N.Y.: Oceana Publications, 1985).

Kutler, Stanley I. *Judicial Power and Reconstruction Politics* (Chicago: University of Chicago Press, 1968).

McKitrick, Eric. *Andrew Johnson and Reconstruction* (Chicago: University of Chicago Press, 1960).

McPherson, James M. *Battle Cry of Freedom: The Civil War Era* (New York: Oxford University Press, 2003).

Neely, Mark E., Jr. *The Fate of Liberty: Abraham Lincoln and Civil Liberties* (New York: Oxford University Press, 1991).

Nelson, William E. *The Fourteenth Amendment: From Political Principle to Judicial Doctrine* (Cambridge, Mass.: Harvard University Press, 1988).

Randall, James G. *Constitutional Problems under Lincoln* (Urbana: University of Illinois Press, 1951).

Ross, Michael A. *Justice of Shattered Dreams: Samuel Freeman Miller and the Supreme Court during the Civil War Era* (Baton Rouge: Louisiana State University Press, 2003).

Swisher, Carl B. *History of the Supreme Court of the United States. Volume 5: The Taney Period* (New York: Macmillan, 1974).

Whittington, Keith E. *Constitutional Construction: Divided Powers and Constitutional Meaning* (Cambridge, Mass.: Harvard University Press, 1999).

Wills, Garry. *Lincoln at Gettysburg: The Words That Remade America* (New York: Simon and Schuster, 1992).

Chapter 7

The Republican Era: 1877–1932

I. Introduction

The Republican victory in 1860 ushered in a new era of American politics. Until their downfall in the midst of the Great Depression in 1932, the Republican Party enjoyed a longer period of dominance of national politics than any other political party had before or has since. But that dominance was never total—and never without political and constitutional debates.

Few guessed that the Republicans would enjoy such lasting success. Abraham Lincoln won over only a minority of voters in 1860, and the party had practically no support in the slaveholding states—nearly half the Union. During the Civil War, Republican dominance depended on the South's retreat and then exclusion from American politics. During Reconstruction, Republicans struggled to hold on to national power by installing friendly governments in the former Confederate states and monitoring developments with federal troops. With the collapse of Reconstruction and the removal of federal troops in 1877, politics returned to "normal"—but not to the politics of the antebellum era. First, Republicans no longer had the votes to act on racial issues. And second, the country increasingly debated the consequences of industrialization and immigration.

The era between Reconstruction and the Great Depression is frequently divided into two periods. The late nineteenth century is known as the Gilded Age. It saw full-scale industrialization, the rapid growth of cities, large-scale immigration from Europe and Asia, and the rise of massive private corporations. These remade the economy, producing an unprecedented array of cheaper goods. Yet they also created shocking individual fortunes, and they triggered violent clashes between capitalists and workers, who were unhappy with wages and working conditions in factories and mines. It was a period of close party competition at the national level, but frequent single-party dominance at the local level. The Gilded Age also saw third-party alternatives. On the whole, national Republicans and Democrats shared a strong commitment to conservative economic values, such as economic development and the protection of rights of property and contract. But Republicans in general interpreted federal power more broadly, while Democrats were more skeptical.

The early twentieth century is known as the Progressive Era. Populist forces led by William Jennings Bryan took over the Democratic Party in 1896. This broke the electoral stalemate between the two major parties and drove the Democrats into national political irrelevance. The Populists had been an independent farmers' movement, advocating inflationary monetary policy and a national income tax. The movement sought extensive federal regulation of banks, railroads, and communications networks. Yet it had limited support outside the South and Midwest. Both parties turned their attention to the problem of managing economic growth and moderating the effects of a generation of economic turmoil. Progressive reformers in both political parties, including Theodore Roosevelt and Woodrow Wilson, were particularly concerned with stamping out corruption in politics and bringing better management to political, social, and economic systems. Political disagreements now turned on the proper shape and scope of social and political reform.

Between Reconstruction and the early 1930s, constitutional understandings and practices were transformed in fundamental ways:

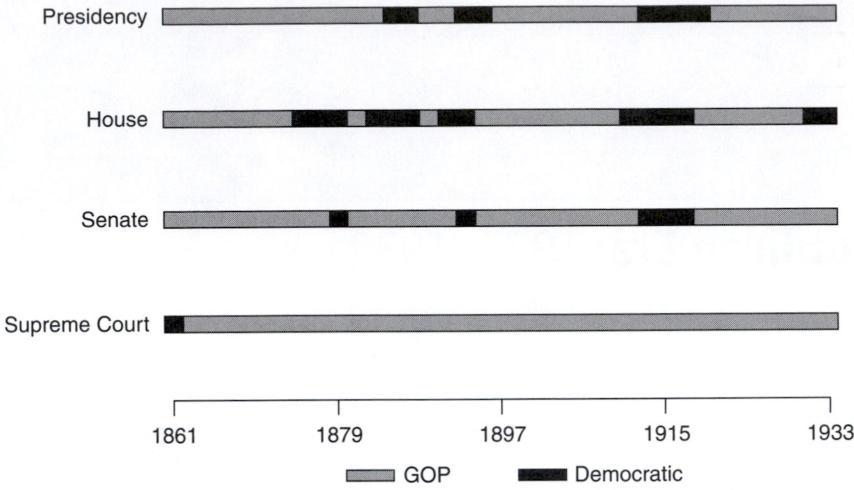

Figure 7-1 Partisan Control of the U.S. Government, 1861–1932

- derailment of protections of civil rights;
- transformation of the Fourteenth Amendment into a restraint on Progressive economic regulation;
- slow and selective recognition of expanded congressional power;
- expanded presidential power in conflicts with Congress;
- support for new methods of governance, such as independent regulatory commissions that blended legislative, executive, and judicial powers;
- use of the commerce clause to support an integrated national market and to inhibit state efforts to interfere;
- American territorial expansion overseas;
- dramatic expansion of federal judicial power; and
- the amendment of the U.S. Constitution to accommodate popular reforms on elections, suffrage, temperance, and taxation.

Partisan Competition in the Gilded Age. The Republican Party that fought the war was a volatile mix of antislavery activists, former Whig nationalists, and pro-Union Democrats. With the end of Reconstruction, the Republicans largely set aside their commitment to end the economic and political exclusion of black freedmen. Congress could debate the issue but not produce legislation. "Home rule" had returned to the South, which meant the return to political dominance there of white Democrats. Republicans thus turned attention more to economic policy and electoral politics.

The Republicans had encouraged industrialization and the growing corporations of the North during the war. Now they dedicated themselves to maintaining a friendly climate for their corporate allies after the war. Protectionist tariffs and a return to the gold standard (or "hard" money, after the wartime experiment with legal tender) were central planks in their economic platform. The postwar Republicans also sought the settlement of the West and the creation of an integrated national market. National railroads and interstate corporations knit distant communities together into a common market. Federal courts prevented states from adopting policies that hampered economic integration.

Electoral calculations likewise shaped the Republican agenda. Civil War pensions to Northern veterans and their widows grew to absorb a huge share of the federal budget. The Grand Army of the Republic, a Union veterans organization, lobbied for pension benefits; it became one of the most influential interest groups in American history and an important ally of Republican politicians. For as long as it remained effective, Republicans did not hesitate to "wave the bloody shirt." They kept reminding northern voters of the Republican role in leading a successful war—and the disloyalty of the Democratic Party so closely tied to the South. When hostility to Chinese immigrants peaked in the West in the latter nineteenth century, Republicans were quick to join Democrats in appealing to nativism, with harsh immigration reform.

When hostility to large corporations grew severe enough, Republicans sought to relieve the pressure through new forms of economic regulation. For exam-

Table 7-1 Major Issues and Decisions of the Republican Era

Major Political Issues	Major Constitutional Issues	Major Court Decisions
Industrialization	Civil Rights	*Slaughterhouse Cases* (1872)
Labor Unrest	Antitrust	*Munn v. Illinois* (1877)
Populism	Income Tax	*Civil Rights Cases* (1883)
Gold Standard	Status of Territories	*Wabash, St. Louis & Pacific Railroad v. Illinois* (1886)
Railroad Regulation	Child Labor	*U.S. v. E. C. Knight* (1895)
Tariffs	Railroad Regulation	*Income Tax Cases* (1895)
Veteran Pensions	State Sovereign Immunity	*Champion v. Ames* (1903)
Workplace Regulation	Appointment Powers	*Lochner v. New York* (1905)
Monopolies	Bureaucracy	*Ex parte Young* (1908)
Immigration	Property Rights	*Hammer v. Dagenhart* (1918)
Spanish–American War	Direct Democracy	*Child Labor Tax Cases* (1922)
World War I	Female Suffrage	

ple, the Interstate Commerce Act regulated interstate railroad rates, and the Sherman Antitrust Act regulated monopolistic business practices. Both the states and the federal government experimented with new policymaking institutions—most notably, independent regulatory commissions.

The end of Reconstruction meant the return of the Democratic South to national politics. The late nineteenth century was perhaps the most competitive political era in the nation's history. The Democrats often won control of the House of Representatives, but large blocs of House seats could swing from election to election. Republicans had taken advantage of their time in power to lock up the U.S. Senate, however. They "packed" the Senate by admitting new states that were often thinly populated but strongly Republican. As a consequence, the Senate was the one elected institution that was not competitive in the latter nineteenth century. It gave Republicans the means to veto Democratic policies that were too damaging to Republican interests—and also to ensure Republican-friendly judicial appointments. Given their small populations, these new states did not help the Republicans much in their struggle for the House, but they did provide a notable boost for Republicans in the Electoral College.

Table 7-2 illustrates this dynamic. The four states admitted in 1889 were admitted by the lame-duck Fiftieth Congress. Democrats still controlled the House and the presidency, but the Republicans took control of both chambers of Congress and the White House in the Fifty-First Congress. Democrats gave in to efforts to admit the four new Republican states, in exchange for the admission of the Democratic Montana. When the Republicans gathered in the Fifty-First Congress, they immediately added two more nearly empty but GOP states in 1890.[1]

Third Parties and Swing Votes. Several third-party movements complicated the picture. The Greenbacks favored inflationary or "soft" money, the Prohibitionists favored alcohol prohibition, and the Populists favored farming interests. Together, third parties often drew over three percent of the national popular vote, more than the margin of victory between the Republican and Democratic presidential nominees. At its peak, the Populists won over 8 percent of the popular

1. On the politics of the admission of new states, see Charles H. Stewart III and Barry R. Weingast, "Stacking the Senate, Changing the Nation: Republican Rotten Boroughs, Statehood Politics, and American Political Development," *Studies in American Political Development* 6 (1992):223; Nolan McCarty, Keith T. Poole, and Howard Rosenthal, "Congress and Territorial Expansion of the United States," in *Party, Process, and Political Change in Congress*, eds. David W. Brady and Mathew D. McCubbins (Stanford: Stanford University Press, 2002).

Table 7-2 Admission of States to the Union, 1863–1890

State	Admission Date	Representation Ratio	Admitting Congress	State Partisan Leaning
West Virginia	1863	3.12	Republican	Republican
Nevada	1864	0.17	Republican	Republican
Nebraska	1867	0.75	Republican	Republican
Colorado	1876	1.01	Republican	Republican
North Dakota	1889	1.16	Divided	Republican
South Dakota	1889	2.13	Divided	Republican
Montana	1889	0.87	Divided	Democratic
Washington	1889	2.16	Divided	Republican
Idaho	1890	0.58	Republican	Republican
Wyoming	1890	0.41	Republican	Republican

Source: Charles Stewart III and Barry R. Weingast, "Stacking the Senate, Changing the Nation: Republican Rotten Boroughs, Statehood Politics and American Political Development," *Studies in American Political Development* 6 (1992):223.

Note: The Representation Ratio is the size of the state population at the time of admission relative to the size of a population entitled to one seat in the House of Representatives at that same time. A Representation Ratio of 1 means that the state's population is equivalent to the size of one congressional district; a Representation Ratio of 2 means that the state's population is equivalent to the size of two congressional districts. Size was a traditional criterion for the admission of a territory as a state. The average Representation Ratio of states admitted before the Civil War was 2.55, and only Oregon had a Representation Ratio below 1 at the time of admission.

vote and 22 electoral votes in the presidential election of 1892 (Table 7-3). As a consequence, no president won the White House with a majority of the popular vote between Grant's reelection in 1872 (with Republicans still in control of the South) and 1896 (when the Republicans took firm control of the presidency).[2] With the House of Representatives and the presidency frequently in play, no party could control the White House and both chambers of Congress for more than two years at a time.

New York, the commercial and financial center of the country, was the critical swing state in the presidential politics of the latter nineteenth century. Democrats responded by catering to New York interests. They nominated a business-friendly New Yorker for every presidential election from the end of the war until 1896, finding success with Grover Cleveland in 1884 and 1892. (He won a popular plurality but not an electoral majority in 1888.) They matched the Republican commitments to a hard currency and an integrated national market. Yet they promised greater fiscal discipline and an end to the political corruption scandals that plagued the Republicans. They also appealed to a different set of business interests, thanks to their commitment to free trade.

In constitutional philosophy, there was little to distinguish the Republicans from the Cleveland Democrats. Both valued property rights and small government, with the Democrats somewhat more inclined to restricting the power of the national government in the name of states' rights. Given their general control of the presidency throughout this period, the Republicans maintained a secure majority on the Supreme Court. Cleveland's appointments to the Court merely served to reinforce its generally conservative tendencies.[3]

The Election of 1896. The elections of 1896 launched a new set of national debates. With the onset of economic depression during Cleveland's second administration, the Democrats fractured between the Populist radicals and business-friendly conservatives. The Republicans

2. In the case of the contested election of 1876, Republican President Rutherford B. Hayes did not even win the plurality of the popular vote. The Democrats agreed to accept Republican claims that Hayes had won a majority of the electoral votes in exchange for full return of home rule in the South.

3. On the centrality of New York to electoral politics and policymaking during this period, see Scott C. James, *Presidents, Parties, and the State* (New York: Cambridge University Press, 2000).

Table 7-3 Percentage of Popular Vote in Presidential Election by Political Party, 1876–1932

Year	Republican	Democrat	Populist	Socialist	Progressive	Other
1876	**48%**	51%				1%
1880	**48%**	48%				3%
1884	48%	**49%**				3%
1888	**48%**	49%				4%
1892	43%	**46%**	9%			2%
1896	**51%**	47%				2%
1900	**52%**	46%	0%	1%		2%
1904	**56%**	38%	1%	3%		2%
1908	52%	43%		3%		3%
1912	23%	**42%**		6%	27%	2%
1916	46%	**49%**		3%		1%
1920	**60%**	34%		3%		2%
1924	**54%**	29%			17%	1%
1928	**58%**	41%		1%		0%
1932	40%	**57%**		2%		1%

Note: Winning party marked in bold.

swept into both chambers of Congress in the 1894 midterm elections, and strike-breaking and the gold standard became the administration's most visible accomplishments. While the Republicans held to their long-standing commitments to nationalism and business, Populists temporarily captured the Democratic Party. Under William Jennings Bryan of Nebraska, the Democratic platform made new pledges to use government power to improve the condition of the common man.

On the eve of the election, the Supreme Court effectively threw itself in with the conservatives. Particularly important were three decisions of 1895. First, *United States v. E. C. Knight* (1895) sharply limited the reach of the Sherman Anti-Trust Act. (This act, passed during the Republican administration of Benjamin Harrison, was largely unused during the second Cleveland administration.) While the Populists strongly opposed monopolies, the Court ruled that the Constitution constrained what the federal government could do about them. Next, *Pollock v. Farmers' Loan & Trust Co.* (1895) struck down the income tax provisions of the Tariff Act of 1894. Tariff reform was a central legislative initiative of the Cleveland administration, but there was little support in Congress for lowering duties. The tariff bill did, however, impose for the first time a peacetime federal income tax on the wealthy. What the Populists had won in Congress, however, they lost in Court. Finally, *In re Debs* (1895) upheld a contempt citation against labor leader Eugene Debs. The Court ruled that Debs had violated an injunction and obstructed interstate commerce in the Pullman railroad strike, which the Cleveland administration had violently put down the year before.

The Supreme Court thus raised constitutional barriers to central elements of the new Democratic program. The Populists responded in turn with fierce denunciations of the Court and calls for judicial reform. The electorate sided with the conservatives. In 1896, the Republican Party finally broke the national electoral logjam. William McKinley, the Republican candidate, won the White House with a majority of the popular vote, as the Republicans solidified their hold over Congress. As Figure 7-2 illustrates, both the Democrats and the GOP solidified their hold over their core regions of support after 1896, reducing the number of closely divided states to a mere handful. Moreover, while the Democrats retained their hold on the South and reached into the rural Midwest, the Republicans had

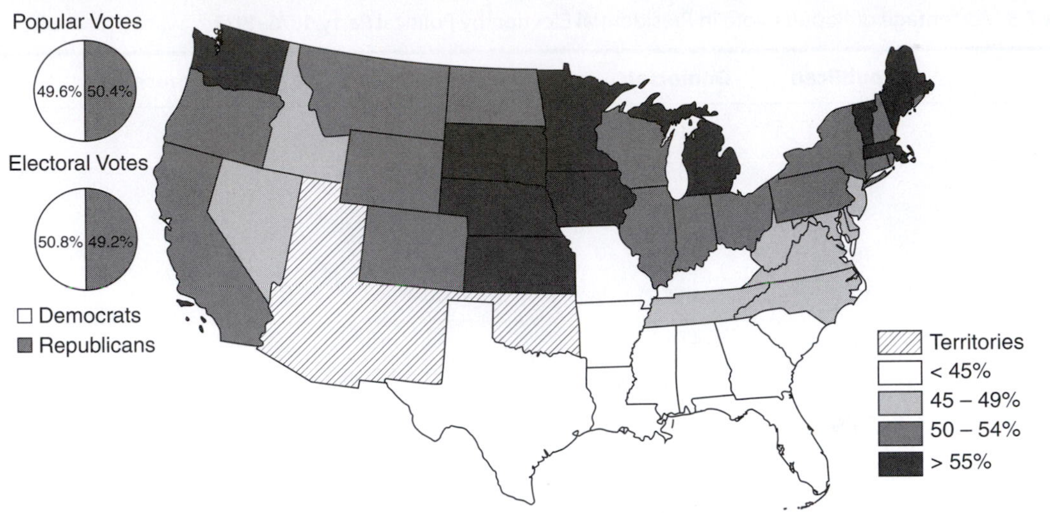

Figure 7-2 Average Republican Party Vote, 1876–1892

Note: State-by-state shading reflects average Republican Party share of the two-party vote, against next largest party in any given election in that state.

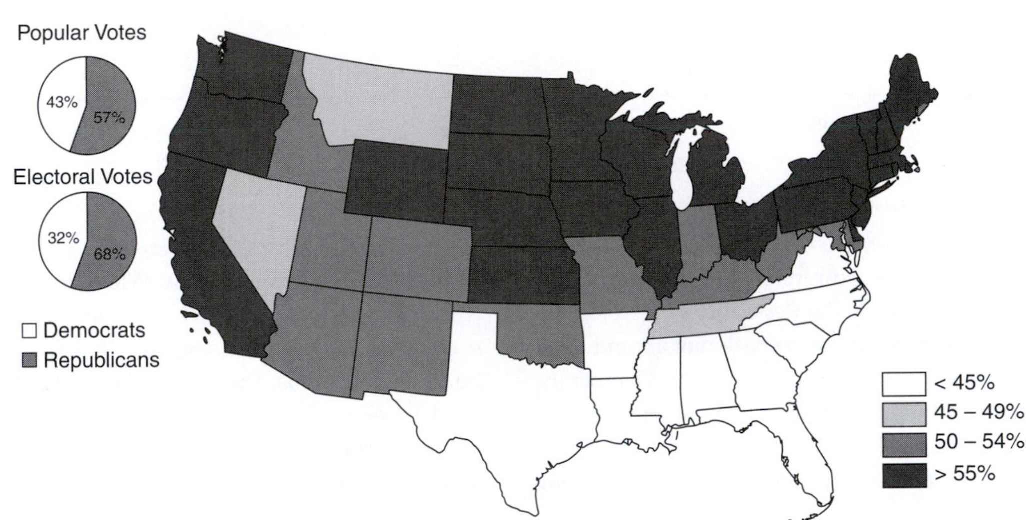

Figure 7-3 Average Republican Party Vote, 1896–1928

Note: State-by-state shading reflects average Republican Party share of the two-party vote, against next largest party in any given election in that state. Figure excludes the election of 1912.

a firm hold on the populous industrial states of the North. When the GOP was united, its advantage in the Electoral College was nearly insurmountable.

Developments in the Progressive Era. Two issues defined the political and judicial agenda in the Progressive Era—the purposes of government and the scope of government power when it came to the economy. Theodore Roosevelt spoke for many reformers in his belief that "the sphere of the State's action may be vastly increased without in any way diminishing the happiness of either the many or the few."[4] The Court often supported conservative politicians in resisting pressures for a more expansive state. Yet the

4. Theodore Roosevelt, "National Life and Character," in *The Works of Theodore Roosevelt*, ed. Francis Vinton Greene, vol. 1 (New York: G. P. Putnam, 1897), 316.

Box 7-1 A Partial Cast of Characters of the Republican Era

Stephen J. Field	■ Conservative Democrat ■ Justice on California supreme court (1857–63) ■ Appointed by Abraham Lincoln to the U.S. Supreme Court (1863–97) ■ Known for his belief in a strong role for judicial review, strict limits on federal power, and broad protections for the rights of private property
William Howard Taft	■ Republican ■ Federal circuit court judge (1892–1900) ■ Civil governor of the Philippines (1901–03) ■ Secretary of War (1904–08) ■ President of the United States (1909–13) ■ Appointed by Warren Harding to be Chief Justice of the United States (1921–30) ■ Known as a reformer but ultimately collided with the Progressives in his own party ■ Defeated for reelection when Theodore Roosevelt ran an independent campaign for the White House in 1912, and became an influential and active chief justice
Oliver Wendell Holmes, Jr.	■ Republican ■ An influential Boston legal scholar and a precursor to the "legal realist" movement ■ Served on the Supreme Judicial Court of Massachusetts (1882–1902) ■ Appointed by Theodore Roosevelt to the U.S. Supreme Court (1902–1932) ■ Known for his view that the law evolved over time and that courts should generally be deferential to what political majorities decide, wrote most famously in dissent
Theodore Roosevelt	■ Progressive Republican ■ Governor of New York (1899–1900) ■ Vice president of the United States (1901) ■ President of the United States (1901–09) ■ Known for his commitment to reform causes, active government, national power, and a strong executive ■ Unsuccessfully ran an independent campaign for the White House in 1912 as a Progressive, emphasizing themes of reform and direct democracy.
John Marshall Harlan	■ Whig and Republican ■ Slaveholding unionist from Kentucky who joined the Union army ■ Kentucky attorney general (1863–67) ■ Republican member of the presidential election commission of 1877 and subsequently appointed by Benjamin Hayes to the U.S. Supreme Court (1877–1911) ■ Critic of the Court's decisions on race and congressional power, wrote most famously in dissent

justices often approved innovative state and federal legislation.

During the early twentieth century, the Progressive movement won many legislative and intellectual victories, influencing both major political parties, though it was kept in check politically by conservative forces. Progressive-minded Republicans in Congress frequently criticized the Supreme Court for being too conservative and hostile to labor unions, and they twice broke party ranks in the presidential campaign. President William Howard Taft, a Republican, was himself known as a reformer, but he was still seen as too conservative by

Progressives within his own party and by his predecessor, Theodore Roosevelt. In 1912, Roosevelt's independent run on the Progressive Party ticket drew more votes than Taft, which allowed Woodrow Wilson, a moderate Democrat, to win with less than 42 percent of the popular vote. In 1924, Republican Wisconsin senator Robert LaFollette drew almost 17 percent of the popular vote for president running under the Progressive banner. (The conservative Republican incumbent, Calvin Coolidge, still won a popular and electoral majority in that year.) Herbert Hoover's nomination in 1928 helped reconcile the Progressive and conservative wings of the Republican Party. Yet four years later the nation was mired in the Great Depression, and Franklin Roosevelt was able to paint Hoover as an arch-conservative.

The early twentieth century was a period of political reform. Civil service reform at the national level finally took root (but not before President James Garfield was assassinated in 1881 by a disappointed office seeker). States and localities went even further. They experimented with nonpartisan elections, initiatives, referendums, direct primaries, and recall elections, among other things. States also shifted away from the party ballot—a ballot printed and distributed by the political parties, who naturally listed only their own candidates. Voters could then simply choose a ballot and place it in the official ballot box. The party ballot was replaced by the "Australian" ballot, a ballot printed by the government that listed all qualified candidates. Now voters could secretly mark the candidates they favored. However, ballot reform was accompanied by other changes that tended to dampen voter participation. These changes included voter registration requirements and literacy tests—and, in the South, legal and extralegal means to keep blacks from the polls.[5]

Some reforms altered the face of the Constitution, with four amendments added between 1913 and 1920. The Sixteenth Amendment authorized a federal income tax, nearly two decades after the Supreme Court had struck down such a tax. And the amendment was part of a change in the political environment as well: Mainstream politicians had grown far more likely to support the tax. The other three amendments provided for the direct election of senators, national Prohibition, and women's suffrage. All followed similar popular Progressive reforms in the states.

It was also a time of political turbulence. Not only did the Progressives splinter the Republican Party. The Socialist Party emerged as a significant political force, winning local office and a notable portion of the popular vote for president. Cities grew, and new waves of European immigrants brought immigration reform, along with social and economic dislocation. They also fueled radical political movements, such as the socialism and anarchism.

The Spanish-American War in 1898 marked America's emergence as a global power and left the United States with its first overseas possessions, some temporary (such as Cuba and the Philippines) and others more permanent (such as Puerto Rico and Hawaii). World War I, the failure of the League of Nations, and debates over isolationism left Americans disillusioned and unsure about their place in the world. World War I and the Wilson administration in the 1910s opened the door to a significant increase in the regulatory power and activity of the federal government, and government only partly retreated from that high point in the 1920s.

David J. Brewer, **"The Nation's Safeguard"** (1893)[6]

After serving extended stints on the Kansas state supreme court and in the federal circuit courts, the Republican David J. Brewer was appointed to the U.S. Supreme Court by President Benjamin Harrison in 1890. He served on the Court for twenty years. The son of Christian missionaries, Brewer was known for his religious conviction, his dedication to the protection of property rights, and for his frequent forays into public speaking. Although an early dissenter on the Fuller Court, the conservative trajectory of the Court soon brought him into the majority and converted his dissents into constitutional doctrine.

In this speech, delivered to the annual meeting of the New York Bar Association in Albany, Brewer voiced the growing concern with "lawlessness" that was animating the legal community at the turn of the twentieth century. The populist backlash against industrial and commercial advancement posed, in his view, the looming danger of

5. On reforms in democratic politics during this period, see Michael E. McGerr, *The Decline of Popular Politics* (New York: Oxford University Press, 1986); Alexander Keyssar, *The Right to Vote* (New York: Basic Books, 2000); J. Morgan Kousser, *The Shaping of Southern Politics* (New Haven: Yale University Press, 1974).

6. Excerpt taken from David J. Brewer, "The Nation's Safeguard," in *Proceedings of the New York State Bar Association, Sixteenth Annual Meeting* (New York: New York State Bar Association, 1893), 37–47.

the coming years. Just two years before he would write the Court's opinion upholding the federal government's actions to break up the Pullman Strike, and in the immediate aftermath of the bloody Homestead Strike at a Pennsylvania steel mill, Brewer warned of a growing belief in "coercion" and "force" that was willing to throw aside law and rights.

...I do not propose to discuss the foot-pad or the burglar; they are vulgar and brutal criminals in whose behalf there has as yet been organized no political party. I wish rather to notice that movement of "coercion," and which by the mere force of numbers seeks to diminish protection to private property. It is a movement which in spirit, if not in letter, violates both the eighth [thou shalt not steal] and tenth [thou shalt not covet] commandments; a movement, which seeing that which a man has attempts to wrest it from him and transfer it to those who have not. It is the unvarying law, that the wealth of the community will be in the hands of a few...and hence it has always been, and until human nature is remodeled always will be true, that the wealth of a nation is in the hands of a few, while the many subsist upon the proceeds of their daily toil. But security is the chief end of government, and other things being equal, that government is best which protects to the fullest extent each individual, rich or poor, high or low, in the possession of his property and the pursuit of his business....

...

This movement expresses itself in two ways. First, in the improper use of the labor organizations to destroy the freedom of the laborer and control the uses of capital....

...

The other form of this movement assumes the guise of a regulation of the charges for the use of property subjected, or supposed to be, to a public use.... [I]t subjects all property to and its uses to the will of the majority... [and] robs property of its value....

...

It is said that the will of the people would often be delayed or thwarted and that this is against the essential idea of government of and by the people. But for what are written constitutions? They exist, not simply to prescribe modes of action, but because of the restraints and prohibitions they contain. Popular government may imply, generally speaking, that the present will of the majority should be carried into effect; but this is true in no absolute or arbitrary sense, and the limitations and checks which are found in all written constitutions are placed there to secure the rights of the minority. Constitutions are generally, and ought always to be, formed in times free from excitement. They represent the deliberate judgment of the people as to the provisions and restraints which, firmly and fully enforced, will secure to each citizen the greatest liberty and utmost protection. They are rules prescribed by Philip sober to control Philip drunk. When difficulties arise, when the measures and laws framed by a majority are challenged as a violation of these rules and a trespass upon the rights of the minority, common justice demands that the tribunal to determine the question shall be as little under the influence of either as is possible....

...

...I am firmly persuaded that the salvation of the nation, the permanence of government of and by the people, rests upon the independence and vigor of the judiciary. To stay the waves of popular feeling, to restrain the greedy hand of the many from filching from the few that which they have honestly acquired, and to protect in every man's possession and enjoyment, be he rich or poor, that which he hath, demands a tribunal as strong as is consistent with the freedom of human action and as free from all influences and suggestions other than is compassed in the thought of justice, as can be created out of infirmities of human nature....

Woodrow Wilson, "The Meaning of Democracy" (1912)[7]

The 1912 presidential race was split four ways. The Republicans were divided between the incumbent, William Howard Taft, and the insurgent ex-president Theodore Roosevelt. With a sizable following but still a distinct fourth was the Socialist Eugene Debs. New Jersey governor and transplanted Virginian Woodrow Wilson was the Democratic Party nominee. Wilson's nomination helped shed the party's image of Populist radicalism, but the contours of his own moderate Progressivism were not well defined. The central question of the campaign was how to deal with the powerful corporations that had rapidly arisen in the late nineteenth and early twentieth centuries and now seemed to dominate the economy.

Advised by labor lawyer Louis Brandeis, whom he later appointed to the Supreme Court, Wilson sought to distinguish

7. Excerpt taken from Scranton Speech, September 23, 1912, *The Papers of Woodrow Wilson* Project Records, Swem Collection, Box 457, Department of Rare Books and Special Collections, Princeton University Library.

"Adopt the philosophy of limitation of governmental power and you will turn the industrial life of this country into a chaotic scramble of selfish interests, each bent on plundering the others, and all bent on oppressing the wage-worker."—ROOSEVELT at San Francisco.

Illustration 7-1 Constitutional Limits in the Campaign of 1912

In a campaign speech in 1912, Democrat Woodrow Wilson said that the "history of liberty is a history of the limitation of governmental power," which Progressives lampooned as enfeebling government and empowering industrial giants. Wilson himself questioned whether liberty can "come from the government" and questioned whether reformers associated with the Republican Party, like either Theodore Roosevelt or William Howard Taft, had too many "entangling alliances" with big business to be trusted to "set our government free."[8]

Source: Boston Journal (September 10, 1912), 6. Library of Congress, Washington, D.C.

himself from both Taft and Roosevelt. Wilson proposed to address the problem of monopoly by active government intervention to recreate the conditions of economic competition, whereas Roosevelt accepted monopolies as inevitable and proposed subjecting them to perpetual government supervision and administration. Where Wilson offered "industrial liberty," he charged that Roosevelt offered "industrial absolutism." The "history of liberty," Wilson declared, "is a history of limitation of governmental power, not the increase of it." Roosevelt promptly responded that, "the limitation of governmental power, of governmental action, means the enslavement of the people by the great corporations who can only be held in check by the extension of governmental power."[9] *He accused Wilson*

8. Arthur S. Link, *The Papers of Woodrow Wilson*, vol. 25 (Princeton: Princeton University Press, 1978), 124, 125, 119.

9. John Wells Davidson, ed., *A Crossroads of Freedom* (New Haven: Yale University Press, 1956), 130; Howard Gillman, *The Constitution Besieged* (Durham, NC: Duke University Press, 1993), 151.

of being a proponent of "laissez faire." Wilson could hardly let such a charge go unanswered. In this campaign address delivered in Scranton, Pennsylvania, on September 23, 1912, Wilson explained his own philosophy of activist government.

...You know that it was Jefferson who said that the best government is that which does as little governing as possible, which exercises its power as little as possible. That was said in a day when...all that was necessary was that the government should withhold its hand and see to it that every man got an opportunity to act if he would. But that time is past. America is not now, and cannot in the future be, a place for unrestricted individual enterprise. It is true that we have come upon an age of great cooperative industry.

...

...[T]reatment of labor by the great corporations is not now what it was in Jefferson's time. Who in this great audience knows his employer? I mean among those who go down into the mines or go into the mills and factories. You never know, you practically never deal with, the president of the corporation....The only thing you know is that by the score, by the hundred, by the thousand, you are employed with your fellow workmen by some agent of an invisible employer. Therefore, whenever bodies of men employ bodies of men, it ceases to be a private relationship....The dealing of great bodies of men with other bodies of men is a matter of public scrutiny, and should be a matter of public regulation.

Similarly, it was no business of the law in the time of Jefferson to come into my house and see how I kept my house. But when my house, when my property, when my so-called private property, became a great mine, and men went along dark corridors amidst every kind of danger to dig out the bowels of the earth things necessary for the industries of the whole nation, and when it was known that no individual owned these mines, that they were owned by great stock corporations...then all the old analogies absolutely collapsed and it became the right of the government to go down into those mines and see whether human beings were properly treated or not....

...[W]e are accused of wishing to minimize the powers of the government of the United States. I am not afraid of the utmost exercise of the powers of the government of Pennsylvania, or of the Union, provided they are exercised with patriotism and intelligence and really in the interest of the people who are living under them. But when it is proposed to set up guardians over those people to take care of them by a process of tutelage and supervision in which they play no active part, I utter my absolute objection....

...

...There is no man, there is no group of men, there is no class of men, big enough or wise enough to take care of a free people. If the free people can't take care of itself, then it isn't free. It hasn't grown up. That is the very definition of freedom. If you are afraid to trust any and every man to put forth his powers as he pleases, then you are afraid of liberty itself. I am willing to risk liberty to the utmost, and I am not willing to risk anything else....

II. Judicial Power and Constitutional Authority

MAJOR DEVELOPMENTS

- Expansion of federal judicial review of the states
- Growth of constitutional litigation in state and federal courts
- Debate over judicial deference to legislatures
- Proposals to recall judges and judicial decisions

The judiciary took on added significance during the Republican Era. Its role in regulating society and arbitrating disputes was newly contested. Its uniquely American function of exercising the power of judicial review ceased to be exceptional and marginal to American constitutionalism. The courts moved to the center of the American constitutional enterprise.

The primary role of state and federal courts had always been to regulate society. Whether implementing statutory rules, inventing new doctrines, or extending and applying inherited principles, courts transmitted the force of the state and maintained law and order. Industrialization and urbanization put that traditional role under new pressures. New technologies, such as the railroads, and the new economy that followed forced judges to grapple with a host of new legal problems—with profound economic and social implications. When corporations were unable to pay their debts, should they be dismantled and their individual assets sold for cash, as was traditional? Or should they be kept intact under the authority of the bankruptcy judge? In other words, were they more valuable as a working economic unit than as a mere

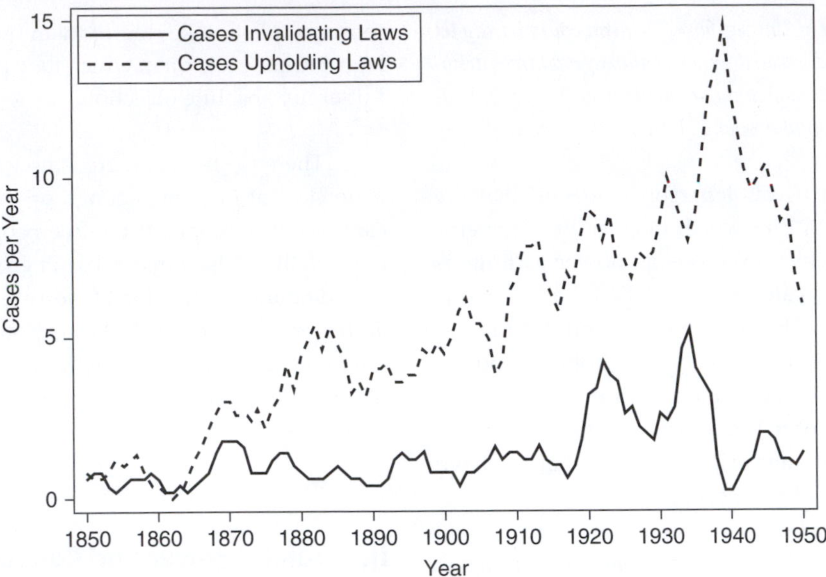

Figure 7-4 Supreme Court Review of Federal Laws, 1850–1950

Source: Keith E. Whittington, The Judicial Review of Congress dataset.

Note: Centered, five-year moving averages.

set of machines, buildings, and surplus steel?[10] When individuals were injured by the normal operation of new machines and factories, should traditional theories of liability be applied even when this hampered economic progress?[11] New social movements created similar difficulties, challenging traditional legal understandings and tools. Were individuals guilty of a conspiracy to restrain trade if they encouraged workers to walk off a job? What if they collectively demanded higher wages? Could judges enjoin labor leaders from interfering with business and threaten them with criminal prosecution?

Judicial Review in the Republican Era. Judicial review came into its own during this period. The very term "judicial review" was an invention of this era, for the practice had become common enough to need a name. Congress debated whether to give courts the power to review regulatory actions. Administrative agencies had grown, but were their actions consistent with statute? Deciding this would mean further judicial supervision of the executive branch. Both state and federal courts became more aggressive in exercising judicial review. And as governments expanded their reach into society, private individuals and organizations became more aggressive in seeking judicial review of elected politicians.

Figures 7-4 and 7-5 illustrate the new importance of judicial review during the Republican era and beyond. Figure 7-4 tracks Supreme Court review of federal statutes. It includes both cases in which the Court upheld the application of a federal law against a constitutional challenge and cases in which the Court invalidated an application of a law. Most of the time, the Court rejected the constitutional challenge and upheld the law, allowing the federal government to grow and exercise power in new and creative ways. The Court did regularly strike down federal laws as unconstitutional, however, and during the 1870s, 1920s, and 1930s did so actively. After the Civil War, the Court also became far more active in striking down state laws as unconstitutional, as seen in Figure 7-5. It made use of both the new tools contained in the Fourteenth Amendment and the text of the original Constitution. Throughout the latter decades of the nineteenth century, the Court regularly struck down state laws, and it did so at a faster rate than it struck down federal laws. During the Progressive Era, when

10. See, e.g., Gerald Berk, *Alternative Tracks* (Baltimore: Johns Hopkins University Press, 1994).

11. See, e.g., Howard Schweber, *The Creation of American Common Law, 1850–1880* (New York: Cambridge University Press, 2004); John Fabian Witt, *The Accidental Republic* (Cambridge: Harvard University Press, 2004).

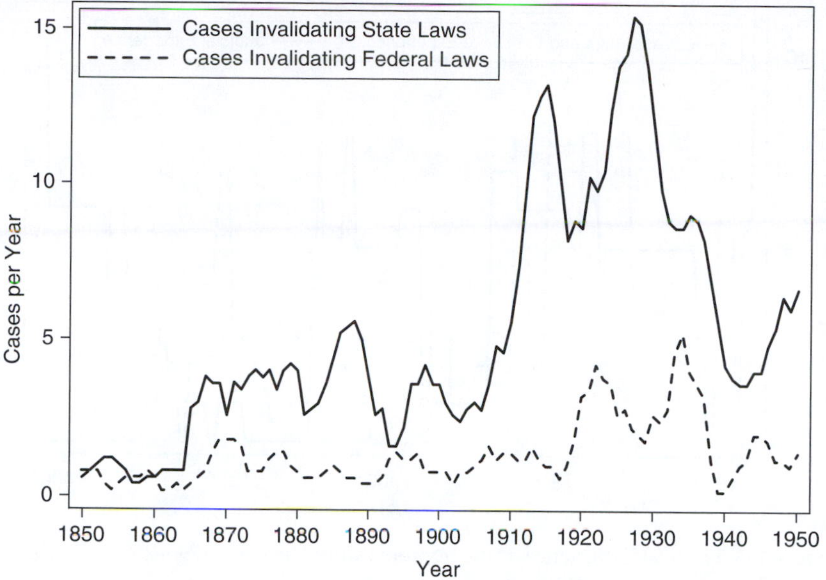

Figure 7-5 Supreme Court Invalidation of State and Federal Laws, 1850–1950

Source: Congressional Research Service, *The Constitution of the United States of America, Analysis and Interpretation* (Washington, DC: Government Printing Office, 2004); Keith E. Whittington, The Judicial Review of Congress dataset.

Note: Centered, five-year moving averages.

states experimented with forms of social and economic regulation, the Court reached new heights of activity, foreshadowing and dwarfing what it would do with federal laws. After 1937, the Court swiftly retreated as the Republican Era gave way to the New Deal. Laws ranging from the federal income tax to alcohol prohibition and minimum wage were challenged in the courts, placing the judiciary and the power of judicial review at the center of political controversy.

Reforming the Federal Judiciary in the Republican Era. The Republicans took a new approach to federal judicial selection, laying the foundation for the work that they expected the Supreme Court to do. As seen in Figure 7-6, the justices of the Jacksonian period were notable for their substantial experience in the legislative and executive branch, though they often had significant judicial experience as well. Secretary of Treasury Roger Taney, Postmaster General John McLean, and U.S. Representative Philip P. Barbour all had significant experience in the political arena before Andrew Jackson placed them on the Court. The Republicans took a different tack.

During the Republican Era, significant political experience became increasingly rare for Supreme Court appointees. Republican selections for the Court had instead made their careers as private lawyers and as judges. They had spent their time grappling with the same questions that they were expected to address on the bench—thorny questions of private law, property, and regulation. Melville Fuller was a Chicago litigator; David Brewer was a Kansas supreme court judge and federal circuit court judge; Oliver Wendell Holmes was chief justice of the Massachusetts supreme court. It was not until the New Deal that politicians once again made their way to the Court, as Franklin Roosevelt, Harry Truman, John Kennedy, and Lyndon Johnson looked to political allies when making judicial appointments.

The expansion of judicial power was not just the creation of eager judges. In the wake of the midterm elections of 1874, where Democrats regained control of the House of Representatives, the lame-duck Republican leaders in 1875 quickly introduced a bill to expand the jurisdiction of federal courts. The Judiciary and Removal Act of 1875 redirected litigation involving national commercial interests—*out* of state courts and *into* the more conservative (Republican) federal judiciary. Technically, this meant granting the federal judiciary "federal questions" jurisdiction—that is, the

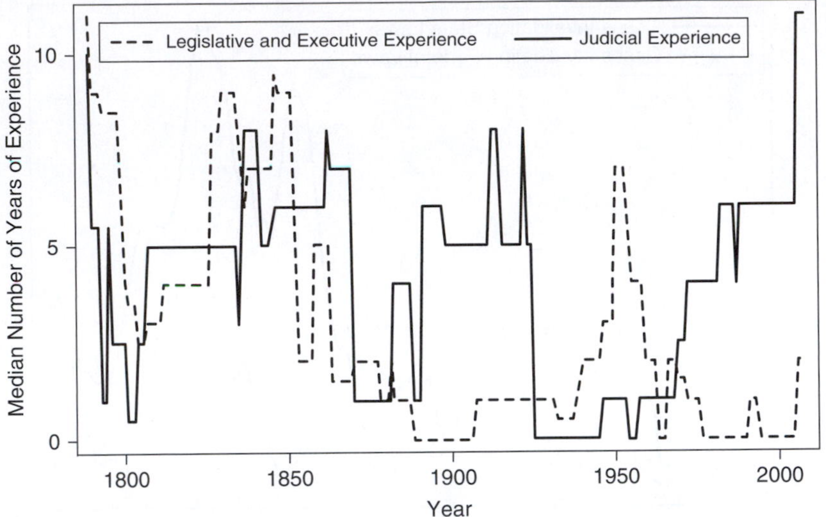

Figure 7-6 Political Experience of the Supreme Court Justices, 1790–2008

Source: Lee Epstein, Jeffrey A. Segal, Harold J. Spaeth, and Thomas G. Walker, *The Supreme Court Compendium*, 4th ed. (Washington, DC: CQ Press, 2007), Tables 4.8, 4.9.

authority to have original jurisdiction in all civil and criminal cases "arising under" the laws of the United States. It also granted "removal jurisdiction": Lawsuits that began in state courts could be "removed" into federal courts if the case involved issues of federal law or parties from different states. The Act attempted to prevent obstruction of removal in two ways. First, it authorized federal judges to hold plaintiffs in default if a state court blocked removal. Second, a state court clerk who refused to effectuate a removal was now guilty of a misdemeanor, punishable by a year of imprisonment and a $1,000 fine.

In sum, federal judicial power expanded, and federal courts became increasingly embroiled in political controversy. However, this expansion came about not just because of the parties in power in the national government. Senator George D. Robinson of Massachusetts spoke from the floor of Congress in 1880, in debates over the pro-farmer Granger Movement:

> In the West there have been granger laws and granger excitement that have led people to commit enormities in legislation and extravagances in practice; and in the South—why, sir, history is too full for me to particularize. Capital is needed to restore the waste places of the South and to build up the undeveloped West; it must flow largely from the old States of the East and from foreign lands. But it will not be risked in the perils of sectional bitterness, narrow prejudices, or local indifference to integrity and honor. I say then, let us stand by the national courts; let us preserve their power.[12]

A. Judicial Review

The Republican Era saw a dramatic expansion of judicial review. Both state courts and federal courts became more active in exercising the power of judicial review in the years after the Civil War. The Fourteenth Amendment to the U.S. Constitution provided one important, but ill-defined, tool for lawyers to use to draw judges into political battles. This crucial Reconstruction amendment gave the federal courts a new basis on which to judge state actions, and over time it became one of the most litigated pieces of text in the U.S. Constitution. But state and federal courts also became more active in practicing horizontal judicial review and evaluating the actions of the other branches of their own government.

Along with the increase in judicial scrutiny of legislation came a growing controversy over whether and how courts used the power to interpret the Constitution and review statutes. Advocates of judicial review, who were mostly on the political right during this

12. *Congressional Record*, 46th Cong., 2nd sess. (Feb. 12, 1880), 850.

period, argued that independent courts were important guardians of rights and should carefully scrutinize legislation. Critics of judicial review, who were mostly on the political left, argued that the courts needed to be checked and that judges should be highly deferential to legislative decisions.

Slaughter-House Cases, 83 U.S. 36 (1873)

The Supreme Court's first opportunity to interpret the Fourteenth Amendment (ratified in 1870) came, not in a case involving black civil rights, but in a dispute over the butchering of animals in New Orleans. In 1869 the Republican state legislature of Louisiana passed a law incorporating the Crescent City Live-Stock Landing and Slaughtering Company and requiring all butchering of animals to be done in the one "grand slaughterhouse" controlled by this company. Prior to the law, about 1,000 butchers were scattered across the 1,154 square miles surrounding New Orleans, and their activities represented a health risk in an era before modern refrigeration and at a time when it was common for butchers to dump remains and waste in waterways. The legislature asserted that moving all of this activity into one central, regulated location was a justifiable exercise of the state's "police power." That is, a legislature had the traditional authority to pass laws that promote public health, safety, or morality.

However, the law also inconvenienced those butchers who had been working on their own property. It also threatened the livelihood of other butchers who had been operating their own slaughterhouse facilities. Outrage at the newly created "monopoly" was fueled by the fact that the new corporation created by the legislature was controlled by a group of seventeen wealthy and politically influential individuals. This fed southern Democrats' anger at "carpet bagging" Republicans. They saw Republican legislatures as corrupt and more interested in conferring special privileges on favored groups than in promoting the general interest.

Before passage of the Fourteenth Amendment, federal courts would have had no opportunity to address this sort of dispute. There was a well-developed body of constitutional law in the states dealing with the scope of the "police powers." These laws distinguished between the legitimate promotion of public health, safety, and morality and the illegitimate use of legislative power to confer special privileges. The latter included "partial" laws designed to benefit some classes at the expense of other classes. However, this case law was elaborated by state courts and was anchored in state constitutional provisions that attempted to define what it meant for a state legislature to operate under "the law of the land" or "due process of law." Until 1870 there were no federal constitutional provisions that could be used by federal courts to impose national standards on state exercises of the police powers.

This changed a year after passage of the Louisiana law, when the Fourteenth Amendment imposed new federal restrictions on the behavior of state governments. Disgruntled butchers hired high-powered counsel to help them get a favorable hearing in the U.S. Supreme Court. Their lawyer was former associate justice of the Supreme Court John A. Campbell, who resigned the Court in 1861 after his state seceded from the Union. Campbell emphasized three provisions of the Fourteenth Amendment:

- *First, he pointed out that the Fourteenth Amendment prohibited states from enforcing "any law which shall abridge the privileges and immunities of citizens of the United States." Campbell argued that one of the privileges and immunities of U.S. citizens was the right to labor freely in an honest avocation.*
- *Second, he noted that the Fourteenth Amendment prohibited states from denying any person "equal protection of the laws." Here he argued that this monopoly was unequal because it bestowed artificial privileges on some butchers at the expense of others.*
- *Finally, he noted that the Fourteenth Amendment declared that states shall not "deprive any person of life, liberty, or property, without due process of law." He argued that the legislation's interference with the ability of butchers to pursue an honest living essentially deprived them of their liberty to work and deprived them of the value of their property.*

For good measure, this son of the Confederacy added, the Thirteenth Amendment prohibited a scheme in which butchers had to pay monopolists a set fee in order to conduct their business. Campbell called it a form of "involuntary servitude."

Was this a legitimate promotion of public health or the conferring of illegitimate privilege? Elements of both were at work, which may help explain why the justices split 5–4, with the majority opinion written by Justice Miller and separate dissents written by Justices Field, Bradley, and Swayne. The majority opinion drew a controversial (but still authoritative) distinction between the "privileges or immunities" of state citizens and U.S. citizens. It also read narrowly the protections associated with the due process and equal protection clauses. In this way, Justice Miller temporarily maintained a more traditional understanding of the separate spheres of national and state authority in the federal system. He also prevented overburdened federal judges from having to review all disputed exercises of state police powers.

However, over the next few decades, as national conservatives became more concerned about the response of state legislatures to farmers' protests, the Populist movement, and labor agitation, conservative judges and lawyers would draw on the views of the Slaughter-House *dissenters in support of greater judicial monitoring of state legislatures.*

Justice MILLER delivered the opinion of the court.

These cases... arise out of the efforts of the butchers of New Orleans to resist the Crescent City Live-Stock Landing and Slaughter-House Company in the exercise of certain powers conferred by the charter which created it, and which was granted by the legislature of that State....

...

This statute is denounced not only as creating a monopoly and conferring odious and exclusive privileges upon a small number of persons at the expense of the great body of the community of New Orleans, but it is asserted that it deprives a large and meritorious class of citizens—the whole of the butchers of the city—of the right to exercise their trade, the business to which they have been trained and on which they depend for the support of themselves and their families, and that the unrestricted exercise of the business of butchering is necessary to the daily subsistence of the population of the city.

But a critical examination of the act hardly justifies these assertions....

It is not, and cannot be successfully controverted, that it is both the right and the duty of the legislative body—the supreme power of the State or municipality—to prescribe and determine the localities where the business of slaughtering for a great city may be conducted. To do this effectively it is indispensable that all persons who slaughter animals for food shall do it in those places and nowhere else.

The statute under consideration defines these localities and forbids slaughtering in any other. It does not, as has been asserted, prevent the butcher from doing his own slaughtering. On the contrary, the Slaughter-House Company is required, under a heavy penalty, to permit any person who wishes to do so, to slaughter in their houses; and they are bound to make ample provision for the convenience of all the slaughtering for the entire city. The butcher then is still permitted to slaughter, to prepare, and to sell his own meats; but he is required to slaughter at a specified place and to pay a reasonable compensation for the use of the accommodations furnished him at that place.

The wisdom of the monopoly granted by the legislature may be open to question, but it is difficult to see a justification for the assertion that the butchers are deprived of the right to labor in their occupation, or the people of their daily service in preparing food, or how this statute, with the duties and guards imposed upon the company, can be said to destroy the business of the butcher, or seriously interfere with its pursuit.

The power here exercised by the legislature of Louisiana is, in its essential nature, one which has been, up to the present period in the constitutional history of this country, always conceded to belong to the States....

This [police] power is, and must be from its very nature, incapable of any very exact definition or limitation. Upon it depends the security of social order, the life and health of the citizen, the comfort of an existence in a thickly populated community, the enjoyment of private and social life, and the beneficial use of property.... The regulation of the place and manner of conducting the slaughtering of animals, and the business of butchering within a city, and the inspection of the animals to be killed for meat, and of the meat afterwards, are among the most necessary and frequent exercises of this power....

It cannot be denied that the statute under consideration is aptly framed to remove from the more densely populated part of the city, the noxious slaughter-houses, and large and offensive collections of animals necessarily incident to the slaughtering business of a large city, and to locate them where the convenience, health, and comfort of the people require they shall be located. And it must be conceded that the means adopted by the act for this purpose are appropriate, are stringent, and effectual. But it is said that in creating a corporation for this purpose, and conferring upon it exclusive privileges—privileges which it is said constitute a monopoly—the legislature has exceeded its power....

It can readily be seen that the interested vigilance of the corporation created by the Louisiana legislature will be more efficient in enforcing the limitation prescribed for the stock-landing and slaughtering business for the good of the city than the ordinary efforts of the officers of the law.

Unless, therefore, it can be maintained that the exclusive privilege granted by this charter to the corporation, is beyond the power of the legislature of Louisiana, there can be no just exception to the validity of the statute....

....

The plaintiffs in error...allege that the statute is a violation of the Constitution of the United States in these several particulars:

That it creates an involuntary servitude forbidden by the thirteenth article of amendment;

That it abridges the privileges and immunities of citizens of the United States;

That it denies to the plaintiffs the equal protection of the laws; and,

That it deprives them of their property without due process of law; contrary to the provisions of the first section of the fourteenth article of amendment. This court is thus called upon for the first time to give construction to these articles.

We do not conceal from ourselves the great responsibility which this duty devolves upon us. No questions so far-reaching and pervading in their consequences, so profoundly interesting to the people of this country, and so important in their bearing upon the relations of the United States, and of the several States to each other and to the citizens of the States and of the United States, have been before this court during the official life of any of its present members. We have given every opportunity for a full hearing at the bar; we have discussed it freely and compared views among ourselves; we have taken ample time for careful deliberation, and we now propose to announce the judgments which we have formed in the construction of those articles, so far as we have found them necessary to the decision of the cases before us, and beyond that we have neither the inclination nor the right to go....

The most cursory glance at these articles discloses a unity of purpose, when taken in connection with the history of the times, which cannot fail to have an important bearing on any question of doubt concerning their true meaning. Nor can such doubts, when any reasonably exist, be safely and rationally solved without a reference to that history;.... Fortunately that history is fresh within the memory of us all, and its leading features, as they bear upon the matter before us, free from doubt.

The institution of African slavery, as it existed in about half the States of the Union, and the contests pervading the public mind for many years, between those who desired its curtailment and ultimate extinction and those who desired additional safeguards for its security and perpetuation, culminated in the effort, on the part of most of the States in which slavery existed, to separate from the Federal government, and to resist its authority. This constituted the war of the rebellion, and whatever auxiliary causes may have contributed to bring about this war, undoubtedly the overshadowing and efficient cause was African slavery....

...

...on the most casual examination of the language of these amendments, no one can fail to be impressed with the one pervading purpose found in them all, lying at the foundation of each, and without which none of them would have been even suggested; we mean the freedom of the slave race, the security and firm establishment of that freedom, and the protection of the newly-made freeman and citizen from the oppressions of those who had formerly exercised unlimited dominion over him....

We do not say that no one else but the negro can share in this protection. Both the language and spirit of these articles are to have their fair and just weight in any question of construction.... [I]n any fair and just construction of any section or phrase of these amendments, it is necessary to look to the purpose which we have said was the pervading spirit of them all, the evil which they were designed to remedy, and the process of continued addition to the Constitution, until that purpose was supposed to be accomplished, as far as constitutional law can accomplish it.

The first section of the fourteenth article, to which our attention is more specially invited, opens with a definition of citizenship—not only citizenship of the United States, but citizenship of the States. No such definition was previously found in the Constitution, nor had any attempt been made to define it by act of Congress.... But it had been held by this court, in the celebrated *Dred Scott* case, only a few years before the outbreak of the civil war, that a man of African descent, whether a slave or not, was not and could not be a citizen of a State or of the United States. This decision, while it met the condemnation of some of the ablest statesmen and constitutional lawyers of the country, had never been overruled; and if it was to be accepted as a constitutional limitation of the right of citizenship, then all the negro race who had recently been made freemen, were still, not only not citizens, but were incapable of becoming so by anything short of an amendment to the Constitution.

To remove this difficulty primarily, and to establish a clear and comprehensive definition of citizenship which should declare what should constitute citizenship of the United States, and also citizenship of a State, the first clause of the first section was framed.

> "All persons born or naturalized in the United States, and subject to the jurisdiction thereof, are citizens of the United States and of the State wherein they reside."

The first observation we have to make on this clause is, that it puts at rest both the questions which we stated to have been the subject of differences of opinion. It declares that persons may be citizens of the United States without regard to their citizenship of a particular State, and it overturns the *Dred Scott* decision by making all persons born within the United States and subject to its jurisdiction citizens of the United States....

The next observation is more important in view of the arguments of counsel in the present case. It is, that the distinction between citizenship of the United States and citizenship of a State is clearly recognized and established....

We think this distinction and its explicit recognition in this amendment of great weight in this argument, because the next paragraph of this same section, which is the one mainly relied on by the plaintiffs in error, speaks only of privileges and immunities of citizens of the United States, and does not speak of those of citizens of the several States. The argument, however, in favor of the plaintiffs rests wholly on the assumption that the citizenship is the same, and the privileges and immunities guaranteed by the clause are the same.

The language is, "No State shall make or enforce any law which shall abridge the privileges or immunities of citizens of the United States." It is a little remarkable, if this clause was intended as a protection to the citizen of a State against the legislative power of his own State, that the word citizen of the State should be left out when it is so carefully used, and used in contradistinction to citizens of the United States, in the very sentence which precedes it. It is too clear for argument that the change in phraseology was adopted understandingly and with a purpose....

Fortunately we are not without judicial construction of this clause of the Constitution. The first and the leading case on the subject is that of *Corfield v. Coryell*, decided by Justice Washington in the Circuit Court for the District of Pennsylvania in 1823. "The inquiry," he says, "is, what are the privileges and immunities of citizens of the several States? We feel no hesitation in confining these expressions to those privileges and immunities which are fundamental; which belong of right to the citizens of all free governments, and which have at all times been enjoyed by citizens of the several States which compose this Union, from the time of their becoming free, independent, and sovereign. What these fundamental principles are, it would be more tedious than difficult to enumerate. They may all, however, be comprehended under the following general heads: protection by the government, with the right to acquire and possess property of every kind, and to pursue and obtain happiness and safety, subject, nevertheless, to such restraints as the government may prescribe for the general good of the whole."...

It would be the vainest show of learning to attempt to prove by citations of authority, that up to the adoption of the recent amendments, no claim or pretence was set up that those rights depended on the Federal government for their existence or protection, beyond the very few express limitations which the Federal Constitution imposed upon the States—such, for instance, as the prohibition against ex post facto laws, bills of attainder, and laws impairing the obligation of contracts. But with the exception of these and a few other restrictions, the entire domain of the privileges and immunities of citizens of the States, as above defined, lay within the constitutional and legislative power of the States, and without that of the Federal government. Was it the purpose of the fourteenth amendment, by the simple declaration that no State should make or enforce any law which shall abridge the privileges and immunities of citizens of the United States, to transfer the security and protection of all the civil rights which we have mentioned, from the States to the Federal government? And where it is declared that Congress shall have the power to enforce that article, was it intended to bring within the power of Congress the entire domain of civil rights heretofore belonging exclusively to the States?

All this and more must follow, if the proposition of the plaintiffs in error be sound. For not only are these rights subject to the control of Congress whenever in its discretion any of them are supposed to be abridged by State legislation, but that body may also pass laws in advance, limiting and restricting the exercise of legislative power by the States, in their most ordinary and usual functions, as in its judgment it may think proper on all such subjects. And still further, such a construction followed by the reversal of the judgments of the Supreme Court of Louisiana in these cases, would constitute this court a perpetual censor upon all legislation of the States, on the civil rights of their own citizens, with authority to nullify such as it did not approve as consistent with those rights, as they existed at the time of the adoption of this amendment. The argument we admit is not always the most conclusive which is drawn from the consequences urged against the adoption of a particular construction of an instrument. But when, as in the case before us, these consequences are so serious, so far-reaching and pervading, so great a departure from the structure and spirit of our institutions; when the effect is to fetter and degrade the State governments by subjecting them to the control of Congress, in the exercise of powers heretofore universally conceded to them of the most ordinary and fundamental character; when in fact it radically changes the whole theory of the relations of the State and Federal governments to each other and of both these governments to the people; the argument has a force that is irresistible, in the absence of language which expresses such a purpose too clearly to admit of doubt.

We are convinced that no such results were intended by the Congress which proposed these amendments, nor by the legislatures of the States which ratified them.

Having shown that the privileges and immunities relied on in the argument are those which belong to citizens of the States as such, and that they are left to the State governments for security and protection, and not by this article placed under the special care of the Federal government, we may hold ourselves excused from defining the privileges and immunities of citizens of the United States which no State can abridge, until some case involving those privileges may make it necessary to do so.

But lest it should be said that no such privileges and immunities are to be found if those we have been considering are excluded, we venture to suggest some which owe their existence to the Federal government, its National character, its Constitution, or its laws.

One of these is well described in the case of *Crandall v. Nevada* (1868). It is said to be the right of the citizen of this great country, protected by implied guarantees of its Constitution, "to come to the seat of government to assert any claim he may have upon that government, to transact any business he may have with it, to seek its protection, to share its offices, to engage in administering its functions. He has the right of free access to its seaports, through which all operations of foreign commerce are conducted, to the subtreasuries, land offices, and courts of justice in the several States." ...

Another privilege of a citizen of the United States is to demand the care and protection of the Federal government over his life, liberty, and property when on the high seas or within the jurisdiction of a foreign government. Of this there can be no doubt, nor that the right depends upon his character as a citizen of the United States.... To these may be added the rights secured by the thirteenth and fifteenth articles of amendment, and by the other clause of the fourteenth, next to be considered....

> "All persons born or naturalized in the United States, and subject to the jurisdiction thereof, are citizens of the United States and of the State wherein they reside. No State shall make or enforce any law which shall abridge the privileges or immunities of citizens of the United States; nor shall any State deprive any person of life, liberty, or property without due process of law, nor deny to any person within its jurisdiction the equal protection of its laws."

The argument has not been much pressed in these cases that the defendant's charter deprives the plaintiffs of their property without due process of law, or that it denies to them the equal protection of the law. The first of these paragraphs has been in the Constitution since the adoption of the fifth amendment, as a restraint upon the Federal power. It is also to be found in some form of expression in the constitutions of nearly all the States, as a restraint upon the power of the States. This law then, has practically been the same as it now is during the existence of the government, except so far as the present amendment may place the restraining power over the States in this matter in the hands of the Federal government.

We are not without judicial interpretation, therefore, both State and National, of the meaning of this clause. And it is sufficient to say that under no construction of that provision that we have ever seen, or any that we deem admissible, can the restraint imposed by the State of Louisiana upon the exercise of their trade by the butchers of New Orleans be held to be a deprivation of property within the meaning of that provision.

"Nor shall any State deny to any person within its jurisdiction the equal protection of the laws."

In the light of the history of these amendments, and the pervading purpose of them, which we have already discussed, it is not difficult to give a meaning to this clause. The existence of laws in the States where the newly emancipated negroes resided, which discriminated with gross injustice and hardship against them as a class, was the evil to be remedied by this clause, and by it such laws are forbidden.

If, however, the States did not conform their laws to its requirements, then by the fifth section of the article of amendment Congress was authorized to enforce it by suitable legislation. We doubt very much whether any action of a State not directed by way of discrimination against the negroes as a class, or on account of their race, will ever be held to come within the purview of this provision. It is so clearly a provision for that race and that emergency, that a strong case would be necessary for its application to any other....

...Under the pressure of all the excited feeling growing out of the war, our statesmen have still believed that the existence of the State with powers for domestic and local government, including the regulation of civil rights—the rights of person and of property—was essential to the perfect working of our complex form of government, though they have thought proper to impose additional limitations on the States, and to confer additional power on that of the Nation.

But whatever fluctuations may be seen in the history of public opinion on this subject during the period of our national existence, we think it will be found that this court, so far as its functions required, has always held with a steady and an even hand the balance between State and Federal power, and we trust that such may continue to be the history of its relation to that subject so long as it shall have duties to perform which demand of it a construction of the Constitution, or of any of its parts. The judgments of the Supreme Court of Louisiana in these cases are

AFFIRMED.

Justice FIELD, with Chief Justice CHASE, Justice SWAYNE, and Justice BRADLEY, dissenting.

I am unable to agree with the majority of the court in these cases, and will proceed to state the reasons of my dissent from their judgment....

...[U]nder the pretence of prescribing a police regulation the State cannot be permitted to encroach upon any of the just rights of the citizen, which the Constitution intended to secure against abridgment.

In the law in question there are only two provisions which can properly be called police regulations—the one which requires the landing and slaughtering of animals below the city of New Orleans, and the other which requires the inspection of the animals before they are slaughtered. When these requirements are complied with, the sanitary purposes of the act are accomplished. In all other particulars the act is a mere grant to a corporation created by it of special and exclusive privileges by which the health of the city is in no way promoted....The health of the city might require the removal from its limits and suburbs of all buildings for keeping and slaughtering cattle, but no such object could possibly justify legislation removing such buildings from a large part of the State for the benefit of a single corporation. The pretence of sanitary regulations for the grant of the exclusive privileges is a shallow one, which merits only this passing notice....

The act of Louisiana presents the naked case, unaccompanied by any public considerations, where a right to pursue a lawful and necessary calling, previously enjoyed by every citizen, and in connection with which a thousand persons were daily employed, is taken away and vested exclusively for twenty-five years, for an extensive district and a large population, in a single corporation, or its exercise is for that period restricted to the establishments of the corporation, and there allowed only upon onerous conditions....

The question presented is, therefore, one of the gravest importance, not merely to the parties here, but to the whole country. It is nothing less than the question whether the recent amendments to the Federal Constitution protect the citizens of the United States against the deprivation of their common rights by State legislation. In my judgment the fourteenth amendment does afford such protection, and was so intended by the Congress which framed and the States which adopted it....

The amendment does not attempt to confer any new privileges or immunities upon citizens, or to enumerate or define those already existing. It assumes that there are such privileges and immunities which belong of right to citizens as such, and ordains that they shall not be abridged by State legislation. If this inhibition has no reference to privileges and immunities of this character, but only refers, as held by the majority of the court in their opinion, to such privileges and immunities as were before its adoption specially designated in the Constitution or necessarily implied as belonging to citizens of the United States, it was a vain and idle enactment, which accomplished nothing, and most unnecessarily excited Congress and the people on its passage. With privileges and immunities thus designated or implied no State could ever have interfered by its laws, and no new constitutional provision was required to inhibit such interference. The supremacy of the Constitution and the laws of the United States always controlled any State legislation of that character. But if the amendment refers to the natural and inalienable rights which belong to all citizens, the inhibition has a profound significance and consequence.

What, then, are the privileges and immunities which are secured against abridgment by State legislation?...

The terms, privileges and immunities, are not new in the amendment; they were in the Constitution before the amendment was adopted. They are found in the second section of the fourth article, which declares that "the citizens of each State shall be entitled to all privileges and immunities of citizens in the several States," and they have been the subject of frequent consideration in judicial decisions. In *Corfield v. Coryell*, Justice Washington said he had "no hesitation in confining these expressions to those privileges and immunities which were, in their nature, fundamental; which belong of right to citizens of all free governments, and which have at all times been enjoyed by the citizens of the several States which compose the Union, from the time of their becoming free, independent, and sovereign;" and, in considering what those fundamental privileges were, he said that perhaps it would be more tedious than difficult to enumerate them, but that they might be "all comprehended under the following general heads: protection by the government; the enjoyment of life and liberty, with the right to acquire and possess property of every kind, and to pursue and obtain happiness and safety, subject, nevertheless, to such restraints as the government may justly prescribe for the general good of the whole." This appears to me to be a sound construction of the clause in question. The privileges and immunities designated are those which of right belong to the citizens of all free governments. Clearly among these must be placed the right to pursue a lawful employment in a lawful manner, without other restraint than such as equally affects all persons. In the discussions in Congress upon the passage of the Civil Rights Act repeated reference was made to this language of Justice Washington. It was cited by Senator Trumbull with the observation that it enumerated the very rights belonging to a citizen of the United States set forth in the first section of the act, and with the statement that all persons born in the United States, being declared by the act citizens of the United States, would thenceforth be entitled to the rights of citizens, and that these were the great fundamental rights set forth in the act; and that they were set forth "as appertaining to every freeman."...

...The privileges and immunities of citizens of the United States, of every one of them, is secured against abridgment in any form by any State. The fourteenth amendment places them under the guardianship of the National authority. All monopolies in any known trade or manufacture are an invasion of these privileges, for they encroach upon the liberty of citizens to acquire property and pursue happiness, and were held void at common law in the great Case of Monopolies, decided during the reign of Queen Elizabeth....

The common law of England, as is thus seen, condemned all monopolies in any known trade or manufacture, and declared void all grants of special privileges whereby others could be deprived of any liberty which they previously had, or be hindered in their lawful trade....The common law of England is the basis of the jurisprudence of the United States. It was brought to this country by the colonists, together with the English statutes, and was established here so far as it was applicable to their condition....

So fundamental has this privilege of every citizen to be free from disparaging and unequal enactments, in the pursuit of the ordinary avocations of life, been regarded, that few instances have arisen where the principle has been so far violated as to call for the interposition of the courts. But whenever this has occurred, with the exception of the present cases from Louisiana, which are the most barefaced and flagrant of all, the enactment interfering with the privilege of the citizen has been pronounced illegal and void....

In all these cases there is a recognition of the equality of right among citizens in the pursuit of the ordinary avocations of life, and a declaration that all grants of exclusive privileges, in contravention of this equality, are against common right, and void.

This equality of right, with exemption from all disparaging and partial enactments, in the lawful pursuits of life, throughout the whole country, is the distinguishing privilege of citizens of the United States. To them, everywhere, all pursuits, all professions, all avocations are open without other restrictions than such as are imposed equally upon all others of the same age, sex, and condition. The State may prescribe such regulations for every pursuit and calling of life as will promote the public health, secure the good order and advance the general prosperity of society, but when once prescribed, the pursuit or calling must be free to be followed by every citizen who is within the conditions designated, and will conform to the regulations. This is the fundamental idea upon which our institutions rest, and unless adhered to in the legislation of the country our government will be a republic only in name. The fourteenth amendment, in my judgment, makes it essential to the validity of the legislation of every State that this equality of right should be respected. How widely this equality has been departed from, how entirely rejected and trampled upon by the act of Louisiana, I have already shown. And it is to me a matter of profound regret that its validity is recognized by a majority of this court, for by it the right of free labor, one of the most sacred and imprescriptible rights of man, is violated. As stated by the Supreme Court of Connecticut, in the case cited, grants of exclusive privileges, such as is made by the act in question, are opposed to the whole theory of free government, and it requires no aid from any bill of rights to render them void. That only is a free government, in the American sense of the term, under which the inalienable right of every citizen to pursue his happiness is unrestrained, except by just, equal, and impartial laws.

...

Justice BRADLEY, also dissenting:

...

The fourteenth amendment to the Constitution of the United States, section 1, declares that no State shall make or enforce any law which shall abridge the privileges and immunities of citizens of the United States....

If a State legislature should pass a law prohibiting the inhabitants of a particular township, county, or city, from tanning leather or making shoes, would such a law violate any privileges or immunities of those inhabitants as citizens of the United States, or only their privileges and immunities as citizens of that particular State? Or if a State legislature should pass a law of caste, making all trades and professions, or certain enumerated trades and professions, hereditary, so that no one could follow any such trades or professions except that which was pursued by his father, would such a law violate the privileges and immunities of the people of that State as citizens of the United States, or only as citizens of the State? Would they have no redress but to appeal to the courts of that particular State?

This seems to me to be the essential question before us for consideration. And, in my judgment, the right of any citizen to follow whatever lawful employment he chooses to adopt (submitting himself to all lawful regulations) is one of his most valuable rights, and one which the legislature of a State cannot invade, whether restrained by its own constitution or not....

I think sufficient has been said to show that citizenship is not an empty name, but that, in this country at least, it has connected with it certain incidental rights, privileges, and immunities of the greatest importance. And to say that these rights and immunities attach only to State citizenship, and not to citizenship of the United States, appears to me to evince a very narrow and insufficient estimate of constitutional history and the rights of men, not to say the rights of the American people....

But even if the Constitution were silent, the fundamental privileges and immunities of citizens, as such, would be no less real and no less inviolable than they now are. It was not necessary to say in words that the citizens of the United States should have and exercise all the privileges of citizens; the privilege of buying, selling, and enjoying property; the privilege of engaging in any lawful employment for a livelihood; the privilege of resorting to the laws for redress of injuries, and the like. Their very citizenship conferred these privileges, if they did not possess them before. And these privileges they would enjoy whether they were citizens of any State or not. Inhabitants of Federal territories and new citizens, made such by annexation of territory or naturalization, though without any status as citizens of a State, could, nevertheless, as citizens of the United States, lay claim to every one of the privileges and immunities which have been enumerated; and among these none is more essential and fundamental than the right to follow such profession or employment as each one may choose, subject only to uniform regulations equally applicable to all....

The keeping of a slaughter-house is part of, and incidental to, the trade of a butcher—one of the ordinary occupations of human life. To compel a butcher, or rather all the butchers of a large city and an extensive district, to slaughter their cattle in another person's slaughter-house and pay him a toll therefore, is such a restriction upon the trade as materially to interfere with its prosecution. It is onerous, unreasonable, arbitrary, and unjust. It has none of the qualities of a police regulation. If it were really a police regulation, it would undoubtedly be within the power of the legislature. That portion of the act which requires all slaughter-houses to be located below the city, and to be subject to inspection, etc., is clearly a police regulation. That portion which allows no one but the favored company to build, own, or have slaughter-houses is not a police regulation, and has not the faintest semblance of one. It is one of those arbitrary and unjust laws made in the interest of a few scheming individuals, by which some of the Southern States have, within the past few years, been so deplorably oppressed and impoverished. It seems to me strange that it can be viewed in any other light....

If my views are correct with regard to what are the privileges and immunities of citizens, it follows conclusively that any law which establishes a sheer monopoly, depriving a large class of citizens of the privilege of pursuing a lawful employment, does abridge the privileges of those citizens.

The amendment also prohibits any State from depriving any person (citizen or otherwise) of life, liberty, or property, without due process of law.

In my view, a law which prohibits a large class of citizens from adopting a lawful employment, or from following a lawful employment previously adopted, does deprive them of liberty as well as property, without due process of law. Their right of choice is a portion of their liberty; their occupation is their property. Such a law also deprives those citizens of the equal protection of the laws, contrary to the last clause of the section....

It is futile to argue that none but persons of the African race are intended to be benefited by this amendment. They may have been the primary cause of the amendment, but its language is general, embracing all citizens, and I think it was purposely so expressed....

[E]ven if the business of the National courts should be increased, Congress could easily supply the remedy by increasing their number and efficiency. The great question is, What is the true construction of the amendment? When once we find that, we shall find the means of giving it effect. The argument from inconvenience ought not to have a very controlling influence in questions of this sort. The National will and National interest are of far greater importance.

In my opinion the judgment of the Supreme Court of Louisiana ought to be reversed.

Justice SWAYNE, dissenting:

I concur in the dissent in these cases and in the views expressed by my brethren, Justice Field and Justice Bradley. I desire, however, to submit a few additional remarks.

The first eleven amendments to the Constitution were intended to be checks and limitations upon the government which that instrument called into existence. They had their origin in a spirit of jealousy on the part of the States, which existed when the Constitution was adopted.... These [Reconstruction] amendments are a new departure, and mark an important epoch in the constitutional history of the country. They trench directly upon the power of the States, and deeply affect those bodies. They are, in this respect, at the opposite pole from the first eleven.

Fairly construed these amendments may be said to rise to the dignity of a new Magna Charta....

These amendments are all consequences of the late civil war. The prejudices and apprehension as to the central government which prevailed when the Constitution was adopted were dispelled by the light of experience. The public mind became satisfied that there was less danger of tyranny in the head than of anarchy and tyranny in the members. The provisions of this section are all eminently conservative in their character. They are a bulwark of defence, and can never be made an engine of oppression.... The construction adopted by the majority of my brethren is, in my judgment, much too narrow. It defeats, by a limitation not anticipated, the intent of those by whom the instrument was framed and of those by whom it was adopted. To the extent of that limitation it turns, as it were, what was meant for bread into a stone. By the Constitution, as it stood before the war, ample protection was given against oppression by the Union, but little was given against wrong and oppression by the States. That want was intended to be supplied by this amendment. Against the former this court has been called upon more than once to interpose. Authority of the same amplitude was intended to be conferred as to the latter. But this arm of our jurisdiction is, in these cases, stricken down by the judgment just given. Nowhere, than in this court, ought the will of the nation, as thus expressed, to be more liberally construed or more cordially executed. This determination of the majority seems to me to lie far in the other direction. I earnestly hope that the consequences to follow may prove less serious and far-reaching than the minority fear they will be.

Theodore Roosevelt, "A Charter of Democracy" (1912)[13]

Theodore Roosevelt launched himself back into presidential politics in 1912 with an attack on judges. He had been out of the White House for four years, and during that time he had become increasingly radical. He was frustrated with the more conservative administration of his successor, William Howard Taft. As the 1912 election approached, Roosevelt, still an extremely popular figure, decided to challenge Taft and retake command of the country. Taft refused to back down, however, and won renomination from the Republican Party. Roosevelt made an independent, "Bull Moose" run with the Progressive Party. Roosevelt bested Taft at the polls, but badly trailed Democratic nominee Woodrow Wilson, who won the presidency with less than 42 percent of the popular vote.

Roosevelt's attack on the courts instantly put him on the front page of the papers, but it proved to be a mixed bag politically. His first political speech in 1912 was an address to the Ohio state constitutional convention as he toured through the state, where he endorsed the application of the recall to judges and elaborated at length on the need to subject judicial decisions to popular check. He developed the theme at length in the early goings of his campaign, but gradually pulled back from it in favor of other themes as the campaign wore on. The issue clearly separated Roosevelt from Taft, but the New York Times *reported that many Republicans thought judicial recall was "veriest nonsense" and it editorialized that the recall was the "craziest of all suggestions that have come out of the bosom of Progressivism."[14] The Ohio convention itself voted down the judicial recall proposal.*

13. Excerpt taken from Theodore Roosevelt, *Progressive Principles* (New York: Progressive National Service, 1913), 46–83.

14. "Taft Will Answer Roosevelt Speech," *New York Times* (February 23, 1912):1; "The Pathology of the Progressives," *New York Times* (February 15, 1912):10.

Mr. President and Members of the Ohio Constitutional Convention:

I believe in pure democracy. With Lincoln, I hold that "this country, with its institutions, belongs to the people who inhabit it. Whenever they shall grow weary of the existing Government, they can exercise their Constitutional right of amending it."

...

I am emphatically a believer in constitutionalism, and because of this fact I no less emphatically protest against any theory that would make of the Constitution a means of thwarting instead of securing the absolute right of the people to rule themselves and to provide for their own social and industrial well-being.

All Constitutions, that of the States no less than that of the Nation, are designed, and must be interpreted and administered so as to fit human rights.

Lincoln so interpreted and administered the National Constitution. Buchanan attempted the reverse, attempted to fit human rights to, and limit them by, the Constitution. It was Buchanan who treated the courts as a fetish, who protested against and condemned all criticism of the judges for unjust and unrighteous decisions, and upheld the Constitution as an instrument for the protection of privilege and of vested wrong. It was Lincoln who appealed to the people against the judges when the judges went wrong, who advocated and secured what was practically the recall of the *Dred Scott* decision, and who treated the Constitution as a living force for righteousness.

....

I therefore very earnestly ask you clearly to provide in this Constitution means which will enable the people readily to amend it if at any point it works injustice, and also means which will permit the people themselves by popular vote, after due deliberation and discussion, but finally and without appeal, to settle what the proper construction of any Constitutional point is.

...

There remains the question of the recall of judges....

...

An independent and upright judiciary which fearlessly stands for the right, even against popular clamor, but which also understands and sympathizes with popular needs, is a great asset of popular government.

There is no public servant and no private man whom I place above a judge of the best type, and very whom

I rank beside him. I believe in the cumulative value of the law and in its value as an impersonal, disinterested basis of control... But I agree with every great jurist, from Marshall downwards, when I say that every judge is bound to consider two separate elements in his decision of a case, one the terms of the law, and the other the conditions of actual life to which the law is applied.... Both the law and life are to be considered in order that the law and the Constitution shall become, in John Marshall's words, "a living instrument and not a dead letter."... Moreover, never forget that the judge is just as much the servant of the people as any other official....

...

But either the recall will have to be adopted or else it will have to be made much easier than it now is to get rid, not merely of a bad judge, but of a judge who, however virtuous, has grown so out of touch with social needs and facts that he is unfit longer to render good service on the bench.

...

...[W]hen a judge decides a Constitutional question, when he decides what the people as a whole can or cannot do, the people should have the right to recall that decision if they think it wrong. We should hold the judiciary in all respect; but it is both absurd and degrading to make a fetish of a judge or of anyone else. Abraham Lincoln said in his first inaugural:

> "If the policy of the Government upon vital questions affecting the whole people is to be irrevocably fixed by decisions of the Supreme Court,... the people will have ceased to be their own rulers, having to that extent practically resigned their Government into the hands of that eminent tribunal. Nor is there in this view any assault upon the courts or the judges."

...

William Howard Taft, Veto of Arizona Statehood (1912)[15]

William Howard Taft's early career in public office had been in and around the judiciary. He had served as an Ohio Superior Court judge, as U.S. solicitor general (the deputy attorney general who represented the federal government in court), and a U.S. circuit court judge before giving up that position to hold a series of executive offices in the federal government culminating in his election as president in 1908. Even as president, however, he still cherished his lifelong ambition of being chief justice on the U.S. Supreme Court, an appointment that he finally won in 1921.

During Taft's political career, judges were both condemned and revered. Radicals, Populists, Progressives, labor leaders, and others harshly criticized the federal and state judiciaries, their powers, and their jurisprudence. For them, the courts were a reactionary and unaccountable force in politics in need of legislative and constitutional checks on their powers. Conservatives in the Democratic and, especially, the Republican Party replied aggressively. The defense of the judiciary was one of the few political issues that truly inspired Taft, and the perceived threat to the courts was what led him to seek renomination and reelection for the presidency, an office which he found otherwise tiresome. Although the Democrat Woodrow Wilson captured the White House in 1912, Taft had accomplished his major aim of keeping a more radical Theodore Roosevelt from taking back the Republican Party and returning to the presidency after a four-year absence.

The "recall" of elected officials was one of several popular institutional reforms that swept through the states during the Progressive Era. Like the initiative and referendum, the recall promised to put in the hands of the people another tool for maintaining popular control of the government. Recall provisions in state constitutions allowed voters to petition for the removal of government officials before the natural end of their term of office. If enough signatures were collected on such a petition, a special election would be held to determine whether the official in question would retain office or be immediately removed. In 1910, popular conventions were held in the territories of Arizona and New Mexico to draft proposed constitutions as part of the process of applying for statehood. The Arizona constitution, dominated by Democrats, included many of the popular institutional features of the era, including initiative, referendum, and recall provisions. The constitution was ratified by Arizona voters and forwarded to Congress and the president for their approval and admission for statehood. In August 1911, President Taft vetoed statehood because the recall provision of the Arizona constitution applied to judges as well as other elected officials. The recall provision was quickly modified, and Arizona was admitted as a state in February 1912. Later that year, the voters of the state approved a constitutional amendment to restore the judicial recall. When a county judge later

15. Excerpt taken from William Howard Taft, Veto Message, August 22, 1911, in *A Compilation of the Messages and Papers of the Presidents*, ed. James D. Richardson, vol. 17 (New York: Bureau of National Literature, 1916), 7636–44.

challenged his recall, the Arizona supreme court upheld the recall provisions of the state constitution as raising matters that "pertain to the sovereign powers of the people in their political aspect, have been unalterably settled, and may not be changed except in the manner provided by the Constitution" [Abbey v. Green, *28 Ariz. 53 (1925)].*

To the House of Representatives:

I return herewith, without my approval, House joint resolution No. 14, "To admit the Territories of New Mexico and Arizona as States into the Union on an equal footing with the original States."

...

...Under the Arizona constitution all elective officers, and this includes county and State judges, six months after their election are subject to recall....

This provision of the Arizona constitution, in its application to county and State judges, seems to me so pernicious in its effect, so destructive of independence in the judiciary, so likely to subject the rights of the individual to the possible tyranny of a popular majority, and, therefore, to be so injurious to the cause of free government, that I must disapprove a constitution containing it....

A government is for the benefit of all the people....A popular government is not a government of a majority, by a majority, for a majority of the people. It is a government of the whole people, by a majority of the whole people under such rules and checks as will secure a wise, just, and beneficent government for all the people....Constitutions are checks on the hasty action of the majority. They are self-imposed restraints of a whole people upon a majority of them to secure sober action and a respect to other individuals, and in his relation to the whole people in their character as a state or government.

...The executive and legislative branches are representative of the majority of the people which elected them in guiding the course of the Government within the limits of the Constitution....But the judicial branch of the Government is not representative of a majority of the people in any such sense, even if the mode of selecting the judges is by popular election....They are not popular representatives. On the contrary, to fill their office properly, they must be independent....

...In order to maintain the rights of the minority and the individual and to preserve our constitutional balance we must have judges with courage to decide against the majority when justice and law require.

By the recall in the Arizona constitution it is proposed to give the majority the power to remove arbitrarily, and without delay, any judge who may have the courage to render an unpopular decision....We can not be blind to the fact that often an intelligent and respectable electorate may be so roused upon an issue that it will visit with condemnation the decision of a just judge, though exactly in accord with the law governing the case, merely because it affects unfavorably their contest....Supporters of such a system seem to think that it will work only in the interest of the poor, the humble, the weak and the oppressed; that it will strike down only the judge who is supposed to favor rich corporations and be affected by the corrupting influence of the rich. Nothing could be further from the ultimate result. The motive it would offer to unscrupulous combinations to seek to control politics in order to control judges is clear. Those would profit by the recall who have the best opportunity of rousing the majority of the people to action on a sudden impulse. Are they likely to be the wisest or the best people in a community? Do they not include those who have money enough to employ the firebrands and slanderers in a community and the stirrers-up of social hate?...The character of the judges would deteriorate to that of trimmers and time-servers, the independent judicial action would be a thing of the past....

...

B. Constitutional Litigation

Although the courts in the Republican Era were increasingly active and important in interpreting the Constitution and exercising the power of judicial review, they still thought of themselves as courts resolving individual cases involving the legal rights of injured parties. By the Progressive period, Congress had given the federal courts a wide-open jurisdiction over "federal questions" of national statutes, treaties, or the U.S. Constitution, and the Supreme Court had been granted a largely discretionary docket so that the justices could choose which cases they would take to hear and decide. Organized interest groups began to form to take advantage of the courts and push constitutional litigation forward on a regular basis.

One question that judges had to confront was how much they would loosen traditional doctrines of standing in order to allow a wider array of parties and issues into court. The leading case of the pre–New

Deal period was *Frothingham v. Mellon* (1923), where the U.S. Supreme Court drew a line against so-called taxpayer suits. These kinds of suits sought to challenge a government policy simply on the basis of the charge that the government was allegedly spending funds in an unconstitutional way. The taxpayer was said to have an interest in seeing that the government spent its revenue in a constitutionally appropriate manner. *Frothingham* held that the taxpayer's injury was too nebulous and indistinguishable from that of any other citizen to give standing for a lawsuit. The courts were not to be drawn into mere political disputes.

Frothingham v. Mellon, 262 U.S. 447 (1923)

The 1921 federal Maternity Act authorized a cooperative arrangement with the states by which the federal government would provide money and support to those states that joined the federal program to protect the health of mothers and infants. The state of Massachusetts filed an original suit on behalf of itself and its citizens in the U.S. Supreme Court to block the implementation of the statute. Frothingham filed suit as a federal taxpayer in federal court in the District of Columbia to prevent any federal expenditures under the law. Her suit was dismissed on jurisdictional grounds, and she appealed. Both suits sought to enjoin Secretary of Treasury Carnegie Mellon from spending federal funds under the act, and both argued that the Maternity Act involved the federal government in policies that were within the exclusive province of the states. The Court heard both cases together.

The Court never reached the substantive constitutional question in these cases. Instead, the unanimous Court dismissed both cases on the grounds that neither the state nor the taxpayer had standing, on those bases alone, to initiate a federal case. In dismissing the cases, the Court explained this standard and how the question of proper standing helped distinguish a court from a legislature. Legislatures could respond to grievances that were common to the people as a whole. Courts existed to resolve claims of individual injury, even when the plaintiffs were raising constitutional objections to a federal law. The power of judicial review was simply a part of the judicial obligation to resolve cases. The courts did not have a general commission to correct constitutional errors or adjust the political relationship between the federal government and the states. Why would the courts decline to accept these types of suits? Are these suits significantly different from other types of suits that the courts did resolve?

JUSTICE SUTHERLAND delivered the opinion of the Court.

...

It is asserted that those appropriations are for purposes not national, but local to the States, and together with numerous similar appropriations constitute an effective means of inducing the States to yield a portion of their sovereign rights. It is further alleged that the burden of the appropriations provided by this act and similar legislation falls unequally upon the several States, and rests largely upon the industrial States, such as Massachusetts, that the act is a usurpation of power not granted to Congress by the Constitution—an attempted exercise of the power of local self-government reserved to the States by the Tenth Amendment... and that, although the State has not accepted the act, its constitutional rights are infringed by the passage thereof and the imposition upon the State of an illegal and unconstitutional option either to yield to the Federal Government a part of its reserved rights or lose the share which it would otherwise be entitled to receive of the moneys appropriated....

We have reached the conclusion that the cases must be disposed of for want of jurisdiction without considering the merits of the constitutional questions.

...

...Under Article III, sec. 2 of the Constitution, the judicial power of this Court extends "to controversies... between a State and citizens of another State" and the Court has original jurisdiction "in all cases... in which a State shall be party." The effect of this is not to confer jurisdiction upon the Court merely because a State is a party, but only where it is a party to a proceeding of judicial cognizance. Proceedings not of a justiciable character are outside the contemplation of the constitutional grant....

...

.... [In the case before us] plaintiff alleges... that she is a taxpayer of the United States, and her contention, though not clear, seems to be that the effect of the appropriations complained of will be to increase the burden of future taxation and thereby take her property, without due process of law. The right of a taxpayer to enjoin the execution of a federal appropriation act, on the ground that it is invalid and will result in taxation for illegal purposes, has never been passed upon by this Court....

.... If one taxpayer may champion and litigate such a cause, then every other taxpayer may do the same, not only in respect of the statute here under review but also in respect of every other appropriation act and statute whose administration requires the outlay of public money, and whose validity may be questioned. The bare suggestion of such a result, with its attendant inconveniences, goes far to sustain the conclusion which we have reached, that a suit of this character cannot be maintained....

...We have no power per se to review and annul acts of Congress on the ground that they are unconstitutional....The party who invokes the power must be able to show not only that the statute is invalid but that he has sustained or is immediately in danger of sustaining some direct injury as the result of its enforcement, and not merely than he suffers in some indefinite way in common with people generally. If a case for preventive relief be presented the court enjoins, in effect, not the execution of a statute, but the acts of the official, the statute notwithstanding. Here the parties plaintiff have no such case. Looking through forms of words to the substance of their complaint, it is merely that officials of the executive department of the government are executing and will execute an act of Congress asserted to be unconstitutional, and this we are asked to prevent. To do so would be not to decide a judicial controversy, but to assume a position of authority over the governmental acts of another and co-equal department, an authority which plainly we do not possess.

[Dismissed.]

III. Powers of the National Government

MAJOR DEVELOPMENTS

- Limited federal power to remedying state discrimination
- Growth of federal regulation of immigration
- Struggle over federal regulation of interstate commerce
- Struggle over federal taxing authority
- Acceptance of wartime draft
- Ambiguous status of territories

The federal government tested the limits of its constitutional powers in new ways in the Republican Era. Both the Republican and Democratic parties proved somewhat ambivalent about federal power. The Democratic inheritance of strict constructionism and limited government was still present through the Cleveland presidency, though they were more supportive of some federal regulatory efforts than their antebellum predecessors had been. With the populist turn of the Democratic Party after 1896, the Democrats significantly weakened their historic commitment to strict constructionism. Twentieth-century Democrats instead emphasized the potential power of democratic government. As William Jennings Bryan concluded, "predatory corporations...have tried to hide behind State rights," and the Democrat platform thereafter demanded "that federal legislation be *added to, not subtracted from*, State legislation."[16] It was a philosophy that the Cleveland Democrats could not abide. For the new Democratic Party of the early twentieth century, party heroes Thomas Jefferson and Andrew Jackson were to be celebrated not for their strict construction of government powers but for their commitment to democracy with a small "d" and to the dignity and interests of the common man.

The Republican Party had divisions of its own on this issue. The Republicans had inherited both Whigs and Democrats during the war. The Whig lineage was the stronger, and the Republicans had a natural attraction to the nationalist constitutional philosophy of Daniel Webster and Henry Clay, and before them of John Marshall, Joseph Story, and Alexander Hamilton. They were likewise far more trusting of the federal government than the old Democrats had been. As President Calvin Coolidge observed, "a government without power is a contradiction in terms."[17] But at the same time, the Republicans were conservative by disposition and distrusting of change and what they saw as democratic excess. The incremental growth of federal power was far more acceptable to most Republicans than reformist bursts of activity.

Both major parties were confronted with startling new social problems and political movements. Problems of race, class conflict, and agricultural dislocation seemed nearly intractable and repeatedly intruded into national politics. International wars gave the United States control over foreign territory and created new pressure to mobilize resources to fight foreign powers on a global scale. Over the course of these decades, social reformers

---

16. William Jennings Bryan, quoted in John Gerring, *Party Ideologies in America, 1828–1996* (New York: Cambridge University Press, 1998), 206.

17. Calvin Coolidge, *Foundations of the Republic* (New York: Charles Scribner's Sons, 1926), 92.

crusaded for causes ranging from alcohol and drug prohibition to the end of child labor to women's rights to the stamping out of pornography and prostitution. Independent political parties and internal factions pressured the national Republicans and the Democrats to respond to social ills with campaign promises and new legislation.

A. Federal Power to Enforce Civil Rights

Note: From the Civil Rights Act to the Civil Rights Cases

Within a year of the 1875 Civil Rights Act's passage, two decisions were handed down that signaled the end of consistent and strong federal intervention to protect former slaves. In *U.S. v. Reese* (1876) a unanimous Court declared unconstitutional sections 3 and 4 of the Civil Rights or Enforcement Act of 1870, which made it a federal offense for state election inspectors to refuse to receive or count votes or to obstruct any citizen from voting. In his opinion for the Court, Chief Justice Waite emphasized that under the Fifteenth Amendment Congress had the authority to pass a law that addressed racial discrimination in voting but not to protect voting rights more generally, as the language of the statute seemed to do. Even though, in this case, the prosecution alleged that the denial of voting rights was based on discrimination on account of race, the justices concluded that the foundation of this prosecution was a statute whose terms were overly broad. It was a damaging blow to federal protection of black voting rights.

There was a similar outcome in *U.S. v. Cruikshank* (1876), which involved a series of federal indictments alleging conspiracy "to injure, oppress, threaten or intimidate any citizen, with intent to prevent or hinder his free exercise and enjoyment of any right or privilege granted or secured to him by the Constitution or laws of the United States." A mob of whites attacked a black posse that was attempting to occupy a courthouse under the authority of a sheriff who had been commissioned by the state's Republican governor. Between sixty and one hundred blacks were killed in what became known as the Colfax Massacre. Almost one hundred whites were indicted for violating Section 6 of the Enforcement Act of 1870, but only a handful were eventually arrested and tried. In a previous case, *U.S. v. Hall*, 26 F. Cas. 701 (CCSD Ala. 1871), Circuit Judge William B. Woods had established a precedent allowing such indictments. However, by 1876 the political climate had changed so much that a unanimous Supreme Court was ready to put a stop to federal prosecutions.

In his opinion for the Court, the Chief Justice held that the rights at issue were protected against infringement by state and federal authorities, not against infringement by private individuals. Because there was no indication that the defendants were acting as agents of the state there was no authority for the federal government to intervene under the Civil War Amendments; instead, it was the responsibility of the state governments to respond to acts of private individuals.

From a later vantage point this decision might seem to represent a reactionary obstruction of an important feature of the agenda of the postwar Republican Party. In fact, very few contemporaneous commentators, North or South, Democrat or Republican, objected to the outcome in *Cruikshank*. Only a few Republican papers warned that the gutting of the Enforcement statutes meant a new "opportunity for serious abuses, and perhaps terrorism in the South." There is no question that an intensification of such violence was one of the most important and predictable results of the decision. A year after these two decisions, President Hayes followed through on the agreement reached with Democratic Party leaders and withdrew the army from Louisiana and South Carolina. Within a few years, congressional Democrats were able to pass a law prohibiting United States marshals from using military forces in the execution of election laws. Black voting in the South, which had been robust in the decade following the end of the Civil War, plummeted in the wake of these decisions by a Court dominated by loyal Republicans adjusting to the new normalcy.[18]

Civil Rights Cases, 109 U.S. 3 (1883)

Several cases raising questions about the application and constitutionality of the Civil Rights Act of 1875 were consolidated in one hearing before the Supreme Court. The Civil Rights Act of 1875 was the last act passed by the Reconstruction Congress, though its provisions had been

18. Charles Warren, *The Supreme Court in United States History*, vol. 2 (Boston: Little, Brown, 1926), 600–22; Charles Fairman, *History of the Supreme Court of the United States*, vol. 6: *Reconstruction and Reunion, 1864–88* (New York: Macmillan, 1971), 1207–1300; Pamela Brandwein, "The Civil Rights Cases and the Lost Language of State Neglect," in *The Supreme Court and American Political Development*, eds. Ronald Kahn and Ken I. Kersch (Lawrence: University Press of Kansas, 2006).

advocated for several years by some Republican legislators. The 1875 act extended federal protection against racial discrimination in public accommodations, including inns, trains, ships, and theaters and in the selection of juries. In doing so, it pushed harder on the question of what exactly the Reconstruction Amendments covered and how far they reached beyond the equal protection of property and persons contained in the Civil Rights Act of 1866 or the protection of political liberties such as voting. It did so, however, just as Reconstruction was nearing its end. With the settlement of the disputed presidential election of 1876, the Republicans largely withdrew from the legislative and executive project of reconstructing the South.

The cases came from across the United States, though not the Deep South, with cases from New York, California, Tennessee, Missouri, and Kansas, and involved accommodations in theaters and railroad cars. In defending the constitutionality of the law, the United States emphasized that although those charged under the act were private individuals, the businesses involved were devoted to a public use and affected with a public interest. Drawing on the Court's earlier opinion in Munn v. Illinois (1877), *upholding the state regulation of grain elevators, the plaintiffs contended that the conduct of such occupations had especially public implications and consequently were particularly subject to governmental control.*

While the Fourteenth Amendment dramatically expanded federal authority, by an 8–1 margin the Court's decision in The Civil Rights Cases *ensured that most of this expanded power would be exercised by federal judges rather than federal legislators. Justice Bradley's majority opinion established a lasting precedent for the proposition that Congress had no power under the Civil War Amendments to prohibit discrimination in privately owned public accommodations. The opinion launched the state action doctrine, that the amendments limit government actors but not private actors. This limited view of federal civil rights authority has been so successfully entrenched that, almost a century later, Congress chose to rely on other sources of legislative power to pass the Civil Rights Act of 1964. Does the sole dissenter, John Marshall Harlan, offer a persuasive critique of this doctrine? Harlan felt so strongly that the majority had erred that he decided to write his dissent with the same pen and inkwell that Chief Justice Taney used to write the* Dred Scott *opinion.*

JUSTICE BRADLEY delivered the opinion of the Court.

. . .

The essence of the law is, not to declare broadly that all persons shall be entitled to the full and equal enjoyment of the accommodations, advantages, facilities, and privileges of inns, public conveyances, and theatres; but that such enjoyment shall not be subject to any conditions applicable only to citizens of a particular race or color, or who had been in a previous condition of servitude....

Has Congress constitutional power to make such a law? Of course, no one will contend that the power to pass it was contained in the Constitution before the adoption of the last three amendments. The power is sought, first, in the Fourteenth Amendment, and the views and arguments of distinguished Senators, advanced whilst the law was under consideration, claiming authority to pass it by virtue of that amendment, are the principal arguments adduced in favor of the power.....

. . .

[In that amendment it] is State action of a particular character that is prohibited. Individual invasion of individual rights is not the subject-matter of the amendment....[T]he last section of the amendment invests Congress with power to enforce it by appropriate legislation. To enforce what? To enforce the prohibition. To adopt appropriate legislation for correcting the effects of such prohibited State laws and State acts, and thus to render them effectually null, void, and innocuous. This is the legislative power conferred upon Congress, and this is the whole of it. It does not invest Congress with power to legislate upon subjects which are within the domain of State legislation; but to provide modes of relief against State legislation, or State action, of the kind referred to....

[I]n the present case, until some State law has been passed, or some State action through its officers or agents has been taken, adverse to the rights of citizens sought to be protected by the Fourteenth Amendment, no legislation of the United States under said amendment, nor any proceeding under such legislation, can be called into activity: for the prohibitions of the amendment are against State laws and acts done under State authority. Of course, legislation may, and should be, provided in advance to meet the exigency when it arises; but it should be adapted to the mischief and wrong which the amendment was intended to provide against....

An inspection of the law shows that it makes no reference whatever to any supposed or apprehended violation of the Fourteenth Amendment on the part of the States. It is not predicated on any such view.

It proceeds *ex directo* to declare that certain acts committed by individuals shall be deemed offences, and shall be prosecuted and punished by proceedings in the courts of the United States. It does not profess to be corrective of any constitutional wrong committed by the States; it does not make its operation to depend upon any such wrong committed. It applies equally to cases arising in States which have the justest laws respecting the personal rights of citizens, and whose authorities are ever ready to enforce such laws, as to those which arise in States that may have violated the prohibition of the amendment. In other words, it steps into the domain of local jurisprudence, and lays down rules for the conduct of individuals in society towards each other, and imposes sanctions for the enforcement of those rules, without referring in any manner to any supposed action of the State or its authorities.

If this legislation is appropriate for enforcing the prohibitions of the amendment, it is difficult to see where it is to stop. Why may not Congress with equal show of authority enact a code of laws for the enforcement and vindication of all rights of life, liberty, and property? . . . The truth is, that the implication of a power to legislate in this manner is based upon the assumption that if the States are forbidden to legislate or act in a particular way on a particular subject, and power is conferred upon Congress to enforce the prohibition, this gives Congress power to legislate generally upon that subject, and not merely power to provide modes of redress against such State legislation or action. The assumption is certainly unsound. It is repugnant to the Tenth Amendment of the Constitution, which declares that powers not delegated to the United States by the Constitution, nor prohibited by it to the States, are reserved to the States respectively or to the people.

. . .

. . . [C]ivil rights, such as are guaranteed by the Constitution against State aggression, cannot be impaired by the wrongful acts of individuals, unsupported by State authority in the shape of laws, customs, or judicial or executive proceedings. The wrongful act of an individual, unsupported by any such authority, is simply a private wrong, or a crime of that individual . . . but if not sanctioned in some way by the State, or not done under State authority, his rights remain in full force, and may presumably be vindicated by resort to the laws of the State for redress. . . . .

. . .

. . . This is not corrective legislation; it is primary and direct; it takes immediate and absolute possession of the subject of the right of admission to inns, public conveyances, and places of amusement. It supersedes and displaces State legislation on the same subject, or only allows it permissive force. It ignores such legislation, and assumes that the matter is one that belongs to the domain of national regulation. Whether it would not have been a more effective protection of the rights of citizens to have clothed Congress with plenary power over the whole subject, is not now the question. What we have to decide is, whether such plenary power has been conferred upon Congress by the Fourteenth Amendment; and, in our judgment, it has not.

. . .

But the power of Congress to adopt direct and primary, as distinguished from corrective legislation, on the subject in hand, is sought, in the second place, from the Thirteenth Amendment, which abolishes slavery. . . .

. . . Conceding the major proposition to be true, that Congress has a right to enact all necessary and proper laws for the obliteration and prevention of slavery with all its badges and incidents, is the minor proposition also true, that the denial to any person of admission to the accommodations and privileges of an inn, a public conveyance, or a theatre, does subject that person to any form of servitude, or tend to fasten upon him any badge of slavery? If it does not, then power to pass the law is not found in the Thirteenth Amendment.

. . .

The long existence of African slavery in this country gave us very distinct notions of what it was, and what were its necessary incidents. Compulsory service of the slave for the benefit of the master, restraint of his movements except by the master's will, disability to hold property, to make contracts, to have a standing in court, to be a witness against a white person, and such like burdens and incapacities, were the inseparable incidents of the institution. Severer punishments for crimes were imposed on the slave than on free persons guilty of the same offences. Congress, as we have seen, by the Civil Rights Bill of 1866, passed in view of the Thirteenth Amendment, before the Fourteenth was adopted, undertook to wipe out these burdens and disabilities, the necessary incidents of slavery, constituting its substance and visible form; and to secure to all citizens of every race and color, and without regard to previous servitude, those fundamental rights which are the essence of civil freedom. . . .

...

The only question under the present head, therefore, is, whether the refusal to any persons of the accommodations of an inn, or a public conveyance, or a place of public amusement, by an individual, and without any sanction or support from any State law or regulation, does inflict upon such persons any manner of servitude, or form of slavery, as those terms are understood in this country?...

...

...[W]e are forced to the conclusion that such an act of refusal has nothing to do with slavery or involuntary servitude, and that if it is violative of any right of the party, his redress is to be sought under the laws of the State; or if those laws are adverse to his rights and do not protect him, his remedy will be found in the corrective legislation which Congress has adopted, or may adopt, for counteracting the effect of State laws, or State action, prohibited by the Fourteenth Amendment. It would be running the slavery argument into the ground to make it apply to every act of discrimination which a person may see fit to make as to the guests he will entertain, or as to the people he will take into his coach or cab or car, or admit to his concert or theatre, or deal with in other matters of intercourse or business....

When a man has emerged from slavery, and by the aid of beneficent legislation has shaken off the inseparable concomitants of that state, there must be some stage in the progress of his elevation when he takes the rank of a mere citizen, and ceases to be the special favorite of the laws, and when his rights as a citizen, or a man, are to be protected in the ordinary modes by which other men's rights are protected. There were thousands of free colored people in this country before the abolition of slavery, enjoying all the essential rights of life, liberty and property the same as white citizens; yet no one, at that time, thought that it was any invasion of his personal status as a freeman because he was not admitted to all the privileges enjoyed by white citizens, or because he was subjected to discriminations in the enjoyment of accommodations in inns, public conveyances and places of amusement. Mere discriminations on account of race or color were not regarded as badges of slavery....

On the whole we are of opinion, that no countenance of authority for the passage of the law in question can be found in either the Thirteenth or Fourteenth Amendment of the Constitution; and no other ground of authority for its passage being suggested, it must necessarily be declared void, at least so far as its operation in the several States is concerned.

...

It is so ordered.

JUSTICE HARLAN, dissenting.

The opinion in these cases proceeds, it seems to me, upon grounds entirely too narrow and artificial. I cannot resist the conclusion that the substance and spirit of the recent amendments of the Constitution have been sacrificed by a subtle and ingenious verbal criticism. "It is not the words of the law but the internal sense of it that makes the law: the letter of the law is the body; the sense and reason of the law is the soul." Constitutional provisions, adopted in the interest of liberty, and for the purpose of securing, through national legislation, if need be, rights inhering in a state of freedom, and belonging to American citizenship, have been so construed as to defeat the ends the people desired to accomplish, which they attempted to accomplish, and which they supposed they had accomplished by changes in their fundamental law....

The Thirteenth Amendment, it is conceded, did something more than to prohibit slavery as an institution, resting upon distinctions of race, and upheld by positive law. My brethren admit that it established and decreed universal civil freedom throughout the United States. But did the freedom thus established involve nothing more than exemption from actual slavery? Was nothing more intended than to forbid one man from owning another as property? Was it the purpose of the nation simply to destroy the institution, and then remit the race, theretofore held in bondage, to the several States for their protection, in their civil rights, necessarily growing out of freedom, as those States, in their discretion, might choose to provide?...

That there are burdens and disabilities which constitute badges of slavery and servitude, and that the power to enforce by appropriate legislation the Thirteenth Amendment may be exerted by legislation of a direct and primary character, for the eradication, not simply of the institution, but of its badges and incidents, are propositions which ought to be deemed indisputable....I do not contend that the Thirteenth Amendment invests Congress with authority, by legislation, to define and regulate the entire body of the civil rights which citizens enjoy, or may enjoy, in the several States. But I hold that since slavery...was the moving or principal cause of the adoption of that amendment, and since that institution rested wholly upon the inferiority, as a race, of those held in bondage, their freedom necessarily involved immunity from, and protection against, all discrimination against them, because of their race, in respect of such civil rights as belong to freemen of other races....

...[T]he right of a colored person to use an improved public highway, upon the terms accorded to freemen of other races, is as fundamental, in the state of freedom established in this country, as are any of the rights which my brethren concede to be so far fundamental as to be deemed the essence of civil freedom. "Personal liberty consists," says Blackstone, "in the power of locomotion, of changing situation, or removing one's person to whatever places one's own inclination may direct, without restraint, unless by due course of law." But of what value is this right of locomotion, if it may be clogged by such burdens as Congress intended by the act of 1875 to remove? They are burdens which lay at the very foundation of the institution of slavery as it once existed. They are not to be sustained, except upon the assumption that there is, in this land of universal liberty, a class which may still be discriminated against, even in respect of rights of a character so necessary and supreme, that, deprived of their enjoyment in common with others, a freeman is not only branded as one inferior and infected, but, in the competitions of life, is robbed of some of the most essential means of existence; and all this solely because they belong to a particular race which the nation has liberated. The Thirteenth Amendment alone obliterated the race line, so far as all rights fundamental in a state of freedom are concerned.

...

...[A] keeper of an inn is in the exercise of a quasi-public employment. The law gives him special privileges and he is charged with certain duties and responsibilities to the public. The public nature of his employment forbids him from discriminating against any person asking admission as a guest on account of the race or color of that person.

...[P]laces of public amusement, within the meaning of the act of 1875, are such as are established and maintained under direct license of the law. The authority to establish and maintain them comes from the public....

...

I am of the opinion that such discrimination practiced by corporations and individuals in the exercise of their public or quasi-public functions is a badge of servitude the imposition of which Congress may prevent under its power, by appropriate legislation, to enforce the Thirteenth Amendment; and, consequently, without reference to its enlarged power under the Fourteenth Amendment, the act of March 1, 1875, is not, in my judgment, repugnant to the Constitution.

It remains now to consider these cases with reference to the power Congress has possessed since the adoption of the Fourteenth Amendment....

...

The assumption that this amendment consists wholly of prohibitions upon State laws and State proceedings in hostility to its provisions, is unauthorized by its language. The first clause of the first section—"All persons born or naturalized in the United States, and subject to the jurisdiction thereof, are citizens of the United States, and of the State wherein they reside"—is of a distinctly affirmative character....

The citizenship thus acquired, by that race, in virtue of an affirmative grant from the nation, may be protected, not alone by the judicial branch of the government, but by congressional legislation of a primary direct character; this, because the power of Congress is not restricted to the enforcement of prohibitions upon State laws or State action....

It is, therefore, an essential inquiry what, if any, right, privilege or immunity was given, by the nation, to colored persons, when they were made citizens of the State in which they reside?...There is one, if there be no other—exemption from race discrimination in respect of any civil right belonging to citizens of the white race in the same State. That, surely, is their constitutional privilege when within the jurisdiction of other States. And such must be their constitutional right, in their own State, unless the recent amendments be splendid baubles, thrown out to delude those who deserved fair and generous treatment at the hands of the nation. Citizenship in this country necessarily imports at least equality of civil rights among citizens of every race in the same State. It is fundamental in American citizenship that, in respect of such rights, there shall be no discrimination by the State, or its officers, or by individuals or corporations exercising public functions or authority, against any citizen because of his race or previous condition of servitude....

...

...It was perfectly well known that the great danger to the equal enjoyment by citizens of their rights, as citizens, was to be apprehended not altogether from unfriendly State legislation, but from the hostile action of corporations and individuals in the States. And it is to be presumed that it was intended, by that section, to clothe Congress with power and authority to meet that danger....

...

...It is, I submit, scarcely just to say that the colored race has been the special favorite of the laws. The statute of 1875, now adjudged to be unconstitutional, is for the benefit of citizens of every race and color. What the nation through Congress, has sought to accomplish in reference to that race, is—what had already been done in every State of the Union for the white race—to secure and protect rights belonging to them as freemen and citizens; nothing more. It was not deemed enough "to help the feeble up, but to support him after." The one underlying purpose of congressional legislation has been to enable the black race to take the rank of mere citizens....At every step, in this direction, the nation has been confronted with class tyranny.... To-day, it is the colored race which is denied, by corporations and individuals wielding public authority, rights fundamental in their freedom and citizenship. At some future time, it may be that some other race will fall under the ban of race discrimination. If the constitutional amendments be enforced, according to the intent with which, as I conceive, they were adopted, there cannot be, in this republic, any class of human beings in practical subjection to another class, with power in the latter to dole out to the former just such privileges as they may choose to grant. The supreme law of the land has decreed that no authority shall be exercised in this country upon the basis of discrimination, in respect of civil rights, against freemen and citizens because of their race, color, or previous condition of servitude. To that decree—for the due enforcement of which, by appropriate legislation, Congress has been invested with express power—everyone must bow, whatever may have been, or whatever now are, his individual views as to the wisdom or policy, either of the recent changes in the fundamental law, or of the legislation which has been enacted to give them effect.

For the reasons stated I feel constrained to withhold my assent to the opinion of the court.

Congressional Debate on Lynching[19]

Although lynch law had always existed in the United States, lynching became increasingly racial, sectional, and brutal after the Civil War. More than 4,000 persons were lynched between Reconstruction and the Second World War, the vast majority of lynching victims were persons of color, and the vast majority of lynchings took place in former slave states. In sharp contrast to pre–Civil War lynchings, which were largely summary affairs, southern lynch mobs typically devised grotesque tortures for the African-American victims. One account observed

> *The two Negroes...were tied to trees and while the funeral pyres were being prepared [they were to be burned alive], they were forced to hold out their hands while one finger at a time was chopped off. The fingers were distributed as souvenirs. The ears...were cut off. [One of the victims] was beaten severely, his skull fractured and one of his eyes, knocked out with a stick, hung by a shred from the socket.*[20]

Although lynch mobs functioned openly, participants rarely faced arrest, much less conviction. One study found that southern states were fifty times more likely to achieve convictions in ordinary homicides, where perpetrators typically made some attempt to cover their tracks, than in lynchings, which were done in public—sometimes on courthouse lawns.[21]

Most American elites during the Progressive Era condemned resort to extra-legal punishments and barbarisms. "Lynching," a prominent politician stated, "is the darkest blot upon an otherwise splendid civilization."[22] *What could be done to remove this stain was more controversial. Several Reconstruction measures aimed at safeguarding persons of color from lynching either had been declared unconstitutional or had been repealed, and justice department officials thought inadequate those measures that were still on the books. Whether revised measures could pass constitutional muster was an open question. Even Moorfield Storey, the main constitutional litigator for the National Association for the Advancement of Colored People (NAACP) during the Progressive Era initially had doubts about the constitutionality of federal anti-lynching legislation.*

The movement for such legislation, however, picked up steam after World War I. Some prominent political elites

19. Excerpt taken from House Committee on the Judiciary, *Constitutionality of a Federal AntiLynching Law*, 67th Cong., 1st Sess. (1921):16; *Congressional Record* 67th Cong., 2nd Sess. (1922):1290.

20. Barbara Holden-Smith, "Lynching, Federalism, and the Intersection of Race and Gender in the Progressive Era," *Yale Journal of Law & Feminism* 8 (1996):31.

21. James Harmon Chadbourn, *Lynching and the Law* (Chapel Hill: University of North Carolina Press, 1933), 13–14.

22. *Congressional Record* 62 (1922):1276 (statement of Representative Burton).

were horrified by racial violence against persons of color that broke out in the war's aftermath. The return of the Republican Party, the political coalition more sympathetic to persons of color, improved the chances of favorable legislation. The Republican Party platform in 1920 "urge[d] Congress to consider the most effective means to end lynching in this country which continues to be a terrible blot on our American civilization," and similar language was used in the Republican party platform in 1924 and 1928. Nevertheless, although anti-lynching bills were routinely introduced in Congress, none became law. In fact, no civil rights legislation would be passed by Congress from 1876 until 1957, which meant that a Republican-dominated Supreme Court was never asked to consider the fairly broad understanding of federal power underlying various anti-lynching measures.

The Dyer Bill was the best hope proponents of federal anti-lynching legislation had for securing favorable law. Proposed by Representative Leonidas Dyer of Missouri, the measure passed the House in 1922 but was defeated by a filibuster in the Senate. Unlike previous Reconstruction measures, the Dyer Bill focused on state officers who either made no effort to prevent or participated in lynchings. States were deemed to have denied persons equal protection of the law if they "fail[ed], neglect[ed], or refuse[d] to provide and maintain protection to the life of any person within its jurisdiction against a mob or riotous assemblage. State officers who did not make "reasonable efforts" to prevent lynching or punish lynchers were subject to severe criminal sanctions. The Dyer Bill also authorized federal attorneys to try as criminals any private persons who conspired with a state official during a lynching. Significantly, these offenses could be tried in federal courts when state courts refused to convict.

Proponents of the Dyer Bill insisted that Section 5 of the Fourteenth Amendment permitted Congress to legislate against both state action and state inaction that violated constitutional rights. This constitutional understanding was supported by the Harding Administration. Opponents of the measure insisted that Congress could constitutionally punish only positive state action that was consistent with discriminatory state law. Did Justice Bradley's opinion in The Civil Rights Cases *make clear whether the federal government could punish state actors who failed to protect fundamental rights? Can a state violate the equal protection clause, not just by engaging in discriminatory conduct itself, but by virtue of a sufficient level of disregard for protecting certain classes of people? How far might that principle be extended?*

Letter of Attorney General H. M. Daugherty to Representative A. J. Volstead (Republican, Minnesota) (1921)

...

Considerable discussion has taken place as to the constitutionality of the proposed legislation, it being contended that the fourteenth amendment gave Congress power to legislate so as to prevent a denial of the equal protection of the laws by the States and not as to acts of individuals not clothed with State authority.

...It will be observed that...the State may act through its legislative, its judicial, or its executive authorities, and the act of any one these is the act of the State....

...

> "The constitutional provision, therefore, must mean that no agency of the State, or of the officers or agents by whom its powers are exerted, shall deny to any person within its jurisdiction the equal protection of the laws. Whoever, by virtue of public position under a State government, deprives another of property, life, or liberty without due process of law or denies or takes away the equal protection of the laws, violates the constitutional inhibition, and as he acts in the name and for the State and is clothed with the State's power his act is that of the State. This must be so or the constitutional prohibition has no meaning. Then the State has clothed one of its agents with power to annul or to evade it." *Ex parte Virginia* (1879)

...To my mind there can be no doubt that negativity on the part of the State may be, as well as any act of a positive nature by such State, a denial of the equal protection of the laws and thus be within the prohibition of the fourteenth amendment so as to give Congress power to act with reference to it....

...

Section 12 and section 13 provide for the punishment of State and municipal officers who fail in their duty to prevent lynchings or who suffer persons accused of crime to be taken from their custody for the purpose of lynching. These sections seem to me to strike at the heart of the evil, namely, the failure of State officers to perform their duty in such cases. The fourteenth amendment recognizes as preexisting the right to due process of law and to the equal protection of the law and guarantees against State infringement of those rights. A State officer charged with the protection of those rights who fails or refuses to do all in his power to protect an accused person against mob action denies to such person due process of law and the equal protection of the laws in every sense of the term....

...

Speech of Representative HAWES (Democrat, Missouri)

...

[The Fourteenth Amendment] relates to the laws of a State, does not relate, nor was it intended to relate, to the individual action of a citizen, nor was it directed toward the malfeasance or nonfeasance of a State officer.

...

Mob violence is a criminal offense in all States. Persons who form part of a mob which takes human life are guilty of murder. Penalties are provided for unlawful assemblage. Penalties are provided for interfering with an officer in the discharge of his duty or taking a prisoner from an officer. There is no State, whose laws in this respect have been questioned by a single proponent of this bill.

The fourteenth amendment does not relate to the acts of individuals or the acts of official agents of a State where the acts of such agents were outside the pale of the law and not in conformity with the law of the Commonwealth. The fourteenth amendment deals directly with the State and the agencies of the State performing certain specific acts for the State.

...

If the Federal Government assumes the right to punish an officer of a State for failure to prevent a crime, or a prosecuting attorney for failure to prosecute a crime, then the Federal Government can go into the business of prosecuting the chicken thief, the crap shooter, the card player, the drunkard, the wife beater, or the thief.

It was never intended that the fourteenth amendment should apply other than to the acts of States or the agents of States, in so far as they complied with the laws of the State. It is not the act of the official, or his omission to act, that is controlled by the fourteenth amendment, but it is the State law that controls the act and provides the things guaranteed in the fourteenth amendment.

...

B. Power to Regulate Commerce

In the late nineteenth century, Congress became more active in trying to regulate national economic actors and activity. One of the landmark regulatory acts of the period after the Civil War was the passage of the Interstate Commerce Act of 1887 and the creation of the Interstate Commerce Commission to regulate the routes and prices of interstate railroads. Interstate railroad regulation was a relatively clear-cut use of the interstate commerce clause, but other actions that Congress wanted to take to regulate economic and social behavior were less clear-cut. The railroads were not the only corporations whose activities reached across state lines, and politicians felt pressure to respond to a variety of economic and social complaints.

The U.S. Supreme Court struggled to develop doctrines to help make sense of this new legislative and economic landscape and provide guidance about the limits of congressional power under the interstate commerce clause. *United States v. E. C. Knight* (1895) made a categorical distinction between commercial activities (the transport and trading of goods), which Congress could regulate, and other sorts of productive activities (such as farming, mining or manufacturing), which Congress could not. Moreover, *E. C. Knight* distinguished between local commercial activities that had a direct or indirect affect on interstate commerce. The former could be regulated by Congress. The latter could not. (Congress could always regulate interstate commercial activities, such as the interstate shipment of goods on railroads.) *Swift v. United States* (1905) supplemented this doctrine by distinguishing between local activities that were inside or outside of the interstate "stream of commerce." *Champion v. Ames* (1903) indicated that Congress had a kind of police power when operating within the boundaries of the commerce clause, and it could regulate items in interstate commerce for a variety of purposes and with a variety of means. But *Hammer v. Dagenhart* (1918) suggested some limits to that doctrine, such that Congress could not use the power to regulate interstate commerce as a back door to regulating production.

The Gilded Age and the Progressive Era were particularly active periods for both Congress and the courts in considering the limits of national power under the interstate commerce clause. The Supreme Court had rarely considered the commerce clause from the perspective of congressional power prior to the Civil

War, although some basic boundaries had been laid down in congressional debates, executive documents, and Chief Justice John Marshall's opinion in *Gibbons v. Ogden* (1824). As Table 7-4 indicates, the Court was confronted with a wider array of questions in the latter part of the nineteenth century and in the twentieth century, and the justices almost always upheld congressional power. But the decisions either way were controversial, and federal statutes expanded further into the economic arena and into social policy.

Table 7-4 Selection of U.S. Supreme Court Cases Reviewing Federal Laws under the Interstate Commerce Clause

Case	Vote	Outcome	Decision
Gibbons v. Ogden, 22 U.S. 1 (1824)	7–0	Upheld	Federal law licensing coastal ships to transport passengers upheld
The Daniel Bell, 77 U.S. 557 (1870)	9–0	Upheld	Federal law requiring inspection of steam ships in the "navigable waters of the United States" extended to local vessels carrying goods bound for interstate markets
In re Rahrer, 140 U.S. 545 (1891)	9–0	Upheld	Federal law subjecting alcohol transported through interstate commerce to local prohibition laws when they reach their destination upheld
United States v. E. C. Knight, 156 U.S. 1 (1895)	8–1	Struck down	Federal law regulating anti-competitive behavior could not be applied to the merger of manufacturers
Champion v. Ames, 188 U.S. 321 (1903)	5–4	Upheld	Federal law prohibiting the shipment of lottery tickets across state lines upheld
Northern Securities Company v. United States, 193 U.S. 197 (1904)	5–4	Upheld	Federal law regulating anti-competitive behavior could be applied to the merger of interstate railroads
Hammer v. Dagenheart, 247 U.S. 251 (1918)	5–4	Struck down	Federal law prohibiting the shipment of goods produced by child labor across state lines struck down
Stafford v. Wallace, 258 U.S. 495 (1922)	7–1	Upheld	Federal law regulating anticompetitive behavior in stockyards upheld as part of the "stream" of interstate commerce

(Continued)

Table 7-4 *Continued*

Case	Vote	Outcome	Decision
Brooks v. United States, 267 U.S. 432 (1925)	9–0	Upheld	Federal law punishing the movement of stolen cars across state lines upheld
Carter v. Carter Coal Co., 298 U.S. 238 (1936)	5–4	Struck down	Federal law regulating hours and wages in mining struck down
National Labor Relations Board v. Jones & Laughlin Steel Corp., 301 U.S. 1 (1937)	5–4	Upheld	Federal law regulating labor conditions of industrial plants upheld
Wickard v. Filburn, 317 U.S. 111 (1942)	8–0	Upheld	Federal law setting production quotas for wheat constitutional as applied to self-sustaining farm
United States v. Sullivan, 332 U.S. 689 (1948)	6–3	Upheld	Federal law punishing alteration of drug labels constitutional as applied to local druggist who transferred pills from a bulk bottle to a pill box for his customers
Katzenbach v. McClung, 379 U.S. 294 (1964)	9–0	Upheld	Federal law prohibiting discrimination in public accommodations constitutional as applied to local restaurant
Perez v. United States, 402 U.S. 146 (1971)	8–1	Upheld	Federal law punishing loan sharking upheld
Fry v. United States, 421 U.S. 542 (1975)	7–1	Upheld	Federal law imposing national wage freeze could be constitutionally applied to state employees
United States v. Lopez, 514 U.S. 549 (1995)	5–4	Struck down	Federal law punishing the possession of a firearm in a school zone struck down
Gonzales v. Raich, 545 U.S. 1 (2005)	6–3	Upheld	Federal law punishing the intrastate production and use of marijuana under state regulation is constitutional as applied

Senate Debate on the Sherman Anti-Trust Act[23]

Rapid industrialization set the stage for the rise of large corporations that had the capacity to exert dominating influence over important aspects of the national economy. Of particular concern was the developing practice of the most powerful companies to create "trust" agreements whereby they gained control over competing firms by combining them into one large firm. Critics believed that these so-called "trusts" or combinations undermined the advantages of capitalism by establishing monopolies within particular industries. Since these trusts operated on a nationwide scale there was pressure put on Congress to devise mechanisms to break up those trusts that were designed to restrict competition. This sort of direct federal regulation of American industry was unprecedented in American history, but then again, before the late nineteenth century American industry mostly operated at the local level and thus was considered best overseen by state and local governments.

Did the congressional authority "to regulate commerce...among the states" include the power to regulate the business practices of companies large enough to have an impact on the operations of national markets, or was it limited to regulating the actual movement of goods across state lines? Did it cover control over "manufacturing" or "production" that took place in just one state as long as the goods were headed for a national market? Or did it only include the subsequent "transportation" or "distribution" of goods among the states? This controversy would preoccupy legislators and judges for more than forty years, culminating in a historic clash between the Supreme Court and Franklin Delano Roosevelt in the 1930s.

The discussion began in earnest during congressional debates over the passage of the Sherman Anti-Trust Act in 1890. The first federal statute of its kind, the act sought to prohibit anti-competitive, monopolistic business practices. Proponents of the bill such as Ohio Republican John Sherman pushed for an expansive reading of the Constitution that would give Congress the explicit power to regulate manufacturing, but critics such as Republican Judiciary Committee Chair George Edmunds questioned whether Congress should make promises that it could not constitutionally keep, that were "purely deceptive and illusory, mere dust and ashes," and worked to produce a more vaguely worded but narrower statute.[24]

23. Excerpt taken from *Congressional Record*, 51st Congress, 1st session (1890), 1768–71, 2460–62, 3147–48.

24. *Congressional Record*, 51st Congress, 1st session (March 27, 1890), 2728.

Debate on Sherman's bill "to declare unlawful trusts and combinations in restraint of trade or production"

Mr. GEORGE (Democrat, Mississippi)

...Mr. President, I now proceed to show that the bill is utterly unconstitutional.

This task is an easy one, since the principles applicable to this examination have again and again been settled by the Supreme Court. I warn Senators now that no attempt will be made to show the bill unconstitutional upon that narrow and strict theory of State rights which they may suppose is entertained by the Southern people and by them only. In all I shall say on this subject, I shall plant my argument on an exposition of the Constitution made by the tribunal which the Constitution itself appoints to perform that duty....

The power to enact the bill is claimed in the bill itself under the commercial clause of the Constitution: the power "to regulate commerce with foreign nations and among the States."

...So far as this bill is concerned, it is needful only to specify the acts...which constitute interstate or foreign commerce. They embrace purchase, sale, exchange, barter, transportation, and intercourse for the purpose of trade in all its forms....

...But, Mr. President, among these commercial acts are not manufactures or any other kind of production, nor sales, nor transportation purely within a State or wholly outside the territorial jurisdiction of the United States. The bill proceeds on the idea that as to interstate commerce the jurisdiction of Congress extends to the regulation of the production and manufacture of articles taking place in a State, if only it be intended, that, after such manufacture or production shall be complete, all or a portion of the articles shall become subjects of interstate commerce, and shall in fact be transported as such.

This basis of the bill is expressly confuted by the decisions I shall quote.

The Supreme Court in *Veazie v. Moor* (1852) speaking of the commercial clause of the Constitution, says it can not "be properly concluded that because the products of domestic enterprise in agriculture or manufactures or in the arts may ultimately become the subjects of foreign (or interstate) commerce, the control of the means or the encouragements by which enterprise is fostered and protected is legitimately within the import of the phrase 'foreign commerce,' or fairly implied by any investiture of the power to regulate such commerce. A pretension so far reaching as this would extend to contracts between citizen and citizen of the same State; would control the pursuits of the planter, the grazier, the manufacturer, the mechanic, the immense operations of the collieries and mines and furnaces of the country; for there is not one of these vocations the results of which may not become the subject of foreign (interstate) commerce."

...The Constitution is a reasonable instrument, designed to specify powers delegated to a general government. So far as these powers are granted expressly or by necessary implication for the execution of express powers, they are full and complete, as well as supreme; but the Constitution neither authorizes nor tolerates the absurdity of the exercise of a power as a necessary incident to and in aid of the execution of an express power when no attempt is made to execute the express power....

Mr. SHERMAN (Republican, Ohio)

...I respectfully submit that, in his subtle argument, [Sen. GEORGE] has entirely overlooked the broad jurisdiction conferred by the Constitution upon courts of the United States in ordinary cases of law and equity between certain parties, as well as cases arising under the Constitution, laws, and treaties of the United States....

...All the combinations at which this bill aims are combinations embracing persons and combinations of several States. Each State can deal with a combination within the State, but only the General Government can deal with combinations reaching not only the several States, but the commercial world. This bill does not include combinations within a State....

...By the Constitution of the United States this jurisdiction of the courts of the United States extends to all cases in law and equity between certain parties. What is meant by the words of "cases in law and equity?" Does this include only cases growing out of the Constitution, statutes, and treaties of the United States? It has been held over and over again that, by these words, the Constitution has adopted as a rule of remedial justice the common law of England as administered by courts of law and equity.

...I submit that this bill as it stands, without any reference to specific powers granted to Congress by the Constitution, is clearly authorized under the judicial article of the Constitution. This bill declares a rule of public policy in accordance with the rule of the common law.

...One would think that with this conception of the evil to be dealt with he would for once turn his telescope upon the Constitution to find out power to deal with so great a wrong, and not, as usual, to reverse it, to turn the little end of the telescope to the Constitution, and then, with subtle reasoning, to dissipate the powers of the Government into thin air....

...What is the meaning of the word "commerce?" It means the exchange of commodities between different places or communities....The power of Congress extends to all this commerce, except only that limited within the bounds of a State.

...

...It is said that commerce does not commence until production ends and the voyage commences. This may be true as far as the actual ownership or sale of articles within a State is subject to State authorities....This bill does not propose to deal with property within a State or with combinations within the State, but only when a combination extends to two or more States or engages in either State or foreign commerce.

...If their productions competed with those of similar partnerships or corporations in other States it would be all right. But to prevent such competition they unite the interests of all these partnerships and corporations into a combination, sometimes called a trust, sometimes a new corporation located in a city remote from the places of production, and then regulate and control the sale and transportation of all the products of many States....Sir, the object aimed at by this bill is to secure competition of the productions of different States which necessarily enter into interstate and foreign commerce.

...In no respect does the work of our fathers in framing the Constitution of the United States appear more like the work of the Almighty Ruler of the Universe rather than the conception of human minds than by the gradual development and application of the powers conferred by it upon different branches of the Federal Government. Many of these powers have remained dormant, unused, but plainly there, awaiting the growth and progress of our country, and when the time comes and the occasion demands we find in that instrument...all the powers necessary to govern a continental empire....

On Judiciary Committee's revised bill to "protect trade and commerce against unlawful restraints and monopolies"

Mr. GEORGE.

Mr. President, I am afraid we have got into this condition about the pending bill, that we have a disposition to do something, and that very speedily, whether that something amounts to much or not. I am afraid that there will be a great disappointment among the people of this country about the effects of this bill when it shall become a law. It covers professedly a very narrow territory, leaving a very large number of these institutions, these trusts, or whatever we may call them, entirely without the purview of the bill.

That is not the fault of the committee, Mr. President. The bill has been very ingeniously and properly drawn to cover every case which comes within what is called the commercial power of Congress. There is a great deal of this matter outside of that. This bill being of that character, it necessarily will be a disappointing measure to the people of this country.

Mr. EDMUNDS (Republican, Vermont).

We all felt it, and the [Judiciary] committee, I think unanimously, including my friend from Mississippi [Sen. GEORGE], thought that if we were really in earnest in wishing to strike at these evils broadly, in the first instance, as a new line of legislation, we would frame a bill that should be clearly within our constitutional power, that we should make its definitions out of terms that were well known to the law already, and would leave it to the courts in the first instance to say how far they could carry it or its definitions as applicable to each particular case as it might arise.

United States v. E. C. Knight Company, 156 U.S. 1 (1895)

The American Sugar Refining Company, incorporated in New Jersey, manufactured about 65 percent of the refined sugar sold in the United States. In 1892, it acquired through an exchange of stock control over four Philadelphia-based sugar refineries, including E. C. Knight, which together accounted for another 33 percent of the national sugar market. The "sugar trust" was among the most notorious in the country at the time, and the Democratic Cleveland administration yielded to political pressure to prosecute the trust. The United States Department of Justice charged that the acquisition violated the 1890 Sherman Anti-Trust Act by creating a combination in restraint of trade and asked the federal circuit court to void the sale. The circuit court declined to do so, and the government appealed to the Supreme Court. In order to determine whether the Sherman Act could reach the sugar trust, the Court had to determine the scope of congressional authority under the commerce clause. In an 8–1 ruling, the Court held that Congress could not regulate the production of goods under the commerce clause and that the executive could not use the Sherman Act to block the operation of the sugar trust. Justice John Marshall Harlan filed the lone dissent. What work did the Court's interpretation of the commerce clause leave for Congress? Is E. C. Knight *consistent with what legislators might have expected? Is it consistent with the Marshall Court's approach to the commerce clause in* Gibbons v. Ogden *(1824)?*

CHIEF JUSTICE FULLER delivered the opinion of the Court.

. . .

The fundamental question is, whether conceding that the existence of a monopoly in manufacture is established by the evidence, that monopoly can be directly suppressed under the act of Congress in the mode attempted by this bill.

It cannot be denied that the power of a State to protect the lives, health, and property of its citizens, and to preserve good order and the public morals, "the power to govern men and things within the limits of its dominion," is a power originally and always belonging to the States, not surrendered by them to the general government, nor directly restrained by the Constitution of the United States, and essential exclusive. The relief of the citizens of each State from the burden of monopoly and the evils resulting from the restraint of trade among such citizens was left with the States to deal with, and this court has recognized their possession of that power even to the extent of holding that an employment or business carried on by private individuals, when it becomes a matter of such public interest and importance as to create a common charge or burden upon the citizens, in other words, when it becomes a practical monopoly, to which the citizen is compelled to resort and by means of which a tribute can be exacted from the community, is subject to regulation by state legislative power. On the other hand, the power of Congress to regulate commerce among the several States is also exclusive. The Constitution does not provide that interstate commerce shall be free, but, by the grant of this exclusive power to regulate it, it was left free except as Congress might impose restraints....

The argument is that the power to control the manufacture of refined sugar is a monopoly over a necessary of life, to the enjoyment of which by a large part of the population of the United States interstate commerce is indispensable, and that, therefore, the general government in the exercise of the power to regulate commerce may repress such monopoly directly and set aside the instruments which have created it. But this argument cannot be confined to the necessaries of life merely, and must include all articles of general consumption....

It is vital that the independence of the commercial power and of the police power, and the delimitation between them, however sometimes perplexing, should always be recognized and observed, for while the one furnishes the strongest bond of union, the other is essential to the preservation of the autonomy of the States as required by our dual form of government, and acknowledged evils, however grave and urgent they may appear to be, had better be borne, than the risk be run, in the effort to suppress them, of more serious consequences by resort to expedients of even doubtful constitutionality.

...The regulation of commerce applies to the subjects of commerce and not to matters of internal police. Contracts to buy, sell, or exchange goods to be transported among the several States, the transportation and its instrumentalities, and articles bought, sold, or exchanged for the purposes of such transit among the States, or put in the way of transit, may be regulated, but this is because they form part of interstate trade or commerce. The fact that an article is manufactured for export to another State does not itself make it an article of interstate commerce, and the intent of the manufacturer does not determine the time when the article or product passes from the control of the State and belongs to commerce....

...[I]n *Kidd v. Pearson* (1888) where the question was discussed whether the right of a State to enact a statute prohibiting within its limits the manufacture of intoxicating liquors, except for certain purposes, could be overthrown by the fact that the manufacturer intended to export the liquors when made, it was held that the intent of the manufacturer did not determine the time when the article or product passed from the control of the State and belonged to commerce, and that, therefore, the statute, in omitting to except from its operation the manufacture of intoxicating liquors within the limits of the State for export, did not constitute an unauthorized interference with the right of Congress to regulate commerce. And [Justice] Lamar remarked "No distinction is more popular to the common mind, or more clearly expressed in economic and political literature, than that between manufacture and commerce. Manufacture is transformation—the fashioning of raw materials into a change of form for use. The functions of commerce are different. The buying and selling and the transportation incidental thereto constitute commerce, and the regulation of commerce in the constitutional sense embraces the regulation at least of such transportation. If it be held that the term includes the regulation of all such manufacturers as are intended to be the subject of commercial transactions in the future, it is impossible to deny that it would also include all productive industries that contemplate the same thing. The result would be the Congress would be invested, to the exclusion of the States, with the power to regulate, not only manufactures, but also agriculture, horticulture, stock raising, domestic fisheries, mining—in short, every branch of human industry...."

...[T]he contracts and acts of the defendants related exclusively to the acquisition of the Philadelphia refineries and the business of sugar refining in Pennsylvania, and bore no direct relationship to commerce between the States or with foreign nations....[I]t does not follow that an attempt to monopolize, or the actual monopoly of, the manufacture was an attempt...to monopolize commerce, even though, in order to dispose of the product, the instrumentality of commerce was necessarily invoked. There was nothing in the proofs to indicate any intention to put a restraint upon trade or commerce....The subject-matter of the sale was shares of manufacturing stock,...yet the act of Congress only authorized the Circuit Courts to proceed by way of preventing and restraining violations of the act in respect to contracts, combinations, or conspiracies in restraint of interstate or international trade or commerce....

The Circuit Court declined, upon the pleadings and proofs, to grant the relief prayed, and dismissed the bill, and we are of the opinion that the Circuit Court of Appeals did not err in affirming that decree.

JUSTICE HARLAN, dissenting.

...If this combination, so far as its operations necessarily or directly affect interstate commerce, cannot be restrained or suppressed under some power granted to Congress, it will be cause for regret that the patriotic statesmen who framed the Constitution did not foresee the necessity of investing the national government with power to deal with gigantic monopolies holding in their grasp, and injuriously controlling for their own interest, the entire trade *among the States* in food products that are essential to the comfort of every household in the land.

The court holds it to be vital in our system of government to recognize and give effect to both the commercial power of the nation and the police powers of the States, to the end that the Union be strengthened and the autonomy of the States preserved. In this view I entirely concur. Undoubtedly, the preservation of the just authority of the States is an object of deep concern to every lover of his country. No greater calamity could befall our free institutions than the destruction of that authority, by whichever means such a result might be accomplished....But it is equally true that the preservation of the just authority of the General Government is essential as well to the safety of the States as to the attainment of the important ends for which that government was ordained by the People of the United States, and the destruction of *that* authority would be fatal to the peace and well-being of the American people. The Constitution which enumerates the power committed to the nation for the objects of interest to the people of all the States should not, therefore, be subjected to an interpretation so rigid, technical, and narrow, that those objects cannot be accomplished....

Congress is invested with power to regulate commerce with foreign nations and among the several States....

...

...It would seem to be indisputable that no *combination* of corporations or individuals can, *of right*, impose unlawful restraints upon *interstate* trade, whether upon transportation or upon such interstate intercourse and traffic as precede transportation, any more than it can, of right, impose unreasonable restraints upon the completely internal traffic of a State....

...The jurisdiction of the general government extends over every foot of territory within the United States. Under the power with which it is invested, Congress may remove unlawful obstructions, of whatever kind, to the free course of trade among the States. In so doing it would not interfere with the "autonomy of the States," because the power thus to protect interstate commerce is expressly given by the people of all the States....Any combination, therefore, that disturbs or unreasonably obstructs freedom in buying and selling articles manufactured to be sold to persons in other States or to be carried to other States—a freedom that cannot exist if the right to buy and sell is fettered by unlawful restraints that crush out competition—affects, not incidentally, but directly, the people of all the States, and the remedy for such an evil is found only in the exercise of powers confided to a government which, this court as said, was the government of all, exercising powers delegated by all, representing all, acting for all. *McCulloch v. Maryland* (1819).

...There is no dispute here as to the lawfulness of the business of refining sugar, *apart from the undue restraint which the promoters of such business, who have combined to control prices, seek to put upon the freedom of interstate traffic in that article.*

It may be admitted that an act which did nothing more than forbid, and which had no other object than to forbid, the *mere* refining of sugar in any State, would be in excess of any power granted to Congress. But the act of 1890 is not of that character. It does not strike at the manufacture simply of articles that are legitimate or recognized subjects of commerce, but at *combinations* that unduly restrain, because they monopolize, *the buying and selling of articles* which are to go into interstate commerce.

...It is said that manufacture precedes commerce and is not a part of it. But it is equally true that when manufacture ends, that which has been manufactured becomes a subject of commerce, that buying and selling succeed manufacture, come into existence after the process of manufacture is completed, precede transportation, and are as much commercial intercourse, where articles are bought *to be* carried from one State to another, as is the manual transportation of such articles after they have been so purchased. The distinction was recognized by this court in *Gibbons v. Ogden* (1824), where the principal question was whether commerce included navigation. Both the court and counsel recognized buying and selling or barter *as included in commerce*....

....

...The end proposed to be accomplished by the act of 1890 is the protection of trade and commerce among the States against unlawful restraints. Who can say that that end is not legitimate or is not within the scope of the

Constitution? The means employed are the suppression, by legal proceedings, of combinations, conspiracies, and monopolies, which by their inevitable and admitted tendency, improperly restrain trade and commerce among the States. Who can say that such means are not appropriate to attain the end of freeing commercial intercourse among the States from burdens and exactions imposed upon it by combinations which, under principles long recognized in this country as well as at the common law, are illegal and dangerous to the public welfare? What clause of the Constitution can be referred to which prohibits the means thus prescribed in the act of Congress?

...While the opinion of the court in this case does not declare the act of 1890 to be unconstitutional, it defeats the main object for which it was passed. For it is, in effect, held that the statute would be unconstitutional if interpreted as embracing such unlawful restraints upon the purchasing of goods in one State to be carried to another State as necessarily arise from the existence of combinations formed for the purpose and with the effect, not only of monopolizing the ownership of all such goods in every part of the country, but of controlling the prices for them in all the States.... In my judgment, the general government is not placed by the Constitution in such a condition of helplessness that it must fold its arms and remain inactive while capital combines, under the name of a corporation, to destroy competition, not in one State only, but throughout the entire country.... The doctrine of the autonomy of the States cannot properly be invoked to justify a denial of power in the national government to meet such an emergency.

...The common government of all the people is the only one that can adequately deal with a matter which directly and injuriously affects the entire commerce of the country, which concerns equally all the people of the Union, and which, it must be confessed, cannot be adequately controlled by any one State. Its authority should not be so weakened by construction that it cannot reach and eradicate evils that, beyond all question, tend to defeat an object which that government is entitled, by the Constitution, to accomplish.

Note: Federalism, the Sherman Act, and the Unions

The Pullman strike of 1894 was one of the biggest in the nation's history, and the extensive federal intervention that included the use of the federal courts and the military to get the trains running again was unusual. The strike convinced Attorney General Richard Olney and others that reforms were needed to head off future disruption of the railroads. This led to the passage of the 1898 Erdman Act that encouraged arbitration of railroad labor disputes. Eugene Debs, who had led the Pullman strike, emerged as a charismatic leader of the labor movement, later running five times for the presidency under the Socialist Party banner. His best showing came in 1912, when he won 6 percent of the popular vote.

Although businesses charged under the Sherman Act frequently appealed to *E. C. Knight* in order to argue that they too were beyond the reach of Congress, the Court rarely looked on those arguments with favor. Railroads proved to be the easy case for federal regulation (since they were in the business of moving goods across state lines), but the Court was equally willing to grant federal authority over such varied enterprises as the selling of cast iron pipes (*Addyston Pipe & Steel Co. v. United States* [1899]), the dealing of tiles and grates brought in from out-of-state (*W. W. Montague & Co. v. Lowry* [1904]), the buying, slaughtering, and shipping of livestock (*Swift & Co. v. United States* [1905]), and the refining, transportation, and selling of oil (*Standard Oil Company of New Jersey v. United States* [1910]). The political climate in favor of anti-trust activity also changed when the "trust-buster" Teddy Roosevelt succeeded McKinley as president in 1901.

In 1908, the Court overruled a lower court in order to allow a hat manufacturer in Danbury, Connecticut, to proceed under the Sherman Act with its civil suit against the United Hatters of North America, a labor union within the American Federation of Labor. The manufacturer alleged that United Hatters had threatened that, unless it unionized its workforce, they would mount a national boycott campaign not only against the manufacturer but against any wholesaler who dealt its hats. The Court held that labor unions were as liable under the Sherman Act as any commercial business for combinations and conspiracies to restrain interstate trade. Moreover, it was the "object and intention of the combination [that] determined its legality." As a consequence, "although some of the means whereby the interstate traffic was to be destroyed were acts within a state... the acts must be considered as a whole.... If the purposes of the combination were, as alleged, to prevent any interstate transportation at all, the fact that the means operated at one end before physical transportation commenced, and, at the other end, after the physical transportation ended, was immaterial" (*Loewe v. Lawlor*, 208 U.S. 274, 301 [1908]).

By the 1920s, the significance of this "object and intention" test was apparent. When the Supreme Court first heard a case arising out of the violent 1914 miner strike at a coal mine in Arkansas, the justices were skeptical that the purely local strike was subject to federal law. By the time the case reached the Court for a second time (*Coronado Coal Co. v. United Mine Workers of America* [1925]), they thought the mine company had assembled the factual record that it needed to invoke the Sherman Act.

> The mere reduction in the supply of an article to be shipped in interstate commerce by the illegal or tortious prevention of its manufacture or production is ordinarily an indirect and remote obstruction to that commerce. But when the intent of those unlawfully preventing the manufacture or production is shown to be to restrain or control the supply entering and moving in interstate commerce, or the price of it in interstate markets, their action is a direct violation of the Anti-Trust Act.... We think there was substantial evidence at the second trial in this case tending to show that the purpose of the destruction of the mines was to stop the production of non-union coal and prevent its shipment to markets of other states than Arkansas, where it would by competition tend to reduce the price of the commodity and affect injuriously the maintenance of wages for union labor in competing mines....

Mining, like manufacturing and agriculture, was not "commerce" and thus, according to *E. C. Knight*, was normally subject only to state regulation. However, the justices held that the obstruction of local mining operations could fall under federal authority when the obstruction was intended to prevent the coal from reaching the national market. Does this conclusion reflect a judicial double standard between the treatment of labor and capital with respect to restraints on interstate commerce? Had the Court's view of the interstate commerce clause generally changed by the 1920s? Or did the results in individual cases depend on the specific situation in each case?

Champion v. Ames ["The Lottery Case"], 188 U.S. 321 (1903)

Lotteries, as devices to raise money for expensive public works projects, had a long and controversial history in the United States. Some states and localities found them to be a valuable source of revenue, but there was a mobilized opposition that saw them as harmful to the poor, to families and to the public morals. With lotteries on the wane, anti-gambling activists finally succeeded in winning a federal ban on the interstate traffic in lottery tickets in 1895. It was the first significant foray into morals legislation by the federal government, and it potentially opened the door to a wider range of federal regulations on topics that had been the traditional purview of states. Did the power to "regulate" interstate commerce include the power to prohibit certain items from moving in interstate commerce? Did it depend on the nature of the item? Could it give Congress an indirect power to regulate manufacturing? Did anything that moved across state lines become subject to congressional regulation? Could Congress, for example, use the interstate commerce clause to pass federal laws against the movement of prostitutes or adulterers or kidnappers across state boundaries? In Hoke and Economides v. United States (1913) *the Court soon indicated that the answer was "yes," but the justices were less certain about using this power to regulate the production of goods.*

When C. F. Champion was indicted and arrested for attempting to smuggle tickets of the Pan-American Lottery Company, based in Paraguay, from Texas to California in a sealed container to be carried by the Wells-Fargo Express Company, he challenged his detention as unconstitutional. Note that the Court's opinion was written by Justice Harlan, who was the lone dissenter in the E. C. Knight *case. In* Champion v. Ames, *he wrote for a 5–4 majority upholding the statute.*

JUSTICE HARLAN delivered the opinion of the Court.

...

If a State, when considering legislation for the suppression of lotteries within its own limits, may properly take into view the evils that inhere in the raising of money, in that mode, why may not Congress, invested with the Power to regulate commerce among the several States, provide that such commerce shall not be polluted by the carrying of lottery tickets from one State to another? In this connection it must not be forgotten that the power of Congress to regulate commerce among the States is plenary, is complete in itself, and is subject to no limitations except such as may be found in the Constitution.....

...

...Congress, by that act, does not assume to interfere with traffic or commerce in lottery tickets carried on exclusively within the limits of any State, but has in view only commerce of that kind among the several States.... It said, in effect, that it would not permit the declared policy of the States, which sought to protect their people against the mischiefs of the lottery business, to be overthrown or disregarded by the agency of interstate commerce. We should hesitate long before adjudging that an evil of such appalling character, carried on through interstate commerce, cannot be met and crushed by the only power competent to that end....

That regulation may sometimes appropriately assume the form of prohibition is... illustrated by the case of diseased cattle, transported from one State to another. Such cattle may have, notwithstanding their condition, a value in money for some purposes, and yet it cannot be doubted that Congress, under its power to regulate commerce, may either provide for their being inspected before transportation begins, or, in its discretion, may prohibit their being transported from one State to another....

...

It is said, however, that if, in order to suppress lotteries carried on through interstate commerce, Congress may exclude lottery tickets from such commerce, that principle leads necessarily to the conclusion that Congress may arbitrarily exclude from commerce among the States any article, commodity or thing, of whatever kind or nature, or however useful or valuable, which it may choose, no matter with what motive, to declare shall not be carried from one State to another. It will be time enough to consider the constitutionality of such legislation when we must do so. The present case does not require the court to declare the full extent of the power that Congress may exercise in the regulation of commerce among the States. We may, however, repeat, in this connection, what the court has heretofore said, that the power of Congress to regulate commerce among the States, although plenary, cannot be deemed arbitrary, since it is subject to such limitations or restrictions as are prescribed by the Constitution. This power, therefore may not be exercised so as to infringe rights secured or protected by that instrument.... But, as often said, the possible abuse of a power is not an argument against its existence. There is probably no governmental power that may not be exerted to the injury of the public. If what is done by Congress is manifestly in excess of the powers granted to it, then upon the courts will rest the duty of adjudging that its action is neither legal nor binding upon the people.

The judgment is *Affirmed*.

CHIEF JUSTICE FULLER, with whom JUSTICE BREWER, JUSTICE SHIRAS and JUSTICE PECKHAM join, dissenting.

...

The power of the State to impose restraints and burdens on persons and property in conservation and promotion of the public health, good order and prosperity is a power originally and always belonging to the States, not surrendered by them to the General Government nor directly restrained by the Constitution of the United States, and essentially exclusive, and the suppression of lotteries as a harmful business falls within this power, commonly called of police....

It is urged, however, that because Congress is empowered to regulate commerce between the several States, it, therefore, may suppress lotteries by prohibiting the carriage of lottery matter. Congress may indeed make all laws necessary and proper for carrying the powers granted to it into execution, and doubtless an act prohibiting the carriage of lottery matter would be necessary and proper to the execution of a power to suppress lotteries; but that power belongs to the States and not to Congress. To hold that Congress has general police power would be to hold that it may accomplish objects not entrusted to the General Government, and to defeat the operation of the Tenth Amendment....

...

Is the carriage of lottery tickets from one State to another commercial intercourse?

The lottery ticket purports to create contractual relations and to furnish the means of enforcing a contract right.

This is true of insurance policies, and both are contingent in their nature. Yet this court has held that the issuing of fire, marine, and life insurance policies, in one State, and sending them to another, to be there delivered to the insured on payment of premium, is not interstate commerce....

In *Paul v. Virginia* (1869), Justice Field, in delivering the unanimous opinion of the court, said: ... "They are, then, local transactions, and are governed by the local law. They do not constitute a part of the commerce between the States any more than a contract for the purchase and sale of goods in Virginia by a citizen of New York whilst in Virginia would constitute a portion of such commerce."

...

If a lottery ticket is not an article of commerce, how can it become so when placed in an envelope or box or other covering, and transported by an express company? To say that the mere carrying of an article which is not an article of commerce in and of itself nevertheless becomes such the moment it is to be transported from one State to another, is to transform a non-commercial article into a commercial one simply because it is transported. I cannot conceive that any such result can properly follow.

It would be to say that everything is an article of commerce the moment it is taken to be transported from place to place, and of interstate commerce if from State to State.

An invitation to dine, or to take a drive, or a note of introduction, all become articles of commerce under the ruling in this case, by being deposited with an express company for transportation. This in effect breaks down all the differences between that which is, and that which is not, an article of commerce, and the necessary consequence is to take from the States all jurisdiction over the subject so far as interstate communication is concerned. It is a long step in the direction of wiping out all traces of state lines, and the creation of a centralized Government.

...

The power to prohibit the transportation of diseased animals and infected goods over railroads or on steamboats is an entirely different thing, for they would be in themselves injurious to the transaction of interstate commerce, and, moreover, are essentially commercial in their nature.... However enticing that business may be, we do not understand these pieces of paper themselves can communicate bad principles by contact.

...

I regard this decision as inconsistent with the views of the framers of the Constitution, and of Marshall, its great expounder. Our form of government may remain notwithstanding legislation or decision, but, as long ago observed, it is with governments, as with religions, the form may survive the substance of the faith.

...

Hammer v. Dagenhart, 247 U.S. 251 (1918)

The prohibition of child labor was an international cause of Progressive reformers at the turn of the twentieth century. Most states adopted child labor laws, but the laws varied in what they prohibited, and enforcement was uneven. Established manufacturers in northern states were particularly concerned about growing competition from the economically less developed South, where child labor laws, as with other labor regulation, were often looser. The reform campaign turned to the federal government to impose a national, uniform standard. Facing a tough reelection campaign in which Progressive activists could play a pivotal role, President Woodrow Wilson swallowed his doubts about the constitutionality of the measure. He helped convince southern senators not to filibuster the measure for the good of the Democratic Party, and in 1916 he signed into law the Keating–Owen Act, banning the interstate shipment of goods produced with child labor.

The law was quickly challenged, when a North Carolina father sought an injunction so that his two minor sons could continue working in a local cotton mill. Since its decision in E. C. Knight *(1895) the Court had characterized Congress' control over the movement of goods across state lines as "plenary." It had allowed Congress to prohibit the interstate shipment of lottery tickets and the interstate transportation of women for immoral purposes. Could there be any doubt that Congress could prohibit the interstate shipment of goods made by child labor? On what grounds could such a prohibition be considered unconstitutional? A sharply divided 5–4 Court struck down the statute as inconsistent with the interstate commerce clause.*

Congress tried to get around the decision by using its taxation power to discourage goods produced with child labor, but the Court struck that down also in Bailey v. Drexel Furniture Co. (1922). *Congress passed a constitutional amendment empowering the federal government to regulate child labor in 1924, but ratification bogged down in the southern states. By the end of the 1920s, child labor had dramatically declined in the United States, but it was not federally regulated until the New Deal.*

JUSTICE DAY delivered the opinion of the Court.

...

The controlling question for decision is: Is it within the authority of Congress in regulating commerce among the States to prohibit the transportation in interstate commerce of manufactured goods, the product of a factory in which, within thirty days prior to their removal therefrom, children under the age of fourteen have been employed or permitted to work....

...

...The thing intended to be accomplished by this statute is the denial of the facilities of interstate commerce to those manufacturers in the States who employ children within the prohibited ages. The act in its effect does not regulate transportation among the States, but aims to standardize the ages at which children may be employed in mining and manufacturing within the States. The goods shipped are of themselves harmless. The act permits them to be freely shipped after thirty days from the time of their removal from the factory. When offered for shipment, and before transportation begins, the labor of their production is over, and the mere fact that they were intended for interstate commerce transportation does not make their production subject to federal control under the commerce power.

Commerce "consists of intercourse and traffic... and includes the transportation of persons and property, as well as the purchase, sale and exchange of commodities." The making of goods and the mining of coal are not commerce, nor does the fact that these things are to be afterwards shipped or used in interstate commerce, make their production a part thereof....

Over interstate transportation, or its incidents, the regulatory power of Congress is ample, but the production of articles, intended for interstate commerce, is a matter of local regulation.

When the commerce begins is determined, not by the character of the commodity, nor by the intention of the owner to transfer it to another state for sale, nor by his preparation of it for transportation, but by its actual delivery to a common carrier for transportation, or the actual commencement of its transfer to another state.... If it were otherwise, all manufacture intended for interstate shipment would be brought under federal control to the practical exclusion of the authority of the States, a result certainly not contemplated by the framers of the Constitution when they vested in Congress the authority to regulate commerce among the States....

It is further contended that the authority of Congress may be exerted to control interstate commerce in the shipment of child-made goods because of the effect of the circulation of such goods in other States where the evil of this class of labor has been recognized by local legislation, and the right to thus employ child labor has been more rigorously restrained than in the State of production. In other words, that the unfair competition, thus engendered, may be controlled by closing the channels of interstate commerce to manufacturers in those States where the local laws do not meet what Congress deems to be the more just standard of other States.

There is no power vested in Congress to require the States to exercise their police power so as to prevent possible unfair competition. Many causes may cooperate to give one State, by reason of local laws or conditions, an economic advantage over others. The Commerce Clause was not intended to give to Congress a general authority to equalize such conditions....

The grant of power to Congress over the subject of interstate commerce was to enable it to regulate such commerce, and not to give it authority to control the States in their exercise of the police power over local trade and manufacture.

The grant of authority over a purely federal matter was not intended to destroy the local power always existing and carefully reserved to the States in the Tenth Amendment to the Constitution.

...

We have neither authority nor disposition to question the motives of Congress in enacting this legislation. The purposes intended must be attained consistently with constitutional limitations and not by an invasion of the powers of the States. This court has no more important function than that which devolves upon it the obligation to preserve inviolate the constitutional limitations upon the exercise of authority, federal and state, to the end that each may continue to discharge, harmoniously with the other, the duties entrusted to it by the Constitution.

In our view the necessary effect of this act is, by means of a prohibition against the movement in interstate commerce of ordinary commercial commodities, to regulate the hours of labor of children in factories and mines within the States, a purely state authority. Thus the act in a twofold sense is repugnant to the Constitution. It not only transcends the authority delegated to Congress over commerce but also exerts a power as to a purely local matter to which the federal authority does not extend. The far reaching result of upholding the act cannot be more plainly indicated than by pointing out that if Congress can thus regulate matters entrusted to local authority by prohibition of the movement of commodities in interstate commerce, all freedom of commerce will be at an end, and the power of the States over local matters may be eliminated, and thus our system of government be practically destroyed....

Affirmed.

JUSTICE HOLMES, with whom JUSTICE MCKENNA, JUSTICE BRANDEIS, and JUSTICE CLARKE join, dissenting.

....

The first step in my argument is to make plain what no one is likely to dispute—that the statute in question is within the power expressly given to Congress if considered only as to its immediate effects and that if invalid it is so only upon some collateral ground. The statute confines itself to prohibiting the carriage of certain goods in interstate or foreign commerce. Congress is given power to regulate such commerce in unqualified terms. It would not be argued today that the power to regulate does not include the power to prohibit. Regulation means the prohibition of something....

The question then is narrowed to whether the exercise of its otherwise constitutional power by Congress can be pronounced unconstitutional because of its possible reaction upon the conduct of the States in a matter upon which I have admitted that they are free from direct control. I should have thought that that matter had been disposed of so fully as to leave no room for doubt....

The manufacture of oleomargarine is as much a matter of state regulation as the manufacture of cotton cloth. Congress levied a tax upon the compound when colored so as to resemble butter that was so great as obviously to prohibit the manufacture and sale. In a very elaborate discussion the present Chief Justice excluded any inquiry into the purpose of an act which apart from that purpose was within the power of Congress....Fifty years ago a tax on state banks, the obvious purpose and actual effect of which was to drive them, or at least their circulation, out of existence, was sustained, although the result was one that Congress had no constitutional power to require. The Court made short work of the argument as to the purpose of the act....And to come to cases upon interstate commerce, notwithstanding *United States v. E. C. Knight Co.* (1895)...the Sherman Act has been made an instrument for the breaking up of combinations in restraint of trade and monopolies, using the power to regulate commerce as a foothold, but not proceeding because that commerce was the end actually in mind. The objection that the control of the States over production was interfered with was urged again and again but always in vain....

...

The act does not meddle with anything belonging to the States. They may regulate their internal affairs and their domestic commerce as they like. But when they seek to send their products across the state line they are no longer within their rights. If there were no Constitution and no Congress their power to cross the line would depend upon their neighbors. Under the Constitution such commerce belongs not to the States but to Congress to regulate. It may carry out its views of public policy whatever indirect effect they may have upon the activities of the States. Instead of being encountered by a prohibitive tariff at her boundaries the State encounters the public policy of the United States which it is for Congress to express. The public policy of the United States is shaped with a view to the benefit of the nation as a whole. If, as has been the case within the memory of men still living, a State should take a different view of the propriety of sustaining a lottery from that which generally prevails, I cannot believe that the fact would require a different decision from that reached in *Champion v. Ames* (1903). Yet in that case it would be said with quite as much force as in this that Congress was attempting to intermeddle with the State's domestic affairs. The national welfare as understood by Congress may require a different attitude within its sphere from that of some self-seeking State. It seems to me entirely constitutional for Congress to enforce its understanding by all the means at its command.

C. Taxing and Spending Power

As we have seen in the context of the commerce clause, reformers demanded that Congress expand its powers over wealth and corporate power, and conservatives grew anxious about the effect that expanded federal power would have on rights to property. As in *E. C. Knight* (1895) and *Debs* (1895), a conservative majority readily took sides in the controversy over the federal income tax of 1894. Although relatively small, the tax was a prominent feature of the Populist platform. The addition of an income tax into a major tariff bill was the primary achievement of William Jennings Bryan during his brief career in Congress.

Article I of the Constitution requires that "direct" taxes be apportioned among the states by population. The income tax case turned on whether taxes on income qualified as "direct" taxes and as a result were subject to this constitutional requirement. If they were a direct tax, then the law as written would be unconstitutional and any income tax scheme would likely be unworkable. A central issue for the justices was how to interpret the Court's own prior decisions and to what degree earlier decisions should settle constitutional disputes. In striking down the income tax provisions of the 1894 statute over the course of two highly controversial decisions in *Pollock v. Farmers' Loan and Trust Company* (1894), the Court helped mobilize William Jennings Bryan and the Populists to take over the Democratic Party in the 1896 convention and delay the adoption of a federal income tax for a generation.

The Court was also confronted with the question of how Congress could use the taxing power. In particular, could Congress use the internal taxing power as a regulatory tool? The broader debate was an old one. The Jacksonian Democrats had denounced protectionist tariffs as unconstitutional since they were designed to regulate and manage the economy rather than raise revenue. Whigs had responded that Congress had broad authority to regulate international trade and in any case the taxation power was "plenary," or unrestricted. *The Child Labor Tax Case* (1922) struck down an effort by Congress to tax goods made with child labor that crossed state borders. The Court was convinced that the tax was designed purely as a regulatory measure and not as a revenue measure, and moreover it was attempting to regulate something that was otherwise outside the scope of federal power in the early twentieth century (labor conditions in manufacturing). Congress could not do indirectly with the taxation power what it was prohibited from doing directly with the regulatory power under the interstate commerce clause.

Pollock v. Farmers' Loan and Trust Company, 157 U.S. 429 (1894)

Charles Pollock, a citizen of Massachusetts, filed suit as a shareholder against the Farmers' Loan and Trust Company of New York to prevent it from paying the federal income tax that was instituted as part of the Wilson Tariff of 1894. The Tariff Act imposed a two-percent tax on corporate income and various sources of personal income over $4,000. The suit argued that these components of the Tariff Act were unconstitutional as imposing a direct tax that was not apportioned among the states, a duty that was not uniform throughout the United States, and a tax on income derived from county and municipal bonds. Pollock *was heard together with the similar case of* Hyde v. Continental Trust Company. *In the first hearing of the income tax cases, the Court was able to decide (by a 6–2 vote) that a tax on rental income from real estate was a direct tax and (unanimously) that the federal government could not tax income from municipal bonds. In the absence of the ailing Justice Howell Jackson the Court split evenly on the remaining questions, which were later reargued before the full bench.*

The Court's decision delayed imposition of a federal income tax for almost twenty years, until passage of the Sixteenth Amendment, which reads: "The Congress shall have power to lay and collect taxes on incomes, from whatever source derived, without apportionment among the several States, and without regard to any census or enumeration."

Mr. ATTORNEY GENERAL for the United States.

...

Taxation...is an uncommonly practical affair. The power to tax is for practical use and is necessarily to be adapted to the practical conditions of human life. These are never the same for any two persons, and for any community, however small, are infinitely diversified. Regard being paid to them, nothing is more evident, nothing has been oftener declared by courts and jurists, than that absolute equality of taxation is impossible....

...

...In its essence and in the last analysis, [this lawsuit] is nothing but a call upon the judicial department of government to supplant the political in the exercise of the taxing power; to substitute its discretion for that of Congress in respect of the subjects of taxation, the plan of taxation, and all the distinctions and discriminations by which taxation is sought to be equitably adjusted to the resources and capacities of the different classes of society. Such an effort, however, weightily supported, cannot, I am bound to believe, be successful. It is inevitably predestined to failure unless the court shall, for the first time in its history, overlook and overstep the bounds which separate the judicial from the legislative power—bounds, the scrupulous observance of which it has so often declared to be absolutely essential to the integrity of our constitutional system of government.

Mr. JAMES C. CARTER for Continental Trust Company.

...

It is alleged by the counsel for the appellant that the income tax—and this they consider its most monstrous form of injustice—falls upon two per cent only of the population of the United States; but what must we think of the fact that this two per cent have been paying but a trifle...? At the same time, another impressive and startling fact, not adverted to by them, has also been receiving more and more of the attention of the people of the country—I mean the growing concentration of large masses of wealth in an ever diminishing number of persons.

...At last the party complaining of these things gained an ascendancy in the legislative counsels, and efforts were made to devise a remedy. This income tax is part of that remedy.

...Some general criticisms made by way of objection to the law, and supposed to be sufficient to condemn it, are wholly lacking in merit: they amount to clamor only. It is said to be class legislation, and to make a distinction between the rich and the poor. It certainly does. It certainly is class legislation in that sense. That was its very object and purpose. This is a distinction that should always be looked to in the business of taxation. Unfortunately heretofore it has been observed in the wrong direction,...and the poorer class prodigiously over-burdened.

...

Mr. JOSEPH H. CHOATE for appellant.

...I believe there are private rights of property here to be protected....The act of Congress which we are impugning before you is communistic in its purposes and tendencies, and is defended here upon principles as communistic, socialistic—what shall I call them—populistic as ever have been addressed to any political assembly in the world.

...

...If it goes out as the edict of this judicial tribunal that a combination of States, however numerous, however unanimous, can unite against the safeguards provided by the Constitution in imposing a tax which is to be paid by the people in four States or three States or in two States, but of which combination is to pay almost no part, while in the spending of it they are to have the whole control, it will be impossible to take any backward step. You cannot here after exercise any check if you now say that Congress is untrammeled and uncontrollable.

...

CHIEF JUSTICE FULLER delivered the opinion of the Court.

...Since the opinion in *Marbury v. Madison* (1803) was delivered, it has not been doubted that it is within judicial competency, by express provisions of the Constitution or by necessary inference and implication, to determine whether a given law of the United States is or is not made in pursuance of the Constitution, and to hold it valid or void accordingly....Necessarily the power to declare a law unconstitutional is always exercised with reluctance; but the duty to do so, in a proper case, cannot be declined, and must be discharged in accordance with the deliberate judgment of the tribunal in which the validity of the enactment is directly drawn into question.

...The Constitution provides that representatives and direct taxes shall be apportioned among the several States according to numbers, and that no direct tax shall be laid except according to the enumeration provided for; and also that all duties, imposts and excises shall be uniform throughout the United States.

...

...The States were about, for all national purposes embraced in the Constitution, to become one....But...they were careful to see to it that taxation and representation should go together, so that the sovereignty reserved should not be impaired, and that when Congress, and especially the House of Representatives, where it was specifically provided that all revenue bills must originate, voted a tax upon property, it should be with the consciousness, and under the responsibility, that in so doing the tax so voted would proportionately fall upon the immediate constituents of those who imposed it....

Thus, in the matter of taxation, the Constitution recognizes two great classes of direct and indirect taxes, and lays down two rules by which their imposition must be governed, namely: The rule of apportionment as to direct taxes, and the rule of uniformity as to duties, imposts and excises.

...[I]t is clear that the rule to govern each of the great classes into which taxes were divided was prescribed in view of the commonly accepted distinction between them and of the taxes directly levied under the systems of the States. And that the difference between direct and indirect taxation was fully appreciated is supported by the congressional debates after the government was organized.

...

...In *Hylton v. United States* (1796)...this court held the [carriage tax] to be constitutional, because not laying a direct tax....

Justice Chase said that he was inclined to think, but of this he did not "give a judicial opinion," that "the direct taxes contemplated by the Constitution, are only two, to wit, a capitation, or poll tax, simply, without regard to property, profession, or any other circumstance; and a tax on land;" and that he doubted "whether a tax, by a general assessment of personal property, within the United States, is included within the term direct tax." But he thought that "an annual tax on carriages for the conveyance of persons, may be considered as within the power granted to Congress to lay duties.... It seems to me, that a tax on expense is an indirect tax; and I think an annual tax on a carriage for the conveyance of persons, is of that kind; because a carriage is a consumable commodity; and such annual tax on it, is on the expense of the owner."

Justice Patterson said that "...Whether direct taxes, in the sense of the Constitution, comprehend any other tax than a capitation tax, and taxes on land, is a questionable point.... But as it is not before the court, it would be improper to give any decisive opinion on it." And he concluded: "All taxes on expenses or consumption are indirect taxes."

...Justice Iredell said: "...A land or a poll tax may be considered of this description.... In regard to other articles, there may possibly be considerable doubt. It is sufficient, on the present occasion, for the court to be satisfied, that this is not a direct tax contemplated by the Constitution, in order to affirm the present judgment."

It will be perceived that each of the justices, while suggesting doubt whether anything but a capitation or a land tax was a direct tax within the meaning of the Constitution, distinctly avoided expressing an opinion upon that question or laying down a comprehensive definition, but confined his opinion to the case before the court.

The general line of observation was obviously influenced by Mr. [Alexander] Hamilton's brief for the government, in which he said: "The following are presumed to be the only direct taxes: Capitation or poll taxes, taxes on lands and buildings, general assessments, whether on the whole property of individuals, or on their whole real or personal estate. All else must of necessity be considered as indirect taxes."

....

...From the foregoing it is apparent: 1. That the distinction between direct and indirect taxation was well understood by the framers of the Constitution and those who adopted it. 2. That under the state systems of taxation all taxes on real estate or personal property or the rents or income thereof were regarded as direct taxes. 3. That the rules of apportionment and of uniformity were adopted in view of that distinction and those systems. 4. That whether the tax on carriages was direct or indirect was disputed, but the tax was sustained as a tax on the use and an excise. 5. That the original expectation was that the power of direct taxation would be exercised only in extraordinary exigencies, and down to August 15, 1894, this expectation has been realized....

We proceed then to examine certain decisions of this court under the acts of 1861 and following years, in which it is claimed that this court has heretofore adjudicated that taxes like those under consideration are not direct taxes and subject to the rule of apportionment, and that we are bound to accept the rulings thus asserted to have been made as conclusive in the premises. Is this contention well founded as respects the question now under examination? Doubtless the doctrine of stare decisis is a salutary one, and to be adhered to on all proper occasions, but it only arises in respect of decisions directly upon the points in issue.

....

Let us examine the cases referred to in light of these observations.

In *Pacific Insurance Co. v. Soule* (1868) the validity of a tax which was described as "upon the business of an insurance company" was sustained on the ground that it was "a duty or excise," and came within the decision in *Hylton's case*.... [T]he decision rested on narrow ground, and turned on the distinction between an excise duty and a tax strictly so termed, regarding the former a charge for a privilege, or on the transaction of business, without any necessary reference to the amount of property belonging to those on whom the charge might fall....

In *Veazie Bank v. Fenno* (1869) a tax was laid on the circulation of state banks or national banks paying out the notes of individuals or state banks, and it was held that it might well be classed under the head of duties, and as falling within the same category as *Soule's case*. It was declared to be of the same nature as excise taxation on freight receipts, bills of lading, and passenger tickets issued by a railroad company.

...In *Railroad Company v. Collector* (1880) the validity of a tax collected of a corporation upon the interest paid to it upon its bonds was held to be "essentially an excise on the business of the class of corporations mentioned in the statute." And Justice Miller, in delivering the opinion, said: "As the sum involved in this suit is small, and the law under which the tax in question was collected has long since been repealed, the case is of little consequence as regards any principle involved in it as a rule of future action."

....

...[W]e are considering the rule *stare decisis*, and we must decline to hold ourselves bound to extend the scope of decisions—none of which discussed the question whether a tax on the income from personalty is equivalent to a tax on that personalty, but all of which held real estate liable to direct taxation only—so as to sustain a tax on the income of realty on the ground of being an excise or duty.

...[I]s there any distinction between the real estate itself or its owners in respect of it and the rents or income of the real estate coming to the owners as a natural and ordinary incident or ownership?

If the Constitution had provided that Congress should not levy any tax upon the real estate of any citizen of any State, could be it be contended that Congress could put an annual tax for five or any other number of years upon the rent or income of the real estate?

...Unless, therefore, a tax upon rents or income issuing out of lands is intrinsically so different from a tax on the land itself that it belongs to a wholly different class of taxes, such taxes must be regarded as falling within the same category as a tax on real estate *eo nomine*. The name of the tax is unimportant. The real question is, is there any basis upon which to rest the contention that real estate belongs to one of the two great classes of taxes, and the rent or income which is the incident of its ownership belongs to the other? We are unable to perceive any ground for the alleged distinction.

....

We are of opinion that the law in question, so far as it levies a tax on the rents and income of real estate, is in violation of the Constitution, and is invalid.

Another question directly presented by the record as to the validity of the tax levied by the act upon the income derived from municipal bonds....

The Constitution contemplates the independent exercise by the Nation and the State, severally, of their constitutional powers.

As the States cannot tax the powers, the operations, or the property of the United States, nor the means which they employ to carry their powers into execution, so it has been held that the United States have no power under the Constitution to tax either the instrumentalities or the property of a State.

...

Upon each of the other questions argued at the bar, to wit, 1, Whether the void provisions as to rents and income from real estate invalidated the whole act? 2, Whether as to the income from personal property as such, the act is unconstitutional as laying direct taxes? 3, Whether any part of the tax if not considered as a direct tax, is invalid for want of uniformity on either of the grounds suggested?—the justices who heard the argument are equally divided, and, therefore, no opinion is expressed.

JUSTICE FIELD, concurring.

...

The income tax law under consideration is marked by discriminating features which affect the whole law. It discriminates between those who receive an income of four thousand dollars and those who do not....The legislation, in the discrimination it makes, is class legislation. Whenever a distinction is made in the burdens a law imposes or in the benefits it confers on any citizens by reason of their birth, or wealth, or religion, it is class legislation, and leads inevitably to oppression and abuses, and to general unrest and disturbance in society. It was hoped and believed that the great amendments to the Constitution which followed the late civil war had rendered such legislation impossible for all future time. But the objectionable legislation appears in the act under consideration....Under wise and constitutional legislation every citizen should contribute his proportion, however small the sum, to the support of the government, and it is no kindness to urge any of our citizens to escape from that obligation.

....

...This inherent limitation upon the taxing power forbids the imposition of taxes which are unequal in their operation upon similar kinds of property, and necessarily strikes down the gross and arbitrary distinctions in the income law as passed by Congress. The law, as we have seen, distinguishes in the taxation between corporations by exempting the property of some of them from taxation and levying the tax on the property of others when the corporations do not materially differ from one another in the character of their business or in the protection required by the government.

. . . The present assault upon capital is but the beginning. It will be but the stepping-stone to others, larger and more sweeping, till our political contests will become a war of the poor against the rich; a war constantly growing in intensity and bitterness.

. . . There is no safety in allowing the limitations to be adjusted except in strict compliance with the mandates of the Constitution which require its taxation, if imposed by direct taxes, to be apportioned among the Sates according to their representation, and if imposed by indirect taxes, to be uniform in operation and, so far as practicable, in proportion to their property, equal upon all citizens. Unless the rule of the Constitution governs, a majority may fix the limitation at such rate as will not include any of their own number.

I am of the opinion that the whole law of 1894 should be declared void and without any binding force.

JUSTICE WHITE, with whom JUSTICE HARLAN joins, dissenting.

My brief judicial experience has convinced me that the custom of filing long dissenting opinions is one "more honored in the breach than in the observance." The only purpose which an elaborate dissent can accomplish, if any, is to weaken the effect of the opinion of the majority, and thus engender want of confidence in the conclusions of courts of last resort. This consideration would impel me to content myself with simply recording my dissent in the present case, were it not for the fact that I consider that the result of the opinion of the court just announced is to overthrow a long and consistent line of decisions, and to deny to the legislative department of the government the possession of a power conceded to it by universal consensus for one hundred years, and which has been recognized by repeated adjudications of this court.

. . . .

In considering whether we are to regard an income tax as "direct" or otherwise, it will, in my opinion, serve no useful purpose, at this late period of our political history, to seek to ascertain the meaning of the word "direct" in the Constitution by resorting to the theoretical opinions on taxation found in the writings of some economists prior to the adoption of the Constitution or since. . . . I say it will serve no useful purpose to examine these writers, because whatever may have been the value of their opinions as to the economic sense of the word "direct," they cannot now afford any criterion for determining its meaning in the Constitution, inasmuch as an authoritative and conclusive construction has been given to that term, as there used by an interpretation adopted shortly after the formation of the Constitution by the legislative department of the government, and approved by the Executive; by the adoption of that interpretation from that time to the present without question, and its exemplification and enforcement in many legislative enactments, and its acceptance by the authoritative text-writers on the Constitution; by the sanction of that interpretation, in a decision of this court rendered shortly after the Constitution was adopted; and finally by the repeated reiteration and affirmance of that interpretation, so that it has become imbedded in our jurisprudence, and therefore may be considered almost a part of the written Constitution itself.

. . . By the act of June 5, 1794, Congress levied, without reference to apportionment, a tax on carriages "for the conveyance of persons."

. . . The carriage tax was defended by a few on the ground that it was a tax on consumption. Mr. Madison opposed it as unconstitutional, evidently upon the conception that the word "direct" in the Constitution was to be considered as having the same meaning as that which had been attached to it by some economic writers. His view was not sustained, and the act passed by a large majority—forty-nine to twenty-two. It received the approval of Washington. The Congress which passed this law numbered among its members many who sat in the convention which framed the Constitution. . . . The tax having been imposed without apportionment, it follows that those who voted for its enactment must have given to the word direct, in the Constitution, a different significance from that which is affixed to it by the economists referred to.

The validity of this carriage tax was considered by this court in *Hylton v. The United States* (1796). . . .

. . . These opinions strongly indicate that the real convictions of the justices were that only capitation taxes and taxes on land were direct within the meaning of the Constitution, but they doubted whether some other objects of a kindred nature might not be embraced in that word. . . .

. . . .

. . . This doctrine has become a part of the hornbook of American constitutional interpretation, has been taught as elementary in all the law schools, and has never since then been anywhere authoritatively questioned.

....

...And now, after a hundred years, after long-continued action by other departments of the government, and after repeated adjudications of this court, this interpretation is overthrown, and the Congress is declared not to have a power of taxation which may at some time, as it has in the past, prove necessary to the very existence of the government. By what process of reasoning is this to be done? By resort to theories, in order to construe the word "direct" in its economic sense, instead of in accordance with its meaning in the Constitution....In view of all that has taken place and of the many decisions of this court, the matter at issue here ought to be regarded as closed forever.

....

...My inability to agree with the court in the conclusions which it has just expressed causes me much regret. Great as is my respect for any view by it announced, I cannot resist the conviction that its opinion and decree in this case virtually annuls its previous decisions in regard to the powers of Congress on the subject of taxation, and is therefore fraught with danger to the court, to each and every citizen, and to the republic. The conservation and orderly development of our institutions rests on our acceptance of the results of the past, and their use as lights to guide our steps in the future. Teach the lesson that settled principles may be overthrown at any time, and confusion and turmoil must ultimately result. In the discharge of its function of interpreting the Constitution, this court exercises an august power. It sits removed from the contentions of political parties and the animosities of factions....If the permanency of its conclusions is to depend upon the personal opinions of those who, from time to time, may make up its membership, it will inevitably become a theatre of political strife, and its action will be without coherence or consistency....Break down this belief in judicial continuity, and let it be felt that on great constitutional questions this court is to depart from the settled conclusions of its predecessors, and to determine them all according to the mere opinion of those who temporarily fill its bench, and our Constitution will, in my judgment, be bereft of value and become a most dangerous instrument to the rights and liberties of the people.

In regard to the right to include in an income tax the interest upon the bonds of municipal corporations, I think the decisions of this court, holding that the Federal government is without power to tax the agencies of the state government, embrace such bonds, and that this settled line of authority is conclusive upon my judgment here.

JUSTICE HARLAN, dissenting.

Pollock v. Farmers' Loan and Trust Company (Rehearing), 158 U.S. 601 (1894)

In granting a rehearing of Pollock *before the full Court, the Court acceded to the attorney general's request that all the issues from the first case be reargued, including the constitutionality of the tax on rental income and income from municipal bonds that a majority of the justices had been able to resolve before. The Court heard arguments a month after issuing its initial decision and issued opinions just two weeks later.*

The Court had been tied 4–4 on the major question after the first hearing. Justice Howell Jackson, who had missed the first hearing, seemed to hold the result in his hands. Jackson now voted to uphold the law, but surprisingly he wound up in dissent. Chief Justice Melville Fuller wrote for a 5–4 majority to strike down the income tax. One of the justices changed his mind during the reargument in order to give Fuller a majority, most likely either George Shiras or Horace Gray. Speculation centered on the Pennsylvania Republican Shiras at the time, and he was bitterly denounced by politicians and the press.

CHIEF JUSTICE FULLER delivered the opinion of the Court.

....

It is said that a tax on the whole income of property is not a direct tax in the meaning of the Constitution, but a duty, and, as a duty, leviable without apportionment, whether direct or indirect. We do not think so. Direct taxation was not restricted in one breath, and the restriction blown to the winds in another.

...In the thirty-sixth number [of the *Federalist*], while still adopting the division of his opponents, he says: "The taxes intended to be comprised under the general denomination of internal taxes, may be subdivided into those of the *direct* and those of the *indirect* kind....As to the latter, *by which must be understood duties and excises on articles of consumption*, one is at a loss to conceive, what can be the nature of the difficulties apprehended." Thus we find Mr. Hamilton, while writing to induce the adoption of the Constitution, *first*, dividing the power of taxation into *external* and *internal*, putting into the former the power of imposing duties on imported articles and into the latter all remaining powers; and, *second*, dividing the latter into *direct* and *indirect*, putting into the latter, duties and excises on articles of consumption.

It seems to us to inevitably follow that in Mr. Hamilton's judgment at that time all internal taxes, except duties and excises on articles of consumption, fell into the category of direct taxes.

...

...We have unanimously held in this case that, so far as this law operates on the receipts from municipal bonds, it cannot be sustained, because it is a tax on the power of the States, and on their instrumentalities to borrow money, and consequently repugnant to the Constitution. But if, as contended, the interest when received has become merely money in the recipient's pocket, and taxable as such without reference to the source from which it came, the question is immaterial whether it could have been originally taxed at all or not. This was admitted by the Attorney General with characteristic candor; and it follows that, if the revenue derived from municipal bonds cannot be taxed because the source cannot be, the same rule applies to revenue from any other source not subject to the tax....

...

We are not here concerned with the question whether an income tax be or be not desirable, nor whether such a tax would enable the government to diminish taxes on consumption and duties on imports, and to enter upon what may be believed to be a reform of its fiscal and commercial system. Questions of that character belong to the controversies of political parties, and cannot be settled by judicial decision. In these cases our province is to determine whether this income tax on the revenue from property does or does not belong to the class of direct taxes. If it does, it is, being unapportioned, in violation of the Constitution, and we must so declare.

....

Our conclusions may, therefore, be summed up as follows:

First. We adhere to the opinion already announced, that, taxes on real estate being indisputably direct taxes, taxes on the rents or income of real estate are equally direct taxes.

Second. We are of opinion that taxes on personal property, or on the income of personal property, are likewise direct taxes.

Third. The tax imposed by sections twenty-seven to thirty-seven, inclusive, of the act of 1894, so far as it falls on the income of real estate and of personal property, being a direct tax within the meaning of the Constitution, and, therefore, unconstitutional and void because not apportioned according to representation, all those sections, constituting one entire scheme of taxation, are necessarily invalid.

The decrees hereinbefore entered in this court will be vacated; the decrees below will be reversed, and the cases remanded, with instructions to grant the relief prayed.

JUSTICE HARLAN, dissenting.

...

...From this history of legislation and of judicial decisions it is manifest –

...That from the foundation of the government, until 1861, Congress following the declarations of the judges in the *Hylton case*, restricted direct taxation to real estate and slaves, and in 1861 to real estate exclusively, and has never, by any statute, indicated its belief that personal property, however assessed or valued, was the subject of "direct taxes" to be apportioned among the States;

...

That in 1861 and subsequent years Congress imposed, without apportionment among the States on the basis of numbers, but by the rule of uniformity, duties on *income* derived *from every kind of property, real and personal*, including income derived from rents, and from trades, professions, and employments, etc.; and, lastly,

That upon every occasion when it has considered the question whether a duty on *incomes* was a direct tax within the meaning of the Constitution, this court has, without *a dissenting voice*, determined it in the negative, always proceeding on the ground that capitation taxes and taxes on land were the only direct taxes contemplated by the framers of the Constitution.

....

...The practice of a century, in harmony with the decisions of this court, under which uncounted millions have been collected by taxation, ought to be sufficient to close the door against further inquiry, based upon the speculations of theorists, and the varying opinions of statesmen who participated in the discussions, sometimes very bitter, relating to the form of government to be established in place of the Articles of Confederation under which, it has been well said, Congress could declare everything and do nothing.

...It seems to me that the court has not given to the maxim of *stare decisis* the full effect to which it is entitled. While obedience to that maxim is not expressly enjoined by the Constitution, the principle that decisions, resting upon a particular interpretation of that instrument, should not be lightly disregarded where such interpretation has been long accepted and acted upon by other branches of the government and by the public, underlies our American jurisprudence.... While, in a large sense, constitutional questions may not be considered as finally settled, unless settled rightly, it is certain that a departure by this court from a settled course of decisions on grave constitutional questions, under which vast transactions have occurred, and under which the government has been administered during great crises, will shake public confidence in the stability of the law.

....

In my judgment—to say nothing of the disregard of the former adjudications of this court, and of the settled practice of the government—this decision may well excite the gravest apprehensions. It strikes at the very foundations of national authority, in that it denies to the general government a power which is, or may become, vital to the very existence and preservation of the Union in a national emergency, such as that of war with a great commercial nation, during which the collection of all duties upon imports will cease or be materially diminished. It tends to reestablish that condition of helplessness in which Congress found itself during the period of the Articles of Confederation.

...If this new theory of the Constitution, as I believe it to be, if this new departure from the safe way marked out by the fathers and so long followed by this court, is justified by the fundamental law, the American people cannot too soon amend their Constitution.

...

...The vast powers committed to the present government may be abused, and taxes may be imposed by Congress which the public necessities do not in fact require, or which may be forbidden by a wise policy. But the remedy for such abuses is to be found at the ballot-box, and in a wholesome public opinion which the representatives of the people will not long, if at all, disregard, and not in the disregard by the judiciary of powers that have been committed to another branch of the government.

...

I cannot assent to an interpretation of the Constitution that impairs and cripples the just powers of the National Government in the essential matter of taxation, and at the same time discriminates against the greater part of the people of our country.

JUSTICE BROWN, dissenting.

....

...It is difficult to overestimate the importance of these cases. I certainly cannot overstate the regret I feel at the disposition made of them by the court. It is never a light thing to set aside the deliberate will of the legislature, and in my opinion it should never be done, except upon the clearest proof of its conflict with the fundamental law....

....

As I cannot escape the conviction that the decision of the court in this great case is fraught with immeasurable danger to the future of the country, and that it approaches the proportions of a national calamity, I feel it a duty to enter my protest against it.

JUSTICE JACKSON, dissenting.

....

It seems to me the court in this case adopts a wrong method of arriving at the true meaning of the words "direct tax" as employed in the Constitution. It attaches too much weight and importance to detached expressions of individuals and writers on political economy, made subsequent to the adoption of the Constitution....

...

...The framers of the Constitution proceeded upon the theory entertained by all political writers of that day, that there was some relation, more or less direct, between population and land. But there is no connection, direct or proximate, between rents of land and incomes of personalty and population—none whatever. They did not have any relation to each other at the time the Constitution was adopted, nor have they ever had since, and perhaps never will have.

...Again, we cannot attribute to the framers of the Constitution an intention to make any tax a direct tax which it was impossible to apportion. If it cannot be apportioned without gross injustice, we may feel assured that it is a tax never contemplated by the Constitution as a direct tax. No tax, therefore, can be regarded as a direct tax, in the sense of that instrument, which is incapable of apportionment by the rule of numbers.

...

...Considered in all its bearings, this decision is, in my judgment, the most disastrous blow ever struck at the constitutional power of Congress. It strikes down an important portion of the most vital and essential power of the government in practically excluding any recourse to incomes from real and personal estate for the purpose of raising needed revenue to meet the government's wants and necessities under any circumstances.

I am therefore compelled to enter my dissent to the judgment of the court.

JUSTICE WHITE, dissenting.

...

Bailey v. Drexel Furniture Company ["The Child Labor Tax Case"], 259 U.S. 20 (1922)

After Hammer v. Dagenhart (1918), *reformers looked for a new approach to winning a federal ban on child labor. The result was the 1919 Child Labor Tax Law, which imposed an excise tax equivalent to 10 percent of net profits on any business employing child labor, but excused employers who could demonstrate that they did not know the age of the minor employee, and authorized the recently created Department of Labor to conduct inspections of a wide variety of businesses that might employ child labor. Drexel Furniture Company of North Carolina was charged such a tax for employing a boy under the age of fourteen in its factory. Drexel Furniture sued to recover the tax, arguing that the federal statute was unconstitutional. There were some precedents to support the claim that Congress' taxing power was broader than its regulatory authority under the commerce clause. For example, in* McCray v. U.S. (1904) *the Court upheld a tax on oleomargarine that was designed to make the product noncompetitive with butter. Would the Court be more accommodating of this strategy for addressing child labor? Keep in mind that the act was passed by the lame-duck Sixty-Fifth Congress. By the time the Court heard the case, the Democrats had lost control of not only Congress but also the presidency. The Court's opinion was written by former Republican president William Howard Taft, over the dissent of just one justice, who chose not to write an opinion. Three of the dissenters from* Dagenhart, *including the great Progressives Oliver Wendell Holmes and Louis Brandeis, joined the majority in the tax case.*

CHIEF JUSTICE TAFT delivered the opinion of the Court.

...

The law is attacked on the ground that it is a regulation of the employment of child labor in the States—an exclusively state function under the Federal Constitution and within the reservations of the Tenth Amendment. It is defended on the ground that it is a mere excise tax levied by the Congress of the United States under its broad power of taxation conferred by Section 8, Article I, of the Federal Constitution. We must construe the law and interpret the intent and meaning of Congress from the language of the act. The words are to be given their ordinary meaning unless the context shows that they are differently used. Does this law impose a tax with only that incidental restraint and regulation which a tax must inevitably involve? Or does it regulate by the use of the so-called tax as a penalty?...[A] court must be blind not to see that the so-called tax is imposed to stop the employment of children within the age limits prescribed. Its prohibitory and regulatory effect and purpose are palpable. All others can see and understand this. How can we properly shut our minds to it?

It is the high duty and function of this court in cases regularly brought to its bar to decline to recognize or enforce seeming laws of Congress, dealing with subjects not entrusted to Congress but left or committed by the supreme law of the land to the control of the States....

Out of a proper respect for the acts of a coordinate branch of the Government, this court has gone far to sustain taxing acts as such, even though there has been ground for suspecting from the weight of the tax it was intended to destroy its subject. But, in the act before us, the presumption of validity cannot prevail, because the proof of the contrary is found on the very face of its provisions. Grant the validity of this law, and all that Congress would need to do, hereafter, in seeking to take over to its control and one of the great number of subjects of public interest, jurisdiction of which the States have never parted with, and which are reserved to them by the Tenth Amendment, would be to enact a detailed measure of complete regulation of the subject and enforce it by a so-called tax upon departures from it. To give such magic to the word "tax" would be to break down all constitutional limitation of the powers of Congress and completely wipe out the sovereignty of the States.

The difference between a tax and a penalty is sometimes difficult to define and yet the consequences of the distinction in the required method of their collection often are important.... [T]here comes a time in the extension of the penalizing features of the so-called tax when it loses its character as such and becomes a mere penalty with the characteristics of regulation and punishment. Such is the case in the law before us....

The case before us cannot be distinguished from that of *Hammer v. Dagenhart* (1918)....Congress there enacted a law to prohibit transportation in interstate commerce of goods made at a factory in which there was employment of children within the same ages and for the same number of hours a day and days in a week as are penalized by the act in this case. This court held the law in that case to be void....

...

But it is pressed upon us that this court has gone so far in sustaining taxing measures the effect or tendency of which was to accomplish purposes not directly within congressional power that we are bound by authority to maintain this law.

...

The next case is that of *McCray v. United States* (1904)....It was the same principle as that applied in the *Veazie Bank Case* (1869). This was that Congress in selecting its subjects for taxation might impose the burden where and as it would and that a motive disclosed in its selection to discourage sale or manufacture of an article by a higher tax than on some other did not invalidate the tax. In neither of these cases did the law objected to show on its face as does the law before us the detailed specifications of a regulation of a state concern and business with a heavy exaction to promote the efficacy of such regulation.

...

The court said that the act could not be declared invalid just because another motive than taxation, not shown on the face of the act, might have contributed to its passage. This case does not militate against the conclusion we have reached in respect of the law now before us. The court, there, made manifest its view that the provisions of the so-called taxing act must be naturally and reasonably adapted to the collection of the tax and not solely to the achievement of some other purpose plainly within state power.

For the reasons given, we must hold the Child Labor Tax Law invalid and the judgment of the District Court is *Affirmed*.

JUSTICE CLARKE, dissenting.

D. Treaty Power

The federal power to enter into treaties with foreign nations has not received a great deal of attention from the Supreme Court. One of the difficult questions posed by the treaty power, especially for American constitutionalism as it existed in the nineteenth and early twentieth centuries, was whether the federal government could do things through the treaty power that they could not do through other enumerated powers. In particular, could the president and the Senate acting together negotiate and ratify a treaty that regulated the internal affairs of the country in ways that Congress could not otherwise regulate through normal legislation? Or was the treaty power implicitly limited by other features of the Constitution, such as federal structure and the reserved powers of the states?

The issue came to a head in *Missouri v. Holland* (1920), when the Court heard a case arising out of a lengthy effort to create national hunting regulations. Traditionally, the states had presumptive constitutional authority to regulate game hunting within their borders. The Woodrow Wilson administration sought a way around the states by negotiating a treaty with Canada that empowered the Department of Agriculture to regulate bird hunting. In writing the decision upholding the federal government, Justice Oliver Wendell Holmes, Jr., made a classic defense of a living Constitution that grew and adapted to the changing needs of the times.

Missouri v. Holland, 252 U.S. 416 (1920)

*Since the late nineteenth century, conservationists had lobbied the states to regulate game hunting, winning a U.S. Supreme Court case recognizing the constitutional power of the states to prohibit hunters from taking their game out of state on the theory that wild game was the common property of the citizens of the state in which they were found and could be regulated by the state government for the benefit of its own citizens (*Geer v. Connecticut *[1896]). But by the early twentieth century, conservationists had tired of wrestling with holdout states that favored hunters, and they turned to the federal government to trump them. Early bills to impose national restrictions on bird hunting went nowhere in Congress, but supporters of the regulation were* *able to attach such a measure as an amendment to an Agriculture Department appropriations bill in 1912. The provision was immediately challenged in court, and a federal district court judge in Arkansas held it to be an unconstitutional infringement on states' rights. Fearing that it would likely lose the case in the U.S. Supreme Court, the Woodrow Wilson administration moved to create a new constitutional basis for the rule. It approached the Canadian government about the possibility of negotiating a treaty that would empower Congress to regulate migratory birds.*

In 1916, the United States and Great Britain completed a treaty committing each nation to regulating the hunting of birds that migrated between the United States and Canada. (Great Britain still had official authority over Canada.) Congress was reluctant, but in 1918, on the basis of the treaty, it passed the Migratory Bird Treaty Act. This empowered the Secretary of Agriculture to create a national hunting season for such birds and made the violation of those regulations a federal crime. In most of the United States, states changed their own policies to match the new federal restrictions, and state game wardens cooperated with the relatively few federal game wardens to enforce the laws. But cooperation was not universal, and many hunters flouted the federal laws in the Midwest and the South.

Missouri attorney general Frank McAllister was among those who opposed the federal limitations on hunting. When federal game warden Ray Holland received a tip that McAllister was going with friends on an out-of-season hunt, Holland was eager to set an example. He arrested McAllister (who had bagged seventy-six ducks), resulting in a fine. McAllister responded by having the state file suit in U.S. district court to prevent Holland from enforcing the federal regulations, which were in conflict with both the state's own hunting laws and the state's traditional property rights to wild game within its borders. The district court upheld the federal act, concluding that the regulation of migratory birds was not "remote" from the natural subject matter of international treaties and could be seen as benefiting "all the states." Missouri appealed to the U.S. Supreme Court.

The Supreme Court's opinion upholding the ruling of the district court and the Migratory Bird Treaty Act is famous for its broad reading of the federal treaty power as a source of congressional authority in domestic affairs that supplemented the powers enumerated in Article I, Section 8, of the Constitution. The decision came in the immediate aftermath of World War I and the debates over American involvement in the League of Nations. It was handed down just a few months before Warren G. Harding won the presidency and returned the federal government to the Republican Party calling for a return to "normalcy," which meant in part the demobilization of the military and a withdrawal of the United States from European affairs. Others, with some success, would urge American "isolationism" from the international economic and diplomatic arena. The Supreme Court was not going to force that choice. Instead, it gave a free hand to Congress and the president to take the actions that they thought were in the national interest, even if those actions trenched on the traditional authority of the states to regulate persons and property within their borders.

The opinion by Justice Oliver Wendell Holmes, Jr., in this case is also famous for its bold declaration of the philosophy of a living Constitution, an "organism" that could grow beyond the expectations of those who drafted it. Even before joining the Court, Holmes was a leading advocate of a "realistic" view of the law. In keeping with the evolutionary theories that were prominent in his day and as likely to be applied to social phenomenon (i.e., "Social Darwinism") as biological ones, Holmes argued that law did not embody timeless principles faithfully handed down from ancient sources but instead reflected the changing needs of contemporary society. As you read the opinion consider whether he could have reached the same conclusion without relying on the metaphor of the living Constitution.

JUSTICE HOLMES delivered the opinion of the Court.

...

To answer this question it is not enough to refer to the Tenth Amendment, reserving the powers not delegated to the United States, because by Article II, Section 2, the power to make treaties is delegated expressly, and by Article VI treaties made under the authority of the United States, along with the Constitution and laws of the United States made in pursuance thereof, are declared the supreme law of the land. If the treaty is valid there can be no dispute about the validity of the statute under Article I, Section 8, as a necessary and proper means to execute the powers of the Government. The language of the Constitution as to the supremacy of treaties being general, the question before us is narrowed to an inquiry into the ground upon which the present supposed exception is placed.

It is said that a treaty cannot be valid if it infringes the Constitution, that there are limits, therefore, to the treaty-making power, and that one such limit is that what an act of Congress could not do unaided, in derogation of the powers reserved to the States, a treaty cannot do. An earlier act of Congress that attempted by itself and not in pursuance of a treaty to regulate the killing of migratory birds within the States had been held bad in the District Court.... Those decisions were supported by arguments that migratory birds were owned by the States in their sovereign capacity for the benefit of their people, and that under cases like *Geer v. Connecticut* (1896), this control was one that Congress had no power to displace. The same argument is supposed to apply now with equal force.

...Acts of Congress are the supreme law of the land only when made in pursuance of the Constitution, while treaties are declared to be so when made under the authority of the United States. It is open to question whether the authority of the United States means more than the formal acts prescribed to make the convention. We do not mean to imply that there are no qualifications to the treaty-making power; but they must be ascertained in a different way. It is obvious that there may be matters of the sharpest exigency for the national well being that an act of Congress could not deal with but that a treaty followed by such an act could, and it is not lightly to be assumed that, in matters requiring national action, "a power which must belong to and somewhere reside in every civilized government" is not to be found.... [W]hen we are dealing with words that also are a constituent act, like the Constitution of the United States, we must realize that they have called into life a being the development of which could not have been foreseen completely by the most gifted of its begetters. It was enough for them to realize or to hope that they had created an organism; it has taken a century and has cost their successors much sweat and blood to prove that they created a nation. The case before us must be considered in the light of our whole experience and not merely in that of what was said a hundred years ago. The treaty in question does not contravene any prohibitory words to be found in the Constitution. The only question is whether it is forbidden by some invisible radiation from the general terms of the Tenth Amendment. We must consider what this country has become in deciding what that Amendment has reserved.

The State as we have intimated founds its claim of exclusive authority upon an assertion of title to migratory birds, an assertion that is embodied in statute. No doubt it is true that as between a State and its inhabitants the State may regulate the killing and sale of such birds, but it does not follow that its authority is exclusive of paramount powers. To put the claim of the State upon title is to lean upon a slender reed. Wild birds are not in the possession of anyone; and possession is the beginning of ownership. The whole foundation of the State's rights is the presence within their jurisdiction of birds that yesterday had not arrived, tomorrow may be in another State and in a week a thousand miles away. If we are to be accurate we cannot put the case of the State upon higher ground than that the treaty deals with creatures that for the moment are within the state borders, that it must be carried out by officers of the United States within the same territory, and that but for the treaty the State would be free to regulate this subject itself.

As most of the laws of the United States are carried out within the States and as many of them deal with matters which in the silence of such laws the State might regulate, such general grounds are not enough to support Missouri's claim. Valid treaties of course "are as binding within the territorial limits of the States as they are elsewhere throughout the dominion of the United States."... No doubt the great body of private relations usually fall within the control of the State, but a treaty may override its power. We do not have to invoke the later developments of constitution law for this proposition; it was recognized as early as *Hopkirk v. Bell* (1806), with regard to statutes of limitation, and even earlier, as to confiscation, in *Ware v. Hylton* (1796)....

Here a national interest of very nearly the first magnitude is involved. It can be protected only by national action in concert with that of another power. The subject-matter is only transitorily within the State and has no permanent habitat therein. But for the treaty and the statute there soon might be no birds for any powers to deal with. We see nothing in the Constitution that compels the Government to sit by while a food supply is cut off and the protectors of our forests and our crops are destroyed. It is not sufficient to rely upon the States. The reliance is vain, and were it otherwise, the question is whether the United States is forbidden to act. We are of opinion that the treaty and statute must be upheld.

Decree affirmed.

JUSTICE VAN DEVANTER and JUSTICE PITNEY dissent without an opinion

E. Necessary and Proper Clause

In the post–Civil War period, the Court and commentators gave less attention to the necessary and proper clause than they had in the Jacksonian Era. Key constitutional debates focused on more specific provisions, such as the commerce clause or the taxing provisions, rather than the "sweeping" clause that had provoked such controversy since *McCulloch v. Maryland* (1819). But the necessary and proper clause continued to play a supplemental role in the constitutional arguments of the period, and the *Selective Draft Law Cases* (1918) are a prime example. When the federal government imposed a military draft during World War I, the question of its constitutionality finally reached the Supreme Court. The key enumerated power at issue was the congressional power "to raise and support armies." There was little question that Congress was empowered to put armies in the field. The question is what specific means are included within that enumerated power to "raise and support" a military force. What does "raise and support" mean, and does it include the specific choice to use a draft? Are there limits on how a draft might be structured? The tandem of the specific enumerated power and the general necessary and proper clause provided the starting point for considering how Congress goes about fulfilling its constitutional responsibilities, and how the menu of choices that Congress faces might be shaped by other constitutional features, such as the structure of the federal union or the rights of individuals.

Selective Draft Law Cases (Arver et al. v. U.S.), 245 U.S. 366 (1918)

The federal government's authority to draft citizens for military duty was not tested until after passage of the Selective Service Act of 1917. World War I was not the first time that Congress imposed a military draft, but it was the first time that the Supreme Court heard a constitutional challenge to the congressional power to adopt such a law. The law authorized the president to call to military duty all male citizens between the ages of twenty-one and thirty, and it authorized the president to create local draft boards to register those eligible for the draft and consider claims of possible exemption from service. The statute provided for a number of exemptions, but those who had religious objections to engaging in war were still subject to the draft and assignment to noncombat duties. Those who were convicted of violating the act challenged its constitutionality on a variety of grounds, including the Thirteenth Amendment's prohibition against involuntary servitude. They also challenged whether the power to compel military service was among the delegated powers of Congress, as well as whether the state militias alone had the power to compel military service. The justices wasted no time upholding law with a unanimous opinion delivered by the Chief Justice. As you read the opinion consider how the Court's opinion can be reconciled with the framers' concerns about "standing armies."

CHIEF JUSTICE WHITE delivered the opinion of the Court.

. . .

The possession of authority to enact the statute must be found in the clauses of the Constitution giving Congress power "to declare war;... to raise and support armies, but no appropriation of money to that use shall be for a longer term than two years;... to make rules for the government and regulation of the land and naval forces." Article I, Section 8. And of course the powers conferred by these provisions like all other powers given carry with them as provided by the Constitution the authority "to make all laws which shall be necessary and proper for carrying into execution the foregoing powers." Article I, Section 8.

As the mind cannot conceive an army without the men to compose it, on the face of the Constitution the objection that it does not give power to provide for such men would seem to be too frivolous for further notice. It is said, however, that since under the Constitution as originally framed state citizenship was primary and United States citizenship but derivative and dependent thereon, therefore the power conferred upon Congress to raise armies was only coterminous with United States citizenship and could not be exerted so as to cause that citizenship to lose its dependent character and dominate state citizenship. But the proposition simply denies to Congress the power to raise armies which the Constitution gives. That power by the very terms of the Constitution, being delegated, is supreme.... It is argued, however, that although this is abstractly true, it is not concretely so because as compelled military service is repugnant to a free government and in conflict with all the great guarantees of the Constitution as to individual liberty, it must be assumed that the authority to raise armies was intended to be limited to the right to call an army into existence counting alone upon the willingness of the citizen to do his duty in time of public need, that is, in time of war. But the premise of this proposition is so devoid of foundation that it leaves not even a shadow of ground upon which to base the conclusion....

When the Constitution came to be formed it may not be disputed that one of the recognized necessities for its adoption was the want of power in Congress to raise an army and the dependence upon the states for their quotas....

...[It is contended] that although it be within the power to call the citizen into the army without his consent, the army into which he enters after the call is to be limited in some respects to services for which the militia it is assumed may only be used.... The fallacy of the argument results from confounding the constitutional provisions concerning the militia with that conferring upon Congress the power to raise armies. It treats them as one while they are different. This is the militia clause:

> The Congress shall have power:... To provide for calling for the militia to execute the laws of the nation, suppress insurrections and repel invasions; to provide for organizing, arming and disciplining the militia, and for governing such part of them as may be employed in the service of the United States, reserving to the states, respectively, the appointment of the officers, and the authority of training the militia according to the discipline prescribed by Congress. Article I, Section 8.

The line which separates it from the army power is not only inherently plainly marked by the text of the two clauses, but will stand out in bolder relief by considering the condition before the Constitution was adopted and the remedy which it provided for the military situation with which it dealt. The right on the one hand of Congress under the Confederation to call on the states for forces and the duty on the other of the states to furnish when called, embraced the complete power of government over the subject. When the two were combined and were delegated to Congress all governmental power on that subject was conferred, a result manifested not only by the grant made but by the limitation expressly put upon the states on the subject. The army sphere therefore embraces such complete authority. But the duty of exerting the power thus conferred in all its plenitude was not made at once obligatory but was wisely left to depend upon the discretion of Congress as to the arising of the exigencies which would call it in part or in whole into play....

And upon this understanding of the two powers the legislative and executive authority has been exerted from the beginning. From the act of the first session of Congress carrying over the army of the government under the Confederation to the United States under the Constitution... down to 1812 the authority to raise armies was regularly exerted as a distinct and substantive power, the force being raised and recruited by enlistment....

So the course of legislation from that date to 1861 affords no ground for any other than the same conception of legislative power which we have already stated.... [I]t soon became manifest that more men were required [than the initial volunteer force]. As a result the Act of March 3, 1863 was adopted entitled "An act for enrolling and calling out the national forces and for other purposes." By that act which was clearly intended to directly exert upon all the citizens of the United States the national power which it had been proposed to exert in 1814 on the recommendation of the then Secretary of War, Mr. Monroe, every male citizen of the United States between the ages of 20 and 45 was made subject by the direct action of Congress to be called by compulsory draft to service in a national army at such time and in such numbers as the President in his discretion might find necessary.... It would be childish to deny the value of the added strength which was thus afforded. Indeed in the official report of the Provost Marshal General, just previously referred to in the margin, reviewing the whole subject it was stated that it was the efficient aid resulting from the forces created by the draft at a very critical moment of the civil strife which obviated a disaster which seemed impending and carried that struggle to a complete and successful conclusion.

Brevity prevents doing more than to call attention to the fact that the organized body of militia within the states as trained by the states under the direction of Congress became known as the National Guard. Act of January 21, 1903...

...

Finally, as we are unable to conceive upon what theory the exaction by government from the citizen of the performance of his supreme and noble duty of contributing to the defense of the rights and honor of the nation as the result of a war declared by the great representative body of the people can be said to be the imposition of involuntary servitude in violation of the prohibitions of the Thirteenth Amendment, we are constrained to the conclusion that the contention to that effect is refuted by its mere statement.

Affirmed.

F. Territorial Acquisition and Governance

After the Civil War, the territorial expansion of the United States took on a different character. Wars with neighboring powers such as Mexico or British Canada had either been fought or averted. Manifest Destiny had been accomplished. The primary borders of the country had been fixed. Over the course of the late nineteenth and early twentieth centuries, Congress continued to debate when and how to admit western territories into the Union as states, but there was little question that eventually the West would be settled and become part of the United States just as the territory along the Mississippi River had.

The constitutionally more complicated situation arose outside the boundaries of the continental United States. The Spanish-American War at the end of the nineteenth century made the United States into a global empire with foreign territories. Some of those territories, such as the Philippines, were not expected to remain in American possession for long. Others, such as Puerto Rico, were likely to remain in American possession—but were not likely to be candidates for statehood any time soon. With peace established, what was the status of those territories and how were they to be governed? Were they foreign spaces to be controlled by a different set of rules, or were they part of the United States subject to the same rules as applied to any other territory? The decision would not only have implications for military policy, local governance, and potential independence of those territories, but it would also have immediate implications for tax and trade policy. Neither the country nor the Court could come to very satisfying conclusions.

Insular Cases [Downes v. Bidwell, 182 U.S. 244 (1901)]

From the beginning of the Republic there was a strong shared conviction that the United States of America faced west and that it was inevitable that it would expand across the continent. By 1845 this sentiment found expression in the claim of journalist John O'Sullivan that it "is by the right of our manifest destiny to overspread and to possess the whole of the continent which Providence has given us for the development of the great experiment of liberty and federated self-government entrusted to us."[25] *However, in 1890 the official report of the U.S. Census declared that there was no longer an American frontier—after a century the continent had been settled. In the wake of this finding, some (including future president Theodore Roosevelt) began to argue that the future of American expansion would be overseas—and, in fact, the United States soon embarked upon a period of overseas territorial acquisition. Hawaii was annexed in 1898 by a simple congressional resolution rather than a treaty of cession or conquest (as is usually required by international law). That same year, the Treaty of Paris, which ended the Spanish–American War, acknowledged American control over the Philippines, Puerto Rico, and Guam. Unlike the conquest of the continent, these territories had extensive populations of non-white people who could not be displaced or relocated.*

The acquisition of these island-related, or insular, territories triggered an important debate over whether the protections and guarantees of the Constitution applied in these settings. In the language of the day, people argued over whether "the Constitution follows the flag." For example, if these territories were considered part of the United States, then Congress could not impose tariffs on the importation of goods from these places because the tariff power only applied to "foreign" countries. More fundamentally, did the provisions of the Bill of Rights apply to these territories or was it acceptable to approach these areas as occupied foreign lands, controlled by the United States but not part of the United States? Dred Scott, *among other antebellum cases, had made clear that the Constitution did apply to territories, and that conclusion had not been repudiated during the Civil War. Influencing all of these debates were assumptions about what it meant to be an American, and these assumptions were widely shaped by notions of racial and cultural superiority. For many, the view that the Constitution should not follow the flag was premised on the belief that the people in these territories were not "fit" for the blessings of liberty and self-government.*

The Court addressed these issues in a series of thirty-five cases starting in 1901 that, collectively, became known as The Insular Cases. *The most important early case was* Downes v. Bidwell. *By a 5–4 vote, the Court concluded that Congress could impose duties on goods imported from Puerto Rico; however, the justices could not agree on a rationale. Justice Brown issued a "statement" announcing the decision of the Court. Must it be true, in the words of one of the justices, that "whether savages or civilized" the people of these territories are "entitled to all the rights, privileges, and immunities of citizens"? Should we take comfort in the view that, even without constitutional protections, these people have nothing to fear because "there are certain principles of natural justice inherent in the Anglo-Saxon character, which need no expression in constitutions or statutes to give them effect or to secure depen-*

25. Quoted in Paul Kens, "A Promise of Expansion," in *The Louisiana Purchase and American Expansion, 1803–1898*, eds. Sanford Levinson and Bartholomew H. Sparrow (Lanham, MD: Rowman & Littlefield, 2005), 139.

dencies against legislation manifestly hostile to their real interests"? A range of competing views is outlined in the following reading. As you consider who has the strongest case do not be influenced by the knowledge that years later, in Balzac v. Puerto Rico *(1922), the justices unanimously embraced the approach suggested by Justice White. Is it fair to say that these decisions help facilitate policies of American imperialism? The legacy of these decisions reverberates in more modern debates about the relationship of territories such as Guantanamo Bay to the American constitutional tradition. The Court's decision led Chicago editor Finley Dunne to quip, "No matter whether the country follows the flag or not, the Supreme Court follows the election returns."*

Statement by JUSTICE BROWN:

...The case also involves the broader question whether the revenue clauses of the Constitution extend of their own force to our newly acquired territories. The Constitution itself does not answer the question. Its solution must be found in the nature of the government created by that instrument, in the opinion of its contemporaries, in the practical construction put upon it by Congress, and in the decisions of this court.

...[A] new Constitution was formed in 1787 by "the people of the United States" "for the United States of America," as its preamble declares. All legislative powers were vested in a Congress consisting of representatives from the several states, but no provision was made for the admission of delegates from the territories, and no mention was made of territories as separate portions of the Union, except that Congress was empowered "to dispose of and make all needful rules and regulations respecting the territory or other property belonging to the United States."...

...[I]t can nowhere be inferred that the territories were considered a part of the United States. The Constitution was created by the people of the United States, as a union of states, to be governed solely by representatives of the states;...In short, the Constitution deals with states, their people, and their representatives.

The Thirteenth Amendment to the Constitution, prohibiting slavery and involuntary servitude "within the United States, or in any place subject to their jurisdiction," is also significant as showing that there may be places within the jurisdiction of the United States that are no part of the Union....

Upon the other hand, the Fourteenth Amendment, upon the subject of citizenship, declares only that "all persons born or naturalized in the United States, and subject to the jurisdiction thereof, are citizens of the United States, and of the state wherein they reside." Here there is a limitation to persons born or naturalized in the United States, which is not extended to persons born in any place "subject to their jurisdiction."

The question of the legal relations between the states and the newly acquired territories first became the subject of public discussion in connection with the purchase of Louisiana in 1803....[The treaty] evidently committed the government to the ultimate, but not to the immediate, admission of Louisiana as a state, and postponed its incorporation into the Union to the pleasure of Congress. In regard to this, Mr. Jefferson, in a letter to Senator Breckinridge of Kentucky, of August 12, 1803, used the following language: "This treaty must, of course, be laid before both Houses, because both have important functions to exercise respecting it....The Constitution has made no provision for holding foreign territory, still less for incorporating foreign nations into our Union. The Executive, in seizing the fugitive occurrence which so much advances the good of our country, have done an act beyond the Constitution."

...

...[The] statutes [eventually passed by Congress] may be taken as expressing the views of Congress, first, that territory may be lawfully acquired by treaty, with a provision for its ultimate incorporation into the Union; and, second, that a discrimination in favor of certain foreign vessels trading with the ports of a newly acquired territory is no violation of that clause of the Constitution (Article I, Section 9) that declares that no preference shall be given to the ports of one state over those of another. It is evident that the constitutionality of this discrimination can only be supported upon the theory that ports of territories are not ports of state within the meaning of the Constitution....

So, too, in the act annexing the Republic of Hawaii, there was a provision continuing in effect the customs relations of the Hawaiian islands with the United States and other countries, the effect of which was to compel the collection in those islands of a duty upon certain articles, whether coming from the United States or other countries, much greater than the duty provided by the general tariff law then in force....

The very treaty with Spain under discussion in this case contains similar discriminative provisions, which are apparently irreconcilable with the Constitution, if that instrument be held to extend to these islands immediately upon their cession to the United States....

The researches of counsel have collated a large number of other instances in which Congress has in its enactments recognized the fact that provisions intended for the states did not embrace the territories, unless specially mentioned....

The decisions of this court upon this subject have not been altogether harmonious. Some of them are based upon the theory that the Constitution does not apply to the territories without legislation. Other cases, arising from territories where such legislation has been had, contain language which would justify the inference that such legislation was unnecessary, and that the Constitution took effect immediately upon the cession of the territory to the United States....

...

Eliminating, then, from the opinions of this court all expressions unnecessary to the disposition of the particular case, and gleaning therefrom the exact point decided in each, the following propositions may be considered as established:

1. That the District of Columbia and the territories are not states within the judicial clause of the Constitution giving jurisdiction in cases between citizens of different states;
2. That territories are not states within the meaning of Rev. Stat. 709, permitting writs of error from this court in cases where the validity of a state statute is drawn in question;
3. That the District of Columbia and the territories are states as that word is used in treaties with foreign powers, with respect to the ownership, disposition, and inheritance of property;
4. That the territories are not within the clause of the Constitution providing for the creation of a supreme court and such inferior courts as Congress may see fit to establish;
5. That the Constitution does not apply to foreign countries or to trials therein conducted, and that Congress may lawfully provide for such trials before consular tribunals, without the intervention of a grand or petit jury;
6. That where the Constitution has been once formally extended by Congress to territories, neither Congress nor the territorial legislature can enact laws inconsistent therewith.

...

Indeed, the practical interpretation put by Congress upon the Constitution has been long continued and uniform to the effect that the Constitution is applicable to territories acquired by purchase or conquest, only when and so far as Congress shall so direct....

We are also of opinion that the power to acquire territory by treaty implies, not only the power to govern such territory, but to prescribe upon what terms the United States will receive its inhabitants, and what their status shall be in what Chief Justice Marshall termed the "American empire." There seems to be no middle ground between this position and the doctrine that if their inhabitants do not become, immediately upon annexation, citizens of the United States, their children thereafter born, whether savages or civilized, are such, and entitled to all the rights, privileges and immunities of citizens. If such be their status, the consequences will be extremely serious. Indeed, it is doubtful if Congress would ever assent to the annexation of territory upon the condition that its inhabitants, however foreign they may be to our habits, traditions, and modes of life, shall become at once citizens of the United States. In all its treaties hitherto the treaty-making power has made special provision for this subject....In all these cases there is an implied denial of the right of the inhabitants to American citizenship until Congress by further action shall signify its assent thereto.

Grave apprehensions of danger are felt by many eminent men,—a fear lest an unrestrained possession of power on the part of Congress may lead to unjust and oppressive legislation in which the natural rights of territories, or their inhabitants, may be engulfed in a centralized despotism. These fears, however, find no justification in the action of Congress in the past century, nor in the conduct of the British Parliament towards its outlying possessions since the American Revolution. Indeed, in the only instance in which this court has declared an act of Congress unconstitutional as trespassing upon the rights of territories (the Missouri Compromise), such action was dictated by motives of humanity and justice, and so far commanded popular approval as to be embodied in the Thirteenth Amendment to the Constitution. There are certain principles of natural justice inherent in the Anglo-Saxon character, which need no expression in constitutions or statutes to give them effect or to secure dependencies against legislation manifestly hostile to their real interests....

...

It is obvious that in the annexation of outlying and distant possessions grave questions will arise from differences of race, habits, laws, and customs of the people, and from differences of soil, climate, and production, which may require action on the part of Congress that would be quite unnecessary in the annexation of contiguous territory inhabited only by people of the same race, or by scattered bodies of native Indians.

We suggest, without intending to decide, that there may be a distinction between certain natural rights enforced in the Constitution by prohibitions against interference with them, and what may be termed artificial or remedial rights which are peculiar to our own system of jurisprudence. Of the former class are the rights to one's own religious opinions and to a public expression of them, or, as sometimes said, to worship God according to the dictates of one's own conscience; the right to personal liberty and individual property; to freedom of speech and of the press; to free access to courts of justice, to due process of law, and to an equal protection of the laws; to immunities from unreasonable searches and seizures, as well as cruel and unusual punishments; and to such other immunities as are in-dispensable to a free government. Of the latter class are the rights to citizenship, to suffrage, and to the particular methods of procedure pointed out in the Constitution, which are peculiar to Anglo-Saxon jurisprudence, and some of which have already been held by the states to be unnecessary to the proper protection of individuals.

Whatever may be finally decided by the American people as to the status of these islands and their inhabitants,—whether they shall be introduced into the sisterhood of states or be permitted to form independent governments,—it does not follow that in the meantime, a waiting that decision, the people are in the matter of personal rights unprotected by the provisions of our Constitution and subject to the merely arbitrary control of Congress. Even if regarded as aliens, they are entitled under the principles of the Constitution to be protected in life, liberty, and property....We do not desire, however, to anticipate the difficulties which would naturally arise in this connection, but merely to disclaim any intention to hold that the inhabitants of these territories are subject to an unrestrained power on the part of Congress to deal with them upon the theory that they have no rights which it is bound to respect.

...

...A false step at this time might be fatal to the development of what Chief Justice Marshall called the American empire. Choice in some cases, the natural gravitation of small bodies towards large ones in others, the result of a successful war in still others, may bring about conditions which would render the annexation of distant possessions desirable. If those possessions are inhabited by alien races, differing from us in religion, customs, laws, methods of taxation, and modes of thought, the administration of government and justice, according to Anglo-Saxon principles, may for a time be impossible; and the question at once arises whether large concessions ought not to be made for a time, that ultimately our own theories may be carried out, and the blessings of a free government under the Constitution extended to them. We decline to hold that there is anything in the Constitution to forbid such action.

We are therefore of opinion that the island of Porto Rico is a territory appurtenant and belonging to the United States, but not a part of the United States within the revenue clauses of the Constitution; that the Foraker act is constitutional, so far as it imposes duties upon imports from such island, and that the plaintiff cannot recover back the duties exacted in this case.

The judgment of the Circuit Court is therefore *affirmed*.

JUSTICE WHITE, with whom concurred JUSTICE SHIRAS and JUSTICE MCKENNA, uniting in the judgment of affirmance:

...

The sole and only issue, then, is not whether Congress has taxed Porto Rico without representation,—for, whether the tax was local or national, it could have been imposed although Porto Rico had no representative local government and was not represented in Congress,—but is whether the particular tax in question was levied in such form as to cause it to be repugnant to the Constitution. This is to be resolved by answering the inquiry, Had Porto Rico, at the time of the passage of the act in question, been incorporated into and become an integral part of the United States?

...

While no particular provision of the Constitution is referred to, to sustain the argument that it is impossible to acquire territory by treaty without immediate and absolute incorporation, it is said that the spirit of the Constitution excludes the conception of property or dependencies possessed by the United States and which are not so completely incorporated as to be in all respects a part of the United States; that the theory upon which the Constitution proceeds is that of confederated and independent states, and that no territory, therefore, can be acquired which does not contemplate statehood, and excludes the acquisition of any territory which is not in a position to be treated as an integral part of the United States. But this reasoning is based on political, and not judicial, considerations. Conceding that the conception upon which the Constitution proceeds is that no territory, as a general rule, should be acquired unless the territory may reasonably be expected to be worthy of statehood, the determination of when such blessing is to be bestowed is wholly a political question, and the aid of the judiciary cannot be invoked to usurp political discretion in order to save the Constitution from imaginary or even real dangers. The Constitution may not be saved by destroying its fundamental limitations.

...

A practical illustration will at once make the consequences clear. Suppose Congress should determine that the millions of inhabitants of the Philippine islands should not continue appurtenant to the United States, but that they should be allowed to establish an autonomous government, outside of the Constitution of the United States, coupled, however, with such conditions providing for control as far only as essential to the guaranty of life and property and to protect against foreign encroachment. If the proposition of incorporation be well founded, at once the question would arise whether the ability to impose these conditions existed, since no power was conferred by the Constitution to annex conditions which would limit the disposition. And if it be that the question of whether territory is immediately fit for incorporation when it is acquired is a judicial, and not a legislative one, it would follow that the validity of the conditions would also come within the scope of judicial authority, and thus the entire political policy of the government be alone controlled by the judiciary.

...

...[T]he sovereignty of the United States may be extended over foreign territory to remain paramount until, in the discretion of the political department of the government of the United States, it be relinquished. This method, then, of dealing with foreign territory, would in any event be available. Thus, the enthralling of the treaty-making power, which would result from holding that no territory could be acquired by treaty of cession without immediate incorporation, would only result in compelling a resort to the subterfuge of relinquishment of sovereignty, and thus indirection would take the place of directness of action,—a course which would be incompatible with the dignity and honor of the government.

...

JUSTICE GRAY, concurring:

....

The civil government of the United States cannot extend immediately, and of its own force, over territory acquired by war. Such territory must necessarily, in the first instance, be governed by the military power under the control of the President as Commander in Chief.... There must, of necessity, be a transition period.

In a conquered territory, civil government must take effect either by the action of the treaty-making power, or by that of the Congress of the United States. The office of a treaty of cession ordinarily is to put an end to all authority of the foreign government over the territory, and to subject the territory to the disposition of the government of the United States.

...

So long as Congress has not incorporated the territory into the United States, neither military occupation nor cession by treaty makes the conquered territory domestic territory, in the sense of the revenue laws; but those laws concerning "foreign countries" remain applicable to the conquered territory until changed by Congress....

...

The system of duties temporarily established by that act during the transition period was within the authority of Congress under the Constitution of the United States.

CHIEF JUSTICE FULLER, with whom concurred JUSTICE HARLAN, JUSTICE BREWER, and JUSTICE PECKHAM, dissenting:

...

Conceding that the power to tax for the purposes of territorial government is implied from the power to govern territory, whether the latter power is attributed to the power to acquire or the power to make needful rules and regulations, these particular duties are nevertheless not local in their nature, but are imposed as in the exercise of national powers. The levy is clearly a regulation of commerce, and a regulation affecting the states and their people as well as this territory and its people. The power of Congress to act directly on the rights and interests of the people of the states can only exist if and as granted by the Constitution. And by the Constitution Congress is vested with power "to regulate commerce with foreign nations, and among the several states, and with the Indian tribes." The territories are indeed not mentioned by name, and yet commerce between the territories and foreign nations is covered by the clause, which would seem to have been intended to embrace the entire internal as well as foreign commerce of the country.

. . .

The government of the United States is the government ordained by the Constitution, and possesses the powers conferred by the Constitution. "This original and supreme will organizes the government, and assigns to different departments their respective powers. It may either stop here, or establish certain limits not to be transcended by those departments. The government of the United States is of the latter description. The powers of the legislature are defined and limited; and that those limits may not be mistaken or forgotten, the Constitution is written. To what purpose are powers limited, and to what purpose is that limitation committed to writing, if these limits may, at any time, be passed by those intended to be restrained?" *Marbury v. Madison* (1803)...

From *Marbury v. Madison* to the present day, no utterance of this court has intimated a doubt that in its operation on the people, by whom and for whom it was established, the national government is a government of enumerated powers, the exercise of which is restricted to the use of means appropriate and plainly adapted to constitutional ends, and which are "not prohibited, but consist with the letter and spirit of the Constitution."

The powers delegated by the people to their agents are not enlarged by the expansion of the domain within which they are exercised. When the restriction on the exercise of a particular power by a particular agent is ascertained, that is an end of the question.

To hold otherwise is to overthrow the basis of our constitutional law, and moreover, in effect, to reassert the proposition that the states, and not the people, created the government.

. . .

The concurring opinion recognizes the fact that Congress, in dealing with the people of new territories or possessions, is bound to respect the fundamental guaranties of life, liberty, and property, but assumes that Congress is not bound, in those territories or possessions, to follow the rules of taxation prescribed by the Constitution....

That theory assumes that the Constitution created a government empowered to acquire countries throughout the world, to be governed by different rules than those obtaining in the original states and territories, and substitutes for the present system of republican government a system of domination over distant provinces in the exercise of unrestricted power.

. . .

But it must be remembered that, as Marshall and Story declared, the Constitution was framed for ages to come, and that the sagacious men who framed it were well aware that a mighty future waited on their work. The rising sun to which Franklin referred at the close of the convention, they well knew, was that star of empire whose course Berkeley had sung sixty years before.

They may not, indeed, have deliberately considered a triumphal progress of the nation, as such, around the earth, but as Marshall wrote: "It is not enough to say that this particular case was not in the mind of the convention when the article was framed, nor of the American people when it was adopted. It is necessary to go further, and to say that, had this particular case been suggested, the language would have been so varied as to exclude it, or it would have been made a special exception."

This cannot be said, and on the contrary, in order to the successful extension of our institutions, the reasonable presumption is that the limitations on the exertion of arbitrary power would have been made more rigorous.

. . .

Tested by those rules our conviction is that the imposition of these duties cannot be sustained.

JUSTICE HARLAN, dissenting:

I concur in the dissenting opinion of the Chief Justice.... I agree in holding that Porto Rico—at least after the ratification of the treaty with Spain—became a part of the United States within the meaning of the section of the Constitution enumerating the powers of Congress, and providing the "all duties, imposts, and excises shall be uniform throughout the United States."

. . .

. . . I take leave to say that if the principles thus announced [in the statement by Justice Brown] should ever receive the sanction of a majority of this court, a radical and mischievous change in our system of government will be the result. We will, in that event, pass from the era of constitutional liberty guarded and protected by a written constitution into an era of legislative absolutism.

Although from the foundation of the government this court has held steadily to the view that the government of the United States was one of enumerated powers, and that no one of its branches, nor all of its branches combined, could constitutionally exercise powers not granted, or which were not necessarily implied from those expressly granted (*Martin v. Hunter's Lessee* [1816]) we are now informed that Congress possesses powers outside of the Constitution, and may deal with new territory, acquired by treaty or conquest, in the same manner as other nations have been accustomed to act with respect to territories acquired by them. In my opinion, Congress has no existence and can exercise no authority outside of the Constitution. Still less is it true that Congress can deal with new territories just as other nations have done or may do with their new territories. This nation is under the control of a written constitution, the supreme law of the land and the only source of the powers which our government, or any branch or officer of it, may exert at any time or at any place. Monarchical and despotic governments, unrestrained by written constitutions, may do with newly acquired territories what this government may not do consistently with our fundamental law. To say otherwise is to concede that Congress may, by action taken outside of the Constitution, engraft upon our republican institutions a colonial system such as exists under monarchical governments. Surely such a result was never contemplated by the fathers of the Constitution. If that instrument had contained a word suggesting the possibility of a result of that character it would never have been adopted by the people of the United States. The idea that this country may acquire territories anywhere upon the earth, by conquest or treaty, and hold them as mere colonies or provinces,—the people inhabiting them to enjoy only such rights as Congress chooses to accord to them,—is wholly inconsistent with the spirit and genius, as well as with the words, of the Constitution.

. . .

The wise men who framed the Constitution, and the patriotic people who adopted it, were unwilling to depend for their safety upon what, in the opinion referred to, is described as "certain principles of natural justice inherent in Anglo-Saxon character, which need no expression in constitutions or statutes to give them effect or to secure dependencies against legislation manifestly hostile to their real interests." They proceeded upon the theory—the wisdom of which experience has vindicated— that the only safe guaranty against governmental oppression was to withhold or restrict the power to oppress. . . . Hence, the Constitution enumerates the powers which Congress and the other departments may exercise,—leaving unimpaired, to the states or the People, the powers not delegated to the national government nor prohibited to the states. That instrument so expressly declares in the 10th Article of Amendment. It will be an evil day for American liberty if the theory of a government outside of the supreme law of the land finds lodgment in our constitutional jurisprudence. No higher duty rests upon this court than to exert its full authority to prevent all violation of the principles of the Constitution.

. . .

. . . Whether a particular race will or will not assimilate with our people, and whether they can or cannot with safety to our institutions be brought within the operation of the Constitution, is a matter to be thought of when it is proposed to acquire their territory by treaty. A mistake in the acquisition of territory, although such acquisition seemed at the time to be necessary, cannot be made the ground for violating the Constitution or refusing to give full effect to its provisions. The Constitution is not to be obeyed or disobeyed as the circumstances of a particular crisis in our history may suggest the one or the other course to be pursued. The People have decreed that it shall be the supreme law of the land at all times. When the acquisition of territory becomes complete, by cession, the Constitution necessarily becomes the supreme law of such new territory, and no power exists in any department of the government to make "concessions" that are inconsistent with its provisions. . . . The Constitution is supreme over every foot of territory, wherever situated, under the jurisdiction of the United States, and its full operation cannot be stayed by any branch of the government in order to meet what some may suppose to be extraordinary emergencies. If the Constitution is in force in any territory, it is in force there for every purpose embraced by the objects for which the government was ordained. Its authority cannot be displaced by concessions, even if it be true, as asserted in argument in some of these cases, that if the tariff act took effect in the Philippines of its own force, the inhabitants of Mandanao, who live on imported rice, would starve, because the import duty is many fold more than the ordinary cost of the grain to them. The meaning of the Constitution cannot depend upon accidental circumstances arising out of the products of other countries or of this country. We cannot violate the Constitution in order to serve particular interests in our own or in foreign lands....

...

We heard much in argument about the "expanding future of our country." It was said that the United States is to become what is called a "world power;" and that if this government intends to keep abreast of the times and be equal to the great destiny that awaits the American people, it must be allowed to exert all the power that other nations are accustomed to exercise. My answer is, that the fathers never intended that the authority and influence of this nation should be exerted otherwise than in accordance with the Constitution. If our government needs more power than is conferred upon it by the Constitution, that instrument provides the mode in which it may be amended and additional power thereby obtained. The People of the United States who ordained the Constitution never supposed that a change could be made in our system of government by mere judicial interpretation. They never contemplated any such juggling with the words of the Constitution as would authorize the courts to hold that the words "throughout the United States," in the taxing clause of the Constitution, do not embrace a domestic "territory of the United States" having a civil government established by the authority of the United States. This is a distinction which I am unable to make, and which I do not think ought to be made when we are endeavoring to ascertain the meaning of a great instrument of government.

...

It would seem, according to the theories of some, that even if Porto Rico is in and of the United States for many important purposes, it is yet not a part of this country with the privilege of protesting against a rule of taxation which Congress is expressly forbidden by the Constitution from adopting as to any part of the "United States." And this result comes from the failure of Congress to use the word "incorporate" in the Foraker act....

I am constrained to say that this idea of "incorporation" has some occult meaning which my mind does not apprehend. It is enveloped in some mystery which I am unable to unravel.

In my opinion Porto Rico became, at least after the ratification of the treaty with Spain, a part of and subject to the jurisdiction of the United States in respect of all its territory and people, and that Congress could not thereafter impose any duty, impost, or excise with respect to that island and its inhabitants, which departed from the rule of uniformity established by the Constitution.

IV. Federalism

MAJOR DEVELOPMENTS

- Rise of the dormant commerce clause
- Constitutional innovation in the states
- Development of police powers jurisprudence
- Modification of state sovereign immunity

The states played many roles in the constitutional developments of the Republican era. For Populist and Progressive reformers, the states were potential sources of political power that might be used to discipline economic forces. In many places, state governments proved relatively easy for popular movements to influence or capture, and they created the first opportunity to test new policies to control corporations and redistribute wealth. In other places, state governments did not seem responsive enough, and reformers created new democratic tools with which to influence state policymaking. As Progressive justice Louis Brandeis enthused, states were "laboratories of democracy," where courageous citizens could "try novel social and economic experiments without risk to the rest of the country."[26] Minimum wage and maximum working hours, workplace safety regulations, consumer health protection, price controls, railroad regulation, business and occupational licensing, alcohol prohibition, and much more were pioneered in the states.

For conservatives, this was precisely the danger. Conservatives raised the Federalist specter of exces-

26. *New State Ice v. Liebmann*, 285 U.S. 262, 311 (1932) (Brandeis, J., dissenting).

sively democratic states abusing government power at the expense of traditional legal rights and unpopular minorities (though not all minorities were of equal concern, with propertied interests taking a much higher priority than racial minorities, for example). Moreover, conservatives rejected Brandeis's premise that state experimentation posed no risk its neighbors or to the nation at large. Political movements to protect local economic interests—whether farmers and workers or local businesses—from national competition hobbled the new interstate corporations that could realize great efficiencies and gains in production through economies of scale. These movements also threatened the creation of an integrated national market on which workers and businesses in other parts of the country depended.

Dormant Commerce Clause. Debates over federalism in the late nineteenth and early twentieth centuries focused on just how much space the states should have to go their own way in deciding social and economic policy. These debates grew more pointed in the aftermath of the Civil War and in an increasingly tight-knit national economy. What constraints did the U.S. Constitution place on how the state governments responded to the demands of their local constituents and interests? How far could the states go in regulating what occurred in their own borders? Could the federal courts act on their own to monitor the actions of the states, or did Congress have to act to preempt state economic regulations?

Railroad regulation was a particular flashpoint for national economic debates in the late nineteenth century. Railroads were tying the country together, exposing local economies to national economic forces. Local railroads faced competition from national railroads, and local producers often felt vulnerable to the transportation costs that they faced. Faced with different costs and levels of competition, railroads often charged different rates for "long-haul" freights than for "short-haul" freights. State legislatures, particularly in the Midwest, responded with various schemes to regulate railroad rates, from banning discriminatory rates to establishing regulatory commissions that set a schedule of fares.

Unlike the state legislatures in the Midwest, whose constituents were largely united against discriminatory fares, Congress faced competing pressures. Unable to balance the conflicting demands of railroads, big shippers and small shippers, Congress remained silent on the issue of railroad rates. There was no federal law in place that could preempt state action such as that of Illinois. Nevertheless, in an adaptation of the conclusion in *Cooley v. Board of Wardens* (1852) that some issues are best addressed by a national law, the Court created the doctrine of the "dormant commerce clause." In *Wabash, St. Louis and Pacific Railway Company v. Illinois* (1886) the Court determined that it would strike down state laws that interfered with the dormant (that is, as-yet-unexpressed) authority of the federal government. Consequently, when it came to the free flow of goods across a national market, the Court's presumption was that the United States be treated internally as a free trade zone. The states could not regulate interstate commerce in a manner that would obstruct the free flow of goods without explicit congressional authorization. If Congress was frozen by competing interests, the Court would make sure that the states would be frozen also. Large economic interests in the east hailed the Court's decision as "fundamental to the existence of the Union and to the existence of trade."[27]

The dormant commerce clause was an important tool with which the federal judiciary, on its own initiative, would help construct a national market, creating the constitutional basis for weaving together regional economies into a single, interconnected national economy in which goods could flow freely from the Pacific to the Atlantic.[28] Large corporations would flourish to take full advantage of economies of scale and drive down the cost of goods. It was a constitutional project that was resisted by Populists and localists but that was fundamental to the vision of conservative Democrats and Republicans alike.

Constitutional Innovation in the States. The late Gilded Age and Progressive Eras were periods of policy, institutional, and constitutional innovation in the states. Some of those innovations were later nationalized, whether in the form of statutes, judicial opinions or constitutional amendments. Four amendments were added to the U.S. Constitution between 1913 and 1920, the Sixteenth through the Nineteenth. They were the first constitutional amendments since Reconstruction, and they were almost prefigured by reforms that had been

27. *The Nation* (October 28, 1886), 339.

28. In other cases, such as *Chicago, Milwaukee and St. Paul Railway Company v. Minnesota* (1890) and *Smyth v. Ames* (1898), the Court used the Fourteenth Amendment's due process clause to limit the ability of the states to regulate railroad rates.

occurring in the states. Female suffrage, alcohol prohibition, and direct election of U.S. senators had all been extensively tried at the state level before a constitutional amendment passed through Congress. The income tax was different. Wisconsin was a leader in developing an income tax, but most states passed on the idea, arguing that the tax was unenforceable and would only lead wealthy taxpayers to flee to neighboring states.[29]

Other constitutional innovations were not adopted at the federal level. Some did not need to be. States controlled election procedures. The spread of the "Australian" or long ballot that was printed by the government and listed all the candidates on a single ballot (instead of a party ballot that was distributed each political party and only listed its candidates) was done entirely at the state and local level. Similarly, the increased use of literacy tests, poll taxes, and voter registration requirements in the late nineteenth and early twentieth centuries were state and local decisions.

The states also experimented with new forms of democratic decision-making. In an initiative, a statute is placed by petition on a ballot, for citizens to accept or reject). In a referendum, it is the legislature that places the statute on a ballot. Both were reforms designed to check legislatures that were viewed as overly influenced by special interests or political parties. Populists and Progressives, especially in the young Western states, embraced these mechanisms of "direct legislation" as a vehicle for a politics free from corruption and partisanship. South Dakota was the first state to adopt a state-level initiative and referendum process in 1898, but other states soon followed. By 1918, when the first wave of reform stalled out, twenty-four states had adopted the mechanisms.

In *Rice v. Foster*, 4 Harr. 479 (Del. 1847), Delaware Chief Justice James Booth, a Whig, had delivered a well-known critique of direct democracy. The case held unconstitutional the state legislature's "local option" statute, which allowed the people of a county to vote on whether liquor licenses would be issued. In his view, the legislature was not only shirking its own constitutional responsibility. It in fact invited the dangers of democracy that republican government was meant to forestall. After all, the framers

> had been taught by the lessons of history, that equal and indeed greater dangers resulted from a pure democracy, than from an absolute monarchy. Each leads to despotism. Wherever the power of making laws, which is the supreme power in a State, has been exercised directly by the people under any system of polity, and not by representation, civil liberty has been overthrown.... In every government founded on popular will, the people, although intending to do right, are the subject of impulse and passion; and have been betrayed into acts of folly, rashness and enormity, by the flattery, deception, and influence of demagogues. A triumphant majority oppresses the minority; each contending faction, when it obtains the supremacy, tramples on the rights of the weaker: the great aim and objects of civil government are prostrated amidst tumult, violence and anarchy.... To guard against these dangers and the evil tendencies of a democracy, our republican government was instituted by the consent of the people. The characteristic which distinguishes it from the miscalled republics of ancient and modern times, is, that none of the powers of sovereignty are exercised by the people; but all of them by separate, co-ordinate branches of government in whom those powers are vested by the constitution. These co-ordinate branches are intended to operate as balances, checks and restraints, not only upon each other, but upon the people themselves; to guard them against their own rashness, precipitancy, and misguided zeal; and to protect the minority against the injustice of the majority.... The sovereign power therefore, of this State, resides with the legislative, executive, and judicial departments. Having thus transferred the sovereign power, the people cannot resume or exercise any portion of it. To do so, would be an infraction of the constitution, and a dissolution of the government.

In a highly influential decision in *Kadderly v. Portland*, 44 Ore. 118 (1903), the Oregon supreme court rejected Judge Booth's reasoning from the antebellum *Rice* decision and gave its blessing to the

29. Alabama's experience was typical, with the state auditor complaining in 1883, "Taxes upon salaries...are regarded with disfavor by almost every taxpayer.... They are in the very nature of things attained by processes inquisitorial in character, and therefore to most persons exceedingly obnoxious. In addition to this the law has never been and probably never will be properly executed, and consequently does not bear equally alike upon all.... I do not hesitate therefore to give it as my opinion that it should be repealed." Alabama dropped the income tax—a holdover from the Civil War—the next year. Edwin R. A. Segliman, *The Income Tax* (New York: Macmillan, 1914), 411.

initiative-and-referendum process. In *Pacific States Telephone and Telegraph Co. v. Oregon* (1912), the U.S. Supreme Court was asked whether the "Oregon System" was consistent with the republican guarantee clause of the U.S. Constitution. The Court decided that this was a "political question" and could not be answered by the courts. In the meantime, state courts across the country followed *Kadderly*. They accepted the initiative-and-referendum system as consistent with a republican form of government—so long as some form of representative government and constitutional limitations on government powers remained in place.

Police Powers Jurisprudence. In the late nineteenth and early twentieth centuries, treatise writers and state and federal judges spent a great deal of time thinking through what became known as the "police powers" of the legislature. There was a great deal of controversy over whether the federal government possessed police powers, but the police powers were at the heart of state politics. Police powers jurisprudence had two sides. One side was positive, concerned with what the state was empowered to do. The other side was negative, concerned with the limitations on how the legislative power could be used.

On the positive side, the traditional police powers inherited from the English common law recognized the obligation of the state to act to protect the safety, order, and morals of the people. Judges recognized this essential power of state and local governments in a wide variety of cases, despite specific constitutional restrictions on legislative power. It was this general reservoir of the police powers, according to the U.S. Supreme Court in the *Slaughter-House Cases* (1873), that authorized the state of Louisiana to establish a single slaughterhouse in the city of New Orleans as a public health measure, despite the addition of the Fourteenth Amendment to the U.S. Constitution. Likewise, the Supreme Court looked to police powers to explain why Massachusetts could adopt mandatory vaccination laws in order to secure the general health of the citizenry (*Jacobson v. Commonwealth of Massachusetts* [1905]). Special police powers could also be used to justify the heightened regulation of businesses "affected with a public interest" (*Munn v. Illinois* [1877]).

On the negative side, the courts indicated that there were intrinsic limits to the legislature's police powers. The Michigan Supreme Court judge Thomas Cooley emphasized the idea that legislation could not be "arbitrary."[30] The Illinois Supreme Court struck down a law that prohibited companies from paying employees with store credit, contending that the police power did not authorize the legislature to create "class legislation." The legislature could not play favorites and make "arbitrary" distinctions among social groups (*Frorer v. People*, 141 Ill. 171 [1893]). Such thinking famously informed the U.S. Supreme Court's interpretation of the Fourteenth Amendment's due process clause in cases such as *Lochner v. New York* (1903), in which the Court struck down a state's maximum working hour law for bakers.

State Sovereign Immunity. The Eleventh Amendment had been passed in response to the U.S. Supreme Court's decision in *Chisholm v. Georgia* (1793), and made clear the claim that the states had some form of sovereign immunity under the new U.S. Constitution. The Eleventh Amendment protected states from federal lawsuits by citizens of other states. But the Eleventh Amendment left some questions unanswered. Did the amendment carve out an exception to federal jurisdiction over the states, or did it give explicit recognition to a general principle of state sovereign immunity? Did the Reconstruction Amendments change the situation?

State debts piled up from the Civil War, Reconstruction, and postwar economic development schemes. Many states looked for ways to lessen their debt burdens and avoid having to fully repay their creditors. At the same time, individuals were turning to the federal courts in order to assert their rights under the new Fourteenth Amendment. Both situations put pressure on the Court to clarify the status of the states and their ability to be sued after Reconstruction.

In *Hans v. Louisiana* (1890), the Court addressed the problem of whether a state's own citizens could sue the state in federal court to collect a debt. In particular, Hans was asserting a violation of the contracts clause of the U.S. Constitution by the state of Louisiana and demanding payment on the state bonds that he held. The Court concluded that a general state sovereign immunity was part of the background assumption to the writing of the U.S. Constitution. The Eleventh Amendment only reaffirmed that general principle. Hans held that citizens

---

30. Thomas M. Cooley, *A Treatise on the Constitutional Limitations which Rest upon the Legislative Power of the States of the American Union*, 1st ed. (Boston: Little, Brown, 1868), 393.

could not sue their own states to collect debts. The "obligations of a State rest for their performance upon its honor and good faith," not on its judicial enforcement.

Ex parte Young (1908) significantly modified the doctrine of state sovereign immunity. *Young* held that individual government officials could be sued to prevent the enforcement of an allegedly unconstitutional law. State sovereign immunity did not prevent the federal courts from hearing claims of potential rights violations and from hearing those claims in the timeliest manner possible. The courts were reluctant to allow suits that would require state officials to withdraw funds from the state treasury. But *Young* opened the federal courthouse door to citizens seeking injunctions against state and local officials who might violate rights.

A. States and the Commerce Clause

In the decades after the Civil War, the federal courts were deeply concerned not only with how much power Congress could exercise under the interstate commerce clause but also with what restrictions the existence of the interstate commerce clause put on the state governments. Congress might not be able to regulate the internal affairs of the states, but Congress alone could regulate the transportation and exchange of goods across state borders. For the Court of the Gilded Age and Progressive Era, that meant that the states should be prevented from interfering with the creation of a national marketplace. That marketplace was still in its infancy in the late nineteenth century, with interstate railroads and telegraphs being rapidly built and local economies being increasingly woven into a national economy. The federal courts used the interstate commerce clause to protect the construction of a single national market within the United States and to prevent the states from carving out protected regional economies or industries. Making those basic decisions was controversial enough. Following through on that mission involved the courts in making many more fine-grained decisions in trying to decide when a state was unduly interfering with interstate commerce.

Wabash, St. Louis and Pacific Railway Company v. Illinois, 118 U.S. 557 (1886)

In the latter half of the nineteenth century, the economics of railroads provoked bitter political struggles in the Midwest. The railroads were subject to fierce competition on long-haul routes across the country, but frequently held monopolies on the short-haul branches that linked to these longer railways. That often meant that farmers, ranchers, and small merchants and producers in the small towns and the countryside frequently paid higher rates on a per-mile basis to ship goods than did the big economic players who operated on a national scale and shipped between the major cities. Competition on the long-haul lines could drive prices below the costs of operating the lines; the short-haul business subsidized the long-haul routes, helping the railroads maintain overall profitability. Short-haul shippers demanded an equalization of rates, ending the price discrimination between shippers, and state governments responded.

The Illinois legislature took the direct route, prohibiting rates that discriminated between short-haul and long-haul shippers. Railroads could not charge more for the transportation of any passenger or freight within the state than it charged for an equivalent shipment "over a greater distance." The Wabash, St. Louis and Pacific Railway Company was charged with violating the act for charging ten cents per hundred pounds more for shipping goods to New York City from Gilman, Illinois, than from Peoria, Illinois, even though the trip from Peoria was eighty-six miles longer within the state than was the trip from Gilman. The railway company was found guilty in state court, and the verdict was affirmed by the state supreme court. From there, the railway company appealed to the U.S. Supreme Court, arguing that the shipments from the cities in Illinois to New York City were part of interstate commerce and that the Illinois legislature could not constitutionally regulate such acts. In a 6–3 decision, the U.S. Supreme Court agreed, reversing the judgment of the state court.

JUSTICE MILLER delivered the opinion of the Court.

. . .

If the Illinois statute could be construed to apply exclusively to contracts for a carriage which begins and ends within the State, disconnected from a continuous transportation through or into other States, there does not seem to be any difficulty in holding it to be valid. For instance, a contract might be made to carry goods for a certain price from Cairo to Chicago, or from Chicago to Alton. The charges for these might be within the competency of the Illinois Legislature to regulate. The reason for this is that both the charge and the actual transportation in such cases are exclusively confined to the limits of the territory of the State, and is not commerce among the States, or interstate commerce, but is exclusively commerce within the State.

So far, therefore, as this class of transportation, as an element of commerce, is affected by the statute under consideration, it is not subject to the constitutional provision concerning commerce among the States....

...

The Supreme Court of Illinois does not place its judgment in the present case on the ground that the transportation and the charge are exclusively State commerce, but, conceding that it may be a case of commerce among the States, or interstate commerce, which Congress would have the right to regulate if it had attempted to do so, argues that this statute of Illinois belongs to that class of commercial regulations which may be established by the laws of a State until Congress shall have exercised its power on that subject...

In *Munn v. Illinois* (1877), the language of this court upon that subject is as follows:

> ...The warehouses of these plaintiffs in error are situated and their business carried on exclusively within the limits of the State of Illinois....Their regulation is a thing of domestic concern, and certainly, until Congress acts in reference to their interstate relations, the State may exercise all the powers of government over them, even though in so doing it may indirectly operate upon commerce outside its immediate jurisdiction. We do not say that a case may not arise in which it will be found that a State, under the form of regulating its own affairs, has encroached upon the exclusive domain of Congress in respect to interstate commerce, but we do say that, upon the facts as they are represented to us in this record, that has not been done.

...[I]t must be admitted that, in a general way, the court treated the cases then before it as belonging to that class of regulations of commerce which, like pilotage, bridging navigable rivers, and many others, could be acted upon by the States in the absence of any legislation by Congress on the same subject.

By the slightest attention to the matter it will be readily seen that the circumstances under which a bridge may be authorized across a navigable stream within the limits of a State, for the use of a public highway, and the local rules which shall govern the conduct of the pilots of each of the varying harbors of the coasts of the United States, depend upon principles far more limited in their application and importance than those which should regulate the transportation of persons and property across the half or the whole of the continent, over the territories of half a dozen States, through which they are carried without change of car or breaking bulk.

...

It cannot be too strongly insisted upon that the right of continuous transportation from one end of the country to the other is essential in modern times to that freedom of commerce from the restraints which the State might choose to impose upon it, that the commerce clause was intended to secure. This clause, giving to Congress the power to regulate commerce among the States and with foreign nations, as this court has said before, was among the most important of the subjects which prompted the formation of the Constitution....And it would be a very feeble and almost useless provision, but poorly adapted to secure the entire freedom of commerce among the States which was deemed essential to a more perfect union by the framers of the Constitution, if at every stage of the transportation of goods and chattels through the country, the State within whose limits a part of this transportation must be done could impose regulations concerning the price, compensation, or taxation, or any other restrictive regulation interfering with and seriously embarrassing this commerce.

The argument on this subject can never be better stated than it is by Chief-Justice Marshall in *Gibbons v. Ogden* (1824). He there demonstrates that commerce among the States, like commerce with foreign nations, is necessarily a commerce which crosses State lines, and extends into the States, and the power of Congress to regulate it exists wherever that commerce is found....

...

We must, therefore, hold that it is not, and never has been, the deliberate opinion of a majority of this court that a statute of a State which attempts to regulate the fares and charges by railroad companies within its limits, for a transportation which constitutes a part of commerce among the States, is a valid law.

...

....That this species of regulation is one which must be, if established at all, of a general and national character, and cannot be safely and wisely remitted to local rules and local regulations, we think is clear from what has already been said. And if it be a regulation of commerce, as we think we have demonstrated it is, and as the Illinois court concedes it to be, it must be of that national character, and the regulation can only appropriately exist by general rules and principles, which demand that it should be done by the Congress of the United States under the commerce clause of the Constitution.

The judgment of the Supreme Court of Illinois is therefore reversed, and the case remanded to that court for further proceedings in conformity with this opinion.

JUSTICE BRADLEY, with whom THE CHIEF JUSTICE and JUSTICE GRAY join, dissenting.

...

The principal question in this case... is whether, in the absence of congressional legislation, a State legislature has the power to regulate the charges made by the railroads of the State for transporting goods and passengers to and from places within the State, when such goods or passengers are brought from, or carried to, points without the State, and are, therefore, in the course of transportation from another State, or to another State.... We think that the State does not lose its power to regulate the charges of its own railroads in its own territory, simply because the goods or persons transported have been brought from or are destined to a point beyond the State in another State.

...

... Does it follow... that because Congress has the power to regulate this matter (though it has not exercised that power), therefore the State is divested of all power of regulation? That is the question before us.

We had supposed that this question was concluded by the previous decisions of this court: that all local arrangements and regulations respecting highways, turnpikes, railroads, bridges, canals, ferries, dams, and wharves, within the State, their construction and repair, and the charges to be made for their use, though materially affecting commerce, both internal and external, and thereby incidentally operating to a certain extent as regulations of interstate commerce, were within the power and jurisdiction of the several States. That is still our opinion.

...

The doctrines announced in these cases apply not only to dams in, and bridges over, navigable streams, but to all structures and appliances in a state which may incidentally interfere with commerce, or which may be erected or created for the furtherance of commerce, whether by water or by land. It is matter of common knowledge that from the beginning of the government the States have exercised almost exclusive control over roads, bridges, ferries, wharves, and harbors. No one has doubted their right to do so....

...

There is a class of subjects, it is true, pertaining to interstate and foreign commerce, which require general and uniform rules for the whole country, so as to obviate unjust discriminations against any part, and in respect of which local regulations made by the States would be repugnant to the power vested in Congress, and, therefore, unconstitutional; but there are other subjects of local character and interest which not only admit of, but are generally best regulated by, State authority. This distinction is pointed out and enforced in the case of *Cooley v. The Port Wardens of Philadelphia* (1852)....

...

Now, since every railroad may be, and generally is, a medium of transportation for interstate commerce, and affects that commerce; and since the charges of fare and freight for such transportation affect and incidentally regulate that commerce; and since the railroad could not be built, and the charges upon it could not be exacted, without authority from the State, it follows as a necessary consequence that the State, in the exercise of its undoubted functions and sovereignty, does, in the establishment and regulation of railroads, to a certain and a very material extent, not only do that which affects but incidentally regulates commerce. It does so by the very act of authorizing the construction of railroads and the collection of fares and freights thereon. No one doubts its powers to do this. The very being of the plaintiffs in error, the very existence of their railroad, the very power they exercise of charging fares and freights, are all derived from the State. And yet, according to the argument of the plaintiffs in error, pursued to its legitimate consequences, the act of the State in doing all this ought to be regarded as null and void because it operates as a regulation of commerce among the States.... And since its being, its franchises, its powers, its road, its right to charge, all come from the State, and are the creation of State law, how can it be contended that the State has no power of regulation over those charges, and over the conduct of the company in the transaction of its business whilst acting within the State and using its railroad lying within the bounds of the State?...

....

To sum up the matter in a word: we hold it to be a sound proposition of law, that the making of railroads and regulating the charges for their use is not such a regulation of commerce as to be in the remotest degree repugnant to any power given to Congress by the Constitution, so long as that power is dormant, and has not been exercised by Congress....

...

The inconveniences which it has been supposed in argument would follow from the execution of the laws of Illinois, we think have been greatly exaggerated. But if it should be found to present any real difficulty in the modes of transacting business on through lines, it is always in the power of Congress to make such reasonable regulations as the interests of interstate commerce may demand, without denuding the States of their just powers over their own roads and their own corporations.

B. Police Powers

Police powers are the most basic powers of the state governments to make laws to protect the health, safety, morals, and welfare of the community. The general power is implicit in the legislative power of the state governments, and it is among the reserved powers of the states protected in the Tenth Amendment. While Congress legislates in reference to a set of specific enumerated powers, the states legislate in reference to the general police powers.

The police powers provide a broad justification for state and local legislation, but they are not unlimited. Specific constitutional limitations can trump the police powers. Some nineteenth-century lawyers and judges argued that the due process clauses in state constitutions and in the Fourteenth Amendment pointed to the implicit limits on the police powers. According to this argument, states could legislate to advance the general welfare of the community, but they could not constitutionally pass a law simply to help their friends or hurt their foes. The legislative power of the state could only be legitimately used for the public benefit, not for private gain. The due process clause indicated "factional" or "class" (or we might say, "special interest") legislation that abused the legislative process was unconstitutional.

Thomas M. Cooley, **Constitutional Limitations** (1868)[31]

Thomas Cooley was among the most influential state jurists in the late nineteenth and early twentieth centuries. A Locofoco Democrat (a libertarian and reformist wing of the party), Cooley was a law professor at the University of Michigan and the reporter for the Michigan state supreme court when he was selected to serve as a justice on that court in 1864. After two decades on the court and in the law school, he left Michigan in the 1880s to work on national issues of railroad regulation and bankruptcy and served as the first chairman of the Interstate Commerce Commission.

A prolific writer and orator, he published in 1868 his most important treatise, Constitutional Limitations, *which quickly became a standard reference on American constitutional law. Unlike most treatises of constitutional law at the time, Cooley's was particularly notable for its focus on the constitutional constraints on government power and their judicial enforcement. First published just as the Fourteenth Amendment was being ratified,* Constitutional Limitations *detailed and systematized the state and federal constitutional provisions limiting government and how they had been interpreted and applied by the courts, ranging widely over liberties of speech, religion, and criminal process but giving extensive consideration to the areas of greatest judicial development, rights of property. The unifying theme of these limitations, Cooley argued, was the ban on the arbitrary use of government power. Along with later treatises by Christopher Tiedeman and Ernst Freund, Cooley gave shape to the emerging police powers jurisprudence and gave content to the due process clauses (and their frequent equivalent in state constitutions, the law of the land clauses) as significant limitations on political power.*

...

What is meant by "the due process of law," and "the law of the land," ... and in what cases can legislative action be annulled as not being "the law of the land," or judicial or ministerial action set aside as not being "due process of law" in the constitutional sense?

...

... It is entirely correct ... in assuming that a legislative enactment is not necessarily the law of the land. The words "by the law of the land," as used in the Constitution, do not mean a statute passed for the purpose of working the wrong. That construction would render the restriction absolutely nugatory, and turn this part of the Constitution into mere nonsense. The people would be made to say to the two houses: "You shall be vested with the legislative power of the State, but no one shall be disenfranchised or deprived of any of the rights or privileges of a citizen, unless you pass a statute for that purpose. In other words, you shall not do the wrong, unless you choose to do it." ...

31. Excerpt taken from Thomas M. Cooley, *A Treatise on the Constitutional Limitations which Rest upon the Legislative Power of the States of the American Union*, 1st ed. (Boston: Little, Brown, 1868), 353–58, 390–93.

...[W]e think we shall find that general rules may sometimes be as obnoxious as special, when in their results they deprive parties of vested rights. While every man has a right to require that his own controversies shall be judged by the same rules which settle those of his neighbors, the whole community is also entitled at all times to demand the protection of the ancient principles which shield private rights against arbitrary interference, even though such interference may be under a rule impartial in its application. It is not the partial character of the rule, so much as its arbitrary and unusual nature, which condemns it as unknown to the law of the land....

The principles, then, upon which the process is based are to determine whether it is "due process" or not, and not any considerations of mere form....

...

Laws public in their objects may be general or local in their application; they may embrace many subjects or one, and they may extend to all citizens or be confined to particular classes, as minors, or married women, bankers or traders, and the like. The power that legislates for the State at large must determine whether particular rules shall extend to the whole State and all its citizens, or to a part of the State or a class of its citizens only....

But a statute would not be constitutional which should proscribe a class or party for opinion's sake, or which should select particular individuals from a class or locality, and subject them to peculiar rules, or impose upon them special obligations or burdens, from which others in the same locality or class are exempt.

...

...The doubt might also arise whether a regulation made for any one class of citizens, entirely arbitrary in its character, and restricting their rights, privileges, or legal capacities in a manner before unknown to the law, could be sustained, notwithstanding its generality. Distinctions in these respects should be based upon some reason which renders them important,—like the want of capacity in infants, and insane persons; but if the legislature should undertake to provide that persons following some specified lawful trade or employment should not have capacity to make contracts, or to receive conveyances, or to build such houses as others were allowed to erect, or in any other way to make such use of their property as was permissible to others, it can scarcely be doubted that the act would transcend the due bounds of legislative power, even if it did not come in conflict with express constitutional provisions. The man or the class forbidden the acquisition or enjoyment of property in the manner permitted to the community at large would be deprived of *liberty* in particulars of primary importance to his or their "pursuit of happiness."

Munn v. State of Illinois, 94 U.S. 113 (1877)

In the early 1870s an agrarian political movement known as the Patrons of Husbandry, a.k.a. "the Grange," developed in the Midwest in response to the economic power of railroads, corporations, and other property-owners who were in a position to take advantage of farmers. Farmers were especially upset at the rates set by railroads for hauling crops to market and by owners of grain elevators for storing the waiting crops. In Illinois, Iowa, Minnesota, and Wisconsin, state legislatures responded by regulating the maximum prices that railroads and grain elevators could charge. The maximum rate law at issue in Munn *applied to grain elevators, and was challenged on the grounds that, by preventing property-owners from setting their own prices, the legislature had effectively deprived them of property without due process of law, in violation of the Fourteenth Amendment.*

The Court handed down its 7–2 decision on March 1, 1877, the day before President Rutherford B. Hayes was declared elected by the Electoral Commission that was charged with resolving the disputed 1876 presidential election. In a decision written by the Chief Justice, with substantial help from Bradley (a dissenter in the Slaughter-House Cases*), the Court ruled that property that is "clothed with a public interest"—in the sense that it is "used in a manner to make it of public consequence, and affect the community at large"—could be regulated "by the public for the common good." Field—the most stridently conservative of this generation of justices—filed a dissent for himself and Justice Strong (who voted with the majority in* Slaughter-House*). One key issue for the justices was how broadly the category of businesses "affected with a public interest" should be understood. The common law had long recognized an expanded role for state regulation of such enterprises, and the Fourteenth Amendment's due process clause might be assumed to take into account that traditional distinction. But how strictly should the category be interpreted? Did grain elevators merit that heightened level of government regulation?*

As in the Slaughter-House Cases *(1873), a majority of the justices understood the importance of property rights but felt obligated to be cautious about the reach of federal judicial power under the newly passed Fourteenth Amendment. As it turned out, by the late 1870s most of these so-called Granger laws were being removed from the books by state legislatures, without having been ordered to do so by federal judges. Nevertheless, many conservatives were extremely disappointed by the result in* Munn. *At one point Field became so frustrated with his brethren's apparent disregard for property rights that he explored a run for the presidency in 1884 as a way to "have placed on the Bench able and conservative men and thus have brought back the decisions of the Court to that line from which they should not have departed."*[32] *Field also arranged for well-known conservative lawyers, such as John Norton Pomeroy, to write articles for prominent legal journals criticizing decisions such as* Munn v. Illinois *for striking "at the stability of private property," a right that represented "the very foundation of modern society and civilization."*[33] *The conservative American Bar Association was also formed around the time of* Munn *so as to organize elite commercial bar advocacy for more sympathetic judicial decision making.*

It would take only thirteen years for the Court, led by a new Chief Justice, to declare in Chicago, Milwaukee & St. Paul Railway v. Minnesota [The Minnesota Rate Case] *(1890) that judges were obligated under the due process clause to protect the property rights of investors or corporations by reviewing the reasonableness of any rates set by state authorities—thus essentially overruling* Munn v. Illinois. *Chief Justice Waite ended his opinion in* Munn *by declaring, "For protection against abuses by legislatures the people must resort to the polls, not to the courts." By the turn of the century, property owners were successfully resorting to the federal courts.*

CHIEF JUSTICE WAITE delivered the opinion of the Court.

...

Every statute is presumed to be constitutional. The courts ought not to declare one to be unconstitutional, unless it is clearly so. If there is doubt, the expressed will of the legislature should be sustained.

The Constitution contains no definition of the word "deprive," as used in the Fourteenth Amendment['s due process clause]. To determine its signification, therefore, it is necessary to ascertain the effect which usage has given it, when employed in the same or a like connection.

While this provision of the amendment is new in the Constitution of the United States, as a limitation upon the powers of the States, it is old as a principle of civilized government. It is found in Magna Charta, and, in substance if not in form, in nearly or quite all the constitutions that have been from time to time adopted by the several States of the Union. By the Fifth Amendment, it was introduced into the Constitution of the United States as a limitation upon the powers of the national government, and by the Fourteenth, as a guaranty against any encroachment upon an acknowledged right of citizenship by the legislatures of the States....

When one becomes a member of society, he necessarily parts with some rights or privileges which, as an individual not affected by his relations to others, he might retain. "A body politic," as aptly defined in the preamble of the Constitution of Massachusetts, "is a social compact by which the whole people covenants with each citizen, and each citizen with the whole people, that all shall be governed by certain laws for the common good." This does not confer power upon the whole people to control rights which are purely and exclusively private,...but it does authorize the establishment of laws requiring each citizen to so conduct himself, and so use his own property, as not unnecessarily to injure another. This is the very essence of government, and has found expression in the maxim sic utere tuo ut alienum non laedas ["one should use his own property in such a manner as not to injure that of another"]. From this source come the police powers, which, as was said by Chief Justice Taney in the *License Cases* (1847), "are nothing more or less than the powers of government inherent in every sovereignty,...that is to say,...the power to govern men and things." Under these powers the government regulates the conduct of its citizens one towards another, and the manner in which each shall use his own property, when such regulation becomes necessary for the public good. In their exercise it has been customary in England from time immemorial, and in this country from its first colonization, to regulate ferries, common carriers, hackmen, bakers, millers, wharfingers, innkeepers, etc., and in so doing to fix a maximum of charge to be made for services rendered, accommodations furnished, and articles sold. To this day, statutes are to be found in many of the States upon some or all these subjects; and we think it has never yet been successfully contended

32. Howard Jay Graham, "Four Letters of Mr. Justice Field," *Yale Law Journal* 47 (1938):1107.

33. John Norton Pomeroy, "The Supreme Court and State Repudiation," *American Law Review* 17 (1883):712.

that such legislation came within any of the constitutional prohibitions against interference with private property....

From this it is apparent that, down to the time of the adoption of the Fourteenth Amendment, it was not supposed that statutes regulating the use, or even the price of the use, of private property necessarily deprived an owner of his property without due process of law....

This brings us to inquire as to the principles upon which this power of regulation rests, in order that we may determine what is within and what without its operative effect. Looking, then, to the common law, from whence came the right which the Constitution protects, we find that when private property is "affected with a public interest, it ceases to be juris privati only." This was said by Lord Chief Justice Hale more than two hundred years ago...and has been accepted without objection as an essential element in the law of property ever since. Property does become clothed with a public interest when used in a manner to make it of public consequence, and affect the community at large. When, therefore, one devotes his property to a use in which the public has an interest, he, in effect, grants to the public an interest in that use, and must submit to be controlled by the public for the common good, to the extent of the interest he has thus created. He may withdraw his grant by discontinuing the use; but, so long as he maintains the use, he must submit to the control....

...It remains only to ascertain whether the warehouses of these plaintiffs in error, and the business which is carried on there, come within the operation of this principle.

For this purpose we accept as true the statements of fact contained in the elaborate brief of one of the counsel of the plaintiffs in error. From these it appears that "...The quantity [of grain] received in Chicago has made it the greatest grain market in the world....The grain warehouses or elevators in Chicago are immense structures, holding from 300,000 to 1,000,000 bushels at one time, according to size. They are divided into bins of large capacity and great strength....They are located with the river harbor on one side and the railway tracks on the other; and the grain is run through them from car to vessel, or boat to car, as may be demanded in the course of business...."...

Under such circumstances it is difficult to see why, if the common carrier, or the miller, or the ferryman, or the innkeeper, or the wharfinger, or the baker, or the cartman, or the hackney-coachman, pursues a public employment and exercises "a sort of public office," these plaintiffs in error do not. They stand, to use again the language of their counsel, in the very "gateway of commerce," and take toll from all who pass. Their business most certainly "tends to a common charge, and is become a thing of public interest and use."...Certainly, if any business can be clothed "with a public interest, and cease to be juris privati only," this has been. It may not be made so by the operation of the Constitution of Illinois or this statute, but it is by the facts.

We also are not permitted to overlook the fact that, for some reason, the people of Illinois, when they revised their Constitution in 1870, saw fit to make it the duty of the general assembly to pass laws "for the protection of producers, shippers, and receivers of grain and produce," art. 13, sect. 7; and by sect. 5 of the same article, to require all railroad companies receiving and transporting grain in bulk or otherwise to deliver the same at any elevator to which it might be consigned, that could be reached by any track that was or could be used by such company, and that all railroad companies should permit connections to be made with their tracks, so that any public warehouse, etc., might be reached by the cars on their railroads. This indicates very clearly that during the twenty years in which this peculiar business had been assuming its present "immense proportions," something had occurred which led the whole body of the people to suppose that remedies such as are usually employed to prevent abuses by virtual monopolies might not be inappropriate here. For our purposes we must assume that, if a state of facts could exist that would justify such legislation, it actually did exist when the statute now under consideration was passed. For us the question is one of power, not of expediency. If no state of circumstances could exist to justify such a statute, then we may declare this one void, because is excess of the legislative power of the State. But if it could, we must presume it did. Of the propriety of legislative interference within the scope of legislative power, the legislature is the exclusive judge....

We know that this is a power which may be abused; but that is no argument against its existence. For protection against abuses by legislatures the people must resort to the polls, not to the courts....

Judgment *affirmed*.

JUSTICE FIELD, dissenting.

I am compelled to dissent from the decision of the court in this case, and from the reasons upon which that decision is founded. The principle upon which the opinion of the majority proceeds is, in my judgment, subversive of the rights of private property, heretofore believed to be protected by constitutional guaranties against legislative interference, and is in conflict with the authorities cited in its support....

The question presented...is one of the greatest importance,—whether it is within the competency of a State to fix the compensation which an individual may receive for the use of his own property in his private business, and for his services in connection with it.

The declaration of the [state] Constitution of 1870, that private buildings used for private purposes shall be deemed public institutions, does not make them so. The receipt and storage of grain in a building erected by private means for that purpose does not constitute the building a public warehouse. There is no magic in the language, though used by a constitutional convention, which can change a private business into a public one, or alter the character of the building in which the business is transacted....One might as well attempt to change the nature of colors, by giving them a new designation. The defendants were no more public warehousemen, as justly observed by counsel, than the merchant who sells his merchandise to the public is a public merchant, or the blacksmith who shoes horses for the public is a public blacksmith; and it was a strange notion that by calling them so they would be brought under legislative control....

...But it would seem from its opinion that the court holds that property loses something of its private character when employed in such a way as to be generally useful. The doctrine declared is that property "becomes clothed with a public interest when used in a manner to make it of public consequence, and affect the community at large;" and from such clothing the right of the legislature is deduced to control the use of the property, and to determine the compensation which the owner may receive for it. When Sir Matthew Hale, and the sages of the law in his day, spoke of property as affected by a public interest, and ceasing from that cause to be juris privati solely, that is, ceasing to be held merely in private right, they referred to property dedicated by the owner to public uses, or to property the use of which was granted by the government, or in connection with which special privileges were conferred. Unless the property was thus dedicated, or some right bestowed by the government was held with the property, either by specific grant or by prescription of so long a time as to imply a grant originally, the property was not affected by any public interest so as to be taken out of the category of property held in private right. But it is not in any such sense that the terms "clothing property with a public interest" are used in this case. From the nature of the business under consideration—the storage of grain—which, in any sense in which the words can be used, is a private business, in which the public are interested only as they are interested in the storage of other products of the soil, or in articles of manufacture, it is clear that the court intended to declare that, whenever one devotes his property to a business which is useful to the public,—"affects the community at large,"— the legislature can regulate the compensation which the owner may receive for its use, and for his own services in connection with it....

If this be sound law, if there be no protection, either in the principles upon which our republican government is founded, or in the prohibitions of the Constitution against such invasion of private rights, all property and all business in the State are held at the mercy of a majority of its legislature. The public has no greater interest in the use of buildings for the storage of grain than it has in the use of buildings for the residences of families, nor, indeed, anything like so great an interest; and, according to the doctrine announced, the legislature may fix the rent of all tenements used for residences, without reference to the cost of their erection. If the owner does not like the rates prescribed, he may cease renting his houses....The public is interested in the manufacture of cotton, woollen, and silken fabrics, in the construction of machinery, in the printing and publication of books and periodicals, and in the making of utensils of every variety, useful and ornamental; indeed, there is hardly an enterprise or business engaging the attention and labor of any considerable portion of the community, in which the public has not an interest in the sense in which that term is used by the court in its opinion; and the doctrine which allows the legislature to interfere with and regulate the charges which the owners of property thus employed shall make for its use, that is, the rates at which all these different kinds of business shall be carried on, has never before been asserted, so far as I am aware, by any judicial tribunal in the United States.

...All that is beneficial in property arises from its use, and the fruits of that use; and whatever deprives a person of them deprives him of all that is desirable or valuable in the title and possession....

No State "shall deprive any person of life, liberty, or property without due process of law," says the Fourteenth Amendment to the Constitution.... By the term "liberty," as used in the provision, something more is meant than mere freedom from physical restraint or the bounds of a prison. It means freedom to go where one may choose, and to act in such manner, not inconsistent with the equal rights of others, as his judgment may dictate for the promotion of his happiness; that is, to pursue such callings and avocations as may be most suitable to develop his capacities, and give to them their highest enjoyment.

The same liberal construction which is required for the protection of life and liberty, in all particulars in which life and liberty are of any value, should be applied to the protection of private property. If the legislature of a State, under pretence of providing for the public good, or for any other reason, can determine, against the consent of the owner, the uses to which private property shall be devoted, or the prices which the owner shall receive for its uses, it can deprive him of the property as completely as by a special act for its confiscation or destruction....

The power of the State over the property of the citizen under the constitutional guaranty is well defined. The State may take his property for public uses, upon just compensation being made therefore. It may take a portion of his property by way of taxation for the support of the government. It may control the use and possession of his property, so far as may be necessary for the protection of the rights of others, and to secure to them the equal use and enjoyment of their property. The doctrine that each one must so use his own as not to injure his neighbor—sic utere tuo ut alienum non laedas—is the rule by which every member or society must possess and enjoy his property; and all legislation essential to secure this common and equal enjoyment is a legitimate exercise of State authority. Except in cases where property may be destroyed to arrest a conflagration or the ravages of pestilence, or be taken under the pressure of an immediate and overwhelming necessity to prevent a public calamity, the power of the State over the property of the citizen does not extend beyond such limits....

...

...The business of a warehouseman was, at common law, a private business, and is so in its nature. It has no special privileges connected with it, nor did the law ever extend to it any greater protection than it extended to all other private business. No reason can be assigned to justify legislation interfering with the legitimate profits of that business, that would not equally justify an intermeddling with the business of every man in the community, so soon, at least, as his business became generally useful.

I am of opinion that the judgment of the Supreme Court of Illinois should be reversed.

JUSTICE STRONG, dissenting.

C. Representation of State Interests

The U.S. Constitution specified that the members of the U.S. Senate will be chosen by the legislatures of the states. The Seventeenth Amendment, ratified in 1913, changed that mode of selection to direct election of senators by the people of each state.

The movement for the direct election of senators built slowly over time before it won final victory with the passage of the Seventeenth Amendment. Resistance to direct election was strongest in the Northeast, but state legislatures and state referenda elsewhere ran strongly in favor of direct election and by 1900 were taking the form of calls for a federal constitutional convention. In 1901, Oregon effectively established direct election on its own by requiring state legislative candidates to pledge to vote for the U.S. Senate candidate (whose name also appeared on the state ballot) who received the most popular votes. Half the states quickly followed suit, with state legislatures ratifying the selection of the voters by the time the Seventeenth Amendment finally passed Congress. Unsurprisingly, the argument for direct election rested in part on a preference for a more democratic political system. But proponents of direct election also emphasized a goal of taking the choice of U.S. senators out of state politics. An upcoming senatorial vote could overshadow local issues in state legislative elections. Partisan and personal turmoil of the senatorial voice had on occasion disrupted state legislative sessions and encouraged the corruption of legislators.

George F. Hoar, "Direct Election of Senators" (1893)[34]

George Hoar, Republican from Massachusetts, was a leading member of the Senate from the end of Reconstruction until his death in 1904, and had been the chair of the Senate

34. Excerpt taken from *Congressional Record*, 53rd Cong., special sess., vol. 25 (April 3, 6, and 7, 1893):101.

Judiciary Committee before the Democrats gained a majority of the Senate in the elections of 1892. When a proposed constitutional amendment first passed the House of Representatives in 1893, Hoar rose to oppose it when it reached the Senate, providing one of the most developed arguments against direct election. Hoar particularly emphasized the value of indirect elections for federalism and moderation. Others, such as former Republican senator George Edmunds of Vermont, emphasized the value of having senators who represented the diverse interests of the state legislature, rather than the median voter of a popular election.

...

I, do not, of course, claim that the people cannot now amend, or that they cannot now improve, our Constitution. That Constitution itself would be a failure if the experience of a hundred years under its operation found the people unfitted to improve it. The lives of our fathers would have been of little worth if, under the Constitution they framed, there had not grown up and flourished a people who were also fit to deal with the great and fundamental constitutional principles of the state.... But they must bring to them the same wisdom and courage and virtue. They must dare to tell the people plain truths. They must possess the wisdom of deliberate action, and arise to the austere virtue of self-restraint.

Mr. President, wherever there can be found an expression of admiration for the American Constitution in the works of any great writer or thinker at home or abroad it will be found that the admiration is based upon that part of its mechanism which secures the deliberate and indirect action of the popular will instead of its immediate, rapid, inconsiderate, and direct action. The parts of it which are everywhere the most praised and by which its framers sought especially to commend it to the confidence of the people were the constitution of the Senate and the constitution of the Supreme Court.

...

I am not afraid to say to the American people that it is dangerous to trust any great power of government to their direct or inconsiderate control. I am not afraid to tell them not only that their sober second thought is better than their hasty action, but that a government which is exposed to the hasty action of a people is the worst and not the best government on earth. No matter how excellent may be the individual, the direct, immediate, hasty action of any mass of individuals on earth is the pathway to ruin and not to safety....

...

It is a poor, cheap flattery of the people, this notion that suffrage is to be deified and that the results of suffrage are to be degraded; that the people have all wisdom and all honesty, but that their trusted agents are to be bought or cajoled. Will it not be the same people who choose the senators and who choose the legislatures? Is there any evil influence which will operate upon the legislature which will not operate with like effect upon the convention?

...

The state legislatures are the bodies of men most interested of all others to preserve state jurisdiction—more than the governors, who may be expected to aspire to national employments. It is well that the members of one branch of the legislature should look to them for their re-election, and it is a great security for the rights of the states. The state legislatures will be made of men whose duty will be the administration of the state authority of their several state interests and the framing of laws for the government of the state which they represent. The popular conventions, gathered for the political purpose of nominating senators, may be quite otherwise composed or guided. Here, in the state legislature, is to be found the great security against the encroachment upon the rights of the states.

...

The Senator from Oregon... goes on to announce, as to the foundations of his argument, the principle that no system can be properly termed free or popular which deprives the individual voter of his right to cast his vote directly for the man of his choice for any office.... And the logic of his position compels him to avow this doctrine. So that, if the people go with him, this amendment must be followed by others, under which the United States judiciary and the president and the vice-president are to be chosen by the action of direct popular majority. This may be sound policy; but when it is established, the Constitution of the United States is gone.

...

V. Separation of Powers

MAJOR DEVELOPMENTS

- Struggle over presidential appointment and removal power
- Expanding unilateral activity by the president
- Expanded rulemaking activity by the executive branch

The late nineteenth century was the era of congressional government. The early twentieth century witnessed the birth of the modern presidency. In between was struggle.

Congress was the seat of party power in the nineteenth century. Most of the government's business was conducted through statute, which only the legislature produced. The discretionary raising and spending of government funds through taxes and appropriations were the most important things that the government did, and the power of the purse was firmly in the hands of the legislature. The rewarding of patronage with government offices large and small was the lifeblood of the mass political parties. Even though presidents officially made nominations to fill those offices, legislators demanded control over how offices were allocated to their friends and foes. The president often felt like a glorified clerk.

This state of affairs gradually changed over the course of the Republican Era. Presidents fought Congress for control of the power of executive appointment and removal. Civil service reform at the turn of the century reduced the number of offices available for political allocation and the political importance of patronage. The rise of the regulatory state and the increasing complexity of government policy even in such traditional domains as the setting of taxes meant that legislatures were no longer the only, or necessarily even the primary, site of policymaking. Independent regulatory bodies and agencies within the executive branch were increasingly important players on the policy stage. Foreign affairs were becoming a routine and significant part of the federal government's agenda, and the president had an outsized role. (President Theodore Roosevelt won a Nobel Peace Prize in 1906 for his role in resolving international disputes, including a peace treaty between Russia and Japan.) The president naturally assumed a leadership role in times of crisis, and as the nineteenth century became the twentieth the opportunities for crisis management multiplied. The integrated economy gave local events new national significance.

The railroads and the radio gave the president new opportunities to speak to a national audience and bring his message to the masses. The scope of federal government activities and the stresses of an urban, industrialized society focused greater attention on the president's leadership. All these changes affected the constitutional division, and balance, of powers.

A. Appointment and Removal Power

The Supreme Court finally found an opportunity to weigh in on the question of the presidential power to remove executive branch officials from office in *Myers v. United States* (1926). There was a lot of water under the bridge by the time the Supreme Court took action. The First Congress had given (or recognized) the power to the president to remove executive officers. The Jacksonians had adopted the spoils system and mass dismissals of lower-level officials after an election. The Reconstruction Congress had sought to control President Andrew Johnson by requiring Senate approval before a cabinet officer could be removed. Civil service reform had limited the ability of presidents to remove low-level officials at their discretion. *Myers* allowed former president William Howard Taft to add the Supreme Court's voice to those debates. The statutory provision at issue in *Myers* was particularly restrictive—requiring Senate approval for the removal of a postmaster general—and it provided an opportunity for Taft to lend the Court's support to the White House in its struggles with Congress over the appointment and removal power. But in the early twentieth century, the more Progressive justices dissented and sided with Congress against the Woodrow Wilson White House on this issue, voicing their view that Congress should be able to impose the statutory controls on lower level government officials that it wants.

Myers v. United States, 272 U.S. 52 (1926)

In the midst of its battle with Andrew Johnson over the control of the policy and administration of the federal government, Congress passed the Tenure of Office Act of 1867, which barred the president from removing from office executive-branch officials without the consent of the Senate. The Tenure of Office Act was later repealed, but Congress adopted new measures that imposed similar restrictions on the presidential removal power. An 1876 statute provided that postmasters could be "removed by the President by and with the advice and consent of the Senate."

Frank S. Myers had been appointed postmaster at Portland, Oregon, by Woodrow Wilson in 1917 to a four-year term. In 1920, several months before the expiration of that four-year term, Wilson ordered, without explanation, that Myers be removed from office, and the president failed to notify the Senate of the removal. Myers protested his *removal and brought suit in the Court of Claims to recover the amount of his salary from the date of the removal order, a total of $8,838.71. Meanwhile, the president had filled Myers's office through a recess appointment. The Court of Claims dismissed the suit on the grounds that he did not file it sufficiently promptly. Myers appealed to the Supreme Court, which accepted his suit as timely (the government did not contest that issue). Since Solicitor General James Beck was arguing, on behalf of the administration, that the statute was unconstitutional, the Court invited Senator George Pepper to participate in the case. Myers died during the litigation, and the suit was continued by his estate.*

Arising at the end of the Progressive Era, the case pointed to a tension in Progressive sensibilities about government administration. On the one hand, by the 1920s the civil service system was well established; the Jacksonian spoils system, and freewheeling executive discretion to make removals and appointments for political reasons, had been firmly rejected. On the other hand, there was a heightened appreciation of the value of the power of the executive branch under unified leadership. A "chief executive officer" could marshal that power to ensure efficient and effective administration.

For both the parties before the Court and the justices, the question of whether Congress could restrict the president's removal power largely turned on the question of what practical construction had been given to the power by government action over time. The value and meaning of the House debate over the removal power in 1789 and of the Tenure of Office Act of 1867 were important points of disagreement among the justices. Was the restriction on the removal of postmasters a break from historical practice or an embodiment of it? Do restrictions on the president's ability to remove executive-branch officials undercut the president's ability to meet his Article II responsibilities? Keep in mind that the majority opinion was written by William Howard Taft—the only justice who had also been President of the United States. Taft wrote for a 6–3 majority striking down the statutory restrictions on the presidential removal power. The opinion sustained Woodrow Wilson's right to fire the postmaster without seeking Senate approval.

CHIEF JUSTICE TAFT delivered the opinion of the Court.

This case presents the question whether under the Constitution the President has the exclusive power of removing executive officers of the United States whom he has appointed by and with the advice and consent of the Senate.

. . .

The question where the power of removal of executive officers appointed by the President by and with the advice and consent of the Senate was vested, was presented early in the first session of the First Congress. There is no express provision respecting removals in the Constitution, except...for removal from office by impeachment....

. . .

[In the First Congress] the exact question which the House voted upon was whether it should recognize and declare the power of the President under the constitution to remove the Secretary of Foreign Affairs without the advice and consent of the Senate....[T]he vote was, and was intended to be, a legislative declaration that the power to remove officers appointed by the President and the Senate vested in the President alone, and until the Johnson Impeachment trial in 1868, its meaning was not doubted even by those who questioned its soundness....

. . .

...[T]he Constitution was so framed as to vest in the Congress all legislative powers therein granted, to vest in the President the executive power, and to vest in one Supreme Court and such inferior courts as Congress might establish, the judicial power. From this division on principle, the reasonable construction of the Constitution must be that the branches should be kept separate in all cases in which they were not expressly blended, and the Constitution should be expounded to blend them no more than it affirmatively requires....

. . .

The vesting of the executive power in the President was essentially a grant of the power to execute the laws. But the President alone and unaided could not execute the laws. He must execute them by the assistance of subordinates. This view has since been repeatedly affirmed by this Court....As he is charged specifically to take care that they be faithfully executed, the reasonable implication, even in the absence of express words, was that as part of his executive power he should select those who were to act for him under his direction in the execution of the laws. The further implication must be, in the absence of any express limitation respecting removals, that as his selection of administrative officers is essential to the execution of the laws by him, so must be his power of removing those for whom he can not continue to be responsible....It was urged that the natural meaning of the term "executive power" granted the President included the appointment and removal of executive subordinates. If such appointments and removals were not an exercise of the executive power, what were they? They certainly were not the exercise of legislative or judicial power in government as usually understood.

....

The requirement of the second section of Article II that the Senate should advise and consent to the Presidential appointments, was to be strictly construed....

...

A reference of the whole power of removal to general legislation by Congress is quite out of keeping with the plan of government devised by the framers of the Constitution. It could never have been intended to leave to Congress unlimited discretion to vary fundamentally the operation of the great independent executive branch of government and thus most seriously to weaken it. It would be a delegation by the Convention to Congress of the function of defining the primary boundaries of another of the three great divisions of government. The inclusion of removals of executive officers in the executive power vested in the President by Article II, according to its usual definition, and the implication of his power of removal of such officers from the provision of section 2 expressly recognizing in him the power of their appointment, are a much more natural and appropriate source of the removing power.

...

...To Congress under its legislative power is given the establishment of offices, the determination of their functions and jurisdiction, the prescribing of reasonable and relevant qualifications and rules of eligibility of appointees, and the fixing of the term for which they are to be appointed, and their compensation—all except as otherwise provided by the Constitution.

...

Made responsible under the Constitution for the effective enforcement of the law, the President needs as an indispensable aid to meet it the disciplinary influence upon those who act under him of a reserve power of removal.....

...

We come now to a period in the history of the Government when both Houses of Congress attempted to reverse this constitutional construction and to subject the power of removing executive officers appointed by the President and confirmed by the Senate to the control of the Senate—indeed, finally, to the assumed power in Congress to place the removal of such officers anywhere in the Government.

...

The extreme provisions of all this [Reconstruction-era] legislation were a full justification for the considerations so strongly advanced by Mr. Madison and his associates in the First Congress for insisting that the power of removal of executive officers by the President alone was essential in the division of powers between the executive and the legislative bodies. It exhibited in a clear degree the paralysis to which a partisan Senate and Congress could subject the executive arm and destroy the principle of executive responsibility and separation of the powers, sought for by the framers of our Government, if the President had no power of removal save by consent of the Senate. It was an attempt to re-distribute the powers and minimize those of the President.

...

The attitude of the Presidents on this subject has been unchanged and uniform to the present day whenever an issue has clearly been raised....

...

An argument ab *inconvenienti* has been made against our conclusion in favor of the executive power of removal by the President, without the consent of the Senate—that it will open the door to a reintroduction of the spoils system. The evil of the spoils system aimed at in the civil service law and its amendments is in respect of inferior offices. It has never been attempted to extend that law beyond them. Indeed, Congress forbids its extension to appointments confirmed by the Senate, except with the consent of the Senate....

...

...When, on the merits, we find our conclusion strongly favoring the view which prevailed in the First Congress, we have no hesitation in holding that conclusion to be correct; and it therefore follows that the Tenure of Office Act of 1867, in so far as it attempted to prevent the President from removing executive officers who had been appointed by him by and with the advice and consent of the Senate, was invalid, and that subsequent legislation of the same effect was equally so.

For the reasons given, we must therefore hold that the provision of the law of 1876, by which the unrestricted power of removal of first class postmasters is denied to the President, is in violation of the Constitution, and invalid. This leads to an affirmance of the judgment of the Court of Claims.

JUSTICE HOLMES, dissenting.

...

The arguments drawn from the executive power of the President, and from his duty to appoint officers of the United States (when Congress does not vest the appointment elsewhere), to take care that the laws be faithfully executed, and to commission all officers of the United States, seem to me spider's webs inadequate to control the dominant facts.

We have to deal with an office that owes its existence to Congress and that Congress may abolish tomorrow. Its duration and the pay attached to it while it lasts depend on Congress alone. Congress alone confers on the President the power to appoint to it and at any time may transfer the power to other hands. With such power over its own creation, I have no more trouble in believing that Congress has power to prescribe a term of life for it free from any interference than I have in accepting the undoubted power of Congress to decree its end.... The duty of the President to see that the laws be executed is a duty that does not go beyond the laws or require him to achieve more than Congress sees fit to leave within his power.

JUSTICE McREYNOLDS, dissenting.

...

May the President oust at will all postmasters appointed with the Senate's consent for definite terms under an Act which inhibits removal without consent of that body? May he approve a statute which creates an inferior office and prescribes restrictions on removal, appoint an incumbent, and then remove without regard to the restrictions?...I think there is no such power. Certainly it is not given by any plain words of the Constitution; and the argument advanced to establish it seems to me forced and unsubstantial.

A certain repugnance must attend the suggestion that the President may ignore any provision of an Act of Congress under which he has proceeded. He should promote and not subvert orderly government. The serious evils which followed the practice of dismissing civil officers as caprice or interest dictated, long permitted under congressional enactments, are known to all. It brought the public service to a low estate and caused insistent demand for reform.....

...

Nothing short of language clear beyond serious disputation should be held to clothe the President with authority wholly beyond congressional control arbitrarily to dismiss every officer whom he appoints except a few judges. There are no such words in the Constitution, and the asserted inference conflicts with the heretofore accepted theory that this government is one of carefully enumerated powers under an intelligible charter....

If the phrase "executive power" infolds the one now claimed, many others heretofore totally unsuspected may lie there awaiting future supposed necessity; and no human intelligence can define the field of the President's permissible activities. "A masked battery of constructive powers would complete the destruction of liberty."

...

I find no suggestion of the theory that "the executive power" of Art. II, Sec. 1, includes all possible federal authority executive in nature unless definitely excluded by some constitutional provision, prior to the well-known House debate of 1789, when Mr. Madison seems to have given it support....

...

Judgment should go for the appellant.

JUSTICE BRANDEIS, dissenting.

In 1833 Justice Story, after discussing in §§ 1537–1543 of his *Commentaries on the Constitution* the much debated question concerning the President's power of removal, said in § 1544:

> If there has been any aberration from the true constitutional exposition of the power of removal (which the reader must decide for himself), it will be difficult, and perhaps impracticable, after forty years' experience, to recall the practice to the correct theory. But, at all events, it will be a consolation to those who love the Union, and honor a devotion to the patriotic discharge of duty, that in regard to "inferior officers" (which appellation probably includes ninety-nine out of a hundred of the lucrative offices in the government), the remedy for any permanent abuse is still within the power of Congress, by the simple expedient of requiring the consent of the Senate to removals in such cases.

Postmasters are inferior officers. Congress might have vested their appointment in the head of the department. The Act of July 12, 1876, c. 176, § 6, 19 Stat. 78, 80, reenacting earlier legislation, provided that "postmasters of the first, second, and third classes shall be appointed and may be removed by the President by and with the advice and consent of the Senate, and shall hold their offices for four years unless sooner removed or suspended according to law." That statute has been in force unmodified for half a century. Throughout the period, it has governed a large majority of all civil offices to which appointments are made by and with the advice and consent of the Senate. May the President, having acted under the statute in so far as it creates the office and authorizes the appointment, ignore, while the Senate is in session, the provision which prescribes the condition under which a removal may take place?

...

To imply a grant to the President of the uncontrollable power of removal from statutory inferior executive offices involves an unnecessary and indefensible limitation upon the constitutional power of Congress to fix the tenure of inferior statutory offices....

...

The separation of the powers of government did not make each branch completely autonomous. It left each, in some measure, dependent upon the others, as it left to each power to exercise, in some respects, functions in their nature executive, legislative and judicial. Obviously the President cannot secure full execution of the laws, if Congress denies to him adequate means of doing so. Full execution may be defeated because Congress declines to create offices indispensable for that purpose. Or, because Congress, having created the office, declines to make the indispensable appropriation. Or, because Congress, having both created the office and made the appropriation, prevents, by restrictions which it imposes, the appointment of officials who in quality and character are indispensable to the efficient execution of the law. If, in any such way, adequate means are denied to the President, the fault will lie with Congress. The President performs his full constitutional duty, if, with the means and instruments provided by Congress and within the limitations prescribed by it, he uses his best endeavors to secure the faithful execution of the laws enacted....

...

B. Inherent Presidential Power

What power do executive officers have to take action beyond the authority that is given to them in statute? Does the Constitution separately empower judges and executive officers, or are they handcuffed by the statutory authority that Congress has thought to provide them? Presidents and their advisors had confronted such questions before, usually in abstract or political contexts. In the case of U.S. Marshal David Neagle the question had immediate legal implications. Neagle was ordered by the attorney general to serve as a bodyguard to Justice Stephen Field, and in the course of his duties killed David Terry on a train in California. Whether Neagle would be tried in state court for murder or be released by a federal court depended on whether the attorney general's order was legal, and federal statutes were not much help. If the attorney general's order was legal, and if Neagle was entitled to the protection that it offered, then it must be because the attorney general was pursuing a constitutional duty. A majority of the justices were willing to recognize such a duty in *In re Neagle* (1890). The presidents themselves built on similar claims when considering the scope of their power and whether they could properly take action in the absence of statutory authority, and sometimes against congressional preferences. The late nineteenth and early twentieth centuries were a period of struggle, as presidents sought to emerge from the shadow of Congress and gain control over the executive branch and an important voice in setting national policy. Developing arguments on behalf of the inherent powers of the president to take action when needed was an important part of that process.

Presidents on Presidential Power

At the turn of the century, the president emerged from the shadow of Congress. The growing importance of foreign policy, the administrative state, interest groups, the railroads and the radio all created opportunities for the president to influence politics. In this period, the presidents were unusually thoughtful and articulate about the powers, duties and responsibilities of the White House. They often found that they had to justify their actions and the powers that they claimed for themselves. In the Jacksonian Era, the Democrats and Whigs had developed contrasting views on presidential power. Now the differences were institutional rather than partisan. Presidents of both parties pushed the power of the executive forward; congressional leaders of both parties resisted. As Teddy Roosevelt explained to his supporters, "I believe in a strong executive; I believe in power."[35]

35. Theodore Roosevelt, *Theodore Roosevelt and His Time Shown in His Own Letters*, ed. Joseph Bucklin Bishop, vol. 2 (New York: Charles Scribner's Sons, 1920), 94.

Of particular note is the so-called "stewardship theory" of presidential power. Teddy Roosevelt argued that "every executive officer, and above all every executive officer in high position, was a steward of the people bound actively and affirmatively to do all he could for the people." As you will see, the more judicially minded Taft—whose reelection campaign in 1912 was derailed by Roosevelt's decision to run as a third party candidate—strongly disagreed with Roosevelt's views.

Grover Cleveland, "The Independence of the Executive" (1904)[36]

In the scheme of our national Government the Presidency is preeminently the people's office. Of course, all offices created by the Constitution, and all government agencies existing under its sanction, must be recognized, in a sense, as the offices and agencies of the people.... When, however, I now speak of the Presidency as preeminently the people's office, I mean that it is especially the office related to the people as individuals, in no general, local, or other combination, but standing on the firm footing of manhood and American citizenship. The Congress may enact laws; but they are inert and vain without executive impulse.... [U]nder the constitutional mandate that the President "shall take care that the laws be faithfully executed," every citizen, in the day or in the night, at home or abroad, is constantly within the protection and restraint of the Executive power....

...[I]t is only in the selection of the President that the body of the American people can by any possibility act together and directly in the equipment of their national Government. Without at least this much of participation in that equipment, we could hardly expect that a ruinous discontent and revolt could be long suppressed among a people who had been promised a popular and representative government.

...

The Constitution declares: "The executive power shall be vested in a President of the United States of America," and this is followed by a recital of the specific and distinctly declared duties with which he is charged, and the powers with which he is invested. The members of the convention were not willing, however, that the executive power which they had vested in the President should be cramped and embarrassed by any implication that a specific statement of certain granted powers and duties excluded all other executive functions; nor were they apparently willing that the claim of such exclusion should have countenance in the strict meaning which might be given to the words "executive power." Therefore we find that the Constitution supplements a recital of the specific powers and duties of the President with this impressive and conclusive additional requirement: "He shall take care that the laws be faithfully executed." This I conceive to be equivalent to a grant of all the power necessary to the performance of his duty in the faithful execution of the laws.

...

...[S]o it is likewise apparent that the convention was not content to rest the sworn obligation of the President solely upon his covenant to "faithfully execute the office of President of the United States," but added hereto the mandate that he should preserve, protect, and defend the Constitution, to the best of his judgment and power, or, as it was afterward expressed, to the best of his ability. Thus is our President solemnly required not only to exercise every power attached to his office, to the end that the laws may be faithfully executed, and not only to render obedience to the demands of the fundamental law and executive duty, but to exert all his official strength and authority for the preservation, protection, and defense of the Constitution.

Theodore Roosevelt, An Autobiography (1913)[37]

The most important factor in getting the right spirit in my Administration, next to the insistence upon courage, honesty, and a genuine democracy of desire to serve the plain people, was my insistence upon the theory that the executive power was limited only by specific restrictions and prohibitions appearing in the Constitution or imposed by the Congress under its Constitutional powers. My view was that every executive officer, and above all every executive officer in high position, was a steward of the people bound actively and affirmatively to do all he could for the people,

36. Excerpt taken from Grover Cleveland, *Presidential Problems* (New York: The Century Company, 1904), 10–17.

37. Excerpt taken from Theodore Roosevelt, *An Autobiography* (New York: Charles Scribner's Sons, 1913), 388–389, 504, 514–516.

and not to content himself with the negative merit of keeping his talents undamaged in a napkin. I declined to adopt the view that what was imperatively necessary for the Nation could not be done by the President unless he could find some specific authorization to do it. My belief was that it was not only his right but his duty to do anything the needs of the Nation demanded unless such action was forbidden by the Constitution or by the laws. Under this interpretation of executive power I did and caused to be done many things not previously done by the President and the heads of the departments. I did not usurp power, but I did greatly broaden the use of executive power. In other words, I acted for the public welfare, I acted for the common well-being of all our people, whenever and in whatever manner was necessary, unless prevented by direct constitutional or legislative prohibition....

...

[O]ccasionally great national crises arise which call for immediate and vigorous executive action, and that in such cases it is the duty of the President to act upon the theory that he is the steward of the people, and that the proper attitude for him to take is that he is bound to assume that he has the legal right to do whatever the needs of the people demand, unless the Constitution or the laws expressly forbid him to do it.

...

So great was that public interest in the Coal Strike of 1902, so deeply and strongly did I feel the wave of indignation which swept over the whole country that had I not succeeded in my efforts to induce the operators to listen to reason, I should reluctantly but none the less decisively have taken a step which would have brought down upon my head the execrations of many of "the captains of industry," as well as of sundry "respectable" newspapers who dutifully take their cue from them.... The mines were in the State of Pennsylvania. There was no duty whatever laid upon me by the Constitution in the matter, and I had in theory no power to act directly unless the Governor of Pennsylvania... should notify me as commander-in-chief of the army of the United States to intervene to keep order.

[But first, the president tried to negotiate a settlement himself, eventually getting the agreement of the miner union and the mine operators for him to appoint an arbitration commission, which was successful in ending the strike.]

... The method of action upon which I had determined in the last resort was to get the Governor of Pennsylvania to ask me to keep order. Then I would put in the army under the command of some first-rate general.... I sent for him, telling him that if I had to make use of him it would be because the crisis was only less serious than that of the Civil War, that the action taken would be practically a war measure, and that if I sent him he must act in a purely military capacity under me as commander-in-chief, paying no heed to any authority, judicial or otherwise, except mine.... Although there would have been plenty of muttering, nothing would have been done to interfere with the solution of the problem which I had devised, until the solution was accomplished and the problem ceased to be a problem. Once this was done, and when people were no longer afraid of a coal famine... then my enemies would have plucked up heart and begun a campaign against me. I doubt if they could have accomplished much anyway, for the only effective remedy against me would have been impeachment, and that they would not have ventured to try.

William Howard Taft, Our Chief Magistrate and His Powers (1916)[38]

... In theory, the Executive power and the Legislative power are independent and separate, but it is not always easy to draw the line and to say where Legislative control and direction to the Executive must cease, and where his independent discretion begins. In theory, all the Executive officers appointed by the President directly or indirectly are his subordinates, and yet Congress can undoubtedly pass laws definitely limiting their discretion and commanding a certain course by them which it is to within the power of the Executives to vary. Fixing the method in which Executive power shall be exercised is perhaps one of the chief functions of Congress....

...

Two principles, limiting Congressional interference with the Executive powers, are clear. *First*, Congress may not exercise any of the powers vested in the President, and *second*, it may not prevent or obstruct the use of means given him by the Constitution for the exercise of those powers.

38. Excerpt taken from William Howard Taft, *Our Chief Magistrate and Their Problems* (New York: Columbia University Press, 1916), 125–126, 129, 139–140, 145–146.

...

The President is made Commander-in-Chief of the army and navy by the Constitution evidently for the purpose of enabling to defend the country against invasion, to suppress insurrection and to take care that the laws be faithfully executed. If Congress were to attempt to prevent his use of the army for any of these purposes, the action would be void.... Congress could not take away from him that discretion and place it beyond his control in any of his subordinates, nor could they themselves, as the people in Athens attempted to, carry on campaigns by votes in the market-place.

...

The true view of the Executive functions is, as I conceive it, that the President can exercise no power which cannot be fairly and reasonably traced to some specific grant of power or justly implied and included within such express grant as proper and necessary to its exercise. Such specific grant must be either in the Federal Constitution or in an act of Congress passed in pursuance thereof. There is no undefined residuum of power which he can exercise because it seems to him to be in the public interest, and there is nothing in the *Neagle* case and its definition of a law of the United States, or in other precedents, warranting such an inference. The grants of Executive power are necessarily in general terms in order not to embarrass the Executive within the field of action plainly marked for him, but his jurisdiction must be justified and vindicated by affirmative constitutional or statutory provision, or it does not exist. There have not been wanting, however, eminent men in high public office holding a different view and who have insisted upon the necessity for an undefined residuum of Executive power in the public interest....

...

My judgment is that the view of... Mr. Roosevelt, ascribing an undefined residuum of power to the President is an unsafe doctrine and that it might lead under emergencies to results of an arbitrary character, doing irremediable injustice to private right. The mainspring of such a view is that the Executive is charged with responsibility for the welfare of all the people in a general way, that he is to play the part of a Universal Providence and set all things right, and that anything that in his judgment will help the people he ought to do, unless he is expressly forbidden not to do it. The wide field of action that this would give to the Executive one can hardly limit. It is enough to say that Mr. Roosevelt has expressly stated how far he thought this principle would justify him in going in respect to the coal famine and the Pennsylvania anthracite strike which he did so much useful work in settling. What was actually done was the result of his activity, his power to influence public opinion and the effect of the prestige of his great office in bringing the parties to the controversy, the mine owners and the strikers, to a legal settlement by arbitration. No one has a higher admiration for the value of what he did there than I have. But if he had failed in this, he says he intended to take action on his theory of the extent of the executive power already state...

Now it is perfectly evident that Mr. Roosevelt thinks he was charged with the duty, not only to suppress disorder in Pennsylvania, but to furnish coal to avoid the coal famine in New York and New England, and therefore he proposed to use the army of the United States to mine the coal which should prevent or relieve the famine. It was his avowed intention to take the coal mines out of the hands of their lawful owners and to mine the coal which belonged to them and sell it in the eastern market, against their objection, without any court proceeding of any kind and without any legal obligation on their part to work the mines at all. It was an advocacy of the higher law and his obligation to execute it which is a little startling in a constitutional republic.... The benevolence of his purpose no one can deny, but no one who looks at it from the standpoint of a government of law could regard it as anything but lawless. I venture to think however, that Mr. Roosevelt is mistaken in what he thinks he would have done. Mr. Roosevelt in office was properly amenable to the earnest advice of those whom he trusted, and there were men about him who would probably have dissuaded him from such a course.

Woodrow Wilson, Constitutional Government in the United States (1908)[39]

... The makers of the Constitution constructed the federal government upon a theory of checks and balances which was meant to limit the operation of each part and allow to no single part or organ of it a dominating force; but no government can be successfully conducted upon

39. Excerpt taken from Woodrow Wilson, *Constitutional Government in the United States* (New York: Columbia University Press, 1908), 54, 60, 66–67, 70.

so mechanical a theory. Leadership and control must be lodged somewhere; the whole art of statesmanship is the art of bringing the several parts of government into effective cooperation for the accomplishment of particular common objects,—and party objects at that....

...

...You cannot compound a successful government out of antagonisms. Greatly as the practice and influence of Presidents have varied, there can be no mistaking the fact that we have grown more and more inclined from generation to generation to look to the President as the unifying force in our complex system, the leader of both his party and of the nation. To do so is not inconsistent with the actual provisions of the Constitution; it is only inconsistent with the very mechanical theory of its meaning and intentions....

...

As legal executive, his constitutional aspect, the President cannot be thought of alone. He cannot execute laws. Their actual daily execution must be taken care of by the several executive departments and by the now innumerable body of federal officials throughout the country. In respect of the strictly executive duties of his office the President may be said to administer the presidency in conjunction with the members of his cabinet, like the chairman of a commission....His executive powers are in commission, while his political powers more and more centre and accumulate upon him and are in their very nature personal and inalienable.

...

He cannot escape being the leader of his party except by incapacity and lack of personal force, because he is at once the choice of the party and of the nation. He is the party nominee, and the only party nominee for whom the whole nation votes. Members of the House and Senate are representatives of localities, are voted for only by sections of voters, or by local bodies of electors like the members of the state legislatures. There is no national party choice except that of President. No one else represents the people as a whole, exercising a national choice...the President represents not so much the party's governing efficiency as its controlling ideas and principles....He can dominate his party by being spokesman for the real sentiment and purpose of the country, by giving direction to opinion, by giving the country at once the information and the statements of policy which will enable it to form its judgments alike of parties and of men.

...

Some of our Presidents have deliberately held themselves off from using the full power they might legitimately have used, because of conscientious scruples, because they were more theorists than statesmen. They have held the strict literary theory of the Constitution, the Whig theory, the Newtonian theory, and have acted as if they thought that Pennsylvania Avenue should have been even longer than it is; that there should be no intimate communication of any kind between the Capitol and the White House....But the makers of the Constitution were not enacting Whig theory, they were not making laws with the expectation that, not the laws themselves, but their opinions, known by future historians to lie back of them, should govern the constitutional action of the country....The President is at liberty, both in law and conscience, to be as big a man as he can. His capacity will set the limit; and if Congress be overborne by him, it will be no fault of the makers of the Constitution,—it will be from no lack of constitutional powers on its part, but only because the President has the nation behind him, and Congress has not....

C. Nondelegation of Legislative Power

According to Article I of the U.S. Constitution, "all legislative Powers herein granted shall be vested in a Congress of the United States." This vesting clause suggests that Congress alone must exercise the legislative powers of the federal government. Congress cannot delegate the federal legislative powers, or a part of them, to someone else. Moreover, in order to exercise the legislative power effectively, Congress must pass a law that actually specifies some legally meaningful directive. If Congress passes a law that does not indicate clearly what government officials and citizens are supposed to do in order to comply with that law, then either the law might not be regarded as effective and enforceable at all or it might be regarded as an attempt to delegate the important decisions to someone else.

The nondelegation doctrine is concerned with statutes that either explicitly delegate too much discretion to another institution or fail to provide sufficient guidance to other actors on how to implement the statute. The nondelegation doctrine has been developed by the courts to address the separation-of-powers problems associated with legislatures delegating too much lawmaking authority to other actors. Judges and bureaucrats may exercise judgment and discretion to implement and administer the policy set in statutes, but they must be guided by a legislative decision made by the legislature.

The challenge for the courts is in determining what standards to use in identifying an unacceptable delegation of lawmaking authority. The growth of the bureaucracy and administrative agencies in the decades after the Civil War put pressure on traditional ideas about the nondelegation doctrine. Statutes were often broadly worded, and administrative agencies were often called upon to engage in extensive rule making in order to fulfill their missions. When did permissible administrative rulemaking become impermissible lawmaking? When did permissible delegations of executive discretion become impermissible delegations of legislative authority? A particularly influential answer emerged from the Taft Court in *J. W. Hampton, Jr. & Co. v. United States* (1928), which held that so long as Congress provided an "intelligible principle" for the executive and the courts to follow, then the delegation was permissible.

J. W. Hampton, Jr. & Co. v. United States, 276 U.S. 394 (1928)

The Republican Party of the nineteenth and early twentieth centuries was dedicated to a policy of protectionism, setting high tariff rates on imported goods that might compete with domestic products. The Republicans were convinced that protectionism was good economic policy in order to protect large, established corporations from international competition. It was also good politics, as the owners of and workers in these corporations were an important component of the Republican electoral coalition and the financiers of party activities.

The subject of intense negotiation and political interest, detailed tariff rates were traditionally fixed in statute by Congress. The Tariff Act of 1922 took a different approach, including a "flexible" tariff provision in its section 315. This section authorized the president to raise tariff rates on any given item by up to 50 percent of the amount set in the statute if the United States Tariff Commission determined that such an adjustment was needed in order to equalize the costs of production in the United States and in foreign countries.

In 1924, President Calvin Coolidge issued a proclamation under this provision raising the import tax on barium dioxide from four cents per pound to six cents per pound, a 50 percent increase that was the maximum allowed by the law. J. W. Hampton, Jr. & Co. filed a protest in the United States Customs Court to the additional tax collected on shipment of barium dioxide. The company argued that the flexible tariff was an unconstitutional delegation of the taxing power of Congress to the executive branch and that the protective tariff was a constitutionally impermissible use of the taxing power. In a unanimous and wide-ranging decision authored by former Republican president William Howard Taft, the Court upheld the flexible tariff. So long as Congress laid down an "intelligible principle" that could guide executive decision making, it had adequately performed its legislative function. Disallowing this kind of flexibility, Taft argued, would at best hamper federal policymaking and at worst render some kinds of regulatory policies effectively impossible. Decided a year before the Great Depression, the case would become a vital precedent in support of the regulatory approach that would be adopted by FDR in the as-yet-unimagined New Deal.

CHIEF JUSTICE TAFT delivered the opinion of the Court.

...

...[T]hey argue that the section is invalid in that it is a delegation to the President of the legislative power, which by article I, Section 1 of the Constitution, is vested in Congress, the power being that declared in section 8 of article I, that the Congress shall have power to lay and collect taxes, duties, imposts and excises....

First, it seems clear what Congress intended by section 315. Its plan was to secure by law the imposition of customs duties on articles of imported merchandise which should equal the difference between the cost of producing in a foreign country the articles in question and laying them down for sale in the United States, and the cost of producing and selling like or similar articles in the United States, so that the duties not only secure revenue, but at the same time enable domestic producers to compete on terms of equality with foreign producers in the markets of the United States. It may be that it is difficult to fix with exactness this difference, but the difference which is sought in the statute is perfectly clear and perfectly intelligible. Because of the difficulty in practically determining what the difference is, Congress seems to have doubted that the information in its possession was such as to enable it to make the adjustment accurately, and also to have apprehended that with changing conditions the difference might vary in such a way that some readjustments would be necessary to give effect to the principle on which the statute proceeds. To avoid such difficulties, Congress adopted in section 315 the method of describing with clearness what its policy and plan was and then authorizing a member of the executive branch to carry out its policy and plan and to find the changing difference from time and time and to make the adjustments necessary to conform the duties to the standard underlying that policy and plan....

...

...[I]t is a breach of the national fundamental law if Congress gives up its legislative power and transfers it to the President, or to the judicial branch, or if by law it attempts to invest itself or its members with either executive power or the judicial power.... In determining what it may do in seeking assistance from another branch, the extent and character of that assistance must be fixed according to common sense and the inherent necessities of the governmental co-ordination.

...

.... As Judge Ranney of the Ohio Supreme Court in *Cincinnati, Wilmington & Zanesville Railroad Co. v Commissioners*, 1 Ohio St. 77, 88 (1852), said in such a case:

> The true distinction, therefore, is between the delegation of power to make the law, which necessarily involves a discretion as to what it shall be, and conferring an authority or discretion as to its execution, to be exercised under and in pursuance of the law. The first cannot be done, to the latter no valid objection can be made.

Again, one of the great functions conferred on Congress by the Federal Constitution is the regulation of interstate commerce and rates to be exacted by interstate carriers for the passenger and merchandise traffic. The rates to be fixed are myriad. If Congress were to be required to fix every rate, it would be impossible to exercise this problem at all. Therefore, common sense requires that in the fixing of such rates Congress may provide a Commission, as it does, called the Interstate Commerce Commission, to fix those rates, after hearing evidence and argument concerning them from interested parties, all in accord with a general rule that Congress first lays down that rates shall be just and reasonable considering the service given and not discriminatory.

...

...If Congress shall lay down by legislative act an intelligible principle to which the person or body authorized to fix such rates is directed to conform, such legislative action is not a forbidden delegation of legislative power. If it is thought wise to vary the customs duties according to changing conditions of production at home and abroad, it may authorize the Chief Executive to carry out this purpose, with the advisory assistance of a Tariff Commission appointed under congressional authority...

...

The judgment of the Court of Custom Appeals is *affirmed*.

D. Elections and Political Parties

Note: Crisis of 1876 and the Electoral Count Act of 1887

During the Civil War and Reconstruction, Republican control of national politics was extremely tenuous, and largely dependent on the imposition of a series of military districts on the former Confederate states. Southern Democrats who sought an end to federal control and the reestablishment of "home rule" were known as "Redeemers," and by 1870 their campaign to end Reconstruction was in full swing. Part of this campaign involved the use of intimidation and violence against blacks and their Republican supporters. Killings occurred throughout the Deep South, as in the Colfax Massacre of 1873. In one seven-month period in Louisiana more than 1,081 political murders took place, mostly of freedmen. By 1874 southern Democrats had regained enough political strength to help the Democratic Party retake the U.S. House of Representatives.

The election of 1876 was a momentous battle. Rutherford B. Hayes, the Republican governor of Ohio, ran against Democrat Samuel J. Tilden, the Democratic governor of New York. The Electoral College vote was so close that problems in just a few key states could hold up the final count. Tilden believed that he had received more popular votes. He was also concerned that the outcomes in key states would not be properly reported, since those state governments and local canvassing boards were controlled by Republicans. In Florida, for example, Republicans declared some returns fraudulent, changing a 94-vote lead by Tilden into a 922-vote margin for Hayes. In December, the outgoing Republican governor of Florida certified the Hayes electors as duly appointed, but in January a Florida court ruled that the Tilden electors should be certified. In response the new Democratic governor sent a new certification to the Congress that gave the state to Tilden. Similar stories unfolded in Louisiana and South Carolina. Republicans countered by pointing out that the outcomes in all of these states were questionable because of ongoing threats of violence against Republican voters.

Not counting these three states, Tilden had 184 electoral votes and Hayes had 165. To win the presidency a candidate needed 185 electoral votes. Florida, Louisiana, and South Carolina—the states where the electoral results were disputed—collectively had 20 electoral votes.

Normally Congress would be in a position to resolve the dispute as part of the process by which electoral votes were certified and counted. However, Congress itself was divided between the two parties, with the Democrats controlling the House and the Republicans controlling the Senate. The Constitution provides that "the President of the Senate shall, in the presence of the Senate and House of Representatives, open all the [electoral] certificates [sent by the states], and the votes shall then be counted." Republicans argued that the power to count the votes rested exclusively with the President of the Senate (conveniently a Republican); Democrats objected, saying that no vote should be counted except by the concurrence of both houses.

On January 29, 1877—a little more than two months before the President was to be sworn into office—the Congress created a fifteen-member commission charged with settling the disputed election. Five members would come from each house of Congress and another five from the Supreme Court. The House would appoint three Democrats and two Republicans, the Senate three Republicans and two Democrats, and the Supreme Court two Democrats and two Republicans—with the fifth Supreme Court appointment being selected by these four. The justices first selected independent Justice David Davis, but just as the bill was passing Congress the Illinois legislature appointed him to the Senate. Davis immediately resigned from the Court. The justices instead selected Republican Justice Joseph P. Bradley. This meant that the commission was composed of eight Republicans and seven Democrats.

In the end, two days before the presidential inauguration, after a series of 8–7 party-line votes, the commission gave all disputed electoral votes to Hayes. He was inaugurated two days later, after having received 4,034,311 popular votes to Tilden's 4,288,546. This resolution was facilitated by the so-called Compromise of 1877, whereby Hayes agreed that, in exchange for receiving the disputed electoral votes and becoming president, he would give the Democrats what they most wanted: the removal of federal troops from the South. This moment marks the formal end of Reconstruction and the triumph of the Redeemers. Jim Crow soon followed.

In the wake of the Hayes–Tilden controversy, Congress spent several years debating how to create a more regular process for handling disputed presidential elections. The result was the Electoral Count Act of 1887. The act was designed to place the burden on the states themselves. The states were encouraged to resolve all disputes within six days of the scheduled Electoral College vote—"by judicial or other methods or procedures" that were based on "laws enacted prior to the day fixed for the appointment of the electors." If they could, then Congress would not challenge their electoral votes. If there was still a controversy, and more than one slate of electors was sent to Congress, then the slate of electors that was "certified by the executive of the State" would be counted, unless both houses of Congress decided differently. If for some reason this did not resolve the election (perhaps because of a dispute over which slate of electors was properly certified) then the two houses of Congress would meet until a decision could be reached.

No provision was made for federal judicial involvement in a disputed presidential election. In fact, none was ever imagined—until the U.S. Supreme Court chose to insert itself into the 2000 presidential election between Democrat Al Gore and Republican George W. Bush.

Suggested Readings

Beth, Loren P. The *Development of the American Constitution, 1877–1917* (New York: Harper & Row, 1971).

Carpenter, Daniel P. *The Forging of Bureaucratic Autonomy: Reputations, Networks, and Policy Innovation in Executive Agencies, 1862–1928* (Princeton: Princeton University Press, 2001).

Clemens, Elisabeth S. *The People's Lobby: Organizational Innovation and the Rise of Interest Group Politics in the United States, 1890–1925* (Chicago: University of Chicago Press, 1997).

Fiss, Owen M. *History of the Supreme Court of the United States, vol. 8, Troubled Beginnings of the Modern State, 1888–1910* (New York: Macmillan, 1993).

Gillman, Howard. *The Constitution Besieged: The Rise and Demise of Lochner Era Police Powers Jurisprudence* (Durham, NC: Duke University Press, 1993).

Hamm, Richard F. *Shaping the Eighteenth Amendment: Temperance Reform, Legal Culture and the Polity, 1880–1920* (Chapel Hill: University of North Carolina Press, 1995).

Hoffer, Williamjames Hull. *To Enlarge the Machinery of Government: Congressional Debates and the Growth of the American State, 1858–1891* (Baltimore: Johns Hopkins University Press, 2007).

James, Scott C. *Presidents, Parties, and the State: A Party System Perspective on Democratic Regulatory Choice, 1884–1936* (New York: Cambridge University Press, 2000).

Keller, Morton. *Affairs of State: Public Life in Late Nineteenth Century America* (Cambridge: Harvard University Press, 1977).

Keller, Morton. *Regulating a New Economy: Public Policy and Economic Change in America, 1900–1933* (Cambridge: Harvard University Press: 1990).

Kens, Paul. *Justice Stephen Field: Shaping American Liberty from the Gold Rush to the Gilded Age* (Lawrence: University Press of Kansas, 1997).

Mason, Alpheus T. *William Howard Taft: Chief Justice* (New York: Simon and Schuster, 1965).

Milkis, Sidney M. *Theodore Roosevelt, the Progressive Party, and the Transformation of American Democracy* (Lawrence: University Press of Kansas, 2009).

Paul, Arnold M. *Conservative Crisis and the Rule of Law: Attitudes of Bar and Bench, 1887–1895* (Ithaca, NY: Cornell University Press, 1960).

Purcell, Edward A., Jr. *Brandeis and the Progressive Constitution: Erie, the Judicial Power, and the Politics of the Federal Courts in Twentieth-Century America* (New Haven: Yale University Press, 2000).

Ross, William G. *A Muted Fury: Populists, Progressives, and Labor Unions Confront the Courts, 1890–1937* (Princeton: Princeton University Press, 1994).

Skowronek, Stephen. *Building a New American State: The Expansion of National Administrative Capacity, 1877–1920* (New York: Cambridge University Press, 1982).

Sparrow, Bartholomew H. *The Insular Cases and the Emergence of American Empire* (Lawrence: University Press of Kansas, 2006).

Swisher, Carl B. *Stephen Field: Craftsman of the Law* (Chicago: University of Chicago Press, 1930).

Wiebe, Robert H. *The Search for Order, 1877–1920* (New York: Hill and Wang, 1966).

Wood, Stephen B. *Constitutional Politics in the Progressive Era: Child Labor and the Law* (Chicago: University of Chicago Press, 1968).

Chapter 8

The New Deal and Great Society Era: 1933–1968

I. Introduction

The period from 1933 to 1968 was the heyday of political and constitutional liberalism. Franklin Roosevelt was first elected to the presidency in 1932, and he brought large Democratic majorities with him to Washington. The policies of Roosevelt and his allies were deeply controversial, but liberals won the major debates. American politics after 1940 was largely a contest between those who would expand and those who would merely maintain the liberal programs established during President Franklin Roosevelt's first two terms of office. Democratic presidential candidates promised new exercises of federal power aimed alleviating poverty, promoting economic security, and, during the 1960s, achieving racial equality. Franklin Roosevelt's shifting bundle of proposals to get the United States out of the Great Depression in the 1930s was known as the New Deal. Subsequent Democratic presidents offered ambitious plans of their own, most famously Lyndon Johnson's Great Society in the 1960s, which expanded the social safety net and launched new civil rights initiatives. Republicans such as Dwight Eisenhower and Richard Nixon promised to manage those programs better than Democrats. Liberal Democrats and liberal Republicans in Congress enthusiastically endorsed the New Deal and Great Society. Conservative Republicans and southern Democrats acted as temporary brakes, slowing and moderating liberal policies.

After Roosevelt's reelection in 1936, the Supreme Court and the administration fought their final battles over the constitutionality of the New Deal. In a series of decisions in 1937, known as the "New Deal Revolution," the Court approved the New Deal. The old conservatives soon left the bench and were replaced by justices committed to the new constitutional order. The debate going forward was between stronger and more moderate liberals over how to understand the legacy of the New Deal. For most of the post–New Deal period, the justices were concerned with allowing the president and Congress to create a "workable government" that could respond to the problems of the modern world as they understood it. John Marshall Harlan, generally considered the leading conservative on the Warren Court, mig ht well have been considered a strong liberal in other historical periods. The leading voice for judicial restraint in the 1960s consistently voted to declare segregation unconstitutional, wrote several of the Court's most important decisions striking down restrictions on free speech, supported the right to an attorney in *Gideon v. Wainwright* (1964), and led the judicial fight to grant married persons a right to use birth control. Neither Harlan nor any other justice appointed by Presidents Roosevelt, Truman, Eisenhower, Kennedy, or Johnson ever suggested that national powers were significantly hampered by concerns over enumerated powers or states' rights.

Two fundamental and related principles lay at the core of the New Deal/Great Society constitutional vision. The first principle was that the national government was responsible for resolving all national economic and, increasingly, all social problems. New Dealers often quoted from the Virginia Plan to the Constitutional Convention, insisting that the national government was constitutionally authorized "to legislate in all cases to which the separate States are incompetent, or in which the harmony of the United States may be interrupted by the exercise of individual Legislation."[1] The second principle was that the national government

1. Max Farrand, ed., *The Records of the Federal Convention of 1787*, vol. 1 (New Haven: Yale University Press, 1966), 23.

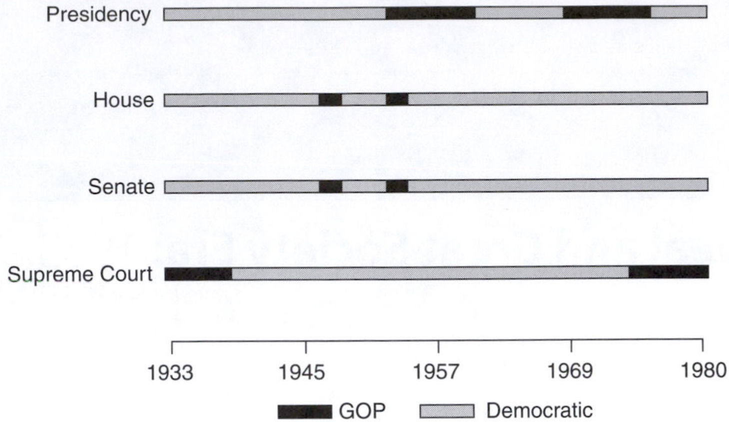

Figure 8-1 Partisan Control of the U.S. Government, 1933–1980

was responsible for guaranteeing to all American citizens a broad array of both positive and negative freedoms. Proponents of the New Deal and Great Society argued that negative rights (protections from government) such as free speech and equal protection had not yet been given sufficient breadth. They added economic security to the positive rights (duties on government) that they believed warranted constitutional protection. While courts played an increasing role in protecting these freedoms, the Constitution vested primary responsibility in the national executive and legislature.

Initial opposition to this constitutional vision questioned whether the national government was authorized to resolve such a wide range of social and economic problems. By the 1950s and 1960s, critics had largely shifted ground. They instead focused on the liberal vision of constitutional rights. The Warren Court and Great Society, in their view, expanded constitutional rights far beyond their original understanding and, in the guise of constitutional interpretation, created both positive and negative rights that did not exist. In the eyes of conservative critics, the liberal justices were acting as a "super-legislature" and "making policy from the bench," just as New Dealers had once complained that conservative justices had done.

Developments. The American constitutional system underwent one of its great transformations during this period. The written text of the state and federal constitutions received only minor adjustments from the 1930s to the 1960s. The great battles occurred over how to interpret those constitutional texts, how to implement the terms of those texts, and what practices to pursue under those constitutions.

The biggest battle took place on the national stage. Franklin Roosevelt entered the White House in 1932 with a large congressional majority, a mobilized base of supporters, and plans for restructuring the government and the economy. His administration and the Congress took unprecedented steps to get the country out of the Depression and to address long-standing liberal goals. The U.S. Supreme Court reacted with alarm. During FDR's first term, the conservative Court struck down federal laws in thirteen cases and state laws in another thirty cases. The Court was often closely divided, issuing 5–4 and 6–3 decisions, while striking down high-profile, newly passed statutes. In his second term, the president struck back, proposing a plan to "reorganize" the federal judiciary by adding new justices to the Supreme Court and new judges to the lower courts. The controversial plan did not pass Congress, but during the legislative debates in 1937 the centrist justices on the Court switched sides. The Court never again struck down a New Deal statute. President Roosevelt soon replaced the conservative judges by normal means.

The constitutional transformation was sweeping. The federal government grew larger and exercised more authority to regulate activities affecting the economy. The federal government took on more taxing-and-spending authority, launching a new era of "cooperative federalism" in which state and local governments receive a large portion of their revenue from the national government. The president took on new authority in the domestic and especially the foreign arena. The courts retreated from strong enforcement of enumerated powers or property

Table 8-1 Major Issues and Decisions of the New Deal and Great Society Era

Major Political Issues	Major Constitutional Issues	Major Court Decisions
New Deal	National Regulatory Authority	*Carter v. Carter Coal Co.* (1936)
World War II	Property Rights	*United States v. Curtiss-Wright Export Corp.* (1936)
Cold War	Presidential War Powers	*National Labor Relations Board v. Jones & Laughlin Steel* (1937)
Domestic Security	Legislative Investigation Powers	*Palko v. Connecticut* (1937)
Korean War	Executive Privilege	*Wickard v. Filburn* (1942)
Civil Rights Movement	Judicial Review	*Youngstown Sheet & Tube Co. v. Sawyer* (1952)
Vietnam War	Civil Rights	*Brown v. Board of Education* (1954)
	Civil Liberties	*Baker v. Carr* (1962)

Note: A host of more detailed civil liberties and civil rights issues became the subject of controversy during this period, and these are explored in more detail in Volume 2 of this set.

rights, but became more active in enforcing separation of powers and civil liberties.

Partisan Coalitions in the New Deal and Great Society Era. Democrats dominated national politics during this period. The Great Depression scrambled party allegiances and damaged the Republican Party for a generation. Democrats routed Republicans in Congress in the midterm elections under President Herbert Hoover in 1930. Franklin Roosevelt solidified Democratic gains in 1932. Roosevelt went on to win an unprecedented four terms as president. His vice president, Harry Truman, won a presidential term on his own in 1948. Republicans regained control of the White House for eight years in the 1950s by nominating the centrist war hero, Dwight Eisenhower, but Democrats returned to the presidency in 1960 for eight more years with John F. Kennedy and Lyndon Johnson. The Democratic grip over Congress loosened only briefly during this entire period. All told, Democrats won seven of nine presidential elections from 1932 until 1968, and sixteen of eighteen congressional elections. Democrats often won those elections by large majorities.

The New Deal coalition was an uneasy partnership of diverse groups. Roosevelt and the New Deal Democrats banded together southern whites, farmers, labor unions and working class voters, ethnic minorities, and northern urban voters. Labor unions grew in size and political significance over the course of the 1930s and 1940s. The Democratic Party successfully challenged the Republicans for the African-American vote in regions of the country where suffrage could be freely exercised. The result was a powerful electoral coalition that shared many common interests and a willingness to expand the national government to pursue them.

The Democratic Party was ideologically split between its dominant liberal wing and its minority conservative wing. Liberals drove the intellectual and political leadership of the Party during this period. The New Deal and Great Society were promoted by liberals. Interest groups such as the Americans for Democratic Action (ADA) began to score congressional voting records to identify and reward liberal legislators. The Party also held a significant group of more conservative legislators. Many were southern members with substantial seniority. They sometimes allied with Republican members to form a "Conservative Coalition" that obstructed liberal reforms ranging from Franklin Roosevelt's Court-packing plan to Harry Truman's national health insurance proposal. At the extreme, such dissenters could split the party, as with South Carolina Senator Strom Thurmond's "Dixiecrat" run for the White House in 1948. As a result, liberals frequently complained that they were not able to get as much done as they wanted, even when the Democrats were in the majority. In the

Box 8-1 A Partial Cast of Characters of the New Deal–Great Society Era

Franklin D. Roosevelt	■ Democrat ■ Assistant secretary of the navy (1913–20) ■ Governor of New York (1929–32) ■ President of the United States (1933–45) ■ Longest-serving president in U.S. history, served through both the Great Depression and World War II ■ Built a new Democratic coalition of labor and agriculture and launched an aggressive and controversial program of active government, expanded central power, and stronger executive power in both domestic and foreign affairs
Earl Warren	■ Republican ■ California attorney general (1939–43) ■ California governor (1943–53) ■ Appointed by Eisenhower to be Chief Justice of the United States (1953–69) ■ An exceedingly popular California politician; was simultaneously nominated by the Republican, Democratic and Progressive Parties for statewide office ■ Led an increasingly liberal Court that supported congressional and presidential power and carved out new civil rights and civil liberties
Robert H. Jackson	■ Democrat ■ Successful New York lawyer who joined Franklin Roosevelt's justice department ■ U.S. solicitor general (1938–40) ■ U.S. attorney general (1940–41) ■ Appointed by Roosevelt to Supreme Court (1941–54) ■ U.S. chief counsel for Nuremberg trials (1945) ■ Known for his pragmatic, functionalist approach to constitutional problems ■ Last person appointed to the Supreme Court who did not graduate from a law school
Hugo Black	■ Democrat ■ U.S. senator (1927–37) ■ Appointed by Roosevelt to Supreme Court (1937–71) ■ A liberal New Dealer, Black was a supporter of the Court-packing plan while in the Senate ■ On the Court he was known for his textualism, appeals to history, and his simultaneous emphasis on judicial restraint and firm defense of civil liberties
Charles Evans Hughes	■ Republican ■ Governor of New York (1907–10) ■ Appointed by Taft to the Supreme Court (1910–1916) ■ Resigned to run for president against Woodrow Wilson in 1916 ■ Secretary of State (1921–25) ■ Appointed by Hoover to be Chief Justice of the United States (1930–41) ■ Started his career as a progressive reformer but later gained a more conservative reputation ■ Guided the Supreme Court through the Court-packing challenge, and wrote key decisions upholding the New Deal
William Brennan	■ Democrat ■ New Jersey supreme court (1951–56) ■ Appointed by Eisenhower to U.S. Supreme Court (1956–90) ■ Chosen by Eisenhower as part of a reelection bid to appeal to Catholic Democrats, Brennan became one of the most significant justices of the twentieth century ■ Wrote many of the landmark decisions of the Warren Court and continued to be a major influence in the Burger Court known for his strong advocacy of active judicial review and expansive liberal interpretation of constitutional rights

midst of the Kennedy administration, the New Deal presidential scholar James MacGregor Burns wrote of the "deadlock of democracy" and called for vigorous presidential leadership to overcome congressional roadblocks.[2]

Republicans were likewise a diverse coalition. On the whole, the GOP was more conservative than the Democrats, but the party included both liberals and conservatives. The liberal wing of the Republican Party was centered in the northeast. The conservative wing was centered in the Midwest. Over time, the GOP attempted to pull white southerners away from the Democratic Party, even as African-American voters shifted their loyalties away from the party of Lincoln and to the party of the New Deal and the Great Society. Republicans did manage to win the White House for two terms by nominating the moderate Eisenhower, who had also been courted by the Democratic Party. More often, they failed. Sometimes they were competitive, as when they nominated the liberal New Yorker Thomas Dewey in 1948. Sometimes they were crushed, as when they nominated the conservative Arizonian Barry Goldwater in 1964. Republican influence in Congress during this period depended on taking advantage of Democratic disagreements.

The Federal Judiciary in the New Deal and Great Society. The federal judiciary underwent a great ideological transformation during this period. The federal courts, led by the U.S. Supreme Court, had been dominated by conservatives for many decades. Many of those judges were skeptical of the constitutionality of Progressive reform legislation passed in the first decades of the twentieth century, and they were likewise skeptical of the constitutionality of the New Deal in first years of Franklin Roosevelt's administration. By the end of the Roosevelt presidency, the Supreme Court had been remade. Franklin Roosevelt by himself made nine appointments to the Supreme Court, and the New Deal Court dramatically reshaped constitutional law in the late 1930s and 1940s. In the 1950s and 1960s, the Warren Court pushed constitutional law in new directions, generating great controversy but also setting landmarks that remain central to law and society today. During these decades, the Supreme Court was the most closely allied with the political left as it has ever been.

The transformation of the courts did not come easily. When Roosevelt and the New Deal Democrats won Congress and the presidency in 1930 and 1932, the Supreme Court included only two justices nominated by a Democratic president. The start of the New Deal was marked by some of the greatest conflicts between the Court and the elected branches in American history. Between 1932 and 1936, the Supreme Court struck down more federal laws in more cases over a shorter period of time than it had at any prior point in its history. Moreover, these were not minor provisions of unimportant statutes. During Roosevelt's first term of office, the Court struck down key provisions of many of the cornerstone statutes of the New Deal. Congress and the President responded with proposals to rein in the Court. The most important of these was President Roosevelt's "Court-packing" plan of 1937, which he unveiled just after his reelection. Roosevelt proposed that Congress pass a statute that would create additional seats on the Court, giving him an immediate majority. After an acrimonious debate, the plan was defeated in Congress, in part because the Court had already reversed itself and started to rule in favor of New Deal policies. Soon after, the strongest conservatives left the bench, and Roosevelt made his appointments by the usual means. The constitutionality of the New Deal was no longer an open question in the courts.

The New Deal Court under the successive leadership of Chief Justice Charles Evans Hughes, Harlan Fiske Stone, and finally Fred Vinson embraced the constitutional changes that were taking place in the 1930s and 1940s. Under the commerce clause, the justices accepted that the federal government could regulate all economic activity when doing so was in the national interest. Under the spending clause, the justices accepted that the federal government could make expenditures that Congress believed served the general welfare without regard to their connection to an enumerated power or any Tenth Amendment restriction. In the name of facilitating a "workable government," the Court approved as consistent with the separation of powers legislation that made broad delegations of power to the executive branch or administrative agencies. In the interest of alleviating judicial oversight of legislative policymaking, the Court adopted a defer-

2. James MacGregor Burns, *The Deadlock of Democracy* (Englewood Cliffs, NJ: Prentice-Hall, 1963).

ential standard for reviewing government regulations that were said to interfere with the contracts or due process clause of the Constitution.

Under the leadership of Chief Justice Earl Warren, the Supreme Court in the 1950s and 1960s advanced in new directions. Building on some earlier cases, the Warren Court launched a "rights revolution" across a wide range of issues. In numerous cases, primarily involving state law and often arising in the South, the Warren Court extended individual rights ranging from free speech to religious free exercise to constitutional criminal procedure to sexual liberty. The Court likewise embarked on new efforts to address racial civil rights and restructure legislative apportionment.

- *United States v. Carolene Products Co.* (1938) established that economic regulations were "presumptively constitutional."
- *Wickard v. Filburn* (1942) established that any activity that has a "substantial economic effect on interstate commerce" can be regulated by Congress.
- *Youngstown Sheet & Tube Co. v. Sawyer* (1952) established that there were boundaries to executive power when Congress had created a specific statutory framework.
- *Brown v. Board of Education* (1954) prohibited racial segregation in public schools.
- *Reynolds v. Sims* (1964) disallowed malapportioned state legislative districts.
- *Engel v. Vitale* (1962) prohibited organized school prayer.
- *Griswold v. Connecticut* (1965) recognized a right to privacy and struck down a state restriction on sales of birth control.
- *Miranda v. Arizona* (1966) imposed rules on police arrests and interrogations to prevent unconstitutional forced confessions.

The Court's work during this period was important, prominent, and controversial. During these decades, the Court addressed basic social and political questions, and often issued bold decisions calling for the reform of social and political institutions. Those efforts were not always successful, but many decisions remain landmarks in constitutional law. The Court's work generated heated controversy and sometimes successful resistance. But the Court also had numerous allies, generally including the leadership of the national government and a growing number of liberal interest groups dedicated to litigating constitutional cases.

Legacies. The New Deal and Great Society reshaped the constitutional landscape. Commentators at the time referred to the events of the New Deal as a constitutional revolution. The court decisions, statutes, and political mobilization of the 1950s and 1960s are often referred to as a rights revolution. Constitutional scholar Bruce Ackerman has aptly characterized the post–New Deal era as a "third republic" in American history, as distinctive and as notable as the periods after the founding and after Reconstruction.[3] Many of the constitutional debates that were familiar throughout American history came to an end during these revolutions. Other debates were transformed, and still other debates began. Constitutionally speaking, we live in a post–New Deal world.

As you read the materials in this chapter, you will want to consider how these decisions changed the terms of debate. How much and in what ways did they transform the constitutional order? Where are the points of continuity with what came before? How familiar are these arguments and debates compared to earlier materials? How persuasive are they as acts of constitutional interpretation? What accounts for the points of change and continuity, and what implications do these decisions have for the future?

The New Deal coalition came under increasing strain in the 1960s. The labor unions that had been strong Democratic supporters went into decline, and non-union workers were less supportive of Democrats. The growing number of professional and white collar workers, by contrast, fed Republican support. The once "Solid South" became a battleground, as southern whites increasingly supported the GOP and the Voting Rights Act of 1965 opened the door for southern blacks to support Democrats. By the end of the 1960s, the New Deal coalition had achieved extraordinary success in the electoral and policy arenas. Further successes would be much more difficult.

3. Bruce Ackerman, *We the People*, vol. 1 (Cambridge: Harvard University Press, 1991).

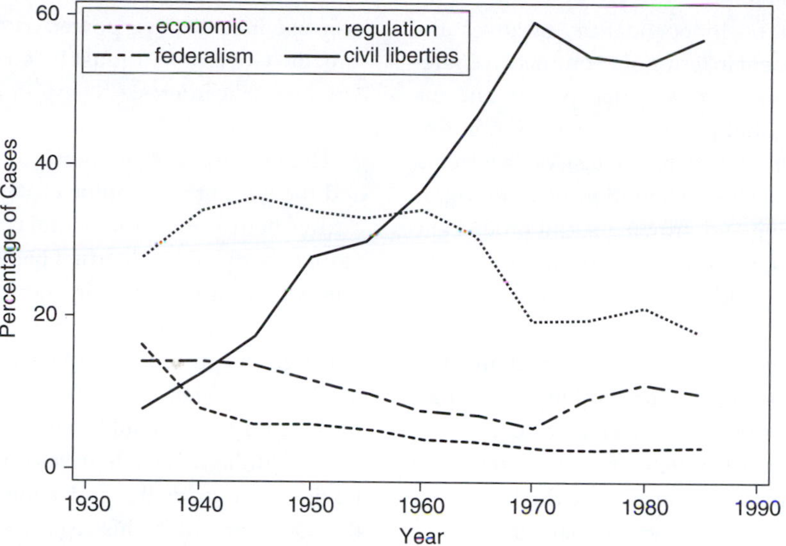

Figure 8-2 Agenda Change on the U.S. Supreme Court, 1933–1988

Source: Richard L. Pacelle, Jr., *The Transformation of the Supreme Court's Agenda* (Boulder, CO: Westview Press, 1991), Table 3.1.

Note: Five-year intervals averaged.

Franklin D. Roosevelt, Commonwealth Club Address (1932)[4]

As both a presidential candidate and a president, Franklin Roosevelt consistently advanced two themes: the need for "bold, persistent experimentation" by the national government to restore prosperity and the social and political commitment to providing economic and personal security for all citizens. Roosevelt first articulated these sentiments during a speech at the Commonwealth Club in San Francisco, delivered during his 1932 campaign for the presidency. The speech laid out a vision of a new "economic constitutional order" that was as concerned with checking private power and marshaling the power of government to advance the public good as with preventing the abuse of political power. Roosevelt's Commonwealth Club Address appeals to traditional constitutional concerns such as the protection of the individual and the inappropriateness of "class legislation" that exploits public power to benefit private interests, while emphasizing the need to reevaluate inherited constitutional commitments and the new constitutional challenges to realizing those ideals in an age of democracy and industrialization. In the election of 1932, he assembled the electoral coalition that enabled him to begin to act on that vision.

4. Excerpt taken from Franklin D. Roosevelt, President's Personal File Speeches, Franklin D. Roosevelt Presidential Library.

. . .

A glance at the situation today only too clearly indicates that equality of opportunity as we have known it no longer exists. Our industrial plant is built; the problem just now is whether under existing conditions it is not overbuilt. Our last frontier has long since been reached, and there is practically no more free land. . . .

. . .

Clearly, all this calls for a reappraisal of values. A mere builder of more industrial plants, a creator of more railroad systems, and organizer of more corporations, is as likely to be a danger as a help. The day of the great promoter or the financial Titan, to whom we granted anything if only he would build, or develop, is over. . . . The day of enlightened administration has come.

. . . In other times we dealt with the problem of an unduly ambitious central Government by modifying it gradually into a constitutional democratic Government. So today we are modifying and controlling our economic units.

As I see it, the task of Government in its relation to business is to assist the development of an economic declaration of rights, an economic constitutional order. This is the common task of statesman and business man. It is the minimum requirement of a more permanently safe order of things.

. . .

The Declaration of Independence discusses the problem of Government in terms of a contract.... Under such a contract rulers were accorded power, and the people consented to that power on consideration that they be accorded certain rights. The task of statesmanship has always been the redefinition of these rights in terms of a changing and growing social order. New conditions impose new requirements upon Government and those who conduct Government.

...

I feel that we are coming to a view through the drift of our legislation and our public thinking in the past quarter century that private power is, to enlarge an old phrase, a public trust as well. I hold that continued enjoyment of that power by any individual or group must depend upon the fulfillment of that trust....

The terms of that contract are as old as the Republic, and as new as the new economic order.

Every man has a right to life; and this means that he has also a right to make a comfortable living. He may by sloth or crime decline to exercise that right; but it may not be denied him....

Our Government formal and informal, political and economic, owes to every one an avenue to possess himself of a portion of that plenty sufficient for his needs, through his own work.

Every man has a right to his own property; which means a right to be assured, to the fullest extent attainable, in the safety of his savings.... In all thought of property, this right is paramount; all other property rights must yield to it. If, in accord with this principle, we must restrict the operations of the speculator, the manipulator, even the financier, I believe we must accept the restriction as needful, not to hamper individualism but to protect it.

...

This implication is, briefly, that the responsible heads of finance and industry instead of acting each for himself, must work together to achieve the common end. They must, where necessary, sacrifice this or that private advantage; and in reciprocal self-denial must seek a general advantage. It is here that formal Government—political Government, if you choose—comes in. Whenever in the pursuit of this objective the lone wolf, the unethical competitor... declines to join in achieving an end recognized as being for the public welfare, and threatens to drag the industry back to a state of anarchy, the Government may properly be asked to apply restraint. Likewise, should the group ever use its collective power contrary to public welfare, the Government must be swift to enter and protect the public interest.

...

The final term of the high contract was for liberty and the pursuit of happiness. We have learnt a great deal of both in the past century. We know that individual liberty and individual happiness mean nothing unless both are ordered in the sense that one man's meat is not another man's poison. We know that the old "rights of personal competency"—the right to read, to think, to speak to choose and live a mode of life, must be respected at all hazards. We know that liberty to do anything which deprives others of those elemental rights is outside the protection of any compact; and that Government in this regard is the maintenance of a balance, within which every individual may have a place if he will take it; in which every individual may find safety if he wishes it; in which every individual may attain such power as his ability permits, consistent with his assuming the accompanying responsibility.

Dwight Eisenhower, Letter to Edgar Newton Eisenhower (1954)[5]

The Republican Party, battered across multiple national elections, increasingly accepted the central constitutional features of the emerging New Deal state. The Republican Party Platform of 1940, while complaining about the "relative expansion of the power of the Federal government over the everyday life of the farmer, the industrial worker and the businessman," devoted most of its fire to how "waste, discrimination and politics" were preventing New Deal measures from achieving their goals. The Republican presidential candidate that year, Wendell Willkie, ran on a platform that called for an "extension" of benefits provided by Social Security, federal grants to states for relief, maintenance of the National Labor Relations Act, and benefit payments to farmers. Unlike the Democratic Party Platform of 1940, Republicans that year endorsed the Equal Rights Amendment for women and called for a ban on race discrimination. The only New Deal measures the Republican convention continued to denounce as unconstitutional

5. Excerpt taken from *The Papers of Dwight David Eisenhower*, ed. Louis Galambos and Daun van Van Ee, vol. 15 (Baltimore: Johns Hopkins University Press, 1996), 391.

in 1940 were laws giving the president control over the currency and the power to allocate radio frequencies.

In 1952, Dwight Eisenhower became the first Republican to be elected president during the New Deal Era. Eisenhower was by no means a traditional Republican. Educated at West Point, he was an army lifer, who rose to national prominence when leading the D-Day assault against Nazi Germany. Eisenhower had no partisan profile before his nomination for the presidency, and had previously been approached by Harry Truman about the possibility of running as a Democratic candidate. When running his first campaign, Eisenhower sought to redefine the Republican Party in his own image, as a "middle-of-the-road Republican." A key feature of Eisenhower's New Republicanism was its acceptance of the legitimacy of the New Deal. His Republican Party offered more competent and fiscally conscious management of the liberal state, not an ideological or constitutional alternative to it. Eisenhower emphasized this point privately as well as publicly, particularly when pressed by his more conservative brother, Edgar, who took the president to task for not returning to the pre–New Deal constitutional state. The president pointed to the only Constitution that he thought mattered, the one laid down by the current Supreme Court and, implicitly, the one sustained by voters in the previous national elections.

. . .

You keep harping on the Constitution; I should like to point out that the meaning of the Constitution is what the Supreme Court says it is. Consequently no powers are exercised by the Federal government except where such exercise is approved by the Supreme Court (lawyers) of the land.

I admit that the Supreme Court has in the past made certain decisions in this general field that have been astonishing to me. A recent case in point was the decision in the Phillips case.[6] Others, and older ones, involved "interstate commerce." But until some future Supreme Court decision denies the right and responsibility of the Federal government to do certain things, you cannot possibly remove them from the political activities of the Federal government.

Now it is true that I believe this country is following a dangerous trend when it permits too great a degree of centralization of governmental functions. I oppose this—in some instances the fight is a rather desperate one. But to attain any success it is quite clear that the Federal government cannot avoid or escape responsibilities which the mass of the people firmly *believe* should be undertaken by it. The political processes of our country are such that if a *rule of reason* is not applied in this effort, we will lose everything—even to a possible and drastic change in the Constitution. This is what I mean by my constant insistence upon "moderation" in government. Should any political party attempt to abolish social security, unemployment insurance, and eliminate labor laws and farm programs, you would not hear of that party again in our political history. There is a tiny splinter group, of course, that believes you can do these things. Among them are H. L. Hunt (you possibly know his background),[7] a few other Texas oil millionaires, and an occasional politician or business man from other areas. Their number is negligible and they are stupid.

To say, therefore, that in some instances the policies of this Administration have not been radically changed from those of the last is perfectly true. . . .

. . .

No matter what the party is in power, it must perforce follow a program that is related to these general purposes and aspirations. But the *great difference is in how it is done and, particularly, in the results achieved.*

II. Judicial Power and Constitutional Authority

MAJOR DEVELOPMENTS

- The struggle over judicial supremacy in constitutional interpretation
- The struggle over how courts should use the power of judicial review
- The lowering of procedural barriers to bringing disputes into courts
- The application of the federal Bill of Rights to the states

Constitutional struggles over judicial power during the New Deal/Great Society Era reflected constitutional struggles over national power. During the early years of the New Deal, from 1933 to 1937, New Deal liberals tried to wrest control over the federal judiciary from both conservatives and older-style Progressives. The

6. *Phillips Petroleum Co. v. Wisconsin*, 347 U.S. 672 (1954) held that the Natural Gas Act extended beyond the companies that operated interstate pipelines and included companies that were producers of natural gas.

7. H. L. Hunt was at the time one of the wealthiest men in the world and a sponsor of hard right political causes.

four most conservative members of the Supreme Court during this period were known as the "Four Horsemen." Justices Butler, McReynolds, Sutherland, and Van Devanter strongly opposed economic regulations being adopted by the state and federal governments in the early 1930s. Old-style Progressives like Justice Brandeis and Cardozo were much more sympathetic to government intervention in the economy, but they were often skeptical about the centralized political power that they saw in the New Deal. Chief Justice Hughes and Justice Roberts occupied more centrist roles on the Court.

From 1933 to 1937, the four conservatives often won over at least one of the moderates on the Court, and sometimes carried additional votes as well. The key victory for the New Deal came when Justice Roberts and Chief Justice Hughes swung decisively away from the conservatives in 1937. The constitutionality of the New Deal was no longer an open question on the Court. Those who doubted the New Deal soon left the bench and were replaced by Roosevelt appointees.

From 1937 to 1968, the central questions over judicial power concerned debates within the New Deal/Great Society coalition. Some argued that the New Deal was committed to legislative supremacy in most areas of public policy and that judges should generally defer to both federal and state elected officials. Justice Felix Frankfurter, a former Harvard law professor who served on the Supreme Court from 1939 until 1962, is the person most associated with this view of judicial power. Others insisted that the New Deal was committed to national supremacy and that state officials should not receive the same deference from judges that federal officials should receive. Advocates of this position often argued that judges should make democracy work better and protect those who were not adequately protected in the democratic process. Justice Hugo Black, a former U.S. senator from Alabama who served on the Supreme Court from 1937 until 1971, is the person most associated with this view of judicial power. Frankfurter found important support for his views on the Court and played a key role in restraining the Court until his retirement in 1962. When President John F. Kennedy chose famed labor lawyer Arthur Goldberg to replace Frankfurter, the initial core of the liberal wing of the Warren Court was in place. The Warren Court embarked on a new activist phase that lasted through Chief Justice Earl Warren's retirement in 1969.

Years of Turmoil. These were years of substantial turmoil for the Court. Figure 8-3 shows the number of cases decided each year in which the Supreme Court formally overruled one of its prior precedents. The

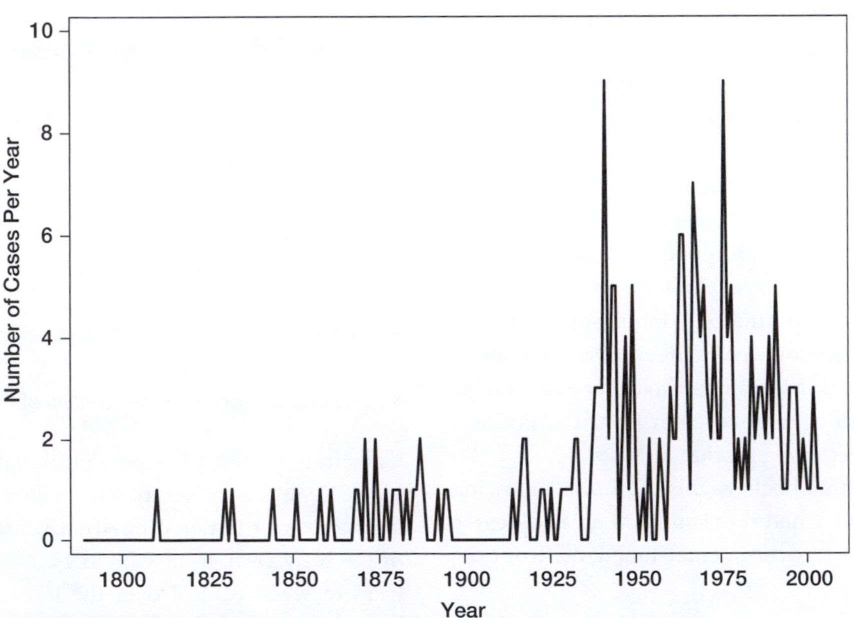

Figure 8-3 Precedents Overruled by the U.S. Supreme Court, 1790–2004

Source: Congressional Research Service, *The Constitution of the United States of America, Analysis and Interpretation* (Washington, DC: Government Printing Office, 2004).

Court has other, less dramatic ways of rejecting its precedents. The Court can simply ignore its earlier decisions and allow them to fall into silent disuse. The Court can "distinguish" current cases from earlier ones, holding that the precedent is not applicable to the current case and rendering precedents increasingly irrelevant to ongoing disputes. But officially overturned precedents are one quite visible sign of legal change on the Court. The New Deal Court marked its constitutional revolution by announcing that a record number of earlier decisions were no longer good law. By the early 1950s, that work had been done, and the Court briefly returned to a historically more normal pattern.

The Warren Court of the 1960s went back to the task of remaking the law and throwing out old precedents. The Court has only gradually retreated since then. The more conservative Courts of the 1980s and 1990s continued to overturn precedents at a pace that would have been surprising before 1937. As might have been expected, the liberal Courts of the New Deal and Great Society Era primarily overturned the precedents set by the more conservative, pre–New Deal Courts. The more conservative Courts since the 1970s have been skeptical of the liberal decisions handed down during the New Deal and Great Society Era.

Figure 8-4 tracks the number of cases that invalidated the application of state and federal laws on constitutional grounds during this period. The struggle over the constitutionality of the New Deal is reflected on the bottom left. The number of cases in which the Court struck down federal laws briefly surged in the early 1930s before collapsing after the reversal of 1937. The Court gradually became more active in enforcing constitutional restrictions on congressional power, peaking again in the early 1970s. Even though the Warren Court came to an end in 1969, the Court continued to strike down laws at a rapid pace well into the 1970s under Chief Justice Warren Burger. The most notable feature of judicial review in the 1960s and 1970s was the Court's focus on state laws. The Court struck down state laws in more cases during this period than in any earlier period in its history. The Warren and early Burger Courts made their mark from the late 1950s through the early 1970s striking down state laws, in cases ranging from *Brown v. Board of Education* (1954) on racial segregation in schools to *Roe v. Wade* (1973) on

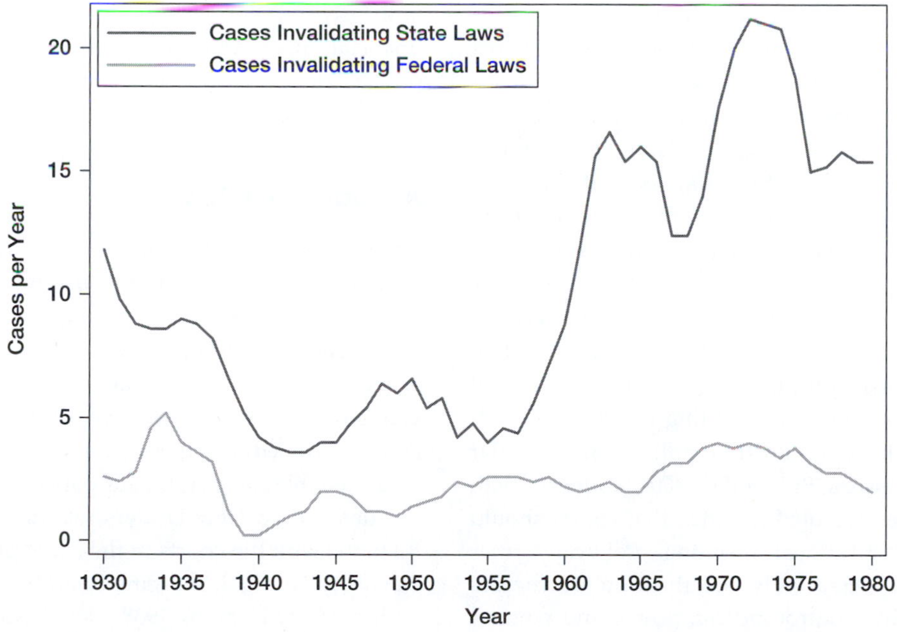

Figure 8-4 U.S. Supreme Court Invalidation of State and Federal Laws, 1930–1980

Source: Congressional Research Service, *The Constitution of the United States of America, Analysis and Interpretation* (Washington, DC: Government Printing Office, 2004); Keith E. Whittington, The Judicial Review of Congress dataset.

Note: Centered, five-year moving averages.

abortion. These cases generated a great deal of national controversy, both over the substance of what the Court had done and over the authority of the Court to do it.

A Commitment to Judicial Supremacy. A renewed constitutional commitment to judicial supremacy was perhaps the most surprising legacy of the New Deal/Great Society Era. As was the case with most presidents who rose to power challenging the fundamental constitutional commitments of an earlier regime, Franklin Roosevelt aggressively challenged the authority of the federal judiciary. He was privately prepared to ignore a possible judicial decision striking down his policy suspending gold payments, and he did little to keep this resolve a secret. After achieving a landslide victory during the 1936 presidential election, Roosevelt proposed a Court-packing plan that would have guaranteed a friendly, pro–New Deal Court. The effort to pack the Court with different justices rather than limit their jurisdiction or weaken their powers highlights how New Dealers were more committed to changing the direction of judicial decision making than challenging judicial authority per se.

Although New Dealers and Great Society liberals disagreed about how the Court should use its power, by the 1950s a broad consensus existed that the Supreme Court had the final authority to determine what the Constitution meant. All nine justices signed the opinion in *Cooper v. Aaron* (1958) which asserted that all elected officials are obligated to obey the Constitution as interpreted by the Supreme Court. President Eisenhower had already endorsed this idea before the Court heard the case. The Warren Court's decisions were often controversial. Conservative opponents of the Warren Court criticized individual decisions. Occasionally, they proposed constitutional amendments or legislation limiting the ability of federal courts to intrude into state politics on particular constitutional issues. But by the 1960s, leaders of both political parties accepted the idea that courts should determine constitutional meaning. Political battles over the courts increasingly took the form of struggles over who would control judicial power and when it ought to be used.

Proponents of the New Deal and Great Society promoted litigation as an appropriate means for resolving contested constitutional questions. An early New Deal measure, the Federal Declaratory Judgment Act of 1934, enabled parties to litigate legal and constitutional issues before an actual injury took place. Declaratory relief statutes allowed courts to rule on the constitutionality of a law without requiring that businesses or individuals actually violate the law, opening more avenues to judicial review. The fact that Roosevelt chose to attack the judiciary through a Court-packing plan showed that the administration was more interested in putting a liberal majority on the Court than in weakening judicial power. Some progressive-minded justices, such as Louis Brandeis and Felix Frankfurter, insisted that judges should avoid resolving constitutional questions whenever possible. Those views seemed antiquated to later liberals.

In the 1960s, the Warren Court sought to lower the barriers to constitutional litigation and judicial resolution of constitutional issues. *Baker v. Carr* (1962) and *Powell v. McCormick* (1969) demonstrated that the justices took a narrow view of the "political questions" doctrine. *Flast v. Cohen* (1968) indicated that the justices might find standing for non-traditional injuries, when doing so enabled the judges to address constitutional wrongs. National elected officials during the Great Society promoted courts as constitutional decision makers by expanding the size of the federal judiciary, appointing sympathetic justices, creating financial incentives for litigation, and supporting public interest groups that were litigating constitutional claims.

A. Judicial Review

The proper use of the power of judicial review—and whether courts even ought to use the power of judicial review at all—was a central question for the New Deal generation. Progressive intellectuals, left-wing activists and liberal politicians had criticized conservative courts throughout the early twentieth century and questioned whether judicial review could ever be a valuable and legitimate part of modern American democracy. New Dealers fought their own painful battle with the courts in the early 1930s, but by the Fall of 1937 the U.S. Supreme Court had fallen into line with the New Deal. By 1938, New Dealers were being appointed to the Court. The New Dealers were torn on how to respond to the new situation. Some continued to urge across-the-board judicial deference. Others began to focus on what a "reinvigorated judiciary" might do for liberal causes. *United States v. Carolene*

Products (1938) provided one important vision of the way forward after 1937. On the one hand, the Court announced that it would defer to legislatures with mere "rationality review" on social and economic policy. On the other hand, the famous "Footnote Four" of the opinion indicated that the Court would not defer across-the-board. There might be cases in which the protection of explicit constitutional provisions, the processes of democracy, or "discrete and insular minorities" required heightened judicial scrutiny.

United States v. Carolene Products, 304 U.S. 144 (1938)

Carolene Products, *decided after the Supreme Court's "switch in time that saved nine" of 1937, emphasized the Court's new deference to economic regulation by the state and federal governments. Filled milk is made by compounding skimmed milk with a fat or oil other than milk fat, usually vegetable oil. The Filled Milk Act of 1923 banned filled milk from interstate commerce. Filled milk was declared by the statute to be an "adulterated article of food, injurious to the public health," and a "fraud upon the public."*

Upholding the Filled Milk Act was not itself a departure for the Court. The Court had upheld similar laws at the state and federal levels well before 1937. Nonetheless, a federal district court in Illinois thought the law reached beyond congressional authority when it heard the case in 1934. Since even the congressional findings only supported the conclusion that filled milk was problematic when falsely labeled by local retailers but was not itself harmful, the district court found that Congress was really attempting to exercise local police powers and therefore the act was at odds with the child labor cases, most notably Hammer v. Dagenhart (1918). *Moreover, since filled milk was itself harmless, Congress was taking property without due process of law by simply declaring filled milk to be a "fraud upon the public" and banning it outright rather than allowing individual cases of fraudulent sales to be tried in the courts.*

After quickly disposing of the interstate commerce issue, the Supreme Court took the opportunity to emphasize a new standard by which it would evaluate economic regulations. Henceforth, the Court would ask only whether the legislature had a rational basis for imposing the constraints that it did on market freedoms, and the Court would generally presume that the legislature had such a rational basis. As was immediately apparent, it was effectively impossible for the government to fail such a test.

After conviction, Carolene Products brought a new appeal, which reached the Supreme Court in 1944. The Court again rejected the constitutional arguments against the application of the Filled Milk Act to Carolene Products, observing that it was sufficient that the congressional hearings had shown that it was least "disputable" as to whether outright prohibition was useful to prevent fraudulent retail sales, and that was enough for the Court. Justice Reed wrote for a unanimous Court in Carolene Products Co. v. United States *(1944):"The power was in Congress to decide its own course. We need look no further."*

The Carolene Products *decision gained new fame during the Warren Court Era for "Footnote Four" of the Court's opinion. Footnote Four sketched in brief one theory of where the Court should direct its energy, having retreated from many of its traditional concerns in 1937. As the Warren Court became increasingly active in the 1960s, many commentators looked to Footnote Four as both a justification for and a guide to a liberal-minded judicial review. In this way, liberal justices could avoid the perceived sins of the judicial review of the so-called Lochner era of the early twentieth century. As you read, consider whether Footnote Four solves the "double standard" problem of justifying what liberals on the Warren Court were doing while explaining why conservatives of the early twentieth century were wrong in how they exercised judicial review. Does it provide an adequate and persuasive guide to how judicial review should be exercised?*

JUSTICE STONE delivered the opinion of the Court.

...

The prohibition of shipment of appellee's product in interstate commerce does not infringe the Fifth Amendment. Twenty years ago this Court, in *Hebe Co. v. Shaw* (1919), held that a state law which forbids the manufacture and sale of a product assumed to be wholesome and nutritive, made of condensed skimmed milk, compounded with coconut oil, is not forbidden by the Fourteenth Amendment. The power of the legislature to secure a minimum of particular nutritive elements in a widely used article of food and to protect the public from fraudulent substitutions, was not doubted; and the Court thought that there was ample scope for the legislative judgment that prohibition of the offending article was an appropriate means of preventing injury to the public.

We see no persuasive reason for departing from that ruling here, where the Fifth Amendment is concerned; and since none is suggested, we might rest decision wholly on the presumption of constitutionality. But affirmative evidence also sustains the statute. In twenty years evidence has steadily accumulated of the danger to the public health from the general consumption of foods which have been stripped of elements essential to the maintenance of health. The Filled Milk Act was adopted by Congress after committee hearings, in the course of which eminent scientists and health experts testified....

There is nothing in the Constitution which compels a legislature, either national or state, to ignore such evidence, nor need it disregard the other evidence which amply supports the conclusions of the Congressional Committees that the danger is greatly enhanced where an inferior product, like appellee's, is indistinguishable from a valuable food of almost universal use, thus making fraudulent distribution easy and protection of the consumer difficult.

...Whether in such circumstances the public would be adequately protected by the prohibition of false labels and false branding imposed by the Pure Food and Drugs Act, or whether it was necessary to go farther and prohibit a substitute food product thought to be injurious to health if used as a substitute when the two are not distinguishable, was a matter for the legislative judgment and not that of courts. *Hebe Co.* v. *Shaw; South Carolina* v. *Barnwell Bros. Inc.* (1938). It was upon this ground that the prohibition of the sale of oleomargarine made in imitation of butter was held not to infringe the Fourteenth Amendment in *Powell* v. *Pennsylvania* (1888)....Compare *McCray* v. *United States* (1904).

Appellee raises no valid objection to the present statute by arguing that its prohibition has not been extended to oleomargarine or other butter substitutes in which vegetable fats or oils are substituted for butter fat. The Fifth Amendment has no equal protection clause, and even that of the Fourteenth, applicable only to the states, does not compel their legislatures to prohibit all like evils, or none. A legislature may hit at an abuse which it has found, even though it has failed to strike at another....

...Even in the absence of such aids [as legislative committee reports] the existence of facts supporting the legislative judgment is to be presumed, for regulatory legislation affecting ordinary commercial transactions is not to be pronounced unconstitutional unless in the light of the facts made known or generally assumed it is of such a character as to preclude the assumption that it rests upon some rational basis within the knowledge and experience of the legislators.[8]...

...Here the demurrer challenges the validity of the statute on its face and it is evident from all the considerations presented to Congress, and those of which we may take judicial notice, that the question is at least debatable whether commerce in filled milk should be left unregulated, or in some measure restricted, or wholly prohibited. As that decision was for Congress, neither the finding of a court arrived at by weighing the evidence, nor the verdict of a jury can be substituted for it.

...

Reversed.

JUSTICE BLACK, concurring in part.

JUSTICE McREYNOLDS thinks that the judgment should be affirmed.

JUSTICE CARDOZO and JUSTICE REED took no part in the decision of this case.

JUSTICE BUTLER, concurring.

...If [the statutory provisions are] construed to exclude from interstate commerce wholesome food

---

8. [Footnote Four in original] There may be narrower scope for operation of the presumption of constitutionality when legislation appears on its face to be within a specific prohibition of the Constitution, such as those of the first ten amendments, which are deemed equally specific when held to be embraced within the Fourteenth. See *Stromberg* v. *California* (1931); *Lovell* v. *Griffin* (1938).

It is unnecessary to consider now whether legislation which restricts those political processes which can ordinarily be expected to bring about repeal of undesirable legislation, is to be subjected to more exacting judicial scrutiny under the general prohibitions of the Fourteenth Amendment than are most other types of legislation. On restrictions upon the right to vote, see *Nixon* v. *Herndon* (1927); *Nixon* v. *Condon* (1932); on restraints upon the dissemination of information, see *Near* v. *Minnesota ex rel. Olson* (1931); *Grosjean* v. *American Press Co.* (1936); *Lovell* v. *Griffin*; on interferences with political organizations, see *Stromberg* v. *California; Fiske* v. *Kansas* (1927); *Whitney* v. *California* (1927); *Herndon* v. *Lowry* (1937); and see Holmes, J., in *Gitlow* v. *New York* (1925); as to prohibition of peaceable assembly, see *De Jonge* v. *Oregon* (1937).

Nor need we enquire whether similar considerations enter into the review of statutes directed at particular religious, *Pierce* v. *Society of Sisters* (1925), or national, *Meyer* v. *Nebraska* (1923); *Bartels* v. *Iowa* (1923); *Farrington* v. *Tokushige* (1927), or racial minorities, *Nixon* v. *Herndon; Nixon* v. *Condon*: whether prejudice against discrete and insular minorities may be a special condition, which tends seriously to curtail the operation of those political processes ordinarily to be relied upon to protect minorities, and which may call for a correspondingly more searching judicial inquiry. Compare *McCulloch* v. *Maryland* (1819), at 428; *South Carolina* v. *Barnwell Bros.* (1938), at 184 n. 2, and cases cited.

products that demonstrably are neither injurious to health nor calculated to deceive, they are repugnant to the Fifth Amendment. *Weaver* v. *Palmer Bros. Co.* (1926). See *People* v. *Carolene Products Co.*, 345 Ill. 166 (IL 1931) . . . . The allegation of the indictment that Milnut "is an adulterated article of food, injurious to the public health," tenders an issue of fact to be determined upon evidence.

B. Judicial Supremacy

The conflicts between the Supreme Court and the Roosevelt administration over the constitutionality of the New Deal provoked a vigorous response from the administration. President Roosevelt criticized the majority of the justices as wrong on the constitutional merits and out of touch with the needs of the nation. For an early case on the administration's suspension of the gold standard, FDR prepared a speech in case the government lost, announcing that he would not comply with the Court's decision. The government won that case, but the highlights of the speech were leaked to the press. As Roosevelt entered his second term, he argued that the president, not the Court, had a better grasp of the people's understanding of the Constitution, and that it was time to bring the Court into line. His proposal to "reorganize" the Court by adding new justices to it would have immediately given him the majority that he needed to validate the New Deal. The proposal failed to pass the Senate, but in the meantime the Court changed its mind on key features of constitutional doctrine and endorsed revised New Deal statutes. Roosevelt was soon able to appoint justices who shared his vision of the Constitution. A dramatic alteration of the constitutional landscape had taken place. The White House contended that this was simply a return to the original, broad terms of the Constitution. Critics moaned that the inherited Constitution had been ripped apart without benefit of a constitutional amendment. What authority do presidential and popular understandings of the Constitution have? Should judges defer to the constitutional views of others, or do they have a responsibility to act on their constitutional understandings? How far can political actors go to get around a Court that they believe is wrong? Must they seek a constitutional amendment to correct a "mistaken" Court, or is it appropriate to use other means to correct judicial errors?

Franklin Roosevelt, Undelivered Speech on the Gold-Clause Cases (1935)[9]

In the economic crisis of the 1930s, the supply of goods outstripped the demand for them. The causes for this situation are various and debatable, but the results were devastating—deflation (declining prices, or the declining value of goods relative to the currency), unemployment, bankruptcies, and debt repudiations. Among his first acts as president, Roosevelt halted trading in gold and soon thereafter took the United States off the gold standard, opening the door to various inflationary policies. In June 1933, a congressional joint resolution declared that any contract "which purports to give the obligee a right to require payment in gold" or a gold-equivalent in U.S. currency "is declared to be against public policy" and void. Public and private debts were to be repaid only in current dollars, gold clauses notwithstanding. Progressive Republican Senator William Borah, a supporter of the measure, argued that bondholders may "suffer, and suffer extremely [but] . . . it devolves upon the Government of the United States to find an escape from the present condition of affairs in some way or other. . . . We must cease to pay tribute to the gold standard at the expense of the average citizen of the United States."[10]

Several constitutional challenges to the suspension of the gold clauses made their way to the Supreme Court. It was the first major challenge to Roosevelt's policies, and both Washington and the financial markets were aflame with speculation about what the Court would do—and how the administration would respond. The attorney general, who argued the case personally before the Supreme Court, emphasized the economic consequences of an adverse ruling as much as the legal supports for the government's actions. As the justices met to discuss the case, congressmen and administration officials publicly discussed what would happen if the government lost. Common suggestions included a constitutional convention, the immediate addition of new justices to the Court and a rehearing of the case, and the declaration of martial law.[11]

When the Court finally handed down its decision in the Gold Clause Cases *(1935), the government had won on a technicality. The justices were clearly uncomfortable with*

9. Excerpt taken from Franklin D. Roosevelt, "Proposed Gold Clause Statement, June 27, 1935," President's Personal File Speeches, Franklin D. Roosevelt Library, Hyde Park, New York.

10. *Cong. Rec.*, 73rd Cong., 1st sess. (June 3, 1933):4905–6.

11. See David Glick, "Conditional Strategic Retreat: The Court's Concession in the 1935 Gold Clause Cases," *Journal of Politics* 71 (2009):800.

and critical of the suspension, but they concluded that the bondholders had no legal remedy and dismissed the suits. President Roosevelt had prepared a draft for a speech to be delivered in case the government had lost. In that speech he would have announced that the President's higher obligation was "to protect the people of the United States," even from the Supreme Court. The draft does not specify the precise actions that the administration would have taken to negate the effects of the Court's decision, though several options were under active consideration, perhaps depending on the substance of the Court's decision. The existence of the speech was leaked to the press just after the Court issued its ruling. Might the justices have been influenced by this charged political environment? Would the president have been justified in taking extreme actions to prevent enforcement of the Court's decision in this case? Roosevelt quotes Lincoln's inaugural address in his speech (see "Lincoln on Departmentalism" in Chapter Six). Were Lincoln's arguments appropriate to the situation facing FDR?

Two years ago the welfare of all our citizens in every section of the United States was endangered by increasing bankruptcies and bank failures. In the short space of the previous three and one half years the purchasing power of the dollar had increased about sixty percent. This meant that debtors of all kinds... were being called on to pay their creditors in currency worth sixty percent more in purchasing power than the money which had been loaned to them.

...

But on the day of my inauguration, any attempt to collect in substance one hundred and sixty cents for every dollar owed would have brought universal bankruptcy.

During the past twenty-three months we have moved rapidly toward establishing and maintaining a dollar of stable purchasing power.... All of our legislation of the past two years has been aimed at creating a currency of sound and standard purchasing power and then maintaining it.

In working toward our broad objective, the American currency was first taken off what is commonly known as the Gold Standard....

The decisions of the Supreme Court are, of course, based on the legal proposition that the exact terms of a contract must be literally enforced.

Let me for a moment analyze the effect of the present decision by giving a few simple illustrations:

...

Consider the plight of the individual who is buying a home for himself and his family and paying each month a specified sum representing interest and reduction of the mortgage. If there is a gold clause in his mortgage—and most mortgages contain this clause—this decision would compel him to increase his payments 69% each month from now on, and perhaps to pay 69% more on some payments already made. Home owners, whether city workers or farmers, could not meet such a demand.

Consider now the other two decisions relating to government obligations on gold notes, gold certificates and gold clause bonds. An old lady came to see me the other day. She is dependent heavily on the income from government bonds which she owns; and her total income is about $800 a year. She owns $10,000 of government gold clause bonds. Under this new decision she would be entitled to ask the Treasury for $16,900. Being the right type of citizen, she volunteered to tell me that she does not consider herself entitled to more than the $10,000 which she had saved and invested.

The actual enforcement of the gold clause against the Government of the United States will not bankrupt the Government. It will increase our national debt by approximately nine billions of dollars. It means that this additional sum must eventually be raised by additional taxation. In our present major effort to get out of the depression, to put people to work, to restore industry and agriculture, the literal enforcement of this opinion would not only retard our efforts, but would put the Government and 125,000,000 people into an infinitely more serious economic plight than we have yet experienced.

...

I do not seek to enter into any controversy with the distinguished members of the Supreme Court of the United States who have participated in this (majority) decision. They have decided these cases in accordance with the letter of the law as they read it. But it is appropriate to quote a sentence from the First Inaugural Address of President Lincoln:

> At the same time, the candid citizen must confess that if the policy of the government, upon vital questions affecting the whole people, is to be irrevocably fixed by decisions of the Supreme Court, the instant they are made, in ordinary litigation between parties in personal actions, the people will have ceased to be their own rulers, having to that extent practically resigned their government into the hands of that eminent tribunal.

It is the duty of the Congress and the President to protect the People of the United States to the best of their ability. It is necessary to protect them from the unintended construction of voluntary acts, as well as from intolerable burdens involuntarily imposed. To stand idly by and to permit the decision of the Supreme Court to be carried through to its logical, inescapable conclusion would so imperil the economic and political security of this nation that the legislative and executive officers of the Government must look beyond the narrow letter of contractual obligations, so that they may sustain the substance of the promise originally made in accord with the actual intention of the parties.

For the value received the same value should be repaid. That is the spirit of the contract and of the law. . . . That would seem to be a decision in accordance with the Golden Rule, with the precepts of the Scriptures, and the dictates of common sense.

In order to attain this reasonable end, I shall immediately take such steps as may be necessary, by proclamation and by message to the Congress of the United States.

In the meantime, I ask every individual, every trustee, every corporation and every bank to proceed on the usual course of their honorable and legitimate business. They can rest assured that we shall carry on the business of the country tomorrow just as we did last week or last month, on the same financial basis, on the same currency basis, and in the same relationship of debtor and creditor as before.

Franklin Roosevelt, Fireside Chat on Court-Packing Plan (1937)[12]

During the first Roosevelt administration, intense conflict took place between the judicial and executive branches of government. Roosevelt believed the Depression created the need for substantial national regulation of the economy. By 5–4 and 6–3 majorities, the Supreme Court declared many of these policies unconstitutional. Judicial casualties included the Agricultural Adjustment Act and the National Industrial Recovery Act. Concerned that such measures as the National Labor Relations Act and the Social Security Act might not pass constitutional muster, the Roosevelt Administration decided to take preemptive measures. Although some administration officials were inclined to seek a constitutional amendment to give the government more power, Roosevelt rejected that choice. An amendment was likely to be difficult to draft and ratify, might be seen as an admission that the justices were correctly interpreting the existing Constitution, and would ultimately leave the fate of the New Deal in the hands of the same judges as before. Instead, Roosevelt proposed the Court-packing plan.

Disingenuously claiming that the central problem was that the justices on the bench were too old and getting behind in their work, Roosevelt proposed allowing the president to appoint an additional justice for each sitting justice who reached the age of seventy, so long as the sitting justice had served at least ten years. The maximum size of the Court was set at fifteen under this scheme. The plan would have given FDR an immediate and large pro–New Deal majority on the Court. In this fireside chat, Roosevelt more honestly addressed the real political conflicts that were responsible for the Court-packing plan.

Despite the overwhelming Democratic majorities in Congress and the president's own dominating reelection, the Court-packing plan was defeated in Congress partly for reasons laid out by the Senate judiciary committee. But, beginning in 1937, key swing justices began consistently supporting New Deal measures. The combination of that "switch in time" and a series of judicial appointments through the normal process of retirements and death made the Court-packing plan irrelevant. Whether the Court-packing plan had any influence on the New Deal turnaround is controversial. Several scholars claim that it had no impact. The 1937 decisions, they insist, were consistent with the previous decisions striking down federal laws and, besides, Justice Roberts had actually made the crucial switch before the Court-packing plan was announced. Others believe that some combination of the election of 1936 and the numerous court-curbing proposals that were introduced in Congress and discussed in the press played crucial roles in the decision Justice Roberts and Chief Justice Hughes made to become consistent supporters of New Deal policies.[13]

12. Excerpt taken from Franklin D. Roosevelt, "Fireside Chat on the Reorganization of the Judiciary, March 9, 1937," President's Personal File Speeches, Franklin D. Roosevelt Library, Hyde Park, New York.

13. On the significance of the Court–packing plan, see William E. Leuchtenburg, *The Supreme Court Reborn* (New York: Oxford University Press, 1995); Barry Cushman, *Rethinking the New Deal Court* (New York: Oxford University Press, 1998); Bruce Ackerman, *We the People: Transformations* (Cambridge: Harvard University Press, 1998); Barry Friedman, *The Will of the People* (New York: Oxford University Press, 2009); Daniel E. Ho and Kevin M. Quinn, "Did a Switch in Time Save Nine?," *Journal of Legal Analysis* 2 (Spring 2010):69.

MY FRIENDS, last Thursday I described in detail certain economic problems which everyone admits now face the nation....

I am reminded of that evening in March, four years ago, when I made my first radio report to you. We were then in the midst of the great banking crisis.

Soon after, with the authority of the Congress, we asked the nation to turn over all of its privately held gold, dollar for dollar, to the government of the United States.

Today's recovery proves how right that policy was.

But when, almost two years later, it came before the Supreme Court its constitutionality was upheld only by a five-to-four vote. The change of one vote would have thrown all the affairs of this great nation back into hopeless chaos. In effect, four justices ruled that the right under a private contract to exact a pound of flesh was more sacred than the main objectives of the Constitution to establish an enduring nation.

...

The American people have learned from the depression. For in the last three national elections an overwhelming majority of them voted a mandate that the Congress and the president begin the task of providing that protection—not after long years of debate, but now.

The courts, however, have cast doubts on the ability of the elected Congress to protect us against catastrophe by meeting squarely our modern social and economic conditions.

...

Last Thursday I described the American form of government as a three-horse team provided by the Constitution to the American people so that their field might be plowed. The three horses are, of course, the three branches of government—the Congress, the executive, and the courts. Two of the horses, the Congress and the executive, are pulling in unison today; the third is not. Those who have intimated that the president of the United States is trying to drive that team, overlook the simple fact that the president, as chief executive, is himself one of the three horses.

It is the American people themselves who are in the driver's seat. It is the American people themselves who want the furrow plowed. It is the American people themselves who expect the third horse to fall in unison with the other two.

I hope that you have re-read the Constitution of the United States in these past few weeks. Like the Bible, it ought to be read again and again.

...In its Preamble, the Constitution states that it was intended to form a more perfect union and promote the general welfare; and the powers given to the Congress to carry out those purposes can best be described by saying that they were all the powers needed to meet each and every problem which then had a national character and which could not be met by merely local action.

But the framers of the Constitution went further. Having in mind that in succeeding generations many other problems then undreamed of would become national problems, they gave to the Congress the ample broad powers "to levy taxes... and provide for the common defense and general welfare of the United States."

...

For nearly twenty years there was no conflict between the Congress and the Court. Then in 1803 Congress passed a statute which the Court said violated an express provision of the Constitution. The Court claimed the power to declare it unconstitutional and did so declare it. But a little later the Court itself admitted that it was an extraordinary power to exercise and through Mr. Justice Washington laid down this limitation upon it: he said, "It is but a decent respect due to the wisdom, the integrity and the patriotism of the legislative body, by which any law is passed, to presume in favor of its validity until its violation of the Constitution is proved beyond all reasonable doubt."

But since the rise of the modern movement for social and economic progress through legislation, the Court has more and more often and more and more boldly asserted a power to veto laws passed by the Congress and by state legislatures in complete disregard of this original limitation which I have just read.

In the last four years the sound rule of giving statutes the benefit of all reasonable doubt has been cast aside. The Court has been acting not as a judicial body, but as a policymaking body.

When the Congress has sought to stabilize national agriculture, to improve the conditions of labor, to safeguard business against unfair competition, to protect our national resources, and in many other ways, to serve our clearly national needs, the majority of the Court has been assuming the power to pass on the wisdom of these acts of the Congress—and to approve or disapprove the public policy written into these laws.

That is not only my accusation. It is the accusation of most distinguished justices of the present Supreme Court....

...

In the face of these dissenting opinions, there is no basis for the claim made by some members of the Court that something in the Constitution has compelled them regretfully to thwart the will of the people.

In the face of such dissenting opinions, it is perfectly clear that, as Chief Justice Hughes has said, "We are under a Constitution, but the Constitution is what the judges say it is."

The Court in addition to the proper use of its judicial functions has improperly set itself up as a third house of the Congress—a super-legislature, as one of the justices has called it—reading into the Constitution words and implications which are not there, and which were never intended to be there.

We have, therefore, reached the point as a nation where we must take action to save the Constitution from the Court and the Court from itself....

I want—as all Americans want—an independent judiciary as proposed by the framers of the Constitution. That means a Supreme Court that will enforce the Constitution as written, that will refuse to amend the Constitution by the arbitrary exercise of judicial power—in other words by judicial say-so. It does not mean a judiciary so independent that it can deny the existence of facts which are universally recognized.

...

When I commenced to review the situation with the problem squarely before me, I came by a process of elimination to the conclusion that, short of amendments, the only method which was clearly constitutional, and would at the same time carry out other much needed reforms, was to infuse new blood into all our courts. We must have men worthy and equipped to carry out impartial justice. But, at the same time, we must have judges who will bring to the courts a present-day sense of the Constitution—judges who will retain in the courts the judicial functions of a court, and reject the legislative powers which the courts have today assumed.

It is well for us to remember that in forty-five out of the forty-eight states of the Union, judges are chosen not for life but for a period of years. In many states judges must retire at the age of seventy....

...

[My] plan has two chief purposes. By bringing into the judicial system a steady and continuing stream of new and younger blood, I hope, first, to make the administration of all federal justice, from the bottom to the top, speedier and, therefore, less costly; secondly, to bring to the decision of social and economic problems younger men who have had personal experience and contact with modern facts and circumstances under which average men have to live and work. This plan will save our national Constitution from hardening of the judicial arteries.

...

Those opposing this plan have sought to arouse prejudice and fear by crying that I am seeking to "pack" the Supreme Court and that a baneful precedent will be established.

...

If by that phrase "packing the Court" it is charged that I wish to place on the bench spineless puppets who would disregard the law and would decide specific cases as I wished them to be decided, I make this answer: that no president fit for his office would appoint, and no Senate of honorable men fit for their office would confirm, that kind of appointees to the Supreme Court.

But if by that phrase the charge is made that I would appoint and the Senate would confirm justices worthy to sit beside present members of the Court, who understand modern conditions, that I will appoint justices who will not undertake to override the judgment of the Congress on legislative policy, that I will appoint justices who will act as justices and not as legislators—if the appointment of such justices can be called "packing the Courts," then I say that I and with me the vast majority of the American people favor doing just that thing—now.

Is it a dangerous precedent for the Congress to change the number of the justices? The Congress has always had, and will have, that power. The number of justices has been changed several times before, in the administrations of John Adams and Thomas Jefferson—both of them signers of the Declaration of Independence—in the administrations of Andrew Jackson, Abraham Lincoln, and Ulysses S. Grant.

I suggest only the addition of justices to the bench in accordance with a clearly defined principle relating to a clearly defined age limit. Fundamentally, if in the future, America cannot trust the Congress it elects to refrain from abuse of our constitutional usages, democracy will

Illustration 8-1 "Three's A Crowd!"
Cartoon critical of President Franklin Roosevelt's Court-packing plan.
Source: Cincinnati Times Star (February 16, 1937). ©2003 New Deal Network

have failed far beyond the importance to democracy of any kind of precedent concerning the judiciary.

...

During the past half-century the balance of power between the three great branches of the federal government has been tipped out of balance by the courts in direct contradiction of the high purposes of the framers of the Constitution. It is my purpose to restore that balance. You who know me will accept my solemn assurance that in a world in which democracy is under attack, I seek to make American democracy succeed. You and I will do our part.

Senate Judiciary Committee Report on President Roosevelt's Court-Packing Plan (1937)[14]

The Senate Judiciary Committee, like the Senate itself, had a solid Democratic majority. The president's bill to "reorganize" the federal judiciary was sent to the Judiciary Committee on a fast track for consideration. Republicans generally kept their silence during the debate over the Court-packing plan and allowed Democrats to argue among themselves. The bulk of the opposition to the Court-packing plan came from more conservative Democrats, but the opposition also included some high-profile liberals who had been strong supporters of the New Deal and critics of the Court. The Senate Judiciary Committee came out with a strongly worded negative report on the bill. Pro–New Deal Washington Post *columnist Ray Clapper wrote in his diary that the committee report read "almost like a bill of impeachment."*[15] *Senate majority leader Joseph Robinson struggled to save the bill on the floor of the Senate, but suffered a fatal heart attack before the bill was finally laid to rest in the summer of 1937.*

The Committee on the Judiciary, to whom was referred the bill (S. 1392) to reorganize the judicial branch of the Government, after full consideration, having unanimously amended the measure, hereby reports the bill adversely with the recommendation that it does not pass....

The committee recommends that the measure be rejected for the following primary reasons:

The bill does not accomplish any one of the objectives for which it was originally offered.

It applies force to the judiciary and in its initial and ultimate effect would undermine the independence of the courts.

It violates all precedents in the history of our Government and would in itself be a dangerous precedent for the future.

The theory of the bill is in direct violation of the spirit of the American Constitution and its employment would permit alteration of the Constitution without the people's consent or approval; it undermines the protection our constitutional system gives to minorities and is subversive of the rights of individuals.

14. Excerpt taken from Report No. 711, U.S. Senate, Committee on the Judiciary, 75th Cong., 1st sess. (1937).

15. Quoted in Leuchtenburg, 146.

...

Shall we now, after 150 years of loyalty to the constitutional ideal of an untrammeled judiciary, duty bound to protect the constitutional rights of the humblest citizen even against the Government itself, create the vicious precedent which must necessarily undermine our system? The only argument for the increase which survives analysis is that Congress should enlarge the Court so as to make the policies of this administration effective.

We are told that a reactionary oligarchy defies the will of the majority, that this is a bill to "unpack" the Court and give effect to the desires of the majority; that is to say, a bill to increase the number of Justices for the express purpose of neutralizing the views of some of the present members. In justification we are told, but without authority, by those who would rationalize this program, that Congress was given the power to determine the size of the Court so that the legislative branch would be able to impose its will upon the judiciary. This amounts to nothing more than the declaration that when the Court stands in the way of a legislative enactment, the Congress may reverse the ruling by enlarging the Court. When such a principle is adopted, our constitutional system is overthrown!

This, then is the dangerous precedent we are asked to establish. When proponents of the bill assert, as they have done, that Congress in the past has altered the number of Justices upon the Supreme Court and that this is reason enough for our doing it now, they show how important precedents are and prove that we should now refrain from any action that would seem to establish one which could be followed hereafter whenever a Congress and an executive should become dissatisfied with the decisions of the Supreme Court.

This is the first time in the history of our country that a proposal to alter the decisions of the court by enlarging its personnel has been so boldly made. Let us meet it. Let us now set a salutary precedent that will never be violated. Let us, of the Seventy-fifth Congress, in words that will never be disregarded by any succeeding Congress, declare that we would rather have an independent Court, a fearless Court, a Court that will dare to announce its honest opinions in what it believes to be the defense of the liberties of the people, than a Court that, out of fear or sense of obligation to the appointing power, or factional passion, approves any measure we may enact. We are not the judges of the judges. We are not above the Constitution.

Even if every charge brought against the so-called "reactionary" members of this Court be true, it is far better that we await orderly but inevitable change of personnel than that we impatiently overwhelm them with new members. Exhibiting this restraint, thus demonstrating our faith in the American system, we shall set an example that will protect the independent American judiciary from attack as long as this Government stands....

The Southern Manifesto (1956)[16]

The Supreme Court in Brown v. Board of Education I (1954) *declared racially segregated public schools to be unconstitutional. In* Brown v. Board of Education II (1955), *the justices ordered all communities to desegregate their public schools with "all deliberate speed." Massive resistance followed. Many states in the South responded by passing ordinances declaring* Brown *itself to be null and void. Most Southern representatives in Congress signed the Southern Manifesto, which urged resistance to the Supreme Court's decision ordering desegregation. Lyndon Johnson, the Senate majority leader at the time, was not asked to sign. The Manifesto was designed in part to pressure moderates into joining a united front and declaring their support for segregation in the face of the Supreme Court's decision. Especially in the Deep South, the Manifesto lent support to governors, state legislators, school administrators, and judges seeking to delay or obstruct the implementation of desegregation in schools and elsewhere.*

We regard the decisions of the Supreme Court in the school cases as a clear abuse of judicial power. It climaxes a trend in the Federal Judiciary undertaking to legislate, in derogation of the authority of Congress, and to encroach upon the reserved rights of the States and the people.

The original Constitution does not mention education. Neither does the 14th Amendment nor any other amendment. The debates preceding the submission of the 14th Amendment clearly show that there was no intent that it should affect the system of education maintained by the States.

In the case of *Plessy* v. *Ferguson* in 1896 the Supreme Court expressly declared that under the 14th Amendment no person was denied any of his rights if the States provided separate but equal facilities....

This interpretation, restated time and again, became a part of the life of the people of many of the States and confirmed their habits, traditions, and way of life. It is founded on elemental humanity and commonsense, for parents should not be deprived by Government of the right to direct the lives and education of their own children.

Though there has been no constitutional amendment or act of Congress changing this established legal principle almost a century old, the Supreme Court of the United States, with no legal basis for such action, undertook to exercise their naked judicial power and substituted their personal political and social ideas for the established law of the land.

...Without regard to the consent of the governed, outside mediators are threatening immediate and revolutionary changes in our public schools systems. If done, this is certain to destroy the system of public education in some of the States.

We reaffirm our reliance on the Constitution as the fundamental law of the land.

We decry the Supreme Court's encroachment on the rights reserved to the States and to the people, contrary to established law, and to the Constitution.

We commend the motives of those States which have declared the intention to resist forced integration by any lawful means.

We appeal to the States and people who are not directly affected by these decisions to consider the constitutional principles involved against the time when they too, on issues vital to them may be the victims of judicial encroachment.

Even though we constitute a minority in the present Congress, we have full faith that a majority of the American people believe in the dual system of government which has enabled us to achieve our greatness and will in time demand that the reserved rights of the States and of the people be made secure against judicial usurpation.

We pledge ourselves to use all lawful means to bring about a reversal of this decision which is contrary to the Constitution and to prevent the use of force in its implementation.

16. Excerpt taken from *Congressional Record*, 84th Cong., 2nd sess. (1956): 4515.

Dwight Eisenhower, Address to the Nation on the Introduction of Troops in Little Rock (1957)[17]

President Eisenhower was ambivalent about Brown v. Board of Education. *He signed the amicus brief urging the Supreme Court to declare segregated schools unconstitutional, supported northern liberals in his Justice Department, and appointed justices to the Supreme Court who were committed to the* Brown *precedent. But he refrained from praising the substantive result in* Brown *or claiming credit for the outcome. Eisenhower had made some significant electoral gains in the South, and he was convinced that incrementalism and quiet diplomacy with moderates in the South would be more effective in achieving desegregation than confrontation.*

His public statements on Brown *emphasized that the judicial decision was the law of the land, that judicial orders had to be obeyed, and that the president had no choice but to enforce them. When Governor Orval Faubus defied a federal judicial order and blocked the desegregation of Central High School in Little Rock, Arkansas, Eisenhower sent federal troops to enforce the judicial order. In contrast to the Southern Manifesto, Eisenhower emphasized judicial supremacy in interpreting the Constitution. The duty of citizens and officials was to obey, regardless of their "personal opinions" about what the Court had done. Is this a reasonable strategy to take in the wake of a controversial decision or should Eisenhower have come out squarely in favor of the Court's decision?*

Good Evening, My Fellow Citizens: For a few minutes this evening I want to speak to you about the serious situation that has arisen in Little Rock. To make this talk I have come to the President's office in the White House. I could have spoken from Rhode Island, where I have been staying recently, but I felt that, in speaking from the house of Lincoln, of Jackson and of Wilson, my words would better convey both the sadness I feel in the action I was compelled today to take and the firmness with which I intend to pursue this course until the orders of the Federal Court at Little Rock can be executed without unlawful interference. In that city, under the leadership of demagogic extremists, disorderly mobs have deliberately prevented the carrying out of proper orders from a Federal Court. Local authorities have not eliminated that violent opposition and, under the law, I yesterday issued a Proclamation calling upon the mob to disperse.... It is important that the reasons for my action be understood by all our citizens. As you know, the Supreme Court of the United States has decided that separate public educational facilities for the races are inherently unequal and therefore compulsory school segregation laws are unconstitutional. Our personal opinions about the decision have no bearing on the matter of enforcement; the responsibility and authority of the Supreme Court to interpret the Constitution are very clear. Local Federal Courts were instructed by the Supreme Court to issue such orders and decrees as might be necessary to achieve admission to public schools without regard to race—and with all deliberate speed.... The very basis of our individual rights and freedoms rests upon the certainty that the President and the Executive Branch of Government will support and insure the carrying out of the decisions of the Federal Courts, even, when necessary, with all the means at the President's command. Unless the President did so, anarchy would result. There would be no security for any except that which each one of us could provide for himself. The interest of the nation in the proper fulfillment of the law's requirements cannot yield to opposition and demonstrations by some few persons. Mob rule cannot be allowed to override the decisions of our courts.... A foundation of our American way of life is our national respect for law. In the South, as elsewhere, citizens are keenly aware of the tremendous disservice that has been done to the people of Arkansas in the eyes of the nation, and that has been done to the nation in the eyes of the world. At a time when we face grave situations abroad because of the hatred that Communism bears toward a system of government based on human rights, it would be difficult to exaggerate the harm that is being done to the prestige and influence, and indeed to the safety, of our nation and the world. Our enemies are gloating over this incident and using it everywhere to misrepresent our whole nation. We are portrayed as a violator of those standards of conduct which the peoples of the world united to proclaim in the Charter of the United Nations. There they affirmed "faith in fundamental human rights" and "in dignity and worth of the human person" and they did so "without distinction as to race, sex, language or religion." And so, with deep confidence, I call upon the citizens of the State of Arkansas to assist in bringing to an immediate end all

17. Excerpt taken from Dwight D. Eisenhower, *Public Papers of the Presidents of the United States, 1957* (Washington, DC: Government Printing Office, 1958), 689.

interference with the law and its processes. If resistance to the Federal Court orders ceases at once, the further presence of Federal troops will be unnecessary and the City of Little Rock will return to its normal habits of peace and order and a blot upon the fair name and high honor of our nation in the world will be removed. Thus will be restored the image of America and of all its parts as one nation, indivisible, with liberty and justice for all. Good night, and thank you very much.

Cooper v. Aaron, 358 U.S. 1 (1958)

In Little Rock, Arkansas, federal troops were needed to protect the few children of color attending a formerly all-white high school. The school board had moved promptly after Brown I *to adopt a desegregation plan, but a state constitutional amendment was subsequently adopted instructing state officials to use all legal means to oppose the "unconstitutional"* Brown *decision. The governor called out the National Guard to block desegregation, but federal troops eventually allowed the school year to continue on a desegregated basis.*

Before the start of the next school year, the school board petitioned the federal district court to allow it to suspend the desegregation plan. Fearing more violence and chaos, the judge ordered the local desegregation plan to be suspended for two and a half years. That order was reversed by a federal circuit court. An appeal was taken to the Supreme Court. As the case was pending before the Supreme Court, President Eisenhower announced that he still believed that the Court had the responsibility to say what the Constitution means and that he was prepared to send troops back to Little Rock to support the courts if needed.

A unanimous Supreme Court agreed that the desegregation plan had to be reinstated immediately. In an unprecedented opinion, signed individually by every member of the court, the justices declared that Brown v. Board of Education *was the law of the land and that all elected officials were obligated to obey the Constitution as interpreted by the Supreme Court.* Cooper *is the first case that clearly cites* Marbury v. Madison *(1803) as establishing judicial supremacy as well as judicial review. Judicial decisions, the justices explicitly declared, bind all elected officials, even those who were not parties to the case before the Court, because the Supreme Court is specially authorized to determine what the Constitution means.*

CHIEF JUSTICE WARREN delivered the opinion of the Court.

As this case reaches us it raises questions of the highest importance to the maintenance of our federal system of government. It necessarily involves a claim by the Governor and Legislature of a State that there is no duty on state officials to obey federal court orders resting on this Court's considered interpretation of the United States Constitution. Specifically it involves actions by the Governor and Legislature of Arkansas upon the premise that they are not bound by our holding in *Brown* v. *Board of Education*....

...

The constitutional rights of respondents are not to be sacrificed or yielded to the violence and disorder which have followed upon the actions of the Governor and Legislature.... The record before us clearly establishes that the growth of the Board's difficulties to a magnitude beyond its unaided power to control is the product of state action. Those difficulties, as counsel for the Board forthrightly conceded on the oral argument in this Court, can also be brought under control by state action.

The controlling legal principles are plain. The command of the Fourteenth Amendment is that no "State" shall deny to any person within its jurisdiction the equal protection of the laws. "A State acts by its legislative, its executive, or its judicial authorities. It can act in no other way. The constitutional provision, therefore, must mean that no agency of the State, or of the officers or agents by whom its powers are exerted, shall deny to any person within its jurisdiction the equal protection of the laws. Whoever, by virtue of public position under a State government,... denies or takes away the equal protection of the laws, violates the constitutional inhibition; and as he acts in the name and for the State, and is clothed with the State's power, his act is that of the State. This must be so, or the constitutional prohibition has no meaning."...

What has been said, in the light of the facts developed, is enough to dispose of the case. However, we should answer the premise of the actions of the Governor and Legislature that they are not bound by our holding in the *Brown* case. It is necessary only to recall some basic constitutional propositions which are settled doctrine.

Article VI of the Constitution makes the Constitution the "supreme Law of the Land." In 1803, Chief Justice Marshall, speaking for a unanimous Court, referring to the Constitution as "the fundamental and paramount law of the nation," declared in the notable case of *Marbury* v. *Madison*,...that "It is emphatically the province and duty of the judicial department to say what the law is." This decision declared the basic principle that the federal judiciary is supreme in the exposition of the law of the Constitution, and that principle has ever since been respected by this Court and the Country as a permanent and indispensable feature of our constitutional system. It follows that the interpretation of the Fourteenth Amendment enunciated by this Court in the *Brown* case is the supreme law of the land, and Art. VI of the Constitution makes it of binding effect on the States "any Thing in the Constitution or Laws of any State to the Contrary notwithstanding." Every state legislator and executive and judicial officer is solemnly committed by oath taken pursuant to Art. VI, cl. 3, "to support this Constitution." Chief Justice Taney, speaking for a unanimous Court in 1859, said that this requirement reflected the framers' "anxiety to preserve it [the Constitution] in full force, in all its powers, and to guard against resistance to or evasion of its authority, on the part of a State...."

No state legislator or executive or judicial officer can war against the Constitution without violating his undertaking to support it. Chief Justice Marshall spoke for a unanimous Court in saying that: "If the legislatures of the several states may, at will, annul the judgments of the courts of the United States, and destroy the rights acquired under those judgments, the constitution itself becomes a solemn mockery...." A Governor who asserts a power to nullify a federal court order is similarly restrained. If he had such power, said Chief Justice Hughes, in 1932, also for a unanimous Court, "it is manifest that the fiat of a state Governor, and not the Constitution of the United States, would be the supreme law of the land; that the restrictions of the Federal Constitution upon the exercise of state power would be but impotent phrases...."

...The basic decision in *Brown* was unanimously reached by this Court only after the case had been briefed and twice argued and the issues had been given the most serious consideration. Since the first *Brown* opinion three new Justices have come to the Court. They are at one with the Justices still on the Court who participated in that basic decision as to its correctness, and that decision is now unanimously reaffirmed. The principles announced in that decision and the obedience of the States to them, according to the command of the Constitution, are indispensable for the protection of the freedoms guaranteed by our fundamental charter for all of us. Our constitutional ideal of equal justice under law is thus made a living truth.

JUSTICE FRANKFURTER, concurring.

While unreservedly participating with my brethren in our joint opinion, I deem it appropriate also to deal individually with the great issue here at stake.

...

...Every act of government may be challenged by an appeal to law, as finally pronounced by this Court. Even this Court has the last say only for a time. Being composed of fallible men, it may err. But revision of its errors must be by orderly process of law. The Court may be asked to reconsider its decisions, and this has been done successfully again and again throughout our history. Or, what this Court has deemed its duty to decide may be changed by legislation, as it often has been, and, on occasion, by constitutional amendment.

...

The duty to abstain from resistance to "the supreme Law of the Land," U.S. Const., Art. VI 2, as declared by the organ of our Government for ascertaining it, does not require immediate approval of it nor does it deny the right of dissent. Criticism need not be stilled. Active obstruction or defiance is barred. Our kind of society cannot endure if the controlling authority of the Law as derived from the Constitution is not to be the tribunal specially charged with the duty of ascertaining and declaring what is "the supreme Law of the Land."...Particularly is this so where the declaration of what "the supreme Law" commands on an underlying moral issue is not the dubious pronouncement of a gravely divided Court but is the unanimous conclusion of a long-matured deliberative process. The Constitution is not the formulation of the merely personal views of the members of this Court, nor can its authority be reduced to the claim that state officials are its controlling interpreters. Local customs, however hardened by time, are not decreed in heaven....

...

...Compliance with decisions of this Court, as the constitutional organ of the supreme Law of the Land, has often, throughout our history, depended on active support by state and local authorities. It presupposes such support. To withhold it, and indeed to use political power to try to paralyze the supreme Law, precludes the maintenance of our federal system as we have known and cherished it for one hundred and seventy years.

...

Note: Court-Curbing and the Warren Court

Conservatives opposed to the increasing liberalism of the Warren Court frequently proposed legislation during the 1950s, 1960s, and 1970s aimed at restricting judicial power. The most common proposals were aimed at limiting federal jurisdiction over particular issues. In the 1950s, efforts were made to prevent the U.S. Supreme Court from adjudicating cases involving communism and domestic security. In the 1960s, many jurisdiction-stripping bills focused on blocking the courts from requiring legislative reapportionment. In the 1970s, conservatives looked to prevent the federal courts from ordering busing in school desegregation cases, interfering in school prayer cases, or striking down state regulations of abortion. "Impeach Earl Warren" billboards dotted the highways in the 1950s, although there was little congressional support for such a move. Justices Douglas and Fortas came under more serious impeachment threats in the 1960s. Fortas resigned under an ethics cloud due to financial improprieties.

Fierce debates took place over whether jurisdiction-stripping bills were constitutional. Proponents insisted that the clause in Article III authorizing Congress to provide exceptions to the appellate jurisdiction of the Supreme Court permitted Congress to prohibit federal courts from adjudicating particular issues on the merits. The Reconstruction Era case of *Ex parte McCardle* (1869), in this view, provided support for the principle that Congress had complete control over the appellate jurisdiction of the Supreme Court. Opponents insisted that the exceptions clause did not permit Congress to strip the entire federal court system of jurisdiction over constitutional issues. Rather, they believed that Congress could determine only whether the Supreme Court should exercise appellate or original jurisdiction in constitutional cases. Harvard Law Professor Henry Hart offered an influential argument that at least one federal court had to have jurisdiction over a federal issue. Federal issues such as the interpretation of the U.S. Constitution could not be left entirely to the state courts.[18] Opponents of court-curbing bills also argued that once Congress vested the Supreme Court with jurisdiction to hear a given case, they could not limit the remedies that the courts might apply to resolve the case. Congress might have control over whether the federal courts had jurisdiction to hear a case involving the racial segregation of schools, but according to this argument Congress did not have the authority to tell judges how to right the constitutional wrongs in the cases that came before them.

Many court-curbing measures came close to passing, but none became law. Such proposals almost always came from the conservatives in Congress during the Warren Court years, and they were typically blocked by the liberal members of Congress and the executive branch. The Eisenhower Administration, for example, condemned court-curbing efforts as "threaten[ing] the independence of the judiciary."[19] Many bouts of court-curbing were short-lived. Congressional efforts to prevent the justices from enforcing reapportionment decisions ended, not surprisingly, immediately after a new Congress was elected using the newly drawn legislative districts.

Still, many observers believe that court-curbing measures had their intended influence on the federal judiciary. After a court-curbing measure almost became law in 1958, the Warren Court demonstrated more deference to Congress in domestic security and Communist cases. The Supreme Court was largely absent from the battle over desegregation for a decade after it issued the *Brown II* decision, leaving the district and circuit courts in the South to work through the problems of massive resistance.

The Warren Court became bolder in the 1960s when it gained stronger support from the other branches of the federal government and drew in some additional justices who favored using judicial power to accomplish liberal goals. Opposition to the Warren Court increased in the late 1960s, and conservative proposals to rein in the Court rose steeply by the beginning of the Nixon administration.[20]

C. Constitutional Litigation

Article III of the U.S. Constitution extends "the judicial power" to "all cases" and "controversies" meeting

18. Henry M. Hart, Jr., "The Power of Congress to Limit Jurisdiction of Federal Courts: An Exercise in Dialectic," *Harvard Law Review* 66 (1953):1362.

19. Lucas A. Powe, Jr., *The Warren Court and American Politics* (Harvard University Press: Cambridge, 2000), 131.

20. On the influence of court-curbing, see Walter F. Murphy, *Congress and the Court* (Chicago: University of Chicago Press, 1962); Lee Epstein and Jack Knight, *The Choices Justices Make* (Washington, DC: CQ Press, 1998); Tom S. Clark, *The Limits of Judicial Independence* (New York: Cambridge University Press, 2010).

certain requirements, including "all Cases, in Law and Equity, arising under this Constitution." The Supreme Court is given original jurisdiction over a small set of cases, and appellate jurisdiction over other cases meeting the Article III requirements, subject to "such Exceptions, and under such Regulations as the Congress shall make." The Supreme Court can only resolve a claim or interpret a provision of the Constitution if a proper case comes before it. The Court cannot act unless it has jurisdiction over the dispute.

Whether a constitutional dispute can be framed into a proper case that can appeal to the judicial power depends both on congressional statutes and judicial doctrines. Should the judicial power be applied expansively, jurisdiction be read broadly, and the meaning of cases and controversies be interpreted liberally in order to allow judges to intervene in as many constitutional disputes as possible? Or should judicial power be confined to a narrower class of disputes, and jurisdictional requirements read more strictly in order to control how often and under what circumstances judges interfere with other government officials?

During this period, the justices wrestled with the question of how easy it should be to have access to the courts. On the U.S. Supreme Court, Felix Frankfurter was the leading advocate for the view that judicial power should be restrained. He advocated a variety of procedural devices for keeping disputes out of the courts. His protégé, constitutional scholar Alexander Bickel, referred to these as the "passive virtues" that helped guide the Court on when it should do nothing—and when it should take action.[21] William O. Douglas was a leading advocate for the view that judicial power should be activist. He advocated eliminating the procedural obstacles that prevented judges from hearing about and trying to correct constitutional abuses. Frankfurter and Douglas were both committed New Dealers, but they had different views of the New Deal legacy. Frankfurter was able to win a narrow majority for his ideas through the 1950s. Douglas gained important allies over time with the addition of new justices such as Earl Warren, William Brennan, and Abe Fortas.

In cases such as *Baker v. Carr* (1962) and *Flast v. Cohen* (1968), the Warren Court spelled out more liberal doctrines for standing and political questions. Such cases helped open the doors of the courts to a wider range of disputes, and encouraged more litigants to bring cases to the courts. Such decisions were part of a broader set of changes that were taking place in and around the courts. The Supreme Court was choosing to hear a large number of cases each year. Lower court judges heard the signal and made innovative decisions of their own. Interest groups were created and mobilized to make use of the courts to affect policy. Congress passed statutes that encouraged and subsidized litigation.

21. Alexander M. Bickel, *The Least Dangerous Branch* (Indianapolis: Bobbs–Merrill, 1962).

Note: Declaratory Judgments

During the first third of the twentieth century, many states passed declaratory judgment acts, which permitted persons to bring lawsuits before suffering an actual legal injury. The Federal Declaratory Judgment Act of 1934 gave the federal courts a similar power to hear such suits and announce what legal rights a party had.

Such measures served useful purposes in both civil and criminal law. When disputes existed over the meaning of contract terms or the constitutionality of legislation, parties no longer had to exercise what they believed to be their legal or constitutional rights at their own risk. Instead, they could have their legal dispute adjudicated before the critical behavior took place. The crucial constitutional question was whether federal courts could, when statutorily authorized, issue declaratory judgments consistent with the requirement in Article III that jurisdiction be exercised only in "cases or controversies." Were declaratory judgments, like advisory opinions, an inappropriate use of the judicial power?

The justices in *Nashville, C. & St. L. R.Y. v. Wallace* (1933) unanimously found declaratory judgment statutes constitutional. The crucial passage of Justice Stone's opinion asserted,

> the Constitution does not require that the case or controversy should be presented by traditional forms of procedure, invoking only traditional remedies. The judiciary clause of the Constitution defined and limited judicial power, not the particular method by which that power might be invoked. It did not crystallize into changeless form the procedure of 1789 as the only possible means for presenting a case or controversy otherwise cognizable by the federal courts. Whenever the judicial power is

> invoked to review a judgment of a state court, the ultimate constitutional purpose is the protection, by the exercise of the judicial function, of rights arising under the Constitution and laws of the United States... so long as the case retains the essentials of an adversary proceeding, involving a real, not a hypothetical, controversy, which is finally determined by the judgment below.

As long as the controversy was "real and substantial," Justice Stone concluded, courts could exercise jurisdiction. When upholding the Federal Declaratory Judgment Act of 1934 in *Aetna Life Ins. Co. v. Haworth* (1937), Chief Justice Hughes announced that Congress could provide standing as long as the controversy was "appropriate for judicial determination," not "a difference or dispute of a hypothetical or abstract character," but "definite and concrete, touching the legal relations of parties having adverse legal interests."

Declaratory judgments had their greatest immediate impact outside the context of the criminal law, but the Warren Court extended the implications of the statutes to halt criminal prosecutions as well. In *Dombrowski v. Pfister* (1965), a bare judicial majority ruled that members of a civil rights organization in Louisiana could obtain a declaratory judgment forbidding their prosecution under state anti-communist laws. Justice Brennan's opinion for the Court declared that federal courts should issue injunctions against state court criminal prosecutions when state statutes seem to restrict constitutionally protected speech and the litigants challenged the "good faith of the appellees in enforcing the statutes, claiming that they have invoked, and threaten to continue to invoke, criminal process without any hope of ultimate success, but only to discourage appellants' civil rights activities."

Dombrowski was sharply limited six years later in *Younger v. Harris* (1971). Justice Black's majority opinion asserted that federal injunctions against state criminal procedures threatened constitutional federalism. Injunctions should only be invoked when a state statute could not possibly be given a constitutional reading or when litigants demonstrated that the statutes were being used solely to harass them.

Flast v. Cohen, 392 U.S. 83 (1968)

For most of American history, "taxpayer suits" were frowned on. Taxpayers could, of course, insist that their tax assessments were unconstitutional or illegal. In such cases, they could establish the standing necessary for a "case or controversy" under Article III by demonstrating a personal stake in the law, distinctive from other citizens who might not pay that particular tax or taxes at all. If they were successful, their tax payments would be refunded. Taxpayers could not, however, challenge governmental expenditures simply because they were taxpayers. One reason for this practice was that governments rarely earmark taxes for specific expenditures. Hence, insufficient connections exist between the admittedly constitutional tax and the allegedly unconstitutional expenditure. More important, taxpayers do not suffer distinctive harms as taxpayers when governments spend money unconstitutionally.

To the extent that the federal government spends money when unconstitutionally procuring instruments for torture, for example, the action equally affects all taxpayers and citizens. Standing, conventional accounts suggest, requires that plaintiffs demonstrate a particularized injury. Traditional accounts suggest that the person who was tortured is in the best position to develop the facts and arguments to present to the courts and to benefit from and help shape any judicial order, not the random taxpayer who happens to find their way into federal court.

Such limitations on access to federal courts, strictly upheld, practically prevent all legal attacks on certain claimed constitutional wrongs. If the President, for example, fails to deliver a State of the Union address, no one suffers any particularized injury. Hence, no lawsuit may be brought. Many justices were not troubled by this limit on constitutional litigation. In their view, such alleged constitutional wrongs were political questions that could not be adjudicated by federal courts for a variety of reasons and were best resolved elsewhere. As Baker v. Carr *(1962) suggests, many Warren Court justices were not fond of the political question doctrine and other procedural issues that prevent various constitutional wrongs from being litigated. Supreme Court efforts to expand the scope of the Bill of Rights might bear little fruit if few persons met the constitutional standing requirements necessary to assert those rights.*

Flast v. Cohen *provided an occasion for expanding traditional standing doctrine as it had been developed in cases like* Frothingham v. Mellon *(1923). The Elementary and Secondary Education Act of 1965 authorized federal officials to provide educational assistance to low-income families. Some funds were dispensed to pay for education in sectarian and religious schools. Believing this practice violated the Establishment Clause of the First Amendment, Protestants and other Americans United for Separation of Church and*

State (now known simply as "Americans United"), along with other public interest groups, sought to construct a lawsuit that would bar such federal expenditures.

Seven families were recruited to serve as plaintiffs. Each maintained they had standing to bring the lawsuit solely because they were federal taxpayers and that their tax revenues were being spent unconstitutionally. They filed for an injunction against Secretary of Health, Education and Welfare Wilbur J. Cohen. A divided three-judge district court panel dismissed the suit on the basis of Frothingham. *Florance Flast and the other plaintiffs appealed directly to the Supreme Court. The Warren Court proved receptive, and allowed the suit in an 8–1 ruling. In practice, however, taxpayer suits under the* Flast *doctrine have been largely limited to constitutional challenges under the Establishment Clause, and* Flast *has been narrowed in its implications by later courts.*[22]

CHIEF JUSTICE WARREN delivered the opinion of the Court.

. . . For reasons explained at length below, we hold that appellants do have standing as federal taxpayers to maintain this action, and the judgment below must be reversed.

. . .

This Court first faced squarely the question whether a litigant asserting only his status as a taxpayer has standing to maintain a suit in a federal court in *Frothingham v. Mellon* (1923), and that decision must be the starting point for analysis in this case. The taxpayer in *Frothingham* attacked as unconstitutional the Maternity Act of 1921, . . . which established a federal program of grants to those States which would undertake programs to reduce maternal and infant mortality. The taxpayer alleged that Congress, in enacting the challenged statute, had exceeded the powers delegated to it under Article I of the Constitution and had invaded the legislative province reserved to the several States by the Tenth Amendment. . . . The Court noted that a federal taxpayer's "interest in the moneys of the Treasury . . . is comparatively minute and indeterminable" and that "the effect upon future taxation, of any payment out of the [Treasury's] funds, . . . [is] remote, fluctuating and uncertain." . . . As a result, the Court ruled that the taxpayer had failed to allege the type of "direct injury" necessary to confer standing. . . .

. . .

The jurisdiction of federal courts is defined and limited by Article III of the Constitution. In terms relevant to the question for decision in this case, the judicial power of federal courts is constitutionally restricted to "cases" and "controversies." . . . Embodied in the words "cases" and "controversies" are two complementary but somewhat different limitations. In part those words limit the business of federal courts to questions presented in an adversary context and in a form historically viewed as capable of resolution through the judicial process. And in part those words define the role assigned to the judiciary in a tripartite allocation of power to assure that the federal courts will not intrude into areas committed to the other branches of government. Justiciability is the term of art employed to give expression to this dual limitation placed upon federal courts by the case-and-controversy doctrine.

. . .

. . . [T]he Government's position is that the constitutional scheme of separation of powers, and the deference owed by the federal judiciary to the other two branches of government within that scheme, present an absolute bar to taxpayer suits challenging the validity of federal spending programs. The Government views such suits as involving no more than the mere disagreement by the taxpayer "with the uses to which tax money is put." According to the Government, the resolution of such disagreements is committed to other branches of the Federal Government and not to the judiciary. Consequently, the Government contends that, under no circumstances, should standing be conferred on federal taxpayers to challenge a federal taxing or spending program. An analysis of the function served by standing limitations compels a rejection of the Government's position.

. . .

. . . The fundamental aspect of standing is that it focuses on the party seeking to get his complaint before a federal court and not on the issues he wishes to have adjudicated. The "gist of the question of standing" is whether the party seeking relief has "alleged such a personal stake in the outcome of the controversy as to assure that concrete adverseness which sharpens the presentation of issues upon which the court so largely depends for illumination of difficult constitutional questions." . . . In other words, when standing is

22. See *Valley Forge Christian College v. Americans United for Separation of Church and State, Inc.*, 454 U.S. 464 (1982); *Hein v. Freedom from Religion Foundation*, 551 U.S. 587 (2007).

placed in issue in a case, the question is whether the person whose standing is challenged is a proper party to request an adjudication of a particular issue and not whether the issue itself is justiciable. Thus, a party may have standing in a particular case, but the federal court may nevertheless decline to pass on the merits of the case because, for example, it presents a political question.... So stated, the standing requirement is closely related to, although more general than, the rule that federal courts will not entertain friendly suits... or those which are feigned or collusive in nature....

When the emphasis in the standing problem is placed on whether the person invoking a federal court's jurisdiction is a proper party to maintain the action, the weakness of the Government's argument in this case becomes apparent. The question whether a particular person is a proper party to maintain the action does not, by its own force, raise separation of powers problems related to improper judicial interference in areas committed to other branches of the Federal Government. Such problems arise, if at all, only from the substantive issues the individual seeks to have adjudicated.... A taxpayer may or may not have the requisite personal stake in the outcome, depending upon the circumstances of the particular case. Therefore, we find no absolute bar in Article III to suits by federal taxpayers challenging allegedly unconstitutional federal taxing and spending programs. There remains, however, the problem of determining the circumstances under which a federal taxpayer will be deemed to have the personal stake and interest that impart the necessary concrete adverseness to such litigation so that standing can be conferred on the taxpayer *qua* taxpayer consistent with the constitutional limitations of Article III.

... [O]ur decisions establish that, in ruling on standing, it is both appropriate and necessary to... determine whether there is a logical nexus between the status asserted and the claim sought to be adjudicated.... Whether such individuals have standing to maintain that form of action turns on whether they can demonstrate the necessary stake as taxpayers in the outcome of the litigation to satisfy Article III requirements.

The nexus demanded of federal taxpayers has two aspects to it. First, the taxpayer must establish a logical link between that status and the type of legislative enactment attacked. Thus, a taxpayer will be a proper party to allege the unconstitutionality only of exercises of congressional power under the taxing and spending clause of Art. I, § 8, of the Constitution. It will not be sufficient to allege an incidental expenditure of tax funds in the administration of an essentially regulatory statute.... Secondly, the taxpayer must establish a nexus between that status and the precise nature of the constitutional infringement alleged. Under this requirement, the taxpayer must show that the challenged enactment exceeds specific constitutional limitations imposed upon the exercise of the congressional taxing and spending power and not simply that the enactment is generally beyond the powers delegated to Congress by Art. I, § 8. When both nexuses are established, the litigant will have shown a taxpayer's stake in the outcome of the controversy and will be a proper and appropriate party to invoke a federal court's jurisdiction.

The taxpayer-appellants in this case have satisfied both nexuses to support their claim of standing under the test we announce today. Their constitutional challenge is made to an exercise by Congress of its power under Art. I, § 8, to spend for the general welfare, and the challenged program involves a substantial expenditure of federal tax funds. In addition, appellants have alleged that the challenged expenditures violate the Establishment and Free Exercise Clauses of the First Amendment. Our history vividly illustrates that one of the specific evils feared by those who drafted the Establishment Clause and fought for its adoption was that the taxing and spending power would be used to favor one religion over another or to support religion in general. James Madison, who is generally recognized as the leading architect of the religion clauses of the First Amendment, observed in his famous Memorial and Remonstrance Against Religious Assessments that "the same authority which can force a citizen to contribute three pence only of his property for the support of any one establishment, may force him to conform to any other establishment in all cases whatsoever."...

The allegations of the taxpayer in *Frothingham v. Mellon*... were quite different from those made in this case, and the result in *Frothingham* is consistent with the test of taxpayer standing announced today. The taxpayer in *Frothingham* attacked a federal spending program and she, therefore, established the first nexus required. However, she lacked standing because her constitutional attack was not based on an allegation that Congress, in enacting the Maternity Act of 1921, had breached a specific limitation upon its taxing and spending power. The taxpayer in *Frothingham* alleged essentially that Congress, by enacting the challenged statute, had exceeded the general powers delegated to it by Art. I, § 8, and that Congress had thereby invaded the legislative province reserved to the States by the Tenth Amendment. To be sure, Mrs. Frothingham made the additional allegation that her tax liability would be increased as a result of the allegedly unconstitutional enactment, and she framed that allegation in terms of a deprivation of property without due process of law. However, the Due Process Clause of the Fifth Amendment does not protect taxpayers against increases in tax liability, and the taxpayer in *Frothingham* failed to make any additional claim that the harm she alleged resulted from a breach by Congress of the specific constitutional limitations imposed upon an exercise of the taxing and spending power....

...

JUSTICE DOUGLAS, concurring.

...It would...be the part of wisdom...to be rid of *Frothingham* here and now.

...

Taxpayers can be vigilant private attorneys general. Their stake in the outcome of litigation may be *de minimis* by financial standards, yet very great when measured by a particular constitutional mandate. My Brother HARLAN's opinion reflects the British, not the American, tradition of constitutionalism. We have a written Constitution; and it is full of "thou shalt nots" directed at Congress and the President as well as at the courts. And the role of the federal courts is not only to serve as referee between the States and the center but also to protect the individual against prohibited conduct by the other two branches of the Federal Government.

There has long been a school of thought here that the less the judiciary does, the better. It is often said that judicial intrusion should be infrequent, since it is "always attended with a serious evil, namely, that the correction of legislative mistakes comes from the outside, and the people thus lose the political experience, and the moral education and stimulus that come from fighting the question out in the ordinary way, and correcting their own errors"; that the effect of a participation by the judiciary in these processes is "to dwarf the political capacity of the people, and to deaden its sense of moral responsibility."...

The late Edmond Cahn, who opposed that view, stated my philosophy. He emphasized the importance of the role that the federal judiciary was designed to play in guarding basic rights against majoritarian control....

The judiciary is an indispensable part of the operation of our federal system. With the growing complexities of government it is often the one and only place where effective relief can be obtained. If the judiciary were to become a super-legislative group sitting in judgment on the affairs of people, the situation would be intolerable. But where wrongs to individuals are done by violation of specific guarantees, it is abdication for courts to close their doors.

...

We have a Constitution designed to keep government out of private domains. But the fences have often been broken down; and *Frothingham* denied effective machinery to restore them. The Constitution even with the judicial gloss it has acquired plainly is not adequate to protect the individual against the growing bureaucracy in the Legislative and Executive Branches. He faces a formidable opponent in government, even when he is endowed with funds and with courage. The individual is almost certain to be plowed under, unless he has a well-organized active political group to speak for him. The church is one. The press is another. The union is a third. But if a powerful sponsor is lacking, individual liberty withers—in spite of glowing opinions and resounding constitutional phrases.

I would not be niggardly therefore in giving private attorneys general standing to sue. I would certainly not wait for Congress to give its blessing to our deciding cases clearly within our Article III jurisdiction. To wait for a sign from Congress is to allow important constitutional questions to go undecided and personal liberty unprotected.

There need be no inundation of the federal courts if taxpayers' suits are allowed. There is a wise judicial discretion that usually can distinguish between the frivolous question and the substantial question, between cases ripe for decision and cases that need prior administrative processing, and the like. When the judiciary is no longer "a great rock" in the storm, as Lord Sankey once put it, when the courts are niggardly in the use of their power and reach great issues only timidly and reluctantly, the force of the Constitution in the life of the Nation is greatly weakened.

...

JUSTICE STEWART, concurring.

I join the judgment and opinion of the Court, which I understand to hold only that a federal taxpayer has standing to assert that a specific expenditure of federal funds violates the Establishment Clause of the First

Amendment. Because that clause plainly prohibits taxing and spending in aid of religion, every taxpayer can claim a personal constitutional right not to be taxed for the support of a religious institution....

...

JUSTICE FORTAS, concurring.

I would confine the ruling in this case to the proposition that a taxpayer may maintain a suit to challenge the validity of a federal expenditure on the ground that the expenditure violates the Establishment Clause....

JUSTICE HARLAN, dissenting.

The problems presented by this case are narrow and relatively abstract, but the principles by which they must be resolved involve nothing less than the proper functioning of the federal courts, and so run to the roots of our constitutional system. The nub of my view is that the end result of *Frothingham v. Mellon*...was correct, even though, like others, I do not subscribe to all of its reasoning and premises. Although I therefore agree with certain of the conclusions reached today by the Court, I cannot accept the standing doctrine that it substitutes for *Frothingham*, for it seems to me that this new doctrine rests on premises that do not withstand analysis. Accordingly, I respectfully dissent.

...

...[T]he United States holds its general funds, not as stakeholder or trustee for those who have paid its imposts, but as surrogate for the population at large. Any rights of a taxpayer with respect to the purposes for which those funds are expended are thus subsumed in, and extinguished by, the common rights of all citizens....

...

It is surely clear that a plaintiff's interest in the outcome of a suit in which he challenges the constitutionality of a federal expenditure is not made greater or smaller by the unconnected fact that the expenditure is, or is not, "incidental" to an "essentially regulatory" program....

Presumably the Court does not believe that regulatory programs are necessarily less destructive of First Amendment rights, or that regulatory programs are necessarily less prodigal of public funds than are grants-in-aid, for both these general propositions are demonstrably false....Apparently the Court has repudiated the emphasis in *Frothingham* upon the amount of the plaintiff's tax bill, only to substitute an equally irrelevant emphasis upon the form of the challenged expenditure.

The Court's second criterion is similarly unrelated to its standard for the determination of standing. The intensity of a plaintiff's interest in a suit is not measured, even obliquely, by the fact that the constitutional provision under which he claims is, or is not, a "specific limitation" upon Congress' spending powers....I am quite unable to understand how, if a taxpayer believes that a given public expenditure is unconstitutional, and if he seeks to vindicate that belief in a federal court, his interest in the suit can be said necessarily to vary according to the constitutional provision under which he states his claim.

...

Although the Court does not altogether explain its position, the essence of its reasoning is evidently that a taxpayer's claim under the Establishment Clause is "not merely one of ultra vires," but one which instead asserts "an abridgment of individual religious liberty" and a "governmental infringement of individual rights protected by the Constitution."...

The difficulties with this position are several. First, we have recently been reminded that the historical purposes of the religious clauses of the First Amendment are significantly more obscure and complex than this Court has heretofore acknowledged....In particular, I have not found, and the opinion of the Court has not adduced, historical evidence that properly permits the Court to distinguish, as it has here, among the Establishment Clause, the Tenth Amendment, and the Due Process Clause of the Fifth Amendment as limitations upon Congress' taxing and spending powers.

The Court's position is equally precarious if it is assumed that its premise is that the Establishment Clause is in some uncertain fashion a more "specific" limitation upon Congress' powers than are the various other constitutional commands....

Even if it is assumed that such distinctions may properly be drawn, it does not follow that federal taxpayers hold any "personal constitutional right" such that they may each contest the validity under the Establishment Clause of all federal expenditures....[A]ppellants challenge an expenditure, not a tax. Where no such tax is involved, a taxpayer's complaint can consist only of an allegation that public funds have been, or shortly will be, expended for purposes inconsistent with the Constitution. The taxpayer cannot ask the return of any portion of his previous tax payments, cannot prevent the collection of any existing tax debt, and cannot demand an adjudication of the propriety of any particular level of taxation. His tax payments are received for the general purposes of the United States, and are, upon proper receipt, lost in the general revenues.... The interests he represents, and the rights he espouses, are, as they are in all public actions, those held in common by all citizens. To describe those rights and interests as personal, and to intimate that they are in some unspecified fashion to be differentiated from those of the general public, reduces constitutional standing to a word game played by secret rules.

It seems to me clear that public actions, whatever the constitutional provisions on which they are premised, may involve important hazards for the continued effectiveness of the federal judiciary.... There is every reason to fear that unrestricted public actions might well alter the allocation of authority among the three branches of the Federal Government. It is not, I submit, enough to say that the present members of the Court would not seize these opportunities for abuse, for such actions would, even without conscious abuse, go far toward the final transformation of this Court into the Council of Revision which, despite Madison's support, was rejected by the Constitutional Convention. I do not doubt that there must be "some effectual power in the government to restrain or correct the infractions" of the Constitution's several commands, but neither can I suppose that such power resides only in the federal courts....

...This Court has previously held that individual litigants have standing to represent the public interest, despite their lack of economic or other personal interests, if Congress has appropriately authorized such suits.... Any hazards to the proper allocation of authority among the three branches of the Government would be substantially diminished if public actions had been pertinently authorized by Congress and the President. I appreciate that this Court does not ordinarily await the mandate of other branches of the Government, but it seems to me that the extraordinary character of public actions, and of the mischievous, if not dangerous, consequences they involve for the proper functioning of our constitutional system, and in particular of the federal courts, makes such judicial forbearance the part of wisdom....

...

Baker v. Carr, 369 U.S. 186 (1962)

New Deal and Great Society liberals waged a long campaign against malapportioned state and federal legislative districts. Through a combination of legislative gerrymandering and inertia, the population in most legislative districts by the end of World War II varied dramatically. Quite frequently, the population of one district would be ten times more than the population of another district with the same power to elect one representative. Liberals opposed these malapportionments for two reasons. First, malapportioned districts were inconsistent with the general democratic principles and commitment to equality underlying mid-twentieth century liberalism. Second, malapportionment often favored conservative rural voters at the expense of more liberal urban voters. This gave an electoral and legislative edge to Republicans and conservative Democrats. Political efforts to dramatically reapportion legislatures faced stiff resistance from many incumbent politicians and interests.

Federal litigation initially proved no more successful. A 4–3 majority in Colegrove v. Green *(1946) refused to determine whether malapportioned congressional districts in Illinois violated the "guarantee of republican government" clause in the Constitution. Justice Frankfurter's opinion for the short-handed Court was joined by only two other justices:*

> *The short of it is that the Constitution has conferred upon Congress exclusive authority to secure fair representation by the States in the popular House and left to that House determination whether States have fulfilled their responsibility. If Congress failed in exercising its powers, whereby standards of fairness are offended, the remedy ultimately lies with the people. Whether Congress faithfully discharges its duty or not, the subject has been committed to the exclusive control of Congress. An aspect of government from which the judiciary, in view of what is involved, has been excluded by the clear intention of the Constitution cannot be entered by the federal courts because Congress may have been in default in exacting from States obedience to its mandate.*

"Courts ought not to enter this political thicket," Frankfurter concluded. Justice Rutledge's concurring opinion declared that the justices might be able to adjudicate this dispute in some circumstances, but that those circumstances were not present in the case before the Court.

A decade later, proponents of reapportionment made another effort, one that focused on Tennessee. Although the Tennessee Constitution provided that seats in the state legislature should be apportioned by population every ten years, the state legislature had not attempted a reapportionment in a half a century. One consequence was that one state legislator represented 2,000 voters in some rural counties, while one state legislator represented almost 50,000 voters in some urban counties. Backed by a variety of interest groups, Charles Baker and other voters filed suit in federal district court against Tennessee Secretary of State Joe Carr. They sought a declaration that the existing state statutes apportioning the legislative districts violated the equal protection clause of the Fourteenth Amendment and an injunction blocking the state from holding any future elections under that apportionment scheme. A three-judge district court panel dismissed the suit as a political question. An appeal was made to the U.S. Supreme Court. The Kennedy administration threw its support behind the interest groups seeking to reapportion the Tennessee state legislature.

In a 6–2 decision, the Court distinguished Colegrove *and struck down the state apportionment law. Justice Brennan's majority opinion set out the modern formulation of the political question doctrine, even as it narrowed the scope of that doctrine by accepting the reapportionment cases as appropriate for judicial resolution. What was the significance of this change in the constitutional foundation of the claim against malapportioned legislative districts? You might also note that Justice Clark's concurring opinion in the case began as a dissent. Clark changed his mind when writing, concluding that judicial intervention was the only remedy available.*

JUSTICE BRENNAN delivered the opinion of the Court.

...

We hold that the District Court has jurisdiction of the subject matter of the federal constitutional claim asserted in the complaint.

...We hold that the appellants do have standing to maintain this suit...

These appellants seek relief in order to protect or vindicate an interest of their own, and of those similarly situated. Their constitutional claim is, in substance, that the 1901 statute constitutes arbitrary and capricious state action, offensive to the Fourteenth Amendment in its irrational disregard of the standard of apportionment prescribed by the State's Constitution or of any standard, effecting a gross disproportion of representation to voting population. The injury which appellants assert is that this classification disfavors the voters in the counties in which they reside, placing them in a position of constitutionally unjustifiable inequality *vis-à-vis* voters in irrationally favored counties. A citizen's right to a vote free of arbitrary impairment by state action has been judicially recognized as a right secured by the Constitution, when such impairment resulted from dilution by a false tally, cf. *United States* v. *Classic* (1941)....

...

In holding that the subject matter of this suit was not justiciable, the District Court relied on *Colegrove v. Green,* and subsequent *per curiam* cases....We understand the District Court to have read the cited cases as compelling the conclusion that since the appellants sought to have a legislative apportionment held unconstitutional, their suit presented a "political question" and was therefore nonjusticiable. We hold that this challenge to an apportionment presents no nonjusticiable "political question." The cited cases do not hold the contrary.

Of course the mere fact that the suit seeks protection of a political right does not mean it presents a political question. Such an objection "is little more than a play upon words."...

We hold that the claim pleaded here neither rests upon nor implicates the Guaranty Clause and that its justiciability is therefore not foreclosed by our decisions of cases involving that clause. The District Court misinterpreted *Colegrove* v. *Green* and other decisions of this Court on which it relied. Appellants' claim that they are being denied equal protection is justiciable, and if "discrimination is sufficiently shown, the right to relief under the equal protection clause is not diminished by the fact that the discrimination relates to political rights."

...[I]n the Guaranty Clause cases and in the other "political question" cases, it is the relationship between the judiciary and the coordinate branches of the Federal Government, and not the federal judiciary's relationship to the States, which gives rise to the "political question."

We have said that "In determining whether a question falls within [the political question] category, the appropriateness under our system of government of attributing finality to the action of the political departments and also the lack of satisfactory criteria for a judicial determination are dominant considerations." *Coleman* v. *Miller* (1939)....The nonjusticiability of a political question is primarily a function of the separation of powers. Much confusion results from the capacity of the "political question" label to obscure the need for case-by-case inquiry. Deciding whether a matter has in any measure been committed by the Constitution to another branch of government, or whether the action of that branch exceeds whatever authority has been committed, is itself a delicate exercise in constitutional interpretation, and is a responsibility of this Court as ultimate interpreter of the Constitution....

Foreign relations: There are sweeping statements to the effect that all questions touching foreign relations are political questions. Not only does resolution of such issues frequently turn on standards that defy judicial application, or involve the exercise of a discretion demonstrably committed to the executive or legislature; but many such questions uniquely demand single-voiced statement of the Government's views. Yet it is error to suppose that every case or controversy which touches foreign relations lies beyond judicial cognizance.... For example, though a court will not ordinarily inquire whether a treaty has been terminated, since on that question "governmental action...must be regarded as of controlling importance," if there has been no conclusive "governmental action" then a court can construe a treaty and may find it provides the answer.

Dates of duration of hostilities: Though it has been stated broadly that "the power which declared the necessity is the power to declare its cessation, and what the cessation requires,"...here too analysis reveals isolable reasons for the presence of political questions, underlying this Court's refusal to review the political departments' determination of when or whether a war has ended. Dominant is the need for finality in the political determination, for emergency's nature demands "A prompt and unhesitating obedience."...But deference rests on reason, not habit. The question in a particular case may not seriously implicate considerations of finality—*e. g.*, a public program of importance (rent control) yet not central to the emergency effort....

Validity of enactments: In *Coleman* v. *Miller* (1939), this Court held that the questions of how long a proposed amendment to the Federal Constitution remained open to ratification, and what effect a prior rejection had on a subsequent ratification, were committed to congressional resolution and involved criteria of decision that necessarily escaped the judicial grasp....

The status of Indian tribes: This Court's deference to the political departments in determining whether Indians are recognized as a tribe, while it reflects familiar attributes of political questions,...also has a unique element in that "the relation of the Indians to the United States is marked by peculiar and cardinal distinctions which exist nowhere else.... [The Indians are] domestic dependent nations...in a state of pupilage. Their relation to the United States resembles that of a ward to his guardian." *The Cherokee Nation* v. *Georgia* (1831).... Yet, here too, there is no blanket rule. While "'It is for [Congress]..., and not for the courts, to determine when the true interests of the Indian require his release from [the] condition of tutelage'..., it is not meant by this that Congress may bring a community or body of people within the range of this power by arbitrarily calling them an Indian tribe...." Able to discern what is "distinctly Indian,"...the courts will strike down any heedless extension of that label. They will not stand impotent before an obvious instance of a manifestly unauthorized exercise of power.

It is apparent that several formulations which vary slightly according to the settings in which the questions arise may describe a political question, although each has one or more elements which identify it as essentially a function of the separation of powers. Prominent on the surface of any case held to involve a political question is found a textually demonstrable constitutional commitment of the issue to a coordinate political department; or a lack of judicially discoverable and manageable standards for resolving it; or the impossibility of deciding without an initial policy determination of a kind clearly for nonjudicial discretion; or the impossibility of a court's undertaking independent resolution without expressing lack of the respect due coordinate branches of government; or an unusual need for unquestioning adherence to a political decision already made; or the potentiality of embarrassment from multifarious pronouncements by various departments on one question.

But it is argued that this case shares the characteristics of decisions that constitute a category not yet considered, cases concerning the Constitution's guaranty, in Art. IV, § 4, of a republican form of government. A conclusion as to whether the case at bar does present a political question cannot be confidently reached until we have considered those cases with special care. We shall discover that Guaranty Clause claims involve those elements which define a "political question," and for that reason and no other, they are nonjusticiable. In particular, we shall discover that the nonjusticiability of such claims has nothing to do with their touching upon matters of state governmental organization.

...

...[S]everal factors were thought by the Court in *Luther v. Borden* (1849) to make the question there "political": the commitment to the other branches of the decision as to which is the lawful state government; the unambiguous action by the President, in recognizing the charter government as the lawful authority; the need for finality in the executive's decision; and the lack of criteria by which a court could determine which form of government was republican.

But the only significance that *Luther* could have for our immediate purposes is in its holding that the Guaranty Clause is not a repository of judicially manageable standards which a court could utilize independently in order to identify a State's lawful government....

...

We come, finally, to the ultimate inquiry whether our precedents as to what constitutes a nonjusticiable "political question" bring the case before us under the umbrella of that doctrine. A natural beginning is to note whether any of the common characteristics which we have been able to identify and label descriptively are present. We find none: The question here is the consistency of state action with the Federal Constitution. We have no question decided, or to be decided, by a political branch of government coequal with this Court. Nor do we risk embarrassment of our government abroad, or grave disturbance at home if we take issue with Tennessee as to the constitutionality of her action here challenged. Nor need the appellants, in order to succeed in this action, ask the Court to enter upon policy determinations for which judicially manageable standards are lacking. Judicial standards under the Equal Protection Clause are well developed and familiar, and it has been open to courts since the enactment of the Fourteenth Amendment to determine, if on the particular facts they must, that a discrimination reflects *no* policy, but simply arbitrary and capricious action.

This case does, in one sense, involve the allocation of political power within a State, and the appellants might conceivably have added a claim under the Guaranty Clause. Of course, as we have seen, any reliance on that clause would be futile. But because any reliance on the Guaranty Clause could not have succeeded it does not follow that appellants may not be heard on the equal protection claim which in fact they tender. True, it must be clear that the Fourteenth Amendment claim is not so enmeshed with those political question elements which render Guaranty Clause claims nonjusticiable as actually to present a political question itself. But we have found that not to be the case here.

...

We conclude that the complaint's allegations of a denial of equal protection present a justiciable constitutional cause of action upon which appellants are entitled to a trial and a decision. The right asserted is within the reach of judicial protection under the Fourteenth Amendment.

JUSTICE CLARK, concurring.

...I would not consider intervention by this Court into so delicate a field if there were any other relief available to the people of Tennessee. But the majority of the people of Tennessee have no "practical opportunities for exerting their political weight at the polls" to correct the existing "invidious discrimination." Tennessee has no initiative and referendum. I have searched diligently for other "practical opportunities" present under the law. I find none other than through the federal courts. The majority of the voters have been caught up in a legislative strait jacket. Tennessee has an "informed, civically militant electorate" and "an aroused popular conscience," but it does not sear "the conscience of the people's representatives." This is because the legislative policy has riveted the present seats in the Assembly to their respective constituencies, and by the votes of their incumbents a reapportionment of any kind is prevented. The people have been rebuffed at the hands of the Assembly; they have tried the constitutional convention route, but since the call must originate in the Assembly it, too, has been fruitless. They have tried Tennessee courts with the same result, and Governors have fought the tide only to flounder. It is said that there is recourse in Congress and perhaps that may be, but from a practical standpoint this is without substance. To date Congress has never undertaken such a task in any State. We therefore must conclude that the people of Tennessee are stymied and without judicial intervention will be saddled with the present discrimination in the affairs of their state government.

...

...It is well for this Court to practice self-restraint and discipline in constitutional adjudication, but never in its history have those principles received sanction where the national rights of so many have been so clearly infringed for so long a time. National respect for the courts is more enhanced through the forthright enforcement of those rights rather than by rendering them nugatory through the interposition of subterfuges. In my view the ultimate decision today is in the greatest tradition of this Court.

JUSTICE DOUGLAS, concurring.

...

JUSTICE STEWART, concurring.

...

JUSTICE FRANKFURTER, with whom JUSTICE HARLAN joins, dissenting.

The Court today reverses a uniform course of decision established by a dozen cases, including one by which the very claim now sustained was unanimously rejected only five years ago. The impressive body of rulings thus cast aside reflected the equally uniform course of our political history regarding the relationship between population and legislative representation—a wholly different matter from denial of the franchise to individuals because of race, color, religion or sex. Such a massive repudiation of the experience of our whole past in asserting destructively novel judicial power demands a detailed analysis of the role of this Court in our constitutional scheme. Disregard of inherent limits in the effective exercise of the Court's "judicial Power" not only presages the futility of judicial intervention in the essentially political conflict of forces by which the relation between population and representation has time out of mind been and now is determined. It may well impair the Court's position as the ultimate organ of "the supreme Law of the Land" in that vast range of legal problems, often strongly entangled in popular feeling, on which this Court must pronounce. The Court's authority—possessed of neither the purse nor the sword—ultimately rests on sustained public confidence in its moral sanction. Such feeling must be nourished by the Court's complete detachment, in fact and in appearance, from political entanglements and by abstention from injecting itself into the clash of political forces in political settlements.

A hypothetical claim resting on abstract assumptions is now for the first time made the basis for affording illusory relief for a particular evil even though it foreshadows deeper and more pervasive difficulties in consequence. The claim is hypothetical and the assumptions are abstract because the Court does not vouchsafe the lower courts—state and federal—guidelines for formulating specific, definite, wholly unprecedented remedies for the inevitable litigations that today's umbrageous disposition is bound to stimulate in connection with politically motivated reapportionments in so many States. In such a setting, to promulgate jurisdiction in the abstract is meaningless. It is as devoid of reality as "a brooding omnipresence in the sky," for it conveys no intimation what relief, if any, a District Court is capable of affording that would not invite legislatures to play ducks and drakes with the judiciary. For this Court to direct the District Court to enforce a claim to which the Court has over the years consistently found itself required to deny legal enforcement and at the same time to find it necessary to withhold any guidance to the lower court how to enforce this turnabout, new legal claim, manifests an odd—indeed an esoteric—conception of judicial propriety.... Even assuming the indispensable intellectual disinterestedness on the part of judges in such matters, they do not have accepted legal standards or criteria or even reliable analogies to draw upon for making judicial judgments. To charge courts with the task of accommodating the incommensurable factors of policy that underlie these mathematical puzzles is to attribute, however flatteringly, omnicompetence to judges. The Framers of the Constitution persistently rejected a proposal that embodied this assumption and Thomas Jefferson never entertained it.

...In effect, today's decision empowers the courts of the country to devise what should constitute the proper composition of the legislatures of the fifty States. If state courts should for one reason or another find themselves unable to discharge this task, the duty of doing so is put on the federal courts or on this Court, if State views do not satisfy this Court's notion of what is proper districting.

We were soothingly told at the bar of this Court that we need not worry about the kind of remedy a court could effectively fashion once the abstract constitutional right to have courts pass on a state-wide system of electoral districting is recognized as a matter of judicial rhetoric, because legislatures would heed the Court's admonition. This is not only a euphoric hope. It implies a sorry confession of judicial impotence in place of a frank acknowledgment that there is not under our Constitution a judicial remedy for every political mischief, for every undesirable exercise of legislative power. The Framers carefully and with deliberate forethought refused so to enthrone the judiciary. In this situation, as in others of like nature, appeal for relief does not belong here. Appeal must be to an informed, civically militant electorate. In a democratic society like ours, relief must come through an aroused popular conscience that sears the conscience of the people's representatives. In any event there is nothing judicially more unseemly nor more self-defeating than for this Court to make *in terrorem* pronouncements, to indulge in merely empty rhetoric, sounding a word of promise to the ear, sure to be disappointing to the hope.

...

The *Colegrove* doctrine, in the form in which repeated decisions have settled it, was not an innovation. It represents long judicial thought and experience. From its earliest opinions this Court has consistently recognized a class of controversies which do not lend themselves to judicial standards and judicial remedies. To classify the various instances as "political questions" is rather a form of stating this conclusion than revealing of analysis. Some of the cases so labeled have no relevance here. But from others emerge unifying considerations that are compelling.

1. The cases concerning war or foreign affairs, for example, are usually explained by the necessity of the country's speaking with one voice in such matters. While this concern alone undoubtedly accounts for many of the decisions, others do not fit the pattern. It would hardly embarrass the conduct of war were this Court to determine, in connection with private transactions between litigants, the date upon which war is to be deemed terminated.... A controlling factor in such cases is that, decision respecting these kinds of complex matters of policy being traditionally committed not to courts but to the political agencies of government for determination by criteria of political expediency, there exists no standard ascertainable by settled judicial experience or process by reference to which a political decision affecting the question at issue between the parties can be judged....

This may be, like so many questions of law, a matter of degree. Questions have arisen under the Constitution to which adjudication gives answer although the criteria for decision are less than unwavering bright lines. Often in these cases illumination was found in the federal structures established by, or the underlying presuppositions of, the Constitution. With respect to such questions, the Court has recognized that, concerning a particular power of Congress put in issue, "...effective restraints on its exercise must proceed from political rather than from judicial processes." *Wickard* v. *Filburn* (1942).... But this is merely to acknowledge that particular circumstances may differ so greatly in degree as to differ thereby in kind, and that, although within a certain range of cases on a continuum, no standard of distinction can be found to tell between them, other cases will fall above or below the range. The doctrine of political questions, like any other, is not to be applied beyond the limits of its own logic, with all the quiddities and abstract disharmonies it may manifest....

2. The Court has been particularly unwilling to intervene in matters concerning the structure and organization of the political institutions of the States. The abstention from judicial entry into such areas has been greater even than that which marks the Court's ordinary approach to issues of state power challenged under broad federal guarantees." We should be very reluctant to decide that we had jurisdiction in such a case, and thus in an action of this nature to supervise and review the political administration of a state government by its own officials and through its own courts. The jurisdiction of this court would only exist in case there had been...such a plain and substantial departure from the fundamental principles upon which our government is based that it could with truth and propriety be said that if the judgment were suffered to remain, the party aggrieved would be deprived of his life, liberty or property in violation of the provisions of the Federal Constitution."

3. The cases involving Negro disfranchisement are no exception to the principle of avoiding federal judicial intervention into matters of state government in the absence of an explicit and clear constitutional imperative. For here the controlling command of Supreme Law is plain and unequivocal. An end of discrimination against the Negro was the compelling motive of the Civil War Amendments. The Fifteenth expresses this in terms, and it is no less true of the Equal Protection Clause of the Fourteenth....

4. The Court has refused to exercise its jurisdiction to pass on "abstract questions of political power, of sovereignty, of government."... The "political question" doctrine, in this aspect, reflects the policies underlying the requirement of "standing": that the litigant who would challenge official action must claim infringement of an interest particular and personal to himself, as distinguished from a cause of dissatisfaction with the general frame and functioning of government—a complaint that the political institutions are awry.... The crux of the matter is that courts are not fit instruments of decision where what is essentially at stake is the composition of those large contests of policy traditionally fought out in non-judicial forums,

by which governments and the actions of governments are made and unmade....

...

5. The influence of these converging considerations—the caution not to undertake decision where standards meet for judicial judgment are lacking, the reluctance to interfere with matters of state government in the absence of an unquestionable and effectively enforceable mandate, the unwillingness to make courts arbiters of the broad issues of political organization historically committed to other institutions and for whose adjustment the judicial process is ill-adapted—has been decisive of the settled line of cases, reaching back more than a century, which holds that Art. IV, § 4, of the Constitution, guaranteeing to the States "a Republican Form of Government," is not enforceable through the courts.

...

The present case involves all of the elements that have made the Guarantee Clause cases non-justiciable. It is, in effect, a Guarantee Clause claim masquerading under a different label. But it cannot make the case more fit for judicial action that appellants invoke the Fourteenth Amendment rather than Art. IV, § 4, where, in fact, the gist of their complaint is the same—unless it can be found that the Fourteenth Amendment speaks with greater particularity to their situation....

...

What, then, is this question of legislative apportionment? Appellants invoke the right to vote and to have their votes counted. But they are permitted to vote and their votes are counted. They go to the polls, they cast their ballots, they send their representatives to the state councils. Their complaint is simply that the representatives are not sufficiently numerous or powerful—in short, that Tennessee has adopted a basis of representation with which they are dissatisfied. Talk of "debasement" or "dilution" is circular talk. One cannot speak of "debasement" or "dilution" of the value of a vote until there is first defined a standard of reference as to what a vote should be worth. What is actually asked of the Court in this case is to choose among competing bases of representation—ultimately, really, among competing theories of political philosophy—in order to establish an appropriate frame of government for the State of Tennessee and thereby for all the States of the Union.

In such a matter, abstract analogies which ignore the facts of history deal in unrealities; they betray reason. This is not a case in which a State has, through a device however oblique and sophisticated, denied Negroes or Jews or redheaded persons a vote, or given them only a third or a sixth of a vote. That was *Gomillion* v. *Lightfoot* (1960). What Tennessee illustrates is an old and still widespread method of representation—representation by local geographical division, only in part respective of population—in preference to others, others, forsooth, more appealing. Appellants contest this choice and seek to make this Court the arbiter of the disagreement. They would make the Equal Protection Clause the charter of adjudication, asserting that the equality which it guarantees comports, if not the assurance of equal weight to every voter's vote, at least the basic conception that representation ought to be proportionate to population, a standard by reference to which the reasonableness of apportionment plans may be judged.

To find such a political conception legally enforceable in the broad and unspecific guarantee of equal protection is to rewrite the Constitution.... Certainly "equal protection" is no more secure a foundation for judicial judgment of the permissibility of varying forms of representative government than is "Republican Form."...

...

Manifestly, the Equal Protection Clause supplies no clearer guide for judicial examination of apportionment methods than would the Guarantee Clause itself. Apportionment, by its character, is a subject of extraordinary complexity, involving—even after the fundamental theoretical issues concerning what is to be represented in a representative legislature have been fought out or compromised—considerations of geography, demography, electoral convenience, economic and social cohesions or divergencies among particular local groups, communications, the practical effects of political institutions like the lobby and the city machine, ancient traditions and ties of settled usage, respect for proven incumbents of long experience and senior status, mathematical mechanics, censuses compiling relevant data, and a host of others. Legislative responses throughout the country to the reapportionment demands of the 1960 Census have glaringly confirmed that these are not factors that lend themselves to evaluations of a nature that are the staple of judicial determinations or for which judges are equipped to adjudicate by legal training or experience or native wit. And this is the more so true because in every strand of this complicated, intricate web of values meet the contending forces of partisan politics. The practical significance of apportionment is that the next election results may differ because of it. Apportionment battles are overwhelmingly party or intra-party contests. It will add a virulent source of friction and tension in federal-state relations to embroil the federal judiciary in them.

Although the District Court had jurisdiction in the very restricted sense of power to determine whether it could adjudicate the claim, the case is of that class of political controversy which, by the nature of its subject, is unfit for federal judicial action. The judgment of the District Court, in dismissing the complaint for failure to state a claim on which relief can be granted, should therefore be affirmed.

JUSTICE HARLAN, with whom JUSTICE FRANKFURTER joins, dissenting.

...

I can find nothing in the Equal Protection Clause or elsewhere in the Federal Constitution which expressly or impliedly supports the view that state legislatures must be so structured as to reflect with approximate equality the voice of every voter. Not only is that proposition refuted by history, as shown by my Brother FRANKFURTER, but it strikes deep into the heart of our federal system. Its acceptance would require us to turn our backs on the regard which this Court has always shown for the judgment of state legislatures and courts on matters of basically local concern.

...

D. Federal Review of the States

Note: The Incorporation of the Bill of Rights

Judicial decisions determining whether the privileges and immunities or the due process clauses of the Fourteenth Amendment required states to honor the liberties set out in the first eight amendments of the Constitution provoked important and heated debates between political liberals over the proper role of federal courts during the post–New Deal period. The controversy involved issues of federalism, constitutional interpretation, judicial power, and, most important, the best justification of the New Deal constitutional regime. Many of these debates played out in the context of the rights of suspected criminals, though there were implications for a broader range of rights and groups.

Central to these debates was not only the question of what rights individuals should have within the American constitutional system in the mid-twentieth century, but also how active the federal courts should be in defining and enforcing those rights. Was the meaning and legacy of the New Deal that democratic majorities should be given wide space to experiment? Could they make pragmatic adjustments to advance the public good as they understood it? Or should a new generation of federal judges monitor government for violations of human rights and human dignity?

Justices Felix Frankfurter and John Marshall Harlan repeatedly insisted that states had no specific obligation to respect liberties set out in the Bill of Rights. The New Deal regime, in their view, was constitutionally committed to allowing elected officials to determine the criminal process that best promoted truth and justice, as long as that local criminal process was "fundamentally fair." Justice Hugo Black just as vigorously insisted that states were obligated to respect all the liberties set out in the Bill of Rights. The Bill of Rights, in his judgment, set the American standard for what was constitutionally fair. Judicial notions of equity and fairness were not enough.

Judicial liberals initially agreed that the Fourteenth Amendment required states to honor fundamental principles of liberty and fairness, but not every provision in the Bill of Rights. Justice Benjamin Cardozo's opinion in *Palko v. Connecticut* (1937), joined by every member of the Hughes Court except Justice Butler, insisted that the Fourteenth Amendment protected only those rights that were "of the very essence of a scheme of ordered liberty." Such rights, he continued, had to be derived from a "principle of justice so rooted in the traditions and conscience of our people as to be ranked as fundamental." Free speech was the best example of a right so central to American liberty. That freedom, Cardozo declared, was "the matrix, the indispensable condition, of nearly every other form of freedom." The specific provisions in the Bill of Rights that provided constitutional protections to criminal suspects were not deemed nearly as vital. New Deal justices in 1937 thought that due process was satisfied as long as criminal suspects were given a trial that was "not a sham or a pretense."

Justice Black signed the *Palko* opinion but soon regretted his vote. By the late 1940s Black, joined by Justices Wiley Rutledge, Frank Murphy, and William

Illustration 8-2 Justices Felix Frankfurter and Hugo Black

Source: Library of Congress Prints and Photographs Division, LC-USZ62-36966 and LC-USZ62-52112.

Douglas, had reached the conclusion that the Fourteenth Amendment required that states honor all the liberties in the Bill of Rights. The idea that justices could determine what rights were "of the very essence of a scheme of ordered liberty," Black argued, required precisely the sort of subjective judgments underlying judicial decisions declaring New Deal measures unconstitutional. In *Adamson v. California* (1947), Black derided the fundamental freedoms approach as a "natural law" theory that was subject to expansion and contraction at the will of the judges. He began to lay out his argument that a proper historical understanding of the original meaning of the Fourteenth Amendment required a total incorporation of the Bill of Rights. The justices should not pick and choose which rights were "incorporated" into the requirements of the Fourteenth Amendment and enforced against the states. According to Black, the federal Bill of Rights provided a complete and exhaustive list of rights covered by the Fourteenth Amendment. The blanket application of the details of the Bill of Rights to the states might require more federal judicial oversight of the state governments, but it imposed limits on how they would exercise that oversight.

Justice Frankfurter vigorously opposed what became known as "total incorporation." His opinions repeatedly declared that justices who required states to respect every liberty in the Bill of Rights were the ones engaging in the same sort of activism underlying judicial decisions declaring New Deal measures unconstitutional. According to Frankfurter, Black would impose more restrictions on the states than the Constitution warranted.

The justices never adopted Black's view that the Fourteenth Amendment totally incorporated every aspect of the Bill of Rights. However, Warren Court majorities adopted so liberal a construction of what rights were "of the very essence of a scheme of ordered liberties" that Black could largely endorse it. The result has become known as "selective incorporation," or "selective incorporation plus." The "plus" reflects the "unenumerated" fundamental freedoms that have supplemented the Court's rights jurisprudence. Justice Black dissented, for example, from the Court's ruling in *Griswold v. Connecticut* (1965), which found a generalized right to privacy in the Constitution that was sufficient to strike down Connecticut's anti-contraceptive law. Incorporation was "selective" because not every provision of the federal Bill of Rights was enforced against the states.

By the end of the 1960s, the Supreme Court had ruled that the Fourteenth Amendment incorporated every provision of the Bill of Rights except the Second Amendment, the Third Amendment, the grand jury provision of the Sixth Amendment, the Seventh Amendment, and the excessive bail provision of the Eighth Amendment, despite disagreements about how best to justify those actions (see, for example, *Duncan v. Louisiana* [1968]). Although law professors continued to fight over the original intentions of the persons responsible for the Fourteenth Amendment, a more conservative federal judiciary did not return to earlier views that narrowly defined incorporation.

III. Powers of the National Government

MAJOR DEVELOPMENTS

- The expansion of national regulatory powers under the commerce clause
- Clarification and expansion of federal powers to enforce civil rights
- Acceptance of broad use of the tax-and-spend power to advance national policies

Proponents of the New Deal and Great Society believed that the Constitution vested the national government with the powers necessary to resolve all national problems. In their view, the Constitution implicitly incorporated the provision of the proposed Virginia Plan that gave power to Congress "to legislate in all cases for the general interests of the union, and also in those to which the states are separately incompetent, or in which the harmony of the United States may be interrupted by the exercise of individual legislation."[23] "[O]ur Constitution tells us," Franklin Roosevelt informed Congress in 1934, that "our Federal Government was established among other things 'to promote the general welfare.'"[24]

Franklin Roosevelt and his allies during the New Deal drew inspiration from the language of Article I of the Constitution and insisted that the Constitution granted ample authority to the federal government to regulate the national economy. Lyndon Johnson and his allies during the Great Society drew inspiration from the language of the post–Civil War Amendments and insisted that the Constitution granted ample authority to the federal government to eradicate racial discrimination and poverty. Liberals during this period disagreed over whether and how individual rights provisions of the Constitution limited the exercise of federal power, but they agreed that the Tenth Amendment and principles of enumerated powers did not impose significant limits on federal power. If Congress thought a statute addressed a national problem, then that was sufficient for the judiciary.

Transforming the Size and Scope of Government. The result was a radical transformation in the size and scope of the federal government. Table 8-2 and Figure 8-5 give some indication of the practical effects of the change, as well as its timing. Table 8-2 tracks government spending over the course of the first several decades of the twentieth century. Although the size of government spending grew throughout the period, so did the size of the economy. The more telling question is how large of a share of the economy the government occupied over time. At the beginning of the century, the states and localities outspent the federal government by a significant margin, and both occupied a relatively small share of the economy. During the New Deal, as the economy shrank and government spending grew, both levels of government expanded significantly. State and local government spending stabilized at this new level, growing somewhat in recent decades. The federal government took another significant leap during the Second World War and never returned to prewar, let alone pre–New Deal, levels of spending. In contrast to the pre–New Deal era, the modern federal government routinely outpaces the spending of the state and local governments by a significant margin.

The same story appears in Figure 8-5, which tracks over the twentieth century the civilian employees of the federal government, the employees needed to design and implement federal regulations and process federal spending. Although the size of the government

23. Robert L. Stern, "The Commerce Clause and the National Economy, 1933–1946: Part Two," *Harvard Law Review* 59 (1946):947.

24. *Public Papers and Addresses of Franklin D. Roosevelt*, ed. Samuel I. Rosenman, vol. 3 (New York: Random House, 1950), 291.

Table 8-2 Federal and State and Local Government Spending, 1902–1980

Year	Federal (in millions of $)	Federal (% GDP)	State/Local (in millions of $)	State/Local (% GDP)
1902	565	3	1095	5
1913	958	3	2257	6
1922	3645	5	5652	8
1932	4034	7	8403	14
1936	8257	10	8501	10
1940	9177	9	11,240	11
1944	99,662	45	10,914	5
1950	42,429	14	27,905	9
1955	70,342	10	40,375	10
1960	90,289	17	69,999	12
1965	118,996	17	86,686	12
1970	184,933	18	148,052	14
1975	291,889	18	268,242	16
1980	526,329	19	432,327	15

Source: Historical Statistics of the United States (New York: Cambridge University Press, 1997), Tables Ea10–23, Ca9–19.

expanded significantly during the New Deal, it doubled in size again after the Second World War. The constitutional disputes over the powers of the national government were accompanied by a fundamental restructuring of the political system that had been inherited from earlier generations.

Constitutional debate during the New Deal focused on what laws were necessary and proper regulations of interstate commerce, although controversies also arose over the scope of the spending power, the taxing power, and the federal power to regulate the currency. Immediately upon taking office in 1933, Franklin Roosevelt called for a more aggressive use of federal power than any other previous administration. Congress from 1933–1936 generally complied with administration requests, passing legislation that dramatically expanded federal oversight of prices, wages, industrial production, agriculture, and employer–employee relationships. The federal judiciary proved less obliging. Lower federal courts issued hundreds of injunctions against New Deal programs. Important programs were declared unconstitutional by the Supreme Court. While some Roosevelt programs were struck down by bare 5–4 majorities, progressive justices such as Louis Brandeis and Benjamin Cardozo in several cases also insisted that Congress was attempting to exercise powers not delegated to the national government. The Supreme Court struck down federal laws in more cases during Roosevelt's first term of office than in any other four-year period up to that point. The most important of those decisions came in 1935 and 1936, when the Court struck down key provisions of the National Industrial Recovery Act, Agricultural Adjustment Act, and the Bituminous Coal Act in cases such as *Panama Refining Co. v. Ryan* (1935), *Schechter Poultry v. United States* (1935), *United States v. Butler* (1936), and *Carter v. Carter Coal* (1936).

Judicial resistance finally melted after Roosevelt's reelection in 1936. At first, the justices claimed to be following precedents. When Chief Justice Hughes upheld the National Labor Relations Act in the *Jones & Laughlin Steel* decision (1937), he maintained that the statute respected the traditional distinction between commerce and production and was properly limited in scope to interstate economic activity. Despite this conventional rhetoric, many liberal and conservative commentators insisted that a "Constitutional Revolu-

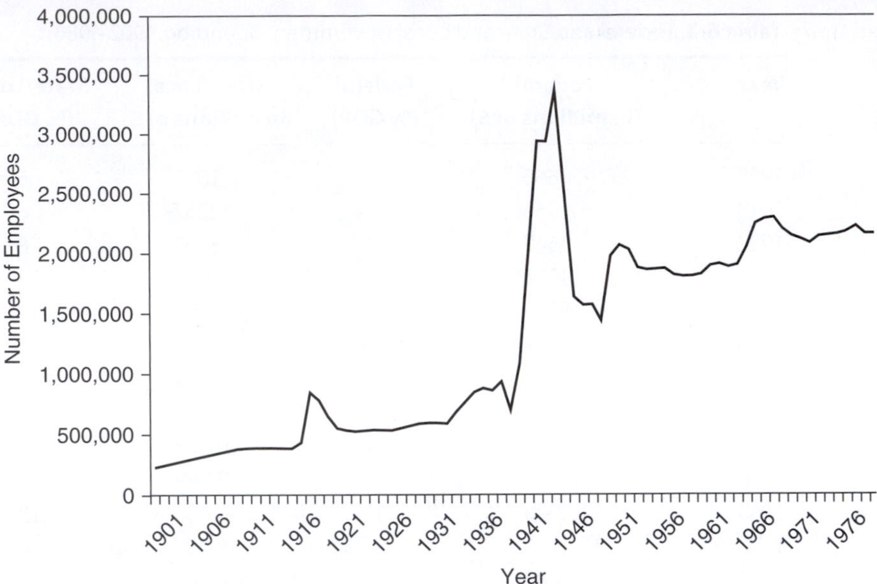

Figure 8-5 Civilian Employees of the Federal Government, 1901–1980

Source: Statistical Abstract of the United States (Washington, DC: Government Printing Office, 2007), HS–50: Federal Government—Employment, 1901–2002 (Total Executive Branch Civilian Employment).

Note: Years 1902–1907 estimated.

tion" had taken place, that the justices were now committed to sustaining New Deal measures regardless of whether they satisfied past constitutional standards.[25] By the early 1940s, a new constitutional regime was unquestionably in place. Roosevelt's judicial appointees felt no need to invoke constitutional rules announced before 1936 when justifying the administration's policies. Most of those justices had themselves been appointed since 1936 and had previously been involved in drafting or defending those New Deal policies. *United States v. Darby* (1941) and *Wickard v. Filburn* (1942) established federal power to regulate all activity that, standing alone or in combination with similar activity, affected interstate commerce in some way. Relying on this standard, the courts for decades rejected every claim that Congress was exceeding its enumerated powers.

The Great Society built upon the constitutional legacy of the New Deal. Following New Deal liberals, Great Society liberals insisted that the commerce clause gave the federal government broad power to regulate interstate commerce, even when the national government was more concerned with regulating social than economic ills. The Civil Rights Act of 1964, which barred racial discrimination in places of public accommodation, was passed and judicially sustained as a regulation of interstate commerce in *Heart of Atlanta Motel, Inc. v. United States* (1964) and *Katzenbach v. McClung* (1964). Some argued that Congress had the power under the post–Civil War Amendments to pass legislation that prevented private racial discrimination. Congress, in their view, could pass any legislation that a rational person might think furthered a legitimate national end. Some passages in *Katzenbach v. Morgan* (1966) indicated that Congress had a limited power to determine the meaning of the Fourteenth Amendment as well as enforce judicially determined rules.

A. Power to Regulate Commerce

The commerce clause was one of the major constitutional battlegrounds of the New Deal. Over the course of the Republican Era, the Court's commerce-clause doctrine evolved. The Court continued to try to maintain its core distinctions between the federal authority

25. Edward S. Corwin, *Constitutional Revolution, Ltd.* (Claremont, CA: Claremont College, 1941).

to regulate interstate commerce and the state authority to regulate local commerce and manufacturing. Deciding when federal regulations of large corporations (the most common problem) exceeded federal authority and became a regulation of manufacturing or local commercial activity was a persistent challenge. The Court developed a two-part test for evaluating commerce-clause claims, asking whether the regulated activity was itself in the "stream of commerce" that crossed state boundaries or whether it directly affected, injured, or hampered interstate commercial activity.

The New Deal posed a basic challenge to that constitutional scheme. The first set of New Deal policies created a comprehensive set of economic regulations, affecting the local shopkeeper as much as the interstate corporation, productive activity as much as commercial activity. New Dealers first attempted to bend the old doctrines to cover the new statutes. They failed to persuade the Court in *Schechter Poultry* (1935) (known as the "sick chicken case" because the government claimed that the Schechter brothers sold sick poultry) or *Carter Coal* (1936) or *U.S. v. Butler* (1936) or even *Railroad Retirement Board v. Alton Railroad Co.* (1935). *Butler* focused mostly on the spending clause in striking down the Agriculture Adjustment Act (AAA), but Justice Owen Roberts also made clear that Congress did not have the power under the commerce clause to regulate farm production. Even in railroad regulation, where the federal government had traditionally had a wide berth, New Dealers lost. In a 5–4 decision in *Railroad Retirement Board,* Justice Roberts concluded that an act establishing a retirement and pension system for railroad employees "is not in purpose or effect a regulation of interstate commerce within the meaning of the Constitution." The statute was "really and essentially related solely to the social welfare of the worker, and therefore remote from any regulation of commerce as such." The government won some important judicial victories during Roosevelt's first term, but the message from the Court was clear: The New Deal did not fit under the commerce clause.

Chief Justice Charles Evan Hughes and Justice Owen Roberts switched their votes to side with the government in the decisive case of *Jones & Laughlin Steel Corp.* (1937). Over the next two years, the Supreme Court made clear in cases such as *Santa Cruz Fruit Packing Co. v. National Labor Relations Board* (1938), *Mulford v. Smith* (1939), and *United States v. Rock Royal Co-Operative, Inc.* (1939) that Congress could regulate businesses that shipped goods in interstate commerce or purchased goods to be shipped in interstate commerce, even if those businesses were located entirely within one state. The remaining conservatives continued to dissent from these decisions. Once the New Dealers had a solid majority on the Court, they abandoned the old doctrine and explicitly overruled the old precedents in *Darby* (1941) and *Wickard* (1942). The new doctrine no longer talked about the stream of commerce and direct and indirect effects on commerce. Instead, Congress simply had the power to regulate any activity that in the aggregate had a substantial economic affect on interstate commerce. The combination of an expanded understanding of interstate commerce and what was necessary and proper to regulate it opened the door to a wide range of national economic regulations.

Schechter Poultry Corp. v. United States, 295 U.S. 495 (1935)

Many liberals believed that the Great Depression required the national government to take a larger role in regulating the economy. One popular proposal was championed by Senator Hugo Black, who would later be Roosevelt's first appointment to the Supreme Court. This mandated a thirty-hour week as a means for reducing unemployment by spreading available work. Although the measure passed the Senate, many thought the bill was unconstitutional. Surprisingly, President Roosevelt shared this assessment. As an alternative to the Black Bill, the administration proposed the National Industrial Recovery Act (NIRA). NIRA allowed industries to establish wage and hours regulations themselves. Once an agreement was reached on wages, hours, and other working conditions, that agreement would be enforced by the national government. This greater flexibility, administration officials believed, would enable NIRA to pass constitutional muster. They were wrong.

Schechter *was a poor case for the government to test the constitutionality of NIRA. The Schechter brothers owned slaughterhouses in New York City, where they killed and sold chickens to local stores. They acquired many of their live chickens from out of state. They had been convicted in federal district court of violating the fair competition standards set by the National Recovery Administration, and their conviction had been affirmed by the appeals court. In* Schechter, *a unanimous Supreme Court ruled that the commerce clause did not allow the national government to determine the wages and hours of local butchers. Chief Justice Charles*

Evan Hughes concluded that the activities of local butchers did not directly affect interstate commerce and could not be controlled by Congress.

One reason for the unanimity may have been poor government presentation. The government brief never explained the effect local slaughtering practices had on interstate commerce. As important, the more progressive justices on the Hughes Court were not as enamored as Roosevelt with central planning. The progressive Justice Louis Brandeis was so offended by NIRA provisions that he called the government lawyers into his office for a tongue lashing immediately after the decision was announced. "This is the end of this business of centralization, and I want you to go back and tell the President that we're not going to let this government centralize everything. It's come to an end. As for your young men, you call them together and tell them to get out of Washington—tell them to go home, back to the states. That is where they must do their work."[26]

Schechter *was one of several early losses for the New Deal in the Supreme Court. As you read Hughes' opinion, consider how large of a defeat this might have seemed. How accommodating is this opinion for national economic regulation?*

CHIEF JUSTICE HUGHES delivered the opinion of the Court.

...We are told that the provision of the statute authorizing the adoption of codes must be viewed in the light of the grave national crisis with which Congress was confronted. Undoubtedly, the conditions to which power is addressed are always to be considered when the exercise of power is challenged. Extraordinary conditions may call for extraordinary remedies. But the argument necessarily stops short of an attempt to justify action which lies outside the sphere of constitutional authority. Extraordinary conditions do not create or enlarge constitutional power. The Constitution established a national government with powers deemed to be adequate, as they have proved to be both in war and peace, but these powers of the national government are limited by the constitutional grants. Those who act under these grants are not at liberty to transcend the imposed limits because they believe that more or different power is necessary. Such assertions of extra-constitutional authority were anticipated and precluded by the explicit terms of the Tenth Amendment,—"The powers not delegated to the United States by the Constitution, nor prohibited by it to the States, are reserved to the States respectively, or to the people."

...

(1) Were these transactions *"in"* interstate commerce? Much is made of the fact that almost all the poultry coming to New York is sent there from other States. But the code provisions, as here applied, do not concern the transportation of the poultry from other States to New York, or the transactions of the commission men or others to whom it is consigned, or the sales made by such consignees to defendants. When defendants had made their purchases, whether at the West Washington Market in New York City or at the railroad terminals serving the City, or elsewhere, the poultry was trucked to their slaughterhouses in Brooklyn for local disposition. The interstate transactions in relation to that poultry then ended. Defendants held the poultry at their slaughterhouse markets for slaughter and local sale to retail dealers and butchers who in turn sold directly to consumers. Neither the slaughtering nor the sales by defendants were transactions in interstate commerce....

The undisputed facts thus afford no warrant for the argument that the poultry handled by defendants at their slaughterhouse markets was in a *"current"* or *"flow"* of interstate commerce and was thus subject to congressional regulation. The mere fact that there may be a constant flow of commodities into a State does not mean that the flow continues after the property has arrived and has become commingled with the mass of property within the State and is there held solely for local disposition and use. So far as the poultry here in question is concerned, the flow in interstate commerce had ceased. The poultry had come to a permanent rest within the State....

(2) Did the defendants' transactions directly *"affect"* interstate commerce so as to be subject to federal regulation? The power of Congress extends not only to the regulation of transactions which are part of interstate commerce, but to the protection of that commerce from injury. It matters not that the injury may be due to the conduct of those engaged in intrastate operations. Thus, Congress may protect the safety of those employed in interstate transportation "no matter what may be the source of the dangers which threaten it."...

...

26. Philippa Strum, *Louis D. Brandeis* (New York: Schocken Books, 1984), 352.

...This is not a prosecution for a conspiracy to restrain or monopolize interstate commerce in violation of the Anti-Trust Act. Defendants have been convicted, not upon direct charges of injury to interstate commerce or of interference with persons engaged in that commerce, but of violations of certain provisions of the Live Poultry Code and of conspiracy to commit these violations. Interstate commerce is brought in only upon the charge that violations of these provisions—as to hours and wages of employees and local sales—"affected" interstate commerce.

In determining how far the federal government may go in controlling intrastate transactions upon the ground that they "affect" interstate commerce, there is a necessary and well-established distinction between direct and indirect effects. The precise line can be drawn only as individual cases arise, but the distinction is clear in principle. Direct effects are illustrated by the railroad cases we have cited, as *e.g.*, the effect of failure to use prescribed safety appliances on railroads which are the highways of both interstate and intrastate commerce, injury to an employee engaged in interstate transportation by the negligence of an employee engaged in an intrastate movement, the fixing of rates for intrastate transportation which unjustly discriminate against interstate commerce. But where the effect of intrastate transactions upon interstate commerce is merely indirect, such transactions remain within the domain of state power. If the commerce clause were construed to reach all enterprises and transactions which could be said to have an indirect effect upon interstate commerce, the federal authority would embrace practically all the activities of the people and the authority of the State over its domestic concerns would exist only by sufferance of the federal government. Indeed, on such a theory, even the development of the State's commercial facilities would be subject to federal control....

...

The question of chief importance relates to the provisions of the Code as to the hours and wages of those employed in defendants' slaughterhouse markets. It is plain that these requirements are imposed in order to govern the details of defendants' management of their local business. The persons employed in slaughtering and selling in local trade are not employed in interstate commerce. Their hours and wages have no direct relation to interstate commerce. The question of how many hours these employees should work and what they should be paid differs in no essential respect from similar questions in other local businesses which handle commodities brought into a State and there dealt in as a part of its internal commerce....If the federal government may determine the wages and hours of employees in the internal commerce of a State, because of their relation to cost and prices and their indirect effect upon interstate commerce, it would seem that a similar control might be exerted over other elements of cost, also affecting prices, such as the number of employees, rents, advertising, methods of doing business, etc. All the processes of production and distribution that enter into cost could likewise be controlled. If the cost of doing an intrastate business is in itself the permitted object of federal control, the extent of the regulation of cost would be a question of discretion and not of power.

The Government also makes the point that efforts to enact state legislation establishing high labor standards have been impeded by the belief that unless similar action is taken generally, commerce will be diverted from the States adopting such standards, and that this fear of diversion has led to demands for federal legislation on the subject of wages and hours. The apparent implication is that the federal authority under the commerce clause should be deemed to extend to the establishment of rules to govern wages and hours in intrastate trade and industry generally throughout the country, thus overriding the authority of the States to deal with domestic problems arising from labor conditions in their internal commerce.

It is not the province of the Court to consider the economic advantages or disadvantages of such a centralized system. It is sufficient to say that the Federal Constitution does not provide for it. Our growth and development have called for wide use of the commerce power of the federal government in its control over the expanded activities of interstate commerce, and in protecting that commerce from burdens, interferences, and conspiracies to restrain and monopolize it. But the authority of the federal government may not be pushed to such an extreme as to destroy the distinction, which the commerce clause itself establishes, between commerce "among the several States" and the internal concerns of a State. The same answer must be made to the contention that is based upon the serious economic situation which led to the passage of the Recovery Act,—the fall in prices, the decline in wages and employment, and the curtailment of the market for commodities. Stress is laid upon the great importance of maintaining wage distributions which would provide the necessary stimulus in starting "the cumulative forces making for expanding commercial activity." Without in any way disparaging this motive, it is enough to say that the recuperative efforts of the federal government must be made in a manner consistent with the authority granted by the Constitution.

We are of the opinion that the attempt through the provisions of the Code to fix the hours and wages of employees of defendants in their intrastate business was not a valid exercise of federal power.

JUSTICE CARDOZO, with JUSTICE STONE, concurring.

...

National Labor Relations Board v. Jones & Laughlin Steel Corp., 301 U.S. 1 (1937)

The Court's half-century-long effort to shield production and manufacturing from federal authority continued through 1936. In Carter v. Carter Coal Company *a majority of the justices struck down the Bituminous Coal Conservation Act of 1935, which authorized the creation of fair competition standards and labor regulations in the coal industry. Even though compliance was voluntary (with tax refunds being used as incentives to follow the regulations) Justice Sutherland declared that Congress was impermissibly trying to control "local evils over which the federal government has no legislative control," since federal commerce power "does not attach until interstate commercial intercourse begins."*

Two events took place between the Carter Coal *decision and the next Supreme Court decision interpreting the commerce clause. The first was Roosevelt's landslide victory in the 1936 national election, an election that also gave Democrats over three-quarters of the seats in Congress. The second was the announcement and controversy over Roosevelt's Court-packing plan. Justices making decisions in this political environment were aware that political retaliation might (but might not) take place should the justices continue opposing the New Deal.*

The first issue on the judicial agenda after the election of 1936 was the constitutionality of the Wagner Act. The Wagner Act required that businesses recognize unions and pay minimum wages. Unlike some previous New Deal statutes, the Wagner Act was specifically limited to businesses engaged in interstate commerce. The Act established the National Labor Relations Board (NLRB) to monitor and penalize unfair labor practices. A better organized Justice Department prosecuted five test cases, carefully selected to represent a range of important interstate industries. The cases were heard and decided together.

Jones & Laughlin Steel Corp. *provided an ideal test case for the government. The corporation was based in Pennsylvania, but it was one of the largest producers of steel in the United States. Through the ownership and management of various subsidiaries, it ran a fully integrated operation, from mining to transportation by rail and barge to smelting and manufacturing and finally to distribution, storage, and sales throughout the United States and Canada. The NLRB had charged Jones & Laughlin Steel with interfering with unionization efforts at its plant in Aliquippa, Pennsylvania, which processed raw materials gathered from other states to manufacture steel for sale nationally. In each of the cases decided and argued with* Jones & Laughlin Steel, *the government and the majority emphasized the tight relationship between the particular plant being regulated by the NLRB and the stream of national commerce. Hughes and Roberts switched sides to join the dissenters from* Carter Coal *to give a 5–4 victory to the government. In* Washington, Virginia & Maryland Coach Co. v. NLRB *(1937), involving an interstate bus service, the justices were unanimous in upholding congressional authority to regulate the labor and wages of company employees.*

The result was a major victory for the Roosevelt Administration. NLRB v. Jones & Laughlin Steel Corp. *and the companion cases were the first decisions to sustain a major New Deal program under the commerce clause. Hughes insisted that the majority was just following earlier precedents in upholding the Wagner Act. The dissenters strongly disagreed. Who has the stronger argument?*

CHIEF JUSTICE HUGHES delivered the opinion of the Court.

...The authority of the federal government may not be pushed to such an extreme as to destroy the distinction, which the commerce clause itself establishes, between commerce "among the several States" and the internal concerns of a State. That distinction between what is national and what is local in the activities of commerce is vital to the maintenance of our federal system.

...

We think it clear that the National Labor Relations Act may be construed so as to operate within the sphere of constitutional authority. The jurisdiction conferred upon the Board, and invoked in this instance, is found in §10 (a), which provides:

> SEC. 10 (a). The Board is empowered, as hereinafter provided, to prevent any person from engaging in any unfair labor practice (listed in section 8) affecting commerce.

The Act specifically defines the "commerce" to which it refers (§2(6)):

> The term "commerce" means trade, traffic, commerce, transportation, or communication among the several States, or between the District of Columbia or any Territory of the United States and any State or other Territory, or between any foreign country and any State, Territory, or the District of Columbia, or within the District of Columbia or any Territory, or between points in the same State but through any other State or any Territory or the District of Columbia or any foreign country.

There can be no question that the commerce thus contemplated by the Act (aside from that within a Territory or the District of Columbia) is interstate and foreign commerce in the constitutional sense.

. . .

. . . The grant of authority to the Board does not purport to extend to the relationship between all industrial employees and employers. Its terms do not impose collective bargaining upon all industry regardless of effects upon interstate or foreign commerce. It purports to reach only what may be deemed to burden or obstruct that commerce and, thus qualified, it must be construed as contemplating the exercise of control within constitutional bounds. It is a familiar principle that acts which directly burden or obstruct interstate or foreign commerce, or its free flow, are within the reach of the congressional power. Acts having that effect are not rendered immune because they grow out of labor disputes. . . . It is the effect upon commerce, not the source of the injury, which is the criterion. . . . We are thus to inquire whether in the instant case the constitutional boundary has been passed.

[I]n its present application, the statute goes no further than to safeguard the right of employees to self-organization and to select representatives of their own choosing for collective bargaining or other mutual protection without restraint or coercion by their employer.

That is a fundamental right. Employees have as clear a right to organize and select their representatives for lawful purposes as the respondent has to organize its business and select its own officers and agents. Discrimination and coercion to prevent the free exercise of the right of employees to self-organization and representation is a proper subject for condemnation by competent legislative authority. . . .

Respondent says that whatever may be said of employees engaged in interstate commerce, the industrial relations and activities in the manufacturing department of respondent's enterprise are not subject to federal regulation. The argument rests upon the proposition that manufacturing in itself is not commerce. . . .

. . .

We do not find it necessary to determine whether these features of defendant's business dispose of the asserted analogy to the "stream of commerce" cases. The instances in which that metaphor has been used are but particular, and not exclusive, illustrations of the protective power which the Government invokes in support of the present Act. The congressional authority to protect interstate commerce from burdens and obstructions is not limited to transactions which can be deemed to be an essential part of a "flow" of interstate or foreign commerce. Burdens and obstructions may be due to injurious action springing from other sources. The fundamental principle is that the power to regulate commerce is the power to enact "all appropriate legislation" for "its protection and advancement." . . . That power is plenary and may be exerted to protect interstate commerce "no matter what the source of the dangers which threaten it." . . . Although activities may be intrastate in character when separately considered, if they have such a close and substantial relation to interstate commerce that their control is essential or appropriate to protect that commerce from burdens and obstructions, Congress cannot be denied the power to exercise that control. . . . Undoubtedly the scope of this power must be considered in the light of our dual system of government and may not be extended so as to embrace effects upon interstate commerce so indirect and remote that to embrace them, in view of our complex society, would effectually obliterate the distinction between what is national and what is local and create a completely centralized government.... The question is necessarily one of degree....

...[I]n the first *Coronado* case (1922) the Court... said that "if Congress deems certain recurring practices, though not really part of interstate commerce, likely to obstruct, restrain or burden it, it has the power to subject them to national supervision and restraint."...

It is thus apparent that the fact that the employees here concerned were engaged in production is not determinative. The question remains as to the effect upon interstate commerce of the labor practice involved. In the *Schechter* case (1935), we found that the effect there was so remote as to be beyond the federal power. To find "immediacy or directness" there was to find it "almost everywhere," a result inconsistent with the maintenance of our federal system. In the *Carter* case (1936), the Court was of the opinion that the provisions of the statute relating to production were invalid upon several grounds.... These cases are not controlling here.

...[T]he stoppage of [the respondent steel company's] operations by industrial strife would have a most serious effect upon interstate commerce. In view of respondent's far-flung activities, it is idle to say that the effect would be indirect or remote. It is obvious that it would be immediate and might be catastrophic. We are asked to shut our eyes to the plainest facts of our national life and to deal with the question of direct and indirect effects in an intellectual vacuum. Because there may be but indirect and remote effects upon interstate commerce in connection with a host of local enterprises throughout the country, it does not follow that other industrial activities do not have such a close and intimate relation to interstate commerce as to make the presence of industrial strife a matter of the most urgent national concern. When industries organize themselves on a national scale, making their relation to interstate commerce the dominant factor in their activities, how can it be maintained that their industrial labor relations constitute a forbidden field into which Congress may not enter when it is necessary to protect interstate commerce from the paralyzing consequences of industrial war? We have often said that interstate commerce itself is a practical conception. It is equally true that interferences with that commerce must be appraised by a judgment that does not ignore actual experience.

Experience has abundantly demonstrated that the recognition of the right of employees to self-organization and to have representatives of their own choosing for the purpose of collective bargaining is often an essential condition of industrial peace. Refusal to confer and negotiate has been one of the most prolific causes of strife. This is such an outstanding fact in the history of labor disturbances that it is a proper subject of judicial notice and requires no citation of instances.... But with respect to the appropriateness of the recognition of self-organization and representation in the promotion of peace, the question is not essentially different in the case of employees in industries of such a character that interstate commerce is put in jeopardy from the case of employees of transportation companies. And of what avail is it to protect the facility of transportation, if interstate commerce is throttled with respect to the commodities to be transported!

...Instead of being beyond the pale, we think that it presents in a most striking way the close and intimate relation which a manufacturing industry may have to interstate commerce and we have no doubt that Congress had constitutional authority to safeguard the right of respondent's employees to self-organization and freedom in the choice of representatives for collective bargaining.

[The next part of the opinion concludes that the NLRA of 1935 did not violate property rights protected by the Fifth Amendment.]

Reversed

JUSTICE McREYNOLDS, dissenting.[27]

JUSTICE VAN DEVANTER, JUSTICE SUTHERLAND, JUSTICE BUTLER and I are unable to agree with the decisions just announced.

...

The Court, as we think, departs from well-established principles followed in *Schechter Corp.* v. *United States*... and *Carter* v. *Carter Coal Co*. Upon the authority of those decisions, the Circuit Courts of Appeals of the Fifth, Sixth and Second Circuits in the causes now before us have held the power of Congress under the commerce clause does not extend to relations between employers and their employees engaged in manufacture, and therefore the Act conferred upon the National

---

27. As noted above, *Jones & Laughlin Steel* was one of five National Labor Relations Board cases decided by the Supreme Court on April 12, 1937. Justices McReynolds, Van Devanter, Sutherland and Butler dissented in all cases. Their actual dissenting opinion was appended to *NLRB v. Friedman–Harry Marks Clothing Co.*, 301 U.S. 58 (1937).

Labor Relations Board no authority in respect of matters covered by the questioned orders. Every consideration brought forward to uphold the Act before us was applicable to support the Acts held unconstitutional in causes decided within two years. And the lower courts rightly deemed them controlling.

...

Any effect on interstate commerce by the discharge of employees shown here, would be indirect and remote in the highest degree, as consideration of the facts will show. In [*Jones & Laughlin*] ten men out of ten thousand were discharged; in the other cases only a few. The immediate effect in the factory may be to create discontent among all those employed and a strike may follow, which, in turn, may result in reducing production, which ultimately may reduce the volume of goods moving in interstate commerce. By this chain of indirect and progressively remote events we finally reach the evil with which it is said the legislation under consideration undertakes to deal. A more remote and indirect interference with interstate commerce or a more definite invasion of the powers reserved to the states is difficult, if not impossible, to imagine.

The Constitution still recognizes the existence of states with indestructible powers; the Tenth Amendment was supposed to put them beyond controversy.

We are told that Congress may protect the "stream of commerce" and that one who buys raw material without the state, manufactures it therein, and ships the output to another state is in that stream. Therefore it is said he may be prevented from doing anything which may interfere with its flow.

This, too, goes beyond the constitutional limitations heretofore enforced. If a man raises cattle and regularly delivers them to a carrier for interstate shipment, may Congress prescribe the conditions under which he may employ or discharge helpers on the ranch? The products of a mine pass daily into interstate commerce; many things are brought to it from other states. Are the owners and the miners within the power of Congress in respect of the miners' tenure and discharge?...

And if this theory of a continuous "stream of commerce" as now defined is correct, will it become the duty of the Federal Government hereafter to suppress every strike which by possibility may cause a blockade in that stream?...

There is no ground on which reasonably to hold that refusal by a manufacturer, whose raw materials come from states other than that of his factory and whose products are regularly carried to other states, to bargain collectively with employees in his manufacturing plant, directly affects interstate commerce. In such business, there is not one but two distinct movements or streams in interstate transportation. The first brings in raw material and there ends. Then follows manufacture, a separate and local activity. Upon completion of this, and not before, the second distinct movement or stream in interstate commerce begins and the products go to other states. Such is the common course for small as well as large industries. It is unreasonable and unprecedented to say the commerce clause confers upon Congress power to govern relations between employers and employees in these local activities....

It is gravely stated that experience teaches that if an employer discourages membership in "any organization of any kind" "in which employees participate, and which exists for the purpose in whole or in part of dealing with employers concerning grievances, labor disputes, wages, rates of pay, hours of employment or conditions of work," discontent may follow and this in turn may lead to a strike, and as the outcome of the strike there may be a block in the stream of interstate commerce. Therefore Congress may inhibit the discharge! Whatever effect any cause of discontent may ultimately have upon commerce is far too indirect to justify Congressional regulation. Almost anything—marriage, birth, death—may in some fashion affect commerce.

...

That Congress has power by appropriate means, not prohibited by the Constitution, to prevent direct and material interference with the conduct of interstate commerce is settled doctrine. But the interference struck at must be direct and material, not some mere possibility contingent on wholly uncertain events; and there must be no impairment of rights guaranteed....

...

Wickard v. Filburn, 317 U.S. 111 (1942)

Wickard v. Filburn *demonstrated how far the Supreme Court was willing to go after 1937 to find a sufficient relationship to interstate commerce when considering the constitutionality of federal regulations of economic activity. The Agricultural Adjustment Act (AAA) of 1938 penalized farmers who harvested more than a specified quota of acres for wheat. Roscoe Filburn exceeded his quota, but did not sell the excess wheat he grew in either local or national markets. Instead, the wheat was used solely to feed his family and their livestock on his small farm in Ohio. The case was not one that the government would have preferred to bring to the Court, but Filburn filed for an injunction in federal district court to block Secretary of Agriculture Claude Wickard and others from enforcing the AAA quotas against him and for a declaration that the Act was unconstitutional. A divided district court panel ruled in favor of Filburn. A unanimous Supreme Court reversed the lower court and found that his activities could be federally regulated. Justice Jackson relied on a pragmatic approach when evaluating the scope of federal power. His opinion set down a new doctrinal standard, asking whether an activity considered in the aggregate exerts a substantial economic effect on interstate commerce.*

Wickard *marked the last of the landmark New Deal commerce clause cases, and it laid down the doctrinal formulations that would guide Congress and the judiciary through the remainder of the twentieth century. As you read the opinion, consider the following: Could the federal government limit people to five at-home dinners a week in order to increase commerce in restaurants? Could the federal government limit the extent to which people make their own clothes? Can the federal government mandate that individuals buy health insurance?*

JUSTICE JACKSON delivered the opinion of the Court.

...

It is urged that under the Commerce Clause of the Constitution, Article I, § 8, clause 3, Congress does not possess the power it has in this instance sought to exercise. The question would merit little consideration since our decision in *United States* v. *Darby* (1941),... sustaining the federal power to regulate production of goods for commerce, except for the fact that this Act extends federal regulation to production not intended in any part for commerce but wholly for consumption on the farm.... [M]arketing quotas not only embrace all that may be sold without penalty but also what may be consumed on the premises.... Penalties do not depend upon whether any part of the wheat, either within or without the quota, is sold or intended to be sold....

...

... We believe that a review of the course of decision under the Commerce Clause will make plain... that questions of the power of Congress are not to be decided by reference to any formula which would give controlling force to nomenclature such as "production" and "indirect" and foreclose consideration of the actual effects of the activity in question upon interstate commerce.

At the beginning Chief Justice Marshall described the federal commerce power with a breadth never yet exceeded. *Gibbons* v. *Ogden* (1824).... He made emphatic the embracing and penetrating nature of this power by warning that effective restraints on its exercise must proceed from political rather than from judicial processes....

...

Not long after the decision of *United States v. Knight Co.* (1895),... Mr. Justice Holmes, in sustaining the exercise of national power over intrastate activity, stated for the Court that "commerce among the States is not a technical legal conception, but a practical one, drawn from the course of business." *Swift & Co.* v. *United States* (1905).... It was soon demonstrated that the effects of many kinds of intrastate activity upon interstate commerce were such as to make them a proper subject of federal regulation. In some cases sustaining the exercise of federal power over intrastate matters the term "direct" was used for the purpose of stating, rather than of reaching, a result; in others it was treated as synonymous with "substantial" or "material"; and in others it was not used at all. Of late its use has been abandoned in cases dealing with questions of federal power under the Commerce Clause.

In the *Shreveport Rate Cases* (1914),... the Court held that railroad rates of an admittedly intrastate character and fixed by authority of the state might, nevertheless, be revised by the Federal Government because of the economic effects which they had upon interstate commerce. The opinion of Mr. Justice Hughes found federal intervention constitutionally authorized because of "matters having such a close and substantial relation to interstate traffic that the control is essential or appropriate to the security of that traffic, to the efficiency of the interstate service, and to the maintenance of conditions under which interstate commerce may be conducted upon fair terms and without molestation or hindrance."...

The Court's recognition of the relevance of the economic effects in the application of the Commerce Clause, exemplified by this statement, has made the mechanical application of legal formulas no longer feasible. Once an economic measure of the reach of the power granted to Congress in the Commerce Clause is accepted, questions of federal power cannot be decided simply by finding the activity in question to be "production," nor can consideration of its economic effects be foreclosed by calling them "indirect."...

Whether the subject of the regulation in question was "production," "consumption," or "marketing" is, therefore, not material for purposes of deciding the question of federal power before us. That an activity is of local character may help in a doubtful case to determine whether Congress intended to reach it. The same consideration might help in determining whether in the absence of Congressional action it would be permissible for the state to exert its power on the subject matter, even though in so doing it to some degree affected interstate commerce. But even if appellee's activity be local and though it may not be regarded as commerce, it may still, whatever its nature, be reached by Congress if it exerts a substantial economic effect on interstate commerce, and this irrespective of whether such effect is what might at some earlier time have been defined as "direct" or "indirect."

...

The maintenance by government regulation of a price for wheat undoubtedly can be accomplished as effectively by sustaining or increasing the demand as by limiting the supply. The effect of the statute before us is to restrict the amount which may be produced for market and the extent as well to which one may forestall resort to the market by producing to meet his own needs. That appellee's own contribution to the demand for wheat may be trivial by itself is not enough to remove him from the scope of federal regulation where, as here, his contribution, taken together with that of many others similarly situated, is far from trivial....

It is well established by decisions of this Court that the power to regulate commerce includes the power to regulate the prices at which commodities in that commerce are dealt in and practices affecting such prices. One of the primary purposes of the Act in question was to increase the market price of wheat, and to that end to limit the volume thereof that could affect the market. It can hardly be denied that a factor of such volume and variability as home-consumed wheat would have a substantial influence on price and market conditions. This may arise because being in marketable condition such wheat overhangs the market and, if induced by rising prices, tends to flow into the market and check price increases. But if we assume that it is never marketed, it supplies a need of the man who grew it which would otherwise be reflected by purchases in the open market. Home-grown wheat in this sense competes with wheat in commerce. The stimulation of commerce is a use of the regulatory function quite as definitely as prohibitions or restrictions thereon. This record leaves us in no doubt that Congress may properly have considered that wheat consumed on the farm where grown, if wholly outside the scheme of regulation, would have a substantial effect in defeating and obstructing its purpose to stimulate trade therein at increased prices.

...

Reversed.

Illustration 8-3 Justice Robert H. Jackson

Source: Library of Congress Prints and Photographs Division, LC-USZ62-38828.

Justice Robert Jackson, Memo on Wickard (1942)[28]

The case of Wickard v. Filburn *reached the Supreme Court soon after Attorney General Robert H. Jackson was appointed to the bench by President Franklin Roosevelt. Although a staunch defender of the New Deal, the* Wickard *case left Jackson uneasy. By 1942, the justices had no doubt that the application of the Agricultural Adjustment Act to Roscoe Filburn would be upheld as constitutional. The difficulty was with how to justify it. The majority opinion that Jackson eventually wrote for the Court that autumn cemented the New Deal Court's constitutional revolution in regards to federalism. The case was also the biggest obstacle for those who wished to see greater judicial scrutiny of federal legislation on commerce clause grounds.*

In the spring of 1942, Jackson confessed to Chief Justice Stone that he remained "baffled" as to how to resolve the case without leaving the Court with "no function but to stamp this Act O.K." and in the process render the "federal compact…pretty meaningless if Congress is to be the sole judge of the extent of its own commerce power." In the summer, Jackson began the process of drafting an opinion with a memo to his law clerk. The memo offers a more frank and political explanation for the Court's actions in the case than the does the opinion that was eventually issued by the Court. As he wrote to his clerk in this memo, "If we sustain the present Act, I don't see how we can ever sustain states' rights again as against a Congressional exercise of the commerce power." Or as he summed up the case to Justice Sherman Minton after the opinion was handed down, "When we admit that it is an economic matter, we pretty nearly admit that it is not a matter which courts may judge."[29] The Court sent that same message in other cases as well, most notably in United States v. Carolene Products *(1938).*

Memorandum for Mr. Costello

Re: *Wickard* Case

[June 19, 1942]

The question of the right of the Federal Government under the power to regulate interstate commerce to say that a farmer may not plant wheat for his own consumption and consume on the farm what he produces presents a good deal of a problem to me. It seems idle to disguise it, for it appears to be a regulation of production and of production not for commerce either actually or in contemplation.…

I have little doubt that had this question arisen prior to the *Shreveport* case it would have been held within the exclusive control of the state. This for the reason that political considerations dominated the thinking of the Court. The Court was politically subdivided and it sought to impress the political divisions upon economic life.

The *Shreveport* line of cases began a different mode of thinking. It allowed the judicial to be determined by the economic effects, and thus shaped the political system by the pattern of the underlying economic system.

The difficulty with this is that the political lines were definitely drawn. Economic lines are not. Economic effects are exceedingly difficult to trace beyond immediate effects, and when they reach out into the sphere where they are mingled with other considerations.

…The formulation of standards as to what would answer the judicial requirements in order to extend federal control have not been clear, and in the *Darby* case following many older cases it is said that Congress may regulate what is "appropriate" for regulation in connection with interstate commerce. Such a test has no real value, as this case amply demonstrates. The only appropriateness to the regulation of home-consumed wheat shown by the stipulation in this case is administrative convenience because of the difficulty of checking it. I suppose another real reason is to compel those who want to consume wheat to buy it in the open market and thereby to sustain the market. All of this raises seriously the question whether the extent of power under the commerce clause is appropriate for judicial decision and brings us to the question of whether Congress by determining what is "appropriate" to its own regulatory schemes may in effect define the extent of its own power under the commerce clause.

Some reasons why we might hold that Congress may define its own powers would be these:

1. That since the economic test is to be applied, the extent of the commerce power is no longer a legal question but an economic, and hence policy, one.
2. That the judicial standards or legal standards for determining the limit of Congressional power are so tenuous and vague that they constitute no protection to the states in any event and that while

28. Excerpt from unpublished memo in the Robert Jackson Papers, Library of Congress.

29. Quoted in Barry Cushman, *Rethinking the New Deal Court* (New York: Oxford University Press, 1998), 215, 221.

the pretense of review has some effect in relieving Congress of its own ultimate responsibility, it is a shadow without substance. I suppose as presently constituted the Court would not decline to hold any law unconstitutional. It might be far better to place responsibility for intelligent and moderate use of this power on Congress than to keep up the pretense of sharing the responsibility which we have no standards for measuring.

On the contrary, it may be urged that this is certainly not the concept of the fathers who sought to have the rights of the states safeguarded equally with the rights of the nation. It would be a strange compact which gave both to the federal and to the constituent governments certain rights, but left the extent to the option of one of the parties. I think it was never so intended, but the trouble is that the forefathers' intentions do not control the course of history. If we sustain the present Act, I don't see how we can ever sustain states' rights again as against a Congressional exercise of the commerce power. Perhaps we should not. But if we have really reached the point where we are dealing only with the shadow of judicial review, I think we should not allow ourselves to stand as a symbol to protection of states' rights which have vanished.

...

It is perhaps time that we recognize that the introduction of economic determinism into constitutional law of interstate commerce marked the end of judicial control of the scope of federal activity. There is no use for us in our day to repeat the mistake of denying that the world is round because we have a preference for a flat one. A frank holding that the interstate commerce power has no limits except those which Congress sees fit to observe might serve a wholesome purpose. In order to be unconstitutional by the judicial process if this Act is sustained, the relation between interstate commerce and the regulated activity would have to be so absurd that it would be laughed out of Congress.

...

It might not do harm... to frankly say that the Supreme Court cannot stand between the two governments when the impact of events and necessity happens to be all on the side of the extension of federal power, and that when the events and necessity have become sufficiently strong and apparent to impress Congress and the Executive, this Court can no longer deny that it is appropriate that the attempted regulation be permitted. Federal power can, of course, discredit itself by attempting more than is just or can break down attempting more than it has capacity to organize or administer. Its excesses and irresponsibilities it must answer for at the polls.

...

B. Federal Power to Enforce Civil Rights

For decades, southern legislators in Congress managed to block efforts to pass significant federal racial civil rights legislation. Both before and after the New Deal, such legislation was a low priority. Advocates of racial civil rights reform had to settle for executive or judicial actions, state and local efforts, or private action.

The situation finally changed in the early 1960s. The civil rights movement mobilized northern public opinion behind reform, and both political parties increasingly found themselves unable to bridge the divide between their diverse coalition partners. With large, liberal majorities in Congress, the Democratic leadership threw its support behind civil rights. The opposition came primarily from southern Democrats. The result, most notably, was the Civil Rights Act of 1964 and the Voting Rights Act of 1965. The Civil Rights Act barred racial segregation in employment, public accommodations, and schools. The Voting Rights Act prohibited the adoption of discriminatory practices affecting voting.

One question confronting advocates of civil rights reform was how federal legislation could be constitutionally justified. The obvious textual inspiration for civil rights reform was the Reconstruction Amendments. The question was whether the Reconstruction Amendments gave Congress the power to do everything that civil rights advocates wanted. In particular, the U.S. Supreme Court had long held that the Reconstruction Amendments only empowered Congress to address "state actions." When state and local governments discriminated on the basis of race, they were in violation of the Reconstruction Amendments, and Congress could intervene. When private individuals engaged in racial discrimination, there was no state action and the Reconstruction Amendments might not provide a legal basis for congressional action. The U.S. Supreme Court had already indicated that those amendments did not authorize Congress to prohibit private racial discrimination in the *Civil Rights Cases*

(1883). One option for the Great Society reformers was to hope that the Warren Court would overturn the *Civil Rights Cases*.[30] A second, potentially safer option was to turn to existing precedent. Since the New Deal, the commerce clause provided the easiest path for defending legislation. Leaders of the executive and legislative branch decided to pin their constitutional hopes for civil rights legislation on the commerce clause in 1964.

The Warren Court upheld everything that Congress did in the name of civil rights in the 1960s. The justification for upholding federal law shifted between the commerce clause and the Reconstruction Amendments depending on who Congress was attempting to regulate. When Congress wanted to regulate private actors, it used the commerce clause. When Congress wanted to regulate government officials, it used the Fourteenth and especially the Fifteenth Amendment. In *Heart of Atlanta Motel, Inc. v. United States* (1964) and *Katzenbach v. McClung* (1964), the Supreme Court upheld the Civil Rights Act of 1964 under the commerce clause. In *South Carolina v. Katzenbach* (1966), the Court turned to Section 5 of the Fifteenth Amendment to justify the Voting Rights Act. The same year, the Court handed down *Katzenbach v. Morgan* (1966), which concluded that Congress could bar states from employing a voting rule that discriminated against Spanish speakers, even though the Court itself had never ruled that such discrimination was a constitutional violation. Section 5 of the Fourteenth Amendment was a "positive grant of legislative power" to Congress that allowed Congress "to enforce" but never "to restrict, abrogate, or dilute" the guarantees of the Fourteenth Amendment. By 1968, there were few apparent limits to congressional power to enforce civil rights under the Reconstruction Amendments.[31]

30. The New Deal Court had also indicated a way of undermining without overturning the *Civil Rights Cases*. In *Shelley v. Kraemer* (1948), the Court held that "racial covenants" (restrictions in housing contracts that prevented real estate in a neighborhood from being sold to members of a designated group) could not be judicially enforced. The judicial enforcement of the contractual provisions would be an unconstitutionally discriminatory "state action" under the Fourteenth Amendment.

31. Congress would encounter such a limit two years later when it passed a 1970 amendment to the Voting Rights Act granting eighteen-year-olds the right to vote in state and federal elections. The Court struck down this extension of voting rights to state elections in *Oregon v. Mitchell* (1970). Congress responded by passing the Twenty-Sixth Amendment to the Constitution.

Congressional Debate over the Civil Rights Act of 1964[32]

Liberals in both the Democratic and the Republican Party relied primarily on the commerce power when passing the Civil Rights Act of 1964, but they relied on Section 5 of the Fourteenth Amendment when passing the Voting Rights Act of 1965. Several years later, Congress passed and President Johnson signed a new bill forbidding discrimination in the housing market. The Supreme Court sustained all of these measures. Only a later amendment to the Voting Rights Act that lowered the voting age in state elections to eighteen met with defeat in the Supreme Court. That decision was reversed by the Twenty-Sixth Amendment to the Constitution.

The congressional debate over the Civil Rights Act was the longest in American history up to that time. Support for civil rights was bipartisan, with only southern Democrats and more libertarian Republicans raising objections. The measure passed easily in the House, with almost four-fifths of all Republicans joining northern Democrats in support of the bill. Senate passage was more difficult, given the usual filibuster by southern Democrats. Senator Everett Dirksen of Illinois, the Republican minority leader, proved crucial. Although a political conservative, Dirksen was personally disturbed by the brutal southern reaction to civil rights protests and aware of the strong civil rights vote in the north. After agreeing to a few compromises, he worked to provide the Republican support necessary to break the southern filibuster. The filibuster was broken on June 10, 1964. Within two weeks, the Senate voted to pass the Civil Rights Act of 1964. Shortly thereafter, the House agreed to the Senate's revisions. The measure became law on July 2, 1964. Title II of the Civil Rights Act prohibited racial discrimination in places of public accommodation, the key provision of the Civil Rights Act of 1875.

MR. HUMPHREY (Democrat, Minnesota)

. . .

It is difficult for most of us to fully comprehend the monstrous humiliations and inconveniences that racial discrimination imposes on our Negro fellow citizens. If a white man is thirsty on a hot day, he goes to the nearest soda fountain. If he is hungry, he goes to the nearest restaurant. If he needs a restroom, he can go to

32. Excerpt taken from *Congressional Record*, 88th Cong., 2nd sess. (March 30, 24, 1964), 6531, 6080.

the nearest gas station. If it is night and he is tired, he takes his pick of the available motels and hotels.

But for a Negro the picture is different. Trying to get a glass of iced tea at a lunch counter may result in insult and abuse, unless he is willing to go out of his way, perhaps to walk across town. He can never count on using a restroom, on getting a decent place to stay, on buying a good meal. These are trivial matters in the life of a white person, but for some 20 million American Negroes, they are important considerations that must be planned for in detail. They must draw up travel plans much as a general advancing across hostile territory would establish his logistical support.

. . .

The American Negro does not seek to be set apart from the community of American life. He seeks participation in it. He does not seek separation. Instead, he seeks participation and inclusion. These Americans want to be full citizens, to enjoy all the rights and privileges, and to assume the duties and burdens. Surely Congress can do nothing less than to permit them to do their job, to be parts of the total community, and to be parts of the life of this Nation. America has become great because Americans are a united people. The American Negroes seek to be part of that society; and they are asking that it be made a legal reality. . . .

. . .

There has been considerable discussion as to whether the constitutional bases of the public accommodations provisions of H.R. 7152 should be the commerce clause or the 14th amendment. The contention will even be made that no constitutional authority whatsoever supports the legislation. I think there is little doubt that, with the careful changes that have been made during the course of its development, this bill finds firm support in both the commerce clause and the 14th amendment, and is not prohibited by any other provision of the Constitution.

. . . [T]hat title II does embody a moral judgment should not be a reason for failing to rely on our power to regulate commerce.

In fact, the Constitution of the United States is the Constitution of a Nation. All its provisions are properly available to effectuate the moral judgments of that Nation. That is why it is wholly appropriate to use any relevant constitutional authority with respect to a national problem. If more than one provision of the Constitution provides that authority, so much the better.

In fact, we have not hesitated to use the power to tax as an instrument against gambling and the narcotic traffic. We have not hesitated to use the power to regulate commerce to fight the white slavery trade.

. . .

Moreover, reliance on the commerce clause is not merely a legal device. The evil of racial discrimination with which title II is concerned has clear economic consequences. . . .

Among other things, that clause gives Congress authority to deal with conditions adversely affecting the allocation of resources. Discrimination and segregation on racial grounds have a substantial adverse effect on the interstate flow of goods, capital, and of persons. Skilled or educated men who are apt to be victims of discrimination in an area are reluctant to settle there even if opportunities are available. For this and other reasons, capital is reluctant to invest in such a region and, therefore the flow of goods to, and their sale within, such an area is similarly reduced. . . .

. . .

One hundred and ninety years have passed since the Declaration of Independence, and 100 years since the Emancipation Proclamation. Surely the goals of this bill are not too much to ask of the Senate of the United States.

MR. WILLIS (Democrat, Louisiana)

. . . [T]he commerce clause does not say that Congress has the right to regulate habits, customs, human behavior, morals, or attitudes; it can only regulate interstate commerce.

You will hear about court cases concerning the manufacture of goods and farming operations, and so on. There is no doubt that the courts have gone far in this field. But you can at least see and feel corn and wheat; you can measure and buy these grains by the ton, and you can put them in a truck or a boxcar and ship them across State lines. But that is a far cry from what the proponents of this bill would twist the commerce clause to mean. And so even to those of you who are not lawyers, I ask you to remember the simple provision of the powers of Congress under the commerce clause, that is to regulate commerce among the several States.

In respect of "commerce" title II indulges the presumption that transients generate "commerce" and that offers to serve travelers affect "commerce." In the area of the 14th Amendment and the concomitant requirement of some sort of "State action," it equates "custom and usage" to affirmative action by a State. In both respects, title II constitutes a novel and dangerous experiment in political theory. Its adoption could work a revolutionary change in the existing balance of Federal–State relationships.

In my opinion, however, the attempted utilization of the 14th amendment and the commerce clause to support title II cannot be defended on constitutional grounds. You are well aware of the decision of the Supreme Court in the *Civil Rights* cases which held squarely and unequivocally that the act of Congress of 1875, entitled "An act to protect all citizens in their civil and legal rights" and proposed to do exactly what is proposed to be done by title II, was unconstitutional and could not be supported under the 14th amendment.

Since my guess is as good as anyone's, I venture to say that the reason no effort was made to base the 1875 Statute on, or to justify it under, the commerce clause was because of the feeling that there was far less chance to support its constitutionality on the commerce clause than there was to have its constitutionality upheld under the 14th amendment.

Heart of Atlanta Motel, Inc. v. United States, 379 U.S. 241 (1964)

Proponents and opponents of the Civil Rights Act of 1964 were eager for an immediate court test, and they found no shortage of possible litigants. The Heart of Atlanta Motel was a large motel located near downtown Atlanta, Georgia. Three-quarters of its guests were from out of state. The motel did not rent rooms to blacks. Given that policy, the owners of the motel sought a declaratory judgment that the Civil Rights Act of 1964 unconstitutionally prohibited private discrimination in places of public accommodation, including motels. The motel owners argued that Congress had exceeded its authority under the interstate commerce clause in trying to reach a business such as the motel, violated the due process and takings clauses of the Fifth Amendment by attempting to direct them how to operate their business, and violated the Thirteenth Amendment by forcing them against their will to rent their rooms to African-Americans. A three-judge district court panel upheld the statute against the constitutional challenge, and the motel owners appealed to the Supreme Court. The justices focused only on the commerce-clause issue and unanimously upheld the law.

Heart of Atlanta *was heard with* Katzenbach v. McClung *(1964), which involved Ollie's Barbecue, a local restaurant in Birmingham, Alabama, that did not serve African-Americans. The federal district court found that Ollie's Barbecue primarily served local patrons and would lose much of its business if forced to integrate. The federal government appealed, arguing that a significant quantity of the food and supplies used in the restaurant had crossed state boundaries at some point. That was sufficient, the appeal continued, to subject the restaurant's service policies to federal regulation under the interstate commerce clause. The Supreme Court held that no direct evidence was needed that a particular restaurant interfered with the flow of interstate commerce. It was enough that Congress had concluded that the existence of segregated accommodations discouraged travel and economic development. A few years later, in* Daniel v. Paul *(1969), the Court ruled that even a snack bar at a private park had enough of a connection to interstate commerce to trigger the Civil Rights Act and desegregate the park, prompting Justice Black to dissent.*

JUSTICE CLARK delivered the opinion of the Court.

. . .

The sole question posed is, therefore, the constitutionality of the Civil Rights Act of 1964 as applied to these facts. The legislative history of the Act indicates that Congress based the Act on § 5 and the Equal Protection Clause of the Fourteenth Amendment as well as its power to regulate interstate commerce under Art. I, § 8, cl. 3, of the Constitution.

The Senate Commerce Committee made it quite clear that the fundamental object of Title II was to vindicate "the deprivation of personal dignity that surely accompanies denials of equal access to public establishments." At the same time, however, it noted that such an objective has been and could be readily achieved "by congressional action based on the commerce power of the Constitution." . . . Our study of the legislative record, made in the light of prior cases, has brought us to the conclusion that Congress possessed ample power in this regard, and we have therefore not considered the other grounds relied upon. This is not to say that the remaining authority upon which it acted was not adequate, a question upon which we do not pass, but merely that since the commerce power is sufficient for our decision here we have considered it alone.

. . .

In light of our ground for decision, it might be well at the outset to discuss the *Civil Rights Cases* (1883), which declared provisions of the Civil Rights Act of 1875 unconstitutional. We think that decision inapposite, and without precedential value in determining the constitutionality of the present Act. Unlike Title II of the present legislation, the 1875 Act broadly proscribed discrimination in "inns, public conveyances on land or water, theaters, and other places of public amusement," without limiting the categories of affected businesses to those impinging upon interstate commerce. In contrast, the applicability of Title II is carefully limited to enterprises having a direct and substantial relation to the interstate flow of goods and people, except where state action is involved. Further, the fact that certain kinds of businesses may not in 1875 have been sufficiently involved in interstate commerce to warrant bringing them within the ambit of the commerce power is not necessarily dispositive of the same question today. Our populace had not reached its present mobility, nor were facilities, goods and services circulating as readily in interstate commerce as they are today. Although the principles which we apply today are those first formulated by Chief Justice Marshall in *Gibbons* v. *Ogden* (1824), the conditions of transportation and commerce have changed dramatically, and we must apply those principles to the present state of commerce. The sheer increase in volume of interstate traffic alone would give discriminatory practices which inhibit travel a far larger impact upon the Nation's commerce than such practices had on the economy of another day. Finally, there is language in the *Civil Rights Cases* which indicates that the Court did not fully consider whether the 1875 Act could be sustained as an exercise of the commerce power. Though the Court observed that "no one will contend that the power to pass it was contained in the Constitution before the adoption of the last three amendments [Thirteenth, Fourteenth, and Fifteenth]," the Court went on specifically to note that the Act was not "conceived" in terms of the commerce power and expressly pointed out:

> Of course, these remarks [as to lack of congressional power] do not apply to those cases in which Congress is clothed with direct and plenary powers of legislation over the whole subject, accompanied with an express or implied denial of such power to the States, as in the regulation of commerce with foreign nations, among the several States, and with the Indian tribes.... In these cases Congress has power to pass laws for regulating the subjects specified in every detail, and the conduct and transactions of individuals in respect thereof.

Since the commerce power was not relied on by the Government and was without support in the record it is understandable that the Court narrowed its inquiry and excluded the Commerce Clause as a possible source of power. In any event, it is clear that such a limitation renders the opinion devoid of authority for the proposition that the Commerce Clause gives no power to Congress to regulate discriminatory practices now found substantially to affect interstate commerce.

We, therefore, conclude that the *Civil Rights Cases* have no relevance to the basis of decision here where the Act explicitly relies upon the commerce power, and where the record is filled with testimony of obstructions and restraints resulting from the discriminations found to be existing. We now pass to that phase of the case.

...

While the Act as adopted carried no congressional findings the record of its passage through each house is replete with evidence of the burdens that discrimination by race or color places upon interstate commerce.... This testimony included the fact that our people have become increasingly mobile with millions of people of all races traveling from State to State; that Negroes in particular have been the subject of discrimination in transient accommodations, having to travel great distances to secure the same; that often they have been unable to obtain accommodations and have had to call upon friends to put them up overnight.... These exclusionary practices were found to be nationwide, the Under Secretary of Commerce testifying that there is "no question that this discrimination in the North still exists to a large degree" and in the West and Midwest as well....

...

[T]he determinative test of the exercise of power by the Congress under the Commerce Clause is simply whether the activity sought to be regulated is "commerce which concerns more States than one" and has a real and substantial relation to the national interest. Let us now turn to this facet of the problem.

That the "intercourse" of which the Chief Justice spoke included the movement of persons through more States than one was settled as early as 1849, in the *Passenger Cases*.... Again in 1913 Mr. Justice McKenna, speaking for the Court, said: "Commerce among the States, we have said, consists of intercourse and traffic between their citizens, and includes the transportation of persons and property." *Hoke* v. *United States*

(1913)...Nor does it make any difference whether the transportation is commercial in character.

...

That Congress was legislating against moral wrongs in many of these areas rendered its enactments no less valid. In framing Title II of this Act Congress was also dealing with what it considered a moral problem. But that fact does not detract from the overwhelming evidence of the disruptive effect that racial discrimination has had on commercial intercourse. It was this burden which empowered Congress to enact appropriate legislation, and, given this basis for the exercise of its power, Congress was not restricted by the fact that the particular obstruction to interstate commerce with which it was dealing was also deemed a moral and social wrong.

It is said that the operation of the motel here is of a purely local character. But, assuming this to be true, "if it is interstate commerce that feels the pinch, it does not matter how local the operation which applies the squeeze." *United States* v. *Women's Sportswear Mfrs. Assn.* (1949)...As Chief Justice Stone put it in *United States* v. *Darby*:

> The power of Congress over interstate commerce is not confined to the regulation of commerce among the states. It extends to those activities intrastate which so affect interstate commerce or the exercise of the power of Congress over it as to make regulation of them appropriate means to the attainment of a legitimate end, the exercise of the granted power of Congress to regulate interstate commerce. See *McCulloch* v. *Maryland*, 4 Wheat. 316, 421.

...

We find no merit in the remainder of appellant's contentions, including that of "involuntary servitude."...

JUSTICE DOUGLAS, concurring.

Though I join the Court's opinions, I am somewhat reluctant here, as I was in *Edwards* v. *California* (1941) to rest solely on the Commerce Clause. My reluctance is not due to any conviction that Congress lacks power to regulate commerce in the interests of human rights. It is rather my belief that the right of people to be free of state action that discriminates against them because of race, like the "right of persons to move freely from State to State"..."occupies a more protected position in our constitutional system than does the movement of cattle, fruit, steel and coal across state lines."...

Hence I would prefer to rest on the assertion of legislative power contained in § 5 of the Fourteenth Amendment which states: "The Congress shall have power to enforce, by appropriate legislation, the provisions of this article"—a power which the Court concedes was exercised at least in part in this Act.

A decision based on the Fourteenth Amendment would have a more settling effect, making unnecessary litigation over whether a particular restaurant or inn is within the commerce definitions of the Act or whether a particular customer is an interstate traveler. Under my construction, the Act would apply to all customers in all the enumerated places of public accommodation. And that construction would put an end to all obstructionist strategies and finally close one door on a bitter chapter in American history.

...

JUSTICE GOLDBERG, concurring.

I join in the opinions and judgments of the Court, since I agree "that the action of the Congress in the adoption of the Act as applied here...is within the power granted it by the Commerce Clause of the Constitution, as interpreted by this Court for 140 years."

The primary purpose of the Civil Rights Act of 1964, however, as the Court recognizes, and as I would underscore, is the vindication of human dignity and not mere economics. The Senate Commerce Committee made this quite clear:

> The primary purpose of...[the Civil Rights Act], then, is to solve this problem, the deprivation of personal dignity that surely accompanies denials of equal access to public establishments. Discrimination is not simply dollars and cents, hamburgers and movies; it is the humiliation, frustration, and embarrassment that a person must surely feel when he is told that he is unacceptable as a member of the public because of his race or color....

Moreover, that this is the primary purpose of the Act is emphasized by the fact that while § 201 (c) speaks only in terms of establishments which "affect commerce," it is clear that Congress based this section not only on its power under the Commerce Clause but also on § 5 of the Fourteenth Amendment....

South Carolina v. Katzenbach, 383 U.S. 301 (1966)

The ink was hardly dry on the Civil Rights Act of 1964 when President Lyndon Johnson proposed the Voting Rights Act of 1965. Two events made passage of a comprehensive voting rights bill almost inevitable. The first was the overwhelming Democratic landslide in the 1964 election. Barry Goldwater campaigned against the Civil Rights Act of 1964, and his overwhelming defeat was interpreted by most politicians as settling both the constitutionality and desirability of legislation securing racial equality. Second, continued televised footage of southern police attacking peaceful civil rights protesters, combined with the Klan murders of three civil rights workers in Mississippi, furthered Northern determination to end Jim Crow permanently. The conventional Southern filibuster was half-hearted and easily defeated.

The Voting Rights Act barred some literacy tests and other registration requirements that had been used to suppress the black vote and required that states and localities covered by the Voting Rights Act receive preclearance from the Justice Department before changing voting rules or electoral procedures in the future. South Carolina sought an injunction against the U.S. attorney general preventing the enforcement of the Voting Rights Act. The bill of complaint was filed directly in the U.S. Supreme Court under its original jurisdiction. The Court invited other states to join the suit as friends of the court and proceeded directly to arguments (since no issues of fact were in dispute).

The Supreme Court easily brushed aside South Carolina's constitutional challenges to the Voting Rights Act, with Justice Black dissenting only on the preclearance provisions. The justices had previously ruled in Lassiter v. Northampton County v. Board of Elections *(1959) that literacy tests, per se, did not violate the Constitution. In* South Carolina v. Katzenbach, *the Court made clear that the national legislation could outlaw literacy tests on the basis of its own legislative fact-finding about their use and effects.* South Carolina *established the principle that Congress could supply the facts to show that a state practice was unconstitutional and could act on that conclusion under the Reconstruction Amendments.*

Notice when you read the opinion how Chief Justice Warren uses McCulloch v. Maryland *(1819) to justify federal powers. Was there any difference between how courts might monitor how Congress exercised power under the commerce clause and how Congress exercised power under the Reconstruction Amendments? You might also consider why southern Democrats were so successful in preventing the passage of civil rights legislation in the early twentieth century, but not as successful in preventing in seating justices on the Court who were sympathetic to civil rights legislation.*

The Voting Rights Act proved effective. African-American voting rates increased dramatically immediately after passage, and southern states began electing some African-Americans to state and national office. A great many controversies remained to be settled, but the days when elections were for whites only ended.

CHIEF JUSTICE WARREN delivered the opinion of the Court.

...

The Voting Rights Act was designed by Congress to banish the blight of racial discrimination in voting, which has infected the electoral process in parts of our country for nearly a century. The Act creates stringent new remedies for voting discrimination where it persists on a pervasive scale, and in addition the statute strengthens existing remedies for pockets of voting discrimination elsewhere in the country. Congress assumed the power to prescribe these remedies from § 2 of the Fifteenth Amendment, which authorizes the National Legislature to effectuate by "appropriate" measures the constitutional prohibition against racial discrimination in voting. We hold that the sections of the Act which are properly before us are an appropriate means for carrying out Congress' constitutional responsibilities and are consonant with all other provisions of the Constitution....

Two points emerge vividly from the voluminous legislative history of the Act contained in the committee hearings and floor debates. First: Congress felt itself confronted by an insidious and pervasive evil which had been perpetuated in certain parts of our country through unremitting and ingenious defiance of the Constitution. Second: Congress concluded that the unsuccessful remedies which it had prescribed in the past would have to be replaced by sterner and more elaborate measures in order to satisfy the clear commands of the Fifteenth Amendment....

...

According to the evidence in recent Justice Department voting suits, [literacy tests are] now the principal method used to bar Negroes from the polls. Discriminatory administration of voting qualifications has been found in all eight Alabama cases, in all nine Louisiana cases, and in all nine Mississippi cases which have gone to final judgment. Moreover, in almost all of these cases, the courts have held that the discrimination was pursuant to a widespread "pattern or practice." White applicants for registration have often been excused altogether from the literacy and understanding tests or have been given easy versions, have received extensive help from voting officials, and have been registered despite serious errors in their answers. Negroes, on the other hand, have typically been required to pass difficult versions of all the tests, without any outside assistance and without the slightest error. The good-morals requirement is so vague and subjective that it has constituted an open invitation to abuse at the hands of voting officials. Negroes obliged to obtain vouchers from registered voters have found it virtually impossible to comply in areas where almost no Negroes are on the rolls.

In recent years, Congress has repeatedly tried to cope with the problem by facilitating case-by-case litigation against voting discrimination....

Despite the earnest efforts of the Justice Department and of many federal judges, these new laws have done little to cure the problem of voting discrimination. According to estimates by the Attorney General during hearings on the Act, registration of voting-age Negroes in Alabama rose only from 14.2% to 19.4% between 1958 and 1964; in Louisiana it barely inched ahead from 31.7% to 31.8% between 1956 and 1965; and in Mississippi it increased only from 4.4% to 6.4% between 1954 and 1964. In each instance, registration of voting-age whites ran roughly 50 percentage points or more ahead of Negro registration.

...

The ground rules for resolving this question [of the constitutionality of the Voting Rights Act] are clear. The language and purpose of the Fifteenth Amendment, the prior decisions construing its several provisions, and the general doctrines of constitutional interpretation, all point to one fundamental principle. As against the reserved powers of the States, Congress may use any rational means to effectuate the constitutional prohibition of racial discrimination in voting....

The basic test to be applied in a case involving § 2 of the Fifteenth Amendment is the same as in all cases concerning the express powers of Congress with relation to the reserved powers of the States. Chief Justice Marshall laid down the classic formulation, years before the Fifteenth Amendment was ratified:

> Let the end be legitimate, let it be within the scope of the constitution, and all means which are appropriate, which are plainly adapted to that end, which are not prohibited, but consist with the letter and spirit of the constitution, are constitutional. *McCulloch v. Maryland* (1819)....

...

We therefore reject South Carolina's argument that Congress may appropriately do no more than to forbid violations of the Fifteenth Amendment in general terms—that the task of fashioning specific remedies or of applying them to particular localities must necessarily be left entirely to the courts. Congress is not circumscribed by any such artificial rules under § 2 of the Fifteenth Amendment. In the oft-repeated words of Chief Justice Marshall, referring to another specific legislative authorization in the Constitution, "This power, like all others vested in Congress, is complete in itself, may be exercised to its utmost extent, and acknowledges no limitations, other than are prescribed in the constitution." *Gibbons v. Ogden* (1824)....

...Congress had found that case-by-case litigation was inadequate to combat widespread and persistent discrimination in voting, because of the inordinate amount of time and energy required to overcome the obstructionist tactics invariably encountered in these lawsuits. After enduring nearly a century of systematic resistance to the Fifteenth Amendment, Congress might well decide to shift the advantage of time and inertia from the perpetrators of the evil to its victims. The question remains, of course, whether the specific remedies prescribed in the Act were an appropriate means of combating the evil, and to this question we shall presently address ourselves.

...The Act intentionally confines these remedies to a small number of States and political subdivisions which in most instances were familiar to Congress by name. This, too, was a permissible method of dealing with the problem. Congress had learned that substantial voting discrimination presently occurs in certain sections of the country, and it knew no way of accurately forecasting whether the evil might spread elsewhere in the future. In acceptable legislative fashion, Congress chose to limit its attention to the geographic areas where immediate action seemed necessary.... The doctrine of the equality of States, invoked by South Carolina, does not bar this approach, for that doctrine applies only to the terms upon which States are admitted to the Union, and not to the remedies for local evils which have subsequently appeared....

It is irrelevant that the coverage formula excludes certain localities which do not employ voting tests and devices but for which there is evidence of voting discrimination by other means. Congress had learned that widespread and persistent discrimination in voting during recent years has typically entailed the misuse of tests and devices, and this was the evil for which the new remedies were specifically designed.... Legislation need not deal with all phases of a problem in the same way, so long as the distinctions drawn have some basis in practical experience. See *Williamson v. Lee Optical Co.* (1955)....

We now arrive at consideration of the specific remedies prescribed by the Act for areas included within the coverage formula. South Carolina assails the temporary suspension of existing voting qualifications, reciting the rule laid down by *Lassiter v. Northampton County Bd. of Elections* (1959) that literacy tests and related devices are not in themselves contrary to the Fifteenth Amendment. In that very case, however, the Court went on to say, "Of course a literacy test, fair on its face, may be employed to perpetuate that discrimination which the Fifteenth Amendment was designed to uproot."... The record shows that in most of the States covered by the Act, including South Carolina, various tests and devices have been instituted with the purpose of disenfranchising Negroes, have been framed in such a way as to facilitate this aim, and have been administered in a discriminatory fashion for many years. Under these circumstances, the Fifteenth Amendment has clearly been violated....

...

After enduring nearly a century of widespread resistance to the Fifteenth Amendment, Congress has marshaled an array of potent weapons against the evil, with authority in the Attorney General to employ them effectively. Many of the areas directly affected by this development have indicated their willingness to abide by any restraints legitimately imposed upon them. We here hold that the portions of the Voting Rights Act properly before us are a valid means for carrying out the commands of the Fifteenth Amendment. Hopefully, millions of non-white Americans will now be able to participate for the first time on an equal basis in the government under which they live. We may finally look forward to the day when truly "the right of citizens of the United States to vote shall not be denied or abridged by the United States or by any State on account of race, color, or previous condition of servitude."

JUSTICE BLACK, concurring in part and dissenting in part.

...

Though, as I have said, I agree with most of the Court's conclusions, I dissent from its holding that every part of § 5 of the Act is constitutional. Section 4 (a), to which § 5 is linked, suspends for five years all literacy tests and similar devices in those States coming within the formula of § 4 (b). Section 5 goes on to provide that a State covered by § 4 (b) can in no way amend its constitution or laws relating to voting without first trying to persuade the Attorney General of the United States or the Federal District Court for the District of Columbia that the new proposed laws do not have the purpose and will not have the effect of denying the right to vote to citizens on account of their race or color. I think this section is unconstitutional on at least two grounds.

[Justice Black first declared that federal courts could not constitutionally provide preclearance, because that was not a case or controversy under Article III.]

My second and more basic objection to § 5 is that Congress has here exercised its power under § 2 of the Fifteenth Amendment through the adoption of means that conflict with the most basic principles of the Constitution. As the Court says the limitations of the power granted under § 2 are the same as the limitations imposed on the exercise of any of the powers expressly granted Congress by the Constitution.... Section 5, by providing that some of the States cannot pass state laws or adopt state constitutional amendments without first being compelled to beg federal authorities to approve their policies, so distorts our constitutional structure of government as to render any distinction drawn in the Constitution between state and federal power almost meaningless. One of the most basic premises upon which our structure of government was founded was that the Federal Government was to have certain specific and limited powers and no others, and all other power was to be reserved either "to the States respectively, or to the people." Certainly if all the provisions of our Constitution which limit the power of the Federal Government and reserve other power to the States are to mean anything, they mean at least that the States have power to pass laws and amend their constitutions without first sending their officials hundreds of miles away to beg federal authorities to approve them. Moreover, it seems to me that § 5 which gives federal officials power to veto state laws they do not like is in direct conflict with the clear command of our Constitution that "The United States shall guarantee to every State in this Union a Republican Form of Government." I cannot help but believe that the inevitable effect of any such law which forces any one of the States to entreat federal authorities in far-away places for approval of local laws before they can become effective is to create the impression that the State or States treated in this way are little more than conquered provinces. And if one law concerning voting can make the States plead for this approval by a distant federal court or the United States Attorney General, other laws on different subjects can force the States to seek the advance approval not only of the Attorney General but of the President himself or any other chosen members of his staff. It is inconceivable to me that such a radical degradation of state power was intended in any of the provisions of our Constitution or its Amendments. Of course I do not mean to cast any doubt whatever upon the indisputable power of the Federal Government to invalidate a state law once enacted and operative on the ground that it intrudes into the area of supreme federal power. But the Federal Government has heretofore always been content to exercise this power to protect federal supremacy by authorizing its agents to bring lawsuits against state officials once an operative state law has created an actual case and controversy. A federal law which assumes the power to compel the States to submit in advance any proposed legislation they have for approval by federal agents approaches dangerously near to wiping the States out as useful and effective units in the government of our country. I cannot agree to any constitutional interpretation that leads inevitably to such a result.

...

C. Taxing and Spending Power

The New Deal made creative use of the taxing and spending powers of the federal government, as well as its regulatory powers. Large taxes were used to enforce the provisions of the Bituminous Coal Conservation Act of 1935. The Agriculture Adjustment Act of 1933 (AAA) used a scheme of special taxes and payments to manage how many acres of crops farmers planted. The Social Security Act of 1935 created a system of taxes on employers and employees and grants in aid to support state unemployment, old-age, and dependent assistance programs.

In each case, questions arose as to whether Congress was using its taxing and spending power to encroach on the jurisdiction of the state governments, rather than to fund the legitimate activities of the national government. The Court was initially concerned as well. In *United States v. Butler* (1936) and *Carter v. Carter Coal* (1936), the majority of the justices distinguished a "tax" from a "penalty." Taxes that were used to regulate economic activity, like those in the Bituminous Coal Conservation Act, were simply to be judged under the interstate commerce clause. Taxes that existed to raise revenue for the government might be evaluated by a more generous standard. As part of the 1937 revolution, the Court upheld the unemployment provisions of the Social Security Act in *Steward Machine Co. v. Davis* (1937).

On the same day as *Steward Machine*, the Court upheld the old-age pension provisions of the Social Security Act in *Helvering v. Davis* (1937) by a 7–2 vote. Justice Cardozo wrote the majority opinion in both cases, arguing for a broad reading of the spending clause and observing, "The existence of such a [state pension] system is a bait to the needy and dependent elsewhere, encouraging them to migrate and seek a haven of repose. Only a power that is national can serve the interests of all." Butler and McReynolds dissented, without writing an opinion.

United States v. Butler, 297 U.S. 1 (1936)

Agriculture had long been a national problem. Even when business was generally good during the 1920s, American farmers were suffering a recession. The Great Depression replaced distress with misery. Farm income plunged by two-thirds and mortgages were foreclosed on 20,000 farms every month. New Dealers believed overproduction was the source of these evils. In an effort to keep farmers solvent and prices stable, the Agricultural Adjustment Act (AAA) devised a scheme in which a tax was placed on the processing of various agricultural commodities and the revenues used to pay farmers not to grow crops on part of their land.

William M. Butler was the appointed receiver of the bankrupt textile mill, Hoosac Mills Corp. Butler was also a former chairman of the national Republican committee and an advisor to former president Calvin Coolidge. When the government presented the bill for the AAA tax on the cotton processed by the mill, Butler refused to pay. A federal district court found in favor of the government, but a circuit court overturned that decision and the government appealed.

The Supreme Court declared this scheme unconstitutional by a 6–3 vote. Justice Owen Roberts endorsed the Hamiltonian claim that Congress, when spending money for the general welfare, was not constrained by the enumerated powers in Article I, Section 8. Nonetheless, he insisted that the effort to influence agricultural production violated state prerogatives protected by the Tenth Amendment. Franklin Roosevelt quoted Justice Harlan Fiske Stone's sharp dissent when proposing the Court-packing plan after his reelection. Privately, Stone declared that the Court's performance in Butler *was embarrassing. Consider when reading the opinion, why Stone might have thought this opinion significantly worse than the others you have read.*

JUSTICE ROBERTS delivered the opinion of the Court.

. . .

The tax can only be sustained by ignoring the avowed purpose and operation of the act, and holding it a measure merely laying an excise upon processors to raise revenue for the support of government. Beyond cavil the sole object of the legislation is to restore the purchasing power of agricultural products to a parity with that prevailing in an earlier day; to take money from the processor and bestow it upon farmers who will reduce their acreage for the accomplishment of the proposed end, and, meanwhile to aid these farmers during the period required to bring the prices of their crops to the desired level.

The tax plays an indispensable part in the plan of regulation. As stated by the Agricultural Adjustment Administrator, it is "the heart of the law"; a means of "accomplishing one or both of two things intended to help farmers attain parity prices and purchasing power." . . .

The statute not only avows an aim foreign to the procurement of revenue for the support of government, but by its operation shows the exaction laid upon processors to be the necessary means for the intended control of agricultural production.

. . .

It is inaccurate and misleading to speak of the exaction from processors prescribed by the challenged act as a tax, or to say that as a tax it is subject to no infirmity. A tax, in the general understanding of the term, and as used in the Constitution, signifies an exaction for the support of the Government. The word has never been thought to connote the expropriation of money from one group for the benefit of another. We may concede that the latter sort of imposition is constitutional when imposed to effectuate regulation of a matter in which both groups are interested and in respect of which there is a power of legislative regulation. But manifestly no justification for it can be found unless as an integral part of such regulation. The exaction cannot be wrested out of its setting, denominated an excise for raising revenue and legalized by ignoring its purpose as a mere instrumentality for bringing about a desired end. To do this would be to shut our eyes to what all others than we can see and understand. . . .

We conclude that the act is one regulating agricultural production; that the tax is a mere incident of such regulation and that the respondents have standing to challenge the legality of the exaction.

It does not follow that as the act is not an exertion of the taxing power and the exaction not a true tax, the statute is void or the exaction uncollectible. . . .

. . . The Government asserts that even if the respondents may question the propriety of the appropriation embodied in the statute their attack must fail because Article I, § 8 of the Constitution authorizes the contemplated expenditure of the funds raised by the tax. This contention presents the great and the controlling question in the case. . . .

There should be no misunderstanding as to the function of this court in such a case. It is sometimes said that the court assumes a power to overrule or control the action of the people's representatives. This is a misconception. The Constitution is the supreme law of the land ordained and established by the people. All legislation must conform to the principles it lays down. When an act of Congress is appropriately challenged in the courts as not conforming to the constitutional mandate the judicial branch of the Government has only one duty,—to lay the article of the Constitution which is invoked beside the statute which is challenged and to decide whether the latter squares with the former. All the court does, or can do, is to announce its considered judgment upon the question. The only power it has, if such it may be called, is the power of judgment. This court neither approves nor condemns any legislative policy. Its delicate and difficult office is to ascertain and declare whether the legislation is in accordance with, or in contravention of, the provisions of the Constitution; and, having done that, its duty ends.

The question is not what power the Federal Government ought to have but what powers in fact have been given by the people. It hardly seems necessary to reiterate that ours is a dual form of government; that in every state there are two governments,—the state and the United States. Each State has all governmental powers save such as the people, by their Constitution, have conferred upon the United States, denied to the States, or reserved to themselves. The federal union is a government of delegated powers. It has only such as are expressly conferred upon it and such as are reasonably to be implied from those granted. In this respect we differ radically from nations where all legislative power, without restriction or limitation, is vested in a parliament or other legislative body subject to no restrictions except the discretion of its members.

. . .

The clause thought to authorize the legislation,—the first,—confers upon the Congress power "to lay and collect Taxes, Duties, Imposts and Excises, to pay the Debts and provide for the common Defence and general Welfare of the United States. . . ." It is not contended that this provision grants power to regulate agricultural production upon the theory that such legislation would promote the general welfare. The Government concedes that the phrase "to provide for the general welfare" qualifies the power "to lay and collect taxes." The view that the clause grants power to provide for the general welfare, independently of the taxing power, has never been authoritatively accepted. Mr. Justice Story points out that if it were adopted "it is obvious that under color of the generality of the words, to 'provide for the common defence and general welfare,' the government of the United States is, in reality, a government of general and unlimited powers, notwithstanding the subsequent enumeration of specific powers." The true construction undoubtedly is that the only thing granted is the power to tax for the purpose of providing funds for payment of the nation's debts and making provision for the general welfare.

. . .

Since the foundation of the Nation sharp differences of opinion have persisted as to the true interpretation of the phrase. Madison asserted it amounted to no more than a reference to the other powers enumerated in the subsequent clauses of the same section; that, as the United States is a government of limited and enumerated powers, the grant of power to tax and spend for the general national welfare must be confined to the enumerated legislative fields committed to the Congress. In this view the phrase is mere tautology, for taxation and appropriation are or may be necessary incidents of the exercise of any of the enumerated legislative powers. Hamilton, on the other hand, maintained the clause confers a power separate and distinct from those later enumerated, is not restricted in meaning by the grant of them, and Congress consequently has a substantive power to tax and to appropriate, limited only by the requirement that it shall be exercised to provide for the general welfare of the United States. . . . Mr. Justice Story, in his *Commentaries*, espouses the Hamiltonian position. We shall not review the writings of public men and commentators or discuss the legislative practice. Study of all these leads us to conclude that the reading advocated by Mr. Justice Story is the correct one. While, therefore, the power to tax is not unlimited, its confines are set in the clause which confers it, and not in those of § 8 which bestow and define the legislative powers of the Congress. It results that the power of Congress to authorize expenditure of public moneys for public purposes is not limited by the direct grants of legislative power found in the Constitution.

But the adoption of the broader construction leaves the power to spend subject to limitations.

. . .

We are not now required to ascertain the scope of the phrase "general welfare of the United States" or to determine whether an appropriation in aid of agriculture falls within it. Wholly apart from that question, another principle embedded in our Constitution prohibits the enforcement of the Agricultural Adjustment Act. The act invades the reserved rights of the states. It is a statutory plan to regulate and control agricultural production, a matter beyond the powers delegated to the federal government. The tax, the appropriation of the funds raised, and the direction for their disbursement, are but parts of the plan. They are but means to an unconstitutional end.

From the accepted doctrine that the United States is a government of delegated powers, it follows that those not expressly granted, or reasonably to be implied from such as are conferred, are reserved to the states or to the people. To forestall any suggestion to the contrary, the Tenth Amendment was adopted. The same proposition, otherwise stated, is that powers not granted are prohibited. None to regulate agricultural production is given, and therefore legislation by Congress for that purpose is forbidden.

. . .

If the taxing power may not be used as the instrument to enforce a regulation of matters of state concern with respect to which the Congress has no authority to interfere, may it, as in the present case, be employed to raise the money necessary to purchase a compliance which the Congress is powerless to command? The Government asserts that whatever might be said against the validity of the plan if compulsory, it is constitutionally sound because the end is accomplished by voluntary co-operation. There are two sufficient answers to the contention. The regulation is not in fact voluntary. The farmer, of course, may refuse to comply, but the price of such refusal is the loss of benefits. The amount offered is intended to be sufficient to exert pressure on him to agree to the proposed regulation. The power to confer or withhold unlimited benefits is the power to coerce or destroy. . . .

. . .

But if the plan were one for purely voluntary co-operation it would stand no better so far as federal power is concerned. At best it is a scheme for purchasing with federal funds submission to federal regulation of a subject reserved to the states.

. . .

Congress has no power to enforce its commands on the farmer to the ends sought by the Agricultural Adjustment Act. It must follow that it may not indirectly accomplish those ends by taxing and spending to purchase compliance. The Constitution and the entire plan of our government negative any such use of the power to tax and to spend as the act undertakes to authorize. It does not help to declare that local conditions throughout the nation have created a situation of national concern; for this is but to say that whenever there is a widespread similarity of local conditions, Congress may ignore constitutional limitations upon its own powers and usurp those reserved to the states. If, in lieu of compulsory regulation of subjects within the states' reserved jurisdiction, which is prohibited, the Congress could invoke the taxing and spending power as a means to accomplish the same end, clause 1 of § 8 of Article I would become the instrument for total subversion of the governmental powers reserved to the individual states.

. . .

JUSTICE STONE, with JUSTICE BRANDEIS and JUSTICE CARDOZO, dissenting.

The power of courts to declare a statute unconstitutional is subject to two guiding principles of decision which ought never to be absent from judicial consciousness. One is that courts are concerned only with the power to enact statutes, not with their wisdom. The other is that while unconstitutional exercise of power by the executive and legislative branches of the government is subject to judicial restraint, the only check upon our own exercise of power is our own sense of self-restraint. For the removal of unwise laws from the statute books appeal lies not to the courts but to the ballot and to the processes of democratic government.

The constitutional power of Congress to levy an excise tax upon the processing of agricultural products is not questioned. The present levy is held invalid, not for any want of power in Congress to lay such a tax to defray public expenditures, including those for the general welfare, but because the use to which its proceeds are put is disapproved.

As the present depressed state of agriculture is nationwide in its extent and effects, there is no basis for saying that the expenditure of public money in aid of farmers is not within the specifically granted power of Congress to levy taxes to "provide for the . . . general welfare." The opinion of the Court does not declare otherwise.

. . .

It is with these preliminary and hardly controverted matters in mind that we should direct our attention to the pivot on which the decision of the Court is made to turn. It is that a levy unquestionably within the taxing power of Congress may be treated as invalid because it is a step in a plan to regulate agricultural production and is thus a forbidden infringement of state power. The levy is not any the less an exercise of taxing power because it is intended to defray an expenditure for the general welfare rather than for some other support of government. Nor is the levy and collection of the tax pointed to as effecting the regulation. While all federal taxes inevitably have some influence on the internal economy of the states, it is not contended that the levy of a processing tax upon manufacturers using agricultural products as raw material has any perceptible regulatory effect upon either their production or manufacture. The tax is unlike the penalties which were held invalid in the *Child Labor Tax Case* (1922), in *Hill* v. *Wallace* (1922), in *Linder* v. *United States* (1925), and in

United States v. *Constantine* (1935), because they were themselves the instruments of regulation by virtue of their coercive effect on matters left to the control of the states. Here regulation, if any there be, is accomplished not by the tax but by the method by which its proceeds are expended, and would equally be accomplished by any like use of public funds, regardless of their source.

...

Of the assertion that the payments to farmers are coercive, it is enough to say that no such contention is pressed by the taxpayer, and no such consequences were to be anticipated or appear to have resulted from the administration of the Act. The suggestion of coercion finds no support in the record or in any data showing the actual operation of the Act. Threat of loss, not hope of gain, is the essence of economic coercion. Members of a long depressed industry have undoubtedly been tempted to curtail acreage by the hope of resulting better prices and by the proffered opportunity to obtain needed ready money....

...The presumption of constitutionality of a statute is not to be overturned by an assertion of its coercive effect which rests on nothing more substantial than groundless speculation.

It is upon the contention that state power is infringed by purchased regulation of agricultural production that chief reliance is placed.

...

...The spending power of Congress is in addition to the legislative power and not subordinate to it. This independent grant of the power of the purse, and its very nature, involving in its exercise the duty to insure expenditure within the granted power, presuppose freedom of selection among diverse ends and aims, and the capacity to impose such conditions as will render the choice effective. It is a contradiction in terms to say that there is power to spend for the national welfare, while rejecting any power to impose conditions reasonably adapted to the attainment of the end which alone would justify the expenditure.

...

The power to tax and spend is not without constitutional restraints. One restriction is that the purpose must be truly national. Another is that it may not be used to coerce action left to state control. Another is the conscience and patriotism of Congress and the Executive. "It must be remembered that legislators are the ultimate guardians of the liberties and welfare of the people in quite as great a degree as the courts."

A tortured construction of the Constitution is not to be justified by recourse to extreme examples of reckless congressional spending which might occur if courts could not prevent—expenditures which, even if they could be thought to effect any national purpose, would be possible only by action of a legislature lost to all sense of public responsibility. Such suppositions are addressed to the mind accustomed to believe that it is the business of courts to sit in judgment on the wisdom of legislative action. Courts are not the only agency of government that must be assumed to have capacity to govern. Congress and the courts both unhappily may falter or be mistaken in the performance of their constitutional duty. But interpretation of our great charter of government which proceeds on any assumption that the responsibility for the preservation of our institutions is the exclusive concern of any one of the three branches of government, or that it alone can save them from destruction is far more likely, in the long run, "to obliterate the constituent members" of "an indestructible union of indestructible states" than the frank recognition that language, even of a constitution, may mean what it says: that the power to tax and spend includes the power to relieve a nationwide economic maladjustment by conditional gifts of money.

...

Steward Machine Co. v. Davis, 310 U.S. 548 (1937)

Franklin Roosevelt was committed to a national relief program, both on general principles and because he rightly predicted that a well-designed relief measure would attach millions of Americans to the New Deal regime. He worried, however, that direct federal payments would be declared unconstitutional. Supreme Court Justice Louis Brandeis, aware of this problem, suggested a solution. Brandeis noted that the Court had previously sustained a federal estate tax, with a proviso that taxpayers in states with a local estate tax could deduct their state payments from their federal tax payments. By doing so, Congress prevented Florida and other states from becoming a haven for retirees simply by abolishing the state estate tax.

Unemployment compensation would work similarly. The federal government would place a tax on employment to be paid by employers and employees. Taxpayers could get up to a 90 percent credit, however, for all taxes they paid to a state unemployment fund, provided that the fund met certain conditions. One of those conditions was that the moneys in the state employment fund would be deposited in the Treasury of the United States until they were used or the state elected not to participate in the federal program.

An Alabama steel services company, Steward Machine, paid the federal unemployment tax of $46.14 and then sued an internal revenue official in federal district court to have the payment returned on the grounds that the statute was unconstitutional. The district court upheld the statute, and the circuit court affirmed that ruling. Steward Machine appealed to the Supreme Court.

The Supreme Court by a 5–4 vote sustained this program. Justice Cardozo's opinion declared that the program was entirely voluntary and, in fact, may have increased state freedom of choice. Chief Justice Hughes and Justice Roberts, who had voted to strike down the Agricultural Adjustment Act, joined Cardozo's opinion. Justices Sutherland and Butler objected only to the provisions requiring states to deposit moneys with the federal government. Justices Butler and McReynolds objected to the entire scheme. Consider when you read the opinions whether Justice Cardozo convincingly distinguishes Steward *from* Butler. *Is there some reason why four justices (Hughes, Cardozo, Van Deventer, Roberts) thought that the federal government had no power to regulate agricultural production, but did have the right to provide assistance to the unemployed?*

JUSTICE CARDOZO delivered the opinion of the Court.

...We are told that the relation of employment is one so essential to the pursuit of happiness that it may not be burdened with a tax.

...We learn that employment for lawful gain is a "natural" or "inherent" or "inalienable" right, and not a "privilege" at all. But natural rights, so called, are as much subject to taxation as rights of less importance. An excise is not limited to vocations or activities that may be prohibited altogether....

...

The excise is not void as involving the coercion of the States in contravention of the Tenth Amendment or of restrictions implicit in our federal form of government.

...

To draw the line intelligently between duress and inducement there is need to remind ourselves of facts as to the problem of unemployment that are now matters of common knowledge. *West Coast Hotel Co.* v. *Parrish* (1937)....Of the many available figures a few only will be mentioned. During the years 1929 to 1936, when the country was passing through a cyclical depression, the number of the unemployed mounted to unprecedented heights. Often the average was more than 10 million; at times a peak was attained of 16 million or more. Disaster to the breadwinner meant disaster to dependents. Accordingly the roll of the unemployed, itself formidable enough, was only a partial roll of the destitute or needy. The fact developed quickly that the states were unable to give the requisite relief. The problem had become national in area and dimensions. There was need of help from the nation if the people were not to starve. It is too late today for the argument to be heard with tolerance that in a crisis so extreme the use of the moneys of the nation to relieve the unemployed and their dependents is a use for any purpose narrower than the promotion of the general welfare. Cf. *United States* v. *Butler* (1936)....

In the presence of this urgent need for some remedial expedient, the question is to be answered whether the expedient adopted has overleapt the bounds of power. The assailants of the statute say that its dominant end and aim is to drive the state legislatures under the whip of economic pressure into the enactment of unemployment compensation laws at the bidding of the central government. Supporters of the statute say that its operation is not constraint, but the creation of a larger freedom, the states and the nation joining in a cooperative endeavor to avert a common evil. Before Congress acted, unemployment compensation insurance was still, for the most part, a project and no more. Wisconsin was the pioneer. Her statute was adopted in 1931....In 1936, twenty-eight other states fell in line, and eight more the present year. But if states had been holding back before the passage of the federal law, inaction was not owing, for the most part, to the lack of sympathetic interest. Many held back through alarm lest, in laying such a toll upon their industries, they would place themselves in a position of economic disadvantage as compared with neighbors or competitors....Two consequences ensued. One was that the freedom of a state to contribute its fair share to the solution of a national problem was paralyzed by fear. The other was that in so far as there was failure by the states to contribute relief according to the measure of their capacity, a disproportionate burden, and a mountainous one, was laid upon the resources of the Government of the nation.

The Social Security Act is an attempt to find a method by which all these public agencies may work together to a common end....

Who then is coerced through the operation of this statute? Not the taxpayer. He pays in fulfillment of the mandate of the local legislature. Not the state. Even now she does not offer a suggestion that in passing the unemployment law she was affected by duress....For all that appears she is satisfied with her choice, and would be sorely disappointed if it were now to be annulled. The difficulty with the petitioner's contention is that it confuses motive with coercion. "Every tax is in some measure regulatory. To some extent it interposes an economic impediment to the activity taxed as compared with others not taxed."...In like manner every rebate from a tax when conditioned upon conduct is in some measure a temptation. But to hold that motive or temptation is equivalent to coercion is to plunge the law in endless difficulties. The outcome of such a doctrine is the acceptance of a philosophical determinism by which choice becomes impossible....

In ruling as we do, we leave many questions open. We do not say that a tax is valid, when imposed by act of Congress, if it is laid upon the condition that a state may escape its operation through the adoption of a statute unrelated in subject matter to activities fairly within the scope of national policy and power. No such question is before us. In the tender of this credit Congress does not intrude upon fields foreign to its function....We do not fix the outermost line. Enough for present purposes that wherever the line may be, this statute is within it. Definition more precise must abide the wisdom of the future.

...

United States v. *Butler*...is cited by petitioner as a decision to the contrary....The decision was by a divided court, a minority taking the view that the objections were untenable. None of them is applicable to the situation here developed.

(a) The proceeds of the tax in controversy are not earmarked for a special group.

(b) The unemployment compensation law which is a condition of the credit has had the approval of the state and could not be a law without it.

(c) The condition is not linked to an irrevocable agreement, for the state at its pleasure may repeal its unemployment law, § 903 (a) (6), terminate the credit, and place itself where it was before the credit was accepted.

(d) The condition is not directed to the attainment of an unlawful end, but to an end, the relief of unemployment, for which nation and state may lawfully cooperate.

...The statute does not call for a surrender by the states of powers essential to their quasi-sovereign existence.

...

There is argument again that the moneys when withdrawn are to be devoted to specific uses, the relief of unemployment, and that by agreement for such payment the quasi-sovereign position of the state has been impaired, if not abandoned. But again there is confusion between promise and condition. Alabama is still free, without breach of an agreement, to change her system over night. No officer or agency of the national Government can force a compensation law upon her or keep it in existence. No officer or agency of that Government, either by suit or other means, can supervise or control the application of the payments.

Finally and chiefly, abdication is supposed to follow from § 904 of the statute and the parts of § 903 that are complementary thereto....By these the Secretary of the Treasury is authorized and directed to receive and hold in the Unemployment Trust Fund all moneys deposited therein by a state agency for a state unemployment fund....

The same pervasive misconception is in evidence again. All that the state has done is to say in effect through the enactment of a statute that her agents shall be authorized to deposit the unemployment tax receipts in the Treasury at Washington....The statute may be repealed. The consent may be revoked. The deposits may be withdrawn. The moment the state commission gives notice to the depositary that it would like the moneys back, the Treasurer will return them. To find state destruction there is to find it almost anywhere. With nearly as much reason one might say that a state abdicates its functions when it places the state moneys on deposit in a national bank.

...

Affirmed.

JUSTICE SUTHERLAND, with whom JUSTICE VAN DEVANTER joins, concurring in part and dissenting in part.

With most of what is said in the opinion just handed down, I concur. I agree that the payroll tax levied is an excise within the power of Congress; that the devotion of not more than 90% of it to the credit of employers in states which require the payment of a similar tax under so-called unemployment-tax laws is not an unconstitutional use of the proceeds of the federal tax; that the provision making the adoption by the state of an unemployment law of a specified character a condition precedent to the credit of the tax does not render the law invalid. I agree that the states are not coerced by the federal legislation into adopting unemployment legislation. The provisions of the federal law may operate to induce the state to pass an employment law if it regards such action to be in its interest. But that is not coercion. If the act stopped here, I should accept the conclusion of the court that the legislation is not unconstitutional.

But the question with which I have difficulty is whether the administrative provisions of the act invade the governmental administrative powers of the several states reserved by the Tenth Amendment. A state may enter into contracts; but a state cannot, by contract or statute, surrender the execution, or a share in the execution, of any of its governmental powers either to a sister state or to the federal government, any more than the federal government can surrender the control of any of its governmental powers to a foreign nation. The power to tax is vital and fundamental, and, in the highest degree, governmental in character. Without it, the state could not exist. Fundamental also, and no less important, is the governmental power to expend the moneys realized from taxation, and exclusively to administer the laws in respect of the character of the tax and the methods of laying and collecting it and expending the proceeds.

...

The precise question, therefore, which we are required to answer by an application of these principles is whether the congressional act contemplates a surrender by the state to the federal government, in whole or in part, of any state governmental power to administer its own unemployment law or the state payroll-tax funds which it has collected for the purposes of that law. An affirmative answer to this question, I think, must be made.

I do not, of course, doubt the power of the state to select and utilize a depository for the safekeeping of its funds; but it is quite another thing to agree with the selected depository that the funds shall be withdrawn for certain stipulated purposes, and for no other. Nor do I doubt the authority of the federal government and a state government to cooperate to a common end, provided each of them is authorized to reach it. But such cooperation must be effectuated by an exercise of the powers which they severally possess, and not by an exercise, through invasion or surrender, by one of them of the governmental power of the other.

...

The force of what has been said is not broken by an acceptance of the view that the state is not *coerced* by the federal law. The effect of the dual distribution of powers is completely to deny to the states whatever is granted exclusively to the nation, and, conversely, to deny to the nation whatever is reserved exclusively to the states....

...If we are to survive as the United *States*, the balance between the powers of the nation and those of the states must be maintained. There is grave danger in permitting it to dip in either direction, danger—if there were no other—in the precedent thereby set for further departures from the equipoise. The threat implicit in the present encroachment upon the administrative functions of the states is that greater encroachments, and encroachments upon other functions, will follow.

JUSTICE McREYNOLDS, dissenting.

...[T]he States [should be] free to exercise governmental powers, not delegated or prohibited, without interference by the Federal Government through threats of punitive measures or offers of seductive favors. Unfortunately, the decision just announced opens the way for practical annihilation of this theory; and no cloud of words or ostentatious parade of irrelevant statistics should be permitted to obscure that fact.

...

No defense is offered for the legislation under review upon the basis of emergency. The hypothesis is that hereafter it will continuously benefit unemployed members of a class. Forever, so far as we can see, the States are expected to function under federal direction concerning an internal matter. By the sanction of this adventure, the door is open for progressive inauguration of others of like kind under which it can hardly be expected that the States will retain genuine independence of action. And without independent States a Federal Union as contemplated by the Constitution becomes impossible.

...

Ordinarily, I must think, a denial that the challenged action of Congress and what has been done under it amount to coercion and impair freedom of government by the people of the State would be regarded as contrary to practical experience. Unquestionably our federate plan of government confronts an enlarged peril.

JUSTICE BUTLER, dissenting.

I think that the objections to the challenged enactment expressed in the separate opinions of JUSTICE McREYNOLDS and JUSTICE SUTHERLAND are well taken. I am also of opinion that, in principle and as applied to bring about and to gain control over state unemployment compensation, the statutory scheme is repugnant to the Tenth Amendment.... The Constitution grants to the United States no power to pay unemployed persons or to require the States to enact laws or to raise or disburse money for that purpose. The provisions in question, if not amounting to coercion in a legal sense, are manifestly designed and intended directly to affect state action in the respects specified. And, if valid as so employed, this "tax and credit" device may be made effective to enable federal authorities to induce, if not indeed to compel, state enactments for any purpose within the realm of state power, and generally to control state administration of state laws.

...

When the federal Act was passed Wisconsin was the only State paying unemployment compensation. Though her plan then in force is by students of the subject generally deemed the best yet devised, she found it necessary to change her law in order to secure federal approval. In the absence of that, Wisconsin employers subject to the federal tax would not have been allowed any deduction on account of their contribution to the state fund....

Federal agencies prepared and took draft bills to state legislatures to enable and induce them to pass laws providing for unemployment compensation in accordance with federal requirements, and thus to obtain relief for the employers from the impending federal exaction. Obviously the Act creates the peril of federal tax not to raise revenue but to persuade. Of course, each State was free to reject any measure so proposed. But, if it failed to adopt a plan acceptable to federal authority, the full burden of the federal tax would be exacted. And, as federal demands similarly conditioned may be increased from time to time as Congress shall determine, possible federal pressure in that field is without limit. Already at least 43 States, yielding to the inducement resulting immediately from the application of the federal tax and credit device, have provided for unemployment compensation in form to merit approval of the Social Security Board. Presumably the remaining States will comply whenever convenient for their legislatures to pass the necessary laws.

The terms of the measure make it clear that the tax and credit device was intended to enable federal officers virtually to control the exertion of powers of the States in a field in which they alone have jurisdiction and from which the United States is by the Constitution excluded.

I am of opinion that the judgment of the Circuit Court of Appeals should be reversed.

IV. Federalism

MAJOR DEVELOPMENTS

- The decline of the Tenth Amendment
- The rise of federal judicial review of states outside of economic regulation
- The rise of cooperative federalism

When the Supreme Court abandoned dual federalism after 1936, the justices abandoned the notion that the Constitution vested states with control over specifically delineated social policies. Up through the early twentieth century, many lawyers and politicians argued that the states and national government occupied separate spheres and were each limited to their own area of responsibilities. This was the vision of dual federalism, which the Court often tried to enforce. New Deal nationalists insisted that the federal government was constitutionally authorized to act on any matter where states were deemed incompetent. Equally important, Congress was the branch of government that determined when federal action was necessary. Chief Justice Harlan Fiske Stone stated basic New Deal constitutional commitments when, in *United States v. Darby* (1941), he described the Tenth Amendment as "but a truism that all is retained which has not been surrendered." The Tenth Amendment was not an independent barrier to congressional action; nor did it indicate principles that might affect how the Court evaluated congressional power.

The New Deal Court largely freed the states to adopt economic regulations without regard to the contracts, takings, or due-process clauses. But the Court imposed new restrictions on the states derived from other rights provisions, as well as from judicious use of the "dormant" commerce clause and the preemption of state laws based on perceived conflicts with federal statutes and policy commitments.

The expansion of congressional power under the commerce clause in cases like *Darby* meant that the Court needed to reconsider the logic of the dormant commerce clause as well. If the commerce clause gave Congress a vast regulatory sphere after 1937, then the dormant commerce clause might imply that the states were extremely restricted in what they could do even if Congress took no action at all. The Court responded by focusing on how discriminatory a state regulation might be. Initially, the New Deal Court suggested in *South Carolina State Highway Department v. Barnwell Brothers* (1938) that it might be deferential to state legislative judgments on public safety. But soon the Court turned to its effort to balancing the local benefits of regulations with the disruption to national commercial activity and the discriminatory effect against out-of-state economic actors. As the conservative jurists before him did, New Deal Justice Felix Frankfurter worried about the possibility of a "crazy-quilt of State laws" that would impose "unreasonable burdens on commerce" if the Court did not intervene to police state regulations.[33]

Preempting state laws that conflicted with federal statutes provided another tool for the post–1937 Supreme Court to limit the states. In *Pennsylvania v. Nelson* (1956), for example, the Supreme Court used the existence of the federal government's anti-subversive Smith Act of 1940 to declare that Congress had "occupied the field of sedition." As a consequence, "no room has been left for the States to supplement it. Therefore, a state sedition statute is superseded regardless of whether it purports to supplement the federal law."

Pennsylvania's prosecution of the admitted Communist Steve Nelson was struck down, but the Court did not rely on the First Amendment to do it. Instead, it pointed to the possibility of a "conflict with the administration of the federal program" by such "sporadic local prosecutions." All state sedition laws were preempted by the existence of a federal law on the subject. Such maneuvers leave an opening for Congress to respond with legislation explicitly authorizing state prosecutions, but new legislation is not easy to pass and would itself be subject to further judicial interpretation. (The three dissenters in *Nelson* thought it was plain that the Smith Act had not itself been intended to preempt state sedition statutes.) The combination of a robust preemption doctrine, the use of the dormant commerce clause, and an expanding set of civil rights and civil liberties meant that the states and localities came under increasing supervision from the federal courts in the 1950s and 1960s.

Although federalism was not a constitutional value during the New Deal/Great Society Era, many commentators insisted that the policies adopted during this period invigorated state governments. New Deal and Great Society programs frequently provided states with substantial sums of money that states used to improve the education, health, and welfare of local citizens. Still, the same Supreme Court decisions that sustained federal power to spend for the general welfare also sustained federal power to attach any conditions to the expenditure of federal funds that national officials thought necessary. States remained laboratories of democracy in the middle of the twentieth century, but only when national elected officials and the Supreme Court believed diversity more important than uniformity.

The period marked the heyday of "cooperative" federalism, with the federal and state government working together to formulate and administer joint policies and with states and localities coming to rely on federal grants to fund a significant portion of their programs. In light of these developments, many scholars argued the American system was better described as one of "marble cake federalism" than of "dual federalism," with overlapping state and federal responsibilities rather than clearly separated ones. Notably, many of the constitutional and judicial challenges to the growth of the national government during and after the New Deal came not from the state governments themselves but from private individuals and businesses who were being taxed or regulated.

As Table 8-3 illustrates, the U.S. Supreme Court has a long and active history of reviewing state laws under the interstate commerce clause. The laws that come under challenge before the Court change over time, reflecting new technologies, government responsibilities, and combinations of interests. The Court has sometimes

33. *Morgan v. Virginia*, 328 U.S. 373, 388 (1946).

changed the particular doctrinal lens with which it views these state laws, but the justices have long pursued the same basic goals of protecting the national marketplace from local legislation that unreasonably discriminates against outside economic actors or disrupts the efficient flow of goods across the nation. Though the Court has often upheld state statutes against constitutional challenges, the interstate commerce clause has proven to be an important independent source of authority for the federal judiciary to evaluate state policies.

V. Separation of Powers

MAJOR DEVELOPMENTS

- The limitation on presidential removal power of independent commissioners
- The decline of the nondelegation doctrine
- The expansion of presidential war powers and executive privilege
- The judicial retreat from limiting congressional investigatory powers

Table 8-3 Selection of U.S. Supreme Court Cases Reviewing State Laws under the Interstate Commerce Clause

Case	Vote	Outcome	Decision
Gibbons v. Ogden, 22 U.S. 1 (1824)	6–0	Struck down	State law regulating navigation of interstate waterways trumped by federal statute
Brown v. Maryland, 25 U.S. 419 (1827)	6–0	Struck down	State license on importers trumped by federal statute
Mayor of New York v. Miln, 36 U.S. 102 (1837)	5–1	Upheld	State law requiring captains of out-of-state ships to indemnify state for passengers who go on poor relief is an internal police regulation
The Passenger Cases, 48 U.S. 283 (1849)	5–4	Struck down	State laws imposing a tax on every out-of-state passenger brought into port are unconstitutional
Cooley v. Board of Wardens, 53 U.S. 299 (1851)	8–1	Upheld	State law requiring large ships to pay for a local pilot to guide them into port does not interfere with interstate commerce since no uniform national policy is necessary
Wabash, St. Louis & Pacific Railroad Company v. Illinois, 118 U.S. 557 (1886)	6–3	Struck down	Because the regulation of goods traveling across state lines requires a uniform national policy, a state law regulating railroad rates for such goods unconstitutionally interferes with interstate commerce even in the absence of a federal law
Kidd v. Pearson, 128 U.S. 1 (1888)	8–0	Upheld	State law prohibiting the manufacture of liquor, even if intended for out-of-state sale, is within the internal police power of the state
Seaboard Air Line Railway v. Blackwell, 244 U.S. 310 (1917)	6–3	Struck down	State law regulating the stops and speeds of trains places a direct burden on interstate commerce and is unconstitutional
Bradley v. Public Utilities Commission of Ohio, 289 U.S. 92 (1933)	9–0	Upheld	State law regulating the licensing of common carrier motor vehicles, in order to promote public safety and reduce traffic congestion, is a valid exercise of police power

Continued

Table 8-3 *Continued*

Case	Vote	Outcome	Decision
Baldwin v. G. A. F. Seelig, Inc., 294 U.S. 511 (1935)	9–0	Struck down	State law regulating the sale of out-of-state purchased milk, with the effect of excluding it, is an act of economic isolation and unconstitutionally discriminatory
South Carolina State Highway Department v. Barnwell Brothers, Inc., 303 U.S. 177 (1938)	7–0	Upheld	State law regulating weight and width of trucks on highways is not an undue burden on interstate commerce
Parker v. Brown, 317 U.S. 341 (1942)	9–0	Upheld	California raisin program designed to prop up prices only has indirect effect on interstate commerce and is not inconsistent with congressional policy
Dean Milk Co. v. City of Madison, Wisconsin, 340 U.S. 349 (1951)	6–3	Struck down	Local ordinance restricting the sale of non-local milk, even in the interest of promoting public safety, unconstitutionally discriminates against interstate commerce when less restrictive alternatives are available
City of Philadelphia v. New Jersey, 430 U.S. 141 (1977)	7–2	Struck down	State law prohibiting the importation of most out-of-state solid or liquid waste without legitimate reason is discriminatorily protectionist
Hunt v. Washington State Apple Advertising Commission, 432 U.S. 333 (1977)	8–0	Struck down	State law prohibiting the display of any state apple inspection grades unconstitutionally discriminates against commerce from states with more rigorous standards and burdens interstate commerce
Exxon Corp. v. Governor of Maryland, 437 U.S. 117 (1978)	7–1	Upheld	State law prohibiting oil producers and refiners from operating gasoline stations is not discriminatory or impermissibly burdensome to interstate commerce
White v. Mass. Council of Construction Employers, 460 U.S. 204 (1983)	7–2	Upheld	Mayoral order requiring city-funded construction projects to employ a minimum number of city residents is valid because city is acting as a market participant rather than a regulator
Maine v. Taylor, 477 U.S. 131 (1986)	8–1	Upheld	State law prohibiting the importation of live baitfish serves a legitimate local concern that cannot be reasonably served by nondiscriminatory alternatives
Oregon Waste Systems, Inc. v. Department of Environmental Quality of Oregon, 511 U.S. 93 (1994)	7–2	Struck down	State law imposing a surcharge on solid waste generated out-of-state and disposed of within the state is discriminatory on its face, and without evidence that no less discriminatory means are available to forward some legitimate local interest, is unconstitutional
Granholm v. Heald, 544 U.S. 460 (2005)	5–4	Struck down	State laws restricting the ability of out-of-state wineries to directly ship alcohol to consumers discriminate against interstate commerce
United Haulers Association v. Oneida-Herkimer Solid Waste Management Authority, 550 U.S. 330 (2007)	6–3	Upheld	County ordinances requiring locally produced garbage to be delivered to local publicly owned processing facilities does not interfere with interstate commerce

Franklin Roosevelt in his first inaugural address declared that he would "ask the Congress for the one remaining instrument to meet the crisis—broad Executive power to wage war against the emergency, as great as the power that would be given to me if we were in fact invaded by a foreign foe."[34] Walter Lippmann, an influential thinker and newspaper columnist of the period, thought the president might have to go further. In a private conversation, Lippman informed president-elect Roosevelt that he might "have no alternative but to assume dictatorial power."[35] Within weeks, Congress had granted the executive branch dramatically increased powers to combat the Depression. Roosevelt and his successors in the White House soon exercised dramatically increased powers in foreign affairs as well. By the end of the New Deal/Great Society Era, numerous commentators were complaining of an "imperial presidency" that was exercising executive, legislative, and sometimes judicial power.[36]

Presidential power during the New Deal/Great Society regime was fueled by the administrative state, foreign affairs, and electoral politics. As the federal government played a more active role in national life, Congress increasingly passed legislation aimed more at empowering administrative agencies than at establishing precise legal rules. One consequence of this practice was an increase in executive policy-making, with the president frequently giving direction to the many administrative agencies.

Lawmaking in the modern administrative state differed from the nineteenth-century practice as well. Congressional regulation before and immediately after the Civil War was usually quite specific. Congress, for example, would determine the exact price at which public lands would be sold or devise a detailed schedule for duties on common goods. Regulation at the turn of the century was much less specific. The Sherman Anti-Trust Act of 1890, for example, prohibited "contracts in restraint of trade," leaving courts with the burden of determining when contracts restrained trade. Crucial New Deal measures added a new dimension of imprecision. Congress often simply declared a vague goal, such as establishing fair competition, and then authorized the president or a department of the executive branch to make specific rules for achieving that end. The size of the executive branch was greatly expanded in order to implement these new directives.

Presidents also benefited from the increased American presence in world affairs. Presidents had historically been granted more leeway in foreign policy than in domestic policy. As international affairs became more important to American life in the twentieth century, the presidency became a more important institution. From 1932 until 1968, congressional majorities generally supported most important executive policy initiatives and generally supported increases in presidential power. When presidents acted unilaterally, they usually could rely on their legislative supporters to prevent a constitutional crisis. Presidents did not always get their way, but the normal expectation was that Congress and the White House would generally be united by party, ideology, and policy goals.

The Supreme Court initially resisted this increase in executive power. In cases such as *Panama Refining Co. v. Ryan* (1935) and *Schechter Poultry Corp. v. United States* (1935), both conservative and progressive justices insisted that Congress could not essentially give the president a blank check to make policy. This ban on legislative delegations was another casualty of the Constitutional Revolution of 1937. By 1940, the justices effectively abandoned any effort to limit congressional decisions to increase executive authority. Separation-of-powers debates for the next thirty years were largely hypothetical. Presidents and members of Congress frequently disputed the precise scope of their authority, but Congress did not directly challenge most executive initiatives. President Roosevelt, for example, asserted that Congress had no constitutional right to include a legislative veto in the legislation granting the president power to make arms deals with the allied powers, but Congress never exercised that veto. The one exception to this practice was when President Truman seized steel mines during the Korean War. When the Supreme Court rejected this exercise of executive power in the *Steel Seizure Case* (1952), Truman backed down, thus avoiding a potential constitutional crisis.

---

34. David M. Kennedy, *Freedom From Fear* (New York: Oxford University Press, 1999), 134.

35. Ibid., 111.

36. See especially, Arthur M. Schlesinger, Jr., *The Imperial Presidency* (Boston: Houghton Mifflin, 1973).

A. General Principles

Youngstown Sheet & Tube Co. v. Sawyer, 343 U.S. 579 (1952) ["Steel Seizure Case"]

The New Deal increased American involvement in world affairs, and the nature of twentieth-century military struggles raised basic questions about the viability of eighteenth-century notions of separation of powers in a twentieth-century world. These issues were at the heart of Youngstown Sheet & Tube, *a decision that has acquired canonical status as the leading modern expression of contemporary constitutional understandings of executive capacity to act unilaterally. One school of thought, exemplified by Justice Black, insists that the Constitution of 1789 clearly spells out the division of powers between the President and Congress. The other school of thought, exemplified by Justices Frankfurter and Jackson, insists that the constitutional text has very little to say about modern problems; constitutional standards must therefore be worked out through analysis of historical developments and pragmatic accommodations. The latter view has become increasingly dominant in American constitutionalism. Jackson's three-part categorization of separation-of-powers situations set the standard for judicial thinking about conflicts between Congress and the President.*

In December 1951, during the Korean War, the United Steelworkers of America gave notice of their intention to strike when the collective bargaining agreement between the steel mills and their employees expired at the end of that year. Federal mediation failed to resolve the impasse. In April 1952, the union called for a nationwide strike. President Harry Truman responded with an executive order directing Secretary of Commerce Charles Sawyer to take control of the steel mills and keep them operational, arguing that the continued production of steel was essential to the war effort and that the president had intrinsic constitutional authority under Article II to take such an action to secure the national interest. The Commerce Secretary, in turn, took possession of the steel mills and directed their management to keep them running in accord with his directives. The president reported his orders to Congress, but Congress took no immediate action. The steel companies complied with the order but sought an injunction restraining the enforcement of the order. In an expedited process, the district court for the District of Columbia issued the injunction, which was then stayed by the Court of Appeals. The Supreme Court heard arguments in the case less than two weeks later.

At the time of the Steel Seizure Case, *the Court included four Truman appointees, individuals who had also been political intimates of the president's. The Truman justices split evenly, with two joining the majority (Burton and Clark) against the president and two in dissent (Vinson and Minton). In 1952, the justices also had a significant amount of personal experience with the challenges of presidential policy and administration. Notably, Jackson and Clark were former attorneys general, who had grappled with these kinds of legal issues from the perspective of the executive branch, and Vinson was a former Secretary of Treasury. Two others, Black and Burton, had come from the other end of Pennsylvania Avenue, both having served in the U.S. Senate. Clark had prepared a memo as Truman's attorney general defending inherent presidential power and advocating presidential seizures of key industrial plants during labor disputes as a good policy during wartime. Vinson had directly advised President Truman that a seizure of the steel mills would be constitutional. He might well have expected his dissenting opinion to have commanded the votes of the majority of the justices.*

JUSTICE BLACK delivered the opinion of the Court.

...

The President's power, if any, to issue the order must stem either from an act of Congress or from the Constitution itself. There is no statute that expressly authorizes the President to take possession of property as he did here. Nor is there any act of Congress to which our attention has been directed from which such a power can fairly be implied. Indeed, we do not understand the Government to rely on statutory authorization for this seizure. There are two statutes which do authorize the President to take both personal and real property under certain conditions. However, the Government admits that these conditions were not met and that the President's order was not rooted in either of the statutes. The Government refers to the seizure provisions of one of these statutes ... as "much too cumbersome, involved, and time-consuming for the crisis which was at hand."

Moreover, the use of the seizure technique to solve labor disputes in order to prevent work stoppages was not only unauthorized by any congressional enactment; prior to this controversy, Congress had refused to adopt that method of settling labor disputes....

It is clear that if the President had authority to issue the order he did, it must be found in some provisions of the Constitution. And it is not claimed that express constitutional language grants this power to the President. The contention is that presidential power should be implied from the aggregate of his powers under the Constitution. Particular reliance is placed on provisions in Article II which say that "the executive Power shall be vested in a President..."; that "he shall take Care that the Laws be faithfully executed"; and that he "shall be Commander in Chief of the Army and Navy of the United States."

The order cannot properly be sustained as an exercise of the President's military power as Commander in Chief of the Armed Forces. The Government attempts to do so by citing a number of cases upholding broad powers in military commanders engaged in day-to-day fighting in a theater of war. Such cases need not concern us here. Even though "theater of war" be an expanding concept, we cannot with faithfulness to our constitutional system hold that the Commander in Chief of the Armed Forces has the ultimate power as such to take possession of private property in order to keep labor disputes from stopping production. This is a job for the Nation's lawmakers, not for its military authorities.

Nor can the seizure order be sustained because of the several constitutional provisions that grant executive power to the President. In the framework of our Constitution, the President's power to see that the laws are faithfully executed refutes the idea that he is to be a lawmaker. The Constitution limits his functions in the lawmaking process to the recommending of laws he thinks wise and the vetoing of laws he thinks bad. And the Constitution is neither silent nor equivocal about who shall make laws which the President is to execute....

The President's order does not direct that a congressional policy be executed in a manner prescribed by Congress—it directs that a presidential policy be executed in a manner prescribed by the President....The power of Congress to adopt such public policies as those proclaimed by the order is beyond question..... The Constitution did not subject this lawmaking power of Congress to presidential or military supervision or control.

...

The Founders of this Nation entrusted the lawmaking power to the Congress alone in both good and bad times. It would do no good to recall the historical events, the fears of power and the hopes for freedom that lay behind their choice. Such a review would but confirm our holding that this seizure order cannot stand.

JUSTICE JACKSON, concurring.

That comprehensive and undefined presidential powers hold both practical advantages and grave dangers for the country will impress anyone who has served as legal adviser to a President in time of transition and public anxiety. While an interval of detached reflection may temper teachings of that experience, they probably are a more realistic influence on my views than the conventional materials of judicial decision which seem unduly to accentuate doctrine and legal fiction....The tendency is strong to emphasize transient results upon policies—such as wages or stabilization—and lose sight of enduring consequences upon the balanced power structure of our Republic.

A judge, like an executive adviser, may be surprised at the poverty of really useful and unambiguous authority applicable to concrete problems of executive power as they actually present themselves. Just what our forefathers did envision, or would have envisioned had they foreseen modern conditions, must be divined from materials almost as enigmatic as the dreams Joseph was called upon to interpret for Pharaoh. A century and a half of partisan debate and scholarly speculation yields no net result but only supplies more or less apt quotations from respected sources on each side of any question. They largely cancel each other....

The actual art of governing under our Constitution does not and cannot conform to judicial definitions of the power of any of its branches based on isolated clauses or even single Articles torn from context. While the Constitution diffuses power the better to secure liberty, it also contemplates that practice will integrate the dispersed powers into a workable government. It enjoins upon its branches separateness but interdependence, autonomy but reciprocity. Presidential powers are not fixed but fluctuate, depending upon their disjunction or conjunction with those of Congress. We may well begin by a somewhat over-simplified grouping of practical situations in which a President may doubt, or others may challenge, his powers, and by distinguishing roughly the legal consequences of this factor of relativity.

1. When the President acts pursuant to an express or implied authorization of Congress, his authority is at its maximum, for it includes all that he possesses in his own right plus all that Congress can delegate. In these circumstances, and in these only, may he be said

(for what it may be worth), to personify the federal sovereignty. If his act is held unconstitutional under these circumstances, it usually means that the Federal Government as an undivided whole lacks power. A seizure executed by the President pursuant to an Act of Congress would be supported by the strongest of presumptions and the widest latitude of judicial interpretation, and the burden of persuasion would rest heavily upon any who might attack it.

2. When the President acts in absence of either a congressional grant or denial of authority, he can only rely upon his own independent powers, but there is a zone of twilight in which he and Congress may have concurrent authority, or in which its distribution is uncertain. Therefore, congressional inertia, indifference or quiescence may sometimes, at least as a practical matter, enable, if not invite, measures on independent presidential responsibility. In this area, any actual test of power is likely to depend on the imperatives of events and contemporary imponderables rather than on abstract theories of law.[37]

3. When the President takes measures incompatible with the expressed or implied will of Congress, his power is at its lowest ebb, for then he can rely only upon his own constitutional powers minus any constitutional powers of Congress over the matter. Courts can sustain exclusive Presidential control in such a case only by disabling the Congress from acting upon the subject.[38] Presidential claim to a power at once so conclusive and preclusive must be scrutinized with caution, for what is at stake is the equilibrium established by our constitutional system.

Into which of these classifications does this executive seizure of the steel industry fit? It is eliminated from the first by admission, for it is conceded that no congressional authorization exists for this seizure....

Can it then be defended under flexible tests available to the second category? It seems clearly eliminated from that class because Congress has not left seizure of private property an open field but has covered it by three statutory policies inconsistent with this seizure.... None of these were invoked. In choosing a different and inconsistent way of his own, the President cannot claim that it is necessitated or invited by failure of Congress to legislate upon the occasions, grounds and methods for seizure of industrial properties.

This leaves the current seizure to be justified only by the severe tests under the third grouping, where it can be supported only by any remainder of executive power after subtraction of such powers as Congress may have over the subject. In short, we can sustain the President only by holding that seizure of such strike-bound industries is within his domain and beyond control by Congress....

I did not suppose, and I am not persuaded, that history leaves it open to question, at least in the courts, that the executive branch, like the Federal Government as a whole, possesses only delegated powers. The purpose of the Constitution was not only to grant power, but to keep it from getting out of hand. However, because the President does not enjoy unmentioned powers does not mean that the mentioned ones should be narrowed by a niggardly construction. Some clauses could be made almost unworkable, as well as immutable, by refusal to indulge some latitude of interpretation for changing times. I have heretofore, and do now, give to the enumerated powers the scope and elasticity afforded by what seem to be reasonable practical implications instead of the rigidity dictated by a doctrinaire textualism.

The Solicitor General seeks the power of seizure in three clauses of the Executive Article, the first reading, "The executive Power shall be vested in a President of the United States of America." Lest I be thought to exaggerate, I quote the interpretation which his brief puts upon it: "In our view, this clause constitutes a grant of all the executive powers of which the Government is capable." If that be true, it is difficult to see why the forefathers bothered to add several specific items, including some trifling ones.

....I cannot accept the view that this clause is a grant in bulk of all conceivable executive power but regard it as an allocation to the presidential office of the generic powers thereafter stated.

The clause on which the Government next relies is that "The President shall be Commander in Chief of the Army and Navy of the United States...." These cryptic

37. Since the Constitution implies that the writ of habeas corpus may be suspended in certain circumstances but does not say by whom, President Lincoln asserted and maintained it as an executive function in the face of judicial challenge and doubt. *Ex parte Merryman*.... Congress eventually ratified his action....

38. President Roosevelt's effort to remove a Federal Trade Commissioner was found to be contrary to the policy of Congress and impinging upon an area of congressional control, and so his removal power was cut down accordingly. *Humphrey's Executor v. United States*.... However, his exclusive power of removal in executive agencies, affirmed in *Myers v. United States*...continued to be asserted and maintained.

words have given rise to some of the most persistent controversies in our constitutional history.... Hence, this loose appellation is sometimes advanced as support for any Presidential action, internal or external, involving use of force, the idea being that it vests power to do anything, anywhere, that can be done with an army or navy.

....

I cannot foresee all that it might entail if the Court should indorse this argument. Nothing in our Constitution is plainer than that declaration of a war is entrusted only to Congress. Of course, a state of war may in fact exist without a formal declaration. But no doctrine that the Court could promulgate would seem to me more sinister and alarming than that a President whose conduct of foreign affairs is so largely uncontrolled, and often even is unknown, can vastly enlarge his mastery over the internal affairs of the country by his own commitment of the Nation's armed forces to some foreign venture. I do not, however, find it necessary or appropriate to consider the legal status of the Korean enterprise to discountenance argument based on it.

Assuming that we are in a war *de facto*, whether it is or is not a war *de jure*, does that empower the Commander-in-Chief to seize industries he thinks necessary to supply our army? The Constitution expressly places in Congress power "to raise and *support* Armies" and "to *provide* and *maintain* a Navy." (Emphasis supplied.) This certainly lays upon Congress primary responsibility for supplying the armed forces....

There are indications that the Constitution did not contemplate that the title Commander-in-Chief of the Army and Navy will constitute him also Commander-in-Chief of the country, its industries and its inhabitants. He has no monopoly of "war powers," whatever they are. While Congress cannot deprive the President of the command of the army and navy, only Congress can provide him an army or navy to command.

...

We should not use this occasion to circumscribe, much less to contract, the lawful role of the President as Commander-in-Chief. I should indulge the widest latitude of interpretation to sustain his exclusive function to command the instruments of national force, at least when turned against the outside world for the security of our society. But, when it is turned inward, not because of rebellion but because of a lawful economic struggle between industry and labor, it should have no such indulgence....

...

The Solicitor General lastly grounds support of the seizure upon nebulous, inherent powers never expressly granted but said to have accrued to the office from the customs and claims of preceding administrations. The plea is for a resulting power to deal with a crisis or an emergency according to the necessities of the case, the unarticulated assumption being that necessity knows no law.

...

The appeal, however, that we declare the existence of inherent powers ex necessitate to meet an emergency asks us to do what many think would be wise, although it is something the forefathers omitted. They knew what emergencies were, knew the pressures they engender for authoritative action, knew, too, how they afford a ready pretext for usurpation. We may also suspect that they suspected that emergency powers would tend to kindle emergencies. Aside from suspension of the privilege of the writ of habeas corpus in time of rebellion or invasion, when the public safety may require it, they made no express provision for exercise of extraordinary authority because of a crisis. I do not think we rightfully may so amend their work, and, if we could, I am not convinced it would be wise to do so, although many modern nations have forthrightly recognized that war and economic crises may upset the normal balance between liberty and authority. Their experience with emergency powers may not be irrelevant to the argument here that we should say that the Executive, of his own volition, can invest himself with undefined emergency powers.

....

[The] contemporary foreign experience may be inconclusive as to the wisdom of lodging emergency powers somewhere in a modern government. But it suggests that emergency powers are consistent with free government only when their control is lodged elsewhere than in the Executive who exercises them. That is the safeguard that would be nullified by our adoption of the "inherent powers" formula. Nothing in my experience convinces me that such risks are warranted by any real necessity, although such powers would, of course, be an executive convenience.

In the practical working of our Government we already have evolved a technique within the framework of the Constitution by which normal executive powers may be considerably expanded to meet an emergency. Congress may and has granted extraordinary authorities which lie dormant in normal times but may be called into play by the Executive in war or upon proclamation of a national emergency. In 1939, upon congressional request, the Attorney General listed ninety-nine such separate statutory grants by Congress of emergency or war-time executive powers. They were invoked from time to time as need appeared. Under this procedure we retain Government by law—special, temporary law, perhaps, but law nonetheless....

In view of the ease, expedition and safety with which Congress can grant and has granted large emergency powers, certainly ample to embrace this crisis, I am quite unimpressed with the argument that we should affirm possession of them without statute. Such power either has no beginning or it has no end. If it exists, it need submit to no legal restraint. I am not alarmed that it would plunge us straightway into dictatorship, but it is at least a step in that wrong direction.

....

But I have no illusion that any decision by this Court can keep power in the hands of Congress if it is not wise and timely in meeting its problems. A crisis that challenges the President equally, or perhaps primarily, challenges Congress. If not good law, there was worldly wisdom in the maxim attributed to Napoleon that "The tools belong to the man who can use them." We may say that power to legislate for emergencies belongs in the hands of Congress, but only Congress itself can prevent power from slipping through its fingers.

...

JUSTICE BURTON, concurring.

...

JUSTICE CLARK, concurring.

...

The limits of presidential power are obscure. However, Article II, no less than Article I, is part of "a constitution intended to endure for ages to come, and, consequently, to be adapted to the various crises of human affairs." Some of our Presidents, such as Lincoln, "felt that measures otherwise unconstitutional might become lawful by becoming indispensable to the preservation of the Constitution through the preservation of the nation." Others, such as Theodore Roosevelt, thought the President to be capable, as a "steward" of the people, of exerting all power save that which is specifically prohibited by the Constitution or the Congress. In my view—taught me not only by the decision of Chief Justice Marshall in *Little v. Barreme* (1804)...but also by a score of other pronouncements of distinguished members of this bench—the Constitution does grant to the President extensive authority in times of grave and imperative national emergency. In fact, to my thinking, such a grant may well be necessary to the very existence of the Constitution itself. As Lincoln aptly said, "(is) it possible to lose the nation and yet preserve the Constitution?" In describing this authority I care not whether one calls it "residual," "inherent," "moral," "implied," "aggregate," "emergency," or otherwise. I am of the conviction that those who have had the gratifying experience of being the President's lawyer have used one or more of these adjectives only with the utmost of sincerity and the highest of purpose.

I conclude that where Congress has laid down specific procedures to deal with the type of crisis confronting the President, he must follow those procedures in meeting the crisis; but that in the absence of such action by Congress, the President's independent power to act depends upon the gravity of the situation confronting the nation. I cannot sustain the seizure in question because...Congress had prescribed methods to be followed by the President in meeting the emergency at hand.

...

JUSTICE DOUGLAS, concurring.

There can be no doubt that the emergency which caused the President to seize these steel plants was one that bore heavily on the country. But the emergency did not create power; it merely marked an occasion when power should be exercised. And the fact that it was necessary that measures be taken to keep steel in production does not mean that the President, rather than the Congress, had the constitutional authority to act. The Congress, as well as the President, is trustee of the national welfare. The President can act more quickly than the Congress. The President with the armed services at his disposal can move with force as well as with speed. All executive power—from the reign of ancient kings to the rule of modern dictators—has the outward appearance of efficiency.

Legislative power, by contrast, is slower to exercise. There must be delay while the ponderous machinery of committees, hearings, and debates is put into motion. That takes time; and while the Congress slowly moves into action, the emergency may take its toll in wages, consumer goods, war production, the standard of living of the people, and perhaps even lives. Legislative action may indeed often be cumbersome, time-consuming, and apparently inefficient. But as Mr. Justice Brandeis stated in his dissent in *Myers v. United States* (1926)..."The doctrine of the separation of powers was adopted by the Convention of 1787 not to promote efficiency but to preclude the exercise of arbitrary power...."

...

The legislative nature of the action taken by the President seems to me to be clear. When the United States takes over an industrial plant to settle a labor controversy, it is condemning property. The seizure of the plant is a taking in the constitutional sense....

...

....Some future generation may...deem it so urgent that the President have legislative authority that the Constitution will be amended. We could not sanction the seizures and condemnations of the steel plants in this case without reading Article II as giving the President not only the power to execute the laws but to make some. Such a step would most assuredly alter the pattern of the Constitution.

We pay a price for our system of checks and balances, for the distribution of power among the three branches of government. It is a price that today may seem exorbitant to many. Today a kindly President uses the seizure power to effect a wage increase and to keep the steel furnaces in production. Yet tomorrow another President might use the same power to prevent a wage increase, to curb trade unionists, to regiment labor as oppressively as industry thinks it has been regimented by this seizure.

JUSTICE FRANFURTER, concurring.

...

A constitutional democracy like ours is perhaps the most difficult of man's social arrangements to manage successfully. Our scheme of society is more dependent than any other form of government on knowledge and wisdom and self-discipline for the achievement of its aims....[History] sheds a good deal of light not merely on the need for effective power, if a society is to be at once cohesive and civilized, but also on the need for limitations on the power of governors over the governed.

To that end they rested the structure of our central government on the system of checks and balances. For them the doctrine of separation of powers was not mere theory; it was a felt necessity. Not so long ago it was fashionable to find our system of checks and balances obstructive to effective government. It was easy to ridicule that system as outmoded—too easy. The experience through which the world has passed in our own day has made vivid the realization that the Framers of our Constitution were not inexperienced doctrinaires. These long-headed statesmen had no illusion that our people enjoyed biological or psychological or sociological immunities from the hazards of concentrated power. It is absurd to see a dictator in a representative product of the sturdy democratic traditions of the Mississippi Valley. The accretion of dangerous power does not come in a day. It does come, however slowly, from the generative force of unchecked disregard of the restrictions that fence in even the most disinterested assertion of authority.

...

The issue before us can be met, and therefore should be, without attempting to define the President's powers comprehensively....

The question before the Court comes in this setting. Congress has frequently—at least 16 times since 1916—specifically provided for executive seizure of production, transportation, communications, or storage facilities. In every case it has qualified this grant of power with limitations and safeguards. This body of enactments...demonstrates that Congress deemed seizure so drastic a power as to require that it be carefully circumscribed whenever the President was vested with this extraordinary authority....

...

...The utmost that the Korean conflict may imply is that it may have been desirable to have given the President further authority, a freer hand in these matters. Absence of authority in the President to deal with a crisis does not imply want of power in the Government. Conversely the fact that power exists in the Government does not vest it in the President. The need for new legislation does not enact it. Nor does it repeal or amend existing law.

...

It is not a pleasant judicial duty to find that the President has exceeded his powers and still less so when his purposes were dictated by concern for the Nation's wellbeing, in the assured conviction that he acted to avert danger. But it would stultify one's faith in our people to entertain even a momentary fear that the patriotism and the wisdom of the President and the Congress, as well as the long view of the immediate parties in interest, will not find ready accommodation for differences on matters which, however close to their concern and however intrinsically important, are overshadowed by the awesome issues which confront the world.

...

CHIEF JUSTICE VINSON, with whom JUSTICE REED and JUSTICE MINTON join, dissenting.

...

In passing upon the question of Presidential powers in this case, we must first consider the context in which those powers were exercised.

Those who suggest that this is a case involving extraordinary powers should be mindful that these are extraordinary times. A world not yet recovered from the devastation of World War II has been forced to face the threat of another and more terrifying global conflict.

Accepting in full measure its responsibility in the world community, the United States was instrumental in securing adoption of the United Nations Charter, approved by the Senate by a vote of 89 to 2. The first purpose of the United Nations is to "maintain international peace and security, and to that end: to take effective collective measures for the prevention and removal of threats to the peace, and for the suppression of acts of aggression or other breaches of the peace,..." In 1950, when the United Nations called upon member nations "to render every assistance" to repel aggression in Korea, the United States furnished its vigorous support. For almost two full years, our armed forces have been fighting in Korea, suffering casualties of over 108,000 men. Hostilities have not abated. The "determination of the United Nations to continue its action in Korea to meet the aggression" has been reaffirmed. Congressional support of the action in Korea has been manifested by provisions for increased military manpower and equipment and for economic stabilization....

...The need for mutual security is shown by the very size of the armed forces outside the free world. Defendant's brief informs us that the Soviet Union maintains the largest air force in the world and maintains ground forces much larger than those presently available to the United States and the countries joined with us in mutual security arrangements. Constant international tensions are cited to demonstrate how precarious is the peace.

Even this brief review of our responsibilities in the world community discloses the enormity of our undertaking. Success of these measures may, as has often been observed, dramatically influence the lives of many generations of the world's peoples yet unborn. Alert to our responsibilities, which coincide with our own self preservation through mutual security, Congress has enacted a large body of implementing legislation....

...

Congress recognized the impact of these defense programs upon the economy. Following the attack in Korea, the President asked for authority to requisition property and to allocate and fix priorities for scarce goods. In the Defense Production Act of 1950, Congress granted the powers requested and, in addition, granted power to stabilize prices and wages and to provide for settlement of labor disputes arising in the defense program.... [A Senate] Committee emphasized that the shortage of steel, even with the mills operating at full capacity, coupled with increased civilian purchasing power, presented grave danger of disastrous inflation.

The President has the duty to execute the foregoing legislative programs. Their successful execution depends upon continued production of steel and stabilized prices for steel. Accordingly, when...a strike shutting down the entire basic steel industry was threatened, the President acted to avert a complete shutdown of steel production....

Twelve days passed [after the initial executive order] without action by Congress. On April 21, 1952, the President sent a letter to the President of the Senate in which he again described the purpose and need for his action and again stated his position that "The Congress can, if it wishes, reject the course of action I have followed in this matter." Congress has not so acted to this date.

...

One is not here called upon even to consider the possibility of executive seizure of a farm, a corner grocery store or even a single industrial plant. Such considerations arise only when one ignores the central fact of this case—that the Nation's entire basic steel production would have shut down completely if there had been no Government seizure. Even ignoring for the moment whatever confidential information the President may possess as "the Nation's organ for foreign affairs," the uncontroverted affidavits in this record amply support the finding that "a work stoppage would immediately jeopardize and imperil our national defense."

. . .

This comprehensive grant of the executive power [in Article II] to a single person was bestowed soon after the country had thrown the yoke of monarchy. Only by instilling initiative and vigor in all of the three departments of Government, declared Madison, could tyranny in any form be avoided. Hamilton added: "Energy in the Executive is a leading character in the definition of good government."...It is thus apparent that the Presidency was deliberately fashioned as an office of power and independence. Of course, the Framers created no autocrat capable of arrogating any power unto himself at any time. But neither did they create an automaton impotent to exercise the powers of Government at a time when the survival of the Republic itself may be at stake.

In passing upon the grave constitutional question presented in this case, we must never forget, as Chief Justice Marshall admonished, that the Constitution is "intended to endure for ages to come, and consequently, to be adapted to the various crises of human affairs," and that "(i)ts means are adequate to its ends." Cases do arise presenting questions which could not have been foreseen by the Framers. In such cases, the Constitution has been treated as a living document adaptable to new situations. But we are not called upon today to expand the Constitution to meet a new situation. For, in this case, we need only look to history and time-honored principles of constitutional law—principles that have been applied consistently by all branches of the Government throughout our history. It is those who assert the invalidity of the Executive Order who seek to amend the Constitution in this case.

. . .

A review of executive action demonstrates that our Presidents have on many occasions exhibited the leadership contemplated by the Framers when they made the President Commander in Chief, and imposed upon him the trust to "take Care that the Laws be faithfully executed." With or without explicit statutory authorization, Presidents have at such times dealt with national emergencies by acting promptly and resolutely to enforce legislative programs, at least to save those programs until Congress could act. Congress and the courts have responded to such executive initiative with consistent approval.

. . . .

In an action furnishing a most apt precedent for this case, President Lincoln without statutory authority directed the seizure of rail and telegraph lines leading to Washington. Many months later, Congress recognized and confirmed the power of the President to seize railroads and telegraph lines and provided criminal penalties for interference with Government operation. This Act did not confer on the President any additional powers of seizure. Congress plainly rejected the view that the President's acts had been without legal sanction until ratified by the legislature. Sponsors of the bill declared that its purpose was only to confirm the power which the President already possessed. Opponents insisted a statute authorizing seizure was unnecessary and might even be construed as limiting existing Presidential powers.

. . .

. . .

Some six months before Pearl Harbor, a dispute at a single aviation plant at Inglewood, California, interrupted a segment of the production of military aircraft. In spite of the comparative insignificance of this work stoppage to total defense production as contrasted with the complete paralysis now threatened by a shutdown of the entire basic steel industry, and even though our armed forces were not then engaged in combat, President Roosevelt ordered the seizure of the plant "pursuant to the powers vested in (him) by the Constitution and laws of the United States, as President of the United States of America and Commander in Chief of the Army and Navy of the United States." The Attorney General [Robert Jackson] vigorously proclaimed that the President had the moral duty to keep this Nation's defense effort a "going concern." His ringing moral justification was coupled with a legal justification equally well stated:

> The Presidential proclamation rests upon the aggregate of the Presidential powers derived from the Constitution itself and from statutes enacted by the Congress.
>
> The Constitution lays upon the President the duty "to take care that the laws be faithfully executed." Among the laws which he is required to find means to execute are those which direct him to equip an enlarged army, to provide for a strengthened navy, to protect Government property, to protect those who are engaged in carrying out the business of the Government....For the faithful execution of such laws the President has back of him not only each general law-enforcement power conferred by

the various acts of Congress but the aggregate of all such laws plus that wide discretion as to method vested in him by the Constitution for the purpose of executing the laws.

The Constitution also places on the President the responsibility and vests in him the powers of Commander in Chief of the Army and of the Navy. These weapons for the protection of the continued existence of the Nation are placed in his sole command and the implication is clear that he should not allow them to become paralyzed by failure to obtain supplies for which Congress has appropriated the money and which it has directed the President to obtain.

...

This is but a cursory summary of executive leadership. But it amply demonstrates that Presidents have taken prompt action to enforce the laws and protect the country whether or not Congress happened to provide in advance for the particular method of execution.... [T]he fact that Congress and the courts have consistently recognized and given their support to such executive action indicates that such a power of seizure has been accepted throughout our history.

History bears out the genius of the Founding Fathers, who created a Government subject to law but not left subject to inertia when vigor and initiative are required.

...

The absence of a specific statute authorizing seizure of the steel mills as a mode of executing the laws—both the military procurement program and the anti-inflation program—has not until today been thought to prevent the President from executing the laws. Unlike an administrative commission confined to the enforcement of the statute under which it was created, or the head to a department when administering a particular statute, the President is a constitutional officer charged with taking care that a "mass of legislation" be executed. Flexibility as to mode of execution to meet critical situations is a matter of practical necessity....

There is no statute prohibiting seizure as a method of enforcing legislative programs....

Whatever the extent of Presidential power on more tranquil occasions, and whatever the right of the President to execute legislative programs as he sees fit without reporting the mode of execution to Congress, the single Presidential purpose disclosed on this record is to faithfully execute the laws by acting in an emergency to maintain the status quo, thereby preventing collapse of the legislative programs until Congress could act. The President's action served the same purposes as a judicial stay entered to maintain the status quo in order to preserve the jurisdiction of a court.... [T]here is no evidence whatever of any Presidential purpose to defy Congress or act in any way inconsistent with the legislative will.

...The Framers knew, as we should know in these times of peril, that there is real danger in Executive weakness. There is no cause to fear Executive tyranny so long as the laws of Congress are being faithfully executed. Certainly there is no basis for fear of dictatorship when the Executive acts, as he did in this case, only to save the situation until Congress could act.

...

The diversity of views expressed in the six opinions of the majority, the lack of reference to authoritative precedent, the repeated reliance upon prior dissenting opinions, the complete disregard of the uncontroverted facts showing the gravity of the emergency and the temporary nature of the taking all serve to demonstrate how far afield one must go to affirm the order of the District Court.

The broad executive power granted by Article II to an officer on duty 365 days a year cannot, it is said, be invoked to avert disaster. Instead, the President must confine himself to sending a message to Congress recommending action. Under this messenger-boy concept of the Office, the President cannot even act to preserve legislative programs from destruction so that Congress will have something left to act upon. There is no judicial finding that the executive action was unwarranted because there was in fact no basis for the President's finding of the existence of an emergency; under this view, the gravity of the emergency and the immediacy of the threatened disaster are considered irrelevant as a matter of law.

...

As the District Judge stated, this is no time for "timorous" judicial action. But neither is this a time for timorous executive action. Faced with the duty of executing the defense programs which Congress had enacted and the disastrous effects that any stoppage in steel production would have on those programs, the President acted to preserve those programs by seizing the steel mills. There is no question that the possession was other than temporary in character and subject to congressional direction—either approving, disapproving or regulating the manner in which the mills were to be administered and returned to the owners. The President immediately informed Congress of his action and clearly stated his intention to abide by the legislative will. No basis for claims of arbitrary action, unlimited powers or dictatorial usurpation of congressional power appears from the facts of this case. On the contrary, judicial, legislative and executive precedents throughout our history demonstrate that in this case the President acted in full conformity with his duties under the Constitution. Accordingly, we would reverse the order of the District Court.

B. Appointment and Removal Powers

Both Democrats and Republicans were nervous about how much control the president should have over the executive branch at the start of the New Deal. There had been hard-fought battles in the late nineteenth century for the principle of a nonpartisan and professional civil service. The reality of a professional civil service was still being built in the early twentieth century, and the number of employees in the federal government was quite small. The New Deal brought a massive influx of new recruits into the government and a welter of new agencies. Many worried that the New Deal had created a political army under the command of the President, and that Roosevelt could use these new executive officials located all across the country to hurt his political enemies, whether they were Republicans or fellow Democrats. One response was the Hatch Act of 1939, which imposed new legal restrictions on the political activities of federal employees. Another was the Executive Reorganization Act of 1939, which allowed the president to create the Executive Office of the President to assist in policy development and management of the executive bureaucracy. A 1937 proposal for reorganizing the executive branch that would have gone further in increasing presidential influence and reducing congressional influence over executive agencies was defeated.

Independent regulatory commissions were one point of tension in the New Deal era. The commissions had been favored by the Progressive reformers in the late nineteenth and early twentieth centuries. Ideally, they were structured to be free of the everyday influence of political parties and the elected branches of government. The commissions had multiple members, who served lengthy staggered terms. The members often had special expertise in the subject matter being regulated by the commission, and often operated under rules limiting the partisanship of the commission. The commissions, such as the Interstate Commerce Commission and the Federal Trade Commission, both made regulatory policy and enforced it in individual cases.

When possible, Roosevelt preferred to create executive agencies inside Cabinet departments to manage new programs. Such agencies could be staffed with presidential appointees and supervised by other presidential appointees. When Congress insisted, new commissions were created such as the Securities and Exchange Commission or the Federal Communications Commission. Newly created commissions at least created an opportunity for President Roosevelt to dominate the process of appointing the commissioners. Old commissions, such as the Federal Trade Commission, posed more of a problem for the administration. Like the courts, they were still staffed by Republicans. The president was impatient for them to vacate their positions. He tried to force the issue by removing a Republican member of the Federal Trade Commission before his term was complete. In *Humphrey's Executor* (1935), the Supreme Court rebuffed the president, upholding the independence of the commissioners.

Humphrey's Executor v. United States, 295 U.S. 602 (1935)

The Federal Trade Commission (FTC), created in 1914, is one of many so-called independent regulatory commissions. Such commissions were designed to be insulated from partisan and legislative politics, and they were armed with broad policymaking authority. The goal was to allow disinterested experts to make and administer the policies that would most be in the national interest. The core mission of the FTC is to correct anticompetitive and fraudulent business practices. The FTC is composed of five commissioners. The commissioners are appointed by the president and confirmed by the Senate, and they serve staggered, seven-year terms. No more than three commissioners may be of the same political party. By statute, the commissioners may be removed from office by the president only for "inefficiency, neglect of duty, or malfeasance in office."

William Humphrey was a commissioner appointed by President Herbert Hoover. His term was set to expire in

September 1938. When Franklin Roosevelt assumed the presidency in 1933 he asked for Humphrey's resignation on the grounds that the "aims and purposes of the Administration" would be better served if the members of the FTC were "personnel of my own choosing." Humphrey refused, and the President responded that "you are hereby removed from the office." Humphrey died a few months later, but his estate brought a suit against the government to collect his unpaid salary for the period between his "removal" by the president and his death. The suit was filed in the U.S. Court of Claims, which certified the constitutional questions to the U.S. Supreme Court for resolution before it proceeded with the rest of the case.

The administration pointed to Myers v. United States *(1926) as providing support for an unconstrained presidential removal power of executive officers. In* Myers, *the Supreme Court had held that the President could remove a postmaster without having to get the consent of the Senate. The administration argued that independent commissioners were no different than postmasters, and their fixed term of office was no different than the requirement that the President go back to the Senate before making a removal. Any restriction on the presidential removal power was unconstitutional. If the President had the constitutional authority to remove Humphrey despite the statutory terms of his office, then the removal would have been legal and the government would owe nothing to his estate.*

The Supreme Court unanimously decided in favor of Humphrey's estate, upholding the terms of the Federal Trade Commission Act and restricting the removal power of the president. This decision marked a serious blow to the President's efforts to gain immediate control over the powerful independent regulatory commissions and furthered Roosevelt's resolve to move against the Court at some point. Would the Myers *Court have decided this case differently? Notice that* Humphrey's Executor *may have been an easier case for the progressives on the federal bench than for the conservatives. Justice Brandeis had long been a champion of independent regulatory agencies. Should the decision have been as easy for the conservatives on the federal bench? What constitutional theories can be used to make a place for independent regulatory agencies in the constitutional scheme?*

JUSTICE SUTHERLAND delivered the opinion of the court.

...

The commission is to be nonpartisan; and it must, from the very nature of its duties, act with entire impartiality. It is charged with the enforcement of no policy except the policy of the law. Its duties are neither political nor executive, but predominantly *quasi*-judicial and *quasi*-legislative. Like the Interstate Commerce Commission, its members are called upon to exercise the trained judgment of a body of experts "appointed by law and informed by experience."...

The legislative reports in both houses of Congress clearly reflect the view that a fixed term was necessary to the effective and fair administration of the law....

...

The debates in both houses demonstrate that the prevailing view was that the Commission was not to be "subject to anybody in the government but...only to the people of the United States"; free from "political domination or control" or the "probability or possibility of such a thing"; to be "separate and apart from any existing department of the government—not subject to the orders of the President."

...

...To support its contention that the removal provision...is an unconstitutional interference with the executive power of the President, the government's chief reliance is *Myers v. United States* (1926)....[T]he narrow point actually decided [in *Myers*] was only that the President had power to remove a postmaster of the first class, without the advice and consent of the Senate as required by act of Congress. In the course of the opinion of the court, expressions occur which tend to sustain the government's contention, but these are beyond the point involved and, therefore, do not come within the rule of stare decisis. In so far as they are out of harmony with the views here set forth, these expressions are disapproved....

The office of a postmaster is so essentially unlike the office now involved that the decision in the *Myers* Case cannot be accepted as controlling our decision here. A postmaster is an executive officer restricted to the performance of executive functions. He is charged with no duty at all related to either the legislative or judicial power. The actual decision in the *Myers* Case finds support in the theory that such an officer is merely one of the units in the executive department and, hence, inherently subject to the exclusive and illimitable power of removal by the Chief Executive, whose subordinate and aid he is....

The Federal Trade Commission is an administrative body created by Congress to carry into effect legislative policies embodied in the statute in accordance with the legislative standard therein prescribed, and to perform other specified duties as a legislative or as a judicial aid. Such a body cannot in any proper sense be characterized as an arm or an eye of the executive. Its duties are performed without executive leave and, in the contemplation of the statute, must be free from executive control. In administering the provisions of the statute in respect of "unfair methods of competition," that is to say, in filling in and administering the details embodied by that general standard, the commission acts in part *quasi*-legislatively and in part *quasi*-judicially.... To the extent that it exercises any executive function, as distinguished from executive power in the constitutional sense, it does so in the discharge and effectuation of its *quasi*-legislative or *quasi*-judicial powers, or as an agency of the legislative or judicial departments of the government.

...

The fundamental necessity of maintaining each of the three general departments of government entirely free from the control or coercive influence, direct or indirect, of either of the others, has often been stressed and is hardly open to serious question. So much is implied in the very fact of the separation of the powers of these departments by the Constitution; and in the rule which recognizes their essential coequality. The sound application of a principle that makes one master in his own house precludes him from imposing his control in the house of another who is master there....

The power of removal here claimed for the President falls within this principle, since its coercive influence threatens the independence of a commission, which is not only wholly disconnected from the executive department, but which, as already fully appears, was created by Congress as a means of carrying into operation legislative and judicial powers, and as an agency of the legislative and judicial departments.

...

In *Marbury v. Madison* (1803)...it is made clear that Chief Justice Marshall was of opinion that a justice of the peace for the District of Columbia was not removable at the will of the President; and that there was a distinction between such an officer and officers appointed to aid the President in the performance of his constitutional duties. In the latter case, the distinction he saw was that "their acts are his acts" and his will, therefore, controls....

The result of what we now have said is this: Whether the power of the President to remove an officer shall prevail over the authority of Congress to condition the power by fixing a definite term and precluding a removal except for cause will depend upon the character of the office; the *Myers* decision, affirming the power of the President alone to make the removal, is confined to purely executive officers; and as to officers of the kind here under consideration, we hold that no removal can be made during the prescribed term for which the officer is appointed, except for one or more of the causes named in the applicable statute. To the extent that, between the decision in the *Myers* case, which sustains the unrestrictable power of the President to remove purely executive officers, and our present decision that such power does not extend to an office such as that here involved, there shall remain a field of doubt, we leave such cases as may fall within it for future consideration and determination as they may arise.

C. Nondelegation of Legislative Powers

The extent to which Congress could delegate power to the executive branch provoked the first clash between President Roosevelt and the Hughes Court. In the wake of the Great Depression, Congress vested administrative agencies with extensive power to regulate various forms of economic life that had often been regulated solely by states, if regulated at all. Congress rarely provided administrators with much detailed guidance. More commonly, federal statutes mandated only that administrative agencies, often with the cooperation of the regulated industries, develop codes of competition that were fair. The National Industrial Recovery Act was typical of these measures. Section 3 of the NIRA declared:

> (u)pon the application to the President by one or more trade or industrial associations or groups, the President may approve a code or codes of fair competition for the trade or industry or subdivision thereof, represented by the applicant or applicants, if the President finds...that such code or codes are not designed to promote monopolies or to eliminate or oppress small enterprises and will not operate to discriminate against them, and will tend to effectuate the policy of this title:...
>
> After the President shall have approved any such code, the provisions of such code shall be the standards of fair competition for such trade or industry or subdivision thereof. Any violation of such standards in any transaction in or affecting interstate

or foreign commerce shall be deemed an unfair method of competition in commerce.

Not surprisingly, the lawyers who attacked these laws began by proclaiming "Congress has set up no intelligible policies to govern the President, no standards to guide and restrict his action, and no procedure for making determinations in conformity with due process of law." In doing so, they appealed to the standards for the nondelegation doctrine that the Supreme Court had established in cases such as *Field v. Clark* (1892) and *J. W. Hampton & Co. v. United States* (1928). These cases emphasized that Congress could not delegate legislative power to the executive branch, but Congress could allow the executive to exercise discretion in implementing policy as long as there were intelligible policies to guide and limit the executive.

These attacks on legislative delegations were initially successful in *Panama Refining Co. v. Ryan* (1935) and *Schechter Poultry v. United States* (1935). After 1937, the Supreme Court largely abandoned any effort to police apparently cooperative arrangements between the legislative and executive branches of the national government. If Congress was to control the details of domestic policymaking, Congress would have to take the initiative to do so. In key cases like *Yakus v. United States* (1944), the New Deal Court adopted a loose standard for evaluating the delegation of lawmaking authority to the executive branch on domestic policy. Meanwhile, in the foreign policy realm, the Supreme Court indicated a greater scope for executive action in cases such as *Curtiss-Wright Export* (1936) even before it loosened the reins in the domestic realm. Such cases effectively put an end to constitutional challenges to federal statutes based on the nondelegation doctrine.

Schechter Poultry Corp. v. United States, 295 U.S. 495 (1935)

In Schechter Poulty Corp. *the Supreme Court declared unconstitutional both the delegation of congressional power and, as noted in the section on national powers, the congressional effort to regulate local butchers under the interstate commerce clause. This defeat effectively killed the National Industrial Recovery Act as an effective administrative tool. The following excerpt focuses on that part of the opinion discussing the issue of the delegation of legislative power. As in* Panama Refining, *Chief Justice Hughes wrote the majority opinion for the Court. Justice Cardozo became more critical of the NIRA. Cardozo had written the lone dissent in* Panama Refining, *but in* Schechter *he wrote a concurring opinion agreeing with Hughes that the NIRA violated the separation of powers.*

CHIEF JUSTICE HUGHES delivered the opinion of the Court.

[Regarding the delegation of legislative power, the] Constitution provides that "All legislative powers herein granted shall be vested in a Congress of the United States, which shall consist of a Senate and House of Representatives." Art I, § 1. And the Congress is authorized "To make all laws which shall be necessary and proper for carrying into execution" its general powers. Art. I, § 8, par. 18. The Congress is not permitted to abdicate or to transfer to others the essential legislative functions with which it is thus vested. We have repeatedly recognized the necessity of adapting legislation to complex conditions involving a host of details with which the national legislature cannot deal directly.... [T]he Constitution has never been regarded as denying to Congress the necessary resources of flexibility and practicality, which will enable it to perform its function in laying down policies and establishing standards, while leaving to selected instrumentalities the making of subordinate rules within prescribed limits and the determination of facts to which the policy as declared by the legislature is to apply. But... the constant recognition of the necessity and validity of such provisions, and the wide range of administrative authority which has been developed by means of them, cannot be allowed to obscure the limitations of the authority to delegate, if our constitutional system is to be maintained....

...

What is meant by "fair competition" as the term is used in the Act? Does it refer to a category established in the law, and is the authority to make codes limited accordingly? Or is it used as a convenient designation for whatever set of laws the formulators of a code for a particular trade or industry may propose and the President may approve (subject to certain restrictions), or the President may himself prescribe, as being wise and beneficent provisions for the government of the trade or industry in order to accomplish the broad purposes of rehabilitation, correction and expansion which are stated in the first section of Title I?

The Act does not define "fair competition." ... Unfairness in competition has been predicated of acts which lie outside the ordinary course of business and are tainted by fraud, or coercion, or conduct otherwise prohibited by law. But it is evidence that in its widest range, "unfair competition," as it has been understood in the law, does not reach the objectives of the codes which are authorized by the National Industrial Recovery Act. The codes may, indeed, cover conduct which existing law condemns, but they are not limited to conduct of that sort....

...

The Government urges that the codes will "consist of rules of competition deemed fair for each industry by representative members of that industry—by the persons most vitally concerned and most familiar with its problems." Instances are cited in which Congress has availed itself of such assistance; as *e.g.*, in the exercise of its authority over the public domain, with respect to the recognition of local customs or rules of miners as to mining claims, or, in matters of a more or less technical nature, as in designating the standard height of drawbars. But would it be seriously contended that Congress could delegate its legislative authority to trade or industrial associations or groups so as to empower them to enact the laws they deem to be wise and beneficent for the rehabilitation and expansion of their trade or industries? Could trade or industrial associations or groups be constituted legislative bodies for that purpose because such associations or groups are familiar with the problems of their enterprises? And, could an effort of that sort be made valid by such a preface of generalities as to permissible aims as we find in section 1 of title I? The answer is obvious. Such a delegation of legislative power is unknown to our law and is utterly inconsistent with the constitutional prerogatives and duties of Congress.

...Congress cannot delegate legislative power to the President to exercise an unfettered discretion to make whatever laws he thinks may be needed or advisable for the rehabilitation and expansion of trade or industry....

...

Such a sweeping delegation of legislative power finds no support in the decisions upon which the Government especially relies. By the Interstate Commerce Act, Congress has itself provided a code of laws regulating the activities of the common carriers subject to the Act, in order to assure the performance of their services upon just and reasonable terms, with adequate facilities and without unjust discrimination. Congress from time to time has elaborated its requirements, as needs have been disclosed. To facilitate the application of the standards prescribed by the Act, Congress has provided an expert body. That administrative agency, in dealing with particular cases, is required to act upon notice and hearing, and its orders must be supported by findings of fact which in turn are sustained by evidence.... When the Commission is authorized to issue, for the construction, extension or abandonment of lines, a certificate of "public convenience and necessity," or to permit the acquisition by one carrier of the control of another, if that is found to be "in the public interest," we have pointed out that these provisions are not left without standards to guide determination. The authority conferred has direct relation to the standards prescribed for the service of common carriers and can be exercised only upon findings, based upon evidence, with respect to particular conditions of transportation....

...

To summarize and conclude upon this point: Section 3 of the Recovery Act is without precedent. It supplies no standards for any trade, industry or activity. It does not undertake to prescribe rules of conduct to be applied to particular states of fact determined by appropriate administrative procedure. Instead of prescribing rules of conduct, it authorizes the making of codes to prescribe them. For that legislative undertaking, § 3 sets up no standards, aside from the statement of the general aims of rehabilitation, correction and expansion described in section one. In view of the scope of that broad declaration, and of the nature of the few restrictions that are imposed, the discretion of the President in approving or prescribing codes, and thus enacting laws for the government of trade and industry throughout the country, is virtually unfettered. We think that the code-making authority thus conferred is an unconstitutional delegation of legislative power.

JUSTICE CARDOZO, concurring.

...Here, in the case before us, is an attempted delegation not confined to any single act nor to any class or group of acts identified or described by reference to a standard. Here in effect is a roving commission to inquire into evils and upon discovery correct them.

I have said that there is no standard, definite or even approximate, to which legislation must conform. Let me make my meaning more precise. If codes of fair competition are codes eliminating "unfair" methods of competition ascertained upon inquiry to prevail in one industry or another, there is no unlawful delegation of legislative functions when the President is directed to inquire into such practices and denounce them when discovered. For many years a like power has been committed to the Federal Trade Commission with the approval of this court in a long series of decisions.... The industries of the country are too many and diverse to make it possible for Congress, in respect of matters such as these, to legislate directly with adequate appreciation of varying conditions. Nor is the substance of the power changed because the President may act at the instance of trade or industrial associations having special knowledge of the facts.... When the task that is set before one is that of cleaning house, it is prudent as well as usual to take counsel of the dwellers.

But there is another conception of codes of fair competition, their significance and function, which leads to very different consequences, though it is one that is struggling now for recognition and acceptance. By this other conception a code is not to be restricted to the elimination of business practices that would be characterized by general acceptation as oppressive or unfair. It is to include whatever ordinances may be desirable or helpful for the well-being or prosperity of the industry affected. In that view, the function of its adoption is not merely negative, but positive; the planning of improvements as well as the extirpation of abuses. What is fair, as thus conceived, is not something to be contrasted with what is unfair or fraudulent or tricky. The extension becomes as wide as the field of industrial regulation. If that conception shall prevail, anything that Congress may do within the limits of the commerce clause for the betterment of business may be done by the President upon the recommendation of a trade association by calling it a code. This is delegation running riot. No such plenitude of power is susceptible of transfer. The statute, however, aims at nothing less, as one can learn both from its terms and from the administrative practice under it. Nothing less is aimed at by the code now submitted to our scrutiny.

The code does not confine itself to the suppression of methods of competition that would be classified as unfair according to accepted business standards or accepted norms of ethics. It sets up a comprehensive body of rules to promote the welfare of the industry, if not the welfare of the nation, without reference to standards, ethical or commercial, that could be known or predicted in advance of its adoption....

...

United States v. Curtiss-Wright Export Corporation, 299 U.S. 304 (1936)

The delegation of power over foreign affairs to the president was less controversial during the early New Deal than the delegation of power over domestic policy. Many nineteenth-century conservatives worried that an increased American presence in international affairs would unconstitutionally increase national powers and aggrandize the executive branch. In contrast, many twentieth-century conservatives insisted on a sharp difference between constitutional authority in domestic and foreign affairs. During World War I, the conservative Republican Senator George Sutherland wrote an important book detailing why the federal government and the President had more authority in foreign policy than in domestic policy.[39] *He was soon given an opportunity to write those views into constitutional law when he was appointed to the U.S. Supreme Court in 1922. Sutherland's opinion in the* Curtiss-Wright *case became the source of the "sole organ" doctrine, that the president was the "sole organ of the federal government in the field of international relations." Proponents of presidential power have subsequently cited Sutherland's argument as a reason to oppose any significant congressional intervention in foreign policy. Sutherland likewise emphasized in* United States v. Belmont *(1933) the unilateral power of the president to make international executive agreements that could trump state law.*

Curtiss-Wright *began with a 1934 congressional resolution authorizing the president, at his discretion, to prohibit or regulate arms sales to Bolivia and Paraguay, which were engaged in a border war. President Roosevelt immediately issued a proclamation barring the arms sales. The president revoked the order in November 1935. Curtiss-Wright Export Companies and others were indicted in federal district court for violating the arms embargo during the several months that it was in effect. They challenged the indictment on several grounds, including the constitutional objection that Congress had delegated excessive lawmaking authority to the president. The district court agreed, leading the government to appeal to Supreme Court.*

39. George Sutherland, *Constitutional Power and World Affairs* (New York: Columbia University Press, 1919).

The Supreme Court quickly disposed of those constitutional objections. Justice McReynolds aside, no other justice had difficulty with legislation granting the president broad discretion in foreign affairs. As you read this opinion, ask yourself whether Justice Sutherland makes a convincing distinction between constitutional authority over domestic affairs and constitutional authority over foreign affairs.

JUSTICE SUTHERLAND delivered the opinion of the Court.

...

Whether, if the Joint Resolution had related solely to internal affairs, it would be open to the challenge that it constituted an unlawful delegation of legislative power to the Executive, we find it unnecessary to determine. The whole aim of the resolution is to affect a situation entirely external to the United States, and falling within the category of foreign affairs. The determination which we are called to make, therefore, is whether the Joint Resolution, as applied to that situation, is vulnerable to attack under the rule that forbids a delegation of the lawmaking power. In other words, assuming (but not deciding) that the challenged delegation, if it were confined to internal affairs, would be invalid, may it nevertheless be sustained on the ground that its exclusive aim is to afford a remedy for a hurtful condition within foreign territory?

...

The two classes of powers are different, both in respect of their origin and their nature. The broad statement that the federal government can exercise no powers except those specifically enumerated in the Constitution, and such implied powers as are necessary and proper to carry into effect the enumerated powers, is categorically true only in respect of our internal affairs. In that field, the primary purpose of the Constitution was to carve from the general mass of legislative powers then possessed by the states such portions as it was thought desirable to vest in the federal government, leaving those not included in the enumeration still in the states.... That this doctrine applies only to powers which the states had is self-evident. And since the states severally never possessed international powers, such powers could not have been carved from the mass of state powers but obviously were transmitted to the United States from some other source....

...

Not only... is the federal power over external affairs in origin and essential character different from that over internal affairs, but participation in the exercise of the power is significantly limited. In this vast external realm, with its important, complicated, delicate and manifold problems, the President alone has the power to speak or listen as a representative of the nation. He makes treaties with the advice and consent of the Senate; but he alone negotiates. Into the field of negotiation the Senate cannot intrude; and Congress itself is powerless to invade it. As Marshall said in his great argument of March 7, 1800, in the House of Representatives, "The President is the sole organ of the nation in its external relations, and its sole representative with foreign nations." *Annals*, 6th Cong...

It is important to bear in mind that we are here dealing not alone with an authority vested in the President by an exertion of legislative power, but with such an authority plus the very delicate, plenary and exclusive power of the President as the sole organ of the federal government in the field of international relations—a power which does not require as a basis for its exercise an act of Congress, but which, of course, like every other governmental power, must be exercised in subordination to the applicable provisions of the Constitution. It is quite apparent that if, in the maintenance of our international relations, embarrassment—perhaps serious embarrassment—is to be avoided and success for our aims achieved, congressional legislation which is to be made effective through negotiation and inquiry within the international field must often accord to the President a degree of discretion and freedom from statutory restriction which would not be admissible were domestic affairs alone involved. Moreover, he, not Congress, has the better opportunity of knowing the conditions which prevail in foreign countries, and especially is this true in time of war. He has his confidential sources of information. He has his agents in the form of diplomatic, consular and other officials. Secrecy in respect of information gathered by them may be highly necessary, and the premature disclosure of it productive of harmful results....

In the light of the foregoing observations, it is evident that this court should not be in haste to apply a general rule which will have the effect of condemning legislation like that under review as constituting an unlawful delegation of legislative power. The principles which justify such legislation find overwhelming support in the unbroken legislative practice which has prevailed almost from the inception of the national government to the present day.

...

The result of holding that the joint resolution here under attack is void and unenforceable as constituting an unlawful delegation of legislative power would be to stamp [a] multitude of comparable acts and resolutions as likewise invalid. And while this court may not, and should not, hesitate to declare acts of Congress, however many times repeated, to be unconstitutional if beyond all rational doubt it finds them to be so, an impressive array of legislation..., enacted by nearly every Congress from the beginning of our national existence to the present day, must be given unusual weight in the process of reaching a correct determination of the problem. A legislative practice such as we have here, evidenced not by only occasional instances, but marked by the movement of a steady stream for a century and a half of time, goes a long way in the direction of proving the presence of unassailable ground for the constitutionality of the practice, to be found in the origin and history of the power involved, or in its nature, or in both combined.

...

Reversed

JUSTICE McREYNOLDS does not agree. He is of opinion that the court below reached the right conclusion and its judgment ought to be affirmed.

JUSTICE STONE took no part in the decision of this case.

D. Executive Privilege

Executive privilege is the president's claim of a constitutional authority to withhold information from the legislative or judicial branch. The term itself likely dates from the postwar era, but the concept has roots dating back to before the American founding. As the Second World War transitioned into the Cold War, the United States expanded its national security apparatus. Increasing amounts of material were designated as classified and kept off the public record. In the 1940s and 1950s, Justice Department lawyers began to argue that the President and cabinet heads had "an uncontrolled discretion to withhold the information and papers in the public interest."[40] They added the principle that communications among executive branch officials must be privileged so that the President would ultimately receive "candid" advice without fear of future disclosure.

The Truman and Eisenhower administrations repeatedly refused to provide documents and information to Congress. Much of this effort was directed at protecting the executive branch from McCarthy investigations, but the claim of executive privilege was applied against a wide range of congressional and judicial inquiries and continued to be used long after the fall of Senator Joseph McCarthy.[41]

William P. Rogers, Senate Testimony on Executive Privilege (1958)[42]

Congressional investigations, led by the House Un-American Activities Committee and the Senate Internal Security Subcommittee, of the executive branch intensified during the Truman and Eisenhower administrations. By the end of the Eisenhower administration, the search for Communist influence within the ranks of the executive branch had largely ended, but the administration had additional concerns with congressional challenges to military and foreign policy conducted by the executive branch.

One of the points of tension between the two branches was over access to executive documents and the number of documents kept classified by the executive branch. When a bill was introduced in the Senate to require the executive branch to routinely make public a wide variety of internal rules, orders, and opinions, Attorney General William Rogers came to the Senate. His extended testimony explained the rationale for and constitutional basis of executive privilege, an argument that he also publicized in speeches before a variety of public audiences. Rogers provided to the Senate a hundred-page study prepared by a Justice Department lawyer during the Truman administration on the history of the executive privilege. It argued that "the President has the last word on the propriety of withholding the papers," though

40. Herman Wolkinson, "Demands of Congressional Committees for Executive Papers," *Federal Bar Journal* 10 (1949):103.

41. On executive privilege, see Louis Fisher, *The Politics of Executive Privilege* (Durham: Carolina Academic Press, 2004); Raoul Berger, *Executive Privilege* (Cambridge: Harvard University Press, 1974); Mark J. Rozell, *Executive Privilege* (Lawrence: University Press of Kansas, 2010).

42. Excerpt taken from *Freedom of Information and Secrecy in Government: Hearings before the Subcommittee on Constitutional Rights of the Committee on the Judiciary*, U.S. Senate, 85th Cong., 2nd sess. (March 6, 1858), 3–48.

"Well, We Certainly Botched This Job. What'll We Stamp It—'Secret' Or 'Top Secret'?"

Illustration 8-4 "Well, We Certainly Botched This Job. What'll We Stamp It—'Secret' or 'Top Secret'?"
Source: Herblock, *Washington Post*, March 13, 1957. Copyright by The Herb Block Foundation

executive-branch documents have sometimes been furnished to Congress "in a spirit of comity and good will."[43]

...

With reference to the right of the public to know generally as distinguished from the legislative branch, it seems to me that there are four principles which it is well to keep in mind:

1. While the people are entitled to fullest disclosure possible, this right like freedom of speech or press, is not absolute or without limitations. Disclosure must always be consistent with national security and the public interest.
2. In recognizing a right to withhold information, the approach must be not how much can legitimately be withheld, but rather little must necessarily be withheld. We injure no one but ourselves if we do not make thoughtful judgments in the classification process.
3. A determination that certain information should be withheld must be premised upon valid reasons and disclosure should promptly be made when it appears that the factors justifying nondisclosures no longer pertain.
4. Nondisclosure can never be justified as a means of covering mistakes, avoiding embarrassment, or for political, personal, or pecuniary reasons.

All persons agree that information which would adversely affect our national security should not be disclosed. Then too, there are compelling reasons for nondisclosure in the field of foreign affairs, in the area of pending litigation and investigations which may lead to litigation, information made confidential by statute, investigative files, and reports, and, finally, information relating to internal government affairs....

...

...[U]nder the Continental Congress, the Department of Foreign Affairs and its Secretary were almost completely subject to the directions of the Continental Congress. Every member of the Continental Congress was entitled to see anything in the records of the Department of Foreign Affairs, including secret matters. Indeed, he could make a copy of everything, except secret matters.

...

Suffice it to say that it came increasingly to be recognized by the leaders of our country then that the design of that pilot plant had grave and serious defects which made it incapable of serving adequately as the engine of the National Government....

Finally, at the Constitutional Convention in Philadelphia in 1787 that prototypes [*sic*] was redesigned as the engine of government which is still operating today. As we all know, it was designed on the principle that our Federal Government is divided into three equal departments or branches, a political innovation not included in the older Articles of Confederation.

Now let us see what action the opening session of the first Congress of the United States took when it came to create the Department of Foreign Affairs under the Constitution.... Here is no language which makes the books and records of the Department... virtually the books and records of Congress; here is no language which requires the Secretary of this Department shall submit his correspondence to Congress before transmittal. The difference is obvious and fundamental. Under the Constitution the first Congress was creating a Foreign Affairs Department of the Executive branch, pursuant to the grand design of the new Constitution based on the political principle of separation of powers.

... In light of their knowledge of the earlier practice, it can only be concluded that they deliberately recognized that the continuance of the former privilege was incompatible with the grand design of the Constitution for the separation of powers between the three branches.

...

The executive branch should not withhold information unless there are sound reasons for it, for national security or the other reasons I cite. I think it is inherent in the constitutional system that Congress should have available for legislative purposes just as much information as they can get and it is proper to give them, as long as it does not impair the functioning of another branch of the Government.

The fact that we have three coordinate branches of the Government requires an understanding and a cooperative spirit in order to work, and it has worked through the years.

As I say, I think the constant repetition that I see occasionally about secrecy, and all is harmful to the Government. I don't think that that is much of a problem.

43. Ibid., 76.

On the contrary, I think we have, in competing with the Russians, we have some decided disadvantages in that it is difficult to keep any information secret even for a short period of time.

...

Sen. HENNINGS: Do you think, General, the President can delegate to others his power to withhold information from Congress?...

Mr. ROGERS: I think he can delegate it to anybody in the executive branch. I think the leading case is *Marbury v. Madison* (1803), and in that case the Court held he can delegate the power to anybody to act on his behalf, at his direction. As a practical matter, it usually works out the head of the department has to make the final decision if there is a controversy.

...[T]he privilege stems from the constitutional power in the President as the Chief Executive.

Suggested Readings

Ackerman, Bruce A. *We the People*, vol. 2: *Transformations* (Cambridge: Harvard University Press, 1998).

Cushman, Barry. *Rethinking the New Deal Court: The Structure of a Constitutional Revolution* (New York: Oxford University Press, 1998).

Fisher, Louis. *Presidential Conflicts between Congress and the President*, 3rd ed. (Lawrence: University Press of Kansas, 1991).

Fisher, Louis. *Presidential War Powers*, 2nd ed. (Lawrence: University Press of Kansas, 2004).

Gillman, Howard. *The Constitution Besieged: The Rise and Demise of Lochner Era Police Power Jurisprudence* (Durham, NC: Duke University Press, 1993).

Irons, Peter H. *The New Deal Lawyers* (Princeton: Princeton University Press, 1982).

Keck, Thomas M. *The Most Activist Supreme Court in History: The Road to Modern Judicial Conservatism* (Chicago: University of Chicago Press, 2004).

Klarman, Michael J. *From Jim Crow to Civil Rights: The Supreme Court and the Struggle for Civil Rights* (New York: Oxford University Press, 2004).

Leuchtenberg, William E. *The Supreme Court Reborn: Constitutional Revolution in the Age of Roosevelt* (New York: Oxford University Press, 1995).

McMahon, Kevin J. *Reconsidering Roosevelt on Race: How the Presidency Paved the Road to Brown* (Chicago: University of Chicago Press, 2004).

Murphy, Walter F. *Congress and the Court: A Case Study in the American Political Process* (Chicago: University of Chicago Press, 1962).

Powe, Lucas A. *The Warren Court and American Politics* (Cambridge: Harvard University Press, 2000).

Silverstein, Gordon. *Imbalance of Powers: Constitutional Interpretation and the Making of American Foreign Policy* (New York: Oxford University Press, 1997).

Sundquist, James L. *Decline and Resurgence of Congress* (Washington, DC: Brookings Institution, 1981).

Tushnet, Mark V., ed. *The Warren Court in Historical and Political Perspective* (Charlottesville: University of Virginia Press, 1993).

Whittington, Keith E. *Constitutional Construction: Divided Powers and Constitutional Meaning* (Cambridge: Harvard University Press, 1999).

Whittington, Keith E. *Political Foundations of Judicial Supremacy: The President, the Supreme Court, and Constitutional Leadership in U.S. History* (Princeton: Princeton University Press, 2007).

Chapter 9

Liberalism Divided: 1969–1980

I. Introduction

The New Deal coalition was powerful but unstable. It wedded traditional Democratic constituencies in the white agricultural South with the ethnic, urban working-class of the North. Committed liberals provided much of the energy of the party and drove its agenda. Yet a substantial and powerful group of conservative Democrats imposed limits on what the party could do, especially on issues that affected race. Both major parties were made up of diverse coalitions. Liberals in the Democratic and Republican parties could often agree to advance reform policies. The "conservative coalition" made up of both Democrats and Republicans could often limit how far reforms could go. Despite Democratic majorities in Congress, governing in the postwar era often meant negotiating these diverse groups. Effective political leaders, such as House Speaker Sam Rayburn and Senate majority leader Lyndon Johnson, were best known for their bargaining skills.

The end of the 1960s marked the beginning of the end for the New Deal coalition, which had put Democrat presidents in office and maintained Democratic majorities in Congress. The political parties began the process of sorting themselves out into more ideologically homogeneous but polarized groups, with liberals moving into the Democratic Party and conservatives moving into the Republican Party. The civil rights movement and the Voting Rights Act disrupted the traditional Democratic Party in the South. While they brought new liberal black voters into the Democratic fold, many conservative white voters left. The Vietnam War and a variety of "social issues," including crime and abortion, shuffled allegiances that much more. Changing economic conditions affected voter calculations in the Sunbelt and elsewhere. As the sorting process unfolded, divisions within and between the parties were intensely felt.

As Figure 9-1 illustrates, voters in the South became far more willing to support the Republican Party. Since the formation of the Democratic Party during the Jacksonian Era, the "Solid South" had been an important part of the Democratic electoral and policy calculation. Over the course of the post–World War II period, voters in the South began to look like those in the rest of the nation, shaking the foundations of the Democratic coalition.[1]

Developments. The process was only beginning when Richard Nixon was elected to the presidency in 1968. Nixon came to power in a position of weakness. He was the first president since 1848 whose party did not control at least one chamber of Congress. On the one hand, he and Congress were entangled in persistent conflicts over how he was using presidential power right up until his resignation during the Watergate scandal. Yet Nixon and Congress also extended the legacy of the New Deal and Great Society. They reached agreement on major legislative initiatives, from the Occupational Safety and Health Act of 1970 to the Consumer Product Safety Act of 1972.

Constitutional debates in this period revolved around that legacy. Liberal disillusionment with Vietnam and unhappiness with the Johnson and Nixon administrations led to a reevaluation of presidential power. After decades of enhancing "presidential

1. Donald Green, Bradley Palmquist, and Eric Schickler, *Partisan Hearts and Minds* (New Haven, CT: Yale University Press, 2002); Edward G. Carmines and James A. Stimson, *Issue Evolution* (Princeton: Princeton University Press, 1989).

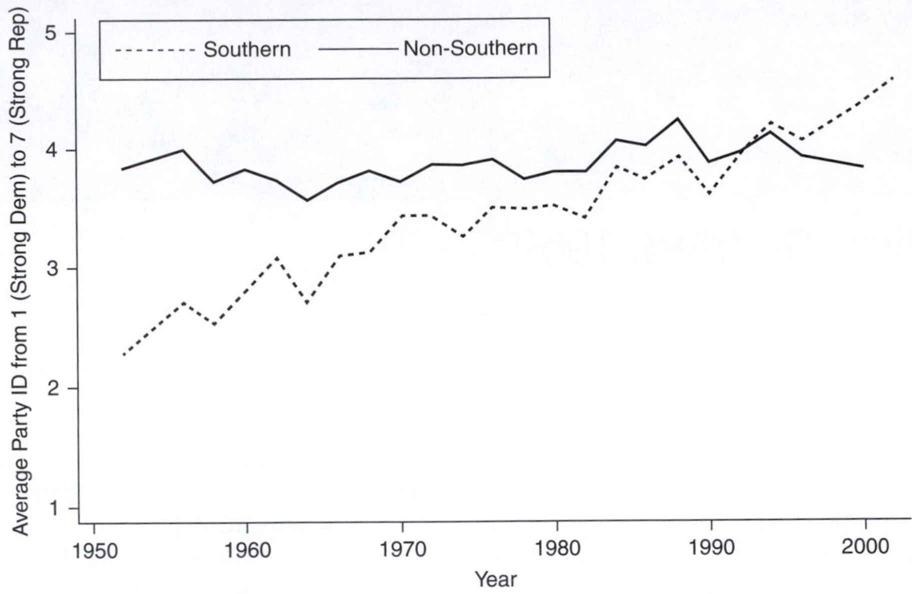

Figure 9-1 Partisan Identification of Southerners and Non-Southerners since 1950
Source: National Election Studies.

leadership," the "imperial presidency" became a new topic of concern. Barry Goldwater's presidential campaign in 1964 reignited debates over "big government" and helped put arguments about federalism and states' rights on the Republican political and legal agenda. Major Warren Court initiatives on crime and race stalled as judges and politicians wrestled over difficult details of implementation and remedies. As the Supreme Court turned its attention to new issues such as sexual liberty, it often found its traditional allies divided. The Court continued to inject itself into major constitutional and political debates, from Watergate to the death penalty to abortion. However, as with the political parties, the dynamics within the Court were becoming more fractured, and the justices' decisions often met with ongoing controversy.

Partisan Coalitions from 1969 to 1980. The Republicans decisively won the presidency in the midst of the Vietnam War in 1968, and Nixon cruised to reelection in 1972. GOP operatives talked hopefully of a new Republican majority that would leave the Democrats to wander in the political wilderness, suffering the same fate as the Republicans after the Great Depression. But Nixon's coattails were not long enough. Nixon won electoral votes in the South, but few Republicans were able to defeat incumbent congressmen there.

From 1968 to 1980, the Democrats had little difficulty retaining control of both houses of Congress. They regained the White House in the first opportunity after Watergate, in the 1976 elections, and had the benefit of unified government. The Democrats elected to Congress after Watergate were strongly liberal and reform-minded, but they found themselves confronting increasingly vocal conservative elements within the party. These internal divisions, combined with an uncertain presidential agenda, undermined the advantage of unified government during Jimmy Carter's single term of office. Instead, conflicts within and between the political parties and between the executive and the legislative branches characterized the period.

The Federal Judiciary from 1969 to 1980. Importantly, Democrats had no opportunity to appoint new members to the Supreme Court during this period, since there were no vacancies during Carter's term. By contrast, Nixon was able to make four appointments to the Court,

Table 9-1 Major Issues and Decisions of the Era of Liberalism Divided

Major Political Issues	Major Constitutional Issues	Major Court Decisions
Vietnam War	Judicial Review	*Powell v. McCormack* (1969)
Civil Rights	Presidential War Powers	*Oregon v. Mitchell* (1970)
Women's Movement	Executive Privilege	*United States v. United States District Court* (1972)
Watergate	Civil Rights	*United States v. Nixon* (1974)
Environmental Movement	Civil Liberties	*National League of Cities v. Usery* (1976)
Stagflation		
Iranian Hostage Crisis		

Note: A host of more detailed civil liberties and civil rights issues became the subject of controversy during this period, and these are explored in further in Volume 2 of this set.

and his successor Gerald Ford was able to make a fifth. Carter had to content himself with making appointments to an expanded lower federal court. As a result, despite the Democratic Party's control over Congress, the U.S. Supreme Court was transformed during this period into a more conservative institution, while the lower federal courts continued to be predominantly liberal.

In making his appointments Richard Nixon tried to score political points by looking either to the South or to Republican judges who were "tough on crime." He was able to make his first two appointments to the Supreme Court soon after his inauguration as president. First he replaced Chief Justice Earl Warren with Warren Burger, a conservative federal circuit court judge and a vocal critic of Supreme Court under Warren's leadership. After a couple of false starts (with the Senate defeating his more aggressively conservative initial choices) the president also managed to replace Justice Abe Fortas with circuit court judge Harry Blackmun. Whereas Fortas was one of the leading liberals on the Court, Blackmun had a reputation as a much more cautious figure.

Nixon next chose Virginia lawyer Lewis Powell to replace New Dealer Hugo Black, who had become a crucial swing vote on the Court. Arch-conservative Justice Department official William Rehnquist replaced the Eisenhower Republican John Marshall Harlan II. After Watergate, Gerald Ford chose a political moderate, John Paul Stevens, to replace the idiosyncratic New Dealer William O. Douglas.

These appointments fractured the newly formed Burger Court. While the Court had shifted decisively to the right, its majority was now in the hands of the Kennedy and Eisenhower moderates. Liberals like William Brennan and Thurgood Marshall could no longer call the shots the way they did on the Warren Court, and conservatives like William Rehnquist did not yet have the votes to make big changes in the law. That left Byron White, Potter Stewart, and Harry Blackmun as critical swing votes. The Court was still capable of issuing important liberal decisions, but justices frequently wrote multiple opinions and had difficulty forming clear majorities.[2]

Legacies. Many of the most prominent constitutional issues of the period revolved around separation of powers. Scholars, politicians, and judges had long supported a more powerful president. Many postwar liberals had wanted a president who could exercise decisive "leadership," respond to crises, and cut through conservative obstructions and compromises in Congress. By the Nixon administration, however, liberals began to worry about an "imperial presidency" that was becoming so powerful that it could

2. Andrew D. Martin, Kevin M. Quinn, and Lee Epstein, "The Median Justice on the United States Supreme Court," *North Carolina Law Review* 83 (2005): 1275; Keith E. Whittington, "The Burger Court: Once More in Transition," in *The Supreme Court of the United States*, ed. Christopher Tomlins (New York: Houghton Mifflin, 2005).

Box 9-1 A Partial Cast of Characters of the Era of Liberalism Divided

Warren Burger	■ Republican ■ Minnesota lawyer ■ Appointed by Dwight Eisenhower to the federal circuit court (1956–69) ■ Appointed by Richard Nixon to be chief justice of the United States (1969–86) ■ A public critic of the Warren Court while serving as a circuit court judge ■ Conservative on social issues and emphasized checks and balances on separation of powers issues, developed a reputation as a weak chief justice
J. William Fulbright	■ Democrat ■ Rhodes Scholar and lawyer from Arkansas ■ President of the University of Arkansas (1939–41) ■ U.S. Representative (1943–45) ■ U.S. Senator (1945–74), long-serving chair of the Senate Foreign Relations Committee ■ Critic of conservative anti-Communists, a sponsor of the Gulf of Tonkin Resolution, he became a leading critic of the Vietnam War and of presidential war powers ■ Defeated in the Democratic primary in 1974
F. Lewis Powell	■ Democrat ■ Virginia lawyer ■ Presided over desegregation of public schools as chair of Richmond school board (1952–61) ■ Facilitated the creation of the Legal Services Program as president of the American Bar Association (1964–65) but also encouraged more active efforts by business to build public and political support for the "free enterprise system" ■ Appointed by Richard Nixon to the Supreme Court (1972–87), where he became an important swing vote on the Burger Court and developed a reputation as a moderate
Byron White	■ Democrat ■ Rhodes Scholar and star professional football player from Colorado before World War II ■ Attended law school after serving in naval intelligence and clerked for Chief Justice Fred Vinson ■ Deputy attorney general (1961–62) ■ Appointed by John F. Kennedy to Supreme Court (1962–93) ■ Known as a pragmatic jurist and a swing vote on the Warren and Burger Courts

short-circuit important checks and balances in the constitutional system. The debate over presidential power reverberated long after the Nixon administration. Not only did Ford and Carter continue to grapple with legislative and administrative reforms in the wake of Vietnam and Watergate, but former Nixon administration officials such as Antonin Scalia and Richard Cheney carried forward their own concerns about the need to protect strong presidential authority. The scope of presidential war powers remained controversial as the United States continued to stand as a global superpower even while the Cold War consensus was collapsing.

Richard M. Nixon, Speech Accepting the Republican Presidential Nomination (1968)

In 1964 the Democrats seemed to have the Republican Party on the ropes. Lyndon Johnson defeated the conservative Republican nominee, Barry Goldwater, in a landslide and liberal Democrats made large gains in the House and the

Senate. Four years later the Democrats were in disarray and there was talk of an "emerging Republican majority." The Democrats held Congress in the 1968 elections, but Richard Nixon successfully launched a presidential bid that emphasized "law and order" and focused his attacks as much on the Warren Court as on the Johnson administration.

...

As we look at America, we see cities enveloped in smoke and flame. We hear sirens in the night. We see Americans dying on distant battlefields abroad. We see Americans hating each other; fighting each other; killing each other at home.

And as we see and hear these things, millions of Americans cry out in anguish;

Did we come all this way for this? Did American boys die in Normandy and Korea and in Valley Forge for this?

Listen to the answers to those questions.

It is another voice, it is a quiet voice in the tumult of the shouting. It is the voice of the great majority of Americans, the forgotten Americans, the non shouters, the non demonstrators. They're not racists or sick; they're not guilty of the crime that plagues the land; they are black, they are white; they're native born and foreign born; they're young and they're old.

...

They're good people. They're decent people; they work and they save and they pay their taxes and they care.

...

If we are to restore prestige and respect for America abroad, the place to begin is at home—in the United States of America.

My friends, we live in an age of revolution in America and in the world. And to find the answers to our problems, let us turn to a revolution...the American Revolution.

The American Revolution was and is dedicated to progress. But our founders recognized that the first requisite of progress is order.

...

And tonight it's time for some honest talk about the problem of order in the United States....

...

Let those who have the responsibility to enforce our laws, and our judges who have the responsibility to interpret them, be dedicated to the great principles of civil rights. But let them also recognize that the first civil right of every American is to be free from domestic violence. And that right must be guaranteed in this country.

...

Jimmy Carter, Inaugural Address (1977)[3]

Jimmy Carter was a dark-horse candidate in 1976. A little-known, post-civil-rights governor from Georgia, Carter offered himself as an outsider to both business-as-usual D.C. politics and to the national Democratic Party. His message often emphasized both personal and national reform and renewal. The message was symbolized by his walking to the White House after delivering his inaugural address. It was reflected less successfully in his "malaise" speech near the end of his term, where he dwelled on the "crisis of the American spirit...all around us." In 1980 he was challenged unsuccessfully for the Democratic nomination for president by the more orthodox liberal Senator Edward Kennedy; he was defeated in the general elections by conservative Republican Ronald Reagan.

...

Let our recent mistakes bring a resurgent commitment to the basic principles of our Nation, for we know that if we despise our own government we have no future. We recall in special times when we have stood briefly, but magnificently, united. In those times no prize was beyond our grasp.

But we cannot dwell upon remembered glory. We cannot afford to drift. We reject the prospect of failure or mediocrity or an inferior quality of life for any person. Our Government must at the same time be both competent and compassionate.

We have already found a high degree of personal liberty, and we are now struggling to enhance equality of opportunity. Our commitment to human rights must be absolute, our laws fair, our natural beauty preserved; the powerful must not persecute the weak, and human dignity must be enhanced.

We have learned that "more" is not necessarily "better," that even our great Nation has its recognized limits, and that we can neither answer all questions nor solve all problems. We cannot afford to do everything,

3. Excerpt taken from Jimmy Carter, *Public Papers of the Presidents of the United States: Jimmy Carter, 1977* (Washington, DC: Government Printing Office, 1977), 1.

nor can we afford to lack boldness as we meet the future. So, together, in a spirit of individual sacrifice for the common good, we must simply do our best.

...

II. Judicial Power and Constitutional Authority

MAJOR DEVELOPMENTS

- Supreme Court vacancies filled with five Republicans and no Democratic appointments, resulting in more conservative decision making
- Active Supreme Court participation in politically-charged cases despite increasing criticism of "judicial activism"
- Maintenance of broad ability of parties to bring constitutional cases to federal courts

The Warren Court came to an abrupt end in 1968. Chief Justice Earl Warren, at the age of 77, did not expect to serve through the term of another presidential administration. He had hoped that his successor would be named by the person that he hoped would be the next president of the United States, Robert Kennedy, but Kennedy was killed in June of 1968. Warren realized that if he waited to retire until after the next president was elected then his replacement would most likely be chosen by his old political rival from California, the Republican Richard Nixon. Worse yet, Nixon was advancing his campaign by specifically criticizing the "activist judges" on the Warren Court. In an attempt to resolve his succession before a new president came into office Warren contacted his ally, President Lyndon Johnson, in June 1968 to inform him that he would resign as soon as a new chief justice was confirmed.

Johnson and Warren agreed that Associate Justice Abe Fortas, a Johnson advisor and one of the most liberal justices (and most skilled lawyers) on the Court, would be a fitting successor. The president rushed the Fortas nomination to the Democratic Senate, hoping for a quick confirmation. It was a disaster. The Republicans and the media denounced the timing of the nomination as inappropriate. South Carolina Democrat Strom Thurmond helped turn the confirmation hearings into a referendum on the Warren Court itself, which by 1968 had at least as many critics as defenders

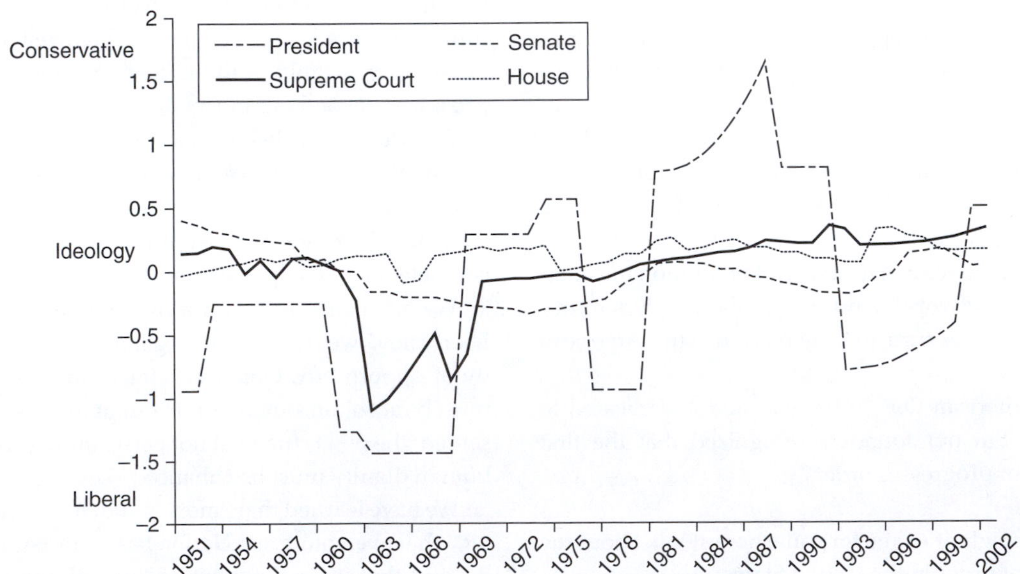

Figure 9-2 Left–Right Location of Supreme Court Relative to Other Branches, 1950–2002

Source: Michael Bailey, "Comparable Preference Estimates across Time and Institutions for the Court, Congress and Presidency," http://www9.georgetown.edu/faculty/baileyma/Data.htm

Note: Median member of each institution placed on common ideological scale based on actual individual votes on cases (Court), bills (Congress), or individual statements about the actions taken by other institutions.

in Congress, especially among southern conservative Democrats. During these hearings Fortas's ethically questionable financial dealings came to light, and the president was forced to withdraw the nomination. Even worse for Johnson and Warren, Fortas was soon forced to resign in the face of an impeachment threat from the Congress. As a consequence, immediately after his inauguration, Richard Nixon was given the opportunity to replace two key liberal members of the Warren Court.

Under the leadership of Chief Justice Warren Burger, the Supreme Court quickly moved in a more conservative direction. One indication of the transition can be seen in Figure 9-2. The figure tracks how conservative or liberal the median members of the various institutions of the federal government have been over the second half of the twentieth century, using one common measure of ideology. The 1960s stands out as an unusually liberal period in the Court's postwar history. By this measure, looking across all the Court's cases, the Court immediately shifted back into a relatively more conservative pattern with the start of the Burger Court—and since then has continued to drift slightly more to the right. Of course, Figure 9-2 also suggests that the Burger Court was only about as conservative as the House of Representatives, which had a Democratic majority, and so it is no surprise that the Burger Court could produce new decisions like *Roe v. Wade* (1973) at the same time that it began to limit the implications of some Warren-era decisions.

Despite Nixon's assault on "judicial activism" the Burger Court showed no hesitation about using the power of judicial review. Both Republicans and Democrats, conservatives and liberals, were committed to the notion that the judiciary should define and enforce constitutional limits. They disagreed, however, about what those limits were—and about how far courts should go in trying to remedy constitutional and policy problems. As a result, the Burger Court in the 1970s struck down state and federal laws in even more cases than did the Warren Court in the 1960s. There may have been fewer landmark cases that laid out new areas of constitutional law in the 1970s, but the Burger Court proved just as willing to nullify the actions of elected officials.

At the same time, conservatives on and off the Court pressed the justices to pare back on the broadened standards of justiciability that the Warren Court had set. Tightening those rules would keep constitutional cases out of the Supreme Court. More importantly, it would keep constitutional issues out of the predominantly liberal lower federal courts. These efforts to shut the courthouse doors were only partly successful. Burger Court majorities did rule that various parties lacked standing to raise challenges to the constitutionality of the Vietnam War, and some of the broader implications of *Flast* were not realized. Nevertheless, as Ronald Reagan entered office, there were still far fewer barriers to constitutional litigation than when Franklin Roosevelt entered office.

A. Constitutional Litigation

One dimension of conflict between conservatives and liberals on the Court was over the rules of constitutional litigation. During the Warren Court, the liberal justices had taken more cases and loosened the doctrines of justiciability so that more issues and disputes could be brought to the federal courts. The Burger Court justices were expected to tighten these rules so that cases could not be so easily brought to the federal courts. The writ of habeas corpus is one mechanism by which federal courts hear legal issues that originate in the states, but the statutes governing when the writ was to be used left a great deal of discretion to the courts. The Warren Court had interpreted that power broadly to facilitate bringing cases into the federal courts. As Justice William Rehnquist argued in the habeas corpus case of *Wainwright v. Sykes* (1977), conservatives wanted the state courts to be the "main event," with federal review of their findings being reserved for exceptional cases. In habeas cases, the Burger Court whittled away at Warren Court precedents so as to give somewhat greater finality to state court decisions.

For cases originating in the federal courts, the Burger Court moved with somewhat less resolve. The Warren Court had established key landmarks regarding questions of standing in *Flast v. Cohen* (1968) and political question doctrine in *Baker v. Carr* (1962). Some expected the Burger Court to dramatically alter those precedents, but they survived largely intact. The federal courts retained discretion to take on a wide range of new constitutional cases that might arise. In essence, the federal judiciary refused invitations to limit its own institutional power.

Powell v. McCormack, 395 U.S. 486 (1969)

Adam Clayton Powell, Jr., was perhaps the most important black congressman of the mid-twentieth century. Early in his career he had broken with his party in order to endorse Dwight Eisenhower, whom he considered preferable on civil rights, but by the 1960s he had become a powerful Democratic legislator under John F. Kennedy and Lyndon Johnson. In 1966 Powell was reelected to his twelfth term as Harlem's congressional representative. During his previous term, a House subcommittee had concluded that, as chairman of the House Committee on Education and Labor, Powell had misused funds and falsified reports. The Democratic caucus voted to strip Powell of his chairmanship. When House members were sworn into office after the 1966 elections, the House resolved by a vote of 363–65 to refuse to administer the oath to Powell and to direct the Speaker of the House to appoint a select committee to determine whether Powell was eligible to serve in the House. After a series of hearings, the committee recommended that Powell be seated as a member but fined, censured, and stripped of his seniority. In a floor vote, the House rejected the recommendation of the committee. It voted 248–176 on the critical amendment to exclude Powell from the House and declare his seat vacant (307–116 on the final vote).

Powell and a group of voters filed suit in federal district court against the Speaker of the House, John McCormack, and other House officers. Powell argued that he met all of the constitutional requirements for office as a member of the House of Representatives (including age, citizenship, and residency), as listed in Article I, Section 2, and he asked for a declaratory judgment that the efforts to exclude him from taking office were unconstitutional. The district court dismissed the suit as a political conflict and not a legal dispute, thus making the case non-justiciable; the Court of Appeals for the District of Columbia Circuit affirmed that decision.

Before the Supreme Court heard the case, Powell was elected to a thirteenth term, and the new Congress seated him but assessed a fine against him. The respondents moved that the case now be dismissed as moot, sine he was no longer excluded from his seat. The justices heard the jurisdictional and substantive arguments together. In an 8–1 vote, the Supreme Court reversed the lower court, ruling both that the courts had the authority to decide such a case and that the House did not have the constitutional authority to exclude a duly elected member who met the minimal qualifications laid out in the text of the Constitution. Even in judging the qualifications of the members of the legislature, the Court, not Congress, was "the ultimate interpreter of the Constitution."

Powell failed to win renomination in his Democratic district in 1970 and so was not elected to a fourteenth term. He died less than two years later.

CHIEF JUSTICE WARREN delivered the opinion of the Court.

. . .

Simply stated, a case is moot when the issues presented are no longer "live" or the parties lack a legally cognizable interest in the outcome. . . . Where one of the several issues presented becomes moot, the remaining live issues supply the constitutional requirement of a case or controversy. . . .

. . .

. . . [E]ven if respondents are correct that petitioners' averments as to injunctive relief are not sufficiently definite, it does not follow that this litigation must be dismissed as moot. . . . There is no suggestion that petitioners' averments as to declaratory relief are insufficient and Powell's allegedly unconstitutional deprivation of salary remains unresolved.

. . .

Respondents assert that the Speech or Debate Clause of the Constitution, Art. I, § 6, is an absolute bar to petitioners' action. . . . The Speech or Debate Clause, adopted by the Constitutional Convention without debate or opposition, finds its roots in the conflict between Parliament and the Crown culminating in the Glorious Revolution of 1688 and the English Bill of Rights of 1689. . . . Although the clause sprang from a fear of seditious libel actions instituted by the Crown to punish unfavorable speeches made in Parliament, we have held that it would be a "narrow view" to confine the protection of the Speech or Debate Clause to words spoken in debate. Committee reports, resolutions, and the act of voting are equally covered, as are "things generally done in a session of the House by one of its members in relation to the business before it." *Kilbourn* v. *Thompson* (1881). . . .

Legislative immunity does not, of course, bar all judicial review of legislative acts. That issue was settled by implication as early as 1803, see *Marbury* v. *Madison*, and expressly in *Kilbourn* v. *Thompson*, the first of this Court's cases interpreting the reach of the Speech or Debate Clause. . . .

. . .

The resolution excluding petitioner Powell was adopted by a vote in excess of two-thirds of the 434 Members of Congress—307 to 116. Article I, § 5, grants the House authority to expel a member "with the Concurrence of two thirds." Respondents assert that the House may expel a member for any reason whatsoever and that, since a two-thirds vote was obtained, the procedure by which Powell was denied his seat in the 90th Congress should be regarded as an expulsion, not an exclusion....

Although respondents repeatedly urge this Court not to speculate as to the reasons for Powell's exclusion, their attempt to equate exclusion with expulsion would require a similar speculation that the House would have voted to expel Powell had it been faced with that question.... The Speaker ruled that the House was voting to exclude Powell, and we will not speculate what the result might have been if Powell had been seated and expulsion proceedings subsequently instituted.

Nor is the distinction between exclusion and expulsion merely one of form. The misconduct for which Powell was charged occurred prior to the convening of the 90th Congress. On several occasions the House has debated whether a member can be expelled for actions taken during a prior Congress and the House's own manual of procedure applicable in the 90th Congress states that "both Houses have distrusted their power to punish in such cases."...

...

Respondents first contend that this is not a case "arising under" the Constitution within the meaning of Art. III. They emphasize that Art. I, § 5, assigns to each House of Congress the power to judge the elections and qualifications of its own members and to punish its members for disorderly behavior.... Thus, respondents maintain, the "power conferred on the courts by article III does not authorize this Court to do anything more than declare its lack of jurisdiction to proceed."

We reject this contention. Article III, § 1, provides that the "judicial Power...shall be vested in one supreme Court, and in such inferior Courts as the Congress may...establish." Further, § 2 mandates that the "judicial Power shall extend to all Cases...arising under this Constitution...." It has long been held that a suit "arises under" the Constitution if a petitioner's claim "will be sustained if the Constitution...[is] given one construction and will be defeated if [it is] given another."...

...

Respondents [maintain] that this case is not justiciable because, they assert, it is impossible for a federal court to "mold effective relief for resolving this case." Respondents emphasize that petitioners asked for coercive relief against the officers of the House, and, they contend, federal courts cannot issue mandamus or injunctions compelling officers or employees of the House to perform specific official acts....

We need express no opinion about the appropriateness of coercive relief in this case, for petitioners sought a declaratory judgment, a form of relief the District Court could have issued. The Declaratory Judgment Act, 28 U. S. C. § 2201, provides that a district court may "declare the rights...of any interested party...whether or not further relief is or could be sought."...We thus conclude that in terms of the general criteria of justiciability, this case is justiciable.

Respondents maintain that even if this case is otherwise justiciable, it presents only a political question. It is well established that the federal courts will not adjudicate political questions....In *Baker* v. *Carr* (1962)...we concluded that on the surface of any case held to involve a political question was at least one of the following formulations:

> a textually demonstrable constitutional commitment of the issue to a coordinate political department; or a lack of judicially discoverable and manageable standards for resolving it; or the impossibility of deciding without an initial policy determination of a kind clearly for nonjudicial discretion; or the impossibility of a court's undertaking independent resolution without expressing lack of the respect due coordinate branches of government; or an unusual need for unquestioning adherence to a political decision already made; or the potentiality of embarrassment from multifarious pronouncements by various departments on one question.

...

In order to determine whether there has been a textual commitment to a co-ordinate department of the Government, we must interpret the Constitution. In other words, we must first determine what power the Constitution confers upon the House through Art. I,

§5, before we can determine to what extent, if any, the exercise of that power is subject to judicial review....

...

Had the intent of the Framers emerged from these materials with less clarity, we would nevertheless have been compelled to resolve any ambiguity in favor of a narrow construction of the scope of Congress' power to exclude members-elect. A fundamental principle of our representative democracy is, in Hamilton's words, "that the people should choose whom they please to govern them." 2 Elliot's Debates 257. As Madison pointed out at the Convention, this principle is undermined as much by limiting whom the people can select as by limiting the franchise itself. In apparent agreement with this basic philosophy, the Convention adopted his suggestion limiting the power to expel.... Unquestionably, Congress has an interest in preserving its institutional integrity, but in most cases that interest can be sufficiently safeguarded by the exercise of its power to punish its members for disorderly behavior and, in extreme cases, to expel a member with the concurrence of two-thirds. In short, both the intention of the Framers, to the extent it can be determined, and an examination of the basic principles of our democratic system persuade us that the Constitution does not vest in the Congress a discretionary power to deny membership by a majority vote.

For these reasons, we have concluded that Art. I, § 5, is at most a "textually demonstrable commitment" to Congress to judge only the qualifications expressly set forth in the Constitution. Therefore, the "textual commitment" formulation of the political question doctrine does not bar federal courts from adjudicating petitioners' claims.

Respondents' alternate contention is that the case presents a political question because judicial resolution of petitioners' claim would produce a "potentially embarrassing confrontation between coordinate branches" of the Federal Government. But, as our interpretation of Art. I, § 5, discloses, a determination of petitioner Powell's right to sit would require no more than an interpretation of the Constitution. Such a determination falls within the traditional role accorded courts to interpret the law, and does not involve a "lack of the respect due [a] coordinate [branch] of government," nor does it involve an "initial policy determination of a kind clearly for nonjudicial discretion." *Baker* v. *Carr*. Our system of government requires that federal courts on occasion interpret the Constitution in a manner at variance with the construction given the document by another branch. The alleged conflict that such an adjudication may cause cannot justify the courts' avoiding their constitutional responsibility....

...Finally, a judicial resolution of petitioners' claim will not result in "multifarious pronouncements by various departments on one question." For, as we noted in *Baker* v. *Carr*, it is the responsibility of this Court to act as the ultimate interpreter of the Constitution. *Marbury* v. *Madison*. Thus, we conclude that petitioners' claim is not barred by the political question doctrine, and, having determined that the claim is otherwise generally justiciable, we hold that the case is justiciable.

...

Further, analysis of the "textual commitment" under Art. I, § 5, has demonstrated that in judging the qualifications of its members Congress is limited to the standing qualifications prescribed in the Constitution. Respondents concede that Powell met these. Thus, there is no need to remand this case to determine whether he was entitled to be seated in the 90th Congress. Therefore, we hold that, since Adam Clayton Powell, Jr., was duly elected by the voters of the 18th Congressional District of New York and was not ineligible to serve under any provision of the Constitution, the House was without power to exclude him from its membership.

Petitioners seek additional forms of equitable relief, including mandamus for the release of petitioner Powell's back pay. The propriety of such remedies, however, is more appropriately considered in the first instance by the courts below....

It is so ordered.

JUSTICE DOUGLAS, concurring.

While I join the opinion of the Court, I add a few words. As the Court says, the important constitutional question is whether the Congress has the power to deviate from or alter the qualifications for membership as a Representative contained in Art. I, § 2, cl. 2, of the Constitution. Up to now the understanding has been quite clear to the effect that such authority does not exist. To be sure, Art. I, § 5, provides that: "Each House shall be the Judge of the Elections, Returns and Qualifications of its own Members...." Contests may arise over whether an elected official meets the "qualifications" of the Constitution, in which event the House is the sole judge. But the House is not the sole judge when "qualifications" are added which are not specified in the Constitution.

A man is not seated because he is a Socialist or a Communist. Another is not seated because in his district members of a minority are systematically excluded from voting. Another is not seated because he has spoken out in opposition to the war in Vietnam. The possible list is long. Some cases will have the racist overtones of the present one. Others may reflect religious or ideological clashes.

At the root of all these cases, however, is the basic integrity of the electoral process. Today we proclaim the constitutional principle of "one man, one vote." When that principle is followed and the electors choose a person who is repulsive to the Establishment in Congress, by what constitutional authority can that group of electors be disenfranchised?

...

JUSTICE STEWART, dissenting.

...

The essential purpose of this lawsuit by Congressman Powell and members of his constituency was to regain the seat from which he was barred by the 90th Congress. That purpose, however, became impossible of attainment on January 3, 1969, when the 90th Congress passed into history and the 91st Congress came into being. On that date, the petitioners' prayer for a judicial decree restraining enforcement of House Resolution No. 278 and commanding the respondents to admit Congressman Powell to membership in the 90th Congress became incontestably moot.

...With the 90th Congress terminated and Powell now a member of the 91st, it cannot seriously be contended that there remains a judicial controversy between these parties over the power of the House of Representatives to exclude Powell and the power of a court to order him reseated....

The petitioners' proposition that conduct of the 91st Congress has perpetuated the controversy is based on the fact that House Resolution No. 2—the same resolution by which the House voted to seat Powell—fined him $25,000 and provided that his seniority was to commence as of the date he became a member of the 91st Congress. That punishment, it is said, "arises out of the prior actions of the House which originally impelled this action." It is indisputable, however, that punishment of a House member involves constitutional issues entirely distinct from those raised by exclusion, and that a punishment in one Congress is in no legal sense a "continuation" of an exclusion from the previous Congress. A judicial determination that the exclusion was improper would have no bearing on the constitutionality of the punishment, nor any conceivable practical impact on Powell's status in the 91st Congress....

...

The passage of time and intervening events have, therefore, made it impossible to afford the petitioners the principal relief they sought in this case. If any aspect of the case remains alive, it is only Congressman Powell's individual claim for the salary of which he was deprived by his absence from the 90th Congress. But even if that claim can be said to prevent this controversy from being moot, which I doubt, there is no need to reach the fundamental constitutional issues that the Court today undertakes to decide.

...

There are, then substantial questions as to whether, on his salary claim, Powell could obtain relief against any or all of these respondents. On the other hand, if he was entitled to a salary as a member of the 90th Congress, he has a certain and completely satisfactory remedy in an action for a money judgment against the United States in the Court of Claims.... Even if the mandatory relief sought by Powell is appropriate and could be effective, the Court should insist that the salary claim be litigated in a context that would clearly obviate the need to decide some of the constitutional questions with which the Court grapples today, and might avoid them altogether....

...If the fundamental principles restraining courts from unnecessarily or prematurely reaching out to decide grave and perhaps unsettling constitutional questions retain any vitality, see *Ashwander* v. *TVA* (1936) (Brandeis, J., concurring), surely there have been few cases more demanding of their application than this one....

Laird v. Tatum, 408 U.S. 1 (1972)

By statute, the president may use the armed forces to help quell insurrections, and President Lyndon Johnson had used federal troops to help put down riots in Detroit in the summer of 1967. From that experience, the army decided that it should better anticipate and plan for civil disorder. Army intelligence thus began compiling reports on meetings and leaders of potentially troublesome groups. While this intelligence gathering primarily involved public information, in 1970 Congress held public hearings, and in response the army severely cut back the program.

Individuals who saw themselves as potentially subject to Army intelligence reports filed suit in federal district court seeking a declaration that the program was an unconstitutional infringement on their First Amendment liberties. The district court dismissed the suit on the grounds that the plaintiffs had suffered no justiciable injury. On appeal, the circuit court agreed that there was no claim that the army's actions were illegal; they were no different from what a "good newspaper reporter would be able to gather" and nothing injurious had been done or was immediately foreseeable. Nonetheless, the circuit court reversed the lower-court ruling. It concluded that the present system "constitutes an impermissible burden on [respondents] and other similarly situated which exercises a present inhibiting effect on their full expression and utilization of their First Amendment rights." This chilling effect created a justiciable injury.

In a 5–4 decision authored by Chief Justice Burger, the Supreme Court reversed the circuit court, agreeing with the district court that the army's actions had not yet created a judicially remediable injury. In the absence of a concrete injury, the plaintiffs had no standing to sue. The majority did indicate, however, that the program was properly subject to judicial review should a litigant with the requisite injury appear before the Court. The Rehnquist Court built on this argument in Lujan v. Defenders of Wildlife *(1992), holding that a party must be "injured in fact" in order to maintain a suit under the Endangered Species Act. A generalized interest in the enforcement of environmental laws was not sufficient to create standing, even with a statute designed to facilitate citizen suits.*

As you read the following opinions, think about whether the justices in the Flast *majority would have found a sufficient injury. What is your best understanding of the legal difference between* Flast *and* Laird*? Does that legal difference explain the different results in the cases? Why might the Burger Court have been interested tightening the rules on who could bring constitutional claims into the federal judiciary as compared to the Warren Court that decided* Flast*?*

CHIEF JUSTICE BURGER delivered the opinion of the Court.

...

Our examination of the record satisfies us that the Court of Appeals properly identified the issue presented, namely, whether the jurisdiction of a federal court may be invoked by a complainant who alleges that the exercise of his First Amendment rights is being chilled by the mere existence, without more, of a governmental investigative and data-gathering activity that is alleged to be broader in scope than is reasonably necessary for the accomplishment of a valid governmental purpose. We conclude, however, that, having properly identified the issue, the Court of Appeals decided that issue incorrectly.

In recent years this Court has found in a number of cases that constitutional violations may arise from the deterrent, or "chilling," effect of governmental regulations that fall short of a direct prohibition against the exercise of First Amendment rights. *E. g., Baird* v. *State Bar of Arizona* (1971); *Keyishian* v. *Board of Regents* (1967).... In none of these cases, however, did the chilling effect arise merely from the individual's knowledge that a governmental agency was engaged in certain activities or from the individual's concomitant fear that, armed with the fruits of those activities, the agency might in the future take some *other* and additional action detrimental to that individual. Rather, in each of these cases, the challenged exercise of governmental power was regulatory, proscriptive, or compulsory in nature, and the complainant was either presently or prospectively subject to the regulations, proscriptions, or compulsions that he was challenging.

...

The decisions in these cases fully recognize that governmental action may be subject to constitutional challenge even though it has only an indirect effect on the exercise of First Amendment rights. At the same time, however, these decisions have in no way eroded the

> established principle that to entitle a private individual to invoke the judicial power to determine the validity of executive or legislative action he must show that he has sustained or is immediately in danger of sustaining a direct injury as the result of that action... *Ex parte Levitt* (1937).

The respondents do not meet this test; their claim, simply stated, is that they disagree with the judgments made by the Executive Branch with respect to the type and amount of information the Army needs and that the very existence of the Army's data-gathering system produces a constitutionally impermissible chilling effect upon the exercise of their First Amendment rights. That alleged "chilling" effect may perhaps be seen as arising from respondents' very perception of the system as inappropriate to the Army's role under our form of government, or as arising from respondents' beliefs that it is inherently dangerous for the military to be concerned with activities in the civilian sector, or as arising from respondents' less generalized yet speculative apprehensiveness that the Army may at some future date misuse the information in some way that would cause direct harm to respondents. Allegations of a subjective "chill" are not an adequate substitute for a claim of specific present objective harm or a threat of specific future harm; "the federal courts established pursuant to Article III of the Constitution do not render advisory opinions." *United Public Workers* v. *Mitchell* (1947).

Stripped to its essentials, what respondents appear to be seeking is a broad-scale investigation, conducted by themselves as private parties armed with the subpoena power of a federal district court and the power of cross-examination, to probe into the Army's intelligence gathering activities, with the district court determining at the conclusion of that investigation the extent to which those activities may or may not be appropriate to the Army's mission. The following excerpt from the opinion of the Court of Appeals suggests the broad sweep implicit in its holding:

> Apparently in the judgment of the civilian head of the Army not everything being done in the operation of this intelligence system was necessary to the performance of the military mission. *If the Secretary of the Army can formulate and implement such judgment based on facts within his Departmental knowledge, the United States District Court can hear evidence, ascertain the facts, and decide what, if any, further restrictions on the complained-of activities are called for* to confine the military to their legitimate sphere of activity and to protect [respondents'] allegedly infringed constitutional rights. 444 F.2d, at 958. (Emphasis added.)

Carried to its logical end, this approach would have the federal courts as virtually continuing monitors of the wisdom and soundness of Executive action; such a role is appropriate for the Congress acting through its committees and the "power of the purse"; it is not the role of the judiciary, absent actual present or immediately threatened injury resulting from unlawful governmental action.

We, of course, intimate no view with respect to the propriety or desirability, from a policy standpoint, of the challenged activities of the Department of the Army; our conclusion is a narrow one, namely, that on this record the respondents have not presented a case for resolution by the courts.

The concerns of the Executive and Legislative Branches in response to disclosure of the Army surveillance activities—and indeed the claims alleged in the complaint—reflect a traditional and strong resistance of Americans to any military intrusion into civilian affairs. That tradition has deep roots in our history and found early expression, for example, in the Third Amendment's explicit prohibition against quartering soldiers in private homes without consent and in the constitutional provisions for civilian control of the military. Those prohibitions are not directly presented by this case, but their philosophical underpinnings explain our traditional insistence on limitations on military operations in peacetime. Indeed, when presented with claims of judicially cognizable injury resulting from military intrusion into the civilian sector, federal courts are fully empowered to consider claims of those asserting such injury; there is nothing in our Nation's history or in this Court's decided cases, including our holding today, that can properly be seen as giving any indication that actual or threatened injury by reason of unlawful activities of the military would go unnoticed or unremedied.

Reversed.

JUSTICE DOUGLAS, with whom JUSTICE MARSHALL joins, dissenting.

If Congress had passed a law authorizing the armed services to establish surveillance over the civilian population, a most serious constitutional problem would be presented. There is, however, no law authorizing surveillance over civilians, which in this case the Pentagon concededly had undertaken. The question is whether such authority may be implied. One can search the Constitution in vain for any such authority.

The start of the problem is the constitutional distinction between the "militia" and the Armed Forces. By Art. I, § 8, of the Constitution the militia is specifically confined to precise duties: "to execute the Laws of the Union, suppress Insurrections and repel Invasions."

. . .

The upshot is that the Armed Services—as distinguished from the "militia"—are not regulatory agencies or bureaus that may be created as Congress desires and granted such powers as seem necessary and proper. The authority to provide rules "governing" the Armed Services means the grant of authority to the Armed Services to govern themselves, not the authority to govern civilians. Even when "martial law" is declared, as it often has been, its appropriateness is subject to judicial review....

...

The claim that respondents have no standing to challenge the Army's surveillance of them and the other members of the class they seek to represent is too transparent for serious argument. The surveillance of the Army over the civilian sector—a part of society hitherto immune from its control—is a serious charge. It is alleged that the Army maintains files on the membership, ideology, programs, and practices of virtually every activist political group in the country, including groups such as the Southern Christian Leadership Conference, Clergy and Laymen United Against the War in Vietnam, the American Civil Liberties Union, Women's Strike for Peace, and the National Association for the Advancement of Colored People. The Army uses undercover agents to infiltrate these civilian groups and to reach into confidential files of students and other groups. The Army moves as a secret group among civilian audiences, using cameras and electronic ears for surveillance. The data it collects are distributed to civilian officials in state, federal, and local governments and to each military intelligence unit and troop command under the Army's jurisdiction (both here and abroad); and these data are stored in one or more data banks.

...

One need not wait to sue until he loses his job or until his reputation is defamed. To withhold standing to sue until that time arrives would in practical effect immunize from judicial scrutiny all surveillance activities, regardless of their misuse and their deterrent effect. As stated in *Flast* v. *Cohen* (1968), "in terms of Article III limitations on federal court jurisdiction, the question of standing is related only to whether the dispute sought to be adjudicated will be presented in an adversary context and in a form historically viewed as capable of judicial resolution." Or, as we put it in *Baker* v. *Carr* (1962), the gist of the standing issue is whether the party seeking relief has "alleged such a personal stake in the outcome of the controversy as to assure that concrete adverseness which sharpens the presentation of issues upon which the court so largely depends for illumination of difficult constitutional questions."

The present controversy is not a remote, imaginary conflict. Respondents were targets of the Army's surveillance....

...

Surveillance of civilians is none of the Army's constitutional business and Congress has not undertaken to entrust it with any such function. The fact that since this litigation started the Army's surveillance may have been cut back is not an end of the matter. Whether there has been an actual cutback or whether the announcements are merely a ruse can be determined only after a hearing in the District Court. We are advised by an *amicus curiae* brief filed by a group of former Army Intelligence Agents that Army surveillance of civilians is rooted in secret programs of long standing....

...

This case involves a cancer in our body politic. It is a measure of the disease which afflicts us. Army surveillance, like Army regimentation, is at war with the principles of the First Amendment. Those who already walk submissively will say there is no cause for alarm. But submissiveness is not our heritage. The First Amendment was designed to allow rebellion to remain as our heritage. The Constitution was designed to keep government off the backs of the people. The Bill of Rights was added to keep the precincts of belief and expression, of the press, of political and social activities free from surveillance. The Bill of Rights was designed to keep agents of government and official eavesdroppers away from assemblies of people. The aim was to allow men to be free and independent and to assert their rights against government. There can be no influence more paralyzing of that objective than Army surveillance. When an intelligence officer looks over every nonconformist's shoulder in the library, or walks invisibly by his side in a picket line, or infiltrates his club, the America once extolled as the voice of liberty heard around the world no longer is cast in the image which Jefferson and Madison designed, but more in the Russian image.

...

JUSTICE BRENNAN, with whom JUSTICE STEWART and JUSTICE MARSHALL join, dissenting.

The Court of Appeals held that a justiciable controversy exists and that respondents have stated a claim upon which relief could be granted....

...

Respondents may or may not be able to prove the case they allege. But I agree with the Court of

Appeals that they are entitled to try. I would therefore affirm the remand to the District Court for a trial and determination of the issues specified by the Court of Appeals.

Rehnquist Memo in Laird v. Tatum, 409 US. 824 (1972)

Having had their circuit court victory reserved by a 5–4 decision in the Supreme Court in Laird v. Tatum, *the appellees petitioned the Court to throw out its earlier decision and rehear the case. They also moved that Justice William Rehnquist (a member of the five-person majority) recuse himself, or decline to sit on the case. Both statute and historical practice may guide recusal, but only the judge or justice in question may decide, and justices rarely offer an explanation for their decision. Rehnquist did respond, however, in filing a memorandum explaining his decision to deny the motion and to continue to participate in the case. He observed that "proof that a Justice's mind at the time he joined the Court was a complete* tabula rasa *in the area of constitutional adjudication would be evidence of lack of qualification, not lack of bias."*

Memorandum of JUSTICE REHNQUIST.

Respondents in this case have moved that I disqualify myself from participation. While neither the Court nor any Justice individually appears ever to have done so, I have determined that it would be appropriate for me to state the reasons which have led to my decision with respect to respondents' motion. In so doing, I do not wish to suggest that I believe such a course would be desirable or even appropriate in any but the peculiar circumstances present here.

...

Respondents in their motion do not explicitly relate their factual contentions to the applicable provisions of 28 U. S. C. § 455. The so-called "mandatory" provisions of that section require disqualification of a Justice or judge "in any case in which he has a substantial interest, has been of counsel, is or has been a material witness...."

Since I have neither been of counsel nor have I been a material witness in *Laird* v. *Tatum*, these provisions are not applicable. Respondents refer to a memorandum prepared in the Office of Legal Counsel for the benefit of JUSTICE WHITE shortly before he came on the Court, relating to disqualification. I reviewed it at the time of my confirmation hearings and found myself in substantial agreement with it. Its principal thrust is that a Justice Department official is disqualified if he either signs a pleading or brief or "if he actively participated in any case even though he did not sign a pleading or brief." I agree. In both *United States* v. *United States District Court* (1972), for which I was not officially responsible in the Department but with respect to which I assisted in drafting the brief, and in *S&E Contractors* v. *United States* (1972), in which I had only an advisory role which terminated immediately prior to the commencement of the litigation, I disqualified myself. Since I did not have even an advisory role in the conduct of the case of *Laird* v. *Tatum*, the application of such a rule would not require or authorize disqualification here.

This leaves remaining the so-called discretionary portion of the section, requiring disqualification where the judge "is so related to or connected with any party or his attorney as to render it improper, in his opinion, for him to sit on the trial, appeal, or other proceeding therein." The interpretation and application of this section by the various Justices who have sat on this Court seem to have varied widely....

Indeed, different Justices who have come from the Department of Justice have treated the same or very similar situations differently. In *Schneiderman* v. *United States* (1943), a case brought and tried during the time Justice Murphy was Attorney General, but defended on appeal during the time that Justice Jackson was Attorney General, the latter disqualified himself but the former did not.

I have no hesitation in concluding that my total lack of connection while in the Department of Justice with the defense of the case of *Laird* v. *Tatum* does not suggest discretionary disqualification here because of my previous relationship with the Justice Department.

However, respondents also contend that I should disqualify myself because I have previously expressed in public an understanding of the law on the question of the constitutionality of governmental surveillance. While no provision of the statute sets out such a provision for disqualification in so many words, it could conceivably be embraced within the general language of the discretionary clause. Such a contention raises rather squarely the question of whether a member of this Court, who prior to his taking that office has expressed a public view as to what the law is or ought to be, should later sit as a judge in a case raising that particular question....

My impression is that none of the former Justices of this Court since 1911 have followed a practice of disqualifying themselves in cases involving points of law with respect to which they had expressed an opinion or formulated policy prior to ascending to the bench.

Justice Black while in the Senate was one of the principal authors of the Fair Labor Standards Act; indeed, it is cited in the popular-name index of the 1970 edition of the United States Code as the "Black–Connery Fair Labor Standards Act."...

Nonetheless, he sat in the case that upheld the constitutionality of that Act, *United States* v. *Darby* (1941)....[T]o my knowledge his Senate role with respect to the Act was never a source of criticism for his participation in the above cases.

Justice Frankfurter had, prior to coming to this Court, written extensively in the field of labor law....Justice Frankfurter had not only publicly expressed his views, but had when a law professor played an important, perhaps dominant, part in the drafting of the Norris–LaGuardia Act....Yet, in addition to sitting in one of the leading cases interpreting the scope of the Act, *United States* v. *Hutcheson* (1941), Justice Frankfurter wrote the Court's opinion.

Justice Jackson in *McGrath* v. *Kristensen* (1950), participated in a case raising exactly the same issue that he had decided as Attorney General (in a way opposite to that in which the Court decided it)....

Two years before he was appointed Chief Justice of this Court, Charles Evans Hughes wrote a book entitled *The Supreme Court of the United States*...[where] he discussed at some length the doctrine expounded in the case of *Adkins* v. *Children's Hospital* (1923). I think that one would be warranted in saying that he implied some reservations about the holding of that case. Nine years later, Chief Justice Hughes wrote the Court's opinion in *West Coast Hotel Co.* v. *Parrish* (1937), in which a closely divided Court overruled *Adkins*. I have never heard any suggestion that because of his discussion of the subject in his book he should have recused himself.

...

Since most Justices come to this bench no earlier than their middle years, it would be unusual if they had not by that time formulated at least some tentative notions that would influence them in their interpretation of the sweeping clauses of the Constitution and their interaction with one another. It would be not merely unusual, but extraordinary, if they had not at least given opinions as to constitutional issues in their previous legal careers. Proof that a Justice's mind at the time he joined the Court was a complete *tabula rasa* in the area of constitutional adjudication would be evidence of lack of qualification, not lack of bias.[4]

...

The oath prescribed by 28 U. S. C. § 453 that is taken by each person upon becoming a member of the federal judiciary requires that he "administer justice without respect to persons, and do equal right to the poor and to the rich," that he "faithfully and impartially discharge and perform all the duties incumbent upon [him]...agreeably to the Constitution and laws of the United States." Every litigant is entitled to have his case heard by a judge mindful of this oath. But neither the oath, the disqualification statute, nor the practice of the former Justices of this Court guarantees a litigant that each judge will start off from dead center in his willingness or ability to reconcile the opposing arguments of counsel with his understanding of the Constitution and the law. That being the case, it is not a ground for disqualification that a judge has prior to his nomination expressed his then understanding of the meaning of some particular provision of the Constitution.

Based on the foregoing considerations, I conclude that respondents' motion that I disqualify myself in this case should be, and it hereby is, denied.

Notes

1. In a footnote to his memorandum, Rehnquist distinguishes between public statements made prior to judicial nomination and public statements made during the nomination process itself. As both a lawyer in the Nixon administration and a Supreme Court justice, Rehnquist worried that nominees were being asked to commit to how they would vote in future cases. When Clarence Thomas was nominated to the

4. In terms of propriety, rather than disqualification, I would distinguish quite sharply between a public statement made prior to nomination for the bench, on the one hand, and a public statement made by a nominee to the bench. For the latter to express any but the most general observation about the law would suggest that, in order to obtain favorable consideration of his nomination, he deliberately was announcing in advance, without benefit of judicial oath, briefs, or argument, how he would decide a particular question that might come before him as a judge. [Eds.—footnote repositioned from the original.]

Supreme Court by President George H. W. Bush in 1991, he was questioned closely by Democratic senators about his views regarding abortion rights. In the aftermath of President Ronald Reagan's failed nomination of Robert Bork to the Supreme Court, the Bush administration was determined to select "stealth nominees," whose views were not as well known. Thomas was advised to evade answering substantive questions about his views during the confirmation process. To the frustration of Democratic senators, he stuck to the script.

Senator Patrick Leahy tried a different angle, noting that *Roe v. Wade* was decided while Thomas was a law student at Yale. Surely "one of the more important cases decided by the U.S. Supreme Court... would have been discussed in the law school while you were there." Thomas refused to take the bait:

JUDGE THOMAS: I was a married student and I worked, I did not spend a lot of time around the law school doing what the other students enjoyed so much, and that's debating all the current cases and all the slip opinions. My schedule was such that I went to classes and generally went to work and went home.... I cannot remember personally engaging in those discussions. The groups that I met with at that time during my years in law school were small study groups.

SENATOR LEAHY: Have you ever had discussion of Roe versus Wade other than in this room? (Laughter.) In the 17 or 18 years it's been there?

JUDGE THOMAS: Only, I guess, Senator, in fact that, in the most general sense, that other individuals express concerns one way or the other and you listen and you try to be thoughtful. If you're asking me whether or not I've ever debated the contents of it, the answer to that is no, Senator.

SENATOR LEAHY: Have you ever, private gathering or otherwise, stated whether you felt that it was properly decided or not?

JUDGE THOMAS: Senator, in trying to recall and recollect on that, I don't recollect commenting one way or the other. There were, again, debates about it in various places, but I generally did not participate. I don't remember or recall participating, Senator.

...

SENATOR LEAHY: Well, was it properly decided or not?

JUDGE THOMAS: Senator, I think that that's where I just have to say what I've said before, that to comment on the holding in that case would compromise my ability to rule....[5]

Given Rehnquist's argument in his memo in *Laird v. Tatum*, is it appropriate, or even necessary, for nominees to refuse to answer substantive questions about constitutional issues during the confirmation process? Did the answer Thomas offered to Leahy's line of questioning satisfy the standards that Rehnquist set out for a qualified jurist?

2. Federal statute requires recusal when "impartiality might reasonably be questioned," but practice helps fill in what questions are reasonable ones. Justice Antonin Scalia is among the most outspoken justices in recent Supreme Court history. Scalia frequently speaks about his constitutional philosophy and the issues of the day. As a result, he recused himself from the 2004 case of *Elk Grove Unified School District v. Newdow* (regarding the use of "under God" in the Pledge of Allegiance as recited in public schools), since he had publicly commented on the merits of the case in an earlier phase of litigation. In 2004, Scalia was asked to recuse himself from the case of *Cheney v. United States District Court for the District of Columbia* (2004) for a different reason: He had recently been on a hunting trip with Vice President Dick Cheney, a party in the case. (The Sierra Club as a respondent in one of the cases consolidated in *Cheney* and filed the motion.) In a memorandum refusing the motion for recusal, Scalia stated that the hunting trip involved a large party and offered "opportunity for private conversation."[6] Scalia noted that his friendship with Cheney dated back to their shared service in the Ford administration, but friendship "has traditionally *not* been a ground for recusal where official action is at issue [as opposed to personal interests], no matter how important the *official action* was to the ambitions or the reputation of the Government officer."

5. Nomination of Judge Clarence Thomas to be Associate Justice of the Supreme Court of the United States; Hearings Before the Senate Committee on the Judiciary, 102d Cong., 1st sess. (1991), 222–23.

6. Memorandum on Justice Scalia, *Cheney v. United States District Court for the District of Columbia* (2004).

Scalia argued that justices were often appointed to the Court precisely because of their personal relations with members of the political elite. It would be "utterly disabling" to adopt a rule by which they could not sit in cases involving the official acts of those friends. Likewise, it would be "quite wrong" for judges to focus on the political implications of the cases that come before them, if only to consider whether those political implications suggest the need for a recusal. Indeed, Scalia saw a slippery slope on which judges could be pressured by public opinion to recuse themselves for "inappropriate (and increasingly silly) reasons," casting unnecessary doubt on the integrity of the judiciary in the process.

How important should even misinformed public perception be in determining whether a judge should grant a recusal motion? Scalia notes that "Washington officials know the rules, and know that discussing with judges pending cases... is forbidden," and similarly that routine "social courtesies"—such as a shared ride on the vice president's plane, a White House dinner, or a sponsored talk at a law school that is also involved in litigation—are not meaningful "gifts" that should raise concerns about a judge's impartiality. Are the social conventions of justices an adequate basis for protecting the integrity of the judicial process? Under what circumstances would a historically accepted practice become unacceptable?

III. Powers of the National Government

MAJOR DEVELOPMENTS

- Continued expansion of national activity in economic and social regulation

The justices had been clear since the 1940s that they were not interested in enforcing boundaries on national power. The Tenth Amendment was a mere "truism." Such "sweeping" clauses as the necessary and proper clause and the spending clause gave Congress ample authority and discretion for creative policymaking. The scope of the commerce clause seemed fairly boundless.

After 1968 Congress launched bold new initiatives, further expanding the scope and size of the federal government. There were few mainstream debates about the constitutional limits of federal authority. An exception was *Oregon v. Mitchell* (1970), which held that Congress could not change the voting age in state and local elections. The result was not unexpected, and Congress quickly responded by passing the Twenty-Sixth Amendment to the Constitution, lowering the voting age to eighteen. But the federal government was expanding its role in a variety of other areas, while giving somewhat less deference to state and local governments. In 1974, for example, Congress amended the Fair Labor Standards Act to remove the exemption that had been given to state and local governments when the act was first passed during the New Deal. The result was a lawsuit that led the Supreme Court to consider whether states were entitled to some constitutional immunity from the application of federal statutes (see *National League of Cities v. Usery* [1976] in Section IV of this chapter). In 1974, Congress passed the Emergency Highway Energy Conservation Act, which used the threat of a reduction of federal highway funds to force states to adopt a national speed limit of 55 miles per hour. In keeping with the "law and order" themes of the Nixon campaign, the federal government continued to expand its role in criminal justice with bills such as the Organized Crime Control Act of 1970 and the Omnibus Crime Control Act of 1970. Regulatory policymaking took on new goals and approaches with the rise of such "social" regulation as the Clean Air Act of 1970 and the Water Pollution Control Act of 1972.

IV. Federalism

MAJOR DEVELOPMENTS

- Expanding use of federal block grants and revenue sharing to fund state and local governments
- Supreme Court experiments with state immunity from federal regulations

Professor Herbert Wechsler provided a good summary of the New Deal and Great Society understanding of federalism in an influential article, "The Political Safeguards of Federalism."[7] Wechsler insisted that New Dealers recognized federalism as

7. Herbert Wechsler, "The Political Safeguards of Federalism: The Role of States in the Composition and Selection of the National Government" *Columbia Law Review* 54 (1954):543. For an update, see Larry D. Kramer, "Putting the Politics Back into the Political Safeguards of Federalism," *Columbia Law Review* 100 (2000):215. For a critique, see John Yoo, "The Judicial Safeguards of Federalism," *Southern California Law Review* 70 (1996):1311.

an important political and constitutional value, but the branches of the government adequately protected these values. In particular, senators and representatives with local party ties could be trusted to protect state interests. In this view, when the national government appeared to step on traditional state prerogatives, it did so because many representatives believed that regulations were in the best interests of the state or were appropriately counterbalanced by other concerns. Courts did not need to intervene to ensure that federalism was maintained within the constitutional system.

Conservatives were more skeptical that national officeholders adequately represented the interests of state and local governments. William Rehnquist was among the conservative skeptics. He and other young Arizona lawyers had played a role in Senator Barry Goldwater's failed presidential campaign in 1964, with its prominent rhetoric of states' rights and denunciation of "big government" in Washington. He later moved into Nixon's Office of Legal Counsel and then to the Supreme Court. One option for reining in the federal power would be to revisit the Court's doctrine on enumerated powers. Rehnquist pursued this option with a group of Reagan- and Bush-appointed justices in the 1990s. In the 1970s, he tried a different strategy. Taking congressional power as a given, he tried to carve out constitutional exceptions for the states. The strategy was somewhat analogous to what the Warren Court had done for some individual rights in the 1960s. Rehnquist won a majority in *National League of Cities v. Usery* (1976), but the victory proved to be limited.

In *National League of Cities*, Rehnquist emphasized that states needed to have the authority and policy space to make diverse choices. In that case, the choices being made involved the wages of local government employees, with potential implications for government budgets and the policy options that they could pursue. The question for the Court and for other national officials is whether the diversity being pursued in the states is desirable, tolerable, or constitutionally preventable. Congress had long tolerated a diverse set of wage policies in the states, but that had come to an end in 1974 when it adopted amendments to the Fair Labor Standards Act applying national standards to state and local governments. States had adopted diverse policies on racial segregation, but the Court and Congress had worked to eliminate many of those in the 1950s and 1960s. States often adopt policies that favor their own residents and protect their own resources, but in a federal system states also

Illustration 9-1 President Richard Nixon presents William Rehnquist with his Commission to be Associate Justice.

Source: Richard Nixon Presidential Library and Museum.

have an obligation to treat the residents of other states fairly. At the tail end of the Warren Court, a majority of the justices led by Justice Brennan argued that residency requirements on welfare payments hampered an interstate right to travel in *Shapiro v. Thompson* (1969). *Shapiro* was part of a broader effort inside and outside the courts to open up access to welfare programs, but it also pointed to the range of uses to which federalism could be put.

A. State Immunity from Federal Regulation

The Tenth Amendment largely ceased to be a source of independent constitutional authority or limitation during the New Deal and Great Society Eras. If Congress was regulating interstate commerce, then evidence that the regulation trenched on traditional state prerogatives or even on attributes of the state government was not constitutionally relevant. As Justice Stone stated in *Darby v. United States* (1941), the Tenth Amendment "states but a truism that all is retained which has not been surrendered." Four years later, in *Fernandez v. Weiner* (1945), the justices more bluntly stated, "[t]he Tenth Amendment does not operate as a limitation upon the powers, express or implied, delegated to the national government." Throughout these years the Supreme Court consistently ruled against states' claims to immunity from federal regulation. *United States v. California* (1936) held that the federal government could regulate state-owned railroads. *New York v. United States* (1946) held that Congress could tax the sale of state goods. *Maryland v. Wirtz* (1946) held that Congress could require that some state employees be paid minimum wages. These decisions were not unanimous. Justice Douglas, in particular, repeatedly insisted that the Tenth Amendment placed some limits on national power. His dissent in *Wirtz* declared the measure "a serious invasion of state sovereignty" that was "not consistent with our constitutional federalism." Interestingly, the majority opinion in *Wirtz* was written by Justice Harlan, who in such national powers cases as *Katzenbach* was far more sympathetic to state concerns than Justice Douglas. The views of the ardent New Dealer William O. Douglas finally gained a bit of traction when the arch conservative William Rehnquist joined the Court in the Nixon era. Rehnquist tried to give teeth to state sovereignty in *National League of Cities v. Usery* (1976), which held that some state entities were immune from some federal regulations.

National League of Cities v. Usery, 426 U.S. 833 (1976)

National League of Cities *was the first case in forty years in which the Supreme Court declared a federal law unconstitutional on Tenth Amendment grounds. The Burger Court declared no other federal law unconstitutional under the Tenth Amendment, and the case was eventually overturned in* Garcia v. San Antonio Metropolitan Transit Authority *(1985).*

In 1974, Congress amended the Fair Labor Standards Act to apply to all state and local employees. A number of cities and states sued the Secretary of Labor to enjoin the enforcement of the new provisions and to have them declared unconstitutional. A three-judge district court panel dismissed the complaint, but the Supreme Court accepted the case for the hearing. In a 5–4 decision the Court declared the 1974 amendments unconstitutional. Justice Rehnquist's majority opinion overruled Wirtz, *holding that the federal government could not regulate the salaries and hours of state employees. Justice Brennan's dissent insisted that states did not need judicial protection, because Congress sufficiently protected state interest. These opinions were particularly remarkable because Justice Rehnquist was then considered the leading proponent of judicial restraint on the Burger Court and Justice Brennan the leading proponent of judicial activism. As you read their opinions consider whether either justice explains the issues. Why is judicial activism justified in some kinds of cases but not others?*

JUSTICE REHNQUIST delivered the opinion of the Court.

. . .

Appellants in no way challenge [past] decisions establishing the breadth of authority granted Congress under the commerce power. Their contention, on the contrary, is that when Congress seeks to regulate directly the activities of States as public employers, it transgresses an affirmative limitation on the exercise of its power akin to other commerce power affirmative limitations contained in the Constitution. Congressional enactments which may be fully within the grant of legislative authority contained in the Commerce Clause may nonetheless be invalid because found to offend against the right to trial by jury contained in the

Sixth Amendment... or the Due Process Clause of the Fifth Amendment. Appellants' essential contention is that the 1974 amendments to the Act, while undoubtedly within the scope of the Commerce Clause, encounter a similar constitutional barrier because they are to be applied directly to the States and subdivisions of States as employers.[8]

This Court has never doubted that there are limits upon the power of Congress to override state sovereignty, even when exercising its otherwise plenary powers to tax or to regulate commerce which are conferred by Art. I of the Constitution. In [*Maryland v.*] *Wirtz*, for example, the Court took care to assure the appellants that it had "ample power to prevent... 'the utter destruction of the State as a sovereign political entity,'" which they feared.... In *Fry* [*v. United States*], the Court recognized that an express declaration of this limitation is found in the Tenth Amendment:

> While the Tenth Amendment has been characterized as a "truism" stating merely that "all is retained which has not been surrendered,"... it is not without significance. The Amendment expressly declares the constitutional policy that Congress may not exercise power in a fashion that impairs the States' integrity or their ability to function effectively in a federal system....

...

...Appellee Secretary argues that the cases in which this Court has upheld sweeping exercises of authority by Congress, even though those exercises pre-empted state regulation of the private sector, have already curtailed the sovereignty of the States quite as much as the 1974 amendments to the Fair Labor Standards Act. We do not agree. It is one thing to recognize the authority of Congress to enact laws regulating individual businesses necessarily subject to the dual sovereignty of the government of the Nation and of the State in which they reside. It is quite another to uphold a similar exercise of congressional authority directed, not to private citizens, but to the States as States. We have repeatedly recognized that there are attributes of sovereignty attaching to every state government which may not be impaired by Congress, not because Congress may lack an affirmative grant of legislative authority to reach the matter, but because the Constitution prohibits it from exercising the authority in that manner. In *Coyle v. Smith* (1911), the Court gave this example of such an attribute:

> The power to locate its own seat of government and to determine when and how it shall be changed from one place to another, and to appropriate its own public funds for that purpose, are essentially and peculiarly state powers. That one of the original thirteen States could now be shorn of such powers by an act of Congress would not be for a moment entertained.

One undoubted attribute of state sovereignty is the States' power to determine the wages which shall be paid to those whom they employ in order to carry out their governmental functions, what hours those persons will work, and what compensation will be provided where these employees may be called upon to work overtime. The question we must resolve here, then, is whether these determinations are "functions essential to separate and independent existence,"... so that Congress may not abrogate the States' otherwise plenary authority to make them.

---

8. JUSTICE BRENNAN's dissent intimates... that guarantees of individual liberties are the only sort of constitutional restrictions which this Court will enforce as against congressional action. It reasons that "Congress is constituted of representatives in both Senate and House elected from the States. ... Decisions upon the extent of federal intervention under the Commerce Clause into the affairs of the States are in that sense decisions of the States themselves."... Precisely what is meant by the phrase "are in that sense decisions of the States themselves" is not entirely clear from this language; it is indisputable that a common constituency of voters elects both a State's Governor and its two United States Senators. It is equally indisputable that since the enactment of the Seventeenth Amendment those Senators are not dependent upon state legislators for their election. But in any event the intimation which this reasoning is used to support is incorrect.

In *Myers v. United States* (1926), the Court held that Congress could not by law limit the authority of the President to remove at will an officer of the Executive Branch appointed by him. In *Buckley v. Valeo* (1976), the Court held that Congress could not constitutionally require that members of the Federal Elections Commission be appointed by officers of the House of Representatives and of the Senate, and that all such appointments had to be made by the President. In each of these cases, an even stronger argument than that made in the dissent could be made to the effect that since each of these bills had been signed by the President, the very officer who challenged them had consented to their becoming law, and it was therefore no concern of this Court that the law violated the Constitution. Just as the dissent contends that "the States are fully able to protect their own interests...,"... it could have been contended that the President, armed with the mandate of a national constituency and with the veto power, was able to protect his own interests. Nonetheless, in both cases the laws were held unconstitutional, because they trenched on the authority of the Executive Branch.

Judged solely in terms of increased costs in dollars, these allegations show a significant impact on the functioning of the governmental bodies involved.... The State of California, which must devote significant portions of its budget to fire-suppression endeavors, estimated that application of the Act to its employment practices will necessitate an increase in its budget of between $8 million and $16 million.

...California asserted that it could not comply with the overtime costs (approximately $750,000 per year) which the Act required to be paid to California Highway Patrol cadets during their academy training program. California reported that it had thus been forced to reduce its academy training program from 2,080 hours to only 960 hours, a compromise undoubtedly of substantial importance to those whose safety and welfare may depend upon the preparedness of the California Highway Patrol.

...

Quite apart from the substantial costs imposed upon the States and their political subdivisions, the Act displaces state policies regarding the manner in which they will structure delivery of those governmental services which their citizens require. The Act, speaking directly to the States qua States, requires that they shall pay all but an extremely limited minority of their employees the minimum wage rates currently chosen by Congress. It may well be that as a matter of economic policy it would be desirable that States, just as private employers, comply with these minimum wage requirements. But it cannot be gainsaid that the federal requirement directly supplants the considered policy choices of the States' elected officials and administrators as to how they wish to structure pay scales in state employment. The State might wish to employ persons with little or no training, or those who wish to work on a casual basis, or those who for some other reason do not possess minimum employment requirements, and pay them less than the federally prescribed minimum wage. It may wish to offer part-time or summer employment to teenagers at a figure less than the minimum wage, and if unable to do so may decline to offer such employment at all. But the Act would forbid such choices by the States. The only "discretion" left to them under the Act is either to attempt to increase their revenue to meet the additional financial burden imposed upon them by paying congressionally prescribed wages to their existing complement of employees, or to reduce that complement to a number which can be paid the federal minimum wage without increasing revenue.

This dilemma presented by the minimum wage restrictions may seem not immediately different from that faced by private employers, who have long been covered by the Act and who must find ways to increase their gross income if they are to pay higher wages while maintaining current earnings. The difference, however, is that a State is not merely a factor in the "shifting economic arrangements" of the private sector of the economy,... but is itself a coordinate element in the system established by the Framers for governing our Federal Union.

...

...[E]ven if we accept appellee's assessments concerning the impact of the amendments, their application will nonetheless significantly alter or displace the States' abilities to structure employer–employee relationships in such areas as fire prevention, police protection, sanitation, public health, and parks and recreation. These activities are typical of those performed by state and local governments in discharging their dual functions of administering the public law and furnishing public services. Indeed, it is functions such as these which governments are created to provide, services such as these which the States have traditionally afforded their citizens. If Congress may withdraw from the States the authority to make those fundamental employment decisions upon which their systems for performance of these functions must rest, we think there would be little left of the States' "separate and independent existence."... Thus, even if appellants may have overestimated the effect which the Act will have upon their current levels and patterns of governmental activity, the dispositive factor is that Congress has attempted to exercise its Commerce Clause authority to prescribe minimum wages and maximum hours to be paid by the States in their capacities as sovereign governments. In so doing, Congress has sought to wield its power in a fashion that would impair the States' "ability to function effectively in a federal system."... This exercise of congressional authority does not comport with the federal system of government embodied in the Constitution. We hold that insofar as the challenged amendments operate to directly displace the States' freedom to structure integral operations in areas of traditional governmental functions, they are not within the authority granted Congress by Art. I, § 8, cl. 3.

...

[In *Fry v. United States*,] the Court held that the Economic Stabilization Act of 1970 was constitutional as applied to temporarily freeze the wages of state and local government employees.... The Court recognized that the Economic Stabilization Act was "an emergency measure to counter severe inflation that threatened the national economy."...

We think our holding today quite consistent with *Fry*. The enactment at issue there was occasioned by an extremely serious problem which endangered the well-being of all the component parts of our federal system and which only collective action by the National Government might forestall. The means selected were carefully drafted so as not to interfere with the States' freedom beyond a very limited, specific period of time. The effect of the across-the-board freeze authorized by that Act, moreover, displaced no state choices as to how governmental operations should be structured, nor did it force the States to remake such choices themselves.... The limits imposed upon the commerce power when Congress seeks to apply it to the States are not so inflexible as to preclude temporary enactments tailored to combat a national emergency....

With respect to the Court's decision in *Wirtz*, we reach a different conclusion....

Wirtz relied heavily on the Court's decision in *United States v. California* (1936). The opinion quotes the following language from that case:

> [We] look to the activities in which the states have traditionally engaged as marking the boundary of the restriction upon the federal taxing power. But there is no such limitation upon the plenary power to regulate commerce. The state can no more deny the power if its exercise has been authorized by Congress than can an individual....

But we have reaffirmed today that the States as States stand on a quite different footing from an individual or a corporation when challenging the exercise of Congress' power to regulate commerce. We think the dicta from *United States v. California*, simply wrong. Congress may not exercise that power so as to force directly upon the States its choices as to how essential decisions regarding the conduct of integral governmental functions are to be made.... We are therefore persuaded that *Wirtz* must be overruled.

JUSTICE BLACKMUN, concurring.

...I may misinterpret the Court's opinion, but it seems to me that it adopts a balancing approach, and does not outlaw federal power in areas such as environmental protection, where the federal interest is demonstrably greater and where state facility compliance with imposed federal standards would be essential.... With this understanding on my part of the Court's opinion, I join it.

JUSTICE BRENNAN, with whom JUSTICE WHITE and JUSTICE MARSHALL join, dissenting.

The Court concedes, as of course it must, that Congress enacted the 1974 amendments pursuant to its exclusive power under Art. I, § 8, cl. 3, of the Constitution "[t]o regulate Commerce...among the several States." It must therefore be surprising that my Brethren should choose this bicentennial year of our independence to repudiate principles governing judicial interpretation of our Constitution settled since the time of Chief Justice John Marshall, discarding his postulate that the Constitution contemplates that restraints upon exercise by Congress of its plenary commerce power lie in the political process and not in the judicial process. For 152 years ago Chief Justice Marshall enunciated that principle to which, until today, his successors on this Court have been faithful.

> [T]he power over commerce...is vested in Congress as absolutely as it would be in a single government, having in its constitution the same restrictions on the exercise of the power as are found in the constitution of the United States. The wisdom and the discretion of Congress, their identity with the people, and the influence which their constituents possess at elections, are...the sole restraints on which they have relied, to secure them from its abuse. They are the restraints on which the people must often rely solely, in all representative governments. *Gibbons v. Ogden*...

Only 34 years ago, *Wickard v. Filburn* (1942),...reaffirmed that "[a]t the beginning Chief Justice Marshall...made emphatic the embracing and penetrating nature of [Congress' commerce] power by warning that effective restraints on its exercise must proceed from political rather than from judicial processes."

My Brethren do not successfully obscure today's patent usurpation of the role reserved for the political process by their purported discovery in the Constitution of a restraint derived from sovereignty of the States on Congress' exercise of the commerce power. Chief Justice Marshall recognized that limitations "prescribed in the constitution,"...restrain Congress' exercise of the power....Thus laws within the commerce power may not infringe individual liberties protected by the First Amendment...or the Sixth Amendment....But there is no restraint based on state sovereignty requiring or permitting judicial enforcement anywhere expressed in the Constitution; our decisions over the last century and a half have explicitly rejected the existence of any such restraint on the commerce power.

We said in *United States v. California* (1936), for example: "The sovereign power of the states is necessarily diminished to the extent of the grants of power to the federal government in the Constitution....[T]he power of the state is subordinate to the constitutional exercise of the granted federal power."...

...

...[M]y Brethren are also repudiating the long line of our precedents holding that a judicial finding that Congress has not unreasonably regulated a subject matter of "commerce" brings to an end the judicial role.

The reliance of my Brethren upon the Tenth Amendment as "an express declaration of [a state sovereignty] limitation,"...not only suggests that they overrule governing decisions of this Court that address this question but must astound scholars of the Constitution. For not only early decisions, *Gibbons v. Ogden* (1824)..., *McCulloch v. Maryland* (1819),...and *Martin v. Hunter's Lessee* (1816),...hold that nothing in the Tenth Amendment constitutes a limitation on congressional exercise of powers delegated by the Constitution to Congress. Rather, as the Tenth Amendment's significance was more recently summarized:

> The amendment states but a truism that all is retained which has not been surrendered....
>
> From the beginning and for many years the amendment has been construed as not depriving the national government of authority to resort to all means for the exercise of a granted power which are appropriate and plainly adapted to the permitted end. *United States v. Darby* (1941)...

...

Today's repudiation of this unbroken line of precedents that firmly reject my Brethren's ill-conceived abstraction can only be regarded as a transparent cover for invalidating a congressional judgment with which they disagree. The only analysis even remotely resembling that adopted today is found in a line of opinions dealing with the Commerce Clause and the Tenth Amendment that ultimately provoked a constitutional crisis for the Court in the 1930's. E.g., *Carter v. Carter Coal Co.* (1936),...*United States v. Butler* (1936),...*Hammer v. Dagenhart* (1918)....

...

My Brethren's treatment of *Fry v. United States* (1975),...further illustrates the paucity of legal reasoning or principle justifying today's result....Obviously the Stabilization Act—no less than every exercise of a national power delegated to Congress by the Constitution—displaced the State's freedom. It is absurd to suggest that there is a constitutionally significant distinction between curbs against increasing wages and curbs against paying wages lower than the federal minimum.

...

My Brethren do more than turn aside longstanding constitutional jurisprudence that emphatically rejects today's conclusion. More alarming is the startling restructuring of our federal system, and the role they create therein for the federal judiciary. This Court is simply not at liberty to erect a mirror of its own conception of a desirable governmental structure....

...

Judicial restraint in this area merely recognizes that the political branches of our Government are structured to protect the interests of the States, as well as the Nation as a whole, and that the States are fully able to protect their own interests in the premises. Congress is constituted of representatives in both the Senate and House elected from the States....Decisions upon the extent of federal intervention under the Commerce Clause into the affairs of the States are in that sense decisions of the States themselves. Judicial redistribution of powers granted the National Government by the terms of the Constitution violates the fundamental tenet of our federalism that the extent of federal intervention into the States' affairs in the exercise of delegated powers shall be determined by States' exercise of political power through their representatives in Congress. See Wechsler, "The Political Safeguards of Federalism".... There is no reason whatever to suppose that in enacting the 1974 amendments Congress, even if it might extensively obliterate state sovereignty by fully exercising its plenary power respecting commerce, had any purpose to do so. Surely the presumption must be to the contrary. Any realistic assessment of our federal political system, dominated as it is by representatives of the people elected from the States, yields the conclusion that it is highly unlikely that those representatives will ever be motivated to disregard totally the concerns of these States....

...

We are left then with a catastrophic judicial body blow at Congress' power under the Commerce Clause. Even if Congress may nevertheless accomplish its objectives— for example, by conditioning grants of federal funds upon compliance with federal minimum wage and overtime standards,... there is an ominous portent of disruption of our constitutional structure implicit in today's mischievous decision. I dissent.

JUSTICE STEVENS, dissenting.

...

The Federal Government may, I believe, require the State to act impartially when it hires or fires the janitor, to withhold taxes from his paycheck, to observe safety regulations when he is performing his job, to forbid him from burning too much soft coal in the capitol furnace, from dumping untreated refuse in an adjacent waterway, from overloading a state-owned garbage truck, or from driving either the truck or the Governor's limousine over 55 miles an hour. Even though these and many other activities of the capitol janitor are activities of the State qua State, I have no doubt that they are subject to federal regulation.

...

My disagreement with the wisdom of this legislation may not, of course, affect my judgment with respect to its validity. On this issue there is no dissent from the proposition that the Federal Government's power over the labor market is adequate to embrace these employees. Since I am unable to identify a limitation on that federal power that would not also invalidate federal regulation of state activities that I consider unquestionably permissible, I am persuaded that this statute is valid. Accordingly, with respect and a great deal of sympathy for the views expressed by the Court, I dissent from its constitutional holding.

B. Interstate Travel

In *United States v. Guest* (1966), the Court affirmed that there was a constitutional right to travel which could be protected by Congress under Section Five of the Fourteenth Amendment. As a result, Congress was able to punish private conspiracies to prevent interstate travel, such as the 1964 murder to the black army reservist Lamuel Penn who was traveling through Georgia. *Edwards v. California* (1941) had struck down an "anti-Okie" law that had made it a crime to transport an "indigent" into the state of California (though Edwards happened to be convicted of bringing his unemployed brother-in-law to the Golden State from Texas). Although the majority struck down the law as an unconstitutional interference with interstate commerce, a four-person concurrence argued that individuals had a fundamental right as members of the union to engage in interstate travel. *Edwards* had deep roots, appealing back to cases such as *Crandall v. Nevada* (1868), which had struck down a Nevada tax on individuals leaving the state on the grounds that citizens had a right to move across state lines unimpeded by legal barriers. *Shapiro v. Thompson* (1969) tested that argument as the Court took up a challenge to the common state laws imposing a residency requirement before individuals could collect welfare. *Shapiro* raised questions about both the extent to which individuals had a "right to welfare" that states could not easily obstruct and the extent to which states could discriminate between long-time residents and new arrivals. If new arrivals were legally worse off than long-time residents, did that impede the constitutional right to travel and violate the structure of a federal constitutional union?

Shapiro v. Thompson, 394 U.S. 618 (1969)

Aid to Families with Dependent Children (AFDC) was a federal welfare program administered through and partly funded by the states. The Connecticut Welfare Department, following state law, denied the application of Vivian Marie Thompson to benefits under AFDC on the grounds that she had not been a resident of the state for a year before filing the application. (Thompson and her infant son had recently moved from Massachusetts to live with her mother in Hartford, Connecticut, but moved into her own apartment soon after her arrival in Hartford). Such state waiting-periods were common, especially as more generous states hoped to avoid becoming "welfare magnets" for the indigent residing in less generous states and as states in general hoped to discourage the poor from migrating into them. A divided federal three-judge panel struck down the provision as a violation of the equal protection clause of the Fourteenth Amendment and a burden on an intrinsic right to travel. Companion cases from the District of Columbia and Pennsylvania raised the same issue and were heard at the same time. The case fragmented the liberals on the Warren Court, in part over the issue of how much deference should be shown to Congress's policy choices and implicit constitutional judgments.

In Shapiro, *at the tail end of the Warren era, the Court took a step toward creating a new right to welfare. The case was first argued in 1967, and the Court voted 6–3 to uphold the residency requirements. Chief Justice Warren's would-be majority opinion, however, provoked strong dissenting opinions from Douglas and Fortas that persuaded Brennan to switch sides (Marshall was the third dissenter in the initial vote) and Stewart to waver. The case was scheduled for reargument, after which Warren was left in dissent. As the senior justice in the new majority, Douglas assigned the opinion to Brennan. Brennan was able to hold together his majority while suggesting that class, like race, was a category of special constitutional concern and that "the very means to subsist" was a fundamental right requiring judicial protection.*

In Shapiro, *the Court emphasized how the relations of federalism imposed limits on the burdens that states could impose on new residents and on those engaging in interstate travel. Residency requirements on welfare benefits ran afoul of a right to interstate travel. The majority and dissent differed, however, on whether such a right had implications for other issues. The Court avoided the question later in the term by dismissing a challenge to state residency requirements for voting as moot since by the time the case reached the Court the plaintiffs had satisfied the residency requirement in* Hall v. Beals *(1969). When might states be able to distinguish between well established and newly arrived residents? Are state policies preferring their own residents consistent with a federal union?*

JUSTICE BRENNAN delivered the opinion of the Court.

...

There is no dispute that the effect of the waiting-period requirement in each case is to create two classes of needy resident families indistinguishable from each other except that one is composed of residents who have resided a year or more, and the second of residents who have resided less than a year, in the jurisdiction. On the basis of this sole difference the first class is granted and the second class is denied welfare aid upon which may depend the ability of the families to obtain the very means to subsist—food, shelter, and other necessities of life. In each case, the District Court found that appellees met the test for residence in their jurisdictions, as well as all other eligibility requirements except the requirement of residence for a full year prior to their applications. On reargument, appellees' central contention is that the statutory prohibition of benefits to residents of less than a year creates a classification which constitutes an invidious discrimination denying them equal protection of the laws.[9] We agree. The interests which appellants assert are promoted by the classification either may not constitutionally be promoted by government or are not compelling governmental interests.

Primarily, appellants justify the waiting-period requirement as a protective device to preserve the fiscal integrity of state public assistance programs. It is asserted that people who require welfare assistance during their first year of residence in a State are likely to become continuing burdens on state welfare programs. Therefore, the argument runs, if such people can be deterred from entering the jurisdiction by denying them welfare benefits during the first year, state programs to assist long-time residents will not be impaired by a substantial influx of indigent newcomers.

There is weighty evidence that exclusion from the jurisdiction of the poor who need or may need relief was the specific objective of these provisions. In the Congress, sponsors of federal legislation to eliminate all residence requirements have been consistently opposed by representatives of state and local welfare agencies who have stressed the fears of the States that elimination of the requirements would result in a heavy influx of individuals into States providing the most generous benefits.... The sponsor of the Connecticut requirement said in its support: "I doubt that Connecticut can and should continue to allow unlimited migration into the state on the basis of offering instant money and permanent income to all who can make their way to the state regardless of their ability to contribute to the economy."...

...

This Court long ago recognized that the nature of our Federal Union and our constitutional concepts of personal liberty unite to require that all citizens be free

9. This constitutional challenge cannot be answered by the argument that public assistance benefits are a "privilege" and not a "right." See *Sherbert* v. *Verner* (1963).

to travel throughout the length and breadth of our land uninhibited by statutes, rules, or regulations which unreasonably burden or restrict this movement. That proposition was early stated by Chief Justice Taney in the *Passenger Cases* (1849):

> For all the great purposes for which the Federal government was formed, we are one people, with one common country. We are all citizens of the United States; and, as members of the same community, must have the right to pass and repass through every part of it without interruption, as freely as in our own States.

We have no occasion to ascribe the source of this right to travel interstate to a particular constitutional provision. It suffices that, as JUSTICE STEWART said for the Court in *United States* v. *Guest* (1966):

> The constitutional right to travel from one State to another...occupies a position fundamental to the concept of our Federal Union. It is a right that has been firmly established and repeatedly recognized.

...

Thus, the purpose of deterring the in-migration of indigents cannot serve as justification for the classification created by the one-year waiting period, since that purpose is constitutionally impermissible. If a law has "no other purpose... than to chill the assertion of constitutional rights by penalizing those who choose to exercise them, then it [is] patently unconstitutional." *United States* v. *Jackson* (1968).

...[T]he class of barred newcomers is all-inclusive, lumping the great majority who come to the State for other purposes with those who come for the sole purpose of collecting higher benefits. In actual operation, therefore, the three statutes enact what in effect are nonrebuttable presumptions that every applicant for assistance in his first year of residence came to the jurisdiction solely to obtain higher benefits. Nothing whatever in any of these records supplies any basis in fact for such a presumption.

More fundamentally, a State may no more try to fence out those indigents who seek higher welfare benefits than it may try to fence out indigents generally. Implicit in any such distinction is the notion that indigents who enter a State with the hope of securing higher welfare benefits are somehow less deserving than indigents who do not take this consideration into account. But we do not perceive why a mother who is seeking to make a new life for herself and her children should be regarded as less deserving because she considers, among others factors, the level of a State's public assistance. Surely such a mother is no less deserving than a mother who moves into a particular State in order to take advantage of its better educational facilities.

Appellants argue further that the challenged classification may be sustained as an attempt to distinguish between new and old residents on the basis of the contribution they have made to the community through the payment of taxes. We have difficulty seeing how long-term residents who qualify for welfare are making a greater present contribution to the State in taxes than indigent residents who have recently arrived.... Appellants' reasoning would logically permit the State to bar new residents from schools, parks, and libraries or deprive them of police and fire protection. Indeed it would permit the State to apportion all benefits and services according to the past tax contributions of its citizens. The Equal Protection Clause prohibits such an apportionment of state services.

We recognize that a State has a valid interest in preserving the fiscal integrity of its programs. It may legitimately attempt to limit its expenditures, whether for public assistance, public education, or any other program. But a State may not accomplish such a purpose by invidious distinctions between classes of its citizens. It could not, for example, reduce expenditures for education by barring indigent children from its schools....

...

...The waiting-period provision denies welfare benefits to otherwise eligible applicants solely because they have recently moved into the jurisdiction. But in moving from State to State or to the District of Columbia appellees were exercising a constitutional right, and any classification which serves to penalize the exercise of that right, unless shown to be necessary to promote a *compelling* governmental interest, is unconstitutional. Cf. *Skinner* v. *Oklahoma* (1942); *Korematsu* v. *United States* (1944); *Bates* v. *Little Rock* (1960); *Sherbert* v. *Verner* (1963).

...

We conclude therefore that appellants in these cases do not use and have no need to use the one-year requirement for the governmental purposes suggested. Thus, even under traditional equal protection tests a classification of welfare applicants according to whether they have lived in the State for one year would seem irrational and unconstitutional. But, of course, the traditional criteria do not apply in these cases. Since the classification here touches on the fundamental right of interstate movement, its constitutionality must be judged by the stricter standard of whether it promotes a *compelling* state interest. Under this standard, the waiting-period requirement clearly violates the Equal Protection Clause.[10]

Connecticut and Pennsylvania argue, however, that the constitutional challenge to the waiting-period requirements must fail because Congress expressly approved the imposition of the requirement by the States as part of the jointly funded AFDC program.

Section 402 (b) of the Social Security Act of 1935, as amended, 42 U. S. C. § 602 (b), provides that:

> The Secretary shall approve any [state assistance] plan which fulfills the conditions specified in subsection (a) of this section, except that he shall not approve any plan which imposes as a condition of eligibility for aid to families with dependent children, a residence requirement which denies aid with respect to any child residing in the State (1) who has resided in the State for one year immediately preceding the application for such aid, or (2) who was born within one year immediately preceding the application, if the parent or other relative with whom the child is living has resided in the State for one year immediately preceding the birth.

On its face, the statute does not approve, much less prescribe, a one-year requirement.... Rather than constituting an approval or a prescription of the requirement in state plans, the directive was the means chosen by Congress to deny federal funding to any State which persisted in stipulating excessive residence requirements as a condition of the payment of benefits.... Both the House and Senate Committee Reports expressly stated that the objective of § 402 (b) was to compel "liberality of residence requirement."...

...

10. We imply no view of the validity of waiting-period *or* residence requirements determining eligibility to vote, eligibility for tuition-free education, to obtain a license to practice a profession, to hunt or fish, and so forth. Such requirements may promote compelling state interests on the one hand, or, on the other, may not be penalties upon the exercise of the constitutional right of interstate travel.

...[E]ven if it could be argued that the constitutionality of § 402 (b) is somehow at issue here, it follows from what we have said that the provision, insofar as it permits the one-year waiting-period requirement, would be unconstitutional. Congress may not authorize the States to violate the Equal Protection Clause... *Katzenbach* v. *Morgan* (1966).

The waiting-period requirement in the District of Columbia Code involved in No. 33 is also unconstitutional even though it was adopted by Congress as an exercise of federal power. In terms of federal power, the discrimination created by the one-year requirement violates the Due Process Clause of the Fifth Amendment. "While the Fifth Amendment contains no equal protection clause, it does forbid discrimination that is "so unjustifiable as to be violative of due process." *Schneider* v. *Rusk* (1964); *Bolling* v. *Sharpe* (1954).

Affirmed.

JUSTICE STEWART, concurring.

...

The Court today does *not* "pick out particular human activities, characterize them as 'fundamental,' and give them added protection...." To the contrary, the Court simply recognizes, as it must, an established constitutional right, and gives to that right no less protection than the Constitution itself demands.

"The constitutional right to travel from one State to another...has been firmly established and repeatedly recognized." *United States* v. *Guest* (1966). This constitutional right, which, of course, includes the right of "entering and abiding in any State in the Union," *Truax* v. *Raich* (1915), is *not* a mere conditional liberty subject to regulation and control under conventional due process or equal protection standards. "The right to travel freely from State to State finds constitutional protection that is quite independent of the Fourteenth Amendment." *United States* v. *Guest*....

CHIEF JUSTICE WARREN, with whom JUSTICE BLACK joins, dissenting.

In my opinion the issue before us can be simply stated: May Congress, acting under one of its enumerated powers, impose minimal nationwide residence requirements or authorize the States to do so? Since I believe that Congress does have this power and has constitutionally exercised it in these cases, I must dissent.

...

The Great Depression of the 1930's exposed the inadequacies of state and local welfare programs and dramatized the need for federal participation in welfare assistance.... The primary purpose of the categorical assistance programs was to encourage the States to provide new and greatly enhanced welfare programs. See, *e. g.*, S. Rep. No. 628, 74th Cong., 1st Sess., 5–6, 18–19 (1935); H. R. Rep. No. 615, 74th Cong., 1st Sess., 4 (1935). Federal aid would mean an immediate increase in the amount of benefits paid under state programs. But federal aid was to be conditioned upon certain requirements so that the States would remain the basic administrative units of the welfare system and would be unable to shift the welfare burden to local governmental units with inadequate financial resources....

...The congressional decision to allow the States to impose residence requirements and to enact such a requirement for the District was the subject of considerable discussion. Both those favoring lengthy residence requirements and those opposing all requirements pleaded their case during the congressional hearings on the Social Security Act. Faced with the competing claims of States which feared that abolition of residence requirements would result in an influx of persons seeking higher welfare payments and of organizations which stressed the unfairness of such requirements to transient workers forced by the economic dislocation of the depression to seek work far from their homes, Congress chose a middle course....

...Residence requirements have remained a part of this combined state-federal welfare program for 34 years. Congress has adhered to its original decision that residence requirements were necessary in the face of repeated attacks against these requirements....

Congress, pursuant to its commerce power, has enacted a variety of restrictions upon interstate travel. It has taxed air and rail fares and the gasoline needed to power cars and trucks which move interstate. Many of the federal safety regulations of common carriers which cross state lines burden the right to travel. And Congress has prohibited by criminal statute interstate travel for certain purposes. Although these restrictions operate as a limitation upon free interstate movement of persons, their constitutionality appears well settled. As the Court observed in *Zemel* v. *Rusk* (1965), "the fact that a liberty cannot be inhibited without due process of law does not mean that it can under no circumstances be inhibited."

...As already noted, travel itself is not prohibited. Any burden inheres solely in the fact that a potential welfare recipient might take into consideration the loss of welfare benefits for a limited period of time if he changes his residence. Not only is this burden of uncertain degree, but appellees themselves assert there is evidence that few welfare recipients have in fact been deterred by residence requirements....

...One fact which does emerge with clarity from the legislative history is Congress' belief that a program of cooperative federalism combining federal aid with enhanced state participation would result in an increase in the scope of welfare programs and level of benefits.... Our cases require only that Congress have a rational basis for finding that a chosen regulatory scheme is necessary to the furtherance of interstate commerce. See, *e. g.*, *Katzenbach* v. *McClung* (1964); *Wickard* v. *Filburn* (1942)....

Appellees suggest, however, that Congress was not motivated by rational considerations. Residence requirements are imposed, they insist, for the illegitimate purpose of keeping poor people from migrating. Not only does the legislative history point to an opposite conclusion, but it also must be noted that "into the motives which induced members of Congress to [act]... this Court may not enquire." *Arizona* v. *California* (1931). We do not attribute an impermissible purpose to Congress if the result would be to strike down an otherwise valid statute.... Since the congressional decision is rational and the restriction on travel insubstantial, I conclude that residence requirements can be imposed by Congress as an exercise of its power to control interstate commerce consistent with the constitutionally guaranteed right to travel.

...Assuming that the constitutionality of § 402 (b) is properly treated by the Court, the cryptic footnote in *Katzenbach* v. *Morgan*, 384 U.S. 641, 651–652, n. 10 (1966), does not support its conclusion. Footnote 10 indicates that Congress is without power to undercut the equal-protection guarantee of racial equality in the guise of implementing the Fourteenth Amendment. I do not mean to suggest otherwise. However, I do not understand this footnote to operate as a limitation upon Congress' power to further the flow of interstate commerce by reasonable residence requirements. Although the Court dismisses § 402 (b) with the remark that Congress cannot authorize the States to violate equal protection, I believe that the dispositive issue is whether under its commerce power Congress can impose residence requirements.

Nor can I understand the Court's implication that other state residence requirements such as those employed in determining eligibility to vote do not present constitutional questions.... If a State would violate equal protection by denying welfare benefits to those who have recently moved interstate, then it would appear to follow that equal protection would also be denied by depriving those who have recently moved interstate of the fundamental right to vote. There is nothing in the opinion of the Court to explain this dichotomy....

The era is long past when this Court under the rubric of due process has reviewed the wisdom of a congressional decision that interstate commerce will be fostered by the enactment of certain regulations. Speaking for the Court in *Helvering* v. *Davis* (1937), Justice Cardozo said of another section of the Social Security Act:

> Whether wisdom or unwisdom resides in the scheme of benefits set forth... is not for us to say. The answer to such inquiries must come from Congress, not the courts. Our concern here, as often, is with power, not with wisdom.

I am convinced that Congress does have power to enact residence requirements of reasonable duration or to authorize the States to do so and that it has exercised this power.

The Court's decision reveals only the top of the iceberg. Lurking beneath are the multitude of situations in which States have imposed residence requirements including eligibility to vote, to engage in certain professions or occupations or to attend a state-supported university. Although the Court takes pains to avoid acknowledging the ramifications of its decision, its implications cannot be ignored. I dissent.

JUSTICE HARLAN, dissenting.

...

In upholding the equal protection argument, the Court has applied an equal protection doctrine of relatively recent vintage: the rule that statutory classifications which either are based upon certain "suspect" criteria or affect "fundamental rights" will be held to deny equal protection unless justified by a "compelling" governmental interest.

The "compelling interest" doctrine, which today is articulated more explicitly than ever before, constitutes an increasingly significant exception to the long-established rule that a statute does not deny equal protection if it is rationally related to a legitimate governmental objective....

I think that this branch of the "compelling interest" doctrine is sound when applied to racial classifications, for historically the Equal Protection Clause was largely a product of the desire to eradicate legal distinctions founded upon race. However, I believe that the more recent extensions have been unwise. For the reasons stated in my dissenting opinion in *Harper* v. *Virginia Bd. of Elections* (1966), I do not consider wealth a "suspect" statutory criterion. And when, as in *Williams* v. *Rhodes* (1968), and the present case, a classification is based upon the exercise of rights guaranteed against state infringement by the Federal Constitution, then there is no need for any resort to the Equal Protection Clause; in such instances, this Court may properly and straightforwardly invalidate any undue burden upon those rights under the Fourteenth Amendment's Due Process Clause.

The second branch of the "compelling interest" principle is even more troublesome. For it has been held that a statutory classification is subject to the "compelling interest" test if the result of the classification may be to affect a "fundamental right," regardless of the basis of the classification....

I think this branch of the "compelling interest" doctrine particularly unfortunate and unnecessary. It is unfortunate because it creates an exception which threatens to swallow the standard equal protection rule. Virtually every state statute affects important rights. This Court has repeatedly held, for example, that the traditional equal protection standard is applicable to statutory classifications affecting such fundamental matters as the right to pursue a particular occupation, the right to receive greater or smaller wages or to work more or less hours, and the right to inherit property. Rights such as these are in principle indistinguishable from those involved here, and to extend the "compelling interest" rule to all cases in which such rights are affected would go far toward making this Court a "super-legislature." This branch of the doctrine is also unnecessary. When the right affected is one assured by the Federal Constitution, any infringement can be dealt with under the Due Process Clause. But when a statute affects only matters not mentioned in the Federal Constitution and is not arbitrary or irrational, I must reiterate that I know of nothing which entitles this Court to pick out particular human activities, characterize them as "fundamental," and give them added protection under an unusually stringent equal protection test.

...

...In light of this undeniable relation of residence requirements to valid legislative aims, it cannot be said that the requirements are "arbitrary" or "lacking in rational justification." Hence, I can find no objection to these residence requirements under the Equal Protection Clause of the Fourteenth Amendment or under the analogous standard embodied in the Due Process Clause of the Fifth Amendment.

...

...I do not minimize the importance of the right to travel interstate. However, the impact of residence conditions upon that right is indirect and apparently quite insubstantial. On the other hand, the governmental purposes served by the requirements are legitimate and real, and the residence requirements are clearly suited to their accomplishment....

I conclude with the following observations. Today's decision, it seems to me, reflects to an unusual degree the current notion that this Court possesses a peculiar wisdom all its own whose capacity to lead this Nation out of its present troubles is contained only by the limits of judicial ingenuity in contriving new constitutional principles to meet each problem as it arises. For anyone who, like myself, believes that it is an essential function of this Court to maintain the constitutional divisions between state and federal authority and among the three branches of the Federal Government, today's decision is a step in the wrong direction....

V. Separation of Powers

MAJOR DEVELOPMENTS

- Congress challenged presidential war powers
- Supreme Court asserted the authority to override executive privilege
- Congress and President struggled over control of executive branch and administrative policymaking

Separation-of-powers issues became more central to American constitutional politics after 1968. Richard Nixon's election began a period of divided government, when increasingly conservative Republican presidents faced increasingly liberal Democratic congresses. Nixon maintained that the president had broad powers to act unilaterally when making both foreign and domestic policy. His decisions to expand the military conflict in Southeast Asia and impound funds appropriated by Congress were aggressively challenged by both national legislators and litigants.

The results of the political crisis that led to Watergate were ambiguous. On the one hand, President Nixon was forced to resign, the Supreme Court rejected his broad claims of executive privilege in *United States v. Nixon* (1974) and his efforts to impound federal funds in *Train v. City of New York* (1975), and the War Powers Act of 1973 limited presidential power to engage in military hostilities abroad. On the other hand, the War Powers Act also recognized an executive authority to initiate military combat that many liberals thought unconstitutional, and the Supreme Court, when it rejected President Nixon's more extreme claims, did give constitutional sanction to both executive privilege and executive immunity. Most important, the Nixon impeachment did not end the era of the imperial presidency. Both Republicans and Democrats who followed would seek to build on the constitutional foundations of the New Deal and Great Society presidency. By the time Ronald Reagan took office, presidents were as likely to wear wigs as espouse William Howard Taft's vision of the passive presidency.

Presidents have asserted that the presence of military conflict or an international crisis expands national and executive power in two ways. First, New Deal and Great Society presidents have asserted the right to take unilateral actions during times of military conflict that they admit would normally be unconstitutional. The Nixon Administration, for example, insisted that the Vietnam War justified that administration's internal surveillance policies. Second, New Deal and Great Society presidents have insisted that war expands national powers in general, even to the point of regulating rights that would be inviolate during peacetime. The Roosevelt Administration made such claims when justifying executive orders providing curfews and the eventual resettlement of Japanese-Americans. For the most part, both Congress and the courts either accepted or did not interfere with Roosevelt's assertions of executive authority during World War II, the one exception being *Ex Parte Endo* (1944), which declared unconstitutional a measure the administration was abandoning. Congress did refuse to grant Truman the power to seize property used to manufacture munitions and the Supreme Court supported that refusal in the *Youngstown* case. Both Congress and the courts more aggressively policed executive power once Richard Nixon took office. Democrats in Congress attempted to restrict the powers Nixon thought necessary for fighting communism, and the Supreme Court further limited executive authority in *United States v. United States District Court* (1972).

Executive action seemed particularly pressing when the United States was involved in foreign combat, which was often the case during the New Deal and Great Society Era. Mark Brandon observes that the United States during the twentieth century was involved in a declared war, an undeclared war, or a significant military action in all but six years.[11] These ongoing military hostilities raised numerous constitutional questions that, by the end of the Great Society Era, were threatening constitutional crises. The most important of these was presidential power to send troops into foreign combat in the absence of a declared war or in the absence of congressional approval. Other questions concerned how military action abroad influenced public policy at home. In particular, Presidents Roosevelt, Truman, and Nixon all claimed that their power as commander-in-chief justified taking unilateral action domestically without congressional approval.

Judicial efforts to limit presidential power were largely limited to circumstances when the justices perceived that Congress had affirmatively rejected the presidential authority in question. Although some language in concurring opinions in the *Youngstown* case suggested greater limits on unilateral executive action, the justices for the most part insisted that Congress clearly disapprove of presidential action before setting constitutional limits. In other words, the Court was as likely to take its cues from congressional politics as from constitutional texts. However, congressional efforts to assert power during the middle of the twentieth century tended to be intermittent, symbolic, or ambiguous. For the most part Congress either acquiesced to Roosevelt Administration policy during World War II or engaged in relatively ineffective grumbling about executive aggrandizement. The national legislature was far more assertive during the Vietnam War, as a Democratic legislature increased controlled by antiwar liberals vigorously condemned President Richard Nixon's military policies in Southeast Asia. Whether the end result of that constitutional dispute, the War Powers Act of 1973, increased or decreased executive authority has been a matter of ongoing disagreement.

11. Mark E. Brandon, "War and American Constitutional Order," *Vanderbilt Law Review* 56 (2003):1815, 1820.

A. Presidential War and Foreign Affairs Powers

During the Second World War and the Cold War there was relative agreement in the political system about how to conduct foreign policy. Presidents were sometimes pushed by members of Congress, either to take a firmer stance against communism or to do more to avoid foreign entanglements, but on the whole they had a great deal of freedom to maneuver. At the extreme, President Harry Truman was able to launch the Korean War without any prior congressional authorization, but presidents routinely engaged in covert and open military missions abroad with implicit congressional support while building a substantial and often secretive national security apparatus to support their activities.

The Vietnam War shattered that consensus. There was less agreement in Washington about geostrategic goals and strategy, and less faith that the White House would make the right calls. Policy disputes triggered constitutional disputes. Congressional reformers challenged presidential authority to initiate and conduct military offenses. Presidential advocates looked to defend established executive prerogatives to exercise discretion to do what was necessary to advance American national interests. The War Powers Act of 1973 was one effort to redefine the relationship between Congress and the president over how military force would be used, recognizing that military forces would continue to be used without prior congressional authorization but seeking to prevent long-term or substantial engagements without explicit legislative involvement. From a different angle, after high-profile congressional hearings investigating the CIA and FBI, the Foreign Intelligence Surveillance Act of 1978 tried to regulate the process by which the executive branch gathered intelligence.

Leonard C. Meeker, The Legality of the United States Participation in the Defense of Viet-Nam (1966)[12]

In 1966, State Department Legal Advisor Leonard Meeker produced a memorandum for submission to the Senate Committee on Foreign Relations explicating the legal basis for the Vietnam War. The memo was wide-ranging, primar-

12. Excerpt taken from *Congressional Record*, 91st Cong., 2nd sess., vol. 116, pt. 15 (June 23, 1970), 20972–77.

ily focusing on international law, American treaty obligations to Vietnam, and the 1964 Gulf of Tonkin Resolutions authorizing the use of military force in Vietnam. It included, however, a constitutional analysis of presidential war powers that later became influential as Congress became disillusioned with the war and began to debate its own proper role in authorizing or ending the use of military force by the United States. The Meeker memo became the starting point for defenders of the presidential direction of the war in Vietnam, not only in the Johnson administration but also in the Nixon administration and in Congress itself.

. . .

Under the Constitution, the President, in addition to being Chief Executive, is Commander in Chief of the Army and Navy. He holds the prime responsibility for the conduct of United States foreign relations. These duties carry very broad powers, including the power to deploy American forces abroad and commit them to military operations when the President deems such action necessary to maintain the security and defense of the United States.

At the Federal Constitutional Convention in 1787, it was originally proposed that Congress have the power "to make war." There were objections that legislative proceedings were too slow for this power to be vested in Congress; it was suggested that the Senate might be a better repository. Madison and Gerry then moved to substitute "to declare war" for "to make war," "leaving to the Executive the power to repel sudden attacks." It was objected that this might make it too easy for the Executive to involve the nation in war, but the motion carried with but one dissenting vote.

In 1787 the world was a far larger place, and the framers probably had in mind attacks upon the United States. In the 20th century, the world has grown much smaller. An attack on a country far from our shores can impinge directly on the nation's security. . . .

Since the Constitution was adopted there have been at least 125 instances in which the President has ordered the armed forces to take action or maintain positions abroad without obtaining prior congressional authorization, starting with the "undeclared war" with France (1798–1800). For example, President Truman ordered 250,000 troops to Korea during the Korean war of the early 1950's. President Eisenhower dispatched 14,000 troops to Lebanon in 1958.

The Constitution leaves to the President the judgment to determine whether the circumstances of a particular armed attack are so urgent and the potential consequences so threatening to the security of the United States that he should act without formally consulting Congress.

. . .

Over a very long period of our history, practice and precedent have confirmed the constitutional authority to engage United States forces in hostilities without a declaration of war . . .

James Madison, one of the leading framers of the Constitution, and Presidents John Adams and Jefferson all construed the Constitution, in their official actions during the early years of the Republic, as authorizing the United States to employ its armed forces abroad in hostilities in the absence of any congressional declaration of war. Their views and actions constitute persuasive evidence as to the meaning and effect of the Constitution. History has accepted the interpretation that was placed on the Constitution by the early Presidents and Congresses in regard to the lawfulness of hostilities without a declaration of war. The instances of such actions in our history are numerous.

. . .

It may be suggested that a declaration of war is the only available constitutional process by which congressional support can be made effective for the use of United States armed forces in combat abroad. But the Constitution does not insist on any rigid formalism. It gives Congress a choice of ways in which to exercise its powers. In the case of Viet-Nam the Congress has supported the determination of the President by the Senate's approval of the SEATO treaty, the adoption of the joint resolution of August 10, 1964, and the enactment of the necessary authorization and appropriations.

. . .

J. William Fulbright, **Congress and Foreign Policy** (1967)[13]

J. William Fulbright, chairman of the Senate Foreign Relations Committee from 1959 through 1974, had ushered the 1964 Gulf of Tonkin Resolution through the Senate, formally launching the Vietnam War. Within a few years, however, Fulbright was pressing for a more active congressional role in the making of foreign policy. The Committee held numer-

13. Excerpt taken from *Congressional Record*, 90th Cong., 1st sess., vol. 113, pt. 15 (July 31, 1967), 20702–706.

ous hearings and issued several reports highlighting what Fulbright viewed as an abdication by Congress of its constitutional role in foreign policy generally and the war powers specifically. Even as he raised those concerns, however, Fulbright and others in Congress struggled with what the practical congressional response could be to the perceived imbalance of power given the nature of American involvement in the world in the latter half of the twentieth century. Those efforts eventually led to the passage of the War Powers Resolution in 1973, but in the late 1960s Fulbright pressed the National Commitments Resolution, which argued that presidents should not promise or commit American resources and support to foreign countries without active congressional approval.

...

The authority of Congress in foreign policy has been eroding since 1940, the year of America's emergence as a major and permanent participant in world affairs, and the erosion has created a significant constitutional imbalance. Many if not most of the major decisions of American foreign policy in this era have been executive decisions.... Since World War II the United States has fought two wars without benefit of Congressional declaration and has engaged in numerous small-scale military activities—in the Middle East, for example, in 1958, and in the Congo on several occasions—without meaningful consultation with the Congress.

New devices have been invented which have the appearance but not the reality of Congressional participation in the making of foreign policy.... One is the joint resolution; another is the congressional briefing session. Neither is a satisfactory occasion for deliberation or the rendering of advice; both are designed to win consent without advice. Their principal purpose is to put the Congress on record in support of some emergency action at a moment when it would be most difficult to withhold support and, therefore, to spare the executive subsequent controversy or embarrassment.

The cause of the constitutional imbalance is crisis. I do not believe that the executive has willfully usurped the constitutional authority of Congress; nor do I believe that the Congress has knowingly given away its traditional authority, although some of its members—I among them, I regret to say—have sometimes shown excessive regard for the executive freedom of action. In the main, however, it has been circumstance rather than design which has given the executive its great predominance in foreign policy. The circumstance has been crisis, an entire era of crisis in which urgent decisions have been required again and again, decisions of a kind that the Congress is ill-equipped to make with what has been thought to be the requisite speed. The President has the means at his disposal for prompt action; the Congress does not.... (I might add that I think there have been many occasions when the need for immediate action has been exaggerated, resulting in mistakes which might have been avoided by greater deliberation.)

The question before us is whether and how the constitutional balance can be restored.... It is improbable that we will soon return to a kind of normalcy in the world, and impossible that the United States will return to its pre-1940 isolation. How then can we in the Congress do what the Constitution does not simply ask of us, but positively requires of us, under precisely the conditions which have resulted in the erosion of our authority? It is not likely that the President... will take the initiative in curtailing his own freedom of action and restoring the constitutional prerogative—that would be too much to expect of him. It is up to the Congress... to re-evaluate its role and to re-examine its proper responsibilities.

...

Prior to redefining our responsibilities, it is important for us to distinguish clearly between two kinds of power, that pertaining to the shaping of foreign policy, to its direction and purpose and philosophy, and that pertaining to the day-to-day conduct of foreign policy. The former is the power which the Congress has the duty to discharge, diligently, vigorously and continuously; the latter, by and large calling for specialized skills, is best left to the executive and its administrative arms....

Our performance in recent years has, unfortunately, been closer to the reverse. We have tended to snoop and pry in matters of detail, interfering in the handling of specific problems in specific places which we happen to chance upon, and, worse still, harassing individuals in the executive departments, thereby undermining their morale and discouraging the creative initiative which is so essential to a successful foreign policy. At the same time we have resigned from our responsibility in the shaping of policy and the defining of its purposes, submitting too easily to the pressures of crisis, giving away things that are not ours to give: the war power of Congress, the treaty power of the Senate and the broader advice and consent power.

...

Permit me to recall some recent crises and the extremely limited role of the Senate in dealing with them.... At the time of the Cuban missile crisis in October 1962, many of us were in our home states campaigning for re-election.... [N]one of us, so far as I know, were given official information until after the Administration had made its policy decisions. President Kennedy called the congressional leadership for a meeting at the White House on Monday, October 22, 1962. The meeting lasted from about 5 p.m. to about 6 p.m.; at 7 p.m. President Kennedy went on national television to announce to the country the decisions which had of course been made before the Congressional leadership were called in. The meeting was not a consultation but a briefing, a kind of courtesy or ceremonial occasion for the leadership of the Congress. At that meeting, the senior Senator from Georgia and I made specific suggestions as to how the crisis might be met; we did so in the belief that we had a responsibility to give the President our best advice on the basis of the limited facts then at our command. With apparent reference to our temerity in expressing our views, Theodore Sorensen in his book on President Kennedy described this occasion as "the only sour note" in an otherwise flawless process of decision making. It is not exaggeration to say that on the one occasion when the world has gone to the very brink of nuclear war... the Congress took no part whatever in the shaping of American policy.

...

On the Senate floor as well as in the Foreign Relations Committee, vigorous and responsible discussion of our foreign relations is essential both to the shaping of wise foreign policy and to the sustenance of our constitutional system. The criteria of responsible and constructive debate are restraint in matters of detail and the day-to-day conduct of foreign policy, combined with diligence and energy in discussing the values, direction and purposes of American foreign policy. Just as it is an excess of democracy when Congress is overly aggressive in attempting to supervise the conduct of foreign policy, it is a failure of democracy when it fails to participate actively in determining policy objectives and in the making of significant decisions.

...

The War Powers Act of 1973

In 1973 Congress passed the War Powers Resolution over President Richard Nixon's veto. For several years, Congress had been debating whether and by what means the legislature should take a more active role in setting foreign policy and initiating military conflict. The continuation and expansion of the Vietnam War, even after congressional sentiment had turned against it, and the weakness of the Nixon administration in the midst of the Watergate scandal and in the final days before his resignation from office spurred Congress to pass the Resolution. The War Powers Resolution was a compromise between those who favored congressional supremacy in this area and those who simply favored greater and more effective congressional participation in the policymaking process. The Resolution called for presidential "consultation" "in every possible instance" with Congress when American troops would be placed in harm's way, a requirement for reporting to Congress on the necessity and authority for presidential action when hostilities did occur, and requiring the president to disengage American forces if Congress either passed a joint resolution calling for such disengagement or failed to authorize the continued use of military force.

Although presidents have formally complied with the terms of the Resolution, they have also consistently maintained that they are not constitutionally required to do so. Congress has provided resolutions authorizing major military operations such as the Iraq war, but other, smaller scale military actions such as the invasion of Grenada, Haiti, and Panama did not have prior congressional authorization. Such actions did not, in the words of President Clinton's assistant attorney general Walter Dellinger, rise to the level of "'war' in the constitutional sense" given their "anticipated nature, scope and duration."[14]

Public Law 93–148

...

SEC. 2. (a) It is the purpose of this joint resolution to fulfill the intent of the framers of the Constitution of the United States and insure that the collective judgment of both the Congress and the President will apply to the introduction of United States Armed Forces into hostilities, or into situations where imminent involvement in hostilities is

14. Walter Dellinger, "Deployment of United States Armed Forces into Haiti, September 27, 1994," 18 Op. O.L.C. 173 (1994).

clearly indicated by the circumstances, and to the continued use of such forces in hostilities or in such situations.

SEC. 2. (b) Under article I, section 8, of the Constitution, it is specifically provided that the Congress shall have the power to make all laws necessary and proper for carrying into execution, not only its own powers but also all other powers vested by the Constitution in the Government of the United States, or in any department or officer thereof.

SEC. 2. (c) The constitutional powers of the President as Commander-in-Chief to introduce United States Armed Forces into hostilities, or into situations where imminent involvement in hostilities is clearly indicated by the circumstances, are exercised only pursuant to (1) a declaration of war, (2) specific statutory authorization, or (3) a national emergency created by attack upon the United States, its territories or possessions, or its armed forces.

SEC. 3. The President in every possible instance shall consult with Congress before introducing United States Armed Forces into hostilities or into situation where imminent involvement in hostilities is clearly indicated by the circumstances, and after every such introduction shall consult regularly with the Congress until United States Armed Forces are no longer engaged in hostilities or have been removed from such situations.

SEC. 4. (a) In the absence of a declaration of war, in any case in which United States Armed Forces are introduced—

(1) into hostilities or into situations where imminent involvement in hostilities is clearly indicated by the circumstances;

(2) into the territory, airspace or waters of a foreign nation, while equipped for combat, except for deployments which relate solely to supply, replacement, repair, or training of such forces; or

(3) (A) the circumstances necessitating the introduction of United States Armed Forces;

(B) the constitutional and legislative authority under which such introduction took place; and

(C) the estimated scope and duration of the hostilities or involvement.

SEC. 4. (b) The President shall provide such other information as the Congress may request in the fulfillment of its constitutional responsibilities with respect to committing the Nation to war and to the use of United States Armed Forces abroad.

SEC. 4. (c) Whenever United States Armed Forces are introduced into hostilities or into any situation described in subsection (a) of this section, the President shall, so long as such armed forces continue to be engaged in such hostilities or situation, report to the Congress periodically on the status of such hostilities or situation as well as on the scope and duration of such hostilities or situation, but in no event shall he report to the Congress less often than once every six months.

. . .

SEC. 5. (b) Within sixty calendar days after a report is submitted or is required to be submitted pursuant to section 4(a)(1), whichever is earlier, the President shall terminate any use of United States Armed Forces with respect to which such report was submitted (or required to be submitted), unless the Congress (1) has declared war or has enacted a specific authorization for such use of United States Armed Forces, (2) has extended by law such sixty-day period, or (3) is physically unable to meet as a result of an armed attack upon the United States. Such sixty-day period shall be extended for not more than an additional thirty days if the President determines and certifies to the Congress in writing that unavoidable military necessity respecting the safety of United States Armed Forces requires the continued use of such armed forces in the course of bringing about a prompt removal of such forces.

SEC. 5. (c) Notwithstanding subsection (b), at any time that United States Armed Forces are engaged in hostilities outside the territory of the United States, its possessions and territories without a declaration of war or specific statutory authorization, such forces shall be removed by the President if the Congress so directs by concurrent resolution.

. . .

SEC. 8. (a) Authority to introduce United States Armed Forces into hostilities or into situations wherein involvement in hostilities is clearly indicated by the circumstances shall not be inferred— (1) from any provision of law (whether or not in effect before the date of the enactment of this joint resolution), including any provision contained in any appropriation Act, unless such provision specifically authorizes the introduction of United States Armed Forces into hostilities or into such situations and stating that it is intended to constitute specific statutory authorization within the meaning of this joint resolution; or (2) from any treaty heretofore or hereafter ratified unless such treaty is implemented by legislation specifically authorizing the introduction of United States Armed Forces into hostilities or into such situations and stating that it is intended to constitute specific statutory authorization within the meaning of this joint resolution.

...

SEC. 8. (d) Nothing in this joint resolution—

(1) is intended to alter the constitutional authority of the Congress or of the President, or the provision of existing treaties; or

(2) shall be construed as granting any authority to the President with respect to the introduction of United States Armed Forces into hostilities or into situations wherein involvement in hostilities is clearly indicated by the circumstances which authority he would not have had in the absence of this joint resolution.

Richard Nixon, **Veto of the War Powers Resolution** (1973)[15]

President Nixon had threatened to veto the War Powers Resolution, but by the time it was passed he was mired in the Watergate scandal and the Vietnam War was regarded as a costly failure exacerbated by an unresponsive executive branch. Nixon was faced with Democratic majorities in both the House and the Senate throughout his time as president, but Congress overrode his veto of the War Powers Resolution with bipartisan support for the bill.

To the House of Representatives:

I hereby return without my approval House Joint Resolution 542—the War Powers Resolution. While I am in accord with the desire of the Congress to assert its proper role in the conduct of our foreign affairs, the restrictions which this resolution would impose upon the authority of the President are both unconstitutional and dangerous to the interests of our Nation.

The proper roles of the Congress and the Executive in the conduct of foreign affairs have been debated since the founding of our country. Only recently, however, has there been a serious challenge to the wisdom of the Founding Fathers in choosing not to draw a precise and detailed line of demarcation between the foreign policy powers of the two branches.

...

Clearly Unconstitutional

House Joint Resolution 542 would attempt to take away, by a mere legislative act, authorities which the President has properly exercised under the Constitution for almost 200 years. One of its provisions would automatically cut off certain authorities after sixty days unless the Congress extended them. Another would allow the Congress to eliminate certain authorities merely by the passage of a concurrent resolution—an action which does not normally have the force of law, since it denies the President his constitutional role in approving legislation.

I believe that both these provisions are unconstitutional. The only way in which the constitutional powers of a branch of the Government can be altered is by amending the Constitution—and any attempt to make such alterations by legislation alone is clearly without force.

Undermining Our Foreign Policy

...I am also deeply disturbed by the practical consequences of this resolution. For it would seriously undermine this Nation's ability to act decisively and convincingly in times of international crisis....

...

Failure to Require Positive Congressional Action

I am particularly disturbed by the fact that certain of the President's constitutional powers as Commander in Chief of the Armed Forces would terminate automatically under this resolution 60 days after they were invoked....In effect, the Congress is here attempting to increase its policymaking role through a provision that it requires it to take absolutely no action at all.

In my view, the proper way for the Congress to make known its will on such foreign policy questions is through a positive action, with full debate on the merits of the issue and with each member taking the responsibility of casting a yes or no vote after considering those

15. Excerpt taken from *Public Papers of the Presidents of the United States: Richard Nixon, 1973* (Washington, DC: Government Printing Office, 1975), 893–95.

merits. The authorization and appropriations process represents one of the ways in which such influence can be exercised.... [The joint resolution] would give every future Congress the ability to handcuff every future President merely by doing nothing and sitting still. In my view, one cannot become a responsible partner unless one is prepared to take responsible action.

United States v. United States District Court, 407 U.S. 297 (1972) [the "Keith Case"]

Robert Plamondon and two co-defendants were charged with the dynamite bombing of a CIA office in Ann Arbor, Michigan. During pretrial motions it was revealed that the government had wiretapped the defendants without first obtaining a search warrant. Plamondon's lawyers argued that this warrantless surveillance violated the Fourth Amendment and that any other evidence obtained as a result of this illegal search should be excluded from the trial. In response, the Justice Department—headed by Attorney General John Mitchell—claimed that the surveillance was lawful as a reasonable exercise of the President's independent Article II power to protect the national security, and that any information so obtained did not have to be disclosed to the defendants. The Nixon administration also relied, in part, on Title III of the Omnibus Crime Control and Safe Streets Act of 1968. This contained a provision that nothing in that law limits the President's constitutional power to protect against the overthrow of the government or against "any other clear and present danger to the structure or existence of the government."

District Court Judge Damon Keith disagreed and ordered the government to disclose the information. The government appealed Judge Keith's ruling (hence the "Keith case"), but its position was unanimously rejected by the Sixth Circuit Court of Appeals. It fared no better before the Supreme Court. In an 8–0 opinion (with newly appointed Justice Rehnquist not participating owing to his prior association with the case in the Justice Department) the justices found that the government's internal security concerns did not justify departure from the customary requirement of judicial approval prior to initiation of a search or surveillance. The justices did not address the question of whether similar requirements were necessary for "foreign surveillance." Is judicial oversight of intelligence gathering consistent with presidential responsibilities for national security? Would the constitutional implications be different if the case involved foreign groups?

JUSTICE POWELL delivered the opinion of the Court.

The issue before us is an important one for the people of our country and their Government. It involves the delicate question of the President's power, acting through the Attorney General, to authorize electronic surveillance in internal security matters without prior judicial approval. Successive Presidents for more than one-quarter of a century have authorized such surveillance in varying degrees, without guidance from the Congress or a definitive decision of this Court. This case brings the issue here for the first time. Its resolution is a matter of national concern, requiring sensitivity both to the Government's right to protect itself from unlawful subversion and attack and to the citizen's right to be secure in his privacy against unreasonable Government intrusion....

During pretrial proceedings, the defendants moved to compel the United States to disclose certain electronic surveillance information and to conduct a hearing to determine whether this information "tainted" the evidence on which the indictment was based or which the Government intended to offer at trial. In response, the Government filed an affidavit of the Attorney General, acknowledging that its agents had overheard conversations in which Plamondon had participated....

...

Together with the elaborate surveillance requirements in Title III, there is the following proviso, *18 U. S. C. § 2511* (3):

> Nothing contained in this chapter or in section 605 of the Communications Act of 1934 (48 Stat. 1143; *47 U. S. C. 605*) shall limit the constitutional power of the President to take such measures as he deems necessary to protect the Nation against actual or potential attack or other hostile acts of a foreign power, to obtain foreign intelligence information deemed essential to the security of the United States, or to protect national security information against foreign intelligence activities. *Nor shall anything contained in this chapter be deemed to limit the constitutional power of the President to take such measures as he deems necessary to protect the United States against the overthrow of the Government by force or other unlawful means, or against any other clear and present danger to the structure or existence of the Government....* (Emphasis supplied.)

The Government relies on § 2511 (3). It argues that "in excepting national security surveillances from the Act's warrant requirement Congress recognized the President's authority to conduct such surveillances without prior judicial approval." The section thus is viewed as a recognition or affirmance of a constitutional authority in the President to conduct warrantless domestic security surveillance such as that involved in this case.

We think the language of § 2511 (3), as well as the legislative history of the statute, refutes this interpretation....

Section 2511 (3)... merely provides that the Act shall not be interpreted to limit or disturb such power as the President may have under the Constitution. In short, Congress simply left presidential powers where it found them....

It is important at the outset to emphasize the limited nature of the question before the Court. This case raises no constitutional challenge to electronic surveillance as specifically authorized by Title III of the Omnibus Crime Control and Safe Streets Act of 1968. Nor is there any question or doubt as to the necessity of obtaining a warrant in the surveillance of crimes unrelated to the national security interest. Further, the instant case requires no judgment on the scope of the President's surveillance power with respect to the activities of foreign powers, within or without this country. The Attorney General's affidavit in this case states that the surveillances were "deemed necessary to protect the nation from attempts of *domestic organizations* to attack and subvert the existing structure of Government" (emphasis supplied). There is no evidence of any involvement, directly or indirectly, of a foreign power....

We begin the inquiry by noting that the President of the United States has the fundamental duty, under Art. II, § 1, of the Constitution, to "preserve, protect and defend the Constitution of the United States." Implicit in that duty is the power to protect our Government against those who would subvert or overthrow it by unlawful means. In the discharge of this duty, the President—through the Attorney General—may find it necessary to employ electronic surveillance to obtain intelligence information on the plans of those who plot unlawful acts against the Government....

But a recognition of these elementary truths does not make the employment by Government of electronic surveillance a welcome development—even when employed with restraint and under judicial supervision. There is, understandably, a deep-seated uneasiness and apprehension that this capability will be used to intrude upon cherished privacy of law-abiding citizens. We look to the Bill of Rights to safeguard this privacy. Though physical entry of the home is the chief evil against which the wording of the Fourth Amendment is directed, its broader spirit now shields private speech from unreasonable surveillance. Our decision in *Katz v. United States* (1967) refused to lock the Fourth Amendment into instances of actual physical trespass. Rather, the Amendment governs "not only the seizure of tangible items, but extends as well to the recording of oral statements... without any 'technical trespass under... local property law.'" That decision implicitly recognized that the broad and unsuspected governmental incursions into conversational privacy which electronic surveillance entails necessitate the application of Fourth Amendment safeguards.

National security cases, moreover, often reflect a convergence of First and Fourth Amendment values not present in cases of "ordinary" crime.... History abundantly documents the tendency of Government—however benevolent and benign its motives—to view with suspicion those who most fervently dispute its policies. Fourth Amendment protections become the more necessary when the targets of official surveillance may be those suspected of unorthodoxy in their political beliefs. The danger to political dissent is acute where the Government attempts to act under so vague a concept as the power to protect "domestic security."...

The price of lawful public dissent must not be a dread of subjection to an unchecked surveillance power. Nor must the fear of unauthorized official eavesdropping deter vigorous citizen dissent and discussion of Government action in private conversation. For private dissent, no less than open public discourse, is essential to our free society....

As the Fourth Amendment is not absolute in its terms, our task is to examine and balance the basic values at stake in this case: the duty of Government to protect the domestic security, and the potential danger posed by unreasonable surveillance to individual privacy and free expression. If the legitimate need of Government to safeguard domestic security requires the use of electronic surveillance, the question is whether the needs of citizens for privacy and free expression may not be better protected by requiring a warrant before such surveillance is undertaken. We must also ask whether a warrant requirement would unduly frustrate the efforts of Government to protect itself from acts of subversion and overthrow directed against it.

...

These Fourth Amendment freedoms cannot properly be guaranteed if domestic security surveillances may be conducted solely within the discretion of the Executive Branch. The Fourth Amendment does not contemplate the executive officers of Government as neutral and disinterested magistrates.... The historical judgment, which the Fourth Amendment accepts, is that unreviewed executive discretion may yield too readily to pressures to obtain incriminating evidence and overlook potential invasions of privacy and protected speech....

It is true that there have been some exceptions to the warrant requirement. But those exceptions are few in number and carefully delineated; in general, they serve the legitimate needs of law enforcement officers to protect their own well-being and preserve evidence from destruction. Even while carving out those exceptions, the Court has reaffirmed the principle that the "police must, whenever practicable, obtain advance judicial approval of searches and seizures through the warrant procedure."

The Government argues that the special circumstances applicable to domestic security surveillances necessitate a further exception to the warrant requirement. It is urged that the requirement of prior judicial review would obstruct the President in the discharge of his constitutional duty to protect domestic security.... It is said that this type of surveillance should not be subject to traditional warrant requirements which were established to govern investigation of criminal activity, not ongoing intelligence gathering.

The Government further insists that courts "as a practical matter would have neither the knowledge nor the techniques necessary to determine whether there was probable cause to believe that surveillance was necessary to protect national security." These security problems, the Government contends, involve "a large number of complex and subtle factors" beyond the competence of courts to evaluate....

We cannot accept the Government's argument that internal security matters are too subtle and complex for judicial evaluation. Courts regularly deal with the most difficult issues of our society. There is no reason to believe that federal judges will be insensitive to or uncomprehending of the issues involved in domestic security cases....

Nor do we believe prior judicial approval will fracture the secrecy essential to official intelligence gathering. The investigation of criminal activity has long involved imparting sensitive information to judicial officers who have respected the confidentialities involved. Judges may be counted upon to be especially conscious of security requirements in national security cases....

Thus, we conclude that the Government's concerns do not justify departure in this case from the customary Fourth Amendment requirement of judicial approval prior to initiation of a search or surveillance. Although some added burden will be imposed upon the Attorney General, this inconvenience is justified in a free society to protect constitutional values....

The judgment of the Court of Appeals is hereby

Affirmed

JUSTICE DOUGLAS, concurring.

While I join in the opinion of the Court, I add these words in support of it.

This is an important phase in the campaign of the police and intelligence agencies to obtain exemptions from the Warrant Clause of the Fourth Amendment. For, due to the clandestine nature of electronic eavesdropping, the need is acute for placing on the Government the heavy burden to show that "exigencies of the situation [make its] course imperative." Other abuses, such as the search incident to arrest, have been partly deterred by the threat of damage actions against offending officers, the risk of adverse publicity, or the possibility of reform through the political process. These latter safeguards, however, are ineffective against lawless wiretapping and "bugging" of which their victims are totally unaware. Moreover, even the risk of exclusion of tainted evidence would here appear to be of negligible deterrent value inasmuch as the United States frankly concedes that the primary purpose of these searches is to fortify its intelligence collage rather than to accumulate evidence to support indictments and convictions. If the Warrant Clause were held inapplicable here, then the federal intelligence machine would literally enjoy unchecked discretion.

Here, federal agents wish to rummage for months on end through every conversation, no matter how intimate or personal, carried over selected telephone lines, simply to seize those few utterances which may add to their sense of the pulse of a domestic underground.

...

That "domestic security" is said to be involved here does not draw this case outside the mainstream of Fourth Amendment law. Rather, the recurring desire of reigning officials to employ dragnet techniques to intimidate their critics lies at the core of that prohibition. For it was such excesses as the use of general warrants and the writs of assistance that led to the ratification of the Fourth Amendment....

...[W]e are currently in the throes of another national seizure of paranoia, resembling the hysteria which surrounded the Alien and Sedition Acts, the Palmer Raids, and the McCarthy era. Those who register dissent or who petition their governments for redress are subjected to scrutiny by grand juries, by the FBI, or even by the military. Their associates are interrogated. Their homes are bugged and their telephones are wiretapped. They are befriended by secret government informers. Their patriotism and loyalty are questioned. Senator Sam Ervin, who has chaired hearings on military surveillance of civilian dissidents, warns that "it is not an exaggeration to talk in terms of hundreds of thousands of...dossiers."... More than our privacy is implicated. Also at stake is the reach of the Government's power to intimidate its critics.

When the Executive attempts to excuse these tactics as essential to its defense against internal subversion, we are obliged to remind it, without apology, of this Court's long commitment to the preservation of the Bill of Rights from the corrosive environment of precisely such expedients....

...We have as much or more to fear from the erosion of our sense of privacy and independence by the omnipresent electronic ear of the Government as we do from the likelihood that fomenters of domestic upheaval will modify our form of governing.

JUSTICE WHITE, concurring.

...I would affirm the Court of Appeals but on the statutory ground urged by defendant-respondents without reaching or intimating any views with respect to the constitutional issue decided by both the District Court and the Court of Appeals....

...Because I conclude that on the record before us the surveillance undertaken by the Government in this case was illegal under the statute itself, I find it unnecessary, and therefore improper, to consider or decide the constitutional questions which the courts below improvidently reached....

B. Executive Privilege

The highest profile assertion of executive privilege came during the Watergate investigation as President Richard Nixon sought to protect tapes of White House conversations from being used in a criminal prosecution. *United States v. Nixon* (1974) is unusual not only because of its extraordinarily dramatic circumstances, but also because it involves a claim of executive privilege in a criminal case in a judicial proceeding. The Supreme Court proved to be particularly unsympathetic to the administration's efforts to completely withhold potential evidence from a criminal investigation in the courts and willing to trust the judgment of a trial court judge to review presidential documents and determine which should remain confidential and which should not. Claims of executive privilege are usually more mundane, and they are more often aimed at the legislature than the courts. Presidents have often argued that their conversations and notes should be confidential if the White House is to function effectively, and ultimately it is the president's judgment of what can be safely revealed that preserves the autonomy and effectiveness of the executive branch. The decision to breach executive privilege is most often a matter of negotiation, rather than mandate. The *Nixon* case posed the question of when the courts might be able to trump the executive's claim of privilege.

United States v. Nixon, 418 U.S. 683 (1974)

The crisis known as Watergate arose as a result of an investigation into potential White House involvement in the burglary and attempted bugging of the Democratic Party's headquarters at the Watergate Hotel on June 17, 1972. This investigation led to inquiries into an alleged secret White House "Special Investigations Unit" known as the "Plumbers." This group was made up of members and former members of America's intelligence community (including former CIA official E. Howard Hunt and former FBI official G. Gordon Liddy) and was created in response to the release of the Pentagon Papers. Their initial job (as plumbers) was to plug leaks. However, before long members of the Plumbers were recruited to engage in a variety of off-the-books campaign activities. These included the sabotaging of Ed Muskie's

"He says he's from the phone company . . ."

Illustration 9-2 "He Says He's from the Phone Company"

Source: Paul Conrad, *Los Angeles Times*, June 1972. Used by permission of the Paul Conrad estate.

presidential campaign by such "dirty tricks" as creating fake banners designed to anger other Democrats, harassing people considered White House "enemies," mugging of demonstrators at Republican events, and conspiring to obstruct justice. The Plumbers were funded by millions of dollars of secret contributions to Nixon's reelection campaign, known as CREEP (the Committee to Reelect the President).

It did not take long before some of Nixon's top aides were implicated in the burglary and the subsequent pre-election cover-up of White House involvement. As District Judge John Sirica was busy presiding over the trial of the Watergate burglars, the Senate established a select committee, chaired by Sam Ervin, to investigate the Watergate affair.

In testimony before this committee it was revealed that Nixon secretly taped all Oval Office conversations. This revelation prompted the Special Watergate Prosecutor, Archibald Cox, to begin legal proceedings to obtain from the President those tapes that were thought likely to contain evidence important for the prosecution of the suspected Watergate conspirators.

In October 1973 Nixon demanded that Cox drop his quest for the White House tapes. When he refused, Attorney General Richardson was ordered to fire Cox. Both Richardson and his deputy refused, citing promises made during Senate confirmation hearings to respect Cox's independence, and so they too were fired by the third-ranking official in the Justice Department, Solicitor General Robert Bork, in what became known as the Saturday Night Massacre.

In response to the political firestorm that followed the "massacre," Nixon informed Sirica that nine tapes would be forthcoming. Unfortunately, the tape of the first conversation between Nixon and Haldeman after the Watergate break-in contained an eighteen-and-a-half-minute gap. While the White House blamed the gap on an innocent mistake made by Nixon's secretary, it was later established that the erasure had been deliberate. One week after Nixon agreed to release these nine (edited) tapes, the House Judiciary Committee began its impeachment inquiry.

In a further attempt to mollify the opposition, Nixon agreed to hire a new Special Prosecutor, Leon Jaworski. Jaworski continued to push for the tapes. Specifically, he wanted an additional sixty-four tapes to use in his prosecution of Mitchell, Haldeman, and Ehrlichman. Nixon refused to turn over the tapes, claiming that they were protected by executive privilege. Jaworski sought a subpoena from the federal courts compelling the president to turn over the tapes.

U.S. v. Nixon *raised a classic separation-of-powers question: How should we balance the president's interest in maintaining the confidentiality of White House conversations against the judiciary's interest in providing due process in a criminal proceeding? Does this issue represent a zero-sum game for these two branches, in the sense that supporting the president's position would make it impossible for the judiciary to carry out its constitutional responsibilities, while (conversely) supporting the judiciary's position would undermine the president's ability to carry out her or his responsibilities?*

As you read the opinion, consider the issues that the Court leaves unanswered. Apparently the need for relevant evidence in a criminal proceeding outweighs the general executive interest in confidential advice. What other competing interests might outweigh a general claim of privilege? Should the president be forced to hand over information whenever the Court or Congress requests it and the president asserts only a general interest in executive confidentiality? Is executive confidentiality less weighty than the judiciary's interest in the operation of the criminal justice system but more weighty than a general congressional interest in administrative oversight? Does the judiciary's interest in relevant information extend to all judicial proceedings or simply those that involve high government officials charged with serious criminal offenses? Does an invocation of executive privilege on the grounds of national security always outweigh the competing interests of the other branches? Who decides whether a president's assertion of executive privilege on grounds of national security is legitimate? The president? The Congress? Certain members of Congress? The courts? Is it properly within the judiciary's sphere of authority to second-guess executive determinations about what will or will not harm national security?

When the tapes were finally released, they revealed that from the very beginning the president and his top advisers conspired to obstruct justice by arranging for millions of dollars in hush money for the Watergate burglars. They also showed that Haldeman intended to use the CIA for political espionage; that Nixon's close friend John Mitchell, the former attorney general and the head of CREEP, originated the break-in of the Watergate hotel; and that Nixon and his advisers discussed contriving a "national security" justification for the break-in. Four days later, as senators of his own political party urged him to leave office, Nixon resigned.

Richard Nixon went 1–3 in the Supreme Court on claims of executive privilege, with two more important cases being heard after Nixon left office. In Nixon v. Administrator of General Services *(1977), the Supreme Court by a 7–2 vote ruled that Congress could pass rules governing the disposal of Nixon's presidential papers, and that a former president could not assert an absolute privilege to keep all presidential papers private. Nixon was more successful when defending against a civil lawsuit by a military analyst, who claimed that he had been illegally fired by the former president in retaliation for his congressional testimony. The Supreme Court by a 5–4 vote in* Nixon v. Fitzgerald *(1982) asserted that the Constitution vested the president with absolute immunity for "acts in performance of particular functions of his office." "Because of the singular importance of the President's duties," Justice Powell's majority opinion declared, "diversion of his energies by concern with private lawsuits would raise unique risks to the effective functioning of government."*

CHIEF JUSTICE BURGER delivered the opinion of the Court.

...

On March 1, 1974, a grand jury of the United States District Court for the District of Columbia returned an indictment charging seven named individuals with various offenses, including conspiracy to defraud the

United States and to obstruct justice. Although he was not designated as such in the indictment, the grand jury named the President, among others, as an unindicted coconspirator. On April 18, 1974, upon motion of the Special Prosecutor, a subpoena *duces tecum* was issued pursuant to Rule 17 (c) to the President by the United States District Court and made returnable on May 2, 1974. This subpoena required the production, in advance of the September 9 trial date, of certain tapes, memoranda, papers, transcripts, or other writings relating to certain precisely identified meetings between the President and others....

[W]e turn to the claim that the subpoena should be quashed because it demands "confidential conversations between a President and his close advisors that it would be inconsistent with the public interest to produce." The first contention is a broad claim that the separation of powers doctrine precludes judicial review of a President's claim of privilege. The second contention is that if he does not prevail on the claim of absolute privilege, the court should hold as a matter of constitutional law that the privilege prevails over the subpoena *duces tecum*.

In the performance of assigned constitutional duties each branch of the Government must initially interpret the Constitution, and the interpretation of its powers by any branch is due great respect from the others. The President's counsel, as we have noted, reads the Constitution as providing an absolute privilege of confidentiality for all Presidential communications. Many decisions of this Court, however, have unequivocally reaffirmed the holding of *Marbury v. Madison* (1803), that "[it] is emphatically the province and duty of the judicial department to say what the law is."...

Notwithstanding the deference each branch must accord the others, the "judicial Power of the United States" vested in the federal courts by Art. III, § 1, of the Constitution can no more be shared with the Executive Branch than the Chief Executive, for example, can share with the Judiciary the veto power, or the Congress share with the Judiciary the power to override a Presidential veto. Any other conclusion would be contrary to the basic concept of separation of powers and the checks and balances that flow from the scheme of a tripartite government. *The Federalist*, No. 47....

In support of his claim of absolute privilege, the President's counsel urges two grounds, one of which is common to all governments and one of which is peculiar to our system of separation of powers. The first ground is the valid need for protection of communications between high Government officials and those who advise and assist them in the performance of their manifold duties; the importance of this confidentiality is too plain to require further discussion. Human experience teaches that those who expect public dissemination of their remarks may well temper candor with a concern for appearances and for their own interests to the detriment of the decisionmaking process. Whatever the nature of the privilege of confidentiality of Presidential communications in the exercise of Art. II powers, the privilege can be said to derive from the supremacy of each branch within its own assigned area of constitutional duties. Certain powers and privileges flow from the nature of enumerated powers; the protection of the confidentiality of Presidential communications has similar constitutional underpinnings.

The second ground asserted by the President's counsel in support of the claim of absolute privilege rests on the doctrine of separation of powers. Here it is argued that the independence of the Executive Branch within its own sphere insulates a President from a judicial subpoena in an ongoing criminal prosecution, and thereby protects confidential Presidential communications.

However, neither the doctrine of separation of powers, nor the need for confidentiality of high-level communications, without more, can sustain an absolute, unqualified Presidential privilege of immunity from judicial process under all circumstances. The President's need for complete candor and objectivity from advisers calls for great deference from the courts. However, when the privilege depends solely on the broad, undifferentiated claim of public interest in the confidentiality of such conversations, a confrontation with other values arises. Absent a claim of need to protect military, diplomatic, or sensitive national security secrets, we find it difficult to accept the argument that even the very important interest in confidentiality of Presidential communications is significantly diminished by production of such material for *in camera* inspection with all the protection that a district court will be obliged to provide.

The impediment that an absolute, unqualified privilege would place in the way of the primary constitutional duty of the Judicial Branch to do justice in criminal prosecutions would plainly conflict with the function of the courts under Art. III. In designing the structure of our Government and dividing and allocating the sovereign power among three co-equal branches, the Framers of the Constitution sought to provide a comprehensive system, but the separate powers were not intended to operate with absolute independence.

> While the Constitution diffuses power the better to secure liberty, it also contemplates that practice will integrate the dispersed powers into a workable government. It enjoins upon its branches separateness but interdependence, autonomy but reciprocity. *Youngstown Sheet & Tube Co.* v. *Sawyer* (1952) (Jackson, J., concurring).

To read the Art. II powers of the President as providing an absolute privilege as against a subpoena essential to enforcement of criminal statutes on no more than a generalized claim of the public interest in confidentiality of nonmilitary and nondiplomatic discussions would upset the constitutional balance of "a workable government" and gravely impair the role of the courts under Art. III.

Since we conclude that the legitimate needs of the judicial process may outweigh Presidential privilege, it is necessary to resolve those competing interests in a manner that preserves the essential functions of each branch....

The expectation of a President to the confidentiality of his conversations and correspondence, like the claim of confidentiality of judicial deliberations, for example, has all the values to which we accord deference for the privacy of all citizens and, added to those values, is the necessity for protection of the public interest in candid, objective, and even blunt or harsh opinions in Presidential decisionmaking. A President and those who assist him must be free to explore alternatives in the process of shaping policies and making decisions and to do so in a way many would be unwilling to express except privately. These are the considerations justifying a presumptive privilege for Presidential communications. The privilege is fundamental to the operation of Government and inextricably rooted in the separation of powers under the Constitution....

But this presumptive privilege must be considered in light of our historic commitment to the rule of law.... We have elected to employ an adversary system of criminal justice in which the parties contest all issues before a court of law. The need to develop all relevant facts in the adversary system is both fundamental and comprehensive. The ends of criminal justice would be defeated if judgments were to be founded on a partial or speculative presentation of the facts. The very integrity of the judicial system and public confidence in the system depend on full disclosure of all the facts, within the framework of the rules of evidence. To ensure that justice is done, it is imperative to the function of courts that compulsory process be available for the production of evidence needed either by the prosecution or by the defense....

In this case the President challenges a subpoena served on him as a third party requiring the production of materials for use in a criminal prosecution; he does so on the claim that he has a privilege against disclosure of confidential communications. He does not place his claim of privilege on the ground they are military or diplomatic secrets. As to these areas of Art. II duties the courts have traditionally shown the utmost deference to Presidential responsibilities....

No case of the Court, however, has extended this high degree of deference to a President's generalized interest in confidentiality. Nowhere in the Constitution, as we have noted earlier, is there any explicit reference to a privilege of confidentiality, yet to the extent this interest relates to the effective discharge of a President's powers, it is constitutionally based.

The right to the production of all evidence at a criminal trial similarly has constitutional dimensions. The Sixth Amendment explicitly confers upon every defendant in a criminal trial the right "to be confronted with the witnesses against him" and "to have compulsory process for obtaining witnesses in his favor." Moreover, the Fifth Amendment also guarantees that no person shall be deprived of liberty without due process of law. It is the manifest duty of the courts to vindicate those guarantees, and to accomplish that it is essential that all relevant and admissible evidence be produced.

In this case we must weigh the importance of the general privilege of confidentiality of Presidential communications in performance of the President's responsibilities against the inroads of such a privilege on the fair administration of criminal justice. The interest in preserving confidentiality is weighty indeed and entitled to great respect. However, we cannot conclude that advisers will be moved to temper the candor of their remarks by the infrequent occasions of disclosure because of the possibility that such conversations will be called for in the context of a criminal prosecution.

On the other hand, the allowance of the privilege to withhold evidence that is demonstrably relevant in a criminal trial would cut deeply into the guarantee of due process of law and gravely impair the basic function of the courts. A President's acknowledged need for confidentiality in the communications of his office is general in nature, whereas the constitutional need for production of relevant evidence in a criminal proceeding is specific and central to the fair adjudication of a particular criminal case in the administration of justice. Without access to specific facts a criminal prosecution may be totally frustrated. The President's broad interest in confidentiality of communications will not be vitiated by disclosure of a limited number of conversations preliminarily shown to have some bearing on the pending criminal cases.

We conclude that when the ground for asserting privilege as to subpoenaed materials sought for use in a criminal trial is based only on the generalized interest in confidentiality, it cannot prevail over the fundamental demands of due process of law in the fair administration of criminal justice. The generalized assertion of privilege must yield to the demonstrated, specific need for evidence in a pending criminal trial....

...We now turn to the important question of the District Court's responsibilities in conducting the *in camera* examination of Presidential materials or communications delivered under the compulsion of the subpoena *duces tecum.*

...It is elementary that *in camera* inspection of evidence is always a procedure calling for scrupulous protection against any release or publication of material not found by the court, at that stage, probably admissible in evidence and relevant to the issues of the trial for which it is sought. That being true of an ordinary situation, it is obvious that the District Court has a very heavy responsibility to see to it that Presidential conversations, which are either not relevant or not admissible, are accorded that high degree of respect due the President of the United States. Chief Justice Marshall, sitting as a trial judge in the *Burr* case (25 Fed. Cas. 30 [C.C.D. Va. 1807]) was extraordinarily careful to point out that

> [in] no case of this kind would a court be required to proceed against the president as against an ordinary individual.

Marshall's statement cannot be read to mean in any sense that a President is above the law, but relates to the singularly unique role under Art. II of a President's communications and activities, related to the performance of duties under that Article. Moreover, a President's communications and activities encompass a vastly wider range of sensitive material than would be true of any "ordinary individual." It is therefore necessary in the public interest to afford Presidential confidentiality the greatest protection consistent with the fair administration of justice. The need for confidentiality even as to idle conversations with associates in which casual reference might be made concerning political leaders within the country or foreign statesmen is too obvious to call for further treatment. We have no doubt that the District Judge will at all times accord to Presidential records that high degree of deference suggested in *United States* v. *Burr,* and will discharge his responsibility to see to it that until released to the Special Prosecutor no *in camera* material is revealed to anyone. This burden applies with even greater force to excised material; once the decision is made to excise, the material is restored to its privileged status and should be returned under seal to its lawful custodian.

Since this matter came before the Court during the pendency of a criminal prosecution, and on representations that time is of the essence, the mandate shall issue forthwith.

JUSTICE REHNQUIST took no part in the decision of these cases.

Suggested Readings

Burgess, Susan A. *Contest for Constitutional Authority* (Lawrence: University Press of Kansas, 1992).

Carmines, Edward G., and James A. Stimson, *Issue Evolution: Race and the Transformation of American Politics* (Princeton: Princeton University Press, 1989).

Ely, John Hart. *War and Responsibility: Constitutional Lessons of Vietnam and Its Aftermath* (Princeton: Princeton University Press, 1993).

Fisher, Louis. *Presidential Conflicts between Congress and the President*, 3rd ed. (Lawrence: University Press of Kansas, 1991).

Fisher, Louis. *Presidential War Powers*, 2nd ed. (Lawrence: University Press of Kansas, 2004).

Keck, Thomas M. *The Most Activist Supreme Court in History: The Road to Modern Judicial Conservatism* (Chicago: University of Chicago Press, 2004).

Kutler, Stanley I. *The Wars of Watergate: The Last Crisis of Richard Nixon* (New York: Norton, 1990).

Ladd, Everett Carll, Jr., with Charles D. Hadley. *Transformations of the American Party System: Political Coalitions from the New Deal to the 1970s* (New York: Norton, 1975).

McGirr, Lisa. *Suburban Warriors: The Origins of the New American Right* (Princeton: Princeton University Press, 2001).

Perlstein, Rick. *Nixonland: The Rise of a President and the Fracturing of America* (New York: Scribner, 2008).

Schwartz, Bernard. *The Ascent of Pragmatism: The Burger Court in Action* (Reading, MA: Addison Wesley, 1990).

Schwartz, Bernard, ed. *The Burger Court: Counter-Revolution or Confirmation?* (New York: Oxford University Press, 1998).

Schlesinger, Arthur M., Jr. *The Imperial Presidency* (Boston: Houghton Mifflin, 1973).

Silverstein, Gordon. *Imbalance of Powers: Constitutional Interpretation and the Making of American Foreign Policy* (New York: Oxford University Press, 1996).

Sundquist, James L. *Decline and Resurgence of Congress* (Washington, DC: Brookings Institution, 1981).

Whittington, Keith E. *Constitutional Construction: Divided Powers and Constitutional Meaning* (Cambridge: Harvard University Press, 1999).

Whittington, Keith E. *Political Foundations of Judicial Supremacy: The President, the Supreme Court, and Constitutional Leadership in U.S. History* (Princeton: Princeton University Press, 2007).

Yalof, David. *Pursuit of Justices: Presidential Politics and the Pursuit of Supreme Court Nominees* (Chicago: University of Chicago Press, 1999).

Part 3 **Contemporary Issues**

Chapter 10

The Reagan Era: 1981–1993

I. Introduction

With the election of Ronald Reagan as president in 1980, the era of the New Deal and the Great Society appeared to have come to an end. It was much less clear what, if anything, had taken its place. The liberal, Democratic order was no longer politically and constitutionally dominant. The ideological and constitutional alternative of the post-Reagan period, however, was neither as well defined nor as politically secure as its predecessors had been.

There had been rumblings within the Democratic order for some time, but Ronald Reagan represented a different level of challenge. Barry Goldwater had managed to capture the Republican Party nomination for a new conservative movement that offered a frontal challenge to liberalism—but incumbent President Lyndon Johnson defeated Goldwater in a landslide in 1964 and launched the Great Society, deepening and expanding the liberal project. The morass of Vietnam and urban race riots politically debilitated Johnson and his vice president and flag bearer in the 1968 presidential election, Hubert Humphrey, opening the door to a victory by Republican Richard Nixon. But Republicans were unable to swing either chamber of Congress in their favor in 1968, and Nixon did not question the foundations of the Great Society, only its perceived excesses. Although Democrats regained the presidency in 1976 with the election of Jimmy Carter, he was not regarded as sufficiently liberal by some Democrats and faced a primary challenge from his left by Senator Edward Kennedy in 1980.

Partisan Coalitions in the Reagan Era. Ronald Reagan's victory in 1980, the "Reagan Revolution," was a true shock to the political system. Reagan was a onetime movie actor who had transformed himself into a political commentator, had gained national prominence during Goldwater's presidential campaign, and had served two terms as governor of California from 1967 to 1975, assembling a record highlighted by aggressive budget cuts, a crackdown on student unrest on state university campuses, a tightening of welfare eligibility, and tax cuts. By the late 1970s, Reagan was the most prominent politician to have emerged out of the conservative movement that Goldwater had spearheaded a decade earlier and was a serious threat to President Gerald Ford's renomination by the Republican Party in 1976. Reagan ran a distinctly conservative campaign in 1980, and his victory shook the New Deal order to its core. As Reagan famously declared in his first inaugural address, "government is not the solution to our problem; government is the problem." This was a sentiment that no major politician since Barry Goldwater would have expressed, and no elected president since before Franklin Roosevelt would have thought.

Reagan's victory was more startling because he was clearly at the head of a successful political movement. In 1980, the Republican Party won a majority in the U.S. Senate for the first time since 1954 with a huge twelve-seat swing. The ranks of the Senate Republicans included a number of freshly elected conservatives willing to challenge establishment Republicans as well as liberal Democrats, including Orrin Hatch (Utah), Jesse Helms (North Carolina), and Dan Quayle (Indiana). Democrats managed to hold on to the House of Representatives in 1980, thanks in part to efforts to insulate incumbents from partisan pressures, but they still lost a large number of seats to conservative Republicans. Conservative southern Democrats, worried about retaining their own seats in the next election, were willing to support Reagan on many of his early legislative initiatives.

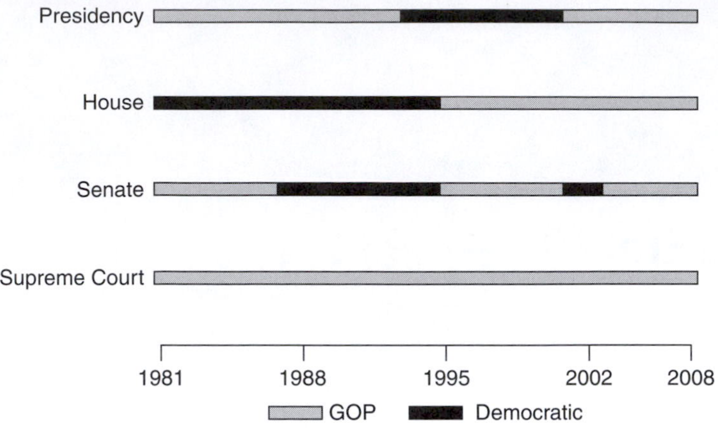

Figure 10-1 Partisan Control of the U.S. Government, 1981–2008

Reagan and the Republicans were not immediately able to consolidate their electoral victories. The 1982 midterm elections came in the midst of one of the most severe recessions in the postwar period, eroding Republican gains in Congress. In 1986, the control of the Senate slipped back into Democratic hands, despite Reagan's own overwhelming reelection in 1984. Even so, the most compelling electoral contest of 1988 was over who was going to inherit Reagan's mantle and carry his legacy forward into a third term in the White House. Once his vice president, George H. W. Bush, convinced conservatives to give him the party nomination, he had little trouble dispatching the Democratic nominee in the general election. Instead of the formation of a new Republican political majority, divided government continued to characterize national politics. The conservatives defined the terms of the debate during the Reagan Era, but they could not capture and hold Congress.

Developments. While the Reagan Era was characterized by conservative policy debates, it lacked the kind of defining constitutional battle or crisis that so often shaped and gave content to the constitutional politics of the past. Constitutional debates were distinctly post–New Deal, both in the sense that they were guided by different political commitments and in the sense that they still took for granted most of the accomplishments of the New Deal.[1] Rather than advocate for a return to pre–New Deal America, the members of the Reagan coalition were reacting against political and social developments that had occurred in the 1960s and 1970s. Within this new context it was possible for mainstream politicians, lawyers, and judges to raise questions about the scope and legitimacy of government power that had been regarded as settled for fifty years. Then again, the most radical challenges to the New Deal constitutional order were usually on the intellectual margins.

The conservative coalition assembled by Reagan drew upon Goldwater's original movement, as well Richard Nixon's successful electoral coalition, Reagan's own experience in California, and those disaffected from the Democratic Party during the 1970s. As a result, the Reagan Republicans had overlapping but divergent interests and beliefs. To the base of "establishment" and "main street" Republicans Reagan and his allies added economic libertarians (who emphasized small government, free markets, and individual liberty), social and religious conservatives (many of whom were newly mobilized into politics by the cultural changes of the 1960s and 1970s), states' rights "federalists," tax cutters, and Cold War hardliners, among others. In the process, Reagan accelerated the shift in the regional center of gravity of the GOP from its birthplace in New England to the South and West.

At the heart of the Reagan-Republican constitutional philosophy was the distrust of the government, and particularly distrust of the federal government. Goldwater's campaign against big government was particularly ill-timed in coming at the high-water mark of public trust in government, but Reagan capitalized on a decade of steady decline in popular faith in government. As Figure 10-2 indicates, the public was ready to listen to Reagan's constitutional philosophy by the late 1970s. Reagan and his successors simultaneously

1. For one description of "the new constitutional order," see Mark V. Tushnet, *The New Constitutional Order* (Princeton: Princeton University Press, 2004).

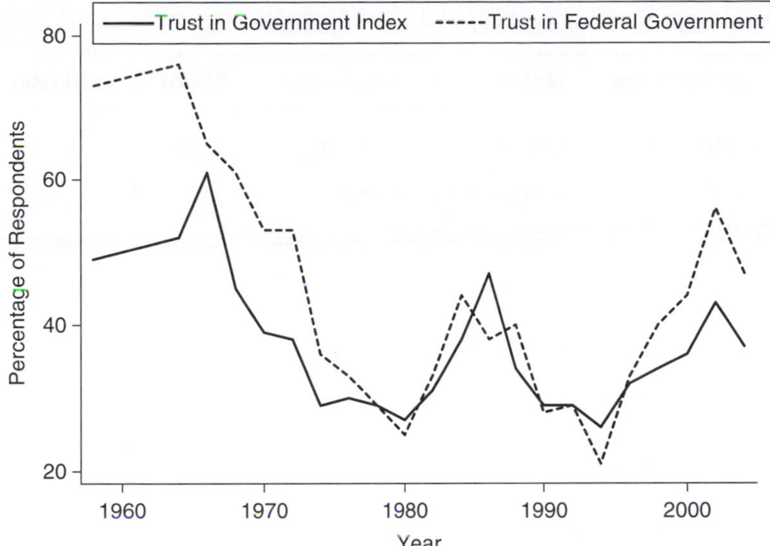

Figure 10-2 Trust in Government Index, 1958–2004

Note: Respondents answering that they trust "most of the time" or "just about always" to a generic trust in government question and a specific trust in the federal government question.

Source: American National Election Studies.

promised to reestablish leadership that would make it once again "morning in America," as Reagan's 1984 reelection campaign put it, but also emphasized that government itself could never be trusted and had to be cut back and carefully limited. Tax cuts, spending cuts, deregulation of the economy, and decentralization of power to the state and local governments were the cornerstones of Reagan's first-term agenda (not all of which were realized in practice even in part), and that policy program had constitutional implications.

Reagan redefined the terms of the political debate, but his political, ideological, and constitutional legacy is complex. The Reagan administration itself found reasons to compromise its philosophical commitments once it became apparent that a significant rearrangement of federal and state responsibilities was not politically feasible. For example, despite originally pledging to dismantle the U.S. Department of Education (created in the waning days of the Carter administration), the "Reaganites" eventually embraced the department as a platform from which to advocate public school reform. Major proposals for amending the constitutional text to accomplish such goals as a balanced federal budget or rolling back abortion rights never won support in Congress.

On the other hand, Reagan did take strong and consistent steps to reenergize presidential power in the wake of Watergate and Vietnam. Conservatives in the 1980s complained about the "fettered presidency," and they advocated for a vision of a president able to control the executive branch and solve national problems without burdensome interference by Congress.[2] Military actions were ordered in Grenada (where a "rescue mission" of American medical students led to the overthrow of the "revolutionary government" that had taken control of the Caribbean island nation in a military coup), Beirut (where a peacekeeping force was eventually removed after a truck bomb of a Marine barracks killed 241 American servicemen), and Libya (where an air strike was carried out in response to a Berlin discotheque bombing by Libyan agents). In none of these cases did the president's unilateral decision lead to any serious conflicts with Congress. Reagan's long-term policies in Latin America were more controversial on Capitol Hill. The administration circumvented congressional attempts to limit its ability to aid the "Contra" rebels who were trying to overthrow the left-wing government of Nicaragua, by allowing the National Security Council to secretly find alternative sources of funding for

2. L. Gordon Crovitz and Jeremy A. Rabkin, eds., *The Fettered Presidency* (Washington, DC: American Enterprise Institute, 1989).

Table 10-1 Major Issues and Decisions of the Reagan Era

Major Political Issues	**Major Constitutional Issues**	**Major Court Decisions**
Deficit Reduction	Presidential War Powers	*Garcia v. SAMTA* (1985)
Tax Reform	Independent Counsel	*INS v. Chadha* (1983)
Social Security Reform	Balanced Budget Amendment	*Morrison v. Olson* (1988)
Drug War	Legislative Delegation	*Haig v. Agee* (1981)
Crime Control	Judicial Review	*South Dakota v. Dole* (1987)
Immigration Reform		
Iran-Contra Scandal		
Cold War		

the rebels. When Congress discovered that this "off the books" operation was partially funded by an "arms for hostages" sale of weapons to the Iranian government, it held a series of hearings that led to resignations and criminal convictions but not impeachment. President George H. W. Bush's decision to lead a United Nations coalition against Saddam Hussein in response to the Iraqi dictator's invasion of Kuwait in 1990 was debated by Congress for two days and eventually supported by both chambers, but the White House insisted that the president had the constitutional authority to proceed even without prior approval. Indeed, Bush did not seek congressional approval before invading Panama and overthrowing General Manuel Noriega in 1989 in order to protect American citizens living in the country.

The Federal Judiciary in the Reagan Era. One response to disappointing outcomes in domestic policy struggles was to turn to courts. One aspect of this strategy focused on judicial appointments. The Reagan administration itself was diligent in advancing judicial nominees for the Supreme Court and the lower courts who shared the president's conservative constitutional philosophy. The 1987 nomination of Judge Robert Bork (then of the District of Columbia Court of Appeals) to the U.S. Supreme Court by President Reagan was the most famous of these episodes. Bork had long been a vocal leader of the conservative legal movement and an articulate spokesman for judicial restraint and originalism, and this made him a lightning rod for opposition. Unfortunately for the White House, Bork's nomination came just after the Republicans had lost control of the Senate in the 1986 midterm elections, and he was defeated in a near party-line vote on the Senate floor. (The more moderate Justice Anthony Kennedy was eventually confirmed to fill that vacancy.) Despite Bork's defeat, Reagan and his successors continued their efforts to work around party opponents in the Senate and install ideologically sympathetic judges on the federal bench. A second aspect of this strategy focused on litigation. Lawyers in the administration mapped out approaches to using the courts proactively to advance White House priorities, whether by rolling back old judicial doctrines which the administration thought were mistaken or by seeking doctrinal innovations that would strengthen the administration's own position.

Ronald Reagan, First Inaugural Address (1981)[3]

In his first inaugural address, President Ronald Reagan offered the country a conservative governing philosophy that was simultaneously distrustful of government and optimistic about the American people and America's place in the world. In doing so, he offered a rather different diagnosis of what ailed society than had Progressives and liberals since

3. Excerpt taken from Ronald Reagan, "Inaugural Address," (Jan. 20, 1981). In *Public Papers of the President of the United States, Ronald Reagan, 1981*, (Washington, DC: Government Printing Office, 1982), 1.

Box 10-1 A Partial Cast of Characters of the Reagan Era

Harry Blackmun	■ Republican ■ Minnesota moderate conservative ■ Appointed to federal circuit court (1959–1970) by Dwight Eisenhower and to the Supreme Court (1970–1994) by Richard Nixon ■ Became a swing vote who often joined the liberal wing on the Burger Court ■ Wrote for the majority in *Roe v. Wade* (1973)
Robert Bork	■ Republican ■ Conservative Yale law professor ■ Solicitor general (1973–1977) ■ Appointed to the D.C. circuit court (1982–1988) by Ronald Reagan ■ Nominated for U.S. Supreme Court by Ronald Reagan and defeated for confirmation in a deeply contested vote in 1987 ■ A leading organizer and spokesman for the conservative legal movement in the 1970s and 1980s and a chief proponent of "originalism"
Edwin Meese	■ Republican ■ Conservative lawyer and businessman ■ A long-time advisor and chief of staff to Ronald Reagan from his days as governor of California ■ Counselor to the President (1981–1985) ■ U.S. Attorney General (1985–1988) ■ A key organizer of legal conservatives in the federal government in the 1980s and a leading spokesman for originalism
Sandra Day O'Connor	■ Republican ■ Arizona moderate conservative ■ Arizona state senate (1969–1974) ■ Judge in Arizona state courts (1975–1981) ■ Appointed to the U.S. Supreme Court (1981–2006) by Ronald Reagan ■ First female Supreme Court justice ■ Became a swing vote on the Burger and Rehnquist Courts, often joining the conservatives on federalism and separation of powers issues
William Rehnquist	■ Republican ■ Arizona conservative ■ Goldwater supporter who joined Nixon Justice Department ■ Deputy attorney general in Office of Legal Counsel (1969–1971) ■ Appointed to be associate justice on the U.S. Supreme Court (1971–1986) by Richard Nixon ■ Appointed to be chief justice on the U.S. Supreme Court (1986–2005) by Ronald Reagan ■ Went from a lone dissenter in the 1970s to a leader of the conservative wing of the Court in the 1980s ■ Advocate of federalism and judicial deference to the exercise of government power

the early twentieth century, and this different diagnosis supported a different political prescription—what was needed now was less government, not more. Rhetorically at least, Reagan offered a frontal challenge to the public philosophy that had guided the nation and influenced constitutional understanding for decades, and he spoke for an organized political and intellectual movement that seemed to be on the cusp of being able to put those ideas into action.

. . .

. . . These United States are confronted with an economic affliction of great proportions. We suffer from the longest and one of the worst sustained inflations in our national history. It distorts our economic decisions, penalizes thrift, and crushes the struggling young and the fixed-income elderly alike. It threatens to shatter the lives of millions of our people.

Idle industries have cast workers into unemployment, causing human misery and personal indignity. Those who do work are denied a fair return for their labor by a tax system which penalizes successful achievement and keeps us from maintaining full productivity.

But great as our tax burden is, it has not kept pace with public spending. For decades, we have piled deficit upon deficit, mortgaging our future and our children's future for the temporary convenience of the present. To continue this long trend is to guarantee tremendous social, cultural, political, and economic upheavals.

. . .

In this present crisis, government is not the solution to our problem; government is the problem. From time to time, we have been tempted to believe that society has become too complex to be managed by self-rule, that government by an elite group is superior to government for, by, and of the people. But if no one among us is capable of governing himself, then who among us has the capacity to govern someone else? All of us together, in and out of government, must bear the burden. The solutions we seek must be equitable, with no one group singled out to pay a higher price.

. . .

It is my intention to curb the size and influence of the Federal establishment and to demand recognition of the distinction between the powers granted to the Federal Government and those reserved to the States or to the people. All of us need to be reminded that the Federal Government did not create the States; the States created the Federal Government.

. . .

It is no coincidence that our present troubles parallel and are proportionate to the intervention and intrusion in our lives that result from unnecessary and excessive growth of government. . . .

. . .

In the days ahead I will propose removing the roadblocks that have slowed our economy and reduced productivity. Steps will be taken aimed at restoring the balance between the various levels of government. Progress may be slow—measured in inches and feet, not miles—but we will progress. Is it time to reawaken this industrial giant, to get government back within its means, and to lighten our punitive tax burden. And these will be our first priorities, and on these principles, there will be no compromise.

. . .

II. Judicial Power and Constitutional Authority

MAJOR DEVELOPMENTS

- New challenges against the Supreme Court as the final authority on the meaning of the Constitution
- Growing support for originalism as the most legitimate method of interpreting the Constitution, and new criticisms of the theory of the "living Constitution"

Paradoxically, over the last thirty years, the power of judicial review is simultaneously as firmly rooted as it has ever been in American history and as controversial. The justices of the U.S. Supreme Court routinely make bold claims on behalf of the power of the courts, and they do not hesitate to wade into intense social and political controversies and develop novel legal theories to resolve them. At the same time, the contemporary era has been marked by unrelenting criticism of the courts. Presidents and politicians routinely voice their opinions on judicial decisions, and presidential candidates are expected to have settled views on the judicial philosophies of those that they might nominate to the federal bench. Interest groups mobilize for and against judicial nominees and particular constitutional positions. Both liberals and conservatives routinely criticize judicial decisions and propose measures to sanction the courts.

The modern Supreme Court has been overwhelmingly shaped by Republican presidents. Beginning with four appointments by Richard Nixon and another by Gerald Ford in the 1970s, the liberal Warren Court was transformed into a divided Burger Court. The Reagan administration made strong efforts to complete a conservative transformation of the judiciary, but divided government and more mundane political considerations complicated this agenda. As a presidential candidate in 1980, Ronald Reagan promised to name a woman to the Supreme Court, which meant that conservatives had to swallow their doubts about Sandra Day O'Connor's mixed record on abortion rights. Conservatives had more freedom when elevating William Rehnquist from associate justice to chief justice when Warren Burger retired in 1986 and then filling Rehnquist's seat with Antonin Scalia. When Republicans lost their Senate majority in the 1986 midterm elections they quickly discovered that they would not be able to easily confirm conservative justices. After conservative intellectual leader Robert Bork was defeated in the Senate in 1987, Reagan eventually settled for Anthony Kennedy, who proved to be a crucial swing vote on the Supreme Court along with Justice O'Connor. President George H. W. Bush succeeded in dividing Senate Democrats to win confirmation for conservative Clarence Thomas, but failed to satisfy conservatives by appointing the relatively unknown "stealth candidate" David Souter, who later aligned with the liberals on the Court. The result was a distinctly more conservative Court, but not a Court that was completely satisfying to either conservatives or liberals.

The period was characterized by vocal and high-profile debates over the proper role of the courts in the constitutional system and how best to interpret the Constitution. These debates extended well beyond law professors and included sitting Supreme Court justices, attorneys general, and senators. Justice William Rehnquist and Judge Robert Bork advocated that the courts be more deferential to elected officials (who were becoming increasingly conservative) and adhere to historical understandings of constitutional meaning (which were, by definition, much less progressive than those advocated by the Warren Court). Liberals such as Justice William Brennan defended the liberal order by urging the courts to be less deferential and adopt an evolving understanding of constitutional meaning. Courts also took on new challenges, with the state courts pushing the envelope on what claims were justiciable.

A. Judicial Supremacy

The Reagan administration renewed or initiated a number of constitutional debates. One of them was the debate over judicial supremacy. Conservatives in and around the administration had a particular interest in challenging the notion that the U.S. Supreme Court was the ultimate interpreter of the U.S. Constitution and that the justices had the final say on the meaning of the Constitution. The Court's decision upholding the right to abortion in *Roe v. Wade* (1973) was the flashpoint for many conservatives in the 1970s and 1980s to argue that the requirements of judge-made constitutional law should be distinguished from the requirements of the Constitution itself. Although they admitted that government officials might be legally bound by specific judicial rulings, they thought that officials should ultimately be guided by the Constitution itself. For citizens, this view might justify civil disobedience and protest, as well as political mobilization and voting decisions. For legislators and executives, it might underwrite efforts to read judicial decisions as narrowly as possible, look for ways to circumvent them or mitigate their effect, look for opportunities to challenge and chip away at existing precedents, and ultimately to appoint judges committed to overturning those precedents.

Edwin Meese, "The Law of the Constitution" (1987)[4]

Edwin Meese was one of Ronald Reagan's longest serving associates and advisors, working with him from his days as governor of California, operating as Reagan's chief of staff during his campaign for president and as his chief policy advisor during his first term of office. During Reagan's second term, Meese served as U.S. attorney general. His tenure as attorney general was notable in part for a series of speeches in which he sought to launch a public discussion of the administration's views on judicial review, including a controversial 1985 speech to the American Bar Association advocating a "jurisprudence of original intention" and questioning the scope of the applicability of the Bill of Rights to the states. Two years later, Meese stirred further controversy with a speech delivered at Tulane Law School that called into question the Supreme Court's assertion in Cooper v. Aaron *(1958) that the Constitution and the constitutional law articulated by the judiciary were of equal authority. Most immediately, Meese's argument provided room for criticizing, and potentially reversing, judicial*

4. Excerpt taken from Edwin A. Meese III, "The Law of the Constitution," *Tulane Law Review* 61 (1987): 679. Reprinted with the permission of the Tulane Law Review Association, which holds the copyright.

decisions with which the administration disagreed, most prominently Roe v. Wade *(1973). Critics denounced the attorney general for inviting legal "chaos," but other legal scholars came to his defense.*[5] *What status should Court opinions interpreting the Constitution have? Should they merely bind the parties in the cases at hand without broader application? Does Meese's view invite chaos, or is he merely explaining why it is legitimate to challenge prevailing precedents in constitutional law?*

...

...I would like to consider a distinction that is essential to maintaining our limited form of government. This is the necessary distinction between the Constitution and constitutional law. The two are not synonymous. What, then, is this distinction?

The Constitution is—to put it simply but one hopes not simplistically—the Constitution. It is a document of our most fundamental law. It begins "We the People of the United States, in Order to form a more perfect Union..." and ends up, some 6,000 words later, with the twenty-sixth amendment....

...

Constitutional law, on the other hand, is that body of law that has resulted from the Supreme Court's adjudications involving disputes over constitutional provisions or doctrines. To put it a bit more simply, constitutional law is what the Supreme Court says about the Constitution in its decisions resolving the cases and controversies that come before it.

This body of law, this judicial handiwork, is in a fundamental way unique in our scheme. For the Court is the only branch of our government that routinely, day in and day out, is charged with the awesome task of addressing the most basic, the most enduring, political questions: What is due process of law? How does the idea of separation of powers affect the Congress in certain circumstances? And so forth. The answers the Court gives are very important to the stability of the law so necessary for good government. Yet as constitutional historian Charles Warren once noted, what's most important to remember is that "[h]owever the Court may interpret the provisions of the Constitution, it is still the Constitution which is the law and not the decision of the Court."

By this, of course, Charles Warren did not mean that a constitutional decision by the Supreme Court lacks the character of law. Obviously it does have binding quality: it binds the parties in a case and also the executive branch for whatever enforcement is necessary. But such a decision does not establish a supreme law of the land that is binding on all persons and parts of government henceforth and forevermore.

This point should seem so obvious as not to need elaboration. Consider its necessity in particular reference to the Court's own work. The Supreme Court would face quite a dilemma if its own constitutional decisions really were the supreme law of the land, binding on all persons and governmental entities, including the Court itself, for then the Court would not be able to change its mind....

...Even so, although the point may seem obvious, there have been those throughout our history—and especially, it seems, in our own time—who have denied the distinction between the Constitution and constitutional law. Such denial usually has gone hand in hand with an affirmation that constitutional decisions are on a par with the Constitution in the sense that they too are the supreme law of the land, from which there is no appeal.

Perhaps the most well-known instance of this denial occurred during the most important crisis in our political history....In the 1858 Senate campaign in Illinois, Stephen Douglas went so far in his defense of *Dred Scott* as to equate the decision with the Constitution. In his third debate with his opponent, Abraham Lincoln, he said:

> It is the fundamental principle of the judiciary that its decisions are final. It is created for that purpose so that when you cannot agree among yourselves on a disputed point you appeal to the judicial tribunal which steps in and decides for you, and that decision is binding on every good citizen.

...

Lincoln, of course, disagreed. In his response to Douglas we can see the nuances and subtleties and the correctness of the position that makes most sense in a constitutional democracy like ours—a position that seeks to maintain the important function of judicial review while at the same time upholding the right of

5. For varying scholarly reactions see, "Perspectives on the Authoritativeness of Supreme Court Decisions," *Tulane Law Review* 61 (1987):991; "Symposium of Executive Branch Interpretation of the Law," *Cardozo Law Review* 15 (1993):21; "Symposium on Constitutional Law," *California Law Review* 92 (2004):959.

the people to govern themselves through the democratic branches of government.

Lincoln said that insofar as the Court "decided in favor of Dred Scott's master and against Dred Scott and his family"—the actual parties in the case—he did not propose to resist the decision. But Lincoln went on to say:

> We nevertheless do oppose *[Dred Scott]*... as a political rule which shall be binding on the voter, to vote for nobody who thinks it wrong, which shall be binding on the members of Congress or the President to favor no measure that does not actually concur with the principles of that decision.

...If a constitutional decision is not the same as the Constitution itself, if it is not binding in the same way that the Constitution is, we as citizens may respond to a decision with which we disagree. As Lincoln in effect pointed out, we can make our responses through the presidents, the senators, and the representatives we elect at the national level. We can also make them through those we elect at the state and local levels. Thus, not only can the Supreme Court respond to its previous constitutional decisions and change them, as it did in *Brown* and has done on many other occasions, but so can the other branches of government, and through them, the American people. As we know, Lincoln himself worked to overturn *Dred Scott* through the executive branch. The Congress joined him in this effort. Fortunately, *Dred Scott*—the case—lived a very short life.

Once we understand the distinction between constitutional law and the Constitution, once we see that constitutional decisions need not be seen as the last words in constitutional construction, once we comprehend that these decisions do not necessarily determine future public policy, once we see all of this, we can grasp a correlative point: constitutional interpretation is not the business of the Court only, but also properly the business of all branches of government. The Supreme Court, then, is not the only interpreter of the Constitution. Each of the three coordinate branches of government created and empowered by the Constitution—the executive and legislative no less than the judicial—has a duty to interpret the Constitution in the performance of its official functions. In fact, every official takes an oath precisely to that effect.

For the same reason that the Constitution cannot be reduced to constitutional law, the Constitution cannot simply be reduced to what Congress or the President say it is either. Quite the contrary.... For as Felix Frankfurter once said, "[t]he ultimate touchstone of constitutionality is the Constitution itself and not what we have said about it."

Some thirty years ago, in the midst of great racial turmoil, our highest Court seemed to succumb to this very temptation. By a flawed reading of our Constitution and *Marbury v. Madison*, and an even more faulty syllogism of legal reasoning, the Court in a 1958 case called *Cooper v. Aaron* appeared to arrive at conclusions about its own power that would have shocked men like John Marshall and Joseph Story.

In this case, in dictum, the Court characterized one of its constitutional decisions as nothing less than "the supreme law of the land." Obviously constitutional decisions are binding on the parties to a case; but the implication of the dictum that everyone should accept constitutional decisions uncritically, that they are judgments from which there is no appeal, was astonishing; the language recalled what Stephen Douglas said about *Dred Scott*. In one fell swoop, the Court seemed to reduce the Constitution to the status of ordinary constitutional law, and to equate the judge with the lawgiver. Such logic assumes, as Charles Evans Hughes once quipped, that the Constitution is "what the judges say it is." The logic of the dictum in *Cooper v. Aaron* was, and is, at war with the Constitution, at war with the basic principles of democratic government, and at war with the very meaning of the rule of law.

...

B. Judicial Review

The conservative legal movement was newly organized during the 1980s and found an institutional home in the Republican White House and Department of Justice of the Reagan and Bush administrations. A central goal of the movement was to change how judicial review was exercised. They had three interrelated objections to how the courts used the power of judicial review during the Warren and early Burger Court years. First, the courts were too activist, too willing to overturn the work of legislatures, and too involved in policy decisions. Second, the courts intervened in a wide range of social and policy debates in order to impose liberal results. Third, in doing so judges were unmoored from any historic understanding of constitutional meaning but were instead pursuing their own personal views of social justice. Conservative lawyers in and around the Nixon administration had voiced similar complaints in the late 1960s and early 1970s, including Earl Warren, William Rehnquist, and Robert Bork, and their proposed solution was to appoint judges who would be "strict constructionists." That solution had apparently not yet taken hold by the 1980s, and the lawyers surrounding the Reagan administration took a more detailed approach. According to the their formula, judges should be more deferential to legislators, they should reach more conservative results in specific areas of law, and they should pay more attention to the original meaning of the Constitution. Attorney General Edwin Meese gave public speeches questioning how the courts were exercising the power of judicial review and advocating a new approach, the Department of Justice prepared detailed litigation guidelines in an effort to identify areas of law that could be pushed in a more conservative direction, and the administration took greater care to identify judicial candidates who shared its constitutional philosophy. Beyond criticizing individual cases, the administration initiated a fierce debate over the purpose and value of judicial review in contemporary American democracy. Those issues were never resolved, but by the end of the 1980s both sides were seeking to lower the volume on the debate.

William H. Rehnquist, "The Notion of a Living Constitution" (1976)[6]

William Rehnquist had mostly operated in the background before his appointment to the U.S. Supreme Court by President Nixon in 1972. A former clerk for Supreme Court Justice Robert Jackson, Rehnquist had become a private lawyer and involved in Republican politics in Phoenix, Arizona, including Barry Goldwater's presidential campaign. When Nixon captured the White House in 1968, some of those Arizona lawyers, including Rehnquist, were pulled into the Justice Department. Rehnquist worked closely with the White House in the Office of Legal Counsel, where he distinguished himself as a brilliant and highly conservative constitutional lawyer. As associate justice, he displayed the same traits. He was the most conservative of the Nixon appointees, and a frequent lone dissenter on the Burger Court.

His speech on the "notion of the living constitution" was one of his first major statements off the bench and of the constitutional and judicial philosophy that influenced the growing conservative legal movement and future Reagan administration. For Rehnquist, both constitutional design and historical experience cautioned judges to exercise judicial restraint, and defer to elected officials for developing solutions to public problems. As you read this excerpt, notice how Rehnquist invokes arguments generally associated with the New Deal, such as the rejection of Lochner v. New York *(1903).*[7] *How much weight does Rehnquist put on original meaning specifically as an alternative to "a living Constitution"?*

...At first blush it seems certain that a living Constitution is better than what must be its counterpart, a dead Constitution.... If we could get one of the major public opinion research firms in the country to sample public opinion concerning whether the United States Constitution should be living or dead, the overwhelming majority of the responses doubtless would favor a living Constitution.

If the question is worth asking a Supreme Court nominee during his confirmation hearings, however, it surely deserves to be analyzed in more than just the public relations context....

...The phrase is really a shorthand expression that is susceptible of at least two quite different meanings.

...

The framers of the Constitution wisely spoke in general language and left to succeeding generations the task of applying that language to the unceasingly changing environment in which they would live. Those who framed, adopted, and ratified the Civil War amendments to the Constitution likewise used what have been aptly described as "majestic generalities" in composing the fourteenth amendment. Merely because a particular activity may not have existed when the Constitution was adopted, or because the framers could not have conceived of a particular method of transacting affairs,

6. Excerpt taken from William H. Rehnquist, "The Notion of a Living Constitution," *Texas Law Review* 54 (1976):693. Reprinted with the permission of the Texas Law Review Association.

7. See also Keith E. Whittington, "William H. Rehnquist: Nixon's Strict Constructionist, Reagan's Chief Justice," in *Rehnquist Justice*, ed. Earl Maltz (Lawrence: University Press of Kansas, 2003); Howard Gillman, "The Collapse of Constitutional Originalism and the Rise of the Notion of the 'Living Constitution' in the Course of American State-Building," *Studies in American Political Development* 11 (1997):191.

cannot mean that general language in the Constitution may not be applied to such a course of conduct. Where the framers of the Constitution have used general language, they have given latitude to those who would later interpret the instrument to make that language applicable to cases that the framers might not have foreseen.

In my reading and travels I have sensed a second connotation of the phrase "living Constitution."... Embodied in its most naked form, it recently came to my attention in some language from a brief that had been filed in a United States District Court on behalf of state prisoners asserting that the conditions of their confinement offended the United States Constitution. The brief argued:

> We are asking a great deal of the Court because other branches of government have abdicated their responsibility.... Prisoners are like other "discrete and insular" minorities for whom the Court must spread its protective umbrella because no other branch of government will do so.... This Court, as the voice and conscience of contemporary society, as the measure of modern conception of human dignity, must declare that the [named prison] and all it represents offends the Constitution of the United States and will not be tolerated.

Here we have a living Constitution with a vengeance. Although the substitution of some other set of values for those which may be derived from the language and intent of the framers is not urged in so many words, that is surely the thrust of the message. Under this brief writer's version of the living Constitution, nonelected members of the federal judiciary may address themselves to a social problem simply because other branches have failed or refused to do so. The same judges, responsible to no constituency whatever, are nonetheless acclaimed as "the voice and conscience of contemporary society."

...

John Marshall's justification for judicial review [in *Marbury v. Madison*] makes the provision for an independent federal judiciary not only understandable but also thoroughly desirable. Since the judges will be merely interpreting an instrument framed by the people, they should be detached and objective. A mere change in public opinion since the adoption of the Constitution, unaccompanied by a constitutional amendment, should not change the meaning of the Constitution. A mere temporary majoritarian groundswell should not abrogate some individual liberty truly protected by the Constitution.

... The Constitution is in many of its parts obviously not a specifically worded document but one couched in general phraseology. There is obviously wide room for honest difference of opinion over the meaning of general phrases in the Constitution; any particular Justice's decision when a decision arises under one of these general phrases will depend to some extent on his own philosophy of constitutional law. One may nevertheless concede all of these problems that inhere in Marshall's justification of judicial review, yet feel that his justification for nonelected judges exercising the power of judicial review is the only one consistent with democratic philosophy of representative government.

...

The brief writer's version [of the living Constitution] seems instead to be based upon the proposition that federal judges, perhaps judges as a whole, have a role of their own, quite independent of the popular will, to play in solving society's problems. Once we have abandoned the idea that the authority of the courts to declare laws unconstitutional is somehow tied to the language of the Constitution that the people adopted, a judiciary exercising the power of judicial review appears in a quite different light. Judges then are no longer the keepers of the covenant; instead they are a small group of fortunately situated people with a roving commission to second-guess Congress, state legislatures, and state and federal administrative officers concerning what is best for the country. Surely there is no justification for a third legislative branch in the federal branch in the federal government, and there is even less justification for a federal legislative branch's reviewing on a policy basis the laws enacted by the legislatures of the fifty states....

...

The second difficulty with the brief writer's version of the living Constitution lies in its inattention to or rejection of the Supreme Court's historical experience gleaned from similar forays into problem solving.

...

One reads the history of these episodes in the Supreme Court to little purpose if he does not conclude that prior experimentation with the brief writer's expansive notion of a living Constitution has done the Court little credit. There remains today those... who appear to cleave nonetheless to the view that the experiments of the Taney Court before the Civil War, and of the Fuller and Taft Courts in the first part of this century, ended in failure not because they sought to bring into the Constitution a principle that the great majority of objective scholars would have to conclude was not there but because they sought to bring into the Constitution the *wrong* extraconstitutional principle.... To the extent that one must, however, go beyond even a generously fair reading of the language and intent of that document in order to subsume these principles, it seems to me that they are not really distinguishable from those espoused in *Dred Scott* and *Lochner*.

The third difficulty with the brief writer's notion of the living Constitution is that it seems to ignore totally the nature of political value judgments in a democratic society. If such a society adopts a constitution and incorporates in that constitution safeguards for individual liberty, these safeguards indeed do take on a generalized moral rightness or goodness.... It is the fact of their enactment that gives them whatever moral claim they have upon us as a society, however, and not any independent virtue they may have in any particular citizen's own scale of values.

Beyond the Constitution and the laws in our society, there simply is no basis other than the individual conscience of the citizen that may serve as a platform for the launching of moral judgments.... Many of us necessarily feel strongly and deeply about our own moral judgments, but they remain only personal moral judgments until in some way given the sanction of law....

...

...It is always time consuming, frequently difficult, and not infrequently impossible to run successfully the legislative gauntlet and have enacted some facet of one's own deeply felt value judgments. It is even more difficult for either a single individual or indeed for a large group of individuals to succeed in having such a value judgment embodied in the Constitution. All of these burdens and difficulties are entirely consistent with the notion of a democratic society. It should not be easy for any one individual or group of individuals to impose by law their value judgments upon fellow citizens who may disagree with those judgments. Indeed, it should not be easier just because the individual in question is a judge....

...

William J. Brennan, "The Constitution of the United States: Contemporary Ratification" (1985)[8]

William Brennan was a Democratic judge on the New Jersey Supreme Court when he was nominated to the U.S. Supreme Court by President Dwight Eisenhower on the eve of the 1956 election, in part to shore up Eisenhower's support among Catholic Democrats. He soon emerged as the intellectual and political leader of the liberal wing of the Warren Court, and he authored many of the Court's landmark decisions on voting rights, religious liberty, free speech, criminal procedure, and civil rights. He remained a potent force on the Court until his retirement in 1990, but his influence waned with the addition of more conservative justices over time.

Brennan and Rehnquist were frequent sparring partners on the bench, offering sharply divergent views across a range of constitutional issues. Justice Brennan took the rise of the Reagan administration and its vocal defense of originalism and judicial restraint as a fundamental challenge to his own constitutional vision and his jurisprudential legacy. In this speech, delivered shortly after Attorney General Edwin Meese's well-publicized address to the American Bar Association on originalism, Brennan offered an alternative vision of the Constitution that frankly embraced judicial activism and an ever-evolving "aspiration to social justice."[9] Is Brennan right that the Court's role is to "adapt" the terms of the Constitution to present values and social needs? Is this role different from the "brief writer's notion" that Rehnquist criticized in the previous excerpt?

...[T]he Constitution embodies the aspiration to social justice, brotherhood, and human dignity that brought this nation into being. The Declaration of Independence, the Constitution and the Bill of Rights solemnly committed the United States to be a country where the dignity and rights of all persons were equal before all authority. In all candor we must concede that part of this egalitarianism in America has been more pretension than realized fact. But we are an aspiring people, a people with faith in progress. Our amended Consti-

8. Excerpt taken from William J. Brennan, in *The Great Debate: Interpreting Our Written Constitution* (Washington, DC: The Federalist Society, 1986). © The Federalist Society. Reprinted with permission.

9. See also Frank I. Michelman, *Brennan and Democracy* (Princeton: Princeton University Press, 1999).

tution is the lodestar for our aspirations. Like every text worth reading, it is not crystalline. The phrasing is broad and the limitations of its provisions are not clearly marked. Its majestic generalities and ennobling pronouncements are both luminous and obscure. This ambiguity of course calls forth interpretation, the interaction of reader and text....

...

There are those who find legitimacy in fidelity to what they call "the intentions of the Framers." In its most doctrinaire incarnation, this view demands that Justices discern exactly what the Framers thought about the question under consideration and simply follow that intention in resolving the case before them. It is a view that feigns self-effacing deference to the specific judgments of those who forged our original social compact. But in truth it is little more than arrogance cloaked as humility. It is arrogant to pretend that from our vantage we can gauge accurately the intent for the Framers on application of principle to specific, contemporary questions. All too often, sources of potential enlightenment such as records of the ratification debates provide sparse or ambiguous evidence of the original intentions. Typically, all that can be gleaned is that the Framers themselves did not agree about the application or meaning of particular constitutional provisions, and hid their differences in cloaks of generality....And apart from the problematic nature of the sources, our distance of two centuries cannot but work as a prism refracting all we perceive....

Perhaps most importantly, while proponents of this facile historicism justify it as a depoliticization of the judiciary, the political underpinnings of such a choice should not escape notice. A position that upholds constitutional claims only if they were within the specific contemplation of the Framers in effect establishes a presumption of resolving textual ambiguities against the claim of constitutional right. It is far from clear what justifies such a presumption against claims of right. Nothing intrinsic in the nature of interpretation—if there is such a thing as the "nature" of interpretation—commands such a passive approach to ambiguity. This is a choice no less political than any other; it expresses antipathy to claims of the minority rights against the majority. Those who would restrict claims of right to the values of 1789 specifically articulated in the Constitution turn a blind eye to social progress and eschew adaptation of overarching principles to changes of social circumstances.

Another, perhaps more sophisticated, response to the potential power of judicial interpretation stresses democratic theory: Because ours is a government of the people's elected representatives, substantive value choices should by and large be left to them. This view emphasizes not the transcendent historical authority of the framers but the predominant contemporary authority of the elected branches of government. Yet it has similar consequences for the nature of proper judicial interpretation. Faith in the majoritarian process counsels restraint. Even under more expansive formulations of this approach, judicial review is appropriate only to the extent of ensuring that our democratic process functions smoothly....

The view that all matters of substantive policy should be resolved through the majoritarian process has appeal under some circumstances, but I think it ultimately will not do. Unabashed enshrinement of majority would permit the imposition of a social caste system or wholesale confiscation of property so long as a majority of the authorized legislative body, fairly elected, approved. Our Constitution could not abide such a situation. It is the very purpose of a Constitution—and particularly of the Bill of Rights—to declare certain values transcendent, beyond the reach of temporary political majorities. The majoritarian process cannot be expected to rectify claims of minority right that arise as a response to the outcomes of that very majoritarian process....

To remain faithful to the content of the Constitution, therefore, an approach to interpreting the text must account for the existence of these substantive value choices, and must accept the ambiguity inherent in the effort to apply them to modern circumstances. The Framers discerned fundamental principles through struggles against particular malefactions of the Crown; the struggle shapes the particular contours of the articulated principles. But our acceptance of the fundamental principles has not and should not bind us to those precise, at times anachronistic, contours. Successive generations of Americans have continued to respect these fundamental choices and adopt them as their own guide to evaluating quite different historical practices. Each generation has a choice to overrule or add to the fundamental principles enunciated by the Framers; the Constitution can be amended or it can be ignored. Yet with respect to its fundamental principles, the text has suffered neither fate....

We current Justices read the Constitution in the only way that we can: as Twentieth Century Americans. We look to the history of the time of the framing and to the intervening history of interpretation. But the ultimate question must be, what do the words of the text mean in our time. For the genius of the Constitution rests not in any static meaning it might have had in a world that is dead and gone, but in the adaptability of its great principles to cope with the current problems and current needs....

Interpretation must account for the transformative purpose of the text. Our Constitution was not intended to preserve a preexisting society but to make a new one, to put in place new principles that the prior political community had not sufficiently recognized....

...[T]he Constitution is a sublime oration on the dignity of man, a bold commitment by a people to the ideal of libertarian dignity protected through law....

...

If we are to be as a shining city upon a hill, it will be because of our ceaseless pursuit of the constitutional ideal of human dignity....As we adapt our institutions to the ever-changing conditions of national and international life, those ideals of human dignity—liberty and justice for all individuals—will continue to inspire and guide us because they are entrenched in our Constitution. The Constitution with its Bill of Rights thus has a bright future, as well as a glorious past, for its spirit is inherent in the aspirations of our people.

The Nomination of Robert H. Bork to the U.S. Supreme Court (1987)

At the time of his nomination to the Supreme Court by Ronald Reagan in 1987, Robert Bork was a judge on the influential Court of Appeals for the District of Columbia, having been easily confirmed to that position early in Reagan's presidency. Within political and legal circles, Bork was among the leading conservative intellectual figures. A well-respected litigator, U.S. solicitor general during the Nixon administration, and a former Yale law professor, Bork had long been a forceful advocate for conservative constitutional and legal causes as a lawyer, public speaker, and writer. As a vocal critic of many of the decisions of the Warren and early Burger Courts, he was particularly known for his support for restraint in the exercise of judicial review and for the use of original intent in guiding constitutional interpretation. His nomination was seen by both supporters and opponents of the Reagan administration to symbolize the ambitions of the conservatives to remake the judiciary and advance a distinct constitutional philosophy through judicial appointments.

Bork's nomination took on added significance not only because he was thought to have the intellectual skills and beliefs to influence the direction of the Court, but also because the vacancy was created by the departure of the moderate Lewis Powell, a swing vote on many issues including abortion and affirmative action. Bork's nomination also came after the midterm elections of 1986, when the Republicans lost their majority in the Senate. Associate Justice William Rehnquist had been elevated to chief justice, and Antonin Scalia had joined the Court, both conservatives, the year before when the Republicans still held the majority.

Given Bork's strong qualifications and the absence of scandal or doubts about his character, the Republicans hoped Bork would be easily confirmed by a bipartisan vote as Scalia had been and as other nominees had been in similar circumstances. Instead, and surprisingly, the confirmation debate focused explicitly on Bork's conservative judicial philosophy, with an organized lobbying campaign complete with television advertisements and a special presidential address. The battle was particularly bitter, with conservatives complaining that the judge's record had been badly misrepresented, remembered afterwards as having been "Borked." His nomination was ultimately defeated in a largely party-line vote on the Senate floor. The vacancy was eventually filled by Anthony Kennedy, a lower profile and more moderate figure who has often been a swing vote on the Rehnquist and Roberts Courts.

Ronald Reagan, "Address to the Nation" (1987)[10]

...

In the last 6½ years I have spoken with you and asked for your help many times. When special interests and power brokers here in Washington balked at cutting your taxes, I asked for your help. You went to your Congressmen and Senators, and the tax cuts passed. And by the way, as a result, at the end of this month we will mark the longest peacetime economic expansion on record.

10. Excerpt taken from Ronald Reagan, "Address to the Nation on the Supreme Court Nomination of Robert H. Bork," (October 14, 1987), in *Public Papers of the President of the United States, Ronald Reagan, 1987: Book II* (Washington, DC: Government Printing Office, 1989), 1177.

Illustration 10-1 "You Were Expecting Maybe Edward M. Kennedy?"

Source: Herblock, *Washington Post*, July 2, 1987. Copyright by *The Herb Block Foundation.*

...Yes, all that America has achieved in the last 6½ years—our record economic expansion, the new pride we have at home, the new strength that may soon bring us history's first agreement to eliminate an entire class of U.S. and Soviet nuclear missiles—all of this has happened because, when the chips were down, you and I worked together.

As you know, I have selected one of the finest judges in America's history, Robert Bork, for the Supreme Court. You've heard that this nomination is a lost cause. You've also heard that I am determined to fight right down to the final ballot on the Senate floor. I'm doing this because what's now at stake in this battle must never in our land of freedom become a lost cause. And whether lost or not, we Americans must never give up this particular battle: the independence of our judiciary.

Back in July when I nominated Judge Bork, I thought the confirmation process would go forward with a calm and sensible exchange of views. Unfortunately, the confirmation process became an ugly spectacle, marred by distortions and innuendos, and casting aside the normal rules of decency and honesty. As Judge Bork said last Friday, and I quote: "The process of confirming Justices for our nation's highest court has been transformed in a way that should not and, indeed, must not be permitted to occur again. The tactics and techniques of national political campaigns have been unleashed on the process of confirming judges. That is not simply disturbing; it is dangerous. Federal judges are not appointed to decide cases according to the latest opinion polls; they are appointed to decide cases impartially, according to law. But when judicial nominees are assessed and treated like political candidates, the effect will be to chill the climate in which judicial deliberations take place, to erode public confidence in the impartiality of courts, and to endanger the independence of the judiciary."

. . .

During the hearings, one of Judge Bork's critics said that among the functions of the Court was reinterpreting the Constitution so that it would not remain, in his words, "frozen into ancient error because it is so hard to amend." Well, that to my mind is the issue, plain and simple. Too many theorists believe that the courts should save the country from the Constitution. Well, I believe it's time to save the Constitution from them. The principal errors in recent years have had nothing to do with the intent of the framers who finished their work 200 years ago last month. They've had to do with those who have looked upon the courts as their own special province to impose by judicial fiat what they could not accomplish at the polls. They've had to do with judges who too often have made law enforcement a game where clever lawyers try to find ways to trip up the police on the rules.

. . .

So, my agenda is your agenda, and it's quite simple: to appoint judges like Judge Bork who don't confuse the criminals with the victims; judges who don't invent new or fanciful constitutional rights for those criminals; judges who believe the courts should interpret the law, not make it; judges, in short, who understand the principle of judicial restraint. That starts with the Supreme Court. It takes leadership from the Supreme Court to help shape the attitudes of the courts in our land and to make sure that principles of law are based on the Constitution. That is the standard to judge those who seek to serve on the courts: qualifications, not distortions; judicial temperament, not campaign disinformation.

In the next several days, your Senators will cast a vote on the Bork nomination. It is more than just one vote on one man: It's a decision on the future of our judicial system. The purpose of the Senate debate is to allow all sides to be heard. Honorable men and women should not be afraid to change their minds based on that debate.

I hope that in the days and weeks ahead you will let them know that the confirmation process must never again be compromised with high-pressure politics. Tell them that America stands for better than that and that you expect them to stand for America. . . .

Thank you, and God bless you all.

Senate Judiciary Committee Hearings on the Nomination of Robert Bork (1987)[11]

Chairman BIDEN (Democrat, Delaware)

. . .

Judge, each generation in some sense has had as much to do to author our Constitution as the 39 men who affixed their signatures to it 200 years ago. Indeed, two years after its signing, following a bitter national debate over its ratification, at the insistence of the people, the Constitution was profoundly ennobled by the addition of what has come to be known as the Bill of Rights.

. . .

America is the promised land because each generation bequeathed to their children a promise, a promise that they might not come to enjoy but which they fully expected their offspring to fulfill. So the words "all men are created equal" took a life of their own, ultimately destined to end slavery and enfranchise women. And the words, "equal protection and due process" inevitably led to the end of the words, "separate but equal," ensuring that the walls of segregation would crumble, whether at the lunch counter or in the voting booth.

. . .

So let's make no mistake about it, the unique importance of this nomination is in part because of the moment in history in which it comes, for I believe that a greater question transcends the issue of this nomination. And that question is, will we retreat from our tradition of progress or will we move forward, continuing to expand and envelope the rights of individuals in a changing world which is bound to have an impact upon the individuals' sense of who they are and what they can do, will these ennobling human rights and human dignity, which is a legacy of the past two centuries, continue to mark the journey of our people?

11. Excerpt taken from "Hearings Before the Committee on the Judiciary, United States Senate, One Hundredth Congress, First Session, on the Nomination of Robert H. Bork to be Associate Justice on the Supreme Court of the United States," (Sept. 15, 16, 17, 18, 19, 21, 22, 23, 25, 28, 29, and 30, 1987), Serial No. J-100–64, (Washington, DC: Government Printing Office, 1989).

. . .

. . . In passing on this nomination to the Supreme Court, we must also pass judgment on whether or not your particular philosophy is an appropriate one at this time in our history.

. . .

You have been a man of significant standing in the academic community and thus in a special way, a vote to confirm you requires, in my view, an endorsement of your basic philosophic views as they relate to the Constitution. And thus the Senate, in exercising its constitutional role of advice and consent, has not only the right in my opinion but the duty to weigh the philosophy of the nominee as it reaches its own independent decision. . . .

. . .

I believe all Americans are born with certain inalienable rights. As a child of God, I believe my rights are not derived from the Constitution. My rights are not derived from any Government. My rights are not derived from any majority. My rights are because I exist I have certain rights. They were given to me and each of my fellow citizens by our creator and they represent the essence of human dignity.

I agree with Justice Harlan, the most conservative jurist and Justice of our era, who stated that the Constitution is, quote, "a living thing" and that "its protections are enshrined in majestic phrases like 'equal protection under the law' and 'due process' and thus cannot be," as he said, and, "reduced to any formula."

It is, as the great Chief Justice John Marshall said, intended, and I quote, "intended to endure for ages to come and consequently to be adapted to the various crises of human affairs, only its great outlines marked," . . .

. . . .

Judge BORK

. . . As you have said, quite correctly, Mr. Chairman, and as others have said here today, this is in large measure a discussion of judicial philosophy, and I want to make a few remarks at the outset on that subject of central interest.

That is, my understanding of how a judge should go about his or her work. That may also be described as my philosophy of the role of a judge in a constitutional democracy.

The judge's authority derives entirely from the fact that he is applying the law and not his personal values. That is why the American public accepts the decisions of its courts, accepts even decisions that nullify the laws a majority of the electorate or of their representatives voted for.

The judge, to deserve that trust and that authority, must be every bit as governed by law as is the Congress, the President, the state governors and legislatures, and the American people. No one, including a judge, can be above the law. Only in that way will justice be done and the freedom of Americans assured.

How should a judge go about finding the law? The only legitimate way, in my opinion, is by attempting to discern what those who made the law intended. The intentions of the lawmakers govern whether the lawmakers are the Congress of the United States enacting a statute or whether they are those who ratified our Constitution and its various amendments.

Where the words are precise and the facts simple, that is a relatively easy task. Where the words are general, as is the case with some of the most profound protections of our liberties—in the Bill of Rights and in the Civil War Amendments—the task is far more complex. It is to find the principle or value that was intended to be protected and to see that it is protected.

As I wrote in an opinion for our court, the judge's responsibility "is to discern how the Framers' values, defined in the context of the world they knew, apply in the world we know."

If a judge abandons intention as his guide, there is no law available to him and he begins to legislate a social agenda for the American people. That goes well beyond his legitimate power.

. . .

Times come, of course, when even a venerable precedent can and should be overruled. The primary example of a proper overruling is Brown against Board of Education, the case which outlawed racial segregation accomplished by Government action. *Brown* overturned the rule of separate but equal laid down 58 years before in Plessy against Ferguson. Yet *Brown*, delivered with the authority of a unanimous Court, was clearly correct and represents perhaps the greatest moral achievement of our constitutional law.

. . .

I can put the matter no better than I did in an opinion on my present court. Speaking of the judge's duty, I wrote: "The important thing, the ultimate consideration, is the constitutional freedom that is given into our keeping. A judge who refuses to see new threats to an established constitutional value and hence provides a crabbed interpretation that robs a provision of its full, fair and reasonable meaning, fails in his judicial duty. That duty, I repeat, is to ensure that the powers and freedoms the Framers specified are made effective in today's circumstances."

But I should add to that passage that when a judge goes beyond this and reads entirely new values into the Constitution, values the Framers and the ratifiers did not put there, he deprives the people of their liberty. That liberty, which the Constitution clearly envisions, is the liberty of the people to set their own social agenda through the processes of democracy.

Conservative judges frustrated that process in the mid-1930's by using the concept they had invented, the Fourteenth Amendment's supposed guarantee of a liberty of contract to strike down laws designed to protect workers and labor unions. That was wrong then and it would be wrong now.

My philosophy of judging, Mr. Chairman, as you pointed out, is neither liberal nor conservative. It is simply a philosophy of judging which gives the Constitution a full and fair interpretation but, where the constitution is silent, leaves the policy struggles to the Congress, the President, the legislatures and executives of the 50 states, and to the American people.

...

Senator HATCH (Republican, Utah)

...

The great danger I see in the impending ideological inquisition is injury to the independence and integrity of the Supreme Court and the whole Federal judiciary. When we undertake to judge a judge according to political rather than legal criteria, we have stripped the judicial office of all that makes it a distinct separated power....

Now, recognizing precisely this danger, the Senate has refused to employ political litmus tests while confirming 53 justices over this past century. Senate precedent does not support subjecting judicial nominees to ideological inquisitions.

Moreover, the Constitution itself does not support that practice. Based on the common sense observation that a diverse congressional body would have difficulty overcoming jealousies and politics to select the best candidate, the Framers...unanimously voted to vest the nomination power in the President. The Senate, however, was given a checking function. In the words of Alexander Hamilton, the advice and consent function was to prevent "nepotism" and "unfit characters." The advice and consent function is a checking function, not a license to exert political influence on another branch, not a license to control the outcome of future cases by overriding the President's prerogatives.

...

This is the reason that politics are injected into this proceeding, because many politicians are hoping to win from unelected judges what they cannot win in the Congress or with the people of the United States of America. My fear, however, is that the price of a politicized judiciary is too high to pay in exchange for a short-term policy set of gains. If judges fear to uphold the Constitution due to political pressures or sense that their judicial careers might be advanced by reading that document in the smokey back rooms of political intrigue, then the Constitution will no longer be the solid anchor holding our nation in place during the times of storm and crisis. Instead, the Constitution will just become part of that political storm, blowing hot and cold whenever the wind changes. That is a price that we in this country cannot afford to pay, and I think it is important that the American people understand that here.

...

Senator KENNEDY (Democrat, Massachusetts)

...

From the beginning, America has set the highest standards for our highest Court. We insist that a nominee should have outstanding ability and integrity. But we also insist on even more: that I those who sit on the Supreme Court must deserve the special title we reserve for only nine Federal judges in the entire country, the title that sums up in one word the awesome responsibility on their shoulders—the title of "Justice."

Historically, America has set this high standard because the Justices of the Supreme Court have a unique obligation: to serve as the ultimate guardians of the Constitution, the rule of law, and the liberty and the equality of every citizen. To fulfill these responsibilities, to earn the title of "Justice," a person must have special qualities:

A commitment to individual liberty as the cornerstone of American democracy.

A dedication to equality for all Americans, especially those who have been denied their full measure of freedom, such as women and minorities.

A respect for justice for all whose rights are too readily abused by powerful institutions, whether by the power of government or by giant concentrations of power in the private sector.

...

These are the standards by which the Senate must evaluate any judicial nominee. And by these standards, Robert Bork falls short of what Americans demand of a man or woman as a Justice on the Supreme Court. Time and again, in his public record over more than a quarter of a century, Robert Bork has shown that he is hostile to the rule of law and the role of the courts in protecting individual liberty.

He has harshly opposed—and is publicly itching to overrule—many of the great decisions of the Supreme Court that seek to fulfill the promise of justice for all Americans.

He is instinctively biased against the claims of the average citizen and in favor of concentrations of power, whether that is governmental or private.

And in conflicts between the legislative and executive branches of Government, he has repeatedly expressed a clear contempt for Congress and an unbridled trust in the power of the President.

...

In Robert Bork's America, there is no room at the inn for blacks and no place in the Constitution for women, and in our America there should be no seat on the Supreme Court for Robert Bork.

Mr. Bork has been equally extreme in his opposition to the right to privacy. In an article in 1971, he said, in effect, that a husband and wife have no greater right to privacy under the Constitution than a smokestack has to pollute the air.

President Reagan has said that this controversy is pure politics, but that is not the case. I and others who oppose Mr. Bork have often supported nominees to the Supreme Court by Republican Presidents, including many with whose philosophy we disagree. I voted for the confirmation of Chief Justice Burger and also Justices Blackmun, Powell, Stevens, O'Connor and Scalia. But Mr. Bork is a nominee of a different stripe. President Reagan has every right to take Mr. Bork's reactionary ideology into account in making the nomination, and the Senate has every right to take that ideology into account in acting on the nomination.

...

...All Americans should realize that the confrontation over this nomination is the result of a deliberate decision by the Reagan Administration. Rather than selecting a real judicial conservative to fill Justice Powell's vacancy, the President has sought to appoint an activist of the right whose agenda would turn us back to the battles of a bitterly divided America, reopening issues long thought to be settled and wounds long thought to be healed.

I for one am proud of the accomplishments of America in moving towards the constitutional ideas of liberty and equality and justice under law. I am also proud of the role of the Senate in ensuring that Supreme Court nominees adhere to the tradition of fairness, impartiality, and the freedom from bias.

I believe the American people strongly reject the Administration's invitation to roll back the clock and relive the more troubled times of the past. I urge the Committee and the Senate to reject the nomination of Mr. Bork.

Note: Modern Court-Curbing

"Court-curbing" has been a part of American constitutional politics from the beginning. Congress has a variety of legitimate tools that it can use to threaten, punish, or weaken the federal judiciary. Legislators have also been willing to threaten to take actions against the Supreme Court that are more constitutionally dubious.

Some forms of court-curbing do not involve legislation. The House of Representatives can impeach and the Senate can convict and remove from office judges for high crimes and misdemeanors. Congress can propose constitutional amendments to alter the power or structure of the Supreme Court and federal judiciary. Congress can hold public hearings to investigate judges or to castigate the courts for their actions. Individual congressmen can give speeches denouncing the judiciary or individual judges. The Senate can rake judicial nominees over the coals during the confirmation process for things that the courts have already done and try to extract promises from them about how they will behave if they are placed on the bench.

Other forms of court-curbing do involve legislation. Congress very rarely passes court-curbing bills, and most of them do not even make it very far into the legislative process. But the possibility that a court-curbing bill will pass is an ever-present threat, and they do sometimes pick up steam in Congress and become real objects of debate and votes. Even when

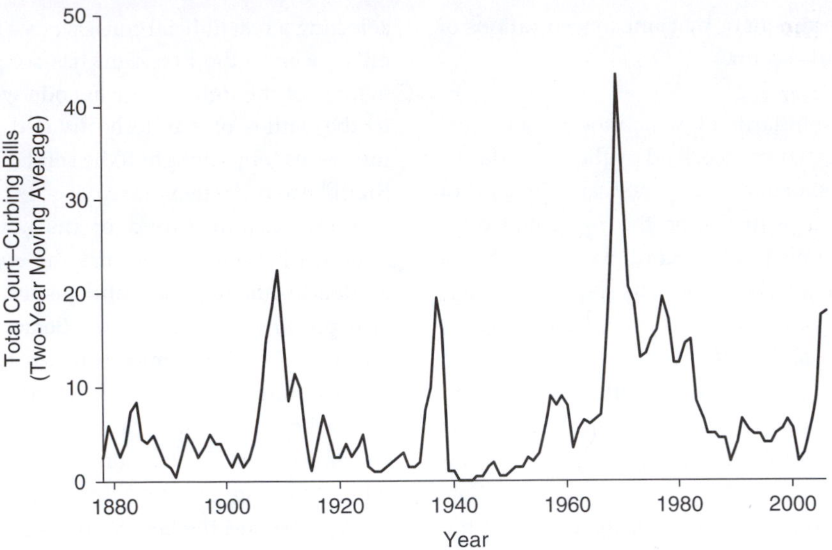

Figure 10-3 Court-Curbing Bills Introduced in Congress, 1877–2007

Source: Courtesy of Tom S. Clark

court-curbing bills do get buried in committee, legislators use them to publicize their complaints about the courts and to try to build political opposition to the judiciary. Court-curbing bills have taken a wide variety of forms over time, though some proposals are particularly common. Legislators have proposed restricting the appellate jurisdiction of the Supreme Court. They have proposed increasing or decreasing the size of the Supreme Court. They have proposed reducing the substantive powers and jurisdiction of the lower federal courts. They have proposed cutting the budget and staff of the federal courts. More questionably, there have even been repeated legislative proposals to alter the number of justices required to strike down a law or to strip the power of judicial review entirely.

The popularity of court-curbing has surged and waned in Congress over time, but it has been common feature of contemporary politics. In the early twentieth century, Progressives—many of whom were on the left wing of the Republican Party—pushed a variety measures to curb the power of the conservative Supreme Court. In the 1930s, liberal Democrats much more successfully proposed a variety of measures challenging the Court, culminating in President Franklin Roosevelt's Court-packing plan. During the Warren Court, conservatives in both the Democratic and the Republican parties backed court-curbing proposals ranging from a noisy but ineffective campaign to impeach Chief Justice Earl Warren to a very close vote to strip part of the Court's appellate jurisdiction. With Ronald Reagan's election in 1980, court-curbing efforts became somewhat more focused. The conservative Senator Jesse Helms of North Carolina found new support for his proposal to strip federal jurisdiction over school prayer cases, forcing an extended debate over the issue on the floor of the Senate in 1982. Senator Helms similarly pushed for legislation declaring that human life begins at the time of conception and limiting the ability of the federal courts to implement the abortion decisions. As Figure 10-3 indicates, court-curbing dropped off after the early Reagan years, but the number of bills introduced in Congress remained high and spiked again after the 2000 elections. Although court-curbing in the late nineteenth and early twentieth centuries primarily came from the political left, the court-curbing since the mid-twentieth century has largely come from the political right. There is some evidence that when legislators rattle the saber by talking about court-curbing, the justices pay attention and adjust their behavior to dissipate the political threat.[12]

---

12. On court-curbing, see Edward Keynes with Randall K. Miller, *The Court vs. Congress* (Durham, NC: Duke University Press, 1989); Tom S. Clark, *The Limits of Judicial Independence* (New York: Cambridge University Press, 2010); Bruce Peabody, ed., *The Judiciary Under Siege* (Baltimore: Johns Hopkins University Press, 2010).

III. Powers of the National Government

MAJOR DEVELOPMENTS

- Growing conservative rhetoric aimed at criticizing the expansion of federal power since the New Deal
- Supreme Court upholds use of federal spending power as a tool to influence state policymaking

The New Deal had settled the questions over the powers of the national government that had roiled constitutional law and politics for decades in the late nineteenth and early twentieth centuries, just as the Civil War and succeeding Republican Era had put an end to many of the debates over national powers that had dominated antebellum politics. Just as some thought—or, perhaps hoped—that the Civil War had finally put an end for all time to *all* disputes over the powers of the national government, so some thought that the New Deal had done so. By the 1960s and 1970s, however, conservatives such as Barry Goldwater on the presidential campaign trail and William Rehnquist on the Supreme Court were raising questions about the scope of the powers of the national government as new issues and new laws appeared on the national agenda.

Such conservatives found new influence after the election of Ronald Reagan. Reagan committed the Republican Party to a conservative constitutional philosophy that reemphasized the idea that there were constitutional limits to the powers of the national government.[13] A conservative legal movement organized both inside the administration—notably in the Department of Justice and the White House Counsel's Office (the president's lawyer within the White House)—and outside of it, through the formation of new organizations such as the Federalist Society (a professional organization of conservative lawyers and law students) and the Institute for Justice and Pacific Legal Foundation (legal advocacy groups). Among the central principles pursued by these conservative lawyers was a rethinking of the powers of the national government.[14] Although the Reagan administration initially emphasized a strategy of legislation and public education to advance its constitutional philosophy on federalism, it eventually turned to judicial nominations and litigation as an alternative strategy that was more likely to be successful in the long-term to advancing its vision of federalism.[15] The strategy seemed to yield its most substantial results once Reagan and George H. W. Bush were able, by the early 1990s, to place five justices on the bench who shared important elements of this constitutional philosophy. The resulting "federalism revolution" of the late 1990s was one of the most distinctive features of the Rehnquist Court.[16] The Reagan–Bush years laid the groundwork for those later judicial innovations.

A. General Principles

Ronald Reagan, Remarks at the National Conference of State Legislatures (1981)[17]

In running for the presidency in 1980, Ronald Reagan distinguished himself from both his Republican and Democratic predecessors in emphasizing the idea that there were firm limits on national power. It was a theme he had inherited from Barry Goldwater, but one that was even more prominent in the Republican platform of 1980 than the Republican platform of 1964. Democrats increasingly emphasized the flexible, malleable, and cooperative relationships between the federal, state, and local governments. The Republican constitutional philosophy after Reagan emphasized the theme of identifying limits on national power and keeping the federal government within those limits, and those ideas were routine features of party platforms and campaign rhetoric.

Reagan thought that many of his economic policies were tied to that constitutional philosophy. Cutting federal taxes, reducing federal spending, deregulation—all were consistent with his goal of returning the federal government to its "proper" bounds, though these initiatives did not involve trying to specify the precise constitutional boundaries of federal power. In other initiatives, Reagan proposed separating

13. Cornell W. Clayton and J. Mitchell Pickerill, *The Supreme Court in the Political Regime* (Chicago: University of Chicago Press, in process).

14. Steven M. Teles, *The Rise of the Conservative Legal Movement* (Princeton: Princeton University Press, 2008).

15. Dawn E. Johnsen, "Ronald Reagan and the Rehnquist Court on Congressional Power: Presidential Influence on Constitutional Change," *Indiana Law Journal* 78 (2003):363.

16. Keith E. Whittington, "Taking What They Give Us: Explaining the Court's Federalism Offensive," *Duke Law Journal* 51 (2001):477.

17. Excerpt taken from Ronald Reagan, "Remarks in Atlanta, Georgia, at the Annual Convention of the National Conference of State Legislatures," (July 30, 1981), in *Public Papers of the President of the United States, Ronald Reagan, 1981* (Washington, DC: Government Printing Office, 1982), 679.

the federal and state role in various policy areas and giving states greater policy discretion in how they implemented shared polices.

Reagan initially looked to state and local government officials as natural allies in his quest to limit the power of the national government. Though they proved interested in his proposals to give them greater discretion in spending federal funds or implementing federal programs, they proved less receptive to his proposals to shift political responsibility downward. Some members of Reagan's own administration were often less interested in federalism issues when those issues could not be combined with other goals, such as budget-cutting and deficit reduction.

...

With the help of these same Americans and with the help of the States, one of our next goals is to renew the concept of federalism....

This Nation has never fully debated the fact that over the past 40 years, federalism—one of the underlying principles of our Constitution—has nearly disappeared as a guiding force in American politics and government. My administration intends to initiate such a debate....

My administration is committed heart and soul to the broad principles of American federalism which are outlined in the Federalist Papers of Hamilton, Madison, and Jay and...they're in that tenth article of the Bill of Rights.

The designers of our Constitution realized that in federalism there's diversity. The Founding Fathers saw the federal system as constructed something like a masonry wall: The States are the bricks, the National Government is the mortar. For the structure to stand plumb with the Constitution, there must be a proper mix of that brick and mortar. Unfortunately, over the years, many people have come increasingly to believe that Washington is the whole wall—a wall that, incidentally, leans, sags, and bulges under its own weight.

The traumatic experience of the Great Depression provided the impetus and the rationale for a government that was more centralized than America had previously known. You had to have lived then, during those depression years, to understand the drabness of that period.

FDR brought the colors of hope and confidence to the era and I, like millions of others, became an enthusiastic New Dealer. We followed FDR because he offered a mix of ideas and movement. A former Governor himself, I believe that FDR would today be amazed and appalled at the growth of the Federal Government's power. Too many in government in recent years have invoked his name to justify what they were doing, forgetting that it was FDR who said, "In the conduct of public utilities, of banks, of insurance, of agriculture, of education, of social welfare—Washington must be discouraged from interfering."

Well, today the Federal Government takes too much taxes from the people, too much authority from the States, and too much liberty with the Constitution.

Americans have at last begun to realize that the steady flow of power and tax dollars to Washington has something to do with the fact that things don't seem to work anymore. The Federal Government is overloaded, muscle-bound, if you will, having assumed more responsibilities than it can properly manage. There's been a loss of accountability as the distinction between the duties of the Federal and State governments have blurred, and the Federal Government is so far removed from the people that Members of Congress spend less time legislating than cutting through bureaucratic red tape for their constituents.

Our economic package, which consists of tax cuts, spending cuts, block grants, and regulatory relief, is a first phase in our effort to revitalize federalism. For too long, the Federal Government has preempted the States' tax base, regulatory authority, and spending flexibility. It has tried to reduce the States to mere administrative districts of a government centralized in Washington. And with our economic proposals, we're staging a quiet federalist revolution. It's a revolution that promises to be one of the most exciting and noteworthy in our generation.

...

B. Taxing and Spending Power

Congress has a general power to spend funds for federal purposes. Congress also has the power to attach various restrictions on how that money is spent. As with all powers, there are questions about the outer bounds of that power. One type of difficulty is the "unconstitutional condition." Congress cannot normally require that someone give up their constitutional rights in order to receive federal funds. It cannot be a condition of federal employment or the receipt of federal funds that someone waive their rights. The Court decided in *Rust v. Sullivan* (1991), for example, that Congress cannot make it a condition for the receipt of federal funds that doctors not advise patients on abortions. The Court observed in *Dolan v. City of Tigard* (1994) that the government can only overcome such difficulties if there is an "essential nexus" between the benefit being offered by the government and the restriction being imposed and the restriction itself is proportionate to the government's need.

In *South Dakota v. Dole* (1987), the Court considered a somewhat different difficulty. Congress not only gives money to individuals and organizations. It also gives money to states and localities, and it attaches restrictions on how those governments can spend federal funds as well. Congress often uses federal funds as political leverage to convince states to cooperate with federal policy goals. The less controversial restriction on federal funds is when Congress specifies where a highway should be built or what quality road materials ought to be used in its construction or even the ethnic diversity and the union membership of the workers who will build the highway. The more controversial restriction on federal funds is when Congress threatens to withhold part of a state's annual highway appropriations unless the state adopts a set of policies that the federal government favors. When is the federal government "buying favors" from the states, and when is it "holding the state hostage"? Does the distinction even matter? Is it an important check on the federal spending power that such restrictions on federal funds must be related to the original purpose of the project? Congress made raising the drinking age a condition for receiving federal highway funds, not federal education funds or federal unemployment funds. Are there state policies that Congress could not influence through restrictions on how federal funds are spent?

South Dakota v. Dole, 483 U.S. 203 (1987)

In 1984, Congress passed the National Minimum Drinking Age Amendment to the Federal Aid Highway Act. The measure directed Secretary of Transportation Elizabeth Dole to withhold 10 percent of a state's allotted federal highway funds if it refused to legislate and enforce a minimum legal drinking age of 21 years. At the time of passage, 31 states had a legal drinking age below 21. In response to the law, every state eventually shifted to the national drinking age set by Congress. Threats to reduce or cut off federal funds to states had been successfully used on other occasions to induce the states to adopt policies that the federal government wanted. Threats to highway funds had been used in the 1970s to induce states to set a national maximum speed limit and were used in the 1990s to encourage states to adopt mandatory seat belt and motorcycle helmet laws, and threats to federal assistance to public schools were used to encourage desegregation in the 1960s. This federal leverage over state policymaking was a side effect of the "fiscal federalism" or "cooperative federalism" that had grown up since the New Deal, and it had shown itself to be quite powerful in driving states to conform to national political preferences.

The drinking age proposal was a favorite of the recently formed and politically highly successful activist group Mothers Against Drunk Driving (MADD), and the Democrats in the House and Senate were pressing the issue hard as a basic safety issue in the 1984 election year. Although President Reagan and Republicans in the Senate were initially opposed to the measure, after House passage Reagan announced that he would not veto the bill. Though the bill might seem "at odds with my philosophical viewpoint that state problems should involve state solutions, and it isn't up to a big and overwhelming Government in Washington to tell the states what to do," this was a "special case" in which the problem of teenage drunk driving was a "national tragedy" and the federal response through the spending power was "judicious" and "limited."[18]

South Dakota sought a declaratory judgment in federal district court that the measure was an invalid exercise of the congressional spending power and a violation of the Twenty-First Amendment (which repealed Prohibition and reserved control over the sale of alcohol to the states). The district court rejected the state's arguments, and a federal circuit court affirmed the ruling of the trial judge. The U.S. Supreme Court heard the case on certiorari.

In a 7–2 decision, the Court affirmed the lower court and upheld Congress's power to use the spending power in this way. Justices Brennan and O'Connor were the lone justices in dissent. This alignment of justices is particularly notable in pitting Chief Justice Rehnquist and Justice O'Connor against one another, normally two strong voices on behalf of states' rights and frequent allies in federalism cases. It was equally unusual for the liberal Brennan and the more conservative O'Connor to find themselves aligned in dis-

18. Ronald Reagan, "Remarks at River Dell High School in Oradell, New Jersey," (June 20, 1984), in *Public Papers of the President of the United States, Ronald Reagan, 1984: Book I* (Washington, DC: Government Printing Office, 1986), 882.

sent together in a federalism case. As you read these opinions, consider how willing Rehnquist and O'Connor were to revisit and unsettle the New Deal precedents relating to the congressional spending power. For Rehnquist, might this case have been an example of the occasional tension between a commitment to "original intent" and a commitment to "judicial restraint"? If the Court had overturned the drinking age law, could the precedent have been easily limited, or would it have necessarily had implications for a wide range of other conditions that Congress might put on receipt of federal grants? Also, if the federal government is given broad authority to use its spending power to influence state behavior, then how meaningful are other limits on federal power over states?

CHIEF JUSTICE REHNQUIST delivered the opinion of the Court.

...

...[W]e need not decide in this case whether [the Twenty-First] Amendment would prohibit an attempt by Congress to legislate directly a national minimum drinking age. Here, Congress has acted indirectly under its spending power to encourage uniformity in the States' drinking ages. As we explain below, we find this legislative effort within constitutional bounds even if Congress may not regulate drinking ages directly.

The Constitution empowers Congress to "lay and collect Taxes, Duties, Imposts, and Excises, to pay the Debts and provide for the common Defense and general Welfare of the United States." Incident to this power, Congress may attach conditions on the receipt of federal funds, and has repeatedly employed the power "to further broad policy objectives by conditioning receipt of federal moneys upon compliance by the recipient with federal statutory and administrative directives." *Fullilove* v. *Klutznick* (1980) (opinion of Burger, C. J.)....The breadth of this power was made clear in *United States* v. *Butler* (1936), where the Court, resolving a longstanding debate over the scope of the Spending Clause, determined that "the power of Congress to authorize expenditure of public moneys for public purposes is not limited by the direct grants of legislative power found in the Constitution." Thus, objectives not thought to be within Article I's "enumerated legislative fields," may nevertheless be attained through the use of the spending power and the conditional grant of federal funds.

The spending power is of course not unlimited....The first of these limitations is derived from the language of the Constitution itself: the exercise of the spending power must be in pursuit of "the general welfare"....In considering whether a particular expenditure is intended to serve general public purposes, courts should defer substantially to the judgment of Congress....Second, we have required that if Congress desires to condition the States' receipt of federal funds, it "must do so unambiguously...enabl[ing] the States to exercise their choice knowingly, cognizant of the consequences of their participation."...Third, our cases have suggested (without significant elaboration) that conditions on federal grants might be illegitimate if they are unrelated "to the federal interest in particular national projects or programs."...Finally, we have noted that other constitutional provisions may provide an independent bar to the conditional grant of federal funds....

...Congress found that the differing drinking ages in the States created particular incentives for young persons to combine their desire to drink with their ability to drive, and that this interstate problem required a national solution. The means it chose to address this dangerous situation were reasonably calculated to advance the general welfare. The conditions upon which States receive the funds, moreover, could not be more clearly stated by Congress....[T]he condition imposed by Congress is directly related to one of the main purposes for which highway funds are expended—safe interstate travel....This goal of the interstate highway system had been frustrated by varying drinking ages among the States.

...

...[W]e think that the language in our earlier opinions stands for the unexceptionable proposition that the [spending] power may not be used to induce the States to engage in activities that would themselves be unconstitutional. Thus, for example, a grant of federal funds conditioned on invidiously discriminatory state action or the infliction of cruel and unusual punishment would be an illegitimate exercise of the Congress' broad spending power. But no such claim can be or is made here....

...

Here Congress has offered relatively mild encouragement to the States to enact higher minimum drinking ages than they would otherwise choose. But the enactment of such laws remains the prerogative of the States not merely in theory but in fact. Even if Congress might lack the power to impose a national minimum drinking age directly, we conclude that encouragement to state action found in § 158 is a valid use of the spending power. Accordingly, the judgment of the Court of Appeals is

Affirmed.

JUSTICE BRENNAN, dissenting.

I agree with Justice O'CONNOR....

JUSTICE O'CONNOR, dissenting.

The Court today upholds the National Minimum Drinking Age Amendment as a valid exercise of the spending power conferred by Article I, § 8. But § 158 is not a condition on spending reasonably related to the expenditure of federal funds and cannot be justified on that ground. Rather, it is an attempt to regulate the sale of liquor, an attempt that lies outside Congress' power to regulate commerce because it falls within the ambit of § 2 of the Twenty-First Amendment.

...We have repeatedly said that Congress may condition grants under the spending power only in ways reasonably related to the purpose of the federal program....In my view, establishment of a minimum drinking age of 21 is not sufficiently related to interstate highway construction to justify so conditioning funds appropriated for that purpose.

...

When Congress appropriates money to build a highway, it is entitled to insist that the highway be a safe one. But it is not entitled to insist as a condition of the use of highway funds that the State impose or change regulations in other areas of the State's social and economic life because of an attenuated or tangential relationship to highway use or safety. Indeed, if the rule were otherwise, the Congress could effectively regulate almost any area of a State's social, political, or economic life on the theory that use of the interstate transportation system is somehow enhanced....

There is a clear place at which the Court can draw the line between permissible and impermissible conditions on federal grants. It is the line identified in the Brief for the National Conference of State Legislatures et al. as *Amici Curiae*:

> Congress has the power to *spend* for the general welfare, it has the power to *legislate* only for delegated purposes....
>
> The appropriate inquiry, then, is whether the spending requirement or prohibition is a condition on a grant or whether it is regulation. The difference turns on whether the requirement specifies in some way how the money should be spent, so that Congress' intent in making the grant will be effectuated. Congress has no power under the Spending Clause to impose requirements on a grant that go beyond specifying how the money should be spent. A requirement that is not such a specification is not a condition, but a regulation, which is valid only if it falls within one of Congress' delegated regulatory powers.

....

Of the other possible sources of congressional authority for regulating the sale of liquor only the commerce power comes to mind. But in my view, the regulation of the age of the purchasers of liquor, just as the regulation of the price at which liquor may be sold, falls squarely within the scope of those powers reserved to the States by the Twenty-First Amendment....

The immense size and power of the Government of the United States ought not obscure its fundamental character. It remains a Government of enumerated powers. Because 23 U. S. C. § 158 cannot be justified as an exercise of any power delegated to the Congress, it is not authorized by the Constitution. The Court errs in holding it to be the law of the land, and I respectfully dissent.

IV. Federalism

MAJOR DEVELOPMENTS

- Court retreats from idea that states were partly exempted from congressional regulatory authority under the commerce clause
- Acceptance of Twenty-Seventh Amendment recognized the possibility of an extended constitutional ratification process

One aspect of federalism that received attention from the U.S. Supreme Court in the latter twentieth century is the possibility that the rights and powers of states imposed limits on congressional power. Justice Rehnquist was not new to the idea, having championed the 1976 *National League of Cities v. Usery* decision, which held that there were limits to congressional authority to regulate the "states qua states." Under that decision, state and local governments were entitled to constitutional exemptions from some national regulations, such as employment regulations. The Tenth Amendment, according to this line of argument, implicitly recognized a special constitutional status for the states, and the national government was necessarily restricted from adopting policies that undermined the independence and functioning of the state governments. If this meant that the federal government could not tax state officials in the nineteenth century (*Collector v. Day* [1871]) or designate where the state capital would be in the early twentieth century (*Coyle v. Smith* [1911]), then perhaps it meant that the federal government could not determine what minimum wage state and local governments paid their employees in the late twentieth century.

Despite the increased interest in federalism and states' rights in the Reagan Era, the Court actually retreated on this issue during the 1980s. Justice Rehnquist could not hold the narrow majority that he had won in the *National League of Cities* decision. In *Garcia v. San Antonio Metropolitan Transit Authority* (1985), Justice Blackmun broke from Rehnquist and overturned *National League of Cities*. The Court would revisit the issue from a different angle and with a new set of justices in the 1990s.

The Burger and early Rehnquist Courts also became more active in applying the dormant commerce clause against the states. In *H. P. Hood & Sons, Inc. v. DuMond* (1949), New Deal Justice Robert Jackson praised the "material success" generated by the "federal free trade unit" that the dormant commerce clause helped protect. Despite such arguments, some of the most conservative justices on the Rehnquist Court have at various times been skeptical of the federal courts exercising their own judgment to determine when the national interest should trump state policies. In a lone dissent in *New Jersey v. City of Philadelphia* (1978), Justice Rehnquist argued that New Jersey should be able to dispose of the solid waste of its own citizens without by that simple fact becoming "the depository for those of every other State" and taking on new health and safety burdens for its own citizens. When dissenting in a case involving the state regulation of truck lengths in *Kassel v. Consolidated Freightways Corp.* (1981), Rehnquist argued that the Court should give a "strong presumption of validity" to the public policy judgments that the state makes to secure the safety and welfare of its residents. The Court's concern should only be with whether such public good arguments are trivial and a mere "pretext for discrimination" and protectionism. The Court's majority, however, concluded that the state regulation unduly interfered with out-of-state shippers. The Court heard a steady diet of such cases in the Burger and early Rehnquist Courts, with the states losing as often as they won. State regulations and taxes were regularly subjected to judicial scrutiny to see whether they imposed an undue burden on interstate commerce and unnecessarily favored local economic actors over out-of-state competitors.

A. States and the Commerce Clause

In 1976, Justice Rehnquist won a surprising majority in *National League of Cities v. Usery* for limiting the power of Congress to regulate the states "qua states" or when performing "traditional governmental functions." States had a limited immunity from the congressional regulatory authority under the commerce clause. It was a narrow 5–4 majority, with Justice Blackmun writing a brief concurring opinion signaling that he would not push *National League of Cities* very far.

With President Reagan appointing pro-federalism Justice Sandra Day O'Connor to replace the retiring Justice Potter Stewart (a member of the original *National League of Cities* majority) in 1981, *National League of Cities* was seemingly secure when the Court heard *Garcia v. San Antonio Metropolitan Transit Authority* in 1985 since the other eight members of the Court were the same ones who had voted in *National League of Cities* and who had ruled in subsequent cases using its principles. In *Garcia*, however, Justice Blackmun switched his vote. He now wrote a 5–4 majority opinion overruling *National League of Cities*, leaving Justice Rehnquist to write a brief dissent hoping that his views would once again "command the support of a majority of this Court." To do so, he would need reinforcements. President Reagan would soon elevate William Rehnquist to the role of chief justice, in part because of his views about federalism, and add Justices Scalia and Kennedy to the Court, but they filled vacancies created by *Garcia* dissenters (Burger and Powell). It was not until the first Bush presidency that any members of the *Garcia* majority left the bench and were replaced (Brennan was replaced by Souter, and then, most importantly, Marshall was replaced by Thomas). The Court has not reconsidered *Garcia* itself, but a decade after *Garcia* it once again began to reconsider the possibility of judicial enforcement of constitutional limits of federal power.

The opinions in *Garcia* herald the competing philosophies that would appear on the Court in the contemporary era. Of particular interest is the division between Justice Blackmun for the majority and Justices Powell and O'Connor in dissent over the adequacy of what has been called "process federalism." In an influential post–New Deal law review article, "The Political Safeguards of Federalism," Herbert Wechsler argued that federalism was adequately protected through the political process and did not require judicial protection through constitutional law, and Justice Blackmun's opinion in *Garcia* reflects this sensibility.[19] By contrast, the dissenters in *Garcia* strongly reject this view in favor of what is sometimes known as "judicially enforced federalism," which calls for judicial intervention in the form of constitutional law and judicial review to protect federalism principles.[20]

Garcia v. San Antonio Metropolitan Transit Authority et al., 469 U.S. 528 (1985)

In 1974, Congress removed the last of the longstanding exemptions to state and local government employees—and particularly public mass transit workers—from the minimum wage and overtime provisions of the Fair Labor Standards Act (FLSA). After the 1976 National League of Cities *decision, the San Antonio Metropolitan Transit Authority (SAMTA) determined that it was constitutionally immune from FLSA and would not comply with its overtime provisions (it paid more than minimum wage regardless of the law). In 1979, the Department of Labor determined that FLSA did apply to SAMTA. SAMTA filed suit in federal district court against the Department of Labor seeking a declaratory judgment that it was immune from the application of the overtime provisions of FLSA, and at the same time the Department of Labor and a number of SAMTA employees, including Joe Garcia, countersued seeking enforcement of the FLSA. The district court granted summary judgment to SAMTA, which was appealed directly to the Supreme Court and remanded for further consideration in light of a recent decision involving a commuter rail service. The district court again ruled in favor of SAMTA, and the ruling was again appealed to the U.S. Supreme Court. This time the Court heard arguments and ruled on the merits, reversing the district court.*

When should the Supreme Court be willing to overturn precedent, according to Justice Blackmun? Is this a persuasive case for doing so? Is the constitutional status of states adequately protected through the political process, or should the judiciary also take an interest in protecting states from federal actions?

JUSTICE BLACKMUN delivered the opinion of the Court.

We revisit in these cases an issue raised in *National League of Cities* v. *Usery*. In that litigation, this Court, by a sharply divided vote, ruled that the Commerce Clause does not empower Congress to enforce the minimum-wage and overtime provisions of the Fair Labor Standards Act (FLSA) against the States "in areas of traditional governmental functions." Although *National League of Cities* supplied some examples of "traditional governmental functions," it did not offer a general explanation of how a "traditional" function is to be distinguished from a "nontraditional" one. Since then, federal and state courts have struggled with the task, thus imposed, of identifying a traditional function for purposes of state immunity under the Commerce Clause.

...

Our examination of this "function" standard applied in these and other cases over the last eight years now persuades us that the attempt to draw the boundaries of state regulatory immunity in terms of "traditional governmental function" is not only unworkable but is also inconsistent with established principles of federalism and, indeed, with those very federalism principles on which *National League of Cities* purported to rest. That case, accordingly, is overruled.

The history of public transportation in San Antonio, Tex., is characteristic of the history of local mass transit in the United States generally. Passenger transportation for hire within San Antonio originally was provided on a private basis by a local transportation company. In 1913, the Texas Legislature authorized the State's municipalities to regulate vehicles providing carriage for hire.... The city continued to rely on such publicly regulated private mass transit until 1959, when

19. Herbert Wechsler, "The Political Safeguards of Federalism: The Role of the States in the Composition and Selection of the National Government," *Columbia Law Review* 54 (1954):543. See also Larry D. Kramer, "Putting the Politics Back into the Political Safeguards of Federalism," *Columbia Law Review* 100 (2000):215.

20. See, e.g., John C. Yoo, "The Judicial Safeguards of Federalism," *Southern California Law Review* 70 (1997):1311; Saikrishna B. Prakash and John C. Yoo, "The Puzzling Persistence of Process-Based Federalism Theories," *Texas Law Review* 79 (2001):1459.

it purchased the privately owned San Antonio Transit Company and replaced it with a public authority....

As did other localities, San Antonio reached the point where it came to look to the Federal Government for financial assistance in maintaining its public mass transit. SATS managed to meet its operating expenses and bond obligations for the first decade of its existence without federal or local financial aid. By 1970, however, its financial position had deteriorated to the point where federal subsidies were vital for its continued operation....

...

Appellees have not argued that SAMTA is immune from regulation under the FLSA on the ground that it is a local transit system engaged in intrastate commercial activity. In a practical sense, SAMTA's operations might well be characterized as "local." Nonetheless, it long has been settled that Congress' authority under the Commerce Clause extends to intrastate economic activities that affect interstate commerce. See, e.g., *Heart of Atlanta Hotel, Inc. v. United States* (1964); *Wickard v. Filburn* (1942). Were SAMTA a privately owned and operated enterprise, it could not credibly argue that Congress exceeded the bounds of its Commerce Clause powers in prescribing minimum wages and overtime rates for SAMTA's employees. Any constitutional exemption from the requirements of the FLSA therefore must rest on SAMTA's status as a governmental entity rather than on the "local" nature of its operations.

...

The controversy in the present cases has focused on the... requirement... that the challenged federal statute trench on "traditional governmental functions." The District Court voiced a common concern: "Despite the abundance of adjectives, identifying which particular state functions are immune remains difficult." Just how troublesome the task has been is revealed by the results reached in other federal cases. Thus, courts have held that regulating ambulance services,... licensing automobile drivers,... operating a municipal airport,... performing solid waste disposal... and operating a highway authority... are functions *protected* under *National League of Cities*. At the same time, courts have held that issuance of industrial development bonds,... regulation of traffic on public roads,... regulation of air transportation,... operation of a telephone system,... operation of a mental health facility,... are *not* entitled to immunity. We find it difficult, if not impossible, to identify an organizing principle that places each of the cases in the first group on one side of a line and each of the cases in the second group on the other side. The constitutional distinction between licensing drivers and regulating traffic, for example, or between operating a highway authority and operating a mental health facility, is elusive at best.

...

...The problem is that neither the governmental/proprietary distinction nor another that purports to separate out important governmental functions can be faithful to the role of federalism in a democratic society. The essence of our federal system is that within the realm of authority left open to them under the Constitution, the States must be equally free to engage in any activity that their citizens choose for the common weal, no matter how unorthodox or unnecessary anyone else—including the judiciary—deems state involvement to be. Any rule of state immunity that looks to the "traditional," "integral," or "necessary" nature of governmental functions inevitably invites an unelected federal judiciary to make decisions about which state policies it favors and which ones it dislikes....

We therefore now reject, as unsound in principle and unworkable in practice, a rule of state immunity from federal regulation that turns on a judicial appraisal of whether a particular governmental function is "integral" or "traditional." Any such rule leads to inconsistent results at the same time that it disserves principles of democratic self-governance, and it breeds inconsistency precisely because it is divorced from those principles.... If there are to be limits on the Federal Government's power to interfere with state functions—as undoubtedly there are—we must look elsewhere to find them....

...

When we look for the States' "residuary and inviolable sovereignty," The Federalist No. 39... (J. Madison), in the shape of the constitutional scheme rather than in predetermined notions of sovereign power, a different measure of state sovereignty emerges. Apart from the limitation on federal authority inherent in the delegated nature of Congress' Article I powers, the principal means chosen by the Framers to ensure the role of the States in the federal system lies in the structure of the Federal Government itself. It is no novelty to observe that the composition of the Federal Government was designed in large part to protect the States from overreaching by Congress. The Framers thus gave the States a role in the selection both of the Executive and the Legislative Branches of the Federal Government. The States were vested with indirect influence over the House of Representatives and the Presidency by their control of electoral qualifications and their role in Presidential elections. They were given more direct influence in the Senate, where each State received equal representation and each Senator was to be selected by the legislature of his State. The significance attached to the States' equal representation in the Senate is underscored by the prohibition of any constitutional amendment divesting a State of equal representation without the State's consent.

...In short, the Framers chose to rely on a federal system in which special restraints on federal power over the States inhered principally in the workings of the National Government itself, rather than in discrete limitations on the objects of federal authority. State sovereign interests, then, are more properly protected by procedural safeguards inherent in the structure of the federal system than by judicially created limitations on federal power.

The effectiveness of the federal political process in preserving the States' interests is apparent even today in the course of federal legislation. On the one hand, the States have been able to direct a substantial proportion of federal revenues into their own treasuries in the form of general and program-specific grants in aid.... Moreover, at the same time that the States have exercised their influence to obtain federal support, they have been able to exempt themselves from a wide variety of obligations imposed by Congress under the Commerce Clause. For example, the Federal Power Act, the National Labor Relations Act, the Labor-Management Reporting and Disclosure Act, the Occupational Safety and Health Act, the Employee Retirement Income Security Act, and the Sherman Act all contain express or implied exemptions for States and their subdivisions. The fact that some federal statutes such as the FLSA extend general obligations to the States cannot obscure the extent to which the political position of the States in the federal system has served to minimize the burdens that the States bear under the Commerce Clause.

We realize that changes in the structure of the Federal Government have taken place since 1789, not the least of which has been the substitution of popular election of Senators by the adoption of the Seventeenth Amendment in 1913, and that these changes may work to alter the influence of the States in the federal political process. Nonetheless, against this background, we are convinced that the fundamental limitation that the constitutional scheme imposes on the Commerce Clause to protect the "States as States" is one of process rather than one of result....

...

We do not lightly overrule recent precedent. We have not hesitated, however, when it has become apparent that a prior decision has departed from a proper understanding of congressional power under the Commerce Clause.... Due respect for the reach of congressional power within the federal system mandates that we do so now.

National League of Cities... is overruled. The judgment of the District Court is reversed, and these cases are remanded to that court for further proceedings consistent with this opinion.

It is so ordered.

JUSTICE POWELL, with whom CHIEF JUSTICE BURGER, JUSTICE REHNQUIST, and JUSTICE O'CONNOR join, dissenting.

...

There are... numerous examples over the history of this Court in which prior decisions have been reconsidered and overruled. There have been few cases, however, in which the principle of *stare decisis* and the rationale of recent decisions were ignored as abruptly as we now witness. The reasoning of the Court in *National League of Cities*, and the principle applied there, have been reiterated consistently over the past eight years. Since its decision in 1976, *National League of Cities* has been cited and quoted in opinions joined by every Member of the present Court.... [T]he five Justices who compose the majority today participated in *National League of Cities* and the cases reaffirming it. The stability of judicial decision, and with it respect for the authority of this Court, are not served by the precipitate overruling of multiple precedents that we witness in these cases.

Whatever effect the Court's decision may have in weakening the application of *stare decisis*, it is likely to be less important than what the Court has done to the Constitution itself.... A unique feature of the United States is the *federal* system of government guaranteed by the Constitution and implicit in the very name of our country. Despite some genuflecting in the Court's opinion to the concept of federalism, today's decision effectively reduces the Tenth Amendment to meaningless rhetoric when Congress acts pursuant to the Commerce Clause....

To leave no doubt about its intention, the Court renounces its decision in *National League of Cities* because it "inevitably invites an unelected federal judiciary to make decisions about which state policies its favors and which ones it dislikes." In other words, the extent to which the States may exercise their authority, when Congress purports to act under the Commerce Clause, henceforth is to be determined from time to time by political decisions made by members of the Federal Government, decisions the Court says will not be subject to judicial review. I note that it does not seem to have occurred to the Court that *it*—an unelected majority of five Justices—today rejects almost 200 years of the understanding of the constitutional status of federalism. In doing so, there is only a single passing reference to the Tenth Amendment. Nor is so much as a dictum of any court cited in support of the view that the role of the States in the federal system may depend upon the grace of elected federal officials, rather than on the Constitution as interpreted by this Court.

...

Much of the Court's opinion is devoted to arguing that it is difficult to define *a priori* "traditional governmental functions." *National League of Cities* neither engaged in, nor required, such a task.... [N]owhere does it mention that *National League of Cities* adopted a familiar type of balancing test for determining whether Commerce Clause enactments transgress constitutional limitations imposed by the federal nature of our system of government. This omission is noteworthy, since the author of today's opinion joined *National League of Cities* and concurred separately to point out that the Court's opinion in that case "[adopts] a balancing approach [that] does not outlaw federal power in areas... where the federal interest is demonstrably greater and where state... compliance with imposed federal standards would be essential."

...

Today's opinion does not explain how the States' role in the electoral process guarantees that particular exercises of the Commerce Clause power will not infringe on residual state sovereignty. Members of Congress are elected from the various States, but once in office they are Members of the Federal Government.[21] Although the States participate in the Electoral College, this is hardly a reason to view the President as a representative of the States' interest against federal encroachment. We noted recently "[the] hydraulic pressure inherent within each of the separate Branches to exceed the outer limits of its power...." The Court offers no reason to think that this pressure will not operate when Congress seeks to invoke its powers under the Commerce Clause, notwithstanding the electoral role of the States.[22]

The Court apparently thinks that the States' success at obtaining federal funds for various projects and exemptions from the obligations of some federal statutes is indicative of the "effectiveness of the federal political process in preserving the States' interests...." But such political success is not relevant to the question whether the political *processes* are the proper means of enforcing constitutional limitations.[23] The fact that Congress generally does not transgress constitutional limits on its power to reach state activities does not make judicial review any less necessary to rectify the cases in which it does do so.[24] The States' role in our system of government is a matter of constitutional law, not of legislative grace. "The powers not delegated to the United States by the Constitution, nor prohibited by it to the States, are reserved to the States, respectively, or to the people." U.S. Const., Amdt. 10.

More troubling than the logical infirmities in the Court's reasoning is the result of its holding, *i. e.*, that federal political officials, invoking the Commerce Clause, are the sole judges of the limits of their own power. This result is inconsistent with the fundamental principles of our constitutional system.... At least since *Marbury* v. *Madison*, it has been the settled province of the federal judiciary "to say what the law is" with

21. One can hardly imagine this Court saying that because Congress is composed of individuals, individual rights guaranteed by the Bill of Rights are amply protected by the political process. Yet, the position adopted today is indistinguishable in principle. The Tenth Amendment also is an essential part of the Bill of Rights.

22. At one time in our history, the view that the structure of the Federal Government sufficed to protect the States might have had a somewhat more practical, although not a more logical, basis. Professor Wechsler, whose seminal article in 1954 proposed the view adopted by the Court today, predicated his argument on assumptions that simply do not accord with current reality....

23. Apparently in an effort to reassure the States, the Court identifies several major statutes that thus far have not been made applicable to state governments.... The Court does not suggest that this restraint will continue after its decision here. Indeed, it is unlikely that special interest groups will fail to accept the Court's open invitation to urge Congress to extend these and other statutes to apply to the States and their local subdivisions.

24. This Court has never before abdicated responsibility for assessing the constitutionality of challenged action on the ground that affected parties theoretically are able to look out for their own interests through the electoral process....

respect to the constitutionality of Acts of Congress. In rejecting the role of the judiciary in protecting the States from federal overreaching, the Court's opinion offers no explanation for ignoring the teaching of the most famous case in our history.

...

The Court emphasizes that municipal operation of an intracity mass transit system is relatively new in the life of our country. It nevertheless is a classic example of the type of service traditionally provided by local government. It is *local* by definition. It is indistinguishable in principle from the traditional services of providing and maintaining streets, public lighting, traffic control, water, and sewerage systems. Services of this kind are precisely those with which citizens are more "familiarly and minutely conversant." The Federalist No. 46....

...

As I view the Court's decision today as rejecting the basic precepts of our federal system and limiting the constitutional role of judicial review, I dissent.

JUSTICE REHNQUIST, dissenting.

I join both Justice POWELL's and Justice O'CONNOR's thoughtful dissents....[But] I do not think it incumbent on those of us in dissent to spell out further the fine points of a principle that will, I am confident, in time again command the support of a majority of this Court.

JUSTICE O'CONNOR, with whom JUSTICE POWELL and JUSTICE REHNQUIST join, dissenting.

The Court today surveys the battle scene of federalism and sounds a retreat. Like JUSTICE POWELL, I would prefer to hold the field and, at the very least, render a little aid to the wounded. I join JUSTICE POWELL's opinion. I also write separately to note my fundamental disagreement with the majority's views of federalism and the duty of this Court.

...

...The true "essence" of federalism is that the States *as States* have legitimate interests which the National Government is bound to respect even though its laws are supreme....If federalism so conceived and so carefully cultivated by the Framers of our Constitution is to remain meaningful, this Court cannot abdicate its constitutional responsibility to oversee the Federal Government's compliance with its duty to respect the legitimate interests of the States.

...

...The Court based the expansion on the authority of Congress [in the twentieth century], through the Necessary and Proper Clause, "to resort to all means for the exercise of a granted power which are appropriate and plainly adapted to the permitted end." *United States* v. *Darby* (1941)....It is worth recalling the cited passage in *McCulloch* v. *Maryland* (1819) that lies at the source of the recent expansion of the commerce power. "Let the end be legitimate, let it be within the scope of the constitution," Chief Justice Marshall said, "and all means which are appropriate, which are plainly adapted to that end, which are not prohibited, but consist with the letter *and spirit* of the constitution, are constitutional" (emphasis added). The *spirit* of the Tenth Amendment, of course, is that the States will retain their integrity in a system in which the laws of the United States are nevertheless supreme....

It is not enough that the "end be legitimate"; the means to that end chosen by Congress must not contravene the spirit of the Constitution. Thus many of this Court's decisions acknowledge that the means by which national power is exercised must take into account concerns for state autonomy. See, e.g., *NLRB v. Jones & Laughlin Steel Corp.* (1937) ("Undoubtedly, the scope of this [commerce] power must be considered in light of our dual system of government and may not be extended so as to embrace effects upon interstate commerce so indirect and remote that to embrace them, in view of our complex society, would effectually obliterate the distinction between what is national and what is local and create a completely centralized government")....

This principle requires the Court to enforce affirmative limits on federal regulation of the States to complement the judicially crafted expansion of the interstate commerce power. *National League of Cities* v. *Usery* represented an attempt to define such limits. The Court today rejects *National League of Cities* and washes its hands of all efforts to protect the States....

...Today, as federal legislation and coercive grant programs have expanded to embrace innumerable activities that were once viewed as local, the burden of persuasion has surely shifted, and the extraordinary has become ordinary....With the abandonment of *National League of Cities*, all that stands between the remaining essentials of state sovereignty and Congress is the latter's underdeveloped capacity for self-restraint.

...It is insufficient, in assessing the validity of congressional regulation of a State pursuant to the commerce power, to ask only whether the same regulation would be valid if enforced against a private party. That reasoning, embodied in the majority opinion, is inconsistent with the spirit of our Constitution. It remains relevant that a *State* is being regulated, as *National League of Cities* and every recent case have recognized....

It has been difficult for this Court to craft bright lines defining the scope of the state autonomy protected by *National League of Cities*. Such difficulty is to be expected whenever constitutional concerns as important as federalism and the effectiveness of the commerce power come into conflict. Regardless of the difficulty, it is and will remain the duty of this Court to reconcile these concerns in the final instance. That the Court shuns the task today by appealing to the "essence of federalism" can provide scant comfort to those who believe our federal system requires something more than a unitary, centralized government. I would not shirk the duty acknowledged by *National League of Cities* and its progeny, and I share JUSTICE REHNQUIST's belief that this Court will in time again assume its constitutional responsibility.

I respectfully dissent.

B. Constitutional Amendment and Ratification

Note: The Validity of the Twenty-Seventh Amendment

The Twenty-Seventh Amendment to the Constitution is the most recent amendment to the U.S. Constitution, and its terms are quite simple: "No law, varying the compensation for the services of the Senators and Representatives, shall take effect, until an election of Representatives shall have intervened." In May 1992 the Archivist of the United States performed his statutory duty of certifying that he had received notices from the constitutionally necessary number of states to ratify the amendment, and both chambers of Congress quickly passed lopsided resolutions declaring that the Constitution had been amended. At the time of the ratification of the "Congressional Pay" Amendment, Congress was under substantial popular pressure. Early that spring the public learned that many members of Congress had routinely been allowed to write checks on empty accounts in a bank operated by the House of Representatives for its members, a scandal that would result in the resignation or defeat of many incumbent legislators. The congressional term limits movement was in full swing, and general concerns about congressional pay and "perks" fed a belief that legislators had lost touch with the people.[25] On the eve of the 1992 elections, Congress was not about to raise questions about the validity of the Congressional Pay Amendment.

There were questions to be raised. The route that the Twenty-Seventh Amendment followed to ratification was unique, and it raises basic questions about the Article V amendment process. The Twenty-Seventh Amendment was approved by the First Congress as one of twelve amendments that were sent to the states for ratification on September 25, 1789, as the original Bill of Rights. Of course, only ten of those twelve amendments received enough votes in the states to be ratified and became the Bill of Rights that we know today. (The other unratified amendment involved the apportionment of the House.) The Congressional Pay Amendment had only been approved by six of the state legislatures when the Bill of Rights won ratification in 1791. That was five states short of what was needed for ratification at the time, and support for the amendment stalled. When congressional pay raise scandals erupted during the Jacksonian Era, the response in the states and Congress was to propose new constitutional amendments—not to try to revive James Madison's amendment from 1789. There was a similar reaction to pay raise scandals in the 1870s, though the Ohio legislature also passed a resolution ratifying the Congressional Pay Amendment at that time. The Ohio governor did not bother notifying the federal government of the state legislature's action. In 1982, a university student and aide to a Texas state legislator took up the cause of the Congressional Pay Amendment and began to lobby state legislatures to ratify it. In 1992, Michigan became the thirty-eighth state to ratify the amendment, 203 years after it had been approved by Congress.[26]

In the case of *Dillon v. Gloss* (1921), upholding the authority of Congress to place explicit time limits on state ratification of proposed constitutional amendments, the U.S. Supreme Court suggested that some

25. See John R. Hibbing and Elizabeth Theiss-Morse, *Congress as Public Enemy* (New York: Cambridge University Press, 1995), 68.

26. For a history of the amendment, see Richard B. Bernstein, "The Sleeper Wakes: The History and Legacy of the Twenty-Seventh Amendment," *Fordham Law Review* 61 (1992):497.

Table 10-2 Timeline of Ratification of Twenty-Seventh Amendment

Year	Number of States Ratifying That Year	Total Number of Ratifying States	Total Number Needed for Ratification That Year
1789	2	2	9
1790	2	4	10
1791	2	6	11
1873	1	7	28
1978	1	8	38
1983	1	9	38
1984	1	10	38
1985	5	15	38
1986	3	18	38
1987	4	22	38
1988	3	25	38
1989	7	32	38
1990	2	34	38
1991	1	35	38
1992	6	41	38

Note: Article V requires ratification by three-quarters of the states. As new states join the union, the number of states required to cross the ratification threshold increases.

sort of time limit was implicit in the principles of the Article V amendment process. The "natural inference" of Article V was that proposal and ratification "are not to be widely separated in time" and that ratification should be "sufficiently contemporaneous in that number of states to reflect the will of the people in all sections at relatively the same period." The Court backed up this argument by noting the common view that it would be "quite untenable" to attempt to take up those amendments—including the Congressional Pay Amendment—"proposed long ago" and "now largely forgotten" and "supplement[]" their ratification totals with "enough more states to make three-fourths by representatives of the present or some future generation." What seemed untenable to the Court, and dominant legal opinion, in 1921, Congress chose not to question in 1992.

On the eve of the 1992 election, President Bush's Office of Legal Counsel produced an opinion for the president agreeing with Congress and approving of the validity of the Twenty-Seventh Amendment.[27] It was easy for the *Dillon* Court to talk about the Congressional Pay Amendment as a dead letter when everyone was treating it that way in political practice. Once state legislatures began to do what the Supreme Court assumed that they would not—take seriously a two-hundred-year-old constitutional amendment—then the vague idea of implicit time limits in Article V and ratification votes "not widely separated in time" became less helpful. The Office of Legal Counsel instead emphasized the value of bright-line rules. The constitutional text did not impose a clear time limit on ratification. "[H]opeless uncertainty" would be introduced if the states had to infer one during the ratification process.

Is it an implicit principle of Article V that proposal and ratification be roughly contemporaneous? In part because the Congressional Pay Amendment did not pass through Congress in the modern era and the campaign to ratify it was a relatively low-profile movement compared to other recent movements to amend the Constitution, the Twenty-Seventh Amendment was also dismissed as a "stealth amendment." Is it inconsistent with the constitutional design or fundamental constitutional values for constitutional change

27. Congressional Pay Amendment, 16 Op. Off. Leg. Counsel 85 (1992).

to occur without broader public debate? Does the passage of the Twenty-Seventh Amendment "settle" the issue of implicit time limits in the ratification process, or is the Twenty-Seventh Amendment an exception? Is it plausible to imagine circumstances in which the states take up and ratify a "largely forgotten" constitutional amendment and Congress would not see it as in its immediate political interest to endorse the amendment as valid?

V. Separation of Powers

MAJOR DEVELOPMENTS

- Disrupted a standard post–New Deal congressional practice by requiring that legislative actions with the force of law be passed by the regular legislative process and submitted for presidential approval
- Continued to recognize a broad authority for the legislature to delegate policymaking discretion to other actors and institutions
- Moved closer to the view that officials performing executive duties be ultimately accountable within the executive branch

It should be no surprise that issues of separation of powers were of particular concern during the Reagan Era. The executive and legislative branches were controlled by different political parties during much of the period. Unlike some earlier periods of divided government, the Democratic and Republican parties of the contemporary era were also ideologically polarized with deep and severe disagreements about the direction that the government should go and in their constitutional philosophies. The result was new forms of institutional conflict and innovation. Richard Nixon tested the boundaries of presidential control over the executive branch and the levers of foreign and domestic policymaking in the early 1970s, and Congress responded by imposing new constraints on executive branch officials and finding new ways to operate so as to leave less discretion in the hands of the administration.[28] Such efforts to seek partisan advantage by building up either Congress or the presidency to circumvent or account for opponents in the other branch have continued since, becoming a major feature of contemporary politics.[29]

The Reagan administration had at least initially hoped that the Republicans would build a new conservative majority. From 1981 to 1993, the GOP controlled the White House, but the Democrats controlled one if not both chambers of Congress. Some observers suggested that the Republicans had an effective electoral lock on the presidency, while the Democrats could not be dislodged from the legislature where "politics is local." The Republicans dug into the institution under their control, building up the executive branch. The Democrats did the same. For the Reagan administration, this included elaborating such arguments as the theory of the "unitary executive" (arguing that the "take care" clause required that all lower level executive branch be accountable to the president) and expanding the use of "signing statements" (whereby presidents, while signing a bill, articulate their own views on the meaning and scope of the new law). For Congress, this included the use of legislative hearings and statutory checks to monitor and limit executive-branch activities and embed Democratic preferences into law.

Conflict between the White House and Congress was a regular feature of the Reagan and Bush years, but the Iran-Contra scandal was perhaps the most serious constitutional and political confrontation between the executive and legislative branches during the 1980s. The Reagan White House was deeply committed to providing aid to anti-Communist governments and groups in Latin America as part of its global Cold War strategy. The Democratic House of Representatives was skeptical of many of these ventures, and a particular flashpoint was American funding for the "Contra" rebels in Nicaragua. Massachusetts Democrat Edward Boland sponsored a series of amendments to defense appropriations bills designed to limit American funding for the Contras. National Security Advisor John Poindexter and his aide, Oliver North, were central in seeking ways to continue to funnel money to the Contras. The most problematic of these efforts was the diversion of funds from a separate project—the secret sale of missiles to Iran. When the arms sale was exposed in the press in the fall of 1986, the money trail and larger covert operation eventually came to light as well.

---

28. See Richard P. Nathan, *The Administrative Presidency* (New York: Wiley, 1983); James L. Sundquist, *The Decline and Resurgence of Congress* (Washington, DC: Brookings Institution, 1981).

29. See Benjamin Ginsberg and Martin Shefter, *Politics by Other Means*, 3rd ed. (New York: Norton, 2002).

With the Democrats in control of both houses of Congress after the 1986 elections, and Reagan entering the final phase of his second term of office, the Iran-Contra scandal was a major blow to his presidency. The administration immediately moved to cooperate with the congressional investigations, to undertake its own internal investigations, and to seek an appointment of an independent counsel. For its part, key members of Congress quickly resolved not to pursue the impeachment of the president. Nonetheless, the scandal severely weakened the administration as it sought, for example, to push forward the Robert Bork nomination. The investigations revealed the extent to which the legislature and the executive had played cat-and-mouse with the power of the purse, with executive officials constantly looking for loopholes and discretionary funds to continue to pursue their favored policies as Congress squeezed their ability to do so. At the extreme, some White House staff tried to run foreign-policy operations completely "off the books" of government financing and eventually used the sale of government assets (the missiles) to fund their enterprise when congressional appropriations were not forthcoming. Like all scandals, Iran-Contra revealed individuals behaving badly, but the episode also showed how difficult it is for one branch of government to control the actions of another.[30]

Constitutional disputes over separation of powers arose both from innovative efforts to get the two elected branches to work together to solve persistent national problems and from new conflicts between the branches. In cases like the legislative veto (by which a chamber of Congress is given the power to veto an action taken by the executive branch) or the balanced budget mechanisms adopted in the 1980s, the courts were faced with questions of whether statutory compromises designed to help implement public policy violated the constitutional scheme of separated powers. In other cases, constitutional questions arose more directly from the conflicts between the elected branches of government and their inability to cooperate with one another.

30. See also Harold Hongju Koh, "Why the President (Almost) Always Wins in Foreign Affairs: Lessons of the Iran-Contra Affair," *Yale Law Journal* 97 (1988):1255; Louis Fisher, "How Tightly Can Congress Draw the Purse Strings?" *American Journal of International Law* 83 (1989):758.

A. Sharing the Legislative Power

Congress during the New Deal and Great Society sought to maintain some measure of control over powers that were being increasingly delegated to the executive branch of the national government. The "legislative veto," first suggested by President Herbert Hoover to facilitate a reorganization of the executive branch, proved a popular device. The national legislature would grant authority to an executive official or an administrative agency to promulgate particular regulations or make certain decisions, but reserve the right to reject those regulations or decisions if they were thought wrong. Sometimes the veto power was lodged in a single chamber of Congress, but other vetoes merely required a majority vote of a legislative committee. By the 1970s, legislative vetoes had become a standard device by which Congress exercised oversight over executive officials and administrative agencies. Indeed, several congressmen routinely attached legislative vetoes to all legislation delegating power to any non-legislative official. When *INS v. Chadha* (1983) was decided, legislative vetoes could be found in more than two hundred laws.

With the increased popularity and use of legislative vetoes came controversy. Many public-interest groups condemned legislative vetoes as a means that enabled Congress to reject environmental and consumer protection regulations adopted by administrative agencies. Presidents signed bills containing legislative vetoes in order to get the broad delegations of authority associated with the device, but they also insisted that, once power had been delegated, Congress could change lawful executive branch decisions only by passing new legislation consistent with Article I's requirement of bicameralism (passage by both houses of the Congress) and presentment (sent to the president for his signature or veto).

Immigration and Naturalization Service v. Chadha, 462 U.S. 919 (1983)

Jaglish Chadha provided an opportunity for opponents of the legislative veto to litigate its constitutionality. Chadha, born in Kenya and holding a British passport, came to the United States as a student. Neither Kenya nor the United Kingdom would permit him to return, however, when his American student visa expired. Chadha then sought permanent resi-

dency in the United States. For more than 150 years, this problem had been dealt with by private legislation. Congress would vote on whether someone like Chadha should be given permanent residency and, if the vote was favorable, the resulting bill would be signed by the President. Overwhelmed with the number of requests, Congress delegated that authority to the attorney general and the Immigration and Naturalization Service, but it reserved the right to veto any decision giving residence. Chadha suffered this fate. His application was initially approved by the Immigration and Naturalization Services, but then "vetoed" by the House of Representatives.

The resulting litigation illustrated how constitutional politics made strange bedfellows. Chadha was represented by Alan Morrison, who was the main attorney for Ralph Nader's consumer protection organization. Nader's group was supported by the Reagan Administration, which sought to free the executive branch from the burden of legislative vetoes. The law professor Antonin Scalia filed a brief for the American Bar Association as an amicus curiae arguing that the legislative veto was unconstitutional. Because the Immigration and Naturalization service did not defend the statute, the Supreme Court asked Congress to intervene. Prominent congressmen wrote the brief in Chadha *and were responsible for oral argument.*

Neither an immigration judge nor the Board of Immigration was willing to address the constitutional issue. Chadha appealed to the federal circuit court, which struck down the legislative veto in the immigration statute as unconstitutional. The INS appealed to the U.S. Supreme Court. A 6–3 Court struck down the legislative veto in Chadha. *Nonetheless, Congress has continued to include legislative vetoes in statutes despite the Court's ruling. Congress has not tried to formally veto executive actions. Instead, it has used the threat of a veto combined with informal pressure to win accommodations from the executive. As a result, these vetoes remain on the books and unchallenged in court. Should the Court be deferential to how Congress and the president work together, or are there larger values and concerns at stake? Is the Court likely to be effective when it interferes with cooperative relationships between the other two branches of government? If this decision was fully enforced, would the effect be to protect congressional authority or expand executive power?*

CHIEF JUSTICE BURGER delivered the opinion of the Court.

. . .

. . . [T]he fact that a given law or procedure is efficient, convenient, and useful in facilitating functions of government, standing alone, will not save it if it is contrary to the Constitution. Convenience and efficiency are not the primary objectives—or the hallmarks—of democratic government and our inquiry is sharpened rather than blunted by the fact that congressional veto provisions are appearing with increasing frequency in statutes which delegate authority to executive and independent agencies. . . .

. . .

Explicit and unambiguous provisions of the Constitution prescribe and define the respective functions of the Congress and of the Executive in the legislative process. Since the precise terms of those familiar provisions are critical to the resolution of these cases, we set them out verbatim. Article I provides:

> All legislative Powers herein granted shall be vested in a Congress of the United States, which shall consist of a Senate *and* House of Representatives. Art. I, § 1. (Emphasis added.)
>
> Every Bill which shall have passed the House of Representatives *and* the Senate, *shall*, before it becomes a law, be presented to the President of the United States. . . . Art. I, § 7, cl. 2. (Emphasis added.)
>
> *Every* Order, Resolution, or Vote to which the Concurrence of the Senate and House of Representatives may be necessary (except on a question of Adjournment) *shall be* presented to the President of the United States; and before the Same shall take Effect, *shall be* approved by him, or being disapproved by him, *shall be* repassed by two thirds of the Senate and House of Representatives, according to the Rules and Limitations prescribed in the Case of a Bill. Art. I, § 7, cl. 3. (Emphasis added.)

. . .

The decision to provide the President with a limited and qualified power to nullify proposed legislation by veto was based on the profound conviction of the Framers that the powers conferred on Congress were the powers to be most carefully circumscribed. It is beyond doubt that lawmaking was a power to be shared by both Houses and the President. . . .

. . .

The President's role in the lawmaking process also reflects the Framers' careful efforts to check whatever propensity a particular Congress might have to enact oppressive, improvident, or ill-considered measures. . . .

...

...The Court also has observed that the Presentment Clauses serve the important purpose of assuring that a "national" perspective is grafted on the legislative process:

> The President is a representative of the people just as the members of the Senate and of the House are, and it may be, at some times, on some subjects, that the President elected by all the people is rather more representative of them all than are the members of either body of the Legislature whose constituencies are local and not countrywide....

The bicameral requirement of Art. I, §§ 1, 7, was of scarcely less concern to the Framers than was the Presidential veto and indeed the two concepts are interdependent. By providing that no law could take effect without the concurrence of the prescribed majority of the Members of both Houses, the Framers reemphasized their belief, already remarked upon in connection with the Presentment Clauses, that legislation should not be enacted unless it has been carefully and fully considered by the Nation's elected officials....

...

[T]he Framers were acutely conscious that the bicameral requirement and the Presentment Clauses would serve essential constitutional functions. The President's participation in the legislative process was to protect the Executive Branch from Congress and to protect the whole people from improvident laws. The division of the Congress into two distinctive bodies assures that the legislative power would be exercised only after opportunity for full study and debate in separate settings....

...

Examination of the action taken here by one House pursuant to § 244(c)(2) reveals that it was essentially legislative in purpose and effect....[T]he House took action that had the purpose and effect of altering the legal rights, duties, and relations of persons, including the Attorney General, Executive Branch officials and Chadha, all outside the Legislative Branch. Section 244(c)(2) purports to authorize one House of Congress to require the Attorney General to deport an individual alien whose deportation otherwise would be canceled under § 244.

...

...Disagreement with the Attorney General's decision on Chadha's deportation—that is, Congress' decision to deport Chadha—no less than Congress' original choice to delegate to the Attorney General the authority to make that decision, involves determinations of policy that Congress can implement in only one way; bicameral passage followed by presentment to the President. Congress must abide by its delegation of authority until that delegation is legislatively altered or revoked.

...

The veto authorized by § 244(c)(2) doubtless has been in many respects a convenient shortcut; the "sharing" with the Executive by Congress of its authority over aliens in this manner is, on its face, an appealing compromise. In purely practical terms, it is obviously easier for action to be taken by one House without submission to the President; but it is crystal clear from the records of the Convention, contemporaneous writings and debates, that the Framers ranked other values higher than efficiency. The records of the Convention and debates in the States preceding ratification underscore the common desire to define and limit the exercise of the newly created federal powers affecting the states and the people. There is unmistakable expression of a determination that legislation by the national Congress be a step-by-step, deliberate and deliberative process.

The choices we discern as having been made in the Constitutional Convention impose burdens on governmental processes that often seem clumsy, inefficient, even unworkable, but those hard choices were consciously made by men who had lived under a form of government that permitted arbitrary governmental acts to go unchecked. There is no support in the Constitution or decisions of this Court for the proposition that the cumbersomeness and delays often encountered in complying with explicit constitutional standards may be avoided, either by the Congress or by the President....With all the obvious flaws of delay, untidiness, and potential for abuse, we have not yet found a better way to preserve freedom than by making the exercise of power subject to the carefully crafted restraints spelled out in the Constitution.

JUSTICE POWELL, concurring.

The Court's decision, based on the Presentment Clauses,...apparently will invalidate every use of the legislative veto. The breadth of this holding gives one pause. Congress has included the veto in literally hundreds of statutes, dating back to the 1930's. Congress clearly views this procedure as essential to controlling the delegation of power to administrative agencies. One reasonably may disagree with Congress' assessment of the veto's utility, but the respect due its judgment as a coordinate branch of Government cautions that our holding should be no more extensive than necessary to decide these cases. In my view, the cases may be decided on a narrower ground. When Congress finds that a particular person does not satisfy the statutory criteria for permanent residence in this country it has assumed a judicial function in violation of the principle of separation of powers. Accordingly, I concur only in the judgment.

...

JUSTICE WHITE, dissenting.

Today the Court not only invalidates § 244(c)(2) of the Immigration and Nationality Act, but also sounds the death knell for nearly 200 other statutory provisions in which Congress has reserved a "legislative veto." For this reason, the Court's decision is of surpassing importance. And it is for this reason that the Court would have been well advised to decide the cases, if possible, on the narrower grounds of separation of powers, leaving for full consideration the constitutionality of other congressional review statutes operating on such varied matters as war powers and agency rulemaking, some of which concern the independent regulatory agencies.

The prominence of the legislative veto mechanism in our contemporary political system and its importance to Congress can hardly be overstated. It has become a central means by which Congress secures the accountability of executive and independent agencies. Without the legislative veto, Congress is faced with a Hobson's choice: either to refrain from delegating the necessary authority, leaving itself with a hopeless task of writing laws with the requisite specificity to cover endless special circumstances across the entire policy landscape, or in the alternative, to abdicate its lawmaking function to the Executive Branch and independent agencies. To choose the former leaves major national problems unresolved; to opt for the latter risks unaccountable policymaking by those not elected to fill that role. Accordingly, over the past five decades, the legislative veto has been placed in nearly 200 statutes. The device is known in every field of governmental concern: reorganization, budgets, foreign affairs, war powers, and regulation of trade, safety, energy, the environment, and the economy.

...

...[T]he legislative veto is more than "efficient, convenient, and useful."...It is an important if not indispensable political invention that allows the President and Congress to resolve major constitutional and policy differences, assures the accountability of independent regulatory agencies, and preserves Congress' control over lawmaking. Perhaps there are other means of accommodation and accountability, but the increasing reliance of Congress upon the legislative veto suggests that the alternatives to which Congress must now turn are not entirely satisfactory.

The history of the legislative veto also makes clear that it has not been a sword with which Congress has struck out to aggrandize itself at the expense of the other branches—the concerns of Madison and Hamilton. Rather, the veto has been a means of defense, a reservation of ultimate authority necessary if Congress is to fulfill its designated role under Art. I as the Nation's lawmaker. While the President has often objected to particular legislative vetoes, generally those left in the hands of congressional Committees, the Executive has more often agreed to legislative review as the price for a broad delegation of authority. To be sure, the President may have preferred unrestricted power, but that could be precisely why Congress thought it essential to retain a check on the exercise of delegated authority.

For all these reasons, the apparent sweep of the Court's decision today is regrettable. The Court's Art. I analysis appears to invalidate all legislative vetoes irrespective of form or subject. Because the legislative veto is commonly found as a check upon rulemaking by administrative agencies and upon broad-based policy decisions of the Executive Branch, it is particularly unfortunate that the Court reaches its decision in cases involving the exercise of a veto over deportation decisions regarding particular individuals. Courts should always be wary of striking statutes as unconstitutional; to strike an entire class of statutes based on consideration of a somewhat atypical and more readily indictable exemplar of the class is irresponsible.

...

The reality of the situation is that the constitutional question posed today is one of immense difficulty over which the Executive and Legislative Branches—as well as scholars and judges—have understandably disagreed. That disagreement stems from the silence of the Constitution on the precise question: The Constitution does not directly authorize or prohibit the legislative veto. Thus, our task should be to determine whether the legislative veto is consistent with the purposes of Art. I and the principles of separation of powers which are reflected in that Article and throughout the Constitution.... From the summer of 1787 to the present the Government of the United States has become an endeavor far beyond the contemplation of the Framers. Only within the last half century has the complexity and size of the Federal Government's responsibilities grown so greatly that the Congress must rely on the legislative veto as the most effective if not the only means to insure its role as the Nation's lawmaker. But the wisdom of the Framers was to anticipate that the Nation would grow and new problems of governance would require different solutions. Accordingly, our Federal Government was intentionally chartered with the flexibility to respond to contemporary needs without losing sight of fundamental democratic principles....

....

...Absent the veto, the agencies receiving delegations of legislative or quasi-legislative power may issue regulations having the force of law without bicameral approval and without the President's signature. It is thus not apparent why the reservation of a veto over the exercise of that legislative power must be subject to a more exacting test. In both cases, it is enough that the initial statutory authorizations comply with the Art. I requirements.

...

...Under the Court's analysis, the Executive Branch and the independent agencies may make rules with the effect of law while Congress, in whom the Framers confided the legislative power, Art. I, § 1, may not exercise a veto which precludes such rules from having operative force. If the effective functioning of a complex modern government requires the delegation of vast authority which, by virtue of its breadth, is legislative or "quasi-legislative" in character, I cannot accept that Art. I—which is, after all, the source of the nondelegation doctrine—should forbid Congress to qualify that grant with a legislative veto.

The Court also takes no account of perhaps the most relevant consideration: However resolutions of disapproval under § 244(c)(2) are formally characterized, in reality, a departure from the status quo occurs only upon the concurrence of opinion among the House, Senate, and President. Reservations of legislative authority to be exercised by Congress should be upheld if the exercise of such reserved authority is consistent with the distribution of and limits upon legislative power that Art. I provides.

...

The central concern of the presentment and bicameralism requirements of Art. I is that when a departure from the legal status quo is undertaken, it is done with the approval of the President and both Houses of Congress—or, in the event of a Presidential veto, a two-thirds majority in both Houses. This interest is fully satisfied by the operation of § 244(c)(2). The President's approval is found in the Attorney General's action in recommending to Congress that the deportation order for a given alien be suspended. The House and the Senate indicate their approval of the Executive's action by not passing a resolution of disapproval within the statutory period. Thus, a change in the legal status quo—the deportability of the alien—is consummated only with the approval of each of the three relevant actors. The disagreement of any one of the three maintains the alien's pre-existing status: the Executive may choose not to recommend suspension; the House and Senate may each veto the recommendation. The effect on the rights and obligations of the affected individuals and upon the legislative system is precisely the same as if a private bill were introduced but failed to receive the necessary approval....

...

...[T]he history of the separation-of-powers doctrine is also a history of accommodation and practicality. Apprehensions of an overly powerful branch have not led to undue prophylactic measures that handicap the effective working of the National Government as a whole. The Constitution does not contemplate total separation of the three branches of Government. "[A] hermetic sealing off of the three branches of Government from one another would preclude the establishment of a Nation capable of governing itself effectively."

...

I regret that I am in disagreement with my colleagues on the fundamental questions that these cases present. But even more I regret the destructive scope of the Court's holding. It reflects a profoundly different conception of the Constitution than that held by the courts which sanctioned the modern administrative state. Today's decision strikes down in one fell swoop provisions in more laws enacted by Congress than the Court has cumulatively invalidated in its history. I fear it will now be more difficult to "[insure] that the fundamental policy decisions in our society

Illustration 10-2 Jagdish Rai Chadha, the respondent in *INS v. Chadha*

Source: © Roger Ressmeyer/CORBIS.

will be made not by an appointed official but by the body immediately responsible to the people."...I must dissent.

JUSTICE REHNQUIST, with whom JUSTICE WHITE joins, dissenting.

.... Over the years, Congress consistently rejected requests from the Executive for complete discretion in this area. Congress always insisted on retaining ultimate control, whether by concurrent resolution, as in the 1948 Act, or by one-House veto, as in the present Act. Congress has never indicated that it would be willing to permit suspensions of deportation unless it could retain some sort of veto.

...

Because I do not believe that [the Court can sever the original grant of power to the executive from the provision of the one-House veto], I would reverse the judgment of the Court of Appeals.

B. Presidential Power to Execute the Law

The "unitary executive" is the theory of separation of powers that holds that *all* the executive power of the federal government is vested in the president of the United States. The president is fully the chief executive, and the constitutional responsibility that the president "take care that the laws be faithfully executed" requires that the president have supervisory control over all lower-level executive officials. The unitary executive envisions the structure of the executive branch as a pyramid, with the president at the top. In particular, the president must have the authority—directly or indirectly—to select, supervise and remove executive branch officers if he is to retain and perform his own constitutional functions.

The idea of the unitary executive has deep roots in American constitutionalism, and it was elaborated in greatest detail by the Jacksonian Democrats in the nineteenth century. It was likewise opposed most aggressively by the Whigs, who argued that executive branch officials up to and including cabinet secretaries were creations of Congress and had independent legal obligations that the president could not control. This might mean that executive branch officials could be insulated from presidential removal or could be given legal responsibilities that the president could not supervise, countermand, or obstruct. It might even mean that officials could be appointed to offices independently of the president. The most extreme forms of these systems of "plural executives" were adopted in some state constitutions, with high-level state executive officers like the attorney general or secretary of treasury being elected independently of the governor.

The idea of the unitary executive found a new set of aggressive advocates in the modern legal conservative movement that gained influence starting particularly with the Reagan administration. During the Reagan years, the theory was developed and expounded in memos and briefs prepared in the Department of Justice, speeches, and publications in think tanks and interest groups, and in academic journals. At the same time, the Reagan administration expanded centralized oversight of the regulatory and other decisions being made throughout the executive branch. Litigation decisions involving the federal government were to be vetted by top officials in the Justice Department. Regulatory decisions with important economic consequences were to follow presidentially specified procedures and be vetted by the Office of Management and Budget, part of the Executive Office of the President.

The argument has gained less traction among the justices on the Supreme Court. Justice Antonin Scalia, who had worked on related arguments himself as a Justice Department lawyer in the aftermath of Watergate, has proven most receptive to such views. The Court as a whole has generally favored a balancing test that focuses on the extent to which congressional action interferes with executive responsibilities. The unitary executive theory is part of a class of arguments about the separation of powers that are classified as "formalist." They emphasize the forms and definitions of the parts of government and look for bright-line rules to guide the constitutional division of powers among offices and levels of government. By contrast, "functionalist" arguments emphasize pragmatic, fluid, less clear-cut, but "workable" approaches to thinking about the structures of government. They focus less on trying to derive logical implications from an overarching theory of a given constitutional office than on trying to maintain set of relationships that more-or-less preserve essential constitutional goals.

The theory of the unitary executive became newly controversial during the George W. Bush administration. Like his predecessors, President Bush defended a strong appointment and removal power over lower-level executive officials, and insisted on supervisory control over executive actors. As in previous administrations, the key pieces of constitutional text that supported the argument was the "vesting" clause of Section 3 of Article II ("executive power shall be vested in a President") and the "take care" clause of Section 3 ("he shall take care that the laws be faithfully executed"). As before, the argument was pressed in bill signing statements, veto messages, and legal briefs and memos. What differed, however, was the context of the War on Terror and the expansiveness of the administration's claims about what executive powers had in fact been vested with the president. At that point, the dispute was less about the extent to which Congress could insulate lower-level executive branch officials from presidential removal or control or give them policy responsibilities that the president could not supervise. The major debate of the Bush administration focused on the extent of presidential war powers under the Constitution and the degree to which Congress can impinge on them.[31]

Bowsher v. Synar, 478 U.S. 714 (1986)

Though not his highest priority, Ronald Reagan campaigned against budget deficits. The federal government had not run an annual budget surplus (when its revenues for the year exceeded its expenditures) since 1969, and on both a dollar basis and as a percentage of the economy the size of the budget deficits of the late 1970s were far larger than any the government had experienced at any time since World War II. The fiscal situation only worsened during Reagan's first term of office. The president and his conservative supporters were successful in winning support for his primary commitments of tax cuts and increased defense spending, but Democrats were successful in protecting their favored domestic programs from spending cuts, and a short but deep recession at the beginning of the Reagan administration further strained the federal budget. By the mid-1980s, the accumulating federal debt was increasingly viewed as a political and economic crisis, threatening economic growth and preventing both parties from pursuing their policy goals.

Reducing the budget deficit required making hard political choices, however, and there was little agreement about the correct choices to make. The most obvious paths toward reducing the deficit threatened core political commitments of one party or the other. Given the continuation of divided government and the ideological divide between the two parties, fiscal politics absorbed the entire legislative calendar but mostly resulted in stalemate. Some had hoped that the 1984 elections would leave a single party in control of the government, but Reagan won a huge personal victory with short coattails that did not bring a Republican majority in the House of Representatives. After the election, the parties looked for a solution that would work within the context of divided government. The Gramm-Rudman-Hollings Act of 1985 was a bipartisan measure, but also something of an internal compromise within Reagan's Republican Party. One Republican sponsor of the measure was New Hampshire's Warren Rudman, a longtime "deficit hawk" and fiscal

31. On the unitary executive, see also Steven G. Calabresi and Christopher S. Yoo, *The Unitary Executive* (New Haven: Yale University Press, 2008); Lawrence Lessig and Cass R. Sunstein, "The President and the Administration," *Columbia Law Review* 94 (1994):1; Robert D. Sloane, "The Scope of Executive Power in the Twenty-First Century: An Introduction," *Boston University Law Review* 88 (2008):341.

conservative within the party. The other Republican sponsor was Phil Gramm, a newly elected member of the Senate from Texas. As a then-Democrat in the House of Representatives, Gramm had broken with his party to support Reagan's early budget initiatives and had become a vocal leader of the tax-cutting wing of the Republican Party.

The central feature of the Gramm-Rudman-Hollings Act was a series of targets for the federal deficits for the next five fiscal years. If the actual deficit were to exceed that target by a specified amount, then an "automatic," across-the-board budget cut would be triggered that would bring the budget within the target. The comptroller general was assigned the responsibility of triggering the automatic cuts, with the president implementing the cuts directed by the comptroller general. After the bill was signed into law, twelve congressmen including Michael Synar filed suit against Charles Bowsher, the comptroller general, in federal district court seeking a declaration that this provision of the act was unconstitutional. A suit was also filed by the National Treasury Employees Union seeking the same, arguing that their members would be injured by an across-the-board spending cut that would reduce the scheduled cost-of-living adjustments to their benefit packages. A special three-judge panel for the district court found that the provision was not an unconstitutional delegation of legislative power but did violate the separation of powers, since a key player in the enforcement of the act, the comptroller general, was not directly accountable to the Chief Executive (since he was removable from office only by congressional resolution). On direct appeal to the U.S. Supreme Court, the justices by a 5–4 decision affirmed the district court and invalidated the provision of the act.

Congress revised the statute in 1987 to avoid the constitutional problem. At least on paper, Congress found ways to meet the budget targets of the act without triggering the automatic cuts. There is some evidence that the act did reduce federal spending and deficits in the late 1980s. It was replaced by a new deficit-reduction structure in 1990, negotiated by Republican President George H. W. Bush and the Democrats, who then held majorities in both houses of Congress. Conservatives accused Bush of breaking his "no new taxes" campaign pledge in order to broker the deal.

CHIEF JUSTICE BURGER delivered the opinion of the Court.

...

It is clear that Congress has consistently viewed the Comptroller General as an officer of the Legislative Branch. The Reorganization Acts of 1945 and 1949, for example, both stated that the Comptroller General and the GAO are "a part of the legislative branch of the Government." Similarly, in the Accounting and Auditing Act of 1950, Congress required the Comptroller General to conduct audits "as an agent of the Congress."

Over the years, the Comptrollers General have also viewed themselves as part of the Legislative Branch.... Comptroller General Warren, who had been a Member of Congress for 15 years before being appointed Comptroller General, testified [in congressional hearings]: "During most of my public life,... I have been a member of the legislative branch. Even now, although heading a great agency, it is an agency of the Congress, and *I am an agent of the Congress*." ...

Against this background, we see no escape from the conclusion that, because Congress has retained removal authority over the Comptroller General, he may not be entrusted with executive powers. The remaining question is whether the Comptroller General has been assigned such powers in the Balanced Budget and Emergency Deficit Control Act of 1985.

The primary responsibility of the Comptroller General under the instant Act is the preparation of a "report." This report must contain detailed estimates of projected federal revenues and expenditures. The report must also specify the reductions, if any, necessary to reduce the deficit to the target for the appropriate fiscal year. The reductions must be set forth on a program-by-program basis.

....

Appellants suggest that the duties assigned to the Comptroller General in the Act are essentially ministerial and mechanical so that their performance does not constitute "execution of the law" in a meaningful sense. On the contrary, we view these functions as plainly entailing execution of the law in constitutional terms. Interpreting a law enacted by Congress to implement the legislative mandate is the very essence of "execution" of the law. Under § 251, the Comptroller General must exercise judgment concerning facts that affect the application of the Act. He must also interpret the provisions of the Act to determine precisely what budgetary calculations are required. Decisions of that kind are typically made by officers charged with executing a statute.

The executive nature of the Comptroller General's functions under the Act is revealed in § 252(a)(3) which gives the Comptroller General the ultimate authority to determine the budget cuts to be made. Indeed, the

Comptroller General commands the President himself to carry out, without the slightest variation (with exceptions not relevant to the constitutional issues presented), the directive of the Comptroller General as to the budget reductions....

...

We conclude that the District Court correctly held that the powers vested in the Comptroller General under § 251 violate the command of the Constitution that the Congress play no direct role in the execution of the laws. Accordingly, the judgment and order of the District Court are affirmed.

Our judgment is stayed for a period not to exceed 60 days to permit Congress to implement the fallback provisions.

It is so ordered.

JUSTICE STEVENS, with whom JUSTICE MARSHALL joins, concurring.

.... I agree with the Court that the "Gramm-Rudman-Hollings" Act contains a constitutional infirmity so severe that the flawed provision may not stand. I disagree with the Court, however, on the reasons why the Constitution prohibits the Comptroller General from exercising the powers assigned to him by § 251(b) and § 251(c)(2) of the Act. It is not the dormant, carefully circumscribed congressional removal power that represents the primary constitutional evil. Nor do I agree with the conclusion of both the majority and the dissent that the analysis depends on a labeling of the functions assigned to the Comptroller General as "executive powers." Rather, I am convinced that the Comptroller General must be characterized as an agent of Congress because of his longstanding statutory responsibilities; that the powers assigned to him under the Gramm-Rudman-Hollings Act require him to make policy that will bind the Nation; and that, when Congress, or a component or an agent of Congress, seeks to make policy that will bind the Nation, it must follow the procedures mandated by Article I of the Constitution—through passage by both Houses and presentment to the President. In short, Congress may not exercise its fundamental power to formulate national policy by delegating that power to one of its two Houses, to a legislative committee, or to an individual agent of the Congress such as the Speaker of the House of Representatives, the Sergeant at Arms of the Senate, or the Director of the Congressional Budget Office. *INS* v. *Chadha* (1983). That principle, I believe, is applicable to the Comptroller General.

...

The Gramm-Rudman-Hollings Act assigns to the Comptroller General the duty to make policy decisions that have the force of law. The Comptroller General's report is, in the current statute, the engine that gives life to the ambitious budget reduction process....It is, in short, the Comptroller General's report that will have a profound, dramatic, and immediate impact on the Government and on the Nation at large.

...

I concur in the judgment.

JUSTICE WHITE, dissenting.

The Court, acting in the name of separation of powers, takes upon itself to strike down the Gramm-Rudman-Hollings Act, one of the most novel and far-reaching legislative responses to a national crisis since the New Deal. The basis of the Court's action is a solitary provision of another statute that was passed over 60 years ago and has lain dormant since that time. I cannot concur in the Court's action. Like the Court, I will not purport to speak to the wisdom of the policies incorporated in the legislation the Court invalidates; that is a matter for the Congress and the Executive, *both* of which expressed their assent to the statute barely half a year ago. I will, however, address the wisdom of the Court's willingness to interpose its distressingly formalistic view of separation of powers as a bar to the attainment of governmental objectives through the means chosen by the Congress and the President in the legislative process established by the Constitution....In attaching dispositive significance to what should be regarded as a triviality, the Court neglects what has in the past been recognized as a fundamental principle governing consideration of disputes over separation of powers:

> The actual art of governing under our Constitution does not and cannot conform to judicial definitions of the power of any of its branches based on isolated clauses or even single Articles torn from context. While the Constitution diffuses power the better to secure liberty, it also contemplates that practice will integrate the dispersed powers into a workable government. *Youngstown Sheet & Tube Co.* v. *Sawyer*, 343 U.S. 579, 635 (1952) (Jackson, J. concurring).

...

The practical result of the removal provision is not to render the Comptroller unduly dependent upon or subservient to Congress, but to render him one of the most independent officers in the entire federal establishment. Those who have studied the office agree that the procedural and substantive limits on the power of Congress and the President to remove the Comptroller make dislodging him against his will practically impossible....

The majority's contrary conclusion rests on the rigid dogma that, outside of the impeachment process, any "direct congressional role in the removal of officers charged with the execution of the laws...is inconsistent with separation of powers." Reliance on such an unyielding principle to strike down a statute posing no real danger of aggrandizement of congressional power is extremely misguided and insensitive to our constitutional role....The Act vesting budget-cutting authority in the Comptroller General represents Congress' judgment that the delegation of such authority to counteract ever-mounting deficits is "necessary and proper" to the exercise of the powers granted the Federal Government by the Constitution; and the President's approval of the statute signifies his unwillingness to reject the choice made by Congress. Under such circumstances, the role of this Court should be limited to determining whether the Act so alters the balance of authority among the branches of government as to pose a genuine threat to the basic division between the lawmaking power and the power to execute the law. Because I see no such threat, I cannot join the Court in striking down the Act.

I dissent.

JUSTICE BLACKMUN, dissenting.

...

...The only relief sought in this case is nullification of the automatic budget-reduction provisions of the Deficit Control Act, and that relief should not be awarded even if the Court is correct that those provisions are constitutionally incompatible with Congress' authority to remove the Comptroller General by joint resolution. Any incompatibility, I feel, should be cured by refusing to allow congressional removal—if it ever is attempted—and not by striking down the central provisions of the Deficit Control Act. However wise or foolish it may be, that statute unquestionably ranks among the most important federal enactments of the past several decades. I cannot see the sense of invalidating legislation of this magnitude in order to preserve a cumbersome, 65-year-old removal power that has never been exercised and appears to have been all but forgotten until this litigation.

...

Morrison v. Olson, 487 U.S. 654 (1988)

Scandal rocked American politics during the last third of the twentieth century. Both presidents and executive officials seemed under constant investigation for criminal misdeeds. These investigations significantly influenced relationships between the two branches of government and national policy. One president, Richard Nixon, was forced to resign. Others suffered significant drops in public opinion that weakened their ability to influence Congress. Many of the investigations were responses to substantial allegations of wrongdoing. As the Watergate, Iran-Contra, and Whitewater affairs indicated, members of the executive branch were not above violating the law. Nevertheless, a good case can be made that no more executive wrongdoing existed from 1970 to the present than at any other time in American history. What differed were the political incentives for emphasizing alleged scandals. In a time of divided government and close partisan divisions among the electorate, many political actors believed they would better gain power by exposing their rivals as corrupt than by proposing new policy initiatives.[32]

Independent counsels were one consequence of the new focus on executive scandals. Concerned that an increasingly politicized Department of Justice would not aggressively pursue allegations of wrongdoing and corruption against executive department officials, Congress passed and President Carter signed the "Ethics in Government Act." Title VI of that measure created a special court, authorized to appoint a special counsel on application from the attorney general. Once appointed, the independent counsel would investigate the particular allegation of wrongdoing largely free from executive interference and could only be removed by a showing of good cause. During the 1980s and 1990s, this device was frequently used and highly controversial. Republicans claimed that independent counsel Lawrence Walsh was overly aggressive in prosecuting members of the Reagan administration during the Iran-Contra scandal. Democrats cried foul when Kenneth Starr investigated President Clinton's behavior during the Whitewater scandal. Justice Scalia's dissent in this case began to seem prescient, and Congress let the independent counsel statute lapse late in

32. See Benjamin Ginsberg and Martin Shefter, *Politics by Other Means*, 3rd ed.(New York: Norton, 2002).

the Clinton era. Presidents have now returned to the earlier practice of using the Department of Justice or appointing a "special prosecutor" under the attorney general to investigate wrongdoing by government officials.

Remarkably, the constitutionality of the independent counsel statute was tested during a more low-level investigation. After a long dispute between the president and Congress, the Reagan Administration agreed to provide Congress with some documents concerning the administration's environmental policies. When Assistant Attorney General Theodore Olson testified before Congress about the role of the Department of Justice during this controversy, many Democrats believed he made false and misleading statements. The chair of the Judiciary Committee repeated these allegations in a public report and passed that information on to the Attorney General of the United States. After a short investigation, the allegations were found sufficiently credible to request the appointment of an independent counsel. The special court appointed James McKay to further investigate the incident and, when McKay resigned, Alexina Morrison was appointed in his place. Morrison sought to obtain a subpoena that would require Olson and two other justice department officials to testify before a grand jury. Olson responded by asserting that the independent counsel statute violated the "appointments clause" (which outlines the process by which these kinds of officers had to be appointed) and the principle of separation of powers, which (under Article II) vests "the executive power" in an executive branch that is controlled by the president. A federal district court upheld the statute, and eventually charged Olson with contempt for refusing to comply with the subpoena. On appeal, the court of appeals reversed the trial court and struck down the independent counsel law as a violation of the separation of powers. In an 8–1 decision, the U.S. Supreme Court reversed the court of appeals and upheld the statute.

After the Whitewater investigations, many liberals came to praise Justice Scalia's dissent as farsighted. How much of his argument is about the "constitutionality" of the independent counsel and how much is about the "policy" of having an independent counsel? How does Scalia differ from Rehnquist in his conception of the separation of powers? Is one approach more obviously helpful to modern conservatives or the presidency than the others?

CHIEF JUSTICE REHNQUIST delivered the opinion of the Court.

This case presents us with a challenge to the independent counsel provisions of the Ethics in Government Act of 1978.... We hold today that these provisions of the Act do not violate the Appointments Clause of the Constitution, Art. II, § 2, cl. 2, or the limitations of Article III, nor do they impermissibly interfere with the President's authority under Article II in violation of the constitutional principle of separation of powers.

...

The Appointments Clause of Article II reads as follows:

> [The President] shall nominate, and by and with the Advice and Consent of the Senate, shall appoint Ambassadors, other public Ministers and Consuls, Judges of the supreme Court, and all other Officers of the United States, whose Appointments are not herein otherwise provided for, and which shall be established by Law: but the Congress may by Law vest the Appointment of such inferior Officers, as they think proper, in the President alone, in the Courts of Law, or in the Heads of Departments....

...The initial question is, accordingly, whether appellant is an "inferior" or a "principal" officer. If she is the latter, as the Court of Appeals concluded, then the Act is in violation of the Appointments Clause.

The line between "inferior" and "principal" officers is one that is far from clear, and the Framers provided little guidance into where it should be drawn....We need not attempt here to decide exactly where the line falls between the two types of officers, because in our view appellant clearly falls on the "inferior officer" side of that line....

First, appellant is subject to removal by a higher Executive Branch official. Although appellant may not be "subordinate" to the Attorney General (and the President) insofar as she possesses a degree of independent discretion to exercise the powers delegated to her under the Act, the fact that she can be removed by the Attorney General indicates that she is to some degree "inferior" in rank and authority. Second, appellant is empowered by the Act to perform only certain, limited duties. An independent counsel's role is restricted primarily to investigation and, if appropriate, prosecution for certain federal crimes....

Third, appellant's office is limited in jurisdiction. Not only is the Act itself restricted in applicability to certain federal officials suspected of certain serious federal crimes, but an independent counsel can only act within the scope of the jurisdiction that has been granted by the Special Division pursuant to a request by the Attorney General. Finally, appellant's office is limited in tenure. There is concededly no time limit on the appointment of a particular counsel. Nonetheless, the office of independent counsel is "temporary" in the sense that an independent counsel is appointed essentially to accomplish a single task, and when that task is over the office is terminated.... In our view, these factors relating to the "ideas of tenure, duration... and duties" of the independent counsel... are sufficient to establish that appellant is an "inferior" officer in the constitutional sense.

...

...Appellees argue that even if appellant is an "inferior" officer, the Clause does not empower Congress to place the power to appoint such an officer outside the Executive Branch. They contend that the Clause does not contemplate congressional authorization of "interbranch appointments," in which an officer of one branch is appointed by officers of another branch. The relevant language of the Appointments Clause is worth repeating. It reads: "...but the Congress may by Law vest the Appointment of such inferior Officers, as they think proper, in the President alone, in the courts of Law, or in the Heads of Departments." On its face, the language of this "excepting clause" admits of no limitation on interbranch appointments. Indeed, the inclusion of "as they think proper" seems clearly to give Congress significant discretion to determine whether it is "proper" to vest the appointment of, for example, executive officials in the "courts of Law."...

...

We do not mean to say that Congress' power to provide for interbranch appointments of "inferior officers" is unlimited. In addition to separation-of-powers concerns, which would arise if such provisions for appointment had the potential to impair the constitutional functions assigned to one of the branches.... In this case, however, we do not think it impermissible for Congress to vest the power to appoint independent counsel in a specially created federal court. We thus disagree with the Court of Appeals' conclusion that there is an inherent incongruity about a court having the power to appoint prosecutorial officers....

...

...Clearly, once it is accepted that the Appointments Clause gives Congress the power to vest the appointment of officials such as the independent counsel in the "courts of Law," there can be no Article III objection to the Special Division's exercise of that power, as the power itself derives from the Appointments Clause, a source of authority for judicial action that is independent of Article III. Appellees contend, however, that the Division's Appointments Clause powers do not encompass the power to define the independent counsel's jurisdiction. We disagree. In our view, Congress' power under the Clause to vest the "Appointment" of inferior officers in the courts may, in certain circumstances, allow Congress to give the courts some discretion in defining the nature and scope of the appointed official's authority. Particularly when, as here, Congress creates a temporary "office" the nature and duties of which will by necessity vary with the factual circumstances giving rise to the need for an appointment in the first place, it may vest the power to define the scope of the office in the court as an incident to the appointment of the officer pursuant to the Appointments Clause....

...

...[O]ne purpose of the broad prohibition upon the courts' exercise of "executive or administrative duties of a nonjudicial nature," is to maintain the separation between the Judiciary and the other branches of the Federal Government by ensuring that judges do not encroach upon executive or legislative authority or undertake tasks that are more properly accomplished by those branches.... The Act simply does not give the Division the power to "supervise" the independent counsel in the exercise of his or her investigative or prosecutorial authority. And, the functions that the Special Division is empowered to perform are not inherently "Executive"; indeed, they are directly analogous to functions that federal judges perform in other contexts, such as deciding whether to allow disclosure of matters occurring before a grand jury.

...

We now turn to consider whether the Act is invalid under the constitutional principle of separation of powers. Two related issues must be addressed: The first is whether the provision of the Act restricting the Attorney General's power to remove the independent counsel to only those instances in which he can show "good cause," taken by itself, impermissibly interferes with the President's exercise of his constitutionally appointed functions. The second is whether, taken as a whole, the Act violates the separation of powers by reducing the President's ability to control the prosecutorial powers wielded by the independent counsel.

...

...[T]his case does not involve an attempt by Congress itself to gain a role in the removal of executive officials other than its established powers of impeachment and conviction. The Act instead puts the removal power squarely in the hands of the Executive Branch; an independent counsel may be removed from office, "only by the personal action of the Attorney General, and only for good cause."...

...

...[W]hether the Constitution allows Congress to impose a "good cause"-type restriction on the President's power to remove an official cannot be made to turn on whether or not that official is classified as "purely executive." The analysis contained in our removal cases is designed not to define rigid categories of those officials who may or may not be removed at will by the President, but to ensure that Congress does not interfere with the President's exercise of the "executive power" and his constitutionally appointed duty to "take care that the laws be faithfully executed" under Article II....

...[T]he real question is whether the removal restrictions are of such a nature that they impede the President's ability to perform his constitutional duty, and the functions of the officials in question must be analyzed in that light.

...

Nor do we think that the "good cause" removal provision at issue here impermissibly burdens the President's power to control or supervise the independent counsel, as an executive official, in the execution of his or her duties under the Act. This is not a case in which the power to remove an executive official has been completely stripped from the President, thus providing no means for the President to ensure the "faithful execution" of the laws. Rather, because the independent counsel may be terminated for "good cause," the Executive, through the Attorney General, retains ample authority to assure that the counsel is competently performing his or her statutory responsibilities in a manner that comports with the provisions of the Act.

...

The final question to be addressed is whether the Act, taken as a whole, violates the principle of separation of powers by unduly interfering with the role of the Executive Branch....

We observe first that this case does not involve an attempt by Congress to increase its own powers at the expense of the Executive Branch....Indeed, with the exception of the power of impeachment—which applies to all officers of the United States—Congress retained for itself no powers of control or supervision over an independent counsel. The Act does empower certain Members of Congress to request the Attorney General to apply for the appointment of an independent counsel, but the Attorney General has no duty to comply with the request, although he must respond within a certain time limit....

...

...[W]e do not think that the Act "impermissibly undermine[s]" the powers of the Executive Branch...or "disrupts the proper balance between the coordinate branches [by] prevent[ing] the Executive Branch from accomplishing its constitutionally assigned functions."...It is undeniable that the Act reduces the amount of control or supervision that the Attorney General and, through him, the President exercises over the investigation and prosecution of a certain class of alleged criminal activity. The Attorney General is not allowed to appoint the individual of his choice; he does not determine the counsel's jurisdiction; and his power to remove a counsel is limited. Nonetheless, the Act does give the Attorney General several means of supervising or controlling the prosecutorial powers that may be wielded by an independent counsel. Most importantly, the Attorney General retains the power to remove the counsel for "good cause," a power that we have already concluded provides the Executive with substantial ability to ensure that the laws are "faithfully executed" by an independent counsel. No independent counsel may be appointed without a specific request by the Attorney General, and the Attorney General's decision not to request appointment if he finds "no reasonable grounds to believe that further investigation is warranted" is committed to his unreviewable discretion. The Act thus gives the Executive a degree of control over the power to initiate an investigation by the independent counsel....Notwithstanding the fact that the counsel is to some degree "independent" and free from executive supervision to a greater extent than other federal prosecutors, in our view these features of the Act give the Executive Branch sufficient control over the independent counsel to ensure that the President is able to perform his constitutionally assigned duties.

JUSTICE SCALIA, dissenting.

...

...[T]he Founders conspicuously and very consciously declined to sap the Executive's strength in the same way they had weakened the Legislature: by dividing the executive power. Proposals to have multiple executives, or a council of advisers with separate authority were rejected.

That is what this suit is about. Power. The allocation of power among Congress, the President, and the courts in such fashion as to preserve the equilibrium the Constitution sought to establish—so that "a gradual concentration of the several powers in the same department"...can effectively be resisted. Frequently an issue of this sort will come before the Court clad, so to speak, in sheep's clothing: the potential of the asserted principle to effect important change in the equilibrium of power is not immediately evident, and must be discerned by a careful and perceptive analysis. But this wolf comes as a wolf....

As a general matter, the Act before us here requires the Attorney General to apply for the appointment of an independent counsel within 90 days after receiving a request to do so, unless he determines within that period that "there are no reasonable grounds to believe that further investigation or prosecution is warranted." As a practical matter, it would be surprising if the Attorney General had any choice (assuming this statute is constitutional) but to seek appointment of an independent counsel to pursue the charges against the principal object of the congressional request, Mr. Olson. Merely the political consequences (to him and the President) of seeming to break the law by refusing to do so would have been substantial. How could it not be, the public would ask, that a 3,000-page indictment drawn by our representatives over 2½ years does not even establish "reasonable grounds to believe" that further investigation or prosecution is warranted with respect to at least the principal alleged culprit? But the Act establishes more than just practical compulsion. Although the Court's opinion asserts that the Attorney General had "no duty to comply with the [congressional] request" that is not entirely accurate. He *had* a duty to comply unless he could conclude that there were "*no reasonable grounds to believe*," not that prosecution was warranted, but merely that "*further investigation*" was warranted....The Court also makes much of the fact that "the courts are specifically prevented from reviewing the Attorney General's decision not to seek appointment, § 592(f)." Yes, but *Congress* is not prevented from reviewing it. The context of this statute is acrid with the smell of threatened impeachment. Where, as here, a request for appointment of an independent counsel has come from the Judiciary Committee of either House of Congress, the Attorney General must, if he decides not to seek appointment, explain to that Committee why.

Thus, by the application of this statute in the present case, Congress has effectively compelled a criminal investigation of a high-level appointee of the President in connection with his actions arising out of a bitter power dispute between the President and the Legislative Branch. Mr. Olson may or may not be guilty of a crime; we do not know. But we do know that the investigation of him has been commenced, not necessarily because the President or his authorized subordinates believe it is in the interest of the United States, in the sense that it warrants the diversion of resources from other efforts, and is worth the cost in money and in possible damage to other governmental interests; and not even, leaving aside those normally considered factors, because the President or his authorized subordinates necessarily believe that an investigation is likely to unearth a violation worth prosecuting; but only because the Attorney General cannot affirm, as Congress demands, that there are *no reasonable grounds to believe* that further investigation is warranted. The decisions regarding the scope of that further investigation, its duration, and, finally, whether or not prosecution should ensue, are likewise beyond the control of the President and his subordinates.

If to describe this case is not to decide it, the concept of a government of separate and coordinate powers no longer has meaning....

...Article II, § 1, cl. 1, of the Constitution provides:

> "The executive Power shall be vested in a President of the United States."

[T]his does not mean *some of* the executive power, but *all of* the executive power. It seems to me, therefore, that the decision of the Court of Appeals invalidating the present statute must be upheld on fundamental separation-of-powers principles if the following two questions are answered affirmatively: (1) Is the conduct of a criminal prosecution (and of an investigation to decide whether to prosecute) the exercise of purely executive power? (2) Does the statute deprive the President of the United States of exclusive control over the exercise of that power? Surprising to say, the Court appears to concede an affirmative answer to both questions, but seeks to avoid the inevitable conclusion that since the statute vests some purely executive power in a person who is not the President of the United States it is void.

The Court concedes that "[t]here is no real dispute that the functions performed by the independent counsel are 'executive'," though it qualifies that concession by adding "in the sense that they are law enforcement functions that typically have been undertaken by officials within the Executive Branch."... There is no possible doubt that the independent counsel's functions fit this description. She is vested with the "full power and independent authority to exercise all *investigative and prosecutorial* functions and powers of the Department of Justice [and] the Attorney General."... Governmental investigation and prosecution of crimes is a quintessentially executive function.

As for the second question, whether the statute before us deprives the President of exclusive control over that quintessentially executive activity: The Court does not, and could not possibly, assert that it does not. That is indeed the whole object of the statute. Instead, the Court points out that the President, through his Attorney General, has at least *some* control. That concession is alone enough to invalidate the statute, but I cannot refrain from pointing out that the Court greatly exaggerates the extent of that "some" Presidential control.... [L]imiting removal power to "good cause" is an impediment to, not an effective grant of, Presidential control.... What we in *Humphrey's Executor* (1935) found to be a means of eliminating Presidential control, the Court today considers the "most importan[t]" means of assuring Presidential control. Congress, of course, operated under no such illusion when it enacted this statute, describing the "good cause" limitation as "protecting the independent counsel's ability to act independently of the President's direct control" since it permits removal only for "misconduct."

...Almost all investigative and prosecutorial decisions—including the ultimate decision whether, after a technical violation of the law has been found, prosecution is warranted—involve the balancing of innumerable legal and practical considerations. Indeed, even political considerations (in the nonpartisan sense) must be considered, as exemplified by the recent decision of an independent counsel to subpoena the former Ambassador of Canada, producing considerable tension in our relations with that country. Another preeminently political decision is whether getting a conviction in a particular case is worth the disclosure of national security information that would be necessary. The Justice Department and our intelligence agencies are often in disagreement on this point, and the Justice Department does not always win.... In sum, the balancing of various legal, practical, and political considerations, none of which is absolute, is the very essence of prosecutorial discretion. To take this away is to remove the core of the prosecutorial function, and not merely "some" Presidential control.

As I have said, however, it is ultimately irrelevant *how much* the statute reduces Presidential control.... It is not for us to determine, and we have never presumed to determine, how much of the purely executive powers of government must be within the full control of the President. The Constitution prescribes that they *all* are.

...

Is it unthinkable that the President should have such exclusive power, even when alleged crimes by him or his close associates are at issue? No more so than that Congress should have the exclusive power of legislation, even when what is at issue is its own exemption from the burdens of certain laws.... No more so than that this Court should have the exclusive power to pronounce the final decision on justiciable cases and controversies, even those pertaining to the constitutionality of a statute reducing the salaries of the Justices.... A system of separate and coordinate powers necessarily involves an acceptance of exclusive power that can theoretically be abused.... While the separation of powers may prevent us from righting every wrong, it does so in order to ensure that we do not lose liberty. The checks against any branch's abuse of its exclusive powers are twofold: First, retaliation by one of the other branch's use of *its* exclusive powers: Congress, for example, can impeach the executive who willfully fails to enforce the laws; the executive can decline to prosecute under unconstitutional statutes.... Second, and ultimately, there is the political check that the people will replace those in the political branches... who are guilty of abuse. Political pressures produced special prosecutors—for Teapot Dome and for Watergate, for example—long before this statute created the independent counsel.

...

[T]he independent counsel is not an inferior officer because she is not *subordinate* to any officer in the Executive Branch (indeed, not even to the President).

Dictionaries in use at the time of the Constitutional Convention gave the word "inferiour" two meanings which it still bears today: (1) "[l]ower in place,...station,...rank of life,...value or excellency," and (2) "[s]ubordinate."...In a document dealing with the structure (the constitution) of a government, one would naturally expect the word to bear the latter meaning—indeed, in such a context it would be unpardonably careless to use the word *unless* a relationship of subordination was intended. If what was meant was merely "lower in station or rank," one would use instead a term such as "lesser officers." At the only other point in the Constitution at which the word "inferior" appears, it plainly connotes a relationship of subordination. Article III vests the judicial power of the United States in "one supreme Court, and in such *inferior* Courts as the Congress may from time to time ordain and establish."

...

Because appellant is not subordinate to another officer, she is not an "inferior" officer and her appointment other than by the President with the advice and consent of the Senate is unconstitutional. ...

Since our 1935 decision in *Humphrey's Executor v. United States*...it has been established that the line of permissible restriction upon removal of principal officers lies at the point at which the powers exercised by those officers are no longer purely executive. Thus, removal restrictions have been generally regarded as lawful for so-called "independent regulatory agencies."...It has often been observed, correctly in my view, that the line between "purely executive" functions and "quasi-legislative" or "quasi-judicial" functions is not a clear one or even a rational one....But at least it permitted the identification of certain officers, and certain agencies, whose functions were entirely within the control of the President. Congress had to be aware of that restriction in its legislation. Today, however, *Humphrey's Executor* is swept into the dustbin of repudiated constitutional principles....

...There are now no lines. If the removal of a prosecutor, the virtual embodiment of the power to "take care that the laws be faithfully executed," can be restricted, what officer's removal cannot? This is an open invitation for Congress to experiment. What about a special Assistant Secretary of State, with responsibility for one very narrow area of foreign policy, who would not only have to be confirmed by the Senate but could also be removed only pursuant to certain carefully designed restrictions? Could this possibly render the President "[un]able to accomplish his constitutional role"?...The Court essentially says to the President: "Trust us. We will make sure that you are able to accomplish your constitutional role." I think the Constitution gives the President—and the people—more protection than that.

The purpose of the separation and equilibration of powers in general, and of the unitary Executive in particular, was not merely to assure effective government but to preserve individual freedom....

Under our system of government, the primary check against prosecutorial abuse is a political one. The prosecutors who exercise this awesome discretion are selected and can be removed by a President, whom the people have trusted enough to elect. Moreover, when crimes are not investigated and prosecuted fairly, nonselectively, with a reasonable sense of proportion, the President pays the cost in political damage to his administration. If federal prosecutors "pick people that [they] thin[k] [they] should get, rather than cases that need to be prosecuted," if they amass many more resources against a particular prominent individual, or against a particular class of political protesters, or against members of a particular political party, than the gravity of the alleged offenses or the record of successful prosecutions seems to warrant, the unfairness will come home to roost in the Oval Office. I leave it to the reader to recall the examples of this in recent years....

That is the system of justice the rest of us are entitled to, but what of that select class consisting of present or former high-level Executive Branch officials?...Can one imagine a less equitable manner of fulfilling the executive responsibility to investigate and prosecute? What would be the reaction if, in an area not covered by this statute, the Justice Department posted a public notice inviting applicants to assist in an investigation and possible prosecution of a certain prominent person? Does this not invite what Justice Jackson described as "picking the man and then searching the law books, or putting investigators to work, to pin some offense on him"? To be sure, the investigation must relate to the area of criminal offense specified by the life-tenured judges. But that has often been (and nothing prevents it from being) very broad—and should the independent counsel or his or her staff come up with something beyond that scope, nothing prevents him or her from asking the judges to expand his or her authority or, if that does not work, referring it to the Attorney General, whereupon the whole process would recommence and, if there was "reasonable basis to believe" that further investigation was warranted, that new offense would be referred to the Special Division, which would in all likelihood assign it to the same independent counsel. It seems to me not conducive to fairness. But even if it were entirely evident that unfairness was in fact the result—the judges hostile to the administration, the independent counsel an old foe of the President, the staff refugees from the recently defeated administration—*there would be no one accountable to the public to whom the blame could be assigned.*

...

The notion that every violation of law should be prosecuted, including—indeed, *especially*—every violation by those in high places, is an attractive one, and it would be risky to argue in an election campaign that that is not an absolutely overriding value. *Fiat justitia, ruat coelum.* Let justice be done, though the heavens may fall. The reality is, however, that it is not an absolutely overriding value, and it was with the hope that we would be able to acknowledge and apply such realities that the Constitution spared us, by life tenure, the necessity of election campaigns. I cannot imagine that there are not many thoughtful men and women in Congress who realize that the benefits of this legislation are far outweighed by its harmful effect upon our system of government, and even upon the nature of justice received by those men and women who agree to serve in the Executive Branch. But it is difficult to vote not to enact, and even more difficult to vote to repeal, a statute called, appropriately enough, the Ethics in Government Act. If Congress is controlled by the party other than the one to which the President belongs, it has little incentive to repeal it; if it is controlled by the same party, it dare not. By its shortsighted action today, I fear the Court has permanently encumbered the Republic with an institution that will do it great harm.

Suggested Readings

Brisbin, Richard A., Jr. *Justice Antonin Scalia and the Conservative Revival* (Baltimore, MD: Johns Hopkins University Press, 1997).

Conlan, Timothy J. *The New Federalism: Twenty-Five Years of Intergovernmental Reform* (Washington, DC: Brookings Institution, 1998).

Craig, Barbara. *Chadha: The Story of an Epic Constitutional Struggle* (New York: Oxford University Press, 1988).

Crovitz, L. Gordon, and Jeremy A. Rabkin, eds., *The Fettered Presidency: Legal Constraints on the Presidency* (Washington, DC: American Enterprise Institute, 1989).

Davis, Sue. *Justice Rehnquist and the Constitution* (Princeton: Princeton University Press, 1989).

Ely, John Hart. *War and Responsibility: Constitutional Lessons of Vietnam and Its Aftermath* (Cambridge: Harvard University Press, 1993).

Fisher, Louis. *Constitutional Conflicts between Congress and the President* (Lawrence: University Press of Kansas, 1997).

Fisher, Louis. *Presidential War Power* (Lawrence: University Press of Kansas, 1995).

Gerhardt, Michael. *The Federal Appointments Process: A Constitutional and Historical Analysis* (Durham, NC: Duke University Press, 2000).

Jones, Charles O. *The Presidency in a Separated System* (Washington, DC: Brookings Institution, 1994).

Keck, Tom. *The Most Activist Supreme Court in History: The Road to Modern Judicial Conservatism* (Chicago: University of Chicago Press, 2004).

Koh, Harold H. *The National Security Constitution: Sharing Powers after the Iran-Contra Affair* (New Haven: Yale University Press, 1990).

Korn, Jessica, *The Power of Separating: American Constitutionalism and the Myth of the Legislative Veto* (Princeton: Princeton University Press, 1996).

Licht, Robert A., and Robert A. Goldwein, eds., *Foreign Policy and the Constitution* (Washington, DC: American Enterprise Institute, 1990).

Maltz, Earl M. *Rehnquist Justice: Understanding the Court Dynamic* (Lawrence: University Press of Kansas, 2003).

Maveety, Nancy. *Justice Sandra Day O'Connor: Strategist on the Supreme Court* (Lanham, MD: Rowman & Littlefield, 1996).

Teles, Steven M. *The Rise of the Conservative Legal Movement: The Battle for the Control of the Law* (Princeton: Princeton University Press, 2008).

Walker, David B. *The Rebirth of Federalism: Slouching Toward Washington* (Chatham, NJ: Chatham House, 1995).

Yarbrough, Tinsley E. *The Rehnquist Court and the Constitution* (New York: Oxford University Press, 2000).

Chapter 11

The Contemporary Era: 1994–Present

I. Introduction

Conservatism seemed ascendant in the Reagan Era, but victory proved elusive. Republicans could not dislodge the Democrats from the House of Representatives or hold the Senate after 1986. Despite high poll numbers early in his term, after the fall of the Berlin Wall and the first Iraq War, President George H. W. Bush proved vulnerable. Bill Clinton seized the White House for the Democrats in 1992, as the economy entered a downturn and businessman H. Ross Perot emerged as an independent candidate. It was, however, the smallest popular vote margin since Woodrow Wilson's victory in the splintered campaign of 1912. Eight years later, Texas governor George W. Bush wrested the White House from Vice President Al Gore after a bruising election dispute that ended in the U.S. Supreme Court. In 2008, the White House again changed hands, as Barack Obama handily won election in the midst of an economic recession.

Clinton had run as a southern moderate against the party's liberal wing. Because the Democrats also retained control of Congress, he enjoyed unified party government for the first time in a dozen years. The "Republican revolution" of 1994, however, came as another electoral shock. The Republicans made stunning gains in the midterm elections, swelled by political novices and conservative firebrands. It marked the first time that the Republicans had controlled the House since the Eisenhower administration.

Politics remains fractured and uncertain. Divided government and slim, unstable congressional majorities have been common. Conservatives were confident that they had captured the public mood in 1994, but Republican numbers dwindled, and they lost their majorities in the House and Senate during George W. Bush's second term. President George W. Bush hoped to build on earlier GOP success and on national security crises, but his second term was mired in war and recession. President Barack Obama won a decisive Democratic victory, but those gains, too, quickly eroded.

Every president since George H. W. Bush has called himself "post-partisan," but in a time of deep partisan division. Voters are more reliable supporters of one party or the other; political combat extends to criminal investigations, public hearings, and impeachment threats. The two parties have become more disciplined, staking out divergent positions on constitutional issues from abortion to federalism.[1]

Presidents Reagan and George H. W. Bush were able to place five justices on the Supreme Court and with Justice Clarence Thomas secured a slim conservative majority. Yet the balance of power was held by Sandra Day O'Connor and Anthony Kennedy, whom conservatives derided as "eighty percenters." Subsequent appointments have largely maintained that balance of power on the Court, with Democratic presidents replacing more liberal justices and Republican presidents replacing more conservative justices.

The Court in the Contemporary Era has been noteworthy for its ideological wobble. A conservative coalition composed of O'Connor, Kennedy, Rehnquist, Scalia, and Thomas issued a series of federalism decisions in the late 1990s, and the conservatives assembled majorities on some other issues as well. But the liberal wing of the Court was also able to peel off swing voters such as

1. Larry M. Bartels, "Partisanship and Voting Behavior, 1952–1996," *American Journal of Political Science* 44 (2000):35; Benjamin Ginsberg and Martin Shefter, *Politics by Other Means* (New York: W. W. Norton, 2002); H. W. Perry, Jr., and L. A. Powe, Jr., "The Political Battle for the Constitution," *Constitutional Commentary* 21 (2004):641.

Table 11-1 Major Issues and Decisions of the Contemporary Era

Major Political Issues	Major Constitutional Issues	Major Court Decisions
Deficit Reduction	Presidential War Powers	*United States v. Lopez* (1995)
Welfare Reform	Independent Counsel	*City of Boerne v. Flores* (1997)
Health Care Reform	Impeachment Power	*Alden v. Maine* (1999)
Terrorism	State Sovereign Immunity	*United States v. Morrison* (2000)
Iraq War	Interstate Commerce Clause	*Hamdi v. Rumsfeld* (2004)
Immigration Reform	Judicial Supremacy	*Gonzales v. Raich* (2005)
	Executive Privilege	*Boumediene v. Bush* (2008)

O'Connor and Kennedy, especially in rights and liberties cases. The Court also struck down laws at an unusually rapid pace, while taking relatively few cases overall. It is assertive in its power of judicial review, but not always ambitious in how it uses that power.[2]

An overriding theme has been "responsible" or "accountable" government. The conservative vision of smaller government, decentralization, and individual responsibility remains influential. The Republican "Contract with America" of 1994, championed by future House Speaker Newt Gingrich, included such populist policies as congressional term limits and balanced budgets. Even a Democratic president, Bill Clinton, declared that the "era of big government is over." Tea Party Republicans have again raised concerns with the cost and growth of government. But both Republicans and Democrats have looked to the federal government for solutions to a variety of social and economic problems, from education to health care. Even "welfare reform" and anti-crime measures were put forth as ways of making government work better. Neither George W. Bush nor Barack Obama made reducing the size of government a goal, and the growth of the national security state has been a constant of the modern era. With the exception of Clarence Thomas, the conservative justices on the Court have little inclination to raise fundamental challenges to the scope of government. With the parties deeply polarized over the proper goals of politics and limits on government power, it remains to be seen how the constitutional politics of the Contemporary Era will be defined.

William J. Clinton, Fourth Annual Message (1996)[3]

Despite running a fairly conservative campaign for his first term of office, President Clinton's early acts were ideologically mixed. He completed the ratification of the North American Free Trade Accord (NAFTA) and passed a deficit reduction package, but he was entangled in debates over homosexuals in the military and failed health care reform. After the Republican takeover of Congress in 1994, Clinton returned to the conservative themes of his first campaign. He claimed welfare reform, originally part of the Republican "Contract with America," as a success. Clinton's willingness to compromise shifted more authority to the states and reduced the sense that income support was an "entitlement"—or even a "right." That led a number of administration officials to resign in protest but helped secure his reelection as a "New Democrat."

. . .

We must answer here three fundamental questions: First, how do we make the American dream of opportunity for all a reality for all Americans who are willing to work for it? Second, how do we preserve our old and enduring values as we move into the future?

2. Thomas M. Keck, *The Most Activist Supreme Court in History* (Chicago: University of Chicago Press, 2004); Mark Tushnet, *A Court Divided* (New York: W. W. Norton, 2005).

3. Excerpt taken from *Public Papers of the Presidents of the United States: William J. Clinton, 1996, Book 1* (Washington, DC: United States Government Printing Office, 1997), 79.

Box 11-1 A Partial Cast of Characters of the Contemporary Era

John Paul Stevens	■ Republican ■ Chicago antitrust lawyer ■ Appointed by Richard Nixon to the federal circuit court (1970–1975), and by Gerald Ford to the U.S. Supreme Court (1975–2010) ■ A consensus, non-political choice for the Court after Watergate, Stevens was not known for a distinctive judicial philosophy but had become a vocal member of the liberal wing as the Court became more conservative over time
Walter Dellinger	■ Democrat ■ Duke law professor and litigator ■ Assistant attorney general and head of the Office of Legal Counsel in the Clinton administration (1993–1996) and acting U.S. solicitor general (1996–1997) ■ Authored a number of opinions on defending presidential power
Anthony Kennedy	■ Republican ■ Moderate conservative ■ California lawyer and lobbyist ■ Appointed by Gerald Ford to federal circuit court (1975–1988), and by Ronald Reagan to U.S. Supreme Court (1988–present) after Robert Bork's nomination failed ■ Became pivotal swing vote on late Rehnquist and Roberts Courts; often votes with conservatives on government powers issues and with liberals on rights and liberties issues
Antonin Scalia	■ Republican ■ Conservative law professor ■ Assistant attorney general and head of the Office of Legal Counsel in the Nixon and Ford administrations (1974–1977) ■ Appointed by Ronald Reagan to the D.C. circuit court (1982–1986) and to the U.S. Supreme Court (1986–present) ■ First Italian-American appointed to the Court ■ An influential leader of the conservative legal movement since the 1970s, and since joining the Court Scalia has become a vocal advocate for "originalism" and a proponent of a formalistic approach to the separation of powers
David Souter	■ Republican ■ Moderate, New Hampshire prosecutor and judge ■ New Hampshire attorney general (1976–1978) and judge on the New Hampshire Supreme Court (1983–1990) ■ Appointed by George H. W. Bush to the federal circuit court (1990) and to the U.S. Supreme Court (1990–2009) ■ Known as a "stealth nominee" with little public record on national or constitutional issues, he was easily confirmed by a Democratic Senate to replace liberal icon William Brennan, emphasizing caution and respect for precedent in his opinions; he soon joined the liberal wing of the Court

(Continued)

Box 11-1 *Continued*

Clarence Thomas	▪ Republican ▪ Conservative lawyer, assistant secretary of education (1981), and director of the Equal Employment Opportunity Commission (1981–1990) during the Reagan and Bush administrations ▪ Appointed by George H. W. Bush to the D.C. circuit court (1990–1991) and to the U.S. Supreme Court (1991–present) ▪ A bruising battle in the Senate ended in one of the closest successful confirmation votes in history; Thomas became the second African-American to serve on the Court ▪ He soon emerged as one of the most conservative members of the Court and a strong advocate for a less deferential brand of originalism than that favored by some of the other conservative justices
John Yoo	▪ Republican ▪ Berkeley law professor ▪ General counsel to the U.S. Senate Judiciary Committee (1995–1996), deputy assistant attorney general in the Office of Legal Counsel (2001–2003) ▪ Authored a number of memos defending presidential power in foreign policy during the George W. Bush administration

And third, how do we meet these challenges together, as one America?

We know big Government does not have all the answers. We know there's not a program for every problem. We know, and we have worked to give the American people a smaller, less bureaucratic Government in Washington. And we have to give the American people one that lives within its means. The era of big Government is over. But we cannot go back to the time when our citizens were left to fend for themselves.

Instead, we must go forward as one America, one nation working together to meet the challenges we face together. Self-reliance and teamwork are not opposing virtues; we must have both. I believe our new, smaller Government must work in an old-fashioned American way, together with all of our citizens through State and local governments, in the workplace, in religious, charitable, and civic associations. Our goal must be to enable all our people to make the most of their own lives, with stronger families, more educational opportunity, economic security, safer streets, a cleaner environment in a safer world.

...

I say to those who are on welfare, and especially to those who have been trapped on welfare for a long time: For too long our welfare system has undermined the values of family and work, instead of supporting them. The Congress and I are near agreement on sweeping welfare reform. We agree on time limits, tough work requirements, and the toughest possible child support enforcement. But I believe we must also provide child care so that mothers who are required to go to work can do so without worrying about what is happening to their children.

I challenge this Congress to send me a bipartisan welfare reform bill that will really move people from welfare to work and do the right thing by our children. I will sign it immediately.

Barack Obama, Inaugural Address (2009)[4]

Barack Obama entered the race for president after having represented Illinois for less than a term in the U.S. Senate. As a young, African-American candidate in a crowded Democratic field, Obama positioned himself as a candidate who did not fit conventional political labels and who stood outside of "politics as usual" in Washington, D.C. After a bruising battle with Hillary Clinton for the Democratic nomination, Obama easily defeated the Republican candidate, John McCain. Although

4. Excerpt taken from *Daily Compilation of Presidential Documents* (Washington, DC: Government Printing Office, January 20, 2009), 1.

McCain had favored the role of the maverick, the long-time senator defended the unpopular Iraq War and ran during a severe economic downturn. The 2008 elections solidified Democratic majorities in Congress as well. Obama avoided laying out a new ideological or constitutional vision in favor of a more pragmatic message of making "hard choices."

...

The question we ask today is not whether our government is too big or too small, but whether it works—whether it helps families find jobs at a decent wage, care they can afford, a retirement that is dignified. Where the answer is yes, we intend to move forward. Where the answer is no, programs will end. And those of us who manage the public's dollars will be held to account, to spend wisely, reform bad habits, and do our business in the light of day, because only then can we restore the vital trust between a people and their government.

Nor is the question before us whether the market is a force for good or ill. Its power to generate wealth and expand freedom is unmatched. But this crisis has reminded us that without a watchful eye, the market can spin out of control. The nation cannot prosper long when it favors only the prosperous. The success of our economy has always depended not just on the size of our gross domestic product, but on the reach of our prosperity, on the ability to extend opportunity to every willing heart—not out of charity, but because it is the surest route to our common good.

As for our common defense, we reject as false the choice between our safety and our ideals. Our Founding Fathers faced with perils that we can scarcely imagine, drafted a charter to assure the rule of law and the rights of man—a charter expanded by the blood of generations. Those ideals still light the world, and we will not give them up for expedience's sake.

...

II. Judicial Power and Constitutional Authority

MAJOR DEVELOPMENTS

- Increasing use of judicial review against federal and state legislation
- Intensifying controversy over judiciary's assertion of supremacy on matters of constitutional meaning
- Enhanced politicization of judicial elections and appointments

Republicans dominated the nomination of Supreme Court justices from the presidency of Richard Nixon in 1969 to the end of the presidency of George H. W. Bush in 1993. Nixon put the Court on a more conservative path with his appointments in the early 1970s, transforming the Warren Court into the Burger Court, but it was not until the end of the George H. W. Bush administration that conservatives seemed to have an occasionally reliable working majority on the Supreme Court (along with supportive judges in the lower courts). Rehnquist, Thomas, and Scalia formed a clear conservative coalition on the late Rehnquist Court. Stevens, Blackmun, and Souter (disappointing conservatives) quickly emerged as a liberal wing. White, O'Connor, and Kennedy were swing votes, often joining the conservatives. Subsequent appointments largely maintained this balance. Clinton appointed Breyer and Ginsburg to replace White and Blackmun. George W. Bush appointed Roberts and Alito to replace Rehnquist and O'Connor. Obama appointed Sotomayor and Kagan to replace Souter and Stevens. Since the beginning of the Clinton administration, the Court has become more polarized, but it remains divided between liberal and conservative wings, and Kennedy is now alone in playing the pivotal role of swing vote.

Both conservatives and liberals have been able to win important cases in the Supreme Court, which cannot be so easily characterized as one or the other. Kennedy often sides with the conservatives on federalism and separation of powers, but with the liberals on rights and liberties. The contemporary Court has emphasized the importance of judicial review. It has insisted that it has the ultimate say on the meaning of the Constitution, even as it has frequently offended both conservatives and liberals when exercising that power. This section reflects debates over the scope of judicial power and constitutional authority.

A. Judicial Review

The phrase "judicial activism" is politically loaded, but its meaning is hard to pin down. Judges might be accused of activism whenever they strike down a law as unconstitutional. They might be "activist" when they overturn established precedents. They might be "activist" when they seem to be engaging in policymaking, when they cannot provide an adequate rationale for their decision, or even when they refuse to

Illustration 11-1 Judicial Nominations

Source: Clay Bennett, *Chattanooga Times Free Press*, May 11, 2010. Used with the permission of Clay Bennett, the Washington Post Writers Group and the Cartoonist Group. All rights reserved.

take any action at all.[5] There may be no objective measure of how *activist* the Supreme Court is, but there is a measure of how *active* it is. This focuses on how many times the Court has struck down laws as unconstitutional. All things being equal, a more active Court is one that strikes down more laws.

Figure 11-1 tracks the number of U.S. Supreme Court cases that invalidate the application of state and federal laws on constitutional grounds since 1970. It continues the story of judicial review by the Court where Figure 8.5 left off. As Figure 8.5 indicated, the Warren and early Burger Courts reached new levels of activity in striking down state laws in the 1960s and 1970s, resulting in a strong political backlash in Congress and elsewhere. When he ran for office in 1968, Richard Nixon pledged to appoint justices who would behave differently, and Ronald Reagan did the same in 1980. Once conservatives won a majority on the Court, the Court decreased the number of state laws that it struck down. That decrease was especially dramatic with the appointment of the Reagan justices in the 1980s. In terms of invalidations of state laws, the Court eventually returned to the low numbers that it had not seen since the dawn of the Warren Court. Meanwhile, the Rehnquist Court in the late 1990s briefly turned its attention to Congress. It stuck down more federal statutory provisions than during any other five years since the New Deal. For a short time, the Court even found itself in the historically unusual circumstance of deciding more cases in which it struck down federal laws than state laws.

The increase in the number of cases in which the Court struck down acts of Congress is the trend that attracted the most attention in the late 1990s. A large number of those decisions—though certainly not all of them—were decided on federalism or separation-of-powers grounds, and conservative justices led the way in many of those cases. For the first time since the New Deal, the Supreme Court enforced limitations on the federal government with regard to the interstate commerce clause, state sovereign immunity, and Section 5 of the Fourteenth Amendment. Liberals began to debate whether it was the conservatives who were engaged in judicial activism. Perhaps judicial restraint—or even

5. Keenan D. Kmiec, "The Origin and Current Meanings of 'Judicial Activism,'" *California Law Review* 92 (2004):1441; Bradley C. Canon, "Defining the Dimensions of Judicial Activism," *Judicature* 66 (1982):236.

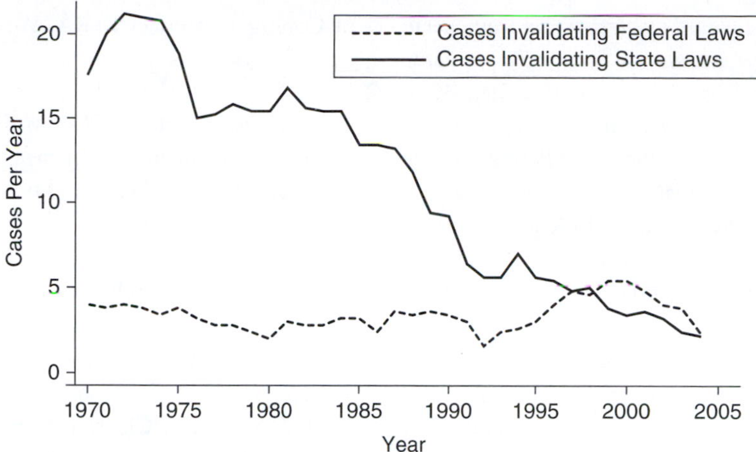

Figure 11-1 Supreme Court Invalidation of State and Federal Laws, 1970–2004

Note: Cases represented by centered, five-year moving average.

Source: Congressional Research Service (state laws); Judicial Review of Congress Database (federal laws).

the elimination of judicial review—might not be a bad thing after all.[6] The pace of invalidations of federal laws began to fall off after the 1990s, however. The Court's review of Congress during that period never had the same kind of huge impact on politics or public policy that it had had during, say, the 1930s.

One feature of the contemporary Court has made it surprisingly active in striking down laws: It invalidated state and federal laws from both the left and the right.[7] Swing justices, such as Sandra Day O'Connor and Anthony Kennedy, joined liberal coalitions to strike down statutes that the conservatives thought should be upheld, but they also joined conservative coalitions to strike down statutes that the liberals thought should be upheld. Some of the most controversial decisions of the Rehnquist and Roberts Courts have favored the left, such as those striking down homosexual sodomy laws (*Lawrence v. Texas* [2003]), military detentions of suspected terrorists (*Boumediene v. Bush* [2008]), and flag-burning laws (*Texas v. Johnson* [1989]). Still others have favored the right, such as those striking down parts of campaign finance reform (*Citizens United v. FEC* [2010]), the District of Columbia's ban on handguns (*District of Columbia v. Heller* [2008]), and parts of the Americans with Disabilities Act (*Board of Trustees of Alabama v. Garrett* [2001]). The Court has drawn criticism from both sides of the political aisle, while making particularly strong claims for its own authority to define constitutional meaning in cases like *City of Boerne v. Flores* (1997).

6. Cass R. Sunstein, *Radicals in Robes* (New York: Basic Books, 2005); Larry D. Kramer, "Popular Constitutionalism, Circa 2004," *California Law Review* 92 (2004):959.

7. Thomas M. Keck, *The Most Activist Supreme Court in History* (Chicago: University of Chicago Press, 2004).

City of Boerne v. Flores, 521 U.S. 507 (1997)

In Sherbert v. Verner *(1963), the Warren Court altered the Court's longstanding understanding of the requirements of the free exercise clause of the First Amendment. Under* Sherbert, *individuals could claim a constitutional exemption from laws that substantially burden religious practices unless they are justified by a compelling government interest. In 1990, a divided Court led by Justice Scalia returned to the earlier standard in* Employment Division v. Smith. *By that standard, it is not constitutionally required that individuals be exempted from neutral, generally applicable laws that only incidentally burden religious practices.*

The Smith *decision sparked an immediate outcry from civil libertarians and religious organizations. An unusual bipartisan and cross-ideological coalition passed the Religious Freedom Restoration Act of 1993 (RFRA), which imposed the* Sherbert *standard by statute. The controversy was over whether Congress could use Section 5 of the Fourteenth Amendment to impose that rule on the states. When the Catholic Archbishop of San Antonio filed suit under RFRA to block the application of the city of Boerne's zoning laws, the district court ruled that Congress had exceeded its constitutional authority by extending RFRA to the states. On appeal, the circuit court reversed. In a 6–3 decision, the Supreme Court reversed the circuit court and struck down RFRA as it applied to the states.*

For members of Congress and the Court, as well as outside observers, RFRA was an effort to reverse a constitutional doctrine by statute. The speed and decisiveness with which Congress responded to the Smith *decision suggested to some that the justices should defer to that legislative judgment as to how best to understand the principles and requirements of the free exercise clause. Even the justices who disagreed with the* Smith *standard were reluctant to accept a rebuke from Congress on a matter of constitutional interpretation, however. RFRA instead led the justices to assert once again that the judiciary, not the legislature, was the ultimate interpreter of the Constitution.*[8]

RFRA and Boerne *were only the first round of responses to the* Smith *decision. Many state legislatures passed their own "mini-RFRAs" that were enforceable in state courts. Congress has explored more targeted legislative options for extending the scope of federal protections in this area, such as the Religious Land Use and Institutionalized Persons Act of 2000. At the same time, there has been a more sustained discussion in Congress and elsewhere about the substantive merits of across-the-board religious exemptions to generally applicable laws and government policies in circumstances ranging from land-use to prison administration.*

Kennedy's opinion for the Court leans on John Marshall's language from Marbury v. Madison *(1803) to emphasize the primacy of the Court's role in interpreting the Constitution. Does* Marbury *determine the result here? To what extent does O'Connor disagree with the majority in* Boerne?

JUSTICE KENNEDY delivered the opinion of the Court.

A decision by local zoning authorities to deny a church a building permit was challenged under the Religious Freedom Restoration Act of 1993 (RFRA)....The case calls into question the authority of Congress to enact RFRA. We conclude the statute exceeds Congress' power.

...

Congress enacted RFRA in direct response to the Court's decision in *Employment Div., Dept. of Human Resources of Ore.* v. *Smith* (1990)....

...

Smith held that neutral, generally applicable laws may be applied to religious practices even when not supported by a compelling governmental interest.

Four Members of the Court disagreed. They argued the law placed a substantial burden on the Native American Church members so that it could be upheld only if the law served a compelling state interest and was narrowly tailored to achieve that end....JUSTICE O'CONNOR concluded Oregon had satisfied the test, while Justice Blackmun, joined by Justice Brennan and Justice Marshall, could see no compelling interest justifying the law's application to the members.

These points of constitutional interpretation were debated by Members of Congress in hearings and floor debates. Many criticized the Court's reasoning, and this disagreement resulted in the passage of RFRA. Congress announced:

> (1) The framers of the Constitution, recognizing free exercise of religion as an unalienable right, secured its protection in the First Amendment to the Constitution;
>
> (2) laws "neutral" toward religion may burden religious exercise as surely as laws intended to interfere with religious exercise;
>
> (3) governments should not substantially burden religious exercise without compelling justification;
>
> (4) in *Employment Division v. Smith*, the Supreme Court virtually eliminated the requirement that the government justify burdens on religious exercise imposed by laws neutral toward religion; and
>
> (5) the compelling interest test as set forth in prior Federal court rulings is a workable test for striking sensible balances between religious liberty and competing prior governmental interests.

The Act's stated purposes are: "(1) to restore the compelling interest test as set forth in *Sherbert v. Verner* (1963)...."

...

8. See "Symposium: Reflections on *City of Boerne v. Flores*," *William and Mary Law Review* 39 (1998):601.

Under our Constitution, the Federal Government is one of enumerated powers.... The judicial authority to determine the constitutionality of laws, in cases and controversies, is based on the premise that the "powers of the legislature are defined and limited; and that those limits may not be mistaken, or forgotten, the constitution is written." *Marbury v. Madison* (1803).

Congress relied on its Fourteenth Amendment enforcement power in enacting the most far reaching and substantial of RFRA's provisions, those which impose its requirements on the States....

...

In defense of the Act respondent contends... that RFRA is permissible enforcement legislation. Congress, it is said, is only protecting by legislation one of the liberties guaranteed by the Fourteenth Amendment's Due Process Clause, the free exercise of religion, beyond what is necessary under *Smith*. It is said the congressional decision to dispense with proof of deliberate or overt discrimination and instead concentrate on a law's effects accords with the settled understanding that Section Five includes the power to enact legislation designed to prevent as well as remedy constitutional violations. It is further contended that Congress' Section Five power is not limited to remedial or preventive legislation.

All must acknowledge that Section Five is "a positive grant of legislative power" to Congress....

Legislation which deters or remedies constitutional violations can fall within the sweep of Congress' enforcement power even if in the process it prohibits conduct which is not itself unconstitutional and intrudes into "legislative spheres of autonomy previously reserved to the States."... For example, the Court upheld a suspension of literacy tests and similar voting requirements under Congress' parallel power to enforce the provisions of the Fifteenth Amendment... as a measure to combat racial discrimination in voting... despite the facial constitutionality of the tests....

It is also true, however, that "as broad as the congressional enforcement power is, it is not unlimited."... In assessing the breadth of Section Five's enforcement power, we begin with its text. Congress has been given the power "to enforce" the "provisions of this article."...

Congress' power under Section Five, however, extends only to "enforcing" the provisions of the Fourteenth Amendment.... The design of the Amendment and the text of Section Five are inconsistent with the suggestion that Congress has the power to decree the substance of the Fourteenth Amendment's restrictions on the States. Legislation which alters the meaning of the Free Exercise Clause cannot be said to be enforcing the Clause. Congress does not enforce a constitutional right by changing what the right is. It has been given the power "to enforce," not the power to determine what constitutes a constitutional violation. Were it not so, what Congress would be enforcing would no longer be, in any meaningful sense, the "provisions of [the Fourteenth Amendment]."

...

If Congress could define its own powers by altering the Fourteenth Amendment's meaning, no longer would the Constitution be "superior paramount law, unchangeable by ordinary means." It would be "on a level with ordinary legislative acts, and, like other acts,... alterable when the legislature shall please to alter it." *Marbury v. Madison* (1803).... Under this approach, it is difficult to conceive of a principle that would limit congressional power.... Shifting legislative majorities could change the Constitution and effectively circumvent the difficult and detailed amendment process contained in Article V.

...

Our national experience teaches that the Constitution is preserved best when each part of the government respects both the Constitution and the proper actions and determinations of the other branches. When the Court has interpreted the Constitution, it has acted within the province of the Judicial Branch, which embraces the duty to say what the law is.... When the political branches of the Government act against the background of a judicial interpretation of the Constitution already issued, it must be understood that in later cases and controversies the Court will treat its precedents with the respect due them under settled principles, including *stare decisis*, and contrary expectations must be disappointed. RFRA was designed to control cases and controversies, such as the one before us; but as the provisions of the federal statute here invoked are beyond congressional authority, it is this Court's precedent, not RFRA, which must control.

JUSTICE STEVENS, concurring.

It is my opinion, the Religious Freedom Restoration Act of 1993 (RFRA) is a "law respecting an establishment of religion" that violates the First Amendment to the Constitution.

...

JUSTICE SCALIA, with whom JUSTICE STEVENS joins, concurring in part.

I write to respond briefly to the claim of Justice O'Connor's dissent...that historical materials support a result contrary to the one reached in *Employment Division, Department of Human Resources of Oregon v. Smith* (1990). We held in *Smith* that the Constitution's Free Exercise Clause "does not relieve an individual of the obligation to comply with a 'valid and neutral law of general applicability on the ground that the law proscribes (or prescribes) conduct that his religion prescribes (or proscribes).'"...The material that the dissent claims is at odds with *Smith* either has little to say about the issue or is in fact more consistent with *Smith* than with the dissent's interpretation of the Free Exercise Clause....

...

JUSTICE O'CONNOR, with whom JUSTICE BREYER joins, dissenting.

I dissent from the Court's disposition of this case. I agree with the Court that the issue before us is whether the Religious Freedom Restoration Act (RFRA) is a proper exercise of Congress' power to enforce Section Five of the Fourteenth Amendment. But as a yardstick for measuring the constitutionality of RFRA, the Court uses its holding in *Employment Division, Department of Human Resources of Oregon v. Smith* (1990), the decision that prompted Congress to enact RFRA as a means of more rigorously enforcing the Free Exercise Clause. I remain of the view that *Smith* was wrongly decided, and I would use this case to reexamine the Court's holding there....

I agree with much of the reasoning set forth in...the Court's opinion. Indeed, if I agreed with the Court's standard in *Smith*, I would join the opinion. As the Court's careful and thorough historical analysis shows, Congress lacks the "power to decree the substance of the Fourteenth Amendment's restrictions on the States." Rather, its power under Section Five of the Fourteenth Amendment extends only to enforcing the Amendment's provisions. In short, Congress lacks the ability independently to define or expand the scope of constitutional rights by statute....

Stare decisis concerns should not prevent us from revisiting our holding in *Smith*. "[S]tare decisis is a principle of policy and not a mechanical formula of adherence to the latest decision, however recent and questionable, when such adherence involves collision with a prior doctrine more embracing in its scope, intrinsically sounder, and verified by experience." *Adarand Constructors, Inc. v. Pena*, 515 U.S. 200, 213 (1995)....This principle is particularly true in constitutional cases where—as this case plainly illustrates—"correction through legislative action is practically impossible."...I believe that, in light of both our precedent and our Nation's tradition of religious liberty, *Smith* is demonstrably wrong. Moreover, it is a recent decision. As such, it has not engendered the kind of reliance on its continued application that would militate against overruling it. Cf. *Planned Parenthood of Southeastern Pennsylvania v. Casey* (1992).

...

I respectfully dissent from the Court's disposition of this case.

JUSTICE SOUTER, dissenting.

...

JUSTICE BREYER, dissenting.

...

The Nomination of Samuel Alito to the U.S. Supreme Court (2006)[9]

Judge Samuel Alito was known as a respected but low-key conservative who had made a career as a prosecutor and judge. He had served in the Reagan administration and been appointed to the Third Circuit Court of Appeals by President George W. Bush. In 2005, he was nominated to fill the vacancy of the retiring Justice Sandra Day O'Connor, and his confirmation hearings were scheduled to follow those of John Roberts, who had been nominated to replace the deceased Chief Justice William Rehnquist.

O'Connor's departure had particular significance because she had cast a critical vote to uphold abortion rights in the 1992 Casey v. Planned Parenthood *decision, which had emphasized the importance of stare decisis, or following precedent, in such cases. Alito's confirmation hearings then became an opportunity for the senators and the nominee to articulate their varying views on the importance of following established precedent in future cases and the conditions under which precedent should be followed or might be set aside. Recent confirmation hearings have also become an opportunity for senators to attempt to influence Supreme*

9. Excerpt taken from United States Senate Judiciary Committee, *Confirmation Hearing on the Nomination of Samuel A. Alito, Jr. to Be Associate Justice of the Supreme Court of the United States*, 109th Cong., 2nd Sess. (January 10–11, 2006).

Court nominees, as well as showcase their own views for their political supporters and constituents in a very public event. The members of the Senate Judiciary Committee tend to be drawn from the ideological extremes, since they have the most interest in the issues that come before the committee. Committee Chairman Arlen Specter was an exception in being a relative moderate from a swing state. At the time of the Alito nomination, Specter was a Republican; he later switched parties after Obama's presidential victory in 2008. By contrast, Republican Sam Brownback was preparing to run a presidential campaign as a social conservative, and Democrat Charles Schumer was organizing the national Democratic campaign for the 2006 midterm Senate elections.

SENATOR SPECTER (Republican, Pennsylvania): Let me move directly into *Casey v. Planned Parenthood* (1992).... How would you weigh that consideration [stare decisis] on the woman's right to choose?

JUDGE ALITO: Well, I think the doctrine of stare decisis is a very important doctrine. It's a fundamental part of our legal system.

And it's the principle that courts in general should follow their past precedents. And it's important for a variety of reasons. It's important because it limits the power of the judiciary. It's important because it protects reliance interests. And it's important because it reflects the view that courts should respect the judgments and the wisdom that are embodied in prior judicial decisions.

It's not an exorable command, but it is a general presumption that courts are going to follow prior precedents....

SPECTER: Let me move on to another important quotation out of *Casey*.

QUOTE: "A terrible price would be paid for overruling *Casey*—or overruling *Roe*. It would seriously weaken the court's capacity to exercise the judicial power and to function as the Supreme Court of a nation dedicated to the rule of law. And to overrule *Roe v. Wade* (1973) under fire would subvert the court's legitimacy."

Do you see the legitimacy of the court being involved in the precedent of *Casey*?

ALITO: Well, I think that the court and all the courts—the Supreme Court, my court, all of the federal courts—should be insulated from public opinion. They should do what the law requires in all instances.

That's why the members of the judiciary are not elected. We have a basically democratic form of government, but the judiciary is not elected. And that's the reason: so that they don't do anything under fire. They do what the law requires....

SPECTER: Judge Alito, let me move to the dissenting opinion by Justice Harlan in *Poe v. Ullman* (1961) where he discusses the constitutional concept of liberty and says, quote, "The traditions from which liberty developed, that tradition is a living thing."

Would you agree with Justice Harlan that the Constitution embodies the concept of a living thing?

ALITO: I think the Constitution is a living thing in the sense that matters...—it sets up a framework of government and a protection of fundamental rights that we have lived under very successfully for 200 years. And the genius of it is that it is not terribly specific on certain things. It sets out—some things are very specific, but it sets out some general principles and then leaves it for each generation to apply those to the particular factual situations that come up.

...

SPECTER: Judge Alito, the commentators have characterized *Casey* as a super-precedent.

...

Do you agree that *Casey* is a super-precedent...?

ALITO: Well, I personally would not get into categorizing precedents as super-precedents or super-duper precedents or any...

SPECTER: Did you say super-duper?

ALITO: Right.

(LAUGHTER)

SPECTER: Good. I like that.

ALITO: Any sort of categorization like that sort of reminds me of the size of the laundry detergent in the supermarket.

I agree with the underlying thought that when a precedent is reaffirmed...each time it's reaffirmed that is a factor that should be taken into account in making the judgment about stare decisis. And when a precedent is reaffirmed on the ground that stare decisis precludes or counsels against reexamination of the merits of the precedent, then I agree that that is a precedent on precedent.

...

SENATOR SCHUMER (Democrat, New York): Now you've tried to reassure us that stare decisis means a great deal to you. You point out that prior Supreme Court precedents, like *Roe*, will stand because of the principle.

...

I just want to ask you this. Stare decisis is not an immutable principle, right?

ALITO: It is a strong principle. And in general courts follow precedents. The Supreme Court needs a special justification for overruling a prior case.

SCHUMER: But they have found them....

In recent years the court has overruled various cases in a rather short amount of time. You mentioned I think it was *National League of Cities* (1976) about fair labor standards, and it was overruled just nine years later by *Garcia* (1985).... *Bowers v. Hardwick* (1986) was overruled by *Lawrence v. Texas* (2003). And of course... *Plessy* (1896) was overruled by *Brown* (1954)....

So the only point I'm making is that despite stare decisis, it doesn't mean a Supreme Court justice who strongly believes in stare decisis won't ever overrule a case. Is that correct? You can give me a yes or no.

ALITO: Yes.

...

SCHUMER: OK....And remember what [Justice Thomas] said when he was sitting in the same chair you're sitting in. He pledged fealty to stare decisis.

Justice Scalia said Justice Thomas, "doesn't believe in stare decisis, period. If a constitutional line of authority is wrong, he would say, 'Let's get it right.'"

Then Justice Scalia said, "I wouldn't"—speaking of himself—"I wouldn't do that."

...

And I'm not saying Justice Thomas was disingenuous with the committee when he was here. I'm just saying that stare decisis is something of an elastic concept that different judges apply in different ways.

...

SENATOR BROWNBACK (Republican, Kansas): Judge Alito, the Supreme Court has gotten a number of things wrong at times, too. That would be correct. And the answer when the court gets things wrong is to overturn the case. –...[T]hat's the way it works, isn't that correct?

ALITO: Well, when the court gets something wrong and there's a prior precedent, then you have to analyze the doctrine of stare decisis. It is an important doctrine, and I've said a lot about it—

BROWNBACK: Wait. Let me just ask you. Was *Plessy* wrong, *Plessy v. Ferguson*?

ALITO: *Plessy* was certainly wrong.

BROWNBACK: OK, I mean, and you've gone through this. *Brown v. Board of Education*, which is in my hometown of Topeka, Kansas.... Fifty years ago, that overturned *Plessy*. *Plessy* had stood on the books since 1896. I don't know if you knew the number. And I've got a chart up here. It was depended upon by a number of people for a long period of time. You've got it sitting on the books for 60 years, twice the length of time of *Roe v. Wade*. You've got these number of cases that considered *Plessy* and uphold *Plessy* to the dependency. And yet *Brown* comes along...And the court looks at this and they say unanimously, that's just not right.

Now, stare decisis would say in the *Brown* case you should uphold *Plessy*. Is that correct?

ALITO:...[C]ertainly it would be a factor that you would consider in determining whether to overrule it. It's a doctrine that you would consider.

BROWNBACK: But obviously—obviously, *Brown* overturned it. And thank goodness it did, correct?

ALITO: Certainly.

BROWNBACK: That it overturned all these super-duper precedents that had been depended upon in this case because the court got it wrong in *Plessy*. Is that correct?

ALITO: The court certainly got it wrong in *Plessy*, and it got it spectacularly wrong in *Plessy*, and it took a long time for that erroneous decision to be overruled.

...

BROWNBACK: I want to give you another number. And that is that in over 200 other cases, the court has revisited and revised earlier judgments. In other words, in some portion or in all the cases, the court got it wrong in some 200 cases. And thank goodness the court's willing to review various cases.

. . .

Settled law? Super-duper precedents? I think there's places where the court gets it wrong, and hopefully they will continue to be willing to revisit it.

. . .

B. Constitutional Litigation

The modern judiciary has become an active player in a wide variety of social, political, and constitutional disputes. Organized interest groups, government officials, and individual actors routinely try to draw the courts into their conflicts. Judicial intervention into a dispute can allow litigants to win a dispute outright and give them the immediate results they desire. More often, the courts can give litigants greater leverage in their ongoing battles in other arenas and put those actors in a better position to advance their long-term agendas.

But before a party can make their case to a judge they have to get their case into court. The contemporary judiciary is quite open to constitutional litigation, but there are still limits to the cases that the courts will accept. In *Massachusetts v. EPA* (2007) a sharply divided U.S. Supreme Court recognized the standing of a state to sue the federal Environmental Protection Agency over its regulatory decisions regarding greenhouse gases. As a result, the courts forced the administration's hand on issuing regulations in a politically sensitive area. On the other hand, the lower federal courts have consistently dismissed cases challenging the constitutionality of military offensives. In the 2003 case of *Doe v. Bush*, for example, a federal circuit court held that a challenge to the constitutionality of the Iraq War was not ripe for judicial resolution. In *Freedom from Religion Foundation v. Perry* (Civil Action H-11–2585) (U.S.D.C. S.D.Tx., July 28, 2011), a federal district court judge dismissed a suit seeking to prevent the governor of Texas from participating in a "prayer rally." In keeping with recent precedents, the judge concluded that the members of the Freedom from Religion Foundation did not suffer the kind of "personal injury" (as opposed to a "generalized grievance") that would entitle them to sue and obtain judicial relief under Article III of the Constitution.[10]

Doe v. Bush, 323 F.3d 133 (1st Cir. 2003)

In 2003, a large group of plaintiffs that included military personnel, their parents (the "John Doe" that provides the name for the case), and Democratic congressmen such as Dennis Kucinich filed suit in a federal district court in Massachusetts. (Kucinich was later a candidate for the 2004 Democratic presidential nomination.) They sought an injunction against President George W. Bush and Secretary of Defense Donald Rumsfeld to prevent them taking military action in Iraq. Such suits have been common since the Vietnam era, but have met with little success. After the district court dismissed the suit, the plaintiffs appealed to the U.S. Court of Appeals for the First Circuit, which unanimously affirmed the dismissal. The three-judge panel for the circuit court included two judges appointed by Republican presidents and one appointed by a Democratic president. The U.S. Supreme Court did not hear the case.

The case, like others before it seeking to declare military actions unconstitutional and illegal, was dismissed as not presenting a justiciable "case or controversy." Often such cases have been dismissed as "political questions," precluding the possibility of judicial review. In Doe, *the circuit court took a somewhat different approach and put off the case as not yet ripe for judicial resolution, leaving open the possibility that judicial intervention might be a possibility in a different case. Ripeness doctrine holds that litigants should be denied standing if their legal claim depends on the outcome of uncertain future events or administrative decision making.*

Should the courts ever be willing to review the constitutionality of military actions? When might a question of whether a president has been authorized to initiate military action become ripe for judicial resolution?

JUDGE LYNCH delivered the opinion of the Court.

In October 2002, Congress passed the Authorization for Use of Military Force Against Iraq Resolution (the "October Resolution"). . . . Plaintiffs argue that the October Resolution is constitutionally inadequate to authorize the military offensive that defendants are now planning against Iraq. See U.S. Const. art. I, § 8,

10. See *Hein v. Freedom of Religion Foundation* (2007); *Freedom from Religion Foundation v. Obama*, 641 F.3d 803 (7th Cir. 2011).

cl. 11 (granting Congress the power "to declare war"). They base this argument on two theories. They argue that Congress and the President are in collision—that the President is about to act in violation of the October Resolution. They also argue that Congress and the President are in collusion—that Congress has handed over to the President its exclusive power to declare war.

...

The case before us is a somber and weighty one. We have considered these important concerns carefully, and we have concluded that the circumstances call for judicial restraint. The theory of collision between the legislative and executive branches is not suitable for judicial review, because there is not a ripe dispute concerning the President's acts and the requirements of the October Resolution passed by Congress. By contrast, the theory of collusion, by its nature, assumes no conflict between the political branches, but rather a willing abdication of congressional power to an emboldened and enlarged presidency. That theory is not fit for judicial review for a different, but related, reason: Plaintiffs' claim that Congress and the President have transgressed the boundaries of their shared war powers, as demarcated by the Constitution, is presently insufficient to present a justiciable issue. Common to both is our assessment that, before courts adjudicate a case involving the war powers allocated to the two political branches, they must be presented with a case or controversy that clearly raises the specter of undermining the constitutional structure.

...

The Constitution reserves the war powers to the legislative and executive branches. This court has declined the invitation to become involved in such matters once before. Over thirty years ago, the First Circuit addressed a war powers case challenging the constitutionality of the Vietnam War on the basis that Congress had not declared war. *Massachusetts v. Laird*, 451 F.2d 26 (1st Cir. 1971). The court found that other actions by Congress, such as continued appropriations to fund the war over the course of six years provided enough indication of congressional approval to put the question beyond the reach of judicial review.

...

The lack of a fully developed dispute between the two elected branches, and the consequent lack of a clearly defined issue, is exactly the type of concern which causes courts to find a case unripe.

In his concurring opinion in *Goldwater v. Carter* (1979), Justice Powell stated that courts should decline, on ripeness grounds, to decide "issues affecting the allocation of power between the President and Congress until the political branches reach a constitutional impasse." A number of courts have adopted Justice Powell's ripeness reasoning in cases involving military powers....

...

...Two factors are used to evaluate ripeness: "the fitness of the issues for judicial decision and the hardship to the parties of withholding court consideration." *Abbott Labs v. Gardner* (1967)....

The hardship prong of this test is most likely satisfied here; the current mobilization already imposes difficulties on the plaintiff soldiers and family members, so that they suffer "present injury from a future contemplated event."...

The fitness inquiry here presents a greater obstacle. Fitness "typically involves subsidiary queries concerning finality, definiteness, and the extent to which resolution of the challenge depends upon facts that may not yet be sufficiently developed."...

...

...The [United Nations] Security Council, now divided on the issue, may reach a consensus. To evaluate this claim now, the court would need to pile one hypothesis on top of another. We would need to assume that the Security Council will not authorize war, and that the President will proceed nonetheless....

Thus, even assuming that plaintiffs correctly interpret the commands of the legislative branch, it is impossible to say yet whether or not those commands will be obeyed. As was the situation in *Goldwater*, "in the present posture of this case, we do not know whether there will ever be an actual confrontation between the Legislative and Executive Branches."

...

According to this second argument, the Constitution deliberately vested power to declare war in the legislative branch as a necessary check on the power of the executive branch, and Congress is not free to upset this careful balance by giving power to the President. This claim of collusion does not align precisely with the test that the political branches have yet to reach a "constitutional impasse"; the claim is that the branches have agreed to an unconstitutional transfer of the "war declaration" powers from Congress to the President....

...

The Supreme Court has recognized a role for judicial review of these types of separation of powers claims even when Congress appears to have agreed to the challenged arrangement.... [One such case was *Clinton v. New York* (1998), involving the constitutionality of a law that gave the president a so-called "Line Item Veto."]

...

There are also, however, significant differences between *Clinton v. New York* (1998) and the case before us. For one, in *Clinton* the President had fully exercised the power that was at issue, which "removed any concern" about ripeness. For another, the Line Item Veto Act contained specific provisions, accepted by both Congress and the President when they enacted the law, which not only permitted judicial review of the statute's validity but created a special expedited process for it....

Perhaps the most important difference is the shared nature of the powers in question here. The Constitution explicitly divides the various war powers between the political branches....

Given this "amalgam of powers," the Constitution overall "envisages the *joint* participation of the Congress and the executive in determining the scale and duration of hostilities." *Laird*, at 31–32 (emphasis added).... [T]here is sometimes a "zone of twilight in which [the President] and Congress may have concurrent authority, or in which its distribution is uncertain.... In this area, any actual test of power is likely to depend on the imperatives of events and contemporary imponderables rather than on abstract theories of law." *Youngstown Sheet & Tube Co. v. Sawyer* (1952).

...

Nor is there clear evidence of congressional abandonment of the authority to declare war to the President. To the contrary, Congress has been deeply involved in significant debate, activity, and authorization connected to our relations with Iraq for over a decade, under three different presidents of both major political parties, and during periods when each party has controlled Congress. It has enacted several relevant pieces of legislation expressing support for an aggressive posture toward Iraq....

It is true that "courts possess power to review either legislative or executive action that transgresses identifiable textual limits" on constitutional power. Questions about the structure of congressional power can be justiciable under the proper circumstances. But courts are rightly hesitant to second-guess the form or means by which the coequal political branches choose to exercise their textually committed constitutional powers. As the circumstances presented here do not warrant judicial intervention, the appropriate recourse for those who oppose war with Iraq lies with the political branches.

Dismissal of the complaint is *affirmed*.

Massachusetts v. Environmental Protection Agency, 549 U.S. 497 (2007)

The Clean Air Act requires the Environmental Protection Agency (EPA) to regulate "the emission of any air pollutant." Numerous environmental organizations in 1999 asked the EPA to regulate those greenhouse gas emissions which the scientific evidence indicated were responsible for increased global warming. While Clinton administration officials were sympathetic, the new Bush administration was not. The EPA in 2003 declared that no authority existed under the Clean Air Act to regulate greenhouse gases and that regulation would not be wise policy. Several states, local governments, and environmental groups brought suit to challenge this ruling. The EPA insisted that the suit could not be heard. First, the state governments were not proper parties to the case; second, no party was suffering the particularized injury necessary for satisfying the case-or-controversy requirement. A divided circuit court ruled in favor of the EPA's discretion under the Clean Air Act. One judge, however, thought the case should have been dismissed as not presenting a justiciable injury. In a 5–4 decision, the Supreme Court reversed the circuit court. It held that the plaintiffs had sufficient standing to litigate the case and that the EPA did indeed have authority to regulate greenhouse gases under existing statutes.

Does Justice Stevens make a convincing case that Massachusetts was an appropriate party and had suffered the constitutionally appropriate particularized injury, or does Chief Justice Roberts correctly claim that this is a matter best settled by the elected branches of government? To what extent do you believe the difference between the justices is over legal questions of standing or the actual existence of global warming? Notice the effort Justice Stevens makes in his majority opinion to appeal to Justice Kennedy, the crucial fifth vote in this case. Why does Chief Justice Roberts not seem to make a similar effort?

JUSTICE STEVENS delivered the opinion of the Court.

Calling global warming "the most pressing environmental challenge of our time," a group of States, local governments, and private organizations, alleged in a petition for certiorari that the Environmental Protection Agency (EPA) has abdicated its responsibility under the Clean Air Act to regulate the emissions of four greenhouse gases, including carbon dioxide. Specifically, petitioners asked us to answer two questions concerning the meaning of § 202(a)(1) of the Act: whether EPA has the statutory authority to regulate greenhouse gas emissions from new motor vehicles; and if so, whether its stated reasons for refusing to do so are consistent with the statute.

In response, EPA, supported by 10 intervening States and six trade associations, correctly argued that we may not address those two questions unless at least one petitioner has standing to invoke our jurisdiction under Article III of the Constitution....

...

Article III of the Constitution limits federal-court jurisdiction to "Cases" and "Controversies." Those two words confine "the business of federal courts to questions presented in an adversary context and in a form historically viewed as capable of resolution through the judicial process." *Flast v. Cohen* (1968)....It is therefore familiar learning that no justiciable "controversy" exists when parties seek adjudication of a political question,...when they ask for an advisory opinion,...or when the question sought to be adjudicated has been mooted by subsequent developments....This case suffers from none of these defects.

...At bottom, "the gist of the question of standing" is whether petitioners have "such a personal stake in the outcome of the controversy as to assure that concrete adverseness which sharpens the presentation of issues upon which the court so largely depends for illumination." *Baker v. Carr* (1962). As JUSTICE KENNEDY explained in his *Lujan* concurrence:

> While it does not matter how many persons have been injured by the challenged action, the party bringing suit must show that the action injures him in a concrete and personal way. This requirement is not just an empty formality. It preserves the vitality of the adversarial process by assuring both that the parties before the court have an actual, as opposed to professed, stake in the outcome, and that the legal questions presented...will be resolved, not in the rarified atmosphere of a debating society, but in a concrete factual context conducive to a realistic appreciation of the consequences of judicial action.

To ensure the proper adversarial presentation, *Lujan* holds that a litigant must demonstrate that it has suffered a concrete and particularized injury that is either actual or imminent, that the injury is fairly traceable to the defendant, and that it is likely that a favorable decision will redress that injury....However, a litigant to whom Congress has "accorded a procedural right to protect his concrete interests," ...—here, the right to challenge agency action unlawfully withheld,—"can assert that right without meeting all the normal standards for redressability and immediacy."...When a litigant is vested with a procedural right, that litigant has standing if there is some possibility that the requested relief will prompt the injury-causing party to reconsider the decision that allegedly harmed the litigant....

...

...Congress has ordered EPA to protect Massachusetts (among others) by prescribing standards applicable to the "emission of any air pollutant from any class or classes of new motor vehicle engines, which in [the Administrator's] judgment cause, or contribute to, air pollution which may reasonably be anticipated to endanger public health or welfare."...Congress has moreover recognized a concomitant procedural right to challenge the rejection of its rulemaking petition as arbitrary and capricious....Given that procedural right and Massachusetts' stake in protecting its quasi-sovereign interests, the Commonwealth is entitled to special solicitude in our standing analysis.

With that in mind, it is clear that petitioners' submissions as they pertain to Massachusetts have satisfied the most demanding standards of the adversarial process. EPA's steadfast refusal to regulate greenhouse gas emissions presents a risk of harm to Massachusetts that is both "actual" and "imminent."...There is, moreover, a "substantial likelihood that the judicial relief requested" will prompt EPA to take steps to reduce that risk....

The harms associated with climate change are serious and well recognized. Indeed, the NRC Report itself—which EPA regards as an "objective and independent assessment of the relevant science," ...—identifies a number of environmental changes that have already inflicted significant harms, including "the global retreat of mountain glaciers, reduction in snow-cover extent, the earlier spring melting of rivers and lakes, [and] the accelerated rate of rise of sea levels during the 20th century relative to the past few thousand years...."

...

That these climate-change risks are "widely shared" does not minimize Massachusetts' interest in the outcome of this litigation.... [R]ising seas have already begun to swallow Massachusetts' coastal land.... Because the Commonwealth "owns a substantial portion of the state's coastal property,"... it has alleged a particularized injury in its capacity as a landowner....

EPA does not dispute the existence of a causal connection between man-made greenhouse gas emissions and global warming. At a minimum, therefore, EPA's refusal to regulate such emissions "contributes" to Massachusetts' injuries.

EPA nevertheless maintains that its decision not to regulate greenhouse gas emissions from new motor vehicles contributes so insignificantly to petitioners' injuries that the agency cannot be haled into federal court to answer for them. For the same reason, EPA does not believe that any realistic possibility exists that the relief petitioners seek would mitigate global climate change and remedy their injuries. That is especially so because predicted increases in greenhouse gas emissions from developing nations, particularly China and India, are likely to offset any marginal domestic decrease.

But EPA overstates its case. Its argument rests on the erroneous assumption that a small incremental step, because it is incremental, can never be attacked in a federal judicial forum. Yet accepting that premise would doom most challenges to regulatory action. Agencies, like legislatures, do not generally resolve massive problems in one fell regulatory swoop.... They instead whittle away at them over time, refining their preferred approach as circumstances change and as they develop a more-nuanced understanding of how best to proceed....

...

In sum—at least according to petitioners' uncontested affidavits—the rise in sea levels associated with global warming has already harmed and will continue to harm Massachusetts. The risk of catastrophic harm, though remote, is nevertheless real. That risk would be reduced to some extent if petitioners received the relief they seek. We therefore hold that petitioners have standing to challenge the EPA's denial of their rule-making petition.

[After finding standing, Justice Stevens ruled that federal statutes authorized the Environmental Protection Agency to regulate greenhouse gases.]

CHIEF JUSTICE ROBERTS, with whom JUSTICE SCALIA, JUSTICE THOMAS, and JUSTICE ALITO join, dissenting.

...

... I would reject these challenges as nonjusticiable. Such a conclusion involves no judgment on whether global warming exists, what causes it, or the extent of the problem. Nor does it render petitioners without recourse. This Court's standing jurisprudence simply recognizes that redress of grievances of the sort at issue here "is the function of Congress and the Chief Executive," not the federal courts. *Lujan v. Defenders of Wildlife* (1992)....

...

Our modern framework for addressing standing is familiar: "A plaintiff must allege personal injury fairly traceable to the defendant's allegedly unlawful conduct and likely to be redressed by the requested relief." *DaimlerChrylser v. Cuno* (2006).... Applying that standard here, petitioners bear the burden of alleging an injury that is fairly traceable to the Environmental Protection Agency's failure to promulgate new motor vehicle greenhouse gas emission standards, and that is likely to be redressed by the prospective issuance of such standards.

...

When the Court actually applies the three-part test, it focuses ... on the State's asserted loss of coastal land as the injury in fact. If petitioners rely on loss of land as the Article III injury, however, they must ground the rest of the standing analysis in that specific injury. That alleged injury must be "concrete and particularized,"... and "distinct and palpable."... Central to this concept of "particularized" injury is the requirement that a plaintiff be affected in a "personal and individual way."...

The very concept of global warming seems inconsistent with this particularization requirement. Global warming is a phenomenon "harmful to humanity at large"... and the redress petitioners seek is focused no more on them than on the public generally—it is literally to change the atmosphere around the world.

...[A]side from a single conclusory statement, there is nothing in petitioners' 43 standing declarations and accompanying exhibits to support an inference of actual loss of Massachusetts coastal land from 20th century global sea level increases. It is pure conjecture.

The Court's attempts to identify "imminent" or "certainly impending" loss of Massachusetts coastal land fares no better.... One of petitioners' declarants predicts global warming will cause sea level to rise by 20 to 70 centimeters by the year 2100.... But the computer modeling program has a conceded average error of about 30 centimeters and a maximum observed error of 70 centimeters.... [A]ccepting a century-long time horizon and a series of compounded estimates renders requirements of imminence and immediacy utterly toothless....

...

Petitioners view the relationship between their injuries and EPA's failure to promulgate new motor vehicle greenhouse gas emission standards as simple and direct: Domestic motor vehicles emit carbon dioxide and other greenhouse gases. Worldwide emissions of greenhouse gases contribute to global warming and therefore also to petitioners' alleged injuries. Without the new vehicle standards, greenhouse gas emissions—and therefore global warming and its attendant harms—have been higher than they otherwise would have been; once EPA changes course, the trend will be reversed.

The Court ignores the complexities of global warming, and does so by now disregarding the "particularized" injury it relied on in step one, and using the dire nature of global warming itself as a bootstrap for finding causation and redressability. First, it is important to recognize the extent of the emissions at issue here. Because local greenhouse gas emissions disperse throughout the atmosphere and remain there for anywhere from 50 to 200 years, it is global emissions data that are relevant.... According to one of petitioners' declarations, domestic motor vehicles contribute about 6 percent of global carbon dioxide emissions and 4 percent of global greenhouse gas emissions.... The amount of global emissions at issue here is smaller still; § 202(a)(1) of the Clean Air Act covers only new motor vehicles and new motor vehicle engines, so petitioners' desired emission standards might reduce only a fraction of 4 percent of global emissions.

This gets us only to the relevant greenhouse gas emissions; linking them to global warming and ultimately to petitioners' alleged injuries next requires consideration of further complexities....

Petitioners are never able to trace their alleged injuries back through this complex web to the fractional amount of global emissions that might have been limited with EPA standards. In light of the bit-part domestic new motor vehicle greenhouse gas emissions have played in what petitioners describe as a 150-year global phenomenon, and the myriad additional factors bearing on petitioners' alleged injury—the loss of Massachusetts coastal land—the connection is far too speculative to establish causation.

...[T]he Court reasons, because any decrease in domestic emissions will "slow the pace of global emissions increases, no matter what happens elsewhere."... Every little bit helps, so Massachusetts can sue over any little bit.

The Court's sleight-of-hand is in failing to link up the different elements of the three-part standing test. What must be likely to be redressed is the particular injury in fact. The injury the Court looks to is the asserted loss of land. The Court contends that regulating domestic motor vehicle emissions will reduce carbon dioxide in the atmosphere, and therefore redress Massachusetts's injury. But even if regulation does reduce emissions—to some indeterminate degree, given events elsewhere in the world—the Court never explains why that makes it likely that the injury in fact—the loss of land—will be redressed. Schoolchildren know that a kingdom might be lost "all for the want of a horseshoe nail," but "likely" redressability is a different matter. The realities make it pure conjecture to suppose that EPA regulation of new automobile emissions will likely prevent the loss of Massachusetts coastal land.

...[P]etitioners' true goal for this litigation may be more symbolic than anything else. The constitutional role of the courts, however, is to decide concrete cases—not to serve as a convenient forum for policy debates....

...

I respectfully dissent.

JUSTICE SCALIA, with whom THE CHIEF JUSTICE, JUSTICE THOMAS, and JUSTICE ALITO join, dissenting.

...

C. Judicial Structure and Selection

Note: Judicial Appointments and Confirmations

The president nominates judicial candidates, and the Senate confirms them. In order to be confirmed, a candidate must receive a majority of the votes cast in the Senate. In the modern Senate, there are two key thresholds that must be passed: the Judiciary Committee, which votes whether to recommend that the full Senate confirm a judicial nominee, and the full Senate, which votes whether to confirm the nominee. Every federal judicial nominee must go through the same process, whether they have been appointed to a district court or the U.S. Supreme Court. Traditionally, the U.S. Supreme Court nominations have attracted the most attention from the full Senate, from the media, and from interest groups, given the importance of that office. Although most Supreme Court nominations are successful and raise little controversy, it has been those nominations that have sometimes led to contentious battles on the floor of the Senate or in committee hearings. In recent years, however, the controversy over judicial appointments has seeped down into the process of filling vacancies on the lower courts as well.

Over the course of American history, there have been twenty-seven failed Supreme Court nominations. In total, 18 percent of the presidential nominations submitted to the Senate for vacancies on the Supreme Court have been withdrawn, voted down, or permanently postponed.[11] Most of those failures occurred in the nineteenth century, and they often occurred when the same party at least nominally held both the White House and the Senate. After a long period of unequaled presidential success, failed nominations have become somewhat more common again in recent decades. Lyndon Johnson, Richard Nixon, Ronald Reagan, and George W. Bush all lost Supreme Court nominees, with Robert Bork's rejection by a Democratic Senate in 1987 being perhaps the most notable.

Perhaps as significant as the reemergence of failed Supreme Court nominations has been the new level of contestation surrounding each vacancy on the Court. Interest groups now routinely mobilize their supporters in the general public and on Capitol Hill whenever a vacancy occurs. The media closely covers the process, and senators are expected to be visible. Potential nominees are carefully scrutinized by the White House both to ensure that they are aligned with the beliefs of the president and to ensure that they do not have any "skeletons in the closet" or an unflattering "paper trail" that might create controversy during the confirmation hearings. Since the 1960s it has become common for even successful Supreme Court nominees to receive a significant number of no votes at their confirmations.[12]

Lower court nominees, especially nominees to the U.S. circuit courts, now get something like the same treatment as Supreme Court nominees. They are carefully vetted by the White House and the Senate. Interest groups mobilize to support or block their nominations. It is now recognized that many important legal decisions are made in the circuit courts, and that the nominees for the circuit courts are both important intellectual and legal figures in their own right and potential future Supreme Court nominees. There are many more ways to block circuit court nominations than Supreme Court nominations, however. Supreme Court nominations are high-profile, and there is a great deal of pressure on senators to move those nominations toward a vote by the full Senate in a timely way. The political battle over lower-court nominations mostly takes place well away from the Senate floor and the public spotlight.

The most effective way to kill a lower-court nomination is to delay it. For most low-profile executive and judicial nominations, opponents of the nomination prefer to obstruct the process and avoid a final vote on confirmation for as long as possible. This might involve a filibuster by a minority of senators to prevent a floor vote on the confirmation. But long before such tactics are necessary it might involve delaying committee hearings through a variety of formal or informal means, or simply delaying the scheduling of a floor vote by the majority party in the Senate. As a result, the time between nomination and successful confirmation of a circuit court judge approached a year during the second half of the Clinton administration and the George W. Bush administration. But, as Figure 11-2 illustrates, successful nominations were hard to come by. Democrats filibustered President George W. Bush's 2001 nomination of Miguel Estrada to the United States Court of Appeals for the District of Columbia, and the nomination was withdrawn in 2003. Minority Republicans filibustered President Barack Obama's 2010 nomination of Goodwin Liu

11. Keith E. Whittington, "Presidents, Senates, and Failed Supreme Court Nominations," *The Supreme Court Review 2006* (2007):401.

12. See Lee Epstein and Jeffrey A. Segal, *Advice and Consent* (New York: Oxford University Press, 2005); Michael J. Gerhardt, *The Federal Appointments Process* (Durham, NC: Duke University Press, 2003).

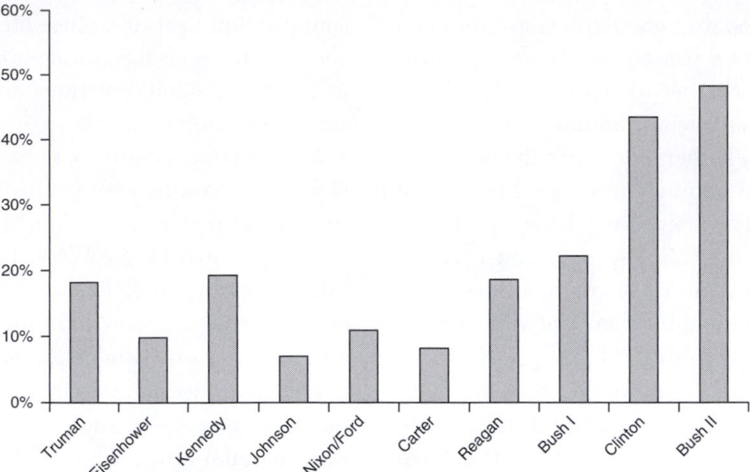

Figure 11-2 Percentage of Federal Circuit Court Nominations Not Confirmed, 1945–2008

Source: Congressional Research Service, *Judicial Nomination Statistics: U.S. District and Circuit Courts, 1945–1976*; Congressional Research Service, *Judicial Nomination Statistics: U.S. District and Circuit Courts, 1977–2003*; American Bar Association, "Article III Judicial Vacancies/Nominations/Confirmations."

to the United States Court of Appeals for the Ninth Circuit, before it was withdrawn in 2011. Both nominees were considered likely future Supreme Court appointments.[13] At stake is the increasing polarization of the political parties and the heightened activist focus on the lower courts. They have led to a near gridlock over circuit court appointments, as each party has sought to aggressively block the nominees of the other.[14]

13. The Estrada and Liu cases were relatively high-profile precisely because they foreshadowed possible battles over Supreme Court nominations. By contrast, a newly created seat on the Fourth Circuit went unfilled for a decade. Republican Senator Jesse Helms of North Carolina favored the appointment of his former aide, District Judge Terrence Boyle, to the vacancy. The Democrats, led by North Carolina Senator John Edwards, blocked a committee vote on Boyle during both Bush administrations. Helms, in turn, blocked a committee vote on any Democratic nominee for the seat during the Clinton administration.

14. See Nancy Scherer, *Scoring Points* (Stanford, CA: Stanford University Press, 2005); Sarah A. Binder and Forrest Maltzman, *Advice & Dissent* (Washington, DC: Brookings, 2009); Roger E. Hartley and Lisa M. Holmes, "The Increasing Senate Scrutiny of Lower Federal Court Nominees," *Political Science Quarterly* 117 (2002):259.

Senate Debate on the "Nuclear Option" (2005)[15]

In George W. Bush's first term as president, the Republican Party held (at most) a slender one-seat majority in the Senate. Given both the circumstances of the contested 2000 presidential election and the increasing polarization of the political parties and judicial nominations of the prior several years, Democrats in the Senate resolved to make the ideological fitness of judicial nominees a consideration in confirmation votes and to use procedural tools to obstruct votes on nominees. Although no Supreme Court vacancies appeared during the first term, this also applied to vacancies on the lower federal courts.

Of particular significance, liberal Democrats were willing to filibuster ideologically objectionable nominees. A "filibuster" is an extended debate by one or more senators on a given subject of Senate business, preventing further action by the Senate on that or other business. In practice, the mere threat of a filibuster is sufficient to prevent an item from coming to the floor, because the modern Senate cannot afford to have its schedule tied up in an extended debate. According to current Senate rules, both legislative bills and nomina-

15. Excerpt taken from *Congressional Record*, 109th Cong. (15 April 2005; 27 April 2005), S3762–64, S4366–68.

tions are subject to filibusters. Debate on any subject can be ended by a successful "cloture" vote, which by current rule requires the support of sixty senators. This means that a minimum of forty senators can maintain a filibuster and prevent a final vote on a piece of legislation or a nomination from taking place.

The cloture rule is itself set by Senate majority and has been changed over time. Until the mid-twentieth century, it was not possible to end debate without the unanimous consent of all the senators. The cloture rule was gradually lowered to the current 60 percent of the senators. At the same time, filibusters became more important as the Senate became busier and the legislative calendar more crowded. The modern Senate could not afford the delay of even a short filibuster, and so even a credible filibuster threat can be enough to block legislation or a nomination. As a result, a modern "filibuster" is less likely to involve someone actually talking on the Senate floor for hours at a time than someone simply announcing that they intend to block a nominee or bill and have enough votes to prevent cloture.

After Bush won reelection in 2004 and Republicans won a larger Senate majority (fifty-five seats), the Democrats continued to filibuster several of the president's judicial nominees, and there was an expectation that they might likewise filibuster a Supreme Court nominee. Senate majority leader Bill Frist responded by proposing the "nuclear option." This would have changed the Senate rule so that a simple majority could invoke cloture on judicial nominations—eliminating the possibility of a minority filibuster of judicial nominees. Although this use of the filibuster may have been new, the filibuster is deeply rooted in Senate tradition. Its elimination would also take a weapon away from the Democrats and future Republicans when they again found themselves in the minority (as they did during the Obama administration). It was uncertain if Frist had the Republican votes to trigger the nuclear option, but it was also uncertain that the liberals could hold forty Democrat votes together against the risk that the elimination of the filibuster might be the response. The stand-off was resolved when a bipartisan group of centrist senators (the "Gang of 14") agreed to abandon both sides. The Democrats would agree to vote for cloture on three of the stalled nominees and the Republicans would agree to vote against the nuclear option. As a result, the filibuster remained an option as the Democrats took over the White House and the Republicans moved into the minority in the Senate. The debate excerpted here is between two members of the Senate Judiciary Committee and staunch members of their respective parties. Should the Senate minority have the ability to filibuster judicial nominees? Should they need the support of at least some members of the majority party in order to sustain a filibuster, or should a portion of the minority party be able to maintain a filibuster on its own?

Senator DURBIN (Democrat, Illinois)...

First, let me say there is one thing that binds every Member of the Senate, Republican or Democrat or Independent.... That oath of office, where we stand solemnly before the Nation, before our colleagues, is an oath where we swear to uphold and defend the Constitution of the United States, this tiny little publication which has guided our Nation and our values for over two centuries.

Though we may disagree on almost everything else, we swear to uphold this document. We swear that at the end of the day we will be loyal to this Constitution of the United States. That, I think, is where this debate should begin, because this Constitution makes it very clear that when it comes to the rules of the Senate, it is the responsibility and authority of the Senate itself to make its rules. I refer specifically to article I, section 5. I quote from the Constitution:

> Each House may determine the rules of its proceedings....

Because of that, most courts take a hands-off attitude. It is their belief that we decide how we conduct business in this Chamber, as the House of Representatives will decide about theirs. That is our constitutional right.

When this Constitution was written, there was a question about whether we could bring together 13 different colonies and they would agree to have one Federal Government.... The Great Compromise said let us resolve this by creating a Senate which will give to every State, large and small, the same number of Senators.... [S]o the Senate would observe the rights of the minority, the smaller populated States, and give them an equal voice on the floor of the Senate.

The Senate rules were written to reflect that unique and peculiar institutional decision. We said within the Senate, following this same value and principle, that our rules would be written so the minority within the Senate would always be respected. We created something called a filibuster, a filibuster which is unique to the Senate but is consistent with the reason for its creation.

...

The reason I tell you this is because at this moment there are those who are planning what I consider to be an assault on the very principles of this Constitution. There are those who wish to change the rules of the Senate and in changing the rules of the Senate, defy tradition, change the rules in the middle of the game, and have a full frontal assault on the unique nature of this institution. That, I think, is an abuse of power. I think it goes way too far. It ignores our Founding Fathers. This nuclear option ignores the Constitution. It ignores the rules of the Senate. For what? So the President of the United States can have every single judicial nominee approved by the Senate.

What is the scorecard? How has President Bush done in sending judicial nominees to the Senate? I can tell you the score as of this moment. Since he was elected President, he has had 215 nominees on the floor for a vote in the Senate and 205 have been approved. That is 205 to 10; over 95 percent of President Bush's judicial nominees have come to the floor and been approved. Only 10 have not been approved. They have been subject to a filibuster, part of the Senate rules.

But this White House and majority party in the Senate have decided 95 percent is not enough. They want it all. They want every nominee. Sadly, they are about to assault this Constitution and the rules of the Senate to try to achieve that goal.

This so-called nuclear option is a power grab. It is an attempt to change the rules of the Senate. It is an assault on the principle and value of checks and balances. It is an attempt by the majority party in the Senate to ram through nominees who will not pledge to protect the most important rights of the American people. It is an attempt to say we cannot demand of the President's nominees that each person be balanced and moderate and committed to the goals of ordinary Americans....

This is not the first President in history who has decided in his second term to take on the courts of our country, to say he wanted to put into that court system men and women who agreed with him politically at any cost. The first was one of our greatest Americans, Thomas Jefferson. Full of victory in his second term, he decided to attempt to impeach a Supreme Court Justice who disagreed with him politically, to show he had the political power, having just been re-elected. His efforts were rejected. They were rejected by his own party, his own party in the Senate, who said: Mr. President, we may be part of your party, but we disagree with this power grab.

We are going to protect the constitutional rights and power of our institution of the Senate.

More recently, President Franklin Delano Roosevelt—one of the greatest in our history—as his second term began, became so frustrated by a Supreme Court that would not agree with him, that he sent to the Senate a proposal to change the composition of the Court to make certain that we filled the bench across the street in the Supreme Court with people who were sympathetic to his political agenda. He sent that legislative proposal to a Congress dominated by his political party, by his Democratic Party. What was their response? They rejected it. They said we stood by you in the election, we will stand by your policies, but we will not allow you to abuse this Constitution. We will not allow you to change the rules so you can have more power over our judges. That was the principle at issue. Frankly, Roosevelt lost the debate when men and women of his own party stood up and opposed him in the Congress.

...

Here we go, again. For the third time in our Nation's history, a President, as he begins his second term, is attempting to change the rules of the Senate to defy the Constitution and to give the Office of the President more power to push through judges, to defy the checks and balances in our Constitution.

...

Senator HATCH (Republican, Utah)...

All we are asking is that the 214-year tradition of the Senate that judicial nominees not be filibustered be followed. That has been the tradition of the Senate up until President Bush became President. All we are asking is that every one of these qualified nominees who have reached the floor receive an up-or-down vote. That is all we are asking.

These are highly qualified nominees. The ABA has ruled they are qualified in every case. They all have a majority bipartisan vote in their favor. If our colleagues on the other side do not want to vote for them, they can vote against them. That will be their right....

The actions of our colleagues on the other side amount to changing that 214-year traditional history of this Senate.

By the way, we never called this the nuclear option. It was called the nuclear option by the Democrats. We called it the constitutional option because the

Constitution says the President has the right to appoint and nominate these people for judicial positions. We have the right to advise and—it is sometimes left off in this body—consent, which means a vote up and down.

. . .

This principle has constitutional roots, historical precedent, and citizen support. I begin with the Constitution because that is where we should always begin. . . .

. . .

Giving judicial nominations reaching the floor an up-or-down vote, that is, exercising our role of advice and consent through voting on nominations, helps us resist the temptation of turning our check on the President's power into a force that can destroy the President's power and upset the Constitution's balance.

Historically, we have followed this standard of everybody who reaches the floor getting an up-or-down vote. When Republicans ran the Senate under President Clinton, we gave each of his judicial nominations reaching the floor a final confirmation decision, an up-or-down vote. We took cloture votes, that is, votes to end debate, on four of the hundreds of nominees reaching us here. All four were confirmed. As a matter of fact, we confirmed 377 judges nominated by President Clinton, almost the same number as the all-time confirmation champion and that was Ronald Reagan, who got 382. But Ronald Reagan had 6 years of a Republican Senate to help him. President Clinton only had 2 years of a Democrat Senate to help him. Yet, with the aid of Republicans on the Judiciary Committee and in this body, he got 377 approved.

In fact, even on the most controversial appeals courts nominations by President Clinton, the Republican leadership used cloture votes to prevent filibusters and ensure up-or-down votes, exactly the opposite of how cloture votes are being used during President Bush's Presidency.

. . .

The purveyors of this fantasy would have us look to President Franklin Delano Roosevelt who, they tell us, wanted to pack the Supreme Court. The Senate rejected his legislative proposal to expand the Court so he could appoint more Justices. By taking this stand, the storytellers say, the Senate kept one-party rule from packing the Court.

Well, as Paul Harvey might say: Here is the rest of the story.

The Senate, even though dominated by President Roosevelt's own party, did not support this legislative plan. And it turns out President Roosevelt did not need any legislative innovations to pack the Supreme Court. He packed it all right, doing it the old-fashioned way, by appointing eight out of nine justices in 6 years. Mind you, during the 75th to the 77th Congress, Democrats outnumbered Republicans by an average of 70 to 20. Now, that is one-party rule.

In those years, from 1937 to 1943, our cloture rule applied only to bills. This meant that ending debate on other things, such as nominations, required unanimous consent. A single Senator in that tiny, beleaguered minority could conduct a filibuster of President Roosevelt's nominations and thwart the real court packing that was in full swing.

Now, if the filibuster were the only thing preventing one-party rule from packing the courts, and the filibuster were so easily used, surely there must be in history filibusters of President Roosevelt's Supreme Court nominations. If the warnings, frantic pleas, and hysterical fundraising appeals we hear today make any sense at all, the filibuster would certainly have been used in FDR's time.

I hate to burst anyone's bubble, but there were no filibusters, not even by a single Senator, not against a single nominee. . . .

Last week, here on the Senate floor, the distinguished Senator from Illinois repeated a selective version of this FDR story and asked what would happen today in a Senate dominated by the President's party. He asked:

> Will they rise in the tradition of Franklin Roosevelt's Senate?

Well, I hope we do. I hope the Senate does exactly what Franklin Roosevelt's Senate did, by debating and voting on the President's judicial nominations. Franklin Roosevelt's Senate did not use the filibuster, even when the minority was much smaller and the filibuster much easier to use, and this Senate should not do so, either.

. . .

III. Powers of the National Government

MAJOR DEVELOPMENTS

- Assertion of new limits to the scope of Congress's power under the commerce
- Heightened restriction on congressional power to enforce rights

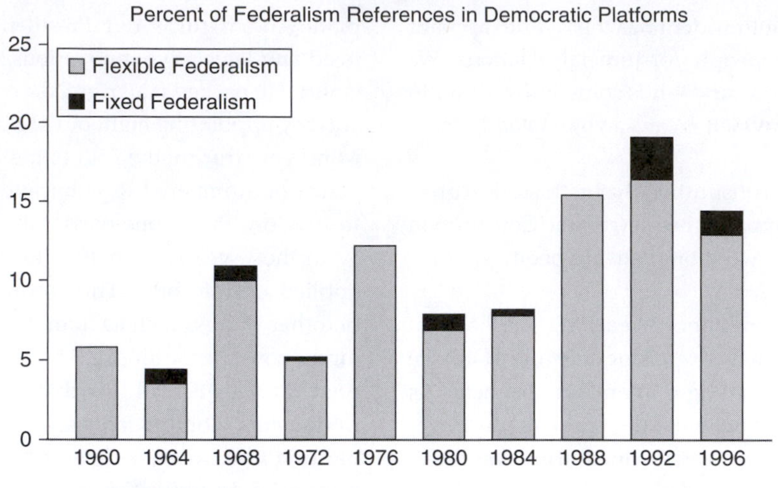

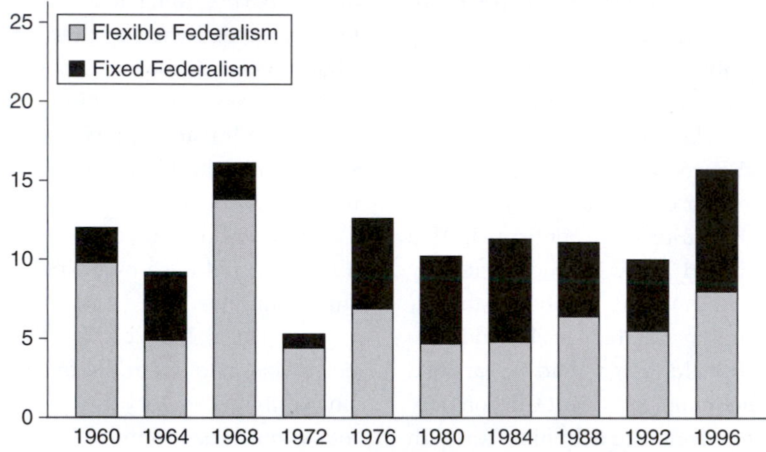

Figure 11-3 Federalism References in Party Platforms, 1960–1996

Source: Cornell W. Clayton and J. Mitchell Pickerill, "Guess What Happened on the Way to Revolution? Precursors to the Supreme Court's Federalism Revolution," *Publius* 34:3 (2004):85. Copyright © 2004, Oxford University Press

The New Deal and World War II had effectively put an end to one set of long-standing debates in American constitutionalism over the scope of national powers. The federal government that emerged from the 1940s was much larger in its scope of activities, share of government revenues, claim on economic resources, and authority to regulate and direct economic activity than what the United States had known previously in its history. The cry of "states' rights" had briefly been a rallying point in the 1950s and early 1960s, but those debates focused mostly on federal authority over racial civil rights.

Conservatives in the Reagan Era sought to reopen the debate over federalism and constitutional powers of the national government. Borrowing themes from Barry Goldwater's 1964 presidential campaign, among other places, conservatives in the 1980s often linked libertarian criticisms of "big government" with a call for greater respect for the limits on national power and for decentralization of power down to states and localities. As Figure 11-3 indicates, Democratic and Republican party platforms diverged in this period. Republicans began to talk more and more about federalism. They often focused on constitutional limitations on national power rather than, for example, the system of federal grants to states and cities. Where Republicans talked about constitutional limits on national power, Democrats called for more effective government and pragmatic solutions to state and local problems. At the extreme, these Republican arguments might mean calling into question the legitimacy of the New Deal itself. There were plenty of more immediate targets, however, such as the creation of the Department of Education during the Carter administration, which conservatives denounced as illegitimate.

Conservatives expected the courts to be a critical battleground on the limits of national power. Starting in the 1980s, lawyers in the Justice Department, in conservative interest groups, and in state governments began to map out strategies for testing those constitutional limits in court. The Reagan administration looked for judicial nominees who shared the president's interest in federalism. Associate Justice William Rehnquist had been a long-time advocate of restricting national power and was elevated to the position of Chief Justice in 1986. Sandra Day O'Connor, Reagan's first choice for the Supreme Court in 1981, was another westerner deeply interested in the issue. When President George H. W. Bush added Clarence Thomas to the bench in 1991, the conservatives for the first time had a slim majority willing to reconsider the scope of national power. At about the same time, Republicans took over the House of Representatives for the first time in decades, and gave brief, but vocal, support for reinvigorating federalism constraints.

The result was a wide-ranging burst of decisions on the U.S. Supreme Court in the late 1990s striking down a variety of provisions of federal statutes and developing several new doctrines limiting congressional power. The pace of these decisions dramatically slowed in the 2000s. It remains unclear the extent to which Chief Justice John Roberts (who replaced Rehnquist) and Justice Samuel Alito (who replaced O'Connor) share an interest in these earlier federalism decisions, despite their generally conservative constitutional philosophy. The Supreme Court developed new doctrine on the commerce clause, state sovereign immunity, the power of the federal government to "commandeer" state government officials, and congressional authority under Section Five of the Fourteenth Amendment to define the rights of individuals vis-à-vis the state governments. Conservatives also pressed for courts to adopt other structural reforms, reining in the congressional spending power and its delegation of lawmaking authority, but with less success.

Republican Party activists have revived calls for a more limited federal government. In 2009 a conservative journalist asked Democratic House Speaker Nancy Pelosi where the Constitution authorized Congress to pass mandatory health care. She replied "Are you serious?" Her press secretary followed up by emphasizing, "That is not a serious question."[16] After Republicans retook control of the House of Representatives in the midterm elections of 2010, they read the text of the Constitution on the floor of the chamber in order to emphasize the limits on federal power. The limitations on the national government have been a common theme of Tea Party manifestos. The Tea Party-backed "Contract from America" from the 2010 campaign included several provisions that touched on federalism themes. The Contract argued, "The purpose of our government is to exercise only those limited powers that have been relinquished to it by the people, chief among these being the protection of our liberties by administering justice and ensuring our safety from threats arising inside or outside our country's sovereign borders." To that end, it pledged that "each bill [be required] to identify the specific provision of the Constitution that gives Congress the power to do what the bill does" and "create a Blue Ribbon taskforce that engages in a complete audit of federal agencies and programs, assessing their Constitutionality, and identifying duplication, waste, ineffectiveness, and agencies and programs better left for the states or local authorities, or ripe for wholesale reform or elimination due to our efforts to restore limited government consistent with the US Constitution's meaning."[17]

In a brief in one of the cases seeking to overturn Obama's health care law, Georgetown law professor Randy Barnett contended,

> The mandate's command to uninsured individuals who are engaging in *no commercial activity* cannot be justified as permissible Commerce Clause regulation. Compelling the uninsured to participate in the commerce of health insurance does not regulate that commerce. Likewise, the status of being uninsured is not a class of economic activities that may be regulated due to its "substantial effect" on commerce. Any argument that the uninsured "affect" the insurance market through their *non-participation*

16. Matt Cover, "When Asked Where the Constitution Authorizes Congress to Order Americans to Buy Health Insurance, Pelosi Says: 'Are You Serious?'" October 22, 2009 (http://www.cnsnews.com/node/55971, last accessed May 23, 2011).

17. The Contract From America (http://www.thecontract.org/the-contract-from-america/).

> is foreclosed by precedent and would eliminate all limits on Congressional power.[18]

By contrast, Yale law professor Jack Balkin has defended the individual mandate provisions of the health care law as well-grounded in post–New Deal constitutional doctrine.

> Congress may regulate economic activity that has a cumulative and substantial effect on interstate commerce. *See Wickard v. Filburn* (1942).... Congress may also regulate local behavior when doing so is "an essential part of a larger regulation of economic activity, in which the regulatory scheme could be undercut unless the intrastate activity were regulated." *Gonzales v. Raich* (2005). Indeed, as Justice Scalia has explained, "Congress may regulate even *noneconomic local activity* if that regulation is a necessary part of a more general regulation of interstate commerce." *Gonzales v. Raich*, 545 U.S. at 37 (Scalia, J., concurring in the judgment) (emphasis added).[19]

New debates over the budget and federal regulation have once again encouraged debates over the proper scope of federal power. How serious those debates might be for policymaking remains to be seen.

This section shows the U.S. Supreme Court once again grappling with the scope of the commerce clause. For the first time since the New Deal, the Court struck down a federal statute for violating the commerce clause in *United States v. Lopez* (1995). Subsequent cases like *United States v. Morrison* (2000) and *Gonzales v. Raich* (2005) helped clarify whether *Lopez* would be the beginning of a dramatic new challenge to federal policymaking or a relatively modest warning to Congress about the need to respect federalism principles. *United States v. Morrison* was also a central case in examining the boundaries of congressional authority to regulate the states under Section 5 of the Fourteenth Amendment. What laws were "appropriate" to enforcing the terms of the Fourteenth Amendment, what rights did the Fourteenth Amendment protect, and who should determine the answers to those questions?

A. Power to Regulate Commerce

After the New Deal cases of the late 1930s and 1940s, the national power to regulate interstate commerce had largely been taken as a settled issue. Congress was understood to have expansive regulatory power under the interstate commerce clause, and the courts were unlikely to question federal authority to regulate activity that occurred within the states.

The commerce power became more interesting when the Supreme Court struck down the federal Gun-Free School Zones Act in *United States v. Lopez* (1995). In this case, the Court reinvigorated the commerce clause as an active restriction on congressional power, emphasizing that Congress could not criminalize mere possession of a firearm which did not have any connection to a commercial transaction or economic activity that in the aggregate could substantially affect interstate commerce.

The immediate effect of striking down the Gun-Free School Zones Act was fairly modest, but what remained uncertain was how many other statutes might be affected by a more restrictive reading of the commerce clause. The narrow 5–4 majority that Chief Justice Rehnquist put together in *Lopez* seemed to reach its limit fairly quickly when it considered the conflict between federal drug regulation and California's acceptance of medical marijuana. In *Gonzales v. Raich* (2005), the Court upheld federal regulations against a commerce clause challenge. Despite *Lopez*, the *Raich* Court concluded that Congress could criminalize mere possession of marijuana within state lines on the grounds that this was necessary as part of a successful national regulatory framework. Commerce clause restrictions on congressional power were on the constitutional agenda in the Contemporary Era, but their ultimate significance remains in doubt.

United States v. Lopez, 514 U.S. 549 (1995)

From 1937 until 1995, the Supreme Court announced no limits on the federal power to regulate interstate commerce. Every claimed exercise of the national commerce power was sustained. This sixty-year trend was broken in 1995 when the justices in United States v. Lopez *declared that Congress had no power to pass the Gun-Free School Zones Act of 1990. The crucial question is whether* Lopez *(and* United States v. Morrison, *noted later) signal a serious effort to*

18. Brief for the Private Plaintiffs-Appellees National Federation of Independent Business, *Florida v. U.S. Department of Health and Human Services, U.S. Court of Appeals for the Eleventh Circuit* (2011), 31.

19. Jack M. Balkin, "The Constitutionality of an Individual Mandate for Health Insurance," *PENNumbra* 158 (2009):106.

declare sharp limitations on federal power or are mere prunings of largely symbolic statutes.

The Gun-Free Schools Zones Act (GFSZA) was passed as part of a broader crime bill in 1990, when the Democrats controlled Congress and Republican George H. W. Bush was in the White House. For the Democrats in Congress, the GFSZA was seen as a modest gun control measure that simply modified the already popular idea of "drug-free school zones." For federal politicians, it allowed them to claim credit for "doing something" about school violence, even though state and local laws already covered much of the same ground as the GFSZA, without the controversy that normally accompanied gun control legislation. No objections—constitutional or otherwise—were raised to the bill in Congress. When twelfth-grader Alfonso Lopez faced federal charges under the GFSZA for carrying a handgun to his San Antonio, Texas, high school, his lawyers argued that Congress did not have the constitutional authority to pass the statute. The district court upheld the law under the commerce clause, and Lopez was convicted and sentenced to six months in prison and two years' supervised release. In a unanimous holding, however, a Fifth Circuit opinion written by a Reagan appointee, but joined by two Carter appointees, struck down the GFSZA as exceeding Congress's power under the commerce clause and marking with no explanation a federal encroachment into the traditional state arena of education. The majority of the justices on the Supreme Court agreed. Lopez *had no effect on the state and local laws regulating guns in schools. Congress responded to the lower court decision by passing the Gun Free Schools Act of 1994, which required schools receiving federal funds to adopt a variety of policies to penalize those found with a gun on school grounds. Congress responded to the Supreme Court decision by passing the Gun Free School Zones Act of 1996, which added a requirement that federal charges could be filed only when the gun had previously moved through interstate commerce.*

Lopez *was notable not only for its powerful symbolism of striking down a federal law on interstate commerce clause grounds but also for locking into place the five-justice majority of Rehnquist, O'Connor, Scalia, Kennedy, and Thomas that would become familiar in numerous federalism cases over the next several years of the Rehnquist Court (most of which did not involve the commerce clause).*

As you read the case, consider the differences between the majority opinion by Chief Justice Rehnquist and the concurring opinion by Justice Thomas. Does Rehnquist work within or significantly challenge the New Deal settlement? In what ways might the Gun-Free School Zones Act be understood to be working at the margins of the New Deal settlement? In what ways might it be understood to be well within the bounds of that settlement?

CHIEF JUSTICE REHNQUIST delivered the opinion of the Court.

In the Gun-Free School Zones Act of 1990, Congress made it a federal offense "for any individual knowingly to possess a firearm at a place that the individual knows, or has reasonable cause to believe, is a school zone." . . . The Act neither regulates a commercial activity nor contains a requirement that the possession be connected in any way to interstate commerce. We hold that the Act exceeds the authority of Congress "to regulate Commerce . . . among the several States. . . ."

. . .

We start with first principles. The Constitution creates a Federal Government of enumerated powers. . . . As James Madison wrote, "the powers delegated by the proposed Constitution to the federal government are few and defined. Those which are to remain in the State governments are numerous and indefinite." . . .

The Constitution delegates to Congress the power "to regulate Commerce with foreign Nations, and among the several States, and with the Indian Tribes." . . . The Court, through Chief Justice Marshall, first defined the nature of Congress' commerce power in *Gibbons* v. *Ogden* (1824):

> Commerce, undoubtedly, is traffic, but it is something more: it is intercourse. It describes the commercial intercourse between nations, and parts of nations, in all its branches, and is regulated by prescribing rules for carrying on that intercourse.

The *Gibbons* Court, however, acknowledged that limitations on the commerce power are inherent in the very language of the Commerce Clause.

> It is not intended to say that these words comprehend that commerce, which is completely internal, which is carried on between man and man in a State, or between different parts of the same State, and which does not extend to or affect other States. Such a power would be inconvenient, and is certainly unnecessary.
>
> Comprehensive as the word "among" is, it may very properly be restricted to that commerce which concerns more States than one. . . . The enumeration

presupposes something not enumerated; and that something, if we regard the language, or the subject of the sentence, must be the exclusively internal commerce of a State....

For nearly a century thereafter, the Court's Commerce Clause decisions dealt but rarely with the extent of Congress' power, and almost entirely with the Commerce Clause as a limit on state legislation that discriminated against interstate commerce.... Under this line of precedent, the Court held that certain categories of activity such as "production," "manufacturing," and "mining" were within the province of state governments, and thus were beyond the power of Congress under the Commerce Clause....

...

Jones & Laughlin Steel (1937), *Darby* (1941), and *Wickard* (1942) ushered in an era of Commerce Clause jurisprudence that greatly expanded the previously defined authority of Congress under that Clause. In part, this was a recognition of the great changes that had occurred in the way business was carried on in this country. Enterprises that had once been local or at most regional in nature had become national in scope. But the doctrinal change also reflected a view that earlier Commerce Clause cases artificially had constrained the authority of Congress to regulate interstate commerce.

But even these modern-era precedents which have expanded congressional power under the Commerce Clause confirm that this power is subject to outer limits. In *Jones & Laughlin Steel*, the Court warned that the scope of the interstate commerce power "must be considered in the light of our dual system of government and may not be extended so as to embrace effects upon interstate commerce so indirect and remote that to embrace them, in view of our complex society, would effectually obliterate the distinction between what is national and what is local and create a completely centralized government."... Since that time, the Court has heeded that warning and undertaken to decide whether a rational basis existed for concluding that a regulated activity sufficiently affected interstate commerce....

...

Consistent with this structure, we have identified three broad categories of activity that Congress may regulate under its commerce power.... First, Congress may regulate the use of the channels of interstate commerce.... Second, Congress is empowered to regulate and protect the instrumentalities of interstate commerce, or persons or things in interstate commerce, even though the threat may come only from intrastate activities.... Finally, Congress' commerce authority includes the power to regulate those activities having a substantial relation to interstate commerce... *i. e.*, those activities that substantially affect interstate commerce....

...

First, we have upheld a wide variety of congressional Acts regulating intrastate economic activity where we have concluded that the activity substantially affected interstate commerce....

Even *Wickard*, which is perhaps the most far reaching example of Commerce Clause authority over intrastate activity, involved economic activity in a way that the possession of a gun in a school zone does not.... The Court said, in an opinion sustaining the application of the Act to Filburn's activity:

> One of the primary purposes of the Act in question was to increase the market price of wheat and to that end to limit the volume thereof that could affect the market. It can hardly be denied that a factor of such volume and variability as home-consumed wheat would have a substantial influence on price and market conditions. This may arise because being in marketable condition such wheat overhangs the market and, if induced by rising prices, tends to flow into the market and check price increases. But if we assume that it is never marketed, it supplies a need of the man who grew it which would otherwise be reflected by purchases in the open market. Home-grown wheat in this sense competes with wheat in commerce....

Section 922(q) [the GFSZA] is a criminal statute that by its terms has nothing to do with "commerce" or any sort of economic enterprise, however broadly one might define those terms. Section 922(q) is not an essential part of a larger regulation of economic activity, in which the regulatory scheme could be undercut unless the intrastate activity were regulated. It cannot, therefore, be sustained under our cases upholding regulations of activities that arise out of or are connected with a commercial transaction, which viewed in the aggregate, substantially affects interstate commerce.

Second, § 922(q) contains no jurisdictional element which would ensure, through case-by-case inquiry, that the firearm possession in question affects interstate commerce. . . . § 922(q) has no express jurisdictional element which might limit its reach to a discrete set of firearm possessions that additionally have an explicit connection with or effect on interstate commerce.

. . .

The Government's essential contention . . . is that we may determine here that § 922(q) is valid because possession of a firearm in a local school zone does indeed substantially affect interstate commerce. . . . The Government argues that possession of a firearm in a school zone may result in violent crime and that violent crime can be expected to affect the functioning of the national economy in two ways. First, the costs of violent crime are substantial, and, through the mechanism of insurance, those costs are spread throughout the population. . . . Second, violent crime reduces the willingness of individuals to travel to areas within the country that are perceived to be unsafe. . . . The Government also argues that the presence of guns in schools poses a substantial threat to the educational process by threatening the learning environment. A handicapped educational process, in turn, will result in a less productive citizenry. That, in turn, would have an adverse effect on the Nation's economic well-being. As a result, the Government argues that Congress could rationally have concluded that § 922(q) substantially affects interstate commerce.

We pause to consider the implications of the Government's arguments. The Government admits, under its "costs of crime" reasoning, that Congress could regulate not only all violent crime, but all activities that might lead to violent crime, regardless of how tenuously they relate to interstate commerce. . . . Similarly, under the Government's "national productivity" reasoning, Congress could regulate any activity that it found was related to the economic productivity of individual citizens: family law (including marriage, divorce, and child custody), for example. Under the theories that the Government presents in support of § 922(q), it is difficult to perceive any limitation on federal power, even in areas such as criminal law enforcement or education where States historically have been sovereign. Thus, if we were to accept the Government's arguments, we are hard pressed to posit any activity by an individual that Congress is without power to regulate.

Although JUSTICE BREYER argues that acceptance of the Government's rationales would not authorize a general federal police power, he is unable to identify any activity that the States may regulate but Congress may not. . . .

. . .

[I]f Congress can, pursuant to its Commerce Clause power, regulate activities that adversely affect the learning environment, then . . . it also can regulate the educational process directly. Congress could determine that a school's curriculum has a "significant" effect on the extent of classroom learning. As a result, Congress could mandate a federal curriculum for local elementary and secondary schools because what is taught in local schools has a significant "effect on classroom learning," . . . and that, in turn, has a substantial effect on interstate commerce.

[A] determination whether an intrastate activity is commercial or noncommercial may in some cases result in legal uncertainty. But, so long as Congress' authority is limited to those powers enumerated in the Constitution, and so long as those enumerated powers are interpreted as having judicially enforceable outer limits, congressional legislation under the Commerce Clause always will engender "legal uncertainty." . . . The Constitution mandates this uncertainty by withholding from Congress a plenary police power that would authorize enactment of every type of legislation. . . . Any possible benefit from eliminating this "legal uncertainty" would be at the expense of the Constitution's system of enumerated powers.

. . .

. . . The possession of a gun in a local school zone is in no sense an economic activity that might, through repetition elsewhere, substantially affect any sort of interstate commerce. Respondent was a local student at a local school; there is no indication that he had recently moved in interstate commerce, and there is no requirement that his possession of the firearm have any concrete tie to interstate commerce.

To uphold the Government's contentions here, we would have to pile inference upon inference in a manner that would bid fair to convert congressional authority under the Commerce Clause to a general police power of the sort retained by the States. Admittedly, some of our prior cases have taken long steps down that road, giving great deference to congressional action. The broad language in these opinions has suggested the possibility of additional expansion, but we decline here to proceed any further. To do so would require us to conclude that the Constitution's enumeration of powers does not presuppose something not enumerated, . . . and that there never will be a distinction between what is truly national and what is truly local. This we are unwilling to do.

JUSTICE KENNEDY, with whom JUSTICE O'CONNOR joins, concurring.

The history of the judicial struggle to interpret the Commerce Clause during the transition from the economic system the Founders knew to the single, national market still emergent in our own era counsels great restraint before the Court determines that the Clause is insufficient to support an exercise of the national power. That history gives me some pause about today's decision, but I join the Court's opinion with these observations on what I conceive to be its necessary though limited holding.

. . .

The history of our Commerce Clause decisions contains at least two lessons of relevance to this case. The first, as stated at the outset, is the imprecision of content-based boundaries used without more to define the limits of the Commerce Clause. The second, related to the first but of even greater consequence, is that the Court as an institution and the legal system as a whole have an immense stake in the stability of our Commerce Clause jurisprudence as it has evolved to this point. *Stare decisis* operates with great force in counseling us not to call in question the essential principles now in place respecting the congressional power to regulate transactions of a commercial nature. That fundamental restraint on our power forecloses us from reverting to an understanding of commerce that would serve only an 18th-century economy, dependent then upon production and trading practices that had changed but little over the preceding centuries; it also mandates against returning to the time when congressional authority to regulate undoubted commercial activities was limited by a judicial determination that those matters had an insufficient connection to an interstate system. Congress can regulate in the commercial sphere on the assumption that we have a single market and a unified purpose to build a stable national economy.

. . .

The statute before us upsets the federal balance to a degree that renders it an unconstitutional assertion of the commerce power, and our intervention is required. . . .

. . .

The statute now before us forecloses the States from experimenting and exercising their own judgment in an area to which States lay claim by right of history and expertise, and it does so by regulating an activity beyond the realm of commerce in the ordinary and usual sense of that term. The tendency of this statute to displace state regulation in areas of traditional state concern is evident from its territorial operation. There are over 100,000 elementary and secondary schools in the United States. . . . Each of these now has an invisible federal zone extending 1,000 feet beyond the (often irregular) boundaries of the school property. In some communities no doubt it would be difficult to navigate without infringing on those zones. Yet throughout these areas, school officials would find their own programs for the prohibition of guns in danger of displacement by the federal authority unless the State chooses to enact a parallel rule.

JUSTICE THOMAS, concurring.

The Court today properly concludes that the Commerce Clause does not grant Congress the authority to prohibit gun possession within 1,000 feet of a school. . . . Although I join the majority, I write separately to observe that our case law has drifted far from the original understanding of the Commerce Clause. In a future case, we ought to temper our Commerce Clause jurisprudence in a manner that both makes sense of our more recent case law and is more faithful to the original understanding of that Clause.

We have said that Congress may regulate not only "Commerce . . . among the several States," . . . but also anything that has a "substantial effect" on such commerce. This test, if taken to its logical extreme, would give Congress a "police power" over all aspects of American life. Unfortunately, we have never come to grips with this implication of our substantial effects formula. Although we have supposedly applied the substantial effects test for the past 60 years, we *always* have rejected readings of the Commerce Clause and the scope of federal power that would permit Congress to exercise a police power; our cases are quite clear that there are real limits to federal power. *New York v. United States* (1992); *Maryland v. Wirtz* (1968). . . .

While the principal dissent concedes that there are limits to federal power, the sweeping nature of our current test enables the dissent to argue that Congress can regulate gun possession. But it seems to me that the power to regulate "commerce" can by no means encompass authority over mere gun possession, any more than it empowers the Federal Government to regulate marriage, littering, or cruelty to animals, throughout the 50 States. Our Constitution quite properly leaves such matters to the individual States, notwithstanding these activities' effects on interstate commerce. Any interpretation of the Commerce Clause that even suggests that Congress could regulate such matters is in need of reexamination.

...

At the time the original Constitution was ratified, "commerce" consisted of selling, buying, and bartering, as well as transporting for these purposes....

As one would expect, the term "commerce" was used in contradistinction to productive activities such as manufacturing and agriculture. Alexander Hamilton, for example, repeatedly treated commerce, agriculture, and manufacturing as three separate endeavors....

Moreover, interjecting a modern sense of commerce into the Constitution generates significant textual and structural problems. For example, one cannot replace "commerce" with a different type of enterprise, such as manufacturing. When a manufacturer produces a car, assembly cannot take place "with a foreign nation" or "with the Indian Tribes." Parts may come from different States or other nations and hence may have been in the flow of commerce at one time, but manufacturing takes place at a discrete site. Agriculture and manufacturing involve the production of goods; commerce encompasses traffic in such articles.

...

In addition to its powers under the Commerce Clause, Congress has the authority to enact such laws as are "necessary and proper" to carry into execution its power to regulate commerce among the several States.... But on this Court's understanding of congressional power under these two Clauses, many of Congress' other enumerated powers under Art. I, § 8, are wholly superfluous. After all, if Congress may regulate all matters that substantially affect commerce, there is no need for the Constitution to specify that Congress may enact bankruptcy laws,... or coin money and fix the standard of weights and measures,... or punish counterfeiters of United States coin and securities, clause 6....

...[I]f a "substantial effects" test can be appended to the Commerce Clause, why not to every other power of the Federal Government? There is no reason for singling out the Commerce Clause for special treatment. Accordingly, Congress could regulate all matters that "substantially affect" the Army and Navy, bankruptcies, tax collection, expenditures, and so on. In that case, the Clauses of § 8 all mutually overlap, something we can assume the Founding Fathers never intended.

Our construction of the scope of congressional authority has the additional problem of coming close to turning the Tenth Amendment on its head. Our case law could be read to reserve to the United States all powers not expressly *prohibited* by the Constitution. Taken together, these fundamental textual problems should, at the very least, convince us that the "substantial effects" test should be reexamined.

...

From the time of the ratification of the Constitution to the mid-1930's, it was widely understood that the Constitution granted Congress only limited powers, notwithstanding the Commerce Clause.... Moreover, there was no question that activities wholly separated from business, such as gun possession, were beyond the reach of the commerce power. If anything, the "wrong turn" was the Court's dramatic departure in the 1930's from a century and a half of precedent.

...

This extended discussion of the original understanding and our first century and a half of case law does not necessarily require a wholesale abandonment of our more recent opinions. It simply reveals that our substantial effects test is far removed from both the Constitution and from our early case law and that the Court's opinion should not be viewed as "radical" or another "wrong turn" that must be corrected in the future. The analysis also suggests that we ought to temper our Commerce Clause jurisprudence.

JUSTICE STEVENS, dissenting.

...

Guns are both articles of commerce and articles that can be used to restrain commerce. Their possession is the consequence, either directly or indirectly, of commercial activity. In my judgment, Congress' power to regulate commerce in firearms includes the power to prohibit possession of guns at any location because of their potentially harmful use; it necessarily follows that Congress may also prohibit their possession in particular markets. The market for the possession of handguns by school-age children is, distressingly, substantial. Whether or not the national interest in eliminating that market would have justified federal legislation in 1789, it surely does today.

JUSTICE SOUTER, dissenting.

In reviewing congressional legislation under the Commerce Clause, we defer to what is often a merely implicit congressional judgment that its regulation addresses a subject substantially affecting interstate commerce "if there is any rational basis for such a finding." ...

The practice of deferring to rationally based legislative judgments "is a paradigm of judicial restraint." ... In judicial review under the Commerce Clause, it reflects our respect for the institutional competence of the Congress on a subject expressly assigned to it by the Constitution and our appreciation of the legitimacy that comes from Congress's political accountability in dealing with matters open to a wide range of possible choices.

...

There is today, however, a backward glance at ... the old pitfalls, as the Court treats deference under the rationality rule as subject to gradation according to the commercial or noncommercial nature of the immediate subject of the challenged regulation. ... The distinction between what is patently commercial and what is not looks much like the old distinction between what directly affects commerce and what touches it only indirectly. ... Thus, it seems fair to ask whether the step taken by the Court today does anything but portend a return to the untenable jurisprudence from which the Court extricated itself almost 60 years ago. The answer is not reassuring. To be sure, the occasion for today's decision reflects the century's end, not its beginning. But if it seems anomalous that the Congress of the United States has taken to regulating school yards, the Act in question is still probably no more remarkable than state regulation of bake shops 90 years ago. In any event, there is no reason to hope that the Court's qualification of rational basis review will be any more successful than the efforts at substantive economic review made by our predecessors as the century began ...

...

JUSTICE BREYER, with whom JUSTICE STEVENS, JUSTICE SOUTER, and JUSTICE GINSBURG join, dissenting.

... In my view, the statute falls well within the scope of the commerce power as this Court has understood that power over the last half century.

In reaching this conclusion, I apply three basic principles of Commerce Clause interpretation. First, the power to "regulate Commerce ... among the several States" ... "encompasses the power to regulate local activities insofar as they significantly affect interstate commerce. ..."

Second, in determining whether a local activity will likely have a significant effect upon interstate commerce, a court must consider, not the effect of an individual act (a single instance of gun possession), but rather the cumulative effect of all similar instances (*i.e.*, the effect of all guns possessed in or near schools). ...

Third, the Constitution requires us to judge the connection between a regulated activity and interstate commerce, not directly, but at one remove. Courts must give Congress a degree of leeway in determining the existence of a significant factual connection between the regulated activity and interstate commerce—both because the Constitution delegates the commerce power directly to Congress and because the determination requires an empirical judgment of a kind that a legislature is more likely than a court to make with accuracy. The traditional words "rational basis" capture this leeway.

...

Applying these principles to the case at hand, we must ask whether Congress could have had a *rational basis* for finding a significant (or substantial) connection between gun-related school violence and interstate commerce. ... As long as one views the commerce connection, not as a "technical legal conception," but as "a practical one," the answer to this question must be yes. Numerous reports and studies—generated both inside and outside government—make clear that Congress could reasonably have found the empirical connection that its law, implicitly or explicitly, asserts. ...

To hold this statute constitutional is not to "obliterate" the "distinction between what is national and what is local," ... nor is it to hold that the Commerce Clause permits the Federal Government to "regulate any activity that it found was related to the economic productivity of individual citizens," to regulate "marriage, divorce, and child custody," or to regulate any and all aspects of education. ... First, this statute is aimed at curbing a particularly acute threat to the educational process—the possession (and use) of life-threatening firearms in, or near, the classroom. ... Second, the immediacy of the connection between education and the national economic well-being is documented by scholars and accepted by society at large in a way and to a degree that may not hold true for other social institutions....

In sum, a holding that the particular statute before us falls within the commerce power would not expand the scope of that Clause. Rather, it simply would apply pre-existing law to changing economic circumstances.

The majority's holding...creates three serious legal problems. First, the majority's holding runs contrary to modern Supreme Court cases that have upheld congressional actions despite connections to interstate or foreign commerce that are less significant than the effect of school violence.

In *Katzenbach* v. *McClung* (1964)...this Court upheld, as within the commerce power, a statute prohibiting racial discrimination at local restaurants, in part because that discrimination discouraged travel by African Americans and in part because that discrimination affected purchases of food and restaurant supplies from other States....It is difficult to distinguish the case before us, for the same critical elements are present. Businesses are less likely to locate in communities where violence plagues the classroom. Families will hesitate to move to neighborhoods where students carry guns instead of books....And (to look at the matter in the most narrowly commercial manner), interstate publishers therefore will sell fewer books and other firms will sell fewer school supplies where the threat of violence disrupts learning. Most importantly...the local instances here, taken together and considered as a whole, create a problem that causes serious human and social harm, but also has nationally significant economic dimensions.

The second legal problem the Court creates comes from its apparent belief that it can reconcile its holding with earlier cases by making a critical distinction between "commercial" and noncommercial "transaction[s]."...

...Although the majority today attempts to categorize...*McClung* and *Wickard* as involving intrastate "economic activity,"...the Courts that decided each of those cases did *not* focus upon the economic nature of the activity regulated. Rather, they focused upon whether that activity *affected* interstate or foreign commerce.

...The third legal problem created by the Court's holding is that it threatens legal uncertainty in an area of law that, until this case, seemed reasonably well settled....

In sum, to find this legislation within the scope of the Commerce Clause would permit "Congress...to act in terms of economic...realities."...Upholding this legislation would do no more than simply recognize that Congress had a "rational basis" for finding a significant connection between guns in or near schools and (through their effect on education) the interstate and foreign commerce they threaten.

Gonzales v. Raich, 545 U.S. 1 (2005)

The Controlled Substances Act of 1970 (CSA, or Title II of the Comprehensive Drug Abuse Prevention and Control Act) consolidated and expanded federal regulation of narcotics. Marijuana is regulated as a "Schedule I" drug under the CSA, with a high potential for abuse and little or no medicinal value. Its manufacture, distribution, or possession is a federal criminal offense, except when preapproved by the federal Food and Drug Administration for a research study.

In 1996, the voters of California approved the Compassionate Use Act which gave "seriously ill Californians" a "right to obtain and use marijuana for medical purposes" and to provide legal protections to doctors who recommend marijuana to such patients and to patients and primary caregivers who cultivate or possess marijuana for such use. The California statute and the litigation challenged the assumption of the federal law that marijuana was of no medicinal value.

Angel Raich and Diane Monson provided a test case for the conflict between these two laws. Both used marijuana for their own medical conditions, though only Monson was physically able to cultivate the plants herself. In 2002, both county deputies and federal Drug Enforcement Agents came to Monson's home. The county determined that Monson was operating within the terms of the Compassionate Use Act. The DEA found her in violation of the Controlled Substances Act and destroyed six marijuana plants. Raich and Monson then filed suit against the United States attorney general seeking an injunction against further enforcement of the CSA and a declaration that CSA was unconstitutional as applied to them. Although the district court initially denied the motion, a divided Ninth Circuit court ruled in favor of Raich and Monson in light of the Supreme Court's recent decisions in Lopez *and* Morrison. *Unlike the conservative Fifth Circuit that decided the original* Lopez *case from Texas, the Ninth Circuit that decided the* Raich *case from California was a liberal court, suggesting the strange political bedfellows that the federalism cases could make.*

The Raich *case was closely watched. Unlike the Gun-Free School Zones Act, the Controlled Substances Act was a central piece of social policy. Invalidating it, even on narrow grounds, would have real policy consequences. The case also pitted the libertarian value of small government against the war on drugs dear to many social conservatives, testing the political and constitutional commitments of the conservative justices. The Supreme Court reversed the Ninth Circuit, and upheld the CSA, on a 6–3 vote, with Justices Kennedy and Scalia switching sides to rule in favor of the federal government and its authority under the commerce clause in this case. As you read this case, consider whether Scalia is persuasive in distinguishing* Raich *from the earlier cases. Does* Raich *signal the repudiation of* Lopez*?*

JUSTICE STEVENS delivered the opinion of the Court.

California is one of at least nine States that authorize the use of marijuana for medicinal purposes. The question presented in this case is whether the power vested in Congress by Article I, § 8, of the Constitution "[t]o make all Laws which shall be necessary and proper for carrying into Execution" its authority to "regulate Commerce with foreign Nations, and among the several States" includes the power to prohibit the local cultivation and use of marijuana in compliance with California law.

...

Respondents in this case do not dispute that passage of the CSA, as part of the Comprehensive Drug Abuse Prevention and Control Act, was well within Congress' commerce power.... Nor do they contend that any provision or section of the CSA amounts to an unconstitutional exercise of congressional authority. Rather, respondents' challenge is actually quite limited; they argue that the CSA's categorical prohibition of the manufacture and possession of marijuana as applied to the intrastate manufacture and possession of marijuana for medical purposes pursuant to California law exceeds Congress' authority under the Commerce Clause.

...

Our case law firmly establishes Congress' power to regulate purely local activities that are part of an economic "class of activities" that have a substantial effect on interstate commerce.... As we stated in *Wickard* (1942), "even if appellee's activity be local and though it may not be regarded as commerce, it may still, whatever its nature, be reached by Congress if it exerts a substantial economic effect on interstate commerce." ... We have never required Congress to legislate with scientific exactitude. When Congress decides that the "'total incidence'" of a practice poses a threat to a national market, it may regulate the entire class.

...

Wickard ... establishes that Congress can regulate purely intrastate activity that is not itself "commercial," in that it is not produced for sale, if it concludes that failure to regulate that class of activity would undercut the regulation of the interstate market in that commodity.

The similarities between this case and *Wickard* are striking. Like the farmer in *Wickard*, respondents are cultivating, for home consumption, a fungible commodity for which there is an established, albeit illegal, interstate market. Just as the Agricultural Adjustment Act was designed "to control the volume [of wheat] moving in interstate and foreign commerce in order to avoid surpluses ..." and consequently control the market price, ... a primary purpose of the CSA is to control the supply and demand of controlled substances in both lawful and unlawful drug markets....

...

In assessing the scope of Congress' authority under the Commerce Clause, we stress that the task before us is a modest one. We need not determine whether respondents' activities, taken in the aggregate, substantially affect interstate commerce in fact, but only whether a "rational basis" exists for so concluding.... Given the enforcement difficulties that attend distinguishing between marijuana cultivated locally and marijuana grown elsewhere, ... and concerns about diversion into illicit channels, we have no difficulty concluding that Congress had a rational basis for believing that failure to regulate the intrastate manufacture and possession of marijuana would leave a gaping hole in the CSA....

To support their contrary submission, respondents rely heavily on two of our more recent Commerce Clause cases....

Those two cases, of course, are *Lopez* (1995) ... and *Morrison* (2000). As an initial matter, the statutory challenges at issue in those cases were markedly different from the challenge respondents pursue in the case at hand. Here, respondents ask us to excise individual applications of a concededly valid statutory scheme. In contrast, in both *Lopez* and *Morrison*, the parties asserted that a particular statute or provision fell outside Congress' commerce power in its entirety.

This distinction is pivotal for we have often reiterated that "[w]here the class of activities is regulated and that class is within the reach of federal power, the courts have no power 'to excise, as trivial, individual instances' of the class."...

...

Unlike those at issue in *Lopez* and *Morrison*, the activities regulated by the CSA are quintessentially economic. "Economics" refers to "the production, distribution, and consumption of commodities."...The CSA is a statute that regulates the production, distribution, and consumption of commodities for which there is an established, and lucrative, interstate market. Prohibiting the intrastate possession or manufacture of an article of commerce is a rational (and commonly utilized) means of regulating commerce in that product....

...

...More fundamentally, if, as the principal dissent contends, the personal cultivation, possession, and use of marijuana for medicinal purposes is beyond the "'outer limits' of Congress' Commerce Clause authority,"...it must also be true that such personal use of marijuana (or any other homegrown drug) for recreational purposes is also beyond those "'outer limits,'" whether or not a State elects to authorize or even regulate such use. Justice Thomas' separate dissent suffers from the same sweeping implications. That is, the dissenters' rationale logically extends to place *any* federal regulation (including quality, prescription, or quantity controls) of *any* locally cultivated and possessed controlled substance for *any* purpose beyond the "'outer limits'" of Congress' Commerce Clause authority. One need not have a degree in economics to understand why a nationwide exemption for the vast quantity of marijuana (or other drugs) locally cultivated for personal use (which presumably would include use by friends, neighbors, and family members) may have a substantial impact on the interstate market for this extraordinarily popular substance. The congressional judgment that an exemption for such a significant segment of the total market would undermine the orderly enforcement of the entire regulatory scheme is entitled to a strong presumption of validity. Indeed, that judgment is not only rational, but "visible to the naked eye,"...under any commonsense appraisal of the probable consequences of such an open-ended exemption.

...

JUSTICE SCALIA, concurring.

...

As we implicitly acknowledged in *Lopez*, Congress's authority to enact laws necessary and proper for the regulation of interstate commerce is not limited to laws directed against economic activities that have a substantial effect on interstate commerce. Though the conduct in *Lopez* was not economic, the Court nevertheless recognized that it could be regulated as "an essential part of a larger regulation of economic activity, in which the regulatory scheme could be undercut unless the intrastate activity were regulated."...

...

Today's principal dissent objects that, by permitting Congress to regulate activities necessary to effective interstate regulation, the Court reduces *Lopez* and *Morrison* to "little more than a drafting guide."...I think that criticism unjustified. Unlike the power to regulate activities that have a substantial effect on interstate commerce, the power to enact laws enabling effective regulation of interstate commerce can only be exercised in conjunction with congressional regulation of an interstate market, and it extends only to those measures necessary to make the interstate regulation effective....

...

The application of these principles to the case before us is straightforward. In the CSA, Congress has undertaken to extinguish the interstate market in Schedule I controlled substances, including marijuana. The Commerce Clause unquestionably permits this....That simple possession is a noneconomic activity is immaterial to whether it can be prohibited as a necessary part of a larger regulation. Rather, Congress's authority to enact all of these prohibitions of intrastate controlled-substance activities depends only upon whether they are appropriate means of achieving the legitimate end of eradicating Schedule I substances from interstate commerce.

By this measure, I think the regulation must be sustained. Not only is it impossible to distinguish "controlled substances manufactured and distributed intrastate" from "controlled substances manufactured and distributed interstate," but it hardly makes sense to speak in such terms. Drugs like marijuana are fungible commodities. As the Court explains, marijuana that is grown at home and possessed for personal use is never more than an instant from the interstate market—and this is so whether or not the possession is for medicinal use or lawful use under the laws of a particular State....Congress need not accept on faith that state law will be effective in maintaining a strict division between a lawful market for "medical" marijuana and the more general marijuana market.... "To impose on [Congress] the necessity of resorting to means which it cannot control, which another government may furnish or withhold, would render its course precarious, the result of its measures uncertain, and create a dependence on other governments, which might disappoint its most important designs, and is incompatible with the language of the constitution."...

...

JUSTICE O'CONNOR, with whom THE CHIEF JUSTICE and JUSTICE THOMAS join in part, dissenting.

...

This case exemplifies the role of States as laboratories. The States' core police powers have always included authority to define criminal law and to protect the health, safety, and welfare of their citizens.... Exercising those powers, California (by ballot initiative and then by legislative codification) has come to its own conclusion about the difficult and sensitive question of whether marijuana should be available to relieve severe pain and suffering. Today the Court sanctions an application of the federal Controlled Substances Act that extinguishes that experiment, without any proof that the personal cultivation, possession, and use of marijuana for medicinal purposes, if economic activity in the first place, has a substantial effect on interstate commerce and is therefore an appropriate subject of federal regulation. In so doing, the Court announces a rule that gives Congress a perverse incentive to legislate broadly pursuant to the Commerce Clause—nestling questionable assertions of its authority into comprehensive regulatory schemes—rather than with precision. That rule and the result it produces in this case are irreconcilable with our decisions in *Lopez* and *United States* v. *Morrison*. Accordingly I dissent.

...

Today's decision allows Congress to regulate intrastate activity without check, so long as there is some implication by legislative design that regulating intrastate activity is essential (and the Court appears to equate "essential" with "necessary") to the interstate regulatory scheme. Seizing upon our language in *Lopez* that the statute prohibiting gun possession in school zones was "not an essential part of a larger regulation of economic activity, in which the regulatory scheme could be undercut unless the intrastate activity were regulated,"... the Court appears to reason that the placement of local activity in a comprehensive scheme confirms that it is essential to that scheme. If the Court is right, then *Lopez* stands for nothing more than a drafting guide: Congress should have described the relevant crime as "transfer or possession of a firearm anywhere in the nation"—thus including commercial and noncommercial activity, and clearly encompassing some activity with assuredly substantial effect on interstate commerce. Had it done so, the majority hints, we would have sustained its authority to regulate possession of firearms in school zones.

...

The Court uses a dictionary definition of economics to skirt the real problem of drawing a meaningful line between "what is national and what is local." It will not do to say that Congress may regulate noncommercial activity simply because it may have an effect on the demand for commercial goods, or because the noncommercial endeavor can, in some sense, substitute for commercial activity. Most commercial goods or services have some sort of privately producible analogue. Home care substitutes for daycare. Charades games substitute for movie tickets. Backyard or windowsill gardening substitutes for going to the supermarket. To draw the line wherever private activity affects the demand for market goods is to draw no line at all, and to declare everything economic. We have already rejected the result that would follow—a federal police power....

In *Lopez* and *Morrison*, we suggested that economic activity usually relates directly to commercial activity.... The homegrown cultivation and personal possession and use of marijuana for medicinal purposes has no apparent commercial character. Everyone agrees that the marijuana at issue in this case was never in the stream of commerce, and neither were the supplies for growing it.... *Lopez* makes clear that possession is not itself commercial activity.... And respondents have not come into possession by means of any commercial transaction; they have simply grown, in their own homes, marijuana for their own use, without acquiring, buying, selling, or bartering a thing of value....

The Court suggests that *Wickard*, which we have identified as "perhaps the most far reaching example of Commerce Clause authority over intrastate activity,"... established federal regulatory power over any home consumption of a commodity for which a national market exists. I disagree. *Wickard* involved a challenge to the Agricultural Adjustment Act of 1938

(AAA), which directed the Secretary of Agriculture to set national quotas on wheat production, and penalties for excess production.... The AAA itself confirmed that Congress made an explicit choice not to reach—and thus the Court could not possibly have approved of federal control over—small-scale, noncommercial wheat farming. In contrast to the CSA's limitless assertion of power, Congress provided an exemption within the AAA for small producers. When Filburn planted the wheat at issue in *Wickard*, the statute exempted plantings less than 200 bushels (about six tons), and when he harvested his wheat it exempted plantings less than six acres.... *Wickard*, then, did not extend Commerce Clause authority to something as modest as the home cook's herb garden. This is not to say that Congress may never regulate small quantities of commodities possessed or produced for personal use, or to deny that it sometimes needs to enact a zero tolerance regime for such commodities. It is merely to say that *Wickard* did not hold or imply that small-scale production of commodities is always economic, and automatically within Congress' reach.

There is simply no evidence that homegrown medicinal marijuana users constitute, in the aggregate, a sizable enough class to have a discernable, let alone substantial, impact on the national illicit drug market—or otherwise to threaten the CSA regime....

...

JUSTICE THOMAS, dissenting.

Respondents Diane Monson and Angel Raich use marijuana that has never been bought or sold, that has never crossed state lines, and that has had no demonstrable effect on the national market for marijuana. If Congress can regulate this under the Commerce Clause, then it can regulate virtually anything—and the Federal Government is no longer one of limited and enumerated powers.

...

...[I]in order to be "necessary," the intrastate ban must be more than "a reasonable means [of] effectuat[ing] the regulation of interstate commerce."... It must be "plainly adapted" to regulating interstate marijuana trafficking—in other words, there must be an "obvious, simple, and direct relation" between the intrastate ban and the regulation of interstate commerce.... *McCulloch v. Maryland* (1819).

...[E]ven assuming Congress has "obvious" and "plain" reasons why regulating intrastate cultivation and possession is necessary to regulating the interstate drug trade, none of those reasons applies to medical marijuana patients like Monson and Raich.

California's Compassionate Use Act sets respondents' conduct apart from other intrastate producers and users of marijuana. The Act channels marijuana use to "seriously ill Californians,"... and prohibits "the diversion of marijuana for nonmedical purposes."... California strictly controls the cultivation and possession of marijuana for medical purposes....

...

Even assuming the CSA's ban on locally cultivated and consumed marijuana is "necessary," that does not mean it is also "proper." The means selected by Congress to regulate interstate commerce cannot be "prohibited" by, or inconsistent with the "letter and spirit" of, the Constitution....

...

Here, Congress has encroached on States' traditional police powers to define the criminal law and to protect the health, safety, and welfare of their citizens.... Further, the Government's rationale—that it may regulate the production or possession of any commodity for which there is an interstate market—threatens to remove the remaining vestiges of States' traditional police powers.

...

...[E]ven a Court interested more in the modern than the original understanding of the Constitution ought to resolve cases based on the meaning of words that are actually in the document. Congress is authorized to regulate "Commerce," and respondents' conduct does not qualify under any definition of that term. The majority's opinion only illustrates the steady drift away from the text of the Commerce Clause.... Federal power expands, but never contracts, with each new locution. The majority is not interpreting the Commerce Clause, but rewriting it.

...

One searches the Court's opinion in vain for any hint of what aspect of American life is reserved to the States. Yet this Court knows that "'[t]he Constitution created a Federal Government of limited powers.'"... That is why today's decision will add no measure of stability to our Commerce Clause jurisprudence: This Court is willing neither to enforce limits on federal power, nor to declare the Tenth Amendment a dead letter. If stability is possible, it is only by discarding the stand-alone substantial effects test and revisiting our definition of "Commerce among the several States." Congress may regulate interstate commerce—not things that affect it, even when summed together, unless truly "necessary and proper" to regulating interstate commerce.

. . .

B. Federal Power to Enforce Civil Rights

Section 5 of the Fourteenth Amendment gives Congress the power "to enforce by appropriate legislation" the other provisions of that amendment. It is, to some extent, the necessary and proper clause of the Fourteenth Amendment. It empowers Congress to pass "appropriate legislation" to carry out other constitutional provisions. It leaves open the question of what kind of legislation counts as "appropriate." Moreover, unlike the necessary and proper clause of Article I, Section 5 of the Fourteenth Amendment is focused on a congressional power "to enforce" the terms of that amendment. How restrictive is the grant of an enforcement power?

At stake in the interpretation of Section 5 of the Fourteenth Amendment is the balance between state and federal authority and between congressional and judicial authority. Section 1 of the Fourteenth Amendment recognizes rights of the individual that are federally protected against state and local governments, or democratic majorities in the states. The more expansive those individual rights are, or might be, the more political issues are nationalized and taken out of the hands of state and local government officials or communities. The more restricted the understanding of those rights are, the more federal channels are closed off to individuals and the more issues are left to states and localities to work out as they will. If Section 5 is read broadly, then it empowers Congress to bring more issues into national politics.

The interpretation of Section 5 also raises a question of the proper balance between judicial and congressional authority. Section 5 authorizes Congress to pass "appropriate" legislation to "enforce" the rights contained in Section 1 of the Fourteenth Amendment. Does that give Congress a role in interpreting the substantive rights provisions contained in Section 1 of the Fourteenth Amendment? Who gets to determine what counts as "appropriate" legislation? Is it a legislative or a judicial judgment as to whether a given piece of legislation is "appropriate," and has Section 5 effectively delegated that judgment to Congress? Should the Court be deferential to whatever Congress does with its Section 5 authority, even if when Congress disagrees with the Court about the meaning of the rights guaranteed by the Fourteenth Amendment and even when Congress imposes more restrictions on the states than the Constitution requires?

In the Warren Court era, the Supreme Court did seem to be deferential to Congress and supportive of the idea that Section 5 empowered Congress to act creatively when it came to racial civil rights. The Rehnquist Court raised new questions about Section 5. There was no controversy over whether Congress could develop remedies for judicially defined Fourteenth Amendment rights. There has been more controversy over whether Congress can pass legislation obstructing or weakening the enforcement of judicially defined rights. The greatest controversy, however, has focused on whether Congress has an independent interpretive role and can question, challenge, or alter the rights that the judiciary finds in the Fourteenth Amendment.

Most notably, *City of Boerne v. Flores* in 1997 picked up on the earlier suggestion of some of the justices that congressional authority to enforce the Constitution under Section 5 had to be limited by the judicial authority to interpret the meaning of the constitutional provisions that are to be enforced.[20] The case involved a very different kind of law than the civil rights statutes that Congress often passed under Section 5. The Religious Freedom Restoration Act of 1993 was passed to overturn the Supreme Court's interpretation of the constitutional requirements of religious liberty. The power to say what the Constitution means, the Court emphasized in *Boerne*, is ultimately a judicial power. The congressional power under Section 5 was to pass a statute "which deters or remedies constitutional violations." Congress cannot "decree the substance of the Fourteenth Amendment's restrictions on the States" or "alter[] the meaning" of the Constitution under the guise of "enforcing" it.[21]

At the end of the 1960s, the Court was primarily interested in freeing Congress to pass expansive new civil rights laws. At the turn of the twentieth-first century, the range of issues that might fall within Section 5 were more diverse, and the Court was more

20. *City of Boerne v. Flores*, 521 U.S. 507 (1997).
21. Ibid., 518, 519.

concerned with reemphasizing its role as the primary interpreter of the Constitution and defining some boundaries on the congressional authority to regulate the states. The Rehnquist Court heard a number of cases raising Section 5 concerns after *Boerne*. Initially, many of the challenged federal statutory provisions failed to pass constitutional muster under this test, and the Court restricted an age discrimination statute in *Kimel v. Florida Board of Regents* (2000) and the Americans with Disabilities Act in *Board of Trustees of the University of Alabama v. Garrett* (2001). By contrast, the Court upheld portions of the Family and Medical Leave Act and other elements of the American with Disabilities Act against Section 5 challenges in *Nevada Department of Human Resources v. Hibbs* (2003) and *Tennessee v. Lane* (2004).

United States v. Morrison, 529 U.S. 598 (2000)

The Violence Against Women Act (VAWA) was passed by the Democratic Congress as part of the Crime Control Act of 1994. In one of its provisions (42 U.S.C § 13981), VAWA followed the model of many civil rights statutes in providing a federal civil remedy for victims of "violence motivated by gender." Under VAWA, such victims could sue those who commit a crime of violence motivated by gender in federal court for compensatory and punitive damages and other forms of relief. The act was controversial, both in analogizing violence against women to civil rights violations and in its expansion of federal authority over such areas of traditional state concern as rape and domestic violence, but with unified Democratic control of Congress it easily passed.

In the fall of 1994, Christy Brzonkala, a freshman at Virginia Tech, was allegedly raped by Antonio Morrison and James Crawford, both members of the Virginia Tech football team. Brzonkala later suffered depression and filed a complaint in 1995 with the university against Morrison and Crawford but did not pursue criminal charges. The university's disciplinary committee found insufficient evidence against Crawford but found Morrison guilty of sexual assault and suspended him for two semesters. When Morrison threatened a legal challenge to the sentence, a second hearing was conducted during the summer which found him guilty only of "using abusive language" but again imposed a two-semester suspension. Given the terms of the conviction, the university senior administration overturned the sentence as excessive in comparison to others convicted of similar offenses. When Brzonkala read in the newspapers that Morrison would be returning to campus in the fall, she withdrew from the university.

In December 1995, Brzonkala filed suit in federal district court against Crawford, Morrison, and Virginia Tech. The suits against Crawford and Morrison were based on the civil remedy provision of VAWA. The district court ruled that that Congress lacked the authority under either the commerce clause or Section 5 of the Fourteenth Amendment to provide for such a suit. A divided circuit court panel reversed the district court, but the full circuit court meeting en banc affirmed the district court in a divided vote. In a 5–4 decision, the U.S. Supreme Court affirmed the circuit court's ruling. The case was particularly notable in being the first after Lopez *in which the Court struck down a federal law on commerce clause grounds and in continuing a line of cases that the Rehnquist Court had begun to develop specifying the limits to congressional power under Section 5 of the Fourteenth Amendment. Brzonkala offered two alternative justifications (the commerce clause and Section 5) for congressional authority to pass the statutory provision under which she hoped to pursue her lawsuit, but the Court did not accept either. In striking down the provision of VAWA allowing for federal civil lawsuits against those thought responsible for violent crimes, the Court's ruling had no effect on other provisions of the statute, which were subsequently expanded, providing federal funds for programs related to violence against women or punishing violence against women that involved interstate travel.*

How deferential should the courts be to congressional definition of rights under the Fourteenth Amendment? How badly would states have to fail in their duty to protect women from crimes in order to justify federal intervention under the Fourteenth Amendment, according to the majority?

CHIEF JUSTICE REHNQUIST delivered the opinion of the Court.

. . .

Due respect for the decisions of a coordinate branch of Government demands that we invalidate a congressional enactment only upon a plain showing that Congress has exceeded its constitutional bounds. See *United States v. Lopez* (1995) (Kennedy, J., concurring).... With this presumption of constitutionality in mind, we turn to the question whether § 13981 falls within Congress' power under Article I, § 8, of the Constitution....

As we discussed at length in *Lopez*, our interpretation of the Commerce Clause has changed as our Nation has developed.... We need not repeat that detailed review of the Commerce Clause's history here; it suffices to say that, in the years since *NLRB v. Jones & Laughlin Steel Corp*. (1937)..., Congress has had considerably greater latitude in regulating conduct and transactions under the Commerce Clause than our previous case law permitted....

Lopez emphasized, however, that even under our modern, expansive interpretation of the Commerce Clause, Congress' regulatory authority is not without effective bounds.

...

With these principles underlying our Commerce Clause jurisprudence as reference points, the proper resolution of the present cases is clear. Gender-motivated crimes of violence are not, in any sense of the phrase, economic activity. While we need not adopt a categorical rule against aggregating the effects of any noneconomic activity in order to decide these cases, thus far in our Nation's history our cases have upheld Commerce Clause regulation of intrastate activity only where that activity is economic in nature....

...

...[T]he concern that we expressed in *Lopez* that Congress might use the Commerce Clause to completely obliterate the Constitution's distinction between national and local authority seems well founded....The reasoning that petitioners advance seeks to follow the but-for causal chain from the initial occurrence of violent crime (the suppression of which has always been the prime object of the States' police power) to every attenuated effect upon interstate commerce. If accepted, petitioners' reasoning would allow Congress to regulate any crime as long as the nationwide, aggregated impact of that crime has substantial effects on employment, production, transit, or consumption. Indeed, if Congress may regulate gender-motivated violence, it would be able to regulate murder or any other type of violence since gender-motivated violence, as a subset of all violent crime, is certain to have lesser economic impacts than the larger class of which it is a part.

...

Because we conclude that the Commerce Clause does not provide Congress with authority to enact § 13981, we address petitioners' alternative argument that the section's civil remedy should be upheld as an exercise of Congress' remedial power under Section Five of the Fourteenth Amendment.

The principles governing an analysis of congressional legislation under Section Five are well settled. Section Five states that Congress may "'enforce,' by 'appropriate legislation' the constitutional guarantee that no State shall deprive any person of 'life, liberty or property, without due process of law,' nor deny any person 'equal protection of the laws.'" *City of Boerne* v. *Flores* (1997)....

Petitioners' Section Five argument is founded on an assertion that there is pervasive bias in various state justice systems against victims of gender-motivated violence. This assertion is supported by a voluminous congressional record. Specifically, Congress received evidence that many participants in state justice systems are perpetuating an array of erroneous stereotypes and assumptions. Congress concluded that these discriminatory stereotypes often result in insufficient investigation and prosecution of gender-motivated crime, inappropriate focus on the behavior and credibility of the victims of that crime, and unacceptably lenient punishments for those who are actually convicted of gender-motivated violence....Petitioners contend that this bias denies victims of gender-motivated violence the equal protection of the laws and that Congress therefore acted appropriately in enacting a private civil remedy against the perpetrators of gender-motivated violence to both remedy the States' bias and deter future instances of discrimination in the state courts.

As our cases have established, state-sponsored gender discrimination violates equal protection unless it serves "important governmental objectives and...the discriminatory means employed" are "substantially related to the achievement of those objectives."...However, the language and purpose of the Fourteenth Amendment place certain limitations on the manner in which Congress may attack discriminatory conduct. These limitations are necessary to prevent the Fourteenth Amendment from obliterating the Framers' carefully crafted balance of power between the States and the National Government. See *Flores*....Foremost among these limitations is the time-honored principle that the Fourteenth Amendment, by its very terms, prohibits only state action. The principle has become firmly embedded in our constitutional law that the action inhibited by the first section of the Fourteenth Amendment is only such action as may fairly be said to be that of the States....

Shortly after the Fourteenth Amendment was adopted, we decided...the *Civil Rights Cases* (1883). In those consolidated cases, we held that the public accommodation provisions of the Civil Rights Act of 1875, which applied to purely private conduct, were beyond the scope of the Section Five enforcement power....

The force of the doctrine of *stare decisis* behind these decisions stems not only from the length of time they have been on the books, but also from the insight attributable to the Members of the Court at that time. Every Member had been appointed by President Lincoln, Grant, Hayes, Garfield, or Arthur—and each of their judicial appointees obviously had intimate knowledge and familiarity with the events surrounding the adoption of the Fourteenth Amendment.

...

Petitioners...argue that, unlike the situation in the *Civil Rights Cases*, here there has been gender-based disparate treatment by state authorities, whereas in those cases there was no indication of such state action. There is abundant evidence, however, to show that the Congresses that enacted the Civil Rights Acts of 1871 and 1875 had a purpose similar to that of Congress in enacting § 13981: There were state laws on the books bespeaking equality of treatment, but in the administration of these laws there was discrimination against newly freed slaves....

But even if that distinction were valid, we do not believe it would save § 13981's civil remedy. For the remedy is simply not "corrective in its character, adapted to counteract and redress the operation of such prohibited state laws or proceedings of state officers." *Civil Rights Cases*. Or, as we have phrased it in more recent cases, prophylactic legislation under Section Five must have a "congruence and proportionality between the injury to be prevented or remedied and the means adopted to that end." *Florida Prepaid Postsecondary Ed. Expense Bd.* v. *College Savings Bank* (1999). Section 13981 is not aimed at proscribing discrimination by officials which the Fourteenth Amendment might not itself proscribe; it is directed not at any State or state actor, but at individuals who have committed criminal acts motivated by gender bias.

In the present cases, for example, § 13981 visits no consequence whatever on any Virginia public official involved in investigating or prosecuting Brzonkala's assault. The section is, therefore, unlike any of the Section Five remedies that we have previously upheld....

Section 13981 is also different from these previously upheld remedies in that it applies uniformly throughout the Nation. Congress' findings indicate that the problem of discrimination against the victims of gender-motivated crimes does not exist in all States, or even most States. By contrast, the Section Five remedy upheld in *Katzenbach* v. *Morgan* (1966) was directed only to the State where the evil found by Congress existed, and in *South Carolina* v. *Katzenbach* (1966) the remedy was directed only to those States in which Congress found that there had been discrimination.

For these reasons, we conclude that Congress' power under Section Five does not extend to the enactment of § 13981.

Petitioner Brzonkala's complaint alleges that she was the victim of a brutal assault. But Congress' effort in § 13981 to provide a federal civil remedy can be sustained neither under the Commerce Clause nor under Section Five of the Fourteenth Amendment. If the allegations here are true, no civilized system of justice could fail to provide her a remedy for the conduct of respondent Morrison. But under our federal system that remedy must be provided by the Commonwealth of Virginia, and not by the United States. The judgment of the Court of Appeals is

Affirmed.

JUSTICE THOMAS, concurring.

...

JUSTICE SOUTER, with whom JUSTICE STEVENS, JUSTICE GINSBURG, and JUSTICE BREYER join, dissenting.

The Court says both that it leaves Commerce Clause precedent undisturbed and that the Civil Rights Remedy of the Violence Against Women Act of 1994, 42 U.S.C. § 13981, exceeds Congress's power under that Clause. I find the claims irreconcilable and respectfully dissent.[22]

Our cases, which remain at least nominally undisturbed, stand for the following propositions. Congress has the power to legislate with regard to activity that, in the aggregate, has a substantial effect on interstate commerce. See *Wickard* v. *Filburn* (1942)....The fact of such a substantial effect is not an issue for the courts in the first instance, but for the Congress, whose institutional capacity for gathering evidence and taking testimony far exceeds ours. By passing legislation, Congress indicates its conclusion, whether explicitly or not, that facts support its exercise of the commerce power. The business of the courts is to review the congressional assessment, not for soundness but simply for the rationality of concluding that a jurisdictional

22. Finding the law a valid exercise of Commerce Clause power, I have no occasion to reach the question whether it might also be sustained as an exercise of Congress's power to enforce the Fourteenth Amendment.

basis exists in fact.... Applying those propositions in these cases can lead to only one conclusion.

One obvious difference from *United States* v. *Lopez*, is the mountain of data assembled by Congress, here showing the effects of violence against women on interstate commerce....

...

The evidence as to rape was similarly extensive [as to domestic violence], supporting these conclusions:

> "[The incidence of] rape rose four times as fast as the total national crime rate over the past 10 years."...
>
> "According to one study, close to half a million girls now in high school will be raped before they graduate."...
>
> ...
>
> "Almost 50 percent of rape victims lose their jobs or are forced to quit because of the crime's severity."...

Based on the data thus partially summarized, Congress found that

> [C]rimes of violence motivated by gender have a substantial adverse effect on interstate commerce, by deterring potential victims from traveling interstate, from engaging in employment in interstate business, and from transacting with business, and in places involved, in interstate commerce... [,] by diminishing national productivity, increasing medical and other costs, and decreasing the supply of and the demand for interstate products.... H. R. Conf. Rep. No. 103–711, p. 385 (1994).

Congress thereby explicitly stated the predicate for the exercise of its Commerce Clause power. Is its conclusion irrational in view of the data amassed? True, the methodology of particular studies may be challenged, and some of the figures arrived at may be disputed. But the sufficiency of the evidence before Congress to provide a rational basis for the finding cannot seriously be questioned.... [23]

...

23. It should go without saying that my view of the limit of the congressional commerce power carries no implication about the wisdom of exercising it to the limit. I and other Members of this Court appearing before Congress have repeatedly argued against the federalization of traditional state crimes and the extension of federal remedies to problems for which the States have historically taken responsibility and may deal with today if they have the will to do so.... [footnote repositioned from original, eds.]

JUSTICE BREYER, with whom JUSTICE STEVENS joins, and with whom JUSTICE SOUTER and JUSTICE GINSBURG join in part, dissenting.

...

... [I]n a world where most everyday products or their component parts cross interstate boundaries, Congress will frequently find it possible to redraft a statute using language that ties the regulation to the interstate movement of some relevant object, thereby regulating local criminal activity or, for that matter, family affairs. See, *e.g.*, Child Support Recovery Act of 1992, 18 U.S.C. § 228. Although this possibility does not give the Federal Government the power to regulate everything, it means that any substantive limitation will apply randomly in terms of the interests the majority seeks to protect. How much would be gained, for example, were Congress to reenact the present law in the form of "An Act Forbidding Violence Against Women Perpetrated at Public Accommodations or by Those Who Have Moved in, or through the Use of Items that Have Moved in, Interstate Commerce"? Complex Commerce Clause rules creating fine distinctions that achieve only random results do little to further the important federalist interests that called them into being. That is why modern (pre-*Lopez*) case law rejected them. See *Wickard v. Filburn* (1942); *United States* v. *Darby* (1941); *Jones & Laughlin Steel Corp.* (1937).

...

I would also note that Congress, when it enacted the statute, followed procedures that help to protect the federalism values at stake. It provided adequate notice to the States of its intent to legislate in an "area of traditional state regulation." And in response, attorneys general in the overwhelming majority of States (38) supported congressional legislation, telling Congress that "our experience as Attorneys General strengthens our belief that the problem of violence against women is a national one, requiring federal attention, federal leadership, and federal funds."...

Moreover, as Justice Souter has pointed out, Congress compiled a "mountain of data" explicitly documenting the interstate commercial effects of gender-motivated crimes of violence. After considering alternatives, it focused the federal law upon documented deficiencies in state legal systems. And it tailored the law to prevent its use in certain areas of traditional state concern, such as divorce, alimony, or child custody....

...

Given my conclusion on the Commerce Clause question, I need not consider Congress' authority under Section Five of the Fourteenth Amendment. Nonetheless, I doubt the Court's reasoning rejecting that source of authority....

...

The majority adds that Congress found that the problem of inadequacy of state remedies "does not exist in all States, or even most States." But Congress had before it the task force reports of at least 21 States documenting constitutional violations. And it made its own findings about pervasive gender-based stereotypes hampering many state legal systems, sometimes unconstitutionally so.... The record nowhere reveals a congressional finding that the problem "does not exist" elsewhere. Why can Congress not take the evidence before it as evidence of a national problem? This Court has not previously held that Congress must document the existence of a problem in every State prior to proposing a national solution. And the deference this Court gives to Congress' chosen remedy under Section Five, suggests that any such requirement would be inappropriate.

Despite my doubts about the majority's Section Five reasoning, I need not, and do not, answer the Section Five question, which I would leave for more thorough analysis if necessary on another occasion. Rather, in my view, the Commerce Clause provides an adequate basis for the statute before us. And I would uphold its constitutionality as the "necessary and proper" exercise of legislative power granted to Congress by that Clause.

IV. Federalism

MAJOR DEVELOPMENTS

- Restriction on state ability to control federal officers and elections
- Restriction on federal ability to control state officers
- Enhanced protection of state and local governments from civil lawsuits

The Rehnquist Court's federalism offensive reexamined the proper scope and limits of national power. Second and closely related, it reexamined the rights and powers of the states to create shields against or exemptions from the exercise of national power. Justice Rehnquist was not new to the idea. As associate justice, he had championed the short-lived 1976 *National League of Cities v. Usery*, which held that there were limits to congressional authority to regulate the "states qua states." Now, as chief justice, he could work with Reagan- and Bush-appointed justices more sympathetic to his concerns. The Court under his leadership thus gave new consideration to the meaning of the Tenth and Eleventh Amendments.

While many Reagan revolutionaries praised federalism, some of their moves to empower states raised no interesting constitutional issues. For example, welfare reform reduced federal involvement, and shifted power to states, but it violated no New Deal constitutional principle. Moreover, as we have seen time and time again, one's views on federalism often depend on the underlying substantive policy issue at stake. Pro-slavery advocates declared their commitment to states rights when they attempted to prevent federal meddling with pro-slavery policies in the southern states, but they quickly turned into strong advocates of national power when debating the scope of federal power to return fugitive slaves from uncooperative northern states. In the previous section we saw that some conservatives articulated a cramped conception of federal power when debating national laws against gun possession near schools, but a more generous conception when defending federal power to regulate narcotics. Gay rights advocates became proponents of federalism when some states passed laws allowing for same-sex marriage. Conservatives who decry federal meddling with traditional state prerogatives were often silent when it came to passage of the national Defense of Marriage Act.

As you review these materials, consider whether advocates articulate positions that they are willing to defend even when their constitutional views conflict with their preferred policy outcomes. Does the constitutional status of states in the federal system depend on political actors separating their policy preferences from their views about federalism? Does it depend on their being consistent in how they treat federalism questions?

This section includes materials on state powers and state immunities. In *U.S. Term Limits v. Thornton* (1995), the U.S. Supreme Court turned back efforts by the states to impose term limits on members of Congress. According to the Court's majority, the states did not have the power to add to the minimum qualifications for federal officeholding in the text of the Constitution. They could not regulate federal elections in a way that disfavored incumbent officeholders. In *Printz v. United States* (1997), Justice Kennedy switched sides. The Court concluded that Congress could not "commandeer" state and local government officials to implement federal policy—in this case, federal background checks on gun purchases. The same narrow majority decided *Alden v. Maine* (1999), one of a string of state sovereign immunity cases. It held that Congress could not subject states to involuntary civil lawsuits under Article I.

A. State Regulation of Federal Elections

Elections of federal officials are regulated by both the state and federal governments. States and localities have the first responsibility for regulating and managing polling places, ballots, ballot access, and voter eligibility for local, state and federal elections. The U.S. Constitution and the federal government through statute put some restrictions on how the states perform those duties. In part of a civil rights statute in 1970, Congress lowered the national voting age to eighteen (most states had set the voting age at twenty-one). In *Oregon v. Mitchell* (1970), the Supreme Court held that Congress could only set the voting age for federal elections, but did not have the constitutional authority to lower the voting age in state and local elections. The Twenty-Sixth Amendment to the Constitution was easily passed and ratified by the summer of 1971 in order to set a national voting age at eighteen for all elections.

Congress has the power to "make or alter" regulations of federal elections, which would allow the national legislature to override most state and local regulations that burden federal elections. The challenge for the Court in the Contemporary Era has been whether there are implicit limits on how the states can regulate federal elections. In particular, *U.S. Term Limits v. Thornton* (1995) addressed the question of whether states could limit ballot access to incumbent federal legislators as part of a scheme for creating term limits. The Court had previously decided in *Powell v. McCormack* (1969) that Congress could not impose additional "qualifications" for federal officeholding beyond the ones listed in the Constitution itself by removing duly elected members from office. Were selective ballot access restrictions a "qualification" for office? Could states regulate who could run for federal office within their borders? A narrowly divided U.S. Supreme Court held that they could not.

U.S. Term Limits v. Thornton, 514 U.S. 779 (1995)

In the 1980s, reelection rates for legislators were unprecedented. Many scholars argued that career-minded incumbents were simply being responsive to voters. Yet many activists began to question whether legislators had instead become too insulated from their constituents.[24] *In the early 1990s, voter initiatives in nearly every state limited the number of terms of office that legislators could serve. (Legislatures rarely voted to adopt term limits on their own.) They hoped that term limits would result in more responsive, accountable, and humble legislators. At the same time, nearly half the states adopted congressional term limits as well, as did the 1994 Republican campaign document, the "Contract with America." Congressional representatives of both parties (but especially Republicans) pledged to leave Congress after a set number of terms. However, a federal constitutional amendment imposing congressional term limits did not pass the Republican House of Representatives, and many members of Congress found reasons to break their pledges. Even so, opposition to terms limits was risky, and Democratic House Speaker Thomas Foley, among others, may have lost reelection because of it.*

In 1995, the Supreme Court closed the door on anything short of a constitutional amendment as a means to enforce congressional term limits. In 1992, Arkansas voters approved a state constitutional amendment. This amendment limited the number of terms that individuals could serve in various state offices or Congress. Democratic Congressman Ray Thornton was among a group of state and federal officeholders who filed suit in state court seeking to have the term limit amendment declared unconstitutional. U.S. Term Limits, an advocacy organization that had been one of the primary sponsors of the Arkansas amendment, joined with the state to defend the amendment. The trial court struck down

24. See, e.g., Stephen Ansolabehere et al., "Old Voters, New Voters, and the Personal Vote: Using Redistricting to Measure the Incumbency Advantage," *American Journal of Political Science* 44 (2000):17; Brandice Canes-Wrone et al., "Out of Step, Out of Office: Electoral Accountability and House Members' Voting," *American Political Science Review* 96 (2002):127.

the amendment, and a divided state supreme court affirmed the trial court. The U.S. Supreme Court heard the case on certiorari, and a 5–4 decision affirmed the decision of the Arkansas Supreme Court. The Court struck down the term limits amendment as inconsistent with the requirements of the U.S. Constitution. Before the end of his term, Thornton left Congress to run successfully for election to the Arkansas Supreme Court.

As you read the opinions in this case, you may notice that Justice Kennedy provides the critical swing vote for the majority, with Justice Thomas in dissent. How does Kennedy's concurring opinion illuminate his approach to the issues raised in U.S. Term Limits? *How does it compare to his views on the scope of national power in* Lopez *or* Alden?

JUSTICE STEVENS delivered the opinion of the Court.

Today's cases present a challenge to an amendment to the Arkansas State Constitution that prohibits the name of an otherwise-eligible candidate for Congress from appearing on the general election ballot if that candidate has already served three terms in the House of Representatives or two terms in the Senate. The Arkansas Supreme Court held that the amendment violates the Federal Constitution. We agree with that holding. Such a state-imposed restriction is contrary to the "fundamental principle of our representative democracy," embodied in the Constitution, that "the people should choose whom they please to govern them."...Allowing individual States to adopt their own qualifications for congressional service would be inconsistent with the Framers' vision of a uniform National Legislature representing the people of the United States. If the qualifications set forth in the text of the Constitution are to be changed, that text must be amended.

...

...[T]he constitutionality of Amendment 73 depends critically on the resolution of two distinct issues. The first is whether the Constitution forbids States to add to or alter the qualifications specifically enumerated in the Constitution. The second is, if the Constitution does so forbid, whether the fact that Amendment 73 is formulated as a ballot access restriction rather than as an outright disqualification is of constitutional significance. Our resolution of these issues draws upon our prior resolution of a related but distinct issue: whether Congress has the power to add to or alter the qualifications of its Members.

...

Powell [v. McCormack] (1969)...establishes two important propositions: first, that the "relevant historical materials" compel the conclusion that, at least with respect to qualifications imposed by Congress, the Framers intended the qualifications listed in the Constitution to be exclusive; and second, that that conclusion is equally compelled by an understanding of the "fundamental principle of our representative democracy...'that the people should choose whom they please to govern them.'"...

...

Petitioners argue that the Constitution contains no express prohibition against state-added qualifications, and that Amendment 73 is therefore an appropriate exercise of a State's reserved power to place additional restrictions on the choices that its own voters may make. We disagree for two independent reasons. First, we conclude that the power to add qualifications is not within the "original powers" of the States, and thus is not reserved to the States by the Tenth Amendment. Second, even if States possessed some original power in this area, we conclude that the Framers intended the Constitution to be the exclusive source of qualifications for Members of Congress, and that the Framers thereby "divested" States of any power to add qualifications.

...

...[T]he power to add qualifications is not part of the original powers of sovereignty that the Tenth Amendment reserved to the States. Petitioners' Tenth Amendment argument misconceives the nature of the right at issue because that Amendment could only "reserve" that which existed before. As Justice Story recognized, "the states can exercise no powers whatsoever, which exclusively spring out of the existence of the national government, which the constitution does not delegate to them....No state can say, that it has reserved, what it never possessed."...

...

Two other sections of the Constitution further support our view of the Framers' vision. First, consistent with Story's view, the Constitution provides that the salaries of representatives should "be ascertained by Law, and paid out of the Treasury of the United States,"...rather than by individual States. The salary provisions reflect the view that representatives owe their allegiance to the people, and not to the States. Second, the provisions governing elections reveal the Framers' understanding that powers over the election of federal officers had to be delegated to, rather than reserved by, the States. It is surely no coincidence that the context of federal elections provides one of the few areas in which the Constitution expressly requires action by the States, namely that "the Times, Places and Manner of holding Elections for Senators and Representatives, shall be prescribed in each State by the Legislature thereof"...[an] express delegation[] of power to the States to act with respect to federal elections.

...

Even if we believed that States possessed as part of their original powers some control over congressional qualifications, the text and structure of the Constitution, the relevant historical materials, and, most importantly, the "basic principles of our democratic system" all demonstrate that the Qualifications Clauses were intended to preclude the States from exercising any such power and to fix as exclusive the qualifications in the Constitution.

...

...Madison...explicitly contrasted the state control over the qualifications of electors with the lack of state control over the qualifications of the elected

> The qualifications of the elected, being less carefully and properly defined by the State constitutions, and being at the same time more susceptible of uniformity, have been very properly considered and regulated by the convention. A representative of the United States must be of the age of twenty-five years; must have been seven years a citizen of the United States; must, at the time of his election be an inhabitant of the State he is to represent; and, during the time of his service must be in no office under the United States. Under these reasonable limitations, the door of this part of the federal government is open to merit of every description, whether native or adoptive, whether young or old, and without regard to poverty or wealth, or to any particular profession of religious faith....

...

Congress' subsequent experience with state-imposed qualifications provides further evidence of the general consensus on the lack of state power in this area....Congress first confronted the issue in 1807 when it faced a challenge to the qualifications of William McCreery, a Representative from Maryland who allegedly did not satisfy a residency requirement imposed by that State. In recommending that McCreery be seated, the Report of the House Committee on Elections noted:

> The committee proceeded to examine the Constitution, with relation to the case submitted to them, and find that *qualifications of members are therein determined, without reserving any authority to the State Legislatures to change, add to, or diminish those qualifications;* and that, by that instrument, Congress is constituted the sole judge of the qualifications prescribed by it, and are obliged to decide agreeably to the Constitutional rules....

...

...[F]inally, state-imposed restrictions, unlike the congressionally imposed restrictions at issue in *Powell*, violate a[n]...idea central to this basic principle: that the right to choose representatives belongs not to the States, but to the people....[T]he Framers, in perhaps their most important contribution, conceived of a Federal Government directly responsible to the people, possessed of direct power over the people, and chosen directly, not by States, but by the people.

...

Permitting individual States to formulate diverse qualifications for their representatives would result in a patchwork of state qualifications, undermining the uniformity and the national character that the Framers envisioned and sought to ensure....

...

...Amendment 73 is an indirect attempt to accomplish what the Constitution prohibits Arkansas from accomplishing directly. As the plurality opinion of the Arkansas Supreme Court recognized, Amendment 73 is an "effort to dress eligibility to stand for Congress in ballot access clothing," because the "intent and the effect of Amendment 73 are to disqualify congressional incumbents from further service."...We must, of course, accept the state court's view of the purpose of its own law: We are thus authoritatively informed that the sole purpose of § 3 of Amendment 73 was to attempt to achieve a result that is forbidden by the Federal Constitution....

...

The merits of term limits, or "rotation," have been the subject of debate since the formation of our Constitution, when the Framers unanimously rejected a proposal to add such limits to the Constitution....It is not our province to resolve this longstanding debate.

We are, however, firmly convinced that allowing the several States to adopt term limits for congressional service would effect a fundamental change in the constitutional framework. Any such change must come not by legislation adopted either by Congress or by an individual State, but rather—as have other important changes in the electoral process—through the amendment procedures set forth in Article V. The Framers decided that the qualifications for service in the Congress of the United States be fixed in the Constitution and be uniform throughout the Nation. That decision reflects the Framers' understanding that Members of Congress are chosen by separate constituencies, but that they become, when elected, servants of the people of the United States. They are not merely delegates appointed by separate, sovereign States; they occupy offices that are integral and essential components of a single National Government. In the absence of a properly passed constitutional amendment, allowing individual States to craft their own qualifications for Congress would thus erode the structure envisioned by the Framers, a structure that was designed, in the words of the Preamble to our Constitution, to form a "more perfect Union."

JUSTICE KENNEDY, concurring.

...

Federalism was our Nation's own discovery. The Framers split the atom of sovereignty. It was the genius of their idea that our citizens would have two political capacities, one state and one federal, each protected from incursion by the other. The resulting Constitution created a legal system unprecedented in form and design, establishing two orders of government, each with its own direct relationship, its own privity, its own set of mutual rights and obligations to the people who sustain it and are governed by it....

A distinctive character of the National Government, the mark of its legitimacy, is that it owes its existence to the act of the whole people who created it.

...

The political identity of the entire people of the Union is reinforced by the proposition, which I take to be beyond dispute, that, though limited as to its objects, the National Government is, and must be, controlled by the people without collateral interference by the States. *McCulloch* (1819) affirmed this proposition as well, when the Court rejected the suggestion that States could interfere with federal powers. "This was not intended by the American people. They did not design to make their government dependent on the States."...The States have no power, reserved or otherwise, over the exercise of federal authority within its proper sphere....That the States may not invade the sphere of federal sovereignty is as incontestable, in my view, as the corollary proposition that the Federal Government must be held within the boundaries of its own power when it intrudes upon matters reserved to the States.

...Nothing in the Constitution or *The Federalist Papers*...supports the idea of state interference with the most basic relation between the National Government and its citizens, the selection of legislative representatives....

...

It is maintained by our dissenting colleagues that the State of Arkansas seeks nothing more than to grant its people surer control over the National Government, a control, it is said, that will be enhanced by the law at issue here. The arguments for term limitations (or ballot restrictions having the same effect) are not lacking in force; but the issue, as all of us must acknowledge, is not the efficacy of those measures but whether they have a legitimate source, given their origin in the enactments of a single State. There can be no doubt, if we are to respect the republican origins of the Nation and preserve its federal character, that there exists a federal right of citizenship, a relationship between the people of the Nation and their National Government, with which the States may not interfere. Because the Arkansas enactment intrudes upon this federal domain, it exceeds the boundaries of the Constitution.

JUSTICE THOMAS, with whom THE CHIEF JUSTICE, JUSTICE O'CONNOR, and JUSTICE SCALIA join, dissenting.

It is ironic that the Court bases today's decision on the right of the people to "choose whom they please to govern them."...Under our Constitution, there is only one State whose people have the right to "choose whom they please" to represent Arkansas in Congress. The Court holds, however, that neither the elected legislature of that State nor the people themselves (acting by ballot initiative) may prescribe any qualifications for those representatives. The majority therefore defends the right of the people of Arkansas to "choose whom they please to govern them" by invalidating a provision that won nearly 60% of the votes cast in a direct election and that carried every congressional district in the State.

I dissent. Nothing in the Constitution deprives the people of each State of the power to prescribe eligibility requirements for the candidates who seek to represent them in Congress. The Constitution is simply silent on this question. And where the Constitution is silent, it raises no bar to action by the States or the people.

Because the majority fundamentally misunderstands the notion of "reserved" powers, I start with some first principles. Contrary to the majority's suggestion, the people of the States need not point to any affirmative grant of power in the Constitution in order to prescribe qualifications for their representatives in Congress, or to authorize their elected state legislators to do so.

Our system of government rests on one overriding principle: All power stems from the consent of the people. To phrase the principle in this way, however, is to be imprecise about something important to the notion of "reserved" powers. The ultimate source of the Constitution's authority is the consent of the people of each individual State, not the consent of the undifferentiated people of the Nation as a whole.

The ratification procedure erected by Article VII makes this point clear. The Constitution took effect once it had been ratified by the people gathered in convention in nine different States. But the Constitution went into effect only "between the States so ratifying the same"; it did not bind the people of North Carolina until they had accepted it....

...

In each State, the remainder of the people's powers—"the powers not delegated to the United States by the Constitution, nor prohibited by it to the States," Amdt. 10—are either delegated to the state government or retained by the people. The Federal Constitution does not specify which of these two possibilities obtains; it is up to the various state constitutions to declare which powers the people of each State have delegated to their state government. As far as the Federal Constitution is concerned, then, the States can exercise all powers that the Constitution does not withhold from them. The Federal Government and the States thus face different default rules: Where the Constitution is silent about the exercise of a particular power—that is, where the Constitution does not speak either expressly or by necessary implication—the Federal Government lacks that power and the States enjoy it.

...

The majority is therefore quite wrong to conclude that the people of the States cannot authorize their state governments to exercise any powers that were unknown to the States when the Federal Constitution was drafted. Indeed, the majority's position frustrates the apparent purpose of the Amendment's final phrase. The Amendment does not preempt any limitations on state power found in the state constitutions, as it might have done if it simply had said that the powers not delegated to the Federal Government are reserved to the States. But the Amendment also does not prevent the people of the States from amending their state constitutions to remove limitations that were in effect when the Federal Constitution and the Bill of Rights were ratified.

...

[W]hile the majority is correct that the Framers expected the selection process to create a "direct link" between Members of the House of Representatives and the people,... the link was between the Representatives from each State and the people of that State; the people of Georgia have no say over whom the people of Massachusetts select to represent them in Congress. This arrangement must baffle the majority, whose understanding of Congress would surely fit more comfortably within a system of nationwide elections. But the fact remains that when it comes to the selection of Members of Congress, the people of each State have retained their independent political identity. As a result, there is absolutely nothing strange about the notion that the people of the States or their state legislatures possess "reserved" powers in this area.

...

...[T]he Constitution's treatment of Presidential elections actively contradicts the majority's position. While the individual States have no "reserved" power to set qualifications for the office of President, we have long understood that they do have the power (as far as the Federal Constitution is concerned) to set qualifications for their Presidential electors—the delegates that each State selects to represent it in the electoral college that actually chooses the Nation's chief executive. Even respondents do not dispute that the States may establish qualifications for their delegates to the electoral college, as long as those qualifications pass muster under other constitutional provisions (primarily the First and Fourteenth Amendments). As the majority cannot argue that the Constitution affirmatively grants this power, the power must be one that is "reserved" to the States. It necessarily follows that the majority's understanding of the Tenth Amendment is incorrect, for the position of Presidential elector surely "'spring[s] out of the existence of the national government.'"...

The provisions that are generally known as the Qualifications Clauses read as follows:

> No Person shall be a Representative who shall not have attained to the age of twenty five Years, and been seven Years a Citizen of the United States, and who shall not, when elected, be an Inhabitant of that State in which he shall be chosen. Art. I, § 2, cl. 2.
>
> No Person shall be a Senator who shall not have attained to the Age of thirty Years, and been nine Years a Citizen of the United States, and who shall not, when elected, be an Inhabitant of that State for which he shall be chosen. Art. I, § 3, cl. 3.

...[T]hese different formulations—whether negative or affirmative—merely establish *minimum* qualifications. They are quite different from an *exclusive* formulation, such as the following:

> Every Person who shall have attained to the age of twenty five Years, and been seven Years a Citizen of the United States, and who shall, when elected, be an Inhabitant of that State in which he shall be chosen, shall be eligible to be a Representative.

At least on their face, then, the Qualifications Clauses do nothing to prohibit the people of a State from establishing additional eligibility requirements for their own representatives.

...

If the people of a State decide that they would like their representatives to possess additional qualifications, however, they have done nothing to frustrate the policy behind the Qualifications Clauses. Anyone who possesses all of the constitutional qualifications, plus some qualifications required by state law, still has all of the federal qualifications. Accordingly, the fact that the Constitution specifies certain qualifications that the Framers deemed necessary to protect the competence of the National Legislature does not imply that it strips the people of the individual States of the power to protect their own interests by adding other requirements for their own representatives.

...

The fact that the Framers did not grant a qualification-setting power to Congress does not imply that they wanted to bar its exercise at the state level. One reason why the Framers decided not to let Congress prescribe the qualifications of its own Members was that incumbents could have used this power to perpetuate themselves or their ilk in office. As Madison pointed out at the Philadelphia Convention, Members of Congress would have an obvious conflict of interest if they could determine who may run against them.... But neither the people of the States nor the state legislatures would labor under the same conflict of interest when prescribing qualifications for Members of Congress, and so the Framers would have had to use a different calculus in determining whether to deprive them of this power.

...

...In fact, the constitutional text supports the contrary inference. As the majority observes,...at the time of the framing some States also imposed religious qualifications on state legislators. The Framers evidently did not want States to impose such qualifications on federal legislators, for the Constitution specifically provides that "no religious Test shall ever be required as a Qualification to any Office or public Trust under the United States."...If the *expressio unius* maxim cuts in any direction in this case, then, it undermines the majority's position: The Framers' prohibition on state-imposed religious disqualifications for Members of Congress suggests that other types of state-imposed disqualifications are permissible....

...

...Today's decision also means that no State may disqualify congressional candidates whom a court has found to be mentally incompetent, who are currently in prison,...or who have past vote-fraud convictions....

...

The voters of Arkansas evidently believe that incumbents would not enjoy such overwhelming success if electoral contests were truly fair—that is, if the government did not put its thumb on either side of the scale. The majority offers no reason to question the accuracy of this belief. Given this context, petitioners portray § 3 of Amendment 73 [forcing multi-term incumbents to run as write-in candidates] as an effort at the state level to offset the electoral advantages that congressional incumbents have conferred upon themselves at the federal level.

...

B. Non-Commandeering

In 1991, the Supreme Court issued a 7–2 ruling authored by Justice O'Connor in *Gregory v. Ashcroft* holding that the application of the federal Age Discrimination in Employment Act to state judges would raise constitutional problems under the Tenth Amendment by interfering with how states organized their basic political offices. In 1992, the Court decided *New York v. United States* in a 6–3 decision authored by Justice O'Connor, holding that Congress could not "commandeer" the states' legislative process by requiring them to adopt a particular regulatory scheme for low-level radioactive waste. Justice Souter, appointed to the Court by the first President Bush in 1990, had joined those early decisions, but subsequently became a dissenter from the conservative federalism decisions of the Rehnquist Court.

The anti-commandeering principles seemed potentially idiosyncratic in *New York v. United States,* but they were tested again in *Printz v. United States* (1997). A 5–4 Court in *Printz* held that Congress could not require that local law enforcement officers perform a federal background check before handgun purchases were finalized. Justice Scalia argued that the Tenth Amendment imposed an independent check on how the federal government could design and implement its laws. The supremacy clause of the Constitution meant that federal laws could preempt conflicting state laws, and state courts were required to recognize and apply federal law in appropriate cases. But it was not the responsibility of state officials to enforce federal laws.

States are often integral to the implementation of federal statutes, and states often have their own reasons for wanting to be involved in how federal policies are administered and enforced. If states are too uncooperative with federal officials, the federal government may seek to enforce federal rules on its own. When the state of Texas in 2010 refused to cooperate with the federal Environmental Protection Agency in the development of new permit requirements for industrial facilities emitting greenhouse gases, the EPA decided to design the permit guidelines on its own without the participation of state regulatory officials and to require companies to obtain the permits directly from federal officials to avoid penalties.[25]

25. James C. McKinley, Jr., "E.P.A. Challenges Texas over Rules on Emissions," *New York Times* (Dec. 22, 2010), A20.

Mandating that states implement federal policies is one way to try to implement federal statutes. The federal government can also try to cajole states into cooperating in the implementation of federal policy, provide financial incentives to states to entice states and localities into participating in federal programs, or simply implement federal policy on its own. In the commandeering cases, the Court indicated that the Tenth Amendment limits how far the federal government can go in mandating that states participate in administering federal policy.

Printz v. United States, 521 U.S. 898 (1997)

After James Brady, Ronald Reagan's press secretary, was permanently disabled in the assassination attempt on the president in 1981, his wife, Sarah Brady, helped found Handgun Control, Inc. to lobby for restrictions on guns, including waiting periods on gun purchases and mandatory background checks on those seeking to purchase guns. The Brady Bill languished until the early 1990s, when Democrats made a major push for the bill. They faced a lobbying campaign by the National Rifle Association, a veto threat from President Bush, and a filibuster in the Senate that defeated the bill. After Bill Clinton won the presidency in 1992, the Democrats pressed the issue again. A bipartisan compromise avoided another filibuster. The NRA and its supporters had proposed a system of "instant background checks." These could keep guns "out of the wrong hands" with no mandatory waiting periods, but the computer database for such a system did not yet exist. The compromise reduced the mandatory waiting period. It also required local law enforcement officers to perform background checks as a temporary measure until the national database for the instant background check came online. Thus, the federal mandate to local officials came from conservative legislators seeking to minimize federal intrusion.

Sheriff Jay Printz of Ravalli County, Montana, objected to Congress adding to the duties of his officers. He filed suit in federal district court challenging the constitutionality of the background check. The trial court agreed, but a divided circuit court reversed. In a 5–4 decision, the Supreme Court reversed the circuit court, striking down the provision of the Brady Act as inconsistent with the anticommandeering principles of the federal system. The local background check provisions of the Brady Act had been set to be replaced by the instant background check system in 1998, and so Congress did not respond to the Court's act in Printz. *Many local law enforcement officials continued to perform background checks on gun purchasers until the federal computer database came online. Is such a principle a necessary part of a two-tiered system of government? What arguments does Scalia use in his majority opinion?*

JUSTICE SCALIA delivered the opinion of the Court.

. . .

. . . [T]he Brady Act purports to direct state law enforcement officers to participate, albeit only temporarily, in the administration of a federally enacted regulatory scheme. Regulated firearms dealers are required to forward Brady Forms not to a federal officer or employee, but to the CLEOs [chief law enforcement officers of the local community], whose obligation to accept those forms is implicit in the duty imposed upon them to make "reasonable efforts" within five days to determine whether the sales reflected in the forms are lawful. While the CLEOs are subjected to no federal requirement that they prevent the sales determined to be unlawful (it is perhaps assumed that their state-law duties will require prevention or apprehension), they are empowered to grant, in effect, waivers of the federally prescribed 5-day waiting period for handgun purchases by notifying the gun dealers that they have no reason to believe the transactions would be illegal.

The petitioners here object to being pressed into federal service, and contend that congressional action compelling state officers to execute federal laws is unconstitutional.

Because there is no constitutional text speaking to this precise question, the answer to the CLEOs' challenge must be sought in historical understanding and practice, in the structure of the Constitution, and in the jurisprudence of this Court. . . .

. . .

The Government observes that statutes enacted by the first Congresses required state courts to record applications for citizenship, . . . to transmit abstracts of citizenship applications and other naturalization records to the Secretary of State, . . . and to register aliens seeking naturalization and issue certificates of registry. . . . Other statutes of that era apparently or at least arguably required state courts to perform functions unrelated to naturalization, such as resolving controversies between a captain and the crew of his ship concerning the seaworthiness of the vessel, . . . hearing the claims of slave owners who had apprehended fugitive slaves and issuing certificates authorizing the slave's forced removal to the State from which he had fled, . . . taking proof of the claims of Canadian refugees who had assisted the United States during the Revolutionary War, . . . and ordering the deportation of alien enemies in times of war. . . .

These early laws establish, at most, that the Constitution was originally understood to permit imposition of an obligation on state *judges* to enforce federal prescriptions, insofar as those prescriptions related to matters appropriate for the judicial power. That assumption was perhaps implicit in one of the provisions of the Constitution, and was explicit in another. In accord with the so-called Madisonian Compromise, Article III, § 1, established only a Supreme Court, and made the creation of lower federal courts optional with the Congress—even though it was obvious that the Supreme Court alone could not hear all federal cases throughout the United States. . . .

For these reasons, we do not think the early statutes imposing obligations on state courts imply a power of Congress to impress the state executive into its service. Indeed, it can be argued that the numerousness of these statutes, contrasted with the utter lack of statutes imposing obligations on the States' executive (notwithstanding the attractiveness of that course to Congress), suggests an assumed *absence* of such power. . . .

Not only do the enactments of the early Congresses, as far as we are aware, contain no evidence of an assumption that the Federal Government may command the States' executive power in the absence of a particularized constitutional authorization, they contain some indication of precisely the opposite assumption. On September 23, 1789—the day before its proposal of the Bill of Rights . . . —the First Congress enacted a law aimed at obtaining state assistance of the most rudimentary and necessary sort for the enforcement of the new Government's laws: the holding of federal prisoners in state jails at federal expense. Significantly, the law issued not a command to the States' executive, but a recommendation to their legislatures. . . .

. . . The Government also invokes the Federalist's . . . observations that the Constitution would "enable the [national] government to employ the ordinary magistracy of each [State] in the execution of its laws" . . . and that it was "extremely probable that in other instances, particularly in the organization of the judicial power, the officers of the States will be clothed in the correspondent authority of the Union" . . . But none of these statements necessarily implies—what is the critical point here—that Congress could impose these responsibilities *without the consent of the States*. They appear to rest on the natural assumption that the States would consent to allowing their officials to assist the Federal Government....

To complete the historical record, we must note that there is not only an absence of executive-commandeering statutes in the early Congresses, but there is an absence of them in our later history as well, at least until very recent years. The Government points to the Act of August 3, 1882,...which enlisted state officials "to take charge of the local affairs of immigration in the ports within such State, and to provide for the support and relief of such immigrants therein landing as may fall into distress or need of public aid"; to inspect arriving immigrants and exclude any person found to be a "convict, lunatic, idiot," or indigent; and to send convicts back to their country of origin "without compensation." The statute did not, however, *mandate* those duties, but merely empowered the Secretary of the Treasury "to *enter into contracts* with such State...officers as *may be designated* for that purpose *by the governor* of any State." (Emphasis added.)

...

The constitutional practice we have examined above tends to negate the existence of the congressional power asserted here, but is not conclusive. We turn next to consideration of the structure of the Constitution, to see if we can discern among its "essential postulates,"...a principle that controls the present cases.

It is incontestible that the Constitution established a system of "dual sovereignty." Although the States surrendered many of their powers to the new Federal Government, they retained "a residuary and inviolable sovereignty."...Residual state sovereignty was also implicit, of course, in the Constitution's conferral upon Congress of not all governmental powers, but only discrete, enumerated ones, which implication was rendered express by the Tenth Amendment's assertion that "the powers not delegated to the United States by the Constitution, nor prohibited by it to the States, are reserved to the States respectively, or to the people."

The Framers' experience under the Articles of Confederation had persuaded them that using the States as the instruments of federal governance was both ineffectual and provocative of federal–state conflict....As Madison expressed it: "The local or municipal authorities form distinct and independent portions of the supremacy, no more subject, within their respective spheres, to the general authority than the general authority is subject to them, within its own sphere."

We have thus far discussed the effect that federal control of state officers would have upon the first element of the "double security" alluded to by Madison: the division of power between State and Federal Governments. It would also have an effect upon the second element: the separation and equilibration of powers between the three branches of the Federal Government itself. The Constitution does not leave to speculation who is to administer the laws enacted by Congress; the President, it says, "shall take Care that the Laws be faithfully executed,"...personally and through officers whom he appoints....The Brady Act effectively transfers this responsibility to thousands of CLEOs in the 50 States, who are left to implement the program without meaningful Presidential control (if indeed meaningful Presidential control is possible without the power to appoint and remove). The insistence of the Framers upon unity in the Federal Executive—to insure both vigor and accountability—is well known....That unity would be shattered, and the power of the President would be subject to reduction, if Congress could act as effectively without the President as with him, by simply requiring state officers to execute its laws.

The dissent of course resorts to the last, best hope of those who defend *ultra vires* congressional action, the Necessary and Proper Clause....What destroys the dissent's Necessary and Proper Clause argument, however, is not the Tenth Amendment but the Necessary and Proper Clause itself. When a "Law...for carrying into Execution" the Commerce Clause violates the principle of state sovereignty reflected in the various constitutional provisions we mentioned earlier, it is not a "Law...*proper* for carrying into Execution the Commerce Clause," and is thus, in the words of The Federalist, "merely [an] act of usurpation" which "deserves to be treated as such."

...

The Government...maintains that requiring state officers to perform discrete, ministerial tasks specified by Congress does not violate the principle of *New York* because it does not diminish the accountability of state or federal officials. This argument fails even on its own terms. By forcing state governments to absorb the financial burden of implementing a federal regulatory program, Members of Congress can take credit for "solving" problems without having to ask their constituents to pay for the solutions with higher federal taxes. And even when the States are not forced to absorb the costs of implementing a federal program, they are still put in the position of taking the blame for its burdensomeness and for its defects....

...

We held in *New York* that Congress cannot compel the States to enact or enforce a federal regulatory program. Today we hold that Congress cannot circumvent that prohibition by conscripting the State's officers directly. The Federal Government may neither issue directives requiring the States to address particular problems, nor command the States' officers, or those of their political subdivisions, to administer or enforce a federal regulatory program. It matters not whether policymaking is involved, and no case-by-case weighing of the burdens or benefits is necessary; such commands are fundamentally incompatible with our constitutional system of dual sovereignty....

JUSTICE O'CONNOR, concurring.

...

JUSTICE THOMAS, concurring.

The Court today properly holds that the Brady Act violates the Tenth Amendment in that it compels state law enforcement officers to "administer or enforce a federal regulatory program."... Although I join the Court's opinion in full, I write separately to emphasize that the Tenth Amendment affirms the undeniable notion that under our Constitution, the Federal Government is one of enumerated, hence limited, powers....

In my "revisionist" view,... the Federal Government's authority under the Commerce Clause, which merely allocates to Congress the power "to regulate Commerce... among the several states," does not extend to the regulation of wholly *intra*state, point-of-sale transactions.... Absent the underlying authority to regulate the intrastate transfer of firearms, Congress surely lacks the corollary power to impress state law enforcement officers into administering and enforcing such regulations....

JUSTICE STEVENS, with whom JUSTICE SOUTER, JUSTICE GINSBURG, and JUSTICE BREYER join, dissenting.

When Congress exercises the powers delegated to it by the Constitution, it may impose affirmative obligations on executive and judicial officers of state and local governments as well as ordinary citizens. This conclusion is firmly supported by the text of the Constitution, the early history of the Nation, decisions of this Court, and a correct understanding of the basic structure of the Federal Government.

...

Indeed, since the ultimate issue is one of power, we must consider its implications in times of national emergency. Matters such as the enlistment of air raid wardens, the administration of a military draft, the mass inoculation of children to forestall an epidemic, or perhaps the threat of an international terrorist, may require a national response before federal personnel can be made available to respond. If the Constitution empowers Congress and the President to make an appropriate response, is there anything in the Tenth Amendment, "in historical understanding and practice, in the structure of the Constitution, [or] in the jurisprudence of this Court,"... that forbids the enlistment of state officers to make that response effective? More narrowly, what basis is there in any of those sources for concluding that it is the Members of this Court, rather than the elected representatives of the people, who should determine whether the Constitution contains the unwritten rule that the Court announces today?

...

The text of the Constitution provides a sufficient basis for a correct disposition of this case.

Article I, § 8, grants the Congress the power to regulate commerce among the States.... [T]here can be no question that that provision adequately supports the regulation of commerce in handguns effected by the Brady Act. Moreover, the additional grant of authority in that section of the Constitution "to make all Laws which shall be necessary and proper for carrying into Execution the foregoing Powers" is surely adequate to support the temporary enlistment of local police officers in the process of identifying persons who should not be entrusted with the possession of handguns. In short, the affirmative delegation of power in Article I provides ample authority for the congressional enactment.

Unlike the First Amendment, which prohibits the enactment of a category of laws that would otherwise be authorized by Article I, the Tenth Amendment imposes no restriction on the exercise of delegated powers....

There is not a clause, sentence, or paragraph in the entire text of the Constitution of the United States that supports the proposition that a local police officer can ignore a command contained in a statute enacted by

Congress pursuant to an express delegation of power enumerated in Article I.

...

...[I]ndeed, the historical materials strongly suggest that the Founders intended to enhance the capacity of the federal government by empowering it—as a part of the new authority to make demands directly on individual citizens—to act through local officials. Hamilton made clear that the new Constitution, "by extending the authority of the federal head to the individual citizens of the several States, will enable the government to employ the ordinary magistracy of each, in the execution of its laws." Hamilton's meaning was unambiguous; the federal government was to have the power to demand that local officials implement national policy programs....

More specifically, during the debates concerning the ratification of the Constitution, it was assumed that state agents would act as tax collectors for the federal government. Opponents of the Constitution had repeatedly expressed fears that the new federal government's ability to impose taxes directly on the citizenry would result in an overbearing presence of federal tax collectors in the States. Federalists rejoined that this problem would not arise because, as Hamilton explained, "the United States...will make use of the State officers and State regulations for collecting" certain taxes....Similarly, Madison made clear that the new central government's power to raise taxes directly from the citizenry would "not be resorted to, except for supplemental purposes of revenue...and that the eventual collection, under the immediate authority of the Union, will generally be made by the officers...appointed by the several States."...

The Court's response to this powerful historical evidence is weak. The majority suggests that "none of these statements necessarily implies...Congress could impose these responsibilities without the consent of the States."...No fair reading of these materials can justify such an interpretation. As Hamilton explained, the power of the government to act on "individual citizens"—including "employing the ordinary magistracy" of the States—was an answer to the problems faced by a central government that could act only directly "upon the States in their political or collective capacities."...

This point is made especially clear in Hamilton's statement that "the legislatures, courts, and magistrates, of the respective members, will be incorporated into the operations of the national government as far as its just and constitutional authority extends; and *will be rendered auxiliary to the enforcement of its laws.*"...It is hard to imagine a more unequivocal statement that state judicial and executive branch officials may be required to implement federal law where the National Government acts within the scope of its affirmative powers.

...

Bereft of support in the history of the founding, the Court rests its conclusion on the claim that there is little evidence the National Government actually exercised such a power in the early years of the Republic....This reasoning is misguided in principle and in fact. While we have indicated that the express consideration and resolution of difficult constitutional issues by the First Congress in particular "provides 'contemporaneous and weighty evidence' of the Constitution's meaning since many of [its] Members...'had taken part in framing that instrument,'"...we have never suggested that the failure of the early Congresses to address the scope of federal power in a particular area or to exercise a particular authority was an argument against its existence....

More importantly, the fact that Congress did elect to rely on state judges and the clerks of state courts to perform a variety of executive functions...is surely evidence of a contemporary understanding that their status as state officials did not immunize them from federal service....

...

The Court's evaluation of the historical evidence, furthermore, fails to acknowledge the important difference between policy decisions that may have been influenced by respect for state sovereignty concerns, and decisions that are compelled by the Constitution. Thus, for example, the decision by Congress to give President Wilson the authority to utilize the services of state officers in implementing the World War I draft...surely indicates that the national legislature saw no constitutional impediment to the enlistment of state assistance during a federal emergency. The fact that the President was able to implement the program by respectfully "requesting" state action, rather than bluntly commanding it, is evidence that he was an effective statesman, but surely does not indicate that he doubted either his or Congress' power to use mandatory language if necessary. If there were merit to the Court's appraisal of this incident, one would assume that there would have been some contemporary comment on the supposed constitutional concern that hypothetically might have motivated the President's choice of language.

...

Perversely, the majority's rule seems more likely to damage than to preserve the safeguards against tyranny provided by the existence of vital state governments. By limiting the ability of the Federal Government to enlist state officials in the implementation of its programs, the Court creates incentives for the National Government to aggrandize itself. In the name of State's rights, the majority would have the Federal Government create vast national bureaucracies to implement its policies. This is exactly the sort of thing that the early Federalists promised would not occur, in part as a result of the National Government's ability to rely on the magistracy of the states....

...

Far more important than the concerns that the Court musters in support of its new rule is the fact that the Framers entrusted Congress with the task of creating a working structure of intergovernmental relationships around the framework that the Constitution authorized. Neither explicitly nor implicitly did the Framers issue any command that forbids Congress from imposing federal duties on private citizens or on local officials. As a general matter, Congress has followed the sound policy of authorizing federal agencies and federal agents to administer federal programs. That general practice, however, does not negate the existence of power to rely on state officials in occasional situations in which such reliance is in the national interest. Rather, the occasional exceptions confirm the wisdom of Justice Holmes' reminder that "the machinery of government would not work if it were not allowed a little play in its joints."...

...

JUSTICE SOUTER, dissenting.

...

In deciding these cases, which I have found closer than I had anticipated, it is The Federalist that finally determines my position. I believe that the most straightforward reading of No. 27 is authority for the Government's position here, and that this reading is both supported by No. 44 and consistent with Nos. 36 and 45.

Hamilton in No. 27 first notes that because the new Constitution would authorize the National Government to bind individuals directly through national law, it could "employ the ordinary magistracy of each [State] in the execution of its laws."... Were he to stop here, he would not necessarily be speaking of anything beyond the possibility of cooperative arrangements by agreement. But he then addresses the combined effect of the proposed Supremacy Clause... and state officers' oath requirement,... and he states that "the Legislatures, Courts and Magistrates of the respective members will be incorporated into the operations of the national government, *as far as its just and constitutional authority extends;* and will be rendered auxiliary to the enforcement of its laws."... The natural reading of this language is not merely that the officers of the various branches of state governments may be employed in the performance of national functions; Hamilton says that the state governmental machinery "will be incorporated" into the Nation's operation, and because the "auxiliary" status of the state officials will occur because they are "bound by the sanctity of an oath."... I take him to mean that their auxiliary functions will be the products of their obligations thus undertaken to support federal law, not of their own, or the States', unfettered choices.

...

In the light of all these passages, I cannot persuade myself that the statements from No. 27 speak of anything less than the authority of the National Government, when exercising an otherwise legitimate power (the commerce power, say), to require state "auxiliaries" to take appropriate action.

...

JUSTICE BREYER, with whom JUSTICE STEVENS joins, dissenting.

I would add to the reasons JUSTICE STEVENS sets forth the fact that the United States is not the only nation that seeks to reconcile the practical need for a central authority with the democratic virtues of more local control. At least some other countries, facing the same basic problem, have found that local control is better maintained through application of a principle that is the direct opposite of the principle the majority derives from the silence of our Constitution. The federal systems of Switzerland, Germany, and the European Union, for example, all provide that constituent states, not federal bureaucracies, will themselves implement many of the laws, rules, regulations, or decrees enacted by the central "federal" body....

Of course, we are interpreting our own Constitution, not those of other nations, and there may be relevant political and structural differences between their systems and our own.... But their experience may nonetheless cast an empirical light on the consequences of different solutions to a common legal problem—in this case the problem of reconciling central authority with the need to preserve the liberty-enhancing autonomy of a smaller constituent governmental entity.... And that experience here offers empirical confirmation of the implied answer to a question JUSTICE STEVENS asks: Why, or how, would what the majority sees as a constitutional alternative—the creation of a new federal gun-law bureaucracy, or the expansion of an existing federal bureaucracy— better promote either state sovereignty or individual liberty?...

C. Sovereign Immunity

Alden v. Maine (1999) was the second in a series of state sovereign immunity cases decided by the Rehnquist Court and part of a broader group of cases in which a narrow five-justice majority emphasized federalism principles in order to invalidate a provision of a congressional statute. The state sovereign immunity cases, or the "Eleventh Amendment cases," are concerned with the conditions under which a state government or government agency can be sued in court by private parties for monetary damages. The Eleventh Amendment itself had made clear that citizens of other states could not make use of "diversity jurisdiction" to sue a state in federal court, and in the 1890 case of *Hans v. Louisiana* the Supreme Court had ruled that state sovereign immunity formed the implicit background principle of the Eleventh Amendment and prevented citizens from suing their own states in federal court to recover debts.

In the late twentieth century, responding in part to a suggestion of the Warren Court, Congress increasingly allowed private lawsuits against state governments as a means of enforcing regulatory policies against the states. The possibility of recovering monetary damages and penalties created incentives for lawyers to take such cases and push them through the courts. Although not posing the same level of threat to the state treasuries as the outstanding revolutionary war debts that led to the passage of the Eleventh Amendment or the bankrupt railroad debts that fed that *Hans* litigation, the "unfunded mandates" and "coercive federalism" of the late twentieth century were a frequent source of complaint and financial concern to state governments.

In 1996, the Supreme Court unexpectedly intervened in *Seminole Tribe of Florida v. Florida*, holding that Congress could not through statute using its Article I powers waive state sovereign immunity in federal courts. *Alden v. Maine* extended *Seminole Tribe*'s logic to state courts, while producing more elaborate opinions explaining the original arguments surrounding *Seminole Tribe*. In subsequent cases, the Court made clear that Congress could abrogate state sovereign immunity when acting under Section 5 of the Fourteenth Amendment (which was passed after the Eleventh Amendment and modified its principle of state sovereignty), but the Court has separately read narrowly the reach of congressional authority under Section 5 in cases like *City of Boerne v. Flores* (1997). The Court later narrowed the implications of *Seminole Tribe* and *Alden* in *Central Virginia Community College v. Katz* (2006), which allowed Congress to abrogate state sovereign immunity when exercising power under the bankruptcy clause of Article I.

Alden v. Maine, 527 U.S. 706 (1999)

In 1992, a group of nearly one hundred state probation officers filed suit in federal district court against their employer, the state of Maine, seeking compensation and monetary damages for violations of the overtime provisions of the federal Fair Labor Standards Act (FLSA). Maine had classified probation officers as professional employees and therefore exempt from federal overtime requirements. The officers had been unsuccessful in persuading the state that court decisions elsewhere had suggested that such a classification was inappropriate. The officers won some key preliminary decisions in district court, leaving the amount of back pay owed by the state as the primary question still to be resolved when Seminole Tribe *was handed down by the U.S. Supreme Court. In light of* Seminole Tribe, *the state promptly moved to have the case dismissed from the federal courts on the grounds of state sovereign immunity, and the district court reluctantly granted the motion. Most of the probation officers then filed their suit in state court, but the state court dismissed the suit on the grounds of sovereign immunity.*

The Maine Supreme Judicial Court affirmed the trial court's ruling. It held that a provision of the FLSA authorizing such private suits against the state governments in state courts without state consent was unconstitutional. The U.S. Supreme Court accepted a cert petition in the case, and a 5–4 decision affirmed the Maine court's ruling. The justices' conflicting views echo debates that were initially rehearsed during the Court's first decade.

After their loss in the courts, the state employees union in Maine took up the probation officers' cause in the legislature. The legislature soon passed a bill appropriating funds to provide back pay and legal expenses for the officers (less than $300,000, a somewhat lower amount than the union had sought) and later passed a bipartisan statute waiving state sovereign immunity for a limited range of similar suits in the future. In general, the state sovereign immunity cases narrowed the ability of individuals to win monetary awards from state governments based on violations of federal statutes that did not relate to civil rights. Congress still had other options to enforce such statutory requirements against the states, including persuading states to waive their sovereign immunity, allowing prospective relief in private lawsuits, and authorizing direct enforcement by federal agencies. Why might Congress try to waive state sovereign immunity to allow private lawsuits to enforce federal statutes? Is immunity from such suits a useful check on congressional power?

JUSTICE KENNEDY delivered the opinion of the Court.

...

We hold that the powers delegated to Congress under Article I of the United States Constitution do not include the power to subject nonconsenting States to private suits for damages in state courts. We decide as well that the State of Maine has not consented to suits for overtime pay and liquidated damages under the FLSA. On these premises we affirm the judgment sustaining dismissal of the suit.

The Eleventh Amendment makes explicit reference to the States' immunity from suits "commenced or prosecuted against one of the United States by Citizens of another State, or by Citizens or Subjects of any Foreign State." We have, as a result, sometimes referred to the States' immunity from suit as "Eleventh Amendment immunity." The phrase is convenient shorthand but something of a misnomer, for the sovereign immunity of the States neither derives from nor is limited by the terms of the Eleventh Amendment. Rather, as the Constitution's structure, and its history, and the authoritative interpretations by this Court make clear, the States' immunity from suit is a fundamental aspect of the sovereignty which the States enjoyed before the ratification of the Constitution, and which they retain today (either literally or by virtue of their admission into the Union upon an equal footing with the other States) except as altered by the plan of the Convention or certain constitutional Amendments.

Although the Constitution establishes a National Government with broad, often plenary authority over matters within its recognized competence, the founding document "specifically recognizes the States as sovereign entities." *Seminole Tribe of Florida* v. *Florida* (1996).... Various textual provisions of the Constitution assume the States' continued existence and active participation in the fundamental processes of governance. See *Printz* v. *United States* (1997).... Any doubt regarding the constitutional role of the States as sovereign entities is removed by the Tenth Amendment, which, like the other provisions of the Bill of Rights, was enacted to allay lingering concerns about the extent of the national power....

The federal system established by our Constitution preserves the sovereign status of the States in two ways. First, it reserves to them a substantial portion of the Nation's primary sovereignty, together with the dignity and essential attributes inhering in that status. The States "form distinct and independent portions of the supremacy, no more subject, within their respective spheres, to the general authority than the general authority is subject to them, within its own sphere." The Federalist No. 39....

Second, even as to matters within the competence of the National Government, the constitutional design secures the founding generation's rejection of "the concept of a central government that would act upon and through the States" in favor of "a system in which the State and Federal Governments would exercise concurrent authority over the people—who were, in Hamilton's words, 'the only proper objects of government.'" *Printz*....

The States thus retain "a residuary and inviolable sovereignty." The Federalist No. 39. They are not relegated to the role of mere provinces or political corporations, but retain the dignity, though not the full authority, of sovereignty.

The generation that designed and adopted our federal system considered immunity from private suits central to sovereign dignity. When the Constitution was ratified, it was well established in English law that the Crown could not be sued without consent in its own courts. See *Chisholm* v. *Georgia* (1793) (Iredell, J., dissenting) (surveying English practice)....

Although the American people had rejected other aspects of English political theory, the doctrine that a sovereign could not be sued without its consent was universal in the States when the Constitution was drafted and ratified. See *Chisholm* (Iredell, J., dissenting); *Hans* v. *Louisiana* (1890).

The ratification debates, furthermore, underscored the importance of the States' sovereign immunity to the American people. Grave concerns were raised by the provisions of Article III which extended the federal judicial power to controversies between States and citizens of other States or foreign nations....

The leading advocates of the Constitution assured the people in no uncertain terms that the Constitution would not strip the States of sovereign immunity....

Despite the persuasive assurances of the Constitution's leading advocates and the expressed understanding of the only state conventions to address the issue in explicit terms, this Court held, just five years after the Constitution was adopted, that Article III authorized a private citizen of another State to sue the State of Georgia without its consent. *Chisholm* v. *Georgia*....

...

The Court's decision "fell upon the country with a profound shock."...

The States, in particular, responded with outrage to the decision. The Massachusetts Legislature, for example, denounced the decision as "repugnant to the first principles of a federal government," and called upon the State's Senators and Representatives to take all necessary steps to "remove any clause or article of the Constitution, which can be construed to imply or justify a decision, that, a State is compellable to answer in any suit by an individual or individuals in any Court of the United States."...

...

...By its terms, then, the Eleventh Amendment did not redefine the federal judicial power but instead overruled the Court...

...Given the outraged reaction to *Chisholm*, as well as Congress' repeated refusal to otherwise qualify the text of the Amendment, it is doubtful that if Congress meant to write a new immunity into the Constitution it would have limited that immunity to the narrow text of the Eleventh Amendment:

> Can we suppose that, when the Eleventh Amendment was adopted, it was understood to be left open for citizens of a State to sue their own state in federal courts, whilst the idea of suits by citizens of other states, or of foreign states, was indignantly repelled? Suppose that Congress, when proposing the Eleventh Amendment, had appended to it a proviso that nothing therein contained should prevent a State from being sued by its own citizens in cases arising under the Constitution or laws of the United States, can we imagine that it would have been adopted by the States? The supposition that it would is almost an absurdity on its face." *Hans*, at 14–15.

...

In short, the scanty and equivocal evidence offered by the dissent establishes no more than what is evident from the decision in *Chisholm*—that some members of the founding generation disagreed with Hamilton, Madison, Marshall, Iredell, and the only state conventions formally to address the matter. The events leading to the adoption of the Eleventh Amendment, however, make clear that the individuals who believed the Constitution stripped the States of their immunity from suit were at most a small minority.

Not only do the ratification debates and the events leading to the adoption of the Eleventh Amendment reveal the original understanding of the States' constitutional immunity from suit, they also underscore the importance of sovereign immunity to the founding generation. Simply put, "The Constitution never would have been ratified if the States and their courts were to be stripped of their sovereign authority except as expressly provided by the Constitution itself." *Atascadero State Hospital* v. *Scanlon* (1985)....

The Court has been consistent in interpreting the adoption of the Eleventh Amendment as conclusive evidence "that the decision in *Chisholm* was contrary to the well-understood meaning of the Constitution," *Seminole Tribe*....As a consequence, we have looked to "history and experience, and the established order of things," rather than "adhering to the mere letter" of the Eleventh Amendment, in determining the scope of the States' constitutional immunity from suit.

...

In this case we must determine whether Congress has the power, under Article I, to subject nonconsenting States to private suits in their own courts. As the foregoing discussion makes clear, the fact that the Eleventh Amendment by its terms limits only "the Judicial power of the United States" does not resolve the question. To rest on the words of the Amendment alone would be to engage in the type of ahistorical literalism we have rejected in interpreting the scope of the States' sovereign immunity since the discredited decision in *Chisholm*....

...In exercising its Article I powers Congress may subject the States to private suits in their own courts only if there is "compelling evidence" that the States were required to surrender this power to Congress pursuant to the constitutional design....

...

A general federal power to authorize private suits for money damages would place unwarranted strain on the States' ability to govern in accordance with the will of their citizens. Today, as at the time of the founding, the allocation of scarce resources among competing needs and interests lies at the heart of the political process. While the judgment creditor of the State may have a legitimate claim for compensation, other important needs and worthwhile ends compete for access to the public fisc. Since all cannot be satisfied in full, it is inevitable that difficult decisions involving the most sensitive and political of judgments must be made. If the principle of representative government is to be preserved to the States, the balance between competing interests must be reached after deliberation by the political process established by the citizens of the State, not by judicial decree mandated by the Federal Government and invoked by the private citizen....

...

This case at one level concerns the formal structure of federalism, but in a Constitution as resilient as ours form mirrors substance. Congress has vast power but not all power. When Congress legislates in matters affecting the States, it may not treat these sovereign entities as mere prefectures or corporations. Congress must accord States the esteem due to them as joint participants in a federal system, one beginning with the premise of sovereignty in both the central Government and the separate States. Congress has ample means to ensure compliance with valid federal laws, but it must respect the sovereignty of the States.

In an apparent attempt to disparage a conclusion with which it disagrees, the dissent attributes our reasoning to natural law. We seek to discover, however, only what the Framers and those who ratified the Constitution sought to accomplish when they created a federal system. We appeal to no higher authority than the Charter which they wrote and adopted. Theirs was the unique insight that freedom is enhanced by the creation of two governments, not one. We need not attach a label to our dissenting colleagues' insistence that the constitutional structure adopted by the founders must yield to the politics of the moment. Although the Constitution begins with the principle that sovereignty rests with the people, it does not follow that the National Government becomes the ultimate, preferred mechanism for expressing the people's will. The States exist as a refutation of that concept. In choosing to ordain and establish the Constitution, the people insisted upon a federal structure for the very purpose of rejecting the idea that the will of the people in all instances is expressed by the central power, the one most remote from their control. The Framers of the Constitution did not share our dissenting colleagues' belief that the Congress may circumvent the federal design by regulating the States directly when it pleases to do so, including by a proxy in which individual citizens are authorized to levy upon the state treasuries absent the States' consent to jurisdiction.

...The judgment of the Supreme Judicial Court of Maine is

Affirmed.

JUSTICE SOUTER, with whom JUSTICE STEVENS, JUSTICE GINSBURG, and JUSTICE BREYER join, dissenting.

In *Seminole Tribe of Florida.* v. *Florida* (1996), a majority of this Court invoked the Eleventh Amendment to declare that the federal judicial power under Article III of the Constitution does not reach a private action against a State, even on a federal question. In the Court's conception, however, the Eleventh Amendment was understood as having been enhanced by a "background principle" of state sovereign immunity (understood as immunity to suit), that operated beyond its limited codification in the Amendment, dealing solely with federal citizen-state diversity jurisdiction. To the *Seminole Tribe* dissenters, of whom I was one, the Court's enhancement of the Amendment was at odds with constitutional history and at war with the conception of divided sovereignty that is the essence of American federalism.

...

The Court rests its decision principally on the claim that immunity from suit was "a fundamental aspect of the sovereignty which the States enjoyed before the ratification of the Constitution," an aspect which the Court understands to have survived the ratification of the Constitution in 1788 and to have been "confirmed" and given constitutional status, by the adoption of the Tenth Amendment in 1791. If the Court truly means by "sovereign immunity" what that term meant at common law, its argument would be insupportable. While sovereign immunity entered many new state legal systems as a part of the common law selectively received from England, it was not understood to be indefeasible or to have been given any such status by the new National Constitution, which did not mention it. See *Seminole Tribe* (Souter, J., dissenting). Had the question been posed, state sovereign immunity could not have been thought to shield a State from suit under federal law on a subject committed to national jurisdiction by Article I of the Constitution. Congress exercising its conceded Article I power may unquestionably abrogate such immunity....

...The conception [of sovereign immunity in the majority opinion] is...not one of common law so much as of natural law, a universally applicable proposition discoverable by reason. This, I take it, is the sense in which the Court so emphatically relies on Alexander Hamilton's reference in The Federalist No. 81 to the States' sovereign immunity from suit as an "inherent" right, a characterization that does not require, but is at least open to, a natural law reading.

...The Court's principal rationale for today's result, then, turns on history: was the natural law conception of sovereign immunity as inherent in any notion of an independent State widely held in the United States in the period preceding the ratification of 1788 (or the adoption of the Tenth Amendment in 1791)?

The answer is certainly no. There is almost no evidence that the generation of the Framers thought sovereign immunity was fundamental in the sense of being unalterable....

...

The only arguable support for the Court's absolutist view that I have found among the leading participants in the debate surrounding ratification was the one already mentioned, that of Alexander Hamilton in The Federalist No. 81, where he described the sovereign immunity of the States in language suggesting principles associated with natural law....

...

There was no unanimity among the Virginians either on state- or federal-court immunity, however, for Edmund Randolph anticipated the position he would later espouse as plaintiff's counsel in *Chisholm v. Georgia* (1793). He contented himself with agnosticism on the significance of what Hamilton had called "the general practice of mankind," and argued that notwithstanding any natural law view of the nonsuability of States, the Constitution permitted suit against a State in federal court: "I think, whatever the law of nations may say, that any doubt respecting the construction that a state may be plaintiff, and not defendant, is taken away by the words *where a state shall be a party*." Randolph clearly believed that the Constitution both could and in fact by its language did trump any inherent immunity enjoyed by the States; his view on sovereign immunity in state court seems to have been that the issue was uncertain ("whatever the law of nations may say").

At the farthest extreme from Hamilton, James Wilson made several comments in the Pennsylvania Convention that suggested his hostility to any idea of state sovereign immunity. First, he responded to the argument that "the sovereignty of the states is destroyed" if they are sued by the United States, "because a suitor in a court must acknowledge the jurisdiction of that court, and it is not the custom of sovereigns to suffer their names to be made use of in this manner." For Wilson, "the answer [was] plain and easy: the government of each state ought to be subordinate to the government of the United States."...

...

At the close of the ratification debates, the issue of the sovereign immunity of the States under Article III had not been definitively resolved, and in some instances the indeterminacy led the ratification conventions to respond in ways that point to the range of thinking about the doctrine. Several state ratifying conventions proposed amendments and issued declarations that would have exempted States from subjection to suit in federal court....

...

...At all events, the state ratifying conventions' felt need for clarification on the question of state suability demonstrates that uncertainty surrounded the matter even at the moment of ratification. This uncertainty set the stage for the divergent views expressed in *Chisholm*.

If the natural law conception of sovereign immunity as an inherent characteristic of sovereignty enjoyed by the States had been broadly accepted at the time of the founding, one would expect to find it reflected somewhere in the five opinions delivered by the Court in *Chisholm* v. *Georgia* (1793). Yet that view did not appear in any of them....

...

The Court's rationale for today's holding based on a conception of sovereign immunity as somehow fundamental to sovereignty or inherent in statehood fails for the lack of any substantial support for such a conception in the thinking of the founding era. The Court cannot be counted out yet, however, for it has a second line of argument looking not to a clause-based reception of the natural law conception or even to its recognition as a "background principle"...but to a structural basis in the Constitution's creation of a federal system....

The National Constitution formally and finally repudiated the received political wisdom that a system of multiple sovereignties constituted the "great solecism of an *imperium in imperio*"....Once "the atom of sovereignty" had been split, *U.S. Term Limits, Inc.* v. *Thornton* (1995) (Kennedy, J., concurring), the general scheme of delegated sovereignty as between the two component governments of the federal system was clear.

Hence the flaw in the Court's appeal to federalism. The State of Maine is not sovereign with respect to the national objective of the FLSA. It is not the authority that promulgated the FLSA, on which the right of action in this case depends. That authority is the United States acting through the Congress, whose legislative power under Article I of the Constitution to extend FLSA coverage to state employees has already been decided, see *Garcia* v. *San Antonio Metropolitan Transit Authority* (1985), and is not contested here.

...

It is symptomatic of the weakness of the structural notion proffered by the Court that it seeks to buttress the argument by relying on "the dignity and respect afforded a State, which the immunity is designed to protect," and by invoking the many demands on a State's fisc. Apparently beguiled by Gilded Era language describing private suits against States as "'neither becoming nor convenient,'" the Court calls "immunity from private suits central to sovereign dignity," and assumes that this "dignity" is a quality easily translated from the person of the King to the participatory abstraction of a republican State....It would be hard to imagine anything more inimical to the republican conception, which rests on the understanding of its citizens precisely that the government is not above them, but of them, its actions being governed by law just like their own. Whatever justification there may be for an American government's immunity from private suit, it is not dignity.

It is equally puzzling to hear the Court say that "federal power to authorize private suits for money damages would place unwarranted strain on the States' ability to govern in accordance with the will of their citizens." So long as the citizens' will, expressed through state legislation, does not violate valid federal law, the strain will not be felt; and to the extent that state action does violate federal law, the will of the citizens of the United States already trumps that of the citizens of the State: the strain then is not only expected, but necessarily intended.

Least of all does the Court persuade by observing that "other important needs" than that of the "judgment creditor" compete for public money. The "judgment creditor" in question is not a dunning bill-collector, but a citizen whose federal rights have been violated, and a constitutional structure that stints on enforcing federal rights out of an abundance of delicacy toward the States has substituted politesse in place of respect for the rule of law.

...

If today's decision occasions regret at its anomalous versions of history and federal theory, it is the more regrettable in being the second time the Court has suddenly changed the course of prior decision in order to limit the exercise of authority over a subject now concededly within the Article I jurisdiction of the Congress....

In 1974, Congress...amended the FLSA, this time "extending the minimum wage and maximum hour provisions to almost all public employees employed by the States and by their various political subdivisions."...[In] *National League of Cities v. Usery* (1976), the Court held the extension of the Act to these employees an unconstitutional infringement of state sovereignty....

But *National League of Cities* was not the last word. In *Garcia*, decided some nine years later,...the Court overruled *National League of Cities*, this time taking the position that Congress was not barred by the Constitution from binding the States as employers under the Commerce Clause.... *Garcia* remains good law, its reasoning has not been repudiated, and it has not been challenged here.

The FLSA has not, however, fared as well in practice as it has in theory. The Court in *Seminole Tribe* created a significant impediment to the statute's practical application by rendering its damages provisions unenforceable against the States by private suit in federal court. Today's decision blocking private actions in state courts makes the barrier to individual enforcement a total one.

...It is true, of course, that the FLSA does authorize the Secretary of Labor to file suit seeking damages, but unless Congress plans a significant expansion of the National Government's litigating forces to provide a lawyer whenever private litigation is barred by today's decision and *Seminole Tribe*, the allusion to enforcement of private rights by the National Government is probably not much more than whimsy. Facing reality, Congress specifically found, as long ago as 1974, "that the enforcement capability of the Secretary of Labor is not alone sufficient to provide redress in all or even a substantial portion of the situations where compliance is not forthcoming voluntarily."...

...

So there is much irony in the Court's profession that it grounds its opinion on a deeply rooted historical tradition of sovereign immunity, when the Court abandons a principle nearly as inveterate, and much closer to the hearts of the Framers: that where there is a right, there must be a remedy....

...

...The resemblance of today's state sovereign immunity to the *Lochner* era's industrial due process is striking. The Court began this century by imputing immutable constitutional status to a conception of economic self-reliance that was never true to industrial life and grew insistently fictional with the years, and the Court has chosen to close the century by conferring like status on a conception of state sovereign immunity that is true neither to history nor to the structure of the Constitution. I expect the Court's late essay into immunity doctrine will prove the equal of its earlier experiment in laissez-faire, the one being as unrealistic as the other, as indefensible, and probably as fleeting.

V. Separation of Powers

MAJOR DEVELOPMENTS

- Rejection of the line-item veto by the Supreme Court
- Debate over presidential power to refuse to enforce statutes
- Controversy over unilaterial presidential actions justified on grounds of national security
- Recognition of some executive immunity from judicial proceedings

Issues involving the separation of powers have been at the center of the constitutional agenda for both the Supreme Court and the elected branches of government throughout the Contemporary Era. This should not be a surprise. First, the two political parties have become increasingly polarized. Conservative Democrats and liberal Republicans were once common, but they are now increasingly rare in the halls of Congress. Political activists in both parties are not merely political professionals; they tend to be ideologically committed. They emphasize issues and principles, and they hold candidates and politicians accountable to them.[26]

Second, divided government has become commonplace. For long periods in American history, unified government—the legislature and the executive controlled by the same political party—has been the norm. The majority party was expected to govern with little assistance from the minority party. In modern politics, divided politics has often been the norm, with no expectation that unified government was just around the corner. Both Congress and the White House have viewed the other branch of government with suspicion, if not outright hostility. They have often looked for ways to work around the other branch or to constrain it.[27]

---

26. Nolan McCarty, Keith T. Poole, and Howard Rosenthal, *Polarized America* (Cambridge, MA: MIT, 2007); Geoffrey C. Layman, Thomas M. Carsey, and Juliana Menasce Horowitz, "Party Polarization in American Politics: Characteristics, Causes, and Consequences," *Annual Review of Political Science* 9 (2006):83.

27. Morris P. Fiorina, "An Era of Divided Government," *Political Science Quarterly* 107 (1992):387; David R. Mayhew, *Divided We Govern* (New Haven: Yale University Press, 2005).

Illustration 11-2 The National Security State

Source: Tom Toles, *Washington Post*, May 18, 2006. © 2006 The Washington Post. Reprinted with permission of UNIVERSAL UCLICK. All rights reserved.

Even as judges and politicians struggle with the consequences of divided government, they have also continued to wrestle with a variety of complicated policy problems. The continued growth of the government, the political power that such growth entails, and the political risks involved in dealing with some political issues (such as deficit reduction) have all led politicians to look for innovative ways to organize policymaking. The justices have sometimes been skeptical about whether those innovations are consistent with constitutional design.

The debates include the power of Congress to create a presidential line-item veto, as well as the authority of the president to refuse to enforce statutory provisions that he regards as unconstitutional. Debates also include the scope of presidential authority during wartime, executive privilege, and the extent to which the president is subject to judicial processes while in office.

A. Sharing the Legislative Power

In the 1980s, the Court had taken a dim view of some of the creative ways that the legislative and executive branch had tried to manipulate the separation of powers in order to manage the complexities of modern government. Most notably, the Court in *INS v. Chadha* (1983) concluded that the common device of the "legislative veto" was unconstitutional. The legislative veto allowed Congress (or a part of Congress) to nullify an executive action under some earlier statutory authority without passing a new statute (in Chadha's case, reversing a decision by the executive branch on whether to deport an individual under existing immigration laws). If Congress wanted to take an action that would have the legal effect, the Court argued, then the legislature must pass a bill and present it to the president for his signature. In *Bowsher v. Synar* (1986), the Court held that the automatic spending cuts mechanism contained in the Gramm-Rudman-Hollings Act of 1985 was unconstitutional. The justices concluded that the statute impermissibly gave a legislative officer, the Comptroller General, an executive function in determining the final cuts to be made if sufficient deficit reduction goals could not be met by the legislature. Such efforts to circumvent the normal legislative process did too much violence to the structure of the Constitution, according to the majority of the justices.

Congress and the president have continued to seek out creative ways to address the administrative and political challenges of modern politics. Each legislative innovation raises its own set of constitutional questions about how well it fits within the constitutional scheme of separation of powers. In *Clinton v. New York* (1998), the Court confronted a statutory "line item veto." Since the founding, the president was understood to have the power to veto or sign entire bills that were presented to him by Congress. This power did not allow the president to mark out, or veto, individual line items from a bill. In the 1990s, Congress tried through statute to give the president a kind of line-item veto power over appropriations bills. The Court held that the line-item veto suffered from the same problem as the legislative veto struck down in *Chadha*. In order for a bill to become law, it must pass through the legislative process outlined in the constitutional text. Congress cannot circumvent that process. As in the 1980s, Congress continues to look for ways to threaten "automatic" budget cuts if the normal legislative process cannot reach an agreement on the federal budget and how best to reduce the debt. Such mechanisms are constrained by the constitutional requirements governing the legislative process and the sharing of powers.[28]

Clinton v. City of New York, 524 U.S. 417 (1998)

Many state constitutions give governors the power to exercise a "line-item veto," the choice to reject individual provisions of a proposed bill and not simply the bill as a whole. In the 1980s, conservatives began to advocate giving the president a similar power in order to fight "wasteful" government spending and promote a smaller government. Some lawyers argued that the president could exercise a line-item veto consistent with the existing terms of the U.S. Constitution. More commonly, it was thought that giving the president a line-item veto power would require a constitutional amendment, but there was not enough support in Congress to pass such an amendment. A "legislative line-item veto" was part of the 1994 Republican Contract with America, and one of the few measures that the Clinton administration supported. The Line Item Veto Act allowed the president to mark out any specific items he disapproved in an enacted spending law. In an expedited procedure, Congress would then vote on a separate "bill of disapproval" containing all the items that the president had lined out. That bill of disapproval would then be subject to the regular presidential veto and possible override. Unless the bill of disapproval passed, the funds for those items from the original appropriations bill would not be spent. The complicated scheme was designed to comply with the Court's earlier decision in Chadha, *while providing something comparable to what could be achieved through a constitutional amendment.*

Senator Robert Byrd, a well-known defender of the prerogatives of the Senate, brought a lawsuit in federal district court seeking to have the Line Item Veto Act declared unconstitutional. The case was dismissed on the grounds that he did not have standing to file suit. When President Clinton vetoed over eighty individual items in tax and spending bills, several parties filed suit. The City of New York, for one, had seen millions of dollars of funds removed. The act was declared invalid in district court, and the Supreme Court heard the case on expedited appeal from the district court. The Supreme Court affirmed the trial court in a 6–3 decision. Did the Line Item Veto Act void the problems with the legislative veto that the Supreme Court identified in INS v. Chadha *(1983)? Are the procedures in the line-item veto consistent with the central values of the constitutional separation of powers?*

JUSTICE STEVENS delivered the opinion of the Court.

. . .

The Line Item Veto Act gives the President the power to "cancel in whole" three types of provisions that have been signed into law: "(1) any dollar amount of discretionary budget authority; (2) any item of new direct spending; or (3) any limited tax benefit."....

. . .

A cancellation takes effect upon receipt by Congress of the special message from the President....If, however, a "disapproval bill" pertaining to a special message is enacted into law, the cancellations set forth in that message become "null and void."...The Act sets forth a detailed expedited procedure for the

28. During the 2011 budget negotiations, law professor Garrett Epps suggested that the president had the unilateral authority to continue to issue government bonds, regardless of the statutory debt limit. Such an assertion of executive authority would at least have significantly changed the negotiating leverage in budget talks. The argument gained little traction in the administration. Garrett Epps, "The Speech Obama Could Give: 'The Constitution Forbids Default,'" *The Atlantic* (April 28, 2011).

consideration of a "disapproval bill,"...but no such bill was passed for either of the cancellations involved in these cases. A majority vote of both Houses is sufficient to enact a disapproval bill. The Act does not grant the President the authority to cancel a disapproval bill...but he does, of course, retain his constitutional authority to veto such a bill.

...

There are important differences between the President's "return" of a bill pursuant to Article I, § 7, and the exercise of the President's cancellation authority pursuant to the Line Item Veto Act. The constitutional return takes place *before* the bill becomes law; the statutory cancellation occurs *after* the bill becomes law. The constitutional return is of the entire bill; the statutory cancellation is of only a part. Although the Constitution expressly authorizes the President to play a role in the process of enacting statutes, it is silent on the subject of unilateral Presidential action that either repeals or amends parts of duly enacted statutes.

There are powerful reasons for construing constitutional silence on this profoundly important issue as equivalent to an express prohibition. The procedures governing the enactment of statutes set forth in the text of Article I were the product of the great debates and compromises that produced the Constitution itself. Familiar historical materials provide abundant support for the conclusion that the power to enact statutes may only "be exercised in accord with a single, finely wrought and exhaustively considered, procedure." Our first President understood the text of the Presentment Clause as requiring that he either "approve all the parts of a Bill, or reject it in toto." What has emerged in these cases from the President's exercise of his statutory cancellation powers, however, are truncated versions of two bills that passed both Houses of Congress. They are not the product of the "finely wrought" procedure that the Framers designed.

...

[We are not] persuaded by the Government's contention that the President's authority to cancel new direct spending and tax benefit items is no greater than his traditional authority to decline to spend appropriated funds....The critical difference between this statute and all of its predecessors, however, is that unlike any of them, this Act gives the President the unilateral power to change the text of duly enacted statutes. None of the Act's predecessors could even arguably have been construed to authorize such a change.

...

JUSTICE KENNEDY, concurring.

...

I write to respond to my colleague JUSTICE BREYER, who observes that the statute does not threaten the liberties of individual citizens, a point on which I disagree....Liberty is always at stake when one or more of the branches seek to transgress the separation of powers.

...

In recent years, perhaps, we have come to think of liberty as defined by that word in the Fifth and Fourteenth Amendments and as illuminated by the other provisions of the Bill of Rights. The conception of liberty embraced by the Framers was not so confined. They used the principles of separation of powers and federalism to secure liberty in the fundamental political sense of the term, quite in addition to the idea of freedom from intrusive governmental acts. The idea and the promise were that when the people delegate some degree of control to a remote central authority, one branch of government ought not possess the power to shape their destiny without a sufficient check from the other two....

It follows that if a citizen who is taxed has the measure of the tax or the decision to spend determined by the Executive alone, without adequate control by the citizen's Representatives in Congress, liberty is threatened. Money is the instrument of policy and policy affects the lives of citizens. The individual loses liberty in a real sense if that instrument is not subject to traditional constitutional constraints.

...

Separation of powers helps to ensure the ability of each branch to be vigorous in asserting its proper authority. In this respect the device operates on a horizontal axis to secure a proper balance of legislative, executive, and judicial authority. Separation of powers operates on a vertical axis as well, between each branch and the citizens in whose interest powers must be exercised. The citizen has a vital interest in the regularity of the exercise of governmental power. If this point was not clear before *INS v. Chadha* (1983), it should have been so afterwards. Though *Chadha* involved the deportation of a person, while the case before us involves the expenditure of money or the grant of a tax exemption, this circumstance does not mean that the vertical operation of the separation of powers is irrelevant here. By increasing the power of the President beyond what the Framers envisioned, the statute compromises the political liberty of our citizens, liberty which the separation of powers seeks to secure.

...

JUSTICE BREYER, with whom JUSTICE O'CONNOR and JUSTICE SCALIA join in part, dissenting.

...

...[T]he Act represents a legislative effort to provide the President with the power to give effect to some, but not to all, of the expenditure and revenue-diminishing provisions contained in a single massive appropriations bill. And this objective is constitutionally proper.

When our Nation was founded, Congress could easily have provided the President with this kind of power. In that time period, our population was less than four million,...federal employees numbered fewer than 5,000,...[and] annual federal budget outlays totaled approximately $4 million....At that time, a Congress, wishing to give a President the power to select among appropriations, could simply have embodied each appropriation in a separate bill, each bill subject to a separate Presidential veto.

Today, however, our population is about 250 million,...the Federal Government employs more than four million people,...the annual federal budget is $1.5 trillion, and a typical budget appropriations bill may have a dozen titles, hundreds of sections, and spread across more than 500 pages of the Statutes at Large....Congress cannot divide such a bill into thousands, or tens of thousands, of separate appropriations bills, each one of which the President would have to sign, or to veto, separately. Thus, the question is whether the Constitution permits Congress to choose a particular novel *means* to achieve this same, constitutionally legitimate, *end*.

...

The background circumstances...mean that we are to interpret nonliteral Separation of Powers principles in light of the need for "workable government." *Youngstown Sheet and Tube Co. v. Sawyer* (1952). If we apply those principles in light of that objective, as this Court has applied them in the past, the Act is constitutional.

...

...Literally speaking, the President has not "repealed" or "amended" anything. He has simply *executed* a power conferred upon him by Congress, which power is contained in laws that were enacted in compliance with the exclusive method set forth in the Constitution....

...

...[T]he delegated power to nullify statutory language was *itself* created and defined by Congress, and included in the statute books on an equal footing with (indeed, as a component part of) the sections that are potentially subject to nullification. As a Pennsylvania court put the matter more than a century ago: "The legislature cannot delegate its power to make a law; but it can make a law to delegate a power."...

...

Because I disagree with the Court's holding of literal violation, I must consider whether the Act nonetheless violates Separation of Powers principles—principles that arise out of the Constitution's vesting of the "executive Power" in "a President,"...and "all legislative Powers" in "a Congress,".... There are three relevant Separation of Powers questions here: (1) Has Congress given the President the wrong kind of power, *i.e.*, "non-Executive" power? (2) Has Congress given the President the power to "encroach" upon Congress' own constitutionally reserved territory? (3) Has Congress given the President too much power, violating the doctrine of "nondelegation?" These three limitations help assure "adequate control by the citizen's representatives in Congress."...And with respect to *this* Act, the answer to all these questions is "no."

Viewed conceptually, the power the Act conveys is the right kind of power. It is "executive." As explained above, an exercise of that power "executes" the Act. Conceptually speaking, it closely resembles the kind of delegated authority—to spend or not to spend appropriations, to change or not to change tariff rates—that Congress has frequently granted the President, any differences being differences in degree, not kind.

...

...And, if an individual Member of Congress, who say, favors aid to Country A but not to Country B, objects to the Act on the ground that the President may "rewrite" an appropriations law to do the opposite, one can respond, "But a majority of Congress voted that he have that power; you may vote to exempt the relevant appropriations provision from the Act; and if you command a majority, your appropriation is safe." Where the burden of overcoming legislative inertia lies is within the power of Congress to determine by rule. Where is the encroachment?

...

In sum, I recognize that the Act before us is novel. In a sense, it skirts a constitutional edge. But that edge has to do with means, not ends. The means chosen do not amount literally to the enactment, repeal, or amendment of a law. Nor, for that matter, do they amount literally to the "line item veto" that the Act's title announces. Those means do not violate any basic Separation of Powers principle. They do not improperly shift the constitutionally foreseen balance of power from Congress to the President. Nor, since they comply with Separation of Powers principles, do they threaten the liberties of individual citizens. They represent an experiment that may, or may not, help representative government work better. The Constitution, in my view, authorizes Congress and the President to try novel methods in this way. Consequently, with respect, I dissent.

JUSTICE SCALIA, with whom JUSTICE O'CONNOR joins, and with whom JUSTICE BREYER joins in part, concurring in part and dissenting in part.

...

Insofar as the degree of political, "law-making" power conferred upon the Executive is concerned, there is not a dime's worth of difference between Congress's authorizing the President to *cancel* a spending item, and Congress's authorizing money to be spent on a particular item at the President's discretion. And the latter has been done since the Founding of the Nation....

The short of the matter is this: Had the Line Item Veto Act authorized the President to "decline to spend" any item of spending contained in the Balanced Budget Act of 1997, there is not the slightest doubt that authorization would have been constitutional. What the Line Item Veto Act does instead—authorizing the President to "cancel" an item of spending—is technically different. But the technical difference does *not* relate to the technicalities of the Presentment Clause, which have been fully complied with; and the doctrine of unconstitutional delegation, which *is* at issue here, is preeminently *not* a doctrine of technicalities. The title of the Line Item Veto Act, which was perhaps designed to simplify for public comprehension, or perhaps merely to comply with the terms of a campaign pledge, has succeeded in faking out the Supreme Court. The President's action it authorizes in fact is not a line-item veto and thus does not offend Art. I, § 7; and insofar as the substance of that action is concerned, it is no different from what Congress has permitted the President to do since the formation of the Union.

...

B. Presidential Power to Execute the Law

Article II of the U.S. Constitution entrusts the president with the "executive power" and charges the president with the duty of taking care that the laws are enforced. The meaning and significance of these constitutional provisions have been contested since the early days of the republic. We now routinely call the president the "chief executive," but what does that title imply within our constitutional system?

One of the more contentious questions that has arisen in the Contemporary Era is the scope of the president's discretion in executing the law. In particular, under what circumstances, if at all, can the president ignore or refuse to enforce a federal statute? The question is not a new one, but recent presidents have been more vocal about their right to refuse to implement unconstitutional statutes. And recent presidents, often at loggerheads with Congress, have perhaps found more occasions to consider what their true duty might be when confronted with bills and statutes that they think might violate constitutional requirements as they understand it. Must the president always enforce an unconstitutional law? When should the president defer to the constitutional judgment of others? Does the president have a particular obligation to protect the prerogatives of the executive branch, as he understands them, against legislative encroachment?

Walter Dellinger, "Presidential Authority to Decline to Execute Unconstitutional Statutes" (1994)[29]

Early in President Bill Clinton's first term of office, law professor Walter Dellinger was named assistant attorney general and head of the Office of Legal Counsel, the primary legal advisor to the attorney general and the president. The Office of Legal Counsel (OLC) helps formulate many of the basic constitutional positions of the administration, especially as regards the powers of the presidency itself.

This memo by Dellinger lays out broad principles for presidential non-enforcement of unconstitutional laws. Dellinger aligned the Clinton administration with previ-

29. Excerpt taken from Office of Legal Counsel, "Presidential Authority to Decline to Enforce Unconstitutional Statutes, November 2, 1994," 18 Op. Off. Legal Counsel 199 (1994).

ous administrations in supporting the view that presidents did in fact have the authority to refuse to enforce laws that the president regarded as unconstitutional. But Dellinger's memo was centrally concerned with distinguishing the Clinton OLC on this issue from its Republican predecessors. An OLC opinion during the George H. W. Bush administration argued, for example, that "unconstitutional statutes are not laws the President must faithfully execute" and that the president was under no obligation to await a judicial determination of a law's constitutionality.[30] *One of Dellinger's colleagues (who was unsuccessfully nominated to head Obama's OLC) characterized this approach as one of "routine" non-enforcement.*[31]

Are presidents obliged to identify constitutional violations in statutes? Lawyers in and around the Reagan and Bush administrations had argued strongly for just that. By the responsibilities of their office, presidents must avoid enforcing laws in a way that would violate constitutional requirements. Liberal critics, in turn, charged that such arguments subverted the special role of the courts. The Constitution, they argued, does not set the president up as a dictator who could "defy" the laws of Congress. Dellinger's approach suggested a more flexible response to constitutional doubts about a law, and it left open judicial resolution of such doubts. As you read the memo, consider whether Dellinger's approach tends to replace constitutional limitations on Congress with judicial limitations on Congress. Does Dellinger still allow for too much executive non-compliance with congressional statutes?[32]

Memorandum Opinion for the Counsel to the President

I have reflected further on the difficult questions surrounding a President's decision to decline to execute statutory provisions that the President believes are unconstitutional, and I have a few thoughts to share with you. Let me start with a general proposition that I believe to be uncontroversial: there are circumstances in which the President may appropriately decline to enforce a statute that he views as unconstitutional.

First, there is significant judicial approval of this proposition. Most notable is the Court's decision in *Myers v. United States* (1926). There the Court sustained the President's view that the statute at issue was unconstitutional without any member of the Court suggesting that the President had acted improperly in refusing to abide by the statute....

Second, consistent and substantial executive practice also confirms this general proposition. Opinions dating to at least 1860 assert the President's authority to decline to effectuate enactments that the President views as unconstitutional. See, e.g., Memorial of Captain Meigs, 9 Op. Att'y Gen. 462, 469–70 (1860) (asserting that the President need not enforce a statute purporting to appoint an officer).... Moreover, numerous Presidents have provided advance notice of their intention not to enforce specific statutory requirements that they have viewed as unconstitutional, and the Supreme Court has implicitly endorsed this practice. See *INS v. Chadha*, 462 U.S. 919, 942 n.13 (1983) (noting that Presidents often sign legislation containing constitutionally objectionable provisions and indicate that they will not comply with those provisions).

While the general proposition that in some situations the President may decline to enforce unconstitutional statutes is unassailable, it does not offer sufficient guidance as to the appropriate course in specific circumstances. To continue our conversation about these complex issues, I offer the following propositions for your consideration.

1. The President's office and authority are created and bounded by the Constitution; he is required to act within its terms. Put somewhat differently, in serving as the executive created by the Constitution, the President is required to act in accordance with the laws—including the Constitution, which takes precedence over other forms of law. This obligation is reflected in the Take Care Clause and in the President's oath of office.

2. When bills are under consideration by Congress, the executive branch should promptly identify unconstitutional provisions and communicate its concerns to Congress so that the provisions can be corrected. Although this may seem elementary, in practice there have been occasions in which the President has been presented with enrolled bills containing constitutional flaws that should have been corrected in the legislative process.

30. William P. Barr, "Issues Raised by Foreign Relations Authorization Bill," 14 Op. Off. Legal Counsel 37, 50 (1990).

31. Dawn E. Johnsen, "Presidential Non-Enforcement of Constitutionally Objectionable Statutes," *Law and Contemporary Problems* 63 (2000):16.

32. See also David Barron, "Constitutionalism in the Shadow of Doctrine: The President's Non-Enforcement Power," *Law and Contemporary Problems* 63 (2000):61.

3. The President should presume that enactments are constitutional. There will be some occasions, however, when a statute appears to conflict with the Constitution. In such cases, the President can and should exercise his independent judgment to determine whether the statute is constitutional. In reaching a conclusion, the President should give great deference to the fact that Congress passed the statute and that Congress believed it was upholding its obligation to enact constitutional legislation. Where possible, the President should construe provisions to avoid constitutional problems.

4. The Supreme Court plays a special role in resolving disputes about the constitutionality of enactments. As a general matter, if the President believes that the Court would sustain a particular provision as constitutional, the President should execute the statute, notwithstanding his own beliefs about the constitutional issue. If, however, the President, exercising his independent judgment, determines both that a provision would violate the Constitution and that it is probable that the Court would agree with him, the President has the authority to decline to execute the statute.

5. Where the President's independent constitutional judgment and his determination of the Court's probable decision converge on a conclusion of unconstitutionality, the President must make a decision about whether or not to comply with the provision. That decision is necessarily specific to context, and it should be reached after careful weighing of the effect of compliance with the provision on the constitutional rights of affected individuals and on the executive branch's constitutional authority. Also relevant is the likelihood that compliance or non-compliance will permit judicial resolution of the issue. That is, the President may base his decision to comply (or decline to comply) in part on a desire to afford the Supreme Court an opportunity to review the constitutional judgment of the legislative branch.

6. The President has enhanced responsibility to resist unconstitutional provisions that encroach upon the constitutional powers of the Presidency. Where the President believes that an enactment unconstitutionally limits his powers, he has the authority to defend his office and decline to abide by it, unless he is convinced that the Court would disagree with his assessment. If the President does not challenge such provisions (*i.e.*, by refusing to execute them), there often will be no occasion for judicial consideration of their constitutionality; a policy of consistent Presidential enforcement of statutes limiting his power thus would deny the Supreme Court the opportunity to review the limitations and thereby would allow for unconstitutional restrictions on the President's authority.

Some legislative encroachments on executive authority, however, will not be justiciable or are for other reasons unlikely to be resolved in court. If resolution in the courts is unlikely and the President cannot look to a judicial determination, he must shoulder the responsibility of protecting the constitutional role of the presidency. This is usually true, for example, of provisions limiting the President's authority as Commander in Chief. Where it is not possible to construe such provisions constitutionally, the President has the authority to act on his understanding of the Constitution.

...

In accordance with these propositions, we do not believe that a President is limited to choosing between vetoing...and executing an unconstitutional provision in it. In our view, the President has the authority to sign legislation containing desirable elements while refusing to execute a constitutionally defective provision.

...

Note: The Bush Administration, Presidential Signing Statements, and the Obligation to Faithfully Execute the Law

When President George W. Bush signed legislation into law, he often issued public statements ("signing statements") at the same time. Signing statements have a long history, and many of the ways in which the Bush administration used signing statements were relatively uncontroversial. Some of their signing statements—both in form and content—were much more controversial.

The Bush administration used presidential signing statements like many other administrations before it had done—to celebrate its legislative achievements and downplay its legislative defeats. The statements that downplay legislative defeats are the more constitutionally interesting. They often seek to provide the president's favored interpretation of the meaning of the bill being signed by the president. These interpretations, crafted by high-level political and legal advisors to the president, are the starting point for the administrative process of interpreting and implementing the law within the executive branch. Administration officials also hope that judges will later pick up on these signing statements, either as persuasive interpretations of the law or as authoritative parts of the legislative record that judges might regard themselves as obliged to follow so as to implement the intent of the lawmakers.

Presidential signing statements have also been used to raise constitutional objections to legislation. As is evident from several readings in this volume, presidents sometimes veto proposed legislation on constitutional grounds. Andrew Jackson's veto of the bill to recharter the Second Bank of the United States is perhaps the most famous. For various reasons, presidents often choose to sign legislation despite possible constitutional objections. Presidents may regard the legislation as a whole as too valuable to veto, despite the presence of individual provisions that might be constitutionally problematic. The president may realize that the proponents of the constitutionally objectionable measure have a "veto-proof" majority in support of it in Congress, and so the president has no hope of stopping the bill by exercising his veto power in any case. The president may fear that the constitutionally objectionable provision is politically popular, and thus the president or his allies may pay a political price for opposing the measure in such a visible way as a veto. The president may simply not regard the constitutionally problematic provision as being substantively important enough to warrant the time and trouble involved in using the veto. It may be easier to fix the problem by other means, including by passing future statutes.

Such constitutional signing statements have become quite common. In their most moderate form, presidential signing statements may simply observe that there are those who hold in good faith constitutional doubts about the legislation that Congress has passed. In a somewhat more aggressive form, the signing statement may call the judiciary's attention to the potential constitutional problem and invite closer judicial scrutiny of the law. In the most aggressive form, the president may declare his own conviction that the aspects of the law are unconstitutional, or that the law could be interpreted in ways such that it would be unconstitutional, and that the administration will avoid implementing the law in a manner that would create constitutional difficulties.

The Bush administration issued signing statements that took all of these forms. What was unusual is that the administration made them routine. Over the course of its first term of office, the Bush administration issued dozens of signing statements that noted hundreds of possible constitutional objections to new federal laws that the president was signing. An individual law could contain a single constitutionally objectionable provision, but more often the administration objected to many particular details in a single large, complex piece of legislation.[33]

Unlike prior presidents, George W. Bush chose to use presidential signing statements as a vehicle for articulating and asserting administration beliefs about constitutional issues. Most administrations have chosen to overlook *possible* constitutional problems in legislation, calling attention to constitutional difficulties in signing statements only in limited circumstances and often when the objection seemed unavoidable. By contrast, the Bush administration seemed determined to highlight issues that might in previous administrations to have been resolved informally, addressed *sub rosa* administratively, or simply left as a hypothetical difficulty to be ignored for the present.

As with most presidents, Bush's signing statements generally emphasized what the administration saw as encroachments on the constitutional authority of the executive branch. There were exceptions. Among those exceptions was, for example, a 2002 law creating a federal "Institute of Education Sciences" in the Department of Education that included among the duties of the director the mandate to create programs to increase the participation of researchers at "historically Black colleges or universities or other institutions of higher education with large numbers of minority students."[34] This was one of several provisions in the law that was singled out for the presidential warning that it would be implemented "in a manner consistent with...the requirements of equal protection

33. For discussion, see Philip J. Cooper, "George W. Bush, Edgar Allan Poe, and the Use and Abuse of Presidential Signing Statements," *Presidential Studies Quarterly* 35 (2005):515; Christopher S. Kelley and Bryan Marshall, "The Last Word: Presidential Power and the Role of Signing Statements," *Presidential Studies Quarterly* 38 (2008); 248; Steven G. Calabresi and Daviel Lev, "The Legal Significance of President Signing Statements," *The Forum* 4 (2006) 8; Curtis A. Bradley and Eric A. Posner, "Presidential Signing Statements and Executive Power," *Constitutional Commentary* 23 (2006):307.

34. 116 Stat. 1947 (2002), PL 107–279.

and due process under the Due Process Clause of the Fifth Amendment."[35] More common, however, were the other types of objections raised to different provisions of that same law. A provision requiring that the Statistics Center being created by the law perform analyses and surveys at the direction of congressional committees was viewed by the administration as running afoul of the principles in *INS v. Chadha* (1983) that congressional committees could not themselves issue binding directives to executive officials. A statutory provision that the director of the Institute of Education Sciences could publish research and reports "without the approval of the Secretary [of Education] or any other office of the Department" was, according to the president, to be implemented "subject to the supervision and direction of the Secretary of Education" so as to accord with the president's own constitutional authority to supervise the conduct of official government actions.

These signing statements aroused little controversy at first, but became the subject of public and political debate in 2006. The issue first attracted attention when the president signed the hotly contested supplemental appropriations bill on December 30, 2005. The appropriations bill included essential funds for continuing operations by the Department of Defense (during the war in Iraq) and aid to the areas recently affected by Hurricane Katrina (which flooded New Orleans). Because the administration regarded the immediate passage of the appropriations bill as essential, it was a perfect vehicle for Congress to attach amendments that the administration opposed. The result was a lengthy signing statement qualifying how various provisions, ranging from the handling of classified information to requirements of congressional committee consultation before certain appropriated funds are actually spent, would be interpreted and implemented by the executive branch.

Most notably, Republican Senator John McCain had included an amendment prohibiting cruel and degrading treatment of military detainees, regardless of where they might be held, by United States personnel. The McCain amendment added legislative pressure in ongoing disputes over the American treatment of detainees in the American military base at Guantanamo Bay in Cuba, as well as detention facilities in Iraq and other countries. The president responded by stating, "The executive branch shall construe [the McCain amendment] in a manner consistent with the constitutional authority of the President to supervise the unitary executive branch and as Commander in Chief and consistent with the constitutional limitations on the judicial power, which will assist in achieving the shared objective of the Congress and the President . . . of protecting the American people from further terrorist attacks."[36]

Republican Senate Judiciary Committee Chairman Arlen Specter held hearings critical of presidential signing statements in the summer of that year. At the same time, the American Bar Association appointed a task force to examine the practice of presidential signing statements and "how they comport with the Constitution."[37] The ABA task force recommended that presidents in the future strive to communicate their constitutional concerns to Congress earlier in the legislative process and that Congress be informed promptly of any signing statements that the president might issue regarding a law. More interesting was the proposal that legislation be enacted to facilitate "judicial resolution" of any presidential claims or interpretations regarding the constitutionality or meaning of a law. (Senator Specter introduced such a bill in the Senate.) Even more controversial was the conclusion that such signing statements were contrary to "our constitutional system of separation of powers." The president's only constitutional options are to exercise the veto power or to enforce the law as written. The president should not "usurp [the] judicial authority as the final interpreter of the constitutionality of congressional acts" or preempt its right to issue "definitive constitutional interpretations."

A number of law professors, many formerly associated with the Office of Legal Counsel in the George H. W. Bush or William Clinton presidencies, objected

35. George W. Bush, "Statement on Signing Legislation to Provide for Improvement of Federal Education Research, Statistics, Evaluation, Information, and Dissemination, and for Other Purposes, November 5, 2002," *Weekly Compilation of Presidential Documents* (November 8, 1995), 1995.

36. George W. Bush, "Statement on Signing H.R. 2863, the "Department of Defense, Emergency Supplemental Appropriations to Address Hurricanes in the Gulf of Mexico, and Pandemic Influenza Act, 2006, December 30, 2005" *Weekly Compilation of Presidential Documents* 41 (January 2, 2006), 1918.

37. American Bar Association, Report of the Task Force on Presidential Signing Statements and the Separation of Powers Doctrine (July 24, 2006), 4.

to the ABA task force report. They argued that the veto-or-enforce-it choice on which the task force insisted ignored longstanding practice, the president's primary obligation to uphold the Constitution itself, and the realities of modern government. For those who were critical of both the task force and the Bush administration (as some of the former Clinton lawyers were), the difficulty with the Bush signing statements was not in the principle of signing statements or of presidential non-enforcement. Their objections to the Bush signing statements were instead to their lack of clarity in stating exactly what the intended administration actions were and to the administration's willingness to set aside clear legislative intent while claiming to be engaged in mere statutory interpretation.

There was little follow-up on the issue of presidential signing statements after the debates of 2006. President Obama brought many of the lawyers from the Clinton administration into his own Justice Department, and he has issued signing statements that included constitutional objections to legislative provisions. President Obama has generally been more measured in issuing constitutional signing statements than the President George W. Bush, however. Some Democrats in Congress have voiced their concern over the continuation of the practice, but the criticisms have been muted.

C. Presidential War and Foreign Affairs Powers

Contemporary controversies over the war powers have revolved around the scope of presidential authority to take action on his own initiative to defend American national security interests. The highest profile and most far-reaching disputes involve the president's authority to launch military offensives and engage in military operations abroad without prior congressional authorization. As commander in chief, the president had operational control of troop movements and both constitutional and statutory responsibilities to protect American lives and property. Only Congress, however, has the constitutional power to "declare war," and the recurring conflict between the legislative and executive branch is whether the congressional power to declare war is enough to prevent presidents from launching de facto wars on their own and whether the exclusive congressional power to declare war limits the ability of the president to respond militarily to national security crises as they arise. The situation has been further complicated in the modern era by the rise of overseas military bases (which put American troops at greater risk of attack than if they remained based in the United States), networks of defense treaties and commitments, changing military technology, and the diversity of military options at the president's command. President George W. Bush received broad congressional authorization for the use of military force in the Persian Gulf, though the vote over the Iraq War was far more controversial than the vote over the war in Afghanistan. But other military offensives, both large and small, have not received explicit prior congressional approval, including the extended bombing campaigns by the Clinton administration in Yugoslavia and the Obama administration in Libya.

A related set of debates concerns *how* presidents exercise the war powers. The decision to initiate military action is one important decision that presidents might make in the name of national security, but the executive routinely makes myriad other decisions in exercising the war powers. How constrained is the president in exercising the war powers, and how far can Congress go in instructing the president or limiting the president in how he acts as commander in chief? Is the constitutional responsibility and power of the president to do what it takes to win the war, once it has been declared? Or can Congress force the president to fight a limited war? Are there other constitutional restrictions on how the president conducts military operations and the workings of the national security state? Are there weapons systems in the American arsenal that the president can be constitutionally prevented from using? Are there intelligence gathering techniques that presidents can be prohibited from employing? Are there battlefield tactics that presidents can be barred from ordering? Such issues gained renewed attention during the George W. Bush administration, when it was revealed that the government was engaging in a wide range of covert activities as part of the War on Terror, from electronic eavesdropping to "enhanced interrogation" that were difficult to justify under current statutes.

Illustration 11-3 War Powers

Source: Nick Anderson, *Houston Chronicle*, June 18, 2011. Used with the permission of Nick Anderson, the Washington Post Writers Group and the Cartoonist Group. All rights reserved.

John Yoo, The President's Constitutional Authority to Conduct Military Operations (2001)[38]

Shortly after the attacks on the World Trade Center and the Pentagon on September 11, 2001, Deputy Assistant Attorney General John Yoo, in the Office of Legal Counsel, produced a memorandum opinion for the deputy counsel to the President, Tim Flanigan. Yoo's memo lays out the president's authority to take a military response to the attacks. By the time the memo was produced, two weeks after the attacks, Congress had passed a joint resolution authorizing the use of military force. The language of the joint resolution itself was the product of discussions with the White House and Office of Legal Counsel, and it gave the president a relatively free hand in responding to the attacks. Although the memo draws on the joint resolution, it primarily relies on inherent presidential power under Article II to launch military operations in the nation's defense. This extends to preemptive military action and military action against governments that were not directly involved in the events of September 11. The memo thus sketches out the second Bush administration's constitutional supports for the developing war on terror.

The memo was not designed for public release, but it did eventually become public. Its bold claims on behalf of presidential war powers made it one of the most famous OLC memos ever produced—along with a series of memos relating to Bush administration war policies. Although the invasion of Iraq in 2003 received separate congressional authorization, the memo had more immediate relevance for American military activity in a range of locales, including the Philippines and Yemen in early 2002.[39] *Is Yoo persuasive that the president has his own constitutional authority to*

38. Excerpt taken from Office of Legal Counsel, "The President's Constitutional Authority to Conduct Military Operations against Terrorists and Nations Supporting Them," September 25, 2001.

39. Yoo has subsequently expanded on this argument; John Yoo, *The Powers of War and Peace* (Chicago: University of Chicago Press, 2006). A critical account of presidential war powers can be found in Louis Fisher, *Presidential War Powers* (Lawrence: University Press of Kansas, 2004).

deploy troops into combat in order to protect national security? What are the limits of such an authority? How can President Obama's bombing of Libya without congressional authorization best be justified?

You have asked for our opinion of the scope of the President's authority to take military action in response to terrorist attacks on the United States on September 11, 2001. We conclude that the President has broad constitutional powers to use military force. Congress has acknowledged this inherent executive power in both the War Powers Resolution...and in the Joint Resolution passed by Congress on September 14, 2001.... Further, the President has the constitutional power not only to retaliate against any person, organization, or State suspected of involvement in terrorist attacks on the United States, but also against foreign States suspected of harboring or supporting such organizations. Finally, the President may deploy military force preemptively against terrorist organizations or the States that harbor or support them, whether or not they can be linked to the specific terrorist incidents of September 11.

...

The President's constitutional power to defend the United States and the lives of its people must be understood in light of the Founders' express intention to create a federal government "clothed with all the powers requisite to [the] complete execution of its trust." *The Federalist* No. 23.... Within the limits that the Constitution itself imposes, the scope and distribution of powers to protect national security must be construed to authorize the most efficacious defense of the Nation and its interests in accordance "with the realistic purposes of the entire instrument." *Lichter v. United States* (1948). Nor is the authority to protect the national security limited to actions necessary for "victories in the field." *Application of Yamashita* (1946). The authority over national security "carries with it the inherent power to guard against the immediate renewal of the conflict." *Id.*

...

Constitutional Text. The text, structure and history of the Constitution establish that the Founders entrusted the President with the primary responsibility, and therefore the power, to use military force in situations of emergency. Article II, Section 2 states that the "President shall be Commander in Chief of the Army and Navy of the United States...." He is further vested with all of "the executive Power" and the duty to execute the laws.... These powers give the President broad constitutional authority to use military force in response to threats to the national security and foreign policy of the United States. During the period leading up to the Constitution's ratification, the power to initiate hostilities and to control the escalation of conflict had been long understood to rest in the hands of the executive branch.

By their own terms, these provisions vest full control of the military forces of the United States in the President. The power of the President is at its zenith under the Constitution when the President is directing military operations of the armed forces, because the power of Commander-in-Chief is assigned solely to the President. It has long been the view of this Office that the Commander-in-Chief clause is a substantive grant of authority to the President and that the scope of the President's authority to commit the armed forces to combat is very broad. *See, e.g.*, Memorandum for Honorable Charles W. Colson, Special Counsel to the President, from William H. Rehnquist, Assistant Attorney General, Office of Legal Counsel, *Re: The President and the War Power: South Vietnam and the Cambodian Sanctuaries* (May 22, 1970).... The President's complete discretion in exercising the Commander-in-Chief power has also been recognized by the courts. In the *Prize Cases* (1862), for example, the Court explained that, whether the President "in fulfilling his duties as Commander in Chief" had met with a situation justifying treating the southern States as belligerents and instituting a blockade, was a question "to be *decided by him*" and which the Court could not question, but must leave to "the political department of the Government to which this power was entrusted."

Some commentators have read the constitutional text differently. They argue that the vesting of the power to declare war gives Congress the sole authority to decide whether to make war. This view misreads the constitutional text and misunderstands the nature of a declaration of war. Declaring war is not tantamount to making war—indeed, the Constitutional Convention specifically amended the working draft of the Constitution that had given Congress the power to make war.... A State constitution at the time of the ratification included provisions that prohibited the governor from "making" war without legislative approval.... If the Framers had wanted to require congressional consent before the initiation of military hostilities, they knew how to write such provisions.

. . .

Constitutional Structure. Our reading of the text is reinforced by analysis of the constitutional structure. First, it is clear that the Constitution secures all federal executive power in the President to ensure a unity of purpose and energy in action. "Decision, activity, secrecy, and dispatch will generally characterize the proceedings of one man in a much more eminent degree than any proceedings of any greater number." *The Federalist* No. 70. . . . The centralization of authority in the president alone is particularly crucial in matters of national defense, war, and foreign policy. . . .

Second, the Constitution makes clear that the process used for conducting military hostilities is different from other government decisionmaking. In the area of domestic legislation, the Constitution creates a detailed, finely wrought procedure in which Congress plays the central role. In foreign affairs, however, the Constitution does not establish a mandatory, detailed, Congress-driven procedure for taking action. Rather, the Constitution vests the two branches with different powers—the President as Commander in Chief, Congress with control over funding and declaring war—without requiring that they follow a specific process in making war. By establishing this framework, the Framers expected that the process for warmaking would be far more flexible, and capable of quicker, more decisive action, than the legislative process. Thus, the President may use his Commander-in-Chief and executive powers to use military force to protect the Nation, subject to congressional appropriations and control over domestic legislation.

Third, the constitutional structure requires that any ambiguities in the allocation of a power that is executive in nature—such as the power to conduct military hostilities—must be resolved in favor of the executive branch. . . . [T]he enumeration in Article II marks the points at which several traditional executive powers were diluted or reallocated. Any *other*, unenumerated executive powers, however, were conveyed to the President by the Vesting Clause.

There can be little doubt that the decision to deploy military force is "executive" in nature, and was traditionally so regarded. It calls for action and energy in execution, rather than the deliberate formulation of rules to govern the conduct of private individuals. . . .

. . .

Conducting military hostilities is a central tool for the exercise of the President's plenary control over the conduct of foreign policy. There can be no doubt that the use of force protects the Nation's security and helps it achieve its foreign policy goals. Construing the Constitution to grant such power to another branch could prevent the President from exercising his core constitutional responsibilities in foreign affairs. . . .

Executive Branch Construction and Practice. The position we take here has long represented the view of the executive branch and the Department of Justice. Attorney General (later Justice) Robert Jackson formulated the classic statement of the executive branch's understanding of the President's military powers in 1941:

> Article II, section 2, of the Constitution provides that the President "shall be Commander in Chief of the Army and Navy of the United States." By virtue of this constitutional office he has supreme command over the land and naval forces of the country and may order them to perform such military duties as, in his opinion, are necessary or appropriate for the defense of the United States. These powers exist in time of peace as well as in time of war.

. . .

The historical practice of all three branches confirms the lessons of the constitutional text and structure. The normative role of historical practice in constitutional law, and especially with regard to separation of powers, is well settled. . . .

. . .

The historical record demonstrates that the power to initiate military hostilities, particularly in response to the threat of an armed attack, rests exclusively with the President. As the Supreme Court has observed, "[t]he United States frequently employs Armed Forces outside the country—over 200 times in our history—for the protection of American citizens or national security." *United States v. Verdugo-Urquidez* (1990). On at least 125 such occasions, the President has acted without prior express authorization from Congress. *See* Bosnia Opinion, 19 Op. O.L.C. at 331. Such deployments, based on the President's constitutional authority alone, have occurred since the Administration of George Washington. . . . Perhaps the most significant deployment without specific statutory authorization took place at the time of the Korean War, when President Truman, without prior authorization from

Congress, deployed United States troops in a war that lasted for over three years and caused over 142,000 American casualties.

Recent deployments ordered solely on the basis of the President's constitutional authority have also been extremely large, representing a substantial commitment of the Nation's military personnel, diplomatic prestige, and financial resources. On at least one occasion, such unilateral deployment has constituted full-scale war. On March 24, 1999, without any prior statutory authorization and in the absence of an attack on the United States, President Clinton ordered hostilities to be initiated against the Republic of Yugoslavia.... In recent decades, no President has unilaterally deployed so much force abroad.

...

The terrorist incidents of September 11, 2001, were surely far graver a threat to the national security of the United States than the 1998 attacks on our embassies (however appalling those events were). The President's power to respond militarily to the later attacks must be correspondingly broader. Nonetheless, President Clinton's action in 1998 illustrates some of the breadth of the President's power to act in the present circumstances.

First, President Clinton justified the targeting of specific groups on the basis of what he characterized as "convincing" evidence of their involvement in the embassy attacks. While that is not a standard of proof appropriate for a criminal trial, it is entirely appropriate for military and political decisionmaking. Second, the President targeted not merely one particular group or leader, but a network of affiliated groups. Moreover, he ordered the action, not only because of particular attacks on United States embassies, but because of a pattern of terrorist activity, aimed at both American and non-Americans, that had unfolded over several years. Third, the President explained that the military action was designed to deter *future* terrorist incidents, not only to punish for past ones. Fourth, the President specifically justified military action on the territory of two foreign states because their governments had "harbor[ed]" and "support[ed]" terrorist groups for years, despite warnings from the United States.

...

...[T]he President can be said to be acting at the apogee of his powers if he deploys military force in the present situation, for he is operating both under his own Article II authority and with the legislative support of Congress. Under the analysis outlined by Justice Jackson in *Youngstown Sheet & Tube Co. v. Sawyer* (1952), the President's power in this case would be "at its maximum."...

The executive branch consistently "has taken the position from the very beginning that section 2(c) of the [War Powers Resolution] does not constitute a legally binding definition of Presidential authority to deploy our armed forces."[40] Moreover, as our Office has noted, "even the defenders of the WPR concede that this declaration [in section 2(c)]—found in the 'Purpose and Policy' section of the WPR—either is incomplete or is not meant to be binding."...

...

The Joint Resolution of September 14, 2001. Whatever view one may take of the meaning of section 2(c)(3) of the WPR, we think it clear that Congress, in enacting the "Joint Resolution [t]o authorize the use of United States Armed Forces against those responsible for the recent attacks launched against the United States,"...has confirmed that the President has broad constitutional authority to respond, by military means or otherwise, to the incidents of September 11.

First, the findings of the Joint Resolution include an express statement that "the President has authority under the Constitution to take action to deter and prevent acts of international terrorism against the United States." This authority is in addition to the President's authority to respond to *past* acts of terrorism. In including this statement, Congress has provided its explicit agreement with the executive branch's consistent position, as articulated in Parts I–III of this memorandum, that the President has the plenary power to use force even before an attack upon the United States actually occurs, against targets and using methods of his own choosing.

...

40. Section 2(c) of the War Powers Resolution states: "The constitutional powers of the President as Commander-in-Chief to introduce United States Armed Forces into hostilities, or into situations where imminent involvement in hostilities is clearly indicated by circumstances, are exercised only pursuant to (1) a declaration of war, (2) specific statutory authorization, or (3) a national emergency created by attack upon the United States, its territories or possessions, or its armed forces." [eds.' note]

Memoranda on Standards of Conduct of Interrogation ["Torture Memos"]

In the months after the attacks of September 11, 2001, advisors to President George W. Bush asked the Office of Legal Counsel (OLC) within the Department of Justice to provide legal guidance on a variety of questions relating to the rapidly expanding war on terrorism. Among the questions asked were the legal limits on interrogation methods that the United States might use on suspected terrorists and those captured on the battlefields of Afghanistan. The OLC produced two memos to the then-White House legal counsel Alberto Gonzales. One, by Assistant Attorney General Jay Bybee, examined the interpretation and limits of treaty and statutory prohibitions on torture. Another, by Deputy Assistant Attorney General John Yoo, further examined the treaty obligations of the United States and the jurisdiction of the International Criminal Court over the interrogation of al Qaeda operatives. Both offered a relatively narrow interpretation of the treaty and statutory provisions, and both memos offered an additional constitutional analysis that limited the extent to which Congress could direct how the president conducted the military campaign.

The legal interpretation of the political appointees within the OLC was met with some consternation among the career legal staff within the Department of Justice and the Pentagon, as well as from some other political appointees. In the summer of 2004, after revelations of the abuse of prisoners in military custody in Iraq became public, these so-called "torture memos" were leaked to the press. By then, Bybee had left the OLC for a seat on a federal circuit court, Yoo had returned to academia, and the White House was in the midst of a reelection campaign. Under international and domestic pressure, President Bush quickly emphasized that the administration was against torture. Gonzales distanced himself and the White House from the memos. He announced that the memos had been withdrawn, and he directed the OLC to produce a new opinion on legal standards affecting interrogations. In December 2004, Acting Assistant Attorney General Daniel Levin produced a new opinion, which was made public. Its broadened definition of torture was to guide administration policy relating to interrogations. After Levin's departure in 2005, the OLC produced new opinions, which were not publicly released, that once again shrank the definition of torture under existing statutes and treaties. These opinions indicated that a wider range of interrogation techniques were legally acceptable.[41] *Does the Levin memo disavow the constitutional analysis in the Bybee and Yoo memos?*

The Bybee memo cites the Supreme Court in Johnson v. Eisentrager *(1950) as recognizing implied presidential powers that are "necessary and proper" to carrying out the "enumerated powers" in Article II of the U.S. Constitution. The language and structure also mirror the constitutional text in Article I. Consider how the Supreme Court has understood the scope of the necessary and proper clause of Article I after the New Deal. What are the implications of that characterization of presidential powers? Are implied powers more confined in the context of separation of powers than they are in the context of federalism?*

The constitutional authority of Congress to limit how the president may use the military forces that Congress supplies to him has been a recurrent issue. During World War I, former president William Howard Taft argued that "Congress could not order battles to be fought on a certain plan, and could not direct parts of the army to be moved from one part of the country to another."[42] *After World War II, Cold War liberals beat back conservative proposals to curtail the president's authority to station troops abroad. During the waning days of the Vietnam War, Congress sought to prevent the use of American air and ground forces in neighboring Cambodia. During the Reagan administration, proposals to prohibit the president from making first use of nuclear weapons were made, and defeated. Having appropriated funds to build weapon systems or create an army, can Congress direct how the president can use those instruments of war? Or do those decisions fall within the discretion of the president as commander in chief?*

Jay S. Bybee, Memo to Alberto R. Gonzales, Counsel to the President (2002)[43]

You have asked for our Office's views regarding the standards of conduct under the Convention Against

41. On the interrogation memos, see also Jack Goldsmith, *The Terror Presidency* (New York: W. W. Norton, 2008); Jane Mayer, *The Dark Side* (Boston: Anchor Books, 2008); John Yoo, *War by Other Means* (Washington, DC: Atlantic Monthly Press, 2006); Karen J. Greenberg and Joshua L. Dratel, eds., *The Torture Papers* (New York: Cambridge University Press, 2005).

42. William Howard Taft, "The Boundaries between the Executive, the Legislative and the Judicial Branches of the Government," *Yale Law Journal* 25 (1915):610.

43. Excerpt taken from Office of Legal Counsel, *Re: Standards for Conduct for Interrogation under 18 U.S.C. §§ 2340–2340A* (August 1, 2002).

Torture and Other Cruel, Inhuman and Degrading Treatment or Punishment as implemented by Sections 2340–2340A of Title 18 of the United States Code. As we understand it, this question has arisen in the context of the conduct of interrogations outside the United States. We conclude below that Section 2340A proscribes acts inflicting, and that are specifically intended to inflict, severe pain or suffering, whether mental or physical. Those acts must be of an extreme nature to rise to the level of torture within the meaning of Section 2340A and the Convention....

...

Even if an interrogation method arguably were to violate Section 2340A, the statute would be unconstitutional if it impermissibly encroached on the President's constitutional power to conduct a military campaign. As Commander-in-Chief, the President has the constitutional authority to order interrogations of enemy combatants to gain intelligence information concerning military plans of the enemy. The demands of the Commander-in-Chief power are especially pronounced in the middle of a war in which the nation has already suffered a direct attack. In such a case, the information gained from interrogations may prevent future attacks by foreign enemies. Any effort to apply Section 2340A in a manner that interferes with the President's direction of such core war matters as the detention and interrogation of enemy combatants thus would be unconstitutional.

...

...[T]he President enjoys complete discretion in the exercise of his Commander-in-Chief authority and in conducting operations against hostile forces. Because both "[t]he executive power and the command of the military and naval forces is vested in the President," the Supreme Court has unanimously stated that it is "*the President alone* who is constitutionally invested with the *entire charge of hostile operations*." *Hamilton v. Dillin*, 88 U.S. 73, 87 (1874) (emphasis added). That authority is at its height in the middle of a war.

In light of the President's complete authority over the conduct of war, without a clear statement otherwise, we will not read a criminal statute as infringing on the President's ultimate authority in these areas. We have long recognized, and the Supreme Court has established a canon of statutory construction that statutes are to be construed in a manner that avoids constitutional difficulties so long as a reasonable alternative construction is available....

In order to respect the President's inherent constitutional authority to manage a military campaign against al Qaeda and its allies, Section 2340A must be construed as not applying to interrogations undertaken pursuant to his Commander-in-Chief authority. As our Office has consistently held during this Administration and previous Administrations, Congress lacks authority under Article I to set the terms and conditions under which the President may exercise his authority as Commander in Chief to control the conduct of operations during a war....

...

It could be argued that Congress enacted 18 U.S.C. § 2340A with full knowledge and consideration of the President's Commander-in-Chief power, and that Congress intended to restrict his discretion in the interrogation of enemy combatants. Even were we to accept this argument, however, we conclude that the Department of Justice could not...enforce Section 2340A against federal officials acting pursuant to the President's constitutional authority to wage a military campaign.

Indeed, in a different context, we have concluded that both courts and prosecutors should reject prosecutions that apply federal criminal laws to activity that is authorized pursuant to one of the President's constitutional powers. This Office, for example, has previously concluded that Congress could not constitutionally extend the congressional contempt statute to executive branch officials who refuse to comply with congressional subpoenas because of an assertion of executive privilege....Although Congress may define federal crimes that the President, through the Take Care Clause, should prosecute, Congress cannot compel the President to prosecute outcomes taken pursuant to the President's own constitutional authority. If Congress could do so, it could control the President's authority through the manipulation of federal criminal law.

...The President's constitutional power to protect the security of the United States and the lives and safety of its people must be understood in light of the Founders' intention to create a federal government "clothed with all the powers requisite to the complete execution of its trust." *The Federalist* No. 23.... Foremost among the objectives committed to that trust by the Constitution is the security of the nation. As Hamilton explained in arguing for the Constitution's adoption, because "the circumstances which may affect the public safety" are not "reducible within certain determinate limits,"

> it must be admitted, as a necessary consequence, that there can be no limitation of that authority, which is to provide for the defense and protection of the community, in any matter essential to its efficacy.

...

The text, structure and history of the Constitution establish that the Founders entrusted the President with the primary responsibility, and therefore the power, to ensure the security of the United States in situations of grave and unforeseen emergencies.... This Office has long understood the Commander-in-Chief Clause in particular as an affirmative grant of authority to the President. *See, e.g.*, Memorandum for Charles W. Colson, Special Counsel to the President, from William H. Rehnquist, Assistant Attorney General, Office of Legal Counsel, *Re: The President and the War Power: South Vietnam and the Cambodian Sanctuaries* (May 22, 1970).... The implication of constitutional text and structure are confirmed by the practical consideration that national security decisions require the unity in purpose and energy in action that characterize the Presidency rather than Congress.

As the Supreme Court has recognized, the Commander-in-Chief power and the President's obligation to protect the nation imply the ancillary powers necessary to their successful exercise. "The first of the enumerated powers of the President is that he shall be Commander-in-Chief of the Army and Navy of the United States. And, of course, the grant of war power includes all that is necessary and proper for carrying those powers into execution." *Johnson v. Eisentrager*, 339 U.S. 763, 788 (1950). In wartime, it is for the President alone to decide what methods to use to best prevail against the enemy.... The President's complete discretion in exercising the Commander-in-Chief power has been recognized by the courts. [See] the *Prize Cases* (1863)....

One of the core functions of the Commander-in-Chief is that of capturing, detaining, and interrogating members of the enemy....

Any effort of Congress to regulate the interrogation of battlefield combatants would violate the Constitution's sole vesting of the Commander-in-Chief authority in the President. There can be little doubt that intelligence operations, such as the detention and interrogation of enemy combatants and leaders, are both necessary and proper for the effective conduct of a military campaign.... Congress can no more interfere with the President's conduct of the interrogation of enemy combatants than it can dictate strategic or tactical decisions on the battlefield. Just as statutes that order the President to conduct warfare in a certain manner or for specific goals would be unconstitutional, so too are laws that seek to prevent the President from gaining the intelligence he believes necessary to prevent attacks upon the United States.

...

John Yoo, Memo to William Haynes II, General Counsel of the Department of Defense (2003)[44]

You have asked our Office to examine the legal standards governing military interrogations of alien unlawful combatants held outside the United States. You have requested that we examine both domestic and international law that might be applicable to the conduct of those interrogations.

...[C]riminal statutes, if they were misconstrued to apply to the interrogation of enemy combatants, would conflict with the Constitution's grant of the Commander in Chief power solely to the President.

...

...The September 11, 2001 terrorist attacks marked a state of international armed conflict between the United States and the al Qaeda terrorist organization. Pursuant to his Commander-in-Chief power, as supported by an act of Congress, the President has ordered the Armed Forces to carry out military operations against al Qaeda, which includes the power both to kill and to capture members of the enemy. Interrogation arises as a necessary and legitimate element of the detention of al Qaeda and Taliban members during an armed conflict.

...

...[T]he text, structure and history of the Constitution establish that the Founders entrusted the President with the primary responsibility, and therefore the power, to protect the security of the United States. The decision to deploy military force in the defense of U.S. interests is expressly placed under

44. Excerpt taken from Office of Legal Counsel, *Re: Military Interrogation of Alien Unlawful Combatants Held Outside the United States* (March 14, 2003).

Presidential authority by the Vesting Clause...and by the Commander-in-Chief Clause....The framers understood the Commander-in-Chef Clause to grant the President the fullest range of power recognized at the time of the ratification as belonging to the military commander. In addition, the structure of the Constitution demonstrates that any power traditionally understood as pertaining to the executive—which includes the conduct of warfare and the defense of the nation—unless expressly assigned to Congress, is vested in the President. Article II, Section 1 makes this clear by stating that the "executive Power shall be vested in a President of the United States of America." This sweeping grant vests in the President the "executive power" and contrasts with the specific enumeration of the powers—those "herein"—granted to Congress in Article I. Our reading of the constitutional text and structure are confirmed by historical practice, in which Presidents have ordered the use of military force more than 100 times without congressional authorization, and by the functional consideration that national security decisions require a unity in purpose and energy that characterizes the Presidency alone.

As the Supreme Court has recognized, the Commander-in-Chief power and the President's obligation to protect the nation imply the ancillary powers necessary to their successful exercise....In wartime, it is for the President alone to decide what methods to use to best prevail against the enemy....The President's complete discretion in exercising the Commander-in-Chief power has been recognized by the courts. In the *Prize Cases* (1863)...the Court explained that whether the President "in fulfilling his duties as Commander in Chief" had appropriately responded to the rebellion of the southern states was a question "to be decided *by him*" and which the Court could not question, but must leave to "the political department of the Government to which this power was entrusted."...

One of the core functions of the Commander in Chief is that of capturing, detaining, and interrogating members of the enemy....It is well settled that the President may seize and detain enemy combatants, at least for the duration of the conflict, and the laws of war make clear that prisoners may be interrogated for information concerning the enemy, its strength, and its plans....Recognizing this authority, Congress has never attempted to restrict or interfere with the President's authority on this score.

...

[T]he Fifth Amendment was not designed to restrict the unique war powers of the President as Commander in Chief. As long ago as 1865, Attorney General Speed explained the unquestioned rule that, as Commander in Chief, the President waging a war may authorize soldiers to engage in combat that could not be authorized as a part of the President's role in enforcing the laws....As Attorney General Speed concluded, the Due Process Clause has no application to the conduct of a military campaign:

> That portion of the Constitution which declares that "no person shall be deprived of his life, liberty, or property without due process of law," has such direct reference to, and connection with, trials for crime or criminal prosecutions that comment upon it would seem to be unnecessary. Trials for offences against the laws of war are not embraced or intended to be embraced in those provisions....The argument that flings around offenders against the laws of war these guarantees of the Constitution would convict all the soldiers of our army of murder; no prisoners could be taken and held; the army could not move. The absurd consequences that would of necessity flow from such an argument show that it cannot be the true construction—it cannot be what was intended by the framers of the instrument. One of the prime motives for the Union and a federal government was to confer the powers of war. If any provisions of the Constitution are so in conflict with the power to carry on war as to destroy and make it valueless, then the instrument, instead of being a great and wise one, is a miserable failure, a felo de se.

...

...If each time the President captured and detained enemy aliens outside the United States, those aliens could bring suit challenging the deprivation of their liberty, such a result would interfere with and undermine the President's capacity to protect the Nation and to respond to the exigencies of war.

The Supreme Court has repeatedly refused to apply the Due Process Clause or even the Just Compensation Clause to executive and congressional actions taken in the direct prosecution of a war effort against enemies of the Nation....

...

[E]ven if the Fifth Amendment applied to enemy combatants in wartime, it is clear that ... the Fifth Amendment does not operate outside the United States to regulate the executive's conduct toward aliens.... As the Supreme Court explained in [*Johnson v.*] *Eisentrager* (1950), construing the Fifth Amendment to apply to aliens who are outside the United States and have no connection to the United States:

> would mean that during military occupation irreconcilable enemy elements, guerrilla fighters, and "werewolves" could require the American Judiciary to assure them freedom of speech, press, and assembly as in the First Amendment, right to bear arms as in the Second, security against "unreasonable" searches and seizures as in the Fourth, as well as rights to jury trial as in the Fifth and Sixth Amendments. Such extraterritorial application of organic law would have been so significant an innovation in the practice of governments that, if intended or apprehended, it could scarcely have failed to excite contemporary comment. Not one word can be cited. No decision of this Court supports such a view.

...

As the Supreme Court has recognized, ... the President enjoys complete discretion in the exercise of his Commander-in-Chief authority in conducting operations against hostile forces. Because both "[t]he executive power and the command of the military and naval forces is vested in the President," the Supreme Court has unanimously stated that it is "*the President alone* [] who is constitutionally invested with the *entire charge of hostile operations.*" *Hamilton v. Dillin* (1874).

...

In the area of foreign affairs and war powers in particular, the avoidance canon has special force. In contrast to the domestic realm, foreign affairs and war clearly place the President in the dominant constitutional position due to his authority as Commander in Chief and Chief Executive and his plenary control over diplomatic relations. There can be little doubt that the conduct of war is a matter that is fundamentally executive in nature, the power over which the Framers vested in a unitary executive.... Correspondingly, during war Congress plays a reduced role in the war effort and the courts generally defer to executive decisions concerning the conduct of hostilities.

...

In order to respect the President's inherent constitutional authority to direct a military campaign against al Qaeda and its allies, general criminal laws must be construed as not applying to interrogations undertaken pursuant to his Commander-in-Chief authority. Congress cannot interfere with the President's exercise of his authority as Commander in Chief to control the conduct of operations during a war.... As we have discussed above, the President's power to detain and interrogate enemy combatants arises out of his constitutional authority as Commander in Chief. Any construction of criminal laws that regulated the President's authority as Commander in Chief to determine the interrogation and treatment of enemy combatants would raise serious constitutional questions whether Congress had intruded on the President's constitutional authority. Moreover, we do not believe that Congress enacted general criminal provisions such as the prohibitions against assault, maiming, interstate stalking, and torture pursuant to any express authority that would allow it to infringe on the President's constitutional control over the operation of the Armed Forces in wartime. In our view, Congress may no more regulate the President's ability to detain and interrogate enemy combatants than it may regulate his ability to direct troop movements on the battlefield. In fact, the general applicability of these statutes belies any argument that these statutes apply to persons under the direction of the President in the conduct of war.

...

Even if these statutes were misconstrued to apply to persons acting at the direction of the President during the conduct of war, the Department of Justice could not enforce this law or any of the other criminal statutes applicable to the special maritime and territorial jurisdictionagainst federal officials acting pursuant to the President's constitutional authority to direct a war. Even if an interrogation method arguably were to violate a criminal statute, the Justice Department could not bring a prosecution because the statute would be unconstitutional as applied in this context....

... Any effort by Congress to regulate the interrogation of enemy combatants would violate the Constitution's sole vesting of the Commander-in-Chief authority in the President. There can be little doubt that intelligence operations, such as the detention and interrogation of enemy combatants and leaders, are both necessary and proper for the effective conduct of a military campaign. Indeed, such operations may be of more importance in a war with an international terrorist organization than one with the conventional armed forces of a nation-state, due to the former's emphasis on covert operations and surprise attacks against civilians. It may be the case that only successful interrogations can provide the information necessary to prevent future attacks upon the United States and its citizens. Congress can no more interfere with the President's conduct of the interrogation of enemy combatants than it can dictate strategic or tactical decisions on the battlefield. Just as statutes that order the President to conduct warfare in a certain manner or for specific goals would be unconstitutional, so too are laws that would prevent the President from gaining the intelligence he believes necessary to prevent attacks upon the United States.

. . .

Daniel Levin, Memo to James B. Comey, Deputy Attorney General (2004)[45]

Torture is abhorrent both to American law and values and to international norms. This universal repudiation of torture is reflected in our criminal law, for example, 18 U.S.C. §§ 2340–2340A; international agreements, exemplified by the United Nations Convention Against Torture (the "CAT"); customary international law; centuries of Anglo-American law; and the longstanding policy of the United States, repeatedly and recently reaffirmed by the President.

This Office interpreted the federal criminal prohibition against torture—codified at 18 U.S.C. §§ 2340–2340A.... The August 2002 Memorandum [the Bybee memo] also addressed a number of issues beyond the interpretation of those statutory provisions, including the President's Commander-in-Chief power, and various defenses that might be asserted to avoid potential liability under sections 2340–2340A....

Questions have since been raised, both by this Office and by others, about the appropriateness and relevance of the non-statutory discussion in the August 2002 Memorandum, and also about various aspects of the statutory analysis, in particular the statement that "severe" pain under the statute was limited to pain "equivalent in intensity to the pain accompanying serious physical injury, such as organ failure, impairment of bodily function, or even death." ... We decided to withdraw the August 2002 Memorandum, a decision you announced in June 2004. At that time, you directed this Office to prepare a replacement memorandum. Because of the importance of—and public interest in—these issues, you asked that this memorandum be prepared in a form that could be released to the public so that interested parties could understand our analysis of the statute.

This memorandum supersedes the August 2002 Memorandum in its entirety. Because the discussion in that memorandum concerning the President's Commander-in-Chief power and the potential defenses to liability was—and remains—unnecessary, it has been eliminated from the analysis that follows. Consideration of the bounds of any such authority would be inconsistent with the President's unequivocal directive that United States personnel not engage in torture.

. . .

The Criminal Division of the Department of Justice has reviewed this memorandum and concurs in the analysis set forth below.

. . .

Caroline D. Krass, Memorandum Opinion on the Authority to Use Military Force in Libya (2011)[46]

In February 2011, widespread popular protests against the military government broke out in Libya, as they had in other Middle Eastern and North African countries in the surrounding months. Libyan leader Muammar Qadhafi responded with aggressive military force, and the country soon collapsed into civil war. As government forces prepared to retake the city of Benghazi on March 17, the United Nations Security Council adopted a resolution imposing a no-fly zone in Libya and authorizing military force to protect civilians. The next day, President Barack Obama announced that Qadhafi would need to implement an immediate ceasefire and withdraw from rebel-controlled areas in order to comply with the UN resolution. On March 19, the

45. Excerpt taken from Office of Legal Counsel, *Re: Legal Standards Applicable Under 18 U.S.C. §§ 2340–2340A* (December 30, 2004).

46. www.fas.org/irp/agency/doj/olc/libya.pdf

United States began air strikes against the Libyan military and government. Congressional leaders were consulted prior to the launch of the American military campaign, and a report was filed with Congress consistent with the War Powers Act indicating that foreign military operations were underway. But the administration denied that the actions in Libya were constrained by the sixty-day limit on "hostilities" without congressional authorization laid out in the War Powers Act.

Before the air strikes began, Principal Deputy Assistant Attorney General Caroline Krass in the Office of Legal Counsel (OLC) provided an informal opinion on the constitutionality of the president launching such an offensive in Libya. Her conclusions were subsequently incorporated into a formal opinion justifying the presidential power to use military force in Libya. The administration offered a variety of documents supporting the legality of those actions, but the Krass opinion provides the key arguments in the most detail. Krass was serving as the acting head of OLC in the spring of 2011, and had been a long-serving national security lawyer in the Bush, Clinton, and Obama administrations.

What type of constitutional arguments does Krass use to build support for her position? Does she adopt a formalist or a functionalist approach to determining when a "war" has begun?

...

The President explained in his March 21, 2011 report to Congress that the use of military force in Libya serves important U.S. interests in preventing instability in the Middle East and preserving the credibility and effectiveness of the United Nations Security Council. The President also stated that he intended the anticipated United States military operations in Libya to be limited in nature, scope, and duration. The goal of action by the United States was to "set the stage" for further action by coalition partners in implementing UNSC Resolution 1973, particularly through destruction of Libyan military assets that could either threaten coalition aircraft policing the UNSC-declared no-fly zone or engage in attacks on civilians and civilian-populated areas. In addition, no U.S. ground forces would be deployed, except possibly for any search and rescue missions, and the risk of substantial casualties for U.S. forces would be low. As we advised you prior to the commencement of military operations, we believe that, under these circumstances, the President had constitutional authority, as Commander in Chief and Chief Executive and pursuant to his foreign affairs powers, to direct such limited military operations abroad, even without prior specific congressional approval.

Earlier opinions of this Office and other historical precedents establish the framework for our analysis. As we explained in 1992, Attorneys General and this Office "have concluded that the President has the power to commit United States troops abroad," as well as to "take military action," "for the purpose of protecting important national interests," even without specific prior authorization from Congress. *Authority to Use United States Military Forces in Somalia*, 16 Op. O.L.C. 6, 9 (1992) ("Military Forces in Somalia"). This independent authority of the President, which exists at least insofar as Congress has not specifically restricted it, see *Deployment of United States Armed Forces into Haiti*, 18 Op. O.L.C. 173, 176 n.4, 178 (1994) ("Haiti Deployment"), derives from the President's "unique responsibility," as Commander in Chief and Chief Executive, for "foreign and military affairs," as well as national security. *Sale v. Haitian Centers Council, Inc.*, 509 U.S. 155, 188 (1993); U.S. Const. art. II, § 1, cl. 1, § 2, cl. 2.

The Constitution, to be sure, divides authority over the military between the President and Congress, assigning to Congress the authority to "declare War," "raise and support Armies," and "provide and maintain a Navy," as well as general authority over the appropriations on which any military operation necessarily depends. U.S. Const. art. I, § 8, cl. 1, 11–14. Yet, under "the historical gloss on the 'executive Power' vested in Article II of the Constitution," the President bears the "'vast share of responsibility for the conduct of our foreign relations,'" *Am. Ins. Ass'n v. Garamendi*, 539 U.S. 396, 414 (2003) (quoting *Youngstown Sheet & Tube Co. v. Sawyer*, 343 U.S. 579, 610–11 (1952) (Frankfurter, J., concurring)), and accordingly holds "independent authority 'in the areas of foreign policy and national security.'" Id. at 429 (quoting *Haig v. Agee*, 453 U.S. 280, 291 (1981)); see also, e.g., *Youngstown Sheet & Tube Co.*, 343 U.S. at 635–36 n.2 (Jackson, J., concurring) (noting President's constitutional power to "act in external affairs without congressional authority")....

This understanding of the President's constitutional authority reflects not only the express assignment of powers and responsibilities to the President and Congress in the Constitution, but also, as noted, the "historical gloss" placed on the Constitution by two centuries of practice. *Garamendi*, 539 U.S. at 414. "Our history," this Office observed in 1980, "is replete with instances of presidential uses of military force abroad in the absence of prior congressional approval." *Presidential Power*, 4A Op. O.L.C. at 187; see generally Richard F. Grimmett, Cong. Research Serv., *Instances of Use of United States Armed Forces Abroad, 1798–2010* (2011). Since then, instances of such presidential initiative have only multiplied, with Presidents ordering, to give just a few examples, bombing in Libya (1986), an intervention in Panama (1989), troop deployments to Somalia (1992), Bosnia (1995), and Haiti (twice, 1994 and 2004), air patrols and airstrikes in Bosnia (1993–1995), and a bombing campaign in Yugoslavia (1999), without specific prior authorizing legislation. This historical practice is an important indication of constitutional meaning, because it reflects the two political branches' practical understanding, developed since the founding of the Republic, of their respective roles and responsibilities with respect to national defense, and because "[m]atters intimately related to foreign policy and national security are rarely proper subjects for judicial intervention." *Haig*, 453 U.S. at 292. In this context, the "pattern of executive conduct, made under claim of right, extended over many decades and engaged in by Presidents of both parties, 'evidences the existence of broad constitutional power.'" *Haiti Deployment*, 18 Op. O.L.C. at 178 (quoting *Presidential Power*, 4A Op. O.L.C. at 187)....

...

We have acknowledged one possible constitutionally-based limit on this presidential authority to employ military force in defense of important national interests—a planned military engagement that constitutes a "war" within the meaning of the Declaration of War Clause may require prior congressional authorization.... In our view, determining whether a particular planned engagement constitutes a "war" for constitutional purposes instead requires a fact-specific assessment of the "anticipated nature, scope, and duration" of the planned military operations. *Haiti Deployment*, 18 Op. O.L.C. at 179. This standard generally will be satisfied only by prolonged and substantial military engagements, typically involving exposure of U.S. military personnel to significant risk over a substantial period. Again, Congress's own key enactment on the subject reflects this understanding. [See, the War Powers Resolution.]...

Applying this fact-specific analysis, we concluded in 1994 that a planned deployment of up to 20,000 United States troops to Haiti to oust military leaders and reinstall Haiti's legitimate government was not a "war" requiring advance congressional approval.... Similarly, a year later we concluded that a proposed deployment of approximately 20,000 ground troops to enforce a peace agreement in Bosnia and Herzegovina also was not a "war," even though this deployment involved some "risk that the United States [would] incur (and inflict) casualties."...

Under the framework of these precedents, the President's legal authority to direct military force in Libya turns on two questions: first, whether United States operations in Libya would serve sufficiently important national interests to permit the President's action as Commander in Chief and Chief Executive and pursuant to his authority to conduct U.S. foreign relations; and second, whether the military operations that the President anticipated ordering would be sufficiently extensive in "nature, scope, and duration" to constitute a "war" requiring prior specific congressional approval under the Declaration of War Clause.

...

In our view, the combination of at least two national interests that the President reasonably determined were at stake here—preserving regional stability and supporting the UNSC's credibility and effectiveness—provided a sufficient basis for the President's exercise of his constitutional authority to order the use of military force....

...

...At the same time, turning to the second element of the analysis, we do not believe that anticipated United States operations in Libya amounted to a "war" in the constitutional sense necessitating congressional approval under the Declaration of War Clause. This inquiry, as noted, is highly fact-specific and turns on no single factor. See *Proposed Bosnia Deployment*, 19 Op. O.L.C. at 334 (reaching conclusion based on specific "circumstances"); *Haiti Deployment*, 18 Op. O.L.C. at 178 (same). Here, considering all the relevant circumstances, we believe applicable historical precedents demonstrate that the limited military operations the President anticipated directing were not a "war" for constitutional purposes.

...The planned operations thus avoided the difficulties of withdrawal and risks of escalation that may attend commitment of ground forces—two factors that this Office has identified as "arguably" indicating "a greater need for approval [from Congress] at the outset," to avoid creating a situation in which "Congress may be confronted with circumstances in which the exercise of its power to declare war is effectively foreclosed." *Proposed Bosnia Deployment*, 19 Op. O.L.C. at 333. Furthermore, also as in prior operations conducted without a declaration of war or other specific authorizing legislation, the anticipated operations here served a "limited mission" and did not "aim at the conquest or occupation of territory." Id. at 332. President Obama directed United States forces to "conduct[] a limited and well-defined mission in support of international efforts to protect civilians and prevent a humanitarian disaster"; American airstrikes accordingly were to be "limited in their nature, duration, and scope." Obama March 21, 2011 Report to Congress....

Accordingly, we conclude that President Obama could rely on his constitutional power to safeguard the national interest by directing the anticipated military operations in Libya—which were limited in their nature, scope, and duration—without prior congressional authorization.

John Cornyn, Speech on Congressional Authorization for the Use of Military Force in Libya (2011)[47]

In April 2011, U.S. Senator John Cornyn of Texas introduced a resolution co-sponsored by a group of Republicans calling on the president to explain the policy objectives in Libya, the plan and expected costs for achieving those objectives, and the limits that the president had imposed on the military operations. It also called on the president to seek congressional authorization for the use of military force in Libya. As usual, the resolution was referred to committee for further consideration.

Cornyn's speech and resolution turned up the heat on the administration to bolster congressional support for the Libyan actions. The conservative Cornyn's co-sponsors ranged from the moderate Susan Collins to the newly elected Tea Party insurgent Mike Lee. By contrast, Tea Party favorite Senator Rand Paul of Kentucky introduced resolutions declaring that the United States was currently at war and requiring that the president immediately cease military operations until Congress provided the necessary authorization. Paul chastised his new colleagues, "The Congress has become not just a rubber stamp for an unlimited Presidency, but, worse, Congress has become a doormat to be stepped upon, to be ignored, and basically to be treated as irrelevant.... There is no excuse for the Senate not to vote on going to war before we go to war."[48] Resolutions introduced by more Democratic groups of senators simply called for the president to submit a plan for achieving his objectives in Libya and to consult regularly with Congress.

Does Cornyn think the United States was at war with Libya? Why might he avoid calling for a vote on authorization for the use of military force himself?

Note that Libyan leader Muammar Qaddafi was captured and killed by rebel forces six months later, after his convoy was attacked by NATO warplanes.

...

...I have grown increasingly concerned that the role of Congress in consultation and in communication with the White House on matters of such grave import to our country and our men and women in uniform as intervening in a foreign country—that the powers of Congress have seemingly been ignored or certainly eroded.

We know this is not new. Since the end of World War II, to my recollection, the U.S. Congress has never exercised its authority under article I, section 8 of the Constitution to declare war. Instead, when our nation has been involved in military operations, we have had something other than a war declared by Congress, but most often with communication and consultation and even authorization by the Congress.

I believe it is imperative, particularly in light of the events subsequent to our intervention in Libya, that the President should submit a plan to Congress on Libya. I believe the President should also come to Congress and ask for a congressional authorization for our continued participation, even in a NATO mission of which the United States bears a disproportionate responsibility.

...

The President watched as Qaddafi forces regained the momentum against those who had taken up arms against the regime. France—France—became the first nation to recognize the Libyan Transitional National Council as the legitimate government of Libya on March 10. And then the Arab League asked that a no-fly zone be imposed over Libya on March 12. Finally, on March 17—this was almost a month after the first protests against Qaddafi in Libya —the United Nations Security Council approved a no-fly zone over Libya, as

47. Excerpt taken from *Cong. Rec.*, 112nd Cong., 1st Sess. (April 14, 2011), S2540.

48. *Cong. Rec.*, 112nd Cong., 1st. Sess. (April 5, 2011), S2110.

well as necessary measures to protect civilians in that country.

U.N. Security Council resolutions take a lot of time to negotiate. There is obviously the need for a lot of consultation between the nations making up the U.N. Security Council. That is why I am only left to wonder why it was during this period of time that the President made so little effort to consult with Congress in a substantive way. I admit he appeared to act like he checked the box once or twice. He sent us a letter on March 21—2 days after Operation Odyssey Dawn began—letting us know what we could have learned from reading the newspaper and watching cable television, that he had ordered strikes on Libya. But the level of consultation with Congress about Libya was nothing like what we had in the years leading up to U.S. military involvement in Iraq and Afghanistan, where Congress issued an explicit authorization for use of military force at the request of the President of the United States.

This is not just a constitutional powers matter. I think this is also a matter of communicating with the American people about the reasons for our intervention in Libya and expressing to the American people what the plan is so they can do what they naturally want to do; that is, provide support for our men and women in uniform, particularly when they are in harm's way.

. . .

So I think the Congress, on behalf of the American people, consistent with our constitutional responsibilities and our shared power in matters as serious as this, deserve a plan from the President of the United States, so he can present it to us and we can have what we sorely need, which is a genuine debate about our role in the future—the way forward in Libya.

So what should that plan look like? I will make a few suggestions. I believe a credible plan should contain a detailed description of U.S. policy objectives in Libya both during and after Qaddafi's rule. It should include a detailed plan to achieve those objectives. And particularly in these times when we are struggling with enormous debt and deficits, it should include a detailed estimate of the costs of U.S. military operations in Libya and any other actions required to implement the plan.

. . .

I think this is, to me, the simplest, the most direct question: If the President's goal was to stop Qaddafi from killing Libyans, civilians rebelling against him and protesting against his tyrannical rule, how in the world do we stop the killing without stopping the killer?

That would be Muammar Qaddafi. How can we stop the killing of civilians until we achieve the objective of removing him by any means necessary?

I think it is also appropriate to inquire as to whether the Pottery Barn rule applies in Libya. Colin Powell, former Secretary of State and Chairman of the Joint Chiefs of Staff, once observed that, Once you break it, you own it, the so-called Pottery Barn rule.

. . .

Finally, I think we need to know, because certainly everything that happens becomes precedent for some future action, whether there is something that one might call an "Obama doctrine." Is it that the United States will use military force when requested by our allies such as France or, perhaps, international bodies such as the Arab League or the United Nations, but not otherwise? Is it something like the United States will protect civilians when they capture the world's media attention, but ignore their suffering otherwise? Is it something that explains why, for example, we are engaged in Libya but not engaged in Syria?

. . .

I believe our debate in the Senate should result in a vote on a congressional authorization for the President's plan, whatever that is, in Libya, but we ought to have a conversation, we ought to communicate, we ought to have a consultation, not allow the President to treat Congress like a potted plant when it comes to intervening in a foreign nation in a military fashion. I believe the President should ask Congress for an authorization, and I believe we should vote on one.

. . .

D. Martial Law and Habeas Corpus

In the wake of the September 11, 2001, attacks on the World Trade Center and the Pentagon and the subsequent war in Afghanistan, President George W. Bush ordered that some individuals detained by the American military during military operations and who were suspected of aiding terrorist organizations were to be held in a military base in Guantanamo Bay, Cuba. The "enemy combatants" were to be detained without trial until they were no longer regarded as a threat to American national security. Other enemy troops captured during battle were detained in camps and prisons in

Afghanistan or elsewhere. The administration subsequently developed a procedure that would allow it to try some of these detainees for war crimes or terrorist activities before special military commissions.

Hamdi v. Rumsfeld (2004) was one of a series of cases on U.S. detention policies. It was issued the same day as *Rasul v. Bush* (2004), which held that federal civilian courts could hear habeas corpus petitions from prisoners detained on a military base in Guantanamo Bay, Cuba. *Hamdan v. Rumsfeld* (2006) concluded that the administration did not have adequate statutory authority to set up military commissions to try detainees and that the design of the trials were in conflict with both statutory and treaty provisions. In *Boumediene v. Bush* (2008), Justice Kennedy wrote for the Court in concluding that Congress must provide some form of adequate judicial review for detainees held in Guantanamo, even if Congress means to restrict the writ of habeas corpus. Although *Hamdan* focused on the possibility of criminal trials for some of the detainees, the other cases have focused on the more basic question of whether the detainees are entitled to some procedure to determine whether they are being properly held and should simply be released. The details of working out and monitoring that procedure have been left to the Court of Appeals for the District of Columbia.

Hamdi was perhaps the most important of these cases in that it came first and signaled that the Court would not simply defer to the administration on detention policies. The *Hamdi* opinion also engaged the most questions of constitutional separation of powers as it asked whether Congress had implicitly authorized the president to detain enemy combatants and what the scope of the combined war power of Congress and the president might be when it comes to detaining individuals captured on the battlefield. The case brought the Court back to some of the fundamental issues raised in *Youngstown Sheet & Tube v. Sawyer* (1952), but here the Court concluded that the legislature and the executive were in agreement. Considering the framework that the Court employed in *Youngstown*, would that divided Court have reached the same result as the majority in *Hamdi*?

Hamdi v. Rumsfeld, 542 U.S. 507 (2004)

Yaser Esam Hamdi was an American citizen, having been born in Louisiana but raised in Saudi Arabia. In 2001, he was captured by Northern Alliance forces in Afghanistan and turned over the American military, which eventually transferred him to a detention facility in Guantanamo Bay, Cuba. Once his status as an American citizen was determined, he was transferred from Guantanamo Bay to a naval brig in Norfolk, Virginia, and later to Charleston, South Carolina. The U.S. government designated Hamdi as an "enemy combatant" to be held indefinitely and without trial. Hamdi's father petitioned for a writ of habeas corpus on his son's behalf, contending that as an American citizen Hamdi could not be held without trial. His father argued that as a relief worker in Afghanistan, he was not a combatant for the Taliban regime or its al-Qaeda allies. The government submitted a report by Defense Department official Michael Mobbs stating that Hamdi had received military training from the Taliban, carried a rifle, and had been captured with his unit on the battlefield. The federal district court ordered the government to produce more evidence to satisfy judicial review of the legality of Hamdi's detention, and the Court of Appeals for the Fourth Circuit reversed that order. Hamdi appealed to the Supreme Court, which vacated the circuit court's order and laid down guidelines governing the battlefield detention of citizens. After the Court's 6–3 decision, the U.S. government agreed to deport Hamdi to Saudi Arabia, and Hamdi agreed to relinquish his American citizenship and accept a variety of international travel restrictions.

Note that Justices Souter and Ginsburg largely rely on statutory grounds to resolve the case, finding that the post–September 11th congressional Authorization for the Use of Military Force did not suspend or alter the 1971 Nondetention Act, which barred the executive branch from indefinitely detaining American citizens except pursuant to an act of Congress.

How critical to the decision is it that Hamdi was a citizen? Could the case have come out differently if Congress had provided more specific statutory support for detentions without judicial review? How many justices fully support the administration's actions?

JUSTICE O'CONNOR announced the judgment of the Court and delivered an opinion, with which CHIEF JUSTICE REHNQUIST, JUSTICE KENNEDY, and JUSTICE BREYER join.

At this difficult time in our Nation's history, we are called upon to consider the legality of the Government's detention of a United States citizen on United States soil as an "enemy combatant" and to address the process that is constitutionally owed to one who seeks to challenge his classification as such.... We hold that although Congress authorized the detention of combatants in the narrow circumstances alleged here, due process demands that a citizen held in the United States as an enemy combatant be given a meaningful opportunity to contest the factual basis for that detention before a neutral decisionmaker.

...

The threshold question before us is whether the Executive has the authority to detain citizens who qualify as "enemy combatants." There is some debate as to the proper scope of this term, and the Government has never provided any court with the full criteria that it uses in classifying individuals as such. It has made clear, however, that, for purposes of this case, the "enemy combatant" that it is seeking to detain is an individual who, it alleges, was "'part of or supporting forces hostile to the United States or coalition partners'" in Afghanistan and who "'engaged in an armed conflict against the United States'" there. We therefore answer only the narrow question before us: whether the detention of citizens falling within that definition is authorized.

The Government maintains that no explicit congressional authorization is required, because the Executive possesses plenary authority to detain pursuant to Article II of the Constitution. We do not reach the question whether Article II provides such authority, however, because we agree with the Government's alternative position, that Congress has in fact authorized Hamdi's detention, through the AUMF [Authorization to Use Military Force].

...

The AUMF authorizes the President to use "all necessary and appropriate force" against "nations, organizations, or persons" associated with the September 11, 2001, terrorist attacks. There can be no doubt that individuals who fought against the United States in Afghanistan as part of the Taliban, an organization known to have supported the al Qaeda terrorist network responsible for those attacks, are individuals Congress sought to target in passing the AUMF. We conclude that detention of individuals falling into the limited category we are considering, for the duration of the particular conflict in which they were captured, is so fundamental and accepted an incident to war as to be an exercise of the "necessary and appropriate force" Congress has authorized the President to use.

The capture and detention of lawful combatants and the capture, detention, and trial of unlawful combatants, by "universal agreement and practice," are "important incident[s] of war." *Ex parte Quirin*, 317 U.S. 1, 28 (1942). The purpose of detention is to prevent captured individuals from returning to the field of battle and taking up arms once again....

There is no bar to this Nation's holding one of its own citizens as an enemy combatant. In *Quirin*, one of the detainees, Haupt, alleged that he was a naturalized United States citizen. We held that "[c]itizens who associate themselves with the military arm of the enemy government, and with its aid, guidance and direction enter this country bent on hostile acts, are enemy belligerents within the meaning of... the law of war."...

In light of these principles, it is of no moment that the AUMF does not use specific language of detention. Because detention to prevent a combatant's return to the battlefield is a fundamental incident of waging war, in permitting the use of "necessary and appropriate force," Congress has clearly and unmistakably authorized detention in the narrow circumstances considered here.

...

Hamdi contends that the AUMF does not authorize indefinite or perpetual detention. Certainly, we agree that indefinite detention for the purpose of interrogation is not authorized. Further, we understand Congress' grant of authority for the use of "necessary and appropriate force" to include the authority to detain for the duration of the relevant conflict, and our understanding is based on longstanding law-of-war principles. If the practical circumstances of a given conflict are entirely unlike those of the conflicts that informed the development of the law of war, that understanding may unravel. But that is not the situation we face as of this date. Active combat operations against Taliban fighters apparently are ongoing in Afghanistan....

Ex parte Milligan (1866) does not undermine our holding about the Government's authority to seize enemy combatants, as we define that term today. In that case, the Court made repeated reference to the fact that its inquiry into whether the military tribunal had jurisdiction to try and punish Milligan turned in large part on the fact that Milligan was not a prisoner of war, but a resident of Indiana arrested while at home there. That fact was central to its conclusion. Had Milligan been captured while he was assisting Confederate soldiers by carrying a rifle against Union troops on a Confederate battlefield, the holding of the Court might well have been different. The Court's repeated explanations that Milligan was not a prisoner of war suggest that had these different circumstances been present he could have been detained under military authority for the duration of the conflict, whether or not he was a citizen.

. . .

Even in cases in which the detention of enemy combatants is legally authorized, there remains the question of what process is constitutionally due to a citizen who disputes his enemy-combatant status. Hamdi argues that he is owed a meaningful and timely hearing and that "extra-judicial detention [that] begins and ends with the submission of an affidavit based on third-hand hearsay" does not comport with the Fifth and Fourteenth Amendments. The Government counters that any more process than was provided below would be both unworkable and "constitutionally intolerable." . . .

Though they reach radically different conclusions on the process that ought to attend the present proceeding, the parties begin on common ground. All agree that, absent suspension, the writ of habeas corpus remains available to every individual detained within the United States. . . .

. . .

. . . [A]s critical as the Government's interest may be in detaining those who actually pose an immediate threat to the national security of the United States during ongoing international conflict, history and common sense teach us that an unchecked system of detention carries the potential to become a means for oppression and abuse of others who do not present that sort of threat. See *Ex parte Milligan*. . . . We reaffirm today the fundamental nature of a citizen's right to be free from involuntary confinement by his own government without due process of law, and we weigh the opposing governmental interests against the curtailment of liberty that such confinement entails.

. . .

Striking the proper constitutional balance here is of great importance to the Nation during this period of ongoing combat. But it is equally vital that our calculus not give short shrift to the values that this country holds dear or to the privilege that is American citizenship. It is during our most challenging and uncertain moments that our Nation's commitment to due process is most severely tested; and it is in those times that we must preserve our commitment at home to the principles for which we fight abroad. . . .

. . .

We therefore hold that a citizen-detainee seeking to challenge his classification as an enemy combatant must receive notice of the factual basis for his classification, and a fair opportunity to rebut the Government's factual assertions before a neutral decisionmaker. See *Cleveland Bd. of Ed.* v. *Loudermill*, 470 U.S. 532, 542 (1985) ("An essential principle of due process is that a deprivation of life, liberty, or property 'be preceded by notice and opportunity for hearing appropriate to the nature of the case' "). . . .

At the same time, the exigencies of the circumstances may demand that, aside from these core elements, enemy combatant proceedings may be tailored to alleviate their uncommon potential to burden the Executive at a time of ongoing military conflict. Hearsay, for example, may need to be accepted as the most reliable available evidence from the Government in such a proceeding. Likewise, the Constitution would not be offended by a presumption in favor of the Government's evidence, so long as that presumption remained a rebuttable one and fair opportunity for rebuttal were provided. . . .

We think it unlikely that this basic process will have the dire impact on the central functions of warmaking that the Government forecasts. The parties agree that initial captures on the battlefield need not receive the process we have discussed here; that process is due only when the determination is made to *continue* to hold those who have been seized. . . . While we accord the greatest respect and consideration to the judgments of military authorities in matters relating to the actual prosecution of a war, and recognize that the scope of that discretion necessarily is wide, it does not infringe on the core role of the military for the courts to exercise their own time-honored and constitutionally mandated roles of reviewing and resolving claims like those presented here. Cf. *Korematsu* v. *United States*, 323 U.S. 214, 233–234 (1944) (Murphy, J., dissenting). . . .

In sum, while the full protections that accompany challenges to detentions in other settings may prove unworkable and inappropriate in the enemy-combatant setting, the threats to military operations posed by a basic system of independent review are not so weighty as to trump a citizen's core rights to challenge meaningfully the Government's case and to be heard by an impartial adjudicator.

In so holding, we necessarily reject the Government's assertion that separation of powers principles mandate a heavily circumscribed role for the courts in such circumstances. Indeed, the position that the courts must forgo any examination of the individual case and focus exclusively on the legality of the broader detention scheme cannot be mandated by any reasonable view of separation of powers, as this approach serves only to *condense* power into a single branch of government. We have long since made clear that a state of war is not a blank check for the President when it comes to the rights of the Nation's citizens. *Youngstown Sheet & Tube v. Sawyer* (1952). Whatever power the United States Constitution envisions for the Executive in its exchanges with other nations or with enemy organizations in times of conflict, it most assuredly envisions a role for all three branches when individual liberties are at stake....

...

There remains the possibility that the standards we have articulated could be met by an appropriately authorized and properly constituted military tribunal. Indeed, it is notable that military regulations already provide for such process in related instances, dictating that tribunals be made available to determine the status of enemy detainees who assert prisoner-of-war status under the Geneva Convention....We anticipate that a District Court would proceed with the caution that we have indicated is necessary in this setting, engaging in a factfinding process that is both prudent and incremental. We have no reason to doubt that courts faced with these sensitive matters will pay proper heed both to the matters of national security that might arise in an individual case and to the constitutional limitations safeguarding essential liberties that remain vibrant even in times of security concerns.

...

The judgment of the United States Court of Appeals for the Fourth Circuit is vacated, and the case is remanded for further proceedings.

JUSTICE SOUTER, with whom JUSTICE GINSBURG joins, concurring in part and dissenting in part.

...

The threshold issue is how broadly or narrowly to read the Non-Detention Act, the tone of which is severe: "No citizen shall be imprisoned or otherwise detained by the United States except pursuant to an Act of Congress." Should the severity of the Act be relieved when the Government's stated factual justification for incommunicado detention is a war on terrorism, so that the Government may be said to act "pursuant" to congressional terms that fall short of explicit authority to imprison individuals?...

...

The fact that Congress intended to guard against a repetition of the World War II internments when it repealed the [Emergency Detention Act of 1950] and gave us [the Non-Detention Act of 1971] provides a powerful reason to think that [the Non-Detention Act] was meant to require clear congressional authorization before any citizen can be placed in a cell. It is not merely that the legislative history shows that [the Non-Detention Act] was thought necessary in anticipation of times just like the present, in which the safety of the country is threatened. To appreciate what is most significant, one must only recall that the internments of the 1940's were accomplished by Executive action....In requiring that any Executive detention be "pursuant to an Act of Congress," then, Congress necessarily meant to require a congressional enactment that clearly authorized detention or imprisonment.

...

The defining character of American constitutional government is its constant tension between security and liberty, serving both by partial helpings of each. In a government of separated powers, deciding finally on what is a reasonable degree of guaranteed liberty whether in peace or war (or some condition in between) is not well entrusted to the Executive Branch of Government, whose particular responsibility is to maintain security. For reasons of inescapable human nature, the branch of the Government asked to counter a serious threat is not the branch on which to rest the Nation's entire reliance in striking the balance between the will to win and the cost in liberty on the way to victory; the responsibility for security will naturally amplify the claim that security legitimately raises. A reasonable balance is more likely to be reached on the judgment of a different branch, just as Madison said in remarking that "the constant aim is to divide and arrange the several offices in such a manner as that each may be a check on the other—that the private interest of every individual may be a sentinel over the public rights." *The Federalist* No. 51. Hence the need for an assessment by Congress before citizens are subject to lockup, and likewise the need for a clearly expressed congressional resolution of the competing claims.

Under this principle of reading [the Non-Detention Act] robustly to require a clear statement of authorization to detain, none of the Government's arguments suffices to justify Hamdi's detention.

. . .

Since the Government has given no reason either to deflect the application of [the Non-Detention Act] or to hold it to be satisfied, I need to go no further; the Government hints of a constitutional challenge to the statute, but it presents none here. I will, however, stray across the line between statutory and constitutional territory just far enough to note the weakness of the Government's mixed claim of inherent, extrastatutory authority under a combination of Article II of the Constitution and the usages of war. It is in fact in this connection that the Government developed its argument that the exercise of war powers justifies the detention, and what I have just said about its inadequacy applies here as well. Beyond that, it is instructive to recall Justice Jackson's observation that the President is not Commander in Chief of the country, only of the military. *Youngstown Sheet & Tube Co.* v. *Sawyer* (1952)....

. . .

...I would...vacate the judgment of the Court of Appeals and remand for proceedings consistent with this view.

Since this disposition does not command a majority of the Court, however, the need to give practical effect to the conclusions of eight members of the Court rejecting the Government's position calls for me to join with the plurality in ordering remand on terms closest to those I would impose.

JUSTICE SCALIA, with whom JUSTICE STEVENS joins, dissenting.

...This case brings into conflict the competing demands of national security and our citizens' constitutional right to personal liberty. Although I share the Court's evident unease as it seeks to reconcile the two, I do not agree with its resolution.

Where the Government accuses a citizen of waging war against it, our constitutional tradition has been to prosecute him in federal court for treason or some other crime. Where the exigencies of war prevent that, the Constitution's Suspension Clause, Art. I, § 9, cl. 2, allows Congress to relax the usual protections temporarily. Absent suspension, however, the Executive's assertion of military exigency has not been thought sufficient to permit detention without charge. No one contends that the congressional Authorization for Use of Military Force, on which the Government relies to justify its actions here, is an implementation of the Suspension Clause. Accordingly, I would reverse the decision below.

The very core of liberty secured by our Anglo-Saxon system of separated powers has been freedom from indefinite imprisonment at the will of the Executive. Blackstone stated this principle clearly:

> Of great importance to the public is the preservation of this personal liberty: for if once it were left in the power of any, the highest, magistrate to imprison arbitrarily whomever he or his officers thought proper...there would soon be an end of all other rights and immunities....To make imprisonment lawful, it must either be, by process from the courts of judicature, or by warrant from some legal officer, having authority to commit to prison....

. . .

The gist of the Due Process Clause, as understood at the founding and since, was to force the Government to follow those common-law procedures traditionally deemed necessary before depriving a person of life, liberty, or property. When a citizen was deprived of liberty because of alleged criminal conduct, those procedures typically required committal by a magistrate followed by indictment and trial....

To be sure, certain types of permissible *non*criminal detention—that is, those not dependent upon the contention that the citizen had committed a criminal act—did not require the protections of criminal procedure. However, these fell into a limited number of well-recognized exceptions—civil commitment of the mentally ill, for example, and temporary detention in quarantine of the infectious. See *Opinion on the Writ of Habeas Corpus*, 97 Eng. Rep. 29, 36–37 (H. L. 1758) (Wilmot, J.). It is unthinkable that the Executive could render otherwise criminal grounds for detention noncriminal merely by disclaiming an intent to prosecute, or by asserting that it was incapacitating dangerous offenders rather than punishing wrongdoing....

The allegations here, of course, are no ordinary accusations of criminal activity. Yaser Esam Hamdi has been imprisoned because the Government believes he participated in the waging of war against the United States. The relevant question, then, is whether there is a different, special procedure for imprisonment of a citizen accused of wrongdoing *by aiding the enemy in wartime.*

JUSTICE O'CONNOR, writing for a plurality of this Court, asserts that captured enemy combatants (other than those suspected of war crimes) have traditionally been detained until the cessation of hostilities and then released. That is probably an accurate description of wartime practice with respect to enemy *aliens*. The tradition with respect to American citizens, however, has been quite different. Citizens aiding the enemy have been treated as traitors subject to the criminal process.

...

The Government argues that our more recent jurisprudence ratifies its indefinite imprisonment of a citizen within the territorial jurisdiction of federal courts. It places primary reliance upon *Ex parte Quirin* (1942), a World War II case upholding the trial by military commission of eight German saboteurs, one of whom, Hans Haupt, was a U.S. citizen. The case was not this Court's finest hour. The Court upheld the commission and denied relief in a brief *per curiam* issued the day after oral argument concluded; a week later the Government carried out the commission's death sentence upon six saboteurs, including Haupt. The Court eventually explained its reasoning in a written opinion issued several months later.

...

But even if *Quirin* gave a correct description of *Milligan*, or made an irrevocable revision of it, *Quirin* would still not justify denial of the writ here. In *Quirin* it was uncontested that the petitioners were members of enemy forces. They were "*admitted* enemy invaders," (emphasis added), and it was "undisputed" that they had landed in the United States in service of German forces. The specific holding of the Court was only that, "upon the *conceded* facts," the petitioners were "plainly within [the] boundaries" of military jurisdiction (emphasis added). But where those jurisdictional facts are *not* conceded—where the petitioner insists that he is *not* a belligerent—*Quirin* left the pre-existing law in place: Absent suspension of the writ, a citizen held where the courts are open is entitled either to criminal trial or to a judicial decree requiring his release.

It follows from what I have said that Hamdi is entitled to a habeas decree requiring his release unless (1) criminal proceedings are promptly brought, or (2) Congress has suspended the writ of habeas corpus. A suspension of the writ could, of course, lay down conditions for continued detention, similar to those that today's opinion prescribes under the Due Process Clause. But there is a world of difference between the people's representatives' determining the need for that suspension (and prescribing the conditions for it), and this Court's doing so.

...

It should not be thought, however, that the plurality's evisceration of the Suspension Clause augments, principally, the power of Congress. As usual, the major effect of its constitutional improvisation is to increase the power of the Court. Having found a congressional authorization for detention of citizens where none clearly exists; and having discarded the categorical procedural protection of the Suspension Clause; the plurality then proceeds, under the guise of the Due Process Clause, to prescribe what procedural protections *it* thinks appropriate....

...It is not the habeas court's function to make illegal detention legal by supplying a process that the Government could have provided, but chose not to. If Hamdi is being imprisoned in violation of the Constitution (because without due process of law), then his habeas petition should be granted; the Executive may then hand him over to the criminal authorities, whose detention for the purpose of prosecution will be lawful, or else must release him.

There is a certain harmony of approach in the plurality's making up for Congress's failure to invoke the Suspension Clause and its making up for the Executive's failure to apply what it says are needed procedures—an approach that reflects what might be called a Mr. Fix-it Mentality. The plurality seems to view it as its mission to Make Everything Come Out Right, rather than merely to decree the consequences, as far as individual rights are concerned, of the other two branches' actions and omissions. Has the Legislature failed to suspend the writ in the current dire emergency? Well, we will remedy that failure by prescribing the reasonable conditions that a suspension should have included. And has the Executive failed to live up to those reasonable conditions? Well, we will ourselves make that failure good, so that this dangerous fellow (if he is dangerous) need not be set free. The problem with this approach is not only that it steps out of the courts' modest and limited role in a democratic society; but that by repeatedly doing what it thinks the political branches ought to do it encourages their lassitude and saps the vitality of government by the people.

Several limitations give my views in this matter a relatively narrow compass. They apply only to citizens, accused of being enemy combatants, who are detained within the territorial jurisdiction of a federal court. This is not likely to be a numerous group.... Where the citizen is captured outside and held outside the United States, the constitutional requirements may be different.... Moreover, even within the United States, the accused citizen-enemy combatant may lawfully be detained once prosecution is in progress or in contemplation....

I frankly do not know whether these tools are sufficient to meet the Government's security needs, including the need to obtain intelligence through interrogation. It is far beyond my competence, or the Court's competence, to determine that. But it is not beyond Congress's. If the situation demands it, the Executive can ask Congress to authorize suspension of the writ—which can be made subject to whatever conditions Congress deems appropriate, including even the procedural novelties invented by the plurality today. To be sure, suspension is limited by the Constitution to cases of rebellion or invasion. But whether the attacks of September 11, 2001, constitute an "invasion," and whether those attacks still justify suspension several years later, are questions for Congress rather than this Court.... If civil rights are to be curtailed during wartime, it must be done openly and democratically, as the Constitution requires, rather than by silent erosion through an opinion of this Court.

...

JUSTICE THOMAS, dissenting.

The Executive Branch, acting pursuant to the powers vested in the President by the Constitution and with explicit congressional approval, has determined that Yaser Hamdi is an enemy combatant and should be detained. This detention falls squarely within the Federal Government's war powers, and we lack the expertise and capacity to second-guess that decision. As such, petitioners' habeas challenge should fail, and there is no reason to remand the case.....

...

The Founders intended that the President have primary responsibility—along with the necessary power—to protect the national security and to conduct the Nation's foreign relations. They did so principally because the structural advantages of a unitary Executive are essential in these domains. "Energy in the executive is a leading character in the definition of good government. It is essential to the protection of the community against foreign attacks." *The Federalist* No. 70....

...

I acknowledge that the question whether Hamdi's executive detention is lawful is a question properly resolved by the Judicial Branch, though the question comes to the Court with the strongest presumptions in favor of the Government. The plurality agrees that Hamdi's detention is lawful if he is an enemy combatant. But the question whether Hamdi is actually an enemy combatant is "of a kind for which the Judiciary has neither aptitude, facilities nor responsibility and which has long been held to belong in the domain of political power not subject to judicial intrusion or inquiry."...

...

In a case strikingly similar to this one, the Court addressed a Governor's authority to detain for an extended period a person the executive believed to be responsible, in part, for a local insurrection. Justice Holmes wrote for a unanimous Court:

> When it comes to a decision by the head of the State upon a matter involving its life, the ordinary rights of individuals must yield to what *he deems* the necessities of the moment. Public danger warrants the substitution of executive process for judicial process. This was admitted with regard to killing men in the actual clash of arms, and we think it obvious, although it was disputed, that the same is true of temporary detention to prevent apprehended harm. *Moyer v. Peabody*, 212 U.S. 78, 85 (1909) (emphasis added).

The Court answered Moyer's claim that he had been denied due process by emphasizing that

> it is familiar that what is due process of law depends on circumstances. It varies with the subject-matter and the necessities of the situation. Thus summary proceedings suffice for taxes, and executive decisions for exclusion from the country.... Such arrests are not necessarily for punishment, but are by way of precaution to prevent the exercise of hostile power. *Id.*, at 84–85.

In this context, due process requires nothing more than a good-faith executive determination. To be clear: The Court has held that an executive, acting pursuant to statutory and constitutional authority may, consistent with the Due Process Clause, unilaterally decide to detain an individual if the executive deems this necessary for the public safety *even if he is mistaken*.

. . .

Undeniably, Hamdi has been deprived of a serious interest, one actually protected by the Due Process Clause. Against this, however, is the Government's overriding interest in protecting the Nation. If a deprivation of liberty can be justified by the need to protect a town, the protection of the Nation, *a fortiori*, justifies it.

I acknowledge that under the plurality's approach, it might, at times, be appropriate to give detainees access to counsel and notice of the factual basis for the Government's determination. But properly accounting for the Government's interests also requires concluding that access to counsel and to the factual basis would not always be warranted. Though common sense suffices, the Government thoroughly explains that counsel would often destroy the intelligence gathering function. Equally obvious is the Government's interest in not fighting the war in its own courts....

E. Executive Privilege

One incident of the party polarization and divided government of the Contemporary Era was a heightened tension between the legislative and executive branches over how policy was formulated and implemented. Congress has a variety of tools that it uses to call the executive branch to account for how it develops and administers policy and to check the president as he tries to impose his will on the executive bureaucracy. Some checks are routine and attempt to make executive branch activities more transparent and open to interest groups, legislators, the media, and the courts. The New Deal–era Administrative Procedures Act, for example, requires that interested parties be heard before administrative agencies make final decisions on many important regulatory decisions. The Watergate-era Federal Advisory Committee Act requires that committees that advised government policymakers disclose information about their members and have open meetings. Other checks are intermittent. Congress can hold hearings to investigate how executive officials implement statutes and can call executive officials to stand for questioning about their conduct.

Normally, such requirements and investigations are part of the routine operation of modern government. Occasionally the executive has pushed back. Most dramatically, the president and his subordinates have sometimes invoked executive privilege in order to avoid the specific demands of legislative oversight. The claim of executive privilege allows the president and his closest advisors to refuse to testify about or divulge documents that are confidential to the internal operation of the White House or perhaps national security. In *In re Sealed Case*, F. 3d 729 (D.C. Cir., 1997), for example, the D.C. Circuit Court held that close presidential advisors could claim an executive privilege for their own communications that could potentially stymie the criminal investigation of a Cabinet secretary. In *Cheney v. United States District Court for the District of Columbia* (2004), the U.S. Supreme Court emphasized that the burden for overcoming legitimate claims of executive privilege were even more difficult outside the context of a criminal trial. Congress confronted its own difficulty with persuading the George W. Bush White House to waive executive privilege claims and agree to let high-level advisors testify in hearings on sensitive matters.

Cheney v. United States District Court for the District of Columbia, 542 U.S. 367 (2004)

Shortly after taking office, President George W. Bush created the National Energy Policy Development Group (NEPDG), chaired by Vice President Dick Cheney, to develop the administration's national energy policy. The NEPDG was composed entirely of high-level executive branch officials. The NEPDG issued a report five months after its creation and disbanded. Afterwards, two interest groups filed suit in federal district court against Cheney and the other members of the NEPDG contending the group had violated the Federal Advisory Committee Act of 1972 (FACA), part of the Watergate-era reforms. FACA imposed a variety of open meeting and disclosure requirements on "advisory committees" that included any nongovernmental employees. The interest groups contended that lobbyists regularly attended meetings of the NEPDG and were de facto members of the group. They also sought an injunction requiring the administration to produce all materials that would have been disclosed if FACA were applicable. Because FACA did not allow private lawsuits to enforce its terms, the district court allowed the suit to proceed against the vice president through a separate statute allowing for a writ of mandamus under limited circumstances.

Since the public record of NEPDG indicated only the official members of the group, the lawsuit began with a discovery motion seeking documents relating to the activities of the NEPDG. The administration responded by claiming that all documents were protected by executive privilege. In the context of a civil lawsuit against the vice president, the administration argued, and the Supreme Court ultimately agreed, a claim to executive privilege could properly be quite broad. The district court approved the discovery request of the interest groups, which a divided circuit court affirmed on appeal. By a 7–2 vote, the Supreme Court reversed the lower courts. Although giving an immediate "victory" to Cheney and the administration, the Court did not directly rule on the administration's argument that it was entitled to blanket immunity from discovery proceedings in this case. The justices instead encouraged the lower courts to narrow any discovery so as not to interfere with the functioning of the executive branch. The circuit court subsequently decided that FACA allowed the president to establish advisory groups, such as the NEPDG. In these groups government employees were the only "voting members," even if non-government employees were also consulted during the process. In this way, the circuit court sought in part to avoid the separation-of-powers concerns identified by the Supreme Court. Given that ruling, no discovery was necessary, and the lawsuit was dismissed.

A key issue for the U.S. Supreme Court was whether to distinguish the claim of executive privilege in U.S. v. Nixon *(1974). Should different standards apply for civil versus criminal proceedings in weighing claims of executive privilege?*

JUSTICE KENNEDY delivered the opinion of the Court.

The United States District Court for the District of Columbia entered discovery orders directing the Vice President and other senior officials in the Executive Branch to produce information about a task force established to give advice and make policy recommendations to the President. This case requires us to consider the circumstances under which a court of appeals may exercise its power to issue a writ of mandamus to modify or dissolve the orders when, by virtue of their overbreadth, enforcement might interfere with the officials in the discharge of their duties and impinge upon the President's constitutional prerogatives.

...

...It is well established that "a President's communications and activities encompass a vastly wider range of sensitive material than would be true of any 'ordinary individual.'" *United States* v. *Nixon*, 418 U.S. 683, 715 (1974). Chief Justice Marshall, sitting as a trial judge, recognized the unique position of the Executive Branch when he stated that "[i]n no case...would a court be required to proceed against the president as against an ordinary individual."...As *Nixon* explained, these principles do not mean that the "President is above the law." Rather, they simply acknowledge that the public interest requires that a coequal branch of Government "afford Presidential confidentiality the greatest protection consistent with the fair administration of justice," and give recognition to the paramount necessity of protecting the Executive Branch from vexatious litigation that might distract it from the energetic performance of its constitutional duties.

...

The distinction *Nixon* drew between criminal and civil proceedings is not just a matter of formalism. As the Court explained, the need for information in the criminal context is much weightier because "our historic[al] commitment to the rule of law...is nowhere more profoundly manifest than in our view that 'the twofold aim [of criminal justice] is that guilt shall not escape or innocence suffer.'"...

The Court also observed in *Nixon* that a "primary constitutional duty of the Judicial Branch [is] to do justice in criminal prosecutions." Withholding materials from a tribunal in an ongoing criminal case when the information is necessary to the court in carrying out its tasks "conflict[s] with the function of the courts under Art. III." Such an impairment of the "essential functions of [another] branch," is impermissible. Withholding the information in this case, however, does not hamper another branch's ability to perform its "essential functions" in quite the same way. The District Court ordered discovery here, not to remedy known statutory violations, but to ascertain whether FACA's disclosure requirements even apply to the NEPDG in the first place. Even if FACA embodies important congressional objectives, the only consequence from respondents' inability to obtain the discovery they seek is that it would be more difficult for private complainants to vindicate Congress' policy objectives under FACA....

A party's need for information is only one facet of the problem. An important factor weighing in the opposite direction is the burden imposed by the discovery orders. This is not a routine discovery dispute. The discovery requests are directed to the Vice President and other senior Government officials who served on the NEPDG to give advice and make recommendations to the President. The Executive Branch, at its highest level, is seeking the aid of the courts to protect its constitutional prerogatives. As we have already noted, special considerations control when the Executive Branch's interests in maintaining the autonomy of its office and safeguarding the confidentiality of its communications are implicated....

Even when compared against *United States* v. *Nixon*'s criminal subpoenas, which did involve the President, the civil discovery here militates against respondents' position. The observation in *Nixon* that production of confidential information would not disrupt the functioning of the Executive Branch cannot be applied in a mechanistic fashion to civil litigation. In the criminal justice system, there are various constraints, albeit imperfect, to filter out insubstantial legal claims. The decision to prosecute a criminal case, for example, is made by a publicly accountable prosecutor subject to budgetary considerations and under an ethical obligation, not only to win and zealously to advocate for his client but also to serve the cause of justice. The rigors of the penal system are also mitigated by the responsible exercise of prosecutorial discretion. In contrast, there are no analogous checks in the civil discovery process here....

...

...Once executive privilege is asserted, coequal branches of the Government are set on a collision course. The Judiciary is forced into the difficult task of balancing the need for information in a judicial proceeding and the Executive's Article II prerogatives. This inquiry places courts in the awkward position of evaluating the Executive's claims of confidentiality and autonomy, and pushes to the fore difficult questions of separation of powers and checks and balances. These "occasion[s] for constitutional confrontation between the two branches" should be avoided whenever possible. *United States* v. *Nixon*

In recognition of these concerns, there is sound precedent in the District of Columbia itself for district courts to explore other avenues, short of forcing the Executive to invoke privilege, when they are asked to enforce against the Executive Branch unnecessarily broad subpoenas....[Here the Court indicated doctrines "to narrow, on its own, the scope of the subpoenas" so as to balance judicial and executive interests.]

...

The judgment of the Court of Appeals for the District of Columbia is vacated, and the case is remanded for further proceedings consistent with this opinion.

It is so ordered.

JUSTICE STEVENS, concurring.

...

...[G]ranting broad discovery in this case effectively prejudged the merits of respondents' claim for mandamus relief—an outcome entirely inconsistent with the extraordinary nature of the writ. Under these circumstances, instead of requiring petitioners to object to particular discovery requests, the District Court should have required respondents to demonstrate that particular requests would tend to establish their theory of the case....

JUSTICE THOMAS, with whom JUSTICE SCALIA joins, concurring in part and dissenting in part.

...

JUSTICE GINSBURG, with whom JUSTICE SOUTER joins, dissenting.

...

The discovery plan drawn by Judicial Watch and Sierra Club was indeed "unbounded in scope." Initial approval of that plan by the District Court, however, was not given in stunning disregard of separation-of-powers concerns. In the order itself, the District Court invited "detailed and precise object[ions]" to any of the discovery requests, and instructed the Government to "identify and explain...invocations of privilege with particularity."...Anticipating further proceedings concerning discovery, the District Court suggested that the Government could "submit [any privileged documents] under seal for the court's consideration," or that "the court [could] appoint the equivalent of a Special Master, maybe a retired judge," to review allegedly privileged documents.

The Government did not file specific objections; nor did it supply particulars to support assertions of privilege. Instead, the Government urged the District Court to rule that Judicial Watch and the Sierra Club could have no discovery at all....

...

...[I]n remanding for consideration of discovery-tailoring measures, the Court apparently rejects [the] no-discovery position. Otherwise, a remand based on the overbreadth of the discovery requests would make no sense. Nothing in the record, however, intimates lower-court refusal to reduce discovery.... In accord with the Court of Appeals, I am "confident that [were it moved to do so] the district court here [would] protect petitioners' legitimate interests and keep discovery within appropriate limits." I would therefore affirm the judgment of the Court of Appeals.

F. Immunity from Judicial Processes

Government officials are sometimes the named party in a lawsuit over government policy because they are the officials in charge of making or enforcing the policy. Such lawsuits are routine, and the individual named in the suit acts simply as a representative of the government in such cases. *Hamdi v. Rumsfeld* (2004) involved Donald Rumsfeld only in his capacity as Secretary of Defense.

Sometimes government officials are sued as individuals, however. They may be sued because of the actions that they took while in government, or they may be sued for a completely unrelated matter. *Clinton v. Jones* (1997) involved the unusual situation of a sitting president being sued in civil court as a result of his personal activities. Presidents are unique since they are a singular office holder at the top of the executive hierarchy, which distinguishes them from a judge or a legislator. Moreover, in the modern era, the president maintains an extraordinarily busy schedule, which puts pressure on his time and energy in ways that would not have been the case even a few decades ago. In such circumstances, was the president implicitly constitutionally immune from a civil lawsuit during the tenure of his office? Should Paula Jones have to wait until after Bill Clinton left the White House to initiate or continue her suit, and should other future claimants and injured parties likewise have to put their disputes on hold if their disputant wins the presidency? If the president did not have a constitutional immunity from civil lawsuits, would the courts be an open door to his political enemies?

Clinton v. Jones, 520 U.S. 681 (1997)

President Bill Clinton was dogged by personal scandal throughout his political career. Some of the accusations were financial. Both he and his spouse, Hillary Rodham Clinton, were accused of taking financial advantage of their official status in the Whitewater Affair, involving land deals and loans in Arkansas. Other accusations were personal. Several women claimed that, during his time in government in office, Clinton had either had affairs with them or had sought to initiate affairs. During his presidential campaign in 1992, Clinton was able to overcome claims that he had had sexual relations with Gennifer Flowers, a former local television reporter and state employee, while governor of Arkansas. The Paula Jones affair had different political and constitutional consequences.

Paula Jones was a minor state employee in Arkansas who accused President Clinton of sexually harassing her when he was governor and then libeling her. Her lawsuit, financed in large part by long-time Clinton rivals, sought more than a half a million dollars in damages. Clinton insisted that the lawsuit be stayed, to be resumed only after he had left the presidency. Relying on past cases, he insisted that presidents could be sued for neither their official nor their unofficial actions while in office. A lower federal court judge in 1994 agreed with Clinton's contention and postponed the trial indefinitely. This postponement was appealed to the Supreme Court of the United States.

In a unanimous decision, the Supreme Court allowed the case to go forward during Clinton's term of office. As a result, Clinton was formally deposed under oath by the lawyers for Paula Jones. During his testimony, he lied about the existence of his affair with Monica Lewinsky, a White House intern, arguably hampering the ability of Jones to build her own case. The revelation of the affair and the false testimony led to Clinton's impeachment by the Republican majority in the House of Representatives in December 1998. He was not convicted by the Senate.

How does the application of constitutional principles turn on factual judgments such as those raised in the majority and concurring opinions? Can trial judges be trusted with the responsibility to balance the president's schedule and the needs of the judicial proceedings?

JUSTICE STEVENS delivered the opinion of the Court.

This case raises a constitutional and a prudential question concerning the Office of the President of the United States. Respondent, a private citizen, seeks to recover damages from the current occupant of that office based on actions allegedly taken before his term began. The President submits that in all but the most exceptional cases the Constitution requires federal courts to defer such litigation until his term ends and that, in any event, respect for the office warrants such a stay. Despite the force of the arguments supporting the President's submissions, we conclude that they must be rejected.

...[Respondent] alleges that [an Arkansas state trooper] persuaded her to leave her desk and to visit...Governor [Clinton] in a business suite at the hotel, where he made "abhorrent" sexual advances that she vehemently rejected. She further claims that her superiors at work subsequently dealt with her in a hostile and rude manner, and changed her duties to punish her for rejecting those advances....

...[I]t is perfectly clear that the alleged misconduct of petitioner was unrelated to any of his official duties as President of the United States and, indeed, occurred before he was elected to that office.

...

...[O]our decision rejecting the immunity claim and allowing the case to proceed does not require us to confront the question whether a court may compel the attendance of the President at any specific time or place. We assume that the testimony of the President, both for discovery and for use at trial, may be taken at the White House at a time that will accommodate his busy schedule, and that, if a trial is held, there would be no necessity for the President to attend in person, though he could elect to do so.

...

The principal rationale for affording certain public servants immunity from suits for money damages arising out of their official acts is inapplicable to unofficial conduct. In cases involving prosecutors, legislators, and judges we have repeatedly explained that the immunity serves the public interest in enabling such officials to perform their designated functions effectively without fear that a particular decision may give rise to personal liability....

This reasoning provides no support for an immunity for *unofficial* conduct. As we explained in *[Nixon v.] Fitzgerald* (1982), "the sphere of protected action must be related closely to the immunity's justifying purposes."...Because of the President's broad responsibilities, we recognized in that case an immunity from damages claims arising out of official acts extending to the "outer perimeter of his authority."...But we have never suggested that the President, or any other official, has an immunity that extends beyond the scope of any action taken in an official capacity....

...

Petitioner's strongest argument supporting his immunity claim is based on the text and structure of the Constitution. He does not contend that the occupant of the Office of the President is "above the law," in the sense that his conduct is entirely immune from judicial scrutiny. The President argues merely for a postponement of the judicial proceedings that will determine whether he violated any law....

...

Rather than arguing that the decision of the case will produce either an aggrandizement of judicial power or a narrowing of executive power, petitioner contends that—as a by-product of an otherwise traditional exercise of judicial power—burdens will be placed on the President that will hamper the performance of his official duties....

Petitioner's predictive judgment finds little support in either history or the relatively narrow compass of the issues raised in this particular case. As we have already noted, in the more than 200-year history of the Republic, only three sitting Presidents have been subjected to suits for their private actions....If the past is any indicator, it seems unlikely that a deluge of such litigation will ever engulf the Presidency. As for the case at hand, if properly managed by the District Court, it appears to us highly unlikely to occupy any substantial amount of petitioner's time.

Of greater significance, petitioner errs by presuming that interactions between the Judicial Branch and the Executive, even quite burdensome interactions, necessarily rise to the level of constitutionally forbidden impairment of the Executive's ability to perform its constitutionally mandated functions....The fact that a federal court's exercise of its traditional Article III jurisdiction may significantly burden the time and attention of the Chief Executive is not sufficient to establish a violation of the Constitution. Two long-settled propositions, first announced by Chief Justice Marshall, support that conclusion.

First, we have long held that when the President takes official action, the Court has the authority to determine whether he has acted within the law....Despite the serious impact of [*Youngstown Sheet & Tube Co. v. Sawyer* (1952)] on the ability of the Executive Branch to accomplish its assigned mission, and the substantial time that the President must necessarily have devoted to the matter as a result of judicial involvement, we exercised our Article III jurisdiction to decide whether his official conduct conformed to the law....

Second, it is also settled that the President is subject to judicial process in appropriate circumstances. Although Thomas Jefferson apparently thought otherwise, Chief Justice Marshall, when presiding in the treason trial of Aaron Burr, ruled that a subpoena *duces tecum* could be directed to the President.... We unequivocally and emphatically endorsed Marshall's position when we held that President Nixon was obligated to comply with a subpoena commanding him to produce certain tape recordings of his conversations with his aides. *United States v. Nixon* (1974)....

...

... Although we have rejected the argument that the potential burdens on the President violate separation of powers principles, those burdens are appropriate matters for the District Court to evaluate in its management of the case. The high respect that is owed to the office of the Chief Executive, though not justifying a rule of categorical immunity, is a matter that should inform the conduct of the entire proceeding, including the timing and scope of discovery.

We add a final comment on two matters that are discussed at length in the briefs: the risk that our decision will generate a large volume of politically motivated harassing and frivolous litigation, and the danger that national security concerns might prevent the President from explaining a legitimate need for a continuance.

We are not persuaded that either of these risks is serious.... Although scheduling problems may arise, there is no reason to assume that the District Courts will be either unable to accommodate the President's needs or unfaithful to the tradition—especially in matters involving national security—of giving "the utmost deference to Presidential responsibilities." Several Presidents, including petitioner, have given testimony without jeopardizing the Nation's security. In short, we have confidence in the ability of our federal judges to deal with both of these concerns.

JUSTICE BREYER, concurring.

I agree with the majority that the Constitution does not automatically grant the President an immunity from civil lawsuits based upon his private conduct....

In my view, however, once the President sets forth and explains a conflict between judicial proceeding and public duties, the matter changes. At that point, the Constitution permits a judge to schedule a trial in an ordinary civil damages action (where postponement normally is possible without overwhelming damage to a plaintiff) only within the constraints of a constitutional principle—a principle that forbids a federal judge in such a case to interfere with the President's discharge of his public duties. I have no doubt that the Constitution contains such a principle applicable to civil suits, based upon Article II's vesting of the entire "executive Power" in a single individual, implemented through the Constitution's structural separation of powers, and revealed both by history and case precedent.

I recognize that this case does not require us now to apply the principle specifically, thereby delineating its contours; nor need we now decide whether lower courts are to apply it directly or categorically through the use of presumptions or rules of administration. Yet I fear that to disregard it now may appear to deny it. I also fear that the majority's description of the relevant precedents de-emphasizes the extent to which they support a principle of the President's independent authority to control his own time and energy.... Further, if the majority is wrong in predicting the future infrequency of private civil litigation against sitting Presidents... acknowledgement and future delineation of the constitutional principle will prove a practically necessary institutional safeguard. For these reasons, I think it important to explain how the Constitution's text, history, and precedent support this principle of judicial noninterference with Presidential functions in ordinary civil damages actions.

...

Article II makes a single President responsible for the actions of the Executive Branch in much the same way that the entire Congress is responsible for the actions of the Legislative Branch, or the entire Judiciary for those of the Judicial Branch. It thereby creates a constitutional equivalence between a single President, on the one hand, and many legislators, or judges, on the other.

The Founders created this equivalence by consciously deciding to vest Executive authority in one person rather than several. They did so in order to focus, rather than to spread, Executive responsibility thereby facilitating accountability. They also sought to encourage energetic, vigorous, decisive, and speedy execution of the laws by placing in the hands of a single, constitutionally indispensable, individual the ultimate authority that, in respect to the other branches, the Constitution divides among many....

...

For present purposes, this constitutional structure means that the President is not like Congress, for

Congress can function as if it were whole, even when up to half of its members are absent.... It means that the President is not like the Judiciary, for judges often can designate other judges, *e.g.*, from other judicial circuits, to sit even should an entire court be detained by personal litigation. It means that, unlike Congress, which is regularly out of session, the President never adjourns.

More importantly, these constitutional objectives explain why a President, though able to delegate duties to others, cannot delegate ultimate responsibility or the active obligation to supervise that goes with it. And the related constitutional equivalence between President, Congress, and the Judiciary, means that judicial scheduling orders in a private civil case must not only take reasonable account of, say, a particularly busy schedule, or a job on which others critically depend, or an underlying electoral mandate. They must also reflect the fact that interference with a President's ability to carry out his public responsibilities is constitutionally equivalent to interference with the ability of the entirety of Congress, or the Judicial Branch, to carry out their public obligations.

...[T]he Constitution protects the President from judicial orders in private civil cases to the extent that those orders could significantly interfere with his efforts to carry out his ongoing public responsibilities.

...

...A Constitution that separates powers in order to prevent one branch of Government from significantly threatening the workings of another could not grant a single judge more than a very limited power to second guess a President's reasonable determination (announced in open court) of his scheduling needs, nor could it permit the issuance of a trial scheduling order that would significantly interfere with the President's discharge of his duties—in a private civil damage action the trial of which might be postponed without the plaintiff suffering enormous harm....I agree with the majority's determination that a constitutional defense must await a more specific showing of need; I do not agree with what I believe to be an understatement of the "danger." And I believe that ordinary case-management principles are unlikely to prove sufficient to deal with private civil lawsuits for damages unless supplemented with a constitutionally based requirement that district courts schedule proceedings so as to avoid significant interference with the President's ongoing discharge of his official responsibilities.

Suggested Readings

Brisbin, Richard A., Jr. *Justice Antonin Scalia and the Conservative Revival* (Baltimore, MD: Johns Hopkins University Press, 1997).

Colucci, Frank J. *Justice Kennedy's Jurisprudence: The Full and Necessary Meaning of Liberty* (Lawrence: University Press of Kansas, 2009).

Fisher, Louis. *Constitutional Conflicts between Congress and the President* (Lawrence: University Press of Kansas, 1997).

Gerhardt, Michael. *The Federal Appointments Process: A Constitutional and Historical Analysis* (Durham, NC: Duke University Press, 2000).

Gibson, James L., and Gregory A. Caldeira. *Citizens, Courts, and Confirmations: Positivity Theory and the Judgments of the American People* (Princeton: Princeton University Press, 2009).

Gillman, Howard. *The Votes that Counted: How the Court Decided the 2000 Presidential Election* (Chicago: University of Chicago Press, 2000).

Keck, Thomas M. *The Most Activist Supreme Court in History: The Road to Modern Judicial Conservatism* (Chicago: University of Chicago Press, 2004).

Maltz, Earl M. *Rehnquist Justice: Understanding the Court Dynamic* (Lawrence: University Press of Kansas, 2003).

Posner, Eric A., and Adrian Vermeule. *The Executive Unbound: After the Madisonian Republic* (New York: Oxford University Press, 2011).

Rosen, Jeffrey. *The Most Democratic Branch: How the Courts Serve America* (New York: Oxford University Press, 2006).

Scherer, Nancy. *Scoring Points: Politicians, Activists, and the Lower Federal Court Appointment Process* (Stanford: Stanford University Press, 2005).

Teles, Steven M. *The Rise of the Conservative Legal Movement: The Battle for the Control of the Law* (Princeton: Princeton University Press, 2008).

Tushnet, Mark. *A Court Divided* (New York: W. W. Norton, 2005).

Tushnet, Mark. *The New Constitutional Order* (Princeton: Princeton University Press, 2003).

Tushnet, Mark, ed. *The Constitution in Wartime: Beyond Alarmism and Complacency* (Durham, NC: Duke University Press, 2005).

Yarbrough, Tinsley E. *The Rehnquist Court and the Constitution* (New York: Oxford University Press, 2000).

Yarbrough, Tinsley E. *David Hackett Souter: Traditional Republican on the Supreme Court* (New York: Oxford University Press, 2005).

Appendix 1

Constitution of the United States of America

We the People of the United States, in Order to form a more perfect Union, establish Justice, insure domestic Tranquility, provide for the common defense, promote the general Welfare, and secure the Blessings of Liberty to ourselves and our Posterity, do ordain and establish this Constitution for the United States of America.

Article. I.

Section. 1. All legislative Powers herein granted shall be vested in a Congress of the United States, which shall consist of a Senate and House of Representatives.

Section. 2. The House of Representatives shall be composed of Members chosen every second Year by the People of the several States, and the Electors in each State shall have the Qualifications requisite for Electors of the most numerous Branch of the State Legislature.

No Person shall be a Representative who shall not have attained to the Age of twenty five Years, and been seven Years a Citizen of the United States, and who shall not, when elected, be an Inhabitant of that State in which he shall be chosen.

[Representatives and direct Taxes shall be apportioned among the several States which may be included within this Union, according to their respective Numbers, which shall be determined by adding to the whole Number of free Persons, including those bound to Service for a Term of Years, and excluding Indians not taxed, three fifths of all other Persons.][1] The actual Enumeration shall be made within three Years after the first Meeting of the Congress of the United States, and within every subsequent Term of ten Years, in such Manner as they shall by Law direct. The number of Representatives shall not exceed one for every thirty Thousand, but each State shall have at Least one Representative; and until such enumeration shall be made, the State of New Hampshire shall be entitled to choose three, Massachusetts eight, Rhode-Island and Providence Plantations one, Connecticut five, New-York six, New Jersey four, Pennsylvania eight, Delaware one, Maryland six, Virginia ten, North Carolina five, South Carolina five, and Georgia three.

When vacancies happen in the Representation from any State, the Executive Authority thereof shall issue Writs of Election to fill such Vacancies.

The House of Representatives shall choose their Speaker and other Officers; and shall have the sole Power of Impeachment.

Section. 3. The Senate of the United States shall be composed of two Senators from each State, [chosen by the Legislature thereof,][2] for six Years; and each Senator shall have one Vote.

Immediately after they shall be assembled in Consequence of the first Election, they shall be divided as equally as may be into three Classes. The Seats of the Senators of the first Class shall be vacated at the Expiration of the second Year, of the second Class at the Expiration of the fourth Year, and of the third Class at the Expiration of the sixth Year, so that one third may be chosen every second Year; [and if Vacancies happen by Resignation, or otherwise, during the Recess of the Legislature of any State, the Executive thereof may make temporary Appointments until the next Meeting of the Legislature, which shall then fill such Vacancies.][3]

1. Changed by Section 2 of the Fourteenth Amendment.

2. Changed by the Seventeenth Amendment.

3. Changed by the Seventeenth Amendment.

No Person shall be a Senator who shall not have attained to the Age of thirty Years, and been nine Years a Citizen of the United States, and who shall not, when elected, be an Inhabitant of that State for which he shall be chosen.

The Vice President of the United States shall be President of the Senate, but shall have no Vote, unless they be equally divided.

The Senate shall choose their other Officers, and also a President pro tempore, in the Absence of the Vice President, or when he shall exercise the Office of President of the United States.

The Senate shall have the sole Power to try all Impeachments. When sitting for that Purpose, they shall be on Oath or Affirmation. When the President of the United States is tried, the Chief Justice shall preside: And no Person shall be convicted without the Concurrence of two thirds of the Members present.

Judgment in Cases of Impeachment shall not extend further than to removal from Office, and disqualification to hold and enjoy any Office of honor, Trust or Profit under the United States: but the Party convicted shall nevertheless be liable and subject to Indictment, Trial, Judgment and Punishment, according to Law.

Section. 4. The Times, Places and Manner of holding Elections for Senators and Representatives, shall be prescribed in each State by the Legislature thereof; but the Congress may at any time by Law make or alter such Regulations, except as to the Places of choosing Senators.

The Congress shall assemble at least once in every Year, and such Meeting shall be [on the first Monday in December,][4] unless they shall by Law appoint a different Day.

Section. 5. Each House shall be the Judge of the Elections, Returns and Qualifications of its own Members, and a Majority of each shall constitute a Quorum to do Business; but a smaller Number may adjourn from day to day, and may be authorized to compel the Attendance of absent Members, in such Manner, and under such Penalties as each House may provide.

Each House may determine the Rules of its Proceedings, punish its Members for disorderly Behavior, and, with the Concurrence of two thirds, expel a Member.

4. Changed by the Twentieth Amendment.

Each House shall keep a Journal of its Proceedings, and from time to time publish the same, excepting such Parts as may in their Judgment require Secrecy; and the Yeas and Nays of the Members of either House on any question shall, at the Desire of one fifth of those Present, be entered on the Journal.

Neither House, during the Session of Congress, shall, without the Consent of the other, adjourn for more than three days, nor to any other Place than that in which the two Houses shall be sitting.

Section. 6. The Senators and Representatives shall receive a Compensation for their Services, to be ascertained by Law, and paid out of the Treasury of the United States. They shall in all Cases, except Treason, Felony and Breach of the Peace, be privileged from Arrest during their Attendance at the Session of their respective Houses, and in going to and returning from the same; and for any Speech or Debate in either House, they shall not be questioned in any other Place.

No Senator or Representative shall, during the Time for which he was elected, be appointed to any civil Office under the Authority of the United States, which shall have been created, or the Emoluments whereof shall have been increased during such time; and no Person holding any Office under the United States, shall be a Member of either House during his Continuance in Office.

Section. 7. All Bills for raising Revenue shall originate in the House of Representatives; but the Senate may propose or concur with Amendments as on other Bills.

Every Bill which shall have passed the House of Representatives and the Senate, shall, before it becomes a Law, be presented to the President of the United States; If he approve he shall sign it, but if not he shall return it, with his Objections to that House in which it shall have originated, who shall enter the Objections at large on their Journal, and proceed to reconsider it. If after such Reconsideration two thirds of that House shall agree to pass the Bill, it shall be sent, together with the Objections, to the other House, by which it shall likewise be reconsidered, and if approved by two thirds of that House, it shall become a Law. But in all such Cases the Votes of both Houses shall be determined by yeas and Nays, and the Names of the Persons voting for and against the Bill shall be entered on the Journal of each House respectively. If any Bill shall not be returned by the President within ten Days (Sundays excepted) after it shall have been presented to him, the Same shall be a Law, in like Manner as if he had signed it, unless the Congress by their Adjournment prevent its Return, in which Case it shall not be a Law.

Every Order, Resolution, or Vote to which the Concurrence of the Senate and House of Representatives may be necessary (except on a question of Adjournment) shall be presented to the President of the United States; and before the Same shall take Effect, shall be approved by him, or being disapproved by him, shall be repassed by two thirds of the Senate and House of Representatives, according to the Rules and Limitations prescribed in the Case of a Bill.

Section. 8. The Congress shall have Power To lay and collect Taxes, Duties, Imposts and Excises, to pay the Debts and provide for the common Defense and general Welfare of the United States; but all Duties, Imposts and Excises shall be uniform throughout the United States;

To borrow Money on the credit of the United States;

To regulate Commerce with foreign Nations, and among the several States, and with the Indian Tribes;

To establish an uniform Rule of Naturalization, and uniform Laws on the subject of Bankruptcies throughout the United States;

To coin Money, regulate the Value thereof, and of foreign Coin, and fix the Standard of Weights and Measures;

To provide for the Punishment of counterfeiting the Securities and current Coin of the United States;

To establish Post Offices and post Roads;

To promote the Progress of Science and useful Arts, by securing for limited Times to Authors and Inventors the exclusive Right to their respective Writings and Discoveries;

To constitute Tribunals inferior to the supreme Court;

To define and punish Piracies and Felonies committed on the high Seas, and Offenses against the Law of Nations;

To declare War, grant Letters of Marque and Reprisal, and make Rules concerning Captures on Land and Water;

To raise and support Armies, but no Appropriation of Money to that Use shall be for a longer Term than two Years;

To provide and maintain a Navy;

To make Rules for the Government and Regulation of the land and naval Forces;

To provide for calling forth the Militia to execute the Laws of the Union, suppress Insurrections and repel Invasions;

To provide for organizing, arming, and disciplining, the Militia, and for governing such Part of them as may be employed in the Service of the United States, reserving to the States respectively, the Appointment of the Officers, and the Authority of training the Militia according to the discipline prescribed by Congress;

To exercise exclusive Legislation in all Cases whatsoever, over such District (not exceeding ten Miles square) as may, by Cession of particular States, and the Acceptance of Congress, become the Seat of the Government of the United States, and to exercise like Authority over all Places purchased by the Consent of the Legislature of the State in which the Same shall be, for the Erection of Forts, Magazines, Arsenals, dock-Yards and other needful Buildings;—And

To make all Laws which shall be necessary and proper for carrying into Execution the foregoing Powers, and all other Powers vested by this Constitution in the Government of the United States or in any Department or Officer thereof.

Section. 9. The Migration or Importation of such Persons as any of the States now existing shall think proper to admit, shall not be prohibited by the Congress prior to the Year one thousand eight hundred and eight, but a Tax or duty may be imposed on such Importation, not exceeding ten dollars for each Person.

The Privilege of the Writ of Habeas Corpus shall not be suspended, unless when in Cases of Rebellion or Invasion the public Safety may require it.

No Bill of Attainder or ex post facto Law shall be passed.

No Capitation, or other direct, Tax shall be laid, [unless in Proportion to the Census or Enumeration herein before directed to be taken.][5]

No Tax or Duty shall be laid on Articles exported from any State.

No Preference shall be given by any Regulation of Commerce or Revenue to the Ports of one State over

5. Changed by Sixteenth Amendment.

those of another: nor shall Vessels bound to, or from, one State, be obliged to enter, clear, or pay Duties in another.

No Money shall be drawn from the Treasury, but in Consequence of Appropriations made by Law; and a regular Statement and Account of the Receipts and Expenditures of all public Money shall be published from time to time.

No Title of Nobility shall be granted by the United States: And no Person holding any Office of Profit or Trust under them, shall, without the Consent of the Congress, accept of any present, Emolument, Office, or Title, of any kind whatever, from any King, Prince, or foreign State.

Section. 10. No State shall enter into any Treaty, Alliance, or Confederation; grant Letters of Marque and Reprisal; coin Money; emit Bills of Credit; make any Thing but gold and silver Coin a Tender in Payment of Debts; pass any Bill of Attainder, ex post facto Law, or Law impairing the Obligation of Contracts, or grant any Title of Nobility.

No State shall, without the Consent of the Congress, lay any Imposts or Duties on Imports or Exports, except what may be absolutely necessary for executing it's inspection Laws: and the net Produce of all Duties and Imposts, laid by any State on Imports or Exports, shall be for the Use of the Treasury of the United States; and all such Laws shall be subject to the Revision and Control of the Congress.

No State shall, without the Consent of Congress, lay any Duty of Tonnage, keep Troops, or Ships of War in time of Peace, enter into any Agreement or Compact with another State, or with a foreign Power, or engage in War, unless actually invaded, or in such imminent Danger as will not admit of delay.

Article. II.

Section. 1. The executive Power shall be vested in a President of the United States of America. He shall hold his Office during the Term of four Years, and, together with the Vice President, chosen for the same Term, be elected, as follows.

Each State shall appoint, in such Manner as the Legislature thereof may direct, a Number of Electors, equal to the whole Number of Senators and Representatives to which the State may be entitled in the Congress: but no Senator or Representative, or Person holding an Office of Trust or Profit under the United States, shall be appointed an Elector.

[The Electors shall meet in their respective States, and vote by Ballot for two Persons, of whom one at least shall not be an Inhabitant of the same State with themselves. And they shall make a List of all the Persons voted for, and of the Number of Votes for each; which List they shall sign and certify, and transmit sealed to the Seat of the Government of the United States, directed to the President of the Senate. The President of the Senate shall, in the Presence of the Senate and House of Representatives, open all the Certificates, and the Votes shall then be counted. The Person having the greatest Number of Votes shall be the President, if such Number be a Majority of the whole Number of Electors appointed; and if there be more than one who have such Majority, and have an equal Number of Votes, then the House of Representatives shall immediately choose by Ballot one of them for President; and if no Person have a Majority, then from the five highest on the List the said House shall in like Manner choose the President. But in choosing the President, the Votes shall be taken by States, the Representation from each State having one Vote; A quorum for this Purpose shall consist of a Member or Members from two thirds of the States, and a Majority of all the States shall be necessary to a Choice. In every Case, after the Choice of the President, the Person having the greatest Number of Votes of the Electors shall be the Vice President. But if there should remain two or more who have equal Votes, the Senate shall choose from them by Ballot the Vice President.][6]

The Congress may determine the Time of choosing the Electors, and the Day on which they shall give their Votes; which Day shall be the same throughout the United States.

No Person except a natural born Citizen, or a Citizen of the United States, at the time of the Adoption of this Constitution, shall be eligible to the Office of President; neither shall any person be eligible to that Office who shall not have attained to the Age of thirty five Years, and been fourteen Years a Resident within the United States.

[In Case of the Removal of the President from Office, or of his Death, Resignation, or Inability to

---

6. Changed by Twelfth Amendment.

discharge the Powers and Duties of the said Office, the Same shall devolve on the Vice President, and the Congress may by Law provide for the Case of Removal, Death, Resignation or Inability, both of the President and Vice President, declaring what Officer shall then act as President, and such Officer shall act accordingly, until the Disability be removed, or a President shall be elected.][7]

The President shall, at stated Times, receive for his Services, a Compensation, which shall neither be increased nor diminished during the Period for which he shall have been elected, and he shall not receive within that Period any other Emolument from the United States, or any of them.

Before he enter on the Execution of his Office, he shall take the following Oath or Affirmation:—"I do solemnly swear (or affirm) that I will faithfully execute the Office of President of the United States, and will to the best of my Ability, preserve, protect and defend the Constitution of the United States."

Section. 2. The President shall be Commander in Chief of the Army and Navy of the United States, and of the Militia of the several States, when called into the actual Service of the United States; he may require the Opinion, in writing, of the principal Officer in each of the executive Departments, upon any Subject relating to the Duties of their respective Offices, and he shall have Power to grant Reprieves and Pardons for Offenses against the United States, except in Cases of Impeachment.

He shall have Power, by and with the Advice and Consent of the Senate, to make Treaties, provided two thirds of the Senators present concur; and he shall nominate, and by and with the Advice and Consent of the Senate, shall appoint Ambassadors, other public Ministers and Consuls, Judges of the supreme Court, and all other Officers of the United States, whose Appointments are not herein otherwise provided for, and which shall be established by Law: but the Congress may by Law vest the Appointment of such inferior Officers, as they think proper, in the President alone, in the Courts of Law, or in the Heads of Departments.

The President shall have Power to fill up all Vacancies that may happen during the Recess of the Senate, by granting Commissions which shall expire at the End of their next Session.

Section. 3. He shall from time to time give to the Congress Information of the State of the Union, and recommend to their Consideration such Measures as he shall judge necessary and expedient; he may, on extraordinary Occasions, convene both Houses, or either of them, and in Case of Disagreement between them, with Respect to the Time of Adjournment, he may adjourn them to such Time as he shall think proper; he shall receive Ambassadors and other public Ministers; he shall take Care that the Laws be faithfully executed, and shall Commission all the Officers of the United States.

Section. 4. The President, Vice President and all civil Officers of the United States, shall be removed from Office on Impeachment for, and Conviction of, Treason, Bribery, or other high Crimes and Misdemeanors.

Article. III.

Section. 1. The judicial Power of the United States, shall be vested in one supreme Court, and in such inferior Courts as the Congress may from time to time ordain and establish. The Judges, both of the supreme and inferior Courts, shall hold their Offices during good Behavior, and shall, at stated Times, receive for their Services, a Compensation, which shall not be diminished during their Continuance in Office.

Section. 2. The judicial Power shall extend to all Cases, in Law and Equity, arising under this Constitution, the Laws of the United States, and Treaties made, or which shall be made, under their Authority;—to all Cases affecting Ambassadors, other public Ministers and Consuls;—to all Cases of admiralty and maritime Jurisdiction;—to Controversies to which the United States shall be a Party;—to Controversies between two or more States;—[between a State and Citizens of another State;—][8] between Citizens of different States,—between Citizens of the same State claiming Lands under Grants of different States, and between a State, or the Citizens thereof, and foreign States, Citizens or Subjects.

In all Cases affecting Ambassadors, other public Ministers and Consuls, and those in which a State shall be Party, the supreme Court shall have original

7. Changed by Twenty-Fifth Amendment.

8. Changed by Eleventh Amendment.

Jurisdiction. In all the other Cases before mentioned, the supreme Court shall have appellate Jurisdiction, both as to Law and Fact, with such Exceptions, and under such Regulations as the Congress shall make.

The Trial of all Crimes, except in Cases of Impeachment; shall be by Jury; and such Trial shall be held in the State where the said Crimes shall have been committed; but when not committed within any State, the Trial shall be at such Place or Places as the Congress may by Law have directed.

Section. 3. Treason against the United States, shall consist only in levying War against them, or in adhering to their Enemies, giving them Aid and Comfort. No Person shall be convicted of Treason unless on the Testimony of two Witnesses to the same overt Act, or on Confession in open Court.

The Congress shall have Power to declare the Punishment of Treason, but no Attainder of Treason shall work Corruption of Blood, or Forfeiture except during the Life of the Person attainted.

Article. IV.

Section. 1. Full Faith and Credit shall be given in each State to the public Acts, Records, and judicial Proceedings of every other State; And the Congress may by general Laws prescribe the Manner in which such Acts, Records and Proceedings shall be proved, and the Effect thereof.

Section. 2. The Citizens of each State shall be entitled to all Privileges and Immunities of Citizens in the several States.

A Person charged in any State with Treason, Felony, or other Crime, who shall flee from Justice, and be found in another State, shall on Demand of the executive Authority of the State from which he fled, be delivered up, to be removed to the State having Jurisdiction of the Crime.

[No Person held to Service or Labor in one State, under the Laws thereof, escaping into another, shall, in Consequence of any Law or Regulation therein, be discharged from such Service or Labor, but shall be delivered up on Claim of the Party to whom such Service or Labor may be due.][9]

Section. 3. New States may be admitted by the Congress into this Union; but no new State shall be formed or erected within the Jurisdiction of any other State; nor any State be formed by the Junction of two or more States, or Parts of States, without the Consent of the Legislatures of the States concerned as well as of the Congress.

The Congress shall have Power to dispose of and make all needful Rules and Regulations respecting the Territory or other Property belonging to the United States; and nothing in this Constitution shall be so construed as to Prejudice any Claims of the United States, or of any particular State.

Section. 4. The United States shall guarantee to every State in this Union a Republican Form of Government, and shall protect each of them against Invasion; and on Application of the Legislature, or of the Executive (when the Legislature cannot be convened) against domestic Violence.

Article. V.

The Congress, whenever two thirds of both Houses shall deem it necessary, shall propose Amendments to this Constitution, or, on the Application of the Legislatures of two thirds of the several States, shall call a Convention for proposing Amendments, which, in either Case, shall be valid to all Intents and Purposes, as Part of this Constitution, when ratified by the Legislatures of three fourths of the several States, or by Conventions in three fourths thereof, as the one or the other Mode of Ratification may be proposed by the Congress; Provided that no Amendment which may be made prior to the Year One thousand eight hundred and eight shall in any Manner affect the first and fourth Clauses in the Ninth Section of the first Article; and that no State, without its Consent, shall be deprived of it's equal Suffrage in the Senate.

Article. VI.

All Debts contracted and Engagements entered into, before the Adoption of this Constitution, shall be as valid against the United States under this Constitution, as under the Confederation.

This Constitution, and the Laws of the United States which shall be made in Pursuance thereof; and

9. Changed by Thirteenth Amendment.

all Treaties made, or which shall be made, under the Authority of the United States, shall be the supreme Law of the Land; and the Judges in every State shall be bound thereby, any Thing in the Constitution or Laws of any State to the Contrary notwithstanding.

The Senators and Representatives before mentioned, and the Members of the several State Legislatures, and all executive and judicial Officers, both of the United States and of the several States, shall be bound by Oath or Affirmation, to support this Constitution; but no religious Test shall ever be required as a Qualification to any Office or public Trust under the United States.

Article. VII.

The Ratification of the Conventions of nine States, shall be sufficient for the Establishment of this Constitution between the States so ratifying the Same.

Done in Convention by the Unanimous Consent of the States present the Seventeenth Day of September in the Year of our Lord one thousand seven hundred and Eighty seven and of the Independence of the United States of America the Twelfth In Witness whereof We have hereunto subscribed our Names,

George Washington—President and deputy from Virginia

New Hampshire — John Langdon, Nicholas Gilman

Massachusetts — Nathaniel Gorham, Rufus King

Connecticut — William Samuel Johnson, Roger Sherman

New York — Alexander Hamilton

New Jersey — William Livingston, David Brearley, William Paterson, Jonathan Dayton

Pennsylvania — Benjamin Franklin, Thomas Mifflin, Robert Morris, George Clymer, Thomas FitzSimons, Jared Ingersoll, James Wilson, Gouverneur Morris

Delaware — George Read, Gunning Bedford, Jr., John Dickinson, Richard Bassett, Jacob Broom

Maryland — James McHenry, Daniel of St. Thomas Jenifer, Daniel Carroll

Virginia — John Blair, James Madison, Jr.

North Carolina — William Blount, Richard Dobbs Spaight, Hugh Williamson

South Carolina — John Rutledge, Charles Cotesworth Pinckney, Charles Pinckney, Pierce Butler

Georgia — William Few, Abraham Baldwin

Attest William Jackson, Secretary

In Convention Monday
September 17th 1787.

Present
The States of

New Hampshire, Massachusetts, Connecticut, Mr. Hamilton from New York, New Jersey, Pennsylvania, Delaware, Maryland, Virginia, North Carolina, South Carolina and Georgia.

Resolved,

That the preceding Constitution be laid before the United States in Congress assembled, and that it is the Opinion of this Convention, that it should afterwards be submitted to a Convention of Delegates, chosen in each State by the People thereof, under the Recommendation of its Legislature, for their Assent and Ratification; and that each Convention assenting to, and ratifying the Same, should give Notice thereof to the United States in Congress assembled. Resolved, That it is the Opinion of this Convention, that as soon as the Conventions of nine States shall have ratified this Constitution, the United States in Congress assembled should fix a Day on which Electors should be appointed by the States which shall have ratified the same, and a Day on which the Electors should assemble to vote for the President, and the Time and Place for commencing Proceedings under this Constitution.

That after such Publication the Electors should be appointed, and the Senators and Representatives elected: That the Electors should meet on the Day fixed for the Election of the President, and should transmit their Votes certified, signed, sealed and directed, as the Constitution requires, to the Secretary of the United States in Congress assembled, that the Senators and Representatives should convene at the Time and Place assigned; that the Senators should appoint a President of the Senate, for the sole Purpose of receiving, opening and counting the Votes for President; and, that after he shall be chosen, the Congress, together with the President, should, without Delay, proceed to execute this Constitution.

By the unanimous Order of the Convention
George WASHINGTON—President

William JACKSON Secretary.

Congress OF THE United States[10] begun and held at the City of New-York, on Wednesday the fourth of March, one thousand seven hundred and eighty nine

THE Conventions of a number of the States, having at the time of their adopting the Constitution, expressed a desire, in order to prevent misconstruction or abuse of its powers, that further declaratory and restrictive clauses should be added: And as extending the ground of public confidence in the Government, will best ensure the beneficent ends of its institution:

RESOLVED by the Senate and House of Representatives of the United States of America, in Congress assembled, two thirds of both Houses concurring, that the following Articles be proposed to the Legislatures of the several States, as Amendments to the Constitution of the United States, all or any of which Articles, when ratified by three fourths of the said Legislatures, to be valid to all intents and purposes, as part of the said Constitution; viz.

ARTICLES in addition to, and Amendment of the Constitution of the United States of America, proposed by Congress, and ratified by the Legislatures of the several States, pursuant to the fifth Article of the original Constitution....

FREDERICK AUGUSTUS MUHLENBERG
Speaker of the House of Representatives.
JOHN ADAMS, Vice-President of the United States and President of the Senate.

ATTEST,
JOHN BECKLEY, Clerk of the House of Representatives.
SAMUEL A. OTIS, Secretary of the Senate.

AMENDMENTS
TO THE CONSTITUTION
OF THE
UNITED STATES OF AMERICA

Amendment I.[11]

Congress shall make no law respecting an establishment of religion, or prohibiting the free exercise thereof; or abridging the freedom of speech, or of the press, or the right of the people peaceably to assemble, and to petition the Government for a redress of grievances.

Amendment II.

A well regulated Militia, being necessary to the security of a free State, the right of the people to keep and bear Arms, shall not be infringed.

---

10. On September 25, 1789, Congress transmitted to the state legislatures twelve proposed amendments, the first two of which, having to do with Congressional representation and congressional pay, were not adopted. The remaining ten amendments became the Bill of Rights. The amendment regarding congressional pay was later ratified and became the Twenty-Seventh Amendment.

11. The first ten Amendments (Bill of Rights) were ratified effective December 15, 1791.

Amendment III.

No Soldier shall, in time of peace be quartered in any house, without the consent of the Owner, nor in time of war, but in a manner to be prescribed by law.

Amendment IV.

The right of the people to be secure in their persons, houses, papers, and effects, against unreasonable searches and seizures, shall not be violated, and no Warrants shall issue, but upon probable cause, supported by Oath or affirmation, and particularly describing the place to be searched, and the persons or things to be seized.

Amendment V.

No person shall be held to answer for a capital, or otherwise infamous crime, unless on a presentment or indictment of a Grand Jury, except in cases arising in the land or naval forces, or in the Militia, when in actual service in time of War or public danger; nor shall any person be subject for the same offence to be twice put in jeopardy of life or limb, nor shall be compelled in any criminal case to be a witness against himself, nor be deprived of life, liberty, or property, without due process of law; nor shall private property be taken for public use without just compensation.

Amendment VI.

In all criminal prosecutions, the accused shall enjoy the right to a speedy and public trial, by an impartial jury of the State and district wherein the crime shall have been committed; which district shall have been previously ascertained by law, and to be informed of the nature and cause of the accusation; to be confronted with the witnesses against him; to have compulsory process for obtaining witnesses in his favor, and to have the assistance of counsel for his defense.

Amendment VII.

In Suits at common law, where the value in controversy shall exceed twenty dollars, the right of trial by jury shall be preserved, and no fact tried by a jury shall be otherwise re-examined in any Court of the United States, than according to the rules of the common law.

Amendment VIII.

Excessive bail shall not be required, nor excessive fines imposed, nor cruel and unusual punishments inflicted.

Amendment IX.

The enumeration in the Constitution of certain rights shall not be construed to deny or disparage others retained by the people.

Amendment X.

The powers not delegated to the United States by the Constitution, nor prohibited by it to the States, are reserved to the States respectively, or to the people.

Amendment XI.[12]

The Judicial power of the United States shall not be construed to extend to any suit in law or equity, commenced or prosecuted against one of the United States by Citizens of another State, or by Citizens or Subjects of any Foreign State.

Amendment XII.[13]

The Electors shall meet in their respective states, and vote by ballot for President and Vice President, one of whom, at least, shall not be an inhabitant of the same state with themselves; they shall name in their ballots the person voted for as President, and in distinct ballots the person voted for as Vice-President, and they shall make distinct lists of all persons voted for as President, and of all persons voted for as Vice-President, and of the number of votes for each, which lists they shall sign and certify, and transmit sealed to the seat of the government of the United States, directed to the President of the Senate;—The President of the Senate shall, in the presence of the Senate and House of Representatives, open all the certificates and the votes shall then be counted;—The person having the greatest number of votes for President, shall be the

12. The Eleventh Amendment was ratified February 7, 1795.

13. The Twelfth Amendment was ratified June 15, 1804.

President, if such number be a majority of the whole number of Electors appointed; and if no person have such majority, then from the persons having the highest numbers not exceeding three on the list of those voted for as President, the House of Representatives shall choose immediately, by ballot, the President. But in choosing the President, the votes shall be taken by states, the representation from each state having one vote; a quorum for this purpose shall consist of a member or members from two-thirds of the states, and a majority of all the states shall be necessary to a choice. [And if the House of Representatives shall not choose a President whenever the right of choice shall devolve upon them, before the fourth day of March next following, then the Vice President shall act as President, as in the case of the death or other constitutional disability of the President—].[14] The person having the greatest number of votes as Vice-President, shall be the Vice-President, if such number be a majority of the whole number of Electors appointed, and if no person have a majority, then from the two highest numbers on the list, the Senate shall choose the Vice-President; a quorum for the purpose shall consist of two-thirds of the whole number of Senators, and a majority of the whole number shall be necessary to a choice. But no person constitutionally ineligible to the office of President shall be eligible to that of Vice President of the United States.

Amendment XIII.[15]

Section 1. Neither slavery nor involuntary servitude, except as a punishment for crime whereof the party shall have been duly convicted, shall exist within the United States, or any place subject to their jurisdiction.

Section 2. Congress shall have power to enforce this article by appropriate legislation.

Amendment XIV.[16]

Section 1. All persons born or naturalized in the United States and subject to the jurisdiction thereof, are citizens of the United States and of the State wherein they reside. No State shall make or enforce any law which shall abridge the privileges or immunities of citizens of the United States; nor shall any State deprive any person of life, liberty, or property, without due process of law; nor deny to any person within its jurisdiction the equal protection of the laws.

Section 2. Representatives shall be apportioned among the several States according to their respective numbers, counting the whole number of persons in each State, excluding Indians not taxed. But when the right to vote at any election for the choice of electors for President and Vice President of the United States, Representatives in Congress, the Executive and Judicial officers of a State, or the members of the Legislature thereof, is denied to any of the male inhabitants of such State, being twenty-one years of age, and citizens of the United States, or in any way abridged, except for participation in rebellion, or other crime, the basis of representation therein shall be reduced in the proportion which the number of such male citizens shall bear to the whole number of male citizens twenty-one years of age in such State.

Section 3. No person shall be a Senator or Representative in Congress, or elector of President and Vice President, or hold any office, civil or military, under the United States, or under any State, who, having previously taken an oath, as a member of Congress, or as an officer of the United States, or as a member of any State legislature, or as an executive or judicial officer of any State, to support the Constitution of the United States, shall have engaged in insurrection or rebellion against the same, or given aid or comfort to the enemies thereof. But Congress may by a vote of two-thirds of each House, remove such disability.

Section 4. The validity of the public debt of the United States, authorized by law, including debts incurred for payment of pensions and bounties for services in suppressing insurrection or rebellion, shall not be questioned. But neither the United States nor any State shall assume or pay any debt or obligation incurred in aid of insurrection or rebellion against the United States, or any claim for the loss or emancipation of any slave; but all such debts, obligations and claims shall be held illegal and void.

Section 5. The Congress shall have power to enforce, by appropriate legislation, the provisions of this article.

14. Changed by the Twentieth Amendment.
15. The Thirteenth Amendment was ratified December 6, 1865.
16. The Fourteenth Amendment was ratified July 9, 1868.

Amendment XV.[17]

Section 1. The right of citizens of the United States to vote shall not be denied or abridged by the United States or by any State on account of race, color, or previous condition of servitude.

Section 2. The Congress shall have power to enforce this article by appropriate legislation.

Amendment XVI.[18]

The Congress shall have power to lay and collect taxes on incomes, from whatever source derived, without apportionment among the several States, and without regard to any census or enumeration.

Amendment XVII.[19]

The Senate of the United States shall be composed of two Senators from each State, elected by the people thereof, for six years; and each Senator shall have one vote. The electors in each State shall have the qualifications requisite for electors of the most numerous branch of the State legislatures.

When vacancies happen in the representation of any State in the Senate, the executive authority of such State shall issue writs of election to fill such vacancies: Provided, That the legislature of any State may empower the executive thereof to make temporary appointments until the people fill the vacancies by election as the legislature may direct.

This amendment shall not be so construed as to affect the election or term of any Senator chosen before it becomes valid as part of the Constitution.

Amendment XVIII.[20]

[Section 1. After one year from the ratification of this article the manufacture, sale, or transportation of intoxicating liquors within, the importation thereof into, or the exportation thereof from the United States and all territory subject to the jurisdiction thereof for beverage purposes is hereby prohibited.

Section 2. The Congress and the several States shall have concurrent power to enforce this article by appropriate legislation.

Section 3. This article shall be inoperative unless it shall have been ratified as an amendment to the Constitution by the legislatures of the several States, as provided in the Constitution, within seven years from the date of the submission hereof to the States by the Congress.]

Amendment XIX.[21]

The right of citizens of the United States to vote shall not be denied or abridged by the United States or by any State on account of sex. Congress shall have power to enforce this article by appropriate legislation.

Amendment XX.[22]

Section 1. The terms of the President and Vice President shall end at noon on the 20th day of January, and the terms of Senators and Representatives at noon on the 3d day of January, of the years in which such terms would have ended if this article had not been ratified; and the terms of their successors shall then begin.

Section 2. The Congress shall assemble at least once in every year, and such meeting shall begin at noon on the 3d day of January, unless they shall by law appoint a different day.

Section 3. If, at the time fixed for the beginning of the term of the President, the President elect shall have died, the Vice President elect shall become President. If a President shall not have been chosen before the time fixed for the beginning of his term, or if the President elect shall have failed to qualify, then the Vice President elect shall act as President until a President shall have qualified; and the Congress may by law provide for the case wherein neither a President elect nor a Vice President elect shall have qualified, declaring who shall then act as President, or the manner in which one

17. The Fifteenth Amendment was ratified February 3, 1870.

18. The Sixteenth Amendment was ratified February 3, 1913.

19. The Seventeenth Amendment was ratified April 8, 1913.

20. The Eighteenth Amendment was ratified January 16, 1919. It was repealed by the Twenty-First Amendment, December 5, 1933.

21. The Nineteenth Amendment was ratified August 18, 1920.

22. The Twentieth Amendment was ratified January 23, 1933.

who is to act shall be selected, and such person shall act accordingly until a President or Vice President shall have qualified.

Section 4. The Congress may by law provide for the case of the death of any of the persons from whom the House of Representatives may choose a President whenever the right of choice shall have devolved upon them, and for the case of the death of any of the persons from whom the Senate may choose a Vice President whenever the right of choice shall have devolved upon them.

Section 5. Sections 1 and 2 shall take effect on the 15th day of October following the ratification of this article.

Section 6. This article shall be inoperative unless it shall have been ratified as an amendment to the Constitution by the legislatures of three-fourths of the several States within seven years from the date of its submission.

Amendment XXI.[23]

Section 1. The eighteenth article of amendment to the Constitution of the United States is hereby repealed.

Section 2. The transportation or importation into any State, Territory, or possession of the United States for delivery or use therein of intoxicating liquors, in violation of the laws thereof, is hereby prohibited.

Section 3. This article shall be inoperative unless it shall have been ratified as an amendment to the Constitution by conventions in the several States, as provided in the Constitution, within seven years from the date of the submission hereof to the States by the Congress.

Amendment XXII.[24]

Section 1. No person who has held the office of President, or acted as President, for more than two years of a term to which some other person was elected President shall be elected to the office of the President more than once. But this Article shall not apply to any person holding the office of President when this Article was proposed by the Congress, and shall not prevent any person who may be holding the office of President, or acting as President, during the term within which this Article becomes operative from holding the office of President or acting as President during the remainder of such term.

Section 2. This article shall be inoperative unless it shall have been ratified as an amendment to the Constitution by the legislatures of three-fourths of the several States within seven years from the date of its submission to the States by the Congress.

Amendment XXIII.[25]

Section 1. The District constituting the seat of Government of the United States shall appoint in such manner as the Congress may direct:

A number of electors of President and Vice President equal to the whole number of Senators and Representatives in Congress to which the District would be entitled if it were a State, but in no event more than the least populous State; they shall be in addition to those appointed by the States, but they shall be considered, for the purposes of the election of President and Vice President, to be electors appointed by a State; and they shall meet in the District and perform such duties as provided by the twelfth article of amendment.

Section 2. The Congress shall have power to enforce this article by appropriate legislation.

Amendment XXIV.[26]

Section 1. The right of citizens of the United States to vote in any primary or other election for President or Vice President, for electors for President or Vice President, or for Senator or Representative in Congress, shall not be denied or abridged by the United States or any State by reason of failure to pay any poll tax or other tax.

Section 2. The Congress shall have power to enforce this article by appropriate legislation.

23. The Twenty-First Amendment was ratified December 5, 1933.

24. The Twenty-Second Amendment was ratified February 27, 1951.

25. The Twenty-Third Amendment was ratified March 29, 1961.

26. The Twenty-Fourth Amendment was ratified January 23, 1964.

Amendment XXV.[27]

Section 1. In case of the removal of the President from office or of his death or resignation, the Vice President shall become President.

Section 2. Whenever there is a vacancy in the office of the Vice President, the President shall nominate a Vice President who shall take office upon confirmation by a majority vote of both Houses of Congress.

Section 3. Whenever the President transmits to the President pro tempore of the Senate and the Speaker of the House of Representatives his written declaration that he is unable to discharge the powers and duties of his office, and until he transmits to them a written declaration to the contrary, such powers and duties shall be discharged by the Vice President as Acting President.

Section 4. Whenever the Vice President and a majority of either the principal officers of the executive departments or of such other body as Congress may by law provide, transmit to the President pro tempore of the Senate and the Speaker of the House of Representatives their written declaration that the President is unable to discharge the powers and duties of his office, the Vice President shall immediately assume the powers and duties of the office as Acting President.

Thereafter, when the President transmits to the President pro tempore of the Senate and the Speaker of the House of Representatives his written declaration that no inability exists, he shall resume the powers and duties of his office unless the Vice President and a majority of either the principal officers of the executive department or of such other body as Congress may by law provide, transmit within four days to the President pro tempore of the Senate and the Speaker of the House of Representatives their written declaration that the President is unable to discharge the powers and duties of his office. Thereupon Congress shall decide the issue, assembling within forty-eight hours for that purpose if not in session. If the Congress, within twenty-one days after receipt of the latter written declaration, or, if Congress is not in session, within twenty-one days after Congress is required to assemble, determines by two-thirds vote of both Houses that the President is unable to discharge the powers and duties of his office, the Vice President shall continue to discharge the same as Acting President; otherwise, the President shall resume the powers and duties of his office.

Amendment XXVI.[28]

Section 1. The right of citizens of the United States, who are eighteen years of age or older, to vote shall not be denied or abridged by the United States or by any State on account of age.

Section 2. The Congress shall have power to enforce this article by appropriate legislation.

Amendment XXVII.[29]

No law, varying the compensation for the services of the Senators and Representatives, shall take effect, until an election of Representatives shall have intervened.

27. The Twenty-Fifth Amendment was ratified February 10, 1967.

28. The Twenty-Sixth Amendment was ratified July 1, 1971.

29. Congress submitted the text of the Twenty-Seventh Amendment to the States as part of the proposed Bill of Rights on September 25, 1789. The Amendment was not ratified together with the first ten Amendments, which became effective on December 15, 1791. The Twenty-Seventh Amendment was ratified on May 7, 1992, by the vote of Michigan.

Appendix 2

Researching and Reading Government Documents

This volume contains a variety of government documents, as well as other types of materials such as political speeches and newspaper articles. Each type of document has its own peculiarities of form and serves its own purposes. Here we provide a brief guide through these sources.

U.S. Supreme Court Opinions

Although the relative importance of the U.S. Supreme Court as an interpreter of the U.S. Constitution has varied over the course of American history, the opinions of the Court are one of the primary sources for understanding how the Constitution has been read and applied over time. Judicial opinions are not always easy to read, even for those who are familiar with their particular style and the technical issues that they discuss. They are unlike any other text that you are likely to encounter in school or in life. You should expect to read and reread them carefully, but the reading becomes easier as you become practiced at it.

The U.S. Supreme Court is primarily an appellate court. It rarely exercises its "original jurisdiction" and serves as the trial court in which the issues of a case are first raised and the facts evaluated (and when it does hear such cases, it usually assigns them to a special master to hear the evidence and make a report to the justices). Instead, the Supreme Court generally hears cases after a trial has already been conducted and most of the issues in the case have already been resolved. The Supreme Court, like other appellate courts, exists to hear disagreements about the meaning and application of the law. The concern with the justices is with setting and clarifying the legal rules that courts will be applying in future cases, not necessarily with doing justice to the parties immediately in front of them.

After accepting a case for its consideration, the Supreme Court issues a decision that specifies how the legal question at issue in the case has been answered and an order that disposes of the case. The opinion in the case supplements these basic elements of the decision, explaining the reasoning of the justices in reaching that outcome. The Supreme Court decides many cases without an opinion, usually because the issues raised in those cases are relatively easy and do not have broader significance beyond that individual case. The Court provides opinions for all of its important decisions, and these opinions both provide a justification for what the Court has done and provides further guidance to lawyers and judges as to how they should understand what the Court has done and what they should do in similar cases in the future.

The decisions and opinions of the U.S. Supreme Court are available from a variety of sources. Initially, Supreme Court opinions were collected and published by private reporters. Because these early private efforts were not always profitable, Congress eventually stepped in to arrange that the official reports of the Court be published at government expense. Opinions in cases are first printed individually as "slip opinions" and later published in bound volumes of the *United States Reports*. The ninety volumes issued before 1875 were often cited by the name of the reporter who produced them (Dallas, Cranch, Wheaton, Peters, Howard, Black, Wallace, and Otto). Since then, they have been known simply as the *U.S. Reports*. Cases are cited by the volume of the *U.S. Reports* in which they appear, the page on which the case starts, and the year in which the case was decided. Thus, the case of *Marbury v. Madison* is cited as *Marbury v. Madison*, 5 U.S.

137 (1803), indicating that the case was decided in 1803 and can be found at page 137 of volume 5 of the *U.S. Reports*. Since the cases reported in the first 90 volumes of the *U.S. Reports* are also known by the individual reporter, *Marbury* can also be cited as 1 Cr. 137 (1803), indicating that the case can be found in the first volume of Cranch's reports (which is the same as volume 5 of the *U.S. Reports*). Both numbering systems can be cited together as 5 U.S. (1 Cr.) 137 (1803).

Besides the official *U.S. Reports*, Supreme Court decisions can also be found in other sources. The *Lawyers' Edition* of the *U.S. Reports* is published by the Lawyers' Cooperative Publishing Company and includes additional notes about the case. These versions are also cited by volume and page number with the abbreviation "L.Ed." indicating the *Lawyers' Edition* ("L.Ed. 2d" for the second series of the *Lawyers' Edition*, which began in 1957). Thus, *Marbury* can be found at 2 L.Ed. 60 (1803). For modern cases, the West Publishing Company also produces the *Supreme Court Reporter*, which is known by the initials "S.Ct.," which appears in print before the slip opinions are collected into the *U.S. Reports* (e.g., *City of Boerne v. Flores*, 117 S.Ct. 2157 [1997]). Three commercial, electronic services also reproduce these Supreme Court cases: Lexis-Nexis, Westlaw, and HeinOnline (the last provides electronic images of the *U.S. Reports* pages). Less complete sets of Supreme Court opinions can also be found on the Internet. The Supreme Court itself provides an electronic version of recent cases at http://www.supremecourtus.gov. Cases are also collected at FindLaw at http://www.findlaw.com/casecode/supreme.html and at Cornell Law School's Legal Information Institute at http://lii.law.cornell.edu. *Shepard's United States Citations* is a reference source that tracks the citation of Supreme Court cases in other opinions written by the Supreme Court and other courts. "Shepardizing" a case by tracking how a decision has been used by subsequent courts provides both a history of the use of that decision and an indication of the current state of the law. A similar service is provided by Westlaw's "KeyCite" system.

When the Supreme Court schedules a case for decision, it will typically accept written briefs from the parties in the case and will often schedule oral arguments as well. The oral arguments were once free-wheeling affairs that could last for days for a single case. They are now tightly regulated by the Court. At oral argument, lawyers are typically allowed thirty minutes to present each side of the case, with the chief justice immediately cutting off the argument when the time has expired. The justices typically ask questions at oral argument, and so the arguments often take the form of an exchange among the justices and the presenting lawyer rather than a monologue by the attorney. The justices also allow some interested parties who are not directly involved in a case to submit amicus curia ("friend of the court") briefs in order to supplement the record and highlight additional features of the case. On occasion, the justices will also allow an amicus to participate in oral arguments (often the U.S. government when the interpretation of a federal law or the Constitution is at issue but the United States is not an official party to the case). Some arguments and attorney briefs can be found in published sources, including Lexis-Nexis and *Landmark Briefs and Arguments of the Supreme Court of the United States*. Early volumes of the *U.S. Reports* often included summaries of the arguments of the attorneys in the case, and they are sometimes excerpted in this volume before the beginning of the Court's opinion. Audio files of some Supreme Court oral arguments can be found at Northwestern University's OYEZ website at http://www.oyez.org.

There are several elements in a typical appellate court decision. It usually begins with a *statement of the facts* in the case and an outline of the *prior history* of the case and how and why it reached the Supreme Court (in this volume, this information is frequently provided in the introductory headnote to the case). It then describes the *legal issue* raised by the case and the question to be resolved by the Court. It then explains the law that is relevant to deciding the case. It is here that the Court will provide its interpretation of the Constitution or other relevant laws that are necessary for deciding the case at hand. It is also here where the Court will describe or articulate the *doctrine* that encapsulates the Court's understanding of the law and that is to guide its application to individual cases. The opinion will then *apply the law* so understood to the particular facts of the case to resolve the questions raised by the case. Finally, the Court will conclude with an *order* disposing of the case.

The form of the order depends on how the case has reached the Court and what the justices have done. Earlier in its history, the judges on a lower court that found themselves divided on some legal question relevant to a case could "certify" those questions for Supreme Court review before a judgment was rendered. In those cases, the Court would answer the questions and send them back to the lower court for it to complete its work and issue a final judgment in the case. More typically, cases reach the Supreme Court after a final judgment has already been rendered in the lower courts, and the appellant in the case wants the Supreme Court to review and revise that judgment. The current route by which cases typically reach the Supreme Court is outlined in Figure A-1. Most cases reach the U.S. Supreme Court from the federal courts, but a significant number come from the state supreme courts. The appellate jurisdiction of the U.S. Supreme Court has been expanded by federal statute over time. Cases may now be appealed from the state courts if they raise a "federal question," a question of the interpretation of federal law, treaties, or the U.S. Constitution. The Court will typically "affirm" what the lower court has done or "reverse" it. In some cases, the order might remand, or send back, the case to the court in which it originated for a final judgment that takes into account what the Supreme Court has done. If the Court finds that it does not have proper jurisdiction to hear and decide the case, it will dismiss the case. The consequence of a dismissal is that the judgment of the lower court will continue to stand. When cases come to the Supreme Court through a petition (e.g., a prisoner's petition for a writ of habeas corpus) or original jurisdiction (e.g., one state bringing suit against another state in a dispute over the location of the state boundary), rather than through an appeal, then the Court will rule directly on the case (e.g., granting or denying the petition) and not simply review the record of the lower court. Since the early twentieth century, the Court's docket has primarily been discretionary. The Court now receives thousands of requests each year that it issue a writ of certiorari (or "cert") scheduling a case to be heard on appeal. As Figure A-2 shows, the Court reached a peak of hearing nearly 300 cases per year in the late nineteenth century, before Congress began to reduce the number of cases that the Court had to hear on mandatory appeal. In recent years, the Court has granted cert in around a hundred cases per year. Thus, not only does the Court review only a tiny fraction of the total number of cases decided each year by the lower federal appellate courts and the state supreme courts, but it agrees to hear only a very small percentage of the cases that it is actively asked to review by the parties involved. Only four justices are needed to grant cert, a practice known as the Rule of Four.

In deciding cases on the merits, the Supreme Court operates on the basis of majority rule. The justices vote on what the judgment of the Court should be in each case, and a majority determines the Court's action. If the Court is equally divided (if, for example, one of the justices does not participate in the case due to illness or a conflict of interest), then the judgment of the lower court stands. The justices discuss each case and vote in private conference after the case has been briefed and argued. By tradition, if the chief justice is a member of

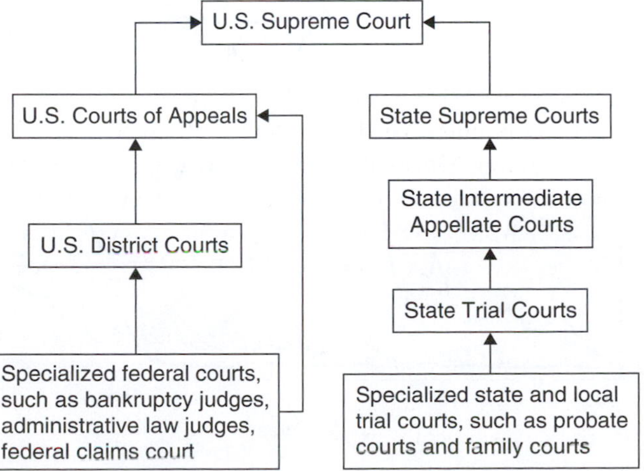

Figure A-1 Getting to the U.S. Supreme Court

Note: In some less common circumstances, cases can reach the U.S. Supreme Court by other routes.

the majority, he may assign which of the members of the majority will write the official opinion of the Court. If the chief justice is a dissenter in the case, then the justice voting with the majority having the most seniority on the Court makes the assignment. After the opinions are drafted, they are circulated to the other justices for comments and revisions. Justices may, and sometimes do, change their votes after the opinions are drafted, and it is possible for enough justices to change their positions to change the outcome in the case. Once the opinions and votes are finalized, then the decision is publicly announced and the slip opinions are published. The decisions are typically announced by the justices orally from the bench, and occasionally the opinions will be read aloud by the justices from the bench (this was once the routine practice, but it is now very rare).

There are four basic types of Supreme Court opinion. The opinion of the Court, or the majority opinion, is the formal opinion of the Court and announces the judgment of the Court in the case. At least a majority of the justices have agreed to the judgment announced in the opinion of the Court, but it is possible that a majority of the justices do not agree with all the legal reasoning contained in the opinion. The majority opinion is signed by an individual justice who is the principal author of the opinion. A per curiam ("by the court") opinion is an unsigned opinion of the Court. These typically reflect the consensus of the entire Court, often in relatively unimportant cases. They have also been used, however, in some important cases in which there was significant disagreement among the justices (for example, in *Bush v. Gore* [2000]). A concurring opinion is written by a member of the Court's majority. A concurrence agrees with the judgment of the Court but disagrees with the legal analysis contained in the majority opinion and provides alternative reasoning for deciding the case. A concurring opinion is typically authored by a single justice but can be "joined" by multiple justices who agree with it. Unlike a concurring opinion, a dissenting opinion is written by a justice who disagrees with judgment reached by the majority of the Court. The dissenting opinion explains why the dissenter(s) think the case should have been decided differently. Like a concurrence, a dissenting opinion is typically authored by a single justice but can be joined by multiple justices. Concurring and dissenting opinions usually do not provide the same detailed statement of the facts of the case or its prior history, and they do not contain an order disposing of the case. The justices are assumed to agree with the majority opinion unless they specify otherwise. The justices are under no obligation to announce publicly that they disagree with the Court's reasoning or its judgment, and justices may announce that they dissent from the majority without writing an opinion explaining the basis of that disagreement. At earlier points in the Court's history, justices frequently refrained from writing separate opinions and often refrained from announcing their disagreement with the majority. Since

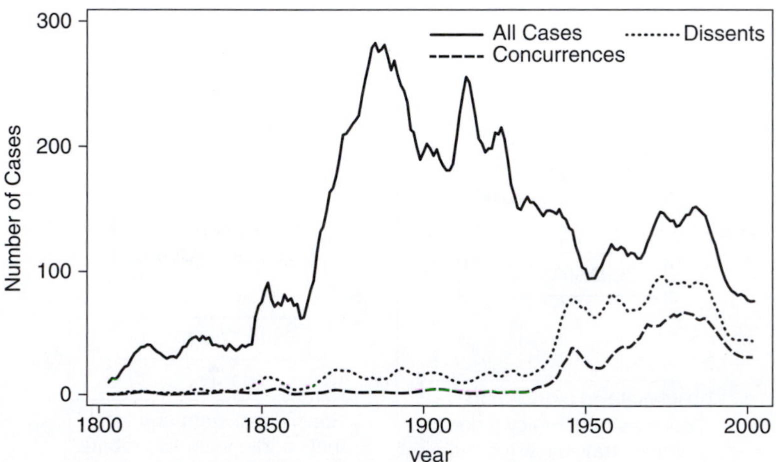

Figure A-2: Number of Supreme Court Cases with Separate Opinions

Source: Lee Epstein, Jeffrey A. Segal, Harold J. Spaeth, Thomas G. Walker, *The Supreme Court Compendium*, 4th ed. (Washington, DC: CQ Press, 2007), Tables 3.2, 3.3.

Note: Centered five-year moving averages.

the early twentieth century, however, the justices have proven very willing to voice their individual opinions in the Court's cases. Figure A-2 shows the number of cases with separate opinions produced by the justices on the Supreme Court over time. Until the late 1930s, a steady 10 percent of the Court cases included a separately authored opinion. Since then, however, the justices have routinely produced dissenting and concurring opinions to supplement the majority opinion. Well over half of all cases decided since World War II include at least one dissenting opinion, and nearly half the cases decided since the mid-1960s include a concurring opinion. Concurring and dissenting opinions have no official standing, and the practice of producing such opinions has been criticized for weakening the authority of the Court and for muddying the state of the law. But separate opinions can be influential either by their own persuasive power or by signaling the possible future trajectory of the Court's majority.

Briefing a Case

Students often find it helpful to "brief" the cases that they read. This is not writing a lawyer's brief, such as those submitted to the Supreme Court. Briefing a case for study is a process of note-taking that identifies and summarizes the key elements in a judicial decision. Some basic elements of a brief are provided next, along with an explanation and an example (in italics) from *United States v. E.C. Knight Company* (1895).

Name of the case—This identifies the parties in the case (some cases also become known by their subject matter, such as *The Legal Tender Cases*). The first party listed is usually the appellant, the party that lost in the lower court and brought the case to the Supreme Court for review. The second party listed is usually the appellee, the party that won in the lower court and is responding to the appeal to the Supreme Court.

U.S. v. E. C. Knight Company

Citation of the case—The citation provides the specific location where the opinion can be found, preferably in the *U.S. Reports*.

156 U.S. 1

Year of the case—The year the case was decided provides important information about the context in which the decision was made.

1895

Vote in the case—The public vote in the case can be determined by identifying the justices who sign on to any dissenting opinions and subtracting them from the total number of justices who participated in the case (giving you the number of justices who must have voted with the majority). Remember that the publicly revealed vote is not necessarily the same as the vote of the justices in their private conference, and note that the decision will indicate if any of the sitting justices did not participate in the case.

8–1

Factual circumstances of the case—What are the key factual details that identify what the dispute is and what triggered the litigation? Note that the Court's opinions often provide more information than is essential for understanding the case. One challenge for the student is learning to identify which facts are critical to the case and help explain the legal and political significance of the case.

The American Sugar Refining Company of New Jersey tried to acquire E. C. Knight Company of Pennsylvania, which would have given the combined company control of 98 percent of the national market in refined sugar. The United States Department of Justice intervened under the authority of the Sherman Anti-Trust Act, petitioning the federal circuit court to void the sale as an illegal restraint of trade.

Legal issue or question raised by the case—What are the legal questions being addressed by the Court in the case? (Note that there may be more than one.) What statutory or constitutional provisions are at issue?

Does Congress have authority under the interstate commerce clause of the U.S. Constitution to prohibit monopolies in the manufacturing of goods?

Outcome of the case—How did the Court dispose of the case, and who won? It is often useful also to know what subsequently happened to the parties and the issue in the case, though this will not of course appear in the Court's own decision.

Affirmed the circuit court. The appellee, E. C. Knight, won.

Legal holding of the case—How did the Court answer the legal question raised in the case?

Congress cannot directly regulate manufacturing.

Doctrine announced or applied in the case—What is the rule for decision that the Court used to resolve the case? This may be a doctrine that the Court invented in this same case, or it may be a doctrine that had been previously announced by the Court and is being used in the case. When the Court is using a previously announced doctrine, you will want to be aware of whether the justices are subtly altering or elaborating that rule as they are deciding this case.

The interstate commerce clause only authorizes Congress to regulate actions that directly affect interstate commerce, not actions that indirectly affect interstate commerce.

Author and legal reasoning of the majority opinion—Even though the majority opinion is formally the opinion of the Court and reflects the input of all the justices in the majority, the core reasoning of the decision will still reflect the particular ideas, commitments and style of the individual justice who wrote the opinion. The legal reasoning used in the majority opinion is frequently the most important aspect of a case, for it will guide future judges seeking to understand what the Court has done and how future cases should be decided. You will want to be able to provide a concise summary of the explanation that the Court offered for its decision and the interpretation of the relevant law that the Court provided.

Fuller. Sherman Anti-Trust Act must be interpreted in light of the constitutional limits on the power of Congress, and therefore cannot be understood to encroach on the police powers of the states. The states have the exclusive authority to regulate manufacturing and prohibit monopolies. Manufacturing affects interstate commerce only "incidentally and indirectly." Federal power extends only to the actual "articles of interstate commerce," and not to goods that are merely intended for interstate commerce. Commerce is the buying, selling and transportation of goods. Manufacturing is the production of goods, and the sale of one sugar refining company to another is a contract relating to manufacturing of sugar, not the interstate sale of sugar.

Author and legal reasoning of any concurring opinions—Concurring opinions are more individual efforts of the justices who write them than are majority opinions, and they provide an alternative legal explanation of how the case was decided. Note that a concurring opinion may attract as many or more justices than the official opinion of the majority, meaning that more members of the Court agree with the legal reasoning of the concurring opinion than agree with the legal reasoning of the "majority" opinion even though it is the majority opinion that has official status and announces the outcome of the case.

None.

Author and legal reasoning of any dissenting opinions—Like concurring opinions, dissenting opinions tend to be much more individualistic than the majority opinion. Justices often write dissenting opinions "for the future," in the hopes that a majority of the Court will eventually change its mind and in some future case adopt the reasoning of the dissent as its own. But dissenting opinions can also be written with a more immediate goal in mind, of attempting to persuade wavering members of the majority to change their votes before the decision is announced. Since the published dissents remain mere dissents, those particular efforts at persuasion were obviously unsuccessful.

Harlan. As decided in Gibbons v. Ogden *(1824) and other decisions, Congress has the authority to regulate "intercourse and traffic" among the states and things that are "incidental" to the interstate buying, selling and transportation of goods. Manufacturing, like transportation, is "incidental" to the buying and selling of goods, and is therefore covered by the interstate commerce clause. Any combination that "disturbs or unreasonably obstructs" interstate commerce directly affects the nation as a whole and can be prohibited by Congress. Prohibiting monopolies in manufacturing is an "appropriate" means for preventing the obstruction of interstate commerce (see* McCulloch v. Maryland *[1819]). Matters that "directly and injuriously affects" national commerce and "cannot be adequately controlled by any one State" can be regulated by Congress.*

Significance of case for American constitutional development—Unlike the other elements of the brief, this will not be obvious within the decision itself; but when reading the case, students should be thinking about why the case was included in the volume and is being taught in this course. Answering this question will often require thinking beyond the case itself and considering the context in which it was decided and its implications for subsequent politics. How did the case clarify or change the meaning of the law? What new issues or ideas were reflected in the case? What disputes or forces does the case reflect? How did the dispute and the outcome in the case fit into the political and social context of the time? How might the case have affected the politics, economy and society of the time? How might it have affected subsequent developments in those fields?

The case significantly limited one of the first and most important efforts of the federal government to control the national economy and imposed significant limits on the ability of the federal government to make future economic policy. The case bolstered conservatives in the Democratic and Republican parties and the emerging interstate corporations, but frustrated populists and their constituencies among farmers, workers, and small businesses. The decision reflected bipartisan conservative commitments (only one dissenter, and opinion author was a Democratic appointee), but came on the eve of the populist takeover of the Democratic Party in the elections of 1896, which also ended Democratic competitiveness in national elections.

Other Court Opinions

This volume contains decisions by a number of other courts besides the U.S. Supreme Courts, and other courts are certainly relevant to American constitutionalism and to legal research. Decisions from other courts excerpted here come from elsewhere in the federal judicial system or from the state judicial systems.

The decisions of federal courts below the U.S. Supreme Court are not reported in the *U.S. Reports*, and as a consequence have a different citation system. Significant decisions from the federal district courts (trial courts at the lowest level of the modern federal judicial system) are reported in the *Federal Supplement*. Those decisions are cited by the volume and page number in which they appear in the *Federal Supplement*, abbreviated as "F.Supp." Early district court cases were reported in *Federal Cases*, abbreviated as "F.Cas." Before the year in which the case was decided in the parenthesis after the page cite, the specific court is identified by "D," meaning district court, and an abbreviation for the state in which the court sits. Thus the citation for *United States v. The William*, an early district court case from Massachusetts, is *United States v. The William*, 28 F. Cas. 614 (D. Mass. 1808). Although there is more than one judge assigned to each federal district, only one sits on any given case (and therefore, there can be no concurring or dissenting opinions). Since district courts are trial courts where cases start, cases decided there generally have no prior history in the judiciary. District court opinions are binding only in the district in which they are issued, and are good law until they are reversed by the same district court, by the circuit court that oversees that district, or by the U.S. Supreme Court.

Significant decisions from the federal circuit courts (the intermediate courts between the district courts and the U.S. Supreme Court, which now operate only as appellate courts but once also operated as trial courts) are reported in the *Federal Reporter*. The *Federal Reporter* is abbreviated as "Fed." or "F.," followed by "2d" or "3d" in the case of the second or third series of that reporter. Instead of "D." and a state, circuit courts are now identified by their circuit number (e.g., 3d Cir.). Early circuit court cases were also reported in *Federal Cases* and were known by the district of the state in which the circuit court was sitting rather than by number (e.g., Cir. Ct. Dist. So. Car., or CCDSC). Thus, *Elkison v. Deliesseline*, an early circuit court case from South Carolina, is *Elkison v. Deliesseline*, 8 F. Cas. 493 (Cir. Ct. Dist. So. Car. 1823). Circuit courts sit in panels of more than one judge, and thus there is a potential for dissenting and concurring opinions (though individual opinions are far more rare in these courts than in the Supreme Court). Circuit court cases are binding law only within the circuits in which they are handed down, and they are good law until overturned by that same circuit court or by the U.S. Supreme Court. Both types of federal cases, district and circuit, can also be found in Lexis-Nexis and Westlaw.

Biographical information about those who have served as federal judges, as well as other information about the federal courts, has been made available on the Internet by the Federal Judicial Center at http://www.fjc.gov.

State judicial systems have a similar structure to the federal judicial system, with trial courts and multi-member appellate courts capped by a highest appellate court for that type of case (some states create separate tracks, and separate supreme courts, for different kinds of cases, such as criminal and civil cases). State court decisions are published in reports maintained within each individual state, and those state reporting systems have sometimes changed over time. Thus, the Pennsylvania Supreme Court case of *Sharpless v. Mayor of Philadelphia*, published in the *Pennsylvania State Reports*, is cited as *Sharpless v. Mayor of Philadelphia*, 21 Pa. 147 (1853). Modern state cases are also collected and published in several regional reporters, such as the *Atlantic Reporter* and the *North Western Reporter*. State court decisions can also be found in Lexis-Nexis and Westlaw. State supreme court decisions are binding only within the state in which they are issued. State supreme courts are the highest authority on the laws and constitutions of their own states, just as the U.S. Supreme Court is the highest authority on federal laws and the U.S. Constitution. Federal laws and the U.S. Constitution are binding within each state and must also be interpreted and applied by state courts when they are relevant to deciding cases that arise within the state judicial systems. When interpreting federal laws or the U.S. Constitution, the state supreme courts can be reviewed and corrected by the U.S. Supreme Court.

Congressional Documents

The most important documents produced by Congress are federal laws. Private laws are legislation intended to benefit particular individuals, such as laws waiving any financial claims that the government might have against an individual or excepting an individual from the usual application of immigration laws. Public laws are legislation that affect the general public. Once a bill becomes a law, it is assigned a public law number reflecting the Congress that passed it and its place in the sequence of laws passed by that Congress (e.g., PL 104–1 was the first law passed by the 104th Congress). Public and private laws and resolutions (pronouncements of one or both chambers of Congress that do not have the force of law) are collected and published in the *U.S. Statutes at Large*, which is cited by volume and page number (e.g., PL 104–1 is printed at 109 Stat. 3). As laws are revised and amended over time, the still valid laws have been consolidated and codified, first in two editions of the *Revised Statutes* in the 1870s and since in several editions of the *United States Code*. The code is cited by subject-matter "title" number, section, and edition (e.g., PL 104–1 was incorporated into 2 USC 1301 [2000]).

Congress also produces a variety of other documents besides statutes and resolutions. The official actions of each chamber of Congress are recorded in constitutionally mandated *Journals*. The debates on the floor of the House of Representatives and the Senate are reported in the *Congressional Record* and its predecessors (*Annals of Congress*, *Register of Debates*, and the *Congressional Globe*). Congressional committees, where most of the work of Congress is done, produce Documents (a wide range of materials that Congress has ordered published, including executive-branch reports and records), Reports (official reports by House and Senate committees to their parent chambers, usually explaining bills being recommended by the committee), and transcripts of Hearings (transcripts of public testimony and discussion that committees gather on topics of interest). These are published separately by the committees. Early Documents and Reports were bound together in the *American State Papers*. Since 1817, Documents and Reports have been collected and published in the *United States Serial Set*. Committee Reports may include reports from both the majority and the minority (from the committee members who disagree with the majority report or the legislative action being recommended). All of these documents are commonly cited by the body that produced it, the title, the type of document, the number of the Congress that produced it, the session number, and the date (e.g., House Report No. 909, "Apportionment Bill," 27th Cong., 2nd sess. [July 16, 1842]). Bill sponsors and the chairmen of the committees reporting legislation are understood to have a privileged voice in explaining the meaning and purpose of a bill, but Congress votes only on the text of the legislation itself, and the body as a whole does not have to approve or agree to anything that is said during legislative debate, written in committee reports, or contained in similar documents created during the legislative process.

Many of these documents are available in the CongressionalUniverse service of Lexis-Nexis and on HeinOnline. Many congressional documents produced through Reconstruction have been placed on the Internet by the Library of Congress at http://lcweb2.loc.gov/ammem/amlaw/lawhome.html. Very recent materials are available at the THOMAS website at http://thomas.loc.gov. Useful biographical information on individuals who have served in Congress can be found in the *Biographical Directory of the U.S. Congress*, available on the Internet at http://bioguide.congress.gov.

Executive Branch Documents

The various components of the federal executive branch produce a vast number and variety of documents.

The president himself produces a variety of documents, all of which have political significance but only some of which have immediate legal effect. The Constitution recognizes only two types of presidential documents. The first are general purpose presidential messages to Congress, the most famous of which is the annual message, or "state of the union address." The second is the veto message to Congress, explaining the president's reasons for vetoing a proposed law. These two constitutionally mandated forms of communication have been supplemented by other formal messages, most notably the inaugural address and the signing statement (remarking on a law being signed by the president, sometimes simply to commemorate the occasion, sometimes to note interpretations of, qualifications to, or concerns about the legislation being signed). Of course, the president also delivers a large number of informal speeches and public statements. Formal messages to Congress have routinely been published in the *Congressional Record*. The messages and speeches of the presidents through the early twentieth century were collected and published in *A Compilation of the Messages and Papers of the Presidents*. Franklin Roosevelt's speeches were published privately in *The Public Papers and Addresses of Franklin Delano Roosevelt*. Those of subsequent presidents have been published by the government in *Public Papers of the Presidents of the United States* and more frequently in *The Weekly Compilation of Presidential Documents*.

The president also produces documents with more immediate legal effect. Executive orders are directives from the president to members of the executive branch (military orders are their counterpart directed to the armed forces). So long as they do not contradict a constitutionally valid statute, these instructions are understood to be binding on subordinate executive officers, directing how they will implement laws and perform executive functions. Presidential proclamations are directed to the general public. Proclamations are often innocuous, declaring days of celebration and the like, but they are sometimes momentous, such as Abraham Lincoln's proclamation calling forth the state militias to put down secession and his Emancipation Proclamation. Executive orders through the early twentieth century were compiled in *Presidential Executive Orders*. They have subsequently been published in the *Federal Register* and compiled in the *Codification of Presidential Executive Orders and Proclamations*. Much of this material is available in HeinOnline. Some of it has been made available on the Internet by the University of California at Santa Barbara's The American Presidency Project at http://www.presidency.ucsb.edu and through the National Archives at http://www.archives.gov/federal-register/index.html.

More routine are regulations and orders produced by executive branch agencies, primarily in the course of interpreting and implementing statutes. These regulations have the immediate force of law and receive substantial deference from the courts. They are published in the *Federal Register* and compiled in the *Code of Federal Regulations*.

Of particular significance to American constitutionalism are the legal opinions of the attorney general. These opinions derive from the constitutional authority of the president to command the written opinion of principal officers of the executive departments upon subjects relating to their office and from the statute originally creating the office of attorney general. The attorney general now routinely provides advisory opinions on legal issues, including constitutional issues. Attorney general opinions have more recently been supplemented by the legal opinions of the Office of Legal Counsel (OLC), which advises the attorney general. Attorney general opinions are compiled in *The Official Opinions of the Attorneys General of the United States*, which is cited by volume, the abbreviation "Op. Att'y Gen.," the page, and the date. A selection of the OLC opinions are published *Opinions of the Office of Legal Counsel*, which is cited in the same fashion with the abbreviation "Op. O.L.C." These formal opinions guide the executive branch in its interpretation and application of the law, including constitutional law, and frequently guide private actors and other government officials, including judges, in their understandings of the law.

State-level executive branch officials perform many of these same functions in the state government. Such state documents are often compiled in equivalent state publications, but they are not always readily accessible and have not generally been collected in the same comprehensive fashion as the federal documents.

Legal Literature

Commentaries on the law produced by private citizens such as law professors or government officials writing in a private capacity have no official status, but they can reflect the currents of legal thinking at the time and exert substantial persuasive power on their own and future generations. As such, they can influence and be cited as authority by government actors who do have formal power, such as judges. Traditionally, scholarly legal treatises that seek to critically synthesize the state of the law have had the greatest influence. Relevant examples of these include St. George Tucker's American edition of William Blackstone's *Commentaries on the Laws of England*

(1803), Joseph Story's *Commentaries on the Constitution of the United States* (1833), John Alexander Jameson's *A Treatise on Constitutional Conventions* (1866), Thomas Cooley's *Constitutional Limitations* (1868), and, more recently, Laurence H. Tribe's *American Constitutional Law* (1978). More diverse is the law review literature, scholarly articles in legal periodicals. An important guide to legal journals is the *Index to Legal Periodicals*. This venerable guide has recently been supplemented by various less comprehensive guides, including LegalTrac. The content of many law reviews is available through services such as Lexis-Nexis, Westlaw, and (with greater historical depth but somewhat less breadth) HeinOnline.

Citation guides for government and legal documents include *The Chicago Manual of Style* (most commonly used in the humanities and social sciences) and *The Bluebook: A Uniform System of Citation* (the most commonly used citation guide in the law schools). A generally helpful resource is the Law Library of Congress's Guide to Law Online, available at http://www.loc.gov/law/public/law-guide.html.

Appendix 3

Chronological Table of Presidents, Congress, and the Supreme Court

Years	President	House of Representatives	U.S. Senate	Supreme Court[1]
1789–1791	G. Washington (F)	Federalist	Federalist	Federalist
1791–1793	G. Washington (F)	Federalist	Federalist	Federalist
1793–1795	G. Washington (F)	Republican[2]	Federalist	Federalist
1795–1797	G. Washington (F)	Federalist	Federalist	Federalist
1797–1799	J. Adams (F)	Federalist	Federalist	Federalist
1799–1801	J. Adams (F)	Federalist	Federalist	Federalist
1801–1803	T. Jefferson (R)	Republican	Republican	Federalist
1803–1805	T. Jefferson (R)	Republican	Republican	Federalist
1805–1807	T. Jefferson (R)	Republican	Republican	Federalist
1807–1809	T. Jefferson (R)	Republican	Republican	Federalist
1809–1811	J. Madison (R)	Republican	Republican	Federalist
1811–1813	J. Madison (R)	Republican	Republican	Federalist
1813–1815	J. Madison (R)	Republican	Republican	Republican
1815–1817	J. Madison (R)	Republican	Republican	Republican
1817–1819	J. Monroe (R)	Republican	Republican	Republican
1819–1821	J. Monroe (R)	Republican	Republican	Republican
1821–1823	J. Monroe (R)	Republican	Republican	Republican
1823–1825	J. Monroe (R)	Republican	Republican[3]	Republican
1825–1827	J. Q. Adams (R)	Republican	Democrat	Republican
1827–1829	J. Q. Adams (R)	Democrat	Democrat	Republican
1829–1831	A. Jackson (D)	Democrat	Democrat	Republican
1831–1833	A. Jackson (D)	Democrat	Democrat	Republican
1833–1835	A. Jackson (D)	Democrat	Whig	Republican

(Continued)

1. Party control of Supreme Court represented by party affiliation of median member.
2. An "Anti-administration" majority that predates the formation of an organized political party.
3. Majority formed from coalition of states' rights Republicans and supporters of Andrew Jackson.

Years	President	House of Representatives	U.S. Senate	Supreme Court
1835–1837	A. Jackson (D)	Democrat	Democrat	Republican
1837–1839	M. Van Buren (D)	Democrat	Democrat	Democrat
1839–1841	M. Van Buren (D)	Democrat	Democrat	Democrat
1841–1843	W. H. Harrison/J. Tyler (W)	Whig	Whig	Democrat
1843–1845	J. Tyler (W)	Democrat	Whig	Democrat
1845–1847	J. Polk (D)	Democrat	Democrat	Democrat
1847–1849	J. Polk (D)	Whig	Democrat	Democrat
1849–1851	Z. Taylor/M. Fillmore (W)	Democrat	Democrat	Democrat
1851–1853	M. Fillmore (W)	Democrat	Democrat	Democrat
1853–1855	F. Pierce (D)	Democrat	Democrat	Democrat
1855–1857	F. Pierce (D)	Republican[4]	Democrat	Democrat
1857–1859	J. Buchanan (D)	Democrat	Democrat	Democrat
1859–1861	J. Buchanan (D)	Democrat	Democrat	Democrat
1861–1863	A. Lincoln (R)	Republican	Republican	Democrat
1863–1865	A. Lincoln (R)	Republican	Republican	Republican
1865–1867	A. Lincoln/A. Johnson (R)	Republican	Republican	Republican
1867–1869	A. Johnson (R)	Republican	Republican	Republican
1869–1871	U. S. Grant (R)	Republican	Republican	Republican
1871–1873	U. S. Grant (R)	Republican	Republican	Republican
1873–1875	U. S. Grant (R)	Republican	Republican	Republican
1875–1877	U. S. Grant (R)	Democrat	Republican	Republican
1877–1879	R. Hayes (R)	Democrat	Republican	Republican
1879–1881	R. Hayes (R)	Democrat	Republican	Republican
1881–1883	J. Garfield/C. Arthur (R)	Republican	Republican	Republican
1883–1885	C. Arthur (R)	Democrat	Republican	Republican
1885–1887	G. Cleveland (D)	Democrat	Republican	Republican
1887–1889	G. Cleveland (D)	Democrat	Republican	Republican
1889–1891	B. Harrison (R)	Republican	Republican	Republican
1891–1893	B. Harrison (R)	Democrat	Republican	Republican
1893–1895	G. Cleveland (D)	Democrat	Democrat	Republican
1895–1897	G. Cleveland (D)	Republican	Republican	Republican
1897–1899	W. McKinley (R)	Republican	Republican	Republican
1899–1901	W. McKinley (R)	Republican	Republican	Republican
1901–1903	W. McKinley/T. Roosevelt (R)	Republican	Republican	Republican
1903–1905	T. Roosevelt (R)	Republican	Republican	Republican
1905–1907	T. Roosevelt (R)	Republican	Republican	Republican
1907–1909	T. Roosevelt (R)	Republican	Republican	Republican

(Continued)

4. Majority formed from coalition of Republican and American (or "Know Nothing") Party members.

Years	President	House of Representatives	U.S. Senate	Supreme Court
1909–1911	W. H. Taft (R)	Republican	Republican	Republican
1911–1913	W. H. Taft (R)	Democrat	Republican	Republican
1913–1915	W. Wilson (D)	Democrat	Democrat	Republican
1915–1917	W. Wilson (D)	Democrat	Democrat	Republican
1917–1919	W. Wilson (D)	Democrat	Democrat	Republican
1919–1921	W. Wilson (D)	Republican	Republican	Republican
1921–1923	W. Harding/C. Coolidge (R)	Republican	Republican	Republican
1923–1925	C. Coolidge (R)	Republican	Republican	Republican
1925–1927	C. Coolidge (R)	Republican	Republican	Republican
1927–1929	C. Coolidge (R)	Republican	Republican	Republican
1929–1931	H. Hoover (R)	Republican	Republican	Republican
1931–1933	H. Hoover (R)	Democrat	Republican	Republican
1933–1935	F. D. Roosevelt (D)	Democrat	Democrat	Republican
1935–1937	F. D. Roosevelt (D)	Democrat	Democrat	Republican
1937–1939	F. D. Roosevelt (D)	Democrat	Democrat	Republican
1939–1941	F. D. Roosevelt (D)	Democrat	Democrat	Democrat
1941–1943	F. D. Roosevelt (D)	Democrat	Democrat	Democrat
1943–1945	F. D. Roosevelt/H. Truman (D)	Democrat	Democrat	Democrat
1945–1947	H. Truman (D)	Democrat	Democrat	Democrat
1947–1949	H. Truman (D)	Republican	Republican	Democrat
1949–1951	H. Truman (D)	Democrat	Democrat	Democrat
1951–1953	H. Truman (D)	Democrat	Democrat	Democrat
1953–1955	D. Eisenhower (R)	Republican	Republican	Democrat
1955–1957	D. Eisenhower (R)	Democrat	Democrat	Democrat
1957–1959	D. Eisenhower (R)	Democrat	Democrat	Democrat
1959–1961	D. Eisenhower (R)	Democrat	Democrat	Democrat
1961–1963	J. Kennedy (D)	Democrat	Democrat	Democrat
1963–1965	J. Kennedy/L. B. Johnson (D)	Democrat	Democrat	Democrat
1965–1967	L. B. Johnson (D)	Democrat	Democrat	Democrat
1967–1969	L. B. Johnson (D)	Democrat	Democrat	Democrat
1969–1971	R. Nixon (R)	Democrat	Democrat	Democrat
1971–1973	R. Nixon (R)	Democrat	Democrat	Democrat
1973–1975	R. Nixon/G. Ford (R)	Democrat	Democrat	Democrat
1975–1977	G. Ford (R)	Democrat	Democrat	Republican
1977–1979	J. Carter (D)	Democrat	Democrat	Republican
1979–1981	J. Carter (D)	Democrat	Democrat	Republican
1981–1983	R. Reagan (R)	Democrat	Republican	Republican
1983–1985	R. Reagan (R)	Democrat	Republican	Republican
1985–1987	R. Reagan (R)	Democrat	Republican	Republican

(Continued)

Years	President	House of Representatives	U.S. Senate	Supreme Court
1987–1989	R. Reagan (R)	Democrat	Democrat	Republican
1989–1991	G. Bush (R)	Democrat	Democrat	Republican
1991–1993	G. Bush (R)	Democrat	Democrat	Republican
1993–1995	W. Clinton (D)	Democrat	Democrat	Republican
1995–1997	W. Clinton (D)	Republican	Republican	Republican
1997–1999	W. Clinton (D)	Republican	Republican	Republican
1999–2001	W. Clinton (D)	Republican	Republican	Republican
2001–2003	G. W. Bush (R)	Republican	Democrat[5]	Republican
2003–2005	G. W. Bush (R)	Republican	Republican	Republican
2005–2007	G. W. Bush (R)	Republican	Republican	Republican
2007–2009	G. W. Bush (R)	Democrat	Democrat	Republican
2009–2011	B. Obama (D)	Democrat	Democrat	Republican
2011–2013	B. Obama (D)	Republican	Democrat	Republican

5. Majority control of the Senate changed three times during the 107th Congress, with the Democrats holding the majority most of the term.

Glossary

acquittal A legal declaration of an accused party's innocence of the charges against it.

adjudicate To preside over, as in a court presiding over a case.

advisory opinion A court statement on the constitutionality of a matter, such as a law or government action, outside the context of a civil or criminal trial. Not accepted in most court systems in the United States.

affidavit A written, sworn statement of fact.

affirm To uphold, as in the decision of a lower court.

affirmative action The giving of preference to members of historically oppressed groups in hiring or school admittance policies.

amicus (or amici) curiae Literally "friend of the court"; a person or entity who is not a party to the case but provides information to the court, whether in a brief or testimony, on behalf of one side.

annul To declare void, to eliminate.

anti-Federalists Those who opposed the ratification of the U.S. Constitution in the late eighteenth century.

appeal To contest the decision of a court before a higher authority, such as a higher court or an executive official.

appellant The party who contests a court's decisions after losing a case by bringing an appeal. Also called the petitioner.

appellate jurisdiction A court's prerogative to hear and decide challenges to the decisions of lower courts, the range of issues and cases that a court can hear on appeal.

appellee The party who responds to the contestation of a court decision that was in their favor. Also called the respondent.

arraignment A hearing in which the court reads the charges against a criminal defendant from the indictment, and the defendant enters a formal plea (i.e., guilty or not guilty).

Articles of Confederation The supreme law that governed the union of the original thirteen states of the United States from 1781 to 1789, predating the Constitution. The Articles of Confederation established a highly federated system in which the states, not the national government, were sovereign.

attitudinal model The theory that one can describe and predict a judge's legal decisions based on one's knowledge of the judge's political beliefs.

balancing test A tool used by courts to decide between competing rights and/or powers. Balancing tests establish frameworks or sets of criteria that take into account multiple factors that must be considered by a judge in determining in the resolution of a dispute in which both sides have some claim to legal authority.

bicameral Two-chambered, as in the U.S. Congress divided between the House of Representatives and the Senate.

bill A piece of proposed legislation.

brief A written statement presented to the court that lays out the argument for one party.

briefing a case A summary and analysis of a case or judicial opinion

case A dispute brought before a court.

case law The body of cases that make up legal precedent.

case or controversy rule The Article III clause that limits the business of courts to resolving active disputes between injured parties, prohibiting, for example, court involvement in speculative questions of legal interpretation.

certiorari (writ of) An appellate court's order to an inferior court to send it the records from a case that the appellate court has agreed to review. Appellants generally ask the U.S. Supreme Court to take a case by asking it to grant this writ.

checks and balances The legal structures that limit the power of government by granting each branch enough power to prevent the tyranny of other branches.

chilling effect A person's or entity's reluctance to act within its constitutional rights and powers due to a law or court ruling punishing similar (but not identical) behavior.

civil law Law pertaining to the relationships among individuals or organizations.

civil right Behavior and government action to which people are legally entitled, such as free speech and equal protection.

class action lawsuit A dispute brought before a court on behalf of a group, members of whom have sustained a common injury or harm.

comity Respect for the decisions of other political entities, especially respect by federal courts for the decisions of state courts.

common law Laws and procedures which are not formally codified in written constitutions or statutes but are instead built through judicial precedent.

compensatory damages Reparations granted to a winning plaintiff in a civil suit that cover the monetary value of losses or injury caused by the defendant.

concurrent powers Jurisdiction shared by national and state governments.

concurring opinion A judge's (or several judges') written statement(s) agreeing with the outcome arrived at by the majority of the court in a case but disagreeing with or adding to the majority's reasoning.

confrontation A defendant's right to hear testimony from and cross-examine the prosecution's witnesses in court.

constitutional law The body of legal decisions pertaining to matters arising under the constitution.

constitutionalism Constitutional interpretation and practice, concerned with the structure of and limitations on government.

contempt Disrespect to or failure to comply with the authority of a court.

contract A legally binding agreement between parties.

criminal law Law pertaining to the regulation of the interaction between individuals and the community or state, and the punishment of infractions thereof.

de facto Literally "in point of fact." As a situation or condition appears in reality, irrespective of legal conditions.

de jure Literally "as a matter of law." As a situation or condition is codified in law.

decree A legal order.

defamation Slander, libel, injury to a person's or an entity's reputation.

defendant The person accused in a criminal suit or sued in a civil suit.

delegation The act of one entity granting its powers to another.

deposition A witness' sworn statement taken out-of-court.

dicta; obiter dicta Language in a judge's opinion that goes beyond what is necessary to reach the judgment and is therefore not considered a part of legal precedent.

direct effects In commerce clause jurisprudence, local actions are subject to federal regulation if they directly affect interstate commerce.

dissenting opinion A judge's (or several judges') written statement(s) disagreeing with the outcome arrived at by the majority of the court in a case.

diversity jurisdiction Cases that the federal courts can hear because the parties involved are from two different states, even though the case may not raise issues of federal law.

docket The list of cases to be heard by a court.

dormant commerce power The implicit prohibition on state governments from regulating interstate commerce even in the absence of conflicting federal regulations.

double jeopardy Trying a party more than once for the same offense. Unconstitutional in the United States.

due process The legal rights and procedures to which individuals are constitutionally entitled before being subjected to legal constraints or disabilities. As outlined in the Fifth, Sixth, and Fourteenth Amendments and in decisions by the Supreme Court, these include (but are not limited to) the right to an attorney, the right to a jury trial, and freedom from double jeopardy.

eminent domain The power of the government to confiscate private property without the owner's consent.

enjoin To prohibit or demand the performance of certain acts.

enumerated powers Those powers of the government that are specifically listed in the Constitution.

equity Principles developed by courts based on fairness and equality that go beyond positive law.

ex post facto law A law that applies retroactively, subjecting parties to criminal sanctions for actions that were not illegal at the time they were committed. Unconstitutional in the United States.

exclusionary rule The prohibition against illegally obtained evidence being used at trial.

exclusive powers Jurisdiction retained by national or state governments and not shared with the other.

federai question jurisdiction Cases that the federal courts can hear because they raise issues under federal law, regardless of who are the parties to the case.

federalism The principle that governing authority is divided between independent national and state governments.

felony A serious crime (in contrast to a misdemeanor), usually punishable by at least a year's incarceration.

gerrymander To design political boundaries in order to intentionally favor a certain political party or interest.

grand jury A body of citizens who decide whether to issue an indictment based on evidence presented to them by a prosecutor.

habeas corpus (writ of) Literally "you have the body." An order brought by or on behalf of a prisoner commanding a review of the lawfulness of the prisoner's detention.

hearsay Second-hand knowledge; information provided by a witness that does not come from the witness' own experiences, but from what the witness has learned from others.

immunity Protection from prosecution for a party's criminal activity, often in exchange for their cooperation with prosecutors.

In re In regard to.

incorporation The process of defining the scope of the due process clause of the Fourteenth Amendment. The debate over incorporation specifically addresses which parts of the federal Bill of Rights are to be applied against the states.

indictment The formal, written charges against a criminal defendant presented by a grand jury.

indirect effects In commerce clause jurisprudence, local actions are not subject to federal regulation if they only indirectly affect interstate commerce.

injunction A court order prohibiting or commanding the performance of certain acts.

intermediate scrutiny The amount of suspicion with which a court examines a regulation that impinges on a constitutional right. To pass intermediate scrutiny, a regulation must further a substantial government interest and the restriction on constitutional rights must be no greater than necessary to the pursuit of that interest. Most notably applied to laws that make sex-based distinctions.

judgment of the court The official decision reached by a court specifying the legal outcome in a case.

judicial activism The philosophy that judges should frequently review and, when necessary, use constitutional grounds to strike down decisions by elected officials or other political figures. Usually has a negative connotation.

judicial restraint The philosophy that judges should show deference to the decisions of political figures, particularly those of elected officials.

judicial review The power of courts to find acts of executive and legislative officials unconstitutional and declare them void.

jurisdiction A government, branch of government, legal body, or person's authority over a certain territory or type of matter or dispute.

jurisprudential Concerning the court system.

justiciable Able to be reviewed and resolved by a court, as in a dispute.

legislative veto The power of the legislature, or portion of the legislature, to nullify an executive or judicial action.

libel Published slander of party's character or reputation.

line-item veto The power of a chief executive to reject part of a bill while approving the larger piece of legislation.

litigant A party to a lawsuit.

majority opinion The written statement detailing the official decision of a court in a case.

mandamus (writ of) A court order demanding the performance of a duty by a public official or government body.

merits The facts of a case or argument, as opposed to the legal or procedural points.

***Miranda* warning** The rights of the accused with which police must acquaint suspects upon their request.

misdemeanor A minor crime (in contrast to a felony), usually punishable by fine, penalty, or confiscation, but little to no jail time.

mistrial A trial that the presiding judge declares void before its completion due to miscarriages of justice.

moot Already-resolved or irrelevant, as in a dispute. Courts will not hear cases in which there is no controversy or in which the parties involved have no direct stake.

motion A request made to the court on behalf of one party in a suit.

natural law The rights of humans that are presumed to exist independent of government.

nonjusticiable Unable to be decided in court.

opinion of the court A written statement detailing the court's decision in a case and its reasoning.

oral argument The hearing before a court of appeals during which lawyers for each side in a case present their spoken legal arguments before the judges and the judges ask questions.

original jurisdiction A government, branch of government, legal body, or person's authority to be the first to decide a matter, as opposed to hearing an appeal.

partisan Pertaining to a political party.

penumbra Rights and powers that are not enumerated in a constitution but are implied by enumerated rights and powers.

per curiam opinion Literally "by the court." A decision by the court acting as a whole, as opposed to an opinion written by individual judges.

petitioner A party who appeals to a court to resolve a dispute. In the appeals process, the party filing the appeal is called the petitioner; the party against whom the appeal is filed is called the respondent.

plaintiff The party who brings suit in a civil case.

plenary Whole or complete, leaving no residuum; as in plenary power.

plurality opinion A written statement detailing the decision supported by the greatest number of judges in a case in which no majority is reached.

police power A government's power to regulate the health, safety, and moral order of people within its territory.

political questions doctrine The philosophy that certain matters are the exclusive domain of the legislative and executive branches of government and should therefore remain free of interference from the judiciary.

popular sovereignty The principle that the ultimate authority in a system of government rests with the people.

precedent A previous court decision on an issue.

preemption Overriding state law with applicable federal law in the case of concurrent powers, particularly the regulation of interstate commerce.

prima facie Literally "on the face of it." Assumed to be true unless effectively disproven.

prior restraint Censorship of speech or publications before their publication or airing.

public forum Places that, according to the Supreme Court, "by long tradition or by government fiat have been devoted to assembly and debate."

punitive damages Reparations granted to a winning plaintiff in a civil dispute that cover no specific costs or losses but are instead intended to punish the respondent and deter similar actions.

rational basis test The lowest level of scrutiny a court will give to a challenged regulation and presumes the constitutionality of government action. To pass a rational basis test, a regulation must be rationally related to a legitimate public purpose. Generally applied when the law does not infringe on any fundamental rights or make use of any suspect classifications.

remand To send back, as in to send a case back to a lower court for review or to send a defendant back to jail pending sentencing.

respondent A party against whom legal action is taken. In the appeals process, the party against whom the appeal is filed is called the respondent; the party filing the appeal is called the petitioner.

reverse To overturn, as in the decision of a lower court.

ripe Ready to be decided by a court. A dispute's "ripeness" is determined by the court based on a number of criteria, including but not limited to level of controversy surrounding the issue at hand and the predicted ability of a legal remedy to resolve the dispute.

selective incorporation The application of individual clauses of the Bill of Rights against the states through the Fourteenth Amendment on a case-by-case basis.

separation of powers The functional division of government powers among independent branches of government in order to prevent any one government official from accumulating too much power and to take advantage of specialization.

solicitor general The Justice Department official who argues cases on behalf of the United States government before the Supreme Court.

sovereign immunity Protection from civil liability for sovereign governments.

standing to sue The right of a party to bring a dispute before a court. In order to have standing, parties must demonstrate that that they have suffered harm due to actions which may be regulated by the court.

stare decisis Literally "to stand by things decided." The judicial principle that courts should respect precedent.

state action Conduct by a state government or official; conduct performed under state law or state authorization.

state courts Courts established under state authority that hear disputes and controversies arising under state law.

statute of limitations The period of time after the committal of a crime within which that crime can be prosecuted.

stay A temporary suspension of court action, for example, a stay of execution.

strategic model The theory that one can describe and predict a judge's legal decisions based on one's knowledge of the judge's political beliefs and the institutional circumstances that constrain the ability of a judge to act on those preferences.

strict construction The narrow reading of constitutional and statutory law.

strict scrutiny The greatest amount of suspicion with which a court examines a regulation that restricts a constitutional right, which presumes that a government action is unconstitutional. To pass strict scrutiny, a regulation must be a narrowly tailored or least restrictive means to achieving a compelling governmental interest. Generally applied when a government action interferes with fundamental rights or employs a suspect classification (such as race).

subpoena An order to give information to a court.

substantive due process Rights that are so fundamental they cannot be infringed without violating the constitutional protection against wrongful and arbitrary government coercion. Often applied to "unenumerated" rights to property or sexual liberty.

test A set of criteria used by courts to determine if actions are legal.

tort A civil wrong.

vacate To annul or eliminate; for example the decision of a lower court by a higher court.

warrant A legal authorization for law enforcement officials to perform a search or an arrest.

writ A legal order.

Index

Note: *t* refers to table, *f* refers to figure, and *b* refers to box.

Cases